ILLUSTRATED ATLAS
OF AMERICAN HISTORY

Table of Contents

Introduction

This illustrated atlas contains dramatic maps and vibrant pictures and graphs to bring your study of American history to life. You can use these pages to compare regions or to make connections between past and present. The atlas has been placed at the front of your textbook, so you will have it as a ready reference throughout the year.

Get up-to-date information about any country in the world. Use the World Desk Reference Online to learn about the world today, practice critical thinking skills, and get updated statistics and data.

UNITED STATES
POLITICAL

Golden Gate Bridge, San Francisco, California

Seattle

Spokane

Olympia

Washington

Portland

Salem

Eugene

Oregon

Great Falls

Helena

Montana

Billings

Boise

Idaho

Pocatello

Minot

Grand Forks

North Dakota

Bismarck

South Dakota

Rapid City

Pierre

Sioux Falls

Wyoming

Casper

Cheyenne

Nebraska

Lincoln

Reno

Carson City

San Francisco

Sacramento

Oakland

San Jose

Nevada

Ogden

Great Salt Lake

Salt Lake City

Utah

Denver

Colorado

Colorado Springs

Kansas

Wichita

California

Las Vegas

125°W

Los Angeles

Long Beach

San Diego

Salton Sea

PACIFIC OCEAN

30°N

115°W

Arizona

Phoenix

Tucson

Santa Fe

Albuquerque

New Mexico

Las Cruces

El Paso

Oklahoma

Oklahoma City

Fort Worth

Texas

Austin

San Antonio

120°W

110°W

160°W

155°W

180°

70°N

170°W

160°W

150°W

140°W

RUSSIA

Honolulu

Hawaii

PACIFIC OCEAN

0 km 100

0 miles 100

Mercator Projection

20°N

160°E

50°N

170°E

Arctic Circle

130°W

Alaska

Fairbanks

60°N

CANADA

Bering Sea

Anchorage

Gulf of Alaska

Juneau

MEXICO

0 km 400

0 miles 400

Albers Conic Equal-Area Projection

105°W

100°W

PACIFIC OCEAN

115°W

110°W

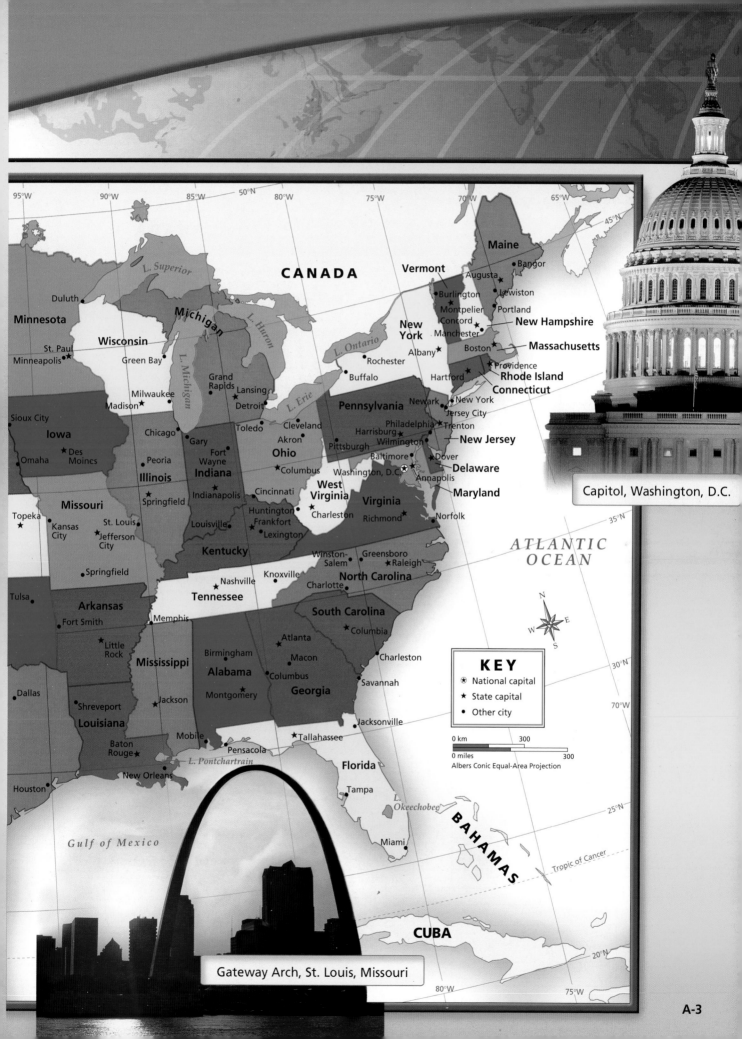

95°W · 90°W · 85°W · 50°N · 80°W · 75°W · 70°W · 65°W · 45°N

Duluth

Minnesota

Wisconsin

St. Paul
Minneapolis ★

Green Bay

L. Superior

Michigan

L. Huron

L. Michigan

Grand
Rapids Lansing

Milwaukee
Madison ★

Sioux City

Iowa

★ Des
Moines
Omaha

Chicago

Gary

Peoria

Illinois

Springfield ★

CANADA

Vermont

Maine

● Bangor

Augusta ★

Burlington ●
Montpelier ★
●Concord

Lewiston ●
● Portland

New Hampshire

**New
York**

L. Ontario

● Rochester

Albany ★

Boston ★

Manchester ●

● Buffalo

Hartford ★

Massachusetts

Providence ★

Rhode Island

Connecticut

Newark ●

● New York

Detroit

Toledo

L. Erie

Pennsylvania

Cleveland ●

Akron ●

Pittsburgh ●

Harrisburg ★

Jersey City ●

● Philadelphia

Trenton ★

● Wilmington

New Jersey

Fort
Wayne

Indiana

Indianapolis ★

Ohio

Columbus ★

Cincinnati ●

**West
Virginia**

Baltimore ●

Washington, D.C. ✪

Dover ★

Delaware

Annapolis ★

Maryland

Missouri

Topeka
★

Kansas
City ●

St. Louis ●
Jefferson ★
City

Springfield ●

Louisville ●

Frankfort ★
● Lexington

Huntington ●

Charleston ★

Virginia

Richmond ★

Norfolk ●

Kentucky

Tennessee

Nashville ★

Winston- ●
Salem

Greensboro ●
● Raleigh ★

Knoxville ●

North Carolina

Tulsa ●

Arkansas

Fort Smith ●

Little ★
Rock

Memphis ●

Charlotte ●

South Carolina

Columbia ★

Atlanta ★

Dallas ●

Shreveport ●

Louisiana

Mississippi

Jackson ★

Birmingham ●

Alabama

Montgomery ★

Macon ●

●Columbus

Georgia

Charleston ●

Savannah ●

**ATLANTIC
OCEAN**

35°N

30°N

70°W

Houston ●

Baton
Rouge ★

Mobile ●

New Orleans

L. Pontchartrain

Pensacola ●

Jacksonville ●

Florida

Tallahassee ★

KEY

✪ National capital

★ State capital

● Other city

0 km ———— 300

0 miles ———— 300

Albers Conic Equal-Area Projection

Gulf of Mexico

Tampa ●

*L.
Okeechobee*

Miami ●

BAHAMAS

25°N

Tropic of Cancer

20°N

CUBA

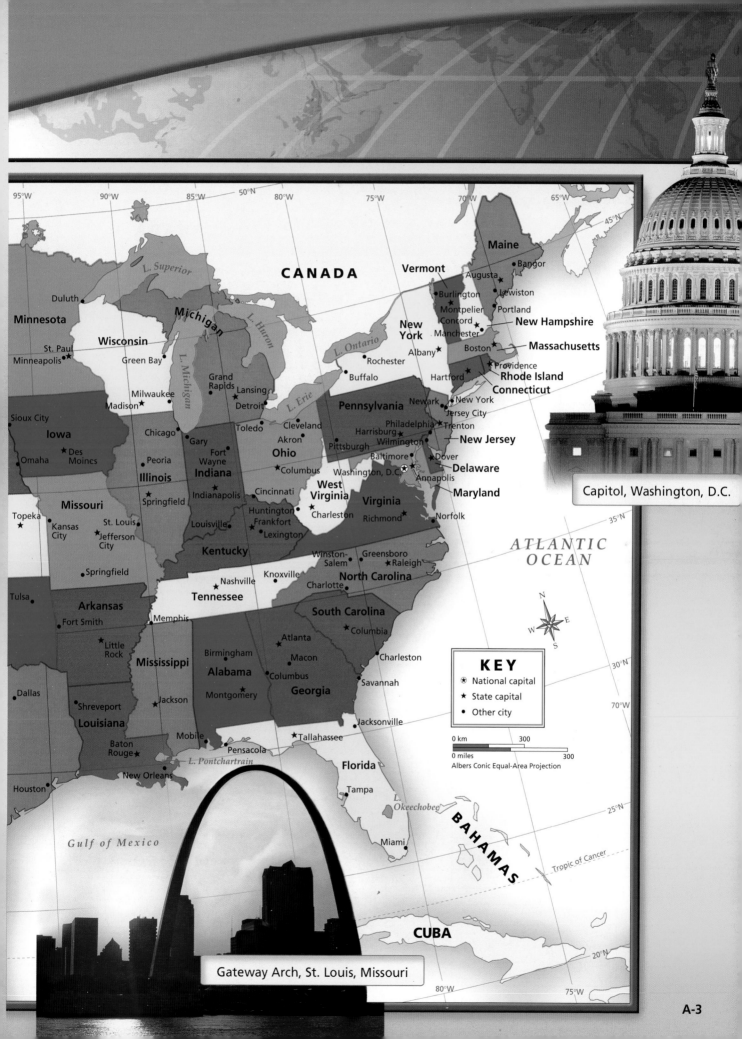

Capitol, Washington, D.C.

Gateway Arch, St. Louis, Missouri

80°W · 75°W

A-3

UNITED STATES
PHYSICAL

Grand Canyon

CANADA

ROCKY MOUNTAINS

CASCADE RANGE

SIERRA NEVADA

GREAT PLAINS

Missouri R.

Missouri R.

Great Salt Lake

Colorado R.

Pikes Peak
(14,110 ft.)

Mt. Whitney
(14,491 ft.)

GRAND CANYON

NORTH

PACIFIC OCEAN

30°N
125°W

Rio Grande

MEXICO

160°W   155°W
PACIFIC OCEAN
Hawaii
20°N
0 km 100
0 miles 100
Mercator Projection

ARCTIC OCEAN
70°N
Arctic Circle
Mt McKinley
(20,320 ft.)
ALASKA RANGE
60°N
25°N

120°W

115°W

110°W

0 km   500
0 miles   500
Albers Conic Equal-Area Projection

Bering Sea

Gulf of Alaska

PACIFIC OCEAN
170°E
180°   170°W   160°W   150°W   140°W   105°W   100°W

125°W   5°W   110°W   105°W   100°W   95°W

Mississippi River

KEY
Land Elevation

Feet		Meters
14,000		4,000
7,000		2,000
1,500		500
700		200
0		0
Below sea level		Below sea level

0 km   300
0 miles   300
Albers Conic Equal-Area Projection

L. Superior

L. Huron

L. Michigan

L. Ontario

L. Erie

Mississippi R.

St. Lawrence R.

Ohio R.

A M E R I C A

A P P A L A C H I A N   M O U N T A I N S

ATLANTIC COASTAL PLAIN

ATLANTIC OCEAN

Mississippi R.

GULF COASTAL PLAIN

Gulf of Mexico

The Everglades, southern Florida

Tropic of Cancer

CUBA

Hispaniola

Caribbean Sea

65°W

60°W

45°N

40°N

35°N

20°N

95°W

90°W

85°W

80°W

75°W

70°W

UNITED STATES
RESOURCES & THE ECONOMY

Grain harvest, an example
of commercial farming

Washington

Oregon

Idaho

Montana

North Dakota

South Dakota

Wyoming

Nevada

Utah

Nebraska

California

Colorado

Kansas

Arizona

New Mexico

Oklahoma

Texas

PACIFIC
OCEAN

45°N

40°N

115°W   110°W   105°W   100°W

Hawaii

RUSSIA

PACIFIC OCEAN

160°W   155°W

0 km   100
0 miles   100
Mercator Projection

20°N

50°N 170°E

PACIFIC
OCEAN

180°   170°W   160°W   150°W   140°W

70°N

Alaska

Bering
Sea

Gulf of
Alaska

130°W
Arctic Circle

CANADA

MEXICO

60°N

0 km   400
0 miles   400
Albers Conic Equal-Area Projection

105°W   100°W

CANADA

Minnesota

L. Superior

Michigan

Wisconsin

L. Huron

L. Michigan

L. Ontario

L. Erie

New York

Vermont

Maine

New Hampshire

Massachusetts

Rhode Island
Connecticut

Iowa

Illinois

Indiana

Ohio

Pennsylvania

New Jersey

Delaware

Maryland

West
Virginia

Virginia

Missouri

Kentucky

North Carolina

Tennessee

Arkansas

South
Carolina

ATLANTIC
OCEAN

Mississippi

Alabama

Georgia

Medical research, a key service
industry in the U.S. economy

Louisiana

Florida

0 km   300
0 miles   300
Albers Conic Equal-Area Projection

N
W   E
S

Gulf of Mexico

KEY

Hunting and gathering	Iron
Forestry	Copper
Livestock raising	Bauxite
Commercial farming	Gold
Manufacturing and trade	Silver
Commercial fishing	Phosphates
Little or no activity	Uranium
Coal	Lead
Petroleum	Nickel
Hydroelectric power	Tungsten

Oil wells pump petroleum,
an important natural resource

95°W 90°W 85°W 80°W 75°W 70°W 65°W 50°N

20°N

75°W

THE WORLD: POLITICAL

100°W   80°W   60°W

Greenland (Den.)

Alaska (U.S.)

60°N

CANADA

NORTH AMERICA

Ottawa

40°N

UNITED STATES

Washington, DC

Bermuda (U.K.)

See inset map

ATLANTIC OCEAN

Tropic of Cancer

Hawaii (U.S.)

20°N

MEXICO

Gulf of Mexico

Mexico City

Caribbean Sea

Caracas

GUYANA

VENEZUELA

Paramaribo

Bogotá

Georgetown

Cayenne

French Guiana (Fr.)

COLOMBIA

SURINAME

Galápagos Is. (Ecuador)

0° Equator

ECUADOR

Quito

SOUTH AMERICA

PACIFIC OCEAN

PERU

Lima

BRAZIL

SAMOA

American Samoa (U.S.)

BOLIVIA

Brasília

French Polynesia (Fr.)

La Paz

Sucre

TONGA

Cook Is. (N.Z.)

20°S

PARAGUAY

Pitcairn I. (U.K.)

Asunción

Tropic of Capricorn

CHILE

Easter Is. (Chile)

URUGUAY

Santiago

Buenos Aires

Montevideo

40°S

International Date Line

ARGENTINA

Falkland Is. (U.K.)

60°S

SOUTHERN OCEAN

Antarctic Circle

ANTARCTICA

Central America and the Caribbean

UNITED STATES

0 km   300

0 miles   300

Azimuthal Projection

Gulf of Mexico

30°N

N

Tropic of Cancer   W   E

Havana

S

BAHAMAS

Nassau

CUBA

20°N

MEXICO

DOMINICAN REPUBLIC

Br. Virgin Is. (U.K.)

HAITI

Puerto Rico (U.S.)

ANTIGUA AND BARBUDA

Belmopan

Kingston

Port-au-Prince

Santo Domingo

BELIZE

JAMAICA

Virgin Islands (U.S.)

Guadeloupe (Fr.)

GUATEMALA

ST. KITTS AND NEVIS

Guatemala

HONDURAS

Caribbean Sea

DOMINICA

Martinique (Fr.)

San Salvador

Tegucigalpa

ST. LUCIA

NICARAGUA

Neth. Antilles (Neth.)

ST. VINCENT AND THE GRENADINES

BARBADOS

EL SALVADOR

Managua

Aruba (Neth.)

GRENADA

COSTA RICA

San José

TRINIDAD AND TOBAGO

10°N

Port of Spain

PACIFIC OCEAN

PANAMA

Panamá

Caracas

ATLANTIC OCEAN

80°W

COLOMBIA

70°W

VENEZUELA

60°W

GUYANA

THE UNITED STATES
A DIVERSE NATION

POLLING PLACE

投票站　CASILLA ELECTORAL
投票所　LUGAR NG BOTOHAN
투표소　PHÒNG PHIẾU

Sign at a California polling place

CANADA

ASIA

UNITED

Asian Migration
According to the 2000 census, 10.2 million Asian Americans make up 3.6 percent of the total U.S. population. Asian immigrants include people from China, Japan, Korea, the Philippines, as well as those from countries in Southeast Asia and South Asia.

N
W E
S

0 km　　　　3,000
0 miles　　　3,000
Mercator Projection

PACIFIC OCEAN

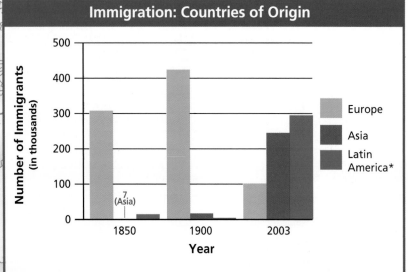

Immigration: Countries of Origin

Number of Immigrants (in thousands)

500
400
300
200
100
7 (Asia)
0

1850　　1900　　2003

Year

Europe
Asia
Latin America*

*Latin America includes the Caribbean, Mexico, and the countries of Central America and South America.

Sources: *Historical Statistics of the United States* and *Statistical Yearbook of the Immigration and Naturalization Service*

European immigrants arriving at Ellis Island, New York

European Migration
The first nonnative settlers to reach North America in the 1500s and 1600s came from Europe. Most immigrants came from northern and western Europe. By the late 1800s, however, the majority of European immigrants were coming from eastern and southern Europe.

EUROPE

STATES

ATLANTIC OCEAN

MEXICO

CENTRAL
AMERICA

AFRICA

A Forced Journey From Africa
Scholars estimate that from the 1500s to the 1800s, more than 10 million enslaved Africans were brought to the Americas. More than 500,000 were transported to Britain's 13 colonies. In 1808, the United States banned the slave trade, but it did not ban slavery until 1865. Today, 34.6 million African Americans make up 12.3 percent of the nation's population.

SOUTH
AMERICA

Latin American Migration
Latin Americans have immigrated to the United States to find jobs. There are 35.3 million Latinos in the United States according to the 2000 Census. A total of 20.6 million of these are Mexican American, while others are from Central and South America and the Caribbean.

UNITED STATES
TERRITORIAL EXPANSION TO 1853

Mandan Village, like the one visited by Lewis and Clark during their exploration of the Louisiana Territory

A covered wagon, the mode of transportation for people moving west in the 1800s

PACIFIC OCEAN

The Alamo, site of a key battle in the war for Texas independence; Texas became part of the Mexican Cession

OREGON COUNTRY
(Agreement with Britain, 1846)

(Ceded by Britain, 1818)

LOUISIANA PURCHASE
(Purchased from France, 1803)

MEXICAN CESSION
(Treaty of Guadalupe-Hidalgo, 1848)

TEXAS ANNEXATION
(Annexed by Congress, 1845)

GADSDEN PURCHASE
(Purchased from Mexico, 1853)

MEXICO

CANADA
(BRITISH TERRITORY)

L. Superior

L. Michigan

L. Huron

Ontario

L. Erie

THE UNITED
STATES,
1783

ATLANTIC
OCEAN

A. M. Willard's *The Spirit of '76*, symbol
of courage during the American Revolution,
fought by the 13 colonies against Great Britain

KEY

Present-day
state boundaries

Original thirteen states

50°W

30°N

0 km   500

0 miles   500

Albers Conic Equal-Area Projection

(Annexed,
1810)

(Annexed,
1812)

FLORIDA
(Ceded by Spain,
1819)

*Gulf of
Mexico*

St. Augustine, oldest permanent
settlement in the United States

60°W

UNITED STATES
POPULATION DENSITY

1870

KEY

Population per square mile

▓	More than 90
▓	45–90
░	18–44
░	6–17
░	2–5
□	Less than 2

Cities

◉ More than 500,000
⊙ 200,000–499,999
● 100,000–199,999
○ 50,000–99,999

Most of the population of the United States was located east of the Mississippi River in 1870.

By 1960, the Midwest and the West had become more populated. A number of large cities had grown in these regions.

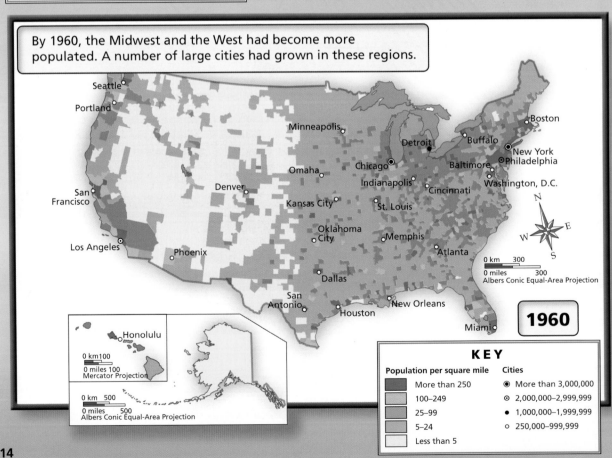

1960

KEY

Population per square mile

▓	More than 250
▓	100–249
░	25–99
░	5–24
□	Less than 5

Cities

◉ More than 3,000,000
⊙ 2,000,000–2,999,999
● 1,000,000–1,999,999
○ 250,000–999,999

In the 1880s, Anaheim, California, outside of Los Angeles was rural. By the twenty-first century Los Angeles, as well as surrounding cities like Anaheim, were modern bustling cities connected by freeways.

Large cities and their suburbs formed huge metropolitan areas by the year 2000. The largest city is New York, followed by Chicago and Los Angeles.

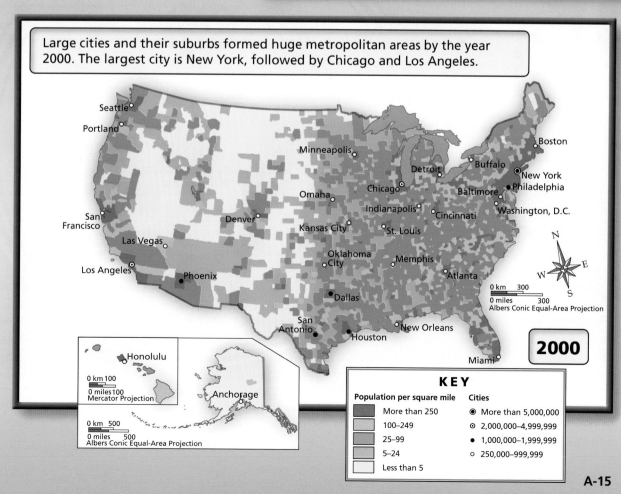

Seattle
Portland
Minneapolis
Detroit
Buffalo
Boston
New York
Philadelphia
Chicago
Baltimore
Washington, D.C.
Omaha
Indianapolis
Cincinnati
San Francisco
Denver
Kansas City
St. Louis
Las Vegas
Oklahoma City
Memphis
Los Angeles
Atlanta
Phoenix
Dallas
San Antonio
New Orleans
Houston
Miami

0 km 300
0 miles 300
Albers Conic Equal-Area Projection

2000

Honolulu
0 km 100
0 miles 100
Mercator Projection

Anchorage
0 km 500
0 miles 500
Albers Conic Equal-Area Projection

KEY

Population per square mile
- More than 250
- 100–249
- 25–99
- 5–24
- Less than 5

Cities
- ◉ More than 5,000,000
- ⊙ 2,000,000–4,999,999
- ● 1,000,000–1,999,999
- ○ 250,000–999,999

SYMBOLS OF OUR NATION

Today's American flag has thirteen red and white stripes representing the original thirteen states. Fifty white stars stand for the current number of states. The first official flag had thirteen stars and was approved in 1777.

Thirteen white stars

American bald eagle

Scroll reading *E Pluribus Unum* ("Out of Many, One")

Olive branch (symbol of peace)

Thirteen arrows (symbol of war)

E PLURIBUS UNUM

The Great Seal of the United States was designed after the American Revolution to represent the new nation, and the values of its founders. The Great Seal appears on the back of the one-dollar bill of the United States.

PENNSYLVANIA

Prentice Hall

AMERICA
HISTORY OF OUR NATION

Authors

James West Davidson

Michael B. Stoff

PEARSON

Prentice Hall

Boston, Massachusetts
Upper Saddle River, New Jersey

THE LANDING OF THE PILGRIMS = 1620   MABELLE L. HOLMES

Acknowledgments appear on page 843, which constitutes an extension of this copyright page.

ISBN 0-13-251352-8

1 2 3 4 5 6 7 8 9 10   09 08 07 06 05

Authors

James West Davidson

Dr. James Davidson is coauthor of *After the Fact: The Art of Historical Detection* and *Nation of Nations: A Narrative History of the American Republic.* Dr. Davidson has taught at both the college and high school levels. He has also consulted on curriculum design for American history courses. Dr. Davidson is an avid canoeist and hiker. His published works on these subjects include *Great Heart,* the true story of a 1903 canoe trip in the Canadian wilderness.

Michael B. Stoff

Dr. Michael Stoff received his Ph.D. from Yale University and teaches history at the University of Texas at Austin. He is the author of *Oil, War, and American Security: The Search for a National Policy on Foreign Oil, 1941–1947,* coauthor of *Nation of Nations: A Narrative History of the American Republic,* and coeditor of *The Manhattan Project: A Documentary Introduction to the Atomic Age.* Dr. Stoff has won numerous grants, fellowships, and teaching awards.

Senior Program Consultants

Albert M. Camarillo

Dr. Albert Camarillo received his Ph.D. in U.S. history from the University of California at Los Angeles. He has been teaching history at Stanford University since 1975. Dr. Camarillo has published six books, including *Chicanos in a Changing Society: From Mexican Pueblos to American Barrios* and *California: A History of Mexican Americans.* His awards for research and writing include a National Endowment for the Humanities Fellowship and a Rockefeller Foundation Fellowship. Dr. Camarillo is the Miriam and Peter Haas Centennial Professor in Public Service.

Diane Hart

Diane Hart is a writer and consultant in history and social studies. She earned bachelor's and master's degrees in history from Stanford University and was a Woodrow Wilson Fellow. As a former teacher at the elementary, secondary, and college levels, Ms. Hart remains deeply involved in social studies education through her active participation in both the National and California Councils for the Social Studies. She has written a number of textbooks for middle school students.

Senior Reading Consultants

Kate Kinsella

Kate Kinsella, Ed.D., is a faculty member in the Department of Secondary Education at San Francisco State University. A specialist in secondary language acquisition and adolescent literacy, she teaches coursework addressing language and literacy development across the secondary curricula. Dr. Kinsella earned her M.A. in TESOL from San Francisco State University and her Ed.D. in Second Language Acquisition from the University of San Francisco.

Kevin Feldman

Kevin Feldman, Ed.D., is the Director of Reading and Early Intervention with the Sonoma County Office of Education (SCOE) and an independent educational consultant. At the SCOE, he develops, organizes, and monitors programs related to K–12 literacy. Dr. Feldman has an M.A. from the University of California, Riverside, in Special Education, Learning Disabilities, and Instructional Design. He earned his Ed.D. in Curriculum and Instruction from the University of San Francisco.

Academic Reviewers

William R. Childs, Ph.D.
Associate Professor of History
Ohio State University
Columbus, Ohio

Theodore DeLaney, Ph.D.
Associate Professor of History
Washington and Lee University
Lexington, Virginia

Wanda A. Hendricks, Ph.D.
Associate Professor of History
University of South Carolina
Columbia, South Carolina

Emma Lapsansky, Ph.D.
Professor of History and Curator
  of Special Collections
Haverford College
Haverford, Pennsylvania

Brendan McConville, Ph.D.
Professor of History
Boston University
Boston, Massachusetts

Gordon Newby, Ph.D.
Chair, Department of Middle Eastern
  and South Asian Studies
Emory University
Atlanta, Georgia

Judy A. Ridner, Ph.D.
Assistant Professor of History
Muhlenberg College
Allentown, Pennsylvania

Teacher Reviewers

Peggy Althof
Social Studies Facilitation, K–12
D-11 Public Schools
Colorado Springs, Colorado

Lon Van Bronkhorst
K–12 Social Studies Curriculum Supervisor
Grand Rapids Public Schools
Grand Rapids, Michigan

Katherine A. Deforge
Chair, Social Studies Department
Marcellus Central Schools
Marcellus, New York

Roceal N. Duke
Social Studies Content Specialist (retired)
District of Columbia Public Schools
Washington, D.C.

Dee Ann Holt
Chair, Social Studies Department
Horace Mann Arts and Science
  Magnet Middle School
Little Rock, Arkansas

Deborah J. Miller
Detroit Public Schools
Detroit, Michigan

Carol Schneider
Curriculum Coordinator
Rock Point Community School
Rock Point, Arizona

Dr. Leigh Tanner
Division of Instructional Support
Pittsburgh Public Schools
Pittsburgh, Pennsylvania

Partnership School Consultants

Melanie Alston
Hackensack Middle School
Hackensack, New Jersey

Matthew Facella
Hackensack Middle School
Hackensack, New Jersey

Karina Koepke
Hackensack Middle School
Hackensack, New Jersey

Richard Yannarelli
Principal
Hackensack Middle School
Hackensack, New Jersey

Content Consultants

Michal Howden
Social Studies Consultant
Zionsville, Indiana

Kathy Lewis-Stewart
Social Studies Consultant
Fort Worth, Texas

Joseph Wieczorek
Social Studies Consultant
Nottingham, Maryland

Differentiated Instruction Consultants

Donald Deshler, Ph.D.
Professor of Special Education (Learning Disabilities)
Director, Center for Research on Learning
University of Kansas
Lawrence, Kansas

Dr. Deshler is the Chair of Prentice Hall's Differentiated Instruction Board. He assembled a distinguished panel of national experts to serve on the board, offering extensive experience in special needs, English language learners, less proficient readers, and gifted and talented students. This team informs Prentice Hall's approach to differentiated instruction and offers guidance on the development of new materials based on this approach.

Anthony S. Bashir, Ph.D.
Coordinator for Academic and Disability Services
Emerson College
Boston, Massachusetts

Cathy Collins Block, Ph.D.
Professor of Curriculum and Instruction
Texas Christian University
Fort Worth, Texas

Anna Uhl Chamot, Ph.D.
Professor of Secondary Education
    ESL and Foreign Language Education
Graduate School of Education and Human
    Development
The George Washington University
Washington, D.C.

Susan Miller, Ph.D.
Professor of Special Education
University of Nevada, Las Vegas
Las Vegas, Nevada

Jennifer Platt, Ed.D.
Associate Dean, College of Education
University of Central Florida
Orlando, Florida

Eric Pyle, Ph.D.
Associate Professor, Geoscience Education
Department of Geology & Environmental Science
James Madison University
Harrisonburg, Virginia

Accuracy Panel

Esther Ratner, Greyherne Information Services
Colleen F. Berg, Greyherne Information Services
Mike Jankowski, M.S. Information Finders
Jane Malcolm, M.L.S. Professional Research
    Services, Tulsa, Oklahoma
Barbara Whitney Petruzzelli, M.L.S.
Amy Booth Raff, M.L.S.
Bernard Rosen, Ph.D.

Table of Contents

Explore the past through the power of technology.

MAP MASTER® Skills Activity

Develop geographic literacy through dynamic map skills instruction. Learn map skills, and interact with every map online and on CD-ROM.

Discovery School Video

Visit the times and places you are studying in American history with a high-impact video program created to enhance your experience of this textbook by our partner Discovery School.

PRENTICE HALL
Student EXPRESS™
Learn · Study · Succeed

Activate your learning with a suite of tools online and on CD-ROM:
• Interactive Textbook
• Reading and Notetaking Study Guide
• Social Studies Skills Tutor
• Web Resources

History Interactive

Launch into an interactive adventure online—using special graphics in this textbook as jumping-off points—to extend your understanding of American history.

UNIT 1 Review:
Beginnings of American History.. 1

Surrender at Yorktown

Table of Contents

The signing of the Constitution

UNIT 3 The New Republic 276

The Lewis and
Clark expedition

Table of Contents

San Francisco, 1850s

Unit 5 Civil War and Reunion 476

The Civil War: African
American soldiers

Table of Contents

The Brooklyn Bridge

Unit 7　A New Role in the World 674

Reference Section

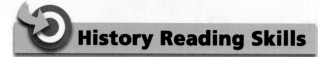

Special Features

History Reading Skills

Enhance your ability to read and understand textbooks through reading skills instruction.

Skills for Life

Build skills that will help you analyze American history content.

Writing Workshop

Develop your writing skills through step-by-step writing instruction and practice.

Links Across Time

Expand your understanding of American history by connecting the past and the present.

LIFE AT THE TIME

Learn more about how people lived at different places and times in history.

Literature

Experience American history through works of literature.

GEOGRAPHY AND HISTORY

Discover the role geography has played in American history.

Links to . . .

Make connections between American history and civics, government, economics, science, geography, and the arts.

Special Features *(continued)*

Biography Quest

Search for answers to mysteries about key people in American history.

Sitting Bull

MAP★MASTER®
Skills Activity

Increase your understanding of American history by studying maps.

Illustrated Atlas of American History

Understand your world by comparing maps of the United States today with historical maps.

Charts, Graphs, and Diagrams

Special Features (continued)

Timelines

Cause and Effect Charts

Political Cartoons

In-Text Sources

Gain insights by examining documents, eyewitness accounts, and other sources.

Special Features (continued)

Primary Sources

Connect to the past through primary sources and literature in the Reference Section.

Tools to help you along the way...

Taking Notes

In history, there's a lot to read about and a lot to understand. Taking good notes is one way to help you remember key ideas and to see the big picture. This program has two ways to help you.

You can keep your notes in the *Interactive Reading and Notetaking Study Guide*. Or you can go online to take your notes. Either way, you will be able to record what you are learning. And, by the end of the year, you'll have created a perfect study tool.

Interactive Textbook

Study Guide *Online*

Complete your Chapter 4 study guide in print or online.

Monitor Your Progress

Progress Monitoring Online

For: Self-test with instant help
Visit: PHSchool.com
Web Code: mya-3046

This program also gives you a chance to make sure you're understanding the material all year long.

At the end of every section and every chapter, you can take a quick practice quiz online. If you get the answers right, that's great! If you miss an answer, you'll get instant help that will show you where you went wrong.

Understanding the Pennsylvania Academic Standards

The **Pennsylvania Academic Standards** describe what you should know and be able to do before completing middle school. The Academic Standards for social studies are divided into four main standards:

- Civics and Government
- Economics
- Geography
- History

Standards Organization

Each of these standards is divided into **standards categories**. The **standards categories** are organized into **grade levels.** You will be working within grade level 9. Each grade level contains a list of **standards statements** with **descriptors** that give the details of what you will learn.

Go to **www.pde.state.pa.us/social_studies** for a full list of Pennsylvania's standards for social studies.

8.1.9.B (3) Different histor-ical perspectives

Reading the Standards

8.1.9.B (3)

8. The Academic Standard
History

1. The Standard Category
Historical Analysis and Skills Development

9. The Grade Level
Grade 9

A. The Standards Statement
Analyze and interpret historical sources

(3) The Descriptor
Different historical perspectives

Alfalfa bales on Pennsylvania farmland.

Why are the Pennsylvania Academic Standards important to me?

By studying the Academic Standards, you will learn basic knowledge and skills that will help you succeed in school, your community, and eventually, the workplace.

Civics and Government

Why do we study civics and government? Learning about civics and government helps you understand the importance of the law and the rights and duties of citizens. In democratic governments, people can enter the political process and influence what governments do. Understanding the rights and responsibilities of citizens helps people recognize ways in which they can participate in their government and society. Knowledge of the laws of American society allows citizens to make informed, responsible decisions as voters, jurors, workers, consumers, and community residents.

Civics and Government
5.1: Principles and Documents of Government
5.2: Rights and Responsibilities of Citizenship
5.3: How Government Works
5.4: How International Relationships Function

Link to Real Life

You are a journalist for a Philadelphia newspaper who has just learned about a factory that has been dumping hazardous waste upstream in the Delaware River.

Why might you need to research the laws of Pennsylvania before writing your article? How might the laws of Pennsylvania affect your community?

▶ To learn more, turn to **How to Read History** on page 412.

Did you know?

After the Civil War, Republicans became the dominant political party in Pennsylvania. Pennsylvania Republicans tended to support big business and industry. During the turn of the 20th century, Republican leaders and activists aided the dramatic development of steel and manufacturing industries in the state.

Economics

Why do we study economics? All people are involved in some type of economic activity. When people buy, sell, trade, produce, or consume goods, they are taking part in an economic activity. Learning about economics helps you understand how the economies of cities, states, nations, and the world directly affect people's lives. By understanding economic systems, people are able to make informed decisions and use resources sensibly as they take part in the economies around them. Many people use economics in the jobs they do. Economists, market analysts, bankers, attorneys, and real estate agents all use economics in their professions.

Economics

6.1: Economic Systems

6.2: Markets and the Functions of Governments

6.3: Scarcity and Choice

6.4: Economic Interdependence

6.5: Work and Earnings

The Susquehanna River winds through eastern Pennsylvania.

Link to Real Life

You want to open a new factory in Pennsylvania, but you are not sure what you want your factory to produce.

Why might it be important to learn about the economy of Pennsylvania? How might factors, such as natural resources, and supply and demand, affect your decision?

▶ To learn more, turn to **Skills for Life** on page 636.

Geography

Why do we study geography? Geography is the study of the physical features of Earth's surface. A region's physical features play a role in the development of economic, political, and social systems. Geographic factors, such as climate, landforms, and natural resources, affect the way people interact with their environment. As countries become increasingly interrelated, it is important to understand how geography affects the relationships among different nations. Learning about geography helps you understand how the world's physical features affect people's lives.

Geography
7.1: Basic Geographic Literacy
7.2: The Physical Characteristics of Places and Regions
7.3: The Human Characteristics of Places and Regions
7.4: The Interactions Between People and Places

Link to Real Life

You are planning to begin managing your family's farm in Luzerne County.

What might you want to learn about the geography of Luzerne County before managing your crops and livestock? How might geographic factors, such as climate, landforms, and natural resources, affect your farm?

▶ To learn more, turn to **Skills for Life** on page 564.

Did you know?

Pennsylvania is the 33rd largest state in the United States. Forests cover a little more than half of the state, serving as home to many different kinds of wildlife such as black bear, white-tailed dear, fox, beavers, rabbits, game birds and songbirds.

History

Why do we study history? Learning about history helps you understand your role in Pennsylvania, the United States, and the world. History is more than a list of dates and events. By analyzing historical events, you can learn from the choices made in the past and use this knowledge to make decisions about the future. Knowledge of history gives people the tools to become participating citizens in their own communities and nations. If you enjoy studying history, you could think about being a historian, librarian, researcher, lawyer, writer, or educator.

History
8.1: Historical Analysis and Skills Development
8.2: Pennsylvania History
8.3: United States History
8.4: World History

Link to Real Life

You are writing a paper about local industries in Pennsylvania. You recently read that many industries are outsourcing labor. This reminds you of changes in industry that occurred at the start of the twentieth century.

Why might it be important to study the history of industry while writing your paper?

▶ To learn more, turn to **How to Read History** on page 642.

Academic Standards

Boathouse Row in Philadelphia reflected in the Schuylkill River

PSSA Skills Review

How will my Social Studies course help me improve on the PSSA?

Many of the skills you practice in social studies—**reading, questioning, analyzing, comparing, interpreting, writing**—are the same skills that will help you succeed on the **Pennsylvania System of School Assessment for Reading and Writing.**

PSSA Skills Review consists of six exercises that will help you practice your reading and writing skills for the PSSA while reviewing your knowledge of social studies. Your teacher will set the pace for the review. For additional help with a skill or topic, turn to the review pages listed below.

Skills Review		

Skills Review	Use After Chapter	Skills Focus	Social Studies Focus	Skills Review	Social Studies Review
1	3	Main Ideas; Cause/Effect	History	28	Chapter 2, Section 1 Chapter 3; Section 1
2	6	Point of View; Make Inferences	Economics	58, 510	Chapter 5, Sections 3, 4, 5
3	11	Compare and Contrast; Cause and Effect	Government	64, 126	Chapter 8, Section 2
4	15	Point of View; Make Inferences	Civics	332	Chapter 14, Section 1
5	18	Compare and Contrast; Sequencing	Culture	222, 338, 480	Chapter 18 Section 4
6	20	Sequencing, Main Ideas	Geography	139	Chapter 20, Section 3

Skyline of Pittsburgh, Pennsylvania

Skills Review 1

 PSSA Skills Review

- **Skills Focus:** Main Ideas; Cause and Effect
- **Social Studies Focus:** History

Read the following passage about the motives of imperialism. Then answer the questions that follow.

> Four main motives can be perceived at work in all the imperial activities of the European peoples during the last four centuries. The first, and perhaps the most potent, has been the spirit of national pride, seeking to express itself in the establishment of its dominion [power] over less highly organized peoples. . . . The second of the blended motives of imperial expansion has been the desire for commercial profits; and this motive has played so prominent [important] a part, especially in our own time, that we are apt to exaggerate its force, and to think of it as the sole motive. . . . A third motive for imperial expansion, which must not be overlooked, is . . . [for people] to propagate [spread] the religious and political ideas which they have adopted. . . . The fourth of the governing motives of imperial expansion is the need of finding new homes for the surplus [excess] population of the colonizing people.
>
> —Ramsay Muir, *The Expansion of Europe: The Culmination of Modern History*

1. According to Muir, which describes a cause of European colonization?

A gaining more wealth

B finding new religions

C learning about other cultures

D creating independent countries

2. What is the main point of the passage?

A Colonization helps increase national pride.

B There are four main motives of colonization.

C Colonization helps people spread religious and political ideas.

D Europe colonized in order to provide homes for its excess population.

3. Which does Muir state as the most important motive for colonization?

A to make profits

B to provide more housing

C to expand power and territory

D to increase religious tolerance

4. According to the passage, as a result of European colonization,

A Europe lost money.

B people found new homes.

C people in the colonies revolted.

D Europe was unable to spread religious ideas.

5. Which of the four motives of European colonization does Muir consider most important?

A social

B cultural

C political

D economic

6. Identify the four motives of European colonization. Choose one motive and explain how it affected the European colonization of North America. Use information from the passage and your knowledge of social studies to support your answer. Write your answer on a separate piece of paper.

Skills Review 2

PA **PSSA Skills Review**

- **Skills Focus:** Point of View; Make Inferences
- **Social Studies Focus:** Economics

Read the following excerpt from a speech given by Patrick Henry previous to the American Revolution. Then answer the questions that follow.

> Sir, we have done everything that could be done to avert the storm which is now coming on. We have petitioned; we have remonstrated [argued]; we have supplicated [pleaded]; we have prostrated [bowed] ourselves before the throne, and have implored its interposition to arrest the tyrannical [over-bearing] hands of the ministry and Parliament. Our petitions have been slighted; our remonstrances [protests] have produced additional violence and insult; our supplications [pleas] have been disregarded. . . .
>
> There is no longer any room for hope. If we wish to be free; if we mean to preserve inviolate those inestimable privileges for which we have been so long contending; . . . we must fight! I repeat it, sir, we must fight!
>
> I know not what course others may take; but as for me— give me liberty or give me death!
>
> —Patrick Henry, March 23, 1775

1. Patrick Henry's view is similar to the views of which group?

A the Whigs

B the Patriots

C the Loyalists

D the Republicans

2. What does Patrick Henry think about war?

A War is needed to gain freedom.

B War will not benefit the colonists.

C War will take away the privileges that have been gained.

D The colonists do not have enough resources to start a war.

3. How does Patrick Henry feel about the colonial government?

A proud

B fearful

C hopeful

D frustrated

4. With which statement would Patrick Henry agree?

A People must hope for the best.

B Freedom is worth fighting for.

C War must be avoided at all costs.

D A controlling government can be tolerated.

5. Henry says the colonists have done everything "to avert the storm which is now coming on." What does "the storm" refer to?

A a revolt

B slavery

C unfair tariffs

D British rule

6. Patrick Henry uses the words "tyrannical hands" to describe the power of the British Parliament. What reasons might Henry have for using these words? How did Parliament treat the colonists? Use information from the passage and your knowledge of social studies to support your answer. Write your answer on a separate piece of paper.

PSSA Skills Review

- **Skills Focus:** Compare and Contrast; Cause and Effect
- **Social Studies Focus:** Government

Read the following passage about America's first political parties. Then answer the questions that follow.

In the late 1780s, political groups began to form in the United States. During this time, people used the term "factions" instead of "political parties." A faction was an organized political group. Many people viewed factions to be unconcerned with the well being of the nation. Despite the efforts of the President and other political leaders, two political parties formed in the early 1790s. These two parties were the Republicans and the Federalists. Each party had strong ideas about how the government should be run. The Republicans were led by Thomas Jefferson and consisted mainly of farmers. Republicans supported strong state governments and believed that the people should have political power. They opposed the national bank, as well as protective tariffs. They wanted the Constitution to be followed exactly. Federalists were led by Alexander Hamilton. They believed that the wealthy and educated should lead the nation and favored a strong central government. Federalists supported the national bank and protective tariffs.

1. How were the Federalists and the Republicans alike?

A They both believed in strong state governments.

B They both put the interests of the nation before their own.

C They were both interested in the creation of a national bank.

D They were both factions that were established in the United States.

2. Why were many farmers part of the Republican party?

A Republicans supported growth of agriculture.

B Republicans supported federal taxation of farmers.

C Republicans supported manufacturing, shipping, and trade.

D Republicans supported a loose interpretation of the Constitution

3. According to the passage, what caused people to dislike factions?

A They thought factions had strong ideas.

B They thought factions were selfish groups.

C They thought factions would raise tariffs.

D They thought factions would create a strong central government.

4. How was political life in America in the early 1780s different from political life in the late 1780s?

A Three political parties existed.

B There were no political parties.

C Americans did not have the power to vote.

D Americans held mainly Republican views.

5. How did the Republicans differ from the Federalists?

A They were in favor of protective tariffs.

B They supported the power of the wealthy.

C They were in favor of strong state governments.

D They supported the power of the central government.

6. Explain how the formation of political parties affected politics in the United States. Use information from the passage and your knowledge of social studies to support your answer. Write your answer on a separate piece of paper.

Skills Review 4

PA PSSA Skills Review

- **Skills Focus:** Point of View; Make Inferences
- **Social Studies Focus:** Civics

Read the following passage about Lincoln's views of the United States before the Civil War. Then answer the questions that follow.

> Under the operation of that policy [slavery], that agitation has not only not ceased [ended], but has constantly augmented [become greater than before]. In my opinion it will not cease until a crisis shall have been reached and passed. "A house divided against itself cannot stand." I believe this government cannot endure permanently, half slave and half free. I do not expect the Union to be dissolved,— I do not expect the house to fall; but I do expect it will cease to be divided. It will become all one thing, or all the other. Either the opponents of slavery will arrest the further spread of it, and place it where the public mind shall rest in the belief that it is in the course of ultimate extinction; or its advocates will push it forward till it shall become alike lawful in all the States, old as well as new, North as well as South.
>
> —Abraham Lincoln, *A House Divided*, 1858

1. What is Abraham Lincoln's opinion about the future of the Union?

A It will resolve its conflicts.

B It will no longer be divided.

C It will dissolve and be taken over.

D It will separate into many pieces.

2. What are Lincoln's feelings about the future of the Union?

A hopeful

B pleased

C saddened

D uncertain

3. Which best tells Lincoln's point of view?

A The Union should remain divided.

B The South should secede from the Union.

C The Union should dissolve and return to British rule.

D The Union should come to an agreement about slavery.

4. Lincoln compares the Union to a house because

A the Union is shaped like a building.

B the Union has the ability to survive while being divided.

C the Union is a place where a group of people lives.

D the Union has many different sections and regions.

5. Lincoln believes that

A conflicts are easily resolved.

B conflicts can tear groups apart.

C conflicts make nations stronger.

D conflicts are necessary for growth.

6. Lincoln states that the Union is divided over the issue of slavery. Why was the nation divided on this issue? What were the pros and cons of slavery? Use information from the passage and your knowledge of social studies to support your answer. Write your answer on a separate piece of paper.

PSSA Skills Review

- **Skills Focus:** Compare and Contrast; Sequencing
- **Social Studies Focus:** Culture

Read the following passage about Mary Antin's experience as an immigrant during the late nineteenth century. Then answer the questions that follow.

> The first meal was an object lesson of much variety. My father produced several kinds of food, ready to eat, without any cooking, from little tin cans that had printing all over them. He attempted to introduce us to a queer, slippery kind of fruit, which he called "banana," but had to give it up for the time being.
>
> With our despised immigrant clothing we shed also our impossible Hebrew names. A committee of our friends, several years ahead of us in American experience, put their heads together and concocted American names for us all. Those of our real names that had no pleasing American equivalents they ruthlessly discarded, content if they retained the initials. My mother, possessing a name that was not easily translatable, was punished with the undignified nickname of Annie. Fetchke, Joseph, and Deborah issued as Frieda, Joseph, and Dora, respectively. As for poor me, I was simply cheated. The name they gave me was hardly new. My Hebrew name being Maryashe in full, Mashke for short, Russianized into Marya *(Mar-ya),* my friends said that it would hold good in English as Mary; which was very disappointing, as I longed to possess a strange-sounding American name like the others.
>
> —Mary Antin, *The Promised Land*

1. When does Mary's family change their names?

A after they learn Hebrew

B before they leave Russia

C after they come to America

D while they travel to America

2. What is different about Mary's life in America?

A her family

B her initials

C her religion

D her clothing

3. How are immigrants that have been in America for several years different from Mary's family?

A They are not as helpful.

B They have Hebrew names.

C They know American names.

D They wear immigrant clothing.

4. When does Mary think she was "simply cheated?"

A after she had to eat food out of a can

B after she shed her "despised immigrant clothing"

C after she was given a strange sounding American name

D after she met friends with more years of American experience

5. The events in this passage most likely happened

A when Mary first came to America.

B after Mary had been in America for several years.

C while Mary's family was coming to America.

D when Mary's family was preparing to leave Russia.

6. How was life different for immigrants in the United States? Use information from the passage and your knowledge of social studies to support your answer. Write your answer on a separate piece of paper.

Skills Review 6

 PSSA Skills Review

- **Skills Focus:** Sequencing; Main Ideas
- **Social Studies Focus:** Geography

Read the following passage about the construction of the Panama Canal. Then answer the questions that follow.

> After the Spanish-American War, the United States gained power in Latin America and the Pacific. To help protect this new overseas empire, President Teddy Roosevelt proposed in 1902 that a canal be built in Panama. The canal would link the Atlantic and Pacific Ocean, which would improve global shipping and aid the U.S. Navy.
>
> Roosevelt proposed that crews dig through the Isthmus of Panama. An isthmus is a slender portion of land that connects to larger portions of land. It would be difficult work. To construct the canal, workers had to not only cut through a mountain, but also dam a river and raise the canal's giant locks.
>
> Making the Gaillard Cut was the most challenging task of the canal process. During the canal construction it was called Culebra Cut, but it was later renamed for Col. David DuBose Gaillard, the engineer who was in charge of this section of the canal work. The Gaillard Cut is an excavated gorge, approximately 9 miles long. The workers had to dig a ditch through the mountains and carve through rock and shale for most of the distance. They worked day after day in the hot sun and drenching rain.

1. According to the passage, work on the Panama Canal began after

  A it was opened in 1914.

  B the Culebra Cut was made.

  C President Roosevelt proposed the idea.

  D David DuBose Gaillard engineered a section.

2. In order to make the Gaillard Cut,

  A workers dammed a river.

  B workers dug a giant ditch.

  C workers created an isthmus.

  D workers raised the canal's giant locks.

3. What is the main point of the last paragraph of the passage?

  A Workers cut a ditch through the mountains and carved through rock.

  B The Gaillard Cut is a ditch through a gorge that is about 9 miles long.

  C Workers faced hot sun and drenching rain while building the Panama Canal.

  D The Gaillard Cut was one of the most challenging jobs in the Panama Canal.

4. According to the passage, the Culebra Cut

  A was renamed the Gaillard Cut.

  B was created after the Gaillard Cut.

  C was created before the Gaillard Cut.

  D was renamed after Teddy Roosevelt.

5. Which information is most important to the meaning of the passage?

  A Workers cut through rock and shale.

  B The Panama Canal was opened in 1914.

  C The Panama Canal was proposed in 1902.

  D Building the Panama Canal was hard work.

6. What were some of the challenges faced by the men working on the creation of the canal? Use information from the passage and your knowledge of social studies to support your answer. Write your answer on a separate piece of paper.

Focus on Writing

Social studies can also help you practice your writing skills for success on the **Pennsylvania System for School Assessment**. The following pages show you how to approach a writing prompt, a sample of a student response, and how to evaluate it.

Sample

Informational Writing Prompt

You will have up to 60 minutes to **plan**, **write**, and **proofread** your response to this writing prompt:

> Write an essay describing one person whom you have studied in history that you would like to meet.

How to Approach a PSSA Writing Prompt

Plan

Before you write:

- Read the prompt carefully so you understand exactly what you are being asked to do.
- Consider the topic, task and audience.
- Think about what you want to write.
- Use scratch paper to organize your thoughts. Use strategies like mapping or outlining.

Write

As you write:

- Maintain a clear and consistent position or claim.
- Include specific details; use examples and reasons to support your ideas.
- Use a variety of well-constructed, complete sentences.
- Use logical organization with an obvious introduction, body and conclusion.

Proofread

After you write:

- Did you support your ideas with specific details?
- Do the point of view and tone of the essay remain consistent?
- Check for capitalization, spelling, sentence structure, punctuation, and usage errors.

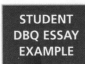

Name: Tushar Avran

Slavery divided the country even before the Civil War. Senator Daniel Webster of Massachusetts had always been against slavery, but he eventually supported making some slavery laws stronger. I would choose to meet Daniel Webster so I could know why he chose to support a compromise between the North and South and why saving the Union was more important than opposing slavery.

In 1850, more territories wanted to become states, but members of Congress had different ideas about if they would be free states or slave states. For example, the North support-ed making California a free state, but the South wanted to make the Fugitive Slave Act stronger.

Senator Henry Clay wanted a compromise between the two positions. Clay met with Webster to discuss this deal, in the hopes they could save the Union and prevent civil war. With Daniel Webster's support, Clay's idea would pass in the Senate. I would like to know what Henry Clay said that was so convincing.

Daniel Webster, however, had always been against slavery. Why, then, would he support a compromise that made it easier to capture people who escaped slavery? Why would he support the chance of new states becoming slave states?

Many people from Webster's home state thought he was a traitor because he had told them he was against slavery, but then seemed to support it. Daniel Webster also seemed to go against his own belief that slavery was wrong, in order to pre-vent civil war

In conclusion, if I met Daniel Webster, it would be easier to understand why it was a good idea to support some of the things that the South wanted in the debate. But maybe I would disagree with Daniel Webster. Still, it might be easier to understand why avoiding civil war was better than getting rid of slavery immediately.

Teacher's Comment:
Good transitions between paragraphs to develop your point, with clear opening and closing paragraphs that develop your idea.

Teacher's Comment:
Adequate, but not sub-stantial details from his-tory to show Webster's conflict of interest. More details could help illus-trate this conflict.

Teacher's Comment:
Suggest answers to the questions you ask, so you can further elaborate on the decisions Daniel Webster faced.

Essay Score: 3 Adequate and/or illustrative content that demonstrates an understanding of the purpose. Sufficient, though not thorough elabora-tion with clearly presented information supported with well-chosen details. Logical order and transitions which develop a controlling idea.

Directions: You will have up to 60 minutes to **plan**, **write**, and **proofread** your response to each writing prompt:

Informational Writing Prompt

Write an essay describing a period in American history in which you would have liked to live.

Persuasive Writing Prompt

Your local school board is holding a meeting to discuss school uniforms. Write a letter to the school board, explaining whether you agree or disagree with requiring school uniforms.

PSSA Scoring Rubric for Informational Writing

Score	Focus	Content Development	Organization	Style
4	• Sharp, distinct controlling point made about a single topic with evident awareness of task and audience.	• Substantial, relevant and illustrative content that demonstrates a clear understanding of the purpose • Thorough elaboration with effectively presented information consistently supported with well-chosen details.	• Effective organizational strategies and structures, such as logical order and transitions, which develop a controlling idea.	• Precise control of the language, stylistic techniques, and sentence structures that creates a consistent and effective tone.
3	• Clear, controlling point made about a single topic with general awareness of task and audience.	• Adequate, specific, and/or illustrative content that demonstrates an understanding of the purpose. • Sufficient elaboration with clearly presented information supported with well-chosen details.	• Organizational strategies and structures, such as logical order and transitions, which develop a controlling idea.	• Appropriate control of language, stylistic techniques and sentence structures that creates a consistent tone.
2	• Vague evidence of a controlling point made about a single topic with an inconsistent awareness of task and audience.	• Inadequate, vague content that demonstrates a weak understanding of the purpose. • Underdeveloped and/or repetitive elaboration with inconsistently supported information. • May be an extended list.	• Inconsistent organizational strategies and structures, such as logical order and transitions, which ineffectively develop a controlling idea.	• Limited control of language and sentence structures that creates interference with tone.
1	• Little or no evidence of a controlling point made about a single topic with a minimal awareness of task and audience.	• Minimal evidence of content that demonstrates a lack of understanding of the purpose. • Superficial, undeveloped writing with little or no support. • May be a bare list.	• Little or no evidence of organizational strategies and structures, such as logical order and transitions, which inadequately develop a controlling idea.	• Minimal control of language and sentence structures that creates an inconsistent tone.

PSSA Scoring Rubric for Persuasive Writing

Score	Focus	Content Development	Organization	Style
4	• Sharp, distinct controlling point presented as a position and made convincing through a clear, thoughtful, and substantiated argument with evident awareness of task and audience.	• Substantial, relevant and illustrative content that demonstrates a clear understanding of the purpose. • Thoroughly elaborated argument that includes a clear position consistently supported with precise and relevant evidence. Rhetorical (persuasive) strategies are evident.	• Effective organizational strategies and structures, such as logical order and transitions, to develop a position supported with a purposeful presentation of content.	• Precise control of language, stylistic techniques, and sentence structures that creates a consistent and effective tone.
3	• Clear, controlling point presented as a position and made convincing through a credible and substantiated argument with general awareness of task and audience.	• Adequate, specific, and/or illustrative content that demonstrates an understanding of the purpose. • Sufficiently elaborated argument that includes a clear position supported with some relevant evidence. Rhetorical (persuasive) strategies may be evident.	• Organizational strategies and structures, such as logical order and transitions, to develop a position supported with sufficient presentation of content.	• Appropriate control of language, stylistic techniques and sentence structures that creates a consistent tone.
2	• Vague evidence of a controlling point presented as a position that may lack a credible and/or substantiated argument with an inconsistent awareness of task and audience.	• Inadequate, vague content that demonstrates a weak understanding of the purpose. • Insufficiently elaborated argument that includes an underdeveloped position supported with little evidence.	• Inconsistent organizational strategies and structures, such as logical order and transitions, to develop a position with inadequate presentation of content.	• Limited control of language and sentence structures that creates interference with tone.
1	• Little or no evidence of a controlling point presented as a position that lacks a credible and/or substantiated argument with minimal awareness of task and audience.	• Minimal evidence of content that demonstrates a lack of understanding of the purpose. • Unelaborated argument that includes an undeveloped position supported with minimal or no evidence.	• Little or no evidence of organizational strategies and structures, such as logical order and transitions, to develop a position with insufficient presentation of content.	• Minimal control of language and sentence structures that creates an inconsistent tone.

PSSA Scoring Rubric for Conventions

4	3	2	1
• Thorough control of sentence formation • Few errors, if any, are present in grammar, usage, spelling and punctuation, but the errors that are present do not interfere with meaning	• Adequate control of sentence formation • Some errors may be present in grammar, usage, spelling and punctuation, but few, if any, of the errors that are present may interfere with meaning	• Limited and/or inconsistent control of sentence formation. Some sentences may be awkward or fragmented • Many errors may be present in grammar, usage, spelling and punctuation, and some of those errors may interfere with meaning	• Minimal control of sentence formation. Many sentences are awkward and fragmented • Many errors may be present in grammar, usage, spelling and punctuation, and many of those errors may interfere with meaning

Historian's Toolkit

Introduction: Studying Our Past

The nation was at war with itself, the North fighting against the South. In July 1863, more than 50,000 soldiers had died at a horrible battle in Gettysburg, Pennsylvania. A few months later, President Abraham Lincoln visited Gettysburg to dedicate the battlefield as a cemetery. Lincoln spoke of the soldiers who had given their lives to keep the nation together:

> **" The world will little note, nor long remember what we say here, but it can never forget what they did here. "**
>
> —Abraham Lincoln, Gettysburg Address

Lincoln was partly right. The world still remembers the soldiers who died during the Civil War. But we also remember what Lincoln said and what he did for the cause of freedom. As you study American history this year, you will be asked to remember all those who came before us—soldiers and Presidents, explorers and inventors, religious leaders and business leaders, the people who wrote our Constitution, and the people who fought to end slavery.

Helping us remember the past is the job of the historian. Historians explore important questions in order to find out how people lived and why they made the decisions they did. Historians also try to understand how history affects our lives today.

On the next few pages, you will learn to think like a historian. You will also get to try out some of the tools historians use. Your Historian's Toolkit can make your study of American history easier and more rewarding.

Union soldier

Think Like a Historian

Historical Evidence

Historians use many types of evidence to learn about the past. This evidence can be divided into primary sources and secondary sources.

Primary Sources A primary source is firsthand information about people or events. Primary sources include official documents, such as laws and public speeches, as well as eyewitness accounts, such as diaries, letters, and autobiographies. Primary sources may also include visual evidence, such as news photographs or videotapes.

Another type of primary source is an artifact. This is an item left behind by people in the past. This might take the form of a statue, a tool, or an everyday object.

Primary sources are valuable because they are created at the time when an event occurs. But this does not necessarily make them "true." Primary sources are created by people, and they may reflect the points of view of the people who created them. The person might not have been aware of certain facts, might have been trying to impress someone, or may even have been lying. So primary sources must be evaluated carefully and considered in relation to other sources on the subject.

Secondary Sources Historians also use secondary sources. These are sources created by someone who did not actually witness events. This textbook, for example, is a secondary source. The authors gathered information from many sources to reach an understanding of what happened and why it happened. Then, they wrote their interpretation of the events. Other secondary sources include news articles and biographies.

Types of Historical Sources

Type of Source	Description	Examples

Primary Sources	• Provide direct evidence about an event
	• Have a limited viewpoint
	• May be reliable or unreliable
	• Include objects left behind by people
		• Official documents
		• Letters and diaries
		• Speeches and interviews
		• Autobiographies
		• Photographs
		• Artifacts
		  • Tools and weapons
		  • Statues and other art

Secondary Sources	• Consist of secondhand information about an event • Use primary sources to create a broader picture • May be reliable or unreliable	• History books • Biographies • Encyclopedias and other reference works • Internet Web sites

Using Historical Sources

Everyone who wants to know about history starts by asking questions. You might be familiar with the types of questions found in your textbook or asked by your teacher. But historians ask questions the way a detective would. Each answer is a clue that leads to another question. The questions and answers bring the historian to an understanding of events in the past.

Consider this situation. Patricia was going through some very old books she found in her great-grandmother's trunk in the attic. Between the pages of one book, she found an old letter on thin, yellowing paper. A copy of the letter is shown here at right.

While reading the letter, Patricia asked herself many questions. Some of her questions are shown at right. Trying to find the answers to the questions is the same sort of thinking that historians use to find out about the past.

June 12, 1849

Dear Sean,

Everyone was happy to get your last letter. After surviving such a long, difficult journey, it must have been wonderful to arrive at last in New York.

Things in our village are not as bad as when you left. But many children and old people are still starving, and too many people have no place to live. You were wise to go to America.

Please tell me more about your plans. After traveling for so long, why would you want to begin a new journey? Where is this place called California? And why are you so sure you can get rich there?

I miss you. I only hope I live long enough to join you someday.

Your loving brother,
Michael

Where did Sean come from? Why was the trip so hard?

What has happened to cause these problems?

How does Sean plan to get rich?

Patricia may follow several steps to find the answers to her questions.

- **Start with what is known.** Patricia knows that her ancestors came to the United States from Ireland many years ago. She thinks this letter might explain why.
- **Read and observe.** Patricia can look for further information in primary and secondary sources. She might look at a map to see where Ireland is and how far it is from New York to California.
- **Speculate.** To help get started, Patricia might make some guesses, called hypotheses, about the answers to her questions.

- **Evaluate evidence.** As Patricia finds more information, she will test her hypotheses against the information that turns up. She can always change her hypotheses as she learns more.
- **Draw conclusions.** Patricia states what she believes are the final answers to her questions.

To start her search, though, Patricia will need to practice her skills of reading like a historian and using maps. The information on the following pages will help you review some of these skills.

Read Informational Texts

Reading a magazine, an Internet page, or a textbook is not the same as reading a novel. The purpose of reading nonfiction texts is to acquire new information. On page HT 7, you'll read about some ⊙ **History Reading Skills** that you'll practice as you read this textbook. Here, we'll focus on a few skills that will help you read nonfiction with a more critical eye.

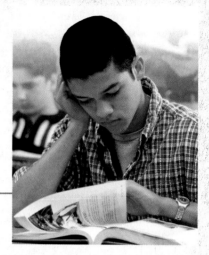

Analyze the Author's Purpose

Different types of materials are written with different purposes in mind. For example, a textbook is written to teach students information about a subject. The purpose of a technical manual is to teach someone how to use something, such as a computer. A newspaper editorial might be written to persuade the reader to accept a particular point of view. An author's purpose influences how the material is presented. Sometimes, an author states his or her purpose directly. More often, the purpose is only suggested, and you must use clues to identify the author's purpose.

Distinguish Between Facts and Opinions

Active reading enables you to distinguish between facts and opinions when reading informational texts. Facts can be proved or disproved, but opinions reflect someone's own point of view.

Because newspaper editorials usually offer opinions on current events and issues, you should watch for bias and faulty logic when reading them. For example, the newspaper editorial at right shows factual statements in blue and opinions in red. Highly charged words are underlined. They reveal the writer's bias.

More than 5,000 people voted last week in favor of building a new shopping center, but the opposition won out. The margin of victory is irrelevant. Those radical voters who opposed the center are obviously self-serving elitists who do not care about anyone but themselves.

This month's unemployment figure for our area is 10 percent, which represents an increase of about 5 percent over the figure for this time last year. These figures mean that unemployment is worsening. But the people who voted against the mall probably do not care about creating new jobs.

Identify Evidence

Before you accept a writer's conclusion, you need to make sure that the writer has based the conclusion on enough evidence and on the right kind of evidence. A writer may present a series of facts to support a claim, but the facts may not tell the whole story. For example, the writer of the newspaper editorial on the previous page claims that the new shopping center would create more jobs. But what evidence is offered? Is it possible that the shopping center might have put many small local stores out of business? This would increase unemployment rather than decreasing it.

Evaluate Credibility

Whenever you read informational texts, you need to assess the credibility of the writer. In other words, you have to decide whether the writer is believable. This is especially true of sites you may visit on the Internet. All Internet sources are not equally reliable. Here are some questions to ask yourself when evaluating the credibility of a Web site:

☐ Is the Web site created by a respected organization, a discussion group, or an individual?

☐ Does the Web site creator include his or her name as well as credentials and the sources he or she used to write the material?

☐ Is the information on the site balanced or biased?

☐ Can you verify the information using two other sources?

☐ Is there a date telling when the Web site was created or last updated?

Build Vocabulary

One of the most important tools in reading informational texts is to make sure you understand the key vocabulary used by the writer. This textbook uses two devices to help you understand important vocabulary terms.

Key Terms

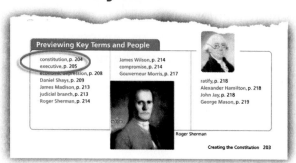

1 Key social studies terms for each chapter are introduced in the chapter opener.

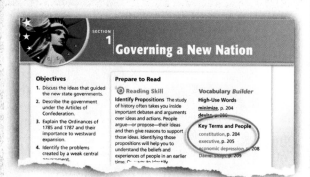

2 They are then listed at the beginning of the section in which they will be used.

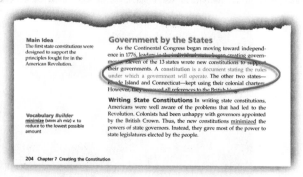

3 Notice that they are always shown in blue type. Their definitions are also in blue.

High-Use Academic Words

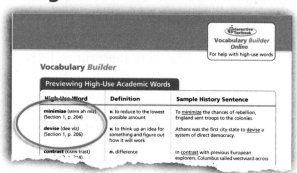

4 High-Use Academic Words appear on the chapter opener in a chart. The chart gives a sample history sentence using each high-use word.

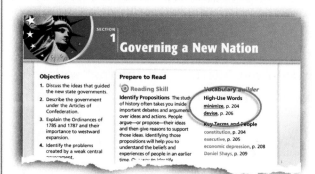

5 The high-use words are then listed at the beginning of the section in which they will appear.

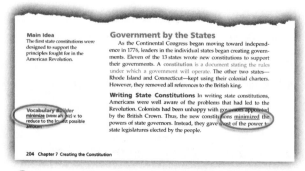

6 High-use words are underlined in the text and defined in the margin.

History Reading Skills

The History Reading Skills described on this page are important in helping you read and understand the information in this book. Each chapter uses a primary or secondary source to teach a reading skill. As you learn to use these skills, you will find that you can apply them to other books you read.

Clarify Meaning You can better understand what you read by using summaries and outlines and by taking notes to help identify main ideas and supporting details. **Chapters 1, 2.**

Compare and Contrast When you compare, you examine the similarities between things. When you contrast, you look at the differences. **Chapters 3, 8.**

Use Context Learn to use context clues to help you understand the meaning of unfamiliar words and words with more than one meaning. **Chapters 4, 17.**

Word Analysis Discover how to analyze words to determine their meanings. **Chapters 6, 18.**

Understand Sequence A sequence is the order in which a series of events occurs. Noting the sequence of important events can help you understand and remember the events. **Chapters 9, 15.**

Analyze Cause and Effect Every event in history has causes and creates effects. You will learn how to identify causes, which are what make events happen, and effects, which are what happen as a result of an event. **Chapters 10, 14.**

Draw Conclusions You will learn how to use details from primary and secondary sources to draw conclusions. **Chapters 5, 12.**

Evaluate Information As you read history, it is important to evaluate how writers' support their propositions, or the ideas they put forth. To do so, it is important to know how to identify and explain central issues and frame good research questions. **Chapters 7, 11, 13, 16, 19, 20.**

MAP★MASTER®

CONTENTS

Go Online PHSchool.com   The maps in this textbook can be found online at **PHSchool.com**, along with map-skills practice.

Geography and History

Historical information is not presented only in written sources. Maps are often a key to understanding what happened and why.

Do you remember when Patricia was asking questions about the letter she found? (See page HT 3.) In addition to using primary and secondary sources, Patricia could have used maps to locate Ireland and to trace Sean's route from New York to California.

In order to get the most out of maps as sources, you need to make sure that your geography map skills are strong. On the next few pages, you can review some of the basic tools historians use to understand maps and geography.

The pictures above show two different geographical regions of the United States. The Midwest (above, left) has fertile plains suitable for farming. The rocky coasts of New England (right) are home to a large fishing industry.

Five Themes of Geography

Studying the history and geography of the United States is a huge task. You can make that task easier by thinking of geography in terms of five themes. The five themes below are tools you can use to organize geographic information and to answer questions about the influence of geography and human history.

Location

1 The exact location of a country or city is expressed in terms of longitude and latitude. Relative location defines where a place is in relation to other places. For example, the exact location of the city of Chicago, Illinois, is 42° north (latitude) and 88° west (longitude). Its relative location could be described as "on the shore of Lake Michigan" or "821 miles north of New Orleans."

Place

2 Location answers the question, "Where is it?" Place answers the question, "What is it like there?" You can identify a place by such features as its landforms, its climate, its plants and animals, or the people who live there. Much of the history of the southeastern United States was shaped by the fact that it had a mild climate and fertile land suitable for large-scale farming of crops such as cotton.

Regions

3 Regions are areas that share common features. Regions may be defined by geography or culture. For example, New York is one of the Middle Atlantic states because it is located on the Atlantic Ocean. In colonial days, it was one of the Middle Colonies. And in the early 1800s, New York was one of the "free states" because slavery was banned there.

Movement

4 Much of history has to do with the movement of people, goods, and ideas from place to place. In Patricia's letter, we saw two examples of movement: the movement of immigrants to the United States from other countries and the movement of Americans from the East to the West. Both played a key role in the history and growth of the United States.

Interaction

5 Human-environment interaction has two parts. The first part has to do with the way an environment affects people. For example, people in the harsh deserts of North Africa developed very different ways of life from those living in the rich farmlands of Italy. The second part of interaction concerns the way people affect their environment. Even in ancient times, people found ways to bring water from rivers to farms or to build roads across mountains.

Practice Geography Skills

Look at the photographs on page HT 8 and read the caption. How do these pictures illustrate the themes of place, region, and interaction?

Build Geography Skills

Globes

A globe is a model of Earth. It shows the actual shape, size, and location of each landmass and body of water.

Globes divide Earth into lines of latitude and longitude. Latitude measures distance north or south of the Equator, which is an imaginary line around the widest part of Earth. Longitude measures distance east or west of the Prime Meridian, which is an imaginary line running from the North Pole to the South Pole. The diagram below shows how lines of longitude and latitude form a grid pattern on a globe.

Using lines of latitude and longitude, you can locate any place on Earth. The location of 38° north latitude and 122° west longitude is written as 38° N/122° W. Only one place on Earth has this location: the city of San Francisco, California.

Practice Geography Skills

Suppose that you wanted to plan a long trip. What would be some advantages and disadvantages of using a globe?

Map Projections

Globes are accurate, but they are not easy to carry around, and they are not useful for showing smaller areas of Earth in detail. So mapmakers had to develop methods to show the curved Earth on a flat surface. These methods are known as map projections. All map projections distort Earth in some way. Below are two common types of map projections.

Mercator Projection

In the 1500s, ocean travelers relied on the Mercator projection, named after mapmaker Gerardus Mercator. The Mercator projection accurately shows direction and the shape of Earth's landmasses. However, it distorts distance and size.

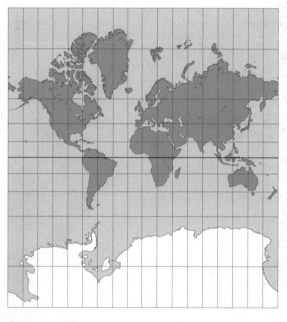

Robinson Projection

The Robinson projection shows the correct shape and size of landmasses for most parts of the world. However, it does not show directions as well as a Mercator projection does. It also distorts the size of the North Pole and South Pole.

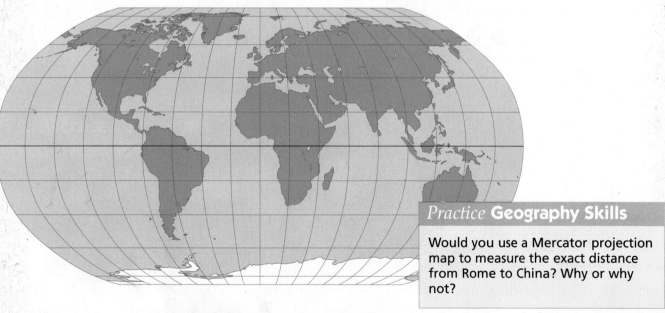

Practice **Geography Skills**

Would you use a Mercator projection map to measure the exact distance from Rome to China? Why or why not?

How to Use a Map

Mapmakers provide several clues to help in understanding the information on a map. Maps provide different clues, depending on their purpose or scale. However, most maps have several clues in common.

Locator
Many maps are shown with locator maps or globes. They show where on Earth the area of the map is located.

Title
Maps have titles. The title tells you the subject of the map.

Key
Often a map has a key, or legend. The key shows the meaning of the symbols and colors used on the map.

Compass rose
Many maps show direction by displaying a compass rose with the directions north, east, south, and west. The letters N, E, S, and W are placed to indicate these directions.

Western United States

KEY
- ⊛ State capital
- • Other city
- — State border

0 km 100
0 miles 100
Albers Conic Equal-Area Projection

Maps of Different Scales

Maps are drawn to different scales, depending on their purpose. Here are three maps drawn to very different scales. Keep in mind that maps showing large areas have smaller scales. Maps showing small areas have larger scales.

▲ Greater Los Angeles

Find the light gray square on the main map of California (left). This square represents the area shown on the map above. It shows Los Angeles in relation to nearby cities, towns, and the Pacific Ocean. It also shows some features near the city, such as the airport and major roadways.

▲ Downtown Los Angeles

Find the gray square on the map of Greater Los Angeles. This square represents the area shown on the map above. This map moves you closer into the center of Los Angeles. Like a zoom on a computer or a camera, this map shows a smaller area, but in greater detail. It has the largest scale. You can use this map to explore downtown Los Angeles.

KEY
■ Point of interest
▨ Park

0 km   2
0 mile   2
Albers Conic Equal-Area Projection

KEY
• Town or neighborhood
✈ Airport
— City or county border
▨ Built-up area

0 km   30
0 miles   30
Albers Conic Equal-Area Projection

Scale bar

A scale bar helps you find the actual distances between points shown on the map. Most scale bars show distances in both miles and kilometers.

Practice Geography Skills

- What part of a map explains the colors used on the map?
- How does the scale bar change depending on the scale of the map?

Build Geography Skills

Political Maps

Historians use many different types of maps. On the next four pages, you will see four maps that relate to American history. Each map shows a different area in a different way and for a different purpose.

One of the most familiar types of map is the political map. Political maps show political divisions, such as borders between countries or states. Colors on a political map help make the differences clear. Political maps also show the location of cities. This map shows the United States in 1790, at the time George Washington was President.

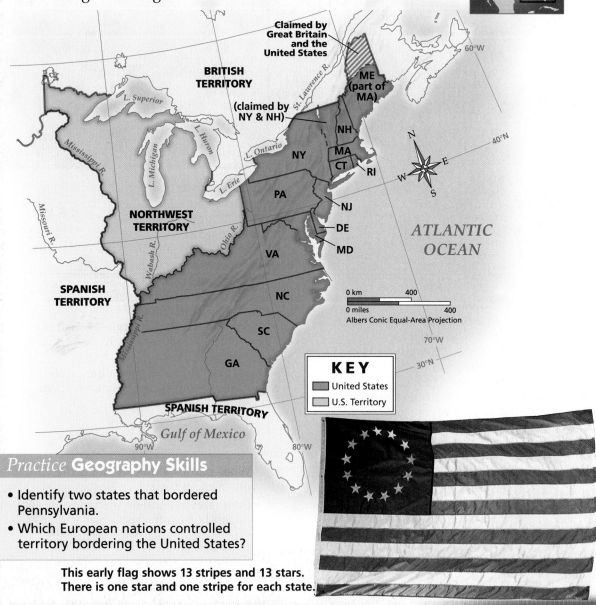

Claimed by Great Britain and the United States

BRITISH TERRITORY

(claimed by NY & NH)

ME (part of MA)

NH

NY

MA

CT

RI

PA

NJ

DE

MD

VA

NC

SC

GA

NORTHWEST TERRITORY

SPANISH TERRITORY

SPANISH TERRITORY

ATLANTIC OCEAN

Gulf of Mexico

L. Superior

L. Huron

L. Michigan

L. Ontario

L. Erie

Mississippi R.

Missouri R.

Wabash R.

Ohio R.

St. Lawrence R.

0 km   400
0 miles   400
Albers Conic Equal-Area Projection

60°W
40°N
70°W
30°N
90°W
80°W

KEY
United States
U.S. Territory

Practice Geography Skills

- Identify two states that bordered Pennsylvania.
- Which European nations controlled territory bordering the United States?

This early flag shows 13 stripes and 13 stars. There is one star and one stripe for each state.

Physical Maps

Physical maps show the major physical features of a region, such as seas, rivers, and mountains. The larger the scale of a physical map, the more detail it can show. For example, the map below shows the rivers that run through the American Southwest. If you compare this map to the physical map in the Atlas at the front of this textbook, you will notice that there are several rivers shown on this map that are not shown on the Atlas map.

Practice Geography Skills

• Identify one river that flows through New Mexico.

• Describe the path of the Colorado River.

The Colorado River formed the Grand Canyon in Arizona.

Special-Purpose Maps
Battle Maps

In addition to political maps and physical maps, there are different types of special-purpose maps. These range from road maps to weather maps to election maps. Some special-purpose maps use arrows to show the movement of people and goods from place to place. The map below shows the battles and troop movements that led up to the Battle of Gettysburg in July 1863.

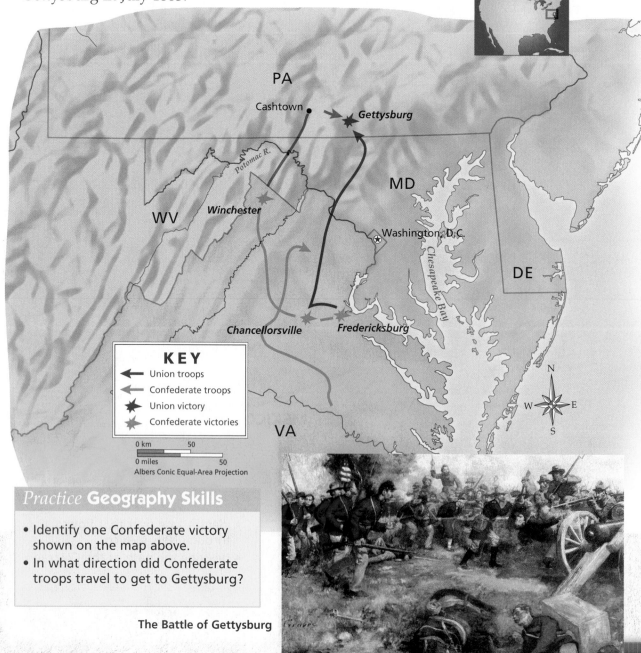

KEY
- ← Union troops
- ← Confederate troops
- ✶ Union victory
- ✶ Confederate victories

0 km 50
0 miles 50
Albers Conic Equal-Area Projection

Practice Geography Skills

- Identify one Confederate victory shown on the map above.
- In what direction did Confederate troops travel to get to Gettysburg?

The Battle of Gettysburg

Election Maps

Have you ever seen a newspaper or watched television during a presidential election? If you have, then you have probably seen an election map. Election maps show all of the states voting in the election. Different colors are used to show which candidates won the vote in which states. The map below shows the election of 1912, when three major candidates were running for President.

KEY

- Theodore Roosevelt
- William Taft
- Woodrow Wilson

Cartoon showing Wilson, Taft, and Roosevelt running for President in 1912

Practice Geography Skills

- Which candidate won in California? In Illinois?
- How many states did Taft win?

Read Visual Information

In this textbook, the information you need to know is presented in written form. Often, however, key information is also summarized in chart form. Charts organize facts and ideas in a visual way that makes them easier to understand.

The next four pages review some of the basic types of visuals you will find in this textbook. Building your ability to analyze visuals will help you get the most out of the information provided.

Timelines

Every chapter in this textbook begins with a timeline. You have used timelines before, but the ones in this book have a few special features. Most of them are made up of two parts:

- **U.S. Events** This is the main part of the timeline. It shows the events that are described in that chapter that took place within the United States.
- **World Events** This part of the timeline shows events that took place in other parts of the world during the same time period. These events are often included because they related to what was going on in the United States.

Timelines make it easier to understand the sequence of events over time. The timelines in this textbook will help you explain how major events are related to one another in time.

Practice **Chart Skills**

- How many years after gold was discovered in California was gold discovered in Australia?
- Which world event was probably related to one of the U.S. events?

U.S. Events

1846 Irish immigration to United States increases.

1849 Gold is discovered in California.

1854 Slavery leads to violence in Kansas.

1840   1850   1860

World Events

1845 Famine strikes Ireland.

1851 Gold is discovered in Australia.

1854 Japan opens ports to foreign ships.

Build Chart Skills

Tables

Tables provide a simple way to organize a large amount of information graphically. A table is arranged in a grid pattern. Columns run vertically, from top to bottom. Rows run horizontally, from left to right.

This sample table summarizes some basic facts about four major wars you will learn about this year. The four wars are listed in the column at the far left, at the beginning of each row. The categories of information given about each war are listed at the top of each column.

Tables can be very large. You may have seen computer spreadsheets that include dozens of columns and rows. Yet, all tables follow the same basic grid pattern shown below.

Four American Wars

War	Dates	Opponents	Results
American Revolution	1775–1781	American colonists vs. Britain	• Colonists win. • United States wins independence.
War of 1812	1812–1814	United States vs. Britain	• No clear winner emerges. • Increased sense of national pride felt.
Mexican-American War	1846–1848	United States vs. Mexico	• United States wins. • United States gains new territory in the West.
Civil War	1861–1865	North vs. South	• North wins. • Union is preserved. • Slavery ends.

Practice Chart Skills

- What were the results of the Mexican-American War?
- In which two wars did Americans fight the same opponent?

Pie Charts

Some charts and graphs in this book show statistical information, that is, information based on exact numbers. Pie charts show statistical information in terms of percentages. The circle, or pie, represents 100 percent of a group. Each wedge of the pie represents one subgroup of the whole. The bigger the wedge is, the larger the group. This pie chart shows how the population of southern states was divided in the year 1850, when slavery was still legal in the South.

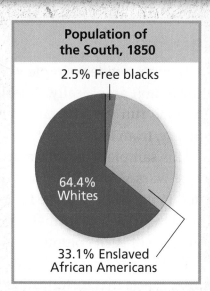

Population of the South, 1850

2.5% Free blacks

64.4% Whites

33.1% Enslaved African Americans

Line Graphs and Bar Graphs

Line graphs and bar graphs show statistical information as it changes over time. The horizontal, or side to side, axis usually tells you the time period covered by the graph. The vertical, or up and down, axis tells you what is being measured. By lining up the points on the graph with the horizontal and vertical axes, you can see how many or how much of something there was at a given time.

On a line graph, the points are connected. On a bar graph, each year is represented by a bar. The line graph (below left) and the bar graph (below right) show the same information: the number of patents, or licenses for new inventions, issued by the U.S. government.

Practice **Chart Skills**

- What percentage of southern society in 1850 was made up of enslaved African Americans?
- About how many patents were issued in 1860? In 1880?

U.S. Patents, 1860–1900

Build Political Cartoon Skills

This textbook also includes a number of political cartoons. Political cartoons are drawings that comment on events and issues through both visual imagery and words. Cartoonists often use symbols and exaggeration to make their points. Learning to analyze cartoons can help you better understand viewpoints on current and historical events.

The first step in analyzing a political cartoon is to identify common symbols. A symbol is an object that represents something besides itself. For example, an eagle or the figure of Uncle Sam may be used to represent the United States. Sometimes, symbols are labeled to make their meaning clear.

Look at the details in the drawing. (In this textbook, we help you focus on certain details by calling them out.) Also, look at the words being spoken by the people in the cartoon. Finally, use both words and pictures to identify the main point the cartoonist is making.

The cartoon below comments on one of the main responsibilities of American citizens: voting.

Practice **Chart Skills**

- Why is the pan labeled "Non-Voters" lower than the pan labeled "Voters"? What does this mean?
- What is the cartoonist's view of people who do not vote?

The cartoon starts with one person who decides not to vote.

The label shows what the scale symbolizes.

Write Like a Historian

You have learned how to use historians' tools to learn about the past. The next step is to write about what you have discovered. Historians share their findings in a variety of ways, including expository essays, narratives, research papers, and persuasive essays or speeches.

At the end of each unit in this textbook, you will find a Writing Workshop. Each Writing Workshop presents detailed instruction about one type of writing. You will have a chance to practice each type.

Expository Essays

An expository essay is a piece of writing that explains something in detail.

1 Select and Narrow Your Topic

Define exactly what you want your essay to do. Do you want to describe a process? Compare and contrast two ideas? Explain the causes and effects of a historical event or development? Explore possible solutions to a problem? You cannot plan your essay until you know what you are trying to do in it.

2 Gather Evidence

Create a graphic organizer that identifies details to include in your essay, such as the one shown below.

3 Write a First Draft

Write a topic sentence, and then organize the essay based on what you are trying to do. If your essay describes a process, write about the steps of the process in order. If your essay explores solutions to a problem, state the problem, and then describe different possible solutions.

4 Revise and Proofread

Make sure that all the details support your topic sentence.

Problem	Suggested Solutions	Evaluation of Solution
The Articles of Confederation left the nation weak because they did not provide for a central authority.	Leave the Articles alone, and persuade other countries and Americans to respect the new nation.	Not practical—what would make more established governments and local rebels accept a weak authority?
	Get rid of the Articles, and create an entirely new plan.	Possible, but it would be a huge task to start all over again.

If you were writing a problem-solution essay, you might create a chart like this to help you organize your ideas.

Narrative Essays

History is like a story. It has characters, both leaders and everyday people. It has a setting where events take place. It even has a plot, in which events unfold, conflicts arise, and resolutions occur.

1 Select and Narrow Your Topic

In this textbook, you will be asked to write narratives about the past. You might be asked to imagine a setting and describe how it affects what is happening. You might be asked to take the point of view of one of history's characters. Or you might be asked to explain the conflict or resolution of a historical situation. First, you must understand what you are being asked to do or who you are asked to be.

Suppose you are asked to imagine you are a pioneer traveling from Missouri to Oregon by wagon train in the 1840s. You can use your imagination and your knowledge of history to create a narrative. For example, how do you feel about the long journey? Would you miss the home you had left behind? Do you think the trip is worth the trouble? Identifying your viewpoint will help you plan your narrative.

2 Gather Details

Brainstorm a list of details you would like to include in your narrative.

3 Write a First Draft

Start by writing a simple opening sentence that conveys the main idea of your essay. Continue by writing a colorful story that has interesting details. Write a conclusion that sums up the main points presented in your essay.

4 Revise and Proofread

Check to make sure you have not begun too many sentences with the word *I*. Replace general words with more colorful ones.

Main idea → Today we rose before dawn and piled into our packed wagons to leave for Oregon. Though excited by the prospect of the journey, I felt sad to leave Missouri. It's

Details → the only home I have ever known. Father says that the trip will be long and difficult—more than 2,000 miles through hard country. He warned that we had to reach Oregon before winter set in. Despite such warnings, I could see how

Summary of viewpoint → excited he was to start our family's new life.

Research Papers

Research papers present information that you have found about a topic.

1 Select and Narrow Your Topic

Choose a topic that interests you. Make sure that your topic is not too broad. For example, instead of writing a report on Native Americans, you might write a report about the Cherokees who were forced to move west in 1837 on a journey known as the Trail of Tears.

2 Acquire Information

Locate several sources of information about the topic from the library or on the Internet. Be sure to evaluate the source. Is it reliable? How does the information compare to what you have found in other sources?

For each resource, create a source index card. Then, take notes using an index card for each detail or subtopic. On the card, note which source the information was taken from. Use quotation marks when you copy exact words from a source.

3 Make an Outline

Use an outline to decide how to organize your research paper. Sort your index cards in the same order.

4 Write a First Draft

Write an introduction, a body, and a conclusion. If you are preparing your first draft by hand, leave plenty of space between lines so you can go back and add details that you may have left out.

5 Revise and Proofread

Be sure to include transition words between sentences and paragraphs. Here are some examples:

- To describe a process: *first, next, then*
- To show a contrast: *however, although, despite*
- To point out a reason: *since, because, if*
- To signal a conclusion: *therefore, as a result, so*

Introduction

The Trail of Tears

How would you feel if soldiers came to your home and forced you to move thousands of miles away? This may sound like an impossible nightmare. But that is what happened to the Cherokee people in 1838.

Conclusion

Therefore, the Trail of Tears was a tragedy for the Cherokees and other Native Americans. Sadly, there would be more clashes with settlers in the years to come.

Persuasive Essays

A persuasive essay is a piece of writing that supports a position or opinion.

1 Select and Narrow Your Topic

Choose a historical topic that has at least two sides or two interpretations. Choose a side. Decide which argument will best persuade your audience to agree with your point of view.

2 Gather Evidence

Create a chart that states your position at the top, and then lists the pros and cons for your position in two columns below. Predict and address the strongest arguments against your viewpoint.

3 Write a First Draft

Write a strong thesis statement that clearly states your position. Continue by presenting the strongest arguments in favor of your position and acknowledging and refuting opposing arguments.

4 Revise and Proofread

Check to make sure you have made a logical argument and that you have not oversimplified the argument.

Practice Your Writing

In this textbook, you will have many opportunities to practice your writing skills. The chart below shows how you can build writing skills in each section, chapter, and unit of this textbook.

Check Your Progress: Writing (end of every section)	Review and Assessment: Writing (end of every chapter)	Writing Workshop (end of every unit)
Helps you build writing skills you will need to complete the unit-level Writing Workshop.	Helps you practice the skills from Check Your Progress and build toward the unit-level Writing Workshop.	Helps you learn and practice the steps needed to write a type of essay—expository, research, or persuasive.
Examples: • Identify causes. • Identify effects. • Use a cause-and-effect chart to organize information.	*Example:* • Write a paragraph describing one cause and one effect of an event.	*Example:* • Expository Composition: Causes and Effects

Unit 1

Across the Atlantic Sailing three small ships across the Atlantic in uncharted waters, Christopher Columbus opened the Americas to regular contact with the people of Europe.

1492

Slave Trade By the late 1600s, a steady stream of ships carried enslaved Africans to the Americas. Most enslaved Africans were forced to work on plantations in the West Indies and in South America. Slavery grew in North America after the plantation system took hold in the South.

LATE 1600s

Review: Beginnings of American History

The Five Nations The Iroquois of the Eastern Woodlands formed the League of the Iroquois to keep the peace among their peoples. The figures on this comb represent the five nations in the League.

1500s

The Pilgrim Community Seeking freedom to practice their religion, Pilgrims founded the colony of Plymouth. In time, the idea of religious freedom for all would become a cornerstone of American democracy.

1620

English Colonies Flourish The English founded 13 colonies along the Atlantic coast of North America. People in the New England, Middle, and Southern colonies developed distinct ways of life. Some children attended school, where they learned reading, writing, and arithmetic.

1750

Roots of the American People
Prehistory–1500

Chapter Preview

For centuries, the Americas were geographically isolated from other parts of the world. Native Americans developed varied ways of life. At the same time, different cultures were developing in Africa, Asia, and Europe.

☑ **What You Will Learn**

Early people spread across the Americas and eventually built great civilizations.

Peoples of North America developed a wide variety of cultures.

A complex trade network linked Africa, Asia, and Europe.

Traditions that came to the Americas from Europe included Judaism, Christianity, and Greek and Roman ideas about government.

| Prehistory | | 1000 | | 1200 |

World Events

20,000–30,000 years ago First people come to the Americas.

1095 Pope calls for crusades to begin.

Quick View Video
View the chapter video for a quick preview of the main ideas.

Hundreds of years ago, Native Americans built these cliff dwellings at Mesa Verde in present-day Colorado.

1200

1200s African empire of Mali rises.

1300s Renaissance begins in Europe.

1400

1400s Aztecs conquer most of Mexico.

1500s Iroquois League is formed.

1600

History Reading Skill Read Actively

How did early Native Americans work together?

In this chapter, you will practice active reading. Read the following description of how the Iroquois people joined together. The side notes suggest ways to read actively.

Introduction About 1570, five Iroquois nations formed the League of the Iroquois. According to Iroquois tradition, a leader named Hiawatha helped found the League. Chief Elias Johnson relates the story of Hiawatha in this selection.

> *Before reading, check features such as an introduction and vocabulary list.*

Vocabulary Before you read the selection, find the meaning of these words in a dictionary: *assembly, tremble, hordes.*

The council met. Hiawatha entered the assembly with even more than ordinary attention. Every eye was fixed upon him when he began to address the council in the following words.

"Friends and Brothers: You being members of many tribes, you have come from a great distance. The voice of war has aroused you up. . . . You tremble for your safety. Believe me, I am with you. . . . To oppose those hordes of northern tribes, singly and alone, would prove certain destruction. . . . We must unite ourselves into one common band of brothers, we must have one voice. . . . This will give us strength."

> *Connect to your own knowledge about ways that working together creates strength.*

—from *Cry of the Thunderbird: The American Indian's Own Story*

READING REVIEW

Why did Hiawatha suggest forming the League?

> *Ask questions or use review questions to set a purpose for reading. Then, read to answer those questions.*

Read Actively
- Preview each section. Read introductory material, headings, and marginal notes. Scan illustrations and graphic material.
- Notice the text organization, and use it to plan a specific reading approach, such as comparing and contrasting.
- Formulate questions based on your preview. Review the questions that appear within the section or at the end of the section. Then, read to find answers to your questions.
- Connect what you read to your prior knowledge or personal experience.

Document-Based Questions
1. How can you tell that the other members of the council respected Hiawatha?
2. What was the goal of the League of the Iroquois?
3. According to Hiawatha, why should the Five Nations band together?

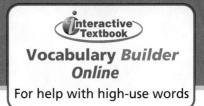
Vocabulary *Builder*

Previewing High-Use Academic Words

High-Use Word	Definition	Sample History Sentence
deprive (dee PRĪV) (Section 1, p. 7)	*v.* to take away	People who were enslaved were <u>deprived</u> of their freedom.
reside (ree ZĪD) (Section 1, p. 8)	*v.* to live; to make one's home in	The people who <u>reside</u> in a city or state make up its population.
currency (KUH rehn see) (Section 2, p. 11)	*n.* items used as money	The dollar is the basic unit of <u>currency</u> in the United States.
distinct (dihs TIHNKT) (Section 2, p. 12)	*adj.* clearly different in quality	There are <u>distinct</u> differences between the climate of Alaska and the climate of Florida.
transmit (trans MIHT) (Section 3, p. 16)	*v.* to pass along; to send	Traders <u>transmitted</u> goods and ideas from one place to another.
sphere (sfeer) (Section 3, p. 17)	*n.* rounded shape	Some early people believed Earth was flat rather than shaped like a <u>sphere</u>.
participate (pahr TIHS uh payt) (Section 4, p. 24)	*v.* to take part in	Adult American citizens have the right to <u>participate</u> in elections.
precise (pree SĪS) (Section 4, p. 27)	*adj.* exact; accurate	Early people were able to create <u>precise</u> calendars based on the sun.

Previewing Key Terms and People

glacier, p. 6
irrigation, p. 7
surplus, p. 7
civilization, p. 8
culture, p. 10
culture area, p. 11

kayak, p. 12
potlatch, p. 12
adobe, p. 12
clan, p. 15
sachem, p. 15
Muhammad, p. 16
Mansa Musa, p. 18
navigation, p. 19
Zheng He, p. 19
monotheism, p. 22
Jesus, p. 23
salvation, p. 23

Vasco da Gama

direct democracy, p. 24
republic, p. 25
feudalism, p. 25
Martin Luther, p. 26
Henry the Navigator, p. 27
Vasco da Gama, p. 27

Kayak

The Earliest Americans

Objectives

1. Understand how people may have first reached the Americas.
2. Find out how people learned to farm.
3. Explore the civilizations of the Mayas, Aztecs, and Incas.

Prepare to Read

Reading Skill

Preview Before Reading The first step in active reading is to preview the text. Read the Prepare to Read information. Scan all the headings and side-margin notes. Read the captions and look at the illustrations. Finally, read the questions that appear at the section's end.

Vocabulary *Builder*

High-Use Words

deprive, p. 7
reside, p. 8

Key Terms

glacier, p. 6
irrigate, p. 7
surplus, p. 7
civilization, p. 8

☆ **Background Knowledge** Tens of thousands of years ago, no humans lived in North America or South America. In this section, you will learn how the first humans may have come to the Americas.

Main Idea
The first people in the Americas came from Asia and eventually learned to farm.

The First Americans

Scientists have various ideas about how people came to the Americas. Some think that people may have come from Asia in large canoes. However, most think that the first humans arrived by land.

The Land Bridge Theory Between 10,000 and 100,000 years ago, much of the world was covered by **glaciers,** or thick sheets of ice. As more and more of the world's water froze, the level of the oceans dropped. Areas that once were covered by shallow water became dry land. One of these areas stretched between Siberia and Alaska. It became a bridge of land many miles wide. The area now lies under a narrow waterway called the Bering Strait.

The land bridge may have appeared and disappeared several times. However, many scientists believe that people first came to North America between 20,000 and 30,000 years ago. They were hunters, possibly following the coast of Siberia as they hunted prehistoric mammals such as the woolly mammoth. Over thousands of years, hunting bands moved over the land. They eventually spread across North America and South America.

Woolly mammoth

Other Theories Not everyone agrees with the land-bridge theory. Some scientists think that people may first have crossed the arctic waters by boat and traveled southward along the Pacific coast. This idea is known as the coastal-route theory.

Many Native Americans also dispute both the land-bridge theory and the coastal-route theory. Each group has its own tradition explaining how they settled in the lands they did. These traditions appear in their creation stories.

Learning to Farm For centuries, early humans could fill most of their needs by hunting. Game animals provided food, furs for clothing, and bones for tools.

In time, many of the larger animals began to disappear. <u>Deprived</u> of their main source of food, hunters had to change their ways of life. In many places, hunters became gatherers. They traveled from place to place, searching for wild plants and small game.

Some 8,000 years ago, gatherers in Mexico began growing food plants, including squash and lima beans. The discovery of farming transformed life. No longer did families have to wander in search of food. In dry regions, farmers developed methods of irrigation. **Irrigation** is a method to water crops by channeling water from rivers or streams. Farmers also learned how to raise animals such as cattle, pigs, and llamas.

With a more dependable food supply, the population grew more rapidly. Once Native Americans produced **surplus,** or extra, food, they traded with others. Some farming communities grew into cities. The cities became centers of government and religious life.

☑**Checkpoint** **How do scientists think people first reached the Americas?**

Vocabulary *Builder*
<u>deprive</u> (dee PRĪV) *v.* to take away

Preview Before Reading
Preview the matter on the following pages under the heading "Three Civilizations." What do the subheadings, images, and captions tell you?

The First Americans Arrive

ASIA

Bering Sea

NORTH AMERICA

PACIFIC OCEAN

ATLANTIC OCEAN

SOUTH AMERICA

180°
160°W
140°W
120°W 100°W 80°W 60°W
80°N
0°
20°W
40°W
60°W
40°N
20°N

KEY
- Glaciers
- Land bridge
- → Land-bridge theory
- → Coastal-route theory

0 km 1,000
0 miles 1,000
Azimuthal Equal-Area Projection

MAP MASTER®
Skills Activity

Scientists think the first people arrived in the Americas about 10,000 to 100,000 years ago.

(a) Interpret a Map According to the land bridge theory, what body of water did Asians cross to reach the Americas?

(b) Draw Inferences Why do you think the population continued to spread southward?

MapMaster ◯nline
For: Interactive map
Visit: PHSchool.com
Web Code: mvp-1011

Explore More Video
To learn more about the
Aztec Empire, view
the video.

Tenochtitlán The Aztecs built
their capital city of Tenochtitlán
on a group of islands in the
middle of a lake. The center of the
city was dominated by a huge
temple (inset). **Critical Thinking:**
*Draw Conclusions How does
this picture support the idea that
the Aztec society was highly
organized?*

Main Idea
The Mayas, Aztecs, and Incas
developed advanced
civilizations in Central and
South America.

Vocabulary *Builder*
<u>reside</u> (ree ZID) *v.* to live; to make
one's home in

Three Civilizations

With the development of cities came the beginnings of civilization. A **civilization** is an advanced culture in which people have developed cities, science, and industries. Over the centuries, several civilizations rose and declined in the Americas. The largest were the civilizations of the Mayas, the Aztecs, and the Incas.

Mayas Between A.D. 250 and A.D. 900, the Mayas built cities in what is now Mexico and Central America. These splendid cities contained large public plazas lined with pyramids, temples, ball courts, and palaces.

The Mayas did more, however. They developed arts, a system of government, and a written language. They also observed the stars. From their study of the heavens, they created the most accurate calendar known until modern times. They also carved stories of their past and their gods into the stones of their buildings.

Around A.D. 900, the Mayas began to abandon their cities. Why this happened remains a mystery. Disease or overpopulation may have caused the decline. Although the Mayan civilization is gone, the Mayan language still forms the root of more than 20 languages of Central America.

Aztecs As Mayan civilization declined, a new civilization was on the rise. The Aztecs built a great capital city, Tenochtitlán (tay noch tee TLAHN), on the site of present-day Mexico City. It was built on a series of islands in a large lake. The city was connected to the mainland by stone roadways. In many parts of Tenochtitlán, farmers raised crops on floating platforms. More than 200,000 people <u>resided</u> in Tenochtitlán at its height, making it perhaps the largest city in the world at that time.

The center of the city was a sacred place with dozens of temples that honored the Aztec gods. This was appropriate because religion dominated Aztec life. To the Aztecs, prosperity depended on the good will of the gods. Like a number of other ancient peoples, the Aztecs practiced human sacrifice as an offering to their gods.

During the 1400s, Aztec armies brought half of modern-day Mexico under their control. The Aztecs proved to be effective but harsh rulers. Conquered tribes were forced to send treasure, food, and prisoners to the Aztec capital. The Aztecs forced the people they conquered to pay high taxes. Resentful subjects would eventually turn on the Aztecs when the empire most needed allies.

Incas In the 1400s, the largest empire was not in Europe or Asia. It was in South America. The vast empire of the Incas stretched down the coast of South America along the Andes, across the Atacama desert, and reached the fringes of the Amazon rain forest.

At the center of the empire was the Inca capital, Cuzco (KOOS koh). Cuzco was linked to other cities and towns by a great network of roads. A Spaniard who traveled the main Inca highway called it "the finest road to be seen in the world."

The Incas constructed buildings of huge stones carefully shaped to fit together. Their engineers built walls to hold soil in their fields, canals to carry water, and bridges over deep canyons. The Incas produced fine weavings and metalwork. Inca rulers wore gold and silver jewelry, and their palaces contained plates of gold.

Figure of an Inca ruler or priest

✓**Checkpoint** Where were the Aztec and Inca civilizations located?

⭐ **Looking Back and Ahead** Most Native Americans did not live in large cities like Tenochtitlán or Cuzco. In the next section, you will learn about the ways of life of people north of Mexico.

Section 1 | **Check Your Progress**

Progress Monitoring ⬤nline

For: Self-test with instant help
Visit: PHSchool.com
Web Code: mva-1011

Comprehension and Critical Thinking

1. **(a) List** Name one skill that people had to learn in order to grow crops.
   (b) Identify Benefits What benefits could farmers get from learning to raise animals?

2. **(a) Define** What is a civilization?
   (b) Apply Information How did the Mayas and Aztecs fit that definition?

🔄 **Reading Skill**

3. **Preview Before Reading** Preview Section 2. Read its headings, study its images and captions, and review its questions. Tell what you think Section 2 will be about. Use the headings to identify the text organization. How can you use this information to plan your reading?

Vocabulary Builder

Answer the following questions in complete sentences that show your understanding of the key terms.

4. How did the growth of glaciers affect water levels in the ocean?
5. Why was learning about irrigation important for farmers?
6. What are the advantages of having a surplus of crops?

Writing

7. Outline a paragraph in response to the following question: How did early civilizations use industry and science to improve their way of life? Then, list four or five supporting details. Next, write a concluding sentence.

Cultures of North America

Objectives

1. Learn about the earliest peoples of North America.
2. Discover what different groups of Native Americans had in common.
3. Explore the impact of geography on Native American cultures.

Prepare to Read

Reading Skill

Apply Prior Knowledge You can prepare for reading by building on and connecting to what you already know. This can be information from an earlier section, chapter, or other reading. It can also be prior knowledge from your own life experience. Applying this knowledge while you are reading helps you interact with and engage in the text. This, in turn, will help you understand and remember what you have read.

Vocabulary *Builder*

High-Use Words

<u>currency</u>, p. 11
<u>distinct</u>, p. 12

Key Terms

culture, p. 10
culture area, p. 11
kayak, p. 12
potlatch, p. 12
adobe, p. 12
clan, p. 15
sachem, p. 15

⭐ **Background Knowledge** In the last section, you explored civilizations in Central America and South America. In this section, you will read about the peoples who settled farther north.

Main Idea
Early cultures developed in the Southwest and the Mississippi Valley.

First Cultures of North America

In North America, as elsewhere, groups of people developed unique **cultures**, or ways of life. Around 3,000 years ago, various groups began to emerge in an area stretching from the Appalachian Mountains to the Mississippi Valley. We call these people Mound Builders because they constructed large piles of earth. Many mounds were burial places, but some served as foundations for public buildings. One group of Mound Builders, the Mississippians, built the first cities in North America. As many as 40,000 people may have lived in the largest Mississippian city, Cahokia, in present-day Illinois.

A far different culture, which we call the Anasazi, emerged in southern Utah, Colorado, northern Arizona, and New Mexico. They built large cliff dwellings, probably to defend against attacks by outsiders such as the Navajos or even the Aztecs. Their largest community housed about 1,000 people. The Anasazis were skilled in making baskets, pottery, and jewelry. They also engaged in trade. Mysteriously, by 1300, the Anasazis had abandoned their cliff dwellings.

Anasazi pottery

From about 300 B.C. to A.D. 1450, highly skilled farmers called the Hohokam dug irrigation canals in the deserts of present-day Arizona. Trade brought them in contact with people who lived on the Gulf of California. The Hohokam traded for seashells, which they used to create jewelry and religious objects.

☑ **Checkpoint**   **For what purposes were mounds built?**

Ways of Life

Scholars classify Native Americans into several culture areas, regions in which groups of people have a similar way of life. Though these cultures were very different from one another, many shared some basic traits.

Meeting Basic Needs Early Native American societies developed a variety of ways to meet their needs. In many areas, women collected roots, wild seeds, nuts, acorns, and berries. Men hunted for game and fished. Wild game was plentiful in regions like the Pacific Coast and the Eastern Woodlands.

In many culture areas, agriculture allowed people to grow and store food. Native Americans learned to grow crops suited to the climate in which they lived. They used pointed sticks for digging. Bones or shells served as hoes. Some used fertilizer, such as dead fish, to make the soil more productive. Where Native Americans lived by farming, their population was much larger than in nonfarming areas.

Trade was a common activity in all the North American cultures. In some areas, items such as seashells or beads were used as <u>currency</u>. Shells, flint for making fires, copper, and salt were all important trade items.

Shared Beliefs Many Native Americans felt a close relationship to the natural world. They believed that spirits dwelled in nature and that these spirits were part of their daily lives.

Traditions reflected these beliefs. For example, the Indians of the Southeast held the Green Corn Ceremony in late summer. The ritual, which could last for more than a week, was a form of natural and spiritual renewal at the end of the growing season. The Pueblo Indians revered spirits known as kachinas. To teach their children about these benevolent spirits, the Pueblos carved kachina dolls.

Native Americans also had a strong oral tradition. Storytellers memorized history and beliefs and then recited them. In this way, their tradition was passed on from generation to generation.

☑ **Checkpoint**   **How did North American cultures meet their needs?**

Main Idea
Many of the varied cultures of North America shared some basic features.

Vocabulary *Builder*
currency (KUH rehn see) *n.* items used as money

Native American Farmers
Early farmers made and used stone tools such as the digging stick and axe shown to the left. **Critical Thinking:** *Clarify Problems Based on this picture, what difficulties might these farmers face?*

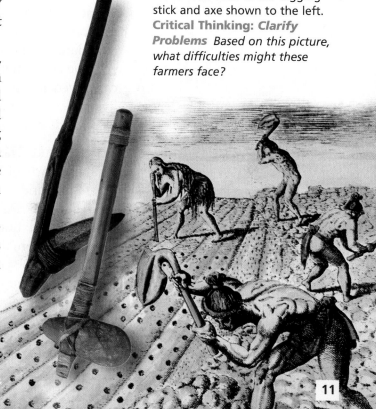

Vocabulary *Builder*
distinct (dihs TIHNKT) *adj.* clearly different in quality

Native Americans of North America

Well before 10,000 B.C., Native Americans had spread across the North American continent. They had adapted to the various climates and living conditions of the lands in which they settled. By A.D. 1500, when the first Europeans reached the Americas, the Native Americans living in North America were a richly diverse group of people with underlined ways of life.

Far North The people of the Arctic lived in a vast and harsh land, some of it covered with ice all year long. The people survived on fish, shellfish, and birds. They also hunted marine mammals, such as whales, seals, and walruses, from **kayaks**, small boats made from skins. In the summer, they fished on the rivers and hunted caribou.

South of the Arctic lay the dense forests of the subarctic region. With a climate too cold for farming, subarctic peoples relied on animals and plants of the forest for food. Most hunted caribou, moose, bear, and smaller animals.

Northwest Many Native Americans lived in the region of the Pacific Northwest, the land that stretches from southern Alaska to northern California. Deer and bears roamed forests rich with roots and berries. Rivers swarmed with salmon. With so much food available, people here were able to live in large, permanent settlements even though they were not farmers.

In many societies of the Northwest, high-ranking people practiced a custom called the potlatch. A **potlatch** was a ceremony at which the hosts showered their guests with gifts such as woven cloth, baskets, canoes, and furs. A family's status was judged by how much wealth it could give away.

Far West The people of the Far West lived in different geographic regions. Winters could be very cold in the forests and grasslands of the north. On the other hand, southern parts could be desertlike. In California, with its warm summers and mild winters, food was abundant. People there ate small game, fish, and berries.

Housing differed, depending on the area. Some Native Americans lived in pit houses, which were dug into the ground. Others lived in cone-shaped houses covered with bark. In the north, houses were made of wooden planks.

Southwest The area that is now Arizona, New Mexico, and the southern parts of Utah and Colorado was dry most of the year. But in late July and August, thunderstorms drenched the desert. All the groups in this area did some farming, although certain groups also followed and hunted animals. Farming peoples had to learn to collect and store the rain for the dry times.

The Pueblo people such as the Hopis and Zunis had stable towns that lasted for hundreds of years. To protect themselves from attack, they built large apartment houses made of **adobe**, or sun-dried brick.

Apply Prior Knowledge
What do you know about apartment life? Use this knowledge to imagine and describe Pueblo homes.

Homes of Native Americans

Native Americans lived in several distinct culture areas. In each region, geography and climate helped shape the people's way of life. **Critical Thinking:** *Apply Information* Look at the map and the pictures. Identify the group that lived in tepees.

Living in the Arctic
The Arctic is bitterly cold throughout the long, harsh winter. Native Americans such as the Inuits kept warm inside igloos made from blocks of ice.

Living in the Eastern Woodlands
With good farmland and plentiful forests, people such as the Iroquois could build sturdier homes. These wood-framed longhouses had separate sections for each family.

Living on the Great Plains
On the grasslands of the western Great Plains, wood was scarce, but buffalo were plentiful. Plains Indians such as the Cheyennes lived in tepees made from buffalo hide.

Inuit

Kutchin

Inuit

Inuit

Hudson Bay

Tlingit

Bella Coola

Kwakuitl

PACIFIC OCEAN

Cree

Blackfeet

Mandan

Dakota

Ojibwa

Algonquin

Montagnais

Huron

Nez Percés

Crow

Iroquois

Coos

Pequot

ATLANTIC OCEAN

Shoshone

Leni-Lenape

Pomos

Miami

Cheyenne

Arapaho

Shawnee

Navajo

Pueblo

Osage

Cherokee

Hohokam

Hopi

Comanche

Natchez

Apache

Gulf of Mexico

Caribbean Sea

KEY

- Arctic / Subarctic
- Northwest Coast
- California / Great Basin / Plateau
- Southwest
- Great Plains
- Eastern Woodlands
- Southeast

The Iroquois Constitution

"Whenever the Confederate Lords shall assemble for the purpose of holding a council, the Onondaga Lords shall open it by expressing their gratitude to their cousin Lords and greeting them, and they shall make an address and offer thanks to the earth where men dwell, to the streams of water . . . to the forest trees for their usefulness, to the animals that serve as food and give their pelts for clothing . . . and to the Great Creator who dwells in the heavens above."

—Iroquois Constitution

The figures on this Seneca comb represent the five Iroquois nations.

Reading Primary Sources
Skills Activity

The constitution of the Iroquois League was at first a spoken rather than a written document. The excerpt above describes how members of the Iroquois League were to begin a meeting.

(a) **Apply Information** What attitude toward nature does this selection reflect?

(b) **Draw Conclusions** Why do you think members of the Iroquois League wanted to begin each meeting with a set ritual?

Great Plains The Great Plains is a vast region stretching between the Mississippi River and the Rocky Mountains. The people of the eastern Plains lived mainly by farming. Women planted corn, beans, and squash in river valleys. Many people lived in earth lodges. These buildings had log frames and were covered with soil.

Much of the western Great Plains was too dry and too matted with grass to be farmed. The treeless land provided few building materials. In the west, some people lived in tepees made of animal skins. Other Plains people dug round pits near their fields for shelter.

Hunting parties followed buffalo across the plains. The Plains people depended on the buffalo for many things. They ate the meat and used the hides to make tepees, robes, and shields. Buffalo bones were made into tools.

Eastern Woodlands Hundreds of years ago, most of what is now the eastern United States was covered by forests of maples, birches, pines, and beeches. The earliest woodlands people lived by hunting, fishing, and foraging for nuts and berries. By about A.D. 1000, a number of woodlands people had taken up farming.

Two groups dominated the Eastern Woodlands. One group spoke Algonquian (al GOHN kee un) languages. The Algonquian people were scattered through southern Canada, the Great Lakes area, and along the Atlantic coast to Virginia. The other groups, speaking Iroquoian (IHR uh kwoy an) languages, lived in what is now New York.

The Iroquois were made up of five distinct nations. Each nation was made up of **clans**, or groups of families that were related to one another. Because membership in a clan was passed from a mother to her children, women had great influence in Iroquois society. They owned all the property that belonged to a clan. Women also chose the clan's **sachem**, or tribal chief.

During the 1500s, the five Iroquois nations went through a period of constant warfare. Finally, Iroquois leaders convinced their people to make peace. They formed a union called the League of the Iroquois. It established a council to make laws to keep the peace. Each tribe was still free to deal with its own affairs.

Southeast The climate in the Southeast was mild, but the summers were steamy and hot. The land and climate supported farming. People such as the Cherokees and Creeks built houses on wooden frames, covered with straw mats. They then plastered the houses with mud clay to keep the interiors cool and dry.

The Natchez people of the Gulf Coast created a complex society. At the top stood the ruler, called the Great Sun, and the nobles. At the bottom were commoners, known as Stinkards. By law, all nobles—including the Great Sun himself—had to marry Stinkards. In this way, membership in each class kept changing.

Cherokee mask

☑**Checkpoint** **In what culture areas was hunting the main way of life?**

☆ **Looking Back and Ahead** In this section, you learned about Native American cultures. In the next sections, you will explore cultures that developed on the other side of the world.

Section 2 | **Check Your Progress**

Progress Monitoring Online
For: Self-test with instant help
Visit: PHSchool.com
Web Code: mva-1012

Comprehension and Critical Thinking

1. (a) Recall What role did nature play in many Native American religious beliefs?
(b) Draw Inferences How does that emphasis on nature reflect the everyday life of the people?

2. (a) Identify Identify two culture areas where farming was the main way of life.
(b) Analyze Cause and Effect Why do you think farming did not develop extensively in the Arctic and the subarctic regions?

Reading Skill

3. Apply Prior Knowledge Reread the first paragraph under the heading "Native Americans of North America." How is your culture group different from others? How is it the same? Use this knowledge to describe how Native American cultures were the same and different.

Vocabulary *Builder*

Fill in the blank in each question with a key term from this section.

4. The _____ of a people includes its customs, beliefs, and ways of making a living.
5. The _____ provided leadership in Iroquois communities.
6. Members of the same _____ shared a common ancestor.

Writing

7. Create a chart that shows how three different groups of Native Americans adapted to the regions in which they lived. Use the following column headings: Region, Way of Life, Diet, Shelter.

Trade Networks of Asia and Africa

Objectives

1. Learn about the role played by Muslims in world trade.
2. Discover how great trading states rose in East Africa and West Africa.
3. Find out how China dominated an important trade route across Asia.

Prepare to Read

Reading Skill

Ask Questions Asking questions when you read will help you organize your reading plan and get involved with the text. You can use your questions, for example, to set a reading purpose— answering the questions. Two ways to generate questions are to restate headings and to study the review questions at the end of the section.

Vocabulary *Builder*

High-Use Words

transmit, p. 16

sphere, p. 17

Key Terms and People

Muhammad, p. 16

Mansa Musa, p. 18

navigation, p. 19

Zheng He, p. 19

★ **Background Knowledge** In the previous section, you learned how important trade was to Native Americans. In this section, you will learn how trade helped link together the people of Asia, Africa, and Europe.

The Muslim Link in Trade

Main Idea
The Muslim world linked traders across three continents.

From earliest times, trade linked groups who lived at great distances from one another. As trade developed, merchants established regular trade routes. These merchants carried their culture with them as they traveled.

By the 1500s, a complex trade network linked Europe, Africa, and Asia. Much of this trade passed through the Arabian Peninsula in the Middle East. Ships from China and India brought their cargoes of spices, silks, and gems to ports on the Red Sea. The precious cargoes were then taken overland to markets throughout the Middle East.

Rise of Islam The growth in trade was also linked to the rise of the religion of Islam. Islam emerged on the Arabian Peninsula in the 600s. Its founder was the prophet **Muhammad.** Muhammad taught that there is one true God. Followers of Islam, called Muslims, believed that the Quran (ku RAHN), the sacred book of Islam, contained the exact word of God as revealed to Muhammad.

Vocabulary *Builder*
transmit (trans MIHT) *v.* to pass along; to send

Islam was <u>transmitted</u> rapidly through conquest and trade. Arab armies swept across North Africa and into Spain. Muslim merchants also spread their religion far into Africa, and from Persia to India. Millions of people across three continents became Muslims.

Advances in Learning Arab scholars made remarkable contributions to mathematics, medicine, and astronomy. They helped develop algebra and later passed it along to Europe. Arab astronomers measured the size of Earth, supporting the Greek belief that Earth was a sphere. Arabs also made important advances in technology. They built ships with large, triangular sails that allowed captains to use the wind even if it changed direction.

☑**Checkpoint** **How did Islam spread?**

The African Link in Trade

Africa has a long history of trade, going back as far as 3100 B.C., when the great civilization of Egypt arose. Egyptian traders sailed throughout the eastern Mediterranean Sea and the Red Sea to bring home cedar logs, silver, and horses. Following routes south from Egypt, they traded for ivory, spices, copper, and cattle.

East African Trade Centers About A.D. 1000, trade centers began to appear in eastern Africa. The most powerful was Zimbabwe (zim BAH bway), which became the center of a flourishing empire in the 1400s. Zimbabwe lay on the trade route between the east coast and the interior of Africa. Traders passing through Zimbabwe had to pay taxes on their goods.

Trade brought prosperity to a number of cities along the east coast of Africa. Kilwa, the chief trading center, attracted merchant ships from as far away as China. Kilwa traders did a brisk trade with the African interior, exchanging cloth, pottery, and manufactured goods for gold, ivory, and furs. An active slave trade also developed between East Africa and Asia across the Indian Ocean.

Vocabulary *Builder*
sphere (sfeer) *n.* rounded shape

Main Idea
Complex trade networks developed in both East Africa and West Africa.

Ask Questions
Preview the headings on the next two pages. Turn them into questions that you would expect to find the answers to as you read.

Merchants in the Middle East

At outdoor bazaars, Muslim merchants bought and sold goods from around the world. Probably the most valuable goods sold at this Persian bazaar were spices from Southeast Asia, such as the ones shown here. **Critical Thinking:** *Link Past and Present* How is this bazaar similar to a modern shopping area? How is it different?

Cardamom

Curry

Cumin

Mansa Musa
1280?–1337

Every Muslim must make a *hajj*, or pilgrimage, to the holy city of Mecca. Mansa Musa's hajj became famous. His escort included 80 camels, each carrying 300 pounds of gold. Thousands of servants and officials accompanied the emperor across the Sahara.

Word of the emperor's hajj reached Europe. A Portuguese mapmaker described Mansa Musa as "the richest and most noble king in all the land."

Biography Quest

How did Mansa Musa's hajj affect the Egyptian economy?

For: The answer to the question about Mansa Musa

Visit: PHSchool.com

Web Code: mvd-1013

West African Trade Centers Trade networks also linked the Middle East and West Africa. Desert nomads guided caravans, or groups of camels and their cargo, across the vast Sahara, the largest desert in the world.

Ghana was the first major center of trade in West Africa. The kingdom was located between the sources of salt in the desert and the gold fields farther south. By the ninth century, the demand for gold had grown in the Middle East. On the other hand, people in West Africa needed salt in their diet to prevent dehydration in the hot tropical climate. As the trade in gold and salt increased, the rulers of Ghana became rich.

Shifting trade routes and disruptions caused by war gradually led Ghana to weaken. In the 1200s, the kingdom was absorbed into the empire of Mali. Mali reached its height under the Muslim ruler **Mansa Musa.** As Mali prospered, its great city of Timbuktu became a center of learning. Merchants from Mali traded throughout the region for kola nuts, food, and, of course, gold.

In the 1400s, Mali had a number of weak rulers. When nomads captured Timbuktu in 1433, the empire had been in decline for some time. It would soon be replaced by Songhai.

The rulers of Songhai captured Timbuktu in 1468. Songhai rulers restored the city as a center of Islamic learning. Trade across the Sahara expanded, which brought wealth to the Songhai Empire. Salt, gold, and captives for sale as slaves passed through Songhai on the way to Muslim markets in the north.

✓**Checkpoint** **What trading kingdoms arose in West Africa?**

The East Asian Link in Trade

Main Idea
China dominated the trade routes that linked East Asia to the Middle East.

As early as 221 B.C., a strong ruler had unified China into a single empire. Later rulers added to the empire until it covered a large part of the continent of Asia. Highways, canals, and a postal system linked China together.

As China's empire expanded, so did its trade. China established trade links with India, Korea, Japan, the Middle East, and Africa. China's trade centers grew into cities. By the 1200s, Hangzhou (HAN JOW) was one of the world's largest cities.

World Traders China had a higher level of technology than any other civilization of the time. Around 1050, the Chinese invented printing with movable type. This was about 400 years before this technology was developed in Europe.

The Chinese made great advances in navigation. Navigation is the science of locating the position and plotting the course of ships. The Chinese invented the magnetic compass, which made it possible for ships to sail out of sight of land and still find their way home.

By the 1300s Chinese ships were sailing trade routes that stretched from Japan to East Africa. The Chinese explorer Zheng He made several voyages with a fleet of more than 300 giant ships. The fleet visited 30 nations throughout Asia and Africa, trading silks and pottery for spices, gems, medicinal herbs, and ivory.

Spice Trade and the Silk Road Chinese silks, bronze goods, pottery, and spices flowed west from China along a route known as the Silk Road. The Silk Road was one of the great trade routes of ancient times. It was not really a single road but a series of routes that stretched about 5,000 miles from Xi'an (SHE AHN) in China to Persia.

Merchants on the Silk Road brought silk and other goods from China across Asia for sale in Middle Eastern and European markets. Along the way they traded in the Middle East for products like cloves, nutmeg, and peppercorns from the Spice Islands in Southeast Asia. The Silk Road declined in importance when alternative sea routes were discovered.

This Chinese figurine is made of jade, a precious trade item.

☑**Checkpoint** **What was the Silk Road?**

⭐ **Looking Back and Ahead** The trade links between Asia and Africa developed at a time when much of Europe was isolated. In the next section, you will learn about the development of Europe. You will also see how Europe began to look toward the riches of Asia.

Section 3 | **Check Your Progress**

Progress Monitoring ⏺nline
For: Self-test with instant help
Visit: PHSchool.com
Web Code: mva-1013

Comprehension and Critical Thinking

1. **(a) Recall** What role did the Muslim world play in trade?
   (b) Interpret Maps Locate the Arabian Peninsula on a world map. Why was its location ideal for a trading center?

2. **(a) Recall** Why were gold and salt important in West African trade?
   (b) Contrast How did trade in East Africa differ from trade in West Africa?

Reading Skill

3. **Ask Questions** Look at the questions you asked, and look at the section review questions. Did the reading answer those questions? How did previewing help you set purposes and increase your understanding?

Vocabulary *Builder*

4. Write two definitions for the key term *navigation*—one a formal definition for a teacher, the other an informal definition for a younger child.

Writing

5. Consider the following thesis statement: The trading network between Asia, Africa, and Europe began a useful exchange of ideas and products. Write one or two paragraphs to develop that thesis.

Global Trade in the Fifteenth Century

For centuries, merchants and traders used land and sea routes to travel between Europe, Africa, and Asia. Before the first European voyages to the Americas, a global trading network linked the major civilizations of three continents. Gold and salt moved east from Africa while silk and spices moved west from China and India. Use the map below to trace the patterns of global trade.

Ivory

Gold

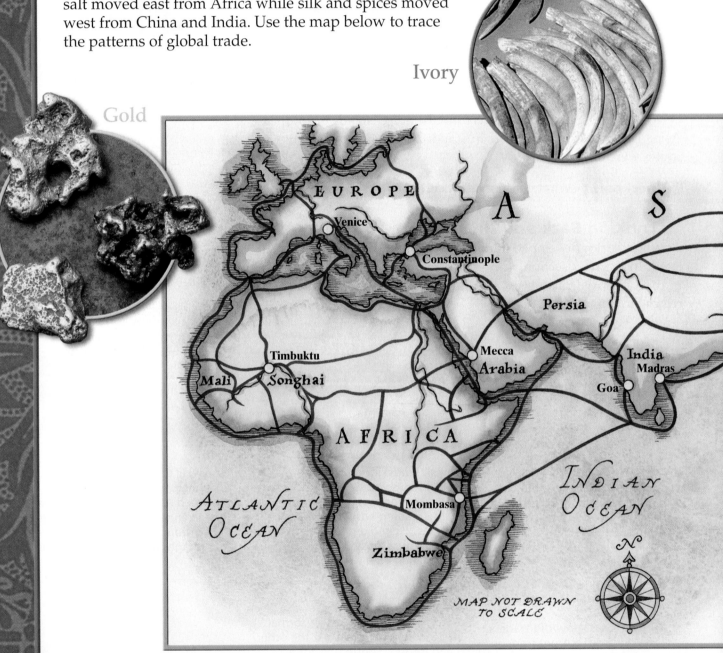

History *Interactive*
Explore Global Trade
Visit: PHSchool.com
Web Code: mvl-1013

Gold, Salt, and Ivory

Trade centers in East and West Africa saw heavy traffic in gold, salt, and ivory. African gold was highly valued in the Middle East.

Salt

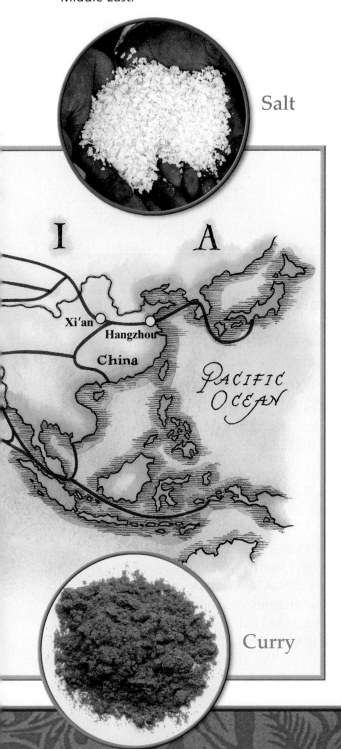

I   A

Xi'an

Hangzhou

China

PACIFIC OCEAN

Curry

Understand Effects:

The Network Expands

When Christopher Columbus sailed west from Spain in 1492, he opened up a new era in global trade. Prior to Columbus's voyage, the Americas were isolated from the flow of goods and ideas that connected Europe, Africa, and Asia. After 1492, the old trade networks expanded across an ocean to a new world of resources.

▲ Trade flourished throughout Asia. Ships from China and India unloaded their cargoes in Arabian ports for overland transport to African or European markets.

Analyze GEOGRAPHY AND HISTORY

Worldwide trade allowed for the exchange of goods and ideas across continents. Write a paragraph describing how West African gold might travel to China.

The European Heritage

Objectives

1. Understand the importance of the Judeo-Christian tradition.

2. Learn how Greece and Rome shaped ideas about government and law.

3. Discover the impact of the Crusades and the Renaissance on Europe.

4. Find out why Europeans began to look beyond their borders.

Prepare to Read

🎧 Reading Skill

Use Graphics to Construct Meaning Textbooks include information beyond the main text that can be useful to your understanding. Nontext material includes maps, tables, charts, photos, and illustrations. In addition, these materials often have accompanying text such as captions or titles. Use this material to gain understanding when you preview, and then refer to it for details as you read.

Vocabulary *Builder*

High-Use Words

<u>participate</u>, p. 24

<u>precise</u>, p. 27

Key Terms and People

monotheism, p. 22

Jesus, p. 23

salvation, p. 23

direct democracy, p. 24

republic, p. 25

feudalism, p. 25

Martin Luther, p. 26

Henry the Navigator, p. 27

Vasco da Gama, p. 27

⭐ **Background Knowledge** In the previous section, you learned how trade influenced civilizations in Asia and Africa. In this section, you will read about how civilization developed in Europe.

The Judeo-Christian Tradition

Main Idea
Judaism and Christianity became the foundation of religious beliefs in Europe.

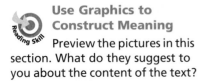
Use Graphics to Construct Meaning
Preview the pictures in this section. What do they suggest to you about the content of the text?

European beliefs and values were shaped by two religions of the ancient Middle East: Judaism and Christianity. The influence of these two religions is known as the Judeo-Christian tradition.

Judaism Around 1700 B.C. a system of beliefs called Judaism arose among the Israelites, a nomadic people of the Middle East. Judaism was the first major world religion to teach monotheism, the idea that there is only one God.

The Israelites credited Moses with bringing God's laws to them. Those laws included the Ten Commandments, a set of religious and moral rules. Jews believed that every Jew must obey the Ten Commandments and other religious and moral laws.

Other early religions regarded rulers as gods. Judaism held that even the most powerful ruler had to obey God's laws. This belief formed the basis for the later view that no person, no matter how powerful or wealthy, is above the law.

Christianity About 2,000 years ago, a Jewish teacher named Jesus of Nazareth began to preach in the region around the Sea of Galilee. Jesus attracted a following. Many believed that he was the Messiah, the Savior chosen by God.

The Gospels, which recount the life of Jesus, tell how crowds flocked to hear Jesus teach and perform miracles. Local officials, however, saw Jesus as a political threat. The Roman rulers of Jerusalem arrested, tried, and crucified Jesus. Followers of Jesus said that he rose from the dead three days later.

The life and teachings of Jesus inspired a new religion, Christianity. Christianity is based on the belief that Jesus was indeed the Messiah, sent by God to save the world. Christians teach that Jesus was, in fact, God in human form.

The teachings of Jesus emphasized love, mercy, and forgiveness. Jesus also taught that all people have an equal chance for salvation, or everlasting life. These beliefs appealed to many people, especially the poor and oppressed. This helped Christianity spread from the Middle East across Europe.

As Christianity spread, the Romans at first viewed it as a threat. Christians were subject to arrest and death. Later, emperors accepted Christianity and made it the official religion of the Roman Empire. As a result, it eventually became the dominant religion of all of Europe.

☑**Checkpoint**   **What does Christianity teach about Jesus?**

The Ten Commandments

❝[I.] I am the Lord your God, who brought you out of the land of Egypt, out of the house of bondage. You shall have no other gods before me. . . .
[III.] You shall not take the name of the Lord your God in vain; . . .
[V.] Honor your father and your mother, that your days may be long in the land which the Lord your God gives you.
[VI.] You shall not kill. . . .
[VIII.] You shall not steal.❞

—Book of Exodus, Revised Standard Version

Painting showing Moses with the Ten Commandments

Reading Primary Sources
Skills Activity

According to the Bible, God gave the Ten Commandments to the Hebrew leader Moses. Five of the Commandments are given above.

(a) Apply Information How does this selection reflect the Judeo-Christian idea of monotheism?

(b) Draw Conclusions How do the Ten Commandments say we should treat other people?

Greek and Roman Traditions

Judaism and Christianity shaped European religious and moral thinking. At the same time, the ancient civilizations of Greece and Rome shaped European political traditions. Greek and Roman ideas would later deeply influence the Founders of the United States.

Athenian Democracy In the fifth century B.C., the Greek city-state of Athens experienced a sudden explosion of learning and creativity. Perhaps its most remarkable achievement was the birth of democracy.

Athens was a direct democracy. **Direct democracy** is a form of government in which an assembly of ordinary citizens makes decisions. This differs from the modern American form of government, in which citizens elect representatives to make laws. Any adult male citizen could <u>participate</u> in the Athenian Assembly. The Athenian leader Pericles described the Athenian idea of democracy:

> ❝Our constitution is named a democracy, because it is in the hands not of the few but of the many. . . . We decide or debate, carefully and in person, all matters of policy.❞
> —Pericles, from *The History of the Peloponnesian War* (Thucydides)

Still, Athenian democracy had limitations. Women, slaves, and foreign-born people could not participate in government.

Athenians believed that a democracy depended on well-rounded, educated citizens. In Athenian schools, boys studied many areas of knowledge, from history and grammar to poetry and music. Because Athenian citizens were expected to voice their opinions in the Assembly, schools also trained students in public speaking.

Roman Government and Law While democracy was developing in ancient Greece, a few small villages in central Italy were growing into the city of Rome. Over time, the Romans developed new traditions in law and government.

Education in Athens
This Greek vase painting shows an Athenian school. At the center, a teacher checks a student's writing tablet. **Critical Thinking: *Interpret Art*** *Identify one other subject that the students at this school are learning.*

Links Across Time

2004 Congress gathers to hear the President speak.

Republican Government

509 B.C. The Roman Republic was established. The elected Senate became the chief governing and law-making body of Rome.

1787 The Founders of the United States admired the Roman Republic. When they wrote the Constitution, they gave lawmaking power to an elected Congress similar to the Roman Senate. But they divided Congress into two separate houses, the Senate and the House of Representatives.

Link to Today ◗nline

Congress Today Today, as in the past, the men and women of Congress make laws that affect the lives of all Americans.

For: Congress in the news
Visit: PHSchool.com
Web Code: mvc-1014

In 509 B.C., the Romans overthrew their king and set up a republic. A **republic** is a form of government in which people choose representatives to govern them. In the Roman Republic, an elected senate and assembly made the laws.

Rome's code of laws defined the rights of citizens. According to the code, everybody was equal under the law. People accused of crimes were considered innocent until proven guilty. These principles form the framework of the American system of justice.

Long years of civil war led to the collapse of the Roman republic. In 27 B.C., a noble named Octavian declared himself emperor. The Roman Empire would last for almost 500 years. During this time, Roman ideas about law and government spread over a wide area.

☑**Checkpoint** How did citizens participate in Greek and Roman government?

New Horizons

After a period of decline, the Roman Empire fell to invaders in A.D. 476. Europe fragmented into many small states. The 1,000-year period after the fall of Rome is known as the Middle Ages.

The Middle Ages By the ninth century, feudalism had arisen in Europe. **Feudalism** is a system in which a ruler grants parts of his land to lords. In exchange, lords owed the king military service and financial assistance. In turn, lords granted land to lesser lords.

Main Idea
The Crusades and the Renaissance inspired Europeans to look beyond their own world.

Copying a Manuscript
In Europe during the Middle Ages, learning was in the hands of the Church. Monks like this one spent hours and hours each day carefully copying books by hand. **Critical Thinking:** *Make Predictions How might the invention of mechanical printing affect learning in Europe?*

The Roman Catholic Church had great power in the Middle Ages. Daily life revolved around the rituals of the Catholic Church. The Catholic Church was also the center of learning. Outside of members of the clergy, few people, even among the nobility, were able to read and write.

The Crusades In 1095, the leader of the Roman Catholic Church, Pope Urban II, declared a crusade, or holy war. Its object was to win back control of the region known as the Holy Land, the land where Jesus had lived and taught. There were nine crusades over the next 200 years. In the end, they failed to win permanent control of the Holy Land.

Still, the Crusades had important long-term effects. They put Europeans in closer contact with the more advanced Muslim civilization. Europeans were attracted by the rich goods they saw in the Holy Land. They tasted strange foods and spices, such as oranges, pepper, and ginger. They also learned about advanced technology used for navigation. In time, the Crusades would help inspire Europeans to look overseas for trade.

The Renaissance Beginning in the 1300s, there was a rebirth of learning that is known as the Renaissance. European scholars rediscovered the classical texts of ancient Greece and Rome. Artists reflected a new interest in subjects that had influenced ancient thinkers.

Science and invention flourished. One invention, in particular, had a great impact on society. In the mid-fifteenth century, Johann Gutenberg invented a printing press. Using movable type, the printing press enabled a printer to produce a large number of identical books in a short time. As books became more available, the ability to read became more widespread.

During the late Middle Ages, powerful nation-states emerged in Europe. Italian cities had long controlled trade on the Mediterranean. The new nations—Spain, Portugal, France, and England—would shift the important trade routes to the Atlantic Ocean.

The Reformation Since the late Roman Empire, most Europeans had belonged to the Roman Catholic Church. Not all were happy with Catholicism, however. In 1517, a German monk named Martin Luther demanded that the Roman Catholic Church reform.

When his demands were rejected, Luther rebelled against the Catholic Church authority. Followers of Luther were called Protestants, because they were protesting certain Catholic Church practices. The movement Luther led is called the Protestant Reformation. Over time, Luther's movement split, and many Protestant churches emerged. The Reformation also plunged Europe into a long series of wars between Catholic and Protestant forces.

✓**Checkpoint** **What was the Renaissance?**

An Age of Exploration Begins

The Renaissance, the rise of nations, and the expansion of trade set the stage for an era of exploration. The person who provided the leadership for this new era was a brother of the king of Portugal, known to history as Prince Henry the Navigator. A deeply religious man, Henry hoped not only to expand Portuguese power but also to spread Christianity to new lands.

In the 1400s, Henry set up a center for exploration at Sagres (SAH greesh) in southern Portugal. He brought mathematicians, geographers, and sea captains to this center to teach his crews everything they needed to know about navigation and mapmaking.

At Sagres, sailors learned how to use the magnetic compass to find their direction at sea. They also learned how to use an instrument called the astrolabe to determine their precise latitude, or distance from the equator.

Using their new skills, Portuguese sailors began sailing southward along the western coast of Africa. By 1498, the Portuguese sailor Vasco da Gama passed the southern tip of Africa and continued north and east to India. Da Gama's course became an important trade route and helped boost Portuguese wealth and power. Later, Portuguese sailors pressed on to the East Indies, the source of trade in spices.

☑ Checkpoint What was Prince Henry's goal?

⭐ Looking Back and Ahead By the time Vasco da Gama reached India, Prince Henry was long dead. However, his work opened the way for European sailors to reach far-flung corners of the globe. In the next chapter, you would see how these sailors linked the long-separated worlds of the east and west.

Main Idea
Portugal led the way in European exploration.

Vocabulary *Builder*
precise (pree sīs) *adj.* exact; accurate

Section 4 | Check Your Progress

Progress Monitoring ⊕nline
For: Self-test with instant help
Visit: PHSchool.com
Web Code: mva-1014

Comprehension and Critical Thinking

1. **(a) Recall** What role did citizens play in Athens?
   (b) Contrast How did Athenian democracy differ from the Roman Republic?

2. **(a) Recall** How did Europeans make greater contact with the outside world?
   (b) Identify Benefits How might Europeans of that time benefit from increased trade?

🔄 Reading Skill

3. **Use Graphics to Construct Meaning** How did previewing visual material in this section help you read more actively? How did this material add detail to your understanding of European civilization?

Vocabulary *Builder*

Answer the following questions in complete sentences that show your understanding of the key terms.

4. How did monotheism differ from other early beliefs?

5. Why were nobles important in feudalism?

6. How are leaders chosen in a republic?

Writing

7. Some of the events covered in this section include the Crusades, feudalism, and the Renaissance. What do you think life was like in Europe before these events happened? How did life in Europe change after these events? Answer the questions in one or two paragraphs.

History books are full of information. Although you cannot remember every fact, you can learn to identify the main ideas and note the details that explain and support them. The following passage is a description such as you might find in a textbook.

> Native Americans developed a variety of ways to meet their basic needs for food, clothing, and shelter. In some culture areas, tribes hunted animals and gathered the nuts and fruits that grew in the wild. Other tribes depended on the sea for food. They made boats out of animal skins or carved canoes out of trees. From their boats and canoes, they speared fish or hunted marine animals such as seals, walruses, and whales.
>
> Whether hunting, fishing, farming, or gathering wild plants, Native Americans had a great respect for the natural world. Their prayers and ceremonies were designed to maintain a balance between people and the forces of nature. They believed that they must adapt their ways to the natural world in order to survive and prosper.

Learn the Skill

Use these steps to learn how to identify main ideas and supporting details.

1. **Find the main idea.** The main idea is what the passage is about. Often, the main idea is stated in the first sentence of a paragraph. However, it can occur in other parts of a paragraph as well.

2. **Restate the main idea.** To be sure you understand the ideas expressed in paragraph, restate the main idea in your own words.

3. **Look for details.** Details might include facts, reasons, explanations, examples, and descriptions that tell more about the main idea.

4. **Make connections.** Note how the details support and expand the main idea.

Practice the Skill

Answer the following questions based on the paragraph above.

1. **Find the main idea.** (a) What is the main-idea sentence in the first paragraph? (b) What is the main-idea sentence in the second paragraph?

2. **Restate the main idea.** Restate the main idea of each paragraph in your own words.

3. **Look for details.** Identify a detail that supports the main idea in each paragraph.

4. **Make connections.** (a) How do the details in the first paragraph help explain its main idea? (b) How do the details in the second paragraph help explain its main idea?

Apply the Skill

See the Review and Assessment at the end of this chapter.

Study Guide *Online*
Complete your Chapter 1
study guide in print or online.

Chapter Summary

Section 1
The Earliest Americans

- Most scientists believe that early people came to the Americas from Asia by way of a land bridge.
- As people learned to farm, they formed permanent settlements.
- The Mayas, Aztecs, and Incas built civilizations in Central America and South America.

Section 2
Cultures of North America

- The Mound Builders were among the earliest cultures of North America.
- People of North America developed varied ways of life, depending upon the environments in which they lived.
- The League of the Iroquois created a pact between warring nations in the Eastern Woodlands.

Section 3
Trade Networks of Asia and Africa

- The Muslim world linked Asia to Africa and Europe through trade.
- Various trading states emerged in both East Africa and West Africa.
- China dominated East Asian trade along the Silk Road.

Section 4
The European Heritage

- Judaism and Christianity formed the foundation for European religious beliefs.
- Greece and Rome shaped ideas about democratic government.
- After the Middle Ages, Europeans began to look beyond their boundaries.

Key Concepts

These notes will help you prepare for questions about key concepts.

Culture Groups of North America

Far North
- Cold climate
- Hunting and fishing

Northwest
- Rich forests
- Permanent settlements

Far West
- Climates vary from desert to mild

Southwest
- Hot, dry climate
- Pueblo people built large settlements

Great Plains
- Farming in east
- Buffalo hunting in west

Eastern Woodlands
- Forests and farming supplied needs
- Iroquois formed league to make peace

Southeast
- Mild climate, hot summers
- Farming communities

Traditions That Came to the Americas From Europe

Judeo-Christian Tradition
- Ideas on justice and morality
- No ruler is above God's law
- Emphasis on love, mercy, and forgiveness

Greek and Roman Civilizations
- Concept of democracy
- Republican system of government
- Roman law in which everyone is equal before the law

Vocabulary *Builder*
Key Terms

1. Draw a table with eight rows and three columns. In the first column, list the following key terms: glacier, irrigate, culture, clan, navigation, monotheism, direct democracy, republic. In the next column, write the definition of each word. In the last column, make a small illustration that shows the meaning of the word.

Comprehension and Critical Thinking

2. **(a) Recall** Describe the land-bridge theory that scientists have developed to explain how people first came to the Americas.
(b) Clarify Problems Some scholars have different ideas about how people first came to the Americas. Why do you think we are not sure about this event?

3. **(a) Describe** How did the Aztecs build a large empire?
(b) Compare What features did the Aztec civilization have in common with civilization of the Incas?
(c) Contrast How did the civilization of the Aztecs differ from other societies of North America?

4. **(a) Recall** What was the purpose of the League of the Iroquois?
(b) Identify Costs and Benefits What did each Iroquois Nation give up by joining the League? What did they gain?
(c) Draw Conclusions Why do you think the Iroquois League succeeded?

5. **(a) Describe** How did trade goods move between West Africa and the Middle East?
(b) Apply Information Describe two ways that goods from China might have reached the trading states of East Africa.
(c) Make Generalizations Based on your reading, write a one-sentence generalization about the importance of trade routes in Asia and Africa.

6. **(a) Summarize** Which Greco-Roman traditions influenced the shaping of government in the United States?
(b) Link Past and Present How do these Greco-Roman ideas directly impact political life in the United States today?

7. **(a) Define** What were the Crusades?
(b) Analyze Cause and Effect What were the long-range effects of the Crusades?
(c) Draw Conclusions Do you think the Crusades were a failure or a success? Explain.

History Reading Skill

8. **Read Actively** Apply what you learned about active reading to the next chapter. Preview the headings and prereading material. Scan the graphic material. Generate two questions to help you guide your reading.

Writing

9. **Write a paragraph on the following topic:** Historical events led to increasing contacts between people in different parts of the world. **Your paragraph should:**
   • begin with a thesis statement that explains the critical events and ideas that started the move toward increasing contacts;
   • support these events or ideas with facts and examples.

10. **Write a Narrative:**
You are a sailor who studied with the navigator Prince Henry. Write a paragraph explaining why you attended Prince Henry's school, what you learned, and your goals after leaving the school.

Skills for Life
Identify the Main Idea
Reread the text following the subheading "Far West" in Section 2, then answer the following questions.

11. What is the main-idea sentence of each paragraph?

12. Summarize the main idea of the two paragraphs in your own words.

13. What details support the main-idea sentence of the first paragraph?

Test Yourself

1. **Native American religious beliefs were based on**

   A the Ten Commandments.

   B the Quran.

   C reverence for nature.

   D the teachings of the Mound Builders.

2. **The Roman Senate was most similar to**

   A the Athenian assembly.

   B the U.S. Congress.

   C the feudal system.

   D the Aztec government.

   Refer to the map at right to answer Question 3.

3. **What do the three civilizations shown on the map have in common?**

   A They were all located in South America.

   B They all traded with the Iroquois.

   C They all disappeared for unknown reasons.

   D They were all very organized societies.

Early Civilizations in the Americas

NORTH AMERICA

ATLANTIC OCEAN

Tenochtitlán
Tikal
Caribbean Sea

PACIFIC OCEAN

SOUTH AMERICA

Cuzco

KEY

Aztec

Maya

Inca

0 km   2,000
0 miles   2,000
Lambert Azimuthal Equal-Area Projection

Document-Based Questions

Task: Look Documents 1 and 2, and answer their accompanying questions. Then, use the documents and your knowledge of history to complete the following writing assignment:

   Write a paragraph describing the influence of geography on the Tlingit society.

Document 1: This photograph shows the land where the people of the Pacific Northwest, such as the Tlingit and Nootka, lived. *Based on this picture, what resources did the Pacific Northwest people have for building homes and finding food?*

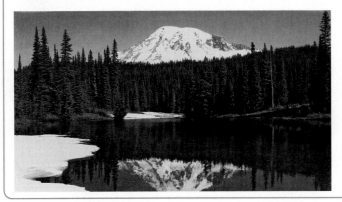

Document 2: In this excerpt from an oral history, a Tlingit boy describes the traditional life of his people. *Why did the Tlingit expect young people to work?*

"Land ownership is one of the biggest laws in the Tlingit culture. You did not fish or hunt on somebody else's land without their permission. If you did and you were caught, your equipment would be broken and you would have to leave. . . .

   The Tlingit people subsisted in seasonal rounds. . . . They hunted black and brown bear with spear and deadfall. For wolf, coyote, and fox they used snares. They used traps to get mink, weasel, and land otter. With bow and arrow, they hunted the mountain goat. They fished Halibut, King salmon, Silver salmon, and Humpy salmon. . . .

   The jobs of young children long ago depended on the mental and physical capabilities. They had to do whatever they could. They had to pick berries, gather roots and plants, and clean fish. The older they got the harder the tasks became. This is how they learned."

Chapter Preview

During the 1400s, two worlds collided when European explorers came into contact with Native Americans. From the 1500s to the 1700s, European nations competed to explore and build settlements in North and South America.

1001
Vikings reach
North America.

1492
Columbus lands
in the West Indies.

**U.S.
Events**

1000

1400

1500

**World
Events**

Discovery SCHOOL

Quick View Video
View the chapter video for a quick preview of the main ideas.

With its long coastline facing the Atlantic Ocean, Portugal funded many journeys of exploration during the 1500s. This monument in Lisbon, Portugal, pays tribute to brave Portuguese explorers.

1539
De Soto begins exploration of what is today the southeastern United States.

1626
New Netherland is settled by the Dutch.

1673
Marquette and Joliet explore the Mississippi River.

1500

1600

1700

1517 Protestant Reformation begins in Germany.

1588 English defeat the Spanish Armada.

1608 French establish settlement in Quebec.

History Reading Skill **Identify Main Ideas and Details**

What did European explorers find in the Americas?

Read the following account by the explorer Christopher Columbus about his first voyage to the Americas. The side notes suggest ways to identify main ideas and their supporting details.

> On August 3, 1492, Christopher Columbus, hoping to find a sea route to Asia, set sail from the Spanish port of Palos with three ships and about 90 men. Read the following account about his arrival, three months later, on the island he named San Salvador.

Primary Source

> Presently, many people of the island assembled. . . . I wanted us to form a great friendship, for I knew they were a people who could be more easily freed and converted to our holy faith by love than by force.

This is the main idea of the paragraph. The main idea gives all the details and information in the text.

These details give more information about the main idea.

> . . .They afterwards came to the ship's boats where they were bringing us parrots, cotton threads in skeins, darts, and many other things. And we exchanged them for other things that we gave them. In time, they took all, and gave what they had with good will. It appeared to me to be a race of people very poor in everything.

> . . .They should be good servants and intelligent, for I saw that they quickly took in what was said to them. I believe that they would easily be made Christians as it appeared to me that they had not religion.

The details of this paragraph reflect an implied main idea. Columbus believes it will be easy to rule these people.

> —Adapted from *The Journal of Christopher Columbus*, 1893

Identify Main Ideas and Details

- Main ideas express the most important ideas in a text. Supporting details give more information about the main ideas.
- Some main ideas are directly stated. Other main ideas are implied and must be figured out by determining what idea fits with all the details.

Document-Based Questions

1. What impresses Columbus most about the people he meets?
2. Why do you think Columbus wanted to make the people he meets Christians?

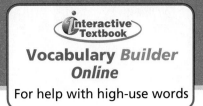
Vocabulary *Builder*

Previewing High-Use Academic Words

High-Use Word	Definition	Sample History Sentence
myth (mihth) (Section 1, p. 37)	*n.* traditional story of unknown authorship	The ancient Greeks developed many <u>myths</u> to explain the world around them.
negative (NEHG ah tihv) (Section 1, p. 41)	*adj.* opposite to something regarded as positive	The arrival of Europeans in the Americas had some <u>negative</u> results for the Native Americans.
factor (FAK tor) (Section 2, p. 45)	*n.* important element of something	A major <u>factor</u> in pushing Spain to explore a sea route to Asia was the control of the land route by Italy.
rigid (RIH jihd) (Section 2, p. 48)	*adj.* not bending; not flexible	European feudalism was a <u>rigid</u> social system that prevented people from rising in society.
restore (ree STOR) (Section 3, p. 50)	*v.* to give back something taken away	Roman senators hoped to <u>restore</u> a republic by assassinating Julius Caesar.
province (PRAHV ahns) (Section 3, p. 51)	*n.* territorial district of a country	Quebec and Alberta are <u>provinces</u> of Canada.
decline (dee KLĪN) (Section 4, p. 54)	*v.* to lessen in force, health, strength, or value	England's defeat of Spain's navy in 1588 signaled the <u>decline</u> of Spain's power.
motive (MOH tihv) (Section 4, p. 55)	*n.* inner drive that causes a person to do something	Most Spanish soldiers' <u>motive</u> for coming to the Americas was to gain wealth.

Previewing Key Terms and People

Christopher Columbus, p. 36
Vasco Núñez de Balboa, p. 39
Ferdinand Magellan, p. 40
strait, p. 40
circumnavigate, p. 40
conquistador, p. 44

Hernando Cortés, p. 44
Moctezuma, p. 44
plantation, p. 47
encomienda, p. 47
Bartolomé de Las Casas, p. 47
mission, p. 47
peninsulare, p. 48
mercantilism, p. 50

John Cabot, p. 51
northwest passage, p. 51
Henry Hudson, p. 52
Samuel de Champlain, p. 53
coureur de bois, p. 54
Jacques Marquette, p. 55
alliance, p. 57

The Age of Exploration

Objectives

1. Explain what happened to the Vikings who explored Newfoundland.

2. Describe the voyages of Christopher Columbus.

3. Describe the expeditions of such Spanish explorers as Vasco Núñez de Balboa and Ferdinand Magellan.

4. Explain the importance of the Columbian Exchange.

Prepare to Read

Reading Skill

Identify Stated Main Ideas Each section in this textbook begins with a paragraph headed **Background Knowledge** that presents information you learned earlier. Then, throughout each section, important ideas are organized by major red headings that look like this: **First Visitors From Europe.** The main idea is also stated in the margin alongside each major heading.

Vocabulary *Builder*

High-Use Words

<u>myth</u>, p. 37

<u>negative</u>, p. 41

Key Terms and People

Christopher Columbus, p. 36

Vasco Núñez de Balboa, p. 39

Ferdinand Magellan, p. 40

strait, p. 40

circumnavigate, p. 40

⭐ **Background Knowledge** In a previous chapter, you learned about changes in Africa, Asia, and Europe that led to increased trade and cultural ties among these lands. While those changes were taking place, cultures in the Americas were unaffected. In this section, you will learn about the first European contacts with the Americas and how those encounters changed both the Americas and Europe.

First Visitors From Europe

Main Idea
Spain agrees to finance Christopher Columbus's voyage to find a sea route to Asia.

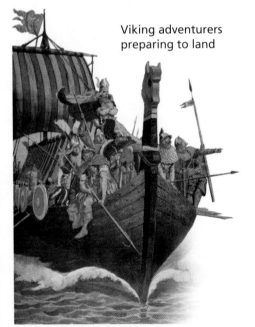

Viking adventurers preparing to land

If you had been in school 50 years ago and your teacher asked "Who discovered America?" you would probably have answered, "Christopher Columbus." But was Columbus really the first?

In a previous chapter, you have read that ancestors of today's Native Americans crossed into the Americas from Asia thousands of years ago. There are also many theories about people from Europe, Asia, and Africa who may have visited the Americas prior to Columbus.

So far, we only have evidence of the arrival of a European people known as the Vikings. The Vikings were a seagoing people who originally lived in the part of northern Europe known as Scandinavia.

In 1963, scientists found the remains of an early Viking settlement in Newfoundland. The findings supported the truth of old Viking stories. According to one story, a Viking named Leif Erikson and 35 others sailed from a colony on Greenland, in 1001, to investigate reports of land farther west. They explored the region and spent the winter in a place they named Vinland.

The Voyages of Columbus Vinland existed only in myths for the next 500 years. Whether Christopher Columbus ever heard the stories is not known. However, Columbus believed he could reach Asia and the East by sailing west across the Atlantic Ocean. He never suspected that a huge landmass was blocking the way.

Christopher Columbus grew up near Genoa, an important port on the west coast of Italy. In the 1470s, he settled in Portugal, which was Europe's leading seafaring nation. Columbus sailed on Portuguese ships, studied maps and charts, and learned about the world beyond Europe. From all this he developed his idea for a voyage to Asia.

Portugal's king showed little interest in Columbus's plan. The king hoped to reach Asia by following the route Bartholomeu Dias and other Portuguese explorers were pioneering around southern Africa. He also believed the world was larger than Columbus had calculated. Thus, in his view, the voyage would be much longer than Columbus expected. For these reasons, Portugal refused to finance such a trip.

Columbus did not give up. He moved to Spain and set his plan before King Ferdinand and Queen Isabella. They liked Columbus's plan. But it took six years before they finally agreed to provide ships for the voyage.

Setting Sail In August 1492, about 90 men—most of them Spaniards—prepared to make the voyage. Columbus's ships—the *Niña*, the *Pinta*, and the *Santa Maria*—were tiny, between 55 and 90 feet long. Sailing with the wind, they covered up to 170 miles per day.

Columbus predicted that they would reach Asia in 21 days. After a month at sea, there was no sight of land. The crew became restless and spoke of mutiny, or soldiers and sailors rebelling against their officers. Columbus held firm against the threat.

Finally, on October 12, a sailor spotted land. Coming ashore in a small boat, Columbus claimed the island for Spain. Curious islanders soon gathered on the beach. Believing he was in the Asian islands known as the Indies, Columbus called these people Indians. The next day he wrote in his journal, "I intend to go see if I can find the island of Japan."

Columbus then sailed southwest to a large island. At first he thought it was Japan. Actually, Columbus was on the island of Cuba. His guides next pointed Columbus west to the island of Hispaniola. Columbus set sail to return to Spain in January 1493.

Vocabulary *Builder*
myth (mihth) *n.* traditional story of unknown authorship

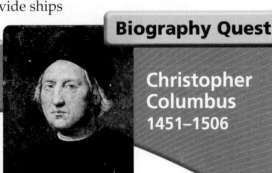

Biography Quest

Christopher Columbus
1451–1506

When Columbus returned to Spain after his first voyage, the king and queen showered him with honors. But after his third voyage, he was led off the ship in chains. Why did his fortunes change?

Columbus managed Spain's colonies poorly. The colonies did not produce much wealth. He also mistreated the Indians. In time, the king and queen ordered his arrest. Columbus set sail for Spain in January 1493.

Biography Quest

How did Columbus trick his crew on his first voyage?

For: The answer to the question about Columbus
Visit: PHSchool.com
Web Code: myd-1012

Early Voyages of Exploration, 1492–1609

During the 1400s and 1500s, a number of daring explorers started the exploration to find a sea route to Asia.
Critical Thinking:
Draw Conclusions
How did technology contribute to the age of exploration?

The Mariner's Astrolabe
Sailors used the mariner's astrolabe to determine latitude, longitude, and time of day. ▶

NORTH AMERICA
Newfoundland
EUROPE
AZTEC EMPIRE
West Indies
ATLANTIC OCEAN
AFRICA
PACIFIC OCEAN
SOUTH AMERICA
INCA EMPIRE
Strait of Magellan
Cape Horn
Cape of Good Hope

N W E S

180°   150°W   60°W   30°W   0°   30°E   60

Identify Stated Main Ideas

Reading Skill

What important idea from the first paragraph following the subheading "Spain Backs More Voyages" is discussed throughout the passage?

Spain Backs More Voyages In Spain, Columbus reported that there were huge amounts of gold in the land he referred to as the West Indies. The grateful monarchs made him governor of all he had claimed for Spain.

In September 1493, he sailed again for the West Indies. This time he commanded 17 ships filled with 1,500 soldiers, settlers, and priests. The Spanish planned to colonize and rule the land they thought was the West Indies. They also intended to convert the people there to Christianity.

On this second voyage, Columbus discovered other islands, including Puerto Rico. He found that the men he had left behind on Hispaniola had been killed by Indians. Not discouraged, Columbus built another settlement nearby and enslaved the local Indians to dig for gold. Within a few months, 12 of his ships returned to Spain, their cargo holds filled with some yellow metal.

On his third expedition in 1498, Columbus reached the northern coast of South America and decided it was the Asian mainland. Spain permitted him to try to prove his claims in a fourth voyage, in 1502.

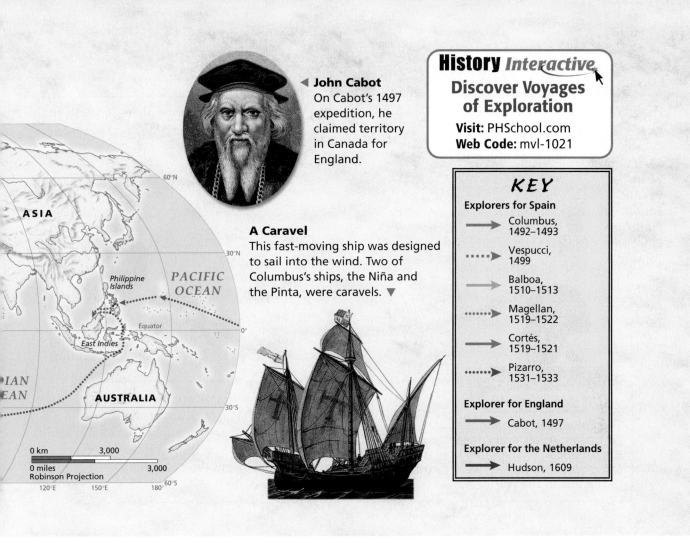

◄ John Cabot
On Cabot's 1497 expedition, he claimed territory in Canada for England.

A Caravel
This fast-moving ship was designed to sail into the wind. Two of Columbus's ships, the Niña and the Pinta, were caravels. ▼

History *Interactive*
Discover Voyages of Exploration
Visit: PHSchool.com
Web Code: mvl-1021

KEY

Explorers for Spain
Columbus, 1492–1493
Vespucci, 1499
Balboa, 1510–1513
Magellan, 1519–1522
Cortés, 1519–1521
Pizarro, 1531–1533

Explorer for England
Cabot, 1497

Explorer for the Netherlands
Hudson, 1609

ASIA

Philippine Islands

PACIFIC OCEAN

Equator

East Indies

AUSTRALIA

0 km 3,000
0 miles 3,000
Robinson Projection
120°E 150°E 180°

He returned to Spain two years later with his beliefs unchanged. Columbus died in 1506, still convinced that he had reached Asia.

☑**Checkpoint** Why were Spain's monarchs interested in the proposal Columbus made to them?

The Continuing Search for Asia

Many explorers followed the route charted by Columbus. Another Italian explorer, Amerigo Vespucci, made two trips to the new lands. His trips convinced Vespucci that the lands he saw were not part of Asia. Upon his return to Europe, he wrote a letter describing a "new world . . . more densely peopled and full of animals than our Europe or Asia or Africa." A German mapmaker labeled the region "the land of Amerigo" on his maps. The name was soon shortened to "America."

Meanwhile, the Spanish continued to explore and colonize. In 1510, Vasco Núñez de Balboa, a Spanish colonist, explored the Caribbean coast of what is now Panama. Hacking his way across the jungle, he became the first European to set eyes on the Pacific Ocean.

Main Idea
The survivors of Magellan's voyage across the Pacific were the first sailors to sail all the way around the globe.

The Columbian Exchange

From Western Hemisphere to Eastern

Maize (corn)
Potato
Sweet potato
Beans
Peanut
Squash
Pumpkin
Pineapple
Tomato
Cocoa
Peppers
Avocado
Turkey

From Eastern Hemisphere to Western

Wheat
Rice
Banana
Peach
Pear
Sugar cane
Watermelon
Lettuce
Horse
Cow
Sheep
Goat
Chicken
Pig
Disease (smallpox, typhus)

Reading Charts
Skills Activity

The Columbian Exchange brought many European, Asian, and African goods to the Americas. At the same time, American crops and livestock were distributed to the rest of the world.

(a) Interpret Charts Identify two kinds of farm animals that Europeans brought to the Americas.

(b) Identify Benefits Who do you think benefited most from the Columbian Exchange? Explain.

The discovery that another ocean lay west of the Americas did not end the search for a water route to Asia. In September 1519, Portuguese explorer Ferdinand Magellan set out to find an Atlantic-Pacific passage.

For more than a year, the small fleet slowly moved down the South American coast looking for a strait, a narrow passage that connects two large bodies of water. As it pushed farther south than earlier expeditions, it encountered penguins and other animals that no European had ever seen before. Finally, near the southern tip of present-day Argentina, Magellan found a narrow passage. After 38 days of battling winds, tides, and currents, his ships exited what today is called the Strait of Magellan. They now entered the large ocean Balboa had seen nine or ten years earlier. Although Magellan did not realize it, Asia was still thousands of miles away.

Magellan finally reached the Philippine Islands. There, he and several others were killed in a battle with Filipinos. The survivors fled in two of the ships. One ship finally reached Spain, in September 1522. Three years after they had begun, the 18 men aboard became first to circumnavigate, or travel around, the entire Earth.

✓Checkpoint **What were the contributions of Balboa and Magellan as explorers?**

The Columbian Exchange

These early Spanish voyages set the stage for a great exchange between the Western and the Eastern hemispheres. The next century began what is now known as the Columbian Exchange, a transfer of people, products, and ideas between the hemispheres.

Many of the changes brought about by the Columbian Exchange were positive. Europeans introduced cows, hogs, and other domestic animals to the Western Hemisphere. Many food plants, such as wheat and oats, also arrived on the ships that brought the Europeans.

The exchange also had <u>negative</u> effects on the Americas. Europeans brought germs to which Native Americans had no immunity, or natural resistance. Smallpox, chickenpox, measles, and other contagious diseases killed Native Americans by the thousands.

The impact of the Americas on Europe was no less important. Europeans in the Americas found plants and animals they had never seen before either. For example, the Americas introduced llamas, turkeys, squirrels, and muskrats to the rest of the world. More important, however, were the crops that Native Americans taught the Europeans to cultivate. Today, plants that once were found only in the Americas account for nearly one third of the world's food supply.

✓ **Checkpoint** **What impact did the Columbian Exchange have on Europe?**

⭐ **Looking Back and Ahead** The voyages of Columbus marked the beginning of a new historical era. The foothold he established in the Caribbean would expand into a vast empire. By 1600, Spain would control much of North and South America and would be one of the world's richest nations.

Main Idea
The Spanish voyages of discovery brought about a huge global exchange of goods and ideas.

Vocabulary *Builder*
<u>negative</u> (NEHG ah tihv) *adj.* opposite to something regarded as positive

---

Section 1 | Check Your Progress

Progress Monitoring ⓸nline
For: Self-test with instant help
Visit: PHSchool.com
Web Code: mva-1021

Comprehension and Critical Thinking
1. **(a) Recall** Who were the Vikings?
   (b) Apply Information What problems might there be with using Viking myths as historical sources?

2. **(a) Recall** What is the Columbian Exchange?
   (b) Support a Point of View Did the Columbian Exchange bring more changes to the Americas or to Europe? Explain your view.

🔄 Reading Skill
3. **Identify Stated Main Ideas** Read the text under the heading "The Columbian Exchange." Identify the stated main idea and explain how the paragraphs support that idea.

Vocabulary *Builder*
Fill in the blanks with the correct key terms.
4. Magellan's ships sailed through a _____ in order to reach the Pacific Ocean.
5. The few survivors of Magellan's crew were the first to _____ Earth.

Writing
6. Create a timeline showing early explorations in the Americas. Choose three entries that you think are most significant. For each choice, write one or two sentences explaining why you made that choice.

Danger at Sea

When Europeans began to make voyages of discovery, they had no idea what they would find. Some of the dangers that they feared did not really exist. Other dangers were all too real. But the more they traveled, the more their views of the world changed.

◀ **Fearsome Sea Monsters**

Popular tales warned that the oceans were filled with dragons, sea serpents, and other monsters. Happily, these dangers turned out to be imaginary.

▲ Storms at Sea

One real danger was bad weather. A violent storm could send a ship and its whole crew to the bottom of the ocean.

▼ Getting Lost

Another real fear was that a ship might get lost in the vast, endless ocean. Fortunately, improved navigational tools, like the sextant and more accurate maps, made this danger less likely.

Sextant

▼ Starvation

Running low on supplies at sea meant disaster. One Spanish sailor described what happened when his ship ran out of food.

"We ... ate only old biscuit reduced to powder, full of grubs and stinking from the dirt which rats had made on it. We drank water that was yellow and stinking."

—Antonio Pigafetta, *Journal*

Piracy ▲

When ships began to carry treasure to Europe, a new danger emerged: piracy. Pirates would attack merchant ships, steal the cargo, and often, murder the crew. Some pirates, such as Captain Kidd (shown above), became legendary for their boldness.

Analyze LIFE AT THE TIME

Imagine you are a European sailor about to go on an ocean voyage. Write a letter explaining your view of the world and why you are going on the voyage in spite of the dangers.

Spain's Empire in the Americas

Objectives

1. Describe how the Spanish were able to defeat the empires of the Aztecs and Incas.

2. Identify Spanish explorations in areas that later became part of the United States.

3. Explain how society was organized in Spain's empire in the Americas.

Prepare to Read

Reading Skill

Identify Supporting Details Text includes details to support a main idea. These details might be examples, reasons, facts, or descriptions. They enable readers to understand a main idea by helping them to picture it or to make sense of its argument or to believe its accuracy. As you read Section 2, look for details that support the main ideas.

Vocabulary *Builder*

High-Use Words

factor, p. 45

rigid, p. 48

Key Terms and People

conquistador, p. 44

Hernando Cortés, p. 44

Moctezuma, p. 44

plantation, p. 47

encomienda, p. 47

Bartolomé de Las Casas, p. 47

mission, p. 47

peninsulare, p. 48

⭐ **Background Knowledge** Even though Columbus never realized that he had reached a region previously unknown to Europeans, his voyages gave Spain a head start on its European rivals in colonizing the Americas. In this section, you will learn how Spain explored and colonized the lands it claimed.

Spanish Conquistadors

Main Idea
The conquests of Cortés and Pizarro helped establish a huge Spanish Empire in the Americas.

By the early 1500s, the Spanish had a firm foothold in the Americas. From Spain's island colonies in the Caribbean, soldier-adventurers called **conquistadors** set out to explore and conquer a world unknown to them. They hoped for riches and glory for themselves and for Spain.

Cortés and Pizarro In 1519, conquistador Hernando Cortés sailed from Cuba to Mexico with more than 500 soldiers. The first Native Americans he met presented him with gifts of gold.

On November 8, 1519, Cortés marched into the Aztec capital city of Tenochtitlán. As the Spaniards moved closer to Tenochtitlán, many Native Americans joined them. Conquered by the Aztecs, they hated the Aztec's brutal rule.

The Aztec leader Moctezuma (mokt uh ZOO muh) (also spelled *Montezuma*) met with Cortés and tried to get him to leave by offering him gold. The gold had the opposite effect. Cortés took Moctezuma hostage and claimed all of Mexico for Spain. However, the Aztecs soon rebelled and forced the Spaniards to flee.

About a year later, Cortés returned with a larger force, recaptured Tenochtitlán, and then destroyed it. In its place he built Mexico City, the capital of the Spanish colony of New Spain.

Cortés used the same methods to subdue the Aztecs in South America that another conquistador, Francisco Pizarro, used. Pizarro landed on the coast of Peru in 1531 to search for the Incas, who were said to have much gold. In September 1532, he led about 170 soldiers through the jungle into the heart of the Inca Empire. Pizarro then took the Inca ruler Atahualpa (ah tuh WAHL puh) prisoner. Although the Inca people paid a huge ransom to free their ruler, Pizarro executed him anyway. By November 1533, the Spanish had defeated the leaderless Incas and captured their capital city of Cuzco.

Why the Spanish Were Victorious How could a few hundred Spanish soldiers defeat Native American armies many times their size? Several <u>factors</u> explain the Spaniards' success. First among these was technology. The Indians' weapons simply were no match for the armor, muskets, and cannons of the Europeans. In addition, many of the Spaniards rode horses, which the Native Americans had never before seen. Finally, the Native Americans were divided among themselves. In Peru, a civil war had just ended. In Mexico, many Native Americans hated the Aztecs.

☑️**Checkpoint** Why were a few Spanish conquistadors able to defeat the larger armies of the Aztecs and Incas?

Vocabulary *Builder*
factor (FAK tor) *n.* important element of something

Spanish Conquistadors
The Spanish soldiers were outnumbered by the Aztecs and the Incas, yet they were able to easily defeat these empires.
Critical Thinking: *Explain Problems Some Native Americans sided with the Spanish against the Aztecs and the Incas. What problems might this have caused between the groups after the battle?*

Discovery SCHOOL

Explore More Video
To learn more about Spanish exploration in the Americas, view the video.

Spanish Explorations in North America

NORTH AMERICA

PACIFIC OCEAN

ATLANTIC OCEAN

Gulf of Mexico

CUBA

Hispaniola

Caribbean Sea

Compostela

Florida

Colorado R.

Mississippi R.

Arkansas R.

Rio Grande

KEY

→ Ponce de León, 1513
→ Cabeza de Vaca/Estevanico, 1528–1536
→ De Soto, 1539–1542
→ Coronado, 1540–1547

0 km 500
0 miles 500
Azimuthal Equal-Area Projection

MAP MASTER®
Skills Activity

Spanish conquistadors explored parts of North America in the 1500s.

(a) Read a Map Key List the explorers represented on the map, and briefly describe the area each one explored.

(b) Link Past and Present Based on this map, in what areas of the present-day United States would you expect to find Latino influence strongest?

MapMaster ⊙nline

For: Interactive map
Visit: PHSchool.com
Web Code: mvp-1022

Main Idea

Spanish explorers believed that the area of what is today the United States contained cities of gold.

Spanish Explorers in North America

The Spanish did not limit themselves to the exploration of what we now call Latin America. In 1513, Juan Ponce de León sailed north from Puerto Rico to investigate reports of a large island. He found beautiful flowers there, so he named the place *La Florida*. Ponce de León became the first Spaniard to set foot in what is now the United States.

Exploration along Florida's west coast began in 1528, when about 400 Spaniards landed near the present-day city of St. Petersburg. Finding none of the gold they had hoped for, they marched into northern Florida. There, under attack by Native Americans, they built five crude boats and set out to sea. About 80 survivors led by Álvar Núñez Cabeza de Vaca eventually landed at present-day Galveston Island on the Texas coast.

Starvation and disease reduced their number to 15 before Indians enslaved them. Finally, only four—including Cabeza de Vaca and Estevanico, an African slave—remained alive. After six years in captivity, they escaped and spent two more years finding their way to Mexico City. In 1536, eight years after landing in Florida, the four survivors of the 400-man expedition returned to Spanish lands.

In Mexico City, the men related stories they had heard from Native Americans about seven great cities filled with gold far to the north. Officials asked the survivors to head an expedition to find these cities. However, only Estevanico was willing to go. In 1539, he led a group into what is now western New Mexico. When Estevanico was killed by Indians, the others returned to Mexico City.

The conquistador Francisco Coronado (koh roh NAH doh) set out with about 1,100 Spaniards and Native Americans to find the golden city. Although he never found the city, he did explore much of what is now New Mexico, Arizona, Texas, and Kansas.

While Coronado was trekking through the southwest, Hernando de Soto was searching for riches in today's southeastern United States. De Soto traveled as far north as the Carolinas and as far west as Oklahoma. He died in what is now Louisiana, in 1542, having found the Mississippi River but no cities of gold.

Native Americans received harsh treatment from Spaniards.

☑ **Checkpoint** **What regions in the present-day United States did Spaniards explore?**

Colonizing Spanish America

At first, Spain let the conquistadors govern the lands they had conquered. However, this was not successful. In order to control its new empire, Spain created a formal system of government to rule its colonies.

Harsh Life for Native Americans Within Spain's vast empire, there was little place for Native Americans except as a source of labor. Government officials granted settlers huge tracts of land to start mines, ranches, and **plantations**—large farms worked by laborers who live on the property. To help Spanish colonists find needed workers, the Spanish government granted *encomiendas* (ehn KOH mee ehn dahz). These were land grants that included the right to demand labor or taxes from Native Americans. The Spanish forced Native Americans to work in the gold and silver mines. Many died when the tunnels caved in. Some Spaniards protested this cruel treatment. The priest **Bartolomé de Las Casas** traveled through New Spain working for reform. Largely due to Las Casas's efforts, the government of Spain ordered reform of the *encomienda* system in the mid-1500s.

Like other Europeans in the Americas, the Spanish believed they had a duty to convert Native Americans to Christianity. They set up **missions**, religious settlements, run by Catholic priests and friars. San Francisco, San Diego, San Antonio, and a number of other U.S. cities got their start as Spanish missions in the 1700s.

Main Idea
The priest Bartolomé de Las Casas spoke out against the cruelty of the *encomienda* system.

The Trade in Humans As the death toll for Native Americans continued to rise, Spanish colonists looked across the Atlantic Ocean for a new source of labor.

In 1517, Spain brought about 4,000 Africans to the Caribbean islands and forced them to work there. By the middle of the 1500s, the Spaniards were shipping about 2,000 enslaved Africans each year to Hispaniola alone. You will read about the growing slave trade in another chapter.

Society in the Spanish Colonies A rigid social system based on birthplace and blood developed in the Spanish colonies. At the top of the social structure were the *peninsulares*, Spanish colonists who had been born in Spain. Almost all government officials came from this class. Colonists born in America of two Spanish parents were called *Creoles*. Generally, Creoles also held important positions. Many of the wealthiest merchants and plantation owners were Creoles.

People of mixed parentage were lower on the social ladder. *Mestizos*, people of Spanish and Indian blood, could achieve economic success as ranchers, farmers, or merchants. But entrance into the upper levels of society was impossible for them. Below mestizos were *mulattos*—people of Spanish and African heritage. Native Americans and African Americans were held at the bottom of society. This rigid class system helped Spain keep control of its empire in the Americas for more than 300 years.

☑ **Checkpoint** How were Native Americans treated under the *encomienda* system?

☆ **Looking Back and Ahead** The resentment and tensions caused by the rigid class system eventually provided the seeds for revolutions in the early 1800s that ended Spain's American empire.

Vocabulary *Builder*
rigid (RIH jihd) *adj.* not bending; not flexible

Identifying Supporting Details
(Reading Skill) Identify two details in these two paragraphs that support the following main idea: *Spain created a formal system of government in America to rule the vast regions it claimed.* Explain how the details support the main idea.

Section 2 | **Check Your Progress**

Progress Monitoring Online
For: Self-test with instant help
Visit: PHSchool.com
Web Code: mva-1022

Comprehension and Critical Thinking

1. (a) Identify What parts of the North American continent did Spanish conquistadors explore?
(b) Apply Information How did the conquistadors help establish the Spanish Empire in the Americas?

2. (a) Identify What was the lasting accomplishment of Bartolomé de Las Casas?
(b) Summarize How would you describe the lives of Native Americans in New Spain?

Reading Skill

3. Identify Supporting Details Read the text following the subheading "Society in the Spanish Colonies." Identify three details that support its main idea: A rigid social system, based on birthplace and blood, developed in Spain's colonies over time. Explain how the details support the main idea.

Vocabulary *Builder*

4. Write two definitions for each of the following key terms: conquistador, plantation, mission, *peninsulare*. First, write a formal definition for your teacher. Second, write a casual definition in everyday English for a classmate.

Writing

5. (a) Prepare an outline you would use to write an essay describing the effects of Spanish colonization in the Americas.
6. (b) Then, write several sentences describing the views of Bartolomé de Las Casas and a conquistador about Spanish rule in the Americas.

Europeans Compete in North America

Objectives

1. Describe the religious and economic conflicts in Europe during the Reformation.

2. Explain why European powers continued to search for a new route to Asia.

3. Describe the outcome of the search by explorers John Cabot and Henry Hudson for a northwest passage around the Americas.

Prepare to Read

Reading Skill

Identify Implied Main Ideas
Sometimes a portion of text does not state the main idea directly. However, the text still has a main idea. This idea is implied, or suggested, by the many details contained in the text. You can identify this idea by reading all the details and developing an idea that fits all of them. State the idea to yourself in a sentence, then reread the text and confirm that the details do support it.

Vocabulary *Builder*

High-Use Words

restore, p. 50

province, p. 51

Key Terms and People

mercantilism, p. 50

John Cabot, p. 51

northwest passage, p. 51

Henry Hudson, p. 52

⭐ **Background Knowledge** Europe in 1500 was in the midst of a great cultural change—the Renaissance. New ideas changed how Europeans thought about their world. Some people, such as Martin Luther, a German priest, boldly called for changes in the Roman Catholic Church. A new movement, the Protestant Reformation began. In this section, you will learn how religious conflict fueled other conflicts that would lead to struggles in the Americas.

Conflicts in Europe

As the appeal of the Reformation increased, the split between the Catholics and the Protestants increased religious and economic tensions between countries in Europe.

Religious Conflicts By 1530, the rulers of Sweden, Denmark, and several European states had split with the Roman Catholic Church and set up Protestant churches in their countries. Elsewhere in Europe, the teachings and writings of Swiss thinker John Calvin had a great influence on the development of Protestant churches in France, Switzerland, Scotland, and the Netherlands.

English Protestants found a supporter in King Henry VIII. Henry was married to Catherine of Aragon, the daughter of King Ferdinand and Queen Isabella of Spain. When Catherine did not produce a male heir to the English throne, Henry sought to divorce her and remarry.

Main Idea
Religious and economic conflicts in Europe increased tensions among the major powers on the continent.

King
Henry VIII

49

Mercantilism

European leaders of the time believed that the purpose of colonies was to benefit the home country. This belief was part of an economic theory known as mercantilism. According to this theory, a nation became strong by building up its gold and silver supply. One way to do this was to take gold and silver from colonies and send it to the royal treasury. **Critical Thinking: *Identify Economic Benefits and Costs** What risks did the home country take in relying on colonies to support its economy?*

Colonies Can trade only with the home country

Raw Materials Such as:
• Gold
• Cotton
• Timber

Home Country Trades to acquire wealth

Manufactured Goods Such as:
• Clothing
• Furniture

Because Catholic law does not permit divorce, Henry asked the pope to annul, or cancel, his marriage. This had occurred before. Popes had annulled royal marriages. The pope's refusal to grant the divorce caused Henry to break with the Roman Catholic Church in 1533. He set up a Protestant church and named it the Church of England.

Economic Conflicts Religious tensions created by the Reformation inflamed rivalries that already existed among the nations of Europe. Wars were common and alliances often shifted. This uncertainty made European rulers believe they could not depend on one another to protect their country's security.

For example, Spain was unwilling to depend on Italian or Portuguese traders. As a result, the Spanish monarchs eagerly supported Columbus's search for a new route to Asia. The Spanish thought that if they could start colonies there, goods from those colonies would make Spain wealthy and powerful. Most importantly, the Spanish hoped Asian colonies would provide gold. Nearly every European nation sought gold to pay for its wars and help strengthen their armies. In fact, Spain required one fifth of all gold that Spaniards found to be sent to the king. This requirement was part of a system widely followed at the time, called mercantilism (MER kuhn tihl ihz uhm). The system of mercantilism held that colonies existed to make the home country wealthy and powerful.

The Spanish Armada England's King Henry VIII died in 1547. He was succeeded by his son Edward, who ruled only a short time before he died, too. The throne then passed to Mary I, who made plans to restore the Roman Catholic Church in England. However, Mary died in 1558 and Elizabeth I, a Protestant, took the throne.

Identify Implied Main Ideas

Reading Skill

What is the implied main idea of the text you have read so far in this section?

Vocabulary *Builder*
restore (ree STOR) *v.* to give back something taken away

The rule of the Protestant Queen Elizabeth I renewed the rivalry with Roman Catholic Spain. Spain's King Phillip II hoped to make England a Catholic nation again. Relations were also strained by English raids on Spanish ships at sea. Many of these ships carried gold from the Americas. The Spanish also resented English assistance to rebels trying to win independence in the Spanish <u>province</u> of Holland.

Vocabulary *Builder*
<u>province</u> (PRAHV ahns) *n.* territorial district of a country

In 1588, Phillip assembled a fleet of 130 warships known as the Spanish Armada. Phillip hoped to force Elizabeth from the throne. A fleet of English ships met the Spanish off the coast of France. The smaller and faster English ships sank many of the Spanish ships. Barely half of the Spanish Armada returned to Spain.

The defeat of the Spanish Armada changed the balance of power in Europe. Spain was weakened and so was its control of the seas. This enabled countries like England and France to found colonies in the Americas. Europe's religious and economic conflicts were not settled by the defeat of the Armada, however. As England and France founded colonies, these conflicts spread to the Americas.

☑ **Checkpoint** **How did economic concerns among European nations lead to conflicts?**

Asia Continues to Beckon

Columbus's return from his first voyage interested another Italian explorer, John Cabot. Cabot decided that a more northern route to Asia would be shorter and easier.

Main Idea
Northern voyages of discovery failed to locate a northwest passage through or around North America.

The Northern Voyages Neither Spain nor Portugal had any interest in Cabot's ideas. However, the English were interested enough to finance a voyage of exploration. Cabot left England with one ship, in May 1497. He crossed the North Atlantic and explored the region around Newfoundland. On a second voyage in 1498, Cabot may have explored the North American coast as far south as Chesapeake Bay. However, we cannot be sure. His ships disappeared without a trace.

Europeans soon realized that the lands Cabot had reached were not Asia, but a land they had never seen. England, France, and Holland all financed voyages of exploration to North America. These voyages focused on finding a **northwest passage,** a sea route from the Atlantic to the Pacific that passed through or around North America.

In 1524, another Italian explorer, Giovanni da Verrazano (vehr rah TSAH noh), searched for such a passage for King Francis I of France. Verrazano explored the Atlantic coastal region from North Carolina to Newfoundland. In doing so, he discovered the mouth of the Hudson River and New York Bay. French explorer Jacques Cartier (kar tee YAY) made three trips to North America for France. In searching for a northwest passage, he discovered the St. Lawrence River and explored it as far as present-day Montreal.

Queen Elizabeth I

English explorer Henry Hudson made four voyages in search of a northwest passage. Two voyages in the Arctic Ocean, during 1607 and 1608, were unsuccessful, and Hudson's English backers gave up on him. However, the Dutch grew interested in his activities and financed a third expedition in 1609. Crossing the Atlantic, Hudson reached what is now New York and explored up the river that today bears his name.

Hudson's discoveries on his third voyage convinced the English to sponsor a fourth voyage in 1610. Hudson again sailed into the Arctic, looking for a passage to the Pacific. He reached as far as Hudson Bay, which also is named for him, before the icy waters forced a halt to the voyage. In the spring of 1611, Hudson's crew, unhappy about spending the winter in this harsh land, grew desperate. They mutinied and set the explorer, his teenage son, and seven loyal crew members adrift in a small boat. The mutineers returned to England. Like John Cabot, Hudson was never heard from again.

With his son and a few loyal crew members, Henry Hudson was set adrift, by mutineers, in Hudson Bay. They died a lonely death somewhere on the bay.

✓Checkpoint **Why did explorers continue to look for routes to Asia?**

☆ **Looking Back and Ahead** Hudson's last voyage marked the end of serious efforts to find a northwest passage. Europe's attention shifted to the lands that the voyagers had explored. In these lands, explorers reported, were vast amounts of timber, fish, and other resources. Europeans began to think of North America not as an obstacle blocking their way to Asia but as a land to be exploited for profit.

Section 3 | **Check Your Progress**

Progress Monitoring ☯nline
For: Self-test with instant help
Visit: PHSchool.com
Web Code: mva-1023

Comprehension and Critical Thinking

1. **(a) Recall** How did the Reformation lead to religious conflict in Europe?
   (b) Apply Information Why do you think the religious tensions that developed during the Reformation among European nations spread to the Americas?

2. **(a) Summarize** How did the defeat of the Spanish Armada change the political balance of power among European countries?

   (b) Analyze Cause and Effect How did the shift in the political balance of power affect the exploration of North America?

Reading Skill

3. **Identify Implied Main Ideas** Find the implied main ideas of the text under the heading "Asia Continues to Beckon." Then, combine this main idea with the main idea you identified under the heading "Conflicts in Europe" to state a single main idea for both of these portions of text.

Vocabulary Builder

Complete each of the following sentences so that the second part further explains the first part and clearly shows your understanding of the key term.

4. Spain's economy was based on the system of mercantilism, under which _____.

5. European explorers searched for a northwest passage, _____.

Writing

6. Why do you think Spain and Portugal refused to support John Cabot's proposed voyage? Write a paragraph explaining your views.

Objectives

1. Describe how the French colony of New France spread into the interior of North America.

2. Explain how the Dutch established a thriving colony along the Hudson River.

3. Explain the influence of these settlements on the Native Americans of the region.

Prepare to Read

Reading Skill

Combine Main Ideas to Construct Meaning Several main ideas are developed in each section in this textbook. Use the red heads to identify the bigger main ideas. The blue heads introduce text that further develops the main ideas. As you read Section 4, identify the main ideas and the ways in which the information helps you to understand these ideas.

Vocabulary *Builder*

High-Use Words

<u>decline</u>, p. 54

<u>motive</u>, p. 55

Key Terms and People

Samuel de Champlain, p. 53

coureur de bois, p. 54

Jacques Marquette, p. 55

alliance, p. 57

⭐ **Background Knowledge** By the early 1600s, England, France, and the Netherlands had each sponsored explorations of North America. Each had staked claims to lands there. In this section, you will learn about the colonies begun by the French and Dutch and how Native American peoples were affected by these colonies.

New France

The French began to settle colonies in the early 1600s. In 1603, Samuel de Champlain made the first of 11 voyages to explore and map the lands along the St. Lawrence River. In 1608, Champlain established a settlement on the banks of the St. Lawrence, which he named Quebec. From this base he ventured east, in 1609, and explored the large lake on the border of present-day Vermont and New York that bears his name. His activities gave the French an influence in the region that lasted 150 years.

Life in New France New France, as the French colony was called, developed in quite different ways than New Spain. As you know, the Spanish sought gold, silver, and other precious minerals. The French, on the other hand, profited from fish and furs. The Spanish forced Native Americans into harsh labor. The French traded with Native Americans for the animal skins so highly valued in Europe. Beaver skins sent to Europe and made into hats were a profitable item.

Main Idea
The major French settlements in North America were based on fur trade with Native Americans.

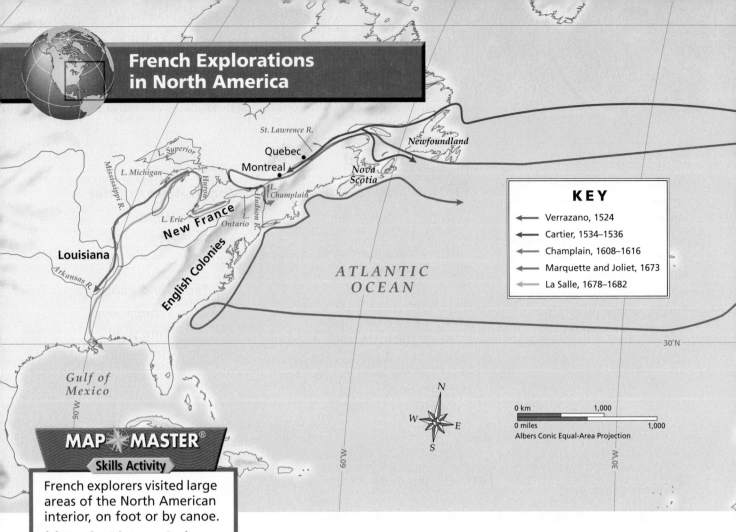

French Explorations in North America

St. Lawrence R.

Quebec
Montreal

Newfoundland

Nova Scotia

L. Superior

L. Michigan

Mississippi R.

L. Huron

New France

L. Erie

L. Ontario

L. Champlain

Hudson R.

Louisiana

Arkansas R.

English Colonies

ATLANTIC OCEAN

KEY

◄— Verrazano, 1524
◄— Cartier, 1534–1536
◄— Champlain, 1608–1616
◄— Marquette and Joliet, 1673
◄— La Salle, 1678–1682

30°N

Gulf of Mexico

90°W

60°W

30°W

N
W   E
S

0 km   1,000
0 miles   1,000
Albers Conic Equal-Area Projection

MAP✦MASTER®
Skills Activity

French explorers visited large areas of the North American interior, on foot or by canoe.

(a) Read a Distance Scale Find the route taken by La Salle. About how many miles did he travel from Montreal to the mouth of the Mississippi River?

(b) Make Predictions What kinds of rivalries do you think the French explorations started?

MapMaster ●nline

For: Interactive map
Visit: PHSchool.com
Web Code: mvp-1024

Vocabulary Builder
decline (dee KLĪN) v. to lessen in force, health, strength, or value

This pattern was set during Champlain's first days in the Americas. He established the colony's first settlement—a trading post—in what is today Nova Scotia, in 1604. As he continued to explore the region, he convinced local Indians to bring pelts to the trading posts established by the French. Trading posts such as Quebec City and Montreal became busy centers of commerce.

Brave employees of the fur companies paddled large canoes into the wilderness to find and acquire pelts from Native Americans. *Coureurs de bois*, the French term for "runners of the woods," were independent traders who lived among the Indians. Many of them married Indian women and started families.

Not until the late 1600s did French colonists begin to farm in large numbers. One reason for this change was that the market for furs in Europe was in decline. Another reason was the disruption that Indian wars brought to the fur trade. Still another was the 3,000 French settlers—including many single young women—that King Louis XIV sent to New France in the 1660s. After the new settlers arrived, the population began to expand. New France had about 5,000 colonists by 1672.

Exploring the Mississippi The same economic and religious motives that established New France also inspired its expansion. By 1670, French missionary Jacques Marquette had founded two missions along the Great Lakes, in present-day Michigan. Meanwhile, French traders explored the Great Lakes area looking for new sources of furs.

In 1673, Father Marquette and Louis Joliet, a French Canadian trader, paddled their canoes along the shores of Lake Michigan to what is now Green Bay, Wisconsin. They made their way west until they reached the Mississippi River. For the next month they followed the river downstream, thinking that it might be the long-sought northwest passage. In July, the group reached Mississippi's junction with the Arkansas River. Convinced that the Mississippi flowed into the Gulf of Mexico and not into the Pacific Ocean, they returned home.

Although Marquette and Joliet did not find a northwest passage, they provided the French with a water route into the heart of North America. The river's exploration was completed in 1682 by René Robert Cavelier, also known as La Salle. Reaching the river's mouth at the Gulf of Mexico, La Salle claimed the entire Mississippi Valley for France. He named the region Louisiana, in honor of King Louis XIV.

☑**Checkpoint** **What was the goal of the voyage of Marquette and Joliet on the Mississippi?**

Vocabulary *Builder*
<u>motive</u> (MOH tihv) *n.* inner drive that causes a person to do something

Combine Main Ideas to Construct Meaning Identify three main ideas from the paragraphs following the subheading "Life in New France." Then, state the big idea of these paragraphs.

Exploring the Mississippi
This drawing shows Father Marquette and Louis Joliet traveling the unknown waters of the Mississippi River. **Critical Thinking:** *Draw Conclusions How would settling the Mississippi Valley benefit New France?*

Links Across Time

Wall Street

Late 1600s Built in 1653, a wall at lower end of Manhattan protected Dutch settlers from outside attacks. Gradually, the path by the wall became an important place for merchants and traders.

1792 The New York Stock Exchange began in lower Manhattan where a group of New York businessmen met daily to buy and sell stocks. Today, Wall Street is part of the thriving commerce of New York City.

Link to Today Online

Wall Street Today How has the role of Wall Street changed in today's financial market? Go online to find out more about Wall Street today.

For: Wall Street in the news
Visit: PHSchool.com
Web Code: mvc-1024

The New York Stock Exchange today

Main Idea
Dutch settlements along the Hudson River valley became a barrier to westward expansion of the English colonies.

New Netherland

Dutch land claims in North America were based on Henry Hudson's exploration of the Hudson River. In 1610, Dutch traders arrived in the Hudson River valley and began a busy trade with Native Americans. The trade was so profitable that the Dutch West India Company decided to establish a permanent colony in what the Dutch called New Netherland.

In 1624, about 300 settlers arrived from the Netherlands. Most of them settled at Fort Orange, a fur-trading post that was later renamed Albany. In 1626, another group settled at the mouth of the Hudson River. The colony's governor, Peter Minuit, purchased the island from nearby Indians. The colonists named their new home New Amsterdam. The town grew steadily as new colonists arrived. By 1653, it had a population of about 800.

New Netherland was a barrier to the English. It kept English settlers from moving westward. In 1664, English forces seized New Netherland. The new territory was renamed New York, after the king's brother, the Duke of York.

☑**Checkpoint** Why did the Dutch establish settlements along the Hudson River?

The Impact on Native Americans

As you have read, Native Americans provided fur pelts to French and Dutch traders. The Europeans gave Native Americans manufactured goods, such as cloth, iron pots and tools, and guns. Ultimately, however, the fur trade had a grave effect on Native Americans.

The French and the Dutch each made alliances with Native American peoples. An **alliance** is an agreement between parties that benefits them both. Long before the Hurons became trading partners with the French, the Iroquois and the Hurons were enemies. The Hurons became partners with the French, and the Dutch had an agreement with the Iroquois. The Iroquois, using guns from the Dutch, began to attack the Hurons. The attacks were devastating to the Hurons.

Even worse were the diseases caused by contact with Europeans. Furthermore, the overtrapping of animals weakened the food chain on which Native Americans depended. As the fur-bearing animals disappeared, the Native Americans' value to the colonists decreased. Instead, Native American land became more valuable to the colonists.

☑Checkpoint **How did the French and Dutch settlements affect Native Americans?**

☆ **Looking Back and Ahead** England did not stand by as France and Holland carved out colonies in North America. As English colonies spread over the Atlantic shores of North America, their competition with New France and New Netherland grew.

Main Idea
The French and Dutch tried to establish peaceful relations with Native Americans, but their presence had a major impact on the Native Americans' future.

Dutch traders with Iroquois

Section 4 | **Check Your Progress**

Progress Monitoring ⬤nline
For: Self-test with instant help
Visit: PHSchool.com
Web Code: mva-1024

Comprehension and Critical Thinking

1. **(a) Describe** How did the colonists in New France support themselves?
   (b) Compare and Contrast How did the economic activities of New France compare with those of New Spain?

2. **(a) Identify** Name two Dutch settlements in the Americas.
   (b) Apply Information How did the geographic location of these settlements contribute to their success?

🔁 Reading Skill

3. **Combine Main Ideas to Construct Meaning** What is the big idea of Section 4? What smaller main ideas work together to support this big idea?

Vocabulary *Builder*

Answer the following questions in complete sentences that show your understanding of the key terms.

4. Who were the *coureurs de bois,* and how did they contribute to the economic success of New France?

5. What were the consequences of the Dutch alliance with the Iroquois for the Hurons?

Writing

6. In Section 2, you read about Bartolomé de Las Casas's observations concerning relations between the Spaniards and the Native Americans. Write similar eyewitness accounts of relations between Native Americans and **(a)** the French and **(b)** the Dutch in the Americas.

When you study history, you generally read about events in the sequence, or order, in which they happened. One way to understand the sequence of historical events is by creating a timeline. A timeline identifies major events and the dates that each took place. You should read a horizontal timeline from left to right. Reading a timeline helps you judge how events could be related in time.

Exploring the Americas

1497: Cabot sails to North America for England.

1524: Verrazano explores along the Atlantic coast for France.

1664: The English take New York from the Dutch.

1450   1500   1550   1600   1650   1700

1492: Columbus sails to islands in the Caribbean Sea for Spain.

1519–1522: Magellan's crew circumnavigates the globe for Spain.

1588: The English navy defeats the Spanish Armada.

1609: Sailing for the Dutch, Hudson reaches New York.

1673: Marquette and Joliet explore the Mississippi River for France.

Learn the Skill

Use these steps to understand sequence.

1 **Identify the time period covered in the timeline.** Look for the beginning date and the ending date.

2 **Figure out the intervals between each date on the timeline.** Timelines are always divided into time periods of equal length, such as 10, 50, or 100 years.

3 **Add additional events.** Include other important historical events on the timeline, based on your reading of the text.

4 **Draw conclusions.** Use the timeline to draw conclusions about the events that took place during a particular period in history. Framing questions based on the timeline can help you draw sound conclusions.

Practice the Skill

Answer the following questions about the timeline on this page.

1 **Identify the time period covered in the timeline.** (a) What is the date of the first event? (b) What is the date of the last event?

2 **Figure out the intervals between each date on the timeline.** How many years are there between each major date on the timeline?

3 **Add additional events.** What other events might you add to this timeline? Why?

4 **Draw conclusions.** How does the timeline show conflict among European nations during this period?

Apply the Skill

See the Review and Assessment at the end of this chapter.

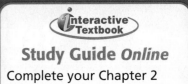

Chapter Summary

Section 1
The Age of Exploration

- The Vikings set up a colony in Newfoundland.
- Christopher Columbus, seeking a sea route to Asia, reached the West Indies in 1492 instead.
- European explorers continued to explore and colonize the Americas.
- The Columbian Exchange resulted in the transfer of products, people, and ideas between Europe and the Americas.

Section 2
Spain's Empire in the Americas

- Spanish conquistadors conquered Native American civilizations in the Americas.
- As the Spanish Empire grew, Native American workers were harshly treated.
- A strict class system developed in Spain's American colonies.

Section 3
Europeans Compete in North America

- During the Reformation, the authority of the Roman Catholic Church was challenged.
- The defeat of the Spanish Armada undermined Spanish control of the seas.
- European explorers continued to seek a northwest passage to Asia.

Section 4
France and the Netherlands in North America

- Colonists in New France established a fur trade with Native Americans.
- The Dutch established permanent settlements in what is now the northeastern United States.
- The French and Dutch settlements had a negative impact on Native American life.

Key Concepts

These notes will help you prepare for questions about key concepts.

European Exploration and Settlement of the Americas

Reasons for Exploration

- Rivalries among European nations sparked a search for an alternate route to Asia.
- Spain backed voyages of exploration to find a western sea route to Asia.
- English, French, and Dutch explorers searched for a northwest passage from the Atlantic to the Pacific that would pass through or around North America.

Results of Exploration

- Christopher Columbus discovered land in the West Indies in 1492.
- Balboa discovered the Pacific Ocean in 1513; Magellan's crew sailed around the world from 1519 to 1522.
- Spanish conquistadors extended Spain's empire in the Americas, from South America into North America.
- During the seventeenth century, the English, French, and Dutch established settlements in the Americas.

Europe's Impact on the Americas

Positive Effects

- The Columbian Exchange brought many new animals and plants to America.
- French and Dutch fur traders gave Native Americans goods, including cloth and iron tools and pots.

Negative Effects

- Europeans brought diseases to the Americas that killed many Native Americans.

Vocabulary *Builder*

Key Terms

Complete each of the following sentences so that the second part further explains the first part and clearly shows your understanding of the key term.

1. Hernando Cortés and Francisco Pizarro were Spanish conquistadors_____.

2. Because Spain's empire in the Americas needed workers, the government issued *encomiendas*_____.

3. In the 1500s and 1600s, many European nations practiced mercantilism_____.

4. During a time of war, it may help to form an alliance_____.

Comprehension and Critical Thinking

5. **(a) Recall** What discoveries did Balboa and Magellan make on their voyages?
   (b) Apply Information How did the achievements of those explorers change the way in which people viewed their world?

6. **(a) Identify** What were some of the products exchanged between Europe and the Americas as a result of the Columbian Exchange?
   (b) Link Past and Present What kinds of cultural and economic exchanges occur between nations today?

7. **(a) Recall** How did the Spanish government bring order to new Spanish settlements being developed in Spanish colonies?
   (b) Apply Information How does the image below show how religion was used to bring order to the settlements?

8. **(a) List** List three ways that French and Dutch colonists affected the lives of Native Americans.
   (b) Explain Problems Why do you think England felt it was a problem when they learned of the presence of French settlements in the valleys of the Ohio and the Mississippi rivers?

9. **(a) Recall** What role did gold play in the economy of Europe during the 1500s?
   (b) Identify Costs How did mercantilism affect the growth of colonies in the Americas?

History Reading Skill

10. **Identify Main Ideas and Details** Identify the main idea of Section 2. Find details to support the main idea.

Writing

11. **Write two paragraphs:**
    Discuss the causes and effects of European exploration in the Americas.
    Your paragraphs should:
    - begin with a thesis statement that expresses a main idea about the beginning of European exploration in the Americas;
    - support the main idea with facts, examples, and other information about the era;
    - use chronological order as much as possible.

12. **Write a Persuasive Speech:**
    The year is 1510. You are an adventurer eager to continue the attempt to find a route to Asia. Prepare a speech you will give to persuade a monarch that spending money on this voyage is a wise decision.

Skills for Life

Understand Sequence

Use the chapter timeline on pages 32–33 to answer the following questions.

13. What time period is covered in the timeline?

14. Into what time intervals is the timeline divided?

15. **(a)** When did the French establish Quebec?
    (b) How many years later did Marquette and Joliet explore the Mississippi?

16. What additional events might you add to the timeline? Why?

17. What trend does this timeline show? Explain.

Test Yourself

1. **Which of the following people was the first Spaniard to set foot in what is now the United States?**

   A Christopher Columbus

   B Juan Ponce de León

   C Francisco Pizarro

   D Francisco Coronado

2. **How did Europe's attitude toward North America change after Henry Hudson's last voyage?**

   A Efforts to find a northwest passage continued.

   B French and Dutch fur traders set up more trading posts.

   C Efforts began to profit from the lands explored.

   D Most countries no longer gained from the system of mercantilism.

3. **In return for the fur pelts, what goods did the Europeans trade with Native Americans?**

   A tobacco

   B food crops

   C cloth and tools

   D pots and silk

4. **Unlike the Spaniards, French claims in North America were largely for**

   A settling farm communities.

   B economic gains.

   C establishing missions and forts.

   D establishing lumber trade posts.

Document-Based Questions

Task: Look at Documents 1 and 2, and answer their accompanying questions. Then, use the documents and your knowledge of history to complete the following writing assignment:

> Write a two-paragraph essay describing positive and negative effects of the Columbian Exchange.

Document 1: The Columbian Exchange involved hundreds of items that enriched people's lives. But one item was deadly—European disease. Bernal Díaz del Castillo, who traveled with Hernando Cortés, describes the scene in the Aztec capital of Tenochtitlán in 1521. *What conditions did the Spanish encounter in Tenochtitlán?*

> "All the houses and stockades in the lake were full of corpses. . . . It was the same in the streets and courts. . . . We could not walk without treading on the bodies and heads of dead Indians. . . . . Indeed, the stench was so bad that no one could endure it . . . and even Cortés was ill from the odors which assailed his nostrils."

Document 2: The arrival of Columbus set off a tragic chain of events for the people of the Americas. Study the graph to see how the population of central Mexico declined after the European arrival. *What happened to the population between 1500 and 1560?*

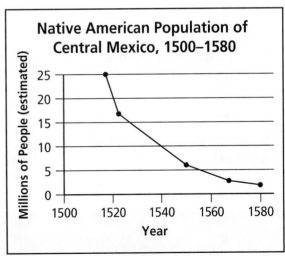

Native American Population of Central Mexico, 1500–1580

Source: Nicolás Sánchez-Albornoz, *The Population of Latin America*

Chapter Preview

As the wealth and power of Spain's empire in the Americas grew, so too did England's push to build a successful empire in North America. English colonists came seeking wealth, religious freedom, and better living conditions. In this chapter, you will learn how the English started their colonies.

U.S. Events

1565 Spain builds first permanent European settlement in North America.

1607 English start colony at Jamestown, Virginia.

1620 Pilgrims sign the Mayflower Compact and settle at Plymouth Bay.

1550

1600

1650

World Events

1558 Elizabeth I becomes queen of England.

1602 Dutch start East India Company.

1640s The English fight a civil war.

This painting shows thankful Pilgrims arriving in Plymouth, Massachusetts, in 1621.

1664
The English take over New Amsterdam from the Dutch.

1682
William Penn founds the colony of Pennsylvania.

1732
Georgia is founded by James Oglethorpe.

1650

1700

1750

1689 William and Mary sign the English Bill of Rights.

1712 Thomas Newcomen's steam engine is put to use in British coal mines.

History Reading Skill **Compare and Contrast**

What was New York City like in the late 1600s?

In this chapter, you will learn how to compare and contrast.

> **Primary Source**
>
> In the 1690s Englishman John Miller lived in New York, where he was the city's only Episcopal minister. He wrote the following description of the city after leaving New York in 1695. Note the spelling differences.
>
> The number of the inhabitants in this Province are about 3000 families whereof almost one halfe are naturally Dutch, a great part English, and the rest French. . . . As to their Religion they are very much divided. . . .
>
> As to their wealth & disposition, thereto ye Dutch are rich & sparing, the English neither very rich nor too great husbands, the French are poor. . . .
>
> The Air of this Province is very good & much like that of the best parts of France. . . . The weather is indeed hotter in summer than one would wish. . . .
>
> He that is not pleased with these advantages may if he please to take a little pains in clearing . . . have good land or pastures. . . . Indeed not all alike for ye land toward the South is generally a sandy soile & not very fruitfull . . . but to the Northward & in the Indian Country the Land is much better. . . .
>
> — John Miller, *New York Considered and Improved,* 1695

The author compares the three population groups without ever stating that he is making a comparison.

The author compares the air of New York to that of France.

The word like *signals the comparison.*

The words not all alike *signal the contrast.*

The author contrasts land in the South with that of the North.

Compare and Contrast
- Look for similarities and differences between people, places, and ideas.
- Remember that some comparisons and contrasts are directly stated in the text, whereas others are unstated.
- One way to find unstated comparisons and contrasts is to connect information from different parts of the text.
- Signal words such as *like* or *unlike* and *similarly* or *in contrast* indicate comparisons and contrasts.

Document-Based Questions
1. Who is the author of this source?
2. How did he gain his knowledge of New York?
3. What evidence in the text might support the assumption that the author has visited the European continent?

Vocabulary *Builder*

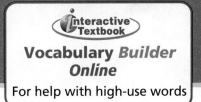

Previewing High-Use Academic Words

High-Use Word	Definition	Sample History Sentence
impose (ihm POHZ) (Section 1, p. 66)	*v.* to place a burden on something or someone	Manufacturers wanted the government to <u>impose</u> a high tax on imports.
sustain (suh STAYN) (Section 1, p. 68)	*v.* to support; to keep going	The colonists were unable at first to grow enough food to <u>sustain</u> themselves.
specify (SPEHS ih fī) (Section 2, p. 73)	*v.* to point out in detail	The government will <u>specify</u> the exact procedures for registering land.
restrict (ree STRIHKT) (Section 2, p. 75)	*v.* to place limitations on something or somebody	Some laws <u>restrict</u> undesirable activities.
fundamental (fuhn duh MEHN tahl) (Section 3, p. 78)	*adj.* most important part	Religious freedom was a <u>fundamental</u> goal of many settlers in colonial America.
accumulate (uh KYOOM yoo layt) (Section 3, p. 81)	*v.* to increase in amount over time	A person who invests wisely may <u>accumulate</u> great wealth.
proprietor (proh PRĪ ah tor) (Section 4, p. 86)	*n.* owner of a business or a colony	Lord Baltimore was the <u>proprietor</u> of Maryland in colonial times.
contrast (KAHN trast) (Section 4, p. 89)	*n.* difference shown between things when compared	The lives of women and men in colonial times provided many <u>contrasts</u>.
function (FUHNK shuhn) (Section 5, p. 91)	*n.* purpose; proper use	The <u>function</u> of government is to serve the people.
convert (kuhn VERT) (Section 5, p. 91)	*v.* to change from one religion to another	European missionaries sought to <u>convert</u> Native Americans to Christianity.

Previewing Key Terms and People

Objectives

1. Explain why England wanted to establish colonies in North America.

2. Describe the experience of the settlers who founded the first permanent English colony in Jamestown.

3. Explain how the Pilgrims managed to survive their first years in the Plymouth Colony.

Prepare to Read

 Reading Skill

Identify Contrasts As you read about early English settlements in North America, think how each of these settlements was unique. How was each different from the other early settlements? For example, you might look at the purpose of the settlements, the conditions each endured, and the composition of the settlers themselves.

Vocabulary *Builder*

High-Use Words

impose, p. 66

sustain, p. 68

Key Terms and People

charter, p. 67

John Smith, p. 67

representative government, p. 69

pilgrim, p. 69

Squanto, p. 70

Main Idea

During the age of exploration, England joined the other European powers in seeking colonies in the Americas.

Vocabulary *Builder*

impose (ihm POHZ) *v.* to place a burden on something or someone

⭐ **Background Knowledge** While Spain, France, and Holland sought colonies in the Americas, England did not remain idle. In this section, you will learn about the first English settlements in North America.

England Seeks Colonies

Like most of Europe in the age of exploration, England was a monarchy. However, in England, the power of the king or queen was limited by law and by a lawmaking body called Parliament.

Ever since the 1200s, English law had limited the king's power to punish people without trial. The law guaranteed the right to trial by jury. Other provisions limited the king's power to impose new taxes. The king could set new taxes only with Parliament's consent. Still, the king's powers were much greater than those of Parliament.

England began to establish colonies in North America in the late 1500s. Colonies would provide new markets for English products and important raw materials for English industries.

Two of the earliest English efforts to establish colonies took place during the 1580s. Both were set up on a small island off the coast of what today is North Carolina. The first colony at Roanoke Island was established in 1585, but it was abandoned a year later. The second colony is one of the great mysteries of American history. It was set up in 1587. The next year, England found itself at war with Spain. No ship was able to visit the Roanoke colony until 1590. By then, the colony was abandoned. It had disappeared without a trace.

☑**Checkpoint** What benefits did England hope to get from establishing colonies in North America?

Founding Jamestown

In 1607, a group of wealthy people made a new attempt to establish an English colony in North America. Eager to gain a share of the wealth of the Americas, they formed the Virginia Company of London. Some of the founders hoped to discover gold or silver. Others expected the colonists to trade with the Indians for furs, which could then be sold in Europe at a profit. Lumber also could be cut from North America's vast forests. Farmers could plant vineyards to grow grapes or mulberry trees to produce silk. England needed all of these products.

England's King James I backed the project. The king granted the merchants a charter to establish a colony called Virginia. A **charter** is a document issued by a government that grants specific rights to a person or company. It gave the Virginia Company authority over a large portion of North America's Atlantic coastline.

The first colonists arrived in Virginia in the spring of 1607. About 100 men sailed into Chesapeake Bay and built a fort they called Jamestown. It would prove to be England's first permanent settlement in North America.

Jamestown barely survived its first year. It was located on a swampy peninsula where insects thrived in warm weather. During the first summer, many colonists caught diseases, such as malaria, and died.

The colony had another serious problem. Many of the colonists had no intention of doing the hard farmwork needed to grow crops. Those men who came to the colony were not farmers. They were skilled in other trades. They spent their time looking for gold, expecting to get the food they needed from the Native Americans. The colonists found no gold. The local people, led by a chief named Powhatan, supplied some food to the colony. But it was not enough. By the spring of 1608, only 38 of the original colonists were still alive.

John Smith Takes Charge Conditions in Jamestown were extremely bad, in part because the colony was poorly led. Then, in the fall of 1608, John Smith was sent out from London to lead the colony. Smith lost no time taking command. He drew up tough, new rules. The most important rule was "He who works not, eats not."

Under Smith's firm leadership, the Jamestown colonists cut timber, put up new

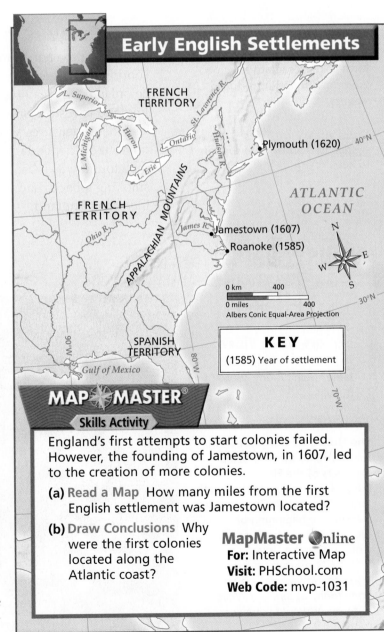

Early English Settlements

FRENCH TERRITORY

L. Superior

L. Michigan

L. Huron

L. Ontario

L. Erie

St. Lawrence R.

Hudson R.

Plymouth (1620)

40°N

ATLANTIC OCEAN

FRENCH TERRITORY

Ohio R.

APPALACHIAN MOUNTAINS

James R.

Jamestown (1607)

Roanoke (1585)

N

W E

S

0 km 400
0 miles 400
Albers Conic Equal-Area Projection

30°N

KEY
(1585) Year of settlement

SPANISH TERRITORY

Gulf of Mexico

90°W

80°W

70°W

MAP MASTER®
Skills Activity

England's first attempts to start colonies failed. However, the founding of Jamestown, in 1607, led to the creation of more colonies.

(a) Read a Map How many miles from the first English settlement was Jamestown located?

(b) Draw Conclusions Why were the first colonies located along the Atlantic coast?

MapMaster ●nline
For: Interactive Map
Visit: PHSchool.com
Web Code: mvp-1031

buildings, and planted crops. Meanwhile, hundreds of new colonists arrived. They included the first English women to settle in Jamestown. To get more food, Smith raided Native American villages. This angered Powhatan, who feared the English intended "to invade my people and possess my country."

The "Starving Time" In the fall of 1609, John Smith returned to England after being injured in an explosion. With Smith gone, conditions in Jamestown quickly worsened. So did relations with the Native Americans. Powhatan decided the time had come to drive the English away. First, he refused to supply them with food. The English settlers quickly ran out of food. The terrible winter of 1609–1610 is called the "starving time." By the spring of 1610, only 60 colonists were still alive.

☑**Checkpoint** **Why did settlers in Jamestown have difficulties at first?**

Main Idea
The Virginia colonists set up a form of representative government and introduced slavery.

Vocabulary *Builder*
sustain (suh STAYN) *v.* to support; to keep going

Jamestown Prospers

During the hard times, the Virginia Company did not give up. It continued to send new colonists and offered free land to keep old colonists from leaving. Most important, it sent new leaders from England to restore order in the colony.

These measures would not have succeeded if the colonists had not found a dependable source of income to sustain the colony. What they found was tobacco, a crop native to the Americas. By the 1580s, smoking tobacco had become popular in several European countries, including England.

Explore More Video
To learn more about the Jamestown Colony, view the video.

The House of Burgesses On July 30, 1619, the 22 elected members of the House of Burgesses first met together at the Jamestown church. That hot day marked the beginning of representative government in what is now the United States.
Critical Thinking: *Link Past and Present* *How would a lawmaking body today be similar? What differences would you expect to see?*

The governor calls the meeting to order.

Soldiers stand guard.

The secretary records what is said at the meeting.

Farmers in Jamestown and nearby settlements in Virginia began planting tobacco in 1612. By the early 1620s, Virginia farmers were selling all the tobacco they could grow. Their success drew new colonists from England.

The House of Burgesses During these years, Virginia developed a tradition of representative government—the form of government in which voters elect people to make laws for them. In 1619, Virginia's lawmaking body, the House of Burgesses, was elected and met for the first time. The House of Burgesses could pass laws and set taxes. However, it shared power with Virginia's appointed governor, who could veto its acts. The House of Burgesses marked the start of representative government in North America.

Africans Come to Virginia In the summer of 1619, a Dutch ship arrived in Virginia from the West Indies. On board were 20 Africans, who had been captured and taken from their homeland. The Africans were sold to the Virginia colonists as slaves. However, that did not necessarily mean they would be enslaved for the rest of their lives. In the early days of the colony, enslaved people had a chance to earn their freedom after working a certain number of years. Some enslaved Africans were able to do this. Permanent slavery for Africans was not established in Virginia until the last part of the 1600s.

African American artist Romare Bearden presents the forced journey enslaved Africans made to the Americas in his painting *Roots Odyssey*.

✓**Checkpoint** **What were the responsibilities of the House of Burgesses?**

The Plymouth Colony

In England during the 1500s, people could be punished for their religious beliefs. In the 1530s, when King Henry VIII declared himself head of the Church of England, everyone was expected to follow the ways of the Church of England.

About the time Jamestown was founded, a group of people in eastern England left their homes and settled in Holland. They wanted to separate from the Church of England and practice Christianity in their own way. These people, called Separatists, were often persecuted or treated badly because of their religion.

Between 1607 and 1609, several groups of Separatists settled in Holland. Although they were allowed to worship as they pleased, they still were not happy. In 1620, one group of Separatists decided to leave Holland and settle in Virginia. They are the people we know today as the Pilgrims. A pilgrim is a person who takes a religious journey.

The Mayflower Compact In September 1620, about 100 Pilgrims sailed for Virginia aboard a ship called the *Mayflower*. After a long voyage, they arrived safely in North America. However, storms had blown them off course, and they landed far to the north in what today is Massachusetts. They called their new home Plymouth, after a port city in England.

Main Idea
The Pilgrims founded the Plymouth Colony in order to practice their religion freely.

Identify Contrasts
How were the Pilgrims' reasons for coming to America different from those of the Jamestown settlers?

Squanto

Because they had landed outside Virginia, the Pilgrims believed they were not bound by the rules of the Virginia Company. But they needed rules of some sort. Before going ashore, 41 adult men signed the Mayflower Compact. It called for a government that would make and follow "just and equal laws." Officeholders would be elected by the colony's adult males.

Thus, a year after the creation of Virginia's House of Burgesses, the Pilgrims had taken a second step toward self-government in the Americas. The Mayflower Compact was the first document in which American colonists claimed a right to govern themselves.

The First Thanksgiving The Pilgrims had a very difficult first winter in Plymouth. They had arrived too late to plant crops and did not have enough food. During the winter of 1620–1621, half the colonists died from hunger or disease.

Conditions improved in the spring of 1621. As had happened at Jamestown, help from local Native Americans sustained the Pilgrims. A local chief gave the Pilgrims some food. Another Native American, named Squanto, brought the Pilgrims seeds of native plants—corn, beans, and pumpkins—and showed them how to plant them. He also taught the settlers how to catch eels from nearby rivers.

In the fall of 1621, the Pilgrims set aside a day to give thanks for their good fortune. Today's Thanksgiving holiday celebrates that occasion.

☑**Checkpoint** Why was the Mayflower Compact important?

☆ **Looking Back and Ahead** The early settlers faced many challenges before they were able to claim success. In the next section, you will read how English settlers established additional colonies in New England.

Section 1 | **Check Your Progress**

Progress Monitoring ⏻nline
For: Self-test with instant help
Visit: PHSchool.com
Web Code: mva-1031

Comprehension and Critical Thinking

1. **(a) Recall** What actions did John Smith take to help Jamestown?
(b) Identify Alternatives What other methods do you think Smith could have used to save the colony?

2. **(a) Identify** Who were the Pilgrims?
(b) Analyze Cause and Effect How did the Pilgrims' experiences in England affect the government they established in the Plymouth Colony?

Reading Skill

3. **Identify Contrasts** How did the government of the Jamestown settlers differ from that of the Plymouth settlers?

Vocabulary *Builder*

Fill in the blanks with the correct key terms.

4. The English king gave the merchants of the Virginia Company a _____ to establish a colony called Virginia.

5. English colonies in North America established a form of _____ based on elections.

Writing

6. Imagine that you are preparing a news report about the founding of Jamestown Colony. Make notes providing background information about this development. Your notes should include the economic benefits of colonialism and the particular details about how Jamestown Colony was founded.

Objectives

1. Describe the geography and climate of the New England Colonies.
2. Describe the Puritan settlement in Massachusetts.
3. Identify the new settlements that developed in New England as a result of Puritan religious practices.
4. Explain the changes that took place in the New England Colonies in the 1600s.

Prepare to Read

 ### Reading Skill

Make Comparisons Despite differences, the New England colonies were alike in many ways. Look for these similarities in this section. For example, how was the climate similar in various colonies? You might also look at the shared reasons colonists had for coming to North America and at the ways that similar government structures evolved throughout New England.

Vocabulary *Builder*

High-Use Words

specify, p. 73
restrict, p. 75

Key Terms and People

John Winthrop, p. 72
toleration, p. 73
Roger Williams, p. 73
Anne Hutchinson, p. 74
Thomas Hooker, p. 74
John Wheelright, p. 75
town meeting, p. 75
Metacom, p. 76

⭐ **Background Knowledge** As you learned in the previous section, Plymouth Colony survived its first winter and began to grow slowly. Meanwhile, new colonies were growing up in this region, which is present-day New England. In this section, you will learn about the challenges the new colonies faced.

Geography of New England

New England is in the northeastern corner of the United States. Massachusetts, Connecticut, and Rhode Island make up southern New England. New Hampshire, Vermont, and Maine make up the northern part.

Much of New England is made up of hills and low mountains. Large areas are covered by forests. The soil is thin and rocky, which makes farming difficult. There are narrow plains located along the Atlantic coast. The Connecticut River, the region's longest river, flows from New Hampshire and Vermont through Massachusetts and Connecticut before reaching the sea. Just off New England's long, jagged coastline are some of the richest fishing grounds in the world.

Winters in New England tend to be long and snowy. Summers are shorter and warm. This helped the early colonists in the region, who caught fewer diseases and lived longer than the colonists in Virginia.

Main Idea
Farming is difficult in New England, but the region has resources like forests and rich fishing grounds.

New Englanders pursue a whale

☑ **Checkpoint** Why would colonists in New England have turned to fishing rather than to farming?

Make Comparisons

Reading Skill Compare the reasons that England's Puritans went to North America with the reasons that the Pilgrims left England. How are they similar?

Puritans in Massachusetts Bay

Similar to the Pilgrims, a group known as the Puritans had disagreements with the Church of England. Rather than split off from the established church, they wanted to reform, or change, it. In the early 1600s, the Puritans were influential in England. Many were important professionals such as merchants, landowners, or lawyers.

The 1620s brought hard times for England's Puritans. King Charles I opposed their movement and persecuted them. Hundreds of Puritan ministers were forced to give up their positions.

The Puritans Leave England A number of Puritans eventually decided to leave England and make the hazardous voyage to North America. In 1630, about 900 Puritans set off in 11 ships. They had formed the Massachusetts Bay Company, which received a charter to establish settlements in what are now Massachusetts and New Hampshire. The Puritans were led by John Winthrop, a respected landowner and lawyer.

In founding their own colony, Puritan leaders believed that their way of life would provide an example to others. As Winthrop said in a sermon during their voyage:

❝Now the only way . . . is . . . to walk humbly with our God. . . . We must consider that we shall be as a City upon a Hill. The eyes of all people are upon us.❞

—John Winthrop, "A Model of Christian Charity," 1630

The Salem Witch Trials

Today, the Salem witch trials show how quickly false accusations can be accepted as true. **Critical Thinking:** *Draw Conclusions Do you think this kind of judgment is possible today? Explain.*

◀ **The Accusers**
Clergymen such as Cotton Mather of Boston helped to feed the hysteria by asserting that the Devil was luring Salem's people into witchcraft.

◀ **The Accused**
An accused woman is strapped to a dunking stool, a common form of punishment.

The Massachusetts Bay Colony The Puritans established several settlements in their colony. The main town was Boston, which was located on an excellent harbor. By 1643, about 20,000 people lived in the Massachusetts Bay Colony.

By the mid-1630s, Massachusetts Bay had an elected assembly, the General Court. Each town sent representatives to the assembly. But voting was limited to adult male members of the Puritan church. Both the General Court and the colony's governor were elected each year.

The Puritans had founded their colony so they could worship as they chose. However, they did not give non-Puritans the same right. The Puritans did not believe in religious **toleration**—recognition that other people have the right to different opinions.

☑**Checkpoint** **Why did the Puritans go to North America?**

New Colonies

Disagreements about religion led to the founding of other colonies in New England. A key dispute involved Roger Williams, minister of a church in the town of Salem. Williams believed the Puritans should split entirely from the Church of England. He also criticized colonists who had seized Native American lands. Williams <u>specified</u> that colonists should pay Native Americans for their land.

Williams was forced to leave Massachusetts Bay in 1635. He moved south, to what today is Rhode Island, where he bought land from Native Americans. In 1636, he founded the town of Providence.

Main Idea
Religious disputes led some people to spread out and start new colonies in New England.

Vocabulary *Builder*
<u>specify</u> (SPEHS ah fī) *v.* to point out in detail

▼ **On Trial**
In 1692, hysteria about witches swept through Salem, Massachusetts. A special court tried dozens of women and men accused of witchcraft.

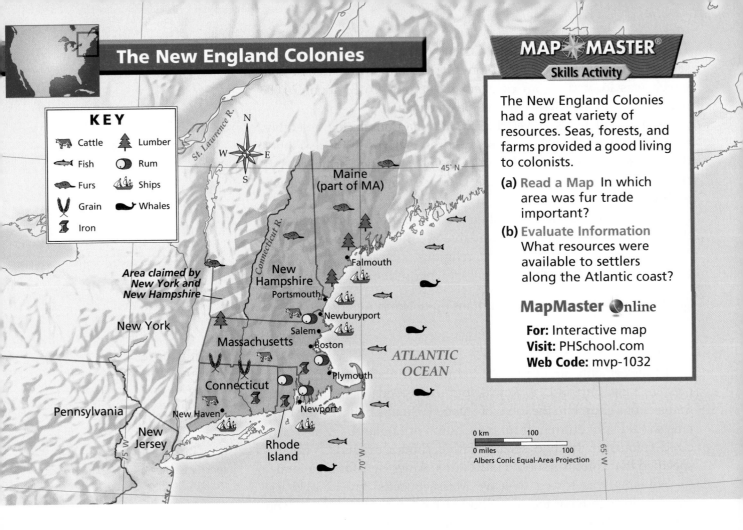

The New England Colonies

KEY

🐄 Cattle
🐟 Fish
🦫 Furs
🌾 Grain
⚒ Iron

🌲 Lumber
🛢 Rum
⛵ Ships
🐋 Whales

Area claimed by New York and New Hampshire

St. Lawrence R.

Connecticut R.

Maine (part of MA)

New Hampshire

Portsmouth

Falmouth

Newburyport

Salem

Boston

Massachusetts

New York

Connecticut

New Haven

Plymouth

Newport

Pennsylvania

New Jersey

Rhode Island

ATLANTIC OCEAN

45° N

70° W

65° W

55° W

0 km 100
0 miles 100
Albers Conic Equal-Area Projection

MAP MASTER®
Skills Activity

The New England Colonies had a great variety of resources. Seas, forests, and farms provided a good living to colonists.

(a) Read a Map In which area was fur trade important?

(b) Evaluate Information What resources were available to settlers along the Atlantic coast?

MapMaster Online

For: Interactive map
Visit: PHSchool.com
Web Code: mvp-1032

In 1644, the colonists in Rhode Island received a charter from the king to govern themselves. In doing so, they made an important contribution to religious toleration. They decided that Rhode Island would have no established church. People of all faiths could worship as they saw fit. Among the people who found religious freedom in Rhode Island were followers of the Jewish faith.

Anne Hutchinson's Dissent A Boston woman, Anne Hutchinson, questioned some of the Puritan teachings. She was put on trial in 1638 and was expelled from Massachusetts. Hutchinson established a settlement on an island that is now a part of Rhode Island. In 1642, she traveled farther south, in what is today New York State.

Settling Connecticut Thomas Hooker, a minister, disagreed with the Puritan leaders. He left Massachusetts with about 100 followers in 1636 and settled in what today is Connecticut. There, he founded the town of Hartford. Hundreds of Puritans followed, and soon Connecticut had several new settlements.

In 1639, the colonists drew up the Fundamental Orders of Connecticut, which established a new government with an elected legislature and governor. In 1662, Connecticut received an official charter from the king granting it self-government.

John Wheelright also was forced to leave Massachusetts. He got into trouble because he agreed with some of Anne Hutchinson's views. In 1638, Wheelright and some followers moved to New Hampshire, where they founded the town of Exeter. For a time, Massachusetts tried to control New Hampshire. Finally, in 1680, a charter from the king made New Hampshire a separate colony.

☑Checkpoint **Why did Roger Williams and Anne Hutchinson leave the Massachusetts Bay Colony?**

Growth and Change

The Puritans believed that towns and churches should manage their own affairs. They also believed that people should work hard and live in strong and stable families.

Each Puritan town governed itself by setting up a town meeting—an assembly of townspeople that decides local issues. Membership in town meetings was <u>restricted</u> to male heads of households. Town meetings set local taxes and elected people to run the towns. New England became a region of towns and villages where neighbors knew one another and participated together in government.

New England families earned their livelihoods in many different ways. Farmers grew crops, but they also made leather goods and other products. Fishers caught cod and other fish that were shipped to customers in Europe. A shipbuilding industry provided many jobs. By the 1660s, more than 300 ships from New England were fishing off the coast or moving products across the Atlantic Ocean.

Main Idea
As the number of colonists in New England grew, the region went through many changes.

Vocabulary *Builder*
restrict (ree STRIHKT) *v.* to place limitations on something or somebody

Links to Civics

The Town Meeting

The New England town meeting was a place to argue important town issues. Questions such as "What roads should be built?" and "How much should the schoolmaster be paid?" were discussed. Town meetings gave New Englanders an opportunity to speak their minds. This early experience encouraged the growth of democratic ideas in New England. Sometimes, as shown here, the exchanges became quite heated. **Critical Thinking: *Interpret Paintings*** *How would you describe the attitude of the artist toward the townspeople he portrays?*

Metacom, known to the English as "King Philip"

King Philip's War By the 1670s, the Native American population was decreasing, mainly because large numbers of Native Americans had died from diseases that they caught from Europeans. By 1670, there were only 12,000 Native Americans in New England, one tenth of their population 100 years earlier.

In 1675, a major conflict erupted. Opponents of the English were led by Metacom, the chief of the Wampanoag, who was also known by his English name, King Philip. His goal was to stop Puritan expansion. Other Native American groups, from Maine to Rhode Island, joined the war, some siding with the settlers. The fighting lasted a year and cost thousands of lives. Metacom and his allies destroyed 12 English towns. The uprising ended in 1676 when Metacom was captured and killed. The war's end left the English colonies free to expand.

Puritan Influence Declines By the 1670s, the outlook of New Englanders was changing. There was a new generation of people born in North America. The new generation had lost some of their parents' religious fervor, as people concentrated on running farms and businesses. In growing towns like Boston, successful merchants were becoming the new community leaders. The English colonies of New England were doing well. But the stern religious rules of the original founders now had less influence over the people who lived there.

☑ **Checkpoint** Why did Metacom declare war on the English colonists?

⭐ **Looking Back and Ahead** As English colonies spread through New England, other colonies were being established to the west and south.

Section 2 | **Check Your Progress**

Progress Monitoring Online
For: Self-test with instant help
Visit: PHSchool.com
Web Code: mva-1032

Comprehension and Critical Thinking

1. **(a) Summarize** What was the geography and climate of New England?
   (b) Identify Economic Costs How did geography affect the New England economy?

2. **(a) Recall** Why did Puritans establish the Massachusetts Bay Colony?

(b) Analyze Cause and Effect How did the lack of religious toleration affect politics in the Massachusetts Bay Colony?

🔄 **Reading Skill**

3. **Make Comparisons** Compare the way the English government treated the Puritans with the way the Puritans treated Anne Hutchinson. How are they similar?

Vocabulary *Builder*

4. Write two definitions for each key term: toleration, town meeting. First, write a formal definition for your teacher. Second, write a casual definition in everyday English for a classmate.

Writing

5. Create a concept web. Label the main oval "Religion." Then, add entries that show how religion played a major role in the settling of the New England Colonies. Add as many secondary ovals as necessary.

Objectives

1. Describe the geography and climate of the Middle Colonies.

2. Describe the early history of New York and New Jersey.

3. Explain how Pennsylvania and Delaware were founded.

4. Explain how the Middle Colonies changed in the 1600s and early 1700s.

Prepare to Read

Reading Skill

Identify Signal Words Signal words help readers spot comparisons and contrasts. For example, when we say, "Kentucky is warm. New York is *also* warm," the word *also* suggests that the two states and climates are similar. If the text reads, "Kentucky is warm. *Instead,* New York is cool," the word *instead* suggests that the two states and climates are different. Look for comparison and contrast signal words as you read this section.

Vocabulary *Builder*

High-Use Words

<u>fundamental</u>, p. 78
<u>accumulate</u>, p. 81

Key Terms and People

proprietary colony, p. 78
royal colony, p. 78
William Penn, p. 78
backcountry, p. 81

⭐ **Background Knowledge** While the New England colonies were growing, important developments were taking place in the region south of New England. In this section, you will learn about this region, which became known as the Middle Colonies.

Geography of the Middle Colonies

Four states made up the Middle Colonies: New York, Pennsylvania, New Jersey, and Delaware. New York, now the largest of these states, also is the farthest north. The scenic Hudson River flows south through eastern New York before reaching the sea at New York City. Long Island, the easternmost piece of New York, extends into the Atlantic Ocean for more than 100 miles. Today, New York City is the most populous city in the country.

Pennsylvania is the region's second-largest state. The southeastern section is a lowland. Philadelphia, Pennsylvania's largest city, is located there, on the Delaware River.

Most of New Jersey is a lowland along the Atlantic coast. Delaware, the region's smallest state, is on the coast directly south of New Jersey.

Middle Colony farmers had an easier time than farmers in New England. The climate was warmer, with a longer growing season. The fertile soil was well suited for crops like wheat, fruits, and vegetables.

Main Idea
With a warmer climate and more fertile soil than New England, the Middle Colonies became a farming region.

Identify Signal Words
What signal words suggest a contrast between the Middle Colonies and the New England Colonies? What contrast is suggested?

☑**Checkpoint** **What conditions in the Middle Colonies favored farming?**

New York and New Jersey

New York began as the Dutch colony of New Netherland. By 1660, it was an economic success. Farmers in the Hudson River valley were prosperous. The colony was the base for a profitable fur trade between the Dutch and Native Americans. The Dutch also made money trading with merchants in the British colonies. This trade violated Britain's mercantile laws and angered the government.

One of New Netherland's major problems was its small Dutch population. Many of the colonists came from Sweden, France, and Portugal. There also were some English Puritans who had settled on Long Island. These people often were hostile to Dutch rule.

Tension also existed between England and Holland. New Netherland separated England's northern colonies from its colonies farther south. Furthermore, England and Holland were rivals at trade.

New Netherland Becomes New York In 1664, England's King Charles II granted the right to all the Dutch lands in North America to his brother James. All that James had to do was conquer the territory. James sent a few warships to do the job, and the Dutch surrendered immediately. The colony was renamed New York, after James, the Duke of York. New Amsterdam, its capital, became New York City. The colony grew slowly. At the end of the 1600s, New York City was still a village on the southern end of Manhattan.

New Jersey New Jersey was established in 1665, when part of southern New York was split off to form a new colony. Like New York and several other English colonies, New Jersey at first was a proprietary colony—a colony created by a grant of land from a monarch to an individual or family. In 1702, New Jersey received a new charter as a royal colony—a colony controlled directly by the English king. New York had become a royal colony in 1685.

☑**Checkpoint** **How did New Jersey become a separate colony?**

Main Idea
Pennsylvania and Delaware were founded by Quakers, who believed in religious toleration.

Vocabulary *Builder*
fundamental (fuhn duh MEHN tahl) *adj.* most important part

Pennsylvania and Delaware

In the 1640s and 1650s, the Quakers were one of a number of new religious groups in England. Their ideas set them apart from most groups, including the Puritans.

The Quakers believed that all people had a direct link, or "inner light," with God. Groups of Quakers, therefore, did not need ministers. Another fundamental Quaker belief was that all people were equal in God's eyes. Thus, they were among the first in England to speak out against slavery. Women were considered equal to men in spiritual matters and often were leaders in Quaker meetings.

By the 1660s, there were thousands of Quakers in England. Many of them refused to pay taxes to support the Church of England. Because of their views, they often suffered from persecution. One Quaker leader was William Penn, a wealthy man who personally knew King Charles II. Penn wanted to find a place for Quakers to live where they would be safe from persecution. He used his connections to get a charter from the king for a new colony in North America. In 1681, he received an area almost as large as England itself, mainly in what is now Pennsylvania.

Penn's "Holy Experiment" Penn arrived in his colony in 1682. To attract settlers, he printed pamphlets in several languages and distributed them in England and on the European continent. Soon, new settlers began arriving from many places—England, Scotland, Wales, and Ireland. Still others came from Germany, Holland, and Switzerland.

Penn considered his colony to be a "holy experiment." His goal was to create a colony in which people from different religious backgrounds could live peacefully. In 1682, Penn wrote his Frame of Government for Pennsylvania. It granted the colony an elected assembly. It also provided for freedom of religion.

Penn tried to deal fairly with Native Americans. He did not allow colonists to settle on land until the Native Americans sold it to them. Relations between settlers and Native Americans in Pennsylvania were far from perfect. However, during Penn's lifetime they were much better in Pennsylvania than in other colonies.

Links to Art

Penn's Treaty With the Indians **by Edward Hicks** Edward Hicks, a Quaker preacher, first painted signs and coaches before he became an artist. In this painting Hicks wanted to show a peaceful meeting between settlers and Native Americans. **Critical Thinking: Detect Points of View** *How might this picture have been different if a Native American artist had painted it?*

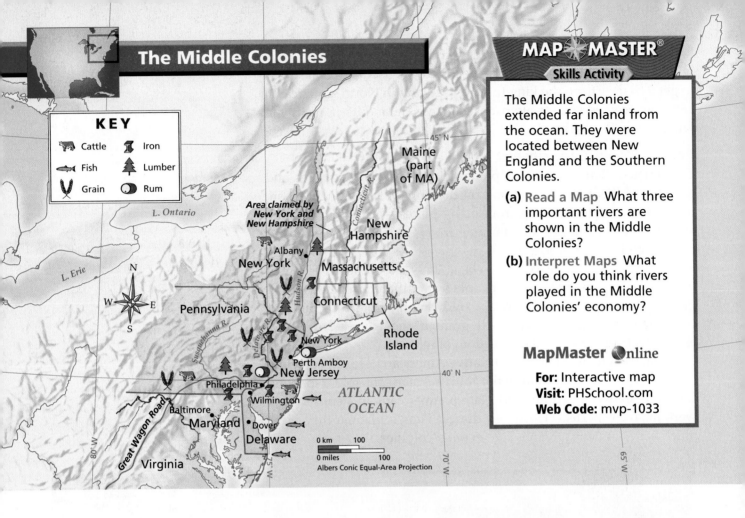

The Middle Colonies

KEY

🐄 Cattle   🔨 Iron
🐟 Fish   🌲 Lumber
🌾 Grain   🛢 Rum

L. Ontario

L. Erie

Area claimed by New York and New Hampshire

Albany

New York

New Hampshire

Maine (part of MA)

Massachusetts

Connecticut

Pennsylvania

New York

Rhode Island

Perth Amboy

New Jersey

Philadelphia

Wilmington

Baltimore

Maryland

Dover

Delaware

Virginia

ATLANTIC OCEAN

Great Wagon Road

0 km   100
0 miles   100
Albers Conic Equal-Area Projection

45° N
40° N
80° W
70° W
65° W

MAP MASTER®
Skills Activity

The Middle Colonies extended far inland from the ocean. They were located between New England and the Southern Colonies.

(a) Read a Map What three important rivers are shown in the Middle Colonies?

(b) Interpret Maps What role do you think rivers played in the Middle Colonies' economy?

MapMaster Online

For: Interactive map
Visit: PHSchool.com
Web Code: mvp-1033

Delaware: A Separate Colony People from Sweden were the first European settlers in Delaware. The Dutch took control of the territory in the 1650s, but they lost it to the English when they lost New York.

Penn's charter for Pennsylvania included Delaware. Because Delaware settlers did not want to send delegates to a distant assembly in Philadelphia, Penn gave the area its own representative assembly. In 1704, Delaware became a separate colony.

✓**Checkpoint** Why did Penn call Pennsylvania "a holy experiment"?

Main Idea

People from many European countries settled in the Middle Colonies during the 1600s and early 1700s.

Growth and Change

By the early 1700s, more than 20,000 colonists lived in Pennsylvania. Fertile soil and hard work made its farms productive. Farmers grew more than they could use and sold the balance. The top cash crop, wheat, was sold to customers in New England and abroad. Because of all its wheat, Pennsylvania was called America's breadbasket. New Jersey also produced large amounts of wheat.

Manufacturing was just beginning in the Middle Colonies during the 1700s. The largest manufacturers produced iron, flour, and paper. Meanwhile, artisans in towns worked as shoemakers, carpenters, masons, weavers, and in many other trades. Among the most important artisans were coopers, who made the barrels used to ship and store flour and other foods.

The Backcountry The western section of Pennsylvania was part of a region called the backcountry. The backcountry was a frontier region extending through several colonies, from Pennsylvania to Georgia.

Many of the people who settled in the backcountry were not English. Thousands were Scotch-Irish. Originally from Scotland, they had settled in Ireland before coming to North America. Large numbers of German immigrants began arriving early in the 1700s. The word these German newcomers used to describe themselves was *Deutsch*, for "German." Americans thought they were saying "Dutch." As a result, German immigrants in Pennsylvania were called the Pennsylvania Dutch.

By the middle of the 1700s, many settlers were pushing south and west along a route that led from Pennsylvania to Georgia. Because they often traveled in covered wagons, the route was called the Great Wagon Road. These backcountry settlers often fought with Native Americans.

Diverse and Thriving Colonies By 1750, the non-English immigrants had made the Middle Colonies the most diverse part of English North America. Philadelphia and New York were accumulating people at such a rate that they had become the largest cities and busiest ports in the colonies. All of the colonies had thriving economies.

Vocabulary Builder
accumulate (uh KYOOM yoo layt)
v. to increase in amount over time

✓**Checkpoint** How was Pennsylvania a breadbasket?

⭐ **Looking Back and Ahead** Both the New England and Middle Colonies had many small family farms. In the next section, you will read that parts of the Southern Colonies developed a plantation economy that was far different.

Section 3 | **Check Your Progress**

Progress Monitoring ⊙nline
For: Self-test with instant help
Visit: PHSchool.com
Web Code: mva-1033

Comprehension and Critical Thinking
1. **(a) Recall** What was the geography and climate of the Middle Colonies?
(b) Identify Economic Benefits What advantages did the geography and climate give to people living in the Middle Colonies?

2. **(a) Summarize** What were William Penn's goals for his colony?
(b) Compare How did Penn's "holy experiment" differ from the Puritans' "city on a hill"?

Reading Skill
3. **Identify Signal Words** What word in the sentence that follows suggests a comparison? What similarity is being identified?
Sentence: Both Pennsylvania and New Jersey produced a lot of wheat.

Vocabulary Builder
Answer the following questions in complete sentences that show your understanding of the key terms.
4. How was New Jersey different after it became a royal colony in 1702?

5. Why did so many people settle in the backcountry?

Writing
6. Imagine that you are a Pennsylvania farmer. Write a letter to a fellow farmer in New England telling him about your life in your new home. Then, write a letter that the New England farmer might send back describing his life in New England.

Landscapes of the 13 Colonies

The physical geography of the 13 British colonies differed widely from region to region. While farmers in New England had difficulty planting crops in thin and rocky soil, farmers in the Middle and Southern colonies had better luck with more fertile soil and warmer climates.

FRENCH TERRITORY

L. Huron

L. Ontario

L. Erie

NH   MA

NY

CT   RI

PA

NJ

Mason-Dixon   Line

MD   DE

VA

APPALACHIAN MOUNTAINS

FRENCH TERRITORY

NC

ATLANTIC OCEAN

SC

TIDEWATER

GA

SPANISH TERRITORY

0   200 KM.
0   200 MI.

KEY
- NEW ENGLAND COLONIES
- MIDDLE COLONIES
- SOUTHERN COLONIES
- CLAIMED BY NH and NY

Three Regions

Although farming was an important economic activity throughout the colonies, poor soil forced people in New England to concentrate on the sea for economic survival. For the colonists to the south, better geography yielded more favorable soils and longer growing seasons.

Understand Effects:
Slavery in the Southern Colonies

Because the climate of the Southern Colonies supported long growing seasons, plantation owners purchased enslaved people and used their labor to harvest rice and sugar crops. As the plantation system grew to dominate the economy of the Southern Colonies, slavery spread throughout the region.

▲ **New England** farmers had to break up rocks in the soil to clear land for crops. Because this was difficult work with only a small chance for financial success, many New Englanders relied upon fishing off the New England coast to provide for their families.

◀ Farmers in the **Middle Colonies** of Pennsylvania and New Jersey had an easier time growing crops. Better soil and a warmer climate in this region rendered huge wheat fields that gave Pennsylvania the nickname America's breadbasket.

◀ The **Southern Colonies** shared a lowland area called the Tidewater. Farmers there grew crops such as sugar, tobacco, and rice (pictured left). These crops thrived in the region's hot, humid environment. Because the Tidewater crops were grown on great stretches of land and required a great deal of labor, large farms, called plantations, developed in the South.

Analyze GEOGRAPHY AND HISTORY

Colonists in each of the three major regions of the 13 colonies learned to adapt to their environments. Write a paragraph describing how physical geography affected the output of food in the colonies.

The Southern Colonies

Objectives

1. Describe the geography and climate of the Southern Colonies.

2. Describe the early history of Virginia.

3. Explain how Maryland, the Carolinas, and Georgia were founded.

4. Identify the factors that produced the Tidewater and backcountry ways of life.

Prepare to Read

🔁 Reading Skill

Compare and Contrast As you read about the Southern Colonies in this section, think about how they are the same and different from one another. What physical features do they share? What human features? In what ways are the communities and places different? Comparing and contrasting will help you better understand the colonies.

Vocabulary *Builder*

High-Use Words
proprietor, p. 86
contrast, p. 89

Key Terms and People
Nathaniel Bacon, p. 85
Lord Baltimore, p. 86
James Oglethorpe, p. 87
debtor, p. 87
plantation, p. 87

⭐ **Background Knowledge** In the previous section, you learned how the Middle Colonies had diverse populations and economies. The Southern Colonies were much less diverse, as you will see in this section.

Main Idea

With a warm climate suited to crops requiring many workers, the Southern Colonies came to depend on slavery.

Concrete marker on the Mason-Dixon line

Geography of the Southern Colonies

During the 1760s, Charles Mason and Jeremiah Dixon were hired to settle a boundary dispute between Maryland and Pennsylvania. They conducted a survey—a careful measuring of an area with scientific instruments using the techniques of mathematics—that took four years to complete. The boundary they drew is known as the Mason-Dixon line. This line on a map marked much more than the boundary between two colonies. After the American Revolution, it was the dividing line between the northern states where slavery was abolished and the southern states where slavery persisted.

Five colonies were located south of the Mason-Dixon line: Maryland, Virginia, North Carolina, South Carolina, and Georgia. They shared a coastal area called the Tidewater, a flat lowland that includes many swampy areas. On its west, the Tidewater blends into a region of rolling hills called the Piedmont.

The climate of these states is warm and humid. Hot summers provide a long growing season that colonial farmers used to raise crops such as tobacco and rice. Both crops required many workers in the fields and thus were partly responsible for helping to spur the early development of slavery.

✔**Checkpoint** What conditions in the Southern Colonies favored the development of a plantation economy?

Virginia Grows

Virginia's population grew gradually during the 1600s. New settlers arriving from Europe made up for the fact that disease and difficult living conditions kept the death rate high. After 1650, the death rate fell, and the population increased more quickly. In 1640, about 10,000 settlers lived in Virginia. By 1670, the number had reached 40,000.

The makeup of Virginia's population also changed. By the 1670s, there were more children because fewer were dying at a young age. The percentage of women in the population rose as well.

Conflicts With Native Americans As Virginia's white population grew, the Native American population shrank. Disease and violence took their toll. In 1607, there had been about 8,000 Native Americans in Virginia. By 1675, only about 2,000 Native Americans were left.

Farmers took over more land to plant tobacco. This led to trouble with the Native Americans. There were two violent confrontations—one in 1622 and the other in 1644. Although the Native Americans killed hundreds of colonists, they were defeated both times. After 1644, the Native Americans living near the coast had to accept English rule.

Bacon's Rebellion There was more trouble to come. Beginning in the 1660s, wealthy Virginia tobacco planters bought most of the good farmland near the coast. That left no land for poorer colonists who wanted to start their own farms. Most of these colonists were young men who were forced to work the land for wealthier farmers. The young men also were angry because without property, they could not vote.

Many poor colonists moved inland to find good farmland. Fighting broke out with Native Americans, and people were killed on both sides. Farmers on the frontier demanded that the governor take strong measures against the Native Americans. However, the governor hesitated. He hoped to avoid an all-out war with the Native Americans, partly because he benefited from his fur trade with them.

Nathaniel Bacon became the leader of the frontier settlers. In 1675, he organized a force of 1,000 westerners and began attacking and killing Native Americans. The governor declared that Bacon and his men were rebels. Bacon reacted by attacking Jamestown, burning it to the ground, and forcing the governor to run away.

The revolt, known as Bacon's Rebellion, collapsed when Bacon became sick and died. The governor hanged 23 of Bacon's followers. Still, he could not stop English settlers from moving onto Native American lands.

☑**Checkpoint** What was the main cause of Bacon's Rebellion?

Main Idea
The Virginia colonists fought Native Americans while sometimes quarreling among themselves.

Bacon's Rebellion
Nathaniel Bacon (center) is shown here taking part in the burning of Jamestown during his 1675 rebellion. **Critical Thinking:** *Explain Problems How did the interests of frontier settlers differ from those of colonists in towns and on plantations?*

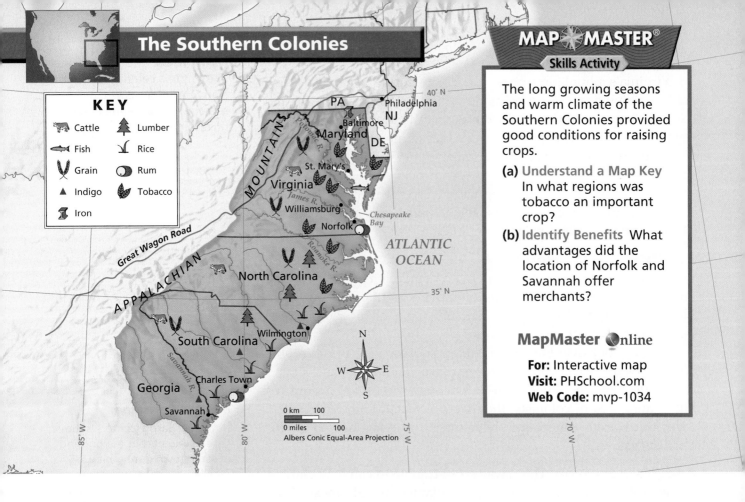

KEY

- 🐄 Cattle
- 🌲 Lumber
- 🐟 Fish
- ⚒ Rice
- 🌾 Grain
- 🛢 Rum
- ▲ Indigo
- 🌿 Tobacco
- ⚒ Iron

ATLANTIC OCEAN

Albers Conic Equal-Area Projection

MAP MASTER®
Skills Activity

The long growing seasons and warm climate of the Southern Colonies provided good conditions for raising crops.

(a) Understand a Map Key In what regions was tobacco an important crop?

(b) Identify Benefits What advantages did the location of Norfolk and Savannah offer merchants?

MapMaster Online

For: Interactive map
Visit: PHSchool.com
Web Code: mvp-1034

Main Idea
Religious toleration among Christians was a key feature of the Maryland Colony.

Vocabulary Builder
proprietor (proh PRĪ ah tor) *n.* owner of a business or a colony

Compare and Contrast
Compare and contrast the population growth, agriculture, and political tensions of Maryland with those of Virginia.

Main Idea
Large plantations took hold in South Carolina, whereas North Carolina and Georgia tended to have small farms.

Religious Toleration in Maryland

In 1632, King Charles I granted a charter for a new colony to George Calvert, an English Catholic. Catholics suffered great discrimination in England. Calvert aimed to set up a colony where Catholics could live safely. His colony, Maryland, lay across Chesapeake Bay from Virginia.

The first settlers included both Catholics and Protestants. They grew tobacco and harvested the sea life of Chesapeake Bay. When George Calvert died, his son, Cecil Calvert, Lord Baltimore, became proprietor. As the charter required, there was a representative assembly similar to the House of Burgesses in Virginia.

Soon there was tension between Protestants and Catholics. Fearing that Catholics might lose their rights, Lord Baltimore got the assembly to pass the Act of Toleration, in 1649. It welcomed all Christians and gave adult male Christians the right to vote and hold office. Although the Toleration Act did not protect people who were not Christian, it was still an important step toward religious toleration in North America.

✓**Checkpoint** Who benefited from Maryland's toleration?

Colonies in the Carolinas and Georgia

By the 1660s, a few settlers from Virginia had moved south beyond the colony's borders. In 1663, King Charles II granted a charter for a new colony to be established there, in the area called Carolina.

The northern part of Carolina developed slowly. It lacked harbors and rivers on which ships could travel easily. Settlers lived on small farms, raising and exporting tobacco. Some produced lumber for shipbuilding.

The southern part of Carolina grew more quickly. Sugar grew well in the swampy lowlands. Many planters came from Barbados in the West Indies. They brought enslaved people to grow sugar. Soon the colonists were using slave labor to grow another crop, rice. It became the area's most important crop.

As rice production spread, Carolina's main city, Charles Town (today's Charleston), eventually became the biggest city in the Southern Colonies. By then, Carolina had become two colonies: North Carolina and South Carolina.

Georgia The last of England's 13 colonies, Georgia was founded for two reasons. First, the English feared that Spain was about to expand its Florida colony northward. An English colony south of Carolina would keep the Spanish bottled up in Florida. Second, a group of wealthy Englishmen led by James Oglethorpe wanted a colony where there would be protection for English debtors— people who owe money. Under English laws, the government could imprison debtors until they paid what they owed.

Georgia's founders wanted Georgia to be a colony of small farms, not large plantations. Therefore, slavery was banned. However, this restriction was unpopular with settlers and did not last. By the 1750s, slavery was legal in Georgia.

Biography Quest

James Oglethorpe 1696–1785

James Oglethorpe was a fighter. A soldier since the age of 16, he fought in many winning battles. Later, as a member of England's Parliament, he fought against slavery and other injustices.

In 1728, a friend of Oglethorpe's died of smallpox while in jail for debt. Oglethorpe organized a committee to investigate conditions in debtors' prisons. Four years later, he founded Georgia as a place where debtors could start a new life.

Biography Quest ◉nline

Why did Georgia colonists later rebel against Oglethorpe?

For: The answer to the question about Oglethorpe
Visit: PHSchool.com
Web Code: mvd-1034

☑**Checkpoint** **Why did Oglethorpe and the other founders establish the colony of Georgia?**

Change in the Southern Colonies

During the 1700s, the Southern Colonies developed two distinct ways of life. People along the coast lived very differently from people who settled inland on the frontier.

The Tidewater Region The most important feature of life along the coast in the Southern Colonies was the plantation, a large farm especially in a hot country where crops such as cotton, sugar, and rice are grown. This led to an economy dominated by plantations in the Tidewater region. The plantation system began in Virginia and Maryland when settlers started growing tobacco. It spread southward when planters found other crops they could export profitably to Europe.

Main Idea
The Tidewater region and the backcountry developed two different ways of life.

Founding of the 13 Colonies

Colony / Date Founded	Leader(s)	Reason(s) Founded
New England Colonies		
■ Massachusetts Plymouth / 1620 Massachusetts Bay / 1630	William Bradford John Winthrop	Religious freedom Religious freedom
■ New Hampshire / 1622	Ferdinando Gorges John Mason	Profit from trade and fishing
■ Connecticut / 1636	Thomas Hooker	Expand trade; religious and political freedom
■ Rhode Island / 1636	Roger Williams	Religious freedom
Middle Colonies		
■ New York / 1624	Peter Minuit	Expand trade
■ Delaware / 1638	Swedish settlers	Expand trade
■ New Jersey / 1664	John Berkeley George Carteret	Expand trade; religious and political freedom
■ Pennsylvania / 1682	William Penn	Profit from land sales; religious and political freedom
Southern Colonies		
■ Virginia / 1607	John Smith	Trade and farming
Maryland / 1634	Lord Baltimore	Profit from land sales; religious and political freedom
■ The Carolinas / 1663 North Carolina / 1712 South Carolina / 1719	Group of eight proprietors	Trade and farming
■ Georgia / 1733	James Oglethorpe	Profit; home for debtors; buffer against Spanish Florida

Reading Charts
Skills Activity

By 1733, England had established 13 colonies on the Atlantic coast of North America. These colonies were founded for a variety of reasons.

(a) **Interpret a Chart** Identify one Middle Colony and one Southern Colony founded for religious reasons.

(b) **Understand Sequence** How many English colonies were there by 1700?

The Tidewater region in South Carolina and Georgia was well suited for rice. However, rice-growing required large numbers of workers laboring in hot, humid, unhealthy conditions. This was one reason rice-farming helped promote the spread of slavery. In time, the enslaved population outnumbered the free population of South Carolina.

The plantation system did not just create a society of slaveholders and enslaved people in the Tidewater. It also divided the white community into a small group of wealthy people and a much larger group with little or no property, most of whom were poor and lived in the backcountry South.

The Backcountry The backcountry was cut off from the coast by poor roads and long distances. Families usually lived on isolated farms. They often did not legally own the land they farmed. Many families lived in simple one-room shacks. Few families had servants or enslaved people to help them with their work. Women and girls worked in the fields with the men and boys.

In the backcountry, people cared less about rank. Life in the backcountry provided a sharp <u>contrast</u> to life near the coast. As a result, backcountry people believed that the colonial governments on the coast did not care about them. They thought that colonial government cared only about protecting the wealth of the Tidewater plantation owners.

Vocabulary *Builder*
<u>contrast</u> (KAHN trast) *n.* difference shown between things when compared

☑ **Checkpoint** How did people live in the backcountry?

⭐ **Looking Back and Ahead** As you have seen, the English colonies developed along distinct regional lines. But Spain, too, was competing for influence in North America. It had started its own colonies long before the English arrived.

Section 4 | **Check Your Progress**

Progress Monitoring Online
For: Self-test with instant help
Visit: PHSchool.com
Web Code: mva-1034

Comprehension and Critical Thinking

1. **(a) Summarize** How did the geography of the Southern Colonies affect the kinds of crops that were grown there?
   (b) Draw Conclusions Why did the struggle for rich farmland affect the colonists in Virginia?

2. **(a) Recall** Why did Lord Baltimore want Maryland's Act of Toleration?
   (b) Compare How would you compare the motives of Lord Baltimore in founding the colony of Maryland with those of James Oglethorpe in founding Georgia?

🎯 **Reading Skill**

3. **Compare and Contrast** Compare and contrast the Tidewater and the backcountry regions of the Southern Colonies.

Vocabulary *Builder*

Read each sentence. If the sentence is true, write YES. If the sentence is not true, write NO and explain why.

4. **Debtors** could not be imprisoned under English law.

5. There were many plantations where crops such as wheat, fruits, and vegetables were grown.

Writing

6. List the different groups of people living in the Southern Colonies between 1620 and the 1700s. Write two or three sentences about each group.

Spanish Colonies on the Borderlands

Objectives

1. Describe Spain's colony in Florida.

2. Explain how Spain established settlements throughout much of North America.

3. Describe the significance of the Spanish missions.

Prepare to Read

Reading Skill

Compare and Contrast Across Sections The colonies discussed in Sections 1 through 4 were settled primarily by people from the British Isles. Section 5 discusses Spain's colonies in North America. Recall information from Sections 1 through 4 in order to compare and contrast the English colonies with those of Spain. Examine the text in Section 5 to ask: How are these similar to or different from the colonies discussed in Sections 1 through 4?

Vocabulary *Builder*

High-Use Words
function, p. 91
convert, p. 91

Key Terms and People
borderland, p. 91
Junípero Serra, p. 92
presidio, p. 92
pueblo, p. 93

⭐ **Background Knowledge** While the English colonies were forming along the coast, Spanish colonies in the Americas were already hundreds of years old. Spain had planted colonies in the Caribbean, Mexico, and South America. Spain's first colonies in the area that is today the United States were established on the peninsula of Florida.

Main Idea
Spain established a colony in Florida decades before English settlers arrived in North America.

Fort at St. Augustine

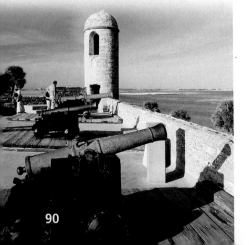

Spanish Florida

Spanish explorers reached Florida early in the 1500s. In 1565, fearing that France might take over the area, Spain built a fort called St. Augustine in northern Florida. It was the first permanent European settlement in what is now the United States.

As English colonies spread southward, Spanish control was threatened. To weaken the English colonies, in 1693, the Spanish announced that enslaved Africans who escaped to Florida would be protected. They would be given land if they helped to defend the colony. During the 1700s, hundreds of enslaved African Americans fled to Florida.

Spain's Florida colony grew slowly. By 1763, there were only three major Spanish settlements there. All were centered around forts, and all were in the north. The Spanish had little control over the rest of Florida.

✓**Checkpoint** Why did the Spanish colonize Florida?

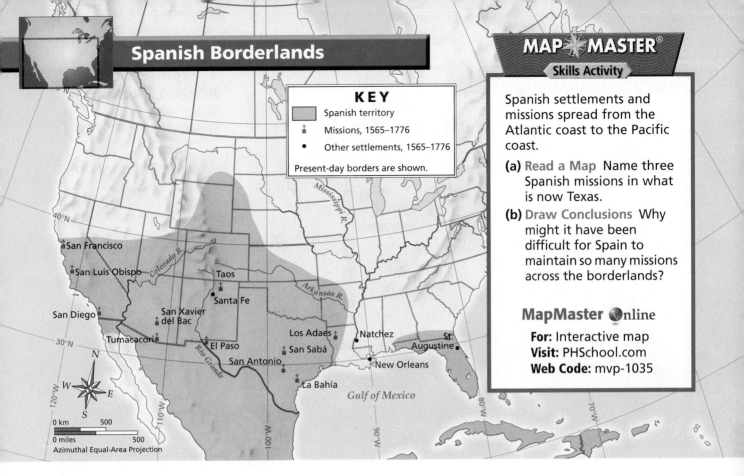

MAP MASTER®
Skills Activity

KEY

Spanish territory

Missions, 1565–1776

Other settlements, 1565–1776

Present-day borders are shown.

Spanish settlements and missions spread from the Atlantic coast to the Pacific coast.

(a) Read a Map Name three Spanish missions in what is now Texas.

(b) Draw Conclusions Why might it have been difficult for Spain to maintain so many missions across the borderlands?

MapMaster Online

For: Interactive map
Visit: PHSchool.com
Web Code: mvp-1035

Settling the Spanish Borderlands

Spain's most important colonies were in Mexico and South America. Its territories north of Mexico were called the borderlands, meaning lands along a frontier. The main <u>function</u> of the Spanish borderlands was to protect Mexico from other European powers.

The borderlands began in the east with Florida. Farther west, they included most of Texas, New Mexico, Arizona, Colorado, Utah, Nevada, and California. This vast area differs greatly from place to place with humid lowlands in Texas and deserts and mountains in New Mexico, Arizona, and Utah. Colorado has highlands and mountains, while California has deserts in its southeast corner.

Juan de Oñate in New Mexico The first Spanish explorers did not start permanent settlements. Then, in 1598, Juan de Oñate (WAN day ohn YAH tay) led an expedition into New Mexico. He aimed to find gold, <u>convert</u> Native Americans to Christianity, and establish a permanent colony. Oñate never found gold, but in 1598 he established Spain's first permanent settlement in the region at Santa Fe.

Oñate brought more than 300 horses. At their settlements, the Spanish used Native Americans to look after the horses. When some Native Americans ran away from the Spanish, they spread the skill of horseback riding from one Native American group to another. This skill forever changed the lives of the Native Americans of the region.

The Native Americans suffered under Spanish rule. In 1680, several groups in New Mexico rebelled and drove the Spanish from the region. After that defeat, the Spanish did not return for more than 10 years.

Main Idea
Spain controlled much of North America during the 1600s and early 1700s.

Vocabulary Builder
<u>function</u> (FUHNK shuhn) *n.* purpose; proper use; official duty

Vocabulary Builder
<u>convert</u> (kuhn VERT) *v.* to change from one religion to another

A Mission: Then and Now

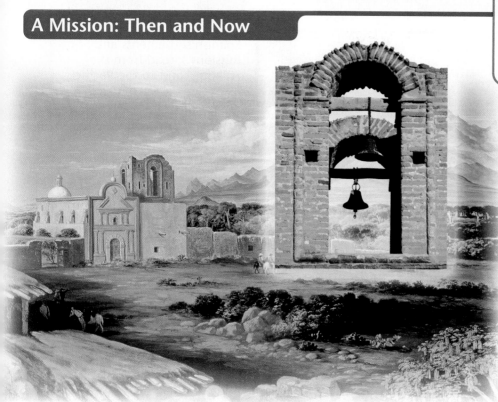

History *Interactive*

Explore an Arizona Mission
Visit: PHSchool.com
Web Code: myp-6152

A Mission: Then and Now
The Tumacácori Mission in southern Arizona was founded in 1691 and rebuilt in 1800. It looks much as it did when Henry Cheever Pratt portrayed it in 1855 (at left). The mission is now a National Historical Park. **Critical Thinking:** *Draw Conclusions Why are abandoned missions like this one considered important to the history of the U.S. Southwest?*

Missions in Texas and Arizona Roman Catholic missionaries played a key role in colonizing the borderlands. To win Native Americans to Christianity, they established missions—religious settlements that aim to spread a religion into a new area. At the missions, priests taught about Catholicism and made Native Americans work by set rules. The missionary who led the way in spreading Spanish influence in what today is Arizona and Texas was Father Eusebio Francisco Kino.

At first, the Spanish had little success. The only early mission that took root in Texas was about 150 miles north of the Rio Grande. Although the mission failed to convert many Native Americans, it did attract Spanish colonists. This mission became the city of San Antonio.

Missions Along the California Coast Spain's California missions were especially important. Spain began colonizing California in 1769. A missionary named Junípero Serra (hoo NEE peh roh SEHR rah) played an important role in that effort. His first mission, just north of today's Mexican-American border, eventually became the city of San Diego. Serra later established other missions, including those located in what is now San Francisco and Los Angeles. Altogether, the Spanish founded almost 20 missions in California between 1769 and 1800.

Presidios and Pueblos Along with missionaries, Spain sent soldiers. They set up presidios—military posts—to defend the missions.

Compare and Contrast Across Sections
Compare and contrast the role of religion in the Spanish settlements with that in the Southern Colonies and New England.

The Spanish also established what they called pueblos—civilian towns. The pueblos were centers of farming and trade. In the middle of the town was a plaza, or public square. Here, townspeople and farmers came to do business or to worship at the church. Church, shops, and homes lined the four sides of the plaza.

✓Checkpoint **What role did missionaries play in Spain's expanding North American empire?**

Life in Spanish Missions

Thousands of Native Americans labored at Spanish missions. They farmed, built churches, and learned a wide range of crafts. The Native Americans were not overworked by Spanish standards of the time. They worked from five to eight hours per day and five or six days per week. They did not work on Sundays or religious holidays.

However, the Native Americans did not have control over their lives. The missionaries punished them harshly if the Native Americans violated mission rules. Native Americans were imprisoned and often kept in shackles or whipped while tied to whipping posts.

Native Americans often rebelled against such treatment. Meanwhile, their population fell as thousands died because of poor living conditions and European diseases.

✓Checkpoint **Why did some Native Americans rebel against rules set by missionaries?**

⭐ **Looking Back and Ahead** Spain had now built a vast empire in the Americas. But the 13 English colonies were destined to grow, too. New frictions would develop within the English Empire as it grew.

Main Idea
Spain established missions to convert Native Americans and to teach them farming and crafts skills.

Section 5 | **Check Your Progress**

Progress Monitoring Online
For: Self-test with instant help
Visit: PHSchool.com
Web Code: mva-1035

Comprehension and Critical Thinking

1. (a) **Identify** Where is Saint Augustine located?
(b) **Draw Conclusions** Why do you think the colony failed to attract settlers?

2. (a) **Summarize** Why were the borderlands important to Spain?
(b) **Apply Information** How did the importance of the borderlands influence the way Spain ruled this region?

3. (a) **Recall** How did Junípero Serra help establish Spain's presence in the Americas?
(b) **Link Past and Present** In what way have the early Spanish missions influenced today's Americans?

Reading Skill

4. **Compare and Contrast Across Sections** Compare and contrast the experiences of Native Americans in Spanish settlements and in English colonies.

Vocabulary *Builder*

5. Draw a table with two rows and three columns. In the first column, list the following key terms from this section: presidio, pueblo. In the next column, write a definition of each word. In the last column, make a small illustration that shows the meaning of each word.

Writing

6. Review the table you created in Vocabulary Builder. Add a column to the table. Write two or three sentences for each key term. Explain how it relates to the settlement of Spanish colonies in the Americas.

Historians use primary sources to find out information about the past from people who lived during that period. A primary source is firsthand information about people or historical events. The following primary source describes events that took place near the Jamestown Colony in 1608.

This selection is from John Smith's book *A Generall Historie of Virginia, New-England, and the Summer Isles,* published in 1624. It describes his capture by Native Americans and his rescue by Pocahontas, the daughter of the Indian chief Powhatan. Using the writing style of this period of history, Smith refers to himself in the third person, using "he" or "him" instead of "I" or "me."

Primary Source

". . . Finding he was beset with 200 savages, two of them he slew still defending himself with the aid of a savage, his guide, . . . yet he was shot in his thigh a little, and had many arrows that stuck in his clothese; but no great hurt, til at last they took him prisoner.

Six or seven weeks those barbarians kept him prisoner, . . . yet he . . . diverted them from surprising the fort . . . [gained] his own liberty, and got himself and his company such estimation among them that those savages admired him more than their own *quiyouckosuchs* [gods]. . . .

1608 At last they brought him to . . . Powhatan, their emperor. . . . Having feasted him after their best barbarous manner they could, a long consultation was held, but the conclusion was: two great stones were brought before Powhatan; then as many as could laid hands on him, dragged him to them, and thereon laid his head, and being ready with their clubs to beat out his brains, Pocahontas, the king's dearest daughter, . . . got his head in her arms, and laid her own upon his to save him from death."

Learn the Skill

Use these steps to read a primary source.

1. **Identify the source.** Ask questions that help you identify the writer or speaker.

2. **Identify the author's purpose for writing.** Often, eyewitnesses might want to inform or persuade the reader to share their views.

3. **Recognize the author's point of view.** Distinguish between facts and the author's opinion.

4. **Evaluate whether the source is reliable.** Consider who wrote the primary source and the information presented. Compare this information with what you know about the subject.

Practice the Skill

Answer the following questions about the primary source on this page.

1. **Identify the source.** (a) Who wrote this excerpt? (b) When did the events occur?

2. **Identify the author's purpose for writing.** Why did the author write this source?

3. **Recognize the author's point of view.** What is the author's opinion of Native Americans?

4. **Evaluate whether the source is reliable.** Is this a reliable source for learning about the history of the Jamestown Colony? Explain.

Apply the Skill

See the Review and Assessment at the end of this chapter.

Interactive Textbook

Study Guide *Online*
Complete your Chapter 3
study guide in print or online.

Chapter Summary

Section 1
The First English Settlements

- The English colony at Jamestown is founded in 1607.
- English Pilgrims seeking religious freedom settled the Plymouth Colony.

Section 2
The New England Colonies

- Puritans seeking religious freedom settled the Massachusetts Bay Colony in 1630.
- People unhappy with the Puritans' religious intolerance founded Rhode Island, Connecticut, and New Hampshire.

Section 3
The Middle Colonies

- After the English takeover, New Netherlands was renamed New York.
- Pennsylvania was founded in 1681 by a Quaker, William Penn.

Section 4
The Southern Colonies

- Maryland was founded as a colony where Catholics could worship freely.
- Large plantations marked the Tidewater region, and small farms dominated the backcountry.

Section 5
Spanish Colonies on the Borderlands

- Spain had large colonies in the Caribbean, Mexico, and South America.
- Spanish missions sought to convert Native Americans to Christianity.
- Spain established presidios and pueblos throughout the borderlands.

Key Concepts

These notes will help you prepare for questions about key concepts.

Why English Colonies Were Founded

- Religious and Political Freedom: Plymouth; Massachusetts Bay; Rhode Island; Connecticut; New Hampshire; New Jersey; Pennsylvania; Maryland; the Carolinas; Georgia
- Economic Reasons (trade; farming): Virginia; the Carolinas; Georgia
- Other Reasons (conquest; political division): New York; New Jersey; Delaware

Why Spanish Colonies Were Founded

- Political Reasons (establish/maintain empire): Florida; Spanish borderlands

Principles of Government in English Colonies

- Elected assemblies
- Right to vote restricted to certain groups of colonists
- Colonial governors
- Town meetings in each Puritan town

How Spain Controlled Colonies in the Americas

- In Florida: forts; settlements
- In borderlands: religious missions; military presidios; pueblos

Vocabulary *Builder*

Key Terms

Answer the following questions in complete sentences that show your understanding of the key terms.

1. How did the charter of the Virginia Company help the colonization of the Americas?

2. What problems resulted because Puritans did not believe in religious toleration?

3. What groups settled in the backcountry?

4. How did town meetings affect the governing of New England colonies?

5. Why was New Jersey a royal colony?

Comprehension and Critical Thinking

6. **(a) Recall** What was the Mayflower Compact?
(b) Apply Information Why do you think the Mayflower Compact is an important part of our country's history?

7. **(a) Identify** Who were the Puritans and the Pilgrims?
(b) Compare and Contrast How would you compare and contrast the Pilgrims and Puritans?
(c) Synthesize Do you think Puritans and Pilgrims would worship together in America? Explain.

8. **(a) Summarize** How does the Edward Hicks painting below show the nature of William Penn's dealings with Native Americans?
(b) Contrast How would you contrast the way colonists in Pennsylvania and in Massachusetts got along with Native Americans?

9. **(a) Identify** How was land farmed in the Tidewater region and in the Virginia backcountry?
(b) Draw Conclusions Would a farmer living in the Tidewater or in the backcountry be more likely to support the Virginia government? Explain.

History Reading Skill

10. **Compare and Contrast** Choose any two colonies from among those discussed in Chapter 3. Make a list of three important features of the colonies. Then, compare and contrast these features in the two colonies you have chosen.

Writing

11. **Write two paragraphs on the following topic:** Describe the factors that led to the establishment of English and Spanish colonies in the Americas.

12. **Write a Dialogue:**
Write a conversation that Roger Williams might have had with William Penn. Include issues about how their colonies were settled.

Skills for Life

Read a Primary Source

Use the primary source below by William Bradford, governor of the Plymouth Colony, to answer the questions that follow.

> [1621] "[What] was most sad and lamentable was that in two or three months' time, half of their company died, . . . being infected with the scurvy and other diseases. . . . [I]n the time of most distress, there were but six or seven sound persons who . . . spared no pains night or day, but with abundance of toil and hazard to their own health fetched them wood, made them fires . . . made their beds . . . and all this willingly . . . without any grudging in the least."
>
> —from the book *Of Plymouth Plantation, 1620–1647*, by William Bradford

13. Who wrote these observations?

14. Why did the author write this source?

15. How does the author show his feeling about the people who cared for the sick colonists?

16. Do you think the author gives an accurate view of the events? Why?

Test Yourself

1. **Which of the following established the right of American colonists to govern themselves?**

   A mercantilism

   B pueblo

   C proprietary colony

   D Mayflower Compact

2. **The followers of Nathaniel Bacon**

   A supported the governor of Virginia.

   B had a profitable fur trade with the Native Americans.

   C were poor farmers seeking good farmland.

   D were fully represented in the House of Burgesses.

3. **What geographical feature helped New England colonists?**

   A long growing seasons

   B mountains

   C natural harbors

   D fertile soil

Refer to the passage below to answer Question 4.

> Roger Williams said that **"**God Land will be as great a God with us English as God Gold was with the Spanish.**"**

4. **Which event can be judged as a result of the colonists' push for land in the Americas?**

   A Spanish missions in Florida

   B King Philip's War

   C the settlement of Pennsylvania

   D the establishment of presidios

Document-Based Questions

Task: Look at Documents 1 and 2, and answer their accompanying questions. Then, use the documents and your knowledge of history to complete this writing assignment:

> Write a short essay explaining why these two documents were important in the development of democratic government in America.

Document 1: The Ordinance for Virginia, dated July 24, 1619, called for the creation of an assembly chosen by and made up of colonists. The House of Burgesses, as the assembly is known, marked the beginning of representative government in America. *What powers did the Burgesses have?*

> **"**And this General Assembly shall have free Power . . . to make, ordain, and enact such general Laws and Orders, for the Behoof [good] of the said Colony, and the good government thereof. . . .**"**

Document 2: In 1620, the Pilgrims arrived in America. While still aboard the *Mayflower,* they drew up and signed the Mayflower Compact. *What powers did the Mayflower Compact give the Plymouth settlers?*

> **"**We . . . combine ourselves together into a civil Body Politick, . . . [to] enact, constitute, and frame, such just and equal Laws, Ordinances, Acts, Constitutions and Offices, from time to time, as shall be thought most meet and convenient for the general Good of the Colony; unto which we promise all due Submission and Obedience.**"**

Chapter Preview

Government and daily life in England's 13 North American colonies were shaped by European ideas. Still, by the mid-1700s, the colonies had developed their own ideas and traditions.

1647
Massachusetts requires large towns to have public schools.

1663
First major slave revolt occurs in Gloucester, Virginia.

1700s
Triangular slave trade brings increasing numbers of enslaved Africans to the colonies.

U.S. Events

1650

World Events

1675

1700

1650s Parliament passes Navigation Acts.

1689 English Bill of Rights is issued.

This needlework depicts the fine clothing and refined manners of wealthy colonists. Most members of colonial society did not enjoy such an elegant lifestyle.

Quick View Video
View the chapter video for a quick preview of the main ideas.

1730s The Great Awakening sweeps through the colonies.

1735 The Zenger case marks a step toward freedom of the press.

1750 Georgia becomes last of colonies to permit slavery.

1700

1725

1750

1700s The Enlightenment influences European intellectual thought.

1748 Montesquieu's *The Spirit of the Laws* argues for separation of powers.

History Reading Skill Determine Meaning From Context

How was life in the colonies dangerous?

In this chapter, you will practice using context to determine word meaning. Read the following description of early life in colonial Virginia. The side notes show you how to use context to determine word meaning.

As you have read, Bacon's Rebellion broke out in 1676 due to a conflict between frontier settlers and the government in colonial Virginia. Below is an excerpt of a report of the incident.

> *Palisades* and *redoubts* are nouns; they must be things used to fortify or protect a home.

In these frightful times the most exposed small families withdrew into our houses, which we <u>fortified</u> with <u>palisades</u> and <u>redoubts</u>. . . . No man stirred out of doors unarmed. Indians were sighted . . . . I rarely heard of any houses burnt, . . . or other injury done, besides murders. . . .

> The familiar word part *fort* suggests that *fortified* means "made strong, like a fort." A preceding clue, *frightful times*, confirms that meaning.

Frequent complaints of bloodshed were sent to Sir William Berkeley, the governor . . . . [The people] grew impatient at the many slaughters of their neighbors. They rose for their own defense, choosing Mr. Bacon for their leader.

> Personal knowledge can help. Artists get *commissions*, army officers get *commissions*; both are payments.

During these delays, with people often slain, the officers and 300 men, led by Mr. Bacon, met. They discussed the danger of going on without a <u>commission</u> on the one part, and the continual murder of their neighbors on the other part. . . . This day ended and no commission came. So they marched into the wilderness in quest of these Indians. . . .

> Unfamiliar word

[T]he Governor sent his proclamation, <u>denouncing</u> all <u>rebels</u> <u>who should not return within a limited time</u>. Most obeyed.

> Read on for information. A description of why someone would be denounced follows. *Denouncing* means "criticizing or condemning, usually in public."

—*Beginning, Progress and Conclusion of Bacon's Rebellion in Virginia.*

Determine Meaning From Context

- Clues such as familiar base words and parts of speech can suggest a word's meaning.
- Surrounding sentences may include examples or descriptions of an unfamiliar word, as well as familiar related words or synonyms.
- Consider how the word is used today.
- Ask: What does the word do?

Document-Based Questions

1. Who might have been the author of these paragraphs?
2. Does the author seem to think Bacon's actions were justified?
3. How might a Native American's report on the same events differ from this text?

Vocabulary *Builder*

Previewing High-Use Academic Words

High-Use Word	Definition	Sample History Sentence
levy (LEHV ee) (Section 1, p. 102)	*v.* to impose (a tax, for example); to force to be paid	In the federal government, Congress holds the power to <u>levy</u> taxes.
retain (ree TAYN) (Section 1, p. 103)	*v.* to keep	The British government <u>retained</u> final say in colonial affairs.
domestic (doh MEHS tihk) (Section 2, p. 108)	*adj.* having to do with the home or household; pertaining to a country's internal affairs	The children busied themselves with <u>domestic</u> duties such as sweeping the floor and cooking dinner.
prospect (PRAHS pehkt) (Section 2, p. 110)	*n.* expectation; something to look forward to happening	The <u>prospect</u> of a brighter future drew many immigrants to America.
maximum (MAK sah mahm) (Section 3, p. 113)	*adj.* largest; highest; greatest	Business people seek to make the <u>maximum</u> possible profit on their investments.
revolt (ree VOHLT) (Section 3, p. 116)	*v.* to rebel; to participate in an uprising	Slave owners feared that angry slaves might <u>revolt</u> against their enslavement.
finance (FĪ nans) (Section 4, p. 120)	*v.* to supply with money; to manage monetary situations	People often seek a bank loan to <u>finance</u> the purchase of a home.
reinforce (ree ihn FORS) (Section 4, p. 122)	*v.* to make stronger; to strengthen; to make more effective	The army <u>reinforced</u> its defenses in anticipation of an attack.

Previewing Key Terms and People

Benjamin Franklin

Governing the Colonies

Objectives

1. Explain how English political traditions influenced the 13 colonies.

2. Describe the responsibilities of early colonial governments.

3. Identify John Peter Zenger's role in establishing freedom of the press.

4. Understand how the Navigation Acts affected the colonies' economy.

Prepare to Read

 Reading Skill

Use Word Clues to Analyze Meaning When you encounter an unfamiliar word, look for clues within the word itself. For example, to understand the term *notable*, the familiar word *note* is helpful. If *note* means "to notice or remember," then *notable* may mean "worth remembering or noticing." Also, consider whether the word seems to be a verb, an adjective, or a noun.

Vocabulary *Builder*

High-Use Words

<u>levy</u>, p. 102

<u>retain</u>, p. 103

Key Terms

legislature, p. 103

bill of rights, p. 103

habeas corpus, p. 104

freedom of the press, p. 105

libel, p. 105

⭐ **Background Knowledge** In the previous chapter, you learned that the New England, the Middle, and the Southern colonies developed in unique ways. However, all three regions shared a common heritage. In this section, we will see how English ideas about government and trade took root in the colonies.

The English Parliamentary Tradition

The English colonists brought with them the idea that they had political rights. This idea was rooted in English history.

Magna Carta In 1215, English nobles forced King John to sign the Magna Carta, the Latin name meaning "great charter." The Magna Carta was the first document to place restrictions on an English ruler's power. It limited the monarch's right to <u>levy</u> taxes without consulting the nobles. It also protected the right to own private property and guaranteed the right to trial by jury:

Main Idea
As English subjects, colonists believed they had political rights and protections.

Vocabulary *Builder*
<u>levy</u> (LEHV ee) *v.* to impose (a tax, for example); to force to be paid

    ❝31. Neither we nor our [officials] shall take, for our castles or for any other work of ours, wood which is not ours, against the will of the owner of that wood. . . .

    39. No free man shall be taken or imprisoned . . . except by the lawful judgment of his peers, or by the law of the land.❞

—Magna Carta

The rights listed in the Magna Carta were at first limited to nobles. Over time, the rights were extended to all English citizens.

Parliament Under the Magna Carta, nobles formed a Great Council to advise the king. This body developed into the English Parliament (PAHR luh mehnt). Parliament was a two-house legislature. A **legislature** is a group of people who have the power to make laws. The House of Lords was made up of nobles, most of whom inherited their titles. Members of the House of Commons were elected. Only a few rich men and landowners had the right to vote for the House of Commons.

Parliament's greatest power was the right to approve new taxes. No monarch could raise taxes without the consent of Parliament. This "power of the purse" gave Parliament a degree of control over the monarch.

In the 1640s, power struggles between King Charles I and Parliament led to the English Civil War. Parliamentary forces eventually won the war, executed the king, and briefly ruled England by itself. In 1660, the monarchy was restored. Still, Parliament <u>retained</u> its traditional rights.

Vocabulary *Builder*
<u>retain</u> (ree TAYN) *v.* to keep

English Bill of Rights An event in 1688 further boosted parliamentary power. Parliament removed King James II from the throne and invited his daughter Mary and her husband William to rule. This was called the Glorious Revolution. In 1689, King William and Queen Mary signed the English Bill of Rights. A **bill of rights** is a written list of freedoms that a government promises to protect.

English Bill of Rights

These selections from the English Bill of Rights deal with the powers of Parliament:

William and Mary

4. **"**That levying money for or to the use of the crown . . . without grant of Parliament . . . is illegal; . . .
6. That the raising or keeping a standing army within the kingdom in time of peace, unless it be with the consent of Parliament, is against the law; . . .
8. That election of members of Parliament ought to be free;
9. That the freedom of speech and debates or proceedings in Parliament ought not to be impeached [challenged] or questioned in any court or place out of Parliament.**"**

—English Bill of Rights

Reading Primary Sources
Skills Activity

The English Bill of Rights was issued under William and Mary in 1689. It guaranteed the powers of Parliament and the basic rights of English citizens.

(a) Interpret a Primary Source Summarize item 4 in your own words.
(b) Draw Conclusions Why do you think Parliament included item 9 in the Bill of Rights?

The English Bill of Rights restated many of the rights granted by the Magna Carta, such as trial by jury. It upheld **habeas corpus,** the principle that a person cannot be held in prison without being charged with a specific crime. Finally, the Bill of Rights required that Parliament meet regularly and declared that no monarch could levy taxes or raise an army without the consent of Parliament.

✓**Checkpoint**   **How was the power of English monarchs limited?**

Colonial Self-Government

Main Idea
White male settlers in the American colonies gained limited rights of self-government.

The legal rights that Englishmen had won over the centuries led the colonists to expect a voice in their government. The ideas of limited monarchy and representative government were dear to them. In their new land, colonists wanted to take part in governing themselves.

Colonial Legislatures As you have read, from 1619 the Virginia Company allowed the House of Burgesses to make laws for the Jamestown Colony. The House of Burgesses became the first legislature in British North America. Massachusetts colonists also set up a legislature called the General Court in 1629. Five years later, Massachusetts colonists gained the right to elect delegates to the General Court.

On the other hand, the British government gave William Penn outright ownership of Pennsylvania. The governor and a large council made laws that an assembly could only approve or reject. But the Pennsylvania colonists wanted to draw up laws themselves. In 1701, they forced Penn to agree that only the General Assembly could make laws. The king could overturn laws passed by the General Assembly, but neither Penn nor his council had any part in lawmaking.

By 1760, every British colony in North America had a legislature of some kind. However, the legislatures still clashed at times with the colonial governors appointed by the king.

Links Across Time

Making State Laws

1619 The House of Burgesses became the first colonial legislature. For the next 155 years, the Burgesses helped govern the affairs of the Virginia Colony.

1776 After the United States declared independence from Britain, Virginia replaced the House of Burgesses with the General Assembly. The other states also set up state legislatures to make laws.

Link to Today   Online

State Legislatures Today   There are 50 separate state legislatures operating in the United States. What issues do these lawmakers face?

For: State legislatures in the news
Visit: PHSchool.com
Web Code: mvc-1041

The Right to Vote In many ways, the colonies offered settlers greater political rights than they would have had in England. From 50 to 75 percent of white males in the American colonies could vote. This was a far greater percentage than in England.

Still, the right to vote did not extend to everyone in the colonies. English women—even those who owned property—could not vote in any colony. Neither could the Native Americans who still lived on land claimed by the colonists. Finally, no Africans, whether free or enslaved, could vote.

✓**Checkpoint**   **Which groups of people were permitted to vote in colonial elections? Which were not permitted to vote?**

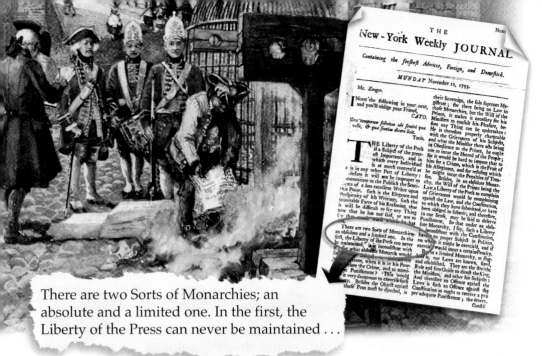

There are two Sorts of Monarchies; an absolute and a limited one. In the first, the Liberty of the Press can never be maintained . . .

Freedom of the Press

The colonists expected to enjoy the traditional rights of English subjects. A notable court case in 1735 helped establish another important right. This was **freedom of the press,** the right of journalists to publish the truth without restriction or penalty.

John Peter Zenger, publisher of the *New York Weekly Journal*, was arrested for printing a series of articles that criticized the governor. Zenger was charged with **libel,** or the publishing of statements that damage a person's reputation. Under modern American law, statements must be untrue in order to be considered libel. However, English law at the time punished writings that criticized the government—even if the statements were true.

At Zenger's trial, Zenger's lawyer, Andrew Hamilton, admitted that Zenger had printed the statements against the governor. However, Hamilton argued that the articles Zenger published were based on fact and, therefore, should not be considered libel. Hamilton told the jury:

> ❝By your verdict, you will have laid a noble foundation for securing to ourselves, our descendants, and our neighbors, the liberty both of exposing and opposing tyrannical power by speaking and writing truth.❞
>
> —Andrew Hamilton, in A Brief Narrative of the Case and Trial of John Peter Zenger

Main Idea
The Zenger trial of 1735 helped to establish the principle that the press can seek and report the truth.

Use Word Clues to Analyze Meaning
Use the familiar base word part *tyrant* as a clue to the meaning of *tyrannical.*

The jurors agreed. They found that Zenger was not guilty of libel.

The Zenger case later helped establish a fundamental principle. A democracy depends on well-informed citizens. Therefore, the press has a right and responsibility to keep the public informed of the truth. Today, freedom of the press is recognized as a basic American liberty.

✓**Checkpoint** **Why was the Zenger case important?**

Main Idea
England's Navigation Acts had a mixed effect, and many colonists came to resent the acts.

A Boston merchant counts up the profits from shipping.

Regulating Trade

As you have read, under the theory of mercantilism, colonies existed in order to serve the economic needs of their parent country. They were a source of raw materials and a place to sell the home country's goods.

In 1651, the English Parliament passed the first of several Navigation Acts to support mercantilism. By these laws: (1) Shipments from Europe to English colonies had to go through England first. (2) Any imports to England from the colonies had to come in ships built and owned by British subjects. (3) The colonies could sell key products, such as tobacco and sugar, only to England. This helped create jobs for English workers.

In many ways, the Navigation Acts benefited the colonies. Colonial traders had a sure market for their goods in England. Also, the law contributed to a booming shipbuilding industry in New England.

Still, as colonial trade expanded, many colonists came to resent the Navigation Acts. In their view, the laws favored English merchants. Colonists felt that they could make more money if they were free to sell to foreign markets themselves. Some colonists got around the Navigation Acts by smuggling—that is, by importing and exporting goods illegally.

☑**Checkpoint** **Why did many colonists resent the Navigation Acts?**

⭐ **Looking Back and Ahead** As the 13 colonies grew, colonists established lawmaking bodies and developed the economy. In the early days, England's monarchy and Parliament influenced the decisions the colonies made. Yet, the colonies were far from England, and colonists were developing their own ideas. In the next section, you will look at the structure of colonial society.

Section 1 | Check Your Progress

Progress Monitoring ⊕nline
For: Self-test with instant help
Visit: PHSchool.com
Web Code: mva-1041

Comprehension and Critical Thinking

1. **(a) Identify** What political rights had England's citizens won by 1688?
   (b) Apply Information Why do you think those living in the 13 colonies believed they were entitled to those rights?

2. **(a) Recall** What were the Navigation Acts?
   (b) Identify Economic Costs and Benefits How did the Navigation Acts affect the colonial economy?

Reading Skill

3. **Use Word Clues to Analyze Meaning** Use its part of speech to help you analyze the meaning of *boomed* in this sentence: As a result of a law that allowed colonists to build their own ships, the shipbuilding industry in New England *boomed*.

Vocabulary *Builder*

Complete each of the following sentences so that the second part further explains the first part and clearly shows your understanding of the key term.

4. Based on English traditions, colonial legislatures _____.

5. The English Bill of Rights protected the rights of individuals, including habeas corpus, _____.

6. John Peter Zenger was accused of libel, _____.

Writing

7. List at least two examples from colonial society to support this main idea: English colonists believed they should have the same freedoms as English citizens.

Colonial Society

Objectives

1. Learn about life on a colonial farm.

2. Describe the roles of men, women, and children in colonial America.

3. List the class differences that existed in colonial society.

Prepare to Read

Reading Skill

Use Sentence Clues to Analyze Meaning To find a word's meaning, you may examine other words within the same sentence for clues. For example, you may find familiar descriptive words near the unfamiliar word or find details that suggest a possible meaning. Ask: How is the unfamiliar word connected to a familiar word in the sentence? How is the word described?

Vocabulary *Builder*

High-Use Words
domestic, p. 108
prospect, p. 110

Key Terms
extended family, p. 107
apprentice, p. 110
gentry, p. 110
middle class, p. 111
indentured servant, p. 111

☆ **Background Knowledge** In this section, we will see how a common culture united American colonists despite their differences.

The Family in Colonial Times

The family played an important role in colonial America. Many people lived with their extended families. An **extended family** is a family that includes, in addition to the parents and their children, other members such as grandparents, aunts, uncles, and cousins.

On a Farm Most colonists lived on farms, where a large family was considered an advantage. Many hands were needed to operate a farm. Usually, farms were widely separated, often by dense forests. This made it necessary for families to be closely knit and self-sufficient. On a farm, each member of the family had many responsibilities. Family members helped plant, cultivate, and harvest crops. There were always fences to mend, animals to tend, and wood to chop.

By today's standards, farmhouses were not very comfortable. Most were made of wood and had few rooms. People sat on stools or benches and slept on planks. Some houses had mattresses of corncobs. There were few utensils, and they were crudely made. In the New England and the Middle colonies winters were cold, and the only source of heat in each house might be a fireplace in the kitchen room. On cold winter nights, the family might huddle around the fire telling stories and shelling nuts.

Main Idea
Colonial Americans lived mainly on farms, often in large extended families.

Tools on colonial farms included hay forks, sickles, and potato shovels.

In a Town In the colonies' few cities and towns, it was easier for single people to sustain themselves. However, family ties were still held in the highest regard. In Puritan New England, single men and women were expected to live with a family as a servant or a boarder.

✓**Checkpoint** **Why was a large family useful on a farm?**

Main Idea
In colonial society, men, women, and children had clearly defined roles.

Men, Women, and Children

The lives of men and women differed. Even on the frontier, where families had to labor together to survive, men and women generally took on different roles. A North Carolina settler wrote:

> "Men are generally of all trades, and women the like within their spheres. . . . Men are generally carpenters, joiners, wheelwrights, coopers, butchers, tanners, shoemakers, tallow-chandlers, watermen, and what not; women soap-makers, starch-makers, dyers, etc. He or she that cannot do all these things, or has not slaves that can, over and above all the common occupations of both sexes, will have but a bad time of it."
>
> —John Urmstone, letter, July 7, 1711

A husband and father controlled a family's income and property. Other family members were expected to accept his authority. In addition to fulfilling their home duties, men represented their families in public life as voters and, sometimes, as officeholders.

Roles of Women In colonial America, most women were expected to marry men chosen by their parents. In choosing, parents considered a man's property, his religion, and their own family interests. Romantic love was not considered the most important reason for marriage. Furthermore, when a woman married, her property and any money she might earn became her husband's. A woman often bore her husband many children. She was expected to be his faithful helper in every way.

Besides childcare, a woman had many <u>domestic</u> responsibilities. She cooked, did the laundry, and spun yarn into cloth that she made into family clothing. Outside, she took care of the garden, milked the cows, tended the chickens, churned butter, and preserved food. If the family had money, she might have help from servants.

Sometimes, however, the line blurred between women's work and men's work. On the western frontier, a woman might help plow or pitch hay. If she lived in a town, she might keep a shop or an inn, or work as a baker, a printer, or even an undertaker. Her husband or sons might help make cloth, if needed.

Women had little or no role in public life. They could not hold office or vote. On the western and southern frontiers, however, the rules were sometimes bent. For example, Mary Musgrove Matthews, a woman of English and Creek ancestry, advised Georgia governor James Oglethorpe on Indian affairs.

Vocabulary *Builder*
<u>domestic</u> (doh MEHS tihk) *adj.* having to do with the home or household; pertaining to a country's internal affairs

COLONIAL WOMEN

Most women in colonial homes were required to handle a wide variety of tasks. In addition to domestic chores, women often worked in the fields along with the men. **Critical Thinking: Compare and Contrast** *How might a woman's responsibilities differ if she lived in a town? How might they be similar?*

History *Interactive*
Explore the Lives of Colonial Women
Visit: PHSchool.com
Web Code: mvl-1042

▲ **Running the Household**
Women were responsible for running the household and caring for the children. Women were not permitted to vote and were not expected to take part in public affairs.

▲ **Making Clothes**
Women's duties included making most of the clothes worn by their families. Among the gentry, women might wear fancier dresses sewed by professional seamstresses.

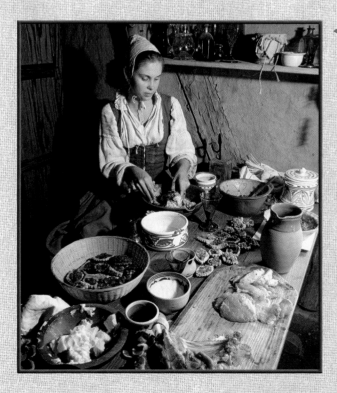

◄ **Preparing a Meal**
In colonial times, preparing meals from scratch took a great deal of time and effort.

▲ **Milking the Cows**
Families that owned cows had fresh milk to use and sell.

Children's dolls were made from cornhusks or from more elaborate materials.

Main Idea
Colonial society was divided into distinct classes, with a small group of gentry at the top.

Vocabulary *Builder*
prospect (PRAHS pehkt) *n.*
expectation; something to look forward to happening

Young People If they survived infancy, colonial children had about seven years before they were required to work. In these years, they could pass the time playing. Children played many games that are still familiar. Marbles, hopscotch, leapfrog, and jump rope were all popular.

The toys colonial children played with were usually homemade. Girls enjoyed dolls made of cornhusks and scraps of cloth, while boys built houses of corncobs. Sometimes, a spinning top would be fashioned out of a bit of leftover wood and string. Children whose families were well-to-do had fine dolls and toy soldiers that were made in Europe.

By the age of seven, most children had work to do. They might do household or farm chores, or, if they were poor, they might become servants in other families. On farms, children were expected to fetch water and wood and to help in the kitchen and in the fields. Older children had greater responsibilities. Boys were expected to work the fields with their fathers, while girls labored beside their mothers learning how to run a house. Parents believed that tasks like these prepared children for adult life.

Boys who were learning trades, such as making shoes or building furniture, began as apprentices. An **apprentice** is someone who learns a trade by working for someone in that trade for a certain period of time. The apprentice would live in the home of a master artisan. At the end of his apprenticeship, the young man was prepared to work independently.

☑**Checkpoint** **How did the jobs of boys and girls differ?**

Social Classes

Many European colonists came to America hoping to build a better life than they could have in Europe. In England and other European countries, land was the main measure of wealth. Land in Europe, however, was in the hands of a relative few. America appeared to have land in abundance, offering immigrants the chance to own land. The possibility of owning land played a large part in the appeal of life in America.

In Europe, a person's prospects were determined by birth. Those who were born wealthy generally stayed wealthy. Those who were born poor had little opportunity to improve their station in life. By contrast, in colonial America there was more social equality among settlers—at least among white settlers. Still, there were many class distinctions.

The Gentry A group known as the gentry were the upper class of colonial society. The gentry included wealthy planters, merchants, ministers, royal officials, and successful lawyers. Prosperous artisans, like goldsmiths, were often considered gentry as well. The gentry were few in number, but they were the most powerful people. For example, in Virginia, some 50 plantation-owning families held most of the land and power.

In New York, wealthy Dutch estate owners lived in luxury. Their homes featured gold mirrors, clocks, richly carved furniture, and jewels. These things were far beyond the means of ordinary colonists.

Because many official jobs paid no salary, few but the gentry could afford to hold office. They felt that serving the community in public office was both their duty and their right, and most people agreed.

The Middle Class The great majority of colonists from Europe were what colonists called "the middling sort." Neither rich nor extremely poor, this middle class was made up of small planters, independent farmers, and artisans. Middle-class men could vote, and a few held office. This middle class was mostly white, but some of its members were of African descent. About 1 percent of African Americans were free during the colonial period.

The growth of the middle class gave the poor something to hope for and work for. The poor who were free might never be rich, but they could always maintain the hope that some day they would be middle class. In this way, the colonies were different from England and the rest of Europe. Not only could people move around the land, they could acquire property and move up the social scale.

Indentured Servants Lower on colonial America's social scale, and just above enslaved Africans, were farmhands and indentured servants. An indentured servant signed a contract to work from 4 to 10 years in the colonies for anyone who would pay for his or her ocean passage to the Americas. In the 1600s, most indentured servants came from England. In the 1700s, a growing number came from Ireland and Germany.

Use Sentence Clues to Analyze Meaning
Who belonged to the middle class in colonial times? What does *middle class* mean?

Life Among the Gentry
The gentry lived a more comfortable life than most colonists. Servants attended to many of their needs. **Critical Thinking: Compare and Contrast** *How do the comforts of the family in this picture compare to those of a middle-class family today?*

An indentured servant assists a colonial bricklayer.

During the time of service, indentured servants had few, if any, rights. They were bound to obey their masters, who could work them almost to death. Those who disobeyed or tried to run away risked being whipped or having time added to the service.

At the end of a term, an indentured servant received a set of clothes, tools, and 50 acres of land. About 1 indentured servant in 10 became a prosperous landowner. Another 1 in 10 became an artisan. The others either returned home to Europe or joined a class of landless, poor whites. The hardships they endured drove many poor whites to resent wealthy landowners.

Free African Americans Free people of African ancestry were never a large portion of the colonial population. By the time the first census was taken in 1790, there were nearly 60,000 free people of African ancestry, compared with more than 757,000 enslaved.

Free African Americans were allowed to own property, even in the South. This permitted them to become slaveholders. Some free blacks purchased relatives who were enslaved and set them free. Still, the lives of free African Americans were restricted. Most African American property owners were not allowed to vote or sit on juries.

☑**Checkpoint** **How might one become a member of the middle class?**

☆ **Looking Back and Ahead** Life in America offered more opportunities than did life in England. This was especially true for the poor and middle class. However, if indentured servants occupied the lowest level of white society in the English colonies, one group was even more disadvantaged. In the next section, you will look in detail at the enslaved Africans who were brought to America against their will.

Section 2 | **Check Your Progress**

Progress Monitoring ⏾nline
For: Self-test with instant help
Visit: PHSchool.com
Web Code: mva-1042

Comprehension and Critical Thinking

1. **(a) Summarize** Describe the responsibilities that children in colonial times were expected to meet.
(b) Link Past and Present How do these responsibilities differ from those of children today?
(c) Draw Conclusions How might you explain this difference?

2. **(a) Recall** Identify the social classes in colonial society.

(b) Apply Information Which two groups had the most privileges and opportunities? Which two groups had the least?

Reading Skill

3. **Use Sentence Clues to Analyze Meaning** Use sentence clues to analyze the meaning of *prospects* in the following sentence: In many countries, a person's *prospects* for success in life are determined by birth.

Vocabulary *Builder*

4. Write two definitions for each key term: extended family, apprentice, gentry, middle class, indentured servant. First, write a formal definition for your teacher. Second, write a casual definition for a classmate.

Writing

5. Write a paragraph describing the importance of work in colonial society.

Slavery in the Colonies

Objectives

1. Describe the conditions under which enslaved Africans came to the Americas.

2. Explain why slavery became part of the colonial economy.

3. Identify the restrictions placed on enslaved Africans in the colonies.

4. Describe how African culture influenced American culture.

Prepare to Read

Reading Skill

Use Paragraph Clues to Analyze Meaning When you encounter an unfamiliar word, read the nearby sentences for clues. You may find clues in examples or descriptions. Sometimes a nearby sentence includes a contrast clue to what the word *does not* mean.

Vocabulary *Builder*

High-Use Words

maximum, p. 113
revolt, p. 116

Key Terms

triangular trade, p. 115
racism, p. 116
slave code, p. 116

⭐ **Background Knowledge** In a previous chapter, you learned how Spanish settlers first brought Africans to the Americas as a source of slave labor. In this section, you will learn about the development of slavery in the English colonies.

The Atlantic Slave Trade

Some scholars estimate that more than 10 million enslaved Africans were transported to the Americas between the 1500s and the 1800s. The Spanish and Portuguese brought the first Africans to the Americas. The British, Dutch, and French also entered the slave trade. In time, English colonists—especially from New England—were actively shipping enslaved Africans across the Atlantic.

Slave traders set up posts along the West African coast. Africans who lived along the coast made raids into the interior, seeking captives to sell to the Europeans. Bound at the leg and neck, captives were forced to march as far as 300 miles to the coast. Half of these captives died along the way.

Middle Passage Once they arrived at the coasts, captives were traded for guns and other goods. They were then loaded onto slave ships and transported across the Atlantic on a brutal voyage that became known as the Middle Passage.

To increase their profits, some slave-ship captains crammed the maximum number of captives on board. As many as 350 people might be bound together in a tiny space below deck, without light or air. Other captains provided better conditions, in the hope that more captives would survive in good health and fetch a higher price.

Main Idea
The Atlantic slave trade became a key part of the colonial economy.

Vocabulary *Builder*
maximum (MAK sah mahm) *adj.*
largest; highest; greatest

The Atlantic Slave Trade

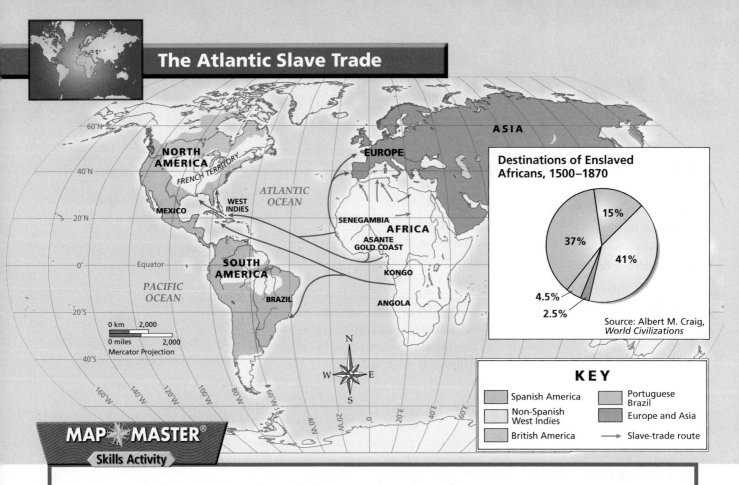

Destinations of Enslaved Africans, 1500–1870

15%
37%
41%
4.5%
2.5%

Source: Albert M. Craig, *World Civilizations*

KEY

Spanish America

Portuguese Brazil

Non-Spanish West Indies

Europe and Asia

British America

→ Slave-trade route

MAP★MASTER®
Skills Activity

The slave trade linked the Americas with Europe and western Africa.

(a) Evaluate Information How did British trade in slaves compare to that of the Spanish and Portuguese?

(b) Identify Costs Did the slave trade help or hurt western Africa? Explain your reasoning.

MapMaster Online

For: Interactive map
Visit: PHSchool.com
Web Code: mvp-1043

Use Paragraph Clues to Analyze Meaning Use the quoted paragraph's description and examples of *inconceivable* to analyze the word's meaning.

Olaudah Equiano told of being captured in western Africa when he was a boy. He later described the conditions aboard a slave ship:

❝The closeness of the place, and the heat of the climate, added to the number in the ship, which was so crowded that each had scarcely room to turn himself, almost suffocated us.... The shrieks of the women, and the groans of the dying, rendered the whole a scene of horror almost inconceivable.❞

—*The Interesting Narrative of the Life of Olaudah Equiano*

As a result of such conditions, from 15 to 20 percent of enslaved Africans died or committed suicide during the Middle Passage.

Once slave ships reached the Americas, healthy men, women, and children were put on the auction block. They might be sold one by one or in groups. Family members were often separated at this stage. The vast majority of those sold ended up on plantations in the Spanish colonies, Brazil, or the Caribbean. (See the pie chart above.) But for some 500,000 enslaved Africans, their final destination was British North America.

Triangular Trade By about 1700, slave traders in the British colonies had developed a regular routine, known as the triangular trade. The **triangular trade** was a three-way trade between the colonies, the islands of the Caribbean, and Africa.

On the first leg of the three-leg voyage, ships from New England carried fish, lumber, and other goods to the Caribbean islands, or West Indies. There, Yankee traders bought sugar and molasses, a dark syrup made from sugar cane. The ships then sailed back to New England, where colonists used the molasses and sugar to make rum.

On the second leg, ships carried rum, guns, and other goods from New England to West Africa. There, merchants traded the goods for enslaved Africans. On the final leg, ships carried their human cargo to the West Indies for sale. With the profits from selling enslaved Africans, traders bought more molasses.

Many New England merchants grew wealthy from the triangular trade. In doing so, they often disobeyed the Navigation Acts, which required them to buy only from English colonies. Because demand for molasses was so high, traders also made purchases from the West Indies. They then smuggled their cargoes into New England.

✔**Checkpoint** **What was the Middle Passage?**

Slavery in the Colonies

Slavery had existed since ancient times. However, in many cultures, slavery was not for life. In some early Christian societies, for example, slaves were freed if they became Christians. In many African societies, people captured in war were often enslaved for only a few years. Then, they were freed and became full members of the community. In the Americas, however, a harsher system of slavery developed over time.

Slavery Takes Root The first Africans who reached Jamestown may have been treated as servants. But by the late 1600s, ships were bringing growing numbers of enslaved Africans.

Why did slavery take root? One reason was the plantation system. The profits that could be made from tobacco and rice led planters to import thousands of enslaved Africans to work the fields. The southern economy came to depend on slavery.

For planters, slaves were preferable to servants. Indentured servants were temporary. Once their terms were over, they could go. Also, as conditions improved in England, fewer servants came to America.

Enslaved for Life As the need for cheap labor grew, colonies made slavery permanent. In 1639, Maryland passed a law stating that baptism did not lead to liberty. This meant people could be enslaved for life. In 1663, a Virginia court held that any child born to a slave was a slave too.

TO BE SOLD on board the Ship *Bance-Island*, on tuesday the 6th of *May* next, at *Afhley-Ferry*; a choice cargo of about 250 fine healthy

NEGROES, juft arrived from the Windward & Rice Coaft. —The utmoft care has already been taken, and fhall be continued, to keep them free from the leaft danger of being infected with the SMALL-POX, no boat having been on board, and all other communication with people from *Charles-Town* prevented.

Auftin, Laurens, & Appleby.

N. B. Full one Half of the above Negroes have had the SMALL-POX in their own Country.

An advertisement for a colonial slave auction

Main Idea
The southern economy came to depend on the labor of enslaved Africans.

Explore More Video
To learn more about slavery in the colonies, view the video.

Slave Labor Preparing tobacco was one of the tasks performed by enslaved workers at a Virginia plantation in the 1700s. **Critical Thinking:** *Draw Conclusions* *How did the cultivation of crops such as tobacco and rice encourage the growth of slavery in North America?*

Vocabulary *Builder*
revolt (ree VOHLT) *v.* to rebel; to participate in an uprising

Early on, there were attempts to stop slavery. In 1652, Rhode Island passed the first antislavery law. However, it did not survive long, because Rhode Island shippers made high profits from the slave trade. Georgia had a ban on slavery until the 1750s and then lifted it. Slavery became legal in all the colonies.

Not every African in America was a slave, but slavery came to be restricted to people of African descent. Thus, slavery was linked to racism. **Racism** is the belief that one race is superior or inferior to another. Most English colonists believed themselves superior to Africans. Also, some colonists believed that they were helping Africans by introducing them to Christianity and European ways.

Resistance to Slavery As the number of enslaved people grew, whites began to worry that they would <u>revolt</u>. The first serious slave revolt took place in 1663, in Gloucester, Virginia. The rebels were betrayed, probably by an indentured servant, and the uprising failed. Soon, other revolts occurred in Connecticut and Virginia.

Fearing more trouble, colonial authorities wrote **slave codes**, or strict laws that restricted the rights and activities of slaves. Under the codes, enslaved people could not meet in large numbers, own weapons, or leave a plantation without permission. It also became illegal to teach enslaved people to read and write. Masters who killed enslaved people could not be tried for murder. Slave codes gave masters more control over enslaved Africans. It also made it harder for escaped slaves to survive.

The new laws did not stop resistance. In 1739, an enslaved Angolan named Jemmy led a revolt in South Carolina. He and his followers killed more than 20 whites before they were defeated. Revolts continued to flare up until slavery itself ended in 1865.

✓Checkpoint **What was the purpose of slave codes?**

116 Chapter 4 Life in the Colonies

African Cultural Influences

The lives of enslaved Africans differed greatly from colony to colony. Only 10 percent of the enslaved population lived north of Maryland. In cities of the North, they were often hired out to work as blacksmiths or house servants. On small farms, they might work alongside the owner. Over time, they might buy their freedom.

Even in the South, the lives of enslaved Africans varied. On rice plantations in South Carolina, Africans saw few white colonists. As a result, more than any other enslaved Africans, these workers kept the customs of West Africa. They reproduced the African grass baskets used to sift rice. They spoke Gullah, a special dialect that was created on the west coast of Africa during slave times. This dialect blended English and several African languages. Even today, some residents of the coastal South speak Gullah.

Enslaved Africans in colonies, such as Virginia and Maryland, were less isolated from white society. Still, many African customs survived. Craftsworkers in cities used African styles to create fine quilts, furniture, carved walking sticks, and other objects. The rhythm of drums used for communication by Africans found its way into American music. The banjo came from Africa as well. African folk tales became a part of American culture.

☑Checkpoint   **What cultural influences did Africans bring to America?**

⭐ **Looking Back and Ahead** In this section, we have seen how millions of Africans were transported to the colonies against their will. In the next section, we shall see how education and religion developed in colonial America.

Main Idea
African culture contributed to music, crafts, and other aspects of American life.

African-style banjo from the 1700s

Section 3 | **Check Your Progress**

Progress Monitoring Online
For: Self-test with instant help
Visit: PHSchool.com
Web Code: mva-1043

Comprehension and Critical Thinking

1. **(a) Recall** Why did fewer indentured servants come to America in the 1700s?
   (b) Analyze Cause and Effect How did the plantation system and the lack of indentured servants affect the status of Africans in America?

2. **(a) Identify** Why did the Gullah dialect develop in South Carolina?
   (b) Compare and Contrast In general, how did the experience of enslaved Africans in the North differ from that of enslaved Africans in the South?

Reading Skill

3. **Use Paragraph Clues to Analyze Meaning** Some paragraphs give you examples and descriptions of unfamiliar words. Reread the second paragraph under the heading "African Cultural Influences." Use paragraph clues to explain the meaning of *dialect* in that context. Explain the clues you used.

Vocabulary *Builder*

Answer the following questions in complete sentences that show your understanding of the key terms.

4. What was triangular trade?

5. How did racism affect the status of Africans in America?

6. Why did white colonists create slave codes?

Writing

7. Create an outline for an essay that discusses the geographic and economic factors that resulted in some colonies using slave labor more than other colonies.

The Spread of New Ideas

Objectives

1. Describe the education colonial children received.
2. Summarize the development of poetry and literature in colonial America.
3. Explain how the Great Awakening affected the colonies.
4. Explain how the colonies were affected by the spread of new ideas.

Prepare to Read

 Reading Skill

Use Context to Determine Meanings When the clues you have tried do not work, broaden the context. Where else might you have encountered this word? Do you remember it from films or books? Was it defined in previous sections? Can you find examples of it elsewhere? Finally, imagine yourself in a situation like the one in which the word appears.

Vocabulary *Builder*

High-Use Words

finance, p. 120
reinforce, p. 122

Key Terms and People

public school, p. 118
dame school, p. 119
Anne Bradstreet, p. 120
Phillis Wheatley, p. 120
Benjamin Franklin, p. 120
Jonathan Edwards, p. 121
natural rights, p. 122
divine right, p. 122
separation of powers, p. 123

⭐ **Background Knowledge** As you have read, the Puritans set up a government based on religion. In this section, you will see the impact of Puritan ideas on education. You will also read about a religious movement that swept the colonies.

The Importance of Education

To Puritans, education went hand in hand with religion. In early New England, everyone was expected to read the Bible.

Puritan Beginnings The Puritans passed laws to promote education. They required parents to teach their children and servants to read. Another law required every town with at least 50 families to start an elementary school. Every town with 100 families had to have a grammar school for older students.

These Massachusetts laws were the beginning of public schools in America. A **public school** is a school supported by taxes. Puritan schools were very different from the public schools of today, however. Puritan schools were run with both private and public money. In addition, Puritan education laws were not completely compulsory. Some towns paid a fine rather than set up a school. Laws that required all children to attend school did not begin until the late 1800s.

Colonial Schools Another difference between colonial schools and modern public schools is that colonial schools included instruction in religion. Most schools in the 1600s were under

Main Idea
Schools and colleges in the early colonies were influenced by religion, and the majority of students were white males.

Use Context to Determine Meaning Use the clues in the surrounding sentences and your own knowledge about education today to determine the meaning of the word *compulsory*.

religious sponsorship. Schools in New Netherland (later New York) were run by the Dutch Reformed Church. Pennsylvania schools were run by the Quakers.

In addition to religion, colonial elementary schools taught basic skills such as reading, writing, and arithmetic. Many students learned lessons from a hornbook, a paddle-shaped board with a printed lesson on top, protected by a transparent piece of animal horn. The hornbook might have the ABCs, the Roman numerals, and the Lord's Prayer so that children could copy and memorize them. A reading book called the *New England Primer,* first published in the 1680s, became widely used.

In the South, people were separated by great distances, so there were few schools. Members of the gentry often hired private tutors to instruct their children. Children from poorer families often received no formal education at all.

Some colonial elementary schools admitted girls. Others taught them only in summers or when boys were not in school. Girls might also attend **dame schools,** schools that women opened in their homes to teach girls and boys to read and write.

Education for African Americans
Most colonial schools were restricted to white children. However, in New York, an Anglican church group ran a school for free African Americans, as well as for Native Americans and poor whites.

Some Quaker and Anglican missionaries taught enslaved people to read. After slave codes in the South outlawed this, some enslaved people passed along their learning in secret. Still others taught themselves from stolen or borrowed books.

Colonial Education
Young children were often educated in dame schools, such as the one shown. **Critical Thinking: Evaluate Information** *Look at the page from the* New England Primer, *below. What kinds of lessons does it include?*

Now the Child being entred in his Letters and Spelling, let him learn these and such like Sentences by Heart, whereby he will be both instructed in his Duty, and encouraged in his Learning.

The Dutiful Child's Promises,

I Will fear GOD, and honour the KING.
I will honour my Father & Mother.
I will Obey my Superiours.
I will Submit to my Elders.
I will Love my Friends.
I will hate no Man.
I will forgive my Enemies, and pray to God for them.
I will as much as in me lies keep all God's Holy Commandments.

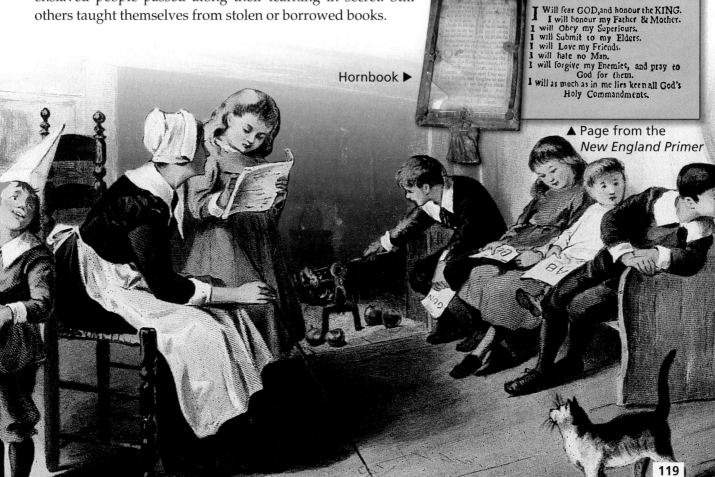

Hornbook ▶

▲ Page from the *New England Primer*

Upper Levels After elementary school, some boys went on to grammar school. Grammar schools were similar to modern high schools. They prepared boys for college. Students learned Greek and Latin, as well as geography, mathematics, and English composition.

The first American colleges were founded largely to educate men for the ministry. The Puritan general council financed what became Harvard College. Opening in 1638, Harvard was the first college in the English colonies. In 1693, colonists in Virginia founded the College of William and Mary, the first college in the South.

Vocabulary *Builder*
finance (Fī nans) *v.* to supply with money; to manage monetary situations

☑**Checkpoint** **How did education differ for girls and boys?**

Roots of American Literature

Main Idea
Colonial literature featured sermons, histories, and poetry as well as writings for a popular audience.

The earliest forms of colonial literature were sermons and histories. Books such as John Smith's *General History of Virginia* and William Bradford's *Of Plymouth Plantation* provided lively accounts of life in the first colonies.

Poetry The first colonial poet was Anne Bradstreet. Her book *The Tenth Muse, Lately Sprung Up in America* was first published in 1650, in England. It was not published in Boston until after her death. Bradstreet's poems, such as "Upon the Burning of Our House" and "To My Dear and Loving Husband," expressed the joys and hardships of life in Puritan New England.

A later poet, Phillis Wheatley, was an enslaved African in Boston. Her first poem was published in the 1760s, when she was about 14. Her works were in a scholarly style that was then popular in Europe.

Ben Franklin Perhaps the best-loved colonial writer was Benjamin Franklin. At age 17, Ben moved from Boston to Philadelphia and started a newspaper, the *Pennsylvania Gazette.* It became the most widely read newspaper in the colonies.

Franklin's most popular work was *Poor Richard's Almanack,* published every year from 1733 to 1753. The *Almanack* was full of pithy sayings that usually had a moral. These included "Eat to live, not live to eat" and "God helps them who help themselves." Franklin also published a vivid autobiography.

Franklin was far more than a writer. He was a businessman, community leader, scientist, inventor, and diplomat. He founded a library and a fire department, made discoveries about electricity, and invented such useful items as bifocal eyeglasses and a stove. As you will see, he also became one of the founders of the United States.

Biography Quest

Phillis Wheatley
1753?–1784

When she was eight, Phillis Wheatley was captured by slave traders in Africa and sent to Boston. But she was luckier than most enslaved Africans. The family she worked for educated her and gave her time to write.

Wheatley won fame as a poet and later gained her freedom. Sadly, her last years were full of hardship. She is recognized today as America's first poet of African descent.

Biography Quest ⏺**nline**

How did Wheatley meet George Washington?

For: The answer to the question about Wheatley

Visit: PHSchool.com

Web Code: mvd-1044

☑**Checkpoint** **How did Ben Franklin contribute to American literature?**

The Great Awakening

From the start, religion played a key role in the 13 English colonies. In Plymouth and Massachusetts Bay, religious leaders set extensive rules on moral and religious matters. Even in colonies that were founded primarily for economic reasons, such as Jamestown, early laws required colonists to attend church regularly.

By the 1700s, rules on religion had become less strict in many of the colonies. The Puritan tradition gradually declined in New England. Still, churches remained centers of faith and community life in all of the colonies.

Religious Revival An emotion-packed Christian movement swept through the colonies in the 1730s and 1740s. This period of religious revival is called the Great Awakening. The Great Awakening began as a reaction against what some Christians saw as a decline of religious zeal in the colonies. Leaders such as Massachusetts preacher Jonathan Edwards called on people to examine their lives and commit themselves to God. In a famous sermon, Edwards warned sinners what would happen to them after they died unless they changed their ways and sought forgiveness:

> ❝The God that holds you over the pit of hell, much as one holds a spider, or some loathesome insect, over a fire, abhors you, and is dreadfully provoked; his wrath towards you burns like fire; he looks upon you as worthy of nothing else, but to be cast into the fire.❞
>
> —Jonathan Edwards, Sinners in the Hands of an Angry God

Forceful preachers quickly spread the Great Awakening throughout the colonies. George Whitefield, an English minister, made several tours of the colonies. His listeners often wept with emotion. After a Whitefield visit to Philadelphia, Benjamin Franklin observed that "one could not walk thro' the Town in an Evening without Hearing Psalms sung in different Families of every Street."

Impact of the Great Awakening

The Great Awakening led to the rise of many new churches. Methodists and Baptists, which had been small sects or groups, grew quickly. The Presbyterian, Dutch Reformed, and Congregationalist churches split between those who followed the new movement and those who did not. In time, the growth of new churches led to more tolerance of religious differences in the colonies.

Main Idea
The Great Awakening led to the rise of new churches and strengthened democratic ideas.

Religious Awakening
Traveling preachers, such as English evangelist George Whitefield (below), provoked a broad religious revival in the 1730s and 1740s. **Critical Thinking:** *Draw Conclusions* *Why might the Great Awakening have unsettled many prominent church leaders of the time?*

Divine Right Versus Natural Rights

	Divine Right	Natural Rights
Where does the right to govern come from?	From God to the ruler	From the people
Where do people's rights come from?	From the ruler	From God to the people
What happens if a government violates people's rights?	People must obey ruler	People can change their government

Reading Charts
Skills Activity

Did the right to rule come from the will of God or from the people? The answer to this question would alter the course of history in nations around the world.

(a) **Read a Chart** Which column represents the views of John Locke?

(b) **Draw Conclusions** Which of those views would be most attractive to the American colonists? Explain.

Vocabulary *Builder*
reinforce (ree ihn FORS) *v.* to make stronger; to strengthen; to make more effective

The Great Awakening was one of the first national movements in the colonies. It <u>reinforced</u> democratic ideas. People thought that if they could decide on their own how to worship God, they could decide how to govern themselves.

✓**Checkpoint** **How did the Great Awakening affect American society?**

Main Idea
The ideas of the Enlightenment in Europe had a far-reaching influence on American political thought.

The Enlightenment

Starting in the late 1600s, a group of European thinkers came to believe that all problems could be solved by human reason. They ushered in a new intellectual movement that became known as the Enlightenment. Enlightenment thinkers looked for "natural laws" that governed politics, society, and economics. The Enlightenment reached its height in France in the mid-1700s. However, some of its key ideas came from an Englishman, John Locke.

Locke In 1690, Locke published *Two Treatises on Government*. In this influential work, Locke argued that people have certain **natural rights,** that is, rights that belong to every human being from birth. These rights include life, liberty, and property. According to Locke, these rights are inalienable, meaning that they cannot be taken away.

Locke challenged the idea of divine right. **Divine right** is the belief that monarchs get their authority to rule directly from God. According to this belief, any rights that people have come to them from the monarch. By contrast, Locke stated that natural rights came from God. He argued that people formed governments in order to protect their rights. They give up some individual freedoms but only to safeguard the rights of the community.

Locke's reasoning led to a startling conclusion. Because government exists to protect the rights of the people, if a monarch violates those rights, the people have a right to overthrow the monarch. This idea would later shape the founding of the United States.

Montesquieu A French thinker, the Baron de Montesquieu (MON tehs kyoo), also influenced American ideas. In his 1748 book *The Spirit of the Laws,* Montesquieu argued that the powers of government should be clearly defined and limited. Furthermore, he favored separation of powers, or division of the power of government into separate branches. Separation of powers, he said, protects the rights of the people because it keeps any individual or group from gaining too much power.

Montesquieu suggested that government should be divided into three branches: a legislative branch to make laws, an executive branch to enforce the laws, and a judicial branch to make judgments based on the law. He wrote:

Montesquieu

> **"**There would be an end to everything, were the same man or the same body . . . to exercise those three powers, that of enacting laws, that of executing the public resolutions, and of trying the causes of individuals.**"**
>
> —Baron de Montesquieu, *The Spirit of the Laws*

As you will see, this division of power would become the basis of government in the United States.

☑ **Checkpoint**   What was the goal of Enlightenment thinkers?

⭐ **Looking Back and Ahead** By the 1770s, educated colonists had come to accept the idea that they were born with certain natural rights. As you will see in the next chapter, this belief would set the stage for conflict with the English king and Parliament.

Section 4 | **Check Your Progress**

Progress Monitoring ⏺nline
For: Self-test with instant help
Visit: PHSchool.com
Web Code: mva-1044

Comprehension and Critical Thinking

1. **(a) Recall** What role did religion play in colonial schools?
   (b) Support Generalizations Find at least two facts to support the following generalization: Education was important to the colonists.

2. **(a) Describe** What was the Great Awakening?

(b) Analyze Cause and Effect What was one effect of the Great Awakening?

🔊 **Reading Skill**

3. **Use Context to Determine Meaning** Reread the quotation by Jonathan Edwards in this section. Use context to determine the meaning of *abhors.* Explain the clues you used.

Vocabulary *Builder*

4. Write two definitions for each key term: public school, dame school, natural rights, separation of powers. First, write a formal definition for your teacher. Second, write a definition in everyday English for a classmate.

Writing

5. Write two to three closing sentences for an essay on the Enlightenment. Focus particularly on the impact of this movement.

How I Became a Printer
by Benjamin Franklin

Introduction

It took Benjamin Franklin 17 years to finish his *Autobiography,* and it was not published until after his death. Today, it is recognized as a classic of early American literature. The book covers only the first 51 years of Franklin's long life, so it does not tell of his later role in the founding of the United States.

Reading Skill

Analyze Autobiographical Approach Writers of autobiographies often convey their attitudes and beliefs as they are conveying a story. As you read, look for clues about Franklin's attitude toward the government. Do you think Franklin approves of the Assembly's actions against James?

Vocabulary *Builder*

As you read this literature selection, look for the following underlined words:

chandler (CHAND ler) *n.* person who makes or sells candles, soap, and other items made from the fat of animals

tedious (TEE dee uhs) *adj.* boring

censure (SEHN sher) *v.* to condemn or criticize

admonish (ad MAHN ihsh) *v.* warn

 Background

Tithing (TĪTH ing) is the practice of giving one tenth of one's earnings to the church annually. Here, Franklin jokingly implies that his father wished to follow this same tradition by giving the tenth of his children, Benjamin, rather than a tenth of his earnings.

I was put to the grammar-school at eight years of age, my father intending to devote me, as the tithe of his sons, to the service of the Church. My early readiness in learning to read (which must have been very early, as I do not remember when I could not read), and the opinion of all his friends, that I should certainly make a good scholar, encouraged him in this purpose of his. . . . But my father, in the mean time, from the view of the expense of a college education, which having so large a family he could not well afford . . . took me from the grammar-school, and sent me to a school for writing and arithmetic. . . . At ten years old I was taken home to assist my father in his business, which was that of tallow-<u>chandler</u> and soapboiler. . . . Accordingly, I was employed in cutting wick for the candles, filling the dipping mold and the molds for cast candles, attending the shop, going of errands etc.

I disliked the trade, and had a strong inclination for the sea, but my father declared against it. However, living near the water, I was much in and about it, learned early to swim well, and to manage boats; and when in a boat or a canoe with other boys, I was commonly allowed to govern, especially in any case of difficulty; and upon other occasions I was generally a leader among the boys. . . .

From a child I was fond of reading, and all the little money that came into my hands was ever laid out in books. . . .

This bookish inclination at length determined my father to make me a printer, though he had already one son (James) of that profession. In 1717 my brother James returned from England with a press and letters to set up his business in Boston. I . . . signed the indenture when I was yet by twelve years old. I was to serve as an apprentice till I was twenty-one years of age, only I was to be allowed journeyman's wages during the last year. In a little time I made great proficiency in the business, and became a useful hand to my brother.

Though a brother, he considered himself as my master, and me as his apprentice, and accordingly, expected the same services from me as he would from another, while I thought he demeaned me too much in some he required of me, who from a brother expected more indulgence. Our disputes were often brought before our father, and I fancy I was either generally in the right, or else a better pleader, because the judgment was generally in my favor. But my brother was passionate, and had often beaten me, which I took extremely amiss; and thinking my apprenticeship very <u>tedious</u>, I was continually wishing for some opportunity of shortening it, which at length offered in a manner unexpected.

One of the pieces in our newspaper on some political point, which I have now forgotten, gave offense to the Assembly. He [James] was taken up, <u>censured</u>, and imprisoned for one month, by the speaker's warrant, I suppose, because he would not discover [reveal] his author. I too was taken up and examined before the council; but, though I did not give them any satisfaction, they contented themselves with <u>admonishing</u> me, and dismissed me. . . .

During my brother's confinement, which I resented a good deal, notwithstanding our private differences, I had the management of the paper; and I made bold to give our rulers some rubs in it, which my brother took very kindly. . . . My brother's discharge was accompanied with an order of the House (a very odd one), that "James Franklin should no longer print the paper called the New England Courant."

There was a consultation held in our printing-house among his friends, . . . it was finally concluded on as a better way, to let it be printed for the future under the name of BENJAMIN FRANKLIN; . . . the contrivance was that my old indenture should be returned to me, with full discharge on the back of it, to be shown on occasion, but to secure to him the benefit of my service, I was to sign new indentures for the remainder of the term, which were to be kept private. A very flimsy scheme it was; however, it was immediately executed, and the paper went on accordingly, under my name for several months.

From *The Autobiography of Benjamin Franklin*,
by Benjamin Franklin. © 2003. Yale University Press.

Ben Franklin (center)

 Analyze Autobiographical Approach

Throughout the story, Franklin conveys his feelings about his brother. When his brother is imprisoned, Franklin takes action by giving the Assembly "some rubs in." Do you think he does this more out of family loyalty or because he supports a free press?

☑ **Checkpoint**   **What plan did Franklin's brother approve to keep publishing the newspaper after his confinement?**

Analyze LITERATURE

Benjamin Franklin disliked being his brother's apprentice. Imagine that you are Franklin. Write a letter to the *New England Courant* expressing your opinion about the fairness or unfairness of being made an apprentice at the age of 12.

If you liked this passage, you might want to read *The Printer's Apprentice* by Stephen Krensky, illustrated by Madeline Sorel. Yearling. 1996.

Compare and Contrast

A Venn diagram is a graphic organizer that shows similarities and differences. You can use a Venn diagram to compare and contrast information about any two items, including time periods, historical events, people, and ideas. Aspects of the two items that are different appear outside the shared area where the circles intersect. Aspects that are similar are listed within the shared area.

Copy and complete the Venn diagram below to compare and contrast information about colonial women and women today. Use information that follows the subheading "Roles of Women" in Chapter 4, Section 2, and your own knowledge about contemporary American women.

Colonial Women
- Did not hold political office or vote
- Parents often chose husbands
- Usually could not own property

Both
- Can have personal opinions about politics
- Work very hard inside and outside the home

American Women Today
- Can hold political office and vote
- Can choose their own husbands
- Able to own property

Learn the Skill

Use these steps to create a Venn diagram.

1 **Identify the subject.** Decide what items you will compare and contrast on the Venn diagram. Write a title summarizing the subject of the organizer.

2 **Identify the differences.** Write the differences between the items being compared in each circle under the appropriate heading.

3 **Identify the similarities.** Write the similarities between the items being compared in the intersecting circle under the heading "Both."

4 **Draw a conclusion about the subject.** Use the information on the Venn diagram to write a sentence summarizing the conclusions.

Practice the Skill

Answer the following questions about the Venn diagram on this page.

1 **Identify the subject.** What is a good title for the Venn diagram on this page?

2 **Identify the differences.** What is a difference between colonial woman and American women today?

3 **Identify the similarities.** What is a similarity between colonial women and American women today?

4 **Draw a conclusion about the subject.** Based on the information in the Venn diagram, what is one conclusion you can draw about colonial women and American women today?

Apply the Skill

See the Review and Assessment at the end of this chapter.

Chapter Summary

Section 1
Governing the Colonies

- The Magna Carta and English Bill of Rights guaranteed the rights of English citizens.
- By 1760, each of the 13 colonies had a legislature to make laws.
- The trial of John Peter Zenger helped establish the idea of freedom of the press.
- England passed the Navigation Acts to regulate colonial trade.

Section 2
Colonial Society

- In colonial society, men, women, and children had clearly defined roles.
- Colonial America offered poor and middle-class whites the opportunity to own land and improve their social status.

Section 3
Slavery in the Colonies

- More than 10 million Africans were transported to the Americas in the Atlantic slave trade.
- The plantation economy of the South became dependent on the labor of enslaved African Americans.
- Slave codes did not stop occasional slave revolts.

Section 4
The Spread of New Ideas

- Education during colonial times was influenced by religion.
- Colonial era literature included poetry, sermons, and popular writing.
- The Great Awakening of the 1730s and 1740s led to the rise of new churches.
- Enlightenment thinkers influenced ideas about government and natural rights.

Key Concepts

These notes will help you prepare for questions about key concepts.

Milestones in the Development of Democracy

1215: Magna Carta
- Limits the power of the English king to tax
- Protects private property
- Guarantees the right to trial by jury
- Creates a Great Council, which later becomes Parliament

1619: House of Burgesses (Virginia)
- Set up in Virginia, becomes the first legislature in British North America

1688: English Bill of Rights
- Upholds habeas corpus, a procedure that prevents unlawful arrest
- Requires Parliament to meet regularly
- Forbids monarchs from raising taxes or an army without the consent of Parliament

1735: Trial of John Peter Zenger
- Establishes freedom of the press in British North America

Effects of Atlantic Slave Trade

- More than 10 million enslaved Africans were forced to come to the Americas.
- Enslaved Africans endured horrible conditions on the Middle Passage journey.
- New England merchants profited from the slave trade.
- Southern plantation owners became dependent on the labor of enslaved Africans.
- Slave revolts resulted in slave codes.

Vocabulary *Builder*

Key Terms

Complete each of the following sentences so that the second part further explains the first part and clearly shows your understanding of the key term.

1. All colonies in British North America had legislatures, _____.

2. The English Bill of Rights guaranteed habeas corpus, _____.

3. On colonial farms, it was important to have an extended family because _____.

4. Many people came to the colonies from Europe as indentured servants, _____.

5. After a time, slave owners enforced slave codes _____.

Comprehension and Critical Thinking

6. **(a) Identify** What rights did the Magna Carta and the English Bill of Rights guarantee?
   (b) Draw Conclusions Why do you think colonists believed they were entitled to the rights guaranteed by the Magna Carta and the English Bill of Rights?
   (c) Link Past and Present Which of these rights do Americans still enjoy today?

7. **(a) Describe** What was life like on a colonial farm?
   (b) Compare and Contrast How were the responsibilities of men and women similar? How were they different?

8. **(a) Identify** What were the various classes into which colonial society was divided?
   (b) Compare In what ways were the poor better off in America than in Europe?
   (c) Explain Problems What were some of the limitations placed on free African Americans? Explain.

9. **(a) Recall** What was the triangular trade?
   (b) Identify Benefits Which groups benefited from this trade?
   (c) Identify Costs Which groups experienced hardships because of this trade?

10. **(a) Describe** What were colonial schools like?
    (b) Frame Questions List at least three questions you would ask a colonial school-age child.

History Reading Skill

11. **Determine Meaning From Context** Find an unfamiliar word in Chapter 4 and use context clues to analyze its meaning. Explain the clues you used.

Writing

12. Write two paragraphs summarizing how the ideas and customs that the colonists brought from England began to change once they left their homeland. Focus on the social and political changes.
    Your paragraphs should:
    • begin with a thesis statement that expresses a main idea;
    • include the ideas that the colonists brought from England;
    • list and discuss the changes that resulted in the colonists changing their views;
    • end by stating how the colonists changed.

13. **Write a Narrative:**
    You are a teacher in a colonial school. Name the colony in which you teach. Describe the school. How many students do you have? What are your goals for your students?

Skills for Life

Compare and Contrast

Review what you have learned about the lives of indentured servants and the lives of enslaved Africans in colonial America. Create a Venn diagram showing some of the similarities and differences. Then, answer the following questions.

14. Identify two differences between enslaved Africans and indentured servants.

15. What was one way in which the life of an indentured servant was similar to the life of an enslaved person?

16. Agree or disagree with the following conclusion: The life of an indentured servant was just as harsh as the life of an enslaved African. Give reasons for your answer.

Test Yourself

1. **The colonies offered the right to vote to**

   A Native Americans.

   B African Americans.

   C white male property owners.

   D any colonist born in England.

2. **One reason that colonists disliked the Navigation Acts was that the laws**

   A prevented colonial merchants from selling their goods in England.

   B led to a decline in the shipbuilding industry.

   C created manufacturing jobs in England.

   D cut colonial merchants off from profitable foreign markets.

3. **What was one result of the Great Awakening in the 13 colonies?**

   A It reinforced the principle of freedom of the press.

   B It led to the decline of the Puritan Church in New England.

   C It led to the formation of new churches.

   D It encouraged colonists to accept royal authority.

4. **According to John Locke, natural rights**

   A cannot be taken away.

   B are granted by the king or queen.

   C apply only to English citizens.

   D apply only to the gentry.

Document-Based Questions

Task: Look at Documents 1 and 2, and answer their accompanying questions. Then, use the documents and your knowledge of history to complete the following writing assignment:

> Write an essay about the treatment of enslaved Africans on the journey to America. How does Document 1 support Equiano's statements about conditions during the journey?

Document 1: These diagrams show the loading plan of a slave ship during the Middle Passage from Africa to the Americas. *Based on this picture, describe the way enslaved Africans were treated on the journey.*

Document 2: Olaudah Equiano, an African who survived the voyage, wrote this description of his experiences. *What were two causes of suffering on the ship?*

"The closeness of the place and the heat of the climate, added to the number in the ship, which was so crowded that each had scarcely room to turn himself, almost suffocated us. . . . The air soon became unfit for respiration . . . and brought on a sickness among the slaves, of which many died. The shrieks of the women, and the groans of the dying, rendered the whole a scene of horror almost inconceivable. Happily perhaps for myself I was soon reduced so low here that it was thought necessary to keep me almost always on deck; and from my extreme youth I was not put in fetters. In this situation I expected every hour to share the fate of my companions, some of whom were almost daily brought upon deck at the point of death, which I began to hope would soon put an end to my miseries. Often did I think many of the inhabitants of the deep much more happy than myself; I envied them the freedom they enjoyed, and as often wished I could change my condition for theirs.

Every circumstance . . . served only to render my state more painful, and heighten my . . . opinion of the cruelty of the whites. One day they had taken a number of fishes, and when they had killed and satisfied themselves with as many as they thought fit . . . they tossed the remaining fish into the sea again, although we begged and prayed for some."

Writing Workshop

Expository Essay
Historical Overview

▶ Introduction

In a historical overview, you survey a particular period or development from history. You present a central idea about the period or development, supporting that idea with facts about that time. A historical overview should have the following characteristics:

- a historical period or development that can be surveyed from beginning to end
- a thesis statement that presents a main idea about that period
- facts and incidences that support the main idea
- interesting descriptions of details and incidents
- an informative tone

Assignment On the following pages, you will learn how to write a historical overview. You will get step-by-step instructions. Each step will include an example from a sample overview about the Age of Exploration.

Read the instructions and the examples. Then, follow each step to plan and write an essay of 500–700 words.

> **Write a historical overview of one region of the 13 colonies from the mid-1600s to the mid-1700s.**

For a review of the steps in the writing process, see the **Historian's Toolkit,** *Write Like a Historian.*

▶ Prewriting

Define the scope of the overview. In writing a historical overview, you start with a well-defined idea of what happened before, during, and after the period you are writing about. It helps to make a timeline showing the major events to be covered.

1100–1300: Crusades take place. Europeans learn new sailing techniques and borrow technology from Muslim sailors.

1420s: Henry the Navigator founds school for sailors.

1519: Magellan circumnavigates the world.

1100   1200   1300   1400   1500   1600

1300s: The Renaissance begins.

1492–1504: Columbus sails to the Americas.

Brainstorm about the "big picture." Focus on the "big picture" rather than on the details of the period. Your goal is to communicate an important central idea about the whole period to your audience.

Write a thesis statement. A thesis statement expresses the main idea of your essay in a sentence or two.

List supporting information. The body of your essay will support and develop your thesis statement with facts, events, and other information. You may have more information than you need. Be sure to choose facts, individuals, and incidents that are most relevant to the idea you are presenting.

> **Sample thesis statement:**
> The age of exploration created a demand in Europe for new goods to consume and new lands to conquer; it opened the way for centuries of colonialism.

▶ Drafting

Choose an organization. Now you need to decide the best order in which to present your information. You have several choices for organizing your historical overview.

One approach is to use chronological order. The advantage of chronological order is that it is easy to stick to and easy for your readers to follow.

You could also modify chronological order by focusing on certain topics, showing how each of these developed during the period.

Introduce your thesis and give background information. Draft an introductory paragraph. Briefly describe the period or development you will be covering, explain why it is important, and lead up to your thesis statement. You could place your thesis statement anywhere in your first paragraph; particularly strong locations are the opening and the closing sentences of the introduction. You may also want to use a quotation or brief incident to catch your readers' interest.

Cover the main developments. Write the body of your essay, following the organization you chose and using your prewriting notes. The body of your essay consists of several paragraphs that support your main idea with facts. You may also need to give your readers some background information about the events you are writing about. For example, it might be helpful to know that Native Americans had never been exposed to diseases that the European settlers brought to the New World.

Pull it together with a strong conclusion. In your final paragraph, restate your main idea and summarize the main support for it. Finish in a powerful way, indicating what lessons this period can teach us or making some other important point.

▶ Student Model

Read the following model of a historical overview. Notice how it includes the characteristics you have learned about.

Spanish Exploration of the Americas

> The introductory paragraph describes the historical period and explains its importance.

During the Renaissance, Europeans became interested in finding new trade routes to Asia. First, the Portuguese sailed east around Africa to Asia and traded goods for gold. Then, Spain's rulers decided to finance voyages to discover a western water route to Asia. These voyages resulted in the exploration of the Americas and the establishment of Spain's empire there.

> The thesis statement expresses the main idea of the essay.

In 1492, the Italian sea captain Christopher Columbus set sail from Spain. His goal was to reach the East Indies by sailing west across the Atlantic Ocean. Instead, Columbus landed on an island in the Caribbean. Convinced that he had reached Asia, Columbus made three more voyages.

> Is this composition organized by chronological order or by the development of certain key topics?

Columbus's discoveries encouraged other Spanish explorers to travel west. In 1513, Juan Ponce de León explored the coasts of Florida. The same year, Vasco Núñez de Balboa crossed the Isthmus of Panama and reached the Pacific Ocean.

> The body of the essay supports the main idea with facts.

Then, in 1519, Ferdinand Magellan set out from Spain with five ships and about 250 crew members. His expedition sailed around the southern tip of South America and started across the Pacific Ocean. Three years later, in 1522, the survivors finally reached Spain after sailing around the world. Magellan never lived to see it, but his sailors had sailed west and finally found the all-water route for Spain.

Spain's search for the western route to Asia started in 1492 and ended successfully in 1522. During this period, Spanish explorers discovered new lands, learned more about Earth's true size, and established Spain's empire in the Americas.

> A strong conclusion restates the main idea and summarizes the main points that support it.

▶ Revising

After completing your draft, read it again carefully to find ways to make your writing better. Here are some questions to ask yourself.

Revise to strengthen your thesis and support
- Does the thesis state your main idea clearly?
- Does each paragraph include reasons and facts that support that main idea?
- Does the essay provide interesting details and descriptions?

Revise to meet written English-language conventions
- Are all sentences complete, with a subject and a verb?
- Are all the words spelled correctly? Use a spell-checker or a dictionary to make sure.
- Are all proper nouns capitalized, including names of people and places?
- Did you use proper punctuation? Check punctuation within sentences as well as at the ends of sentences.

▶ Rubric for Self-Assessment

Evaluate your historical overview using the following rating scale:

	Score 4	Score 3	Score 2	Score 1
Organization	Supports the thesis with a series of logically ordered paragraphs; uses some type of chronological order	Uses a reasonably clear organization to present the supporting information	Chooses an organization not suited to the topic	Shows lack of organizational strategy
Presentation	Supports the main idea effectively with relevant facts and incidents; links all information to the main idea	Supports the main idea adequately with several facts, details, or examples; links most information to the main idea	Does not support the main idea adequately; does not link supporting information to the main idea; includes irrelevant information	Does not provide facts, details, or examples to support the main idea
Use of Language	Varies sentence structure and vocabulary successfully; includes no or very few mechanical errors	Uses some variety in sentence structure and vocabulary; includes few mechanical errors	Uses the same types of sentences without varying them; does not vary vocabulary; includes many mechanical errors	Writes incomplete sentences; uses language poorly; sounds confused; includes many mechanical errors

Unit 2

Think Like a Historian

As you read this unit, think about this question: *How did the colonists break away from Britain and create a republican form of government?*

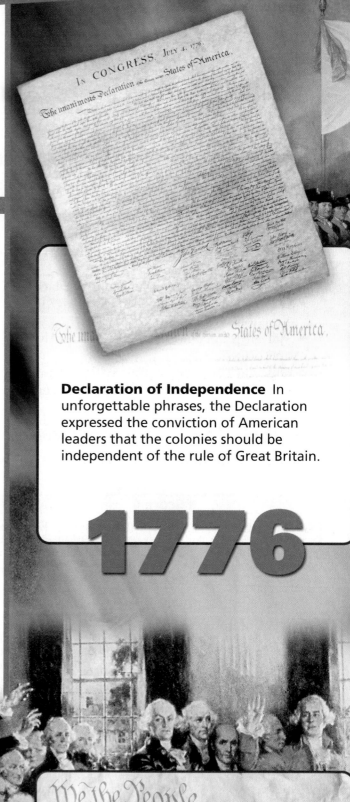

Declaration of Independence In unforgettable phrases, the Declaration expressed the conviction of American leaders that the colonies should be independent of the rule of Great Britain.

1776

Writing the Constitution All through the hot summer of 1787, delegates from the states debated the new shape of the U.S. government. The Constitution created a framework for the government of the United States we enjoy today.

1787

Forming a New Nation

The Final Battle Trapped by American and French forces, the British were forced to surrender at the Battle of Yorktown. The British defeat marked the end of the fighting in the American Revolution.

1781

A Bill of Rights The Bill of Rights was intended to prevent the kind of abuses Americans had suffered under English rule. One of the rights protected was the right of the people peaceably to assemble.

1791

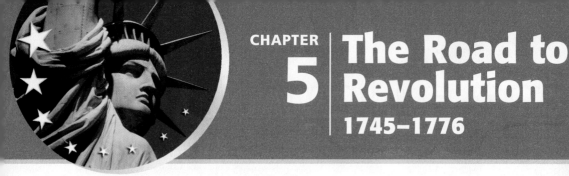

Chapter Preview

As the 13 colonies became increasingly independent throughout the 1700s, it became harder for Britain to control them. The colonists resisted Parliament's and King George III's efforts to control the economy and government of the colonies. Tensions continued to rise, finally erupting in war between Britain and its 13 colonies in 1775.

U.S. Events

1740s English move into Ohio Valley.

1754 French and Indian War begins.

1759 British capture Quebec.

1740   1750   1760

World Events

1748 Britain and France fight to control trade in India.

1756 Seven Years' War breaks out in Europe between France and Britain.

The first shots of the American Revolution were fired on the green at Lexington, April 19, 1775. No one knows who fired the very first shot, but the battle ended with British troops in full retreat toward Boston.

1765
Stamp Act
passed.

1770
Five colonists
die in Boston
Massacre.

1775
Fighting at Lexington
and Concord marks
beginning of American
Revolution.

1760

1770

1780

1769 James Watt
improves the steam
engine in England.

1773 British
Parliament
passes the Tea Act.

History Reading Skill **Draw Inferences and Conclusions**

What conflicts arose between colonists during the American Revolution era?

In this chapter, you will learn how to draw inferences and conclusions. Read the following account of struggle between colonists loyal to England and those seeking independence. The side notes show you how to draw inferences and conclusions.

Primary Source

During the period when many American colonists fought to win independence from Britain, other colonists remained loyal to Britain and its king. Patriot colonists and Loyalist colonists argued passionately. On some occasions, as you will read below, the arguments became violent.

> You can infer that the writer sympathizes with Malcolm.

The most shocking cruelty was exercised a few nights ago upon a poor old man, one Malcolm. A quarrel was picked with him. . . . He was stripped naked on one of the severest cold night this winter. His body was covered all over with tar, then with feathers. . . .

> Details that support the inference: He is loyal to the king and governors. He calls those attacking him "traitors."

The unhappy wretch they say behaved with the greatest bravery. When under torture they demanded of him to curse his masters, the king [King George of Britain], governors, etc., which they could not make him do. He still cried, "Curse all traitors." . . .

They are angry with him, particularly because he was with Governor Tyron [of New York]. . . . The Governor has declared that [Malcolm] was of great service to him in that affair, by his courageous spirit encountering the greatest dangers.

> You can infer that Malcolm is a Loyalist and his attackers are Patriots.

—Ann Hulton, *Letters of a Loyalist: Lady Ann Hulton*

Draw Inferences and Conclusions

- An inference is an idea suggested, but not stated, in the text. Support inferences with details in the text.
- Draw a conclusion by analyzing what you have read and forming an opinion about what it means.
- Add information from previous readings or from personal experience to complete an inference or conclusion.

Document-Based Questions

1. Who wrote this letter?
2. How might the letter have been different if written by a Patriot?

Vocabulary *Builder*

Previewing High-Use Academic Words

High-Use Word	Definition	Sample History Sentence
collide (koh LĪD) (Section 1, p. 140)	*v.* to come into violent conflict	French and British ambitions collided in the Ohio River valley in the 1750s.
resolve (ree SAHLV) (Section 1, p. 143)	*n.* strong determination to succeed in doing something	The goal of gaining land for Spain strengthened Columbus's resolve to find a sea route to Asia.
minimum (MIHN ah muhm) (Section 2, p. 146)	*n.* smallest quantity possible	With the end of the French and Indian War, colonists expected a minimum rise in taxes to the British.
emotional (ee MOH shuhn ahl) (Section 2, p. 147)	*adj.* appealing to the emotions, or feelings, of people	After the French and Indian War, colonial soldiers returned to an emotional homecoming.
prior (PRĪ or) (Section 3, p. 150)	*adj.* preceding in time; earlier; former	Prior to the arrival of Cortés, the Aztecs ruled over a mighty empire.
react (ree AKT) (Section 3, p. 152)	*v.* to act in return	The French reacted strongly to Washington's expedition into the Ohio River valley.
crisis (KRĪ sihs) (Section 4, p. 156)	*n.* time of great danger or trouble	The crisis was eased when the British Parliament repealed the Stamp Act.
restore (ree STOR) (Section 4, p. 158)	*v.* to bring back to a normal state; to put back; to reestablish	By the end of 1763, the French knew there was little opportunity to restore its empire in North America.

Previewing Key Terms and People

John Adams

George Washington, p. 140
militia, p. 140
alliance, p. 141

cede, p. 144
duty, p. 146
boycott, p. 147
petition, p. 147
writ of assistance, p. 148
John Adams, p. 149
Samuel Adams, p. 149
monopoly, p. 151
repeal, p. 152
minuteman, p. 152

blockade, p. 161
mercenary, p. 161

George Washington

Trouble on the Frontier

Objectives

1. Identify the reasons why fighting broke out between France and Britain in North America.

2. Describe the early defeat of the British by the French at the beginning of the French and Indian War.

3. Explain how the British gained victory, and explain the results of the French and Indian War.

Prepare to Read

Reading Skill

Make Inferences When ideas are not actually stated, readers must infer these ideas by analyzing the details and evidence in the text. As you read about the choices and views of both the Americans and the British in colonial times, think about the inferences you can make from their actions.

Vocabulary *Builder*

High-Use Words

<u>collide</u>, p. 140
<u>resolve</u>, p. 143

Key Terms and People

George Washington, p. 140
militia, p. 140
alliance, p. 141
cede, p. 144

Main Idea

A struggle over control of the Ohio River valley led to conflict between England and France.

Vocabulary *Builder*

<u>collide</u> (koh LĪD) *v.* to come into violent conflict

☆ **Background Knowledge** Between 1650 and 1750, American colonists developed a large degree of self-government. Americans were proud of their hard-won rights and intensely loyal to the British monarch. In this section, you will learn how this loyalty was strained by a conflict on the North American frontier.

Competing Empires

By the middle of the 1700s, France and Britain each controlled large areas of North America which bordered on each other for thousands of miles. Each country feared the other and sought to increase the area it controlled. These ambitions <u>collided</u> on the frontier and eventually led to war.

Native Americans lived on most of the territory claimed by France and Britain. There were few French settlers. Therefore, they did not threaten to seize Native American lands. However, the need of British settlers for farmland led to conflict with the Native Americans. By the 1740s, British settlers were pushing into the Ohio River valley lands claimed by the French. The pressure soon led to trouble.

The French and Indian War Begins In 1753, the French began building forts to back their claim to the land between Lake Erie and the Ohio River. This news alarmed the Virginia Colony, which also claimed the Ohio River valley. The governor of Virginia decided to send soldiers to order the French to leave. He chose a 21-year-old surveyor in the Virginia militia, George Washington, as the leader. The militia is a force made up of civilians trained as soldiers but not part of the regular army. Washington made the dangerous journey, returning home to tell the governor that the French had rejected his warning.

The next year, Washington traveled west again with orders to build a fort where the Allegheny and the Monongahela (muh non goh HEEL uh) rivers meet to form the Ohio River.

Washington arrived too late. The French were there already, building their own fort, which they called Fort Duquesne (du KANE). Washington marched south for about 50 miles and built a small fort of his own. He called it Fort Necessity.

Later, Washington's troops attacked and defeated a small French force. However, a larger French army arrived and forced Washington to surrender Fort Necessity. The French allowed Washington and his men to return home to Virginia with the message that they would never give up the Ohio River valley.

The Albany Congress Expecting war to break out soon, the British government called a meeting of colonial leaders. It took place in Albany, New York. The British wanted the colonies to agree to cooperate in defending themselves against the French. The British also invited the Iroquois tribes to the meeting. They hoped to form an alliance with the Iroquois against the French. An **alliance** is an agreement between countries to help each other against other countries.

The Iroquois refused to make an alliance, in part because they expected the French to defeat the British in a war. The colonial leaders tried to work out a plan to defend themselves. Benjamin Franklin of Pennsylvania believed the colonies had to succeed. To make that point, his newspaper, the *Philadelphia Gazette*, published a picture of a snake chopped into pieces with the warning "Join, or Die."

Make Inferences

How did Virginia's governor view George Washington? Give one detail that supports your inference.

Join, or Die

JOIN, or DIE.

Reading Political Cartoons

Skills Activity

Benjamin Franklin's 1754 cartoon was a plea for unity in defending the colonies during the French and Indian War.

(a) Distinguish Relevant Information Identify the eight sets of initials that label the eight pieces of the snake.

(b) Draw Conclusions What point is Franklin making about the importance of colonial unity?

Franklin drew up a plan, called the Albany Plan of Union. It called for a council of representatives elected by the colonial assemblies. The council would have authority over western settlements, relations with Native Americans, and other urgent matters. It also could organize armies and collect taxes to pay its expenses.

The Albany Congress approved Franklin's plan, but the colonial assemblies rejected it. The colonies wanted to control their own taxes and armies. Franklin complained that "everyone cries, union is necessary," but they behave like "weak noodles" when the time comes to take action.

☑**Checkpoint** **Why were the British concerned about French activity in the Ohio River valley?**

Main Idea
The first years of the French and Indian War were marked by a series of military disasters for the British.

Early British Defeats

Soon after Washington's return, the British government decided it had to push the French out of the Ohio River valley. In 1755, it sent General Edward Braddock to Virginia with orders to capture Fort Duquesne. Braddock arrived with a large force of regular British troops and Virginia militia. Colonel George Washington joined Braddock's force as a volunteer.

The French and Indian War

MAP★MASTER®

Skills Activity

On land and on sea, Britain and France battled furiously during the French and Indian War. The victor would win control of most of North America.

(a) Read a Map Key From Fort Oswego, on the western frontier, what two French posts did the British attack?

(b) Draw Conclusions Why was it important to the British to capture Louisbourg and Fort Duquesne?

MapMaster ⚫nline

For: Interactive map
Visit: PHSchool.com
Web Code: mvp-2051

KEY

New France
British Territory
French forts
British forts
British advances

Disaster at Fort Duquesne General Braddock understood military tactics used in Europe, where armies fought in formation on open fields. But he knew nothing about fighting in North America, where conditions were very different. Braddock did not respect colonial soldiers. He did not listen to warnings that soldiers marching down a narrow road through a dense forest in red uniforms were perfect targets for an enemy fighting from behind trees and bushes. When Benjamin Franklin warned him about the danger of ambushes, Braddock said they were no threat to his well-trained troops.

As Braddock's force neared Fort Duquesne in early July, it was ambushed by French troops and their Native American allies. More than half of Braddock's men were killed or wounded, with the general himself among the dead.

General Edward Braddock

More British Defeats The British had other setbacks during 1755. An army led by the governor of Massachusetts failed to take Fort Niagara on Lake Ontario. Further east, an army of British colonists and Native Americans was ambushed and suffered heavy losses near Lake George. These defeats may have strengthened Iroquois leaders' <u>resolve</u> not to ally with Britain.

In May 1756, Britain declared war on France, marking the official beginning of the Seven Years' War between the two countries. Shortly thereafter, French troops led by General Louis de Montcalm captured and destroyed Britain's Fort Oswego on Lake Ontario. In 1757, Montcalm captured Fort William Henry on Lake George.

Vocabulary *Builder*
<u>resolve</u> (ree SAHLV) *n.* strong determination to succeed in doing something

☑**Checkpoint** What fatal errors did General Edward Braddock make?

The British Turn the Tide

The situation improved for Britain during 1757 when William Pitt became prime minister. Pitt sought top generals who had genuine military talent. He chose James Wolfe, who was only 30 years old when he became one of Britain's top generals.

With Pitt's generals in command, the war entered a new phase. In the summer of 1758, Britain scored its first major victory in the war. It captured the fort at Louisbourg. In the fall, the British took Fort Duquesne. The British renamed the post Fort Pitt, in William Pitt's honor. It later became the city of Pittsburgh.

These and other victories led the Iroquois to side with the British. More victories in 1759 set the stage for the British attack on Quebec and the key battle of the war.

Quebec, the capital of New France, was located on a high cliff, overlooking the St. Lawrence River. General Montcalm commanded the French defenders, and General Wolfe led the British attack. At first, the British made little progress. Then, they found an unguarded trail that allowed them to climb the cliffs, protecting the city at night without being discovered. In September 1757, approximately 4,000 British soldiers defeated 4,500 French soldiers on the plains in

Main Idea
New leadership allowed the British to win a series of important victories and led to the French surrender.

The British attack Quebec.

front of the city. More than 2,000 soldiers were killed or wounded in the battle, including both Wolfe and Montcalm.

After losing Quebec, France could no longer defend the rest of its North American territory. Montreal, the other major French city in Canada, fell in 1760. In February 1763, Britain and France signed the Treaty of Paris. France lost almost all of its North American possessions. France ceded, or surrendered, French Canada to Great Britain. Great Britain also gained all other French territory east of the Mississippi, with the exception of New Orleans. Britain also received Spanish Florida. New Orleans, along with all French territory west of the Mississippi, went to Spain.

Native Americans also lost a great deal. Without French help, the Native Americans could not stop British settlers from moving on their lands.

✓**Checkpoint** **What was the outcome of the Battle of Quebec?**

⭐ **Looking Back and Ahead** The defeat of the French left the British in control of a vast area in North America. However, whatever sense of triumph British leaders felt at the war's outcome was soon replaced by a nagging realization. The victory had substituted one set of problems for another.

Section 1 | **Check Your Progress**

Progress Monitoring 🌐nline
For: Self-test with instant help
Visit: PHSchool.com
Web Code: mva-2051

Comprehension and Critical Thinking

1. **(a) Summarize** How did the French and Indian War affect the 13 colonies?
(b) Detect Points of View How did most colonists feel about helping the British? Explain.

2. **(a) Recall** How did the war go for the British before 1757? After 1757?
(b) Make Predictions How might the outcome influence relations between the British and the American colonists?

Reading Skill

3. **Make Inferences** Think about how the Iroquois felt about the Ohio River valley. Why do you think the Iroquois may have preferred to be neutral in the conflict between France and England? What can you infer about how the Iroquois felt about European conflicts in North America?

Vocabulary *Builder*

4. Write two definitions for each key term: militia, alliance. First, write a formal definition for your teacher. Second, write a definition in everyday English for a classmate.

Writing

5. Write two or three sentences identifying the problems facing the Albany Congress. Were these problems solved? Explain your answer in three or four sentences.

The Colonists Resist Tighter Control

Objectives

1. Explain the conflict between Native Americans and British settlers in 1763.
2. Describe how the colonists responded to British tax laws.
3. Describe what happened during the Boston Massacre.

Prepare to Read

Reading Skill

Support Inferences With Details Inferences must be based on information. This information may be details stated in the text. First, make the logical inference, then read the text and identify support for your inference. If you cannot support the inference, adjust it until the evidence will support it.

Vocabulary *Builder*

High-Use Words

<u>minimum</u>, p. 146
<u>emotional</u>, p. 147

Key Terms and People

duty, p. 146
boycott, p. 147
petition, p. 147
writ of assistance, p. 148
John Adams, p. 149
Samuel Adams, p. 149

⭐ **Background Knowledge** By defeating France, Britain solved one problem. However, the outcome of the war created another problem. In this section, you will learn how financial problems led Britain to pass measures that angered American colonists.

Conflict With Native Americans

By 1763, Britain controlled almost all of North America east of the Mississippi River. This enormous territory promised endless room for settlement. However, Native Americans living west of the Appalachian Mountains were desperately trying to keep their lands. Fighting between Native Americans and white settlers began as soon as the French and Indian War ended.

Pontiac's War In the last days of the French and Indian War, the leader of the Ottawa nation, Pontiac, formed an alliance of western Native Americans. In May 1763, Pontiac and his allies attacked British forts and settlements throughout the area. Nearly half a dozen western British forts were destroyed and at least 2,000 backcountry settlers were killed. British settlers reacted with equal viciousness. They killed Native Americans who had not attacked them.

The British finally defeated Pontiac's forces in early August at a battle near Fort Pitt. Pontiac continued to fight for another year, but by the fall of 1764, the war was over.

The Proclamation of 1763 Britain wanted to avoid further wars with Native Americans on the frontier. Therefore, the British government issued the Proclamation of 1763. It banned colonial settlement west of a line drawn along the Appalachian Mountains. Settlers were told they had to move to a location east of that line.

Main Idea
Colonists moving westward into the Ohio River valley spurred a reaction by Native Americans led by Pontiac.

Support Inferences With Details
Use details from the text to support this inference: Chief Pontiac thought that keeping his people's lands and way of life was more important than anything else.

Effects of the French and Indian War

THE FRENCH AND INDIAN WAR

- France loses its North American possessions.

- Britain is left with a large debt.

- Colonists develop a sense of unity.

- Colonists begin settling in the Ohio River valley.

- Native Americans resist colonists settling in the Ohio River valley.

Reading Charts

Skills Activity

The struggle between France and Great Britain to establish an empire in the Americas ended in 1763. The results brought political, social, and economic change to North America.

(a) **Read a Chart** Which nation faced huge expenses after the war?

(b) **Apply Information** How do you think the war impacted relations between Britain and the colonies?

The Proclamation of 1763 angered many colonists who believed they had the right to reside wherever they wanted. The proclamation was widely ignored and proved impossible for the British to enforce.

☑**Checkpoint**   What were the terms of the Proclamation of 1763?

Main Idea
Conflict arose when the British government attempted to impose taxes on the colonists.

Vocabulary *Builder*
minimum (MIHN ah muhm) *n.* smallest quantity possible

British Rule Leads to Conflict

The colonists were proud of their contribution toward winning the French and Indian War. Tens of thousands of men had served as soldiers, and many had died in the war. Massachusetts alone lost more than 1,500 men. The colonists expected Britain to be grateful for their assistance. At best, they expected only a <u>minimum</u> rise in taxes.

Although ties between the colonies had begun to grow before the war, the 13 colonies still were divided in many ways. But the people of those colonies also saw themselves as different from people living in Britain. In 1763, the colonists still considered themselves loyal British subjects. Increasingly, however, they identified more with one another than with Britain.

The British saw things differently. The French and Indian War left Britain deeply in debt. Furthermore, these expenses continued. The British government had to keep troops in North America to make sure France did not try to regain its lost territory and to protect settlers against Native American attacks. British leaders believed the colonists should pay part of the debt.

The Sugar Act The British effort to impose new taxes on the colonies began in 1764 when Parliament passed the Sugar Act, which put a **duty**—or import tax—on several products, including molasses. It also called for harsh punishment of smugglers. Colonial merchants, who sometimes traded in smuggled goods, protested.

The Quartering Act One year later, Parliament passed the Quartering Act. The purpose of the Quartering Act was to save money. To enforce the Proclamation of 1763, Britain kept about 10,000 soldiers in the colonies. The act required colonists to quarter, or house, British troops and provide them with food and other supplies. The colonists protested angrily. Once again, the colonists complained that Parliament was violating their rights.

☑**Checkpoint** **Why did the British impose new taxes on the American colonists?**

The Stamp Act

An even more unpopular law was the Stamp Act, passed by Parliament in early 1765. The Stamp Act required that all colonists buy special tax stamps for all kinds of products and activities. The stamps had to be placed on newspapers, wills, licenses, insurance policies, land titles, contracts, and other documents.

Protests against the Stamp Act were widespread. Virginia's House of Burgesses passed several resolutions declaring that it alone had the right to tax the people of Virginia. Patrick Henry, one of the youngest members of that body, made an <u>emotional</u> speech attacking the law. Henry ended his speech with a reference to the murder of Julius Caesar in ancient Rome. When Henry said that some good American would do the same to King George III, cries of treason were hurled against him. Henry replied, "If this be treason, make the most of it."

Other colonial assemblies followed Virginia's example. Merchants in New York, Boston, and Philadelphia organized a **boycott**—an organized campaign to refuse to buy certain products— of British goods. The protests spread to every colony.

In October, delegates from nine colonies met in New York for the Stamp Act Congress. They sent a **petition**—a written request to a government. Addressed to the king and Parliament, this petition demanded the end of both the Sugar Act and Stamp Act.

The protests worked. In 1766, Parliament repealed the Stamp Act. However, at the same time it passed the Declaratory Act, which said Parliament had total authority over the colonies. That set the stage for further trouble between Britain and her colonies.

☑**Checkpoint** **Why did colonists object to the Stamp Act?**

Main Idea
Protests over the Stamp Act spread throughout the colonies and led the British to repeal the act.

Vocabulary *Builder*
<u>emotional</u> (ee MOH shuhn ahl) *adj.* appealing to the emotions, or feelings, of people

Biography Quest

Patrick Henry
1736–1799

In the days before the American Revolution, the most eloquent spokesperson for independence was Patrick Henry.

Henry gave his famous speech in 1775. He urged Virginians to take up arms in their defense. "I know not what course others may take," he roared, "but as for me, give me liberty or give me death!" He later went on to serve six terms as governor of Virginia.

Biography Quest **Online**

How did a salary dispute make Henry famous?

For: The answer to the question about Patrick Henry
Visit: PHSchool.com
Web Code: mvd-2052

Massacre! An American view of the Boston Massacre shows an organized unit of British troops firing directly into a group of colonists. But, in fact, more than 400 colonists surrounded the troops, cursing them and throwing sticks, rocks, and ice at them. **Critical Thinking: Detect Points of View** *How does the artist show the tension at the scene of the Boston Massacre?*

Main Idea
Attempts to enforce writs of assistance and the Boston Massacre infuriated many colonists.

Protests Spread

British officials sought a means of taxing the colonists in a way that would not anger them. Under the Townshend Acts of 1767, Britain would no longer tax products or activities inside the colonies. It would only tax products brought into the colonies.

Writs of Assistance The Townshend Acts set up a system to enforce the new import duties. To help customs officers find illegal goods, they were allowed to use **writs of assistance**—court orders that allowed officials to make searches without saying for what they were searching. Many colonists saw these writs and the searches they allowed as yet another violation of their rights.

Charles Townshend, the official in charge of the British treasury, also wanted to weaken the colonial assemblies. When the New York assembly refused to supply money to house and feed soldiers under the Quartering Act, Parliament suspended the assembly. The colonists again reacted by boycotting British goods.

The Boston Massacre Once again, the protests worked. The boycott hurt British merchants and manufacturers, who put pressure on Parliament. On March 5, 1770, Parliament repealed all the Townshend duties—except the one on tea. That tax was left in force to demonstrate Parliament's right to tax the colonies.

Parliament had not acted in time. On March 5, 1770, in Boston, an angry crowd of workers and sailors surrounded a small group of soldiers. They shouted at the soldiers and threw snowballs and rocks at them. The frightened soldiers fired into the crowd, killing five and wounding six.

Governor Thomas Hutchinson tried to calm things down by having the nine soldiers involved in the shooting arrested and tried for murder. John Adams, a well-known Massachusetts lawyer, defended them. Adams also was a leading defender of colonial rights against recent British policies. Yet, he took the unpopular case because he believed that in a free country every person accused of a crime had the right to a lawyer and a fair trial. Only two soldiers were convicted of the crime. Their punishment was having their thumbs branded.

Committees of Correspondence
As tensions grew, colonial leaders saw the need to keep in closer contact with people in other colonies. After the Boston Massacre, Samuel Adams, a cousin of John Adams, established what he called a Committee of Correspondence. The aim was to keep colonists informed of British actions. Soon, committees were sprouting in other colonies. The committees wrote letters and pamphlets to spread the alarm whenever Britain tried to enforce unpopular acts of Parliament. In this way, the committees helped unite the colonists against Britain.

Samuel Adams

☑ **Checkpoint** How did colonists react to the Townshend Acts?

⭐ **Looking Back and Ahead** When colonists heard that the Townshend Acts had been repealed, they were overjoyed. But the dispute over taxes was not settled. Before long, colonists would face other crises that would lead to armed resistance.

Section 2 | **Check Your Progress**

Progress Monitoring ⬤nline

For: Self-test with instant help
Visit: PHSchool.com
Web Code: mva-2052

Comprehension and Critical Thinking

1. (a) Recall What was the Proclamation of 1763?
(b) Apply Information Why did the British feel the Proclamation was critical in their relationship with the Native Americans?

2. (a) Describe What happened during the Boston Massacre?
(b) Detect Points of View Why do you think the colonists described this event as a "massacre"?

🔄 Reading Skill

3. Support Inferences With Details Read the text following the subheading "Committees of Correspondence." Give a detail from the text to support the following inference: The colonists believed that the strength of unity would help them.

Vocabulary *Builder*

Answer the following questions in complete sentences that show your understanding of the key terms.

4. How did the American boycott affect Great Britain economically?
5. What did the delegates to the Stamp Act Congress hope to achieve by sending a petition to the British king and Parliament?
6. Why did colonists object to writs of assistance?

Writing

7. As a member of Parliament, you vote against repealing the Stamp Act. Brainstorm one or two possible solutions that you think would work better.

From Protest to Rebellion

Objectives

1. Identify the causes of the Boston Tea Party.

2. Explain how the colonists protested the Intolerable Acts.

3. Describe the events of April 19, 1775, at Lexington and Concord.

Prepare to Read

Reading Skill

Draw Logical Conclusions
Reaching conclusions means analyzing what you have read and forming an opinion about what it means. As with inferences, you can add your own personal knowledge to the information to draw a conclusion. Always ask yourself: Does this conclusion make sense?

Vocabulary *Builder*

High-Use Words
prior, p. 150
react, p. 152

Key Terms
monopoly, p. 151
repeal, p. 152
minuteman, p. 152

⭐ **Background Knowledge** The British policy of taxation had angered American colonists in all the colonies. But the anger stopped short of armed resistance to the British. This section describes how the conflict deepened until the colonists turned to armed rebellion.

Main Idea
Opposition to the British tax on tea led to a dramatic confrontation in Boston Harbor.

A Dispute Over Tea

During the early 1770s, the protests in the colonies against British policies quieted down. However, that did not mean the colonists were satisfied with the British government. Although most of the Townshend duties had been repealed, the one on tea remained. Many colonists drank tea. With every cup they drank, they were paying a tax that Parliament had placed on them without their consent.

The Tea Act In 1773, the British Parliament passed the Tea Act. It was intended to help the British East India Company, one of Britain's most important companies. For many years, the company had made money growing tea in India and selling it in Britain and in the colonies. However, the colonial boycott of tea seriously hurt the company.

Vocabulary *Builder*
prior (PRĪ or) *adj.* preceding in time; earlier; former

The Tea Act actually lowered the price of tea by allowing the East India Company to ship tea directly to the colonies. Prior to the Tea Act, the tea first had to be shipped to Britain. Frederick North, the prime minister of England, felt the colonists should not object to the Tea Act since the price of tea was lowered. However, some colonists reacted angrily to the part of the act that gave the East India

Company a monopoly on selling British tea in the colonies. A **monopoly** is total control of a market for a certain product.

The monopoly hurt colonial merchants. Many of them sold Dutch tea that was smuggled into the colonies. Now, they would not be able to compete with the lower-priced East India Company Tea. Many colonial leaders also argued that even though the price of tea was lowered, colonists still had to pay the tax on tea.

The Boston Tea Party A group of colonists called the Sons of Liberty soon organized in port cities to stop the East India Company tea from being unloaded. They threatened ship captains who were bringing in the tea and colonial tea merchants who said they would buy it. No tea was unloaded in New York, Philadelphia, or other ports. However, in Boston, Governor Thomas Hutchinson decided to make sure that the tea would be unloaded. He refused to give the arriving tea ships papers that would allow them to return to England. So, when the first tea ships from Britain arrived, Hutchinson ordered the cargo to be unloaded.

For more than two weeks, feelings were tense in Boston. Finally, on the night of December 16, 1773, a large crowd gathered in the harbor. Suddenly, a large group of men disguised as Native Americans boarded the tea ship. During the next three hours, they threw 342 cases of tea into the harbor. As the crowd cheered and shouted, the raiders destroyed 90,000 pounds of tea worth thousands of dollars.

☑**Checkpoint** How did Boston colonists show their opposition to the Tea Act?

Boston Tea Party
Members of the Sons of Liberty protested the Tea Act by dumping chests of tea into Boston Harbor. **Critical Thinking: *Apply Information*** *Why do you think the colonists chose to disguise themselves as Native Americans?*

The Intolerable Acts

The Boston Tea Party outraged the British government. King George III called for tough action to make examples of the people of Boston and Massachusetts.

In response, Parliament passed four laws. These laws were so harsh that colonists called them the Intolerable Acts. The first act closed the port of Boston. Two others increased the powers of the royal governor, abolished the upper house of the Massachusetts legislature, and cut the powers of town meetings. Now, anyone accused of murdering a British colonial official could be tried in Britain, rather than in the colonies. Finally, a fourth law strengthened the 1765 Quartering Act.

Parliament also passed the Quebec Act, which set up a government for the territory taken from France in 1763. The Quebec Act claimed land between the Ohio and the Missouri rivers as part of Canada. Quebec's new boundaries took away the western lands claimed by several colonies and blocked colonists from moving west.

Main Idea
The British reaction to the Boston Tea Party outraged colonists and led to the First Continental Congress.

Causes of the Revolution

History *Interactive*

Discover the Events That Led to the Revolution

Visit: PHSchool.com
Web Code: mvl-2054

Roots of the Revolution

Relations between Great Britain and the colonies changed after the French and Indian War. Years of colonial protest against laws passed by Parliament gradually led to open revolt. **Critical Thinking: Explain Problems** *Why did colonists view these laws as attacks on their rights as British citizens?*

French and Indian War (1754–1763)

The Stamp Act (1765)

The Boston Tea Party (1773)

The Intolerable Acts (1774)

Outbreak of the Revolution

Vocabulary Builder
react (ree AKT) *v.* to act in return

Draw Logical Conclusions
What conclusion can you make about how the Congress felt about independence at this time?

Americans in all the colonies <u>reacted</u> by trying to help the people of Boston. Food and other supplies poured into Boston from throughout the colonies. Meanwhile, the Committee of Correspondence organized a meeting to discuss what to do next.

That meeting, known as the First Continental Congress, took place in Philadelphia in September and October 1774. Twelve of the 13 colonies sent delegates. Only Georgia did not send representatives. Among the delegates were John Adams and Samuel Adams from Massachusetts, John Jay of New York, and George Washington and Patrick Henry from Virginia.

The Congress demanded the **repeal**, or official end, of the Intolerable Acts and declared that the colonies had a right to tax and govern themselves. It also called for the training of militias to stand up to British troops if necessary. The Congress also called for a new boycott of British goods. It then voted to meet again in May 1775 if its demands were not met.

✓ Checkpoint **What did the First Continental Congress accomplish?**

Main Idea
The British attempt to seize Patriot arms led to the first open battle of the American Revolution.

The Shot Heard Round the World

The British government had no intention of meeting the demands of the First Continental Congress. It chose, instead, to use force to restore its authority. Meanwhile, the colonists began to arm and form new militia units called **minutemen**—citizen soldiers who could be ready to fight at a minute's notice.

In April, General Thomas Gage, the new governor of Massachusetts, learned the minutemen were storing arms in Concord, about 20 miles from Boston. On April 18, 1775, he sent 700 troops to seize the arms and capture some important colonial leaders. As the troops set out, a signal sent by the Patriots appeared in the steeple of Boston's Old North Church. Two men, Paul Revere and William Dawes, then rode through the night to warn the minutemen.

Five miles from Concord in the town of Lexington, about 77 minutemen were waiting when the British arrived. The British commander ordered the minutemen to go home. They refused. Suddenly, a shot rang out. Nobody knows who fired it, but it turned out to be the first shot of the American Revolution—"the shot heard round the world." The British then opened fire, killing eight Americans.

A larger battle took place in nearby Concord. This time, 400 minutemen fought the British, killing three of them. As the British retreated toward Boston, about 4,000 Americans fired at them from behind trees and fences. By the time the British reached Boston, almost 300 of them had been killed or wounded.

Statue of a minuteman

☑**Checkpoint** What led to the conflict at Lexington and Concord?

☆ **Looking Back and Ahead** News of the battles at Lexington and Concord traveled fast through the colonies. Many colonists saw their hopes of reaching an agreement with Britain fade. For many, the battles were proof that only war would decide the future of the 13 colonies.

Section 3 | Check Your Progress

Progress Monitoring ⊕nline
For: Self-test with instant help
Visit: PHSchool.com
Web Code: mva-2053

Comprehension and Critical Thinking

1. (a) Recall Why did Britain pass the Tea Act?
(b) Identify Alternatives What other ways, besides the Boston Tea Party, might colonists have protested the Tea Act?

2. (a) Summarize What were the Intolerable Acts?
(b) Apply Information How did the Intolerable Acts affect colonial unity?

3. (a) Describe How did the American Revolution begin?
(b) Draw Conclusions Why do you think the first shot fired at Lexington was called "the shot heard round the world"?

⊕ Reading Skill

4. Draw Logical Conclusions Based on the battles of Lexington and Concord, what can you conclude about the colonists' advantage in fighting?

Vocabulary *Builder*

Fill in the blanks with the correct key terms.

5. The _____ were colonists who could prepare to fight in a very short time.

6. Because the East India Company had a _____ on selling British tea in the colonies, other countries could not sell their tea there.

7. The First Continental Congress provided for the training of _____ that could fight the British troops.

Writing

8. One of the decisions of the First Continental Congress was to boycott British goods. In a paragraph, identify the problem that Congress was trying to solve by boycotting British goods. Did the boycott solve the problem? Explain.

A Spirit of Protest

From the Stamp Act to the Boston Tea Party to the outbreak of fighting at Lexington and Concord, a spirit of protest steadily grew in the colonies. This defiant mood expressed itself in many ways.

Boycotting British Goods

Women took a leading role in refusing to buy British goods. In October 1774, a group of women in Edenton, North Carolina, signed a pledge. They promised "not to conform to the Pernicious Custom of Drinking Tea." Above, the women of Edenton pour away tea.

A Warning of Danger

Benjamin Franklin was the first to use a serpent as a symbol of the colonies. (See Section 1.) By 1775, the serpent had become a rattlesnake, which stood for the idea that the colonists would ▼ fight back against tyranny.

DONT TREAD ON ME

The Pen as a Weapon

Mercy Otis Warren of Boston wrote plays that made fun of the British. The plays were not acted in theaters but were circulated privately. In *The Blockheads*, Warren shows how the Patriots made fools of the ▼ British troops after Lexington and Concord. One British soldier says:

Mercy Otis Warren

"Ha, ha, ha,—yankee doodle forever. . . . We were sent here to ransack the country and hang up a parcel of leading fellows for the crows to pick, and awe all others into *peace* and *submission*—instead of this, in our first attempt, we were drove thro' the country, like a pack of *jackasses*."

—Mercy Otis Warren, *The Blockheads*

Violent Protests

The spirit of protest sometimes took a violent turn. The British cartoon below shows a tax official in Boston being tarred and feathered by members of the Sons of Liberty. Hot tar was poured over the body of the victim, who was then covered with chicken feathers. Tarring and feathering was not fatal, but it was painful and humiliating. In the background, colonists pour tea into Boston Harbor.

The first Liberty Tree was an elm in Boston, where dummies representing tax collectors were hanged. Patriots in many colonies raised Liberty Trees or Liberty Poles as symbols of protest.

In addition to being tarred and feathered, the unfortunate tax collector has tea poured down his throat.

Analyze LIFE AT THE TIME

Choose a person pictured on these pages. As that person, write a letter to a friend describing how you feel about the new mood of protest in the colonies.

The War Begins

Objectives

1. Identify the issues facing the Second Continental Congress.

2. Describe the differences between Patriots and Loyalists.

3. Identify the Olive Branch Petition, and explain why it failed.

4. Explain the significance of the Battle at Bunker Hill.

Prepare to Read

 Reading Skill

Identify Supporting Evidence Readers often draw conclusions without even realizing that they are doing so. However, like inferences, conclusions should be supported and challenged and the evidence identified. This ensures that your conclusions are logical and reliable. Remember, you may need to use evidence from prior reading to reach your conclusions.

Vocabulary *Builder*

High-Use Words

crisis, p. 156

restore, p. 158

Key Terms

blockade, p. 161

mercenary, p. 161

⭐ **Background Knowledge** Lexington and Concord were the first battles of the American Revolution. As war loomed, many colonists expected the British to give in quickly and meet the colonists' demands. Instead, a long struggle for independence lay ahead.

The Second Continental Congress

Main Idea
The Second Continental Congress was divided, at first, about what course to take in the dispute with Britain.

Vocabulary *Builder*
crisis (KRĪ sihs) *n.* time of great danger or trouble

Even after the battles of Lexington and Concord, most colonists still did not favor independence. At the same time, many of them were ready to use force, if necessary, to defend their rights against the British.

As the <u>crisis</u> with Britain deepened, the Second Continental Congress came together in Philadelphia in May 1775. The delegates included Thomas Jefferson, a young lawyer from Virginia; Boston merchant John Hancock; and Benjamin Franklin of Philadelphia.

The Congress, at first, was divided about what to do. A group of delegates from New England wanted to declare independence. A more moderate group from the Middle Colonies favored less drastic action. However, nearly all delegates felt they needed to prepare for war. The first step was to form an army.

The Congress chose George Washington as the commander of the newly formed Continental army. He had military experience and was well respected.

The Congress also took steps to pay for its army by printing paper money. The Second Continental Congress was starting to act like a government.

Patriots Against Loyalists By 1775, a split was developing in the American colonies. Colonists who favored independence and were willing to fight for it took the name Patriots. Those who remained loyal to Britain and the king called themselves Loyalists. Most colonists were Patriots. However, as many as one third of the colonists may have had Loyalist sympathies.

The Loyalists came from every colony and all sections of the population. Everywhere, however, they were a minority. During 1774 and 1775, the Patriots took control of local governments.

The Loyalists included some people from the wealthiest families in the colonies. Many leading merchants and large landowners were Loyalists. They feared a rebellion would lead to a change in government and that they would lose their property. Government officials who owed their jobs and place in society to the British Crown often were Loyalists.

At the same time, many enslaved African Americans sided with the British, hoping to win their freedom. So did most Native Americans, who feared they would lose their lands if the colonists won independence.

During the Revolution, thousands of Loyalists fought on the British side. During and after the Revolutionary War, about 100,000 Loyalists left the country forever. Many settled in Canada.

Identify Supporting Evidence

Reading Skill

Give evidence to support the conclusion that Loyalists strongly supported social order.

Lord Dunmore's Declaration

Lord Dunmore sent this declaration to the rebel Patriots in Virginia:

"[So] that the peace and good order of this colony may be again restored . . . I do, [by] the authority to me given by His Majesty, determine to execute martial law. . . . I do require every person capable of bearing arms to resort to His Majesty's standard, or be looked upon as traitors to His Majesty's . . . government, and [subject to] the penalty . . . such as [loss] of life or lands. . . ."

—from Proclamation of Lord Dunmore, November 1775

Boys laughing at a Loyalist

Reading Primary Sources

Skills Activity

In 1775, Patriots had taken over Virginia. In desperation, Lord Dunmore, the Loyalist governor, issued a declaration against the rebel Patriots.

(a) Apply Information According to Dunmore, why are the Patriots a danger to the colony?

(b) Make Predictions Do you think Dunmore's declaration will be obeyed? Explain.

Vocabulary *Builder*
<u>restore</u> (ree STOR) *v.* to bring back to a normal state; to put back; to reestablish

Petitioning the King Even months after Lexington and Concord, many delegates at the Second Continental Congress hoped that peace could be <u>restored</u> between Britain and its American colonies. Two resolutions passed in July showed the uncertainty of Congress. The first resolution was called the Olive Branch Petition and was sent to King George. The petition stated that the colonists were loyal to the king. It asked George to stop the fighting so all disputes between the colonists and Britain could be solved peacefully. The petition got its name from the olive branch, a symbol of peace since ancient times.

The next day, the Congress passed a tougher statement called the Declaration of the Causes and Necessities of Taking Up Arms. Written in part by Thomas Jefferson, the document stated that the colonists were ready "to die freemen rather than to live as slaves."

The effort to make peace failed. King George did not bother to answer the Olive Branch Petition. Instead, he declared the colonies were "in open . . . rebellion." Parliament, meanwhile, voted to send 20,000 soldiers to the colonies to end the revolt.

An Important American Victory On May 10, 1775, the same day the Second Continental Congress began meeting, an important battle took place in northern New York. A daring band of colonists made a surprise attack on Fort Ticonderoga (ti kahn duh ROH guh).

The fort stood at the southern end of Lake Champlain and protected the water route to Canada. Leading the force was Ethan Allen, a blacksmith. Most of his followers came from the nearby Green Mountains of today's Vermont. Because of that, they were known as the Green Mountain Boys.

Ethan Allen demanding the surrender of Fort Ticonderoga

Allen's force of 83 men reached the fort by crossing the lake at night and surprising the British in the early morning. Only 42 British troops guarded the fort, and they surrendered almost immediately.

Fort Ticonderoga was important for two reasons. It controlled the main route between Canada and the Hudson River valley. It also held valuable weapons, especially cannons. The Americans needed the cannons to match the powerful British weapons. When the Green Mountain Boys took the fort, they seized several dozen cannons. Later, those cannons were moved to Boston, where George Washington used them to drive the British from the city.

☑**Checkpoint** How did the divided loyalties of the colonists affect the Second Continental Congress?

Main Idea
The battles at Bunker Hill and Ticonderoga proved Americans could fight and stand up to professional British soldiers.

Early Battles

By June 1775, the British had 6,500 troops in Boston. The Americans had about 10,000 surrounding the city. About 1,600 of these troops occupied Breed's Hill overlooking the city. From this position, they could fire on British ships in Boston harbor. Nearby was Bunker Hill, also controlled by the Americans.

Delivering the Cannons

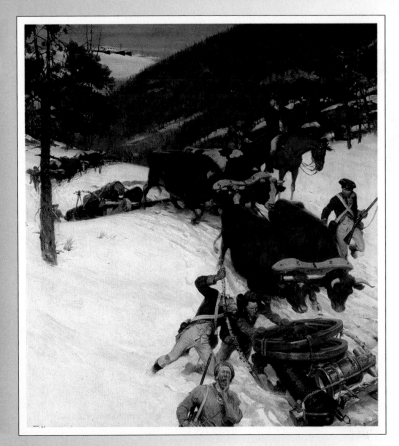

From Fort Ticonderoga to Boston

The difficulty of dragging cannons from Fort Ticonderoga to Boston is evident in this painting of the event. **Critical Thinking: *Apply Information*** *What does this effort indicate about the Continental army's military forces?*

Battle of Bunker Hill The Americans surrounding Boston were farmers and workers, not trained soldiers. Nobody knew if they would stand and fight against tough British troops.

British General William Howe decided to attack straight up the hill. The American commander, Israel Putnam, knew his soldiers did not have much ammunition. The Americans waited until the British were only about 150 feet away. When they opened fire, hundreds of British soldiers fell dead and wounded.

The first British attack failed. So did the second. The third attack succeeded, only because the Americans ran out of ammunition and had to retreat. The British won the battle but at a terrible cost. More than 1000 were killed or wounded. American losses were about 400 killed or wounded. The Americans had proved they could fight and stand up to professional British soldiers.

The Battle of Bunker Hill did not solve Britain's problem in Boston. The city still was surrounded by American forces. In July 1775, George Washington arrived and took charge of the army.

Washington knew he had to build a regular army. Washington also needed powerful weapons to drive the British from Boston. He had the British cannons, which had been seized at Fort Ticonderoga, dragged on sleds across mountains and forests to Boston. That difficult 300-mile journey took three months.

In March, Washington placed the cannons on high ground overlooking Boston. This made it impossible for the British to defend the city. On March 17, 1776, they withdrew from Boston by sea and never returned.

The Battle of Bunker Hill

On June 16, 1775, the colonists occupied Bunker Hill and Breed's Hill, two high points near Charles Town, which was across the harbor from Boston. The battle that took place there the following morning fueled the colonists' determination to fight. After this battle, it is said that "a frenzy of revenge" gripped the colonists. **Critical Thinking: Understand Sequence** *Based on the information on this page and on your reading, describe the sequence of events before, during, and after the battle.*

Building the Fort
The night before battle, as shown in this engraving, the colonists built a fort on Breed's Hill. The colonists hoped to take advantage of the hill when using cannons to attack the British warships in the harbor. ▼

◄ **The Attack**
This painting shows the attack on Bunker Hill and the burning of Charles Town.

◄ **The Battle Begins**
On the morning of June 17, British soldiers took position around the base of Breed's Hill. As shown in this painting, the British soldiers, wearing red coats, marched straight up the hill through tall grass and over fences.

Although the Americans won in Boston, Washington knew that the war was far from over. Britain still held most of the advantages. They had the most powerful navy in the world. They used it to transport troops and supplies and to blockade American ports. A **blockade** is the shutting off of a port by ships to keep people or supplies from moving in or out. The British also strengthened their army by hiring **mercenaries**—soldiers who serve another country for money.

Invading Canada While Washington was training one army outside Boston, two other American armies were moving north into Canada. One, led by Richard Montgomery, left from Fort Ticonderoga. The other, led by Benedict Arnold, moved north through Maine.

Arnold had a terrible journey through the Maine woods in winter. His troops were forced to boil candles, bark, and shoe leather for food. In late December 1775, the Americans attacked Quebec during a severe snowstorm. The attack was turned back. Montgomery was killed, and Arnold was wounded. The Americans stayed outside Quebec until May 1776, when the British landed new forces in Canada. Weakened by disease and hunger, the Americans withdrew, leaving Canada to the British.

✔**Checkpoint** **What did the Battle of Bunker Hill show about the American and British forces?**

⭐ **Looking Back and Ahead** After Bunker Hill, King George III was confident that he could soon restore order in the colonies. Meantime, colonists wondered what chance they had of defeating a well-armed, powerful nation such as Britain.

Section 4 | **Check Your Progress**

Progress Monitoring ●nline
For: Self-test with instant help
Visit: PHSchool.com
Web Code: mva-2054

Comprehension and Critical Thinking

1. **(a) Recall** What were the major achievements of the Second Continental Congress?
(b) Apply Information How did the Second Continental Congress influence the conflict between the colonists and Britain?

2. **(a) Recall** What did the Patriots want?
(b) Apply Information Why do you think Loyalists were described as "having their heads in England . . . but their bodies in America"?

◉ Reading Skill

3. **Identify Supporting Evidence** Give evidence to support the conclusion that the war's momentum shifted after the Battle of Bunker Hill.

Vocabulary *Builder*

Read each sentence below. If the sentence is true, write YES. If the sentence is not true, write NO and explain why.

4. Countries set up **blockades** to help strengthen trade relations.

5. Most **mercenaries** are hired to fight for their own countries.

Writing

6. In a few sentences, describe how a Loyalist might have reacted to the Olive Branch Petition and to the Declaration of the Causes and Necessities of Taking Up Arms as possible solutions to the feud between Britain and the colonies. Then, write a brief response reflecting how a Patriot might have reacted to these documents as a solution to the feud.

You can increase your understanding of history by asking questions about what you see and read. Formulating, or asking, questions helps you become a more effective learner. The better your questions, the more you will learn.

> Patrick Henry presented his views in this excerpt from a speech to the convention that gathered after the Virginia Assembly was suspended.

Primary Source

"Sir, we have done everything to avert the storm which is now coming on. We have petitioned; we have remonstrated; we have supplicated; we have prostrated ourselves before the throne. Our petitions have been slighted; our remonstrances have produced additional violence and insult; our supplications have been disregarded. . . .

There is no longer any room for hope. If we wish to be free; if we mean to preserve inviolate those inestimable privileges for which we have been so long contending; . . . we must fight! I repeat it, sir, we must fight! An appeal to arms and to the God of hosts is all that is left us!

—I know not what course others may take; but as for me,—give me liberty, or give me death!"

—Patrick Henry, March 23, 1775

Learn the Skill

Use these steps to formulate questions.

1 **Examine the material.** Ask basic questions to summarize what you are reading. Formulate questions that begin with *who, what, when, where,* and *how much.*

2 **Think of analytical questions.** These are questions that reflect a thoughtful approach to the information. They might begin with *how* or *why.*

3 **Ask questions that evaluate.** These call for judgments and opinions based on evidence.

4 **Formulate hypothetical questions.** Hypothetical questions involve the word *if.* They suggest possible outcomes: *if this happens, would such and such occur?*

Practice the Skill

Answer the following questions about the primary source.

1 **Examine the material.** What is Patrick Henry's view of the American Revolution?

2 **Think of analytical questions.** (a) How would you describe the tone or feeling? (b) Formulate an analytical question.

3 **Ask questions that evaluate.** (a) Why is this primary source persuasive? Explain. (b) Formulate a question to evaluate the source.

4 **Formulate hypothetical questions.** If the British had won the Revolution, what do you think would have happened to Patrick Henry and those who supported his views?

Apply the Skill

See the Review and Assessment at the end of this chapter.

interactive Textbook

Study Guide *Online*
Complete your Chapter 5 study guide in print or online.

Chapter Summary

Section 1
Trouble on the Frontier

- British settlers moved into lands claimed by the French in the Ohio River valley.
- After early British defeats at Fort Duquesne, Fort Niagara, and Lake George, France was defeated.
- Under the 1763 Treaty of Paris, Britain and Spain took control of all of France's North American possessions.

Section 2
The Colonists Resist Tighter Control

- To avoid conflict with Native Americans, Britain issued the Proclamation of 1763.
- After the end of the war, Britain strengthened its control over the American colonies by imposing a series of new taxes.
- Colonists protested Britain's actions by boycotting British goods.

Section 3
From Protest to Rebellion

- After Parliament passed the Tea Act, American colonists dumped cases of British tea into Boston Harbor.
- The Intolerable Acts further tightened Britain's control over the American colonies.
- The first major conflict between American colonists and British soldiers took place at Lexington and Concord on April 18, 1775.

Section 4
The War Begins

- The Second Continental Congress met in Philadelphia in May 1775 to deal with the deepening crisis with Great Britain.
- The British surrendered Fort Ticonderoga to a small American force led by Ethan Allen.
- When the Olive Branch Petition failed, the Continental Congress approved a more militant statement of purpose.
- Although the Patriots lost the Battle of Bunker Hill, George Washington finally drove the British from Boston.

Key Concepts

These notes will help you prepare for questions about key concepts.

From Protest to Revolution: Major Events

1763: Britain wins French and Indian War

1764–1766: Britain tightens control of American colonies through a series of unpopular acts: Sugar Act; Quartering Act; Stamp Act; Townshend Acts

1770: Boston Massacre increases tensions between colonists and British

1773: Tea Act results in Boston Tea Party

1774: Intolerable Acts punish colonists for Boston Tea Party

April 1775: First battles of Revolution at Lexington and Concord

May 1775: Britain rejects Second Continental Congress's effort to make peace

June 1775: British win Battle of Bunker Hill but suffer heavy losses

March 1776: Americans drive British from Boston

Vocabulary *Builder*

Key Terms

Answer the following questions in complete sentences that show your understanding of the key terms.

1. Why did the British want to form an alliance with the Iroquois during the French and Indian War?

2. How did the role of the militia change after the battles of Lexington and Concord?

3. What did Britain hope to achieve by a blockade of American ports?

4. How did the English king react to the colonists' petition about the Sugar and Stamp Acts?

Comprehension and Critical Thinking

5. **(a) Identify** What were three results of the French and Indian War?
(b) Make Predictions What would have happened if the French had won the French and Indian War?

6. **(a) Recall** What was Pontiac's War?
(b) Draw Conclusions What happened to the relationship between Native Americans and colonists after the French and Indian War? Explain your answer.

7. **(a) Recall** What did the First Continental Congress do?
(b) Recall What did the Second Continental Congress do?
(c) Compare and Contrast Compare and contrast the achievements of the First and Second Continental Congress.

8. **(a) Recall** What were the terms of the Olive Branch Petition?
(b) Identify What was the Declaration of the Causes and Necessities of Taking Up Arms?
(c) Apply Information Given the terms of each document, why might British leaders have felt the colonists were sending mixed messages about independence?

9. **(a) Describe** How did colonists react to the Battle of Bunker Hill?
(b) Make Predictions How do you think this reaction would help colonial forces during the war?

History Reading Skill

10. **Make Inferences and Draw Conclusions** Draw a conclusion about George Washington as a military leader. Use evidence from throughout this chapter to support your conclusion.

Writing

11. **Write two paragraphs on the following topic:** How did the French and Indian War affect the relationship between the 13 colonies and Britain?
Your paragraphs should:
- include a thesis statement that expresses your main idea;
- develop that main idea with facts, examples, and other information;
- conclude by describing the lasting impact of what happened.

12. **Write a Narrative:**
Since 1766, you have been a colonial merchant living in Boston. Write a letter to a friend explaining why you feel it is important to serve on the correspondence committee in your town.

Skills for Life

Formulate Questions

Use the quotation below to answer the questions.

"As to government matters, it is not in the power of Britain to do this continent justice; the business of it will soon be too weighty and intricate to be managed with any tolerable degree of convenience, by a power so distant from us, and so very ignorant of us; for if they cannot conquer us, they cannot govern us. . . .
. . . Freedom have been hunted round the globe. . . . O receive the fugitive, and prepare in time an asylum for mankind."

—Thomas Paine, *Common Sense*, January 1776

13. How does Thomas Paine feel about the American Revolution?

14. **(a)** Why does Thomas Paine compare "freedom" to a "fugitive"?
(b) How would this comparison affect his readers?

Test Yourself

1. How did the Battle at Bunker Hill affect the colonists?

A They needed to train their militia.

B They were proud of having stood their ground against the British soldiers.

C They were proud of their victory.

D They decided to call for a new commanding general.

Refer to the quotation below to answer Question 2.

> "Drive from the Ohio River any European foreigners, and do it in a way that will make them lose all taste for trying to return."

2. The result of this policy by the French government

A ended relations between France and Spain.

B increased tensions between England and Native Americans.

C increased tensions between France and England.

D pushed French colonists farther west.

Refer to the map below to answer Question 3.

North America, 1763

BRITISH TERRITORY

13 Colonies

SPANISH TERRITORY (Louisiana)

0 km 500
0 miles 500
Lambert Azimuthal Equal-Area Projection

3. How did the boundaries after 1763 affect the British?

A British colonists settled in Canada.

B Britain could not expand farther north.

C Britain could not expand farther west.

D Britain offered to buy Louisiana from Spain.

Document-Based Questions

Task: Look at Documents 1 and 2, and answer their accompanying questions. Then, use the documents and your knowledge of history to complete this writing assignment:

Use the evidence in the documents to write a two-paragraph essay explaining the causes and degree of colonial anger.

Document 1: Angered by the Stamp Act, in October 1765, representatives from nine colonies met in the Stamp Act Congress. Challenging Britain's right to tax the colonists, they issued a Declaration of Rights, excerpted below. *According to the delegates, why did Britain not have the right to tax the colonies?*

> "The members of this congress . . . make the following declarations. . . .
>
> That His Majesty's . . . subjects in these colonies are entitled to all the . . . rights and privileges of his natural born subjects [in] Great Britain.
>
> That the people of these colonies are not . . . represented in the House of Commons in Great Britain. . . .
>
> That the only representatives of the people of these colonies are persons chosen . . . by themselves; and that no taxes ever have been or can be constitutionally imposed on them but by their respective legislatures. . . ."

Document 2: Look at the 1774 engraving of the tarring and feathering of a British tax collector in the Life at the Time feature in this chapter. *The fury of the colonists surprised the British. Why do you think this was so?*

Chapter Preview

The American Revolution began as a protest against unfair colonial rule. But after the colonists issued the Declaration of Independence, the war turned into a struggle to create a new nation.

☑ **What You Will Learn**

The Declaration of Independence proclaimed that the colonies were separating from Britain.

The American army faced many difficulties in the early years of the war.

The impact of the war was felt by all Americans in every part of the nation.

After a final victory, the Americans at last achieved independence from British rule.

U.S. Events

1776
Continental Congress issues Declaration of Independence.

1777
American victory at Saratoga marks turning point in war.

1779
American ship *Bonhomme Richard* defeats British ship in naval battle.

1776

1778

1780

World Events

1778 France recognizes the United States.

1779 Spain enters war against Britain.

Discovery SCHOOL

Quick View Video
View the chapter video for a quick preview of the main ideas.

By signing the Declaration of Independence, the Continental Congress proclaimed that the colonies were free of British rule.

1781
British troops surrender to Americans at Battle of Yorktown.

1783
Britain recognizes American independence in Treaty of Paris.

1780

1782

1784

1780 Indians in Peru stage unsuccessful revolution.

1783 Spain regains Florida.

History Reading Skill **Analyze Word Parts**

What was the end of the American Revolution like?

In this chapter, you will learn how to analyze word parts to determine meaning. Read the following journal entry by an American army surgeon in the American Revolution. The side notes show you how to analyze word parts to determine meaning.

Dr. James Thacher served as a surgeon in the Continental Army. He wrote this journal entry to describe the official surrender of British General Cornwallis in 1781.

Primary Source

October 19, 1781

This is to us a most glorious day; but to the English, one of bitter chagrin and <u>disappointment</u>. . . .

> The prefix *dis-* means "not." To *disappoint* comes originally from *not* keeping an appointment.

At about twelve o'clock, the combined army was arranged and drawn up in two lines extending more than a mile in length. The Americans were drawn up in a line on the right side of the road, and the French occupied the left. . . .

The Americans were not all in <u>uniform</u>, nor was their dress so neat. Yet they exhibited an erect, soldierly air, and every [face] beamed with satisfaction and joy. The [crowd] of <u>spectators</u> from the country was . . . probably equal to the military, but universal silence and order prevailed.

> *Uni-* means "one." *Form* means "shape." Thus, *uniforms* all have one shape.

> The word root *spec* means "see." *Spectators* are people who watch.

—James Thacher, *Military Journal During the American Revolution*

Analyze Word Parts

- Use the meanings of familiar prefixes to help you construct meanings for unfamiliar words.
- Combine the meanings of prefixes with those of word roots to build meanings for new words.
- Find word roots that you know, then use them to determine the meanings of unfamiliar words.

Document-Based Questions

1. Who wrote this selection? What was his relationship to the event being described?
2. Identify four groups of people who were present at the event.
3. Why was this event important to the people who were there?
4. Why do you think the crowd greeted the event with "universal silence"?

Vocabulary *Builder*

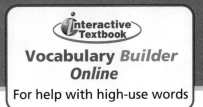

Interactive Textbook

Vocabulary *Builder* Online

For help with high-use words

Previewing High-Use Academic Words

High-Use Word	Definition	Sample History Sentence
prospect (PRAHS pehkt) (Section 1, p. 170)	*n.* possibility; expectation	The <u>prospect</u> of wealth attracted many settlers to the colonies.
logic (LAH jihk) (Section 1, p. 171)	*n.* reason; careful thought	Thinkers of the Enlightenment believed in using <u>logic</u> to support their opinions.
vital (vī tuhl) (Section 2, p. 183)	*adj.* necessary; of great importance	Shipbuilding played a <u>vital</u> role in the New England economy.
transform (trans FORM) (Section 2, p. 183)	*v.* to change from one thing or condition to another	The battles of Lexington and Concord <u>transformed</u> the colonial struggle from a protest to a revolution.
confine (kuhn FĪN) (Section 3, p. 188)	*v.* to keep within certain limits	Captives on slave ships were <u>confined</u> in small, crowded spaces.
resource (REE sors) (Section 3, p. 188)	*n.* supply of something to meet a particular need	For New England shipbuilders, wood was a valuable <u>resource</u>.
efficient (ee FISH ehnt) (Section 4, p. 191)	*adj.* acting effectively, without wasted cost or effort	The printing press provided an <u>efficient</u> way to make books.
option (AHP shuhn) (Section 4, p. 192)	*n.* choice; possible course of action	A poor person who wanted to go to the colonies had the <u>option</u> of becoming an indentured servant.

Previewing Key Terms and People

Thomas Paine, p. 170
Richard Henry Lee, p. 171
resolution, p. 171
preamble, p. 172
grievance, p. 172
Nathan Hale, p. 180
mercenary, p. 181
alliance, p. 183

Marquis de Lafayette, p. 183
cavalry, p. 183
Friedrich von Steuben, p. 183
enlist, p. 187
civilian, p. 187
continental, p. 188
George Rogers Clark, p. 189
Bernardo de Gálvez, p. 189

John Paul Jones, p. 190
privateer, p. 190
Charles Cornwallis, p. 191
guerrilla, p. 191
Francis Marion, p. 191
Nathanael Greene, p. 192
traitor, p. 192

A Nation Declares Independence

Objectives

1. Find out how Thomas Paine stirred support for independence.
2. Understand the meaning and structure of the Declaration of Independence.
3. Learn how Congress finally agreed to separate from England.

Prepare to Read

Reading Skill

Analyze Word Roots Many English words have common word roots or parts. For example, the root *mot* means "move." That root appears in the words *motion, motor, promote,* and *demote.* Those words have different meanings, but all share some connection to movement. Learn to recognize familiar word roots and trace their origins.

Vocabulary *Builder*

High-Use Words

prospect, p. 170

logic, p. 171

Key Terms and People

Thomas Paine, p. 170

Richard Henry Lee, p. 171

resolution, p. 171

preamble, p. 172

grievance, p. 172

Main Idea
Thomas Paine's *Common Sense* helped increase support for independence in the colonies.

Vocabulary *Builder*
prospect (PRAHS pehkt) *n.* possibility; expectation

⭐ **Background Knowledge** In the last chapter, you saw why many Americans became angry with British rule. In this section, you will learn how Patriots moved from protesting injustice to seeking independence.

A Call for Independence

When the year 1776 began, few colonists could have predicted what lay ahead. Most colonists still hoped for a peaceful end to the quarrel with Britain.

Colonists Divided Both Patriots and Loyalists were in a minority at the start of 1776. Many colonists were in the middle, with no strong feelings about the dispute with Britain.

Even within the Continental Congress, support for independence was limited to about one third of the delegates. Patriots such as John Adams found it hard to win others to the cause of independence. Adams complained that Loyalists used the <u>prospect</u> of independence as a way to frighten people into giving up the struggle.

Common Sense In January 1776, a 50-page pamphlet titled *Common Sense* was published in Philadelphia. The pamphlet stimulated broad support for independence.

The author, Thomas Paine, called King George III a "royal brute." Paine ridiculed the very idea of rule by kings. Americans, he said, would be far better off if they governed themselves. (See Reading Primary Sources on the next page.)

Paine's strong <u>logic</u> and powerful words inspired people in all the colonies. Some 500,000 copies of the pamphlet were sold between January and July of 1776. George Washington wrote, "*Common Sense* is working a powerful change in the minds of men."

Vocabulary *Builder*
<u>logic</u> (LAH jihk) *n.* reason; careful thought

Virginia's Resolution Paine's pamphlet increased support for independence within the Continental Congress. In May 1776, Virginia authorized its delegates to support independence. Soon after, Richard Henry Lee introduced a resolution, or formal statement of opinion, to Congress. The Virginia resolution proclaimed that "these United Colonies are, and of right ought to be, free and independent States."

Before voting on Lee's resolution, Congress appointed a committee to draw up a statement stating the reasons for separation from Britain. Thomas Jefferson, a 33-year-old delegate from Virginia, was given the task of composing the declaration. Highly educated but shy, Jefferson spoke little in Congress. However, he was known for his graceful writing style.

In the heat of the Philadelphia summer, Jefferson struggled to find the words that would convince Americans and the world of the rightness of independence. The result was masterful. John Adams and Benjamin Franklin, who were also on the committee, suggested only minor changes.

☑ **Checkpoint** **What proposal did Richard Henry Lee make to Congress?**

Common Sense

"I challenge the warmest advocate for reconciliation, to show a single advantage that this continent can reap, by being connected with Great Britain. I repeat the challenge, not a single advantage is derived. Our corn will fetch its price in any market in Europe, and our imported goods must be paid for, buy them where we will. . . . Whenever a war breaks out between England and any foreign power, the trade of America goes to ruin, because of her connection with Britain. . . . Every thing that is right or natural pleads for separation. The blood of the slain, the weeping voice of nature cries, 'TIS TIME TO PART."

Thomas Paine

—Thomas Paine, *Common Sense*

Reading Primary Sources

Skills Activity

In *Common Sense*, Thomas Paine gives political, military, and moral arguments for breaking away from Britain. In the excerpt above, Paine discusses some economic reasons.

(a) Identify Costs Why does Paine think that association with Britain hurts American trade?

(b) Make Inferences What do you think Paine means by "the blood of the slain"?

The Declaration of Independence

The Declaration of Independence is a brilliant piece of writing. Building on the ideas of the Enlightenment, it uses step-by-step logic to explain why the colonists wanted to break away from British rule. (See the Declaration of Independence following this section.)

The Declaration begins with a preamble, or introduction. It says that "a decent respect to the opinions of mankind" requires that Americans explain why they are breaking away from Britain.

Natural Rights The Declaration is divided into three main sections. The first section states some general ideas about society and government. "We hold these truths to be self-evident," or obvious to all. First among these truths is that "all men are created equal." Jefferson goes on to state that everyone is "endowed by their Creator with certain unalienable rights." This statement is based on John Locke's ideas about natural rights. (See Chapter 4.)

Like Locke, Jefferson goes on to state that governments are created in order to protect people's rights. And, like Locke, he concludes that, if a government violates those rights, the people have a right to abolish their government and create another.

List of Grievances Jefferson's next task was to prove that the British government had, in fact, violated the rights of the colonists. So the next section details a long list of specific grievances, or formal complaints, against King George III of England.

Many grievances accuse the king of ignoring rights that English citizens had enjoyed since the time of the Magna Carta. For example, the Magna Carta had established trial by jury as a basic right. The Declaration thus condemns the king "for depriving us, in many cases, of trial by jury." The Declaration also charges the king with "imposing taxes on us without our consent"—another violation of traditional English rights.

Time after time, says the Declaration, colonists have appealed to the king. But King George has ignored the petitions they sent. He must, therefore, be considered "unfit to be the ruler of a free people."

Dissolving the Bonds After stating the basic principle that the people have a right to abolish an unjust government and showing that the king has violated the rights of the colonists, the Declaration reaches a logical conclusion. It asserts that the colonies are "free and independent states . . . and that all political connection between them and the state of Great Britain is, and ought to be totally dissolved."

The document ends with a solemn pledge: "With a firm reliance on the protection of Divine Providence, we mutually pledge to each other our Lives, our Fortunes, and our sacred Honor." The serious tone shows that, to the Patriots, declaring independence was a serious and deeply felt step.

King George III

✓**Checkpoint** What does the Declaration of Independence say about people's rights?

Impact of the Declaration

When Congress met to debate Lee's resolution, it still was not certain that they would declare independence. But on July 4, 1776, Congress approved the Declaration of Independence. Since then, Americans have celebrated July 4th as Independence Day.

The actual signing of the Declaration took place on August 2. According to tradition, as he stepped up to sign the document, Benjamin Franklin commented, "We must all hang together, or most assuredly we shall all hang separately." Indeed, for the delegates who signed, the personal risk was great. If captured by the British, they could be hanged.

The Declaration of Independence changed the nature of the Revolution. No longer were the Patriots fighting for fairer treatment from Britain. Now, they were fighting to create a new nation. There was no turning back.

Since then, the Declaration of Independence has become one of the world's enduring documents. The statement that "all men are created equal" still inspires Americans and people in other nations. In 1776, these words applied primarily to white, male property owners. Over the years, Americans worked to expand the notion of equality and natural rights.

☑Checkpoint **How did the Declaration change the nature of the American Revolution?**

⭐ **Looking Back and Ahead** Declaring independence from Britain was only a first step. For the Declaration to have real meaning, the Americans would have to win their liberties on the battlefield. In the next section, you will read about the progress of the war for independence.

Thomas Jefferson

| Section 1 | **Check Your Progress** |

Progress Monitoring 🌐 **nline**
For: Self-test with instant help
Visit: PHSchool.com
Web Code: mva-2061

Comprehension and Critical Thinking

1. (a) Recall What was the main idea of Thomas Paine's *Common Sense*?
(b) Draw Conclusions Why do you think *Common Sense* had such an impact on colonists?

2. (a) Identify What are the major parts of the Declaration of Independence?
(b) Apply Information Why is the list of grievances against the king an important part of the Declaration?

Reading Skill

3. Analyze Word Roots Use the word root *spir*, meaning "breathe," to determine the meaning of the word *inspire* in this sentence: The statement that "all men are created equal" still *inspires* Americans and people in other nations.

Vocabulary *Builder*

Complete each sentence so that the second part further explains the first part and clearly shows your understanding of the key term.

4. The Declaration of Independence began with a preamble, or _____.
5. Congress took a step toward independence when Lee introduced Virginia's resolution, or _____.
6. The Declaration includes a list of grievances, or _____.

Writing

7. List two challenges you think Thomas Jefferson faced in writing the Declaration of Independence. Do you think he met these challenges? Explain.

The Declaration
of Independence

By signing the Declaration of Independence, members of the Continental Congress sent a clear message to Britain that the American colonies were free and independent states. Starting with its preamble, the document spells out all the reasons the people of the United States have the right to break away from Britain. **Critical Thinking:** *Detect Points of View How would a Loyalist react to the Declaration of Independence?*

Explore More Video
To learn more about the roots of the Declaration of Independence, view the video.

Preamble
The document first lists the reasons for writing the Declaration.

Protection of Natural Rights
If a government fails to protect people's natural rights, the people have a right to reject it and create another.

Grievances Against the King
King George has violated colonists' rights and ignored their petitions.

Declaring Independence
Therefore, the colonies declare their independence from Great Britain.

IN CONGRESS, JULY 4, 1776.

The unanimous Declaration of the thirteen united States of America,

★ In Congress, July 4, 1776

The Unanimous Declaration of the Thirteen United States of America

When in the Course of human events, it becomes necessary for one people to dissolve the political bands which have connected them with another, and to assume among the powers of the earth, the separate and equal station to which the Laws of Nature and of Nature's God entitle them, a decent respect to the opinions of mankind requires that they should declare the causes which impel them to the separation.

We hold these truths to be self-evident, that all men are created equal, that they are endowed by their Creator with certain unalienable Rights, that among these are Life, Liberty and the pursuit of Happiness. That to secure these rights, Governments are instituted among Men, deriving their just powers from the consent of the governed. That whenever any Form of Government becomes destructive of these ends, it is the Right of the People to alter or to abolish it, and to institute new Government, laying its foundation on such principles and organizing its powers in such form, as to them shall seem most likely to effect their Safety and Happiness. Prudence, indeed, will dictate that Governments long established should not be changed for light and transient causes; and

The Declaration of Independence has four parts: the Preamble, the Declaration of Natural Rights, the List of Grievances, and the Resolution of Independence. The Preamble states why the Declaration was written. The document will explain to the world the reasons why the colonists feel **impelled**, or forced, to separate from Great Britain.

People set up governments to protect their basic rights. These rights are **unalienable**; they cannot be taken away. The purpose of government is to protect these natural rights. When a government does not protect the rights of the people, the people must change the government or create a new one. The colonists feel that the king's repeated **usurpations**, or unjust uses of power, are a form of **despotism**, or tyranny, that has denied them their basic rights.

accordingly all experience hath shown that mankind are more disposed to suffer, while evils are sufferable, than to right themselves by abolishing the forms to which they are accustomed. But when a long train of abuses and usurpations, pursuing invariably the same Object evinces a design to reduce them under absolute Despotism, it is their right, it is their duty, to throw off such Government, and to provide new Guards for their future security. Such has been the patient sufferance of these Colonies; and such is now the necessity which constrains them to alter their former Systems of Government. The history of the present King of Great Britain is a history of repeated injuries and usurpations, all having in direct object the establishment of an absolute Tyranny over these States. To prove this, let Facts be submitted to a candid world.

He has refused his Assent to Laws, the most wholesome and necessary for the public good.

He has forbidden his Governors to pass Laws of immediate and pressing importance, unless suspended in their operation till his Assent should be obtained; and when so suspended, he has utterly neglected to attend to them.

> The List of Grievances details the colonists' complaints against the British government, and King George III in particular. The colonists have no say in determining the laws that govern them and they feel King George's actions show little or no concern for the well being of the people.

He has refused to pass other Laws for the accommodation of large districts of people, unless those people would relinquish the right of Representation in the Legislature, a right inestimable to them and formidable to tyrants only.

> The colonists refuse to **relinquish**, or give up, the right to representation, which they feel is **inestimable**, or priceless.

He has called together legislative bodies at places unusual, uncomfortable, and distant from the depository of their public Records, for the sole purpose of fatiguing them into compliance with his measures.

He has dissolved Representative Houses repeatedly, for opposing with manly firmness his invasions on the rights of the people.

> The king has refused to allow new legislators to be elected. As a result, the colonies have not been able to protect themselves against foreign enemies and **convulsions**, or riots, within the colonies.

He has refused for a long time, after such dissolutions, to cause others to be elected; whereby the Legislative powers, incapable of Annihilation, have returned to the People at large for their exercise; the State remaining in the mean time exposed to all the dangers of invasion from without, and convulsions within.

> The king has tried to stop foreigners from coming to the colonies by refusing to pass naturalization laws. Laws for naturalization of foreigners are laws that set up the process for foreigners to become legal citizens.

He has endeavoured to prevent the population of these States; for that purpose obstructing the Laws for Naturalization of Foreigners; refusing to pass others to encourage their migrations hither, and raising the conditions of new Appropriations of Lands.

He has obstructed the Administration of Justice by refusing his Assent to Laws for establishing Judiciary powers.

> The king alone has decided a judge's **tenure**, or term. This grievance later would result in Article 3, Section 1, of the Constitution, which states that federal judges hold office for life.

He has made Judges dependent on his Will alone, for the tenure of their offices, and the amount and payment of their salaries.

He has erected a multitude of New Offices, and sent hither swarms of Officers to harass our people, and eat out their substance.

He has kept among us, in times of peace, Standing Armies without the Consent of our legislatures.

A Critical Time

Objectives

1. Discover the results of fighting in the Middle States.

2. Understand why the Battle of Saratoga was a turning point in the American Revolution.

3. Learn how foreign nations and volunteers helped the Americans.

Prepare to Read

↻ Reading Skill

Apply the Meanings of Prefixes Prefixes—word parts added to the beginning of words or word roots—can dramatically affect a word's meaning. Applying the meanings of common prefixes will help you define unfamiliar words. Piece together a likely meaning. Check how the word is used within the content of the surrounding text. If necessary, use a dictionary.

Vocabulary *Builder*

High-Use Words
vital, p. 183
transform, p. 183

Key Terms and People
Nathan Hale, p. 180
mercenary, p. 181
alliance, p. 183
Marquis de Lafayette, p. 183
cavalry, p. 183
Friedrich von Steuben, p. 183

☆ **Background Knowledge** In the last section, you saw how the 13 colonies proclaimed their independence. This section describes how American fortunes shifted back and forth on the battlefield in 1776 and 1777.

Retreat From New York

In mid-1776, the heavy fighting shifted from New England to the Middle States. There, the Continental army suffered through the worst days of the war.

Attack and Retreat In June 1776, just as the Continental Congress was considering independence, a large British fleet arrived off New York. Sir William Howe, the British commander, gathered his forces on Staten Island, at the southern edge of New York harbor.

Washington expected Howe's attack. He already had led his forces south from Boston to Brooklyn on Long Island. However, his army was no match for the British. Howe had about 34,000 well-trained troops and 10,000 sailors, as well as ships to ferry them ashore. Washington had fewer than 20,000 poorly trained troops and no navy.

That summer saw a long series of battles and American retreats. In the Battle of Long Island, in August 1776, the British drove Washington's troops out of Brooklyn. The following month, Washington had to abandon New York City. The British pursued the Americans north to White Plains, then west and south across New Jersey.

Main Idea
Washington and the Continental army suffered severe setbacks in New York.

British fleet off Long Island

179

Nathan Hale During the fight for New York, Nathan Hale became an American legend. Hale was a Connecticut officer, and he volunteered for dangerous spy duty. His mission was to collect information about British battle plans on Long Island.

Caught behind British lines, Hale was tried and condemned to death. He was hanged the next morning. Later, it was reported that his last words had been, "I only regret that I have but one life to lose for my country."

✓**Checkpoint** What was the result of the Battle of Long Island?

Main Idea
The surprise victory at Trenton raised American spirits.

Surprises for the British

Under relentless British pursuit, the Continental army kept retreating. In December, it crossed the Delaware River into Pennsylvania. The British now threatened Philadelphia. Patriot spirits were low. Many soldiers deserted. Others seemed ready to go home as soon as their terms of service ended.

The Revolutionary War, 1775–1777

MAP MASTER®
Skills Activity

In the early stages of the American Revolution, the fighting moved from New England to the Middle States.

(a) Understand Sequence What is the earliest military action shown on this map?

(b) Interpret Maps How did sea power help the British capture Philadelphia?

MapMaster Online
For: Interactive map
Visit: PHSchool.com
Web Code: mvp-2062

KEY
⬅ American forces
⬅ British forces
✦ American victories
✦ British victories
⬆ Forts

0 km 200
0 miles 200
Albers Conic Equal-Area Projection

Thomas Paine had retreated with the army through New Jersey. To raise morale, he wrote another pamphlet, *The Crisis*. Paine urged Americans to support the army, despite hard times. He wrote:

> **"**These are the times that try men's souls. The summer soldier and the sunshine patriot will, in this crisis, shrink from the service of his country; but he that stands it now deserves the love and thanks of man and woman.**"**
>
> —Thomas Paine, *The Crisis*

Washington had *The Crisis* read aloud to his troops. At the same time, he made plans for a bold attack.

Crossing the Delaware On Christmas night, 1776, Washington led 2,400 men across the river in small boats. Soldiers huddled in the boats as the spray from the river froze on their faces. So poorly supplied were the troops that some had no shoes. Once across the river, the soldiers marched in the swirling snow. To keep their feet from freezing, the soldiers bound them in rags.

On the far bank, the men trudged several miles with Washington urging them on. Early on December 26, they attacked Trenton from two sides, achieving complete surprise.

An American Victory The attack brought a ringing American victory. The soldiers in Trenton were Hessians (men from Hesse, a small German state). They were among thousands of German mercenaries who were fighting for the British. Mercenaries are soldiers who are paid to fight for a country other than their own. Washington's army captured almost a thousand Hessian mercenaries.

Pursued by the British, Washington used a clever trick to escape. His soldiers made camp near Trenton and lit campfires. After dark, most of the men packed up and quietly withdrew. The British did not discover the trick until daylight, when the main body of soldiers attacked and heavily damaged a British force near Princeton.

☑ **Checkpoint** **How did Washington attack Trenton?**

Saratoga: A Turning Point

British general John Burgoyne came up with a plan he hoped would quickly end the rebellion. His goal was to cut New England off from the rest of the states.

Washington at Trenton
During Washington's surprise attack on Trenton, the commander of the Hessian mercenaries was seriously wounded. In this picture, Washington orders his men to help the dying Hessian officer to his bed. **Critical Thinking: Apply Information** *Why was Washington able to win the battle at Trenton?*

Main Idea
The Battle of Saratoga ended Britain's hopes of a quick victory.

The British Plan Burgoyne's plan called for British forces to drive toward Albany, New York, from three directions. From Canada, an army of 8,000 would move south to capture the forts on Lake Champlain, Lake George, and the upper Hudson River. From the west, a smaller British force would drive through the Mohawk Valley toward Albany. And from the south, General Howe would lead a large army up the Hudson River from New York City.

Burgoyne's plan ran into trouble almost immediately. George III ordered Howe to move south from New York in a misguided attempt to attack Philadelphia. Not until November were Howe's forces ready to march north again. At the same time, American forces cut off the British troops coming through the Mohawk Valley.

An American Victory Burgoyne led the main British force from Canada in June. After recapturing Fort Ticonderoga, they slowly pushed south, dragging a large train of baggage carts through the woods. Supplies were running short.

Americans were rushing to block the British. By September, the American commander in New York, General Horatio Gates, had 6,000 men ready to fight. At the village of Saratoga, New York, the Americans surrounded the British. After suffering heavy casualties, Burgoyne surrendered on October 17, 1777.

Reading Skill

Apply the Meanings of Prefixes
The prefix *mis-* means "badly" or "wrongly." What does the word *misguided* mean?

History Interactive

Explore a Soldier's Life
Visit: PHSchool.com
Web Code: mvl-2062

Revolutionary Soldier

The three-cornered hat, or tricorn, was standard headgear for Continental soldiers.

Every marksman depended on his powder horn, an animal horn used to carry gunpowder.

To load a musket, a soldier first had to fill it with gunpowder. Then, he had to push the ammunition—a lead ball—down the barrel with a ramrod. Only then was the musket ready to fire.

A Continental Soldier

A soldier in the Continental army needed the strength and stamina to travel long distances on foot. Perhaps the most important skill was good marksmanship—the ability to shoot well. **Critical Thinking: *Clarify Problems*** *What do you think were some of the disadvantages of the musket as a military weapon?*

Results of the Battle The Battle of Saratoga marked a major turning point in the war. The American victory ended the British threat to New England and destroyed British hopes of an easy victory. It also lifted Patriot spirits at a time when Washington's army was suffering defeats. Perhaps most important, the Battle of Saratoga helped convince Europeans that the Americans had a sound chance of winning.

✓**Checkpoint** **List two results of the Battle of Saratoga.**

Help From Overseas

Soon after Saratoga, France agreed to openly support American independence. In February 1778, France officially formed an alliance with the United States. An **alliance** is a formal agreement between two powers to work together toward a common goal.

The French Alliance France was eager to weaken Britain. Even before Saratoga, the French had secretly supplied money and arms to the Americans. But the French did not want to take an open stand until it seemed the Americans might win. The Battle of Saratoga convinced the French government to help the struggling young nation. In February 1778, France became the first nation to sign a treaty with the United States.

France and its allies in the Netherlands and Spain also went to war with Britain. By carrying the fight to Europe and the Caribbean, the allies forced Britain to wage war on many fronts. This helped the American cause, because the British could spare fewer troops to fight in North America.

European Volunteers A number of Europeans volunteered to serve with the American forces. They were inspired by the American struggle for liberty.

A French noble, the Marquis de Lafayette (lah fay YET), became a high-ranking officer in Washington's army. He and Washington became close friends. When Lafayette was wounded in battle, Washington told a surgeon, "Treat him as though he were my son."

Volunteers from Poland also made <u>vital</u> contributions to the Patriot war effort. Thaddeus Kosciusko (kawsh CHUSH koh) was an engineer who took charge of building fortifications at West Point. Casimir Pulaski led and trained **cavalry**, or units of troops on horseback.

Baron von Steuben A German baron, Friedrich von Steuben (STOO buhn), helped train the Continental army. Steuben had served in the Prussian army, which was considered the best in Europe.

Before Steuben arrived in early 1778, American troops were often poorly trained and undisciplined. Steuben taught the soldiers how to march, how to improve their aim, and how to attack with bayonets. His methods helped to <u>transform</u> raw recruits into soldiers and shaped the Continental army into a more effective force.

✓**Checkpoint** **How did France aid the Patriot cause?**

Main Idea
Both foreign nations and individuals from Europe gave valuable help to the Patriot cause.

Medals commemorating the American-French alliance

Vocabulary *Builder*
<u>vital</u> (VĪ tuhl) *adj.* necessary; of great importance

Vocabulary *Builder*
<u>transform</u> (trans FORM) *v.* to change from one thing or condition to another

Main Idea
The winter of 1777–1778 was a difficult time for the American army.

Washington at Valley Forge

Valley Forge

Washington's Continental army suffered through the cruel winter of 1777–1778 in a hastily built camp at Valley Forge in Pennsylvania. Meanwhile, some 22 miles away, British officers in Philadelphia danced the winter away in a merry round of parties and balls.

The 11,000 Continental soldiers were not sufficiently fed, clothed, or housed. Many lacked socks, shoes, and even trousers. Throughout the winter, they shivered in drafty huts. At any one time, about one soldier in four was sick with chills, fever, or worse.

Because food was so scarce, the soldiers mainly ate thin soup and dry bread patties. One private later recalled that he went without food for two days. He was so hungry he would have grabbed food away from anyone, even his best friend. Finally, he found half a pumpkin. He cooked it "upon a rock, the skin side up, by making a fire on it."

When Americans learned about conditions at Valley Forge, they sent help. Women collected food, medicine, warm clothes, and ammunition. Some women, including George Washington's wife, Martha, went to Valley Forge to tend the sick and wounded.

Despite its woes, the Continental army used that winter to gather its strength for the battles that lay ahead. Steuben's drills sharpened the soldiers' skills and discipline.

☑Checkpoint **Why was the winter at Valley Forge so difficult?**

⭐ **Looking Back and Ahead** By the spring of 1778, the army at Valley Forge was ready to resume the fight. "The army grows stronger every day," wrote one New Jersey soldier. While soldiers drilled, Washington and his staff planned new campaigns against the British.

Section 2 | **Check Your Progress**

Progress Monitoring 🌐nline
For: Self-test with instant help
Visit: PHSchool.com
Web Code: mva-2062

Comprehension and Critical Thinking

1. **(a) Recall** What happened at Trenton in December 1776?
(b) Draw Inferences What did Washington's actions at the Battle of Trenton show about his character and leadership?

2. **(a) List** What were three important results of the American victory at Saratoga?
(b) Make Predictions What do you think would have happened if the Americans had lost the battle?

🔟 Reading Skill

3. **Apply the Meanings of Prefixes** The prefix *trans-* means "change." The word root *form* means "shape" or "structure." Use this information to explain the meaning of *transform* in this sentence: His methods helped to *transform* raw recruits into soldiers.

Vocabulary *Builder*

Read each sentence below. If the sentence is true, write YES and explain why. If the sentence is not true, write NO and explain why not.

4. German mercenaries helped the British because they believed the king should rule the Americans.
5. After making an alliance with the Americans, France contributed money and arms to the Patriots.
6. The cavalry soldiers fired at the British soldiers from the ground before running away.

Writing

7. In order to gather enough soldiers to fight the battle in America, the British had to hire German mercenaries. List one strong argument for and one strong argument against this solution.

Valley Forge
by Maxwell Anderson

Prepare to Read

Introduction

Maxwell Anderson's play *Valley Forge* depicts the hardships faced by Washington's army in the winter of 1778. One problem the army faced was men trying to go home. Here, Washington hears the complaints of a soldier named Teague.

Reading Skill

Analyze Dramatic Conflict An important element in any drama is conflict, when two characters want different things. As you read this scene, try to identify the source of the conflict between Washington and Teague.

Vocabulary *Builder*

As you read this literature selection, look for the following underlined words:

commissary (KAH muh sehr ee) *n.* food supplies

munitions (myoo NIH shuhns) *n.* weapons and ammunition

TEAGUE: I'm going hungry here and my woman's going hungry at home. You let me go home for the winter, and you won't have to feed me, and that relieves the <u>commissary</u>. I rustle some wild meat for the younguns and the old woman, and they don't starve and I don't starve. More'n that, everybody knows there's two or three thousand men gone home already for that same reason, and if they was here now they'd be chewing the bark off the second-growth birch like so many cottontails. I don't hold it against you and I don't hold it against anybody because I don't know who in thunder to hold it against, but there's nothing to eat here. . . .

WASHINGTON: Well, Master Teague, if they catch you they'll give you seventy-five lashes, and that's a good deal to take and live. On the other hand, you're quite right from your own angle, and if I were you I'd feel as you do. If you go home, and we all go home this winter, you won't need to bother about coming back in the spring. There'll be not fighting to come back to. General Howe will march out of Philadelphia and take over these states of ours. If he knew now how many have deserted, how many are sick, how many unfit for duty on account of the lack of food and clothes and <u>munitions</u>, he'd come back in force and wring our necks one by one, and the neck of our sickly little revolution along with us.

From *America On Stage: Ten Great Plays of American History,*
ed. Stanley Richards. Doubleday & Co., 1976.

Analyze LITERATURE

Do you think that Washington should permit Teague to go home without punishment? Write a paragraph explaining the reasons for your opinion.

 Analyze Dramatic Conflict

What does Teague want? What does Washington want? How are their wishes in conflict?

 If you liked this excerpt and want to learn more about George Washington, you might want to read *George Washington and the Founding of a Nation* by Albert Marrin. Dutton Books, 2001.

Objectives

1. Discover the role that African Americans played in the American Revolution.

2. Find out how the war affected women and other civilians.

3. Learn about the progress of the fighting on the western frontier and at sea.

Prepare to Read

Reading Skill

Analyze Word Roots Word roots can do more than help you define unfamiliar words. They can help you expand your vocabulary. As you read Section 3, use word roots to determine meanings. Then, list other words you know that come from the same word roots. Think about how they share meanings with the text words—and how the meanings differ. Notice the shades of meaning that can derive from a single word root.

Vocabulary *Builder*

High-Use Words
<u>confine</u>, p. 188
<u>resource</u>, p. 188

Key Terms and People
enlist, p. 187
civilian, p. 187
continental, p. 188
George Rogers Clark, p. 189
Bernardo de Gálvez, p. 189
John Paul Jones, p. 190
privateer, p. 190

⭐ **Background Knowledge** You have learned about the early stages of the American Revolution. In this section, you will read how the war affected Americans in all parts of the country.

African Americans in the War

African Americans fought on both sides of the American Revolution. For them, the war meant both danger and opportunity.

Free and Slave From the beginning, free African Americans took part in the war. At least nine served as minutemen at Lexington and Concord. Peter Salem fought at Bunker Hill and Saratoga.

Enslaved people served as well. After fleeing his master in Rhode Island, Jehu Grant served in the American army for nine months. He later recalled:

Main Idea
The promise of freedom led many African Americans to serve in the American Revolution.

> ❝When I saw liberty poles and the people all engaged for the support of freedom, I could not but like and be pleased with such thing. . . . The songs of liberty . . . thrilled through my heart.❞
>
> —Jehu Grant, letter, December 1, 1836

Analyze Word Roots
The word root *port* means "to carry." The prefix *sub-* means "under," and *sub-* becomes *sup-* when used before the letter *p.* Use these word parts to explain the meaning of *support.* List three other words that build on the root *port.*

The British offered freedom to enslaved people who deserted and joined the British. Many thousands did so. They served mainly in support roles as cooks, blacksmiths, and teamsters. However, some people who had formerly been enslaved fought for the British.

On the American side, Washington at first refused to accept African American soldiers. But the British offer of freedom to enslaved people made Washington change his policy. By the end of the war, some 7,000 African Americans had served on the American side, including 2,000 in the navy. African Americans also served in northern militias and state armies. Most southern states, however, refused to accept African American soldiers. Slave owners feared armed slave revolts.

Freedom Beckons During the Revolution, a number of northern states took steps to end slavery. For example, a Pennsylvania law of 1780 provided for a gradual end to slavery. It allowed slaveholders to keep their existing slaves but barred them from getting more.

☑**Checkpoint** **Why did some enslaved African Americans choose to fight for the British?**

The War at Home

Many men **enlisted,** or signed up for duty, in the military. After a set term, usually one year, they were free to leave. Thus, Washington had to struggle constantly to keep the ranks of his army filled.

Civilians, or people not in the military, also faced hardships. They were often subject to food shortages and military attack.

Main Idea
The war brought hardships and new responsibilities to women and others.

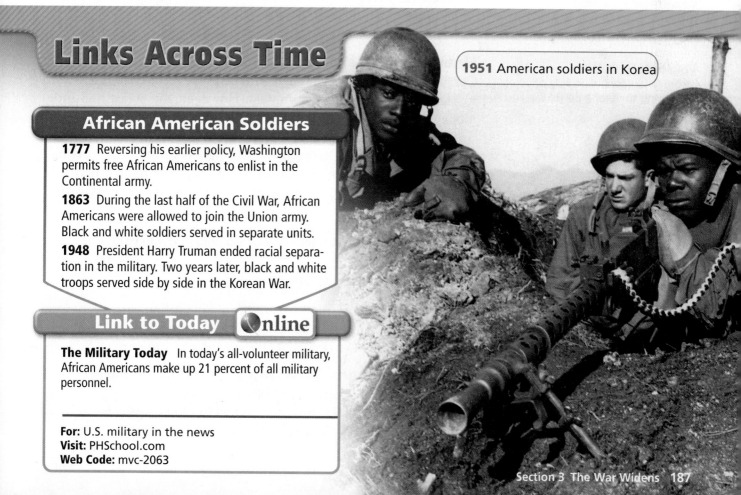

Links Across Time

1951 American soldiers in Korea

African American Soldiers

1777 Reversing his earlier policy, Washington permits free African Americans to enlist in the Continental army.

1863 During the last half of the Civil War, African Americans were allowed to join the Union army. Black and white soldiers served in separate units.

1948 President Harry Truman ended racial separation in the military. Two years later, black and white troops served side by side in the Korean War.

Link to Today 🅞nline

The Military Today In today's all-volunteer military, African Americans make up 21 percent of all military personnel.

For: U.S. military in the news
Visit: PHSchool.com
Web Code: mvc-2063

A Woman in Battle

When her husband was wounded at the Battle of Monmouth, Mary Ludwig Hays dropped her water bucket and took up his cannon. Her heroic actions made her a legendary American hero, known as Molly Pitcher. **Critical Thinking:** *Evaluate Information* *Why do you think Molly Pitcher has become a popular subject for American artists? What image of women does she represent?*

Vocabulary *Builder*
<u>confine</u> (kuhn FĪN) *v.* to keep within certain limits

Vocabulary *Builder*
<u>resource</u> (REE sors) *n.* supply of something to meet a particular need

Women As men went to war, women took over many of their duties. On farms, women planted crops and cared for livestock. In towns, women often ran their husbands' businesses.

Some women accompanied their husbands to military camps. In battles, they cared for the wounded. One woman, Deborah Sampson, joined the army, disguised as a man. Wounded in battle, Sampson tended her own wounds in order to keep her secret.

The added responsibilities of wartime gave many women a new confidence. At a time when women's roles were largely <u>confined</u>, the war opened up new opportunities for many women.

Financial Burdens Paying for the war was a difficult task. Congress had limited <u>resources</u>. With no power to tax, Congress had to plead with the states for money. However, the states had little money themselves.

To pay and supply troops, Congress printed continentals, or paper money. But the more money Congress printed, the less the money was worth. By the end of the war, paper money had lost almost all its value. Something worthless was said to be "not worth a continental."

✔**Checkpoint** **What roles did women play in the Revolution?**

Main Idea
Fighting on the western frontier brought Native Americans into the war.

Fighting in the West

Throughout most of the American Revolution, attention was mainly focused on the 13 states along the Atlantic coast. However, skirmishes and battles occurred on the western frontier as well.

Native Americans Take Sides Americans tried to keep the Native Americans neutral. They offered payments to groups willing to remain at peace. They brought leaders to Philadelphia to impress them with parades of Continental troops.

Still, most Native American groups sided with Britain. They feared that an American victory would mean more settlers moving west or south onto Native American lands.

Defending the Frontier Seeking to defend against attacks on the frontier, Virginia sent George Rogers Clark and a militia force to strike British forts beyond the Appalachian Mountains in 1778. Clark's forces easily captured two Mississippi River outposts, Kaskaskia and Cahokia.

Early in 1779, Clark and his men trudged across 200 miles, at times splashing through icy floodwaters up to their chests. Their midwinter attack on the fort at Vincennes caught the British by surprise. The British and their Native American allies surrendered.

Clark's victories allowed settlers to remain on the frontier. This strengthened the American claim on the Ohio Valley area.

Help From the Spanish The Americans got unofficial help from Spain. At the time, Spain governed Louisiana, the land west of the Mississippi stretching as far north as Canada. The Spanish were eager to get back Florida, which they had lost to Britain at the end of the French and Indian War.

Even before Spain declared war against Britain in 1779, Louisiana governor Bernardo de Gálvez began helping the Americans. He secretly provided money and munitions to George Rogers Clark and other Americans. He also gave American ships safe refuge in New Orleans harbor. From 1779 to 1781, Gálvez played a key role in Spanish attacks that captured British forts on the Mississippi River and the Gulf of Mexico.

In 1781, the Americans sought financial help from the Spanish colony of Cuba. A group of wealthy women, the "Havana's Ladies," were especially generous. They sent some 7 million dollars to the Americans along with a letter saying, "So the American mothers' sons are not born as slaves." Without the contribution of these women, Washington's army might have run short of needed funds at a critical point in the war. A commander in the Continental army later wrote with gratitude of "the generous gesture and solidarity of the Cuban ladies and how they had donated money and jewelry."

✓**Checkpoint** What was the result of the fighting in the West?

The Revolution in the West

KEY

← American forces

← British forces

✳ American victories

⬆ Forts

0 km 200
0 miles 200
Albers Conic Equal-Area Projection

MAP MASTER®

Skills Activity

Several important battles took place west of the Appalachian Mountains, especially in the Ohio Valley.

(a) Interpret Maps Describe the route taken by British troops to Vincennes.

(b) Understand Sequence Use the information on the map to explain the sequence of the three battles shown here.

MapMaster ⬤nline

For: Interactive map
Visit: PHSchool.com
Web Code: mvp-2063

Main Idea

Although Britain blockaded American ports, the American navy won a few victories.

John Paul Jones

The War at Sea

Congress had voted to create a Continental navy as early as 1775. But American shipyards were able to build only a few warships. With only a small navy to go against the powerful British fleet, the Americans became skilled at making hit-and-run attacks on British shipping. Still, Britain dominated the seas. The British fleet blocked most ships from entering or leaving American ports.

The most famous naval battle took place off the coast of England in 1779. The American ship *Bonhomme Richard* (bon ohm ree CHARD), under the command of **John Paul Jones,** fought side by side with the larger British warship *Serapis.* Cannon and musket fire ripped the sails of both ships to shreds and blasted holes in their wooden sides. Though his ship was in tatters, Jones refused to give up. "I have not yet begun to fight," he vowed. Finally, with dozens of sailors dead on each side, the captain of the *Serapis* surrendered.

The navy had help from some 800 privateers that harassed British shipping. **Privateers** were armed civilian ships that had their government's permission to attack enemy ships and keep their goods. Operating like pirate ships, privateers seized cargoes of rum from the West Indies, wool from England, and furs from Canada. Such attacks forced Britain to spend valuable resources protecting merchant ships.

☑**Checkpoint** **How did privateers help the American war effort?**

☆ **Looking Back and Ahead** Despite important battles at sea and in the west, the main war effort was concentrated in the colonies. In the next section, you will read about the final phase of the war.

Section 3 | **Check Your Progress**

Progress Monitoring ◉**nline**
For: Self-test with instant help
Visit: PHSchool.com
Web Code: mva-2063

Comprehension and Critical Thinking

1. **(a) Recall** How did Washington's policy toward African American soldiers change? What was the reason for this change?
(b) Identify Benefits How did African Americans expect to benefit from serving in the military?

2. **(a) Describe** What challenges did the American navy face?
(b) Draw Conclusions Why do you think John Paul Jones is considered a great American hero?

◎ Reading Skill

3. **Analyze Word Roots** The root *fid* means "faith." The prefix *con-* means "with." Use these word parts to determine the meaning of *confidence* in this sentence: The added responsibilities of wartime gave many women a new *confidence.*

Vocabulary *Builder*

4. Draw a table with four rows and three columns. In the first column, list the key terms from this section: enlist, civilian, continental, privateer. In the next column, write the definition of each word. In the last column, make a small illustration that shows the meaning of the word.

Writing

5. Identify the problems facing the Continental Congress during the war. Then, brainstorm one or two possible solutions.

Winning Independence

Objectives

1. Find out how the Americans won the final battle of the Revolution.

2. Learn the terms of the peace treaty with England.

3. Explore the reasons that the Americans were victorious.

4. Examine the effects of the American Revolution.

Prepare to Read

 Reading Skill

Apply the Meanings of the Prefix *re-* Prefixes sometimes have more than one meaning. For example, the prefix *re-* can mean "again" or "anew," but it can also mean "back" or "backward." You must think about the surrounding words and context in which the word is used before deciding which meaning of the prefix to apply.

Vocabulary *Builder*

High-Use Words

<u>efficient</u>, p. 191

<u>option</u>, p. 192

Key Terms and People

Charles Cornwallis, p. 191

guerrilla, p. 191

Francis Marion, p. 191

Nathanael Greene, p. 192

traitor, p. 192

⭐ **Background Knowledge** In the last section, you read about battles at sea and in the West. In this section, you will see how fighting shifted to the South the final stages of Revolution.

Fighting Moves South

The British shifted their attention to the South late in 1778. Their aim was to capture some key cities, win over the local population, and then march north, acquiring one state after another.

British Advance At first, the plan seemed to work. British soldiers moved north from Florida to Georgia. In December 1778, the British took the city of Savannah. Within a month, they controlled most of Georgia.

Moving on to South Carolina, the British captured the main port, Charles Town, and then the rest of the state. The British commander, Lord Charles Cornwallis, then carried the war into North Carolina. It looked as if the British might be unstoppable.

To slow the British advance, Americans used guerrilla tactics. Guerrillas are fighters who work in small bands to make hit-and-run attacks. In South Carolina, Francis Marion led his men silently through the swamps. They attacked without warning, then escaped. Marion's guerrilla attacks were so <u>efficient</u> that he won the nickname the Swamp Fox. Other bands of guerrillas were also active.

Elsewhere in the South, Loyalist bands roamed the backcountry. They plundered and burned Patriot farms, killing men, women, and children. "If a stop cannot be put to these massacres," wrote one Continental general, "the country will be depopulated in a few months more."

Main Idea
After fighting shifted to the South, the war ended with an American victory at Yorktown.

Vocabulary *Builder*
efficient (ee FISH ehnt) *adj.* acting effectively, without wasted cost or effort

Vocabulary *Builder*
<u>option</u> (AHP shuhn) *n.* choice; possible course of action

Brighter Days Patriot fortunes began to improve in October 1780. Some 900 frontier fighters defeated a larger force of British troops and Loyalists atop Kings Mountain in South Carolina.

In December 1780, General Nathanael Greene took over command of the Continental army in the South. Greene split his small army in two. He led 1,200 men into eastern South Carolina, leaving General Daniel Morgan with 800 men in the west.

In January 1781, Morgan won a clear victory at the Battle of Cowpens. He put a small militia force in front, telling the men to fire three shots and then retreat. The British rushed forward, only to be met by charging cavalry and a line of skilled riflemen.

American Traitor Still, the British seemed to have the upper hand in the South. In addition to Cornwallis's forces, the British had troops under the command of an American traitor, Benedict Arnold. A **traitor** is a person who turns against one side in a conflict to help the other side.

Early in the war, Arnold had fought bravely for the Patriots. But Arnold felt Congress undervalued him. He plotted to turn West Point, a key fort on the Hudson River in New York, over to the British. When the plot was discovered in September 1780, Arnold escaped. He and his Loyalist soldiers then staged a series of destructive raids in Virginia.

Final Battle Weakened by battles like Cowpens, Cornwallis headed to Virginia. That gave Greene an excellent opportunity. Over a five-month period, Patriot forces swept through the Deep South. By late summer, only Charles Town and Savannah remained in British hands.

Cornwallis then made a fateful mistake. He moved his main army to the Yorktown peninsula, a tongue of Virginia land poking into Chesapeake Bay. There, he thought, the British fleet could reinforce his position. But at the end of August, the French fleet arrived off Yorktown and chased off British ships.

At the same time, Washington rushed toward Virginia with American and French troops. Cornwallis found himself in a trap. American and French soldiers barred escape by land, while the French fleet blocked escape by sea. After three weeks, Cornwallis had no <u>option</u> but to surrender.

On October 19, 1781, the Americans and French lined up in two facing columns. The British marched glumly between the two columns and tossed their weapons into a large pile on the ground. The victory at Yorktown was the last major battle of the war.

✓**Checkpoint** **How were Cornwallis and his troops trapped at Yorktown?**

Making Peace With Britain

The news from Yorktown caused shockwaves in Britain. Although the king wanted to keep fighting, Parliament voted in favor of peace.

Peace talks began in Paris in 1782. The American delegation included Benjamin Franklin and John Adams. Britain was eager for peace, so the Americans got most of what they wanted.

Treaty of Paris The talks led to an agreement, the Treaty of Paris. Britain recognized the independence of the United States. The boundaries of the new nation were set at the Atlantic on the east, Canada on the north, the Mississippi River on the west, and Florida on the south. Florida itself was returned to Spain.

For its part, the United States agreed to "earnestly recommend" that the states restore rights and property taken from Loyalists during the war. However, most states ignored this pledge.

On April 15, 1783, Congress approved the treaty. The war was officially over. It had been almost exactly eight years since the "shot heard round the world" started the fighting at Lexington.

Main Idea
In the Treaty of Paris, Britain recognized American independence.

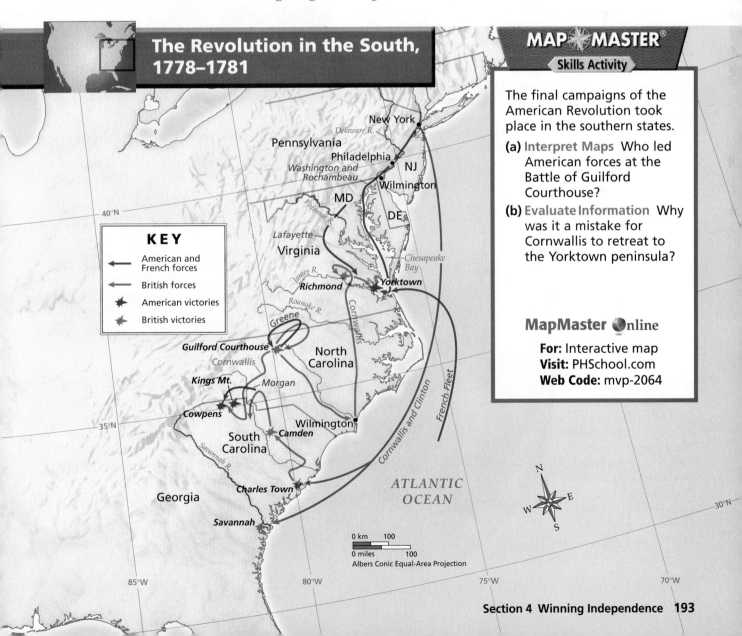

The Revolution in the South, 1778–1781

KEY
- ← American and French forces
- ← British forces
- ✳ American victories
- ✳ British victories

New York
Delaware R.
Pennsylvania
Philadelphia
NJ
Washington and Rochambeau
Wilmington
MD
DE
40°N
Lafayette
Virginia
Chesapeake Bay
James R.
Richmond
Yorktown
Cornwallis
Roanoke R.
Greene
Guilford Courthouse
Cornwallis
North Carolina
Kings Mt.
Morgan
Cowpens
Wilmington
Camden
South Carolina
Savannah R.
Charles Town
Georgia
Savannah
French Fleet
Cornwallis and Clinton
ATLANTIC OCEAN
35°N
30°N
Potomac R.

0 km 100
0 miles 100
Albers Conic Equal-Area Projection

N W E S

85°W   80°W   75°W   70°W

MAP MASTER®
Skills Activity

The final campaigns of the American Revolution took place in the southern states.

(a) Interpret Maps Who led American forces at the Battle of Guilford Courthouse?

(b) Evaluate Information Why was it a mistake for Cornwallis to retreat to the Yorktown peninsula?

MapMaster Online

For: Interactive map
Visit: PHSchool.com
Web Code: mvp-2064

Why Did the Americans Win?

Many factors contributed to the American victory. They fell into four main groups: geographic advantages, help from abroad, patriotic spirit, and skilled leadership.
Critical Thinking: *Evaluate Information What do you think was the most important reason for the American victory?*

Geography

Americans, such as Francis Marion (pictured below), were on their home ground. They knew the forests, hills, and swamps. But British forces were far from their home country. They had to depend on longer supply lines, stretching across the Atlantic Ocean. ▼

Patriotic Spirit ▲

A key asset of the Americans was patriotism. Americans were fighting to create a new nation. Many soldiers stayed in the army for years, at great financial and personal sacrifice. Leaders such as Jefferson and Adams risked their lives and fortunes to champion independence.

Skilled Leadership ►

Despite great odds, George Washington (left) never gave up. Although he sometimes faced sharp criticism in Congress, his courage and knowledge won him broad support in the army. By the end of the war, he was the new nation's most admired hero.

◄ Help From Abroad

The Americans might never have won without French military help. Men such as Lafayette (right) provided needed leadership and support. Money from such countries as Spain and the Netherlands was also crucial.

Washington's Farewell On December 4, 1783, Washington and his ranking officers were reunited for one last meal together at Fraunces Tavern in New York City. In parting, each man, in turn, embraced Washington. One officer wrote, "Such a scene of sorrow and weeping I had never before witnessed."

Washington wished to retire to his plantation. Soon, though, he would again be called to the aid of the nation he had helped create.

☑ **Checkpoint** What was the Treaty of Paris?

Impact of the Revolution

The immediate effect of the American Revolution was to create a new nation of 13 independent states, linked by ties of custom and history. The long-term effects are still being felt today. The Declaration of Independence cemented ideas like equality and liberty in the American mind. Over time, those concepts have gained broader meanings.

The impact of American independence reached beyond the borders of the infant nation. In 1789, revolution shook France. Leaders of the French Revolution, including Lafayette, looked to the American example. They issued the Declaration of the Rights of Man and the Citizen, modeled in part on the Declaration of Independence. The American Revolution also inspired later independence movements in Latin America.

☑ **Checkpoint** How did the American Revolution affect France?

☆ **Looking Back and Ahead** The United States emerged from the American Revolution as a proud nation—but also weak and deeply in debt. In the next chapter, you will read how the new nation met the challenge of forming a democratic government.

Main Idea
The American Revolution affected people both in the United States and around the world.

Apply the Meaning of the Prefix *re*-
The word root *belli* means "war." Apply a meaning of *re*- to determine the meaning of *rebelled*. Identify the prefix meaning that you applied.

Section 4 | Check Your Progress

Progress Monitoring ⓞnline
For: Self-test with instant help
Visit: PHSchool.com
Web Code: mva-2064

Comprehension and Critical Thinking
1. **(a) Recall** What military strategy defeated Cornwallis at Yorktown?
   (b) Apply Information What was one important factor that contributed to the American victory at Yorktown?
2. **(a) Describe** What were the provisions of the Treaty of Paris?
   (b) Identify Benefits Why was setting the nation's western border important economically to the new country?

Reading Skill
3. **Apply the Meanings of the Prefix *re*-** Read the text under the heading "Making Peace With Britain," and find at least two words that use the prefix *re*-. Apply the meanings of the prefix to define those words.

Vocabulary *Builder*
Answer the following questions in complete sentences that show your understanding of the key terms.
4. What advantages did guerrillas have against larger forces?

5. Why did Americans consider Benedict Arnold to be a traitor?

Writing
6. Once the Treaty of Paris was signed, the Americans had to address a new set of problems. Prepare a thesis statement for an essay about the challenges facing the new nation.

By comparing maps from different time periods, you can see how historical changes affected an area. The two maps below show North America before and after the Revolutionary War.

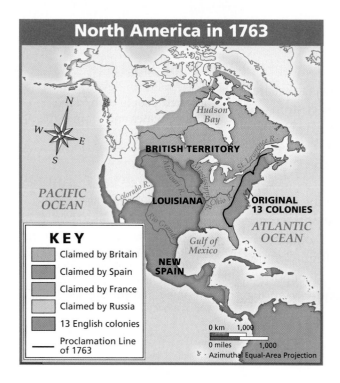

North America in 1763

KEY
- Claimed by Britain
- Claimed by Spain
- Claimed by France
- Claimed by Russia
- 13 English colonies
- Proclamation Line of 1763

0 km   1,000
0 miles   1,000
Azimuthal Equal-Area Projection

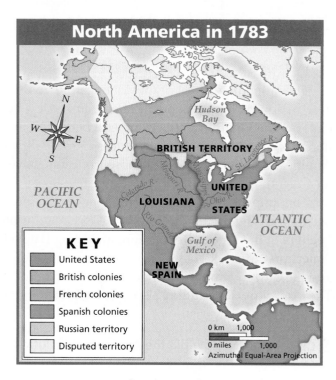

North America in 1783

KEY
- United States
- British colonies
- French colonies
- Spanish colonies
- Russian territory
- Disputed territory

0 km   1,000
0 miles   1,000
Azimuthal Equal-Area Projection

Learn the Skill
Use these steps to compare maps.

1 **Check the subject and area shown on each map.** What do the map titles and labels tell you? Is the same geographical area shown on each map?

2 **Study the map key.** Determine what symbols are used to present specific information that you can compare.

3 **Compare the maps.** Use the data on the maps to make comparisons and note changes over time.

4 **Interpret the maps.** Think over what you already know about this period from other sources. Draw conclusions or make predictions based on your own knowledge and the information on the maps.

Practice the Skill
Answer the following questions about the two maps on this page.

1 **Check the subject and area shown on each map.** (a) What area is shown on both maps? (b) What is the date of each map?

2 **Study the map key.** (a) What do the colors on the 1763 map key represent? (b) What color was added to the map key on the 1783 map?

3 **Compare the maps.** (a) What was the major difference between North America in 1763 and in 1783? (b) How was North America the same in 1763 and in 1783?

4 **Interpret the maps.** How did the 1783 Treaty of Paris affect the distribution of land in North America?

Apply the Skill
See the Review and Assessment at the end of this chapter.

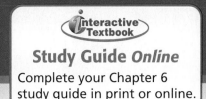

Study Guide *Online*
Complete your Chapter 6
study guide in print or online.

Chapter Summary

Section 1
A Nation Declares Independence

- Thomas Paine's pamphlet *Common Sense* convinced more Americans to support independence from Britain.
- The Declaration of Independence used Enlightenment ideas and careful logic to show why Americans wanted to be free of British rule.

Section 2
A Critical Time

- As fighting moved from New England to the Middle States, American troops faced many setbacks.
- The Battle of Saratoga was a turning point in the war.
- As a result of the American victory at Saratoga, France decided to aid the American cause.

Section 3
The War Widens

- African Americans fought on both sides of the Revolution, often in the hope of gaining freedom.
- As men went to war, women took on added responsibilities.
- Important battles took place on the western frontier and at sea.

Section 4
Winning Independence

- In the final stages of the war, fighting shifted to the South, ending in the British surrender at Yorktown.
- In the Treaty of Paris, Britain recognized American independence.
- The American Revolution and the Declaration of Independence have inspired people in other nations who sought freedom.

Key Concepts

These notes will help you prepare for questions about key concepts.

Major Ideas of the Declaration of Independence

- All men are created equal.
- All people are born with rights that cannot be taken away.
- People form governments to protect people's rights.
- If people are dissatisfied with their government, they have the right to form another.
- The king has violated the rights of the colonists.
- Therefore, the colonies declare their independence.

Some Key Figures of the American Revolution

- **Thomas Paine:** Wrote *Common Sense* and *The Crisis*
- **John Adams:** Led fight for independence in Congress
- **Richard Henry Lee:** Introduced resolution in Congress calling for independence
- **Thomas Jefferson:** Wrote Declaration of Independence
- **George Washington:** Commanded Continental army
- **Nathan Hale:** Executed by British in New York for spying
- **Marquis de Lafayette:** French volunteer; helped Washington
- **Friedrich von Steuben:** Trained American troops
- **George Rogers Clark:** Won victories in West
- **Bernardo de Gálvez:** Spanish governor; supported Americans
- **John Paul Jones:** Won major naval victory
- **Francis Marion:** Led guerrilla attacks on British troops
- **Nathanael Greene:** Commanded troops in South
- **Benedict Arnold:** American general; turned traitor
- **Lord Charles Cornwallis:** British general; surrendered at Yorktown

Vocabulary *Builder*
Key Terms
Complete each of the following sentences so that the second part explains the first part and shows your understanding of the key term.

1. Congress decided to pay the soldiers and buy their food and equipment by printing continentals _____.

2. The Declaration of Independence declared that people have unalienable rights _____.

3. One of the reasons that America won the war was because of its French and Spanish alliances _____.

4. During the Revolution, the small American navy had help from privateers _____.

5. A Polish volunteer led the American cavalry _____.

Comprehension and Critical Thinking

6. **(a) Recall** Why was the publication of *Common Sense* so important?
(b) Describe What was the political importance of the Declaration of Independence?
(c) Draw Conclusions How do you think that *Common Sense* influenced people's reaction to the Declaration of Independence?

7. **(a) Review** How did the course of the war change from June to the end of December 1776?
(b) Analyze Cause and Effect What effect do you think this change had on the Patriots?

8. **(a) Summarize** How did France help America during the Revolution?
(b) Make Predictions What do you think might have happened if France had not come to the aid of America during the Revolution?

9. **(a) Summarize** What financial problems faced Congress during the Revolution?
(b) Identify Alternatives What are some ways the new American government might avoid these same financial problems in the future?

10. **(a) Recall** How did the victories of the militia led by George Clark in the West benefit the frontier settlers?
(b) Identify Benefits What were the economic benefits of these victories for the new nation?

History Reading Skill

11. **Analyze Word Parts** Choose a word that contains any of the word parts discussed in this chapter. Use the word part to define the word. Then, write a sentence that contains the word and clarifies its meaning.

Writing

12. **Write two paragraphs discussing the problem of winning support from other nations for the Patriot cause. Your paragraph should:**
   - include a thesis statement that expresses your main idea;
   - develop the main idea with facts, examples, and other information;
   - conclude by describing the lasting impact of what happened.

13. **Write a Dialogue:**
   It is May 1775. Your family is seriously divided over which course to take. Choose one of the following roles: a parent concerned about the safety of the children, a Loyalist supporter, a Patriot supporter. Write one page of conversation about the situation.

Skills for Life
Compare Maps
Use the maps in Sections 3 and 4 to answer the following questions.

14. **(a)** What areas are shown on both maps?
(b) What is the date of each map?

15. What information is provided in the map key for "The Revolution in the West" that is not included in the map key for "The Revolution in the South"?

16. Based on the information in the maps, how would you compare the success of the British troops in the South and the West?

Test Yourself

1. **Which statement best describes the effects of the American Revolution on women?**

   A The political rights of women were reduced.

   B Women had to take on many new responsibilities.

   C Many women were forced to serve in the army.

   D The Declaration of Independence granted equal rights to women.

2. **One effect of the Treaty of Paris was that Britain**

   A gave up all its colonies in North America.

   B surrendered to the Patriots.

   C recognized American independence.

   D formed an alliance with the United States.

Refer to the map below to answer Question 3.

3. **What battle is shown on the map?**

   A Battle of Saratoga

   B Battle of Cowpens

   C Battle of Yorktown

   D Battle of Trenton

Document-Based Questions

Task: Look at Documents 1 and 2, and answer their accompanying questions. Then, use the documents and your knowledge of history to complete this writing assignment:

> Write an essay comparing the ways in which these two documents proclaim people's basic rights. How do they reflect the Enlightenment ideas of John Locke?

Document 1: This excerpt describes the basic principles behind the Declaration of Independence. *According to the Declaration, what basic rights do people have?*

> "We hold these truths to be self-evident, that all men are created equal, that they are endowed by their Creator with certain unalienable Rights, that among these are Life, Liberty, and the pursuit of Happiness. That to secure these rights, Governments are instituted among Men, deriving their just powers from the consent of the governed."
>
> —Declaration of Independence

Document 2: In 1789, on the eve of the French Revolution, the French Assembly issued the Declaration of the Rights of Man and the Citizen. As you can see from the excerpt below, this document was modeled in part on the American Declaration of Independence. *According to the Declaration of the Rights of Man and the Citizen, what is the aim of government?*

> "The representatives of the French people . . . have determined to set forth in a solemn declaration the natural, unalienable, and sacred rights of man.
>
> 1. Men are born and remain free and equal in rights. . . .
>
> 2. The aim of all political association is the preservation of the natural and imprescriptable rights of man. These rights are liberty, property, security, and resistance to oppression."
>
> —Declaration of the Rights of Man and the Citizen

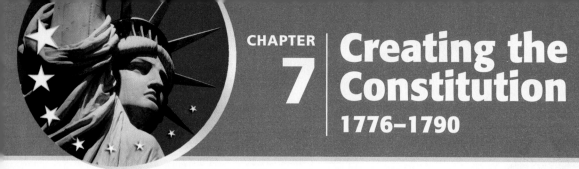

CHAPTER

7 | Creating the Constitution
1776–1790

Chapter Preview

In 1776, the 13 colonies declared their independence from Britain. In the American Revolution, they fought a long, hard battle for freedom. Now they faced another challenge. They had to find a new form of government to replace British rule.

☑ What You Will Learn

Weaknesses in the Articles of Confederation convinced leading Americans that the country needed a strong central government.

After months of intense debate, delegates to the Constitutional Convention agreed on a new plan of government.

The states approved the Constitution, but many of the states insisted that it also include a bill of rights.

The Constitution

U.S. Events

1777
Congress adopts Articles of Confederation.

1781
Articles of Confederation approved by last of 13 states.

1776

1780

1784

World Events

1778 France and United States sign treaty of alliance.

Discovery SCHOOL

Quick View Video
View the chapter video for a quick preview of the main ideas.

Proud of their new nation, American artisans wove this rug featuring important patriotic symbols.

1786
Shays' Rebellion breaks out in Massachusetts.

1787
Constitutional Convention creates new plan of government.

1791
Bill of Rights goes into effect.

1784

1788

1792

1789 French Revolution begins.

1793 Emperor of China rejects British trade.

History Reading Skill **Analyze Propositions and Support**

What arguments had been used to support the American Revolution?

In this chapter, you will learn how to analyze propositions—arguments—and the evidence used to support them.

Primary Source

A leader in the American Revolution, Patrick Henry, argued on the eve of that conflict that England was readying itself for war despite colonial efforts to resolve the problems through diplomacy.

Ask yourselves . . . [about] . . . these warlike preparations which cover our waters and darken our land. Are fleets and armies necessary to a work of love and reconciliation? Have we shown ourselves so unwilling to be reconciled, that force must be called in to win back our love? Let us not deceive ourselves, sir. These are implements of war and subjugation; the last arguments to which kings resort. I ask gentlemen, sir, what means this martial array, if its purpose be not to be to force us into submission? Can gentlemen assign any other possible motives for it? Has Great Britain any enemy, in this quarter of the world, to call for all this accumulation of navies and armies? No, sir, she has none. They are meant for us; they can be meant for no other. . . .

. . . Beside, sir, we have no election [choice]. If we were base enough to desire it, it is now too late to retire from the contest. There is no retreat but in submission and slavery! Our chains are forged! . . . The war is inevitable—and let it come! I repeat it, sir, let it come!

— Patrick Henry, speech to the Second Virginia Convention, March 23, 1775

> These questions support Henry's argument.

> Henry sees that England is massing troops in the colonies and proposes that England is preparing to fight its colonies.

> Here, Henry states the problem that war is unavoidable and proposes that the colonies must prepare for it.

> These are the supporting reasons for Henry's views.

Analyze Propositions and Support

- Ask yourself what problems Patrick Henry identifies and what he proposes in response to those problems.
- Evaluate Henry's propositions and support. Does he support his propositions convincingly? Do you agree with them?

Document-Based Questions

1. When was this speech given?
2. What events were taking place in Massachusetts around this time?
3. What action do you think Henry wants the Virginia Convention to take?

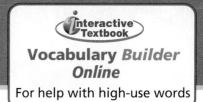

Vocabulary *Builder*

Previewing High-Use Academic Words

High-Use Word	Definition	Sample History Sentence
minimize (MIHN ah mīz) (Section 1, p. 204)	*v.* to reduce to the lowest possible amount	To <u>minimize</u> the chances of rebellion, England sent troops to the colonies.
devise (dee vīz) (Section 1, p. 206)	*v.* to think up an idea for something and figure out how it will work	Athens was the first city-state to <u>devise</u> a system of direct democracy.
contrast (KAHN trast) (Section 2, p. 214)	*n.* difference	In <u>contrast</u> with previous European explorers, Columbus sailed westward across the Atlantic Ocean.
emotion (ee MOH shuhn) (Section 2, p. 214)	*n.* strong feeling about something or someone	The people of Massachusetts reacted with <u>emotion</u> when they heard of the Boston Massacre.
flexible (FLEHKS ah bahl) (Section 3, p. 221)	*adj.* able to change	The Puritans of Massachusetts found it difficult to be <u>flexible</u> on religious matters.
amendment (ah MEHND mehnt) (Section 3, p. 221)	*n.* addition or alteration to a document	The Twenty-sixth <u>Amendment</u> allows citizens who are 18 years old to vote in state and national elections.

James Wilson

Previewing Key Terms and People

constitution, p. 204
executive, p. 205
economic depression, p. 208
Daniel Shays, p. 209
James Madison, p. 213
judicial branch, p. 213
Roger Sherman, p. 214

James Wilson, p. 214
compromise, p. 214
Gouverneur Morris, p. 217

ratify, p. 218
Alexander Hamilton, p. 218
John Jay, p. 218
George Mason, p. 219

Roger Sherman

Governing a New Nation

Objectives

1. Discuss the ideas that guided the new state governments.

2. Describe the government under the Articles of Confederation.

3. Explain the Ordinances of 1785 and 1787 and their importance to westward expansion.

4. Identify the problems created by a weak central government.

Prepare to Read

Reading Skill

Identify Propositions The study of history often takes you inside important debates and arguments over ideas and actions. People argue—or propose—their ideas and then give reasons to support those ideas. Identifying those propositions will help you to understand the beliefs and experiences of people in an earlier time. One way to identify propositions is to ask yourself what problems people had and how they proposed solving those problems.

Vocabulary *Builder*

High-Use Words

minimize, p. 204

devise, p. 206

Key Terms and People

constitution, p. 204

executive, p. 205

economic depression, p. 208

Daniel Shays, p. 209

⭐ **Background Knowledge** You have read about the causes of the American Revolution. Leaders of the new nation remembered what they had hated about British rule. They had seen how the king and Parliament in faraway England had exerted power over elected colonial legislatures. Americans sought instead to create a republic in which the states had more power than the central government.

Main Idea
The first state constitutions were designed to support the principles fought for in the American Revolution.

Government by the States

As the Continental Congress began moving toward independence in 1776, leaders in the individual states began creating governments. Eleven of the 13 states wrote new constitutions to support their governments. A **constitution** is a document stating the rules under which a government will operate. The other two states—Rhode Island and Connecticut—kept using their colonial charters. However, they removed all references to the British king.

Writing State Constitutions In writing state constitutions, Americans were well aware of the problems that had led to the Revolution. Colonists had been unhappy with governors appointed by the British Crown. Thus, the new constitutions <u>minimized</u> the powers of state governors. Instead, they gave most of the power to state legislatures elected by the people.

Vocabulary *Builder*
minimize (MIHN ah mīz) *v.* to reduce to the lowest possible amount

The governor served as the state's executive. In a government, the **executive** is the person who runs the government and sees that the laws are carried out. Governors appointed key state officials, but usually the legislature had to approve the appointments.

The new constitutions allowed more people to vote than in colonial times. Nonetheless, all but a few states barred African Americans (including those who were free) from voting. New Jersey allowed some women to vote until 1807, but women could not vote in any other state. In order to vote, white males had to be 21 or older. In most states, they also had to own a certain amount of property.

Protecting Rights The Declaration of Independence listed ways that Britain had violated the rights of colonists. To prevent such abuses, states sought to protect individual rights. Virginia was the first state to include a bill of rights in its constitution. Virginia's list included freedom of the press and the right to trial by jury, and it also barred "cruel and unusual punishments." The final clause guaranteed freedom of religion:

> “That religion, or the duty which we owe to our Creator, and the manner of discharging it, can be directed only by reason and conviction, not by force or violence; and therefore all men are equally entitled to the free exercise of religion, according to the dictates of conscience.”
>
> —Virginia Bill of Rights, 1776

Many other states followed Virginia's lead. For example, the New York state constitution also included a bill of rights that guaranteed freedom of religion:

> “This convention doth further, in the name and by the authority of the good people of this State, ordain, determine, and declare, that the free exercise and enjoyment of religious profession and worship, without discrimination or preference, shall forever hereafter be allowed, within this State, to all mankind.”
>
> —New York Constitution of 1777

Massachusetts also included freedom of religion in its bill of rights. However, Massachusetts did retain its official church. Massachusetts's bill of rights declared that people have the freedom to worship as they please, so long as they did not disturb the public peace or interfere with other people's freedom of worship.

☑**Checkpoint** Why did many state constitutions limit the power of state governors?

Protecting Rights
Virginia included a bill of rights in its constitution. The Virginia bill of rights became a model for other states and, later, for the national Constitution. **Critical Thinking: Link Past and Present** *Which protections in the Virginia bill of rights are enjoyed by all Americans today?*

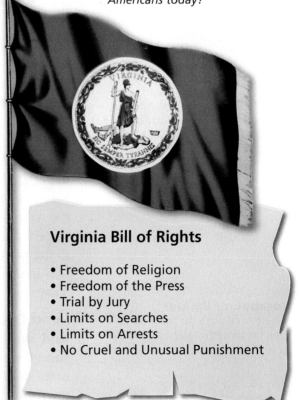

Virginia Bill of Rights

- Freedom of Religion
- Freedom of the Press
- Trial by Jury
- Limits on Searches
- Limits on Arrests
- No Cruel and Unusual Punishment

Main Idea
The Articles of Confederation
were designed to preserve
liberty by restricting the powers
of the federal government.

The Articles of Confederation

While the states were writing their constitutions, the Continental Congress created a plan for the nation as a whole. It was called the Articles of Confederation. Congress adopted the Articles in 1777.

Form of Government Instead of having three branches of government like those of most states, the government under the Articles had just one branch—a one-house legislature, called Congress. There was no executive and no system of national courts.

Within Congress, all states would be equal and each had a single vote. Moreover, for the most important matters, nine states had to agree before a law could go into effect.

Limited Government The framers of the Articles of Confederation kept in mind their complaints against Britain. Parliament had passed laws the colonists considered unfair. The new states did not want to risk giving too much power to a central government far from the people. Thus, the Articles provided for a limited central government.

Under the Articles, most power remained in the hands of the states. Congress could not regulate trade or collect taxes. Instead, it had to ask the states for the money it needed.

Congress did have some powers under the Articles. It could deal with foreign nations and with Native Americans outside the 13 states. It could make laws, declare war, coin or borrow money, and run a postal service. However, the national government had no power to enforce the laws that it made. For that, it depended on the states.

Identify Propositions
What issues concerned the framers when they were drafting the Articles of Confederation? What did they propose in response?

☑**Checkpoint** How did the Articles of Confederation ensure the power of the states?

Main Idea
The ordinances of 1785 and 1787
created a way for national lands
to be sold to the public.

Settling the Western Lands

The Articles had to be approved by all 13 states. But some states would not give their approval until other states dropped their claims to vast areas of land west of the Appalachian Mountains. It took years to get all the states to give up their claims to western lands. In 1781, Virginia was the final state to agree. Only then did Maryland approve the Articles of Confederation, the final state to do so.

The western lands that the states had given up were turned over to the national government. They proved to be very valuable. Land was in great demand. It could be sold off, piece by piece, to private companies seeking to develop western settlements.

Land Ordinance of 1785 Congress had to <u>devise</u> a system for land sales and settlement. Under the Land Ordinance of 1785, surveyors were to divide public lands into townships, 6 miles on each side. This would result in a grid of squares. Within each township there would also be a grid, 1 mile on each side. These 36 sections would be sold for no less than $1 an acre.

Vocabulary *Builder*
<u>devise</u> (dee vīz) *v.* to think up an idea for something and figure out how it will work

Within each township, one section was set aside to support schools. This reflected the belief of the nation's leaders that democracy depended on education. Thomas Jefferson later wrote:

"If a nation expects to be ignorant and free, in a state of civilization, it expects what never was and never will be."

—Thomas Jefferson, letter to Charles Yancey, 1816

Northwest Ordinance of 1787 Investors were eager to buy land in the Northwest Territory, north of the Ohio River. They pressed Congress to determine how this area would be governed. In response, Congress passed the Northwest Ordinance of 1787. It guaranteed basic rights for settlers and banned slavery there.

The Northwest Ordinance set a three-step process for admitting new states. When a territory was just starting to be settled, Congress would appoint a governor, a secretary, and three judges. Once the territory had 5,000 free adult male settlers, it could elect a legislature. When the free population reached 60,000, the territory could ask to become a state. In time, five states—Ohio, Indiana, Illinois, Michigan, and Wisconsin—were carved out of the Northwest Territory. (For more on the settling of the Northwest Territory, see the Geography and History feature.)

✓**Checkpoint** How did the two ordinances turn national land into private holdings?

Western Land Claims

MAP MASTER
Skills Activity

By 1783, several states claimed land west of the Appalachian Mountains.

(a) Read a Map Key Which states had disputed land claims with New York? With North Carolina?

(b) Make Predictions Based on this map, how might western land claims threaten national unity?

MapMaster Online
For: Interactive map
Visit: PHSchool.com
Web Code: myp-2031

KEY
- Original 13 states
- Areas claimed
- (1784) Date ceded to the United States

0 km 500
0 miles 500
Albers Conic Equal-Area Projection

207

Shays' Rebellion
Abigail Adams called the leaders of Shays' Rebellion "ignorant, restless desperadoes without conscience or principles." However, many felt that the Massachusetts farmers had good reason for their anger. Here, farmers attack the Massachusetts statehouse.
Critical Thinking: *Analyze Cause and Effect*
What was the main cause of Shays' Rebellion?

Main Idea
The Articles of Confederation denied the central government the power to deal effectively with several key issues facing the nation.

Growing Problems

Under the Articles of Confederation, the United States had many successes. It waged a successful war for independence, negotiated a peace treaty with Britain, and set up rules for settling new territories. But the United States faced growing problems during the 1780s. Many Americans concluded that the Articles did not give the government enough power to solve these problems.

Economic Problems Under the Articles, each state set its own trade policy. Each state tried to help its own farmers and manufacturers by setting taxes on goods brought in from other states. This practice discouraged trade among the states. In addition, each state printed its own money, making trade between states harder.

Another problem grew from the fact that the central government did not have the power to tax. As a result, there was little money to run the government. The situation grew more desperate every year.

Foreign Affairs Because the United States seemed to be weak, powerful nations viewed it with scorn. British troops continued to occupy forts in the Northwest Territory, although the peace treaty required that the forts be turned over to the United States. The Spanish, who controlled New Orleans, refused to let Americans ship products down the Mississippi River. Therefore, western farmers had to send products along the rugged trails over the Appalachian Mountains, which was far more costly.

Shays' Rebellion In the mid-1780s, a severe economic depression hit the United States. An **economic depression** is a period when business activity slows, prices and wages drop, and unemployment rises. As the depression deepened, there was widespread despair and anger.

The depression hit farmers in Massachusetts especially hard. As crop prices declined, many were unable to pay their taxes. The state government then began seizing some farms and selling them in order to get the back taxes. Angry farmers demanded that the legislature stop the farm sales. They also demanded that the state issue more paper money to make it easier to get loans. Still, the legislators took no action.

In August 1786, a former Revolutionary War captain named Daniel Shays led an uprising of about 1,000 Massachusetts farmers. When the farmers tried to seize arms from a state warehouse, the state called out the militia. Shays and other leaders were arrested.

Although Shays' Rebellion fizzled, it had frightened some leading Americans. They believed that a stronger central government would protect against popular unrest. In response, Congress asked the states to send delegates to a convention in Philadelphia in 1787. Their task was to revise the Articles of Confederation.

✓**Checkpoint** **What did Shays' Rebellion demonstrate about the strength of the national government under the Articles of Confederation?**

⭐ **Looking Back and Ahead** After 10 years of independence, some leading Americans had come to the conclusion that the Articles of Confederation needed improvement. The Philadelphia convention was called to revise the Articles. But were the Articles of Confederation worth saving? Or was an entirely new framework required? This decision would be one of the first issues that the delegates at the Philadelphia convention would confront.

Section 1 | **Check Your Progress**

Progress Monitoring ⏺nline
For: Self-test with instant help
Visit: PHSchool.com
Web Code: mya-2031

Comprehension and Critical Thinking

1. (a) Recall Why did the Continental Congress make the federal government weak when it drew up the Articles of Confederation?
(b) Explain Problems Why did foreign powers treat the U.S. government under the Articles of Confederation with scorn?

2. (a) Recall Why was a section of public land set aside to support public schools under the Land Ordinance of 1785?
(b) Analyze Cause and Effect How does education contribute to a successful democracy?

🔄 **Reading Skill**

3. Identify Propositions Reread the text following the heading "Land Ordinance of 1785." What belief did the nation's leaders have about education? What did they propose to further this belief?

Vocabulary *Builder*

Fill in the blanks with the correct key terms.
4. After the break with Britain, each of the states wrote a new _____, a framework for the state government.

5. The _____ is the person in a government responsible for carrying out the laws.
6. In the 1780s, when business slowed and unemployment rose, the nation entered a period of _____.

Writing

7. Identify two problems caused by the creation of a weak national government under the Articles of Confederation. Write a sentence about each problem, explaining why it was important that it be solved.

Settling the Northwest Territory

By the end of the American Revolution, the United States had acquired a vast territory west of the Appalachian Mountains. Congress passed two land ordinances, one in 1785 and another in 1787. The ordinances served as a framework for moving settlers into—and forming states out of—this Northwest Territory. The states of Ohio, Indiana, Illinois, Michigan, Wisconsin, and part of Minnesota were eventually carved out of the expanse.

NORTHWEST TERRITORY WITH PRESENT-DAY STATE BOUNDARIES

▲ A New Organization

The Land Ordinance of 1785 established a system for settling the Northwest Territory. Surveyors laid out a grid of lines spaced 6 miles apart. These lines marked off townships. Each township was divided into 36 sections, and these 1-mile square sections could be divided into smaller units for sale to farmers.

1 mile

1 mile

Half Section
320 Acres

Quarter
Section
160 Acres

6	5	4	3	2	1
7	8	9	10	11	12
18	17	16*	15	14	13
19	20	21	22	23	24
30	29	28	27	26	25
31	32	33	34	35	36

6 miles

6 miles

* Income reserved to support schools

Understand Effects:
Slavery and the Northwest Ordinance

Congress banned slavery in the Northwest Territory in 1787. Eventually, five free states were formed from the territory. Decades later, the balance between free states and slave states would lead to a national crisis.

▼ An Enduring Landscape

The grid established more than 200 years ago remains the basis for land division across the Midwest. Many roads and property lines still follow the straight lines and right angles the original surveyors laid out.

▲ Support for Education

The 1785 ordinance set aside one section in every township to support public schools. Lands were often reserved for school buildings like the one shown here.

Analyze **GEOGRAPHY AND HISTORY**

Write a pamphlet recruiting settlers to live in the Northwest Territory.

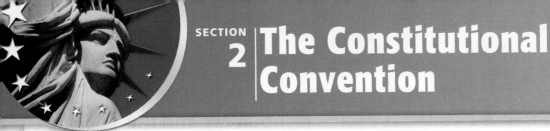

Objectives

1. Describe the proceedings of the Constitutional Convention.

2. Identify the specifics of the Virginia Plan.

3. Explain how the Great Compromise satisfied both large and small states.

4. Describe the disputes over slavery and the compromises that were reached.

5. Discuss the drafting of the new Constitution.

Prepare to Read

Reading Skill

Identify Support for Propositions As you read about the propositions that people from history made to solve their problems and advance their ideas, look for supporting evidence. How did people try to convince those around them to support these propositions? What reasons did they give to explain their views? Identifying supporting evidence helps you understand and respond to propositions.

Vocabulary *Builder*

High-Use Words

contrast, p. 214

emotion, p. 214

Key Terms and People

James Madison, p. 213

judicial branch, p. 213

Roger Sherman, p. 214

James Wilson, p. 214

compromise, p. 214

Gouverneur Morris, p. 217

⭐ **Background Knowledge** In Section 1, you learned that many Americans worried about the weaknesses of the Articles of Confederation. These weaknesses prompted the states to call a meeting in Philadelphia to revise the Articles. In this section, you will learn how the Constitutional Convention instead led to the creation of an entirely new framework of government.

Main Idea

The original aim of the Constitutional Convention was to revise the Articles of Confederation.

The Constitutional Convention Begins

An air of mystery hung over Philadelphia in the summer of 1787. Every day, the nation's great leaders passed in and out of the statehouse. One Philadelphia resident, Susannah Dillwyn, wrote to her father, "There is now sitting in this city a grand convention, who are to form some new system of government or mend the old one."

Aims of the Convention In fact, members of the convention did not have the authority to "form some new system of government." Congress had called the meeting "for the sole and express purpose of revising the Articles of Confederation." However, many delegates argued that revising the Articles would not be enough.

Early on, the delegates voted to keep their debates secret. Despite the heat, windows remained tightly shut. Guards kept out members of the public. The delegates would be free to speak their minds—even if their discussions took the convention far beyond its original aims.

The Delegates In all, 55 delegates from 12 states took part in the convention. Only Rhode Island did not send any representatives.

Some delegates, such as George Washington and Ben Franklin, had been respected leaders of the Revolution. Washington was quickly voted president of the convention. Most delegates, however, were younger. Alexander Hamilton of New York was only 32. Another influential delegate was 36-year-old James Madison of Virginia. Madison took careful notes on the meetings. Published after his death, Madison's notes became a rich source of historical information.

☑Checkpoint **Why did delegates to the Constitutional Convention keep their debates secret?**

The Virginia Plan

On the third day of the convention, Edmund Randolph of Virginia proposed a plan for a new, strong central government. James Madison was the principal author of this Virginia Plan. For the next month, debate focused on this proposal.

Three Branches of Government The Virginia Plan called for the central government to have three separate branches. Congress would continue to be the legislative branch. But two additional branches would be created. The executive branch would carry out the laws. The judicial branch would consist of a system of courts to interpret the law.

Many delegates believed that a strong executive was necessary to correct the weaknesses of the Articles of Confederation. But should the executive be one person or a group of people?

Main Idea
The Virginia Plan set forth an entirely new framework for the national government.

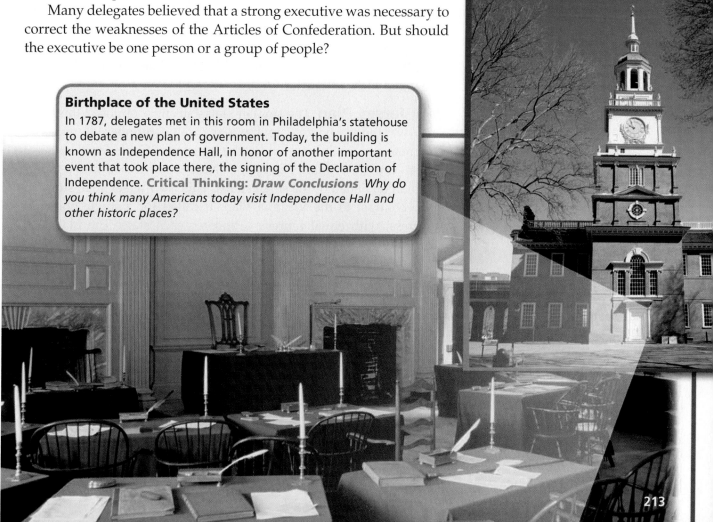

Birthplace of the United States

In 1787, delegates met in this room in Philadelphia's statehouse to debate a new plan of government. Today, the building is known as Independence Hall, in honor of another important event that took place there, the signing of the Declaration of Independence. **Critical Thinking:** *Draw Conclusions* *Why do you think many Americans today visit Independence Hall and other historic places?*

James Wilson

Randolph proposed that Congress appoint three people to serve jointly as chief executive. One person alone, he said, would never be able to win the people's confidence. Others objected. A single executive, they said, could act more quickly when urgent action was required. Eventually, the delegates voted to have one person, called the President, serve as executive.

A Two-House Legislature The Virginia Plan called for a change in the composition of Congress. Rather than a single legislative body, it would consist of two parts—a lower house and an upper house.

Delegates argued long and hard about methods of choosing members of the two houses. Some wanted state legislatures to elect both houses. Roger Sherman of Connecticut said the people "should have as little to do" with the selection process as possible because they can be misled.

On the other hand, James Wilson of Pennsylvania warned against shutting the people out of the process. According to Wilson, election of the legislature by the people was "not only the cornerstone, but the foundation of the fabric."

☑**Checkpoint** How was the national government organized under the Virginia Plan?

Main Idea
After fierce debate, delegates agreed on a plan that satisfied both large and small states.

The Great Compromise

One part of the Virginia Plan nearly tore the convention apart. The plan called for representation based on population. The more people a state had, the more seats it would have in each house. Naturally, this idea drew support from big states like Virginia, Pennsylvania, and Massachusetts.

New Jersey Plan The smaller states strongly opposed this idea. They wanted each state to have the same number of votes in Congress, as was the case under the Articles of Confederation.

On June 15, William Paterson of New Jersey introduced a modified plan on behalf of the small states. This New Jersey Plan stood in sharp <u>contrast</u> to the Virginia Plan. It called for a single house of Congress, with equal representation for each state. The plan also expanded the powers of Congress to raise money and regulate commerce.

In the summer heat, delegates argued day after day over the great issues at stake. <u>Emotions</u> ran so high that some feared the convention would fail and the Union would break apart.

Vocabulary *Builder*
<u>contrast</u> (KAHN trast) *n.* difference

Vocabulary *Builder*
<u>emotion</u> (ee MOH shuhn) *n.* strong feeling about something or someone

Terms of the Compromise Finally, Roger Sherman of Connecticut worked out a compromise that he hoped would satisfy both the large and small states. A **compromise** is an agreement in which each side gives up part of what it wants. On July 16, 1787, delegates narrowly voted to accept Sherman's proposals, which came to be known as the Great Compromise.

The key to Sherman's plan was a two-house Congress. To please the large states, the lower house, called the House of Representatives, was to be based on population. Bigger states would thus have more votes. Representatives would be chosen by a vote of the people to serve two-year terms. To please the small states, each state would have two seats in the upper house, or Senate. State legislatures would choose senators, who would serve six-year terms.

The Great Compromise was a vital step in creating a new Constitution. Now, small-state delegates were willing to support a strong central government.

✓ **Checkpoint** **What was the main difference between the Virginia Plan and the New Jersey Plan?**

Debates Over Slavery

Other issues also divided the delegates—none more so than the question of slavery. The issue touched off bitter debates between northerners and southerners.

Three-Fifths Compromise Southern delegates said that enslaved people should be counted in calculating how many representatives a state should have in Congress. Northern delegates said that because enslaved people could not vote, they should not be counted toward a state's representation.

Finally, Congress agreed to a plan called the Three-Fifths Compromise. Each enslaved person would be counted as three fifths of a free person. Thus, 500 enslaved people would count as 300 free people. The Three-Fifths Compromise was a gain for the South, which got more seats in the House. Northern delegates reluctantly agreed in order to keep the South in the Union.

The Three-Fifths Compromise was a blow to African Americans. It helped preserve slavery in the new Constitution by making a distinction between "free persons" and "all other persons." The compromise was finally overturned when slavery was banned in 1865.

Slave Trade Some northern delegates wanted to ban the buying and selling of people anywhere in the country. Southern delegates protested that a ban would ruin the South's economy.

Once again, a compromise was reached. Ships would be allowed to bring enslaved people into the country for a period of 20 years. After 1808, Congress could bar the importation of enslaved people. But the slave trade *within* the United States was not affected.

✓ **Checkpoint** **What was the Three-Fifths Compromise?**

Identify Support for Propositions
Roger Sherman proposed a two-house Congress, hoping to satisfy both small and large states. What support did he give to show how this solution would meet the needs of all states?

Main Idea
Disputes among the delegates over slavery indicated just how deeply divided the North and the South were.

Links Across Time

Slavery and the Constitution

1787 Slavery was the "unfinished business" of the Constitutional Convention. Compromises postponed the debate over the issue.

1861–1865 Growing disputes between the North and the South finally led to the bloody Civil War. Slavery was banned—and erased from the Constitution—by the Thirteenth Amendment in 1865.

Link to Today

Compromise Today Congress still debates many difficult and troubling issues. What compromises do they reach?

For: Congressional debates in the news
Visit: PHSchool.com
Web Code: myc-2032

Signing the CONSTITUTION

In his *Signing of the Constitution*, painter Howard Chandler Christy captured the moment on September 17, 1787, when delegates signed the historic document that has guided our government for more than 200 years.

1 **Roger Sherman** helped draft the Great Compromise that determined how states would be represented in Congress. After months of bitter debate, the compromise satisfied both large and small states.

2 **George Washington** was voted president of the meeting. His firm leadership held the convention together when it seemed close to breaking up.

3 **Benjamin Franklin,** though frail and ailing, was one of the convention's most respected delegates. At the end, he wrote a masterful speech supporting the Constitution.

4 **James Madison** wrote much of the Constitution and led the fight to get it approved by the states. He is often called the Father of the Constitution.

▶ **The Constitution**

Critical Thinking: *Interpret Paintings*
How does the artist draw attention to certain Framers?

A New Constitution

Main Idea
The Constitution of the United States derives its authority from "We the People of the United States."

After many more weeks of debate, the delegates agreed on all the terms. A so-called Committee of Style was appointed to draw up the final wording of the new Constitution. Gouverneur Morris, a gifted writer, was largely responsible for writing the Preamble, or introduction.

The Preamble highlights a major difference between the Constitution and the Articles of Confederation. The Articles were a pact between separate states. By contrast, the Constitution opens with the words, "We the People of the United States, in order to form a more perfect union, . . . do ordain and establish this Constitution for the United States of America." The Constitution thus claims to take its authority from the people rather than from the states.

The aging Ben Franklin gave some final advice on the day of the signing. Because he was so ill, Franklin remained seated and another delegate read Franklin's speech. Like many other delegates, Franklin had some doubts about parts of the Constitution. Still, he said, "I agree to this Constitution with all its faults," and he urged others to do the same. At last, the delegates stepped forward to place their signatures on the document.

☑Checkpoint **What is the significance of the Constitution's first phrase: "We the People of the United States"?**

⭐ **Looking Back and Ahead** Once the Constitution had been signed, secrecy ended. Public debates began. These debates would stretch over 10 months. And, as the Constitution's supporters soon learned, the battle for approval would be hard-fought and bitter.

Section 2 | Check Your Progress

Progress Monitoring Online
For: Self-test with instant help
Visit: PHSchool.com
Web Code: mya-2032

Comprehension and Critical Thinking

1. (a) Summarize Summarize the arguments for and against having a single executive.
(b) Explain Problems What problems do you think might arise during a crisis if the executive power in the U.S. government was held by three people?

2. (a) Describe How was representation in Congress to be based, according to the terms of the Great Compromise?
(b) Apply Information Why did the small states decide to support a strong central government after the compromise?

Reading Skill

3. Identify Support for Propositions Reread the text following the heading "Slave Trade." What reason did southerners give to support their position against ending the slave trade?

Vocabulary *Builder*

Fill in the blanks with the correct key terms.
4. The Virginia Plan called for a _____, or system of courts to interpret the law.

5. Under a _____ between northern and southern states, Congress could bar slaves from being imported after 1808.

Writing

6. Choose one of the problems that the delegates at the Constitutional Convention had to solve. List several possible solutions for that problem, and then write a few sentences explaining the solution that the convention eventually chose. What were the advantages and disadvantages of this solution?

Debating the Constitution

Objectives

1. Compare the positions of the Federalists and the Antifederalists.

2. Discuss the debate over ratification.

3. Describe the Bill of Rights and how it protects the people.

Prepare to Read

 Reading Skill

Evaluate Support for Propositions When a person argues a proposition using reasons and support, listeners or readers must evaluate that support—that is, whether the evidence given really supports the proposition. As you read, ask yourself if the propositions are well supported and whether or not they convince you.

Vocabulary *Builder*

High-Use Words

flexible, p. 221

amendment, p. 221

Key Terms and People

ratify, p. 218

Alexander Hamilton, p. 218

John Jay, p. 218

George Mason, p. 219

⭐ **Background Knowledge** As you have read, the original purpose of the 1787 convention had been to revise the Articles of Confederation. Instead, the delegates produced an entirely new frame of government. How would the states greet the new Constitution?

Main Idea
Supporters and opponents of the new Constitution argued over the need for a strong central government.

Federalists Versus Antifederalists

The convention had set a process for states to ratify, or approve, the Constitution. Each state was to hold a convention. The Constitution would go into effect once it was ratified by nine states.

The Federalist Position Supporters of the new Constitution called themselves Federalists because they favored a strong federal, or national, government. James Madison, Alexander Hamilton, and John Jay published the *Federalist Papers,* a series of 85 newspaper essays in support of the Constitution.

At the heart of the Federalist position was the need for a stronger central government. For the Union to last, they argued, the national government had to have powers denied to it under the Articles of Confederation, including the power to enforce laws. Hamilton wrote:

Evaluate Support for Propositions
How does Hamilton support the proposition that the national government needed more powers?

    ❝Government implies the power of making laws. It is essential to the idea of a law, that it be attended with . . . a penalty or punishment for disobedience. If there be no penalty . . . the resolutions or commands which pretend to be laws will, in fact, amount to nothing more than advice.❞

    —Alexander Hamilton, *The Federalist* No. 15

The Antifederalist Position Opponents of ratification were called Antifederalists. Leading Antifederalists, such as George Mason and Patrick Henry of Virginia, agreed that the Articles of Confederation were not strong enough. However, they felt the Constitutional Convention had gone too far.

Antifederalists were not all united in their reasons for opposing the Constitution. Some of their most frequent arguments included:

- **Weakening the States** Antifederalists argued that the Constitution dangerously weakened the state governments. They feared that a too-strong central government, like that of England, would wipe out state power and individual freedom. "There never was a government over a very extensive country without destroying the liberties of the people," warned Mason.

- **No Bill of Rights** Some Antifederalists pointed out that the proposed Constitution offered no protections for basic freedoms. Unlike the constitutions of many states, it had no bill of rights.

- **President or King?** Another objection was that the Constitution provided for a President who could be reelected again and again. Said Henry, "Your President may easily become a king."

Biography Quest

George Mason
1725–1792

The author of Virginia's bill of rights, George Mason, went to the Constitutional Convention with hopes of forming "a wise and just government." But Mason quickly became dissatisfied. Though a slave owner himself, he favored an end to slavery and disliked the Three-Fifths Compromise. Mason was even more upset when the convention voted against his proposal to add a bill of rights. In the end, he refused to sign his name to the new Constitution.

Biography Quest **nline**

Why is Mason called "the father of the Bill of Rights"?

For: The answer to the question about Mason

Visit: PHSchool.com

Web Code: myd-2033

☑**Checkpoint** Why did Antifederalists believe that the Constitutional Convention had gone too far?

The Ratification Debate

The debate between Federalists and Antifederalists heated up as states held their ratification conventions. Without the approval of nine states, the Constitution would not go into effect.

Delaware acted first. Its convention unanimously approved the Constitution on December 7, 1787. Pennsylvania, New Jersey, Georgia, and Connecticut quickly followed.

Antifederalists hoped to win in Massachusetts. Opposition to the Constitution was strong in the rural areas from which Shays' Rebellion had drawn its strength. Only a major campaign by Constitution supporters won ratification by the state.

All eyes moved to Virginia. By then, Maryland and South Carolina had ratified, which made a total of eight state ratifications. Only one more was needed. But if large and powerful Virginia rejected the pact, New York and other remaining states might do so, too.

Main Idea
After intense debates, each of the 13 states ratified the Constitution.

United We Stand . . .

United we stand—Divided we fall

A hand reaches from the heavens to put Virginia in place.

New Hampshire was the ninth state to ratify, allowing the Constitution to go into effect.

Reading Political Cartoons
Skills Activity

The cartoon above appeared in an American newspaper in 1788—at a time when the states were debating whether or not to ratify the Constitution.

(a) **Identify Main Ideas** What do the pillars represent? Which pillar is first? What pillars are missing?

(b) **Detect Points of View** Do you think the cartoonist favored the Federalists or the Antifederalists?

Patrick Henry led the attack on the Constitution in Virginia. "There will be no checks, no real balances, in this government," he said. James Madison supported the Constitution and warned of the possible breakup of the Union. In the end, the Federalist view narrowly won out. Virginia's convention approved the Constitution by a vote of 89 to 79.

Meanwhile, in June 1788—while Virginia was still debating—New Hampshire became the ninth state to ratify. The Constitution could now go into effect. In time, New York and North Carolina followed. Finally, in May 1790, Rhode Island became the last of the original 13 states to ratify the Constitution.

On July 4, 1788, Philadelphia celebrated the ratification of the Constitution. A huge parade snaked along Market Street, led by soldiers who had served in the Revolution. Benjamin Rush, a Philadelphia doctor and strong supporter of the Constitution, wrote to a friend, "Tis done. We have become a nation."

✓**Checkpoint** Why was the vote in Virginia so important?

Main Idea
The Bill of Rights aims to protect Americans against unfair use of government powers.

The Bill of Rights

Once the ninth state had ratified the Constitution, Congress took steps to prepare for a new government. George Washington was elected the first President, with John Adams as Vice President.

During the debate on the Constitution, many of the states had insisted that a bill of rights be added. This became one of the first tasks of the new Congress that met in March 1789.

The Framers had provided a way to amend the Constitution. They wanted to make the Constitution <u>flexible</u> enough to change. But they did not want changes made lightly. So, they made the process fairly difficult. (You will read more about the amendment process in the Citizenship Handbook.)

In 1789, the first Congress passed a series of <u>amendments</u>. By December 1791, three fourths of the states had ratified 10 amendments. These amendments are known as the Bill of Rights. The Bill of Rights aims to protect people against abuses by the federal government. Many of them came out of the colonists' struggle with Britain.

The First Amendment guarantees freedom of religion, speech, and the press. The Second Amendment deals with the right to bear arms. The Third Amendment bars Congress from forcing citizens to keep troops in their homes, as Britain had done.

The Fourth Amendment protects citizens from unreasonable searches of their homes or seizure of their property. Amendments Five through Eight protect citizens who are accused of crimes and are brought to trial. The last two amendments limit the powers of the federal government to those that are granted in the Constitution.

✓**Checkpoint** **Why did Congress move quickly to pass the Bill of Rights?**

⭐ **Looking Back and Ahead** The delegates to the Constitutional Convention are often called the Framers because they framed, or shaped, our form of government. The Constitution they wrote established a republic that has thrived for more than 200 years. On the following pages, you will read the actual text of the Constitution and study its meaning in more detail.

Vocabulary *Builder*
<u>flexible</u> (FLEHKS ah bahl) *adj.* able to change

<u>amendment</u> (ah MEHND mehnt) *n.* addition or alteration to a document

---

Section 3 | **Check Your Progress**

Progress Monitoring Online
For: Self-test with instant help
Visit: PHSchool.com
Web Code: mya-2033

Comprehension and Critical Thinking

1. (a) Summarize In complete sentences, list three arguments of the Antifederalists against the Constitution.
(b) Draw Conclusions Why might the Antifederalists think the Constitution would reduce the power of the states?

2. (a) Recall Compare the attitudes of Patrick Henry and James Madison toward ratification.
(b) Apply Information How did the passage of the Bill of Rights help deal with Patrick Henry's concerns?

Reading Skill

3. Evaluate Support for Propositions Patrick Henry led the attack on the Constitution. "There will be no checks, no real balances, in this government," he said. Evaluate his supporting argument. Do you think it is an effective argument?

Vocabulary *Builder*

Answer the following question in a complete sentence that shows your understanding of the key term.
4. Why was it important that Virginia ratify the Constitution?

Writing

5. Write a paragraph discussing the Bill of Rights as the solution to a problem faced by the early U.S. government after the Constitution was ratified. Complete the following topic sentence, and then write four more sentences developing this idea with specific information. **Topic sentence:** In 1789, the first Congress passed 10 amendments to the Constitution, known as the Bill of Rights, in order to protect _____.

Major historical events have both causes and effects. Sometimes causes and effects are short term. They take place shortly before or after the major event. Causes and effects can also be long term. They build up over a period of time.

CAUSES
- King George III had limited colonists' liberty.
- America had fought a revolution to protect freedoms.
- Antifederalists wanted a specific list of rights that protected citizens' basic liberties.
- Some states refused to ratify the Constitution unless a bill of rights was added later.

BILL OF RIGHTS ADDED TO CONSTITUTION IN 1791

EFFECTS
- First 10 amendments identify and guarantee basic rights and freedoms.
- The federal government cannot take away rights spelled out in the Bill of Rights.

Learn the Skill
Use these steps to analyze cause-and-effect relationships.

1 **Read labels.** The labels on the chart tell which event is the focus of study and which statements are the causes and which are the effects.

2 **Identify causes.** Causal statements give reasons why an event occurred. Major events have both long- and short-term causes.

3 **Identify effects.** Effect statements tell what happened because of the events. Major events have both long- and short-term effects.

4 **Analyze cause-and-effect relationships.** Think about why certain causes led to the event and why the event in turn had the results it did.

Practice the Skill
Answer the following questions about cause and effect based on the chart above.

1 **Read labels.** To what event do the causes lead?

2 **Identify causes.** (a) What was one cause of the Bill of Rights? (b) Was this a long- or short-term cause? Explain.

3 **Identify effects.** (a) What was one effect of the Bill of Rights? (b) Was this a long- or short-term effect? Explain.

4 **Analyze cause-and-effect relationships.** How did colonial history lead to a concern about protecting citizens' rights?

Apply the Skill
See the Review and Assessment at the end of this chapter.

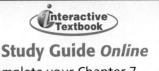

Study Guide *Online*
Complete your Chapter 7 study guide in print or online.

Chapter Summary

Section 1
Governing a New Nation

- Many states added a bill of rights to their constitutions to protect individual freedoms.
- The Northwest Ordinance established a three-stage process for transforming a territory into a state.
- An increasing number of Americans came to believe that a stronger federal government was needed to deal with the country's pressing problems.

Section 2
The Constitutional Convention

- The Virginia Plan, calling for a strong central government with three branches, formed the basis of the U.S. Constitution.
- The Great Compromise set up a Congress with two houses, which pleased both the large and small states.

- As part of the compromise that won support for the Constitution, northern and southern delegates agreed that each enslaved person would count as three fifths of a free person.

Section 3
Debating the Constitution

- Federalists believed that three competing branches of government would keep any one part of the federal government from becoming too strong.
- Antifederalists were concerned that a strong federal government threatened states' rights and individual freedoms.
- A bill of rights was added to the Constitution to protect the people against abuses by the federal government.

Key Concepts

These notes will help you prepare for questions about key concepts.

Weaknesses of the National Government Under the Articles

- No power to tax or regulate trade
- Seen as weak by foreign powers
- Only one branch of government, the Congress
- Congress had few powers
- No means of enforcing its laws
- Unable to put down internal disturbances

Reforms of the National Government by the Constitutional Convention

- Set up three branches of government
- Congress to consist of two houses
- Established a single executive
- Expanded powers to raise money and regulate trade
- Compromise over issues related to slavery
- Constitution based on "we the people," not "we the states"

Federalists Versus Antifederalists

Federalists
- Need a stronger national government

Antifederalists
- Constitutional Convention had no authority to write a new constitution
- Constitution threatens to weaken powers of the states
- No bill of rights to protect individual freedoms
- President may become too powerful

Vocabulary *Builder*

Key Terms

Answer the questions in complete sentences that show your understanding of the key terms.

1. How did the economic depression of the mid-1780s impact farmers?

2. What is the role of the judicial branch in government?

3. What process did the Constitutional Convention set forth for states to ratify the Constitution?

Comprehension and Critical Thinking

4. **(a) Recall** Which powers did the Congress not have under the Articles of Confederation?
(b) Apply Information How did not having these powers make the national government weak?

5. **(a) Recall** List the three stages a territory had to go through to become a state under the Northwest Ordinance of 1787.
(b) Draw Conclusions How did this process help a territory prepare for statehood?

6. **(a) Describe** What were the causes of Shays' Rebellion of 1786?
(b) Detect Points of View Thomas Jefferson called Shays' Rebellion "a medicine necessary for the sound health of government." What do you think he meant?

7. **(a) Contrast** How did the New Jersey Plan differ from the Virginia Plan?
(b) Link Past and Present Which key part of the New Jersey Plan is not part of our Constitution today? Why not?

8. **(a) Recall** Describe one contribution made by each of the following to the writing and ratification of the Constitution: George Washington; James Madison; Roger Sherman; Gouverneur Morris.
(b) Evaluate Information Whose contribution do you think was most important? Give reasons for your answer.

9. **(a) Summarize** Which freedoms and rights are protected in the Bill of Rights?
(b) Draw Conclusions The Bill of Rights limited the powers of the federal government to those granted in the Constitution. Why do you think these limits were included?

History Reading Skill

10. **Analyze Propositions and Support** Reread the text under the heading "The Great Compromise." What did the Virginia Plan propose about representation in Congress? How did delegates from smaller states respond? What support did they give for their different responses? Evaluate that support.

Writing

11. **Write two paragraphs on the following topic:** Explain how the Constitution addressed weaknesses in the Articles of Confederation.
Your paragraphs should:
- include a thesis statement that expresses your main idea;
- develop that main idea with facts, examples, and other information;
- conclude by describing the lasting impact of what happened.

12. **Write a Narrative:**
You are a delegate who has just arrived in Philadelphia in May 1787. Write a letter home explaining your feelings about the upcoming convention.

Skills for Life

Analyze Cause and Effect
Use the information below to answer the questions that follow.

Cause: In 1774, the British Parliament passes an act that forces American colonists to house British troops in their homes.

Event: Bill of Rights, Third Amendment

"No soldier shall, in time of peace, be quartered in any house without the consent of the owner; nor in time of war, but in a manner to be prescribed by law."

---

13. What right does the Third Amendment protect?

14. **(a)** What was one cause of the Third Amendment?
(b) Was this cause long term or short term? Explain.

15. How did the colonists' experiences under British rule influence their decision to change the Constitution?

Test Yourself

1. **The Great Compromise settled a dispute between**

    A the North and the South.

    B Britain and the new United States.

    C the large states and the small states.

    D the President and Congress.

2. **Antifederalists opposed the Constitution because it**

    A did not give the President enough power.

    B weakened the state governments.

    C contained a bill of rights.

    D could not be amended.

Study the political cartoon below to answer Question 3. Consider how it is similar to and different from the cartoon in Section 3.

3. **What event is the creator of this political cartoon celebrating?**

    A the approval of the Constitution

    B the abolition of the slave trade

    C the failure of Shays' Rebellion

    D the passage of the Northwest Ordinance

Document-Based Questions

Task: Look at Documents 1 and 2, and answer their accompanying questions. Then, use the documents and your knowledge of history to complete this writing assignment:

> Write an essay explaining why the writers of the Constitution felt it was necessary to create a new plan of government.

Document 1: This excerpt from the Articles of Confederation defines the limitations on the powers of the national Congress. *According to this excerpt, what is Congress not allowed to do without the consent of the states?*

> "The United States in Congress assembled shall never engage in a war . . . nor coin money, nor regulate the value thereof, nor [spend] the sums and expenses necessary for the defense and welfare of the United States . . . nor borrow money on the credit of the United States . . . nor agree upon the number of vessels of war, to be built or purchased, or the number of land or sea forces to be raised, nor appoint a commander in chief of the army or navy, unless nine States [agree] to the same. . . ."

Document 2: This excerpt from the Constitution defines some of the powers granted to Congress. *Why do you think the Framers of the Constitution gave Congress the power to set standards for weights and measures, rather than leaving it up to each state?*

> **"The Congress shall have power:**
> 1. To lay and collect taxes . . . to pay the debts and provide for the common defense and general welfare of the United States. . . .
> 2. To borrow money on the credit of the United States. . . .
> 3. To coin money, regulate the value thereof, and of foreign coin, and for the standard of weights and measures. . . .
> 4. To declare war. . . .
> 5. To raise and support armies. . . .
> 6. To provide and maintain a navy."

The United States Constitution: An Outline

Original Constitution

Preamble

Article I	Legislative Branch
Section 1	A Two-House Legislature
Section 2	House of Representatives
Section 3	Senate
Section 4	Elections and Meetings
Section 5	Legislative Proceedings
Section 6	Compensation, Immunities, and Disabilities of Members
Section 7	Law-Making Process
Section 8	Powers of Congress
Section 9	Powers Denied to Congress
Section 10	Powers Denied to the States

Article II	Executive Branch
Section 1	President and Vice President
Section 2	Powers of the President
Section 3	Duties of the President
Section 4	Impeachment

Article III	Judicial Branch
Section 1	Courts, Terms of Office
Section 2	Jurisdiction
Section 3	Treason

Article IV	Relations Among the States
Section 1	Full Faith and Credit
Section 2	Privileges and Immunities of Citizens
Section 3	New States and Territories
Section 4	Protection Afforded to States by the Nation

Article V	Provisions for Amendment

Explore More Video
To learn more about the first 10 amendments to the Constitution, view the video.

The Constitution of the United States

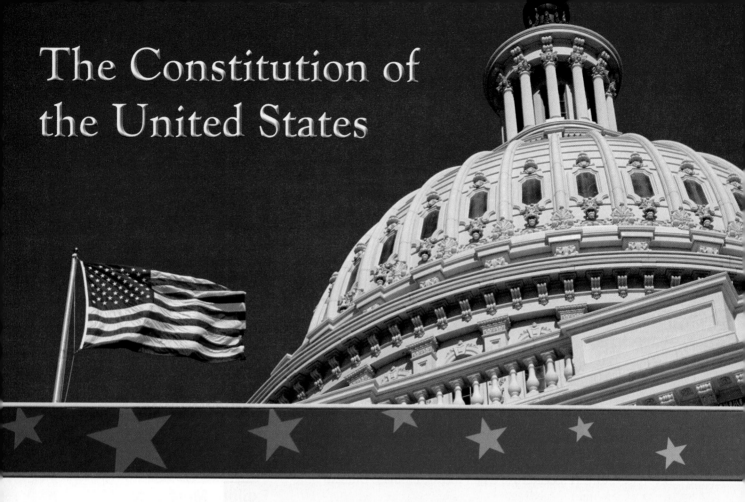

A Note on the Text of the Constitution

The complete text of the Constitution, including amendments, appears on the pages that follow. Spelling, capitalization, and punctuation have been modernized, and headings have been added. Portions of the Constitution altered by later amendments or that no longer apply are printed in blue. Commentary appears in the outside column of each page.

The Preamble The Preamble describes the purpose of the government as set up by the Constitution. Americans expect their government to defend justice and liberty and provide peace and safety from foreign enemies.

Preamble

We the people of the United States, in order to form a more perfect union, establish justice, insure domestic tranquillity, provide for the common defense, promote the general welfare, and secure the blessings of liberty to ourselves and our posterity, do ordain and establish this Constitution for the United States of America.

Article I ★ Legislative Branch

Section 1. A Two-House Legislature

Section 1 The Constitution gives Congress the power to make laws. Congress is divided into the Senate and the House of Representatives.

All legislative powers herein granted shall be vested in a Congress of the United States, which shall consist of a Senate and House of Representatives.

Section 2. House of Representatives

1. Election of Members The House of Representatives shall be composed of members chosen every second year by the people of the several states, and the electors in each state shall have the qualifications requisite for electors of the most numerous branch of the state legislature.

2. Qualifications No person shall be a representative who shall not have attained to the age of twenty-five years, and been seven years a citizen of the United States, and who shall not, when elected, be an inhabitant of that state in which he shall be chosen.

3. Apportionment Representatives and direct taxes shall be apportioned among the several states which may be included within this Union, according to their respective numbers, which shall be determined by adding to the whole number of free persons, including those bound to service for a term of years and excluding Indians not taxed, three fifths of all other persons. The actual enumeration shall be made within three years after the first meeting of the Congress of the United States, and within every subsequent term of ten years, in such manner as they shall by law direct. The number of representatives shall not exceed one for every thirty thousand, but each state shall have at least one representative; and until such enumeration shall be made, the state of New Hampshire shall be entitled to choose three, Massachusetts eight, Rhode Island and Providence Plantations one, Connecticut five, New York six, New Jersey four, Pennsylvania eight, Delaware one, Maryland six, Virginia ten, North Carolina five, South Carolina five, and Georgia three.

4. Filling Vacancies When vacancies happen in the representation from any state, the executive authority thereof shall issue writs of election to fill such vacancies.

5. Officers; Impeachment The House of Representatives shall choose their Speaker and other officers; and shall have the sole power of impeachment.

Section 3. Senate

1. Composition; Term The Senate of the United States shall be composed of two senators from each state chosen by the legislature thereof, for six years, and each senator shall have one vote.

2. Classification; Filling Vacancies Immediately after they shall be assembled in consequence of the first election, they shall be divided as equally as may be into three classes. The seats of the senators of the first class shall be vacated at the expiration of the second year, of the second class at the expiration of the fourth year, and of the third class at the expiration of the sixth year, so that one third may be chosen every second year; and if vacancies happen by resignation, or otherwise, during the recess of the legislature of any State, the executive thereof may make temporary appointments until the next meeting of the legislature, which shall then fill such vacancies.

Clause 1 Electors refers to voters. Members of the House of Representatives are elected every two years. Any citizen allowed to vote for members of the larger house of the state legislature can also vote for members of the House.

Clause 3 The number of representatives each state elects is based on its population. An enumeration, or census, must be taken every 10 years to determine population. Today, the number of representatives in the House is fixed at 435. Clause 3 contains the Three-Fifths Compromise worked out at the Constitutional Convention. Persons bound to service meant indentured servants. All other persons meant slaves. All free people in a state were counted. However, only three fifths of the slaves were included in the population count. This three-fifths clause became meaningless when slaves were freed by the Thirteenth Amendment.

Clause 4 Executive authority means the governor of a state. If a member of the House leaves office before his or her term ends, the governor must call a special election to fill the seat.

Clause 5 The House elects a Speaker. Only the House has the power to impeach, or accuse, a federal official of wrongdoing.

Clause 2 Every two years, one third of the senators run for reelection. The Seventeenth Amendment changed the way of filling vacancies, or empty seats. Today, the governor of a state must choose a senator to fill a vacancy that occurs between elections.

3. Qualifications No person shall be a senator who shall not have attained to the age of thirty years, and been nine years a citizen of the United States, and who shall not, when elected, be an inhabitant of that state for which he shall be chosen.

4. President of the Senate The Vice President of the United States shall be president of the Senate, but shall have no vote, unless they be equally divided.

5. Other Officers The Senate shall choose their other officers, and also a president pro tempore, in the absence of the Vice President, or when he shall exercise the office of the President of the United States.

6. Impeachment Trials The Senate shall have the sole power to try all impeachments. When sitting for that purpose, they shall be on oath or affirmation. When the President of the United States is tried, the Chief Justice shall preside; and no person shall be convicted without the concurrence of two thirds of the members present.

7. Penalty on Conviction Judgment in cases of impeachment shall not extend further than to removal from office, and disqualification to hold and enjoy any office of honor, trust or profit under the United States: but the party convicted shall nevertheless be liable and subject to indictment, trial, judgment, and punishment, according to law.

Section 4. Elections and Meetings

1. Election of Congress The times, places, and manner of holding elections for senators and representatives, shall be prescribed in each state by the legislature thereof; but the Congress may at any time by law make or alter such regulations, except as to the places of choosing senators.

2. Sessions The Congress shall assemble at least once in every year, and such meeting shall be on the first Monday in December, unless they shall by law appoint a different day.

Section 5. Legislative Proceedings

1. Organization Each house shall be the judge of the elections, returns, and qualifications of its own members, and a majority of each shall constitute a quorum to do business; but a smaller number may adjourn from day to day, and may be authorized to compel the attendance of absent members, in such manner, and under such penalties, as each house may provide.

2. Rules Each house may determine the rules of its proceedings, punish its members for disorderly behavior, and with the concurrence of two thirds, expel a member.

3. Record Each house shall keep a journal of its proceedings, and from time to time publish the same, excepting such parts as may in their judgment require secrecy; and the yeas and nays of the members of either house on any question shall, at the desire of one fifth of those present, be entered on the journal.

Clause 5 Pro tempore means temporary. The Senate chooses one of its members to serve as president pro tempore when the Vice President is absent.

Clause 6 The Senate acts as a jury if the House impeaches a federal official. The Chief Justice of the Supreme Court presides if the President is on trial. Two thirds of all senators present must vote for conviction, or finding the accused guilty. No President has ever been convicted. The House impeached President Andrew Johnson in 1868, but the Senate acquitted him of the charges. In 1998–99, President Bill Clinton became the second President to be impeached and acquitted.

Clause 1 Each state legislature can decide when and how congressional elections take place, but Congress can overrule these decisions. In 1842, Congress required each state to set up congressional districts with one representative elected from each district. In 1872, Congress decided that congressional elections must be held in every state on the same date in even-numbered years.

Clause 1 Each house decides whether a member has the qualifications for office set by the Constitution. A quorum is the smallest number of members who must be present for business to be conducted. Each house can set its own rules about absent members.

Portions of the Constitution altered by later amendments or that no longer apply are printed in blue.

4. Adjournment Neither house, during the session of Congress, shall, without the consent of the other, adjourn for more than three days, nor to any other place than that in which the two houses shall be sitting.

Clause 4 Neither house can adjourn, or stop meeting, for more than three days unless the other house approves. Both houses must meet in the same city.

Section 6. Compensation, Immunities, and Disabilities of Members

1. Salaries; Immunities The senators and representatives shall receive a compensation for their services, to be ascertained by law, and paid out of the Treasury of the United States. They shall in all cases, except treason, felony, and breach of the peace, be privileged from arrest during their attendance at the session of their respective houses, and in going to and returning from the same; and for any speech or debate in either house, they shall not be questioned in any other place.

Clause 1 Congress decides the salary for its members. While Congress is in session, a member is free from arrest in civil cases and cannot be sued for anything he or she says on the floor of Congress. This allows for freedom of debate. However, a member can be arrested for a criminal offense.

2. Restrictions on Other Employment No senator or representative shall, during the time for which he was elected, be appointed to any civil office under the authority of the United States, which shall have been created, or the emoluments whereof shall have been increased during such time; and no person holding any office under the United States shall be a member of either house during his continuance in office.

Clause 2 Emolument means salary. A member of Congress cannot hold another federal office during his or her term. A former member of Congress cannot hold an office created while he or she was in Congress. An official in another branch of government cannot serve at the same time in Congress.

Section 7. Law-Making Process

1. Revenue Bills All bills for raising revenue shall originate in the House of Representatives; but the Senate may propose or concur with amendments as on other bills.

Clause 1 Revenue is money raised by the government through taxes. Tax bills must be introduced in the House. The Senate, however, can make changes in tax bills.

2. How a Bill Becomes Law; the Veto Every bill which shall have passed the House of Representatives and the Senate shall, before it become a law, be presented to the President of the United States; if he approve, he shall sign it, but if not, he shall return it, with his objections, to that house in which it shall have originated, who shall enter the objections at large on their journal, and proceed to reconsider it. If after such reconsideration two thirds of that house shall agree to pass the bill, it shall be sent, together with the objections, to the other house, by which it shall likewise be reconsidered, and if approved by two thirds of that house, it shall become a law. But in all such cases the votes of both houses shall be determined by yeas and nays, and the names of the persons voting for and against the bill shall be entered on the journal of each house respectively. If any bill shall not be returned by the President within ten days (Sundays excepted) after it shall have been presented to him, the same shall be a law, in like manner as if he had signed it, unless the Congress by their adjournment prevent its return, in which case it shall not be a law.

Clause 2 A bill, or proposed law, that is passed by a majority of the House and Senate is sent to the President. If the President signs the bill, it becomes law.

A bill can also become law without the President's signature. The President can refuse to act on a bill. If Congress is in session at the time, the bill becomes law 10 days after the President receives it.

The President can veto, or reject, a bill by sending it back to the house where it was introduced. If the President refuses to act on a bill and Congress adjourns within 10 days, then the bill dies. This way of killing a bill without taking action is called the pocket veto.

Congress can override the President's veto if each house of Congress passes the bill again by a two-thirds vote.

3. Resolutions Passed by Congress Every order, resolution, or vote to which the concurrence of the Senate and House of Representatives may be necessary (except on a question of adjournment) shall be presented to the President of the United States; and before the same shall take effect, shall be approved by him, or being disapproved by him, shall be repassed by two thirds of the Senate and House of Representatives, according to the rules and limitations prescribed in the case of a bill.

Congress's power is expressed directly in the Constitution. Numbered from 1 to 18, these powers are also known as enumerated powers.

Clause 1 Duties are tariffs. Imposts are taxes in general. Excises are taxes on the production or sale of certain goods.

Clause 3 Only Congress has the power to regulate foreign and inter-state commerce. This allows a "common market" with a unified set of laws governing trade. This clause has also been interpreted as giving the federal government authority over Native American nations.

Clause 4 Naturalization is the process whereby a foreigner becomes a citizen. Bankruptcy is the condition in which a person or business cannot pay its debts.

Clause 5 Congressional power to coin money and set its value is one of the keys to creating a stable economy.

Clause 6 Counterfeiting is the making of imitation money. Securities are bonds. Congress can make laws to punish counterfeiters.

Clause 11 Only Congress can declare war. Declarations of war are granted at the request of the President. Letters of marque and reprisal were documents issued by a government allowing merchant ships to arm themselves and attack ships of an enemy nation. They are no longer issued.

Clauses 15, 16 The militia is a body of citizen soldiers. Each state has its own militia, today called the National Guard. Normally, the militia is under the command of a state's governor. However, it can be placed under the command of the President.

Portions of the Constitution altered by later amendments or that no longer apply are printed in blue.

Section 8. Powers of Congress

The Congress shall have power

1. To lay and collect taxes, duties, imposts, and excises, to pay the debts and provide for the common defense and general welfare of the United States; but all duties, imposts and excises shall be uniform throughout the United States;

2. To borrow money on the credit of the United States;

3. To regulate commerce with foreign nations, and among the several states, and with the Indian tribes;

4. To establish an uniform rule of naturalization, and uniform laws on the subject of bankruptcies throughout the United States;

5. To coin money, regulate the value thereof, and of foreign coin, and fix the standard of weights and measures;

6. To provide for the punishment of counterfeiting the securities and current coin of the United States;

7. To establish post offices and post roads;

8. To promote the progress of science and useful arts by securing for limited times to authors and inventors the exclusive right to their respective writings and discoveries;

9. To constitute tribunals inferior to the Supreme Court;

10. To define and punish piracies and felonies committed on the high seas and offenses against the law of nations;

11. To declare war, grant letters of marque and reprisal, and make rules concerning captures on land and water;

12. To raise and support armies, but no appropriation of money to that use shall be for a longer term than two years;

13. To provide and maintain a navy;

14. To make rules for the government and regulation of the land and naval forces;

15. To provide for calling forth the militia to execute the laws of the Union, suppress insurrections, and repel invasions;

16. To provide for organizing, arming, and disciplining the militia, and for governing such part of them as may be employed in the service of the United States, reserving to the states, respectively, the appointment of the officers, and the authority of training the militia according to the discipline prescribed by Congress;

17. To exercise exclusive legislation in all cases whatsoever, over such district (not exceeding ten miles square) as may, by cession of particular states, and the acceptance of Congress, become the seat of the government of the United States, and to exercise like authority over all places purchased by the consent of the legislature of the state in which the same shall be, for the erection of forts, magazines, arsenals, dock-yards, and other needful buildings; —and

18. To make all laws which shall be necessary and proper for carrying into execution the foregoing powers, and all other powers vested by this Constitution in the government of the United States, or in any department or officer thereof.

Section 9. Powers Denied to Congress

1. The Slave Trade The migration or importation of such persons as any of the states now existing shall think proper to admit, shall not be prohibited by the Congress prior to the year one thousand eight hundred and eight, but a tax or duty may be imposed on such importation, not exceeding ten dollars for each person.

2. Writ of Habeas Corpus The privilege of the writ of habeas corpus shall not be suspended, unless when in cases of rebellion or invasion the public safety may require it.

3. Bills of Attainder; Ex Post Facto Laws No bill of attainder or ex post facto law shall be passed.

4. Apportionment of Direct Taxes No capitation, or other direct, tax shall be laid, unless in proportion to the census or enumeration herein before directed to be taken.

5. Taxes on Exports No tax or duty shall be laid on articles exported from any state.

6. Special Preference for Trade No preference shall be given by any regulation of commerce or revenue to the ports of one state over those of another; nor shall vessels bound to, or from, one state, be obliged to enter, clear, or pay duties in another.

7. Spending No money shall be drawn from the Treasury, but in consequence of appropriations made by law; and a regular statement and account of the receipts and expenditures of all public money shall be published from time to time.

8. Titles of Nobility No title of nobility shall be granted by the United States; and no person holding any office of profit or trust under them, shall, without the consent of the Congress, accept of any present, emolument, office, or title, of any kind whatever, from any king, prince or foreign state.

Section 10. Powers Denied to the States

1. Unconditional Prohibitions No state shall enter into any treaty, alliance, or confederation; grant letters of marque and reprisal; coin money; emit bills of credit; make any thing but gold and silver coin a tender in payment of debts; pass any bill of attainder, ex post facto law, or law impairing the obligation of contracts, or grant any title of nobility.

2. Powers Conditionally Denied No state shall, without the consent of the Congress, lay any imposts or duties on imports or exports, except what may be absolutely necessary for executing its inspection laws; and the net produce of all duties and imposts, laid by any state on imports or exports, shall be for the use of the Treasury of the United States; and all such laws shall be subject to the revision and control of the Congress.

Clause 18 Clause 18 gives Congress the power to make laws as needed to carry out the first 17 clauses. It is sometimes called the elastic clause because it lets Congress stretch the meaning of its power.

Clause 1 "Such persons" means slaves. In 1808, as soon as Congress was permitted to abolish the slave trade, it did so.

Clause 2 A writ of habeas corpus is a court order requiring government officials to bring a prisoner to court and explain why he or she is being held. A writ of habeas corpus protects people from unlawful imprisonment. The government cannot suspend this right except in times of rebellion or invasion.

Clause 3 A bill of attainder is a law declaring that a person is guilty of a particular crime. An ex post facto law punishes an act which was not illegal when it was committed. Congress cannot pass a bill of attainder or ex post facto laws.

Clause 7 The federal government cannot spend money unless Congress appropriates it, or passes a law allowing it. The government must publish a statement showing how it spends public funds.

Clause 1 The writers of the Constitution did not want the states to act like separate nations, so they prohibited states from making treaties or coining money. Some powers denied to the federal government are also denied to the states.

Clauses 2, 3 Powers listed here are forbidden to the states, but Congress can pass laws that give these powers to the states.
Clause 2 forbids states from taxing imports and exports without the consent of Congress. States may charge inspection fees on goods entering the states. Any profits go to the United States Treasury.

Clause 3 forbids states from keeping an army or navy without the consent of Congress. States cannot make treaties or declare war unless an enemy invades or is about to invade.

Clauses 2, 3 Some writers of the Constitution were afraid to allow the people to elect the President directly. Therefore, the Constitutional Convention set up the electoral college. Clause 2 directs each state to choose electors, or delegates to the electoral college, to vote for President. A state's electoral vote is equal to the combined number of senators and representatives. Each state may decide how to choose its electors. Members of Congress and federal officeholders may not serve as electors. This much of the original electoral college system is still in effect.

Clause 3 Clause 3 called upon each elector to vote for two candidates. The candidate who received a majority of the electoral votes would become President. The runner-up would become Vice President. If no candidate won a majority, the House would choose the President. The Senate would choose the Vice President.

The election of 1800 showed a problem with the original electoral college system. Thomas Jefferson was the Republican candidate for President, and Aaron Burr was the Republican candidate for Vice President. In the electoral college, the vote ended in a tie. The election was finally decided in the House, where Jefferson was chosen President. The Twelfth Amendment changed the electoral college system so that this could not happen again.

Portions of the Constitution altered by later amendments or that no longer apply are printed in blue.

3. Other Denied Powers No state shall, without the consent of Congress, lay any duty of tonnage, keep troops, or ships of war in time of peace, enter into any agreement or compact with another state, or with a foreign power, or engage in war, unless actually invaded, or in such imminent danger as will not admit of delay.

Article II ★ Executive Branch

Section 1. President and Vice President

1. Chief Executive; Term The executive power shall be vested in a President of the United States of America. He shall hold his office during the term of four years, and, together with the Vice President, chosen for the same term, be elected as follows:

2. Electoral College Each state shall appoint, in such manner as the legislature thereof may direct, a number of electors, equal to the whole number of senators and representatives to which the state may be entitled in the Congress: but no senator or representative, or person holding an office of trust or profit under the United States, shall be appointed an elector.

3. Former Electoral Method The electors shall meet in their respective states, and vote by ballot for two persons, of whom one at least shall not be an inhabitant of the same state with themselves. And they shall make a list of all the persons voted for, and of the number of votes for each; which list they shall sign and certify, and transmit sealed to the seat of the government of the United States, directed to the president of the Senate. The president of the Senate shall, in the presence of the Senate and House of Representatives, open all the certificates, and the votes shall then be counted. The person having the greatest number of votes shall be the President, if such number be a majority of the whole number of Electors appointed; and if there be more than one who have such majority, and have an equal number of votes, then the House of Representatives shall immediately choose by ballot one of them for President; and if no person have a majority, then from the five highest on the list the said House shall in like manner choose the President. But in choosing the President, the votes shall be taken by states, the representation from each state having one vote; a quorum for this purpose shall consist of a member or members from two thirds of the states, and a majority of all the states shall be necessary to a choice. In every case, after the choice of the President, the person having the greatest number of votes of the electors shall be the Vice President. But if there should remain two or more who have equal votes, the Senate shall choose from them by ballot the Vice President.

4. Time of Elections The Congress may determine the time of choosing the electors, and the day on which they shall give their votes; which day shall be the same throughout the United States.

5. Qualifications for President No person except a natural-born citizen, or a citizen of the United States at the time of the adoption of this Constitution, shall be eligible to the office of President; neither shall any person be eligible to that office who shall not have attained to the age of thirty-five years, and been fourteen years a resident within the United States.

6. Presidential Succession In case of the removal of the President from office, or of his death, resignation, or inability to discharge the powers and duties of the said office, the same shall devolve on the Vice President, and the Congress may by law provide for the case of removal, death, resignation or inability, both of the President and Vice President, declaring what officer shall then act as President, and such officer shall act accordingly, until the disability be removed, or a President shall be elected.

7. Salary The President shall, at stated times, receive for his services, a compensation, which shall neither be increased nor diminished during the period for which he shall have been elected, and he shall not receive within that period any other emolument from the United States, or any of them.

8. Oath of Office Before he enter on the execution of his office, he shall take the following oath or affirmation:—"I do solemnly swear (or affirm) that I will faithfully execute the office of the President of the United States, and will to the best of my ability, preserve, protect, and defend the Constitution of the United States."

Section 2. Powers of the President

1. Military Powers The President shall be commander in chief of the army and navy of the United States, and of the militia of the several states, when called into the actual service of the United States; he may require the opinion, in writing, of the principal officer in each of the executive departments, upon any subject relating to the duties of their respective offices, and he shall have power to grant reprieves and pardons for offenses against the United States, except in cases of impeachment.

2. Treaties; Appointments He shall have power, by and with the advice and consent of the Senate, to make treaties, provided two thirds of the senators present concur; and he shall nominate, and by and with the advice and consent of the Senate, shall appoint ambassadors, other public ministers and consuls, judges of the Supreme Court, and all other officers of the United States, whose appointments are not herein otherwise provided for, and which shall be established by law: but the Congress may by law vest the appointment of such inferior officers, as they think proper, in the President alone, in the courts of law, or in the heads of departments.

3. Temporary Appointments The President shall have power to fill up all vacancies that may happen during the recess of the Senate, by granting commissions which shall expire at the end of their next session.

Clause 6 The powers of the President pass to the Vice President if the President leaves office or cannot discharge his or her duties. The Twenty-fifth Amendment replaced this clause.

Clause 7 The President is paid a salary. It cannot be raised or lowered during his or her term of office. The President is not allowed to hold any other federal or state position while in office.

Clause 1 The President is the head of the armed forces and the state militias when they are called into national service. So the military is under civilian, or nonmilitary, control. The President can get advice from the heads of executive departments. In most cases, the President has the power to grant reprieves and pardons. A reprieve suspends punishment ordered by law. A pardon prevents prosecution for a crime or overrides the judgment of a court.

Clause 2 The President has the power to make treaties with other nations. Under the system of checks and balances, all treaties must be approved by two thirds of the Senate.

The President has the power to appoint ambassadors to foreign countries and to appoint other high officials. The Senate must confirm, or approve, these appointments.

Section 3. Duties of the President

He shall from time to time give to the Congress information of the state of the Union, and recommend to their consideration such measures as he shall judge necessary and expedient; he may, on extraordinary occasions, convene both houses, or either of them, and in case of disagreement between them, with respect to the time of adjournment, he may adjourn them to such time as he shall think proper; he shall receive ambassadors and other public ministers; he shall take care that the laws be faithfully executed, and shall commission all the officers of the United States.

Section 4. Impeachment

The President, Vice President and all civil officers of the United States, shall be removed from office on impeachment for, and conviction of, treason, bribery, or other high crimes and misdemeanors.

Article III ★ Judicial Branch

Section 1. Courts, Terms of Office

The judicial power of the United States shall be vested in one Supreme Court, and in such inferior courts as the Congress may from time to time ordain and establish. The judges, both of the Supreme and inferior courts, shall hold their offices during good behavior, and shall, at stated times, receive for their services, a compensation, which shall not be diminished during their continuance in office.

Section 2. Jurisdiction

1. Scope of Judicial Power The judicial power shall extend to all cases, in law and equity, arising under this Constitution, the laws of the United States, and treaties made, or which shall be made, under their authority;—to all cases affecting ambassadors, other public ministers and consuls;—to all cases of admiralty and maritime jurisdiction;—to controversies to which the United States shall be a party;—to controversies between two or more states; between a state and citizens of another state; —between citizens of different states;—between citizens of the same state claiming lands under grants of different states, and between a state, or the citizens thereof, and foreign states, citizens, or subjects.

2. Supreme Court In all cases affecting ambassadors, other public ministers and consuls, and those in which a state shall be a party, the Supreme Court shall have original jurisdiction. In all the other cases before mentioned, the Supreme Court shall have appellate jurisdiction, both as to law and fact, with such exceptions, and under such regulations as the Congress shall make.

Section 4
Civil officers include federal judges and members of the Cabinet. High crimes are major crimes. Misdemeanors are lesser crimes. The President, Vice President, and others can be forced out of office if impeached and found guilty of certain crimes.

Clause 1 Jurisdiction refers to the right of a court to hear a case. Federal courts have jurisdiction over cases that involve the Constitution, federal laws, treaties, foreign ambassadors and diplomats, naval and maritime laws, disagreements between states or between citizens from different states, and disputes between a state or citizen and a foreign state or citizen.

Clause 2 Original jurisdiction means the power of a court to hear a case where it first arises. The Supreme Court has original jurisdiction over only a few cases, such as those involving foreign diplomats. More often, the Supreme Court acts as an appellate court. An appellate court does not decide guilt. It decides whether the lower court trial was properly conducted and reviews the lower court's decision.

Portions of the Constitution altered by later amendments or that no longer apply are printed in blue.

3. Trial by Jury The trial of all crimes, except in cases of impeachment, shall be by jury; and such trial shall be held in the state where the said crimes shall have been committed; but when not committed within any state, the trial shall be at such place or places as the Congress may by law have directed.

Section 3. Treason

1. Definition Treason against the United States shall consist only in levying war against them, or in adhering to their enemies, giving them aid and comfort. No person shall be convicted of treason unless on the testimony of two witnesses to the same overt act, or on confession in open court.

> **Clause 1** Treason is clearly defined. An <u>overt act</u> is an actual action.

2. Punishment The Congress shall have power to declare the punishment of treason, but no attainder of treason shall work corruption of blood or forfeiture except during the life of the person attained.

> **Clause 2** Congress has the power to set the punishment for the traitors. Congress may not punish the children of convicted traitors by taking away their civil rights or property.

Article IV ★ Relations Among the States

Section 1. Full Faith and Credit

Full faith and credit shall be given in each state to the public acts, records, and judicial proceedings of every other state. And the Congress may by general laws prescribe the manner in which such acts, records, and proceedings shall be proved, and the effect thereof.

> Each state must recognize the official acts and records of any other state. For example, each state must recognize marriage certificates issued by another state. Congress can pass laws to ensure this.

Section 2. Privileges and Immunities of Citizens

1. Privileges The citizens of each state shall be entitled to all privileges and immunities of citizens in the several states.

2. Extradition A person charged in any state with treason, felony, or other crime, who shall flee from justice, and be found in another state, shall on demand of the executive authority of the state from which he fled, be delivered up, to be removed to the state having jurisdiction of the crime.

> **Clause 2** <u>Extradition</u> means the act of returning a suspected criminal or escaped prisoner to a state where he or she is wanted. State governors must return a suspect to another state. However, the Supreme Court has ruled that a governor cannot be forced to do so if he or she feels that justice will not be done.

3. Fugitive Slaves No person held to service or labor in one state, under the laws thereof, escaping into another, shall in consequence of any law or regulation therein, be discharged from such service or labor, but shall be delivered up on claim of the party to whom such service or labor may be due.

> **Clause 3** "Persons held to service or labor" refers to slaves or indentured servants. This clause required states to return runaway slaves to their owners. The Thirteenth Amendment replaces this clause.

Section 3. New States and Territories

1. New States New states may be admitted by the Congress into this Union; but no new states shall be formed or erected within the jurisdiction of any other state; nor any state be formed by the junction of two or more states, or parts of states, without the consent of the legislatures of the states concerned as well as of the Congress.

> **Clause 1** Congress has the power to admit new states to the Union. Existing states cannot be split up or joined together to form new states unless both Congress and the state legislatures approve. New states are equal to all other states.

2. Federal Lands The Congress shall have power to dispose of and make all needful rules and regulations respecting the territory or other property belonging to the United States; and nothing in this Constitution shall be so construed as to prejudice any claims of the United States, or of any particular state.

Section 4. Protection Afforded to States by the Nation

The United States shall guarantee to every state in this Union a republican form of government, and shall protect each of them against invasion; and on application of the legislature, or of the executive (when the legislature cannot be convened) against domestic violence.

Article V ★ Provisions for Amendment

The Congress, whenever two thirds of both houses shall deem it necessary, shall propose amendments to this Constitution, or, on the application of the legislatures of two thirds of the several states, shall call a convention for proposing amendments, which, in either case, shall be valid to all intents and purposes, as part of this Constitution, when ratified by the legislatures of three fourths of the several states, or by conventions in three fourths thereof, as the one or the other mode of ratification may be proposed by the Congress; provided that no amendment which may be made prior to the year one thousand eight hundred and eight shall in any manner affect the first and fourth clauses in the ninth section of the first Article; and that no state, without its consent, shall be deprived of its equal suffrage in the Senate.

Article VI ★ National Debts, Supremacy of National Law, Oath

Section 1. Validity of Debts

All debts contracted and engagements entered into, before the adoption of this Constitution, shall be as valid against the United States under this Constitution, as under the Confederation.

Section 2. Supremacy of National Law

This Constitution, and the laws of the United States which shall be made in pursuance thereof, and all treaties made, or which shall be made, under the authority of the United States, shall be the supreme law of the land; and the judges in every state shall be bound thereby, anything in the constitution or laws of any state to the contrary notwithstanding.

Section 4 In a republic, voters choose representatives to govern them. The federal government must protect the states from foreign invasion and from domestic, or internal, disorder if asked to do so by a state.

The Constitution can be amended, or changed, if necessary. An amendment can be proposed by (1) a two-thirds vote of both houses of Congress or (2) a national convention called by Congress at the request of two thirds of the state legislatures. (This second method has never been used.) An amendment must be ratified, or approved, by (1) three fourths of the state legislatures or (2) special conventions in three fourths of the states. Congress decides which method will be used.

Congress has proposed each of the 27 amendments to the Constitution by a vote of two-thirds in both houses. The only amendment ratified by constitutional conventions of the states was the Twenty-first Amendment. State legislatures have ratified all other amendments.

Section 2 The "supremacy clause" in this section establishes the Constitution, federal laws, and treaties that the Senate has ratified as the supreme, or highest, law of the land. Thus, they outweigh state laws. A state judge must overturn a state law that conflicts with the Constitution or with a federal law.

Portions of the Constitution altered by later amendments or that no longer apply are printed in blue.

Section 3. Oaths of Office

The senators and representatives before mentioned, and the members of the several state legislatures, and all executive and judicial officers, both of the United States and of the several states, shall be bound by oath or affirmation, to support this Constitution; but no religious test shall ever be required as a qualification to any office or public trust under the United States.

Article VII ★ Ratification of Constitution

The ratification of the conventions of nine states shall be sufficient for the establishment of this Constitution between the states so ratifying the same.

Done in convention by the unanimous consent of the states present the seventeenth day of September, in the year of our Lord one thousand seven hundred and eighty-seven, and of the independence of the United States of America the twelfth. In Witness whereof, we have hereunto subscribed our names.

Article VII During 1787 and 1788, states held special conventions. By October 1788, the required nine states had ratified the United States Constitution.

Attest: William Jackson, SECRETARY
George Washington, PRESIDENT and deputy from Virginia

New Hampshire
John Langdon
Nicholas Gilman

Massachusetts
Nathaniel Gorham
Rufus King

Connecticut
William Samuel Johnson
Roger Sherman

New York
Alexander Hamilton

New Jersey
William Livingston
David Brearley
William Paterson
Jonathan Dayton

Pennsylvania
Benjamin Franklin
Thomas Mifflin
Robert Morris
George Clymer
Thomas Fitzsimons
Jared Ingersoll
James Wilson
Gouverneur Morris

Delaware
George Read
Gunning Bedford, Jr.
John Dickinson
Richard Bassett
Jacob Broom

Maryland
James McHenry
Dan of St. Thomas Jennifer
Daniel Carroll

Virginia
John Blair
James Madison, Jr.

North Carolina
William Blount
Richard Dobbs Spaight
Hugh Williamson

South Carolina
John Rutledge
Charles Cotesworth Pinckney
Charles Pinckney
Pierce Butler

Georgia
William Few
Abraham Baldwin

The Amendments Amendments are changes. The Constitution has been amended 27 times since it was ratified in 1788. The first 10 amendments are referred to as the Bill of Rights. These amendments give rights to the people and states, thus putting limits on the power of government.

First Amendment The First Amendment protects five basic rights: freedom of religion, speech, the press, assembly, and petition. Congress cannot set up an established, or official, church or religion for the nation. It cannot forbid the practice of religion, nor can it force the practice of religion.

Congress may not abridge, or limit, the freedom to speak and write freely. The government may not censor, or review, books and newspapers before they are printed. This amendment also protects the right to assemble, or hold public meetings. Petition means ask. Redress means to correct. Grievances are wrongs. The people have the right to ask the government for wrongs to be corrected.

Second Amendment Americans debate the exact meaning of the Second Amendment. Some believe that it guarantees the right of individuals to own firearms. Others argue that it guarantees the right of each state to maintain a militia. Gun control, or the passage of laws to regulate the ownership and use of firearms, is one of the most controversial issues today.

Third Amendment In colonial times, the British could quarter, or house, soldiers in private homes without permission of the owners. The Third Amendment prevents such abuses.

Portions of the Constitution altered by later amendments or that no longer apply are printed in blue.

Amendments

First Amendment ★

(1791) Freedom of Religion, Speech, Press, Assembly, and Petition

Congress shall make no law respecting an establishment of religion, or prohibiting the free exercise thereof; or abridging the freedom of speech, or of the press; or the right of the people peaceably to assemble, and to petition the government for a redress of grievances.

Second Amendment ★

(1791) Bearing Arms

A well-regulated militia being necessary to the security of a free state, the right of the people to keep and bear arms shall not be infringed.

Third Amendment ★

(1791) Quartering of Troops

No soldier shall, in time of peace, be quartered in any house, without the consent of the owner; nor in time of war, but in a manner to be prescribed by law.

Fourth Amendment ★

(1791) Searches and Seizures

The right of the people to be secure in their persons, houses, papers, and effects, against unreasonable searches and seizures, shall not be violated, and no warrants shall issue, but upon probable cause, supported by oath or affirmation, and particularly describing the place to be searched, and the persons or things to be seized.

Fifth Amendment ★

(1791) Criminal Proceedings; Due Process; Eminent Domain

No person shall be held to answer for a capital, or otherwise infamous, crime, unless on a presentment or indictment of a grand jury, except in cases arising in the land or naval forces, or in the militia, when in actual service in time of war or public danger; nor shall any person be subject for the same offense to be twice put in jeopardy of life and limb; nor shall be compelled, in any criminal case, to be a witness against himself; nor be deprived of life, liberty, or property, without due process of law; nor shall private property be taken for public use, without just compensation.

Sixth Amendment ★

(1791) Criminal Proceedings

In all criminal prosecutions, the accused shall enjoy the right to a speedy and public trial, by an impartial jury of the state and district wherein the crime shall have been committed, which district shall have been previously ascertained by law, and to be informed of the nature and cause of the accusation; to be confronted with the witnesses against him; to have compulsory process for obtaining witnesses in his favor, and to have the assistance of counsel for his defense.

Fourth Amendment This amendment protects Americans from unreasonable searches and seizures. Search and seizure are permitted only if a judge has issued a warrant, or written court order. A warrant is issued only if there is probable cause. This means an officer must show that it is probable, or likely, that the search will produce evidence of a crime.

Fifth Amendment This amendment protects the rights of the accused. Capital crimes are those that can be punished with death. Infamous crimes are those that can be punished with prison or loss of rights. The federal government must obtain an indictment, or formal accusation, from a grand jury to prosecute anyone for such crimes. A grand jury is a panel of between 12 and 23 citizens who decide if the government has enough evidence to justify a trial.

Double jeopardy is forbidden by this amendment. This means that a person cannot be tried twice for the same crime. However, if a court sets aside a conviction because of a legal error, the accused can be tried again. A person on trial cannot be forced to testify, or give evidence, against himself or herself. A person accused of a crime is entitled to due process of law, or a fair hearing or trial.

Finally, the government cannot seize private property for public use without paying the owner a fair price for it.

Sixth Amendment In criminal cases, the jury must be impartial, or not favor either side. The accused is guaranteed the right to a trial by jury. The trial must be speedy. If the government purposely postpones the trial so that it becomes hard for the person to get a fair hearing, the charge may be dismissed. The accused must be told the charges and be allowed to question all witnesses. Witnesses who can help the accused can be ordered to appear in court. The accused must be allowed a lawyer.

Seventh Amendment <u>Common law</u> refers to rules of law established by judges in past cases. This amendment guarantees the right to a jury trial in lawsuits where the sum of money at stake is more than $20. An appeals court can set aside a verdict only if legal errors made the trial unfair.

Eighth Amendment <u>Bail</u> is money that the accused leaves with the court as a pledge to appear for trial. If the accused does not appear, the court keeps the money. This amendment prevents the court from imposing bail or fines that are <u>excessive</u>, or too high. The amendment also forbids cruel and unusual punishments, such as physical torture.

Ninth Amendment The rights of the people are not limited to those listed in the Bill of Rights. In the Ninth Amendment, the government is prevented from claiming these are the only rights people have.

Tenth Amendment Powers not given to the federal government belong to the states. Powers reserved to the states are not listed in the Constitution.

Eleventh Amendment A private citizen from one state cannot sue the government of another state in federal court. However, a citizen can sue a state government in a state court.

Portions of the Constitution altered by later amendments or that no longer apply are printed in blue.

Seventh Amendment ★

(1791) Civil Trials

In suits at common law, where the value in controversy shall exceed twenty dollars, the right of trial by jury shall be preserved, and no fact tried by a jury shall be otherwise re-examined in any court of the United States, than according to the rules of the common law.

Eighth Amendment ★

(1791) Punishment for Crimes

Excessive bail shall not be required, nor excessive fines imposed, nor cruel and unusual punishments inflicted.

Ninth Amendment ★

(1791) Unenumerated Rights

The enumeration in the Constitution, of certain rights, shall not be construed to deny or disparage others retained by the people.

Tenth Amendment ★

(1791) Powers Reserved to the States

The powers not delegated to the United States by the Constitution, nor prohibited by it to the states, are reserved to the states respectively, or to the people.

Eleventh Amendment ★

(1795) Suits Against States

The judicial power of the United States shall not be construed to extend to any suit in law or equity, commenced or prosecuted against one of the United States by citizens of another state, or by citizens or subjects of any foreign state.

Twelfth Amendment ★

(1804) Election of President and Vice President

The electors shall meet in their respective states, and vote by ballot for President and Vice President, one of whom, at least, shall not be an inhabitant of the same state with themselves; they shall name in their ballots the person voted for as President, and in distinct ballots the person voted for as Vice President, and they shall make distinct lists of all persons voted for as President, and of all persons voted for as Vice President, and of the number of votes for each, which lists they shall sign and certify, and transmit sealed to the seat of the government of the United States, directed to the president of the Senate; the president of the Senate shall, in the presence of the Senate and the House of Representatives, open all the certificates and the votes shall then be counted;—the person having the greatest number of votes for President shall be the President, if such number be a majority of the whole number of electors appointed; and if no person have such a majority, then from the persons having the highest numbers not exceeding three on the list of those voted for as President, the House of Representatives shall choose immediately, by ballot, the President.

But in choosing the President, the votes shall be taken by states, the representation from each state having one vote; a quorum for this purpose shall consist of a member or members from two thirds of the states, and a majority of all states shall be necessary to a choice. And if the House of Representatives shall not choose a President whenever the right of choice shall devolve upon them, before the fourth day of March next following, then the Vice President, shall act as President, as in the case of death or other constitutional disability of the President—The person having the greatest number of votes as Vice President, shall be the Vice President, if such a number be a majority of the whole number of electors appointed, and if no person have a majority, then from the two highest numbers on the list, the Senate shall choose the Vice President; a quorum for the purpose shall consist of two thirds of the whole number of senators, and a majority of the whole number shall be necessary to a choice. But no person constitutionally ineligible to the office of President shall be eligible to that of Vice President of the United States.

Twelfth Amendment This amendment changed the way the electoral college voted as outlined in Article II, Clause 3.

This amendment provides that each elector choose one candidate for President and one candidate for Vice President. If no candidate for President receives a majority of electoral votes, the House of Representatives chooses the President. If no candidate for Vice President receives a majority, the Senate elects the Vice President. The Vice President must be a person who is eligible to be President.

This system is still in use today. However, it is possible for a candidate to win the popular vote and lose in the electoral college. This happened in 1888 and in 2000.

Thirteenth Amendment ★

(1865) Slavery and Involuntary Servitude

Section 1. Outlawing Slavery Neither slavery nor involuntary servitude, except as a punishment for crime whereof the party shall have been duly convicted, shall exist within the United States, or any place subject to their jurisdiction.

Section 2. Enforcement Congress shall have power to enforce this article by appropriate legislation.

Thirteenth Amendment The Emancipation Proclamation (1863) freed slaves only in areas controlled by the Confederacy. This amendment freed all slaves. It also forbids involuntary servitude, or labor done against one's will. However, it does not prevent prison wardens from making prisoners work. Congress can pass laws to carry out this amendment.

Fourteenth Amendment, Section 1
This amendment defines citizenship for the first time in the Constitution. It was intended to protect the rights of the freed slaves by guaranteeing all citizens "equal protection under the law."

Fourteenth Amendment, Section 2
This section replaced the three-fifths clause. It provides that representation in the House of Representatives is decided on the basis of the number of people in the state. It also provides that states which deny the vote to male citizens over age 21 will be punished by losing part of their representation in the House. This provision has never been enforced.

Fourteenth Amendment ★

(1868) Rights of Citizens

Section 1. Citizenship All persons born or naturalized in the United States, and subject to the jurisdiction thereof, are citizens of the United States and of the state wherein they reside. No state shall make or enforce any law which shall abridge the privileges or immunities of citizens of the United States; nor shall any state deprive any person of life, liberty, or property, without due process of law; nor deny to any person within its jurisdiction the equal protection of the laws.

Section 2. Apportionment of Representatives Representatives shall be apportioned among the several states according to their respective numbers, counting the whole number of persons in each state, excluding Indians not taxed. But when the right to vote at any election for the choice of electors for President and Vice President of the United States, representatives in Congress, the executive and judicial officers of a state, or the members of the legislature thereof, is denied to any of the male inhabitants of such state, being twenty-one years of age, and citizens of the United States, or in any way abridged, except for participation in rebellion, or other crime, the basis of representation therein shall be reduced in the proportion which the number of such male citizens shall bear to the whole number of male citizens twenty-one years of age in such state.

Section 3. Former Confederate Officials No person shall be a senator or representative in Congress, or elector of President and Vice President, or hold any office, civil or military, under the United States, or under any state, who having previously taken an oath, as a member of Congress, or as an officer of the United States, or as a member of any state legislature, or as an executive or judicial officer of any state, to support the Constitution of the United States, shall have engaged in insurrection or rebellion against the same, or given aid or comfort to the enemies thereof. But Congress may, by a vote of two thirds of each house, remove such disability.

Section 4. Public Debt The validity of the public debt of the United States, authorized by law, including debts incurred for payment of pensions and bounties for services in suppressing insurrection or rebellion, shall not be questioned. But neither the United States nor any state shall assume or pay any debt or obligation incurred in aid of insurrection or rebellion against the United States, or any claim for the loss of emancipation of any slave; but all such debts, obligations and claims shall be held illegal and void.

Section 5. Enforcement The Congress shall have power to enforce, by appropriate legislation, the provisions of this article.

Portions of the Constitution altered by later amendments or that no longer apply are printed in blue.

Fifteenth Amendment ★

(1870) Right to Vote—Race, Color, Servitude

Section 1. Extending the Right to Vote The right of citizens of the United States to vote shall not be denied or abridged by the United States or by any state on account of race, color, or previous condition of servitude.

Section 2. Enforcement The Congress shall have power to enforce this article by appropriate legislation.

Sixteenth Amendment ★

(1913) Income Tax

The Congress shall have power to lay and collect taxes on incomes, from whatever source derived, without apportionment among the several states, and without regard to any census or enumeration.

Seventeenth Amendment ★

(1913) Popular Election of Senators

Section 1. Method of Election The Senate of the United States shall be composed of two senators from each state, elected by the people thereof, for six years; and each senator shall have one vote. The electors in each state shall have the qualifications requisite for electors of the most numerous branch of the state legislatures.

Section 2. Vacancies When vacancies happen in the representation of any state in the Senate, the executive authority of such state shall issue writs of election to fill such vacancies: provided, that the legislature of any state may empower the executive thereof to make temporary appointments until the people fill the vacancies by election as the legislature may direct.

Section 3. Those Elected Under Previous Procedure This amendment shall not be so construed as to affect the election or term of any senator chosen before it becomes valid as part of the Constitution.

Fifteenth Amendment, Section 1 Previous condition of servitude refers to slavery. This amendment gave African Americans, both former slaves and free African Americans, the right to vote. In the late 1800s, southern states used grandfather clauses, literacy tests, and poll taxes to keep African Americans from voting.

Fifteenth Amendment, Section 2 Congress can pass laws to carry out this amendment. The Twenty-fourth Amendment barred the use of poll taxes in national elections. The Voting Rights Act of 1965 gave federal officials the power to register voters where there was voting discrimination.

Sixteenth Amendment Congress has the power to collect taxes on people's income. An income tax can be collected without regard to a state's population. This amendment changed Article 1, Section 9, Clause 4.

Seventeenth Amendment, Section 1 This amendment replaced Article 1, Section 2, Clause 1. Before it was adopted, state legislatures chose senators. This amendment provides that senators are directly elected by the people of each state.

Eighteenth Amendment ★

(1919) Prohibition of Alcoholic Beverages

Section 1. Ban on Alcohol After one year from the ratification of this article, the manufacture, sale, or transportation of intoxicating liquors within, the importation thereof into, or the exportation thereof from the United States and all territory subject to the jurisdiction thereof for beverage purposes is hereby prohibited.

Section 2. Enforcement The Congress and the several states shall have concurrent power to enforce this article by appropriate legislation.

Section 3. Method of Ratification This article shall be inoperative unless it shall have been ratified as an amendment to the Constitution by the legislatures of the several states, as provided in the Constitution, within seven years from the date of the submission hereof to the states by Congress.

Nineteenth Amendment ★

(1920) Women's Suffrage

Section 1. The Right to Vote The right of citizens of the United States to vote shall not be denied or abridged by the United States or by any state on account of sex.

Section 2. Enforcement Congress shall have power to enforce this article by appropriate legislation.

Twentieth Amendment ★

(1933) Presidential Terms; Sessions of Congress; Death or Disqualification of President-Elect

Section 1. Beginning of Terms The terms of the President and Vice President shall end at noon on the 20th day of January, and the terms of senators and representatives at noon on the 3rd day of January, of the years in which such terms would have ended if this article had not been ratified; and the terms of their successors shall then begin.

Section 2. Congressional Sessions The Congress shall assemble at least once in every year, and such meeting shall begin at noon on the 3rd day of January, unless they shall by law appoint a different day.

Eighteenth Amendment This amendment, known as Prohibition, banned the making, selling, or transporting of alcoholic beverages in the United States. Later, the Twenty-first Amendment repealed, or canceled, this amendment.

Nineteenth Amendment Neither the federal government nor state governments can deny the right to vote on account of sex. Thus, women won suffrage, or the right to vote. Before 1920, some states had allowed women to vote in state elections.

Twentieth Amendment, Section 1. The date for the inauguration of the President was changed to January 20th, and the date for Congress to begin its term changed to January 3rd. Prior to this amendment, the beginning of term date was set in March. The outgoing officials with little or no influence on matters were not effective in office. Being so inactive, they were called "lame ducks."

Portions of the Constitution altered by later amendments or that no longer apply are printed in blue.

Section 3. Presidential Succession If, at the time fixed for the beginning of the term of the President, the President-elect shall have died, the Vice President-elect shall become President. If a President shall not have been chosen before the time fixed for the beginning of his term, or if the President-elect shall have failed to qualify, the Vice President-elect shall act as President until a President shall have qualified; and the Congress may by law provide for the case wherein neither a President-elect nor a Vice President-elect shall have qualified, declaring who shall then act as President, or the manner in which one who is to act shall be selected, and such person shall act accordingly until a President or Vice President shall have qualified.

Section 4. Elections Decided by Congress The Congress may by law provide for the case of the death of any persons from whom the House of Representatives may choose a President whenever the right of choice shall have devolved upon them, and for the case of the death of any of the persons from whom the Senate may choose a Vice President whenever the right of choice shall have devolved upon them.

Section 5. Date of Implementation Sections 1 and 2 shall take effect on the 15th day of October following the ratification of this article.

Section 6. Ratification Period This article shall be inoperative unless it shall have been ratified as an amendment to the Constitution by the legislatures of three fourths of the several states within seven years from the date of its submission.

Twentieth Amendment, Section 3. If the President-elect dies before taking office, the Vice President-elect becomes President. If no President has been chosen by January 20 or if the elected candidate fails to qualify for office, the Vice President-elect acts as President, but only until a qualified President is chosen.

Finally, Congress has the power to choose a person to act as President if neither the President-elect nor the Vice President-elect is qualified to take office.

Twenty-first Amendment ★

(1933) Repeal of Prohibition

Section 1. Repeal The eighteenth article of amendment to the Constitution of the United States is hereby repealed.

Section 2. State Laws The transportation or importation into any state, territory, or possession of the United States for delivery or use therein of intoxicating liquors, in violation of the laws thereof, is hereby prohibited.

Section 3. Ratification Period This article shall be inoperative unless it shall have been ratified as an amendment to the Constitution by conventions in the several states, as provided in the Constitution, within seven years from the date of the submission hereof to the states by the Congress.

Twenty-first Amendment, Section 1 The Eighteenth Amendment is repealed, making it legal to make and sell alcoholic beverages. Prohibition ended December 5, 1933.

Twenty-second Amendment ★

(1951) Presidential Tenure

Section 1. Two-Term Limit No person shall be elected to the office of the President more than twice, and no person who has held the office of President, or acted as President, for more than two years of a term to which some other person was elected President shall be elected to the office of President more than once. But this article shall not apply to any person holding the office of President when this article was proposed by the Congress, and shall not prevent any person who may be holding the office of President, or acting as President, during the term within which this article becomes operative from holding the office of President or acting as President during the remainder of such term.

Section 2. Ratification Period This article shall be inoperative unless it shall have been ratified as an amendment to the Constitution by the legislatures of three fourths of the several states within seven years from the date of its submission to the state by the Congress.

Twenty-third Amendment ★

(1961) Presidential Electors for the District of Columbia

Section 1. Determining the Number of Electors The district constituting the seat of government of the United States shall appoint in such manner as the Congress may direct:

A number of electors of President and Vice President equal to the whole number of senators and representatives in Congress to which the district would be entitled if it were a state, but in no event more than the least populous state; they shall be in addition to those appointed by the states, but they shall be considered, for the purposes of the election of President and Vice President, to be electors appointed by a state; and they shall meet in the district and perform such duties as provided by the twelfth article of amendment.

Section 2. Enforcement The Congress shall have power to enforce this article by appropriate legislation.

Twenty-fourth Amendment ★

(1964) Right to Vote in Federal Elections—Tax Payment

Section 1. Poll Tax Banned The right of citizens of the United States to vote in any primary or other election for President or Vice President, for electors for President or Vice President, or for senator or representative in Congress, shall not be denied or abridged by the United States or any state by reason of failure to pay any poll tax or other tax.

Section 2. Enforcement The Congress shall have the power to enforce this article by appropriate legislation.

Twenty-second Amendment, Section 1
This amendment provides that no President may serve more than two terms. A President who has already served more than half of someone else's term can serve only one more full term. Before Franklin Roosevelt became President, no President served more than two terms in office. Roosevelt broke with this custom and was elected to four terms. The amendment, however, did not apply to Harry Truman, who became President after Franklin Roosevelt's death in 1945.

Twenty-third Amendment, Section 1
This amendment gives the residents of Washington, D.C., the right to vote in presidential elections. Until this amendment was adopted, people living in Washington, D.C., could not vote for President because the Constitution had made no provision for choosing electors from the nation's capital. Washington, D.C., now has three electoral votes.

Twenty-fourth Amendment, Section 1
A poll tax is a tax on voters. This amendment bans poll taxes in national elections. Some states used poll taxes to keep African Americans from voting. In 1966, the Supreme Court struck down poll taxes in state elections, also.

Portions of the Constitution altered by later amendments or that no longer apply are printed in blue.

(1967) Presidential Succession, Vice Presidential Vacancy, Presidential Inability

Section 1. President's Death or Resignation In case of the removal of the President from office or of his death or resignation, the Vice President shall become President.

Section 2. Vacancies in Vice Presidency Whenever there is a vacancy in the office of the Vice President, the President shall nominate a Vice President who shall take office upon confirmation by a majority vote of both houses of Congress.

Section 3. Disability of the President Whenever the President transmits to the President pro tempore of the Senate and the Speaker of the House of Representatives his written declaration that he is unable to discharge the powers and duties of his office, and until he transmits to them a written declaration to the contrary, such powers and duties shall be discharged by the Vice President as acting President.

Section 4. Vice President as Acting President Whenever the Vice President and a majority of either the principal officers of the executive departments or of such other body as Congress may by law provide, transmit to the President pro tempore of the Senate and the Speaker of the House of Representatives their written declaration that the President is unable to discharge the powers and duties of his office, the Vice President shall immediately assume the powers and duties of the office as acting President.

Thereafter, when the President transmits to the President pro tempore of the Senate and the Speaker of the House of Representatives his written declaration that no inability exists, he shall resume the powers and duties of his office unless the Vice President and a majority of either the principal officers of the executive department or of such other body as Congress may by law provide, transmit within four days to the President pro tempore of the Senate and the Speaker of the House of Representatives their written declaration that the President is unable to discharge the powers and duties of his office. Thereupon Congress shall decide the issue, assembling within forty-eight hours for that purpose if not in session. If the Congress, within twenty-one days after receipt of the latter written declaration, or, if Congress is not in session, within twenty-one days after Congress is required to assemble, determines by two-thirds vote of both Houses that the President is unable to discharge the powers and duties of his office, the Vice President shall continue to discharge the same as acting President; otherwise, the President shall resume the powers and duties of his office.

Twenty-fifth Amendment, Section 1
If the President dies or resigns, the Vice President becomes President. This section clarifies Article 2, Section 1, Clause 6.

Twenty-fifth Amendment, Section 3
If the President declares in writing that he or she is unable to perform the duties of office, the Vice President serves as acting President until the President recovers.

Twenty-fifth Amendment, Section 4
Two Presidents, Woodrow Wilson and Dwight Eisenhower, fell gravely ill while in office. The Constitution contained no provision for this kind of emergency. Section 3 provided that the President can inform Congress he or she is too sick to perform the duties of office. However, if the President is unconscious or refuses to admit to a disabling illness, Section 4 provides that the Vice President and Cabinet may declare the President disabled. The Vice President becomes the acting President until the President can return to the duties of office. In case of a disagreement between the President and the Vice President and Cabinet over the President's ability to perform the duties of office, Congress must decide the issue. A two-thirds vote of both houses is needed to find the President is disabled or unable to fulfill the duties of office.

Twenty-sixth Amendment ★

Twenty-sixth Amendment, Section 1
In 1970, Congress passed a law allowing 18-year-olds to vote. However, the Supreme Court decided that Congress could not set a minimum age for state elections.

(1971) Right to Vote—Age

Section 1. Lowering the Voting Age The right of citizens of the United States, who are eighteen years of age or older, to vote shall not be denied or abridged by the United States or by any state on account of age.

Section 2. Enforcement The Congress shall have the power to enforce this article by appropriate legislation.

Twenty-seventh Amendment ★

Twenty-seventh Amendment
If members of Congress vote themselves a pay increase, it cannot go into effect until after the next congressional election. This amendment was proposed in 1789. In 1992, Michigan became the thirty-eighth state to ratify it.

(1992) Congressional Pay

No law, varying the compensation for the services of the senators and representatives, shall take effect until an election of representatives shall have intervened.

Independence Hall room where the Constitution was signed

Portions of the Constitution altered by later amendments or that no longer apply are printed in blue.

CITIZENSHIP HANDBOOK

Table of Contents

Key Terms

amend, p. 264
appeal, p. 262
bill, p. 259
censorship, p. 267
checks and balances, p. 257
citizen, p. 270
dictatorship, p. 252
dissent, p. 267
federalism, p. 257
habeas corpus, p. 252
interest group, p. 271
jurisdiction, p. 262
libel, p. 267
limited government, p. 256
naturalization, p. 270
override, p. 259
popular sovereignty, p. 256
private property, p. 252
ratify, p. 264
repeal, p. 255
republic, p. 252
separation of powers, p. 253
unconstitutional, p. 263
veto, p. 259

Ideas Behind the Constitution

The delegates to the Constitutional Convention who gathered in Philadelphia were greatly influenced by past experiments with democracy and natural rights. As they debated the new document for American government, the Founders considered a variety of past political ideas.

Ancient Rome

Earlier in this textbook, you read about the ancient Roman Republic. The Framers of the United States Constitution looked to Rome as a model. Like the early Romans, they sought to create a lasting **republic,** or a government in which citizens rule themselves through elected representatives. American leaders also admired what they saw as the independent thinking and public service of Roman citizens. Romans, Americans said, had been willing to serve in public office out of devotion to the republic.

However, Americans also took the fate of Rome as a warning. The Roman Republic eventually collapsed and became a **dictatorship,** a government in which one person or a small group holds complete authority. American leaders believed that the Roman Republic faltered when citizens began to value luxury and comfort more than freedom and public service. The Framers of the Constitution wanted to avoid Rome's fate. They hoped to build a system in which informed, independent citizens played an active role in their own government.

Two Historic Documents

You also learned earlier about the following two important documents in British history: the Magna Carta, which British nobles forced King John to sign in 1215; and the Bill of Rights, which William and Mary issued in 1689 after the Glorious Revolution. These two documents created an English tradition of liberty, which the colonists brought to America.

The following principles found in the these two documents became part of the American system of government:

King John signing the Magna Carta

- Citizens have rights which the government must protect.
- Even the head of the government must obey the law.
- Taxes cannot be raised without the consent of the people.
- Elections should be held frequently.
- People accused of crimes have the right to trial by jury and the right of **habeas corpus,** meaning no person may be held in prison without being charged with a specific crime.
- People have the right to **private property,** or property owned by an individual.

Teachings of the Enlightenment

Many of the Framers were influenced by the works of European Enlightenment thinkers. In his book *Two Treatises on Government*, the English writer John Locke declared that every individual has natural rights to life, liberty, and property. Locke said government is an agreement between the ruler and the ruled. Further, he argued, if a ruler violates the people's natural rights, the people have a right to rebel.

The French thinker Baron de Montesquieu (MOHN tehs kyoo) suggested a concept known as **separation of powers**—the idea that powers of government must be clearly defined and divided into legislative, executive, and judicial branches. This concept was designed to keep one person or group from gaining too much power.

John Locke

Representative Traditions and the Declaration of Independence

Americans enjoyed a long tradition of representative government. The Virginia colonists set up the House of Burgesses, and the Pilgrims drafted the Mayflower Compact in 1620. The compact was the first document of self-government in North America.

Each of the 13 colonies had a written charter that identified the powers and limits of government granted by the British Crown. In addition to these traditions, the Framers of the Constitution drew on the grievances Thomas Jefferson had listed against George III in the Declaration of Independence. In writing the Constitution, they sought to prevent similar abuses in the new American government.

Baron de Montesquieu

Declaring Independence
Delegates sign the Declaration of Independence.

Assessment

1. Identify two principles of American government that came from the Magna Carta or the English Bill of Rights.

2. How did Montesquieu's ideas affect the crafting of the Constitution?

Structure of the Constitution

The principles of the Constitution have guided the United States for more than 200 years. The Constitution is divided into three main parts: the Preamble, or opening statement; the Articles; and the Amendments. The Preamble begins with the words, "We the people of the United States." These words show that the authority of the government comes from its citizens. The Preamble then goes on to outline six basic goals for the new government. They are shown on the chart below.

Goals of the Preamble

Goals	What It Means to Us
■ To form a more perfect union	All states should work together as a unified nation.
■ To establish justice	Everyone should be treated equally and fairly under the law.
■ To ensure domestic tranquillity	The government has the responsibility to ensure peace and order at home.
■ To provide for the common defense	The government has the responsibility to protect its citizens against foreign attack.
■ To promote the general welfare	The government has the responsibility to promote the well-being of all its citizens.
■ To secure the blessings of liberty	The government should value and protect the rights of its citizens.

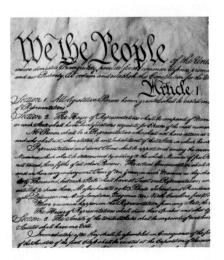

The Constitution

Articles

The main body of the Constitution is divided into seven sections called articles. Together, they establish the framework for American government. The first three articles describe the three branches of the national government: legislative, executive, and judicial. Article 1 establishes the powers and limits on Congress. Articles 2 and 3 do the same for the President and the courts.

Article 4 deals with relations between states. It requires states to honor one another's laws and also sets out a system for admitting new states. Article 5 provides a process to amend the Constitution. Article 6 states that the Constitution is the "supreme law of the land." States cannot make laws that violate the Constitution and federal laws prevail in all disputes. The final article, Article 7, sets up a procedure for the states to ratify the Constitution.

Amendments

The Amendments are formal changes that have been made to the Constitution. Some of these changes added new ideas to the document. Others repealed, or canceled, other parts of the Constitution.

In more than 200 years, only 27 changes have been made to the Constitution. The first 10 amendments, known as the Bill of Rights, were added in 1791. You will read more about the Bill of Rights later in this handbook.

Some later amendments had an immediate and powerful impact on American society. A few of them are illustrated below.

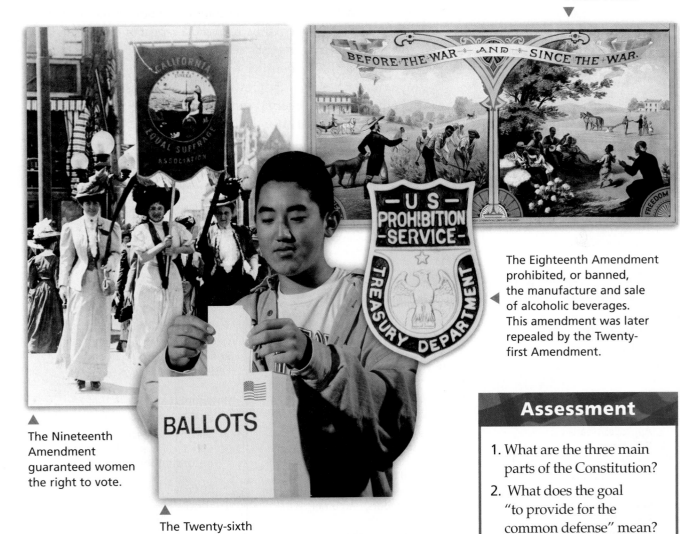

The Thirteenth Amendment ended slavery throughout the United States.

The Nineteenth Amendment guaranteed women the right to vote.

The Twenty-sixth Amendment lowered the minimum voting age from 21 to 18.

The Eighteenth Amendment prohibited, or banned, the manufacture and sale of alcoholic beverages. This amendment was later repealed by the Twenty-first Amendment.

Assessment

1. What are the three main parts of the Constitution?

2. What does the goal "to provide for the common defense" mean? How might this be done?

Principles of the Constitution

The Constitution rests on seven basic principles. They are popular sovereignty, limited government, separation of powers, federalism, checks and balances, republicanism, and individual rights.

- **Popular Sovereignty** The Framers of the Constitution lived at a time when monarchs claimed that their power came from God. The Preamble, which begins "We the people," reflects a revolutionary new idea: a government gets its authority from the people. This principle, known as popular sovereignty, asserts that the people are the primary source of the government's authority.

- **Limited Government** The colonists believed that the British king had ruled them harshly. To avoid a repeat of this rule in their new government, the Framers made limited government a principle of the Constitution. In a limited government, the government has only the powers that the Constitution gives it. Equally important, every citizen of the United States—including the President—must obey the law.

- **Separation of Powers** To further limit the power of the government, the Framers provided for separation of powers. The Constitution divides the government into three branches, and each branch has its own duties. The chart below outlines the duties of each branch of government.

Separation of Powers

Legislative Branch (Congress)	Executive Branch (President)	Judicial Branch (Supreme Court and Other Federal Courts)
Passes Laws	**Carries Out Laws**	**Interprets Laws**
■ Can override President's veto ■ Approves treaties ■ Can impeach and remove President and other high officials ■ Prints and coins money ■ Raises and supports armed forces ■ Can declare war ■ Regulates foreign and interstate trade	■ Proposes laws ■ Can veto laws ■ Negotiates foreign treaties ■ Serves as commander in chief of armed forces ■ Appoints federal judges, ambassadors, and other high officials ■ Can grant pardons to federal offenders	■ Can declare laws unconstitutional ■ Can declare executive actions unconstitutional

Checks and Balances

Legislative Branch
(Congress makes laws)

Checks on the Executive Branch
- Can override President's veto
- Confirms executive appointments
- Ratifies treaties
- Can declare war
- Appropriates money
- Can impeach and remove President

Checks on the Judicial Branch
- Creates lower federal courts
- Can impeach and remove judges
- Can propose amendments to overrule judicial decisions
- Approves appointments of federal judges

Executive Branch
(President carries out laws)

Checks on the Legislative Branch
- Can propose laws
- Can veto laws
- Can call special sessions of Congress
- Makes appointments
- Negotiates foreign treaties

Checks on the Judicial Branch
- Appoints federal judges
- Can grant pardons to federal offenders

Judicial Branch
(Supreme Court interprets laws)

Check on the Executive Branch
- Can declare executive actions unconstitutional

Check on the Legislative Branch
- Can declare acts of Congress unconstitutional

- **Checks and Balances** A system of checks and balances safeguards against abuse of power. Each branch of government has the power to check, or limit, the actions of the other two. This arrangement guarantees that no branch of government will become too powerful. The chart above describes the specific checks each branch has on the other two. The next six pages of this handbook will detail how each branch of government works.

- **Federalism** The Constitution also establishes the principle of federalism, or division of power between the federal government and the states. The Constitution grants specific powers to the federal government and other powers to the states. Powers that are not clearly given to the federal government belong to the states.

- **Republicanism** The Constitution provides for a republican form of government. Instead of direct participation in government, citizens elect representatives to carry out their will.

- **Individual Rights** The Constitution protects individual rights, such as freedom of speech, freedom of religion, and the right to trial by jury. You will learn more about the rights protected by the Constitution later in this handbook.

Assessment

1. How does the Constitution reflect the principle of separation of powers?

2. How can the judicial branch check the powers of the executive and legislative branches?

The first and longest article of the Constitution deals with the legislative, or lawmaking, branch. Article 1 sets up the Congress to make the nation's laws. Congress is made up of two bodies: the House of Representatives and the Senate.

The Senate

The Senate is based on equal representation, with two senators for each state. Senators are elected to six-year terms. The Vice President of the United States is the president of the Senate. The Vice President presides over the Senate—casting a vote when there is a tie—but cannot take part in Senate debates.

The House of Representatives

The larger of the two bodies is the House of Representatives, which currently has 435 members. Representation in the House is based on population, with larger states having more representatives than smaller states. Every state has at least one representative. Representatives are elected by the people of their district for two-year terms. The leader of the House is called the Speaker. The Speaker, who is chosen by the representatives, regulates debates and controls the agenda.

Senate

Office: Senator
Number: 2 per state
Term: 6 years
Requirements: Age 30 or over; citizen for 9 years; resident of state in which elected

House of Representatives

Office: Representative
Number: At least 1 per state; based on population
Term: 2 years
Requirements: Age 25 or over; citizen for 7 years; resident of state in which elected

How a Bill Becomes a Law

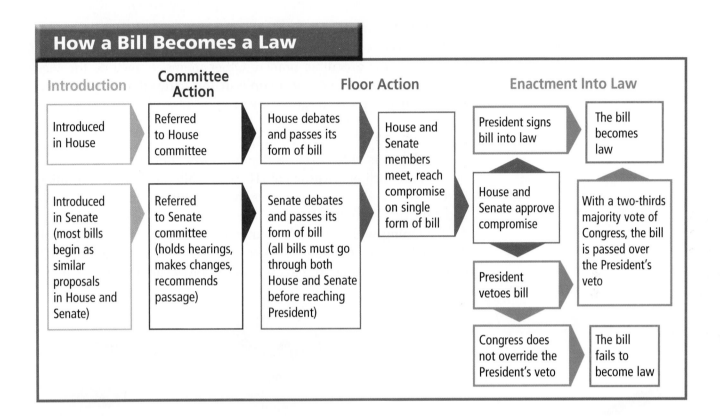

Introduction	Committee Action	Floor Action	Enactment Into Law

Introduced in House → Referred to House committee → House debates and passes its form of bill →

Introduced in Senate (most bills begin as similar proposals in House and Senate) → Referred to Senate committee (holds hearings, makes changes, recommends passage) → Senate debates and passes its form of bill (all bills must go through both House and Senate before reaching President) →

House and Senate members meet, reach compromise on single form of bill →

President signs bill into law → The bill becomes law

House and Senate approve compromise →

With a two-thirds majority vote of Congress, the bill is passed over the President's veto

President vetoes bill →

Congress does not override the President's veto → The bill fails to become law

Powers of Congress

The most important power of Congress is the power to make the nation's laws. A **bill,** or proposal for a new law, may be introduced either in the House or the Senate. After debate and changes, the bill is voted on. If both houses vote to approve the bill, it then goes to the President to be signed. If the President signs the bill, it becomes a law. The President, however, has the power to **veto,** or reject, the bill. Congress may vote to **override,** or pass a law despite a presidential veto. A two-thirds vote is needed to override. (See flowchart above.)

Other powers of Congress are listed in Article 1, Section 8. These include the power to collect taxes, to coin money, to establish post offices, to fix standard weights and measures, and to declare war.

Congressional Committees

Much of the work in Congress is done through committees. Each committee deals with a specific topic. For example, if someone in Congress introduces a bill to improve the nation's railroad service, the bill would first go to the Transportation Committee for study. Other standing committees deal with such areas as defense, education, taxation, foreign affairs, agriculture, or science.

Assessment

1. What are the major differences between membership in the Senate and membership in the House?

2. How can Congress pass a bill over a presidential veto?

Article 2 of the Constitution sets up an executive branch to carry out the laws and run the affairs of the national government. The President is the head of the executive branch. Other members include the Vice President, the Cabinet, and people in the many departments and agencies that help run the government.

Powers of the President

The Framers of the Constitution intended Congress to be the most powerful branch of government. Therefore, although the Constitution is very specific about the powers of the legislature, it offers few details about the powers of the President. (See the graphic organizer below.)

Beginning with George Washington, Presidents have often taken those actions they thought were necessary to carry out their job. Thus, they shaped the presidency to meet the nation's changing needs.

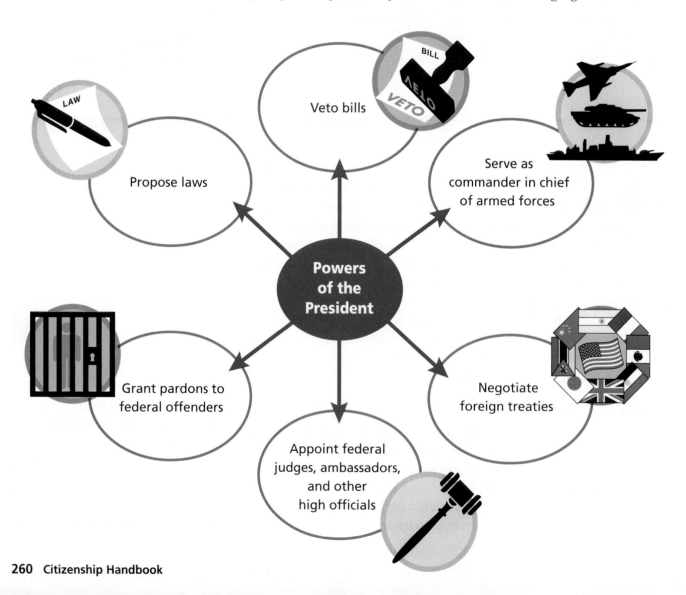

LAW

BILL

VETO

Veto bills

Serve as commander in chief of armed forces

Propose laws

Powers of the President

Grant pardons to federal offenders

Negotiate foreign treaties

Appoint federal judges, ambassadors, and other high officials

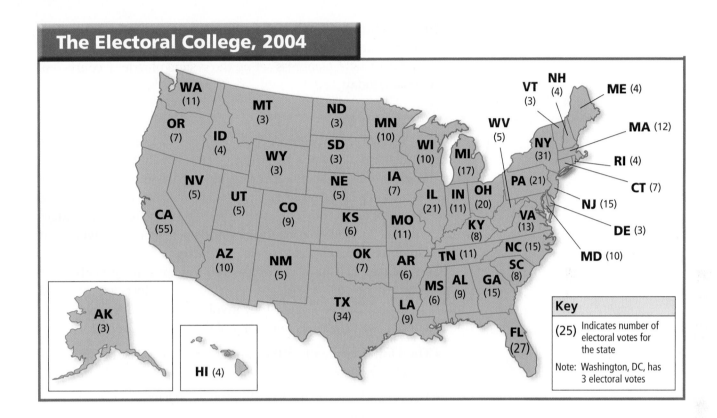

The Electoral College, 2004

WA (11)
OR (7)
MT (3)
ND (3)
MN (10)
VT (3)
NH (4)
ME (4)
WV (5)
ID (4)
WY (3)
SD (3)
WI (10)
MI (17)
NY (31)
MA (12)
NV (5)
UT (5)
CO (9)
NE (5)
IA (7)
IL (21)
IN (11)
OH (20)
PA (21)
RI (4)
CT (7)
CA (55)
KS (6)
MO (11)
KY (8)
VA (13)
NJ (15)
DE (3)
AZ (10)
NM (5)
OK (7)
AR (6)
TN (11)
NC (15)
SC (8)
MD (10)
TX (34)
LA (9)
MS (6)
AL (9)
GA (15)
FL (27)
AK (3)
HI (4)

Key

(25) Indicates number of electoral votes for the state

Note: Washington, DC, has 3 electoral votes

Electing the President

The President is elected for a four-year term. As a result of the Twenty-second Amendment, adopted in 1951, no President may be elected to more than two complete terms.

The Framers set up a complex system for electing the President, known as the electoral college. When Americans vote for President, they do not vote directly for the candidate of their choice. Rather, they vote for a group of "electors" who are pledged to the candidate. The number of a state's electors depends on the number of its senators and representatives. (See the map above.)

A few weeks after Election Day, these electors meet in each state to cast their votes for President. In most states, the candidate with the majority of the popular vote receives all that state's electoral votes. The candidate who receives a majority of the electoral votes nationwide becomes President. Although electors are not required by federal law to vote for their pledged candidate, only a few have broken their pledges and voted for other candidates in past elections.

Assessment

1. Why do you think the Framers chose not to give the President the power to declare war?

2. How many electors does your state have?

The Constitution establishes a Supreme Court and authorizes Congress to establish any other courts that are needed. Under the Judiciary Act of 1789, Congress set up the system of federal courts that is still in place today.

Lower Courts

Most federal cases begin in district courts. Evidence is presented during trials, and a jury or a judge decides the facts of the case. A party that disagrees with the decision of the judge or jury may **appeal** it, that is, ask that the decision be reviewed by a higher court. The next level of court is the appellate court, or court of appeal. Appellate court judges review decisions of district courts to decide whether the lower court judges interpreted and applied the law correctly.

Court cases can be filed under federal or state jurisdiction. **Jurisdiction** is the power to hear and decide cases. Most cases are tried under state jurisdiction because they involve state laws. A case may be placed under federal jurisdiction if any of the following apply:

- The United States is either suing another party or being sued by another party.
- The case is based on the Constitution or on a federal law.
- The case involves disputes between different states.

Federal Court System

State Route → **United States Supreme Court** ← **Federal Route**

State Supreme Court
- Highest state court
- Hears appeals of appellate court cases

Appellate Court
- Hears appeals of trial court cases

Trial Court
- Handles civil and criminal cases

United States Supreme Court
- Nation's highest court
- Reviews the decisions of lower courts
- Decides cases involving U.S. Constitution and federal laws

Court of Appeal
- Hears appeals of cases originating in U.S. district courts
- Can review decisions by federal administrative agencies

District Court
- Federal trial court
- Handles civil and criminal cases

The Supreme Court

At the top of the American judicial system is the Supreme Court.
(See the chart on the facing page.) The Court is made up of a chief justice
and eight associate justices. The President appoints the justices, but
Congress must approve the appointments. Justices serve until they
resign, retire, or die. However, like other federal officials, Supreme
Court justices may be impeached and removed from office.

The main job of the Supreme Court is to serve as the nation's final
court of appeal. It hears the cases that have been tried and appealed in
lower federal and state courts. The Court hears and decides fewer than
100 cases each year.

Decisions rest on a majority vote of at least five justices. One justice
then writes a majority opinion, a document that explains the constitutional reasons for the decision. A justice who voted against the
majority may submit a dissenting opinion, explaining his or her reasons
for disagreeing with the majority opinion.

There is no court of appeal beyond the Supreme Court. However,
if another case dealing with the same issues comes up, the Supreme
Court may sometimes reverse its own past decisions.

Judicial Review

The most important power of the Supreme Court is the power to
decide what the Constitution means. At the beginning of the 1800s, the
Court asserted the right to declare whether acts of the President or laws
passed by Congress are unconstitutional, that is, not allowed under the
Constitution. The landmark 1803 case of *Marbury* v. *Madison* established
this power of judicial review for the Supreme Court.

Assessment

1. How does a case reach
   the United States
   Supreme Court?

2. What is judicial review?

Amending the Constitution

Although the Framers were pleased with the government they had established through the Constitution, some were dissatisfied with the final document. For one thing, while establishing the powers of the state and federal governments, the document said nothing about the rights of the American people. In 1791, the new nation would do something about this omission when it added the Bill of Rights, the first 10 amendments to the Constitution.

This addition was possible because the founders had written a Constitution that allowed for change. The Constitution was flexible enough to be changed but not so flexible that it could be *easily* changed. Article 5 laid out the method for amending, or changing, the Constitution. The flowchart below shows the amendment process.

The Amendment Process

The Constitution can be changed in one of four ways. There are two different procedures for proposing amendments to the Constitution. There are also two different procedures for ratifying, or approving, amendments to the Constitution, the second step in the process.

Proposing an Amendment Congress can propose an amendment if both the House and Senate vote for a change to the Constitution. Each of the Constitution's 27 amendments has been proposed in this way.

The second way to propose an amendment begins at the state level. Currently, the legislatures of 34 states must call for a national convention. It is then up to the national convention to formally propose an amendment.

Ratifying an Amendment An amendment can be ratified through the action of state legislatures. Currently, the yes vote of 38 states is needed. Twenty-six of the 27 amendments to the Constitution have been ratified in this way.

An amendment can also be ratified through the action of state conventions rather than through state legislatures. Conventions, are special meetings that are called to address a specific issue. Only the Twenty-first Amendment was added through the process of state conventions.

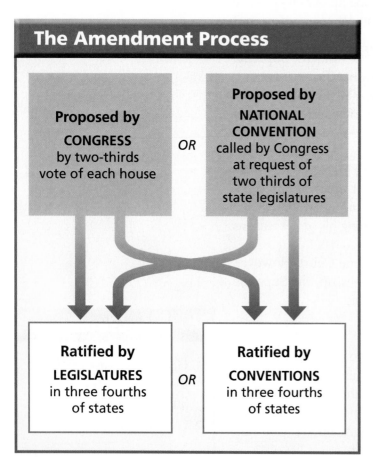

The Amendment Process

Proposed by
CONGRESS
by two-thirds
vote of each house

OR

Proposed by
NATIONAL
CONVENTION
called by Congress
at request of
two thirds of
state legislatures

Ratified by
LEGISLATURES
in three fourths
of states

OR

Ratified by
CONVENTIONS
in three fourths
of states

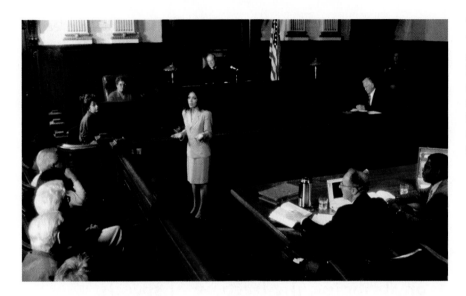

The Sixth Amendment
The right to trial by jury in a criminal case is guaranteed by the Sixth Amendment. It also ensures that a person accused of a crime has the right to be represented by a lawyer and to hear the testimony given by witnesses in the trial.

The Bill of Rights

The Preamble of the Constitution begins with the words, "We the People of the United States." However, the seven articles of the original document deal mostly with issues involving the structure and powers of the branches of government, not with the rights of individuals. The Bill of Rights, the name given to the first 10 amendments to the Constitution, addresses the freedoms guaranteed to citizens.

- *First Amendment:* freedom of religion, speech, and the press; right of petition and assembly (See the following page.)
- *Second Amendment:* right to bear arms
- *Third Amendment:* government cannot force people to quarter troops in their homes
- *Fourth Amendment:* protects against unreasonable search and seizure
- *Fifth Amendment:* rights of people accused of crimes
- *Sixth Amendment:* right to trial by jury in criminal cases
- *Seventh Amendment:* right to trial by jury in civil cases
- *Eighth Amendment:* forbids excessive bail and cruel or unusual punishment
- *Ninth Amendment:* people's rights are not limited to those listed in the Constitution
- *Tenth Amendment:* states or people have all powers not denied or given to federal government by the Constitution

Assessment

1. Which one of the four different two-step processes has most often been used to add amendments to the Constitution?

2. Why do you think the Founders added the Ninth Amendment to the Bill of Rights?

The First Amendment

The colonial past was very much on the minds of American leaders when they set out to write the Bill of Rights in the early 1790s. It is not surprising, therefore, that the colonial experience inspired the very first amendment to the Constitution.

First Amendment

Congress shall make no law respecting an establishment of religion, or prohibiting the free exercise thereof; or abridging the freedom of speech, or of the press; or the right of the people peaceably to assemble, and to petition the government for a redress of grievances.

Freedom of Religion

This painting by Norman Rockwell illustrates the principle of freedom of religion.

Freedom of Religion As you have learned, Pilgrims, Puritans, Quakers, and Catholics had come to North America because they wanted to practice their religion freely. Yet, colonial religious leaders such as Thomas Hooker, Roger Williams, and Anne Hutchinson were later driven from Massachusetts after clashing with community leaders over religious questions. The Founders wanted to avoid such church-versus-state disputes. Thus, the First Amendment affirms freedom of religion as a basic right. Americans are free to follow any religion or no religion, as they choose.

This part of the First Amendment was inspired by the Virginia Statute on Religious Freedom, written by Thomas Jefferson. Jefferson later spoke of a "wall of separation between Church and State." However, not everyone agrees on the nature of that separation. Some people believe that the First Amendment means that religion should play no role in government. Others argue that the Amendment merely says that Congress cannot establish an official, state-supported church or make any laws that interfere with freedom of worship.

Freedom of the Press
American reporters do their jobs without fear of government interference.

Peaceful Assembly
These striking workers are exercising their right of peaceful assembly.

Freedom of Speech and Freedom of the Press Dictators understand that their power depends on silencing dissent, or disagreement. They will often shut down newspapers and jail people who criticize the government. By contrast, the First Amendment protects the right of Americans to speak without fear of punishment.

The First Amendment also protects the press from government censorship. Censorship is the power to review, change, or prevent the publication of news. Freedom of the press also means that journalists cannot be arrested for criticizing the government or public officials. (As you have read, this principle was established in the colonies by the case of John Peter Zenger.)

The Framers knew that a free flow of ideas is vital to a democratic government. Still, freedom of the press is not unlimited. The press has a responsibility to present the news fairly and accurately. Individuals may sue journalists for libel, or the publication of false and malicious information that damages a person's reputation.

Peaceful Assembly and Petition As you have read, King George III and Parliament ignored the colonists' petition protesting the Stamp Act. Such experiences had a powerful effect on the leaders who wrote the Bill of Rights. The First Amendment thus guarantees the right of Americans to assemble in peaceful protest. It also protects their right to petition the government for a change in policy.

Assessment

1. What does the First Amendment say about freedom of religion?

2. Identify two rights of a free press.

The First Amendment 267

State and Local Governments

As you have learned, under the principle of federalism, the Constitution assigns some powers to the government in Washington, D.C., and other powers to the states. You have already read about the role of the federal government in our nation's life. Now you will learn about the role played by state and local governments.

State Governments

In general, the federal government deals with national issues. The states concern themselves with needs within each state.

State governments resemble the federal government in many ways. Each state has a constitution of its own, for example, and each state constitution can be amended. In addition, every state is divided into three branches of government. Each state has a legislature, a governor who serves as the chief executive, and a judiciary. But there are some differences between the state and federal governments. Nebraska, for instance, is the only state in the Union with a one-house legislature.

The Federal System

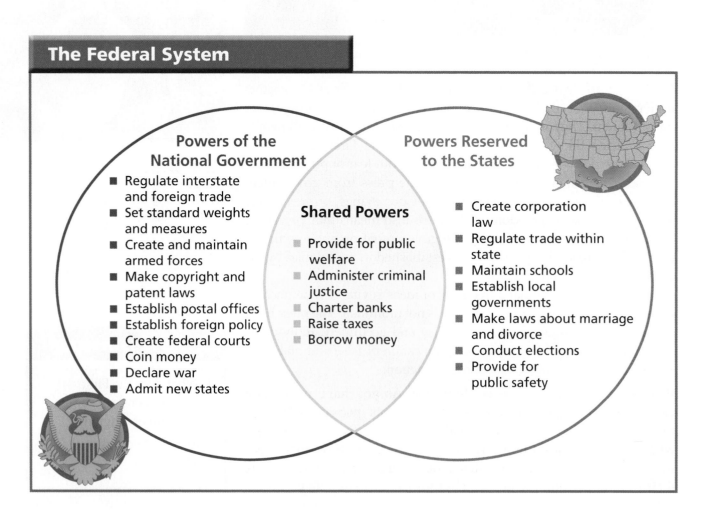

Powers of the National Government
- Regulate interstate and foreign trade
- Set standard weights and measures
- Create and maintain armed forces
- Make copyright and patent laws
- Establish postal offices
- Establish foreign policy
- Create federal courts
- Coin money
- Declare war
- Admit new states

Shared Powers
- Provide for public welfare
- Administer criminal justice
- Charter banks
- Raise taxes
- Borrow money

Powers Reserved to the States
- Create corporation law
- Regulate trade within state
- Maintain schools
- Establish local governments
- Make laws about marriage and divorce
- Conduct elections
- Provide for public safety

Local Government
City or town governments usually set up and fund fire departments.

State Services

Enforcing the law, protecting property, regulating business, building and maintaining highways, and operating state parks are just a few of the many tasks the state oversees. In addition, states supervise public education by setting standards and by funding school programs.

Local Governments

As we have seen, the Constitution carefully identifies the powers of state and federal governments. However, it says nothing about local government. Local governments administer smaller units, such as counties, cities, and towns.

Local governments have budgets just like the federal government and state government. Most of the money in their budgets is spent on education. Cities, towns, or school districts hire teachers and staff, buy books and supplies, and maintain school buildings. But local governments do not have sole control over the school system. They are required by law to meet the state's education standards.

Local government generally plays a more direct role in our lives than federal or state government does. For example, local governments hire people who interact with us on a regular basis, such as firefighters, police officers, and garbage collectors. In addition, local governments maintain local roads and hospitals, provide sewers and water, run libraries, oversee parks and recreational facilities, and conduct safety inspections of buildings.

Assessment

1. Name two powers the federal goverment and state governments share. Name two powers that are reserved to the states.

2. What permits local governments to function even though they are not mentioned in the Constitution? Explain your answer.

What is a citizen? A **citizen** is someone who is entitled to all the rights and privileges of a particular nation. Not everyone who lives in a certain nation is a citizen of that nation. On the other hand, some citizens live outside the nation to which they belong.

Becoming an American Citizen

To become a citizen of the United States, you must fulfill one of the following three requirements:

- You were born in the United States or have at least one parent who is a citizen of the United States.
- You were naturalized. **Naturalization** is the official legal process of becoming a citizen.
- You were 18 years old or younger when your parents were naturalized.

Each year, millions of people born in other countries and living in the United States become naturalized. To become a naturalized citizen, a person must live legally in the United States for at least five years. The person then applies for citizenship. He or she must take a citizenship examination and undergo a series of interviews. Finally, the applicant takes the citizenship oath before a judge, swearing to "support and defend the Constitution and laws of the United States."

A naturalized citizen enjoys every right of a natural-born citizen except one. Only natural-born citizens may serve as President or Vice President.

Naturalization
New citizens of the United States proudly take the citizenship oath.

Rights of Citizens

As you have seen, the Bill of Rights guarantees certain rights to citizens. You have the right to worship as you please, the right to express your opinion, and the right to consult a lawyer if you are arrested. But the Ninth Amendment states that citizens' rights are not limited to those listed in the Constitution. Over the years, federal and state laws have identified other rights. For example, the Constitution does not mention education. But today, laws in every state guarantee that children have the right to an education.

Responsibilities of Citizens

In addition to rights, citizens have responsibilities. Some actions are required of every citizen. For example, all citizens *must*

- obey federal, state, and local laws;
- pay their fair share of taxes;
- serve on juries if called;
- defend the nation if called.

Citizens have other responsibilities that are not required by law. Good citizens *should*

- vote in federal, state, and local elections;
- stay informed on important issues;
- serve the community;
- help to create a just society.

Some citizens participate in the political process through interest groups. An **interest group** is an organization that represents the concerns of a particular group. The American Association of Retired Persons, the National Rifle Association, and the Sierra Club are examples of interest groups that try to influence lawmakers and raise public awareness of certain issues.

Young people, too, can get involved in the political process. For example, in one California community, poor children could not afford to pay for public transportation to school every day. Some students organized to solve this problem. Using their First Amendment rights, they collected signatures on petitions and held public rallies. As a result, the local transportation board took up the issue. Like thousands of other Americans, these students used their rights as citizens to voice their views and help their communities.

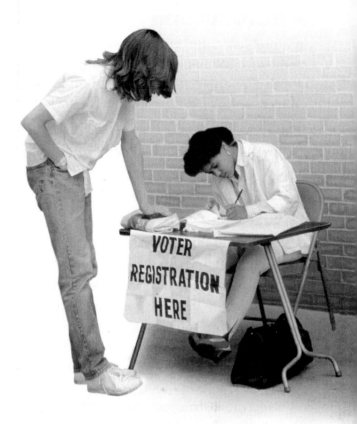

Registering to Vote
Before a U.S. citizen can vote, he or she must register.

Assessment

1. How does a person become an American citizen?

2. Identify three ways that Americans can participate in the political process.

Writing Workshop

Problem-Solution Essay

▶ Introduction

In a problem-solution essay, you analyze a problem and propose a method for solving it. The problem you choose to analyze should be one that offers some challenges but is still possible to resolve. A problem-solution essay should have the following characteristics:

- a problem that needs to be solved
- a thesis statement that identifies the problem and points toward the solution
- identification of several possible solutions
- specific facts, details, examples, and reasons indicating why one solution is best
- an analytical tone

Assignment On the following pages, you will learn how to write a problem-solution essay. You will get step-by-step instructions. Each step will include an example from a sample essay discussing the Articles of Confederation.

Read the instructions and the examples. Then, follow each step to plan and write a 500–700 word essay.

> **Analyze a problem faced by the writers of the Constitution and discuss the solution that the Constitutional Convention chose.**

▶ Prewriting

Define the problem to be solved. In order to write a problem-solution essay, you need to start with a clear vision of the problem itself.

Once you have broken your problem down and looked at it from different angles, sit back and look at the big picture. Think about your ultimate goal in solving the problem.

For a review of the steps in the writing process see the **Historian's Toolkit**, *Write Like a Historian.*

Sample notes about a problem arising from the Articles of Confederation

- The Articles did not include a central executive because the states didn't want to give up power to central authority.

- Congress had to manage everything.

- Nine states had to vote for any action to take place.

- Foreign governments saw the new nation as weak and ignored its demands.

- Americans also defied the national government (Shays' Rebellion).

- It was difficult for Congress to act quickly or make changes in policy.

Sample goal:
The problems with the Articles needed to be solved so that the new nation could survive and adapt to change.

Brainstorm to identify several solutions. Look for as many solutions as you can, even if they solve only part of the problem. List each solution and evaluate it. One good technique is to ask questions. Create a chart like this one to help you evaluate your various solutions.

Write a thesis statement. Write a thesis statement briefly identifying the problem. Your thesis statement may also indicate possible solutions, but you may also save that information for later in your essay.

Gather supporting information. Look for facts, details, and reasons to support your solutions to the problem.

> **Sample thesis statement:**
> The Articles of Confederation left the new nation too weak because they allowed for no central authority besides Congress. The Articles needed to be changed in some way—or something new had to replace them.

Problem	Possible Solution	Evaluation
The Articles of Confederation left the nation weak because there was no central authority.	Leave the Articles as is, persuade other countries and Americans to respect the new nation	Not practical—what would make more established governments and local rebels accept a weak authority?
	Leave the basic Articles in place but have Congress elect a new executive each year, rotating from state to state	Possible, but amendments needed to be agreed on by all the states. Also, how does the central authority work with the Congress, which was used to running everything?
	Get rid of the Articles, create an entirely new plan	Possible, but it would be a huge task to start all over again.

▶ Drafting

Decide how to organize your writing. The simplest way to organize a problem-solution essay is to begin by identifying the problem in the first paragraph, leading up to your thesis statement. Present the solution that you think works best, explaining why it is the most promising one.

Support your thesis with examples and details. Use your lists of supporting information to back up your ideas about the best solution to the problem.

Use an analytical tone. As you write your draft, remember that you are appealing to people's ability to reason, not to their emotions. Describe the problem and the various possible solutions objectively.

Write a strong conclusion. In your final paragraph, restate your ideas about the problem and its solution.

▶ Model Essay

Read the following model of a problem-solution essay. Notice how it
includes the characteristics you have learned about.

The Articles of Confederation: Problems and Solutions

In November 1777, the Continental Congress
approved the first American constitution: the Articles of
Confederation. Soon after the Articles were ratified by the
states in 1781, problems arose. One of the most serious of
these problems was that the Articles of Confederation
left the new nation too weak. It allowed for no central
authority besides Congress.

> The thesis statement identifies the problem.

The Articles of Confederation created a loose
alliance of 13 independent states. No state wanted to
give up its power to a strong central government. Even
Congress had little power. For example, Congress could
pass a law, but nine states had to approve the law before
it went into effect. Congress had no power to tax the
states, so the nation could not pay its war debts.

> This paragraph describes the problem in greater detail.

Recognizing that many problems existed with the
Articles of Confederation, the Continental Congress met
again in 1787. There were a number of solutions they could
have considered. First, Congress could change the Articles
so that Congress would elect a new central authority
each year. Second, Congress could give itself more power.
These solutions might solve some of the nation's
problems, but not all. Finally, Congress could get rid of the
Articles and create an entirely new plan of government.
The delegates saw this as the best solution, but one
that would take a great deal of work.

> Each paragraph describes possible solutions and discusses their pros and cons.

> The analytical tone presents the information fairly, using straightforward language.

Most of the delegates to what became known as the
Constitutional Convention recognized that the Articles of
Confederation had serious weaknesses. Their decision to
formulate a new plan of government was a bold one.
Nevertheless, it proved to be the best solution. The
delegates created a new and lasting form of government
for the United States.

> The conclusion restates the thesis. It shows the importance of solving the problem and explaining why the solution was a good one.

▶ Revising

After completing your draft, read it again carefully to find ways to make your writing better. Here are some questions to ask yourself.

Revise to strengthen your thesis and support
- Do the introduction and thesis statement identify the problem?
- Do the body paragraphs explain the problem thoroughly? Do they examine several solutions and describe the most effective solution clearly?
- Is your proposal supported by convincing reasons, facts, and examples?

Revise to meet written English-language conventions
- Are all sentences complete, with a subject and a verb?
- Are all the words spelled correctly? Use a spell-checker or a dictionary to make sure.
- Are all proper nouns capitalized, including names of people and places?
- Did you use proper punctuation? Check punctuation within sentences as well as at the ends of sentences.

▶ Rubric for Self-Assessment

Evaluate your problem-solution essay using the following rating scale:

	Score 4	Score 3	Score 2	Score 1
Organization	Supports the thesis with a series of paragraphs exploring a problem and its various solutions, ending with a discussion of the one proposed by the writer	Uses a reasonably clear organization, but occasionally wanders from the topic	Chooses an organization not suited to the topic (for example, presents the solution without having explained the problem)	Shows lack of organizational strategy
Presentation	Explores the problem and solutions thoroughly with facts, details, and reasons; links all information to the goal of solving the problem	Explores the problem and solutions adequately with several facts, details, or examples; links most information to the goal of solving the problem	Does not explore the problem and solutions adequately; does not link supporting information to the goal of solving the problem	Does not provide any facts, details, or examples to explore the problem and solutions
Use of Language	Varies sentence structure and vocabulary successfully; includes none or very few mechanical errors	Uses some variety in sentence structure and vocabulary; includes few mechanical errors	Uses the same types of sentences without varying them; repeats words; includes many mechanical errors	Writes incomplete sentences; uses language poorly; sounds confused; includes many mechanical errors

Unit 3

Think Like a Historian

As you read this unit, think about this question: *What problems might a new nation face?*

George Washington After leading U.S. troops to victory against the British, Washington led the new nation as its first President. His actions set precedents that future Presidents would follow.

1789

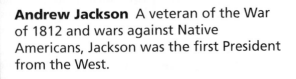

Andrew Jackson A veteran of the War of 1812 and wars against Native Americans, Jackson was the first President from the West.

1828

The New Republic

Exploring the Louisiana Territory
President Thomas Jefferson acquired the Louisiana Territory and sent an expedition to explore lands west of the Mississippi River.

1803

War of 1812 In June 1812, the United States declared war on Great Britain. One reason for war was Britain's refusal to stop seizing U.S. Navy vessels and sailors.

1812

Trail of Tears Forced to move west to Indian Territory under harsh conditions, thousands of Native Americans lost their lives on what became known as the Trail of Tears.

1838

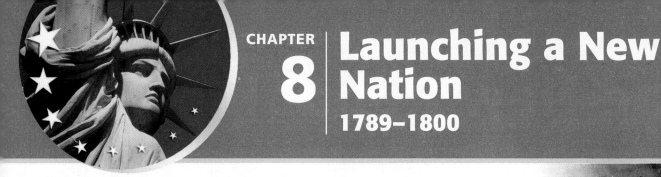

CHAPTER

8 Launching a New Nation
1789–1800

Chapter Preview

The Constitution had created a framework of government. Now the young nation faced many decisions about how to make the plan work. Meanwhile, challenges arose inside the nation's borders and on the high seas.

U.S. Events

1789 George Washington becomes first President of the United States.

1790 Alexander Hamilton announces economic plan.

1794 Whiskey Rebellion is crushed.

1789   1792   1795

World Events

1789 French Revolution begins.

1793 France and Britain go to war. "Reign of Terror" occurs in France.

Quick View Video
View the chapter video for a quick preview of the main ideas.

Washington had to leave his comfortable estate at Mount Vernon, Virginia (below), and move to New York to assume the presidency of the United States.

1795
Senate approves Jay Treaty with Britain.

1798
"XYZ Affair" becomes public. Congress passes Alien and Sedition acts.

1800
France agrees to stop seizing American ships.

1795

1798

1799 Napoleon Bonaparte gains political power in France.

1801

279

How to Read History

 History Reading Skill **Analyze Comparisons**

What questions did America's founders have about their new government?

In this chapter, you will learn how to analyze comparisons made through similes, metaphors, and analogies. Read the following speech given by Benjamin Franklin. The side notes point out the comparisons.

Primary Source

Benjamin Franklin was one of the many state representatives who gathered in Philadelphia in 1787 to create the Constitution. Here, Franklin gives his views about the completed Constitution.

> . . . It . . . astonishes me, Sir, to find this system approaching so near to perfection as it does; and I think it will astonish our enemies, who are waiting with confidence to hear, that our councils are confounded <u>like those of the builders of Babel</u>, and that our States are on the point of separation, only to meet hereafter for the purpose of cutting one another's throats. Thus I consent, Sir, to this Constitution, because I expect no better, and because I am not sure that it is not the best. <u>The opinions I have had of its errors I sacrifice to the public good.</u> I have never whispered a syllable of them abroad. <u>Within these walls they were born, and here they shall die.</u> . . .
>
> —Benjamin Franklin, Closing Speech to the Constitutional Convention, September 17, 1787

The word *like* signals a simile comparing the representatives to the builders of the Tower of Babel.

Franklin draws an analogy between his giving up his views to help the overall good and ancient peoples who made sacrifices to please their gods.

Here, Franklin uses a metaphor, discussing his criticisms as if they were living things.

Analyze Comparisons

- Find similes—comparisons of different things linked by the words *like* or *as.*
- Find metaphors—implied comparisons that do not have the words *like* or *as* but suggest that one thing is like another.
- Draw analogies—find ideas in the text that are connected in some way.

Document-Based Questions

1. Who was Franklin addressing?
2. What was his purpose for giving this speech?
3. Would the reference to "our enemies" help to achieve this purpose? Why or why not?

Vocabulary *Builder*

Previewing High-Use Academic Words

High-Use Word	Definition	Sample History Sentence
invest (ihn VEHST) (Section 1, p. 284)	*v.* to purchase something with the hope that its value will grow	Wealthy Americans <u>invested</u> in land, believing that they could sell it later for a profit.
impose (ihm POHZ) (Section 1, p. 285)	*v.* to place a burden on something or someone	Manufacturers wanted the government to <u>impose</u> a high tax on imports.
hostile (HAHS tihl) (Section 2, p. 291)	*adj.* unfriendly; adverse or opposed	Native Americans were often <u>hostile</u> to colonial settlements established on Native American lands.
fundamental (fuhn duh MEHN tahl) (Section 2, p. 293)	*adj.* basic; most important; forming the foundation of an idea or action; essential	The most <u>fundamental</u> principle of democracy is that the people rule.
cease (sees) (Section 3, p. 296)	*v.* to cause to come to an end; to stop	After hours of battle, the soldiers on both sides <u>ceased</u> their firing.
emphasize (EHM fah sīz) (Section 3, p. 297)	*v.* to stress; to give more importance to	The Declaration of Independence <u>emphasizes</u> equality and the natural rights of humankind.
react (ree AKT) (Section 4, p. 298)	*v.* to act in response to another action; to respond	Delegates to the Constitutional Convention <u>reacted</u> cautiously to Roger Sherman's Great Compromise.
provoke (prah VOHK) (Section 4, p. 301)	*v.* to cause to anger; to excite; to cause an action	When France seized U.S. ships, it must have known that its actions would <u>provoke</u> great anger among the American people.

Previewing Key Terms and People

SECTION
1

Washington Takes Office

Objectives

1. Discuss how the new government was organized during Washington's presidency.

2. Explain why the new nation faced an economic crisis.

3. Identify the three parts of Hamilton's financial plan.

4. Describe how Washington responded to the Whiskey Rebellion.

Prepare to Read

 Reading Skill

Identify Similes Similes use the signal words *like* or *as* to connect two items being compared. The comparison helps the reader to imagine the description more fully. For example, "the gunfire echoed like thunder" creates a mental image of the sound of a battle. Look for similes as you read this section.

Vocabulary *Builder*

High-Use Words

invest, p. 284

impose, p. 285

Key Terms

inauguration, p. 283

precedent, p. 283

bond, p. 284

speculator, p. 284

unconstitutional, p. 285

tariff, p. 286

⭐ **Background Knowledge** In 1789, the United States was one fourth of its size today. All 13 states were in the East. The nation's western border followed the Mississippi River. The enormous Northwest Territory lay between that river and the Appalachian Mountains. In the North, the Great Lakes formed much of the border separating the United States from British-controlled Canada. In the South, the United States bordered on Spanish-controlled Florida and Louisiana.

The American people had a new Constitution. They now had a new Congress and their first President. In this section, you will learn how the nation's leaders made this brand-new government work.

The First President

Main Idea
Congress and the President chose people to run the institutions created by the Constitution.

In April of 1789, George Washington traveled from Virginia to the nation's capital, New York City, to begin his term as the first President of the United States. Washington's journey along bumpy roads took eight days. Large crowds lined the streets. As one newspaper reported, Americans greatly admired the tall, stately war hero:

❝Many persons in the crowd were heard to say they should now die contented—nothing being wanted to complete their happiness . . . but the sight of the savior of his country.❞
—*Gazette of the United States,* April 1789

Washington's **inauguration**—a ceremony in which the President takes the oath of office—was held on April 30, 1789. Despite all he had achieved, Washington was anxious. The country was divided on many issues. Washington understood how much the new nation depended on him. His actions would set a **precedent**—an example to be followed by others in the future.

The Executive Branch The Constitution of the United States provided only a general outline for organizing the government. When the President took office, the entire federal government was made up of little more than 75 post offices, a few clerks, and a tiny army of 672 soldiers.

The first job of the President and the Congress, therefore, was to put a working government in place. First, Congress passed laws to set up three departments for the executive branch: Treasury, State, and War. Each department was to be headed by a secretary nominated by the President. The President would also appoint an attorney general to advise him on legal matters.

Washington appointed four well-known men to take the new posts. He chose Alexander Hamilton to be secretary of the treasury. Hamilton was considered one of the country's outstanding leaders and an expert on economic affairs. Thomas Jefferson, the author of the Declaration of Independence, became secretary of state. His task was to manage relations with foreign countries. Henry Knox, a former general, was Washington's choice for secretary of war. Edmund Randolph, who had played an important role at the Constitutional Convention, became attorney general.

Washington soon began meeting regularly with these leaders as a group. Over time, this group became known as the Cabinet.

Explore More Video
To learn more about George Washington's presidency, view the video.

Washington's Inauguration
George Washington took the oath of office on a balcony of Federal Hall in New York City as well-wishers watched from the street below. **Critical Thinking:** *Link Past and Present Who attended Washington's oath-taking? How would a modern-day President's inauguration be different?*

Establishing the Judiciary The Constitution also called for a judiciary, or court system. The Judiciary Act of 1789 provided for a Supreme Court of 6 justices. Under the Supreme Court were 3 circuit courts and 13 district courts. The main job of the federal courts was to hear appeals from the state courts. Washington appointed John Jay of New York as the first Chief Justice of the Supreme Court.

☑**Checkpoint** What were the new executive departments?

The Nation's First Economic Crisis

The American Revolution had left the nation deeply in debt. The federal government owed $52 million. That debt was mainly in the form of bonds. A **bond** is a certificate issued by a government for an amount of money that the government promises to pay back with interest. Both Americans and foreigners had <u>invested</u> in bonds to help the war effort. Would the government pay back this debt?

The issue was complicated because most people who had originally bought the bonds had sold them for less than they were worth. The buyers were **speculators**—people who invest in a risky venture in the hope of making a large profit. It seemed unfair to many Americans that speculators would make a profit after the original bond-holders had lost money. Also in dispute was whether or not the federal government should pay back state debts.

The government was operating on a shoestring. It did not even have the money for George Washington's move to New York. Washington had to borrow $3,000 to pay his moving expenses.

☑**Checkpoint** Why was there such a large public debt?

Main Idea
The federal government owed millions of dollars but lacked money with which to pay its debts.

Vocabulary Builder
<u>invest</u> (ihn VEHST) *v.* to purchase something with the hope that its value will grow

---

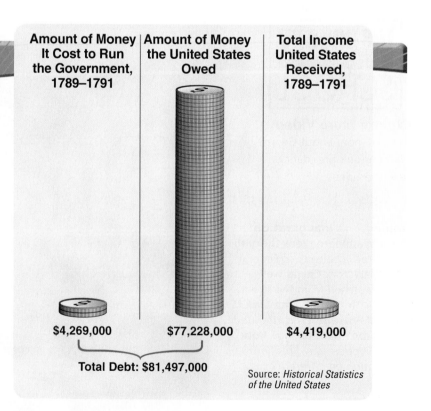

Links to Economics

The Debt Problem

The U.S. government was collecting enough in taxes to pay its expenses, but hardly enough to pay back the debt. Hamilton's financial plan sought to find new sources of income to repay the debt.
Critical Thinking: *Identifying Economic Costs* *Without the amount of money owed, how much would the government have had left over after paying its costs?*

Amount of Money It Cost to Run the Government, 1789–1791	Amount of Money the United States Owed	Total Income United States Received, 1789–1791
$4,269,000	$77,228,000	$4,419,000

Total Debt: $81,497,000

Source: *Historical Statistics of the United States*

Hamilton's Financial Plan

The person responsible for developing a plan to solve the country's financial crisis was Alexander Hamilton, the secretary of the treasury.

Hamilton's program had three parts: (1) The U.S. government would fully assume, or agree to pay, all federal *and* state debts. (2) The U.S. government would charter a national bank for depositing government funds. (3) The government would <u>impose</u> a high tax on goods imported into the country.

Paying the Debt Hamilton knew that paying the debt would be a huge burden on the U.S. government. However, he wanted to prove to people here and abroad that the United States would honor its debts in full. Then, people would be willing to invest again in the future.

Many southerners opposed the plan to repay state debts. Several southern states had paid off their wartime debts on their own. Southerners thought other states should do the same.

Congress debated the plan for six months in 1790. Then, an agreement was reached. Southerners would support Hamilton's plan to have the federal government repay the wartime debt. In return, the government would build its new capital city in the South. The capital would rise along the banks of the Potomac River, between Virginia and Maryland.

A National Bank The second part of Hamilton's plan called for the creation of a privately owned bank of the United States. It would provide a safe place to deposit government funds. The bank would be able to issue paper money that would serve as a national currency.

The debate over the bank of the United States went beyond the bank itself and focused on the powers the government had under the Constitution. Opponents of the bank, such as Thomas Jefferson, insisted that the law establishing the bank was **unconstitutional**—contrary to what is permitted by the Constitution.

Jefferson argued that nowhere in the Constitution was there a provision allowing Congress to set up a national bank. Jefferson's view, that the Constitution permits only what it specifically says, is called a "strict" interpretation of the Constitution. Hamilton argued for a "loose" interpretation. He pointed out that Article 1, Section 8 of the Constitution gave Congress the power to make all laws "necessary and proper" for fulfilling its duties. This suggested that there were things not directly permitted by the Constitution that Congress could do.

Main Idea
Alexander Hamilton proposed a three-part plan to address the economic crisis.

Vocabulary *Builder*
impose (ihm POHZ) *v.* to place a burden on something or someone

Biography Quest

Alexander Hamilton
1755–1804

If not for Aaron Burr, Alexander Hamilton might have made even greater contributions to the nation. In 1804, Burr ran for governor of New York. Hamilton opposed Burr and criticized his character. After losing the election, Burr challenged Hamilton to a duel. Hamilton was against dueling because his son had been killed in a duel. He purposely missed his shot at Burr. However, Burr took careful aim and killed Hamilton.

Biography Quest

Why did Hamilton defend Loyalists in court after the American Revolution?

For: The answer to the question about Hamilton

Visit: PHSchool.com

Web Code: myd-3041

The Whiskey Rebellion

Farmers thought that having to pay a tax on the whiskey they produced from their corn was too heavy a burden. The tax was part of Alexander Hamilton's plan to pay the nation's war debt. **Critical Thinking:** *Detect Points of View* Why did the farmers resist the tax? Why did George Washington think it was important to put down the Whiskey Rebellion?

"We Won't Pay the Tax" ▲
Angry Pennsylvania farmers and militia members tar and feather a would-be tax collector (second from left). Farmers thought it was unfair to tax their "liquid corn," or whiskey.

No Tolerance for Rebellion ▶
George Washington reviews U.S. troops as they start off to Pennsylvania to put down the rebellion. He said the farmers' actions threatened both "the just authority of government" and "the rights of individuals."

In 1791, Congress did pass a law establishing the bank, and the President signed it. However, to this day Americans disagree about whether the Constitution should be interpreted strictly or loosely.

A High Tariff The final part of Hamilton's plan called for a high tariff—a tax on imported goods. It would raise money for the federal government. It would also protect U.S. manufacturers from foreign competition.

The tariff was the only part of Hamilton's plan that Congress did not pass, and that was because southerners opposed it. They argued that a high tariff would help the North, where most industries were located, while making southerners pay more for the goods they bought.

☑**Checkpoint** How did Congress respond to Hamilton's plan?

The Whiskey Rebellion

In 1791, Congress imposed a tax on all whiskey made and sold in the United States. Hamilton hoped this tax would raise funds for the Treasury. Instead, it led to a revolt that tested the strength of the new government.

Many backcountry farmers made extra money by turning the corn they grew into whiskey. Therefore, they bitterly resented the new whiskey tax. Farmers compared it to the hated taxes that Britain had imposed on the colonies before the Revolution. Many farmers organized protests and refused to pay the tax.

In 1794, officials in western Pennsylvania tried to collect the tax. Farmers rebelled, burning down the home of a tax collector. Soon, a large, angry mob was marching through Pittsburgh like a gathering storm. The violent protest became known as the Whiskey Rebellion.

Washington responded quickly to this challenge to federal authority. He sent the militia to Pennsylvania. When the rebels heard that 13,000 troops were marching against them, they quickly scattered. Washington later pardoned the leaders of the rebellion.

The Whiskey Rebellion tested the will of the new government. Washington's forceful response showed Americans that armed rebellion was not acceptable in a republic.

☑ **Checkpoint** **What was the cause of the Whiskey Rebellion?**

☆ **Looking Back and Ahead** George Washington set a firm course for the federal government, while Alexander Hamilton began to attack the debt problem. In the next section, you will read how the nation's first political parties developed.

Main Idea

When Pennsylvania farmers rebelled against a federal tax on whiskey, President Washington responded with armed force.

Identify Similes
Find the simile in this paragraph. What two things are being compared?

Section 1 | Check Your Progress

Progress Monitoring Online
For: Self-test with instant help
Visit: PHSchool.com
Web Code: mya-3041

Comprehension and Critical Thinking

1. **(a) Describe** How did Washington's inauguration reflect the nation's deep respect for him?
(b) Organize Information Create a chart showing the top posts in the executive branch and judiciary at this time. Define each position and name the first person to occupy each post.

2. **(a) Recall** What was the nation's first economic crisis? How was it further complicated?
(b) Explain Problems What was Hamilton's plan to solve the crisis? Why was it controversial?

Reading Skill

3. **Identify Similes** Identify the simile in this sentence: The new President was as tough as nails. What two things does it compare?

Vocabulary *Builder*

4. Write two definitions for each key term: inauguration, precedent, bond, speculator, unconstitutional, tariff. First, write a formal definition for your teacher. Second, write a definition in everyday English for a classmate.

Writing

5. A newspaper account of George Washington's inauguration referred to him as "the savior of his country." That was a reference to Washington's service as commander in chief during the Revolutionary War. If you were to begin reading an essay about the life of George Washington, list five questions you would like it to answer.

The Arts of Early America

After winning independence, Americans began to develop their own styles in the arts. Often, they deliberately turned away from the model of their former British rulers.

Architecture

American architects of the Federal Period (1790–1830) turned away from the influence of England. They looked instead to two ancient civilizations, Greece and Rome. Domes and pillars were common. Buildings were designed to create a sense of harmony and balance. This picture shows the White House as it looked in 1807.

History *Interactive*

Explore Art and Music of the 1800s
Visit: PHSchool.com
Web Code: myp-3047

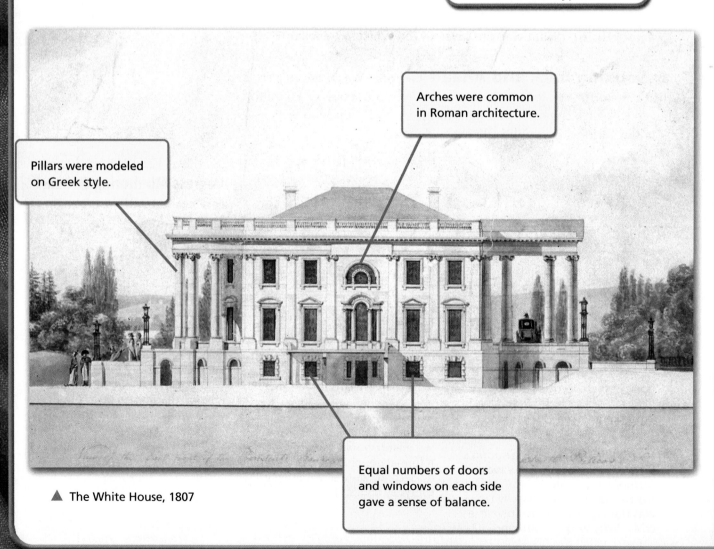

Arches were common in Roman architecture.

Pillars were modeled on Greek style.

Equal numbers of doors and windows on each side gave a sense of balance.

▲ The White House, 1807

Folk Art

Folk art is art created by ordinary people rather than trained artists. Common types of American folk art included hand-stitched samplers, weather vanes, ships' figureheads, and tavern signs. Much of the folk art of this time included patriotic images that revealed pride in the new nation. This Pennsylvania Dutch watercolor shows George Washington and his wife, Martha.

Pennsylvania Dutch watercolor ▶

Music

Many early American popular songs—including "Yankee Doodle"(below, right)—were adapted from old English melodies. In 1796, Americans put a new set of words to "Yankee Doodle" (below, left) to show pride in their democracy.

The Right of Free Elections

Should enemies beset us round,

Of foreign, fierce complexions;

Undaunted we will stand our ground,

Upheld by free elections.

We'll never from our duty swerve,

Let who will make objections;

But while we live, unchanged preserve

The freedom of elections.

Yankee Doodle

There was Captain Washington
Upon a slapping stallion
A-giving orders to his men
I guess there was a million.
Yankee Doodle, keep it up
Yankee Doodle dandy
Mind the music and the step
And with the girls be handy.

Early American flute ▲

Analyze LIFE AT THE TIME

Choose one of the examples of art, architecture, or music shown on these pages. Write a paragraph explaining how it shows a sense of pride in being an American.

Objectives

1. Explain how early political parties emerged.
2. Compare the political views of the Republicans and the Federalists.
3. Discuss the result of the election of 1796.

Prepare to Read

Reading Skill

Infer Meanings of Similes
Similes compare things that may seem unrelated. The comparison helps you to see things in a new way. When you read a simile, think about how the items being compared are similar. Try to determine what point the writer is making.

Vocabulary *Builder*

High-Use Words
hostile, p. 291
fundamental, p. 293

Key Terms and People
faction, p. 290
James Madison, p. 290
Thomas Jefferson, p. 290
Alexander Hamilton, p. 290
John Adams, p. 293

⭐ **Background Knowledge** The arguments over Hamilton's financial plan reflected serious disagreements among the new nation's leaders. In this section, you will learn how those differences led to the formation of political parties in the United States.

Main Idea

Against the expectations of the Framers of the Constitution, two political parties soon came into being.

Political Parties Emerge

The Framers of the Constitution did not expect political parties to develop in the United States. Rather, they thought that government leaders would rise above personal or local interests. The leaders, they believed, would work together for the sake of the country.

In those days, people spoke of *factions* rather than *political parties.* A **faction** was an organized political group, and the word was not complimentary. **James Madison** considered factions to be selfish groups, unconcerned with the well-being of the whole nation. Madison argued in the *Federalist Papers* that an effective national government would prevent the growth of factions. As he put it,

> **"**Among the numerous advantages promised by a well-constructed Union, none deserves to be more accurately developed than its tendency to break and control the violence of faction.**"**
>
> —James Madison, *The Federalist* No. 10, 1787

Infer Meanings of Similes

To what is "the spirit of faction" compared in the final sentence of this paragraph? What does the comparison mean?

Thomas Jefferson and **Alexander Hamilton,** who were rarely in agreement, both disliked factions. Hamilton warned that the "spirit of faction" might work like a spark to bring mob rule and chaos.

No one was more <u>hostile</u> to factions than George Washington. The President watched unhappily as Jefferson and Hamilton, the leading members of his Cabinet, grew apart. Washington tried to reduce the quarreling. In a letter to Henry Lee, he predicted that factions would destroy the "best fabric of human government and happiness."

Despite Washington's efforts, by the early 1790s two political parties were beginning to form. One group supported Thomas Jefferson and his close ally, James Madison. The other supported Alexander Hamilton and his ideas.

✓**Checkpoint**   **Why did many of the nation's leaders dislike political parties?**

Republicans Against Federalists

The two parties that took shape during the first half of the 1790s eventually got the names Republicans and Federalists.

The Republicans took their name from political clubs called Democratic-Republican Societies that had been organized in various parts of the country. They argued that the federal government was growing too strong under President Washington. They wanted to keep most power at the state or local level. They feared that a strong central government would act like a monarchy.

Vocabulary *Builder*
<u>hostile</u> (HAHS tihl) *adj.* unfriendly; adverse or opposed

Main Idea
The Republicans and the Federalists disagreed on how powerful the federal government should be.

Republicans Versus Federalists

Republicans	Federalists
1. Were led by Thomas Jefferson	1. Were led by Alexander Hamilton
2. Believed people should have political power	2. Believed wealthy and educated should lead
3. Favored strong state government	3. Favored strong central government
4. Emphasized agriculture	4. Emphasized manufacturing, shipping, and trade
5. Favored strict interpretation of Constitution	5. Favored loose interpretation of Constitution
6. Were pro-French	6. Were pro-British
7. Opposed national bank	7. Favored national bank
8. Opposed protective tariff	8. Favored protective tariff

Reading Charts

Skills Activity

The nation's first political parties were the Federalists and the Republicans. They took opposing stands on many political issues.

(a) Read a Chart How did the parties differ on federal power?

(b) Apply Information Why did the party that favored strong state governments insist on a strict interpretation of the Constitution?

Links Across Time

Political Parties Then and Now

1790s Political differences between Thomas Jefferson and Alexander Hamilton led to the development of America's first political parties.

1850s By the 1850s, the parties we know today had taken shape. Today's Democratic Party actually traces its roots to Jefferson's Republican Party. The modern Republican Party, which was born during the 1850s over the issue of slavery, has no connection to Jefferson's Republicans.

Link to Today ◉nline

Political Parties Today The two major parties play a leading role in the American political system. How do the parties stand on today's political issues?

For: Political parties in the news
Visit: PHSchool.com
Web Code: myc-3042

The donkey is the modern-day symbol associated with the Democratic Party.

The symbol for today's Republican Party is an elephant.

This early Republican Party drew its main strength from southern planters and northern farmers and artisans. Key leaders were James Madison and Thomas Jefferson. Unhappy with the federal government's policies, Jefferson resigned as secretary of state in 1793.

The Federalists took their name from the people who had supported the adoption of the Constitution after 1787. A prominent leader was Alexander Hamilton. As in the debates over the Constitution, Federalists said the United States needed a strong federal government to hold the country together and deal with its problems.

Federalists drew support mainly from merchants, other property owners, and ordinary workers whose jobs depended on manufacturing and trade. They were especially strong in the North.

Organizing and Arguing At the time that both parties were organizing, the Federalists had an advantage. President Washington usually supported Hamilton and his policies. One Hamilton supporter running for office proudly said, "I am a FEDERALIST, the friend of order, of government, and of the present administration."

A newspaper editor who supported the Republicans saw the situation very differently. In 1792, he printed a series of questions in the *National Gazette* implying that the Federalists wanted to betray the Constitution and bring back a king. "Are not some amongst us . . . advocates for monarchy and aristocracy?" he asked. "Are not the principles of all such [people] hostile to the principles of the constitution?"

Other Disagreements In addition to their <u>fundamental</u> disagreement about the power of the federal government, Federalists and Republicans disagreed about other issues. Federalists favored the national bank and a national tariff. The Republicans opposed both. Federalists favored close ties with England. Republicans were sympathetic to France, where a revolution overthrew the king in 1789. (You will read more about the French Revolution in Section 3.)

Vocabulary *Builder*
<u>fundamental</u> (fuhn duh MEHN tahl) *adj.* basic; most important; forming the foundation of an idea or action; essential

☑ **Checkpoint** How did Federalists and Republicans differ?

The Election of 1796

In 1796, George Washington said he would not seek a third term. This set an important precedent. Not until Franklin Roosevelt ran for and won a third term in 1940 would any President seek more than two terms. (In 1951, the Twenty-second Amendment legally limited the President to two terms.)

The Republican candidate for President in 1796 was Thomas Jefferson. The Federalists nominated John Adams, a New Englander, who had been Washington's Vice President.

In 1796, President and Vice President were not elected together as a ticket, as they are today. Instead, the candidate getting the most votes became President and the second-place candidate became Vice President.

Adams finished first and Jefferson second. The country thus gained a Federalist President and a Republican Vice President. Not surprisingly, this led to serious tensions during the next four years.

Main Idea
The 1796 election gave the United States a Federalist President and a Republican Vice President.

☑ **Checkpoint** Which party won the presidency in 1796?

☆ **Looking Back and Ahead** The Republicans and Federalists had conflicting visions of what the federal government should do. In the next section, you will read how President Washington dealt with challenges at home and abroad.

Section 2 | **Check Your Progress**

Progress Monitoring Online
For: Self-test with instant help
Visit: PHSchool.com
Web Code: mya-3042

Comprehension and Critical Thinking

1. **(a) Describe** How did the Framers of the Constitution feel about political parties?
(b) Draw Conclusions Do you believe having political parties helps or hurts the nation? Explain.

2. **(a) Recall** What was the fundamental difference between the two political parties?

(b) Detect Points of View If you were a worker at a northern textile mill during Washington's presidency, would you have supported the Republicans or the Federalists? Explain.

Reading Skill
3. **Infer Meanings of Similes** Explain the simile in this sentence: Alexander Hamilton acted like a friend to government.

Vocabulary *Builder*
Complete this sentence so it clearly shows your understanding of the key term.
4. As a result of factions, _____.

Writing
5. Use Internet or library resources to find and read an article giving an overview of the life of George Washington. Then, create a timeline showing the most important events in Washington's life.

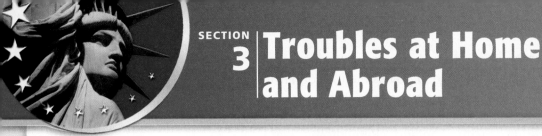

Objectives

1. Discuss the conflicts with Native Americans in the Northwest Territory.

2. Describe how Americans reacted to the French Revolution.

3. Identify the main points of Washington's Farewell Address.

4. Summarize Washington's accomplishments as President.

Prepare to Read

Reading Skill

Infer Meanings of Metaphors
As you read, notice metaphors that speak of one item as if it were another. For example, "he is the foundation of our success" means that his work supports our success, as a foundation supports a building. The word *like* is absent but is suggested by the comparison. As you read this section, look for metaphors.

Vocabulary *Builder*

High-Use Words
cease, p. 296
emphasize, p. 297

Key Terms and People
Anthony Wayne, p. 295
neutral, p. 295
impressment, p. 296
John Jay, p. 296

⭐ **Background Knowledge** The first two sections in this chapter have discussed political divisions within the United States during a turbulent and confusing time. In this section, you will learn how President Washington coped with a variety of other challenges.

Conflicts in the Northwest Territory

Main Idea
Settlers clashed with British-backed Native Americans in the Northwest Territory.

As a result of the Treaty of Paris that ended the American Revolution, the United States won the vast territory north and west of the Ohio River to the Mississippi River. Although the British still had forts in the region, they promised to withdraw within a "reasonable" time. A decade later, the British soldiers were still there. Moreover, the British were supplying Native Americans with guns and ammunition. The British hoped that this would limit American settlement in the Northwest Territory.

A Struggle Over Lands Native Americans in the Northwest Territory wanted to keep their lands. During the 1780s, they attacked many American settlements. Several Native American groups joined together to oppose settlement.

Many American leaders believed that the country's future depended on settling its western lands. Therefore, the federal government tried to force Native Americans in the territories to sell their lands. By 1790, the United States had succeeded in buying Native American lands in most of Kentucky and in part of Tennessee. North of the Ohio River, Native Americans refused to sell. Even there, though, the flow of white settlement continued.

Infer Meanings of Metaphors
Explain the metaphor in the final sentence of this paragraph.

A Series of Battles In 1790, Washington sent a small force to end the Native American attacks on settlers. Warriors led by Little Turtle of the Miami Nation and Blue Jacket of the Shawnees defeated the soldiers. The next year, Washington sent a larger force. This time, Little Turtle won an even bigger victory. More than 900 soldiers were killed or wounded. It was the worst defeat the army would ever suffer in a battle with Native Americans.

Washington then turned to a Revolutionary War hero, General Anthony Wayne, to lead the forces against the Native Americans. Native Americans gathered for battle at a place where fallen trees covered the ground. They thought the trees would cause trouble for Wayne and his soldiers. But in August 1794, Wayne won a major victory at the Battle of Fallen Timbers.

That battle broke the Native American hold on the Northwest. In the 1795 Treaty of Greenville, leaders of the defeated Native American nations gave up most of their lands from the Ohio River in the south to Lake Erie in the north. Today, that is most of the state of Ohio.

☑**Checkpoint** **How were the conflicting claims of settlers and Native Americans resolved?**

Treaty of Greenville

In the Treaty of Greenville, Native Americans gave up, or ceded, territory to the United States. The cessions (lands ceded) are shown in color.

(a) Read a Map How many areas were ceded?

(b) Analyze Cause and Effect What event shown on the map led to the cessions?

MapMaster Online

For: Interactive map
Visit: PHSchool.com
Web Code: myp-3043

KEY

▨ Indian cessions

Miami Indian tribes

The French Revolution

The French Revolution began in 1789. Most Americans at first supported the French revolutionaries. In their eyes, France was following the lead of the United States in fighting monarchy.

Soon, though, the French Revolution became controversial in the United States. One reason was that it became more violent. This process peaked in mid-1793 with a period called the Reign of Terror. The French revolutionaries executed about 17,000 people, including the king and queen. The Federalists denounced the violence. But Jefferson and his supporters argued that in a fight by oppressed people to win freedom, some injustices were to be expected.

Secondly, by early 1793, France and Britain were at war. In that war, said President Washington, the United States would remain neutral—not favoring either side in a dispute.

The United States wanted to trade with both sides. However, each European country feared such trade would benefit the other. Both countries began stopping American ships and seizing their cargoes.

Main Idea

Americans at first welcomed the French Revolution, but they divided over how to respond.

American Reaction to the Reign of Terror

In this excerpt, a British observer describes the reactions of some Americans to the execution of Louis XVI.

In this illustration, an executioner displays the severed head of Louis XVI.

❝Never was the memory of any man so cruelly insulted as that of this mild and humane monarch [Louis XVI]. He was guillotined in effigy [using a dummy to represent a real person], in the capital of the Union [Philadelphia], twenty or thirty times every day, during one whole winter and part of the summer. Men, women, and children flocked to the tragical exhibition, and not a single paragraph appeared in the papers to shame them from it.❞

—William Cobbett, *History of the American Jacobins* (Philadelphia, 1796)

Reading Primary Sources
Skills Activity

During the Reign of Terror, revolutionaries used the guillotine to behead the French king Louis XVI in January 1793. Queen Marie Antoinette was executed in October 1793.

(a) Detect Points of View How did the author view Louis XVI's execution?

(b) Draw Conclusions How do you think Philadelphians who attended the "tragical exhibition" felt about the king's execution? Explain.

The British made matters worse by the **impressment** of sailors on American ships, which meant seizing the sailors and forcing them to serve in the British navy. Some of the sailors were British sailors who had fled the British navy, but many were Americans.

As tensions rose, Hamilton urged the President to stay friendly with Britain. He argued that American prosperity depended on trade with Britain. The British purchased 75 percent of American exports and supplied 90 percent of American imports.

Washington agreed and tried to repair relations with Britain. He sent John Jay to London to try to solve the most serious problems.

Jay returned with a treaty in 1795. In it, the United States agreed to pay debts long owed to British merchants. In return, Britain agreed to pay for the ships it had seized. It also agreed to withdraw its troops from the Northwest Territory and stop aiding Native Americans there. However, the British refused to recognize a U.S. right to trade with France. They also refused to <u>cease</u> impressment of U.S. sailors.

The Jay Treaty angered Republicans. They claimed the United States had given away too much and gotten too little. Federalists, in contrast, liked the treaty because it kept peace with Britain. Since Federalists controlled the Senate, the Jay Treaty won approval by a narrow margin.

Vocabulary *Builder*
<u>cease</u> (sees) *v.* to cause to come to an end; to stop

✓**Checkpoint** How did Americans react to the Jay Treaty?

Washington Retires From Public Life

In 1796, Washington published a letter to fellow Americans that had lasting influence. Washington's Farewell Address made two major points. First, the President warned against political divisions at home. He feared that violent divisions might tear the nation apart.

Washington's second piece of advice concerned foreign policy. In a famous passage, Washington <u>emphasized</u> his belief that the United States must not get entangled in the affairs of Europe. He said:

> **"**Europe has a set of primary interests which to us have none or a very remote relation. . . . Why . . . entangle our peace and prosperity in the toils [traps] of European ambition? . . . It is our true policy to steer clear of permanent alliances with any portion of the foreign world.**"**
>
> —George Washington, Farewell Address, 1796

As he left office, Washington could take pride in his accomplishments: (1) The United States now had a functioning federal government. (2) The economy was improving. (3) Washington had avoided war. (4) The British had been forced to leave their forts in the Northwest Territory, an area that was now safe for settlement.

Still, political divisions were growing and challenges remained.

☑ **Checkpoint** What were Washington's chief accomplishments?

☆ **Looking Back and Ahead** As President, George Washington created conditions for a strong federal government. In the next section, you will read how his successor sought to deal with divisions at home and challenges abroad.

Main Idea
Washington's Farewell Address has had lasting influence.

Vocabulary *Builder*
emphasize (EHM fah sīz) *v.* to stress; to give more importance to

---

Section 3 | Check Your Progress

Progress Monitoring Online
For: Self-test with instant help
Visit: PHSchool.com
Web Code: mya-3043

Comprehension and Critical Thinking

1. **(a) Describe** How did Washington deal with Britain's policy of impressment?
   (b) Compare and Contrast How did Washington's policy on matters at home differ from his foreign policy?

2. **(a) Recall** What were the two main arguments Washington made in his Farewell Address?
   (b) Distinguish Facts From Opinions Support the following opinion with facts from the chapter: George Washington was a great first President.

Reading Skill

3. **Infer Meanings of Metaphors** Identify and explain the metaphor in this sentence: In the heated political atmosphere, this warning had little impact.

Vocabulary *Builder*
Read each sentence that follows. If the sentence is true, write YES. If the sentence is not true, write NO and explain why.

4. As a neutral nation, the United States should trade only with Britain and not France.

5. The Jay Treaty did not end the impressment of American sailors by the British navy.

Writing

6. Based on what you have read about George Washington in this section, write a description of the personality traits he showed as President of the United States. Include at least two specific examples of actions that he took as President.

Objectives

1. Discuss the reasons for tension between the United States and France.

2. Describe the main provisions of the Alien and Sedition acts.

3. Explain how controversy arose over states' rights.

Prepare to Read

Reading Skill

Identify Analogies In an analogy, two pairs of items are connected with the same sort of comparison. For example, both pairs might compare synonyms, or words with similar meanings. You must understand the comparison between the first pair in order to complete the comparison between the second pair. Some common types of analogies are cause-effect, antonyms, and synonyms.

Vocabulary *Builder*

High-Use Words

react, p. 298

provoke, p. 301

Key Terms

alien, p. 300

sedition, p. 300

nullify, p. 301

states' rights, p. 301

⭐ **Background Knowledge** As you have read, John Adams was elected to succeed George Washington as President. Like Washington, he struggled to reduce the country's divisions and to steer a neutral course in foreign policy.

Main Idea
Despite many Americans' desire for war against France, John Adams managed to resolve differences peacefully.

Troubles With France

Adams immediately faced a crisis over relations with France. The French were angered by U.S. neutrality in the war between France and Britain. France had hoped for U.S. support. Had not French assistance been the key to success in the American Revolution? Why didn't Americans show their gratitude by helping the French now?

The Jay Treaty only increased tensions with France. As the French saw it, the treaty put the United States on Britain's side. France reacted late in 1796 by snubbing a U.S. diplomat. Moreover, the French continued to attack American merchant ships.

Vocabulary *Builder*
react (ree AKT) *v.* to act in response to another action; to respond

The XYZ Affair In 1797, Adams sent a new three-person mission to France. Agents of the French government demanded that the United States pay a bribe of $250,000. The agents also wanted the United States to lend France several million dollars.

The Americans said they would pay "not a sixpence [a coin worth six pennies]." Later, that statement led to the slogan, "Millions for defense, but not one sixpence for tribute [a forced payment]."

The bribe attempt was a sensation when it became public. Because the names of the French agents were kept secret, they were called X, Y, and Z. The incident became known as the XYZ Affair.

War Fever The XYZ Affair caused an outbreak of war fever in the United States. Many Federalists demanded that Adams ask Congress to declare war on France.

With war fever rising, Adams asked Congress to increase the size of the army and rebuild the navy. It did both, thus enhancing the power of the central government. Adams also convinced Congress to create a separate department of the navy. Between 1798 and 1800, the United States fought an undeclared naval war with France.

Nonetheless, the President and many other Americans opposed a full-scale war. To avoid war, Adams sent a new mission to France. Napoleon Bonaparte, France's dictator, was busy dealing with war in Europe. In 1800, he agreed to stop seizing American ships.

President Adams had avoided war. But the agreement angered leaders of his own Federalist Party, especially the pro-British Hamilton. This disapproval weakened Adams politically.

Still, Adams was satisfied. He told a friend that he wanted his tombstone to read: "Here lies John Adams, who took upon himself the responsibility of peace with France in the year 1800."

Identify Analogies The phrase *war fever* is an analogy. Think about what having a fever does to a person's body. How is that similar to what the desire for war might do to the country?

☑**Checkpoint** **How did Adams settle differences with France?**

The Alien and Sedition Acts

The war fever deepened the split between Federalists and Republicans. Federalists' fear of revolutionary France spilled over into a mistrust of immigrants. Federalists suspected them of bringing in dangerous ideas and feared that they would back the Republicans.

Main Idea
During the troubles with France, Federalists in Congress passed drastic laws to limit immigration and restrict free speech.

The Five-Headed Monster

The three American representatives declare, "Cease bawling, Monster! We will not give you sixpence."

The five-headed monster represents the French government.

Reading Political Cartoons
Skills Activity

The XYZ Affair stirred anti-French feeling in the United States. This 1798 cartoon shows a five-headed creature demanding a bribe from the three American representatives (at left).

(a) Explain What does the five-headed creature want?

(b) Detect Points of View What opinion do you think the cartoonist has of the French government? What evidence supports your view?

Links to Government

New Life for a Debate

Passage of the Alien and Sedition acts renewed the debate over federal versus state power. Jefferson and Madison wrote the Kentucky and Virginia resolutions in defense of states' rights. **Critical Thinking:** *Detect Points of View According to defenders of states' rights in 1798, what could states do if they disliked a federal law?*

Arguments for States' Rights	Arguments for Federal Power
■ The federal government derives its power from rights given to it by the states. ■ Because the states created the United States, individual states have the power to nullify a federal law.	■ The federal government derives its power from rights given to it by the American people. ■ States have no power to nullify federal laws. ■ States cannot revoke federal powers set forth in the Constitution.

Trouble on the Horizon

Within 25 years of the Alien and Sedition acts, people in New England and South Carolina would threaten to leave the Union because they either disagreed with American foreign policy or opposed laws passed by Congress.

Federalist leaders decided that to restore order at home they must destroy their political opponents. Congress passed a group of laws in 1798 aimed at immigrants. Another 1798 law targeted Republicans.

The laws directed at immigrants were the Alien Act. An **alien** is an outsider or someone from another country. The Alien Act increased the length of time from 5 to 14 years that a person had to live in the United States to become a citizen. The President gained the power to deport or imprison any alien he considered dangerous.

The law targeting Republicans was the Sedition Act. **Sedition** is activity designed to overthrow a government. The Sedition Act probably was the harshest law limiting free speech ever passed in the United States. It made it a crime for anyone to write or say anything insulting or anything false about the President, Congress, or the government in general. During 1798 and 1799, ten people were convicted under the act. Most were Republican editors and printers.

☑Checkpoint **What did the Alien and Sedition acts do?**

Main Idea
Critics of the Alien and Sedition acts argued that states could refuse to obey certain federal laws.

States' Rights

The Republicans denounced the Alien and Sedition acts. They charged that the Sedition Act violated the Constitution, especially the First Amendment, which guarantees freedom of speech.

However, the Republicans faced a problem opposing the law. At the time, it was not clearly established that the Supreme Court had the power to strike down a law as unconstitutional. Because of this, the Republicans expressed their opposition through the state legislatures.

Republicans James Madison and Thomas Jefferson, both Virginians, led the campaign. Madison wrote a resolution attacking the Alien and Sedition acts. It was passed by the Virginia legislature. Jefferson wrote a similar resolution that was passed by the Kentucky legislature. Together, the Virginia and Kentucky resolutions stated that the Alien and Sedition acts were unconstitutional. They declared that states had the right to declare laws passed by Congress to be unconstitutional.

No other states supported Virginia and Kentucky, so the two resolutions had little immediate impact. As for the Alien and Sedition acts, they were not in force for long. The law that gave the President the power to imprison or deport dangerous aliens expired after two years. The Sedition Act expired in 1801. The waiting period for immigrants to become citizens was restored to five years in 1802.

However, over the long term the Virginia and Kentucky resolutions were far more important than the laws that provoked them. The resolutions claimed that states could nullify—deprive of legal force—a law passed by Congress. The resolutions also boosted the idea of states' rights. This is the idea that the union binding "these United States" is an agreement between the states and that they therefore can overrule federal law. In decades to come, a number of states would refuse to obey certain federal laws. States' rights would become the rallying cry for southern defenders of slavery.

✔Checkpoint **Why did the issue of states' rights arise at this time?**

⭐ **Looking Back and Ahead** You have read how the United States got up and running under its first two Presidents. The next chapter deals with the next two Presidents, Thomas Jefferson and James Madison, and the challenges they faced.

James Madison

Vocabulary *Builder*
provoke (prah VOHK) *v.* to cause to anger; to excite; to cause an action

---

Section 4 | **Check Your Progress**

Progress Monitoring Online
For: Self-test with instant help
Visit: PHSchool.com
Web Code: mya-3044

Comprehension and Critical Thinking

1. **(a) Recall** What problem did President Adams face abroad?
(b) Explain Problems How did Adams resolve this problem?

2. **(a) Summarize** Why did the Federalist Congress pass the Alien and Sedition acts?
(b) Analyze Cause and Effect Explain the following statement: State reaction to the Alien and Sedition acts caused further tension between the political parties.

Reading Skill

3. **Identify Analogies** Explain the analogy in this sentence: As the call for war heated up, John Adams tried to be the nation's firefighter.

Vocabulary *Builder*

Answer the following questions in complete sentences that show your understanding of the key terms.
4. Why did Federalists mistrust aliens?
5. Why did newspaper editors accused of sedition tend to be Republicans?

6. Why did Republicans want to nullify the Alien and Sedition acts?
7. How can states' rights be used to oppose federal laws?

Writing

8. Use Internet or library resources to research the life of John Adams. List the principal events in his life. Then, describe the personality traits he displayed as President of the United States. Write a thesis statement that could be used to introduce a biographical essay about Adams.

It is important to be able to tell the difference between facts and opinions when you read historical stories and narratives. A fact is something that can be proved to be true or can be observed. An opinion is a statement that reflects a person's feelings, judgments, or beliefs about a subject.

This diary entry, which is historical fiction, was written by a merchant living in colonial Philadelphia in the 1790s.

February 28

After dinner tonight I finished reading today's edition of the *Gazette of the United States.* The publisher of the newspaper is John Fenno. In my opinion, he is right to favor the Federalist leader, Alexander Hamilton. Of course, I am a merchant and I agree with Hamilton's support of trade and manufacturing. To me it is a more worthwhile policy than Mr. Jefferson's support of the farmers.

I believe that I have Hamilton alone to thank for the National Bank. This Bank, established by Congress in 1791, has the power to make loans to businesses, such as my dry goods store. Of course, the federal Bank is opposed by that friend of the states, Thomas Jefferson, who isn't thinking of our country's future. I only hope that Mr. Hamilton's party wins the next election.

—Isaac Smith

Learn the Skill
Use these steps to identify facts and opinions.

1. **Decide which statements are facts.** Facts are statements that are based on direct evidence and can be proved to be true. Facts tell what really happened. You can look up a statement in a research source to prove it is a fact.

2. **Decide which statements are opinions.** An opinion is a personal interpretation of an event, an idea, or a person. Words such as "I think," "I believe," or "I feel" are often used in a statement of opinion. Look for these words when you read.

3. **Recognize how writers or speakers mix facts and opinions.** Sometimes writers use facts to support their personal opinion. Or, writers use facts and opinions to persuade the reader to support their point of view.

Practice the Skill
Answer the following questions about the journal entry on this page.

1. **Decide which statements are facts.** (a) Find two facts in this journal entry. (b) How can you prove that each statement is a fact?

2. **Decide which statements are opinions.** (a) Find two statements of opinion in this journal entry. (b) How can you tell that each is an opinion?

3. **Recognize how writers or speakers mix facts and opinions.** (a) Find an example of a statement that mixes fact and opinion. What is the fact? What is the opinion? (b) Why do you think the writer mixed fact and opinion in this selection?

Apply the Skill
See the Review and Assessment at the end of this chapter.

CHAPTER **8** | **Quick Study Guide**

interactive
Textbook

Study Guide *Online*
Complete your Chapter 8
study guide in print or online.

Chapter Summary

Section 1
Launching a New Nation

- George Washington was inaugurated as the first President in April of 1789.
- Washington and Congress organized the executive and judiciary branches.
- Alexander Hamilton developed a financial plan to repay the country's large war debt.
- Federal forces put down the Whiskey Rebellion in 1794.

Section 2
The Birth of Political Parties

- Deepening differences between factions led to the first political parties.
- Republicans wanted a limited national government, while Federalists favored a strong federal government.
- John Adams, a Federalist, won the presidency in 1796. Thomas Jefferson, a Republican, won the vice presidency.

Section 3
Troubles at Home and Abroad

- Washington responded forcefully to conflict in the Northwest Territory between settlers and Native Americans.
- The United States remained neutral when France and Britain went to war.
- In his Farewell Address, George Washington warned the nation against disunity and against becoming involved in foreign wars.

Section 4
The Presidency of John Adams

- John Adams was elected President of the United States in 1796.
- The United States and France avoided full-scale war under Adams but fought an undeclared naval war.
- The Federalist-sponsored Alien and Sedition acts provoked a strong reaction by Republicans in favor of states' rights.

Key Concepts

These notes will help you prepare for questions about key concepts.

	George Washington's Presidency	John Adams's Presidency
Key Events at Home	First Cabinet forms	Tension continues between political parties
	National bank opens	Alien Act passes
	Rise of political parties	Sedition Act passes
	Whiskey Rebellion occurs	Issues over states' rights develop
	Battle of Fallen Timbers occurs	Adams's political party does not support him for second term
	Washington retires	
Key Events Abroad	Britain and France ignore U.S. policy of neutrality	XYZ Affair occurs
	Britain signs the Jay Treaty	Navy is enlarged for undeclared war with France

Vocabulary *Builder*

Key Terms

Fill in the blanks with the correct key terms.

1. Many of the customs that Washington started set a _____ for how other Presidents were to act in the future.

2. Jefferson said the national bank was _____ because it was not written in the Constitution that Congress had authority to establish one.

3. Neither France nor Britain agreed that the United States could be a _____ nation and trade with both sides during their war.

4. The _____ Act violated the First Amendment of the Constitution.

Comprehension and Critical Thinking

5. **(a) Recall** What was the purpose of George Washington's Cabinet?
   (b) Link Past and Present Why do you think current Presidents have more advisers than the number required in Washington's day?

6. **(a) Describe** What were two internal problems and their resolutions during Washington's second term as President?
   (b) Explain Problems What does the picture below indicate about Washington's view of the Whiskey Rebellion?

7. **(a) Recall** In Washington's Farewell Address, he talked about neutrality toward European nations. Why did Washington believe that the United States needed to be neutral in the war between France and Britain?
   (b) Draw Conclusions In Washington's Farewell Address, he also talked about national unity. Why was building unity an important goal for Washington?

8. **(a) Recall** Why were the Alien and Sedition acts unpopular with many people?
   (b) Apply Information Would you defend or oppose the government's right to silence people who criticize it? Explain.

History Reading Skill

9. **Analyze Comparisons** George Washington is often referred to as the Father of Our Country. What is the meaning of this metaphor? Do you think this is a valid comparison? Explain.

Writing

10. **Write a paragraph about either George Washington or John Adams.**
    Include major events and describe your subject's personality.

    Your paragraph should:
    • begin with a thesis statement;
    • expand on that main idea with facts, examples, and other information;
    • conclude by stating what you think was your subject's most important contribution to the new nation.

11. **Write a Narrative:**
    Study the pictures, map, and text in Section 1 about the Whiskey Rebellion. Write a two-paragraph narrative describing the rebellion. Write from the point of view of either a farmer or a soldier.

Skills for Life

Distinguish Facts From Opinions

Use the fictional journal entry below to answer the questions that follow.

> "I am grateful that at least our Vice President, Thomas Jefferson, is a Republican. I believe that his policies are the only hope for farmers, such as myself and my neighbors. In my opinion, our political leaders don't have to be rich or well-educated. The people can lead as well as follow. Of course, the Federalist Mr. Hamilton, with his fine clothes, favors the wealthy merchants."

12. **(a)** Identify one fact in the journal entry.
    (b) How can you prove the statement is a fact?

13. **(a)** What is an example of an opinion?
    (b) How can you tell the statement is an opinion?

14. Find a statement that mixes fact and opinion. What is the fact? What is the opinion?

Test Yourself

1. **Which of the following led to tension between France and the United States during Adams's presidency?**

   A Treaty of Greenville

   B Jay Treaty

   C Treaty of Paris

   D Declaration of Independence

Refer to the quotation below to answer Question 2.

> "It is in my judgment necessary under the circumstances of the case to take measures for calling forth the militia in order to . . . cause the laws to be duly executed."

2. **What event is the subject of the quotation?**

   A French Revolution

   B XYZ Affair

   C Battle of Fallen Timbers

   D Whiskey Rebellion

Refer to the chart below to answer Question 3.

The First Political Parties	
Federalists	**Republicans**
Favored strong central government	Favored state government
Emphasized manufacturing, shipping, and trade	Emphasized agriculture
Supported loose interpretation of the Constitution	Supported strict interpretation of the Constitution
Favored national bank	Opposed national bank

3. **Which statement describes a fundamental difference between the two parties?**

   A Federalists believed in a strong central government, and Republicans did not.

   B Federalists believed in a strict interpretation of the Constitution, and Republicans did not.

   C Republicans believed in a strong central government, and Federalists did not.

   D Republicans believed in a loose interpretation of the Constitution, and Federalists did not.

Document-Based Questions

Task: Look at Documents 1 and 2, and answer their accompanying questions. Then, use the documents and your knowledge of history to complete this writing assignment:

> Write a newspaper editorial supporting or attacking President Adams's decision to avoid war with France.

Document 1: In 1797, France began seizing American ships. Enraged Americans called for war, but President John Adams urged a policy of peace. *What action does Adams say he will take toward France?*

> "It is my sincere desire . . . to preserve peace and friendship with all nations; and believing that neither the honor nor the interest of the United States absolutely forbid the repetition of advances for securing these desirable objects with France, I shall institute a fresh attempt at negotiation, and shall not fail to promote and accelerate an accommodation on terms compatible with the rights, duties, interests, and honor of the nation."

Document 2: After the XYZ Affair, newspapers published cartoons such as the one shown below. It depicts the United States as a young woman surrounded by members of the French government. *What is the cartoonist's view of the XYZ Affair?*

PROPERTY PROTECTED à la Françoise.

CHAPTER
9 | **The Era of Thomas Jefferson**
1800–1815

Chapter Preview

By 1800, the Federalists faced many problems. The Alien and Sedition acts had angered many Americans. The party itself was divided. The election of 1800 would mark the end of the Federalist era. A new party took charge of the government, and a period of growth and national pride began.

Section 1	☑ **What You Will Learn**
Jefferson Takes Office Pages 310–313	Thinking of his election as "the Revolution of 1800," President Jefferson hoped to make far-reaching changes in government.
Section 2	
The Louisiana Purchase Pages 314–319	Having acquired a vast expanse of western territory, Jefferson sent Meriwether Lewis and William Clark to explore the region.
Section 3	
A Time of Conflict Pages 322–326	Conflicts with the British at sea and Native Americans in the West led to the War of 1812.
Section 4	
The War of 1812 Pages 327–331	Although the War of 1812 did not resolve British-American disputes, many Americans considered the war a victory.

U.S. Events

1803 United States purchases Louisiana from France.

1804 Lewis and Clark set out to explore Louisiana.

1809 Embargo Act bans foreign trade.

1800   1805   1810

World Events

1804 Napoleon becomes emperor of France.

1810 Mexico declares independence from Spain.

Quick View Video
View the chapter video for a quick preview of the main ideas.

The USS *Philadelphia* burns in Tripoli harbor, 1804. Although Americans wanted no involvement in foreign conflict, they were still drawn into a brief war with North African pirates.

1811
Americans defeat Native Americans at Tippecanoe.

1812
United States declares war on Britain.

1815
Battle of New Orleans is fought.

1810

1815

1820

1815 Napoleon suffers final defeat at Battle of Waterloo.

1819 Simón Bolívar seizes Bogotá from the Spanish.

History Reading Skill **Relate Events in Time**

What did Americans discover as they explored new lands to the west?

In this chapter, you will learn how to relate events in time and understand their sequence. Read this account of an important exploration of the American West in the early 1800s. The side notes show you how to relate events in time and identify their sequence.

Primary Source

In 1804, President Jefferson sent Meriwether Lewis and William Clark to explore the Louisiana Territory. Lewis and Clark kept journals documenting their travels. The first paragraph below is a letter introducing part of those journals. The second paragraph is an excerpt from the journals.

> The dates clarify the sequence.

"They left the Pacific Ocean 23d March, 1806, where they arrived in November, 1805;—and where some Americans had been just before. . . . They have kept an ample journal of their tour, which will be published, and must afford much intelligence."

> Words such as *before, after, next,* and *soon* show sequence.

> Time descriptions tell readers what happened when.

"Here we remained during the day, the wind having risen at twelve so high that we could not proceed. It continued to blow violently all night, with occasional sprinklings of rain from sunset till midnight. On both sides of the river the country is rough and broken, the low grounds becoming narrower; the tops of the hills on the north exhibits some scattered pine and cedar, on the south, the pine has not yet commenced. . . ."

> This verb shows sequence by describing a process.

—Journals of the Lewis and Clark expedition

Relate Events in Time

- Sequence signal words tell you when events happen in time.
- Use sequence verbs to understand the order of events in time.
- Look for dates or times to relate events to one another in time.
- Notice when two or more events occur at the same time.

Document-Based Questions

1. Why did Lewis and Clark keep a journal?
2. What kinds of information did they record? List five specific details in the journal excerpt.
3. Do you think their journals were a good source of information about the American West? Explain.

Vocabulary *Builder*

Previewing High-Use Academic Words

High-Use Word	Definition	Sample History Sentence
prospect (PRAHS pehkt) (Section 1, p. 310)	*n.* expectation; likely outcome	Slaveholders in the southern colonies feared the <u>prospect</u> of a rebellion by enslaved people.
cease (sees) (Section 1, p. 313)	*v.* to stop; to come to an end	With Cornwallis's surrender at Yorktown, all Revolutionary War fighting <u>ceased</u>.
crisis (KRĪ sihs) (Section 2, p. 314)	*n.* turning point or deciding event in history	The Whiskey Rebellion created a <u>crisis</u> for George Washington's presidency.
alter (AWL ter) (Section 2, p. 315)	*v.* to change in some way; to make different	Cornwallis's decision to camp on the Yorktown peninsula <u>altered</u> the course of the American Revolution.
decline (dee KLĪN) (Section 3, p. 324)	*v.* to gradually lose strength or power	The strength of the Continental army <u>declined</u> after Valley Forge.
restore (ree STOR) (Section 3, p. 326)	*v.* to bring back to a former condition	The Loyalists hoped to <u>restore</u> British power to the colonies.
reinforce (ree ihn FORS) (Section 4, p. 328)	*v.* to strengthen with additional troops	At Yorktown, American forces were <u>reinforced</u> by the French navy.
critic (KRIHT ihk) (Section 4, p. 331)	*n.* someone who makes judgments on the value of actions	The Antifederalists were <u>critics</u> of the U.S. Constitution.

Tecumseh

Previewing Key Terms and People

Thomas Jefferson

The Era of Thomas Jefferson 309

Jefferson Takes Office

Objectives

1. Describe the outcome of the election of 1800.

2. Explain Jefferson's policies as President.

3. Discuss the importance of *Marbury* v. *Madison.*

Prepare to Read

 Reading Skill

Understand Sequence of Events A historian must master the sequence of events that make up a historical episode. To understand the sequence, determine what happened first, next, or last. Look for clues such as dates and sequence signal words. Compare when events occurred. This will help you identify connections between events.

Vocabulary *Builder*

High-Use Words

prospect, p. 310

cease, p. 313

Key Terms and People

Thomas Jefferson, p. 310

Aaron Burr, p. 310

laissez faire, p. 311

John Marshall, p. 313

judicial review, p. 313

⭐ **Background Knowledge** In the previous chapter, you learned how the Federalists controlled the national government until the election of 1800. As a result of this election, the new Republican administration of Thomas Jefferson reversed Federalist policies. This led to what Jefferson called the "Revolution of 1800."

Republicans Take Charge

Main Idea
After a bitter election campaign, Thomas Jefferson used his inaugural address to try to bring opposing sides together.

Margaret Smith attended the inauguration of Thomas Jefferson as President of the United States in March 1801. After the inauguration, she wrote a letter explaining how proud she was of the United States. In other countries, the transfer of power usually involved "confusion . . . and bloodshed." However, "in our happy country" that transfer was peaceful and orderly.

Vocabulary *Builder*
prospect (PRAHS pehkt) *n.*
expectation; likely outcome

A Bitter Campaign The presidential election of 1800 was viciously contested. The Federalists raised the prospect of civil war if Jefferson were elected. Republicans accused John Adams of wanting to create a monarchy.

By receiving 73 electoral votes, Jefferson defeated Adams. According to the Constitution, the person who received the next highest total of electoral votes would be Vice President. However, Aaron Burr, Jefferson's running mate, also received 73 votes. It was up to the House of Representatives to decide who would be President. For six days, the House was deadlocked. On the 36th vote, Jefferson won the election.

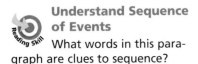 **Understand Sequence of Events**
What words in this paragraph are clues to sequence?

To avoid this situation in the future, the Twelfth Amendment to the Constitution changed how electors voted. Beginning in 1804, electors would vote separately for President and Vice President.

Jefferson's Inauguration Thomas Jefferson was the first President to be inaugurated in Washington, D.C., the country's new capital. Jefferson believed the government should have simple customs. To make the point, he walked to his inauguration instead of riding in a fancy carriage. He also ended the custom of people bowing to the President. Instead, they just shook his hand.

Jefferson used his inaugural address to bring a divided country together. He told the American people:

> " Let us, then, fellow-citizens, unite with one heart and one mind. . . . Every difference of opinion is not a difference of principle. . . . We are all Republicans; we are all Federalists. "
> —Thomas Jefferson, First Inaugural Address, March 4, 1801

✔**Checkpoint** Why did the election of 1800 have to be decided in the House of Representatives?

Jefferson Charts a New Course

Jefferson thought of his election as the "Revolution of 1800." Jefferson's first goal as President was to limit the federal government's power over states and citizens. The new President thought that under Washington and Adams the federal government had become too involved in economic affairs. He believed in the idea known as laissez faire (LEHS ay fehr), from the French term for "let alone." **Laissez faire** means that the government should not interfere in the economy.

New Republican Policies Jefferson put his laissez faire ideas into practice when he reduced the number of people in government. He fired all tax collectors and cut the number of U.S. diplomats.

Main Idea
As President, Thomas Jefferson's main goal was to limit the federal government's power over states and citizens.

Thomas Jefferson's Home
Thomas Jefferson designed his home, Monticello. In the design, he included elements of Greek architecture, such as columns, and Roman architecture, such as domes. **Critical Thinking: *Link Past and Present*** *What elements of Greek and Roman culture are still important to us today?*

Goals and Policies of Thomas Jefferson

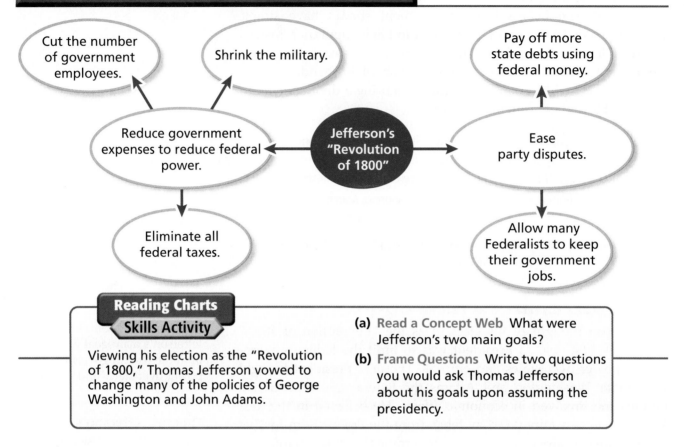

Jefferson's "Revolution of 1800"

- Cut the number of government employees.
- Shrink the military.
- Reduce government expenses to reduce federal power.
- Eliminate all federal taxes.
- Pay off more state debts using federal money.
- Ease party disputes.
- Allow many Federalists to keep their government jobs.

Reading Charts
Skills Activity

Viewing his election as the "Revolution of 1800," Thomas Jefferson vowed to change many of the policies of George Washington and John Adams.

(a) Read a Concept Web What were Jefferson's two main goals?

(b) Frame Questions Write two questions you would ask Thomas Jefferson about his goals upon assuming the presidency.

Larger cuts came from shrinking the military. Jefferson cut the army's budget in half, reducing the army's size from 4,000 to about 2,500 soldiers. At the same time, Jefferson eliminated all federal taxes inside the country. Now, most tax revenue came from the tariff on imported goods.

The Sedition Act was another of Jefferson's targets. As you have read, a number of people had been convicted and fined under the act. Jefferson ordered those fines refunded. Those imprisoned under the Sedition Act were released.

Federalist Policies Remain Jefferson could not reverse all Federalist policies. He believed that the United States had to keep repaying its national debt. He also did not fire most of the Federalist officeholders. He said they could keep their jobs if they did them well and were loyal citizens.

☑**Checkpoint** What action did Jefferson take as President to help those convicted under the Sedition Act?

Main Idea

The Supreme Court ruling in *Marbury* v. *Madison* established the principle of judicial review.

The Supreme Court and Judicial Review

One Federalist who did not keep his job was Judge William Marbury. Adams had appointed Marbury and several other judges in the last hours before he left office. The Republicans argued that these appointments were aimed at maintaining Federalist power.

When Jefferson took office, he ordered James Madison, his secretary of state, to <u>cease</u> work on the appointments. Marbury then sued Madison, citing the Judiciary Act of 1789. This act gave the Supreme Court the power to review cases brought against a federal official.

The outcome of the case forever changed the relationship of the three branches of government. In his ruling, Chief Justice John Marshall spoke for a unanimous Court. He ruled that the Judiciary Act of 1789 was unconstitutional. Marshall stated that the Court's powers came from the Constitution, not from Congress. Therefore, Congress did not have the right to give power to the Supreme Court in the Judiciary Act. Only the Constitution could do that.

The Court's actual decision—that it could not help Marbury gain his commission—was not highly significant. However, the ruling did set an important precedent. Marshall used the case of *Marbury* v. *Madison* to establish the principle of judicial review—the authority of the Supreme Court to strike down unconstitutional laws. Today, judicial review remains one of the most important powers of the Supreme Court.

✔**Checkpoint** What is judicial review?

⭐ **Looking Back and Ahead** Thomas Jefferson had long argued that the federal government's powers were limited to what was set down in the Constitution. The Constitution did not specifically give the government the power to buy land from a foreign country. In the next section, you will read of Jefferson's dilemma when France offered to sell the United States the huge territory known as Louisiana.

Vocabulary *Builder*
cease (sees) *v.* to stop; to come to an end

Section 1 | Check Your Progress

Progress Monitoring ⬤nline
For: Self-test with instant help
Visit: PHSchool.com
Web Code: mya-3051

Comprehension and Critical Thinking

1. (a) Recall How did Jefferson's inauguration demonstrate the changes he planned for the U.S. government?
(b) Apply Information How did Jefferson's policies change the American government?

2. (a) Identify What was Chief Justice Marshall's decision in the case of *Marbury* v. *Madison*?
(b) Make Predictions How did the outcome of *Marbury* v. *Madison* affect the relationship of the three branches of government?

Reading Skill

3. Understand Sequence of Events Read the first paragraph under the heading "Jefferson Charts a New Course." What was Jefferson's *first* priority as President?

Vocabulary *Builder*

Read each sentence below. If the sentence is true, write YES. If the sentence is not true, write NO and explain why.
4. Jefferson believed in laissez faire, the idea that the federal government should not interfere in economic affairs.

5. John Marshall cited judicial review as the reason why only the Senate had the right to decide whether acts of Congress are constitutional.

Writing

6. Based on what you have read in this section about Jefferson's early days in office, write a thesis statement about Jefferson's influence on American government. Then, list the kinds of supporting information that would back up your thesis statement.

The Louisiana Purchase

Objectives

1. Explain the importance of New Orleans and the crisis over its port.

2. Describe how the United States gained the Louisiana Purchase.

3. Discuss Lewis and Clark's expedition.

Prepare to Read

Reading Skill

Distinguish Events in Sequence As you read, it will help you to identify events that occur at about the same time in different locations. Ask yourself if these events share a common cause. Was there any advantage for people to make these events happen at the same time? Would faster communication have changed the sequence at all?

Vocabulary *Builder*

High-Use Words

crisis, p. 314
alter, p. 315

Key Terms and People

expedition, p. 317
Meriwether Lewis, p. 317
William Clark, p. 317
continental divide, p. 318
Zebulon Pike, p. 319

⭐ **Background Knowledge** In the previous section, you learned how Jefferson focused on reducing the size of the federal government upon becoming President. But Jefferson had a lifelong interest in the American West. In this section, you will learn how he expanded the country's borders far to the west.

The Nation Looks West

Main Idea
U.S. leaders worried that France or Spain might close the port of New Orleans to the goods of western farmers.

The tide of westward settlement speeded up in the years after the United States won independence. By 1800, more than one million settlers lived between the Appalachian Mountains and the Mississippi River.

Most western settlers were farmers. Because there were few roads in the West, they relied on the Mississippi River to ship their crops to the port at New Orleans. From there, the goods were loaded on ships and carried to markets in the East.

Spain, which controlled the Mississippi and New Orleans, had several times threatened to close the port to American ships. To prevent this from happening again, in 1795 the United States negotiated a treaty with Spain. The Pinckney Treaty guaranteed the Americans' right to ship their goods down the Mississippi to New Orleans. There, they could be stored until they were transferred to oceangoing ships for the journey east.

Vocabulary *Builder*
crisis (KRĪ sihs) *n.* turning point or deciding event in history

For a time, Americans shipped their goods through New Orleans peacefully. Then, in 1801, a crisis developed. Jefferson discovered that Spain had secretly given New Orleans and the rest of its Louisiana Territory to France.

Jefferson was alarmed by this development. The French ruler, Napoleon Bonaparte, had already set out to conquer Europe. Jefferson feared that he now intended to make France the first power in America as well. If Napoleon controlled Louisiana, the westward expansion of the United States would be blocked.

☑ **Checkpoint** **What important right did the United States gain with the Pinckney Treaty of 1795?**

Buying Louisiana

Even before the transfer of Louisiana to France took place, America's position in Louisiana was threatened. In 1802, the Spanish governor of Louisiana withdrew the right of Americans to ship their goods through New Orleans. Westerners exploded in anger. They demanded that Jefferson go to war to win back their rights.

The situation was explosive. What would happen, Jefferson worried, when the French took over New Orleans?

A Surprise Offer The President decided the best approach was to try to buy the city of New Orleans from the French. He sent his friend James Monroe to France to make a deal. Monroe had the help of Robert Livingston, the American minister in Paris. Jefferson instructed the two men to buy New Orleans and a territory to the east called West Florida.

In Paris, the Americans discovered an <u>altered</u> situation. A revolution led by Toussaint L'Ouverture (too SAN loo vehr TYOOR) had driven the French from their Caribbean colony of Haiti. Without Haiti as a base, the French would have trouble defending Louisiana in the event of a war. At the same time, tensions between France and Britain were again on the rise. War was looming and Napoleon needed money to support the war effort. France offered to sell the United States not only New Orleans but the *entire* Louisiana Territory.

It would take months to get Jefferson's advice. So Livingston and Monroe agreed to buy the whole Louisiana Territory for $15 million— about 4 cents an acre. This included an enormous area stretching from the Gulf of Mexico to Canada and from the Mississippi River to the Rocky Mountains.

Main Idea
The Louisiana Purchase gave the United States a vast area with untold wealth.

Vocabulary *Builder*
alter (AWL ter) *v.* to change in some way; to make different

Haitian Independence
Toussaint L'Ouverture (right) helped lead the Haitian struggle to expel the French. *Critical Thinking: Analyze Cause and Effect Why would France have trouble defending Louisiana if it did not control Haiti?*

Exploring the Louisiana Purchase

KEY

— Present-day state boundaries
← Lewis and Clark, 1804–1805
← Pike, 1805–1806
← Pike, 1806–1807

OREGON COUNTRY
(claimed by Great Britain, Russia, Spain, and the United States)

SPANISH TERRITORY

LOUISIANA PURCHASE

UNITED STATES

SPANISH FLORIDA

PACIFIC OCEAN

ATLANTIC OCEAN

Lemhi Pass · Snake R. · Columbia R. · ROCKY MOUNTAINS · Continental Divide · Pikes Peak · Platte R. · Missouri R. · GREAT PLAINS · Mississippi R. · St. Louis · Arkansas R. · Colorado R. · Santa Fe · Rio Grande · Natchitoches · New Orleans

0 km 400
0 miles 400
Albers Equal-Area Projection

MAP MASTER

Skills Activity

After buying the Louisiana Territory in 1803, Thomas Jefferson was eager to have it explored and mapped.

(a) Read a Map Key Along which rivers did Zebulon Pike travel?

(b) Make Predictions Based on the map, how might the Spanish have felt about the explorations of Pike?

MapMaster Online

For: Interactive map
Visit: PHSchool.com
Web Code: myp-3052

The Louisiana Purchase proved an amazing bargain for the United States. Its area almost doubled the size of the country. Although largely unexplored, the region clearly had millions of acres of fertile farmland and other natural resources. Ownership of Louisiana gave the United States control of the Mississippi River. As Livingston put it, "From this day, the United States take their place among the powers of the first rank."

Jefferson's Dilemma Jefferson was delighted with the deal. At the same time, he had a serious problem. The Constitution nowhere states that the President has the power to buy land from a foreign country. Adding the huge Louisiana Territory would dramatically change the character of the nation.

In the end, Jefferson decided that he did have authority to buy Louisiana. The Constitution, he reasoned, allowed the President to make treaties. The Senate approved the treaty and Congress quickly voted to pay for the land.

☑ **Checkpoint** Why did President Jefferson hesitate to approve the purchase of the Louisiana Territory?

Lewis and Clark Explore the West

In January 1803, even before the United States had bought Louisiana, Jefferson convinced Congress to spend $2,500 on a western expedition (eks puh DISH uhn). An **expedition** is a long and carefully organized journey.

Jefferson chose army captain Meriwether Lewis to lead the exploration. Lewis chose William Clark, also an army officer, as his coleader. The men were ordered to report back on the geography, plants, animals, and other natural features of the region.

The expedition also had other goals. Jefferson wanted Lewis and Clark to make contact with Native Americans who lived in the Louisiana Territory. The President also wanted Lewis and Clark to find out if a waterway existed between the Mississippi River and the Pacific Ocean.

Into the Unknown In the spring of 1804, Lewis and Clark left St. Louis and headed up the Missouri River. Their three boats carried tons of supplies and about 40 men. Most were Americans, although there were several French Canadians. The expedition also included an enslaved African American named York.

In mid-July, the party reached the mouth of the Platte River, a powerful tributary that flows into the Missouri. In early August, they met Native Americans for the first time. Three weeks later, the expedition reached the eastern edge of the Great Plains.

Main Idea
Lewis and Clark brought back valuable information on the area's people, plants, and animals.

Links Across Time

1969 American astronauts Buzz Aldrin (shown here) and Neil Armstrong landed on the moon.

Exploration

1804–1806 Lewis and Clark explored the lands of the Louisiana Purchase. Their journals, maps, and drawings inspired the rapid settlement of the West.

1960s American explorers ventured into the "new frontier" of outer space. On July 20, 1969, the United States became the first nation to land a man on the moon. People around the world watched the landing on television.

Link to Today

Exploration Today The United States has sent additional missions to the moon and beyond. What kinds of exploration are going on today?

For: Recent activities of the U.S. space program
Visit: PHSchool.com
Web Code: mvc-3052

Lewis and Clark: A Hard Journey At times during their travel up the Missouri River, members of the Lewis and Clark party had to carry their boats around rapids and falls. Here, Sacagawea, Clark, Lewis, and York examine the Great Falls in present-day Montana. **Critical Thinking: Apply Information** *What other hazards did Lewis and Clark face on their river voyages?*

In late October 1804, the expedition reached the territory of the Mandan people, in what is now North Dakota. Lewis and Clark decided to camp there for the winter. They were joined in camp by a French Canadian trader and his wife, a Native American named Sacagawea (sahk uh juh WEE uh). She was a Shoshone (shoh SHOH nee) who would travel with them and serve as translator.

Crossing the Rockies In April 1805, the party set out again. By summer they were in what is now Montana. They began to climb the Rockies. By August, they had reached the Continental Divide. A **continental divide** is the place on a continent that separates river systems flowing in opposite directions. The view to the west was beautiful but also deeply disappointing. Lewis had hoped to see a wide river that would take the group to the Pacific. Instead, all he saw were "immense ranges of mountains still to the west."

The next day, Lewis met a group of Shoshone warriors. When Sacagawea arrived to interpret, she was astonished to see that the Shoshone chief was her brother. She jumped up and threw her arms around him. Thanks to Sacagawea, the Shoshones agreed to sell the expedition horses that were needed to cross the mountains.

At the Pacific On the west side of the Rockies, Lewis and Clark reached the Columbia River. Here, they stopped to build canoes for the downriver voyage. At one point, they had to cross a 55-mile stretch of rapids and rough water. Finally, through a dense early November fog, they saw the Pacific Ocean.

The travelers spent the wet and gloomy winter of 1805–1806 near the point where the Columbia River flows into the Pacific. They began the return journey in March 1806. It took the party half a year to return to St. Louis. Their return, however, brought the American people a new awareness of a rich and beautiful part of the continent.

Pike's Expedition At the same time that Lewis and Clark were trekking back home, other Americans also hoped to learn more about the West. From 1805 to 1807, Zebulon Pike explored the southern part of the Louisiana Territory.

Pike led an expedition due west to the Rocky Mountains. There, he tried to climb a mountain that rose out of the Colorado plains. He made it about two thirds of the way to the top. Standing in snow up to his waist, he was forced to turn back. Today, this mountain is known as Pikes Peak.

Pike's return route took him into Spanish New Mexico. Early in 1807, Spanish troops arrested the members of the party as spies. The Spanish feared Pike was gathering information so that the Americans could take over the region. After several months of captivity, the men were released and escorted back to the United States. As the Spanish had feared, Pike's reports about the Spanish borderlands created great American interest in the region.

✓**Checkpoint** **What goals did President Jefferson set for Lewis and Clark's expedition?**

☆ **Looking Back and Ahead** Lewis and Clark and Pike gave the United States detailed knowledge of the West. However, Americans had little time to digest this information. They soon found themselves caught up again in Europe's conflicts.

Distinguish Events in Sequence
What do the words "at the same time" tell you about the sequence of events? What was happening at the same time?

Section 2 | **Check Your Progress**

Progress Monitoring Online
For: Self-test with instant help
Visit: PHSchool.com
Web Code: mya-3052

Comprehension and Critical Thinking

1. **(a) Recall** Why was New Orleans important to the United States?
   (b) Identify Benefits What was the significance of the Louisiana Purchase?

2. **(a) Identify** Who was Sacagawea, and how was she important to the success of the Lewis and Clark expedition?
   (b) Compare and Contrast How was Pike's expedition similar to that of Lewis and Clark's? How was it different?

Reading Skill

3. **Distinguish Events in Sequence** Describe how the sequence of Lewis and Clark's expedition related to that of Zebulon Pike.

Vocabulary *Builder*

4. Draw a table with two rows and two columns. In the first column, list the key terms from this section: expedition, continental divide. In the next column, write the definition of each word.

Writing

5. Use this section and the following items to write a thesis statement about the life of Meriwether Lewis.
   Items: Born in 1774; Virginian; family friend of Jefferson; in 1792 asked by Jefferson to lead exploration of the Northwest; with Clark led expedition through Louisiana Territory; was appointed governor of Louisiana Territory in 1808; died mysteriously in 1809.

Exploring the Louisiana Purchase

An atmosphere of eager anticipation filled the air as Meriwether Lewis and William Clark and their men set out to explore the vast lands that lay west of the Mississippi River. Use the map below to follow Lewis and Clark on their journey to the Pacific Ocean.

5 NOVEMBER 1805: The expedition reaches the Pacific Coast. Upon glimpsing his goal for the first time, Clark notes, "great joy in camp," in his journal.

The expedition follows the Columbia River to the Pacific Coast.

4 AUGUST 1805: Lewis proceeds ahead of main party and walks through Lemhi Pass to cross the Continental Divide.

Lemhi Pass

William Clark

Clark's compass

Understand Effects:

Legacy of the Expedition

The explorers returned to St. Louis in 1806. Though the expedition was a success, it failed to excite the majority of Americans. Over time, however, the journey of Lewis and Clark contributed to a national feeling that Americans had a Manifest Destiny, a duty to expand west across the continent.

Meriwether Lewis

A page from Lewis's journal

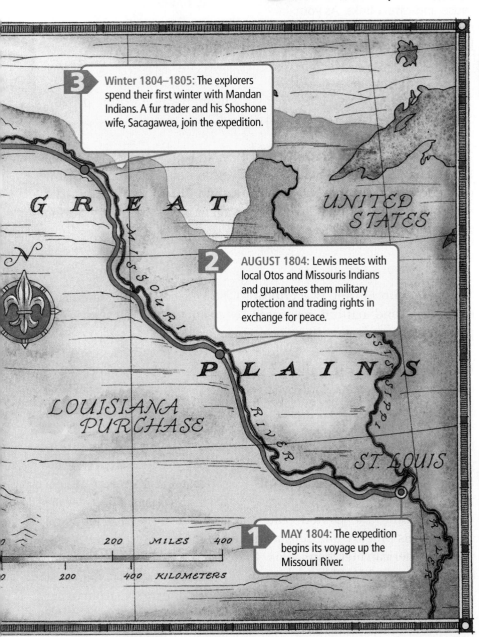

3 Winter 1804–1805: The explorers spend their first winter with Mandan Indians. A fur trader and his Shoshone wife, Sacagawea, join the expedition.

GREAT

UNITED STATES

2 AUGUST 1804: Lewis meets with local Otos and Missouris Indians and guarantees them military protection and trading rights in exchange for peace.

P L A I N S

MISSOURI

MISSISSIPPI

LOUISIANA PURCHASE

RIVER

ST. LOUIS

200   MILES   400

200   400   KILOMETERS

1 MAY 1804: The expedition begins its voyage up the Missouri River.

RIVER

Analyze **GEOGRAPHY AND HISTORY**

Write a journal entry that expresses Lewis and Clark's excitement about crossing the Continental Divide. How did the explorers know they were closer to their goal?

A Time of Conflict

Objectives

1. Discuss how the United States defeated the Barbary pirates.
2. Explain how war in Europe hurt American trade.
3. Discuss the causes and effects of the Embargo Act.
4. Identify the events leading up to the Battle of Tippecanoe.

Prepare to Read

Reading Skill

Explain How Events Are Related in Time Many events that occur in sequence have cause-and-effect relationships. Explaining how events are related in time will help you find these cause-and-effect links. As you read this section, look for events that have this relationship.

Vocabulary *Builder*

High-Use Words

decline, p. 324
restore, p. 326

Key Terms and People

tribute, p. 322
Stephen Decatur, p. 322
embargo, p. 324
smuggle, p. 324
Tecumseh, p. 326
William Henry Harrison, p. 326

⭐ **Background Knowledge** In the previous chapter, you learned how the United States under Washington and Adams became entangled in the dispute between France and Britain. That dispute did not go away. As you will learn, it rose again with added fury during the administration of Thomas Jefferson.

Defeating the Barbary States

Main Idea
Threats to American shipping led the United States to capture Tripoli, stronghold of the Barbary pirates.

Trade with Europe was critical to the U.S. economy. Americans sold crops and natural resources to customers in Europe. They purchased manufactured goods made in Europe.

After the American Revolution, pirates began attacking American ships in the Mediterranean Sea. The pirates came from four small countries on the North African coast—Morocco, Algiers, Tunisia, and Tripoli. Together, these countries were known as the Barbary States.

Barbary pirates raided European and American ships, taking property and enslaving sailors and holding them for ransom. European governments stopped such raids by paying the Barbary States tribute—money paid by one country to another in return for protection. In exchange, their rulers agreed to leave European ships alone.

Explain How Events Are Related in Time
Explain why the United States stopped paying tribute to the Barbary States.

For a time, the United States also paid tribute. But Jefferson stopped this practice and sent warships to the Mediterranean Sea to protect American merchant ships. At first, these military patrols went badly. The warship *Philadelphia* ran aground near the Tripoli coast and its 300-man crew was imprisoned. To keep the pirates from using the ship, 60 American sailors led by Stephen Decatur raided Tripoli harbor and burned the *Philadelphia* down to the waterline.

The next year, a small force of American marines marched 600 miles across the Sahara and captured Tripoli. A line in the U.S. Marine Corps anthem—"To the shores of Tripoli"—recalls that victory. It inspired a wave of confidence in the ability of the United States to deal forcefully with foreign powers that threatened American security and prosperity.

☑ **Checkpoint** How did European nations protect themselves against raids by the Barbary pirates?

American Neutrality Is Challenged

A more serious threat to American overseas trade came from two much more powerful countries, Britain and France. By 1803, the two nations once again were at war. The United States remained neutral.

Because it was neutral, the United States continued trading with both Britain and France. The war in Europe had created opportunities for Americans to sell their products there.

Meanwhile, Britain and France looked for ways to weaken each other. One method was to cut off the other country's foreign trade. British warships started seizing American ships trading with France. French warships did the same to American ships trading with Britain. Between 1803 and 1807, France seized 500 American ships and Britain seized more than 1,000.

Britain badly needed sailors for its war against France. So it turned again to impressment. As a result, thousands of American sailors were forced to serve in the British navy.

Main Idea
Britain and France interfered with American shipping, increasing tensions between the United States and the two European nations.

Impressment
A nineteenth-century woodprint shows unfortunate American sailors being impressed by British gangs. Conditions on board British warships were harsh.
Critical Thinking: *Draw Conclusions* *What impact do you think impressment had on the performance of the British navy?*

George III   Napoleon

Beginning in 1805, Britain and France increased their efforts to attack trade with their foes. No matter what American merchant ships did, they risked being seized by either Britain or France.

✓**Checkpoint** What was impressment, and why did it anger Americans?

Main Idea
The Embargo Act hurt the United States far more than it hurt Britain or France.

Jefferson Responds With an Embargo

The President looked for peaceful methods to force Britain and France to respect American neutrality. He decided to use an **embargo**—a government order that forbids foreign trade. In 1807, Congress passed the Embargo Act. It imposed a total embargo on American ships sailing to any foreign port. Jefferson predicted that both countries would soon cease attacking American ships.

Things did not turn out as Jefferson expected. Indeed, the big loser proved to be the United States. In just one year, American exports fell from $109 million to $25 million. Prices of American crops <u>declined</u>, hurting farmers and planters. Tens of thousands of Americans lost their jobs.

Vocabulary *Builder*
<u>decline</u> (dee KLĪN) *v.* to gradually lose strength or power

Many Americans were outraged by the embargo. Anger was greatest in New England, where merchants depended heavily on foreign trade. Thousands of Americans turned to **smuggling**—the act of illegally importing or exporting goods—in order to evade the embargo.

Congress finally repealed the Embargo Act in 1809, just before Jefferson left office. Then, Congress passed a less severe law that reopened foreign trade with every country except Britain and France. The law stated that the United States would reopen trade with those countries when they started respecting America's trading rights as a neutral nation.

☑ **Checkpoint** **Why did President Jefferson place an embargo on foreign goods in 1807?**

Tecumseh and the Prophet

In the years after the Battle of Fallen Timbers, tens of thousands of settlers moved westward. Ohio became a state in 1803. Americans continued to push into new areas. They settled in the territory of Indiana and other lands farther west.

The tide of settlement had a grave impact on Native Americans. Diseases such as measles, smallpox, and influenza killed thousands of Native Americans who had never been exposed to such diseases before. Settlers took over large parts of the Native American hunting grounds. Deer and other animals the Native Americans depended on were driven away as farmers cleared the forests for planting. The Native American population decreased, and the power of their traditional leaders declined.

Main Idea
Native Americans led by Tecumseh resisted white settlement but suffered a severe setback at the Battle of Tippecanoe.

Land Taken From Native Americans

KEY
- Land taken before 1750
- Land taken 1750–1784
- Land taken 1785–1810

0 km 500
0 miles 500
Azimuthal Equal-Area Projection

Abnakis
Penobscots
Wampanoags
Narragansetts
Iroquois Pequots
Mohegans
Susquehannas
Leni-Lenapes
Powhatans
Kickapoos Eries
Miamis
Illinois
Missouris
Kansas
Osages Shawnees
Cherokees
Chickasaws
Creeks
Natchez
Seminoles
Gulf of Mexico
ATLANTIC OCEAN
L. Superior
L. Michigan
L. Huron
L. Ontario
L. Erie
Mississippi R.
Missouri R.
Ohio R.
Arkansas R.
Red R.

MAP MASTER®
Skills Activity

As settlers moved west, they took over Native American lands.

(a) Read a Map Key When did the Osages lose their land?

(b) Make Predictions Notice the lands shaded purple. What do you think happened to the Native American lands in this area after 1784?

MapMaster ●nline

For: Interactive map
Visit: PHSchool.com
Web Code: myp-3053

New Leaders Take Charge The Shawnee people were hard hit by these developments. After 1805, two Shawnee brothers—Tenskwatawa (tehn SKWAH tuh wuh) and Tecumseh (tih KUHM suh)—began urging Native American resistance. Tecumseh and Tenskwatawa, who was also known as the Prophet, called on Native Americans to preserve traditional ways.

Vocabulary *Builder*
restore (ree STOR) *v.* to bring back to a former condition

Tecumseh organized the western tribes into a league to restore Indian lands. He traveled widely spreading his message.

Harrison's Victory American officials were deeply concerned by Tecumseh's activities. William Henry Harrison, governor of the Indiana Territory, decided to take action. While Tecumseh was traveling in search of allies, Harrison marched a thousand soldiers against Shawnee villages on the Tippecanoe River. In the Battle of Tippecanoe, Harrison defeated the Native Americans.

The Battle of Tippecanoe marked the high point of Native American opposition to settlement. Even though the alliance declined in power after the battle, Tecumseh and his warriors continued their struggle during the next several years.

✓**Checkpoint** What actions did Tecumseh and the Prophet urge on their followers?

⭐ **Looking Back and Ahead** Tensions remained high in the West even after Harrison's victory. Many Americans blamed the British, who continued to send arms to the Native Americans. There were widespread calls for war with Britain. Could the President and Congress resist them?

Section 3 | Check Your Progress

Progress Monitoring Online
For: Self-test with instant help
Visit: PHSchool.com
Web Code: mya-3053

Comprehension and Critical Thinking

1. **(a) Identify** Who were the Barbary pirates?
(b) Identify Costs What was the United States risking when it refused to pay tribute to the Barbary pirates? Why do you think Jefferson believed it was worth the risk?

2. **(a) Describe** How did settlement in the West affect the Native Americans who lived there?
(b) Clarify Problems Why were Native Americans of the West more likely to favor the British than the Americans?

Reading Skill

3. **Explain How Events Are Related in Time** What happened after Congress passed a law to undo the Embargo Act? Explain the connection between the Embargo Act and the new law.

Vocabulary *Builder*

4. Write two definitions for each key term: tribute, embargo, smuggle. First, write a formal definition for your teacher. Second, write a definition in everyday English for a classmate.

Writing

5. Read the following thesis statement: "The last years of Thomas Jefferson's presidency were clouded by international problems." Review the information in this section and choose four facts or details from the section that support this thesis statement. Then, based on the supporting items you chose, write several sentences developing the thesis statement.

The War of 1812

Objectives

1. Explain why the United States declared war on Britain.

2. Describe what happened in the early days of the war.

3. Discuss the American invasion of Canada and the fighting in the South.

4. Identify the events leading to the end of the War of 1812.

Prepare to Read

Reading Skill

Explain How Events Are Related in Time Events can be related in time in many ways. One event may directly cause another or events may unfold over time. As you read this section, try to relate the many events to one another in time. Use the skills you practiced in Sections 1–3 as tools. Also, use sequence verbs as a tool. These verbs describe how events progress over time.

Vocabulary *Builder*

High-Use Words
reinforce, p. 328
critic, p. 331

Key Terms and People
nationalism, p. 327
war hawk, p. 327
blockade, p. 328
Oliver Hazard Perry, p. 329
Andrew Jackson, p. 330
secede, p. 331

☆ **Background Knowledge** In previous sections, you have learned how the first three U.S. Presidents worked hard to avoid war with Britain and France. In this section, you will learn why, despite these efforts, the United States finally went to war.

The Move Toward War

Tension with Britain was high when James Madison took office in 1809. Americans were angry at Britain for arming Native Americans in the Northwest. Americans also resented the continued impressment of American sailors by the British.

To most Americans, the country's honor was at stake. They felt a new sense of American **nationalism**—pride in one's country. In 1810, two strong nationalists, Henry Clay of Kentucky and John C. Calhoun of South Carolina, became leaders in the House of Representatives.

Clay, Calhoun, and their supporters were called **war hawks**— those who were eager for war with Britain. Opposition to war was strongest in New England. Many New Englanders believed war with Britain would harm American trade.

Relations with Britain worsened steadily in the early months of 1812. In the spring, the British told the United States they would continue impressing sailors. Meanwhile, Native Americans in the Northwest began new attacks on frontier settlements. In June, Congress declared war on Britain.

✔**Checkpoint** **In what regions of the United States was the support for war with Britain the strongest?**

Main Idea
Led by the war hawks, Congress declared war on Britain in June 1812.

Andrew Jackson, a young war hawk

Vocabulary *Builder*
reinforce (ree ihn FORS) *v.* to strengthen with additional troops

Early Days of the War

The war did not come at a good time for the British, who were still at war in Europe. However, Britain was not willing to meet American demands to avoid war. Providing Native Americans with support was one way of protecting Canada against an American invasion.

When the war began, Americans were confident that they would win. It soon became apparent that the United States was not prepared for war. Jefferson's spending cuts had weakened American military strength. The navy had only 16 warships ready for action. The army also was small, with fewer than 7,000 men.

In the first days of the war, the British set up a blockade of the American coast. A **blockade** is the action of shutting a port or road to prevent people or supplies from coming into an area or leaving it. By 1814, the British navy had 135 warships blockading American ports. After reinforcing their troops, the British were able to close off all American ports by war's end.

A major sea battle was fought at the beginning of the war. In August 1812, the USS *Constitution* defeated the British warship *Guerrière* (gai ree AIR) in a fierce battle. According to tradition, American sailors nicknamed the *Constitution* "Old Ironsides" because British artillery fire bounced off the ship's thick wooden hull. To the Americans, it seemed as if the *Constitution* were made of iron.

✓**Checkpoint** **Why was the United States unprepared for war?**

"Old Ironsides"

History *Interactive*
**Explore
Old Ironsides**
Visit: PHSchool.com
Web Code: myp-3054

In the most famous sea battle of the War of 1812, the USS *Constitution* engaged the British frigate *Guerrière* in the North Atlantic Ocean.

For nearly an hour, the two ships closed in on each other. Then, the *Constitution* fired a barrage that tore off both of the *Guerrière* masts. Meanwhile, British cannonballs bounced harmlessly off the reinforced hull of the *Constitution*. **Critical Thinking:** *Identify Benefits How were ships like the* Constitution *helpful to the American naval effort?*

A cutaway of the ▶ *Constitution*'s hull.

The ship's hull, which was more than two feet thick at the waterline, was made up of three layers of extremely tough and durable oak wood.

Guerrière

USS Constitution

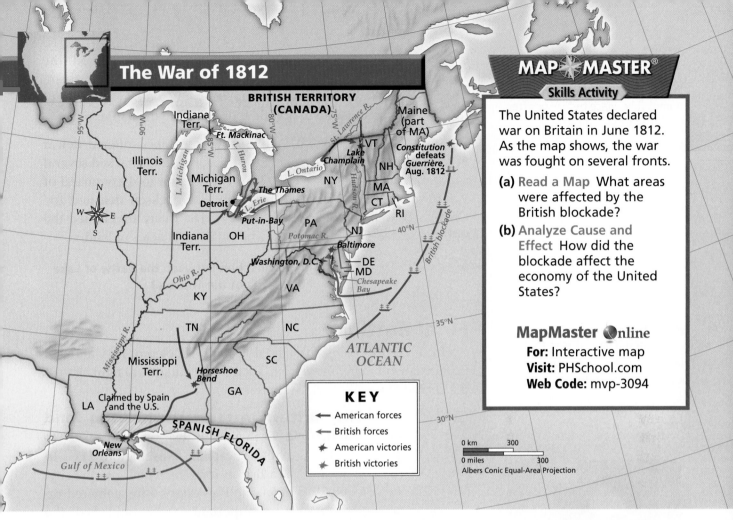

The War of 1812

BRITISH TERRITORY (CANADA)

Indiana Terr.
Ft. Mackinac
Illinois Terr.
L. Michigan
L. Huron
Michigan Terr.
The Thames
Detroit
L. Erie
Put-in-Bay
Indiana Terr.
OH
Maine (part of MA)
VT
Lake Champlain
Constitution defeats Guerrière, Aug. 1812
NH
NY
MA
CT
RI
St. Lawrence R.
L. Ontario
Hudson R.
PA
NJ
Potomac R.
Baltimore
Washington, D.C.
DE
MD
Chesapeake Bay
VA
KY
Ohio R.
TN
NC
SC
Mississippi R.
Mississippi Terr.
Horseshoe Bend
GA
LA
Claimed by Spain and the U.S.
New Orleans
Gulf of Mexico
SPANISH FLORIDA
ATLANTIC OCEAN
British blockade
40°N
35°N
30°N
W-90
W-95
80°W
75°W

KEY
← American forces
← British forces
★ American victories
★ British victories

0 km 300
0 miles 300
Albers Conic Equal-Area Projection

MAP MASTER®
Skills Activity

The United States declared war on Britain in June 1812. As the map shows, the war was fought on several fronts.

(a) Read a Map What areas were affected by the British blockade?

(b) Analyze Cause and Effect How did the blockade affect the economy of the United States?

MapMaster Online
For: Interactive map
Visit: PHSchool.com
Web Code: mvp-3094

The War in the West and South

In the West, the Americans and British fought for control of the Great Lakes and the Mississippi River. Both sides had Native American allies.

Invasion of Canada Even before the war began, war hawks were demanding an invasion of Canada. They expected Canadians to welcome the chance to throw off British rule.

In July 1812, American troops under General William Hull invaded Canada from Detroit. Hull was unsure of himself. Fearing he did not have enough soldiers, he soon retreated.

The British commander, General Isaac Brock, took advantage of Hull's confusion. His army of British soldiers and Native American warriors quickly surrounded Hull's army and forced it to surrender. The British captured more than 2,000 American soldiers. It was a serious defeat for the United States.

American forces had better luck on Lake Erie. Both sides were aware of the importance of controlling the lake. A key three-hour battle took place at Put-In-Bay, in the western part of the lake, in 1813.

During the battle, the American flagship was badly damaged. The American commander, Oliver Hazard Perry, switched to another ship and continued the fight until it was won. Perry announced his victory with a dramatic message: "We have met the enemy and they are ours." With Americans in control of the lake, the British were forced to leave Detroit and retreat back into Canada.

Main Idea
Native Americans suffered severe setbacks during fighting in the West and South during 1814.

Explain How Events Are Related in Time
Did the Battle of the Thames take place before or after the Battle of Lake Erie?

As the British and their Native American allies retreated, the Americans under General William Henry Harrison pursued them. They followed the British into Canada, defeating them in the Battle of the Thames. Tecumseh was among those killed in the battle.

Conflict in the South Native Americans also suffered defeat in the South. In the summer of 1813, Creek warriors attacked several southern American settlements. Andrew Jackson took command of American forces in Georgia. In March 1814, Jackson defeated the Creeks at the Battle of Horseshoe Bend. The treaty that ended the fighting forced the Creeks to give up millions of acres of land.

☑**Checkpoint** What is the connection between the Battle of Lake Erie and the Battle of the Thames?

Main Idea
Although the War of 1812 had no clear victor, Americans gained new confidence after its end.

Final Battles

In 1814, the British finally defeated Napoleon. This allowed Britain to send many more troops across the Atlantic to fight against the United States.

The British Attack Washington and Baltimore The new British strategy was to attack the nation's capital, Washington, D.C. In August 1814, a British force marched into the city. Dolley Madison, the President's wife, gathered up the President's important papers and fled the White House. The British set fire to several government buildings, including the White House. Americans were shocked to learn that their army could not defend Washington.

The British now moved on to Baltimore. Their first objective was Fort McHenry, which defended the city's harbor. British warships bombarded the fort throughout the night of September 13, 1814. Francis Scott Key, a young American, watched the attack. At dawn, Key saw the American flag still flying over the fort. The Americans had beaten off the attack.

On the back of an old envelope, Key wrote a poem that he called "The Star-Spangled Banner." It told the story of his night's watch. The poem became popular and was set to music. In 1931, Congress made it the national anthem of the United States.

The War Ends By 1814, Britain had tired of war. Peace talks began in Ghent (gehnt), Belgium. On Christmas Eve 1814, the two sides signed the Treaty of Ghent, which ended the war. The treaty returned things to the way they had been before the war.

Biography Quest

Tecumseh
1768–1813

The Shawnee war chief Tecumseh challenged the tide of white settlement. Tecumseh visited Native Americans from the Great Lakes to Florida, urging them to unite. He was away recruiting when General Harrison defeated the Shawnee at Tippecanoe. After the battle, Tecumseh allied his forces with the British, hoping that a British victory would mean the return of Native American lands. His death at the Battle of the Thames dealt a blow to Native American resistance.

Biography Quest ⊙nline

Why did Tecumseh issue an angry challenge to his allies, the British?

For: The answer to the question about Tecumseh

Visit: PHSchool.com

Web Code: myd-3054

News of the treaty took several weeks to reach the United States. In that time, the two sides fought one more battle. In January 1815, American forces under General Andrew Jackson won a stunning victory over the British at the Battle of New Orleans.

Protests and Peace From the start, there had been opposition to the War of 1812 within the United States. As the war dragged on, Federalist <u>critics</u> of President Madison spoke out more strongly, criticizing what they called "Mr. Madison's War." New Englanders in particular disliked the war, mainly because the blockade had badly damaged New England trade.

In December 1814, a group of Federalists met in Hartford, Connecticut. Some delegates to the Hartford Convention suggested that the New England states secede, or withdraw, from the United States. While the delegates debated, news of the peace treaty arrived. With the war over, the Hartford Convention quickly ended.

To some Americans, the War of 1812 was the "Second War of Independence." Once and for all, the United States secured its independence from Britain. European nations would now have to treat the young republic with respect. Pride at this achievement brought the confidence of Americans to a new height.

☑**Checkpoint** **What was the purpose of the Hartford Convention?**

⭐ **Looking Back and Ahead** After the War of 1812, Americans entered a new era of confidence. Tensions between regions, which had been high during the war, cooled with the coming of peace. In the postwar period, Americans enjoyed a period of calm and unity. As you will read in the next chapter, this era paved the way for a major expansion of American democracy.

Vocabulary *Builder*
<u>critic</u> (KRIHT ihk) *n.* someone who makes judgments on the value of actions

Section 4 | **Check Your Progress**

Progress Monitoring ⬤nline
For: Self-test with instant help
Visit: PHSchool.com
Web Code: mya-3054

Comprehension and Critical Thinking

1. **(a) Identify** Who were the war hawks? Why did they push for war with Britain?
(b) Draw Conclusions Were the war hawks overconfident? What did they overlook in their evaluation of British power?

2. **(a) Recall** How did the War of 1812 end?
(b) Analyze Cause and Effect What were some results of the war that were not expressly written in the treaty?

🔵 **Reading Skill**

3. **Explain How Events Are Related in Time** What battle was taking place at about the same time that William Hull was invading Canada?

Vocabulary *Builder*

Add a second sentence to each of the following sentences that clearly shows your understanding of the key term.
4. The War of 1812 increased U.S. nationalism. _____.
5. At the Hartford Convention, dissatisfied Federalists made plans

for the New England states to secede. _____.

Writing

6. Read the following notes about First Lady Dolley Madison and rearrange them in the best order for a biographical essay. **Notes:** Died in 1849; stylish woman; married James Madison in 1794; served as President Jefferson's official hostess; saved many valuables from White House when British invaded in 1814; turned Washington from a "dull swamp" into lively social city.

When reading a historical document, it is important to remember that the writer has a particular point of view, or way of looking at a subject. It is also important to consider how events of the time may have influenced the author's feelings.

The Danbury Baptist Association wrote to President Jefferson, asking why he would not establish national days of fasting and thanksgiving, as previous Presidents had done. Jefferson answered the letter in 1802. His carefully worded reply reflects his opinion about the separation of government and religion in the new nation.

Primary Source

"Believing with you that religion is a matter which lies solely between man & his god, that he owes account to none other for his faith or his worship, that the legitimate powers of government reach actions only, and not opinions, I contemplate with sovereign reverence that act of the whole American people which declared that their legislature should make no law respecting an establishment of religion, or prohibiting the free exercise thereof, thus building a wall of separation between church and state."

—Thomas Jefferson, Jan. 1, 1802

Learn the Skill

Use these steps to put historical points of view in context.

1. **Identify the context.** If you know the history of the period when a document was written, you can better understand the writer's point of view.

2. **Identify the main idea.** What main point does the writer make?

3. **Look for important words or phrases.** The writer may use key words or phrases that sum up the point of view being expressed.

4. **Identify point of view.** How does the writer or speaker feel about the subject?

5. **Relate point of view to context.** How was the point of view affected by historical context?

Practice the Skill

Answer the following questions about the primary source on this page.

1. **Identify the context.** (a) Why was this letter written? (b) How did the Bill of Rights address the issue of an American national church?

2. **Identify the main idea.** What is the main point of this letter?

3. **Look for important words or phrases.** What is an example of a key word or phrase that sums up the writer's point of view?

4. **Identify point of view.** How does the writer feel about the subject of the letter?

5. **Relate point of view to context.** How was Jefferson's point of view influenced by the events of the time?

Apply the Skill

See the Review and Assessment at the end of this chapter.

Interactive Textbook

Study Guide *Online*
Complete your Chapter 9 study guide in print or online.

Chapter Summary

Section 1
Jefferson Takes Office

- The Twelfth Amendment was added to the Constitution to prevent the deadlock in government that occurred when Jefferson and Burr received the same number of electoral votes in the election of 1800.
- In *Marbury* v. *Madison,* Chief Justice John Marshall and the Supreme Court established judicial review.

Section 2
The Louisiana Purchase

- In 1803, the United States purchased the Louisiana Territory from France.
- The Louisiana Purchase gave the United States control of the Mississippi River.
- Jefferson sent Lewis and Clark on an expedition to explore the new territory.

Section 3
A Time of Conflict

- In an attempt to punish Britain and France, Jefferson proposed the Embargo Act. The embargo hurt the U.S. economy.
- Native Americans were defeated when they opposed U.S. settlement in the Northwest Territory.

Section 4
The War of 1812

- The war hawks blamed Britain for trouble with the Native Americans and decreased trade.
- The War of 1812 ended without a clear victor, but the United States achieved a new sense of nationalism.

Key Concepts

These notes will help you prepare for questions about key concepts.

Jefferson Charts New Directions

- Becomes President after disputed election of 1800
- Changes Federalist policies
- Attempts to limit federal government's power over states and citizens
- Reduces federal budget
- Cuts size of military

Exploring New Lands

- United States purchases Louisiana Territory from France

- Lewis and Clark explore the Northwest; find route to the Pacific
- Pike explores the Southwest

Foreign Entanglements

- Americans defeat Barbary States at Tripoli
- Jefferson establishes Embargo Act of 1807 against Britain and France
- Embargo hurts Americans more than it does Britain and France

War of 1812

- United States declares war on Britain in 1812
- Many Native Americans ally with Britain
- Treaty of Ghent establishes peace, but no territory is gained by either nation
- Jackson's victory at New Orleans follows peace treaty
- Nationalism rises in the United States

Vocabulary *Builder*

Key Terms

Fill in the blanks with the correct key terms.

1. The principle of _____ gave the Supreme Court a central role in American government.

2. Lewis and Clark's _____ inspired many Americans to move west.

3. When Congress repealed Jefferson's _____ on trade, foreign trade was allowed again with every country except Britain and France.

4. During the Embargo Act, thousands of Americans turned to _____.

5. After crossing the _____ in the Rocky Mountains, Lewis and Clark began traveling on rivers that flowed to the Pacific Ocean.

Comprehension and Critical Thinking

6. **(a) Recall** What was Jefferson's view about the powers the federal government should have?
(b) Clarify Problems How did he apply these views to the situation of buying Louisiana?
(c) Draw Conclusions Use these situations and other information from the chapter to evaluate Jefferson's record as President.

7. **(a) Summarize** Why did Jefferson not want to keep William Marbury and other last-minute appointments of former President Adams on the federal payroll?
(b) Explain Problems How did Chief Justice John Marshall deal with the problem created by James Madison's inaction?

8. **(a) Describe** What obstacles did Lewis and Clark's expedition encounter?
(b) Draw Conclusions In what ways did Lewis and Clark's expedition help western settlers?
(c) Link Past and Present What modern-day explorations compare to Lewis and Clark's and Pike's expeditions?

9. **(a) Recall** What was the Embargo Act of 1807?
(b) Identify Alternatives What did Congress do to ease the economic effects of the embargo?

10. **(a) Summarize** What were the goals of Tecumseh and the Prophet?
(b) Detect Points of View How did settler views differ from Shawnee views?

11. **(a) Recall** Why were many Native Americans allied with the British during the War of 1812?
(b) Identify Costs Do you think siding with the British military helped or hurt the Native American cause? Explain.

History Reading Skill

12. **Relate Events in Time** Read the text under the heading "Lewis and Clark Explore the West." Which of these events happened first: Lewis and Clark headed up the Missouri River, or Lewis and Clark reached the mouth of the Platte River? What signal words offer clues to the sequence?

Writing

13. Write two paragraphs discussing Thomas Jefferson's experiences as President.
Your paragraphs should:
- begin with a thesis statement that expresses your main impressions;
- expand on that main idea with facts, examples, and other information;
- conclude by stating Jefferson's most important contribution to the new nation.

14. **Write a Narrative:**
What would it have been like to be an American sailor impressed by the British? Write a paragraph describing what the experience might have been like. Be sure to describe the conflicting emotions sailors may have felt.

Skills for Life

Detect Historical Points of View
Use the quotation below to answer the questions.

> "I consider the government of the United States as [prevented] by the Constitution from intermeddling religious institutions, their doctrines, discipline, or exercise. This results not only from the provision that no law shall be made respecting the establishment, or free exercise, of religion, but from that also which reserves to the states the powers not delegated to the U.S."
>
> —Thomas Jefferson, to Samuel Miller, Jan. 23, 1808

15. What is Jefferson's point of view?

16. How was Jefferson's point of view affected by historical events?

Test Yourself

1. **Which of the following of Jefferson's policies negatively affected the American ability to fight the British in the War of 1812?**

   A the elimination of federal taxes

   B the Embargo Act of 1807

   C the purchase of the Louisiana Territory

   D the reduction of the military

2. **Which present-day states were formed from the Louisiana Purchase?**

   A Pennsylvania, New York, Massachusetts, and Maine

   B South Dakota, Nebraska, Kansas, and Oklahoma

   C Washington, Oregon, California, and Nevada

   D South Carolina, Virginia, Florida, and Georgia

Refer to the quotation below to answer Question 3.

"Where are the Narragansett, the Mohican, the Pocanet, and other powerful tribes of our people? They have vanished before the avarice and oppression of the white man. . . . Will we let ourselves be destroyed in our turn?. . . Shall we, without a struggle, give up our homes . . .?"

3. **Who was the likely speaker of this quotation?**

   A President Thomas Jefferson

   B Chief Justice John Marshall

   C Native American leader Tecumseh

   D Secretary of State John Quincy Adams

Document-Based Questions

Task: Look at Documents 1 and 2, and answer their accompanying questions. Then, use the documents and your knowledge of history to complete this writing assignment:

Write a draft of a document explaining New England's opposition to the War of 1812 and expressing the region's views on the rights of states to challenge, or even separate from, the federal government.

Document 1: During the War of 1812, the British blockaded American ports. *Based on this map, how would the blockade affect merchants in New England?*

British Blockade, 1812

Document 2: In 1814, New Englanders meeting in the Hartford Convention called for increased states' rights and even considered secession from the Union. *In the portion of the document below, issued by the Hartford Convention, what causes are cited as reasons for separating from the Union?*

"Events may prove that the causes of our calamities are deep and permanent. . . . They may be traced to implacable combinations of individuals, or of states, to monopolize power and office, and to trample without remorse upon the rights and interests of commercial sections of the Union.

Whenever it shall appear that these causes are radical and permanent, a separation, by equitable arrangement, will be preferable to an alliance by constraint, among nominal friends. . . ."

CHAPTER
10 | # A Changing Nation
1815–1840

Chapter Preview

After the War of 1812, American confidence was high. A new period of national pride and identity began. Yet, at the same time, there were forces of division as well as unity at work.

1816
Congress passes Tariff of 1816.

1819
McCulloch v. *Maryland* strengthens federal government.

1823
Monroe Doctrine is issued.

U.S. Events

1810   1818   1826

World Events

1819 Spain cedes Florida to United States.

1821 Spain recognizes independence of Mexico.

Quick View Video
View the chapter video for a quick preview of the main ideas.

Stump Speaker by the American painter George Caleb Bingham captures the energy of an election rally during the era of Jacksonian democracy.

1828
Andrew Jackson is elected President.

1837
Panic of 1837 brings economic collapse.

1838–1839
Cherokees are forced to move to Oklahoma along Trail of Tears.

1826

1834

1842

1841 Act of Union unites Upper and Lower Canada.

History Reading Skill Analyze Cause and Effect

What qualities does a leader need?

In this chapter, you will learn how to analyze cause-and-effect relationships. Read the following letter from Andrew Jackson's mother to her son, in which she advises him on how to be a good man. The side notes show you how to analyze causes and effects.

> Andrew Jackson became U.S. President in 1829. His mother, Elizabeth, a tireless nurse during the Revolutionary War, wrote this letter to him shortly before her death during that war.
>
> **Primary Source**
>
> Dear Andrew,
>   If I should not see you again, I wish you to remember and treasure up some things I have already said to you. In this world, you will have to make your own way. To do that, you must have friends. You can make friends by being honest, and you can keep them by being steadfast. . . .
>   To forget an obligation or be ungrateful for a kindness is a crime. Men guilty of it sooner or later must suffer the penalty.
>   In personal conduct, always be polite, but never obsequious [too eager to please]. No one will respect you more than you respect yourself. Avoid quarrels as long as you can without yielding to imposition. But sustain your manhood always.
>   Never wound the feelings of others. If you ever have to defend your feelings or your honor, do it calmly. If angry at first, wait till your anger cools before you proceed.
>
>   Love,
>   Mother

Jackson needs friends *because* he must make his own way.

Two effects: Being honest *and* steadfast can lead to both making and keeping friends.

Two causes: Forgetting an obligation *or* being ungrateful can both result in a penalty eventually.

Lack of respect for yourself is a cause that can lead to the long-term effect that others don't respect you either.

Analyze Cause and Effect
- Look for words that signal cause-and-effect relationships. Words that signal causes include *caused* and *brought about.* Words that signal effects include *therefore* and *thus.*
- Consider whether a cause has more than one effect and whether an effect has more than one cause.
- Think about whether causes will have immediate or long-term effects, or both.

Document-Based Questions
1. When was this letter written?
2. What kinds of advice does Elizabeth Jackson give to her son?
3. What might have caused her to write the letter?

Vocabulary *Builder*

Previewing High-Use Academic Words

High-Use Word	Definition	Sample History Sentence
circuit (SIR kuht) (Section 1, p. 340)	*n.* circular trip around an area	The sentry made a circuit around the military camp.
infrastructure (IHN frah struhk chahr) (Section 1, p. 343)	*n.* basic public works, like bridges and roads, needed for a society to function	By building new roads and bridges, the planners hoped to improve the country's infrastructure.
province (PRAHV ahns) (Section 2, p. 346)	*n.* governmental division of a country, similar to a state	Quebec is a province of Canada.
domestic (doh MEHS tihk) (Section 2, p. 348)	*adj.* relating to one's country; internal	President Washington was focused on dealing with domestic affairs.
participate (pahr TIHS ah payt) (Section 3, p. 349)	*v.* to take part in; to share in an activity	The delegates to the Constitutional Convention participated in a historic debate over the nature of government.
react (ree AKT) (Section 3, p. 350)	*v.* to act in response to another action	King George III reacted with anger when he heard of the colonists' demands.
voluntary (VAHL ahn tair ee) (Section 4, p. 357)	*adj.* done willingly, of one's own free will	Settlers began a huge voluntary movement westward.
quote (kwoht) (Section 4, p. 357)	*v.* to repeat the exact words spoken or written	The newspaper quoted long excerpts from the President's speech.
enrich (ehn RIHCH) (Section 5, p. 362)	*v.* to make wealthy	After the American Revolution, speculators hoping to enrich themselves bought government bonds.
resolve (ree SAHLV) (Section 5, p. 364)	*v.* to decide; to solve	Debates during the Constitutional Convention did not resolve the issue of slavery.

Previewing Key Terms and People

Building a National Identity

Objectives

1. Describe the feeling of national unity that followed the War of 1812.

2. Explain how Congress tried to strengthen the national economy.

3. Discuss how Supreme Court rulings supported federal power and economic growth.

Prepare to Read

Reading Skill

Analyze Cause and Effect
Events in history are often linked by cause and effect. This means that one event makes another happen. However, you cannot assume that because events occur together or in sequence they have a cause-and-effect link. Ask yourself: Why did this event or result happen? What happened because of this event? The answers will show if a cause-and-effect relationship exists.

Vocabulary *Builder*

High-Use Words

circuit, p. 340

infrastructure, p. 343

Key Terms and People

Henry Clay, p. 341

John C. Calhoun, p. 341

Daniel Webster, p. 341

charter, p. 342

dumping, p. 342

contract, p. 344

capitalism, p. 344

interstate commerce, p. 344

⭐ **Background Knowledge** You have learned how the United States acquired territory west of the Mississippi River and fought Great Britain in the War of 1812. Americans then turned to internal affairs.

Main Idea
The period of national unity following the War of 1812 is known as the Era of Good Feelings.

The Era of Good Feelings

With the end of the War of 1812, the Republicans took firm control of the government. The presidential election of 1816 resulted in a landslide victory for Republican candidate James Monroe of Virginia. He defeated Rufus King, the Federalist candidate, by 183 to 34 electoral votes. Stung by this defeat, the Federalist Party began to lose power. Within a few years, the party had disappeared.

President Monroe wanted to promote national unity. In the spring and summer of 1817, he made a goodwill circuit of the middle and northern sections of the country. He was warmly greeted in Connecticut and Massachusetts, the only states that had not voted for him in 1816. The old arguments over the War of 1812 seemed to have faded away.

Vocabulary *Builder*
circuit (SIR kuht) *n.* circular trip around an area

While Monroe was in Boston, a local newspaper described the new sense of national unity as the "Era of Good Feelings." The name stuck and was used to describe Monroe's two terms in office. When he ran for reelection in 1820, no candidate opposed him.

✓**Checkpoint** What happened to the Federalist Party after the War of 1812?

Building the National Economy

After 1815, many Americans believed the federal government should take action to increase economic prosperity in all regions of the country. Even the Republicans began to see merit in certain federal programs. This was a change, because in previous years Republicans had been known for stressing states' rights. Support for federal measures to promote economic prosperity came from many regions.

These beliefs were expressed by a number of bright young members of Congress from different regions. Outstanding among those who favored federal action were Henry Clay of Kentucky, John C. Calhoun of South Carolina, and Daniel Webster of Massachusetts.

- Clay spoke for people in the West who thought the country needed better roads and canals to transport goods from one region to another.

- Calhoun spoke for the interests of the South. While first a defender of national unity, he later put more emphasis on the idea of states' rights.

- Webster became a spokesperson for the Northeast. At first, he opposed high tariffs, but he later came to support them as a way of protecting industry.

Analyze Cause and Effect
Explain what Americans believed was needed to make national unity grow. What would cause that growth to happen?

Daniel Webster

NORTH

Henry Clay

WEST

SOUTH

John C. Calhoun

New Leaders Speak for Their Regions

During the Era of Good Feelings, three young members of Congress became spokespersons for their regions.

Daniel Webster - Massachusetts
He supported tariffs because they allowed New England's factories to compete against European manufacturers.

John C. Calhoun - South Carolina
He opposed tariffs because they raised the price of goods that southerners bought.

Henry Clay - Kentucky
He supported the construction of roads and canals because they would enable the three regions of the country to trade with one another.

Critical Thinking: *Apply Information Which of the three leaders would you expect to be the strongest supporter of slavery? Explain.*

History *Interactive*

Find Out How Tariffs Work

Visit: PHSchool.com
Web Code: myp-3061

How Tariffs Work

By increasing the cost of imported goods, tariffs helped U.S. manufacturers to compete with foreign manufacturers. But the higher prices hurt consumers. **Critical Thinking:** *Identify Economic Costs Why was the cost of cloth higher in the United States than in Britain?*

	United States	Great Britain
Cost of cloth	$6.00	$5.00
Cost to manufacture final product	$0.85	$0.50
Shipping costs	$0.20	$0.25
Tariff	—	$1.50
Total	**$7.05**	**$7.25**

The Second Bank of the United States As you have read, Congress passed a law in 1791 creating the first Bank of the United States. In 1811, the Bank ceased to exist. Its **charter**—a legal document giving certain rights to a person or company—had run out. Without the Bank, the economy suffered. State banks made too many loans and issued too much money. This caused an increase in spending and led to rising prices.

To cure these problems, Congress established the second Bank of the United States in 1816. Like the first Bank, the new Bank was privately owned and had a charter to operate for twenty years. It lent money to individuals and controlled the money supply. This gave a boost to American businesses.

The Tariff of 1816 Another problem the nation faced after the War of 1812 was foreign competition. Most British goods had been kept out of the United States by the Embargo Act and the War of 1812. This helped American industry grow rapidly. New American factories made textiles, smelted iron, and produced many other products.

After the War of 1812, British manufacturers looked to sell their goods in the United States. They could still produce goods more cheaply than the Americans because they had well-established factories and more customers. This gave the British an opportunity to drive their American competitors out of business by dumping their goods in the United States. **Dumping** is selling goods in another country below market prices.

British dumping caused dozens of New England businesses to fail. As their investments collapsed, angry factory owners turned to Congress for help. They demanded protective tariffs to raise the price of foreign goods.

Congress responded with the Tariff of 1816, which put a tax on foreign textiles, iron, leather goods, paper, and other products. In 1818 and 1824, Congress passed even higher tariffs.

These tariffs were popular in the North, where most factories were located. However, the tariffs were deeply resented in the South, where they forced southerners to pay more for their goods. John C. Calhoun became a bitter foe of tariffs. He argued that they made northern manufacturers rich at the expense of the South.

Clay's American System As the debate over tariffs raged, Henry Clay came up with a plan that he believed would help the economy of each section of the country. He called his plan the American System. It proposed high tariffs and a federal program of public works.

Clay believed that high tariffs helped all regions of the country, not just the North. According to Clay, the wealth produced by tariffs would enable northerners to buy farm products from the West and the South. The tariff also would provide revenue for the federal government. The government could then use the money to build up the infrastructure—roads, bridges, and canals—in the South and West.

Clay's American System never fully became government policy. Presidents Madison and Monroe both refused to support some of Clay's projects. Also, southerners continued to oppose protective tariffs. They were not convinced by Clay's argument that high tariffs would aid the South in the long run.

☑ **Checkpoint** **According to Henry Clay, how would his American System benefit the economy?**

British Leather Boots
The U.S. tariff on imports such as leather goods helped New England manufacturers to compete.

Vocabulary *Builder*
infrastructure (IHN frah struhk chahr) *n.* basic public works, like bridges and roads, needed for a society to function

Three Important Supreme Court Rulings

The Supreme Court also promoted national economic growth and the power of the federal government during this era. Led by Chief Justice John Marshall, a Federalist sympathizer, the Court issued a series of important rulings between 1819 and 1824.

In *McCulloch* v. *Maryland* (1819), the Court protected the second Bank of the United States. The case grew out of an attempt by the state of Maryland to put a tax on the branch of the Bank operating in that state. The Bank refused to pay the tax.

The Court's 1819 decision, written by Marshall, strengthened the power of the federal government. It ruled that states had no power to interfere with federal institutions. A tax, said the Court, was a dangerous interference because "the power to tax involves the power to destroy." Moreover, according to Marshall, a state cannot pass any law that violates a federal law. This reasoning would be used in future years to expand the power of the federal government.

Main Idea
A number of Supreme Court rulings strengthened the federal government and supported economic growth.

Interstate Commerce
No individual state could grant a monopoly to a steamboat company to use a river that divides two states, the Supreme Court ruled in *Gibbons v. Ogden*.

Two other decisions helped shape American life. In *Dartmouth College* v. *Woodward* (1819), the Court ruled that the charter of Dartmouth College in New Hampshire was a private contract. A **contract** is an agreement between two or more parties that can be enforced by law. Since the Constitution protected private contracts, New Hampshire could not change Dartmouth's charter. In protecting private contracts, the Court was protecting private businesses. In doing that, it helped promote **capitalism**—the economic system in which privately owned businesses compete in a free market.

In *Gibbons* v. *Ogden* (1824), the Court again supported federal power. It ruled that New York State could not give a steamboat company a monopoly to carry passengers on the Hudson River. The Court pointed out that travel on the Hudson River included stops in New Jersey as well as New York. Therefore, it was **interstate commerce**—trade between two or more states. Under the Constitution, only Congress can regulate interstate commerce. Again, the Court had strengthened the federal government at the expense of the states.

☑**Checkpoint** How did the Supreme Court ruling in *Dartmouth College* v. *Woodward* support economic growth?

⭐ **Looking Back and Ahead** Americans turned their attention to economic growth after the War of 1812. But while Americans were debating Henry Clay's American System, events in Latin America were drawing the concern of American leaders.

Section 1 | Check Your Progress

Progress Monitoring ⊕nline
For: Self-test with instant help
Visit: PHSchool.com
Web Code: mya-3061

Comprehension and Critical Thinking

1. **(a) Recall** Which groups supported and which opposed tariffs?
   (b) Draw Conclusions Do you think the American System offered a good solution to regional differences? Explain.

2. **(a) Recall** What did *McCulloch* v. *Maryland* decide?
   (b) Compare What did the Supreme Court decisions in *McCulloch* v. *Maryland* and *Gibbons* v. *Ogden* have in common?

Reading Skill

3. **Analyze Cause and Effect** Reread the text following the headings "The Tariff of 1816" and "Clay's American System." What did Clay believe would result from high tariffs?

Vocabulary *Builder*
Fill in the blanks with the correct key terms.
4. To set up the Bank of the United States, the government granted it a ____.
5. Private businesses compete in the American economic system called ____.

Writing

6. Decide which is the best closing sentence for an essay on James Monroe. Explain your choice.
   Sentences:
   (a) James Monroe, the fifth President of the United States, won two landslide victories.
   (b) Clearly, James Monroe deserved to have his presidency called the Era of Good Feelings.
   (c) James Monroe is, without a doubt, one of the greatest men ever elected President.

Dealing With Other Nations

Objectives

1. Explain why Spain ceded Florida to the United States.

2. Describe how Spanish territories in the Americas gained independence.

3. Explain why the Monroe Doctrine was issued.

4. Discuss how Canada became self-governing.

Prepare to Read

Reading Skill

Identify Multiple Effects As you read about historical events, note that some events have multiple, or more than one, effects. Several effects may happen at the same time or one effect may lead to the next. As you read this section, look for multiple effects of each event.

Vocabulary *Builder*

High-Use Words

province, p. 346

domestic, p. 348

Key Terms and People

cede, p. 345

Miguel Hidalgo, p. 346

Simón Bolívar, p. 346

James Monroe, p. 347

John Quincy Adams, p. 347

self-government, p. 348

⭐ **Background Knowledge** In the previous section, you learned how the United States dealt with problems at home after 1815. In this section, you will learn why the United States took a firm position in challenging European influence in the Americas.

Relations With Spain

At the time of the War of 1812, the United States and Haiti were the only parts of the Americas not under European control. Spain controlled more territory in the Americas than any other European country. However, Spain's power had steadily weakened over several hundred years.

Spain's control was especially weak in Florida. Spain could not stop enslaved African Americans who escaped from plantations in Georgia and Alabama from crossing into Florida. Once in Florida, many of the escapees joined the Seminole Nation. The Seminoles often crossed into the United States to raid American settlements.

In 1817, the U.S. government sent Andrew Jackson to recapture those who had escaped slavery. Jackson attacked and destroyed Seminole villages. He then went far beyond his orders. He seized two important Spanish towns and forced the governor to flee Florida.

Jackson's attack on Florida showed that the United States could take over Florida whenever it wanted. Since Spain could not protect Florida, it decided to give up the territory. In the Adams-Onís Treaty of 1819, Spain ceded, or gave up, Florida to the United States.

Main Idea

Spain's inability to defend Florida led it to turn the colony over to the United States.

Identify Multiple Effects

Spain's control was especially weak in Florida. What were all the effects of this situation?

✓ **Checkpoint** What effect did Andrew Jackson's attack on Florida have on the government of Spain?

Main Idea
A series of revolts allowed most Latin American colonies to win their independence from Spain and Portugal.

Vocabulary *Builder*
<u>province</u> (PRAHV ahns) *n.* governmental division of a country, similar to a state

Spanish Colonies Win Independence

By 1810, opposition to Spanish rule ran strong in Spain's American colonies. The American and French revolutions had inspired Latin Americans to want to control their own affairs. Revolutionary movements were growing in almost all of the Spanish colonies. Spain seemed unable to control the pressure for change in Latin America.

Mexico Breaks Away Mexico's struggle for independence began in 1810. In that year, Father Miguel Hidalgo (ee DAHL goh) organized an army of Native Americans that freed several Mexican <u>provinces</u>. However, in 1811, Hidalgo was captured and executed by troops loyal to Spain.

Another revolution broke out in Mexico in 1820. This time, Spain was unable to end the fighting. In 1821, Spain agreed to Mexico's independence.

At first, Mexico was ruled by an emperor. Then, in 1823, the monarchy was overthrown. A new constitution, patterned after the United States Constitution, made Mexico a federal republic of nineteen states and four territories.

Independence for South and Central America South America, too, was affected by revolutionary change. Here, the best-known leader of the struggle for independence from Spain was Simón Bolívar (see MOHN boh LEE vahr).

New Nations of Latin America

MAP MASTER®
Skills Activity

Wars of independence led to the creation of many new countries in Latin America in the first half of the 1800s.

(a) Read a Map What parts of Latin America remained colonies of European nations?

(b) Apply Information Use the world map in the Atlas in this textbook to identify how the border between the United States and Mexico has changed.

MapMaster ●nline

For: Interactive map
Visit: PHSchool.com
Web Code: myp-3062

KEY

New nations

European colonies

0 km 2,000
0 miles 2,000
Azimuthal Equal-Area Projection

Bolívar is often called the Liberator for his role in leading independence movements in the northern part of South America. In August 1819, he led an army on a daring march from Venezuela over the ice-capped Andes Mountains and into Colombia. There, he defeated the Spanish and became president of the independent Republic of Great Colombia. It included today's nations of Venezuela, Colombia, Ecuador, and Panama.

Farther north, the people of Central America declared their independence from Spain in 1821. Two years later, they formed the United Provinces of Central America. It included today's nations of Nicaragua, Costa Rica, El Salvador, Honduras, and Guatemala.

In 1822, Brazil announced its independence from Portugal. Soon after, the United States recognized the independence of Mexico and six other former colonies in Central and South America. By 1825, most parts of Latin America had thrown off European rule.

☑Checkpoint **Why was Miguel Hidalgo important to the history of Mexico?**

Links Across Time

Beyond the Monroe Doctrine

1823 The Monroe Doctrine warned European nations not to interfere in Latin America.

1900s U.S. Presidents cited the Monroe Doctrine to justify armed actions in Latin America. The actions often angered Latin Americans.

1930s President Franklin D. Roosevelt launched a Good Neighbor Policy. It stressed cooperation and trade to promote U.S. interests in the hemisphere.

Link to Today

Connection to Today What is the state of our relations with the countries of Latin America today?

For: U.S. relations with Latin America today
Visit: PHSchool.com
Web Code: myc-3062

The Monroe Doctrine

The future of these new countries was soon clouded. Several European powers, including France and Russia, indicated that they might help Spain regain its colonies.

This worried President James Monroe and Secretary of State John Quincy Adams. It also worried the British. Both nations wanted to protect trade with Latin America. In 1823, Britain suggested that the two countries issue a joint statement. The statement would announce their determination to protect the freedom of the new nations of Latin America.

Adams told President Monroe he thought the United States should take action alone. He believed a joint statement would make the United States look like Britain's junior partner. Monroe agreed.

In a message to Congress in December 1823, the President stated what is known as the Monroe Doctrine. The United States would not allow European nations to create American colonies or interfere with the free nations of Latin America. The United States would consider any attempt to do so "dangerous to our peace and safety."

At the time, the United States was not strong enough to block European action. Only the British navy could do that. As U.S. power grew, however, the Monroe Doctrine boosted the influence of the United States in the region.

☑Checkpoint **What was Adams's advice to Monroe?**

Main Idea
In the Monroe Doctrine, the United States warned European nations against reestablishing colonies in Latin America.

Relations With Canada

Canada remained a British colony after the American Revolution. In 1791, the country was divided into two parts. Upper Canada was mainly English, and Lower Canada was mainly French. In 1837, there were rebellions against British rule in both parts of Canada.

Although the British put down the rebellions, they learned a lesson. They could no longer deny rights to Canadians. Britain would have to give Canadians more powers of self-government—the right of people to rule themselves independently. The Act of Union of 1841 was a major step in that direction. It merged Canada's two parts into a single unit governed by a Canadian legislature. Britain, however, still had ultimate control.

Canada and the United States had their own disagreements. Tensions were particularly high when the United States unsuccessfully tried to invade Canada during the War of 1812.

The situation slowly improved after the war. Between 1818 and 1846, the United States and Britain settled several border disputes regarding Canada. Eventually, the United States and Canada established excellent relations. Their relations remain strong to this day.

☑**Checkpoint** **Why did Britain grant some self-government to Canada?**

⭐ **Looking Back and Ahead** The Monroe Doctrine convinced Americans that their southern borders were safe from European expansion. Treaties with Britain lessened the tensions along the northern border with Canada. With a new sense of confidence, Americans prepared to make great strides on the domestic front. The 1820s and 1830s would see an upsurge in the democratic spirit.

Vocabulary *Builder*
<u>domestic</u> (doh MEHS tihk) *adj.* relating to one's country; internal

---

Section 2 | Check Your Progress

Progress Monitoring Online
For: Self-test with instant help
Visit: PHSchool.com
Web Code: mya-3062

Comprehension and Critical Thinking

1. (a) **Summarize** What was the Monroe Doctrine?
(b) **Clarify Problems** Would the United States have looked weak if it had jointly issued a warning with Britain? Explain.

2. (a) **List** Name six of today's Latin American countries that were independent by 1825.
(b) **Identify Economic Benefits** How did Great Britain and the United States benefit from the independence of Spain's American colonies?

Reading Skill

3. **Identify Multiple Effects** European powers, such as France and Russia, considered helping Spain regain its South and Central American colonies. What were the effects of this situation? Reread the text under the heading "The Monroe Doctrine."

Vocabulary *Builder*

Answer the following questions in complete sentences that show your understanding of the key terms.
4. What did Spain cede to the United States in the Adams-Onís Treaty?

5. How did Canadians benefit when Britain granted them more self-government?

Writing

6. Revise the following sentences to make them flow better. **Sentences:** The Monroe Doctrine stated that the United States would not allow Spain to take back its former colonies. The doctrine helped the new Latin American states remain free. The doctrine supported the cause of democracy in the Western Hemisphere.

The Age of Jackson

Objectives

1. Discuss the conflict between Andrew Jackson and John Quincy Adams over the election of 1824.

2. Explain how the right to vote expanded in the United States.

3. Describe Andrew Jackson's victory in the election of 1828.

Prepare to Read

 Reading Skill

Identify Short-Term Effects
Some events have effects that take place shortly after the event. Other events create changes that last only a short time. Both of these types of effects are short-term effects. As you read Section 3, look for examples of the short-term effects of events.

Vocabulary *Builder*

High-Use Words
<u>participate</u>, p. 349
<u>react</u>, p. 350

Key Terms and People
Andrew Jackson, p. 349
suffrage, p. 351
caucus, p. 352
nominating convention, p. 352
spoils system, p. 354

⭐ **Background Knowledge** Earlier, you read how one party dominated the political scene during the Era of Good Feelings. In this section, you will learn how important changes in American political life during the 1820s and 1830s led to an era of vigorous competition in political life.

Adams and Jackson in Conflict

Andrew Jackson served two terms as President, from 1829 to 1837. His presidency marked the opening of a new and more democratic era in American political life. So great was his influence that the twenty-year period after he became President is often called the Age of Jackson.

Andrew Jackson was a wealthy man by the time he became President. However, he began life with very little. Born in a log cabin on the border of North and South Carolina, he was an orphan by the age of 14. Jackson was ambitious, brave, and tough. He survived smallpox as a child and severe gunshot wounds as an adult.

During a difficult march with his troops in 1812, one soldier described him as "tough as hickory." Hickory trees are extremely strong, and their wood is very hard. The description fit Jackson so well that it stuck as a nickname. Jackson became known as Old Hickory.

Jackson stood for the idea that ordinary people should <u>participate</u> in American political life. As a general and later as President, Andrew Jackson was deeply loved by millions of ordinary Americans. They loved him for his humble beginnings and his firm leadership.

Main Idea
Andrew Jackson was deeply loved by millions of Americans. John Quincy Adams never won the trust of the American people.

Vocabulary *Builder*
<u>participate</u> (pahr TIHS ah payt) v. to take part in; to share in an activity

The Election of 1824

Jackson first ran for President in 1824. His opponents were John Quincy Adams, Henry Clay, and William H. Crawford of Georgia. Jackson received the most electoral votes, but not a majority. According to the Constitution, the House of Representatives would have to decide the election.

The choice was between Jackson and Adams, the two who had received the most votes. As Speaker of the House, Clay had great influence. He told his supporters to vote for Adams. The House then elected Adams on the first ballot.

Jackson <u>reacted</u> with fury. He had won the most popular votes and the most electoral votes, but still had lost the election. When Adams appointed Clay secretary of state, Jackson's supporters claimed the two men had made a "corrupt bargain."

The Presidency of John Quincy Adams

Adams was burdened by the charges of a secret deal. He accomplished little, even though he had ambitious plans for the nation. He supported Clay's American System and wanted the federal government to play a larger role in supporting the American economy.

Adams proposed a national program to build roads and canals and a high tariff to protect industry. He also planned to set up a national university and an observatory for astronomers in Washington, D.C. However, he lacked the political skill to push his programs through Congress. Adams never won the trust of the American people. As a result, he served only one term.

Vocabulary *Builder*
<u>react</u> (ree AKT) *v.* to act in response to another action

▲ *The County Election*, George Caleb Bingham

Despite his failures, Adams was an eloquent supporter of what he saw as America's special place in the world. He stated his ideas in a Fourth of July speech in 1821. He said the United States had no designs on the territory of other nations:

> "Wherever the standard of freedom and independence has been or shall be unfurled, there will her [America's] heart, . . . and her prayers be. But she goes not abroad in search of monsters to destroy. She is the well-wisher to the freedom and independence of all."
>
> —John Quincy Adams, Fourth of July 1821 Address

✓**Checkpoint** **Why did Jackson's supporters claim there had been a "corrupt bargain" in the election of 1824?**

A New Era in Politics

Main Idea
A growing spirit of democracy resulted in more white American males gaining the right to vote.

The election of 1824 disappointed Andrew Jackson and his followers. Still, that election began a new era in American politics.

Back in the 1790s, states had begun extending suffrage—the right to vote. Many states dropped the requirement that men had to own property to be able to vote. Voting requirements varied slightly from state to state. However, almost all adult white males now could vote and hold office.

$\mathscr{D}$emocracy in $\mathscr{A}$ction

Voter Participation in Presidential Elections, 1824–1840

(bar graph showing Percentage of Voters by Year)
- 1824: approximately 28
- 1828: approximately 57
- 1832: approximately 55
- 1836: approximately 58
- 1840: approximately 81

The Age of Jackson saw the first stirrings of democracy in action in the United States. More men could and did vote, and many more people joined political parties and participated in election campaigns.

It would be many years until women and African Americans also gained the right to vote. However, the kinds of political contests that are familiar to Americans today had their beginnings in the presidential elections of the 1820s and 1830s. *Critical Thinking: Draw Conclusions Why would people become more actively involved in political campaigns as the right to vote was extended to new groups?*

◄ Portrait of Andrew Jackson shown inside a souvenir box from an early presidential campaign.

Andrew Jackson
1767–1845

Andrew Jackson was a Tennessee landowner, lawyer, and judge. His military campaigns against the British in the War of 1812 and against Native Americans in Florida made him a war hero. Political opponents called him a country hick. But supporters admired him as a self-made man who spoke out for ordinary people. His election as President was a sign that the United States was becoming a more democratic nation.

Biography Quest 🌐 **Online**

How did Jackson gain a reputation as a supporter of ordinary people?

For: The answer to the question about Jackson
Visit: PHSchool.com
Web Code: myd-3063

Identify Short-Term Effects

What was the immediate effect of using nominating conventions to choose presidential candidates?

States also were changing how they chose presidential electors. Previously, state legislatures chose them. Now, that right went to the voters. In 1824, voters chose the presidential electors in 18 out of 24 states.

Of course, suffrage was still restricted in the United States. Women could not participate in government. Nor could enslaved African Americans, male or female. In most states, even free African Americans could not vote.

Democracy in the Age of Jackson

Extending the right to vote was part of a larger spread of democratic ideas. Supporters of Andrew Jackson believed that ordinary people should vote in elections, hold public office, and do anything else they had the ability to do. Jackson's supporters strongly opposed special privileges for those of high social status.

Wealthy observers were sometimes dismayed by this spirit of equality. One visitor complained, "the rich and the poor, the educated and the ignorant, the polite and the vulgar, all . . . feed at the same table."

Jackson and his supporters did not trust government. They believed it often favored the rich and powerful. The Jacksonians also were suspicious of banks, which they believed favored the rich.

New Political Parties The Age of Jackson brought back the two-party system that had briefly ended during the Era of Good Feelings. During the 1824 election, the Republican Party split. Supporters of Adams called themselves National Republicans. Jackson's supporters used the name Democrats.

In 1831, the National Republicans nominated Henry Clay to run against Jackson. Jackson won easily, with strength in all parts of the country. However, by 1836, the anti-Jackson forces had formed a new party, the Whigs. From then until 1852, the Democrats and the Whigs were the country's two major political parties.

The new parties adopted a new way of choosing their presidential candidates. Previously, a party's members of Congress held a **caucus**—a meeting of members of a political party. These caucuses involved only a small group of people. Beginning in 1831, political parties started holding national **nominating conventions**—large meetings of party delegates to choose candidates for office. National conventions opened the nominating process to many more people and made it more democratic.

✓**Checkpoint** **Which groups did not benefit from increased suffrage in the United States?**

Jackson Becomes President

Three times as many people voted in the election of 1828 as had voted in 1824. Most of these new voters supported Jackson, who easily defeated Adams.

The election revealed growing sectional and class divisions among American voters. Jackson did best in the West and the South, where planters and small farmers supported him. He also did well among small business people, artisans, and workers in cities and towns nationwide. Adams was most popular in his home region of New England.

Jackson's Inauguration Jackson's supporters called the election a victory for the "common man." His inauguration in March 1829 showed what they meant. Thousands of ordinary working people jammed into Washington for the event. After the inauguration at the Capitol, Jackson rode a horse to the White House. A journalist described the scene:

> **❝**As far as the eye could reach, the sidewalks of the Avenue were covered with people on foot . . . with . . . carriages and persons on horseback. . . . For a full half hour, I stood waiting for the stream to run by; but like a never failing fountain people continued pouring forth.**❞**
>
> —Amos Kendall in the *Argus of Western America*,
> March 29, 1829

Main Idea
Andrew Jackson's victory in 1828 was a result of widespread support among farmers, workers, and artisans.

Jackson's Inauguration
Joyful crowds welcomed Andrew Jackson to the White House upon his inauguration in 1829. The artist who created this picture made sly fun of the celebrants. **Critical Thinking: *Apply Information*** *Why were some people upset by what happened at Jackson's inauguration?*

353

Twenty thousand people crowded in and around the White House for a reception in Jackson's honor. They did not all behave well. Some broke furniture, spilled drinks, trampled rugs, and broke several thousand dollars worth of glassware and dishes. Officials finally lured the unruly crowd outside by moving the punch bowl onto the White House lawn.

Jackson's opponents were shocked. One member of the Supreme Court complained about the "reign of King Mob." A Jackson supporter saw things more positively: "It was the People's day, and the People's President, and the People would rule."

The Spoils of Victory Jackson began his term by replacing some government officials with his supporters. Previous Presidents had done the same thing. In fact, during his two terms Jackson replaced only about 20 percent of federal officeholders.

The difference was that Jackson openly defended what he was doing. He claimed putting new people into government jobs furthered democracy. One of his supporters put it more selfishly when he compared the process to a conquering army after a war, saying "to the victors belong the spoils [loot]." People quickly applied the term spoils system to the practice of rewarding government jobs to loyal supporters of the party that wins an election.

✓**Checkpoint** How did Andrew Jackson justify the spoils system?

⭐ **Looking Back and Ahead** As President, Andrew Jackson supported the right of ordinary people to participate in government. Jackson's belief in equality, however, left out many, including Native Americans. In the next section, you will read how government policies denied basic rights to Native Americans.

Section 3 | Check Your Progress

Progress Monitoring Online
For: Self-test with instant help
Visit: PHSchool.com
Web Code: mya-3063

Comprehension and Critical Thinking

1. (a) **Recall** What was the "corrupt bargain"?
   (b) **Evaluate Information** Who benefited from accusations of a "corrupt bargain"?

2. (a) **Recall** How did the United States become more democratic between the 1790s and the 1830s?
   (b) **Draw Conclusions** How did these democratic changes contribute to Jackson's election in 1828?

Reading Skill

3. **Identify Short-Term Effects** What was the immediate effect when Henry Clay told his supporters to vote for Adams?

Vocabulary Builder

Read each sentence below. If the sentence is true, write YES. If the sentence is not true, write NO and explain why.

4. By 1828, suffrage had been extended to white women and African Americans.

5. In 1824, a nominating convention chose John Quincy Adams to run for President.

6. Tens of thousands of ordinary citizens showed up for the caucus celebrating Jackson's victory.

Writing

7. Using vivid, specific words will make your writing livelier and more accurate. Rewrite these sentences using more specific, colorful words. **Sentences:** Many people liked Andrew Jackson, and he was very popular. People liked Jackson better than John Quincy Adams. They felt Jackson was a man of the people and Adams was not a man of the people.

Indian Removal

Objectives

1. Describe the culture of Native Americans in the Southeast.
2. Describe the conflict over land occupied by Native Americans in the Southeast.
3. Discuss the forced removal of Native Americans.

Prepare to Read

Reading Skill

Identify Long-Term Effects
Many historical events have long-term effects—lasting effects that build up over time. As you read Section 4, look for events that have long-term effects. Think about why these causes have had such a lasting effect.

Vocabulary *Builder*

High-Use Words
<u>voluntary</u>, p. 357
<u>quote</u>, p. 357

Key Person
Sequoyah, p. 355

⭐ **Background Knowledge** As a general, Andrew Jackson won great popularity for his victories over Native Americans in Georgia and Florida. As President, Jackson worked to remove Native Americans from their homelands in the Southeast.

Native Americans of the Southeast

When Andrew Jackson became President, more than 100,000 Native Americans still lived east of the Mississippi River. Many of these Native Americans were farmers or lived in towns.

The Choctaw, Chickasaw, Cherokee, and Creek nations lived in parts of Mississippi, Alabama, northern Georgia, western North Carolina, and southern Tennessee. The Seminoles, who lived in Florida, had an unusual origin. They were a combination of Creeks who had moved into Florida in the late 1700s, Florida Native Americans, and escaped African American slaves.

The Cherokees had adopted some white customs. Aside from farming, they ran successful businesses, such as grain and lumber mills. The Cherokees had their own schools, and some could speak and read English. Many had converted to Christianity.

The Cherokees even had a written alphabet for their language. It had been created by a learned leader named Sequoyah (sih KWOY uh). In 1827, the Cherokees established a government based on a written constitution. They claimed status as a separate nation. The next year, they started a newspaper in both English and Cherokee.

☑ **Checkpoint** What were some of the customs and ways of life of the Cherokees?

Main Idea
The Native Americans of the Southeast followed a variety of customs.

Seminole woman

Indian Removal

WISCONSIN
TERRITORY

Sauk

Fox

L. Superior

L. Michigan

L. Huron

L. Ontario

L. Erie

ME

VT

NH

MA

CT

RI

NY

PA

NJ

MD

DE

40° N

MI

IL

IN

OH

VA

MO

Missouri R.

Mississippi R.

Ohio R.

KY

NC

INDIAN
TERRITORY

Ft. Smith

Ft. Gibson

Ft. Coffee

Memphis

TN

SC

ATLANTIC
OCEAN

AR

Red R.

AL

GA

70° W

LA

Vicksburg

MS

New Orleans

FLORIDA TERRITORY

30° N

0 km 200

0 miles 200

Azimuthal Equal-Area Projection

Gulf of Mexico

100° W

90° W

80° W

20° N

KEY

- Ceded to Native Americans
- Ceded by Native Americans
- ← Common removal route
- ← Cherokee removal route (Trail of Tears)
- ← Chickasaw removal route
- ← Choctaw removal route
- ← Creek removal route
- ← Seminole removal route
- ⚑ Forts

N E W S

MAP MASTER®

Skills Activity

In the 1830s, some 100,000 Native Americans of the Southeast were driven from their homes and forced to walk to a new home across the Mississippi River.

(a) Read a Map Which five Southeast nations were affected by the movement?

(b) Apply Information Use the scale of miles and the map above to answer the following question: About how far did the Seminoles have to travel to get from Florida Territory to New Orleans?

MapMaster ●nline

For: Interactive map
Visit: PHSchool.com
Web Code: myp-3064

Conflict Over Land

To government leaders, the presence of Native Americans in the Southeast stood in the way of westward expansion of the United States. Furthermore, the Native Americans lived on fertile land. White farmers wanted that land for growing cotton.

Forced Movement Policies to move Native Americans from their lands dated from the presidency of Thomas Jefferson. Jefferson hoped the movement would be <u>voluntary</u>. He believed that moving west was the only way the Native Americans could preserve their cultures.

After the War of 1812, the federal government signed treaties with several Native American groups of the Old Northwest. Under those treaties, the groups gave up their lands and moved west of the Mississippi River.

However, the Native Americans of the Southeast would not move. In 1825, President James Monroe suggested a plan to move all Native Americans living east of the Mississippi to land west of the river. However, nothing came of the plan. Yet, year by year, the pressure on the Native Americans of the Southeast grew. By the 1820s, many white southerners were demanding that Native Americans be removed by force.

In 1825 and 1827, the state of Georgia passed a law forcing the Creeks to give up most of their land. In 1828, Georgia tried to get the Cherokees to do the same. The state said the Cherokees were not a separate nation and they had to move off their land.

Support for Native Americans Georgia's actions were challenged in two suits that reached the Supreme Court. The decision in the first suit went against the Cherokees. In *Cherokee Nation* v. *Georgia* (1831), the Court refused to stop Georgia from enforcing its law. But in *Worcester* v. *Georgia* (1832), the Court declared that Georgia's laws "can have no force" within Cherokee territory.

Chief Justice John Marshall wrote the Court's majority opinion in *Worcester* v. *Georgia*. He <u>quoted</u> treaties that the United States had signed, guaranteeing certain territory to Native Americans. Under the Constitution, treaties are the supreme law of the land. Therefore, Marshall said, Georgia had no say over Cherokee territory.

Like the state of Georgia, President Jackson wanted to remove the Native Americans from their land. He was furious when he heard of the ruling in *Worcester* v. *Georgia*. "John Marshall has made his decision," he is reported to have said. "Now let him enforce it!"

Jackson was already putting into effect a federal law called the Indian Removal Act of 1830. The law gave him authority to offer Native American nations land west of the Mississippi in exchange for their lands in the East. It also provided money so the law could be carried out.

☑**Checkpoint** **According to Marshall, why was Georgia barred from applying its laws to Cherokee territory?**

Main Idea
Andrew Jackson objected to a Supreme Court ruling in favor of Native Americans.

Vocabulary *Builder*
<u>voluntary</u> (VAHL ahn tair ee) *adj.* done willingly, of one's own free will

Vocabulary *Builder*
<u>quote</u> (kwoht) *v.* to repeat the exact words spoken or written

A Tragic Journey This painting, *Shadow of the Owl*, by Cherokee artist John Guthrie portrays the Trail of Tears. More than 4,000 Cherokees died along the trail. The tombstone of one of them is shown below. **Critical Thinking:** *Interpret Art What do you think the owl in the main picture represents?*

WHITEPATH
CHEROKEE WARRIOR CHIEF
DIED 1838
TRAIL OF TEARS

Main Idea
Native Americans were moved to the West under harsh and dangerous conditions.

On the Trail of Tears

Believing they had no choice, most Native American leaders signed new treaties giving up their lands. They agreed to move to what was called the Indian Territory. Today most of that area is in the state of Oklahoma.

Removal of the Choctaws The Choctaws signed the first treaty in 1830. The Treaty of Dancing Rabbit Creek stated that

> "the United States under a grant . . . shall cause to be conveyed to the Choctaw Nation a tract of country west of the Mississippi river . . . "
>
> —Article II, Treaty of Dancing Rabbit Creek, 1830

Closely guarded by American soldiers, the Choctaws moved west between 1831 and 1833.

The federal government did not provide enough tents, food, blankets, shoes, winter clothes, or other supplies. Heavy rain and snow caused enormous suffering. An army lieutenant wrote that one group "walked for 24 hours barefoot through the snow and ice" before reaching shelter.

Cherokee Removal The Cherokees held out a few years longer. They were still on their land in 1837 when Jackson left office.

Finally, in 1838, President Martin Van Buren forced the Cherokees to move. In the winter of 1838–39, they went to Indian Territory, guarded by 7,000 soldiers. The route is called the Trail of Tears. A soldier's description helps explain why:

"On the morning of November 17th, we encountered a terrific sleet and snow storm with freezing temperatures, and from that day until we reached the end of the fateful journey on March the 26th, 1839, the sufferings of the Cherokee were awful. The trail of the exiles was a trail of death."

—Memoirs of Private John G. Burnett, December 1890

The Cherokees were forced to march hundreds of miles. They had little food or shelter. Many did not survive. Of 15,000 Cherokees who began the trip, 4,000 died along the way.

One group refused to move. The Seminoles fought three wars against removal. However, in the 1840s most Seminoles were forced to move. In their new homes in the Indian Territory, Native Americans struggled to rebuild their lives under very difficult conditions.

✓ **Checkpoint** **What mistakes in planning did the government make before removing Native Americans?**

☆ **Looking Back and Ahead** Andrew Jackson was determined to be a strong President. He defied the Supreme Court by enforcing the Indian Removal Act. In Section 5, you will learn about his stands against the nation's bankers and his dramatic actions to save the Union.

Identify Long-Term Effects
President Jackson sent federal agents to finalize treaties for Native American removal. Summarize the long-term effects of this policy. Explain how the policy affected the Native Americans in the region.

Section 4 | **Check Your Progress**

Progress Monitoring Online
For: Self-test with instant help
Visit: PHSchool.com
Web Code: mya-3064

Comprehension and Critical Thinking

1. **(a) Recall** How did the Supreme Court rule in the case of *Worcester* v. *Georgia*?
(b) Detect Bias Why do you suppose President Jackson objected to the Court's decision?

2. **(a) Compare and Contrast** Describe the removal of the Choctaws and the Cherokees.
(b) Identify Economic Benefits Why would the Cherokees be particularly opposed to removal from their land?

Reading Skill

3. **Identify Long-Term Effects** A long-term effect is an effect that lasts over a long period of time. White farmers wanted the lands belonging to Native Americans of the Southeast. Write three sentences summarizing the long-term effects of this desire for land.

Writing

4. A paragraph should focus on a single topic. Rewrite the following paragraph to get rid of any sentences that stray from the topic. **Paragraph:** By the 1830s, Native Americans had fought several legal battles over land. Many Native Americans wore traditional clothing. The states tried to make the Native Americans move. However, the Supreme Court decided that states could not force them from their homes.

Sequoyah and the Cherokee Alphabet by Robert Cwiklik

Prepare to Read

Introduction

The leader Sequoyah became convinced that the Cherokee needed a system to write in their own language. The following selection is from a biography of Sequoyah. In this excerpt, Sequoyah becomes interested in the "talking leaves" of an English book.

Reading Skill

Analyze Motivation A character's motives are the reason for his or her actions. As you read this excerpt, look for clues that tell why Sequoyah wanted the book.

Vocabulary *Builder*

As you read this literature selection, look for the following underlined words:

leaves (leevz) *n.* pages or sheets

wampum belt (WAHM pum) *n.* belt woven with images made with beads or shells, used to record historic events

pelts (pehltz) *n.* animal skins

bristled (BRIHS ahld) *v.* became angry

⭐ Background

The images on the wampum belt were a record of events in Cherokee history. Details like names of people and places were passed down from one medicine man to the next. The medicine men would tell the history of the tribe based on the images on the belt.

Sequoyah picked up the book to examine it. He saw that it was made of thin <u>leaves</u> of paper. Instead of the pictures on a <u>wampum belt</u>, there were marks of some kind on the paper, like the footprints of a crow. And the marks were in neat rows like the rows of corn planted in a garden. When the reader looked at those rows, the leaves of the book "talked" to him. The reader then told his friends what the leaves said. Sequoyah found these talking leaves fascinating.

Sequoyah mentally compared the markings on the talking leaves to the designs on a wampum belt. The colorful belt was much prettier, but the book was filled with many thin leaves, each covered with markings. It must surely "remember" more than the wampum belt. Wu The had told Sequoyah that books made the white people's medicine powerful. She had said that just one of their books of talking leaves could remember more than all the medicine men of Taskigi together. And the white men had many, many such books. This is why Wu The wanted Sequoyah to learn English—so he could learn the secret of the talking leaves, the secret of the white people's powerful medicine.

Sequoyah was so curious about the talking leaves that he bought the book from the hunter for two good deer <u>pelts</u>. The men laughed, thinking they had again cheated an Indian. Sequoyah knew his pelts were worth more in silver than this book. Still he wished to have it. He wanted to ponder the secret of its talking leaves.

Agi Li and Rabbit Eyes kidded Sequoyah as the three hiked home after the rain stopped, "You gave good pelts for a book you cannot even understand," they said, laughing.

Later the boys fell to talking about the talking leaves. "Surely," Rabbit Eyes said, "it was a magic power of the white man to be able to put his speeches into books."

"Surely," Agi Li said, "one must learn the white man's language to gain the power of the talking leaves."

Sequoyah <u>bristled</u> at this. "Bah," he said. "These are mere scratchings, mere crow's prints. It is not magic. I could invent them for the Cherokee language, and we, too, could have our own talking leaves."

The other boys laughed at this. "How can you do such a thing?" asked Agi Li, chuckling.

Sequoyah picked up a flat stone and scratched out a picture of a deer on it with the blade of his knife. "There," he said, showing them the stone. "That means 'deer,' see?" Then Sequoyah drew an arrow through the deer. "And that means 'to hunt a deer,'" he said.

His friends laughed again. "At this rate, you will be scratching on stones until you are an old man, Sequoyah, to make pictures of every word there is in our language. It is impossible. The talking leaves belong to the white man. They are not meant for us."

Sequoyah stood his ground. "You are wrong," he said. "You think the white man has special medicine. That is why you wear his clothes," Sequoyah said, pointing to their trousers and shirts. "Well, our medicine can be just as strong, if we wish it."

From *Sequoyah and the Cherokee Alphabet,* by Robert Cwiklik.
© 1989 Silver Burdett Press.

Analyze Motivation
At the beginning of the excerpt, Sequoyah's curiosity motivates him to buy the book. What is his motivation for wanting to write his language?

☑**Checkpoint**   **Why did Wu The want Sequoyah to learn English?**

Sequoyah and his
Cherokee alphabet

If you liked this story about Sequoyah, you might want to read more about the Cherokees in *The Cherokee Dragon: A Novel of the Real People* by Robert J. Conley. St. Martin's Press. 2000.

Analyze **LITERATURE**

Sequoyah went on to create an alphabet for the Cherokees. Imagine that you are Sequoyah. Write a paragraph explaining to the Cherokees why they should learn to write.

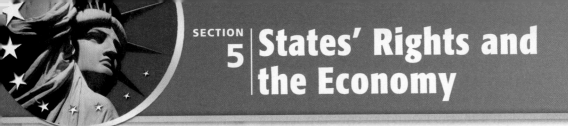

States' Rights and the Economy

Objectives

1. Describe the disagreement over the Bank of the United States.

2. Discuss the differing viewpoints on the balance of federal and state powers.

3. Explain why South Carolina threatened to secede from the Union.

4. Describe the economic crisis that began in 1837.

Prepare to Read

Reading Skill

Identify Multiple Causes Just as events can have multiple effects, so too can they have multiple causes. Major events in history often have many causes. As you read Section 5, look for events that have multiple causes.

Vocabulary *Builder*

High-Use Words

enrich, p. 362

resolve, p. 364

Key Terms and People

nullification, p. 364

Martin Van Buren, p. 366

William Henry Harrison, p. 367

Main Idea

Andrew Jackson opposed the Bank of the United States, saying he believed it gave too much power to the wealthy.

Vocabulary *Builder*

enrich (ehn RIHCH) *v.* to make wealthy

⭐ **Background Knowledge** As you learned in Section 3, Andrew Jackson believed that common people needed support against powerful forces of wealth. This belief led Jackson to take a strong stand against the Bank of the United States.

The Bank War

Between 1816 and the early 1830s, the second Bank of the United States earned strong support from business people. They liked the fact that the Bank made loans to businesses. Moreover, the Bank was a safe place for the federal government to keep its money. The paper money it issued formed a stable currency. Its careful policies helped create confidence in banks all over the country.

On the other hand, many Americans disliked the Bank. They opposed the way the Bank restricted loans made by state banks. Fearing that state banks were making too many loans, Bank directors often limited the amount of money banks could lend. This angered farmers and merchants who wanted to borrow money to buy land. Many southerners and westerners blamed the Bank for the economic crisis that broke out in 1819. In that crisis, many people lost their farms.

The Bank's most powerful enemy was Andrew Jackson, who called the Bank "the Monster." According to Jackson, the Bank allowed a small group of the wealthy people to enrich themselves at the expense of ordinary people. Jackson believed that the wealthy stood for unfair privilege. Jackson especially disliked Nicholas Biddle, the Bank's president. Biddle, who came from a wealthy Philadelphia family, was skilled at doing favors for powerful politicians.

Biddle got Congress to renew the Bank's charter in 1832, although the charter still had four years to go. The news reached Jackson when he was sick in bed. The President vowed, "The Bank . . . is trying to kill me, but I will kill it!"

Jackson immediately vetoed the bill. The fight over the Bank became a major issue in the 1832 presidential election. Henry Clay, who ran against Jackson, strongly supported the Bank. But most voters stood solidly behind Jackson's veto of the Bank bill. Jackson won reelection by a huge margin.

Jackson's victory over the Bank helped to increase the powers of the presidency. It showed that a determined President could stir up the voters and face down powerful opponents in Congress.

The second Bank ceased to exist when its charter ran out in 1836. Unfortunately for Jackson's successor, an economic crisis struck a few months after Jackson left office. Without a Bank of the United States, it was harder for the new President to end the crisis.

☑ **Checkpoint** **What were the arguments for and against the second Bank of the United States?**

The Question of States' Rights

Since the founding of the United States, Americans had debated what should be the balance between the powers of the states and the powers of the federal government.

Main Idea
The balance of federal and state powers had been an issue since the early days of the Union.

King Andrew the First

A king's crown

Trampling on rights

Reading Political Cartoons

Skills Activity

The national press ridiculed Jackson for his quick temper and steely will.

(a) Detect Points of View Name two negative images in the cartoon. Why do you think Jackson is shown stepping on the bank document?

(b) Distinguish Relevant Information Would this cartoon have the same impact in Britain if, instead of Jackson, it showed a British leader? Explain your answer.

The Constitutional Convention of 1787 had created a government based on federalism, the division of power between the national government and the states. The Constitution gave the federal government many significant powers. At the same time, the Tenth Amendment set limits on federal power. It states that any powers not specifically given to the federal government are "reserved to the States respectively, or to the people."

Over the years, the issue of balancing federal and state power had come up repeatedly. The Alien and Sedition acts had raised the issue. So had the Virginia and Kentucky resolutions and the Hartford convention. The issue could never be fully <u>resolved</u>. During Andrew Jackson's presidency, arguments over federal power and states' rights caused a serious crisis.

Vocabulary *Builder*
<u>resolve</u> (ree SAHLV) *v.* to decide; to solve

☑**Checkpoint** **How does the Tenth Amendment limit federal powers?**

Main Idea
Andrew Jackson forcefully opposed South Carolina's threat to leave the Union.

The Nullification Crisis

The crisis erupted when Congress passed a law in 1828 raising the tariff on iron, textiles, and other products. The tariff helped manufacturers in the North and some parts of the West. But it made southerners pay more for manufactured goods. It seemed to southerners that the federal government was forcing them to obey an unfair law.

Vice President John C. Calhoun of South Carolina argued that the states had the right of **nullification,** an action by a state that cancels a federal law to which the state objects. If accepted, Calhoun's ideas would seriously weaken the federal government.

Arguments for Nullification To many southerners, the tariff issue was part of a much larger problem. If the federal government could enforce what they considered an unjust law, could it also use its power to end slavery?

John C. Calhoun had based his theory of nullification on his view of how the Union was formed. He said the Union grew from an agreement between the various states. After the Union was formed, each state kept certain powers. One of them was the power to nullify federal laws the people of the state considered unfair.

Milestones in the States' Rights Debate

1787: The Constitution divides power between the states and federal government.

1814–1815: At the Hartford Convention, opponents of the War of 1812 insist that states have the right to secede.

1787   1802   1817   1832

1798: Kentucky and Virginia claim that states can nullify laws deemed unconstitutional.

1832: South Carolina claims the right to nullify tariffs, but it backs down when President Jackson threatens to use force against it.

Federal Power Versus States' Rights

President Andrew Jackson and Vice President John C. Calhoun took opposing views on states' rights and nullification. They had once been friends. However, by 1830, the two men were fierce enemies. **Critical Thinking:** *Detect Points of View How may Andrew Jackson's views about nullification have been affected by his responsibility as President of the United States?*

"The Union—next to our liberty, the most dear"

"Our Federal Union— It must be preserved"

John C. Calhoun

Andrew Jackson

Arguments Against Nullification The clearest argument against nullification came from Massachusetts Senator Daniel Webster. He argued that the United States had not been formed by the states, but by the entire American people. In a dramatic speech on the floor of the Senate in January 1830, Webster defended his belief, saying "We are all agents of the same supreme power, the people."

A few months later, President Jackson dramatically defended the Union. At a banquet, Jackson stared directly at Vice President Calhoun and said, "Our Federal Union—It must be preserved." Ominously, Calhoun responded: "The Union—next to our liberty, the most dear." The challenge was clear. To Calhoun, states' rights was more important than saving the Union.

South Carolina Threatens to Secede In 1832, Congress passed another tariff law. Although it lowered some tariffs, it passed high tariffs on iron and textiles. South Carolina then called a state convention, which voted to nullify the tariffs. The tariffs of 1828 and 1832, it said, did not apply to South Carolina. The state also warned the federal government not to use force to impose the tariffs. If it did, South Carolina would secede from the Union.

A furious Jackson responded strongly. In December 1832, he put federal troops in South Carolina on alert. Then he issued a "Proclamation to the People of South Carolina." It said that the Union could not be dissolved. It also warned that "disunion by armed force is treason." With tensions running high, Calhoun resigned as Vice President.

Early in 1833, Jackson asked Congress to allow the federal government to collect its tariff in South Carolina by force if necessary. At the same time, he supported a compromise bill that would lower the tariffs. In March 1833, Congress passed both laws.

Unable to win support for its position from other states, South Carolina then repealed its tariff nullification. Many Americans breathed a sigh of relief. The crisis had been settled peacefully.

The Election of 1840

Both the Whigs and the Democrats tried new methods in the presidential election of 1840. They broadened their appeal, hoping to win the vote of the "common man." **Critical Thinking:** *Link Past and Present How are presidential campaigns today similar to the 1840 campaign? How are they different?*

Jackson had successfully defended federal power, while states' rights supporters had suffered a setback. However, the issue of states' rights would not go away. Americans would continue to debate the balance between states' rights and federal powers until the Civil War broke out in 1861.

✓**Checkpoint** **What was the position of Vice President John C. Calhoun on nullification?**

Main Idea

Jackson's successor, Martin Van Buren, faced an economic crisis known as the Panic of 1837.

The End of the Jackson Era

A weary Andrew Jackson retired from office after two terms. Martin Van Buren was Andrew Jackson's choice to succeed him. Van Buren, the son of a New York tavern owner, had played a central role in organizing Jackson's first election victory in 1828. He had been secretary of state during Jackson's first term and Vice President during his second term. He had long been a close political adviser to Jackson.

In the election of 1836, the Whigs ran three candidates, each from a different region of the country. Their goal was to prevent any candidate from receiving a majority of electoral votes. This would throw the election into the House of Representatives. However, the strategy did not work. Van Buren received a majority of both the electoral and the popular vote.

The Panic of 1837 Van Buren took office at a time when the American economy was beginning a severe slump. Because Britain was experiencing an economic slowdown, British manufacturers were buying less cotton. This caused cotton prices to fall sharply. American banks could not collect on the loans they had made to cotton growers. As a result, hundreds of banks went bankrupt.

The result was an economic collapse in the United States called the Panic of 1837. The economic hard times that followed lasted six years. The hardships of those years ruined Van Buren's presidency.

The Election of 1840 Van Buren ran for reelection in 1840 against the Whig candidate, William Henry Harrison. This time the Whigs ran a skillful campaign. They used parades, barbecues, and other forms of entertainment to reach ordinary voters. They portrayed Harrison as a "man of the people" who would feel right at home in a simple log cabin. Helped by his "log cabin" campaign, Harrison easily defeated Van Buren. The Whigs were in power and the Age of Jackson was over.

☑️**Checkpoint** What was the main cause of the Panic of 1837?

⭐ **Looking Back and Ahead** Throughout the administrations of John Quincy Adams, Andrew Jackson, and Martin Van Buren, Americans continued to push westward. By the 1830s, Americans had settled most of the land east of the Mississippi River. By the 1840s, they were crossing the Mississippi in large numbers. You will read about this movement in the next unit.

Identify Multiple Causes
In 1837, the United States experienced an economic collapse. What were two causes of this collapse?

Section 5 | **Check Your Progress**

Progress Monitoring 🌐nline
For: Self-test with instant help
Visit: PHSchool.com
Web Code: mya-3065

Comprehension and Critical Thinking

1. **(a) Recall** Why did states' rights become an issue in the 1820s?
(b) Distinguish Relevant Information Agree or disagree with the following statement and provide relevant facts to support your position: "The issue of states' rights had plagued the nation from the time of the Constitutional Convention."

2. **(a) Summarize** What were John C. Calhoun's and Daniel Webster's positions on nullification?
(b) Detect Points of View What did John C. Calhoun mean when he said, "The Union—next to our liberty, the most dear"?

Reading Skill

3. **Identify Multiple Causes** After the nullification crisis, South Carolina repealed its nullification of the federal tariffs. What were two causes of the state's action?

Vocabulary Builder

4. Write two definitions for the key term nullification. First, write a formal definition for your teacher. Second, write a definition in everyday English for a classmate.

Writing

5. Correct the errors in grammar, spelling, and punctuation in the following passage. **Passage:** The Nullification Crises represent a conflict between the South and the federal government. president Jackson at a banquet said that the Union must be preserved. John Calhoun answered "The Union—next to our liberty, the most dearest."

Bias is slanted writing that communicates a certain point of view about an idea or event. The writer either leaves out information or purposely changes the facts in order to create a certain impression. Bias is different from objective writing, which presents the facts in a balanced way.

The following excerpt, from Andrew Jackson's seventh annual message to Congress, focuses on his Indian removal policy.

Primary Source

". . . The plan of removing the [native] people to . . . country west of the Mississippi River approaches its [conclusion]. . . . All preceding experiments for the improvement of the Indians have failed. It seems now to be an established fact that they can not live in contact with a civilized community and prosper. . . .

The plan for their removal . . . is founded upon the knowledge we have gained of their character and habits, and has been dictated by a spirit of [generosity]. A territory exceeding in extent that [given up] has been granted to each tribe. Of its climate, fertility, and capacity to support an Indian population the representations are highly favorable. . . .

. . . A country west of Missouri and Arkansas has been assigned to them, into which the white settlements are not to be pushed. . . . A barrier has thus been raised for their protection . . . guarding the Indians as far as possible from those evils which have brought them to their present condition."

—Andrew Jackson, December 7, 1835

Learn the Skill
Use these steps to identify bias.

1 **Identify the source.** Knowing the speaker or writer and the audience helps you understand why the point of view might be biased.

2 **Find the main idea.** Summarize the main point in the primary source.

3 **Compare the primary source with objective writing.** Look for differences between the biased writing and an objective account of the same subject. Does the biased writer leave out information or alter facts? Does the biased writer use broad generalizations that support a particular point of view? Does the biased writer use emotionally charged words?

4 **Draw conclusions.** What does the writer or speaker hope to accomplish?

Practice the Skill
Answer the following questions about the primary source on this page.

1 **Identify the source.** (a) Who is the author? (b) Why might the author's position be biased?

2 **Find the main idea.** What is the main point of the speech?

3 **Compare the primary source with objective writing.** Read the information about the government's Indian removal policy in Section 4. (a) What is one way that this account differs from the account in Section 4? (b) What is an example of a broad generalization that creates a biased view? (c) What information about the real reason for Indian removal is not included?

4 **Draw conclusions.** What message does the author want to present to the audience?

Apply the Skill
See the Review and Assessment at the end of this chapter.

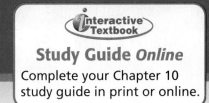

Study Guide *Online*
Complete your Chapter 10 study guide in print or online.

Chapter Summary

Section 1
Building a National Identity

- James Monroe's time as President was called the Era of Good Feelings.
- Tariffs protected northern factories but forced the South to pay more for goods.
- Key Supreme Court decisions strengthened the power of the federal government.

Section 2
Dealing With Other Nations

- The United States acquired Florida in 1819.
- Spanish territories in the Americas revolted and gained their independence.
- Britain granted Canadians more rights.

Section 3
The Age of Jackson

- John Quincy Adams served only one term.
- Democratic reforms allowed more white men to vote.

Section 4
Indian Removal

- The government forced Native Americans to move west of the Mississippi River.
- Thousands of Native Americans died resisting removal or along the journey west.

Section 5
States' Rights and the Economy

- Jackson vetoed a bill to renew the charter of the second Bank.
- South Carolina said that states had the right to nullify federal laws.
- Jackson insisted that states could not nullify federal laws.
- Eventually, South Carolina backed down on nullification.

Key Concepts

These notes will help you prepare for questions about key concepts.

Democratic Reforms in the Age of Jackson

- States dropped property requirements for voting.
- Presidential electors were chosen by voters instead of state legislators.
- Candidates for office were chosen by nominating conventions instead of caucuses.

Key Supreme Court Rulings and Their Impact

McCulloch v. *Maryland*
- The Court ruled that a state law could not go against a federal law.
- The decision strengthened federal power.

Dartmouth College v. *Woodward*
- The Court said the charter of Dartmouth College was a private contract, which New Hampshire could not change.
- The protection of contracts helped promote capitalism.

Gibbons v. *Ogden*
- The Court ruled that only the federal government had the power to regulate interstate commerce.
- The decision further strengthened federal powers.

Vocabulary *Builder*

Key Terms

Answer the following questions in complete sentences that show your understanding of the key terms.

1. How would British dumping hurt American business?

2. What are the advantages of suffrage?

3. Which group of people might hold a caucus?

4. Who did John C. Calhoun believe had the right of nullification?

Comprehension and Critical Thinking

5. **(a) List** How did Henry Clay believe the United States would benefit from his American System?
   (b) Analyze Cause and Effect Which regions of the country were likely to benefit most from the plan? Why?

6. **(a) Explain** Why did President Monroe issue the Monroe Doctrine?
   (b) Apply Information How might the Monroe Doctrine aid Latin American nations?
   (c) Draw Conclusions How do you think Latin American leaders felt about the Monroe Doctrine?

7. **(a) Describe** Why did Andrew Jackson lose the presidential election in 1824?
   (b) Analyze Cause and Effect What changes occurred between 1824 and 1828 that resulted in Jackson winning the 1828 election?

8. **(a) Identify** What was the Trail of Tears?
   (b) Link Past and Present Why does the state of Oklahoma today have a large Native American population?

9. **(a) Describe** How did the spoils system work?
   (b) Draw Conclusions How would it affect a political party?
   (c) Detect Points of View Why did Jackson say the spoils system furthered democracy?

10. **(a) Identify** What was the Panic of 1837?
    (b) Draw Inferences How might the panic have contributed to the election of William Henry Harrison in 1840?

History Reading Skill

11. **Analyze Cause and Effect** Reread the text in Section 1 under the heading "Three Important Supreme Court Rulings." What was the cause of the Supreme Court's decision in *McCulloch* v. *Maryland*? What were the results of the decision? Which results were short-term? Which were long-term?

Writing

12. **Revise the following paragraph to correct the errors in grammar, spelling, and punctuation:** In 1832, congress pass a new law, which lowered some tariffs but continued the high tarriffs on iron and textiles. Generally the South opposed tarifs. South Caroline actually voted to oppose the tariff legislation. Because President Jackson regard this act as a challenge to his authority. He issued a "Proclamation to the People of South Carolina." Which said that leaving the Union would be an act of treeson.

13. **Write a Narrative:**
    Imagine you are a Cherokee in 1838–1839. Write a narrative describing your journey to the Indian Territory.

Skills for Life

Identify Bias

Use the excerpt below to answer the questions.

> "More than eight millions of the stock of this bank are held by foreigners. By this act the American Republic proposes virtually to make them a present of some millions of dollars. . . . If we must have a bank with private stockholders, every consideration of sound policy and every impulse of American feeling admonishes that it should be *purely American*. . . ."
>
> —Andrew Jackson, "Bank Veto Message," July 10, 1832

14. **(a)** Who is the author? **(b)** Why would the author's position be biased?

15. What is the main point of the message?

16. Give an example of emotionally charged words used to support the writer's point of view.

17. What message does the writer want to convey to the audience?

Test Yourself

1. **What was the principal reason Andrew Jackson opposed the second Bank of the United States?**

   A Its policies hurt revenue Jackson expected to get from tariffs.

   B The second Bank refused to loan money to state banks.

   C Jackson believed it gave power to a small group of wealthy people.

   D The second Bank backed John C. Calhoun on the issue of nullification.

2. **Which issue was Andrew Jackson referring to when he said, "John Marshall has made his decision. Now let him enforce it"?**

   A a case about the importance of private contracts

   B a state attempt to apply its laws to Cherokee territory

   C interstate commerce

   D the dumping of goods by Britain in the United States

Refer to the map below to answer Question 3.

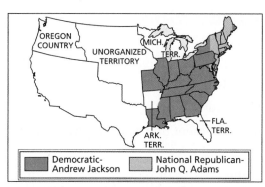

Democratic-Andrew Jackson

National Republican-John Q. Adams

3. **Based on the map above, what was the major reason Jackson won the election of 1828?**

   A Jackson won only the states with large electoral vote totals.

   B New states that joined the Union between 1824 and 1828 voted for Jackson.

   C Many states that had voted for Adams in 1824 switched to Jackson.

   D Jackson swept the electoral votes of states in the South and West.

Document-Based Questions

Task: Look at Documents 1 and 2, and answer their accompanying questions. Then, use the documents and your knowledge of history to complete this writing assignment:

Write a short essay describing how changing political practices reflected new views of democracy that began to take hold during the Age of Jackson.

Document 1: William Henry Harrison's 1840 presidential campaign was filled with advertising, slogans, organized rallies, and campaign songs like this one. *What image of Harrison was this song trying to create?*

"Come swell the throng and join the song,
Make the circle wider
Join the round for Harrison, Log Cabin and Hard Cider.
With Harrison our country's won,
No treachery can divide her.
Thy will be done
With Harrison, Log Cabin and Hard Cider."

Document 2: This campaign poster combines images of a humble log cabin with slogans about Harrison's exploits as a general. *What image of Harrison does this poster create? How does this image compare to Andrew Jackson's image?*

Writing Workshop

Narrative Essay
Biographical Essay

▶ Introduction

In a biographical essay, you write about the life and personality of a person who actually lived. A biographical essay should have the following characteristics:

- a real-life subject
- a thesis statement that states a specific idea about that person's life and achievements
- an account of one or more major events in the subject's life
- a description of the subject's key character traits

Assignment On the following pages, you will learn how to write a biographical essay. You will get step-by-step instructions. Each step will include an example from a sample essay discussing the life of George Washington.

Read the instructions and the examples. Then, follow each step to plan and write a 500–700 word essay.

> **Discuss one of the historical people from Unit 3. Review his or her most important contribution to the nation, giving reasons for your choice.**

For a review of the steps in the writing process, see the **Historian's Toolkit,** *Write Like a Historian.*

▶ Prewriting

Choose your subject. Choose a person whose life seems especially appealing to you. Once you have decided on a subject, make notes about what you already know about his or her life and personality.

Sample notes about George Washington

- "father of his country"
- "first in war, first in peace, first in the hearts of his countrymen"
- Washington's father was a wealthy Virginia planter.
- Washington fought in the French and Indian War.
- led disorganized, poorly funded Continental army in the Revolution against better-trained, better-funded professional British soldiers
- struggled with Continental Congress for money
- encountered many tough situations as President and knew each decision would have impact on the future
- the nation faced financial problems: debt crisis, Hamilton's plan
- faced other crises: Whiskey Rebellion, conflict in Northwest Territory, European wars

Gather information. Once you have reviewed what you know, think about what areas of this person's life you would like to focus on. Then, write down some questions to help you direct your research.

Draw conclusions. Based on your research, make some decisions about your subject's personality. What did he or she value most? Is there a connection between your subject's character traits and his or her role in history?

Write a thesis statement. You have learned more about your subject and reflected on his or her life and personality. You are ready to write a thesis statement.

Sample questions about George Washington:

- What was Washington's family background like? What about his education?

- What qualities made him a good general? Were they the same things that made him a good President?

- How did his soldiers feel about him? How did other leaders feel about him?

- How effective was he as a President?

- What was Washington like as a person?

- What were his personality strengths and weaknesses? What did he do best? What did he not do as well?

Sample thesis statement:
George Washington was not a very imaginative man, but he had a practical, steady mind—a quality that was necessary to give stability to our new nation.

▶ Drafting

Decide how to organize your writing. The simplest way to organize a biographical essay is to cover the main events of the subject's life chronologically.

Another type of organization focuses on a few important events in the person's life, building up to the one that you think is most important.

Write an introduction. The first paragraph of your essay introduces your subject. The introduction leads up to the thesis statement, which expresses the idea you will develop in your essay.

Support your thesis with examples and details. Use the information you have gathered to support and develop your idea about your subject.

Use an informative, lively tone. As you write your draft, enliven your writing with vivid language and colorful details that appeal to the senses.

Write a strong conclusion. In your final paragraph, restate your view of the person about whom you are writing. Tell the reader what this individual has contributed to the country.

Writing Workshop *continued*

▶ Model Essay

Read the following model of a biographical essay about George Washington. Notice how it includes the characteristics you have learned about.

George Washington: A Quiet American Hero

When George Washington was a boy, he liked to make up his own sayings. "Lean not on anyone" was one of them. As he grew older, a strong sense of self-reliance and responsibility—to his family, his soldiers, and his country—shaped Washington's character. It gave him a quiet strength that helped him direct the course of our nation.

Washington grew up on his family's Virginia plantation. As a young man, he decided to learn a trade as a land surveyor. George Washington was only sixteen years old when he set out on his first surveying expedition. Sleeping outdoors and hunting for his food made the teenager more mature. This maturity and sense of responsibility were the perfect qualities for a military leader.

Seven years later, Washington was already a colonel commanding Virginia's colonial troops. At six feet two inches tall, he was a forceful leader who inspired his men to defend the colony's 350-mile western frontier.

In 1775, Washington's leadership was called upon one more time. The Second Continental Congress named him commander in chief of the army. From 1775 to 1783 his strength helped his soldiers overcome many problems. Washington's troops didn't have enough supplies, and many soldiers deserted. The men suffered horribly during the bitterly cold winter at Valley Forge.

After Washington's death, Thomas Jefferson said about the leader, "His integrity was most pure, his justice the most inflexible I have ever known." Without this quiet American hero, with his strong sense of responsibility, our nation's early history would have been very different.

The opening paragraph is an introduction to the subject. It can include an anecdote.

The thesis statement introduces the idea that will be developed in the essay.

Is this essay organized chronologically; by focusing on a few events; or by contrasting the public's opinion with the real man?

Each paragraph includes examples and details to develop ideas about the subject.

The conclusion restates the thesis statement in a new way.

▶ Revising

After completing your draft, read it again carefully to find ways to make your writing better. Here are some of the things you should look for.

Revise to strengthen your thesis
- Do the introduction and thesis statements create a clear, unified impression of the person about whom you are writing?
- Do the body paragraphs develop this impression?

Revise to meet written English-language conventions
- Are all sentences complete, with a subject and a verb?
- Are all the words spelled correctly?
- Are all proper nouns capitalized, including names of people and places?
- Did you use proper punctuation?

▶ Rubric for Self-Assessment

Evaluate your biographical essay using the following rating scale:

	Score 4	Score 3	Score 2	Score 1
Organization	Supports the thesis with a series of logically ordered paragraphs creating a clear impression of a real-life person, organized chronologically, by order or importance, or by character trait	Uses a reasonably clear organization, but occasionally includes less relevant information (for example, anecdotes or facts that wander from the thesis)	Chooses an organization not suited to the topic (for example, presents personality traits without tying them to an overall impression or to the subject's actions)	Shows lack of organizational strategy
Presentation	Discusses the life and personality of the subject in a way that develops a clear impression of the person with facts, details, and anecdotes from the subject's life; links all information to the thesis	Discusses the life and personality adequately with several facts, details, or examples; links most supporting information to the thesis	Does not discuss the life and personality adequately in any detail; does not link supporting information to the thesis	Does not provide any facts, details, or examples about the subject's life and personality
Use of Language	Varies sentence structure and vocabulary successfully; includes no or very few mechanical errors	Uses some variety in sentence structure and vocabulary; includes few mechanical errors	Uses the same types of sentences without varying them; repeats words; includes many mechanical errors	Writes incomplete sentences; uses language poorly; sounds confused; includes many mechanical errors

Unit 4

The Industrial Revolution Samuel Slater's textile mill in Pawtucket, Rhode Island, was the first successful water-powered mill in the United States. Before long, other manufacturers were putting up mills alongside northeastern rivers.

1793

Elizabeth Cady Stanton Stanton (shown here) and Lucretia Mott were the driving forces behind the 1848 Seneca Falls Convention in New York, a convention to advance women's rights.

1848

The Nation Expands and Changes

"Am I Not a Man and a Brother?" An emblem of a man in chains became the symbol of the struggle against slavery. In 1827, Samuel Cornish and John Russwurm set up an abolitionist newspaper called *Freedom's Journal.*

1827

Battle of Buena Vista Outnumbered two to one, an American force under General Zachary Taylor (on his white horse) forced General Santa Anna's Mexican army to retreat under cover of night back into central Mexico.

1847

San Francisco Boom Within a few years of the California gold rush, San Francisco had become a thriving town with rows of houses looking out at a busy waterfront.

1850s

CHAPTER | **North and South**
11 | **Take Different Paths**
1800–1845

Chapter Preview

Americans faced many challenges as the nation expanded westward. Differences between the North and the South grew while the country benefited from the Industrial Revolution.

1794
Eli Whitney patents cotton gin.

1808
Importation of enslaved people is banned.

1812
War of 1812 helps boost American industries.

U.S. Events

1790

1805

1820

World Events

1790 Richard Arkwright builds first steam-powered textile factory in England.

Quick View Video
View the chapter video for a quick preview of the main ideas.

Steam locomotives like the English-built Stourbridge Lion greatly speeded transportation. The Stourbridge Lion was the first full-sized locomotive operated on a railroad track in the United States.

1820
Missouri Compromise highlights disagreements between North and South over slavery.

1830
Peter Cooper builds steam locomotive.

1844
Samuel F. B. Morse tests telegraph.

1820

1835

1850

1845 Famine strikes Ireland.

1848 Revolutions break out in Europe.

History Reading Skill **Identify and Explain Central Issues**

What issues helped to divide the North and South?

In this chapter, you will learn how to identify and explain central issues. You will also learn how to place events in the context of the times and places in which they occurred. Read the following speech given by Virginia Congressman John Randolph, in which he opposes a tariff on manufactured goods. The side notes show you how to analyze central issues and orient them in time and place.

Primary Source

John Randolph spoke out for farmers against the protective tariffs of 1816 and 1817. He believed that these tariffs favored northern industry and unfairly burdened southern farmers.

> It comes down to this: <u>whether you, as a planter, will consent to be taxed in order to hire another man to go to work in a shoemaker's shop or to set up a spinning jenny.</u> For my part, I will not agree to it. No, I will buy where I can get products cheapest. . . .
>
> . . . The cultivators bear the <u>whole brunt of the war and taxation and remain poor, while the others [the manufacturers] run in the ring of pleasure and fatten upon them. The cultivators not only pay all but fight all, while the others run. The manufacturer is the citizen of no place or any place. The cultivator has his property, his lands, his all, his household goods to defend.</u> . . .
>
> . . . The cultivators, the patient drudges of the other orders of society, are now waiting for your resolution.

—Congressman John Randolph, *Annals of Congress*

This paragraph outlines the problem: taxes on manufactured goods are costing farmers money.

It seems there was a lot of tension between southern farmers and northern industrialists.

Here, Randolph refers to the War of 1812, which had recently affected the nation.

Identify and Explain Central Issues

- Look for important issues and problems of a historical period.
- Consider how these issues would affect people in this time period: What challenges or attitudes would these problems and issues create?
- Place the problems and issues in the context of other historical events you know about, such as wars.
- Make generalizations—broad statements—from the issues and problems: People's political views grow out of their personal needs and priorities.

Document-Based Questions

1. Who was John Randolph?
2. Why was he speaking to Congress?
3. What did he want Congress to do? Why?

Vocabulary *Builder*

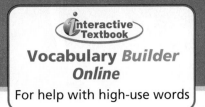
Previewing High-Use Academic Words

High-Use Word	Definition	Sample History Sentence
invest (ihn VEHST) (Section 1, p. 383)	*v.* to supply money for a project in order to make a profit	Shipowners invested in voyages to distant lands.
efficient (ee FISH ehnt) (Section 1, p. 386)	*adj.* acting effectively, without wasted cost or effort	New inventions often led to more efficient ways of doing business.
reign (rayn) (Section 2, p. 393)	*n.* period of dominance or rule	The American Revolution took place during the reign of King George III.
inferior (ihn FIR ee uhr) (Section 2, p. 395)	*adj.* less worthy; less valuable; of lower rank	Old factories are inferior to newer, more modern ones.
devote (dee VOHT) (Section 3, p. 397)	*v.* to commit; to apply (time and energy, for example)	To become a judge, one must devote many years to the study of law.
revolt (ree VOHLT) (Section 3, p. 400)	*n.* uprising; rebellion	Slaveholders feared times when enslaved African Americans would rise up in revolt and fight for freedom.
pursue (per SYOO) (Section 4, p. 402)	*v.* to chase after; to try to capture	Latin American leaders vowed to pursue liberty in their fight for freedom from European control.
isolated (ī sah lay tehd) (Section 4, p. 403)	*adj.* set apart	Lord Cornwallis was trapped on the isolated Yorktown peninsula.

Previewing Key Terms and People

Nat Turner

Industrial Revolution, p. 382
factory system, p. 383
capitalist, p. 383
Francis Cabot Lowell, p. 384
mass production, p. 386
interchangeable parts, p. 386
urbanization, p. 390

telegraph, p. 391
Samuel F.B. Morse, p. 391
famine, p. 394
nativist, p. 394
discrimination, p. 395
cotton gin, p. 396
slave code, p. 399

spiritual, p. 400
Nat Turner, p. 400
Daniel Boone, p. 401
turnpike, p. 402
corduroy road, p. 403
canal, p. 403
Henry Clay, p. 404

The Industrial Revolution

Objectives

1. Explain the changes that the Industrial Revolution brought to American life.

2. Discuss the importance of Samuel Slater's cotton mill.

3. Describe the growth of industry in the United States after 1812.

4. Identify important developments in factories and the problems that factory life produced.

Prepare to Read

 Reading Skill

Identify Central Issues From the Past To effectively study history, you can identify important— or central—issues and then seek to make generalizations from them. To make a generalization, identify main points or ideas in a text. Then, devise a general principle or broad statement that applies to all of them and to other situations.

Vocabulary *Builder*

High-Use Words

invest, p. 383

efficient, p. 386

Key Terms and People

Industrial Revolution, p. 382

factory system, p. 383

capitalist, p. 383

Francis Cabot Lowell, p. 384

mass production, p. 386

interchangeable parts, p. 386

⭐ **Background Knowledge** In the early 1700s, most people worked as farmers. Men worked in the fields to produce food for their families. Women helped in the fields and made simple goods, like candles and soap, at home. In this section, you will see how new inventions began to change the way people lived and worked.

Main Idea

The Industrial Revolution introduced great changes in the way Americans lived.

A Revolution in Technology

In the 1700s, a great change began that we now call the **Industrial Revolution.** Gradually, machines took the place of many hand tools. Much of the power once provided by people and horses began to be replaced, first by flowing water and then by steam engines.

The Industrial Revolution began in Britain, in the textile, or cloth-making, industry. For centuries, workers had spun thread in their homes on spinning wheels. The thread was then woven into cloth on hand looms. Making thread was time-consuming. It took one person, spinning one strand at a time, almost two weeks to produce a pound of cotton thread.

Machines and Factories In the 1760s, the spinning jenny speeded up the thread-making process. The jenny allowed a person to spin many strands at once. However, thread still had to be made by hand.

Then, in 1764, Richard Arkwright invented the water frame, a spinning machine powered by running water rather than human energy. Other inventions speeded up the weaving process. To house the large machines, manufacturers built textile mills on the banks of rivers.

The new mills created a new way of working, known as the factory system. The **factory system** brings workers and machinery together in one place. Instead of spinning at home, textile workers had to go to the factories and begin and end work at specific hours. Workers now had to keep up with the machines instead of working at their own pace.

British mill owners soon recognized the potential of the new water frames and the factory system. However, the system required huge amounts of money to be <u>invested</u> in buildings and machines. Thus, the mill owners turned to **capitalists,** people who invest capital, or money, in a business to earn a profit. Factories proved to be a good investment for the capitalists and mill owners. By 1784, British workers were producing 24 times as much thread as they had in 1765.

Steam Power Building factories on riverbanks had some disadvantages. In a dry season, the machines had no power. Also, most factories were far from cities, and labor was hard to find in rural areas.

In 1790, Arkwright built the first steam-powered textile plant. The steam engine was a reliable source of power. Factories no longer had to be built on riverbanks. They could be built in cities, where young women and children provided cheap labor.

Britain tried to guard the secrets of its industrial success. It forbade anyone to take information about textile machinery out of Britain. Skilled workers were forbidden to leave the country.

☑Checkpoint How did the Industrial Revolution change the way work was performed?

Vocabulary Builder
<u>invest</u> (ihn VEHST) *v.* to supply money for a project in order to make a profit

A Steam Engine

① Cylinder
Steam from boiling water rises into the cylinder.

③ Flywheel
The other end of the beam goes down, moving gears to turn the flywheel.

② Piston rod Pressure from the rising steam pushes the piston rod up and raises one end of the beam.

History *Interactive*
Steam Engine in Action
Visit: PHSchool.com
Web Code: myp-4071

Steam Engine
Steam engines use the energy created by boiling water to push rods and wheels. **Critical Thinking:** *Identify Economic Benefits* What advantage would the steam engine have given to a manufacturer over competitors who depended on water power to operate their machinery?

The American Industrial Revolution

Main Idea
Britain tried but failed to prevent the spread of the new industrial methods.

In 1789, a young apprentice in one of Arkwright's factories decided to immigrate to the United States. Samuel Slater knew that his knowledge of Arkwright's machines could be worth a fortune. He studied hard and memorized the plans of Arkwright's machines. Then, he boarded a ship for New York.

In the United States, Slater joined forces with a wealthy merchant, Moses Brown. Brown had rented a textile mill in Pawtucket, Rhode Island. Relying entirely on his memory, Slater constructed a spinning machine based on Arkwright's. Slater's factory began producing cotton thread at a rate never before seen in the United States.

☑**Checkpoint** **Why did Samuel Slater have to build his machines from memory?**

American Industry Grows

Main Idea
The factory system changed the way Americans worked and encouraged the growth of U.S. industry.

The success of Slater's mill marked the beginning of American industrialization. Industrialization began in the Northeast. The region was home to a class of merchants who had capital to build factories and to buy raw materials.

Still, U.S. industry did not grow significantly until the War of 1812. As the British navy blockaded U.S. ports, Americans had to depend on their own industries to supply goods.

The Lowell Mills Francis Cabot Lowell found a way. Before the war, he had visited England and seen the latest weaving machines. When he returned to the United States, Lowell and an associate built an improved version of the English machines.

With several other capitalists, Lowell opened a mill in Waltham, Massachusetts. The mill was organized in a new way. Instead of obtaining thread from separate spinning mills, Lowell's factory brought together spinning and weaving in one building.

After Lowell died in 1817, his partners expanded the business. Wanting better lives for their workers, the partners built a new town, with boardinghouses, a library, and a hospital. They named their mill town Lowell after their late partner.

Lowell Girls The new factories were staffed with young women from nearby farms. "Lowell girls" lived in boardinghouses under strict supervision. After work, they might attend lectures or visit libraries. As a result, many women gained an education they probably would not have received on their family farms. The British novelist Charles Dickens was amazed when he saw Lowell:

> "Firstly, there is a . . . piano in a great many of the boardinghouses. Secondly, nearly all these young ladies subscribe to circulating libraries. Thirdly, they have [created] a periodical called 'The Lowell Offering.' . . ."
> —Charles Dickens, *American Notes,* 1842

Identify Central Issues From the Past
What generalization can you make about the link between war, trade, and inventiveness?

☑**Checkpoint** How was the Lowell factory system different from the European factory system?

Links Across Time

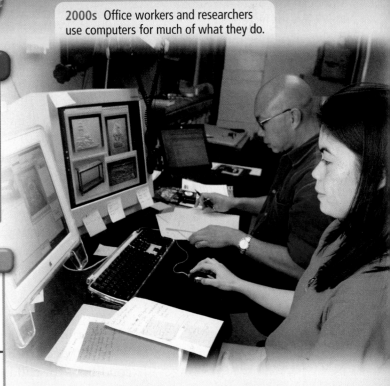

2000s Office workers and researchers use computers for much of what they do.

Technology and Work

1820s The Industrial Revolution opened the way for new developments in technology, which changed the way people worked.

1981–2000s Since the invention of the personal computer, changes in technology have affected not only *how* people work but also *where* they work. With speedy laptops and hand-held devices, workers are able to work successfully at home or at the office.

Link to Today

Technology's Impact Technology continues to advance. How are technological innovations changing people's lives today?

For: Technology in the workplace
Visit: PHSchool.com
Web Code: myc-4071

Factory Workers

This picture shows young girls at work in a textile factory about 1834.
Critical Thinking: *Draw Conclusions* *What were some disadvantages for children who worked in early American factories?*

Main Idea

American inventors developed new ways for factories to produce large amounts of goods quickly.

Vocabulary *Builder*

<u>efficient</u> (ee FISH ehnt) *adj.* acting effectively, without wasted cost or effort

The Revolution Takes Hold

The Lowell system was an example of a unique American outlook. Without a long tradition of doing things a certain way, Americans experimented with new methods. One of the most important developments was **mass production,** or the rapid manufacture of large numbers of identical objects.

Before the 1800s, skilled craftsworkers manufactured clocks, guns, and other mechanical products. Each part of the gun or clock was handcrafted. When a part broke, a craftsworker had to create a unique piece to fit the product. In the 1790s, American inventor Eli Whitney devised a system of **interchangeable parts,** identical pieces that could be assembled quickly by unskilled workers.

Interchangeable parts soon came to be used in the manufacture of other products. Manufacturing became more <u>efficient</u>. The price of many goods dropped. As people bought more goods, U.S. industry expanded to satisfy their needs.

Factory Life As you have read, the Lowell mills treated factory workers in a new and kinder way. However, this was not the general rule. Samuel Slater employed children in his textile mill, as had been done for decades in British factories. As time went on, working conditions for children and adults became harsher.

Child Labor Children routinely worked on family farms in the 1800s. Their labor was often needed to help feed their families. Working on a home farm was different from working in a factory, however. American textile mills, coal mines, and steel foundries employed children as young as 7 or 8. These children had no opportunities for education. They often worked in unsafe conditions. By 1880, more than a million children between the ages of 10 and 15 worked for pay.

Factory Conditions Working conditions were appalling. Factories were poorly lighted. There was little fresh air. Machines were designed to perform a task, not to protect the worker. As a result, many workers were injured on the job. A worker who lost a hand or a foot received no help. He or she needed to depend on family for support. Business owners provided no payments for disabled workers, as they do by law today.

To keep machines running as long as possible, workdays lasted 12 or 14 hours. By 1844, workers were demanding shorter days. "Eight hours for work, eight hours for sleep, and eight hours for God and the brethren" was an early slogan. Conditions gradually improved, but the 8-hour workday was far in the future.

☑**Checkpoint** **How did Eli Whitney's system of interchangeable parts speed up the manufacturing process?**

⭐ **Looking Back and Ahead** Although the new factories were hard on workers, industrialization led to vastly increased production and lower prices. In the next section, you will read how the growth of northern industry helped to widen the gap between the North and the South.

Section 1 | **Check Your Progress**

Progress Monitoring Online
For: Self-test with instant help
Visit: PHSchool.com
Web Code: mya-4071

Comprehension and Critical Thinking

1. **(a) Describe** How did the War of 1812 affect U.S. industry?
   (b) Draw Conclusions Why did advances in industry occur mainly in the North?

2. **(a) Recall** What are interchangeable parts?
   (b) Draw Conclusions How did the system of interchangeable parts affect employment in the United States?

🕮 Reading Skill

3. **Identify Central Issues From the Past** Based on this section, what generalization can you make about the impact of inventiveness during the early Industrial Revolution?

Vocabulary *Builder*

4. Write two definitions for each key term: factory system, capitalist, interchangeable parts. First, write a formal definition for your teacher. Second, write a definition in everyday English for a classmate.

Writing

5. Rewrite the following lists of causes and effects, so that causes are correctly paired up with their effects.

   Causes: Francis Lowell; Arkwright's textile plant; Samuel Slater's emigration; Eli Whitney

   Effects: efficiency in mass production; libraries for factory workers; factories built in cities; increased American production of cotton thread

Mill Workers
by Lucy Larcom

Prepare to Read

Introduction

Lucy Larcom was born in Massachusetts in 1824. After her father died when she was 11, Lucy went to work in the Lowell textile mills. Years later, she wrote about her experiences. The following selection is an excerpt from her memoirs.

Reading Skill

Analyze Setting In literature, a character's actions and attitudes often are affected by his or her surroundings. In the memoir below, we learn how the physical conditions in a textile mill affect Lucy Larcom's outlook on work. As you read, pay attention to her descriptions of the mill.

Vocabulary *Builder*

As you read this literature selection, look for the following underlined words:

bobbin (BAHB ihn) *n.* spool for thread or yarn, used in spinning, weaving, or in a sewing machine

board (bord) *n.* meals provided regularly for pay

drudge (druhj) *n.* person who does hard, menial, or tedious work

Background

Women and girls who worked in northern mills were educated. Some mills published collections of workers' essays and poetry.

I went to my first day's work in the mill with a light heart. The novelty of it made it seem easy, and it really was not hard just to change the bobbins on the spinning-frames every three-quarters of an hour or so, with half a dozen other little girls who were doing the same thing. When I came back at night, the family began to pity me for my long, tiresome day's work, but I laughed and said, "Why, it is nothing but fun. It is just like play."

And for a while it was only a new amusement.... We were not occupied more than half the time. The intervals were spent frolicking around the spinning-frames, teasing and talking to the older girls, or entertaining ourselves with games and stories in the corner, or exploring, with the overseer's permission, the mysteries of the carding-room, the dressing-room, and the weaving-room.

I never cared much for machinery. The buzzing and hissing of pulleys and rollers and spindles and flyers around me often grew tiresome. I could not see into their complications, or feel interested in them. But in a room below us we were sometimes allowed to peer in through a sort of blind door at the great waterwheel that carried the works of the whole mill. It was so huge that we could only watch a few of its spokes at a time, and part of its dripping rim, moving with a slow, measured strength through the darkness that shut it in. It impressed me with something of the awe which comes to us in thinking of the great Power which keeps the mechanism of the universe in motion....

When I took my next three months at the grammar school, everything there was changed, and I too was changed.... It was a great delight to me to study, and at the end of the three months the master told me that I was prepared for the high school.

Lowell girls weaving in a Massachusetts textile mill in the 1850s

But alas! I could not go. The little money I could earn—one dollar a week, besides the price of my <u>board</u>—was needed in the family, and I must return to the mill. . . .

At this time I had learned to do a spinner's work, and I obtained permission to tend some frames that stood directly in front of the windows, with only them and the wall behind me, extending half the length of the mill. . . .

The last window in the row behind me was filled with flourishing houseplants—fragrant-leaved geraniums, the overseer's pets. . . . T[he] perfume and freshness tempted me there often. . . . On the whole, it was far from being a disagreeable place to stay in. The girls were bright looking and neat, and everything was kept clean and shining. The effect of the whole was rather attractive to strangers. . . .

Still, we did not call ourselves ladies. We did not forget that we were working girls, wearing coarse aprons suitable to our work, and that there was some danger to our becoming <u>drudges</u>. I know that sometimes the confinement of the mill became very wearisome to me. In the sweet June weather I would lean far out of the window, and try not to hear the unceasing clash of the sound inside. Looking away to the hills, my whole stifled being would cry out, "Oh that I had wings!"

From *A New England Girlhood,* by Lucy Larcom.
Peter Smith, 1973. First published in 1887 by Macmillan.

✓Checkpoint **Why did Larcom return to the mill after finishing three months at grammar school?**

Analyze LITERATURE

Lucy Larcom's words describe a mill in New England during the 1800s. Consider the sights and sounds around her, and how working in the mill made her feel. Write a paragraph in which you describe what it is like to work in a mill.

⭐ **Background**
The wages paid for millwork offered new opportunities to many women and girls, but workers lived apart from their families and often felt lonely.

Analyze Setting
Lucy's attitude toward the mill changes somewhat over the course of this excerpt. How does setting contribute to this change?

If you liked this passage from *A New England Girlhood,* you might want to read more first-person accounts in *Ordinary Americans: U.S. History Through the Eyes of Everyday People,* edited by Linda R. Monk. Close Up Foundation. 2003.

The North Transformed

Objectives

1. Explain why American cities grew in the 1800s.
2. List the new inventions and advances in agriculture and manufacturing.
3. Describe the improvements in transportation during the early 1800s.
4. Discuss the wave of immigration to the United States in the 1840s and 1850s.
5. Describe the problems African Americans faced in the North.

Prepare to Read

 Reading Skill

Explain Central Issues From the Past As you read about the events of the past, you'll discover that people struggled with issues, much as they do today. Explain those issues to yourself—try to identify what people's concerns were, how they felt about issues, what the issues were about. This will make issues more real and understandable for you.

Vocabulary *Builder*

High-Use Words

<u>reign</u>, p. 393
<u>inferior</u>, p. 395

Key Terms and People

urbanization, p. 390
telegraph, p. 391
Samuel F.B. Morse, p. 391
famine, p. 394
nativist, p. 394
discrimination, p. 395

Main Idea

As cities in the United States grew, Americans faced a variety of urban problems.

⭐ **Background Knowledge** You have read that from colonial times, the North and the South developed as distinct regions. At first these differences were small. But during the Industrial Revolution, the differences between the North and South widened dramatically.

Northern Cities

American cities had long been the centers of commerce and culture. By today's standards, these early cities were small. New York, the largest, had a population of slightly more than 33,000 in 1790. Compared to the major cities of Europe, or even the ancient Aztec capital of Tenochtitl´n, New York was hardly more than a town.

Growth of Cities In the 1800s, however, U.S. cities grew larger. The Industrial Revolution spurred urbanization, or the growth of cities due to movement of people from rural areas to cities. As capitalists built more factories, agricultural workers were attracted to the new types of work available in the cities.

As cities along the eastern coast became crowded, newly arrived immigrants headed west. Pittsburgh, Pennsylvania, had about 23,000 people in 1840. Ten years later, the city had more than doubled in population. Farther west, the Kentucky city of Louisville was also growing. German and Irish immigrants increased the city's population to more than 43,000 by 1850, making Louisville larger than Washington, D.C.

Urban Problems Growing cities faced many problems. Filthy streets, the absence of good sewage systems, and a lack of clean drinking water encouraged the spread of disease.

> "One finds in the streets [of New York] dead cats and dogs, which make the air very bad; dust and ashes are thrown out into the streets, which are swept perhaps once every [two weeks]."
>
> —Baron Axel Klinckowstrom of Sweden

Citywide fires were another common problem. Most structures were made of wood. Volunteer firefighters were often poorly trained and equipped. Insurance companies paid firefighters for saving an insured building. Racing to fire scenes to earn the insurance money, rival fire companies sometimes ended up fighting one another instead of the fire.

✓ **Checkpoint** What problems did cities face in the early 1800s?

The Growth of Northern Industry

New inventions revolutionized communications. The most important was the telegraph, a device that used electrical signals to send messages quickly over long distances.

The Telegraph Samuel F.B. Morse's invention worked by sending electrical signals over a wire. A code devised by Morse used shorter and longer bursts of electricity. In his system, known as the Morse code, each letter of the alphabet is represented by its own mix of short signals ("dots") and long signals ("dashes").

Explain Central Issues From the Past
Explain the link between industrialization and urban problems.

Main Idea
New inventions and other advances in agriculture and manufacturing boosted industrial growth.

Growing Cities
American cities became bustling centers of enterprise during the 1800s. This is a view along Broadway in New York City.
Critical Thinking: *Explain Problems* *What problems did the rapid growth of cities pose for city dwellers?*

Samuel F.B. Morse
1791–1872

Samuel Morse began his career as a painter. By 1835, however, he was working on the invention that would make him famous. For years, he struggled to find funding. In 1843, he convinced Congress to back his efforts.

The following year, he arranged to link the nation's capital and the city of Baltimore with telegraph lines. The historic first message was sent from the Capitol building in Washington, D.C.

Biography Quest

What chance event led Morse to attempt to develop the telegraph?

For: The answer to the question about Morse
Visit: PHSchool.com
Web Code: myd-4072

In 1844, Morse tested his system. He wired a message from Washington, D.C., to his assistant in Baltimore: "What hath God wrought?" A few minutes later, a response came back from Baltimore.

The telegraph soon became part of American life. Thousands of miles of wires were strung across the nation. Factories in the East could communicate with their markets in the West in a matter of hours rather than weeks.

Advances in Agriculture The mechanical reaper, invented by Cyrus McCormick, made it easier for farmers to settle the prairies of the Midwest. The reaper cut stalks of wheat many times faster than a human worker could. This enabled farmers to cultivate more land and harvest their crops with fewer workers.

Improvements in threshers also speeded up the harvesting of grain. Threshers separate the grains of wheat from their stalks. The wheat grains are then ground into flour. Eventually, the mechanical reaper and the thresher were put together into one machine called a combine.

These advances in agriculture also affected industry. Farm laborers who had been replaced by machines went to cities to work in shops and factories. Cities like Cincinnati grew as both agricultural and industrial centers.

Advances in Manufacturing Other inventions revolutionized the way goods were made. In 1846, Elias Howe patented a machine that could sew seams in fabric. A few years later, Isaac Singer improved on Howe's design. The sewing machine made it much more efficient to produce clothing in quantity. As clothes became less expensive, people of modest means began to dress almost as well as wealthier Americans.

By 1860, factories in New England and the Middle Atlantic states were producing most of the nation's manufactured goods. That year, Americans had over $1 billion invested in businesses. Of that total, more than 90 percent was invested in businesses in the North.

☑ **Checkpoint** **What new inventions helped northern industry to grow?**

Main Idea
Advances in transportation made it easier for businesses to obtain raw materials and get goods to market.

A Transportation Revolution

Improvements in transportation spurred the growth of American industry. As transportation became faster and easier, factories could make use of raw materials from farther away. Improved transportation also allowed factory owners to ship their goods to distant markets.

Steamboats and Clipper Ships In 1807, Robert Fulton, an American inventor, used a steam engine to power a boat. Fulton's *Clermont* was the first practical steamboat. It was 133 feet long and had wooden side paddles that pulled it through the water.

Although side-paddle steamboats were ideal for traveling on rivers, they were not suited to ocean travel. In 1850, a new type of American-built ship appeared, the clipper ship. Long and slender, with tall masts, the clipper ships were magnificent, swift vessels. The Yankee clippers, as they were called, were the world's fastest ships. Their reign was brief, however. By the 1850s, Great Britain was producing oceangoing steamships. These ironclad steamships were faster and could carry more cargo.

Railroads Of all forms of transportation, railroads did the most to tie together raw materials, manufacturers, and markets. Steamboats had to follow the paths of rivers, which sometimes froze in winter. Railroads, however, could be built almost anywhere.

America's first railroad, the Baltimore and Ohio, was begun in 1828. As with most European railroads, its cars were drawn along the track by horses. Then, in 1830, Peter Cooper built the first American-made steam locomotive. By 1840, about 3,000 miles of railway track had been built in the United States.

✓**Checkpoint** Why were railroads a better means of transportation than steamboats?

A New Wave of Immigrants

The American population grew rapidly in the 1840s. Millions of immigrants entered the United States, mostly from western Europe. Some came because they had heard of opportunities to buy cheap land. Others believed their skills would serve them well in the United States. Still others had little choice, because they could not survive at home.

Vocabulary Builder
reign (rayn) *n.* period of dominance or rule

Main Idea
Hunger and political unrest in Europe increased immigration to the United States in the 1840s.

Fulton's Steamboat
Robert Fulton's steamboat, the *Clermont,* carried passengers between New York and Albany on the Hudson River. **Critical Thinking:** *Interpret Pictures Why would the* Clermont *not be suitable for ocean travel?*

Irish Immigration, 1845–1853

Number of Immigrants (in thousands) vs **Year**

Source: *Historical Statistics of the United States*

Fleeing the Famine

A famine in the 1840s drove many Irish to the United States. They contributed to a sharp rise in immigration. **Critical Thinking: Draw Inferences** *Why do you suppose the peak did not come immediately after the famine started in 1845?*

The Great Hunger Ireland had long been under British rule. While the best farmland was owned by British landlords, the potato was the staple, or basic, food for most of the population. Then, in 1845, a fungus destroyed the potato crop, leading to famine, or widespread starvation. The years that followed are often called the Great Hunger. More than a million people starved to death. About a million more left Ireland.

Most of the Irish immigrants who came to the United States during this period had been farm laborers at home. The men found work doing the lowliest jobs in construction or laying railroad track in the East and Midwest. Young Irish women were often employed as household workers.

German Newcomers Germans came to America during this period as well. Many had taken part in revolutions against harsh rulers. When the revolutions failed, the Germans fled to the United States.

Unlike the Irish, German immigrants came from many different levels of society. After arriving in the United States, most Germans moved west. Many settled in the Ohio Valley and the Great Lakes region.

Reaction Against Immigrants Some Americans worried about the growing foreign population. These were nativists, or people who wanted to preserve the country for white, American-born Protestants. Nativists especially opposed Irish immigration because most of the Irish were Roman Catholics.

One group of nativists in New York formed a secret group. When asked about their secret order, members replied, "I know nothing." In time, the Know-Nothings became a political party. In 1856, the Know-Nothing candidate for President won 21 percent of the vote. Soon after, the party split over the issue of slavery and dissolved.

✓**Checkpoint** Why did Irish and German immigration to the United States increase in the 1840s?

African Americans in the North

Even more than immigrants, African Americans in the North faced discrimination. Discrimination is the denial of equal rights or equal treatment to certain groups of people.

Slavery had largely ended in the North by the early 1800s. Free African Americans there were joined by new arrivals from the South. Freedom, however, did not grant equal treatment. African Americans were often denied the right to vote. They were not allowed to work in factories or in skilled trades. Even when they sought the least desirable jobs, they were at a disadvantage. Many employers preferred to hire white immigrants rather than African Americans.

Prejudice against African Americans led to the racial segregation of schools and public facilities. Turned away by white congregations, African Americans formed their own churches. For example, people who had been freed from slavery started the African Methodist Episcopal Church in Philadelphia in 1816.

White newspapers often portrayed African Americans as <u>inferior</u>. African Americans responded by starting their own publications. The first newspaper owned and run by African Americans was *Freedom's Journal*, which was established in 1827 in New York. Its editor, John B. Russwurm, had been one of the first African Americans to graduate from an American college.

☑ **Checkpoint** **What obstacles did African Americans face in the North?**

⭐ **Looking Back and Ahead** Northern cities grew with the arrival of immigrants from abroad and African Americans from rural areas. Meanwhile, as you will read in the next section, the South depended more and more on cotton and slavery.

Main Idea
Although slavery ended in the North, free African Americans struggled to overcome discrimination and prejudice.

Vocabulary *Builder*
inferior (ihn FIR ee uhr) *adj.* less worthy; less valuable; of lower rank

---

Section 2 | Check Your Progress

Progress Monitoring ⬤nline
For: Self-test with instant help
Visit: PHSchool.com
Web Code: mya-4072

Comprehension and Critical Thinking

1. (a) Recall What factors led to the growth of cities?
(b) Evaluate Information How did the rapid growth of cities affect urban living conditions?

2. (a) Recall How did the telegraph improve communication?
(b) Identify Economic Benefits How might improved communication help the growing economy?

⟳ Reading Skill

3. Explain Central Issues From the Past Reread the text following the heading "Advances in Agriculture." Explain how changes in agriculture affected workers in the nineteenth century.

Vocabulary *Builder*

Read each sentence below. If the sentence is true, write YES. If the sentence is not true, write NO and explain why.
4. Urbanization is the movement of people from urban areas to farms.

5. More than a million people died in a **famine** during "the Great Hunger" that started in Ireland in 1845.
6. Even though many African Americans living in the North were legally free, they still suffered from **discrimination**.

Writing

7. Based on what you have read in this section, list as many causes as you can for the growth of industry in the North. Put stars next to the causes that you think are most important.

The Plantation South

Objectives

1. Explain the significance of cotton and the cotton gin to the South.

2. Describe what life was like for free and enslaved African Americans in the South.

Prepare to Read

Reading Skill

Explain Problems From the Past Why did problems occur in the past? Try to answer this question as you read. It will help you connect events and understand people's beliefs and actions. Put yourself in the shoes of the people about whom you read. What problems would you have with these same issues? Explain these problems to clarify them.

Vocabulary *Builder*

High-Use Words

<u>devote</u>, p. 397

<u>revolt</u>, p. 400

Key Terms and People

cotton gin, p. 396

slave code, p. 399

spiritual, p. 400

Nat Turner, p. 400

⭐ **Background Knowledge** As you have read, Eli Whitney's system of interchangeable parts revolutionized industry. Another of Whitney's inventions had an equally powerful impact on the rural South.

The Cotton Kingdom

Main Idea
As cotton production expanded in the South to supply the northern textile industry, planters increased their use of slave labor.

As the North became more urban and industrialized, the South remained largely rural. Two events changed life in the South. First, a boom in textiles caused by the Industrial Revolution created a huge demand for cotton. Second, a new invention allowed the South to satisfy that demand.

The Cotton Gin In 1793, Eli Whitney devised a simple machine that speeded the processing of cotton. His **cotton gin** used a spiked cylinder to remove seeds from cotton fibers.

Before the introduction of the cotton gin, the seeds had to be picked out of the cotton fibers by hand. This was a slow process. Working by hand, a laborer could clean only a pound of cotton a day.

The cotton gin was revolutionary technology. A worker could process fifty times more cotton fiber with the gin than by hand. Cotton growing became far more profitable.

Slave Labor To grow more cotton, planters used more slave labor. In 1790, there were about 698,000 enslaved African Americans in the United States. By 1860, the census recorded nearly 4 million. During that time, the price of a slave increased ten or twenty times.

Cotton became the greatest source of wealth for the United States. It enriched planters in the South, as well as bankers and shipowners in the North. Cotton production rose at an astonishing rate. Planters grew one and a half millon pounds of cotton in 1790. In 1820, they grew ten times as much.

Southern states were not all alike. States like Alabama and Mississippi, which depended on cotton, had large populations of enslaved people. Other states, such as Kentucky, <u>devoted</u> less attention to cotton. Fewer enslaved people lived there.

In the southern "Cotton Kingdom," society was dominated by owners of large plantations. This small but wealthy class lived in luxury and sent their children to the finest schools. But more than half of all southern farmers did not have slaves. They grew corn and raised hogs and chickens.

Defending Slavery Most southern whites accepted the system of slavery. Many feared that any weakening of controls over African Americans might encourage violent uprisings. By the 1830s, some people in the North were urging that slavery be banned. (You will read about the movement to end slavery in the next chapter.) In response, southern whites hardened their support for slavery.

Supporters of slavery said it was more humane than the free labor system of the North. Unlike northern factory workers, they argued, enslaved African Americans did not worry about unemployment.

Vocabulary *Builder*
<u>devote</u> (dee VOHT) *v.* to commit; to apply (time and energy, for example)

Explain Problems From the Past
Explain the disagreements between supporters and critics of slavery.

Cotton Production and Slavery

Cotton Production

Source: *Historical Statistics of the United States*

Growth of Slavery

Source: *Historical Statistics of the United States*

Reading Charts
Skills Activity

The rise in cotton production in the South was paralleled by a rise in the number of enslaved African Americans.

(a) Read Graphs How much did cotton production increase between 1800 and 1850? In what 10-year period did slavery grow the fastest?

(b) Make Predictions If cotton production had decreased, would the number of slaves have declined? Explain your reasoning.

Critics of slavery, however, challenged this reasoning. They argued that northern workers were free to quit a job and take another if conditions became too harsh. Also, the critics said, people held in slavery often suffered physical or other abuse from white owners. There was no satisfactory substitute for freedom.

✓**Checkpoint**   How widespread was slave ownership?

Main Idea
Whether free or enslaved, African Americans in the South were subject to harsh rules and unequal treatment.

African Americans in the South

Not all of the 4 million African Americans in the South were enslaved. About 253,000 (or 6 percent) were free. Many had purchased their freedom. A few did well, especially in cities like New Orleans. But most did not share in the prosperity around them.

Restrictions on Free African Americans Laws denied basic rights even to African Americans who were free. By law, they were excluded from all but the most menial jobs. Their children were denied the right to attend public schools. African Americans could not vote, serve on juries, or testify against white defendants in court.

Free African Americans were discouraged from traveling. In a petition, some described the conditions they faced:

> ❝[When] we have occasion to . . . Travel . . . [b]y Steem boat or Stage, we have been exceedingly anoyd And put to very considerable inconvenience and eaven compeled to Leave the boat and thereby entirely defeated from accomplishing our just and lawful business because we have not [had] a certificate from some White person.❞
>
> —petition to Delaware legislature, 1850s

Explore More Video
To learn more about southern plantations, view the video.

Plantation Life Life on a southern plantation showed vast contrasts. The families of large plantation owners enjoyed many luxuries. Families bound to slavery experienced hard work and many cruelties. **Critical Thinking: Compare and Contrast** *How do these pictures support the view that plantation owners and enslaved African Americans lived very*

▼ **A Family on the Patio** A wealthy southern family relaxes on their patio as they survey their estate.

◀ **Keeping Cool** Refreshing breezes from fans like this kept wealthy women cool.

The freedom of African Americans in the South was never secure. Slave catchers prowled the streets looking for escapees. They often kidnapped free African Americans and sold them into slavery.

In spite of all the restrictions placed upon them, many free African Americans made valuable contributions to southern life. Norbert Rillieux revolutionized the sugar industry. His method of refining sugar made the process faster, safer, and less costly. Another African American inventor, Henry Blair, developed a seed-planting device that reduced the time a farmer spent sowing a crop.

Life Under Slavery For all the problems faced by free African Americans, those who were enslaved faced much greater trials. They had no rights at all. Laws known as **slave codes** controlled every aspect of their lives. As a Kentucky court ruled in 1828, ". . . a slave by our code is not treated as a person but as a . . . thing. . . ."

Many enslaved African Americans became skilled workers. Their skills kept the plantations operating efficiently. Others worked in the owners' homes as housekeepers, butlers, or nannies and became trusted house servants.

The vast majority did heavy farm labor. Most slaveholders stopped short of working a laborer to death. Some came close, however. On the large plantations, white overseers administered punishment—often a whipping—for many offenses.

Enslaved African Americans had only one real protection against mistreatment: Owners looked on them as valuable property that they needed to keep healthy and productive.

Families of enslaved African Americans were often broken apart when slave owners sold one or more of their family members. Many children had only the slightest memory of their parents.

◀ **A Family in the Fields**
Children worked in the fields with their enslaved parents. This Georgia family was picking cotton.

◀ **Bonds of Slavery**
Shackles such as these were used to restrain slaves who tried to escape or who otherwise displeased a master.

Nat Turner captured

Vocabulary *Builder*
<u>revolt</u> (ree VOHLT) *n.* uprising;
rebellion

After 1808, it was illegal to import enslaved Africans to the United States. As a result, African Americans had little direct contact with Africa. Nevertheless, African customs, music, and dance survived in their daily lives from one generation to another.

Many African Americans found a message of hope in the Bible. African Americans composed spirituals, religious folk songs that blended biblical themes with the realities of slavery.

Resistance to Slavery Many African Americans did what they could to resist the slaveholders. Some worked slowly or pretended not to understand what they were told to do. Others deliberately broke farm equipment. The most daring fled north to freedom.

Sometimes, resistance became rebellion. Nat Turner led the most famous slave <u>revolt</u> in 1831. Turner said he had a vision that told him to kill whites. He and others killed about 60 whites. In reprisal, many innocent African Americans were executed.

☑**Checkpoint** How did enslaved African Americans adapt to slavery and resist it?

⭐ **Looking Back and Ahead** The more cotton they grew, the more southern planters depended on the labor of enslaved African Americans. At the same time, African Americans in the South struggled to endure or resist slavery. In the next section, you will read how the settling of western areas caused new tensions between North and South.

Section 3 | **Check Your Progress**

Progress Monitoring Online
For: Self-test with instant help
Visit: PHSchool.com
Web Code: mya-4073

Comprehension and Critical Thinking

1. **(a) Summarize** How were northern textile mills and southern cotton plantations linked? What key invention deepened this connection?
(b) Understand Sequence Place the following events in the order in which they happened: population of cotton-producing states triples; Whitney invents the cotton gin; Nat Turner leads slave revolt; the need for slaves increases; northern textile factories have need for cotton; support for slavery hardens among southern whites.

2. **(a) Describe** What might a typical workday be like for an enslaved African American on a southern cotton plantation?
(b) Draw Conclusions Why do you think enslaved people rebelled, even though the risk was so great and the likelihood of success so small?

Reading Skill

3. **Explain Problems From the Past** Connect the problems facing southern planters and southern African Americans.

Vocabulary *Builder*

Answer the following questions in complete sentences that show your understanding of the key terms.

4. How does the cotton gin work?
5. How did slave codes control every aspect of the lives of enslaved African Americans?
6. What would be a common theme of an African American spiritual?

Writing

7. Based on what you have read in this section, list as many effects as you can that resulted from the invention of the cotton gin by Eli Whitney. List the effects in the order in which they happened. If one effect led to another effect, draw an arrow between those two developments.

Objectives

1. Identify the problems Americans moving westward faced.
2. Describe the impact of the building of the Erie Canal.
3. Discuss the debate over slavery and the Missouri Compromise.

Prepare to Read

Reading Skill

Place Events in a Matrix of Time and Place Each event in history takes place in the context of a specific time and place. As you read this textbook or other history textbooks, try to remember additional events from the same time or place. Then, look for possible connections among the events discussed in the different parts of a chapter or unit.

Vocabulary *Builder*

High-Use Words

<u>pursue</u>, p. 402

<u>isolated</u>, p. 403

Key Terms and People

Daniel Boone, p. 401

turnpike, p. 402

corduroy road, p. 403

canal, p. 403

Henry Clay, p. 404

★ **Background Knowledge** You have learned that there was a boom in cotton production after the invention of the cotton gin. Settlers moved west from southern states to find new land for cotton. Farther north, a different stream of settlers headed west, seeking land for other crops.

Moving West

During colonial times, Americans looked on the backcountry between the Atlantic Coast and the Appalachian Mountains as the western frontier. By the 1750s, the Scotch-Irish and the Germans of Pennsylvania had begun to settle the backcountry.

The most famous early pioneer was Daniel Boone. In 1775, Boone and a party of 30 men cleared a new route to the West—the Wilderness Road. It crossed the Appalachian Mountains through the Cumberland Gap into Kentucky. The Wilderness Road became the main route across the Appalachians. In time, pioneers created many other routes for westward travel. (See the map on the next page.)

A Growing Population By the early 1800s, the flow of immigrants to the West had become a flood. As western populations grew, many areas applied to become states. From 1792 to 1819, eight states joined the Union: Kentucky (1792), Tennessee (1796), Ohio (1803), Louisiana (1812), Indiana (1816), Mississippi (1817), Illinois (1818), and Alabama (1819).

Main Idea

During the early 1800s, a flood of settlers pushed the frontier ever farther to the west.

Place Events in a Matrix of Time and Place

Name two important events from the early nineteenth century that contributed to America's growth as a nation. Consider the topics covered in this chapter and in previous chapters.

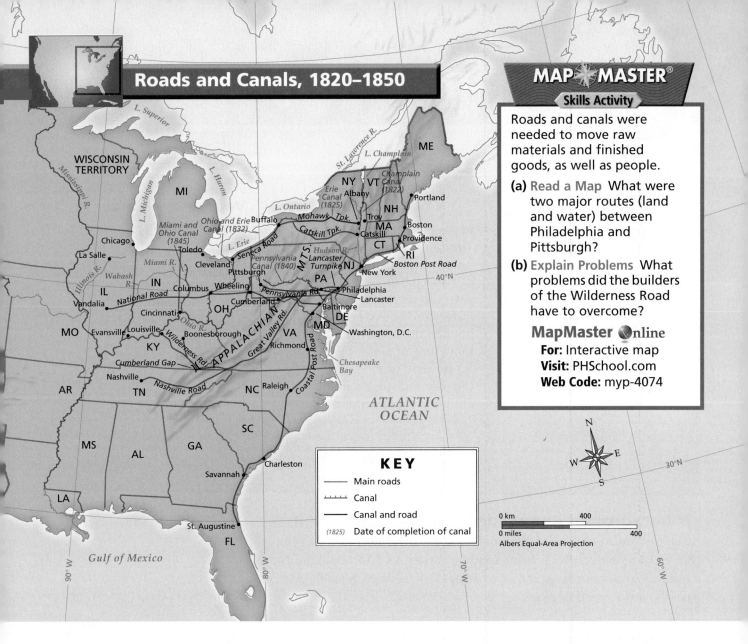

Roads and Canals, 1820–1850

MAP MASTER®

Skills Activity

Roads and canals were needed to move raw materials and finished goods, as well as people.

(a) Read a Map What were two major routes (land and water) between Philadelphia and Pittsburgh?

(b) Explain Problems What problems did the builders of the Wilderness Road have to overcome?

MapMaster ⬤nline
For: Interactive map
Visit: PHSchool.com
Web Code: myp-4074

KEY

⎯⎯ Main roads
⊢⊢⊢⊢ Canal
⎯⎯ Canal and road
(1825) Date of completion of canal

0 km — 400
0 miles — 400
Albers Equal-Area Projection

Vocabulary *Builder*
pursue (per SYOO) *v.* to chase after; to try to capture

Traveling west was not easy. Many early roads began as paths for deer or bison. Indians used these well-worn paths to <u>pursue</u> game. Then, white settlers began to drive their wagons over these paths. Not surprisingly, the roads were terrible. They were unpaved, dotted with tree stumps, and easily washed out by rain.

✔**Checkpoint** How did American settlers heading west reach their new homes?

Main Idea
Both private investors and the government helped to extend the network of American roads.

Roads and Turnpikes

Clearly the nation needed better roads. Farmers and merchants had to have a way to move their goods to market quickly and cheaply. Some capitalists decided to provide that way.

Private companies began to build **turnpikes,** or toll roads. At certain points, a bar on a hinge swung out across the road. The bar resembled a spear, or pike. Travelers would have to stop and pay a toll in order to pass.

In 1795, a private company in Pennsylvania built a turnpike between Lancaster and Philadelphia. The Lancaster Turnpike was the first long-distance stone road in the United States. The road provided cheap, reliable transportation to <u>isolated</u> agricultural areas.

In marshy areas, wagons traveled on **corduroy roads,** roads made of sawed-off logs, laid side by side. This meant a bumpy ride as wagons bounced over each log. Corduroy roads were a hazard to horses, because they could break their legs if they slipped through the logs.

The National Road was the first federally funded road. Begun in 1811 in Cumberland, Maryland, it stretched to Wheeling, in western Virginia, by 1818 and reached Vandalia, Illinois, in 1850. The road crossed hundreds of miles of varying terrain. Bridges carried it over many rivers and streams.

☑ **Checkpoint** **What was the National Road?**

Vocabulary *Builder*
<u>isolated</u> (ī sah lay tehd) *adj.* set apart

Canals

Slow road travel isolated western farmers from eastern markets. The fastest, cheapest way to ship goods was by water. However, the major rivers ran north and south. The solution was to build canals from east to west. A **canal** is a channel that is dug across land and filled with water. Canals allow boats to reach more places.

In 1816, New York Governor DeWitt Clinton proposed a canal from the Hudson River to Lake Erie. Critics scoffed at the idea. Still, work began on "Clinton's Ditch" in 1817.

Building the canal was a challenge for canal engineers—and for workers, who were mostly Irish immigrants. The land in upstate New York is not level. Locks had to be built to raise or lower boats in the canal. Locks are chambers just big enough to hold a boat. When a boat enters a lock, gates close at both ends of the chamber. If the boat is to be raised, water flows into the lock. If the boat must be lowered, water drains out.

At Lockport, five double locks raised the canal 50 feet. One canal traveler wrote:

> ❝As one passes along this deep cavern and sees . . . the rough perpendicular walls pierced in every part with drill-holes used for blasting the rock, he is astonished at the perseverance, labor, and expense which it cost.❞
> —from the *Diary of Jonathan Pearson,* 1833

Within two years of its opening in 1825, the canal had paid for itself. Produce from the Midwest came across Lake Erie, passed through the Erie Canal, and was carried down the Hudson River to New York City. Because of its location at the end of the canal, New York soon became the richest city in the nation.

Main Idea
The Erie Canal was one of many canals built to fill gaps in the nation's system of transportation.

Crazy Over Canals
American popular culture celebrated the new canals with songs, stories, and even jokes.

The success of the Erie Canal sparked a surge of canal building. In 1829, a canal was built through Delaware. Canals were soon underway in Virginia, Pennsylvania, Ohio, Indiana, and Illinois.

☑ **Checkpoint** **How did the building of the Erie Canal help farmers in the interior of the country?**

Main Idea
As new states applied to enter the Union, a renewed debate over slavery added to tensions between the North and the South.

The Extension of Slavery

Westward expansion strengthened the nation. It also caused problems. The most serious problem was the extension of slavery.

Slave and Free States In 1819, the nation consisted of 11 "slave states," which permitted slavery, and 11 "free states," which prohibited slavery. However, Missouri had been seeking admission as a slave state since 1817.

Northerners had reacted strongly. Adding another slave state would upset the balance in the Senate, where each state had two votes. Adding two more senators from a slave state would make the South more powerful than the North.

In 1819, Representative James Tallmadge of New York proposed that Missouri be admitted as a slave state. However, once it was admitted, no more slaves could be brought into the state.

The bill passed the House of Representatives, but it failed in the Senate. Southern senators feared that slavery itself—and thus the South's economic well-being—was being threatened.

The Missouri Compromise In the next session of Congress, Maine applied for admission to the Union. Unlike Missouri, Maine prohibited slavery. The admission of both a free state and a slave state would maintain the balance in the Senate.

In 1820, Senator Henry Clay persuaded Congress to adopt the Missouri Compromise. It permitted Maine to be admitted to the Union as a free state and Missouri to be admitted as a slave state. In addition, the compromise provided that the Louisiana Territory north of the southern border of Missouri would be free of slavery. The compromise had one other important feature. It gave southern slave owners a clear right to pursue escaped fugitives into "free" regions and return them to slavery.

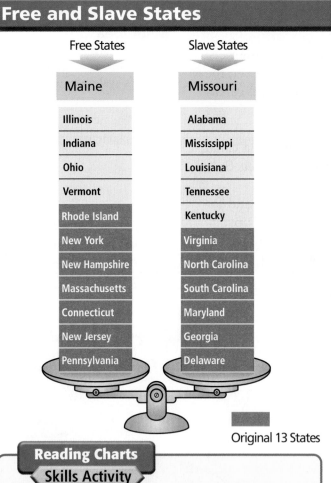

Free and Slave States

Free States	Slave States
Maine	Missouri
Illinois	Alabama
Indiana	Mississippi
Ohio	Louisiana
Vermont	Tennessee
Rhode Island	Kentucky
New York	Virginia
New Hampshire	North Carolina
Massachusetts	South Carolina
Connecticut	Maryland
New Jersey	Georgia
Pennsylvania	Delaware

■ Original 13 States

Reading Charts
Skills Activity

The addition of Missouri to the Union threatened to upset the balance between free states and slave states.

(a) Read a Chart Which of the following was a free state: Kentucky, Tennessee, or Ohio?

(b) Explain Problems Why did northern states wish to have Missouri and Maine enter the Union at the same time?

A Continuing Problem The Missouri Compromise revealed how much sectional rivalries divided the states of the Union. The compromise seemed to balance the interests of the North and the South. However, white southerners were not happy that Congress had given itself the power to make laws regarding slavery. Many northerners, in turn, were angry that Congress had allowed slavery to expand into another state.

Thomas Jefferson was alarmed by the fierce debate over the Missouri Compromise. The former President, much older now, saw that the issues raised by the compromise could tear the nation apart. He wrote to a friend:

> **"** This momentous question, like a firebell in the night, awakened and filled me with terror. I considered it at once as the knell of the Union. . . . [W]e have the wolf by the ears, and we can neither hold him, nor safely let him go. **"**
> —Thomas Jefferson, letter of April 22, 1820

As Jefferson observed, the bitterness of feelings about slavery posed a serious threat to national unity. In time, the issue of slavery would indeed split the nation in two.

☑**Checkpoint** **Why was Jefferson alarmed at the bitterness of the debate over the extension of slavery?**

☆ **Looking Back and Ahead** In this chapter, you learned about increasing differences between North and South. In the next chapter, you will read about the movement to end slavery and other efforts to bring social change.

Section 4 | **Check Your Progress**

Progress Monitoring ◉nline
For: Self-test with instant help
Visit: PHSchool.com
Web Code: mya-4074

Comprehension and Critical Thinking

1. **(a) Recall** How did building better roads and canals transform the United States?
   (b) Identify Economic Benefits How did improved transportation lead to economic growth?

2. **(a) List** What were the main points of the Missouri Compromise?
   (b) Make Predictions Why would the issues addressed by the Missouri Compromise continue to tear the nation apart?

Reading Skill

3. **Place Events in a Matrix of Time and Place** What event in the early nineteenth century led to the creation of the Missouri Territory and later to the state of Missouri? Describe this event.

Vocabulary *Builder*

4. Draw a table with three rows and three columns. In the first column, list the key terms from this section: turnpike, corduroy road, canal. In the next column, write the definition of each term. In the

last column, make a small illustration that shows the meaning of the term.

Writing

5. Based on what you have read in this section, write a thesis statement about the most important change caused by the development of new routes to the West.

Skills for Life

Evaluate Internet Sources

When you are doing research on the Internet, it is important to evaluate the Web sites to determine if the information is valid and objective. The page below is from a Web site about Samuel F.B. Morse.

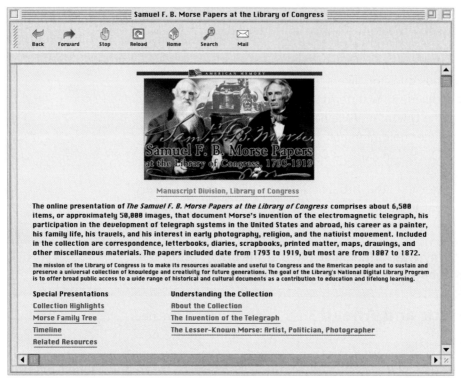

Source: The Library of Congress

Learn the Skill

Use these steps to learn how to evaluate Internet sources.

1 Determine the Web site's purpose. Does the Web site provide information? Is it trying to sell something or to promote a particular point of view?

2 Examine the information. Does the site include visuals? Does it include first-person accounts and other primary source materials?

3 Compare the information to what you already know. Does the information agree with what you have read in a textbook or in another reliable print source? What other information is provided?

4 Evaluate the source. Is the source an established organization? Can you tell who provided the information?

Practice the Skill

Use the information above to answer the following questions.

1 Determine the Web site's purpose. What is the purpose of this Web site?

2 Examine the information. (a) What kinds of information can you find on this page? (b) What other features does it include?

3 Compare the information to what you already know. What additional information does this Web site give that supplements the information in this chapter?

4 Evaluate the source. (a) Who is the provider for this site? (b) If you were writing a paper about Samuel F.B. Morse, do you think you could use the information on this Web site? Why or why not?

Apply the Skill

See the Review and Assessment at the end of this chapter.

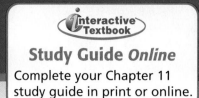

Chapter Summary

Section 1
The Industrial Revolution

- By the end of the 1700s, advances in technology allowed goods to be produced cheaply and quickly by machines.
- In the United States, the Industrial Revolution centered in the Northeast, which had an ample supply of labor and raw materials.
- Factory conditions became increasingly dangerous, and laborers fought for better working conditions.

Section 2
The North Transformed

- Cities grew rapidly during the 1800s, and crowding, disease, and fast-spreading fires were common problems.
- Northern industries grew due to advances in technology.

Section 3
The Plantation South

- Eli Whitney's cotton gin made possible a huge increase in cotton production.
- As cotton production grew, the number and value of enslaved African Americans increased dramatically.
- In the face of cruel conditions, many enslaved African Americans resisted slavery.

Section 4
The Challenges of Growth

- By the early 1800s, a flood of settlers westward helped many territories qualify for statehood.
- Better roads and canals further increased the rate of western settlement.
- Tension arose over slavery in the territories, but the Missouri Compromise settled the issue temporarily.

Key Concepts

These notes will help you prepare for questions about key concepts.

Key Inventions and Innovations

Manufacturing
- Spinning jenny
- Steam engine
- Factory system
- Interchangeable parts and mass production
- Sewing machine

Agriculture
- Mechanical reaper
- Thresher
- Combine
- Cotton gin

Transportation and Communication

Improvements
- Roads are improved.
- Canals link waterways.
- Clipper ships speed traffic over oceans.
- Steamships ply rivers.
- Use of railroads is increased.
- The telegraph speeds communication.

Effects of Improvements
- Goods get to market faster and cheaper.
- People migrate to the West.

Impact of Immigration

Population Movement
- Irish immigrate to the United States due to famine.
- German immigration is sparked by revolutions against harsh rulers.
- Free African Americans in the South move north and west.

Effects of Immigration
- Large numbers of people fill factory jobs.
- Nativists become politically active in reaction to European immigration.

Vocabulary *Builder*

Key Terms

Fill in the blanks with the correct key terms.

1. The _____ was the change in the way people made goods beginning in the late 1700s.

2. People who wanted to keep immigrants out of the country were called _____.

3. African Americans sang _____ to keep hope during their difficult lives.

4. Travelers had to pay tolls on _____ in order to pass.

Comprehension and Critical Thinking

5. **(a) Describe** Who were the Lowell girls?
   (b) Apply Information How do you think the Lowell system affected production?

6. **(a) Identify** What contribution did Eli Whitney make to manufacturing?
   (b) Identify Economic Benefits How did this contribution benefit consumers?

7. **(a) Summarize** How did the physical limitations of steamboats differ from those of railroads?
   (b) Draw Conclusions Why were both means of transportation important to the growth of industry?

8. **(a) Summarize** How did the cotton gin benefit southern planters? How did it benefit northern textile manufacturers?
   (b) Analyze Cause and Effect How did the cotton gin change life for enslaved people?

9. **(a) Contrast** What arguments did some southerners use to defend slavery? What were some points raised by northern critics of slavery to challenge those arguments?
   (b) Apply Information What were some tactics that enslaved African Americans employed in order to endure or resist slavery?

10. **(a) Describe** What were some of the difficulties Americans faced as they traveled west?
    (b) Analyze Cause and Effect How did improved transportation affect western settlement? How did it affect industry?
    (c) Draw Conclusions How were immigrants important to the transportation revolution?

11. **(a) Recall** How was slavery an issue in the debate over Missouri's statehood?
    (b) Detect Points of View Why did northerners believe that it would be damaging to the North if the South became more powerful in the Senate?

History Reading Skill

12. **Identify and Explain Central Issues** Write a paragraph that explains the issues central to the Missouri Compromise. Orient the issues in the context of the times and places in which they occurred.

Writing

13. **Write a paragraph explaining *either* the causes *or* the effects of one of the following developments:**
    - Industrialization of the North
    - The cotton empire of the South

    Your paragraph should:
    - begin with a sentence that expresses your main idea;
    - indicate whether you will focus on the subject's causes or its effects;
    - expand on your main idea with facts, examples, and other information.

14. **Write a Narrative:**
    Choose one of the inventions developed during the first half of the nineteenth century. Write a narrative that describes how people were affected by the invention.

Skills for Life

Evaluate Internet Sources

Visit this Web site: www.eriecanalmuseum.org. Then, use the information to answer the following questions.

15. What seems to be the purpose of this Web site?

16. **(a)** What kinds of information can you find on this page? **(b)** What other features and links does it include?

17. What additional information does this Web site give to supplement the information in your textbook?

18. **(a)** Who is the provider for this site? **(b)** If you were writing a paper about the Erie Canal, do you think you could use the information on this Web site? Why or why not?

Test Yourself

1. Which of the following inventions did the most to advance the connection between goods, raw materials, and markets?

   A interchangeable parts

   B steamboats

   C telegraphs

   D railroads

2. In the mid-1800s, many immigrants came to the United States from Ireland to escape

   A revolutions.

   B famine.

   C political unrest.

   D religious persecution.

Refer to the quotation below to answer Question 3.

"This momentous question, like a firebell in the night, awakened and filled me with terror. I considered it at once as the knell of the Union. . . ."

3. To which issue does this quotation refer?

   A transportation

   B slavery

   C immigration

   D mass production

Document-Based Questions

Task: Look at Documents 1 and 2, and answer their accompanying questions. Then, use the documents and your knowledge of history to complete this writing assignment:

Write an essay describing what life was like for enslaved African Americans in the South. Use information from the graph to explain why slaveholders felt restrictive measures were necessary.

Document 1: This graph gives information about the population of some slave-holding states in 1840. *Use the graph to make a generalization about the South's slave population.*

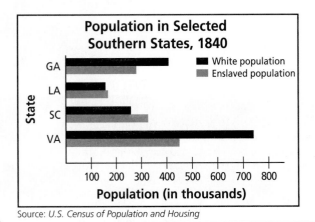

Population in Selected Southern States, 1840

White population
Enslaved population

State: GA, LA, SC, VA

Population (in thousands): 100 200 300 400 500 600 700 800

Source: *U.S. Census of Population and Housing*

Document 2: The excerpt below is from a 1930s interview with Fountain Hughes, born a slave in 1848 near Charlottesville, Virginia. *How does Fountain Hughes describe what it meant to be a slave?*

"Well, I belonged to B., when I was a slave. My mother belonged to B. But we was all slave children. . . .

Now I couldn' go from here across the street . . . [with]out I have a note, or something from my master. . . . Whoever he sent me to, they'd give me another pass an' I'd bring that back so as to show how long I'd been gone. . . . An' when I come back, why I carry it to my master an' give that to him, that'd be all right. But I couldn' jus' walk away like the people does now. . . .

We belonged to people. They'd sell us like they sell horses an' cows an' hogs an' all like that. Have a auction bench, an' they'd put you on, up on the bench an' bid on you jus' same as you bidding on cattle."

CHAPTER 12

An Age of Reform
1820–1860

Chapter Preview

As the country grew, efforts to bring social reforms increased. In the mid-1800s, Americans worked for change in many areas. Meanwhile, American culture flowered as artists and writers began to develop uniquely American styles.

U.S. Events

1826 Charles Finney begins holding religious revival meetings.

1831 William Lloyd Garrison founds antislavery newspaper.

1837 Horace Mann begins campaign to improve public schools.

1820　　1830　　1840

World Events

1822 Colony of Liberia is founded in West Africa.

1833 Slavery is banned in all British colonies.

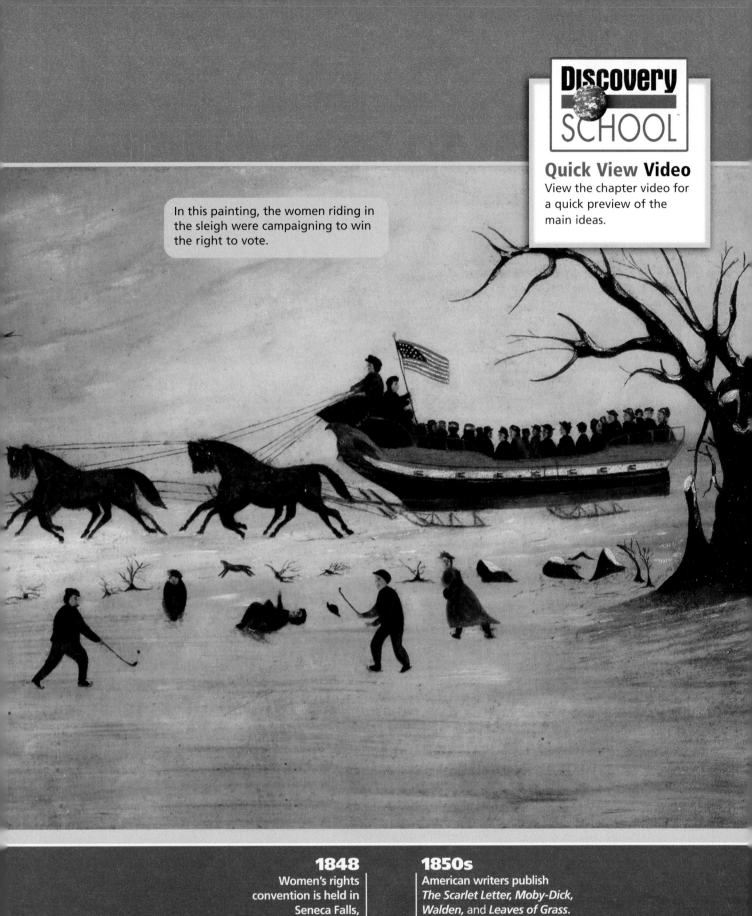

In this painting, the women riding in the sleigh were campaigning to win the right to vote.

1848
Women's rights convention is held in Seneca Falls, New York.

1850s
American writers publish *The Scarlet Letter, Moby-Dick, Walden,* and *Leaves of Grass*.

1840   1850   1860

1845 Britain passes law to reform mental hospitals.

1860 Charles Dickens publishes *Great Expectations*.

History Reading Skill **Draw Conclusions From Sources**

For which rights were nineteenth-century women fighting?

In this chapter, you will learn how to use details to draw conclusions from sources. Read the following selection by women's rights advocate Elizabeth Cady Stanton. The side notes show you how to draw conclusions from sources.

The Declaration of Sentiments was issued in 1848 during a women's rights convention in Seneca Falls, New York.

Primary Source

...We hold these truths to be self-evident: that all men and women are created equal; that they are endowed by their Creator with certain inalienable rights; . . . that to secure these rights governments are instituted, deriving their just powers from the consent of the governed. Whenever any form of government becomes destructive of these ends, it is the right of those who suffer from it to refuse allegiance to it, and to insist upon the institution of a new government. . . .

> This detail shows that Stanton believes action is necessary to win rights for women.

The history of mankind is a history of repeated injuries and usurpations [unlawful seizure of power] on the part of man toward woman, having in direct object the establishment of an absolute tyranny over her. . . .

He has never permitted her to exercise her inalienable right to the elective franchise [right to vote]. . . .

> This detail points out that women could not vote.

He has taken from her all right in property, even to the wages she earns. . . .

> Women did not get the same type of education as men.

He has denied her the facilities [means] for obtaining a thorough education, all colleges being closed against her.

—Elizabeth Cady Stanton,
Declaration of Sentiments

Draw a Conclusion

• Stanton provides details of injustices women have faced.
• You can conclude that Stanton believes women have been denied rights and that they must fight for these rights.

Document-Based Questions

1. Compare this excerpt to the opening of the Declaration of Independence. Identify two similarities in language.
2. Why do you think Stanton deliberately repeated language from the Declaration of Independence?

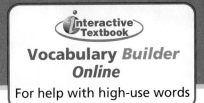
Vocabulary *Builder*

Previewing High-Use Academic Words

High-Use Word	Definition	Sample History Sentence
impulse (IHM puhls) (Section 1, p. 415)	*n.* sudden push or driving force	Reformers had an <u>impulse</u> to try to improve society.
convert (kahn VERT) (Section 1, p. 415)	*v.* to change from one political party, religion, or way of life to another	The preacher's goal was to <u>convert</u> his listeners from a life of sin to a life of good works.
eliminate (ee LIHM ih nayt) (Section 2, p. 422)	*v.* to get rid of	Some people worked to <u>eliminate</u> the problem of alcohol abuse.
via (VEE ah) (Section 2, p. 424)	*prep.* by way of	Settlers went west <u>via</u> the Great Wagon Road.
exclude (ehks KLYOOD) (Section 3, p. 428)	*v.* to keep out or expel; to reject	Most colleges at that time <u>excluded</u> women and African Americans.
emotion (ee MOH shuhn) (Section 4, p. 432)	*n.* strong feeling such as sadness, anger, or love	His speech about the evils of slavery stirred the <u>emotions</u> of the audience.
reproduce (ree prah DYOOS) (Section 4, p. 435)	*v.* to make a copy	In her paintings, she tried to <u>reproduce</u> the beauty of the natural world.

Previewing Key Terms and People

Improving Society

Objectives

1. Discuss what led many Americans to try to improve society in the 1800s.

2. Identify the social problems that reformers tried to solve.

3. Summarize the improvements in public education in the 1800s.

Prepare to Read

 Reading Skill

Assess Evidence for a Conclusion In reading history, you will encounter many descriptive details that help you draw conclusions about historical events. Evaluate the details carefully with questions such as these: Are they accurate and from reliable sources? Do the sources have firsthand knowledge of the situations? What conclusions do the details point to?

Vocabulary *Builder*

High-Use Words

<u>impulse</u>, p. 415

<u>convert</u>, p. 415

Key Terms and People

social reform, p. 414

predestination, p. 415

Charles Finney, p. 415

revival, p. 415

temperance movement, p. 416

prohibition, p. 416

Dorothea Dix, p. 417

public school, p. 417

Horace Mann, p. 418

⭐ **Background Knowledge** As you have read, the presidency of Andrew Jackson was a time of expanding democracy in the United States. This democratic spirit was one factor that helped spark efforts to improve American society. In this section, you will read about some of these efforts.

Main Idea
Political and religious ideas inspired Americans to seek ways to improve society.

The Reforming Spirit

In the 1830s, many Americans became interested in social reform, or organized attempts to improve conditions of life. The effort to create a better society had both political and religious roots.

Jacksonian Democracy The expansion of democracy in the Age of Jackson encouraged reform. Most states dropped property requirements for voting. As a result, more white American men were able to vote than ever before. Political parties also developed a more open way of choosing candidates for President.

In the spirit of Jacksonian democracy, some people worked to make the political system even fairer. A number of reformers believed that all men should vote and be able to hold office. Others supported greater legal rights for women. Increasingly, reformers also spoke out strongly against slavery. They argued that no society that allowed one human being to own another could call itself democratic.

The Second Great Awakening Religious feelings and ideas also sparked the reforming <u>impulse</u>. Beginning in the early 1800s, a new generation of ministers challenged some traditional views. This movement became known as the Second Great Awakening.

Changing religious ideas sparked the Second Great Awakening. In colonial days, many American Protestants believed in **predestination**, the idea that God decided the fate of a person's soul even before birth. But leaders of the Second Great Awakening preached that people's own actions determined their salvation. This "doctrine of free will" blended easily with political ideas about democracy and independence.

The most important of this new generation of preachers was **Charles Finney**. Finney held the first of many religious revivals in 1826. A **revival** is a huge outdoor religious meeting. Before long, Finney and other preachers were conducting revivals across the nation. A single revival might go on for several days or even a week. Ministers of different faiths preached day and night, trying to <u>convert</u> sinners and urging people to reform their lives.

Finney believed that the emotion of a revival could touch even the most hopeless sinner. "All sorts of abandoned characters are awakened and converted," he wrote. "The worst part of human society is softened and reclaimed, and made to appear as a lovely specimen of the beauty of holiness."

Vocabulary *Builder*
impulse (IHM puhls) *n.* sudden push or driving force

Vocabulary *Builder*
convert (kahn VERT) *v.* to change from one political party, religion, or way of life to another

Drinking alcohol is a step toward Hell.

Education is a step toward self-improvement.

At this crossroad, a person may choose to follow one path or the other.

Industry, or hard work, puts a person on the right path.

The Way to Salvation

This symbolic painting, *The Way of Good and Evil,* shows two paths a person can take. One path leads to Hell and the other leads to Heaven. **Critical Thinking: Apply Information** *How does this painting reflect the doctrine of free will that was part of the Second Great Awakening?*

Preaching at a revival meeting

Thus, the religious revivals of the Second Great Awakening encouraged reform. People came to believe that, if they had the power to improve themselves, they could improve society as well.

Utopian Communities The desire to create a more perfect society spurred some reformers to found utopian communities. (*Utopia* was a book about a fictional ideal society.) Utopian reformers hoped their communities would become models for others to follow.

Robert Owen founded a utopian community in Indiana in 1825. He called this colony New Harmony. New Harmony was based on common ownership of property. Residents were to raise their own food and manufacture their own goods. However, New Harmony turned out to be anything but harmonious. Members argued among themselves about goals and actions. The colony dissolved after about two years. Indeed, most utopian communities did not last very long.

☑ **Checkpoint** **What was the goal of the Second Great Awakening?**

Social Reformers at Work

Utopian reformers tried to create perfect, separate communities. However, most reform-minded Americans chose to work within the existing society. The reforming impulse took many forms.

Main Idea
Reformers worked to solve a variety of social problems, including alcohol abuse and poor treatment of prisoners and persons with mental illnesses.

The Temperance Movement Many reformers supported the temperance movement, an organized effort to end alcohol abuse and the problems created by it. Alcohol was widely used in the United States. Whiskey was cheaper than milk or beer. Often, it was safer to drink than water, which was frequently contaminated. As a result, alcohol abuse reached epidemic proportions.

Many women were drawn to the temperance movement. They pointed out how many women and children suffered at the hands of husbands and fathers who drank too much. Such organizations as the American Temperance Society published pamphlets denouncing "strong drink."

Most reformers favored temperance, or moderation in drinking. But others called for prohibition, a total ban on the sale and consumption of alcohol. During the 1850s, supporters of prohibition got nine states to pass laws banning the sale of alcohol. The movement was interrupted by the Civil War but reemerged later.

Prison Reform Other reformers sought to improve the nation's prison system. Prisons had traditionally been harsh places, designed to make people want to stay out of them. Poorly heated buildings, inadequate food, and cramped conditions were typical. Many people in prison were not criminals at all but were people who owed money they could not pay back. Because debtors could seldom earn money while in jail, they often remained locked up for years.

Chains and cages used on prisoners

Dorothea Dix

Reforming Prison Conditions

The two drawings shown at left are from an 1858 magazine article about prison conditions. Such sights led Dorothea Dix (right) and other reformers to call for more humane treatment of prisoners. *Critical Thinking: Frame Questions Based on these drawings, write two questions that you would ask Dorothea Dix to answer.*

Social reformers began investigating conditions in jails. Dorothea Dix, a Massachusetts schoolteacher, was one of those who took up the cause of prison reform. Over the years, she worked to convince state legislatures to build new, more sanitary, and more humane prisons. In addition, debtors were no longer sent to jail.

Reforms for the Mentally Ill Dix was outraged to find that prisons were also used to house individuals with mental illnesses. After a careful investigation, she reported to the Massachusetts legislature on the horrifying conditions she had witnessed: "A woman in a cage . . . [One man] losing the use of his limbs from want of exercise . . . One man and one woman chained."

Dix's shocking report helped persuade the Massachusetts legislature to fund a new mental hospital. She then continued her efforts in other states. She urged city and state governments around the country to create separate institutions, called asylums, for those with mental illnesses. The new asylums provided treatment, rather than punishment.

☑**Checkpoint** How did Dorothea Dix contribute to social reform?

Education Reform

Education was another area of concern to reformers. The first American schools were set up for religious purposes. The Puritans of Massachusetts believed that all people needed to be able to read and understand the Bible. In 1642, they passed a law requiring all large towns to hire teachers and build schools. In this way, Massachusetts set up the first public schools, or free schools supported by taxes.

Need for Better Education By the early 1800s, Massachusetts was still the only state to require public schools. In other states, children from wealthy families were educated privately, whereas poor children generally received no education outside the home. Under these circumstances, many Americans could not read or write.

Main Idea
Gradually, states took steps to improve education and make it available to more people.

Links Across Time

Public Education

1852 Massachusetts became the first state to pass a law that required all children to attend school up to a certain age. This was known as compulsory education.

1918 By this date, compulsory education laws had been passed in every state in the Union. As a result, for the first time, every state required children to attend school at least up to the tenth grade.

Link to Today Online

Education Today Today, billions of dollars in federal, state, and local taxes go to support public education. But not everybody agrees on the best way to spend that money and to educate American children.

For: Education in the news
Visit: PHSchool.com
Web Code: myc-4081

Public school classroom, around 1920

The reforms of the Jacksonian Era increased the number of eligible voters. Reformers grew concerned that the education system was not keeping up with the political system. They argued that education was necessary to ensure that voters were intelligently informed. With immigration on the rise, reformers also pointed out that better schools would help immigrants assimilate, or become part of, American culture.

Mann and Public Education Horace Mann of Massachusetts took the lead in education reform. To Mann, public financing of education was essential for democracy to work. He said:

> "If we do not prepare children to become good citizens; if we do not develop their capacities, if we do not enrich their minds with knowledge . . . then our republic must go down to destruction as others have gone before it."
>
> —Horace Mann, quoted in *A Century of Childhood* (Heininger)

After becoming head of the state board of education in 1837, Mann convinced Massachusetts to improve its public school system. It created colleges to train teachers, raised the salaries of teachers, and lengthened the school year. (To learn more about public education in the 1800s, see the Life at the Time feature.)

Reading Skill

Assess Evidence for a Conclusion
Read the quotation by Horace Mann. Assess the credibility of this source in supporting the following conclusion: Mann believed that strong character, moral behavior, and wide knowledge were equally important qualities. List three examples from the quotation that support this conclusion.

Other states soon followed Massachusetts's example. By the 1850s, public schools had gained much acceptance in the Northeast. Southern and western states lagged behind, however. They would not create their own public school systems until many decades later.

Education for African Americans The improvements in public education did little for African Americans. Southern states prohibited teaching enslaved persons to read. In the North, free black children were seldom admitted to the same schools as white children.

Reformers who tried to improve educational opportunities for African Americans often met with resistance. Prudence Crandall, a Quaker teacher, opened a school for African American girls in Connecticut. Hostile neighbors attacked and destroyed the school.

Still, some opportunities did open up. In major northern cities, free African American educators opened their own schools. In 1855, Massachusetts became the first state to admit African American students to public schools. Some African Americans attended private colleges such as Harvard and Oberlin. In 1854, Pennsylvania chartered Ashmun Institute (later called Lincoln University), the nation's first college for African American men.

☑**Checkpoint** **How did public education improve in the mid-1800s?**

⭐ **Looking Back and Ahead** Inspired by political or religious ideals, reformers tackled many social problems. But one issue towered above all others in the minds of reformers. In the next section, you will read about the growing efforts to end slavery.

Section 1 | **Check Your Progress**

Progress Monitoring ⬤nline
For: Self-test with instant help
Visit: PHSchool.com
Web Code: mya-4081

Comprehension and Critical Thinking

1. **(a) Identify** What were the ideas of predestination and the doctrine of free will?
   (b) Draw Conclusions How might the doctrine of free will promote democracy?

2. **(a) Recall** Which reforms did Horace Mann convince the state of Massachusetts to make?
   (b) Detect Points of View According to Mann, why is it important for a democracy to have educated citizens?

Reading Skill

3. **Assess Evidence for a Conclusion** Assess the quotation that follows by Dorothea Dix. Is the evidence reliable? Does it support the conclusion that the mentally ill were poorly treated? **Quotation:** "[T]wo females . . . lie in wooden bunks filled with straw; always shut up. . . . The use of cages [is] all but universal."

Vocabulary *Builder*

Answer the following questions in complete sentences that show your understanding of the key terms.
4. What did the temperance movement seek?

5. What was the goal of social reform in the 1830s?
6. What is a religious revival?

Writing

7. A topic sentence sets the focus for a single paragraph. A thesis statement expresses a broader idea to be developed in an entire essay. Write three topic sentences for paragraphs that would support and develop the following thesis statement: A powerful reforming spirit swept through this country in the 1830s.

Going to School

Following the lead of Massachusetts, other states in the North began to fund public schools. Not all children were able to attend school, and most of those who did only got as far as the eighth grade. What were these early American classrooms like?

The Classroom

Schools in the early 1800s were not like the large public buildings we know today. In rural areas especially, many children went to one-room schoolhouses, where children of all ages were taught together. Students wrote on chalk slates and were expected to recite their lessons when called upon by the teacher.

History *Interactive*
Explore an Early American Classroom
Visit: PHSchool.com
Web Code: myp-4081

A Popular Textbook ▲

In elementary schools, the most popular text-books were *McGuffey's Eclectic Readers* (Primer through Sixth). First published in 1836, the Readers offered moral lessons along with the "three Rs"—reading, 'riting, and 'rithmetic. The lesson shown above was used to teach children how to read and how to treat pets.

Rewards and Punishments ▶

Discipline was strict in early classrooms. Students who failed to learn their lessons might have to sit in a corner wearing a "dunce cap" (right). But there were also rewards. Students might get certificates for learning their lesson well, for good behavior, or just for coming to school on time (below).

▼

Analyze LIFE AT THE TIME

Look at the pages from *McGuffey's Eclectic Primer* shown at the top of this page. Then, write a lesson for the Primer about the importance of going to school. Use simple language that can be understood by elementary school students.

The Fight Against Slavery

Objectives

1. Describe efforts in the North to end slavery.

2. Discuss the contributions of William Lloyd Garrison, Frederick Douglass, and other abolitionists.

3. Describe the purpose and risks of the Underground Railroad.

4. Explain why many people in the North and South defended slavery.

Prepare to Read

Reading Skill

Form an Opinion Based on Evidence You can use details and evidence in primary and secondary sources to help you form opinions about history. Remember that primary sources come from people who saw or experienced events, whereas secondary sources (such as this textbook) build on many sources to recount historical information.

Vocabulary *Builder*

High-Use Words

eliminate, p. 422

via, p. 424

Key Terms and People

abolitionist, p. 423

William Lloyd Garrison, p. 423

Frederick Douglass, p. 424

Harriet Tubman, p. 424

⭐ **Background Knowledge** As early as colonial times, some Americans had opposed slavery. Most Quakers, in particular, condemned slavery on religious and moral grounds. In this section, you will see how the reforming impulse of the 1800s spurred a vigorous new effort to end slavery.

Roots of the Antislavery Movement

A number of prominent leaders of the early republic, such as Alexander Hamilton and Benjamin Franklin, opposed slavery. They believed that slavery violated the most basic principle of the Declaration of Independence, "that all men are created equal."

Main Idea
Soon after the American Revolution, northern states began to do away with slavery.

Slavery Ends in the North In 1780, Pennsylvania became the first state to pass a law that gradually eliminated slavery. By 1804, every northern state had ended or pledged to end slavery. Congress also outlawed slavery in the Northwest Territory. As a result, when Ohio entered the Union in 1803, it became the first state to ban slavery in its state constitution.

Vocabulary *Builder*
eliminate (ee LIHM ih nayt) *v.* to get rid of

The Colonization Movement The American Colonization Society, established in 1817, was an early antislavery organization. This society proposed that slaves be freed gradually and transported to Liberia, a colony founded in 1822 on the west coast of Africa.

The colonization movement did not work. Most enslaved people had grown up in the United States and did not desire to leave. By 1830 only about 1,400 African Americans had migrated to Liberia.

✓**Checkpoint** How did slavery end in the North?

Growing Opposition to Slavery

The Second Great Awakening inspired further opposition to slavery. Many people were influenced by the preaching of Charles Finney, who condemned slavery. By the mid-1800s, a small but growing number of people were **abolitionists,** reformers who wanted to abolish, or end, slavery. Rejecting gradual emancipation, abolitionists called for a complete and immediate end to slavery.

Garrison One of the most forceful voices for abolition was William Lloyd Garrison. A Quaker, he strongly opposed the use of violence to end slavery. Still, Garrison was more radical than many others, because he favored full political rights for all African Americans.

In 1831, Garrison launched an abolitionist newspaper, the *Liberator.* It became the nation's leading antislavery publication for 34 years, ending only when slavery itself ended.

Garrison cofounded the New England Anti-Slavery Society, which later became the American Anti-Slavery Society. Leaders of this group included Theodore Weld, a minister who had been a pupil of Charles Finney. Weld brought the zeal of a religious revival to anti-slavery rallies. Other members included Sarah and Angelina Grimke, daughters of a South Carolina slaveholder.

African American Abolitionists Prominent African Americans in the North took a leading role in the abolitionist movement. In 1829, David Walker published his *Appeal: to the Coloured Citizens of the World.* This strongly worded pamphlet urged enslaved people to rebel, if necessary, to gain their freedom.

The Liberator

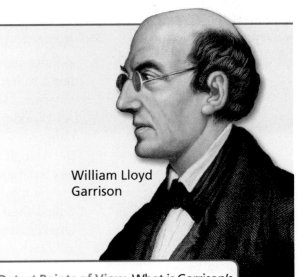

"Let Southern oppressors tremble—let all the enemies of the persecuted blacks tremble. . . . On this subject, I do not wish to think, or to speak, or write, with moderation. No! No! Tell a man whose house is on fire to give a moderate alarm . . . but urge me not to use moderation in a cause like the present. I am in earnest—I will not equivocate—I will not excuse—I will not retreat a single inch—AND I WILL BE HEARD."

—William Lloyd Garrison, *Liberator,* January 1831

William Lloyd Garrison

Reading Primary Sources
Skills Activity

In the above excerpt from the first issue of the *Liberator,* William Lloyd Garrison vows to take a firm stand against slavery.

(a) **Detect Points of View** What is Garrison's attitude toward slaveholders?

(b) **Draw Conclusions** What does Garrison mean when he writes, "Tell a man whose house is on fire to give a moderate alarm"?

Perhaps the most powerful speaker for abolitionism was Frederick Douglass. Born into slavery, Douglass had broken the law by learning to read. He later escaped to freedom in the North. Garrison and other abolitionists encouraged Douglass to describe his experiences at antislavery rallies. Douglass told one crowd:

> **"** I appear this evening as a thief and a robber. I stole this head, these limbs, this body from my master, and ran off with them. **"**
>
> —Frederick Douglass, speech, 1842

By appearing in public, Douglass risked being sent back into slavery. Yet, he continued to speak before larger and larger audiences. He also published his own antislavery newspaper, the *North Star.*

A Former President Takes a Stand Abolitionists won the support of a few powerful people. Former President John Quincy Adams, now a member of Congress, read antislavery petitions from the floor of the House of Representatives. In 1839, Adams proposed a constitutional amendment that would ban slavery in any new state joining the Union. However, the amendment was not passed.

Two years later, Adams made a dramatic stand against slavery. Captive Africans aboard the slave ship *Amistad* had rebelled, killing the captain and ordering the crew to sail back to Africa. Instead, the crew sailed the ship to America. The 73-year-old Adams spoke to the Supreme Court for nine hours and helped the captives regain their freedom.

☑**Checkpoint** **What role did Frederick Douglass play in the abolitionist movement?**

The Underground Railroad

Some courageous abolitionists dedicated themselves to helping people escape from slavery. They established a system known as the Underground Railroad. Despite its name, it was neither underground nor a railroad. It was a network of people—black and white, northerners and southerners—who secretly helped slaves reach freedom.

Working for the Underground Railroad was illegal and dangerous. "Conductors" led fugitive slaves from one "station" to the next. Stations were usually the homes of abolitionists, but might be churches or caves. Supporters helped by donating clothing, food, and money to pay for passage on trains and boats. Many people risked their lives to help runaway slaves. Levi Coffin, an Indiana Quaker, assisted more than 3,000 fugitives.

Harriet Tubman, who had herself escaped from slavery, escorted more than 300 people to freedom <u>via</u> the Underground Railroad. Tubman was nicknamed the Black Moses after the biblical leader who led the Israelites out of slavery in Egypt. She proudly told Frederick Douglass that, in 19 trips to the South, she "never lost a single passenger." Slave owners promised a $40,000 reward for her capture.

Antislavery medallion

Main Idea
Some abolitionists secretly worked to help African Americans escape from slavery.

Vocabulary *Builder*
<u>via</u> (VEE ah) *prep.* by way of

THE Underground Railroad

As many as 50,000 African Americans escaped from slavery in the South to freedom in the North or in Canada via the Underground Railroad.
Critical Thinking: *Identify Costs and Benefits*
What were the risks of helping fugitive slaves escape? Why do you think conductors on the Underground Railroad chose to take those risks?

THE UNDERGROUND RAILROAD

KEY
→ RAILROAD ROUTES
☐ FREE STATES
☐ SLAVE STATES
☐ TERRITORIES

HARRIET TUBMAN 1820-1913

▼ This modern quilt honors Harriet Tubman, the most famous conductor on the Underground Railroad.

The homes of some conductors ▶ had secret rooms to hide runaway slaves. In this room, the bed would be moved to hide the doorway.

▶ This song contained directions for escaping slaves. The "drinking gourd" is the Big Dipper.

"The riverbank makes a very good road.
The dead trees will show you the way.
Left foot, peg foot, traveling on,
If you follow the drinking gourd."

Each year, hundreds of slaves moved along the Underground Railroad to freedom in the North or in Canada. In total, perhaps as many as 50,000 gained their freedom in this way.

☑ **Checkpoint** How did the Underground Railroad work?

Main Idea
Many people in both the North and the South defended slavery.

Opposing Abolition

Abolitionists faced powerful obstacles in the North as well as in the South. Many northerners profited from the existence of slavery. Northern textile mill owners and merchants relied on the cotton produced by southern slave labor. Northern workers feared that freed slaves might come north and take their jobs.

Such fears sometimes prompted violence against abolitionists. Mobs attacked antislavery meetings. In 1835, William Lloyd Garrison was dragged through the streets of Boston with a rope around his neck.

As you have read, southerners had long defended slavery as a positive force. Now, as support for abolition grew louder, they went on the offensive. The state of Georgia offered a $5,000 reward for the arrest and conviction for libel of William Lloyd Garrison. Southerners in Congress won passage of a "gag rule" that blocked discussion of antislavery petitions. John Quincy Adams unsuccessfully fought for repeal of the gag rule.

☑ **Checkpoint** Why did some northerners oppose abolition?

⭐ **Looking Back and Ahead** By the 1840s, the North and the South were increasingly divided by the issue of slavery. Abolitionists succeeded in making converts in the North. Slavery was spreading along with the cotton boom in the South.

Section 2 | Check Your Progress

Progress Monitoring ⬤nline
For: Self-test with instant help
Visit: PHSchool.com
Web Code: mya-4082

Comprehension and Critical Thinking

1. **(a) List** What solutions did the American Colonization Society propose to end slavery?
(b) Explain Problems Why did most African Americans reject the society's goals?

2. **(a) Identify** Which groups in the North were opposed to abolition? Why?
(b) Identify Alternatives How might the concerns of these groups have been calmed?

⬤ Reading Skill

3. **Form an Opinion Based on Evidence** Henry Brown mailed himself to freedom in a crate. What do you think was important to him? Use evidence quoted from his own narrative to form your opinion: "I was . . . placed on my head. . . . In this dreadful position, I remained the space of an hour and a half . . . my eyes were almost swollen out of their sockets, and the veins on my temples seemed ready to burst. I made no noise, however, determining to obtain 'victory or death.'"

Vocabulary Builder

4. Write two definitions for the key term abolitionist. First, write a formal definition for your teacher. Second, write a definition in everyday English for a classmate.

Writing

5. Choose three details from Section 2 that support the topic sentence that follows. Then, write a paragraph developing the topic based on these details.
Topic sentence: Abolitionists used a variety of tactics to oppose slavery.

A Call for Women's Rights

Objectives

1. Explain how the women's suffrage movement began.

2. Describe the goals of the Seneca Falls Convention in 1848.

3. Identify the new opportunities that women gained in the mid-1800s.

Prepare to Read

Reading Skill

State the Meaning of Evidence One way to draw conclusions from source material is to make a statement about the meaning of the evidence. This statement will be a conclusion drawn from the details of the evidence. Your statement should use your own words, fit with all the details, and make sense to you.

Vocabulary *Builder*

High-Use Word

exclude, p. 428

Key Terms and People

Sojourner Truth, p. 427

Lucretia Mott, p. 427

Elizabeth Cady Stanton, p. 428

women's suffrage, p. 428

women's rights movement, p. 429

Susan B. Anthony, p. 429

⭐ **Background Knowledge** You have read how abolitionists fought to rid the country of slavery. In this section, you will see how abolitionism helped spark another reform movement, which was dedicated to rights for women.

The Struggle Begins

In 1820, the rights of American women were limited. They could not vote, serve on juries, attend college, or enter such professions as medicine or law. Married women could not own property or keep their own wages. Most Americans—both men and women—believed that a woman's place was in the private world of the home.

Women who were active in abolition or other social reform movements believed that they had important contributions to make to American society. They began to demand rights as equal citizens. Among these women was Sojourner Truth. Born into slavery in New York State, she was illiterate, but her words inspired the crowds that heard her. Truth became a powerful voice on behalf of both enslaved African Americans and women.

Lucretia Mott, a Quaker, had spent years working in the antislavery movement. Quakers allowed women to take public roles that other religions prohibited. Mott thus had organizing skills and public speaking experience that most women of her day did not.

☑ **Checkpoint** Why did some reformers turn to the issue of women's rights?

Main Idea

Women who were involved in abolition and other reform movements began to speak out about the status of women.

Sojourner Truth

427

Vocabulary *Builder*
exclude (ehks KLYOOD) *v.* to keep out or expel; to reject

Seneca Falls Convention

In 1840, Mott traveled to London to attend an international anti-slavery convention. There, she met another abolitionist, Elizabeth Cady Stanton. Stanton was honeymooning in London with her husband, a delegate to the conference. But when Mott and Stanton tried to attend a meeting, they were told that women were not permitted to take an active role in the proceedings.

Mott and Stanton were infuriated at being excluded. Sitting outside the convention hall, they agreed on the need for a convention to advance women's rights. They followed through on that idea in the summer of 1848. Their convention met in Seneca Falls, New York, "to discuss the social, civil, and religious rights of women." The Seneca Falls Convention attracted over 300 men and women.

Declaration of Sentiments Stanton wrote a Declaration of Sentiments, modeled on the Declaration of Independence. It began, "We hold these truths to be self-evident: that all men and women are created equal. . . ." The declaration then listed injustices women suffered, including being shut out from educational opportunities and good jobs. The Declaration of Sentiments demanded full equality for women in every area of life.

Like the colonial Patriots, Stanton opposed "taxation without representation." In a speech just before the convention, she declared:

> ❝[W]e are assembled to protest against a form of government existing without the consent of the governed—to declare our right to be free as man is free, to be represented in the government which we are taxed to support.❞
>
> —Elizabeth Cady Stanton, speech, July 19, 1848

Call for Suffrage Stanton's argument was the beginning of the long battle for women's suffrage, or the right of women to vote. However, not all of the delegates agreed when Stanton included a call for women's suffrage in the Declaration of Sentiments. Some, such as Frederick Douglass, strongly supported it. Others, including Lucretia Mott, feared that the call for women's suffrage would be so controversial that it would harm their other causes. Still, the convention narrowly voted to support the demand for women's suffrage.

☑**Checkpoint** What was the purpose of the Declaration of Sentiments?

Biography Quest

Elizabeth Cady Stanton
1815–1902

With seven children to care for, Elizabeth Cady Stanton still found time to try to change the world. She began her long political partnership with Susan B. Anthony in 1851. For much of the next 50 years, the two women pooled their talents to try to win women the right to vote. "[I am] a fine writer," Stanton noted. "Miss Anthony is a thorough manager." Sadly, Stanton died 18 years before women finally won the vote.

Biography Quest nline

Why was Stanton's wedding ceremony unusual for its day?

For: The answer to the question about Stanton

Visit: PHSchool.com

Web Code: myd-4083

New Opportunities for Women

The Seneca Falls Convention launched the women's rights movement in the United States. The **women's rights movement** was an organized effort to improve the political, legal, and economic status of women in American society.

Political Victories In the years after the Seneca Falls Convention, Susan B. Anthony became a close ally of Stanton. The two made a dynamic team. As an unmarried woman, Anthony was free to travel and devote herself to reform work. Stanton, the mother of a growing family, more often wrote speeches from her home. Together, they founded the National Woman Suffrage Association in 1869.

The fight for women's suffrage made little progress at first. Yet the women's rights movement won some victories. In 1860, Stanton and Anthony convinced New York to pass a law protecting women's property rights. Many other states followed. Some states revised their laws to allow married women to keep their wages.

Education for Women The women's rights movement focused much attention on education. American schools emphasized education for boys, who would grow up to be voters, citizens, and professionals. Girls seldom studied advanced subjects like math and science.

Even before the Seneca Falls Convention, reformers worked to give girls a chance for a better education. In 1821, Emma Willard started an academy in Troy, New York, that soon became the model for girls' schools everywhere. The Troy Female Seminary attracted the daughters of lawyers and doctors. The first year, 90 students enrolled. By 1831, the seminary had more than 300 students. Many female reformers of this era attended Willard's school.

Mary Lyon began an even bolder experiment when she opened Mount Holyoke Female Seminary in Massachusetts, in 1837. Lyon did not call her school a college. However, Mount Holyoke was, in fact, the first college for women in the United States. The school showed that women could indeed learn subjects like Latin, geometry, and chemistry.

Main Idea
In the mid-1800s, women gained new opportunities for education and careers.

Cause and Effect

CAUSES
- Women could not vote, serve on juries, own property, or divorce abusive husbands.
- Many abolitionists believed that women also deserved equal rights.
- Women were denied equal educational opportunities.
- Seneca Falls Convention launched the women's rights movement.

THE WOMEN'S RIGHTS MOVEMENT

EFFECTS
- Suffragist movement demanded that women get the right to vote.
- States passed laws that protected women's property rights.
- Private schools for women opened, and some colleges accepted women as students.
- Women entered careers once closed to them.

Reading Charts
Skills Activity
The Seneca Falls Convention marked the start of an organized women's rights movement in the United States.

(a) Read a Chart Identify two effects of the women's rights movement.

(b) Analyze Cause and Effect Why is the abolition movement shown as a cause of the women's rights movement?

Maria Mitchell (left) at her telescope

State the Meaning of Evidence
Make a general statement that is supported by the evidence in these three paragraphs.

New Careers Gradually, American society came to accept that girls could be educated and that women could be teachers. More and more schools began hiring women teachers who had been trained at one of the new academies or colleges for women. Some women began trying to enter other professions as well.

Margaret Fuller made a career as a journalist, scholar, and literary critic. She spoke in public for pay at a time when it was illegal for women to do so. In 1845, Fuller published an influential book, *Women in the Nineteenth Century.* "We would have every . . . barrier thrown down. We would have every path laid open to Woman as freely as to Man," she wrote.

Other women excelled in science. Elizabeth Blackwell was admitted to Geneva Medical College in New York. Blackwell graduated first in her class in January 1849, becoming the first woman to graduate from an American medical school. The astronomer Maria Mitchell was the first professor hired at Vassar College. She was also the first woman elected to the American Academy of Arts and Sciences in 1848. A crater on the moon was later named in her honor.

☑**Checkpoint** Give two examples of advances in education for women.

☆ **Looking Back and Ahead** The delegates at the Seneca Falls Convention hesitated to demand women's suffrage. As it turned out, getting the vote was a long struggle. Not until 1920 did a constitutional amendment guarantee women's right to vote. You will read more about the women's suffrage movement in a later chapter.

Section 3 | **Check Your Progress**

Progress Monitoring ⏻nline
For: Self-test with instant help
Visit: PHSchool.com
Web Code: mya-4083

Comprehension and Critical Thinking

1. **(a) Summarize** What were the goals of the women's rights movement?
(b) Compare and Contrast How were the goals of the women's rights movement similar to and different from those of the abolitionist movement?

2. **(a) Recall** Why was it considered more important for boys to get a good education than girls in the early 1800s?
(b) Explain Problems How did the lack of equal educational opportunities hurt women?

Reading Skill

3. **State the Meaning of Evidence** Make a statement about public views regarding women in politics, and then support it with the evidence in this paragraph: "Hers is the domestic altar; there she ministers and commands . . .; let her not seek madly to descend from this eminence to mix with the strife and ambition of the cares of government; the field of politics is not her appropriate arena."

Vocabulary *Builder*

Read each sentence below. If the sentence is true, write YES and explain why. If the sentence is not true, write NO and explain why not.

4. Supporters of women's suffrage opposed the right to vote.

5. The Seneca Falls Convention marked the start of the women's rights movement.

Writing

6. Imagine that you are a reporter in 1848 writing an article about the Seneca Falls Convention. Write a few sentences explaining why the convention met. Then, predict what might be the long-term effects of the convention.

Objectives

1. Identify the common themes in American literature and art in the mid-1800s.
2. Describe the flowering of American literature in the mid-1800s.
3. Discuss the development of unique American styles in art and music.

Prepare to Read

Reading Skill

Draw Logical Conclusions As you review the details and evidence in text, make sure that the conclusions you draw are logical. In other words, they should make sense with all the details and with what you know about the events and about the world. Use your own experience to test, for example, whether particular attitudes make sense in a given situation. Do they fit the historical context?

Vocabulary *Builder*

High-Use Words

<u>emotion</u>, p. 432
<u>reproduce</u>, p. 435

Key Terms and People

transcendentalism, p. 432
Ralph Waldo Emerson, p. 432
individualism, p. 432
Henry David Thoreau, p. 432
civil disobedience, p. 433
Herman Melville, p. 433
Nathaniel Hawthorne, p. 433
Louisa May Alcott, p. 434

⭐ **Background Knowledge** The reformers that you have read about in this chapter all shared a sense of optimism. They believed that individuals could reform themselves and that society could be improved. In this section, you will see how this same optimistic spirit inspired a new generation of American writers.

An American Culture Develops

Before 1800, American writers and artists modeled their work on European styles. Poets used complex, formal language and filled their poems with references to Greek and Roman myths. Most artists trained in Europe and learned European approaches to painting.

American Themes By the mid-1800s, American writers and artists had begun to develop styles that reflected American optimism and energy. Their work explored subjects that were uniquely American. Two early writers, Washington Irving and James Fenimore Cooper, reflected this interest in American themes.

Irving drew upon the Dutch history of New York in his stories "The Legend of Sleepy Hollow" and "Rip Van Winkle." Rip Van Winkle was a lazy farmer who slept through the American Revolution.

Cooper created the popular character Natty Bumppo, a frontiersman who kept moving westward. Uncomfortable with life in cities and towns, Bumppo criticized the destruction of nature. Cooper's novels about Bumppo, such as *The Deerslayer* and *The Last of the Mohicans*, helped American literature gain popularity in Europe.

Main Idea
In the 1800s, American writers explored uniquely American themes and developed new ideas about people and nature.

Transcendentalism By the early 1800s, a new artistic movement took shape in Europe, called Romanticism. Unlike thinkers of the Enlightenment, who emphasized reason, Romantics placed greater value on nature, <u>emotions</u>, and imagination.

A small but influential group of writers and thinkers in New England developed an American form of Romanticism, called transcendentalism (trahnz ehn DEHNT uhl ihzm). **Transcendentalism** was a movement that sought to explore the relationship between humans and nature through emotions rather than through reason. It got its name because its goal was to transcend, or go beyond, human reason.

Transcendentalists believed in a close link between humans and nature. They urged people to live simply and to seek beauty, goodness, and truth within their own souls.

Emerson and Thoreau Ralph Waldo Emerson was the leading transcendentalist. In his popular speeches and essays, Emerson asked Americans to question the value of material goods. Civilization might provide wealth, he said, but nature reflected higher values that came from God. Emerson also stressed **individualism,** the unique importance of each individual. "Trust thyself," he taught. He challenged people to use their "inner light" to guide their lives and improve society.

Henry David Thoreau (thuh ROW) took up Emerson's challenge. He spent two years living in the woods at Walden Pond, meditating on nature. In his 1854 book *Walden*, Thoreau urged people to live

Moby-Dick

Herman Melville's novel *Moby-Dick* tells the story of a sea captain's mad pursuit of a white whale. The novel is still widely read and has been filmed several times. **Critical Thinking:** *Apply Information* *You have read that Melville was interested in extreme, dark emotions. How does the excerpt on the facing page reflect that interest?*

Herman Melville

CHAPTER CXXXIV   THE CHASE—SECOND DAY

AT day-break, the three mast-heads were punctually manned afresh.

"D'ye see him?" cried Ahab, after allowing a little space for the light to spread.

"See nothing, Sir."

simply. "Most of the luxuries, and many of the so-called comforts of life, are not only not indispensable, but positive hindrances to the elevation of mankind," he wrote.

Like Emerson, Thoreau believed that individuals must judge right and wrong for themselves. He encouraged civil disobedience, the idea that people should peacefully disobey unjust laws if their consciences demand it. Thoreau spent a night in jail for refusing to pay a tax that he felt supported slavery. Thoreau's ideas about civil disobedience and nonviolent protest influenced later leaders like Martin Luther King, Jr.

Draw Logical Conclusions Draw a logical conclusion about Thoreau's values from the information and quotation in this paragraph.

✓**Checkpoint**   **What was the goal of transcendentalism?**

Flowering of American Literature

Irving and Cooper set a high standard for American writers. Two later novelists, Herman Melville and Nathaniel Hawthorne, began to change the tone of American literature.

Main Idea
American fiction and poetry reached new heights in the 1840s and 1850s.

Melville and Hawthorne   Both Hawthorne and Melville were fascinated by psychology and extreme emotions. Melville's novel *Moby-Dick* (1851) told the story of a sea captain who is obsessed with pursuing a white whale. In the end, Captain Ahab's mad pursuit destroys himself, his ship, and his crew. *Moby-Dick* was largely ignored when it was first published. Today, however, it is considered one of the greatest American novels.

▼ Captain Ahab tells his crew that he lost his leg because of the white whale Moby Dick.

❝ 'Aye, my hearties all round; it was Moby Dick that dismasted me; Moby Dick that brought me to this dead stump I stand on now. Aye aye,' he shouted with a terrific, loud, animal sob, like that of a heart-stricken moose; 'Aye, aye! it was that accursed white whale that razeed me; made a poor pegging lubber for me for ever and a day!' Then, tossing both arms, with measure-less imprecations he shouted out, 'Aye, aye! and I'll chase him round Good Hope, and round the Horn, and round the Norway Maelstrom, and round perdition's flames before I give him up. And this is what ye have shipped for, men! To chase that white whale on both sides of land, and over all sides of the earth....' ❞

▲ Captain Ahab in a movie version of *Moby-Dick*.

The Hudson River School

This landscape painting by Thomas Cole shows Americans building a home in the middle of the wilderness. Like other paintings of the Hudson River school, it reflects a sense of the beauty and power of nature. **Critical Thinking:** *Evaluate Information* What is the relationship between people and nature in this painting?

Hawthorne was descended from the Puritans of Massachusetts. He often used historical themes to explore the dark side of the mind. In his 1850 novel *The Scarlet Letter*, a young minister is destroyed by secret guilt. The novel paints a grim picture of Puritan life.

Alcott Louisa May Alcott presented a gentler view of New England life. In 1868, Alcott published *Little Women*, a novel based on her own experiences growing up with three sisters. The main character, Jo March, was one of the first young American heroines to be presented as a believable, imperfect person rather than as a shining ideal.

Poets of Democracy Poets helped create a new national voice. Henry Wadsworth Longfellow based poems on American history, such as "Paul Revere's Ride." His long poem *The Song of Hiawatha* was one of the first works to honor Native Americans.

Walt Whitman published *Leaves of Grass* in 1855. This book of poems shocked many readers because it rejected formal rules. But today, Whitman is seen as the poet who best expresses the democratic American spirit. His poetry celebrated common people:

> ❝[T]he policeman travels his beat—the gate-keeper marks who pass; . . .
>
> The clean-hair'd Yankee girl works with her sewing-machine, or in the factory or mill.❞
>
> —Walt Whitman, "Song of Myself"

Some poets used their pens to support social reform. John Greenleaf Whittier, a Massachusetts Quaker, and Frances Watkins Harper, an African American woman from Maryland, wrote poems that described and condemned the evils of slavery.

✓**Checkpoint** How did writers explore the American past?

Art and Music

After 1820, artists also began to create a unique American style. Turning away from European themes, they focused on the landscapes around them or on the daily lives of common Americans.

Painting America A group of artists painted scenes of the Hudson River valley. This group became known as the Hudson River school. Thomas Cole and the other painters of this school reflected the values of Romanticism. They sought to stir emotions by reproducing the beauty and power of nature.

Other American painters were inspired by everyday life. George Caleb Bingham created a timeless picture of life on the great rivers. George Catlin captured the ways and dignity of Native Americans.

Popular Songs Most early American songs, such as "Yankee Doodle," had roots in English, Irish, or Scottish tunes. Over time, a wide variety of new American songs emerged. Many were work songs, chanted by men as they sailed on whaling ships, laid railroad tracks, or hauled barges along canals. The spiritual was a special type of song developed by enslaved African Americans.

The most popular American songwriter of the 1800s was Stephen Foster. Many of his tunes, such as "Camptown Races" and "Old Folks at Home," are still familiar today.

✓ **Checkpoint** **Identify two themes of American painting.**

⭐ **Looking Back and Ahead** American culture of the 1800s had an influence that is still felt today. People still read *Moby-Dick* and *Little Women*. Concepts like individualism and civil disobedience continue to affect people's ideas and actions.

Main Idea
American painters and songwriters also used their skills to explore American life.

Vocabulary *Builder*
reproduce (ree prah DYOOS) *v.* to make a copy of

Section 4 | **Check Your Progress**

Progress Monitoring ⏺nline
For: Self-test with instant help
Visit: PHSchool.com
Web Code: mya-4084

Comprehension and Critical Thinking

1. (a) Recall Before 1800, what models influenced American writers and painters?
(b) Draw Conclusions How did later works like *The Scarlet Letter* and the paintings of the Hudson River school reflect a change in American art and literature?

2. (a) Recall What did Henry David Thoreau mean by "civil disobedience"?
(b) Link Past and Present How did Thoreau's ideas influence Martin Luther King, Jr.?

Reading Skill

3. Draw Logical Conclusions In a novel by James Fenimore Cooper, Natty Bumppo watches as settlers shoot hundreds of pigeons. Based on the following quotation, what conclusion can you draw about Natty's feelings for nature? Explain why your conclusion is logical. **Quotation:** "It's much better to kill only such as you want, without wasting your powder and lead, than to be firing into God's creatures in this wicked manner. . . . Wasn't the woods made for the beasts and birds to harbor in?"

Vocabulary *Builder*

4. Write two definitions for the key term transcendentalism. First, write a formal definition for your teacher. Second, write a definition in everyday English for a classmate.

Writing

5. What is the relationship between artists and society? Using examples from this section, write a paragraph explaining how writers, painters, and musicians reflect the society in which they lived and how they help to influence it.

A summary briefly retells the main ideas of a selection, using different words. It also includes the most important details about the main ideas. Summaries should not include personal opinions about the selection. Read the primary source below, then read summaries A–C.

Primary Source

In 1852, Frederick Douglass, African American abolitionist, was invited to speak at a July 4th gathering in Rochester, New York.

Fellow citizens, pardon me, allow me to ask, why am I called upon to speak here today? What have I, or those I represent, to do with your national independence? Are the great principles of political freedom and of natural justice, embodied in that Declaration of Independence, extended to us? . . . This Fourth of July is yours, not mine. You may rejoice. I must mourn. . . . Do you mean, citizens, to mock me by asking me to speak today? . . . My subject then, fellow citizens, is American slavery. I shall see this day and its popular characteristics from the slave's point of view.

—Frederick Douglass,
Independence Day speech,
Rochester, 1852

Summary A: Douglass believes that all Americans should celebrate the Fourth of July. The freedoms established in the Declaration of Independence are meant for all.

Summary B: Douglass does not feel he is able to speak. He is a poor man who does not enjoy the wealth and good fortune shared by many members of the audience.

Summary C: Douglass reminds his audience that African Americans did not enjoy the freedoms and independence guaranteed in the Declaration of Independence.

Learn the Skill

Use these steps to determine which summary accurately captures the main idea of the speech.

1 **Identify the subject of the selection.** What is the selection about?

2 **Find the main idea of the selection.** Determine the writer or speaker's most important point about the subject.

3 **Find important details.** What details provide key information about the main idea?

4 **Evaluate the summary.** Does it accurately restate the main idea of the original in different words? Does it include important details? Does it communicate the basic meaning of the original text?

Practice the Skill

Answer the following questions about the summaries on this page.

1 **Identify the subject of the selection.** What is the selection about?

2 **Find the main idea of the selection.** What main point does Frederick Douglass make?

3 **Find important details.** What is one detail that provides information about the main idea?

4 **Evaluate the summary.** Which is the best summary of Douglass's speech? Give three reasons for your answer.

Apply the Skill

See the Review and Assessment at the end of this chapter.

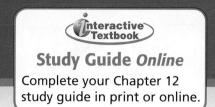

Study Guide *Online*
Complete your Chapter 12 study guide in print or online.

Chapter Summary

Section 1
Improving Society

- Jacksonian democracy encouraged reform by focusing on ideals of liberty and equality.
- In the Second Great Awakening, ministers preached that people had free will and could reform their own lives.
- Reformers tackled a variety of causes, including temperance, prison reform, improved conditions for those with mental illnesses, and public education.

Section 2
The Fight Against Slavery

- Abolitionists such as William Lloyd Garrison and Frederick Douglass called for an end to slavery.
- Conductors on the Underground Railroad helped people escape from slavery to freedom.
- Abolitionists faced strong opposition in both the North and the South.

Section 3
A Call for Women's Rights

- People active in social reform began to demand equal rights for women.
- The Declaration of Sentiments at the Seneca Falls Convention called for women's equality in many areas of public life.
- The women's rights movement focused much of its attention on gaining better education for women.

Section 4
American Literature and Arts

- American writers and artists began to explore American themes in their work.
- Transcendentalists emphasized emotions, nature, and individualism.
- Melville and Hawthorne explored dark areas of psychology, while Whitman wrote poems celebrating democracy.

Key Concepts

These notes will help you prepare for questions about key concepts.

Major Movements of the Early 1800s	
MOVEMENT	**GOAL**
Second Great Awakening	Individuals reform their lives through use of free will
Utopian communities	Perfect humankind by building perfect communities
Temperance movement	End abuses related to alcohol use
Prison and mental hospital reform	Improve conditions in prisons and build separate asylums
Public education	Public financing of education to strengthen democracy
Abolition	End slavery
Underground Railroad	Help slaves escape to freedom
Women's rights	Improve condition of women in society
Transcendentalism	Individuals seek divine within themselves

Vocabulary *Builder*

Key Terms

Complete each of the following sentences so that the second part further explains the first part and clearly shows your understanding of the key term.

1. The doctrine of free will was almost the exact opposite of predestination, the belief that _____.

2. People in the United States who wanted to end slavery were called abolitionists because they wanted to _____.

3. Women who wanted to _____ supported women's suffrage.

Comprehension and Critical Thinking

4. **(a) Describe** Describe two problems Dorothea Dix uncovered.
   (b) Apply Information What did she do to correct them?
   (c) Link Past and Present How do you think Dix's work benefits people today?

5. **(a) List** Give two reasons why Americans opposed slavery.
   (b) Compare and Contrast Compare how northern abolitionists and southern slaveholders viewed slavery.

6. **(a) Recall** Which rights were denied women in the early 1800s?
   (b) Draw Conclusions What rights did women gain as a result of the victories won in the struggle for equal rights in the 1800s?

History Reading Skill

7. **Draw Conclusions From Sources** Based on the following quotation, what conclusion can you draw about the writer's view regarding education? Explain how you reached this conclusion.

"Those who have been blessed with a good common-school education rise to a higher and higher point in the kinds of labor performed and also in the rate of wages paid, while the ignorant sink like dregs and are always found at the bottom."

—Annual Reports of the Secretary of the Board of Education of Massachusetts, 1839–1844

Writing

8. **Read the following poem by Frances Watkins Harper. Then, write a paragraph explaining how this poem is related to the spirit of change that swept the United States in the mid-1800s:**

"I ask no monument, proud and high,
To arrest the gaze of passers-by;
All that my yearning spirit craves,
Is bury me not in a land of slaves."

—Frances Watkins Harper,
"Bury Me in a Free Land"

9. **Write a Narrative:**
   You are a student in the 1850s. Your parents have taken you to a public meeting about temperance, abolition, or women's rights. Write a letter to a friend describing what you saw and heard at the meeting and how it made you feel. Use information from this chapter to create your description.

Skills for Life

Evaluate Summaries

Review Section 3, "A Call for Women's Rights." Then, look at the three summaries below and answer the questions that follow.

Summary A: The Seneca Falls Convention was a failure. American women failed to make any political or economic gains.

Summary B: The Seneca Falls Convention did not change American society overnight. Still, the convention marked the start of a long struggle for women's rights that eventually succeeded.

Summary C: The Seneca Falls Convention was a great success. Before long, many states gave women property rights and passed laws giving women suffrage.

10. What is the main idea of the section?

11. Which is the best summary of the section? Give three reasons for your answer.

Test Yourself

1. **The idea that God decides the fate of each person is called**

   A prohibition.

   B transcendentalism.

   C romanticism.

   D predestination.

2. **Frederick Douglass and William Lloyd Garrison were**

   A founders of the American Colonization Society.

   B leaders of the antislavery movement.

   C conductors on the Underground Railroad.

   D delegates to the Seneca Falls Convention.

Refer to the quotation below to answer Question 3.

> "Most of the luxuries, and many of the so-called comforts of life, are not only not indispensable, but positive hindrances to the elevation of mankind."

3. **The quotation above describes the core ideas of which American author?**

   A Herman Melville

   B Louisa May Alcott

   C Henry David Thoreau

   D James Fenimore Cooper

Document-Based Questions

Task: Look at Documents 1 and 2, and answer their accompanying questions. Then, use the documents and your knowledge of history to complete this writing assignment:

> Write a short essay about the Second Great Awakening. Include details about the emotional and moral impact of the movement.

Document 1: Charles Grandison Finney, a leading figure of the Second Great Awakening, conducted spellbinding revival meetings in many eastern cities. This excerpt is from Finney's Revival Lectures. *According to Finney, what role do revivals play in religion?*

> "Almost all the religion in the world has been produced by revivals. God has found it necessary to take advantage of the excitability there is in mankind, to produce powerful excitements among them, before he can lead them to obey. Men are so spiritually sluggish, there are so many things to lead their minds off from religion, and to oppose the influence of the Gospel, that it is necessary to raise an excitement among them, till the tide rises so high as to sweep away the opposing obstacles. They must be so excited that they will break over these counteracting influences, before they will obey God."

Document 2: Millions of American flocked to revival meetings, sometimes camping at the sites for several days. *Why were so many Americans attracted to the revival movement?*

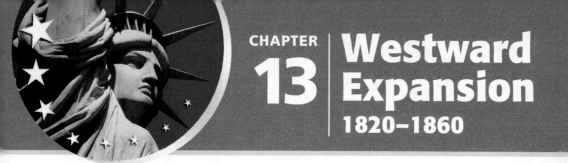

Chapter Preview

The Louisiana Purchase in 1803 had almost doubled the size of the nation. In the years that followed, Americans continued to push westward. New territories, settled by a diverse mix of people, were added to the nation. By 1853, the United States would stretch from coast to coast.

U.S. Events

1821
William Becknell opens Santa Fe Trail.

1830
Joseph Smith founds Mormon Church.

1836
Texas declares independence from Mexico.

1820

1830

1840

World Events

1821 Mexico wins independence from Spain.

1833 Santa Anna becomes president of Mexico.

In this painting, settlers traveling to the West by wagon train pause on their long journey.

1846
Mexican-American War begins.

1849
California gold rush begins.

1853
United States buys land from Mexico in Gadsden Purchase.

1840

1850

1851 Australian gold rush begins.

1860

1858 British government takes control of India.

History Reading Skill Frame Research Questions

What questions could you ask to learn more about the California gold rush?

In this chapter, you will learn how to frame, or ask, questions that can be answered through research. Read the following letter from Louise Amelia Clappe about her experiences as a gold miner in California in 1851. The side notes show you how to frame research questions.

Primary Source

> Nothing of importance has happened since I last wrote you, except that I have become a miner. I can truly say that I am sorry I "learned the trade," for I wet my feet, tore my dress, spoilt a pair of new gloves, nearly froze my fingers, got an awful headache, took cold, and lost a valuable pin in this, my labor of love.
>
> I myself thought . . . that one had but to stroll gracefully along romantic streamlets . . . and to stop now and then to . . . carelessly rinse out a small panful of yellow sand in order to fill one's work bag with the . . . precious mineral. Since I have been here, I have discovered my mistake. . . .
>
> . . . To be sure, there are now and then "lucky strikes." Once a person took $256 out of a single basinful of soil. But such luck is as rare as the winning of a $100,000 prize in a lottery. We are acquainted with many here whose gains have never amounted to much more than wages:—that is, from $6 to $8 a day.
>
> —Louise Amelia Clappe,
> letter of November 25, 1851

Build on a unique event: What happened to the few "lucky strikers"? How did their experience encourage the thousands of gold miners who came to the American West?

Build on the details: What problems did 19th century customs about women's dress present for miners?

Build on her beliefs: Why did miners believe that getting gold would be so easy? How did propaganda play a role in this mistaken belief?

Frame Research Questions

- Ask questions that explain details. These often require you to combine information from the text with information you have from other readings.
- Ask questions that explain attitudes. These often require you to make an inference from the text (figure out information that is not directly stated).
- Ask questions that explore individual situations and how they demonstrate beliefs, values, or other larger ideas.

- Use these question types to frame research questions that go beyond the text. Focus on larger issues, such as cause-effect or comparison of historical situations with present situations.

Document-Based Questions

1. When was this letter written?
2. What was the purpose of the letter?
3. How does Clappe's experience compare with that of immigrants to America today?

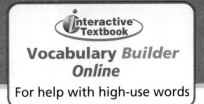

Interactive Textbook

Vocabulary *Builder* Online

For help with high-use words

Vocabulary *Builder*

Previewing High-Use Academic Words

High-Use Word	Definition	Sample History Sentence
manual (MAN yoo ahl) (Section 1, p. 444)	*adj.* done by using one's hands	Mining for gold required people to do a lot of <u>manual</u> labor.
distinct (dihs TIHNKT) (Section 1, p. 446)	*adj.* clear or definite; different in its quality	The Southwest had a <u>distinct</u> culture different from that of other parts of the country.
isolated (ī sah lay tehd) (Section 2, p. 449)	*adj.* set apart; separated	People living in remote parts of the West often led <u>isolated</u> lives.
hostile (HAHS tihl) (Section 2, p. 450)	*adj.* unfriendly; intending to do harm	Native Americans and new settlers from the East were sometimes <u>hostile</u> to one another.
levy (LEHV ee) (Section 3, p. 454)	*v.* to force to be paid	To protect local manufacturers, Congress <u>levied</u> a tax on imports.
provoke (prah VOHK) (Section 3, p. 457)	*v.* to cause to anger; to excite; to cause an action	Laws that forced Native Americans off their land <u>provoked</u> an angry response.
efficient (ee FISH ehnt) (Section 4, p. 463)	*adj.* done in a way that increases production with the least amount of waste	The cotton gin provided a more <u>efficient</u> way of processing cotton.
prospect (PRAHS pehkt) (Section 4, p. 464)	*n.* promise; something looked forward to	The <u>prospect</u> of owning good farmland attracted many settlers to the West.

Previewing Key Terms and People

frontier, p. 444
land grant, p. 446
ranchero, p. 446
expansion, p. 447
William Becknell, p. 448
John Jacob Astor, p. 448
mountain man, p. 449
rendezvous, p. 449

Marcus and Narcissa Whitman, p. 450
Stephen Austin, p. 454
dictatorship, p. 455
siege, p. 455
Sam Houston, p. 455
annex, p. 456
James K. Polk, p. 456

cede, p. 457
John C. Frémont, p. 457
Joseph Smith, p. 462
polygamy, p. 462
Brigham Young, p. 463
forty-niner, p. 464
water rights, p. 464
vigilante, p. 465

The West

Objectives

1. Identify the destinations of settlers heading west in the early 1800s.

2. Describe the unique culture of the Southwest.

3. Explain the meaning of Manifest Destiny.

Prepare to Read

Reading Skill

Ask Analytical Questions
Reading about historical events will often lead you to ask questions. When these questions are analytical—or require you to solve puzzles in the text to answer them—they can yield interesting research. Think about the *why* and *how* of history to help you ask questions about the text and then to frame possible research questions.

Vocabulary *Builder*

High-Use Words
manual, p. 444
distinct, p. 446

Key Terms
frontier, p. 444
land grant, p. 446
ranchero, p. 446
expansion, p. 447

⭐ **Background Knowledge** Since colonial times, settlers had been moving westward from the Atlantic coast toward the Appalachian Mountains. In this section, you will see how settlers in the early 1800s began to look even farther west.

What Was "The West"?

As the nation grew, Americans' idea of "the West" changed. Early Americans thought of the area between the Appalachians and the Mississippi River as the western frontier. A **frontier** is the land that forms the farthest extent of a nation's settled regions. By the 1820s, however, much of the land in this area had been settled. As the population soared, Americans began to look beyond the Mississippi River.

The Great Plains Stretching for seemingly endless miles to the west, the Great Plains lie between the Mississippi River and the Rocky Mountains. The Plains were easy to reach from eastern and southern states. However, settlers in the early 1800s were not attracted to this vast region. Farmers did not consider the land suitable for agriculture. The Plains were covered by grass that was anchored to the ground by deep root systems. Breaking up the dense sod would be hard <u>manual</u> labor.

For many settlers in the early 1800s, the Great Plains were simply a route to the Far West. Some were attracted to the area known as Oregon Country in the Northwest. Others were interested in the Mexican lands of the Southwest.

Main Idea
By the early 1800s, Americans thought of the area beyond the Great Plains as the western frontier.

Vocabulary *Builder*
<u>manual</u> (MAN yoo ahl) *adj.* done by using one's hands

The Northwest In the Northwest, settlers were attracted to the fertile land stretching from beyond the Rocky Mountains to the Pacific Ocean. This region is now occupied by the states of Oregon and Washington as well as by most of British Columbia in Canada. In the early 1800s, the United States, Great Britain, Russia, and Spain all claimed this land as their own.

The Southwest The Mexican settlements in the Southwest were another major destination for settlers heading west. This area, known as the Spanish Borderlands, was part of New Spain. Together with Mexico, these lands had been claimed for Spain in the 1500s.

The lands of the Southwest included present-day California, Utah, Nevada, Arizona, New Mexico, Texas, and about half of Colorado. Ruled first by Spain, then by Mexico, these lands had a culture and history very different from that of the eastern United States.

☑**Checkpoint** What did "the West" mean to Americans in the 1800s?

Ask Analytical Questions
What do you think were the land and climate features that attracted people to the Northwest? Suggest a possible research question to build on this topic.

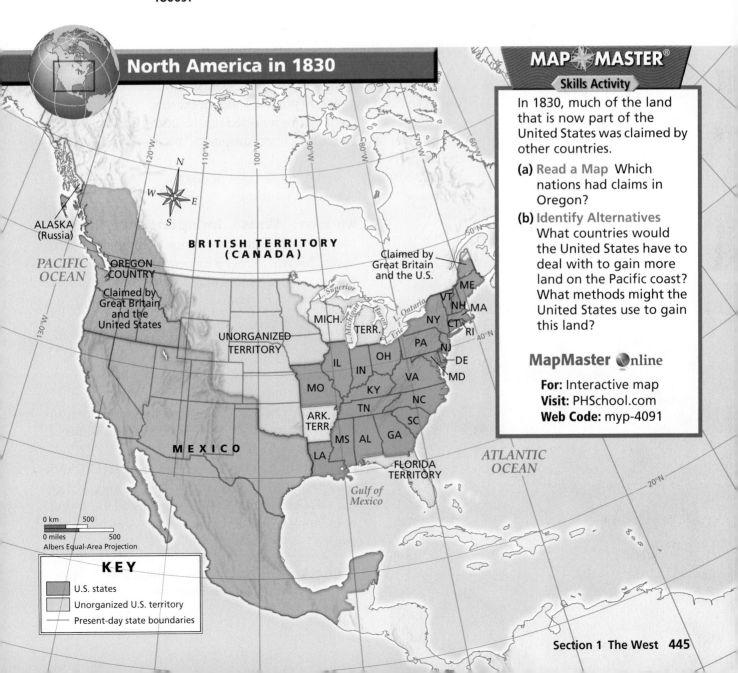

North America in 1830

ALASKA (Russia)

PACIFIC OCEAN

OREGON COUNTRY
Claimed by Great Britain and the United States

BRITISH TERRITORY (CANADA)

Claimed by Great Britain and the U.S.

UNORGANIZED TERRITORY

MICH. TERR.

L. Superior
L. Michigan
L. Huron
L. Ontario
L. Erie

ME.
VT NH MA
NY CT RI
PA NJ
DE
OH
IL IN
VA MD
MO KY
TN NC
ARK. TERR.
SC
MS AL GA
LA

MEXICO

FLORIDA TERRITORY

Gulf of Mexico

ATLANTIC OCEAN

0 km 500
0 miles 500
Albers Equal-Area Projection

KEY
- U.S. states
- Unorganized U.S. territory
- Present-day state boundaries

MAP MASTER®
Skills Activity

In 1830, much of the land that is now part of the United States was claimed by other countries.

(a) Read a Map Which nations had claims in Oregon?

(b) Identify Alternatives What countries would the United States have to deal with to gain more land on the Pacific coast? What methods might the United States use to gain this land?

MapMaster ●nline

For: Interactive map
Visit: PHSchool.com
Web Code: myp-4091

Mission in the Southwest

Old Spanish missions, like this one in California, still dot the Southwest. Native Americans were forced to live and work on the mission grounds, where Spanish priests taught them about Christianity. **Critical Thinking: Apply Information** *How were missions like these an example of cultural blending?*

Mexican Settlements

Like England and France, Spain followed a policy of mercantilism toward its colonies. It was illegal for settlers in New Spain to trade with other countries. Raw materials were sent to Spain. Manufactured goods were shipped to the Spanish colonies for sale.

Over the years, many Spanish settlers, or peninsulares, had children. These American-born children were called creoles. Spanish settlers, Native Americans, and Africans also intermarried. The result was another group, the mestizos. By the 1800s, this combination of ethnic groups had created a <u>distinct</u> Southwestern culture.

Native Americans Spanish missionaries, such as Junípero Serro (ho NEE peh roh SEHR rah) in California, were determined to convert Native Americans to Catholicism. Many Indians in the borderlands were forced to live and work at missions. There, they herded sheep and cattle and raised crops. They also learned about the Catholic religion. In the end, the mission system took a terrible toll on Native Americans. Thousands died from overwork or disease.

Spanish settlers and Native Americans exchanged language, foods, and customs. The Spanish brought their language, religion, and laws to the region. The Indians introduced the Spanish to such foods as beans, squash, and potatoes. Spanish settlers adopted Native American clothing, such as ponchos and moccasins.

Southwestern architecture reflected this blending of cultures. The general style of the buildings was European. However, Native American laborers brought their skills and cultural traditions. Churches and other buildings were made from adobe, or sun-dried brick, a traditional Native American building material.

Mexico Wins Independence In 1821, Mexico won its independence from Spain. Unlike Spain, Mexico allowed its people to trade with the many foreign ships that landed on its shores. Mexico also permitted overland trade with the United States.

Under Spanish rule, **land grants,** or government gifts of land, had been given only to a few peninsulares. Mexico, however, made many grants to individual **rancheros,** or owners of ranches. Mexico also removed the missions from church control and distributed mission lands to rancheros and a few American settlers.

Much of this land belonged to Native Americans. Indians often responded by raiding ranches, but they were soon crushed. By 1850, the Indian population in the Southwest had been drastically reduced.

✅**Checkpoint** **What groups shaped the culture of the Southwest?**

Manifest Destiny

From the beginning, Americans had been interested in westward **expansion,** or extending the nation beyond its existing borders. Thomas Jefferson was one of many who believed that the nation must increase in size to make room for its growing population. As you have read, under Jefferson, the Louisiana Purchase doubled the territory of the nation.

By the 1840s, many Americans strongly favored westward expansion. Newspaper editor John L. O'Sullivan wrote in 1845:

> **"**The American claim is by the right of our manifest [obvious] destiny to overspread and possess the whole of the continent which Providence has given us for the development of the great experiment of liberty and . . . self-government entrusted to us.**"**
>
> —John L. O'Sullivan, *United States Magazine and Democratic Review*

The phrase Manifest Destiny quickly became popular. It described the belief that the United States was destined, or meant, to extend from the Atlantic to the Pacific—"from sea to shining sea."

✔**Checkpoint** **What did Americans mean by Manifest Destiny?**

☆ **Looking Back and Ahead** The drive to achieve Manifest Destiny would become one of the most powerful forces shaping American history. In the next sections, you will see how Americans pursued the goal of Manifest Destiny.

Main Idea
Many Americans believed that the United States should extend to the Pacific Ocean.

Section 1 | Check Your Progress

Progress Monitoring Online
For: Self-test with instant help
Visit: PHSchool.com
Web Code: mya-4091

Comprehension and Critical Thinking

1. **(a) Recall** Why did American farmers prefer to settle in the Northwest rather than the Great Plains?
   (b) Evaluate Information How did the geography of the Great Plains affect U.S. settlement of that region in the early 1800s?

2. **(a) Explain** What is Manifest Destiny?
   (b) Detect Points of View How do you think the Mexican government felt about the idea of Manifest Destiny?

Reading Skill

3. **Ask Analytical Questions** Suggest a possible research question related to this topic: The effect of Native American labor on slavery in Mexican settlements.

Vocabulary *Builder*

Fill in the blanks with the correct key terms.

4. Each time Americans settled farther west, the _____ moved.

5. Under Spanish rule, only peninsulares received _____, but under Mexican rule, rancheros received them as well.

Writing

6. Decide which is the best closing sentence for an essay discussing why Americans were drawn to the lands west of the Mississippi River. Explain your choice.
   Sentences:
   (a) So for many Americans, the West was a promise—of wealth, adventure, and freedom.
   (b) The fertile lands of the Northwest drew many people who wanted to own farms.
   (c) Therefore, the southwestern lands ruled by Mexico had developed a culture very different from that of easterners.

2 | Trails to the West

Objectives

1. Explain how traders and fur trappers helped open the West.

2. List the reasons pioneers traveled along the Oregon Trail and describe the hardships they faced.

3. Discuss the issues for women, Native Americans, and new settlers in the West.

Prepare to Read

Reading Skill

Ask Inferential Questions You can also ask inferential questions to explore a text and generate research ideas. Inferential questions require you to read between the lines. In other words, you have to use clues in the text and your own knowledge to make reasonable guesses about history. You can then conduct research to confirm or disprove your guesses.

Vocabulary *Builder*

High-Use Words

isolated, p. 449
hostile, p. 450

Key Terms and People

William Becknell, p. 448
John Jacob Astor, p. 448
mountain man, p. 449
rendezvous, p. 449
Marcus and Narcissa Whitman, p. 450

Main Idea

Merchants and fur traders blazed important trails to both Oregon and the Southwest.

⭐ **Background Knowledge** As you know, the earliest Europeans who came to the Americas included merchants and Christian missionaries. As Americans moved westward in the 1800s, traders and missionaries continued to play an important role.

Traders Lead the Way

The first Americans to move into the Far West were traders. They were looking for new markets in which to sell their goods. In the process, they blazed important trails for the people who followed.

The Santa Fe Trail As you have read, when Mexico won independence, it began to allow overland trade with the United States. In 1821, Captain William Becknell led a wagon train filled with merchandise from Independence, Missouri, to Santa Fe, New Mexico. The route stretched for about 800 miles.

Becknell crossed treacherous rivers with bottoms of quicksand. He and the traders traveling with him barely survived the desert. Then, he had to find a way through nearly impassable mountains. In spite of these obstacles, Becknell's group reached Santa Fe with their wagons. Other Americans followed Becknell's route. It became known as the Santa Fe Trail. The Santa Fe Trail soon became a busy international trading route.

The Oregon Fur Trade Farther north, fur traders were making huge fortunes. John Jacob Astor, a German immigrant, sent the first American fur-trading expedition to Oregon. Astor established the American Fur Company in 1808 at Fort Astor, now Astoria, Oregon.

448 Chapter 13 Westward Expansion

Astor's expedition consisted of two groups. The first group sailed around South America and up the Pacific coast. The second group traveled across the continent, using information that had been recorded by Lewis and Clark. On the way, they found the South Pass through the Rocky Mountains. This important route helped to open the Northwest for the missionaries and settlers who followed.

Mountain Men The fur trade made Astor the richest man in the country. The trappers who supplied him with furs were also eager to become rich. These **mountain men,** or fur trappers of the Northwest, would become legendary.

For most of the year, trappers led <u>isolated</u>, dangerous lives. They endured bitter cold, intense heat, and attacks from wild animals. Jedediah Smith was once scalped by a grizzly bear. He persuaded a companion to sew his scalp back onto his head and to piece together his severed ear. Several weeks later, Smith returned to his work.

Once a year, trappers would bring their furs to a **rendezvous** (RAHN day voo), a meeting where the trappers would trade furs for supplies. Here, the mountain men would celebrate their time together—singing, laughing, and competing in contests. Then, they got down to serious bargaining. Beaver fur was in great demand in the East, so trappers were able to command high prices for their furs.

By the 1830s, the supply of beavers was nearly exhausted. Most trappers moved back east to become farmers, merchants, or even bankers. Others stayed as guides for the wagon trains that brought thousands of settlers west in the 1840s. One mountain man, an African American named James Beckwourth, discovered a pass through the Sierras that later became a major route to California.

☑**Checkpoint** **Why did the mountain men travel to Oregon?**

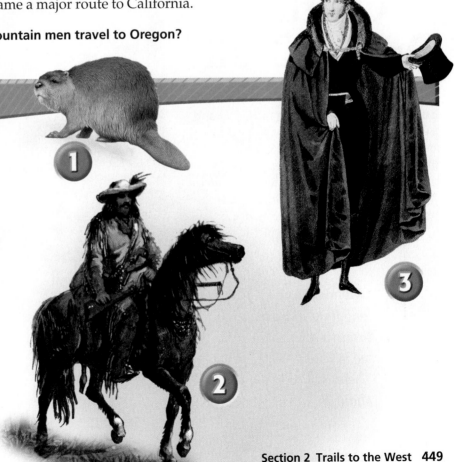

Links to Economics

The Oregon Fur Trade

What do the beaver (1), the mountain man (2), and the man in the fancy cloak (3) have in common? They were all part of the same economic process, called supply and demand. Fashions in the East created a demand for beaver fur, used in hats and fur-lined cloaks. Mountain men supplied the furs to meet the demand. **Critical Thinking: *Draw Conclusions*** *What other people were needed to complete the link between the mountain man and the man wearing the fur cloak?*

Main Idea
Thousands of men and women made the hazardous journey to Oregon.

Vocabulary *Builder*
<u>hostile</u> (HAHS tihl) *adj.* unfriendly; intending to do harm

The Oregon Trail

The first white easterners to build permanent homes in Oregon were missionaries. In the 1830s, they began to travel west for the purpose of bringing their religious beliefs to the Indians.

Missionaries One couple, Marcus and Narcissa Whitman, set up a mission in Oregon to serve the Cayuse Indians. The Whitmans had trouble from the start. The Cayuses mistrusted them, partly because the Whitmans made little effort to understand Cayuse ways.

As more settlers arrived and took over Indian lands, the Cayuses grew increasingly <u>hostile</u>. Then, in 1847, an epidemic of measles killed many Cayuse adults and nearly all their children. Blaming the Whitmans, the Indians killed them along with 12 other settlers.

Still, missionaries like the Whitmans greatly spurred settlement of the West. Their glowing reports of Oregon led more easterners to make the journey west. Farmers sought the free and fertile land, the mild climate, and the plentiful rainfall of the river valleys. Settlers from all over the country were in the grip of "Oregon Fever."

On the Oregon Trail Most settlers followed the Oregon Trail, a route that stretched more than 2,000 miles from Missouri to Oregon. They set out in spring and had to be in Oregon within five months. Travelers caught by winter in the Rockies risked a slow death. The trip itself was hazardous. Disease and accidents killed about one traveler out of every ten on the Oregon Trail.

On the Oregon Trail

To many easterners, Oregon held out the promise of fertile, available farmland and greater freedom. But first, they had to pack their belongings and set off on the long, difficult Oregon Trail. **Critical Thinking:** *Identify Costs and Benefits Do you think the benefits of moving to Oregon out- weighed the risks? Why or why not?*

▲ Covered wagons were designed to carry cargo, not passengers.

"*Monday June 13. This has been a long hard day's travel. Came 30 miles through sand and dust. . . . Tomorrow we will come to the first poison water. There will be no more good water for about 25 miles.*"

— diary of Mrs. Amelia Stewart Knight, 1853

Pioneers on the Oregon Trail banded together for mutual protection. Most traveled in long trains of covered wagons drawn by teams of horses or oxen. The wagons carried food and possessions, while the people walked. They traveled for up to 15 hours each day. At night, wagons were drawn up in a circle to keep the cattle from wandering.

As the miles went by, the horses and oxen tired more easily. People began to discard personal items to lighten their wagons. The trail was scattered with "leeverites," short for "leave 'er right here." There was so much debris that passersby would gather up wagonloads of flour, bacon—even cast-iron stoves!

Dust got into everything. Some people wore masks to keep it out of their faces and lungs. Clean, safe water was hard to find. Francis Parkman, a famous historian, observed the following incident:

> **"**I saw a tall slouching fellow . . . contemplating the contents of his tin cup, which he had just filled with water. 'Look here, you,' said he; 'it's chock full of animals!' The cup . . . exhibited in fact an extraordinary variety and profusion of animal life.**"**
>
> —Francis Parkman, *The Oregon Trail*

Despite such hardships, more than 50,000 people reached Oregon between 1840 and 1860.

✓**Checkpoint** Why did settlers travel by wagon train?

Ask Inferential Questions
Reading Skill Why do you think so many Americans were willing to face the hardships of westward settlement? Suggest a possible research topic to answer this question.

◀ Coffee grinder

Trunk carefully packed with dishware ▶

◀ Butter churn

451

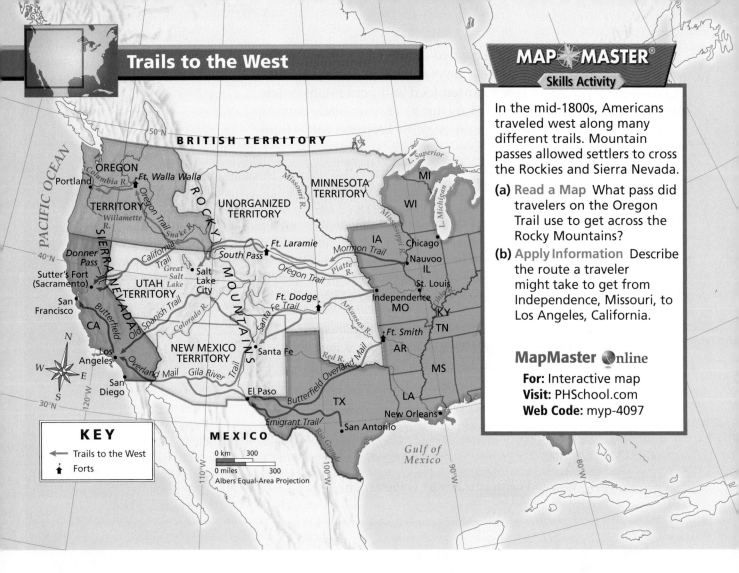

In the mid-1800s, Americans traveled west along many different trails. Mountain passes allowed settlers to cross the Rockies and Sierra Nevada.

(a) Read a Map What pass did travelers on the Oregon Trail use to get across the Rocky Mountains?

(b) Apply Information Describe the route a traveler might take to get from Independence, Missouri, to Los Angeles, California.

MapMaster Online

For: Interactive map
Visit: PHSchool.com
Web Code: myp-4097

KEY
← Trails to the West
↑ Forts

Life in the West

Main Idea
Women enjoyed new status in the West, but settlers faced conflicts with Native Americans already living on the land.

Pioneer life was filled with hardships. Settlers arrived with few possessions. Working only with hand tools, they had to clear the land, plant crops, and build shelters. Disease, accidents, and natural disasters like storms and floods were an ever-present threat.

A. H. Garrison was 15 years old when his family went west in 1846. He later recalled the hardships of their first winter in Oregon.

> "On Christmas day, it began to snow, and it continued until the ground was covered to a depth of twenty inches. . . . At the beginning of the storm, father had thirteen head of oxen, and twelve head of cows, and one fine American mare. There was no feed to be had, and the grass was so covered that the cattle could get nothing to eat. . . . When spring came, we had four oxen and three cows left."
>
> —*Reminiscences of A. H. Garrison*

Some settlers gave up and returned to the East. Others, like John Bidwell of California, met the challenges and went on to live extraordinary lives. Bidwell and his wife Annie each became civic leaders. Annie Bidwell later fought for the right of women to vote.

Women in the West Women in the West worked alongside men to make a success of their family farms. The fact that their labor was necessary for a family's survival raised the status of western women.

Meanwhile, as you have read, women in the East had begun to campaign for greater political and legal rights. Chief among these was the right to vote. On a national level, women's struggle for the vote would take many years. But the West was quicker to reward the hard work of its women. In 1869, the Wyoming Territory became the first area of the United States to grant women the vote.

Native Americans and Settlers Native Americans in Oregon lived in an uneasy peace with the white settlers. Indians in the southern part of Oregon usually got along with whites. In northern Oregon, however, Native Americans were angered by the presence of strangers on their lands.

The discovery of gold in northern Oregon in the 1850s brought large numbers of white and Chinese miners into the area. War broke out there in 1855. The miners killed several dozen Native American men. Three months later, miners massacred an equal number of Indian women, children, and old men.

The Indians fought back, killing white and Chinese alike. The brief war ended when the U.S. government intervened. The Native Americans were forced to accept peace treaties.

Woman harvesting hay on a western farm

✓**Checkpoint** **Why did women enjoy greater equality in the West than in the East?**

⭐ **Looking Back and Ahead** The Oregon and Santa Fe trails created close links between east and west. In the next section, you will see how western lands became part of the United States.

Section 2 | **Check Your Progress**

Progress Monitoring Online
For: Self-test with instant help
Visit: PHSchool.com
Web Code: mya-4092

Comprehension and Critical Thinking

1. **(a) Recall** Why did Americans go to Oregon in the early 1800s?
   (b) Analyze Cause and Effect What factors might have discouraged Americans from traveling to Oregon?

2. **(a) Explain** Why did conflict arise between Native Americans and settlers in Oregon?
   (b) Make Predictions Do you think such conflicts would be likely to continue later in the 1800s? Explain.

Reading Skill

3. **Ask Inferential Questions** Reread the text following the heading "The Oregon Fur Trade." What qualities were needed to be successful as a fur trapper in Oregon? Suggest a possible research question to take this topic further.

Vocabulary Builder

Read each sentence below. If the sentence is true, write YES and explain why. If the sentence is not true, write NO and explain why not.

4. Mountain men made their living by farming the Great Plains.

5. A trapper would often trade his furs for supplies at a rendezvous.

Writing

6. For each of these transitions (connecting words), write a sentence that expresses a cause-effect relationship about the topic in parentheses. **Transitions:**
   (a) *because* (Astor and the Oregon Trail)
   (b) *as a result* (the decline in the fur trade)
   (c) *therefore* (hardships on the Oregon Trail)

Conflict With Mexico

Objectives

1. Explain how Texas became independent from Mexico.

2. Discuss the issues involved in annexing Texas and Oregon.

3. Summarize the main events in the Mexican-American War.

4. Explain how the United States achieved Manifest Destiny.

Prepare to Read

Reading Skill

Ask Questions to Synthesize Information As you read history, recall what you already know about the topic. Consider as well what you know about related topics or experiences— even from modern times. Pull these many pieces of information together to ask and answer questions about the text. Then, use your questions to build research topics.

Vocabulary *Builder*

High-Use Words

levy, p. 454

provoke, p. 457

Key Terms and People

Stephen Austin, p. 454

dictatorship, p. 455

siege, p. 455

Sam Houston, p. 455

annex, p. 456

James K. Polk, p. 456

cede, p. 457

John C. Frémont, p. 457

⭐ **Background Knowledge** Mexico became independent in 1821. That year, American traders began to travel to the Southwest along the Santa Fe Trail. In this section, you will see how increasing tensions between the United States and Mexico led to war.

Texas Wins Independence

Main Idea
Conflicts with the Mexican government led American settlers in Texas to declare independence.

In 1820, the Spanish governor of Texas gave Moses Austin a land grant to establish a small colony in Texas. After Moses died, his son, Stephen Austin, led a group of some 300 Americans into Texas.

Soon after, Mexico won independence from Spain. The Mexican government agreed to honor Austin's claim to the land. In return, Austin and his colonists agreed to become Mexican citizens and to worship in the Roman Catholic Church.

Growing Conflict Thousands of Americans flooded into Texas. They soon came into conflict with the Mexican government. The new settlers were Protestant, not Catholic. Also, many of the settlers were slaveholders from the American South who wanted to grow cotton in Texas. However, Mexico had abolished slavery.

For a while, Mexico tolerated these violations of its laws. Then, in 1830, Mexico banned further American settlement. Still, Americans kept arriving in Texas. Tensions increased as Mexico tried to enforce its laws banning slavery and requiring settlers to worship in the Catholic Church. Mexico also began to levy heavy taxes on American imports.

Vocabulary *Builder*
levy (LEHV ee) *v.* to force to be paid

Declaring Independence American settlers wanted more representation in the Mexican legislature. Some Tejanos (teh HAH nos), Texans of Mexican descent, also hoped for a democratic government that gave less power to the central government.

These hopes were dashed in 1833 when General Antonio López de Santa Anna became president of Mexico. Santa Anna wanted a strong central government, with himself at the head. Soon after, Santa Anna overturned Mexico's democratic constitution and started a **dictatorship,** or one-person rule.

Austin urged Texans to revolt against the Mexican government. In 1836, Texans declared independence from Mexico and created the Republic of Texas.

Texans at War Santa Anna responded with force. His troops laid siege to the Alamo, a mission in San Antonio where about 185 Anglo-Americans and Tejanos were gathered. A **siege** is an attack in which one force surrounds a city or fort. The defenders of the Alamo held out for 12 days under heavy cannon fire. At last, Mexican forces overran the Alamo. All of the defenders were killed in battle or executed afterward. Inspired by the bravery of the Alamo defenders, many American volunteers joined the Texan army.

The following April, the commander of the Texan forces, **Sam Houston,** led a small army in a surprise attack against Santa Anna's army at San Jacinto. Texans shouted "Remember the Alamo!" Within 18 minutes, the Texans had captured Santa Anna. They forced him to sign a treaty recognizing Texan independence.

Discovery SCHOOL

Explore More Video
To learn more about the Texas War for Independence, view the video.

Siege at the Alamo For 12 days, a small group of Texans held off Mexican troops at the Alamo. This print from the 1800s is not an eyewitness portrayal, but it gives an idea of the odds against the defenders of the Alamo. **Critical Thinking: *Detect Points of View*** *Based on this print (right), why do you think many Americans admired the defenders of the Alamo?*

The Alamo today

Ask Questions to Synthesize Information Why was it important whether a new state was a slave state or a free state? Suggest a possible research topic building on this question.

Republic of Texas Sam Houston became president of the new Republic of Texas. He hoped that the United States would annex, or add on, Texas. But public opinion in the United States was divided. Southerners supported annexation of Texas as a slave state. Northerners opposed this, but still hoped for western expansion.

Presidents Andrew Jackson and Martin Van Buren refused to support annexation. Both feared that adding a slave state might spark a huge political fight that could split the Union.

☑**Checkpoint** Why did Texans want independence from Mexico?

Annexing Texas and Oregon

Main Idea
Americans elected a new President in 1844 who promised to expand the territory of the United States.

A decade after Texas won its independence, the annexation of Texas remained an unsettled question. It became a major issue in the presidential election of 1844.

Election of 1844 President John Tyler favored the annexation of Texas. But Tyler was not nominated for a second term. In 1844, the Whigs nominated Henry Clay instead.

Clay hoped to avoid the issue of annexation. But the Democratic candidate, James K. Polk, called for the annexation of both Texas and Oregon. At the time, Oregon was jointly held by Britain and the United States. Polk demanded that the British withdraw from all territory south of latitude 54°40'N. Polk, the candidate of expansion, won the election.

Annexation Shortly before Polk took office, Tyler asked Congress to annex Texas. Congress voted for admission of Texas as a state in 1845, three days before Tyler left office. A convention of Texan delegates quickly met and voted for annexation.

In keeping with his campaign promise, President Polk negotiated a treaty with Britain to divide Oregon. The United States got the lands south of latitude 49°N. Eventually, this territory became the states of Washington, Oregon, and part of Idaho.

Tensions With Mexico The annexation of Texas increased tensions with Mexico. Mexico had never formally recognized Texan independence. The treaty that Santa Anna had been forced to sign at San Jacinto set the southern boundary of Texas at the Rio Grande. The Mexican government claimed that the southern boundary of Texas was the Nueces River, farther to the north.

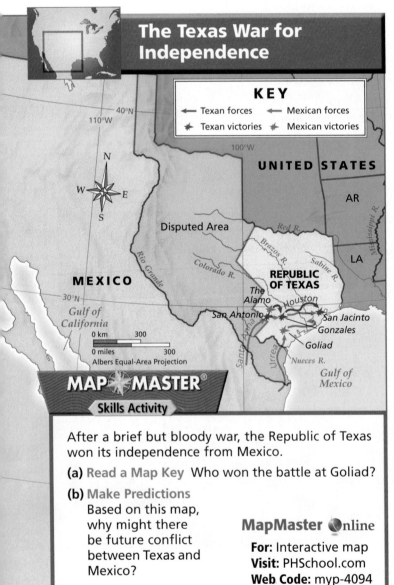

The Texas War for Independence

KEY
← Texan forces ← Mexican forces
✶ Texan victories ✶ Mexican victories

UNITED STATES

AR

Disputed Area

MEXICO

REPUBLIC OF TEXAS

The Alamo

San Antonio

San Jacinto
Gonzales
Goliad

Nueces R.

Gulf of California

0 km   300
0 miles   300
Albers Equal-Area Projection

Rio Grande
Colorado R.
Brazos R.
Red R.
Sabine R.
Mississippi R.
Houston

LA

Gulf of Mexico

MAP✶MASTER®
Skills Activity

After a brief but bloody war, the Republic of Texas won its independence from Mexico.

(a) Read a Map Key Who won the battle at Goliad?

(b) Make Predictions Based on this map, why might there be future conflict between Texas and Mexico?

MapMaster Online
For: Interactive map
Visit: PHSchool.com
Web Code: myp-4094

In fact, Texas had never controlled the area between the two rivers. But setting the Rio Grande as the border between Texas and Mexico would have given Texas much more land. President Polk put pressure on Mexico to accept this claim. Still, Mexico refused.

✔Checkpoint **How did the annexation of Texas increase tensions with Mexico?**

The Mexican-American War

Polk knew that the Mexican government needed cash. He offered money to settle the claim for the Rio Grande border. He also offered to purchase California and the rest of New Mexico. Outraged Mexicans refused the offer. They did not want to cede, or give up, more land to the United States.

Polk then changed his tactics. Hoping to provoke a Mexican attack on U.S. troops, he sent General Zachary Taylor south to the disputed land south of the Nueces. The Mexicans saw this as an act of war. After Mexican troops ambushed an American patrol on the disputed land, Polk asked Congress for a declaration of war. He claimed that Mexico had forced this war by shedding "American blood upon American soil."

Opposition to War Overall, the war with Mexico was very popular among Americans. Support for the war was strongest among southerners and westerners, who were willing to take up arms to gain more land.

Many northerners, however, argued that Polk had provoked the war. They scornfully referred to it as "Mr. Polk's war" and claimed that he was trying to extend slavery. Abraham Lincoln, a member of the House of Representatives from Illinois, pointed out that the land under dispute was not "American soil." He held that General Taylor's troops had invaded Mexico, not the other way around.

Rebellion in California Polk ordered troops under the command of Stephen Kearny to invade and capture Santa Fe, New Mexico. From there, Kearny was to lead his troops into California.

Even before Kearny's troops reached California, settlers near San Francisco had begun their own revolt against Mexico. Taking up arms, they raised a grizzly bear flag and declared California an independent republic. A bold young explorer, John C. Frémont, soon took command of the Bear Flag Rebellion. He moved to join forces with U.S. troops under the command of Kearny.

Main Idea
Expansionists favored war with Mexico, but some Americans disapproved.

Vocabulary *Builder*
provoke (prah VOHK) *v.* to cause to anger; to excite; to cause an action

Biography Quest

John C. Frémont
1813–1890

John C. Frémont changed Americans' view of the West. Frémont led several expeditions to explore the area. During one expedition, he helped to map out the Oregon Trail. For this, he became known as the Great Pathfinder.

It was Frémont's salesmanship that did the most to advance the cause of Manifest Destiny. His published accounts of his journeys excited people's interest in the vast, untapped riches of the Great Plains.

Biography Quest

How did Frémont become involved in the California rebellion?

For: The answer to the question about Frémont

Visit: PHSchool.com

Web Code: myd-4093

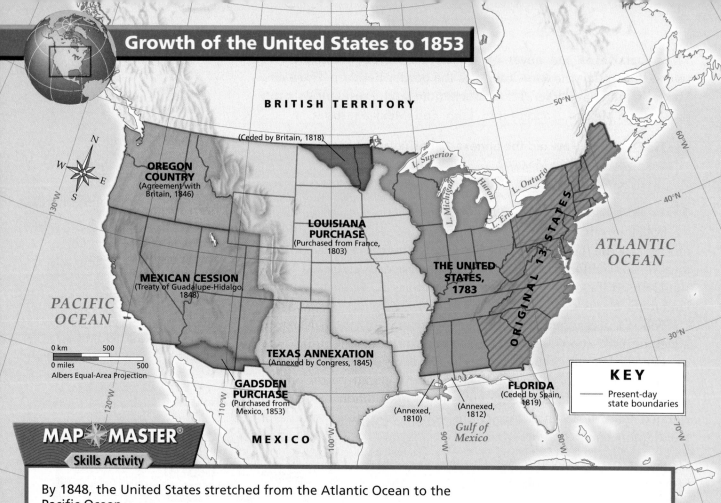

Growth of the United States to 1853

BRITISH TERRITORY

(Ceded by Britain, 1818)

OREGON COUNTRY
(Agreement with Britain, 1846)

LOUISIANA PURCHASE
(Purchased from France, 1803)

MEXICAN CESSION
(Treaty of Guadalupe-Hidalgo, 1848)

THE UNITED STATES, 1783

ORIGINAL 13 STATES

ATLANTIC OCEAN

PACIFIC OCEAN

0 km 500
0 miles 500
Albers Equal-Area Projection

TEXAS ANNEXATION
(Annexed by Congress, 1845)

GADSDEN PURCHASE
(Purchased from Mexico, 1853)

(Annexed, 1810)

(Annexed, 1812)

FLORIDA
(Ceded by Spain, 1819)

Gulf of Mexico

MEXICO

L. Superior
L. Michigan
L. Huron
L. Erie
L. Ontario

KEY
— Present-day state boundaries

N W E S

50°N
60°W
40°N
30°N
70°W
80°W
90°W
100°W
110°W
120°W
130°W

MAP MASTER
Skills Activity

By 1848, the United States stretched from the Atlantic Ocean to the Pacific Ocean.

(a) Read a Map What areas on the map did the United States own in 1853 that it did not own in 1830?

(b) Apply Information Look at a map of the present-day United States. When and how did your state become part of the United States?

MapMaster Online

For: Interactive map
Visit: PHSchool.com
Web Code: myp-4093

Mexico had very little military presence in California. Frémont's forces quickly captured Monterey and San Francisco. Meanwhile, General Kearny's troops captured Santa Fe and San Diego. There they united with naval units to occupy more of California. By early 1847, all of southern California was also under American control.

Invasion of Mexico Moving south from the Rio Grande, General Zachary Taylor captured the Mexican city of Monterrey. Santa Anna attacked Taylor at the Battle of Buena Vista. Though greatly outnumbered, Taylor's forces were better armed. Santa Anna retreated.

An American army under General Winfield Scott captured Veracruz, an important Mexican port. Scott then marched from Veracruz to Mexico City. Scott's army forced the Mexican army into the capital. Still, Santa Anna would not surrender.

Scott's campaign ended at Chapultepec, a stone palace above Mexico City. Like the Texans at the Alamo, the Mexicans fought bravely to defend Chapultepec. Most of them were killed. In Mexico, these young men are still honored for their bravery and patriotism.

After Mexico's defeat at Chapultepec, Santa Anna left Mexico City. The Mexican capital was now in American hands. The United States had won the war. (To learn more about the key battles in the Mexican-American War, see the Geography and History feature.)

☑ **Checkpoint** How did Polk's actions lead to war with Mexico?

Achieving Manifest Destiny

Polk sent a representative, Nicholas Trist, to help General Scott negotiate a treaty with the Mexican government. Despite many difficulties, Trist negotiated the Treaty of Guadalupe-Hidalgo, which was signed in 1848. It formally ended the Mexican-American War.

Under the treaty, Mexico recognized the annexation of Texas and ceded a vast territory to the United States. This territory, known as the Mexican Cession, included present-day California, Nevada, and Utah, as well as parts of Wyoming, Colorado, Arizona, and New Mexico. In return, the United States paid $18 million to Mexico.

In the Gadsden Purchase of 1853, the United States paid Mexico $10 million for a narrow strip of present-day Arizona and New Mexico. Manifest Destiny had been achieved.

☑ **Checkpoint** What was the Mexican Cession?

⭐ **Looking Back and Ahead** By 1853, the United States owned all the territory that would make up the first 48 states. Not until Alaska and Hawaii joined the Union in 1959 would any states outside this area be added.

Main Idea
As a result of the Mexican-American War, the United States gained a huge new territory.

| Section 3 | **Check Your Progress** |

Progress Monitoring ⬤nline
For: Self-test with instant help
Visit: PHSchool.com
Web Code: mya-4093

Comprehension and Critical Thinking

1. **(a) Recall** Why did the Republic of Texas hope the United States would annex Texas?
   (b) Analyze Cause and Effect How would the addition of Texas as a slave state affect the Union? Explain.

2. **(a) Recall** What did the United States gain as a result of the Mexican-American War?
   (b) Draw Conclusions How do you think the Mexican-American War affected the relationship between Mexico and the United States?

Reading Skill

3. **Ask Questions to Synthesize Information** Reread the text following the heading "Invasion of Mexico." Why might Santa Anna have been unwilling to surrender? Suggest a possible research topic to explore this question.

Vocabulary *Builder*

Complete each of the following sentences so that the second part clearly shows your understanding of the key term.

4. Many U.S. senators wanted to annex Texas, _____.

5. In Mexico, Santa Anna established a dictatorship, _____.

6. The Mexicans laid siege to the Alamo, _____.

Writing

7. Rewrite the following paragraph to eliminate sentence errors and improve sentence variety. **Paragraph:** Conflict between Mexicans and Anglo-Americans. There was a difference in religion. Mexicans were Catholics. Many Anglo-Americans Protestants. Mexico had outlawed slavery. but many Anglo-Americans owned slaves. This also created problems. Mexico began to tax American imports. Hostilities finally broke out. When Santa Anna attacked the Alamo.

The Mexican-American War

By 1846, the United States and Mexico stood on the brink of war. Mexicans were furious at the American annexation of Texas the year before. Americans felt that Mexico stood in the way of Manifest Destiny. After a border dispute erupted in hostilities, U.S. troops attacked Mexico on two fronts in order to achieve quick victory.

History *Interactive*

Learn More About the Mexican-American War

Visit: PHSchool.com
Web Code: myp-4095

▶ U.S. soldier at the Battle of Buena Vista

War on Land

American forces invaded Mexico in two directions. John C. Frémont and Stephen Kearny moved west from Fort Leavenworth ❶ to take control of California. They were aided by a revolt of American settlers near San Francisco. Zachary Taylor marched south across the Rio Grande and defeated a large Mexican force at Buena Vista ❷ .

▶ Rebel American settlers declared California a new nation—the Bear Flag Republic.

War at Sea

The U.S. Navy blockaded Mexico's east and west coasts. American sailors helped secure California ❸ while another fleet in the Gulf of Mexico supported the assault at Veracruz ❹. Winfield Scott won a last battle against Mexican soldiers at the Battle of Chapultepec.

The War's Final Days

By the time of General Scott's victory outside Mexico City, U.S. forces had surrounded the Mexican capital. The northern territories of California and New Mexico were under Frémont's and Kearny's control, and Taylor had moved south to press for attack. With the loss of Mexico City, the Mexican government moved to make peace.

WAR AT SEA

KEY
⟵ UNITED STATES FORCES ⟵ MEXICAN FORCES
✦ UNITED STATES VICTORY

UNITED STATES

SAN FRANCISCO
MONTEREY
❸
LOS ANGELES
SAN DIEGO
STOCKTON
SLOAT
Pacific Ocean

MO
TN
AR
MS AL
TEXAS LA
Rio Grande
Nueces R.
DISPUTED AREA

MEXICO
NEW ORLEANS
SCOTT
Gulf of Mexico
❹
SCOTT

MAZATLAN
MEXICO CITY
CHAPULTEPEC
SANTA ANNA
VERACRUZ

0   250   500 MILES
0   250   500 KILOMETERS

◀ The shako cap—topped with a tall plume of feathers—was part of the American uniform during the war.

Analyze **GEOGRAPHY AND HISTORY**

Select a key battle from the Mexican-American War, and write a journal entry about it from a U.S. soldier's point of view.

▲ U.S. Navy ships guard the American landing at Veracruz.

A Rush to the West

Objectives

1. Explain why the Mormons settled in Utah and the issues that divided Mormons and the federal government.

2. Discuss the effects of the 1849 California gold rush.

3. Describe how California's population had changed by 1850.

Prepare to Read

Reading Skill

Ask Questions That Go Beyond the Text Research questions should build on the information you learn in your textbook. Use the many strategies you practiced in Sections 1–3 to build questions that link the text topic to larger issues. For example, you might look at how history fits with modern situations or why the people of history made the decisions they made. Check yourself to be sure that your questions cannot be answered with *yes* or *no*.

Vocabulary *Builder*

High-Use Words

efficient, p. 463

prospect, p. 464

Key Terms and People

Joseph Smith, p. 462

polygamy, p. 462

Brigham Young, p. 463

forty-niner, p. 464

water rights, p. 464

vigilante, p. 465

☆ Background Knowledge You have seen that, as a result of the war with Mexico, the United States gained the lands known as the Mexican Cession. In this section, you will see why large numbers of Americans began to settle in this vast region.

Main Idea
The Mormons journeyed westward seeking a safe place to practice their religion.

Mormons Settle Utah

Even before the end of the war, a group of Americans had begun moving into the part of the Mexican Cession that is today Utah. These were the Mormons, members of the Church of Jesus Christ of Latter-day Saints. The church was founded in 1830 by Joseph Smith, a New York farmer. Smith said that heavenly visions had revealed to him the text of a holy book called the *Book of Mormon*.

Seeking Refuge The Mormon Church grew quickly, but some of its teachings often placed its followers in conflict with their neighbors. For example, Mormons at first believed that property should be held in common. Smith also favored polygamy, the practice of having more than one wife at a time.

Hostile communities forced the Mormons to move from New York to Ohio and then to Missouri. By 1844, the Mormons had settled in Nauvoo, Illinois. There, Joseph Smith was murdered by an angry mob.

Brigham Young, the new Mormon leader, realized that Nauvoo was no longer safe. He had heard about a great valley in the Utah desert, which at the time was still owned by Mexico. In 1847, he led a party of Mormons on a long, hazardous journey to the valley of the Great Salt Lake. Over the next few years, some 15,000 Mormon men, women, and children made the trek to Utah.

Although Utah was a safe refuge, the land was not hospitable. Farming was difficult in the dry desert. Then, in the summer of 1849, enormous swarms of crickets nearly destroyed the Mormons' first harvest. But a flock of seagulls flew in from the Pacific and devoured the crickets. The Mormons then set out to make the desert bloom. Under strict church supervision, they enclosed and distributed farmland and set up an <u>efficient</u> system of irrigation.

Vocabulary *Builder*
efficient (ee FISH ehnt) *adj.* done in a way that increases production with the least amount of waste

Conflict With the Government
In 1848, as a result of the Mexican Cession, Utah became part of the United States. Congress then created the Utah Territory. Mormon leaders immediately came into conflict with officials appointed to govern the territory.

Three issues divided the Mormons and the federal government. First, the Mormon Church controlled the election process in the Utah Territory. Non-Mormons had no say. Second, the church supported businesses that were owned by Mormons. "Outsiders" had difficulty doing business. The third issue was polygamy, which was illegal in the rest of the country.

These issues were not resolved for more than 40 years. In time, Congress passed a law that took control of elections away from the Mormon Church. Church leaders agreed to ban polygamy and to stop favoring Mormon-owned businesses. Finally, in 1896, Utah became a state.

Mormons Come to Utah
Brigham Young (below) led the first wave of Mormons to migrate to Utah. In later years, settlers continued to arrive. Some, like those shown in the painting, were so poor they had to haul their belongings along the Mormon Trail by hand. **Critical Thinking:** *Identify Benefits Identify two benefits these Mormons might look forward to from settling in Utah.*

☑**Checkpoint** **Why did the Mormons leave Illinois?**

The California Gold Rush

When California was ceded to the United States in 1848, about 10,000 Californios, or Mexican Californians, were living in the territory. A handful of wealthy families owned most of the land. They lived an elegant, aristocratic life. Their ranches were worked by poorer Californios or by Native Americans.

After the Mexican Cession, easterners began to migrate to California. The wealthy Californios looked down on the newcomers from the East, and the newcomers felt contempt for the Californios. The two groups rarely mixed or intermarried.

Gold Is Discovered An event in January 1848 would bring a flood of other settlers to California. James Marshall was building a sawmill on John Sutter's land near Sacramento. One morning, he found a small gold nugget in a ditch. Sutter tried to keep his discovery a secret. But the news spread like wildfire throughout the country and abroad. By 1849, the California gold rush had begun.

The <u>prospect</u> of finding gold attracted about 80,000 fortune seekers. The nickname **"forty-niners"** was given to these people who came to California in search of gold. In just two years, the population of California zoomed from 14,000 to 100,000.

Sutter's Mill was just the beginning. Prospectors, or gold seekers, searched throughout the Sacramento Valley for gold. They dug into the land using picks and shovels. They also looked in streams. This process, called placer mining, did not take much labor, money, or skill. Miners washed dirt from a stream in a pan, leaving grains of gold in the bottom. Finding gold was called "hitting pay dirt."

Gold above ground was quickly found. But there was more gold in underground deposits, or lodes. Gold in lodes was difficult and expensive to mine. It required heavy and expensive machinery. As a result, large companies took over the mining of underground lodes.

Water Rights In the gold fields, disputes over water rights were common. **Water rights** are the legal rights to use the water in a river, stream, or other body. California has an abundance of land, but much of it is desert. Settlers needed water for irrigation and mining.

California had kept older Mexican laws regarding water rights. Landowners had the right to use the water that flowed through their land. At the same time, it was illegal to cut off water to one's neighbors. In most gold rush territories, though, the law was ignored. The first people to reach a stream used as much water as they wanted—sometimes even the whole stream! Disputes over water rights often erupted into violence.

Life in Mining Towns Mining towns were not very permanent places. Most sprang up overnight and emptied just as quickly when miners heard news of a gold strike in another place.

Mining towns attracted both miners and people hoping to make money from miners. Miners were often willing to pay high prices for food and supplies. They also needed entertainment. A typical mining town was made up of a row of businesses with a saloon at its center.

Panning for Gold
Forty-niners, like the man in this picture, spent many back-breaking hours sifting through sand at the edge of the river. If they were lucky, their reward was a glimmer of gold in their pan. **Critical Thinking: *Apply Information*** *Based on your reading, what method of gold mining did this prospector use?*

California was not yet a state, so federal law did not apply within the mining towns. To impose some order, miners banded together and created their own rules. Punishment for crimes was often quick and brutal. **Vigilantes,** or self-appointed law enforcers, punished people for crimes, though they had no legal right to do so.

Role of Women Gold rushes were not like other migrations in American history. Most migrations included men and women, young and old. Most forty-niners, however, were young men. By 1850, the ratio of men to women in California was twelve to one!

Still, some women did come to California in search of fortune, work, or adventure. Unlike other areas of the country, California offered women profitable work. Some women mined, but many more stayed in town. They worked in or ran boardinghouses, hotels, restaurants, laundries, and stores.

Drifting and Settling Few forty-niners struck it rich. After the gold rush ended, many people continued to search for gold throughout the West. There were gold or silver strikes in British Columbia, Idaho, Montana, Colorado, Arizona, and Nevada. Other miners gave up the drifting life and settled in the West for good.

✅ **Checkpoint** **Why were water rights an important issue?**

Links Across Time

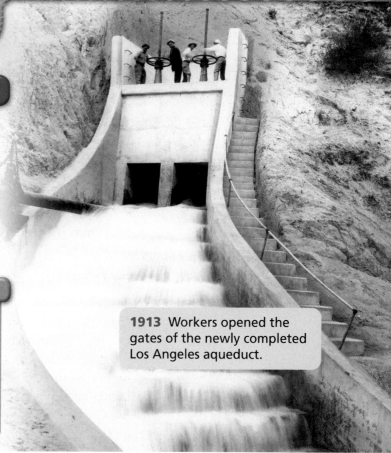

Water Rights in the West

1849 During the gold rush, California law generally gave water rights to the first person to make use of a body of water.

1905 Los Angeles, still a small city, won rights to the Owens River, 200 miles away. Engineers later built aqueducts and dams to carry the water to the city. This water helped Los Angeles grow rapidly. But ranchers and farmers in the Owens Valley protested the loss of their water rights.

Link to Today Online

Connection to Today Water rights remain an issue in many areas of the nation today. Farms and communities still compete to win access to clean, available water.

For: Water rights in the news
Visit: PHSchool.com
Web Code: myc-4094

1913 Workers opened the gates of the newly completed Los Angeles aqueduct.

San Francisco During the Gold Rush

This painting shows San Francisco in the 1850s. "Where there was a vacant piece of ground one day," wrote one witness, "the next saw it covered with half a dozen tents or shanties." **Critical Thinking:** *Distinguish Relevant Information* *What information in this picture supports the conclusion that San Francisco had a diverse population?*

Main Idea
The gold rush permanently altered the makeup of California's population.

California's Changing Population

Many gold rush towns were temporary, but some grew and prospered. San Francisco had only 200 inhabitants in 1848. During the gold rush, immigrants who sailed to California passed through San Francisco's harbor. Its merchants provided miners with goods and services. Many newcomers remained in the city. Others returned to settle there after working in the mines. By 1870, San Francisco had a population of more than 100,000.

An Unusual Mix of People The gold rush brought enormous ethnic diversity to California. People came from Europe, Asia, Australia, and South America. By 1860, the population of California was almost 40 percent foreign-born.

European immigrants often enjoyed more freedom in California than in Europe. They also faced less prejudice than in the East. In some ways, mining societies were more democratic, as men in the gold fields had to rely on one another. One immigrant wrote home:

> **"**We live a free life, and the best thing . . . is that no human being here sets himself up as your lord and master. It is true that we do not have many of the luxuries of life, but I do not miss them.**"**
>
> —quoted in *Land of Their Choice* (Blegen)

Chinese Immigrants China's economy was in trouble in the 1840s. After news reached China of a "mountain of gold," about 45,000 Chinese men went to California. Most hoped to return home to China with enough money to take care of their families.

Chinese laborers faced prejudice. They generally were not given higher-paying jobs in the mines. Instead, they were hired to do menial labor. Some cooked or did laundry. Despite many difficulties, the Chinese worked hard. They helped build railroads and worked on farms. Their labor also helped cities like San Francisco to prosper.

African Americans Several thousand free African Americans lived in California by 1850. They had their own churches and newspapers. Many ran their own businesses. However, they did not have equal rights. They could not vote or serve on juries.

Slavery did not take root in California. Some southerners did bring their slaves with them during the gold rush. However, the other miners objected. They believed that anyone who profited from mining should participate in the hard labor of finding gold.

Native Americans For Native Americans, the gold rush brought even more tragedy. Miners swarmed onto Indian lands to search for gold. Vigilante gangs killed Indians and stole their land. About 100,000 Indians, nearly two thirds of the Native American population of California, died during the gold rush.

Impact on Californios By 1850, only 15 percent of Californians were Mexican. The old ruling families did not have a strong say in the new territorial government. When a constitutional convention was held, only 8 of the 48 delegates were Californios.

Californio politicians could not stop the passage of laws that discriminated against their people. The legislature levied a high tax on ranches and required rancheros to prove that they owned their land. This was often difficult, because most had received their land grants from Spain or Mexico. By the time many Californios could prove ownership, they had had to sell their land to pay legal bills.

☑**Checkpoint** What effects did the gold rush have on Californios?

⭐ **Looking Back and Ahead** California had enough people by 1850 to apply for admission to the Union as a free state. As you will read in the next chapter, California's request for statehood would cause a national crisis.

Ask Questions That Go Beyond the Text Ask a question that explores beyond the text and requires research to answer. You might focus on the ways that the lives of Mexicans in California changed after the gold rush.

Section 4 | **Check Your Progress**

Progress Monitoring Online
For: Self-test with instant help
Visit: PHSchool.com
Web Code: mya-4094

Comprehension and Critical Thinking

1. **(a) Recall** Why did the Mormons decide to move to Utah?
   (b) Identify Alternatives What other options might the Mormons have considered?

2. **(a) List** Which groups migrated to California after 1848?
   (b) Make Inferences Which groups benefited most from the discovery of gold? Which groups suffered most? Explain.

Reading Skill

3. **Ask Questions That Go Beyond the Text** Recall what you just read about California during the gold rush. Ask a question that goes beyond the text and requires research to answer.

Vocabulary *Builder*

4. Write two definitions of the term water rights. First, write a formal definition for your teacher. Second, write a definition in everyday English for a classmate.

Writing

5. Write a short paragraph explaining what happened as a result of the California gold rush in 1849. Then, exchange paragraphs with another student. Check your partner's work for errors. Work together to take the best elements from each paragraph and to create a new version.

Historical evidence comes from many sources. Evaluating the validity of written sources is important in putting together a picture of the past.

The following journal entries, written by Elizabeth Wood, describe portions of her two-and-a-half-month journey from Fort Laramie, Wyoming, to eastern Oregon in 1851.

Primary Source

"July 25. Since last date we camped at the ford where emigrants cross from the south to the north side of the Platte. . . . We stopped near the Red Buttes, where the hills are of a red color, nearly square and have the appearance of houses with flat roofs. . . . We also passed Independence Rock and the Devil's Gate, which is high enough to make one's head swim, and the posts reach an altitude of some 4 or 500 feet."

"Monday, September 15th. . . . Mount St. Elias is in the distance, and is covered with snow, so you can imagine somewhat the beauty and grandeur of the scene. We are now among the tribe of Wallawalla Indians."

—Journal of a Trip to Oregon, Elizabeth Wood

Learn the Skill
Use these steps to evaluate written sources.

1. **Identify the source.** Knowing who the writer is helps you to evaluate that person's account of events.

2. **Note the context.** When was the account written? In what form did it appear? What was the purpose of the account?

3. **Analyze the point of view.** What is the writer trying to say? How does the writer feel about the subject?

4. **Evaluate the validity of the material.** How true is this account? Why do you think so?

Practice the Skill
Answer the following questions to evaluate the source on this page.

1. **Identify the source.** Who wrote these journal entries?

2. **Note the context.** (a) When were these entries written? (b) What was their purpose?

3. **Analyze the point of view.** (a) How does the writer feel about the journey? (b) What words or phrases express the writer's feelings?

4. **Evaluate the validity of the material.** Do you think this journal entry accurately describes the journey west? Why or why not?

Apply the Skill
See the Review and Assessment at the end of this chapter.

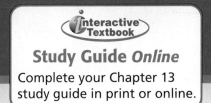

Chapter Summary

Section 1
The West

- By the 1820s, land-hungry Americans often had to look west of the Mississippi River for territory to settle.
- Some Americans moved to the Mexican-controlled lands of the Southwest.
- Manifest Destiny was the idea that the United States had the right to "spread and possess the whole of the continent."

Section 2
Trails to the West

- Traders and trappers helped open the West for settlement.
- Free land and the mild climate attracted settlers from all parts of the United States to Oregon.

Section 3
Conflict With Mexico

- American settlers in Texas rebelled against Mexico and created the independent Republic of Texas.
- American forces defeated Mexican troops in what became known as the Mexican-American War.
- The United States gained vast new territories as a result of the Treaty of Guadalupe-Hidalgo.

Section 4
A Rush to the West

- The Mormons moved west to Utah for religious freedom.
- Gold fever brought thousands of immigrants to California.

Key Concepts

These notes will help you prepare for questions about key concepts.

U.S. Territorial Acquisitions in the West

Oregon
- Also claimed by Britain
- Region divided by agreement with Britain, 1846

Texas
- Won independence from Mexico in 1836; became independent republic
- Annexed by Congress, 1845

Mexican Cession
- Acquired from Mexico after Mexican-American War, 1848
- Included California, Utah, most of Southwest

Gadsden Purchase
- Purchased from Mexico, 1853
- Small portion of southern Arizona and New Mexico

Key Groups That Settled the American West

- Traders—first Americans to move to the West
- Trappers—made their living in the fur trade
- Missionaries—came west to convert Native Americans
- Farmers—attracted to the West by land
- Mormons—moved west for religious freedom
- Forty-niners—flocked to California to hunt for gold

Vocabulary *Builder*

Key Terms

Answer the following questions in complete sentences that show your understanding of the key terms.

1. Why did settlers in California argue over water rights?

2. What did rancheros own?

3. How did wealthy families benefit from land grants?

4. To what did General Santa Anna lay siege in San Antonio during the war for Texas independence?

Comprehension and Critical Thinking

5. **(a) Identify** Who were the peninsulares, the creoles, and the mestizos?
   (b) Draw Inferences Which of these groups were most likely to support Mexican independence from Spain? Why?

6. **(a) Recall** What was Manifest Destiny?
   (b) Identify Economic Benefits What economic benefits could the United States get from following the ideals of Manifest Destiny?

7. **(a) Describe** Describe the life of a mountain man like the one pictured at right.
   (b) Draw Inferences How did these men contribute to the goal of Manifest Destiny?

Mountain man

8. **(a) Explain** What did President James Polk do to bring about Manifest Destiny?
   (b) Draw Conclusions How did Great Britain threaten Manifest Destiny?

9. **(a) Recall** Why did the Mormons immigrate to Utah?
   (b) Compare What other groups in earlier American history came to North America for similar reasons?

10. **(a) Identify** Who were the forty-niners?
    (b) Analyze Cause and Effect How did the forty-niners contribute to California becoming a state?

History Reading Skill

11. **Frame Research Questions** Frame a research question about any aspect of this chapter. Start by reviewing headings and choosing one that interests you. Remember to frame questions that go beyond the text and require research to answer.

Writing

12. **Write two paragraphs discussing the results of the Mexican-American War.** Then, exchange papers with another student.
    As you look at your partner's paragraphs, you should:
    - correct every error you can find;
    - look for places to add transitions to make the sentences flow better and to connect the two paragraphs;
    - find opportunities to mix short and long sentences.

13. **Write a Narrative:**
    You are an easterner in the 1840s trying to decide whether to go to Oregon, Utah, or California. Write a diary entry in which you weigh the possible costs and benefits of such a trip and reach a final decision.

Skills for Life

Evaluate Written Sources

Use the diary entry below to answer the questions.

> "Tuesday May 20th. Travelled 20 miles and camped . . . saw several antelope, and an animal called prairie dogs, which resemble a puppy. There are acres of them . . . they plough the ground up and form little knolls all over the ground. . . ."
>
> —Journal of Travels to Oregon, Amelia Hadley, 1851

14. Who wrote this journal entry?

15. When was it written?

16. How does the writer feel about the journey?

17. Do you think this journal entry accurately describes prairie wildlife? Why or why not?

Test Yourself

1. Which of the following most directly led to achieving Manifest Destiny?

A Women vote in the West.

B Mormons settle Utah.

C Santa Anna establishes dictatorship in Mexico.

D President Polk negotiates a treaty with Great Britain to divide Oregon.

Refer to the quotation below to answer Question 2.

> "I am determined to sustain myself as long as possible and die like a soldier, who never forgets what is due to his honor and that of his country. Victory or Death!"

2. The person who made this statement was mostly likely

A at the Alamo.

B at a rendezvous.

C at John Sutter's sawmill.

D on the Oregon Trail.

Refer to the map below to answer Question 3.

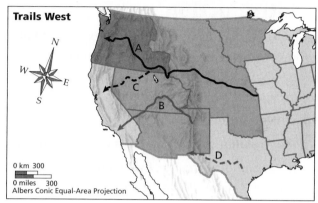

Trails West

0 km 300
0 miles 300
Albers Conic Equal-Area Projection

3. Which of the trails marked on the map led the forty-niners to their final destination?

A trail A

B trail B

C trail C

D trail D

Document-Based Questions

Task: Look at Documents 1 and 2, and answer their accompanying questions. Then, use the documents and your knowledge of history to complete this writing assignment:

> List the reasons for and against the Mexican-American War. Then, write a short essay analyzing the arguments of each side. Draw a conclusion about the validity of each argument.

Document 1: In 1846, President Polk asked Congress to declare war against Mexico. *What does Polk accuse Mexico of doing?*

> "The grievous wrongs perpetrated by Mexico upon our citizens throughout a long period of years remains unredressed. . . . We have tried every effort of reconciliation. . . . But now . . . Mexico has passed the boundary of the United States, has invaded our territory and shed American blood upon the American soil. . . .
>
> . . . I involve the prompt action of Congress to recognize the existence of the war, and to place at the disposition of the Executive the means of prosecuting the war with vigor, and thus hastening the restoration of peace."

Document 2: Abraham Lincoln, then a member of Congress, spoke out against the Mexican-American War. *How does Lincoln challenge Polk's reasons for war with Mexico?*

> "I carefully examined the President's messages. . . . The result of this examination was to make the impression that . . . he falls far short of proving his justification [for the war]. . . . The President . . . declares that the soil was ours on which hostilities were commenced by Mexico. . . .
>
> Let [the President] remember he sits where Washington sat, and so remembering, let him answer as Washington would answer. . . . And if, so answering, he can show that the soil was ours, where the first blood of the war was shed, . . . then I am with him. . . . But if he can not do this . . . then I shall be fully convinced . . . that he is deeply conscious of being in the wrong."

Writing Workshop

Expository Essay
Multiple Causes or Effects

▶ Introduction

In a cause-effect essay, you either explain what caused an event to happen or describe the effects of an event. Most important events in history have several causes and several effects. An essay analyzing multiple causes or effects should have the following characteristics:

- an event or development that has several causes or effects
- a thesis statement that makes a point about these causes or effects
- supporting information that shows how the causes or effects are related to the development (and often to each other)

Assignment   On the following pages, you will learn how to write an essay analyzing multiple causes or effects. You will get step-by-step instructions. Each step will include an example from a sample essay discussing the gold rush.

Read the instructions and the examples. Then, follow each step to plan and write a 500–700 word essay.

> **Write an essay analyzing either the causes or the effects of the antislavery movement.**

▶ Prewriting

Define your subject and brainstorm about its causes and effects. Begin by thinking about the central historical event or development about which you are going to write. Brainstorm about causes or effects using the following guidelines:

If you can choose whether to write about *causes* or *effects*	Decide which seems more interesting or complex. If a development has only one principal cause, it would make more sense to write about its effects.
If you are asked to focus on the *causes* of a historical event	Try to go back as far as you can to find the earliest factors leading to the event. List the various causes in chronological order. See if any of the causes have caused one another, and draw arrows showing these connections.
If you are asked to focus on the *effects* of a historical event	See if any effects can still be felt today. If some of the effects are connected, with one result leading to another, draw arrows between them. Be specific: What seems to be a single effect may turn out to be several different effects.

For a review of the steps in the writing process, see the **Historian's Toolkit**, *Write Like a Historian.*

Decide on the major causes or effects to analyze. Now you need to decide which causes or effects you will actually write about. You can choose from several different approaches.

- Analyze causes or effects that are related to one another in a chain, each one leading to the next.
- Examine in depth two or three most important causes or effects of the historical development.
- Discuss the kinds of causes or effects involved. For example, you could look at the economic, social, and cultural causes or effects.

Write a thesis statement. Once you have chosen the causes or effects you will discuss, you are ready to write a thesis statement expressing an idea about these causes or effects.

> **Sample thesis statement:**
> The California gold rush of 1849 had a number of social, political, economic, and cultural effects on the history of California.

▶ Drafting

Decide how to organize your writing. Essays analyzing causes and effects may be organized chronologically, by order of importance, or according to types of causes or effects.

- **Chronological organization** You could organize a cause-effect essay chronologically, moving from earlier events to later ones.

- **Order of importance** You could also organize your causes or effects by order of importance, saving the most important one for last.

- **Types** You might organize your analysis according to types of causes or effects. For example, in discussing the gold rush, you might look first at the population changes that occurred as thousands of settlers moved to California. Then you could discuss the economic changes and, finally, the cultural changes.

Write an introduction. The first paragraph of your essay introduces your subject to the reader. Lead up to your thesis statement in which you announce your main idea about these causes or effects.

Support your thesis with examples and details. You should devote one or two paragraphs to each of the major causes or effects. Be sure to include relevant facts and details.

Write a strong conclusion. In your final paragraph, show the reader how you have supported your thesis.

Writing Workshop *continued*

▶ Model Essay

Read the following model of an essay discussing the effects of the gold rush. Notice how it includes the characteristics you have learned about.

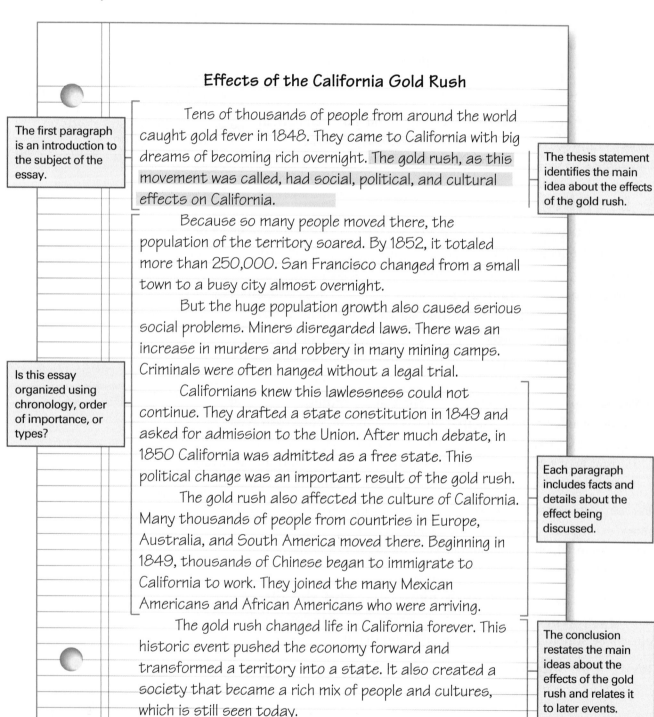

Effects of the California Gold Rush

The first paragraph is an introduction to the subject of the essay.

Tens of thousands of people from around the world caught gold fever in 1848. They came to California with big dreams of becoming rich overnight. The gold rush, as this movement was called, had social, political, and cultural effects on California.

The thesis statement identifies the main idea about the effects of the gold rush.

Because so many people moved there, the population of the territory soared. By 1852, it totaled more than 250,000. San Francisco changed from a small town to a busy city almost overnight.

But the huge population growth also caused serious social problems. Miners disregarded laws. There was an increase in murders and robbery in many mining camps. Criminals were often hanged without a legal trial.

Is this essay organized using chronology, order of importance, or types?

Californians knew this lawlessness could not continue. They drafted a state constitution in 1849 and asked for admission to the Union. After much debate, in 1850 California was admitted as a free state. This political change was an important result of the gold rush.

Each paragraph includes facts and details about the effect being discussed.

The gold rush also affected the culture of California. Many thousands of people from countries in Europe, Australia, and South America moved there. Beginning in 1849, thousands of Chinese began to immigrate to California to work. They joined the many Mexican Americans and African Americans who were arriving.

The gold rush changed life in California forever. This historic event pushed the economy forward and transformed a territory into a state. It also created a society that became a rich mix of people and cultures, which is still seen today.

The conclusion restates the main ideas about the effects of the gold rush and relates it to later events.

▶ Revising

After completing your draft, read it again carefully to find ways to make your writing better. Here are some questions to ask yourself.

Revise to strengthen your thesis and support
- Do the introduction and thesis statement establish a clear relationship between your topic and its causes or effects?
- Do the body paragraphs develop the connection with logical facts, examples, and reasons?

Revise to use helpful transitions and clear language
- Does the essay include transitions showing cause or effect and connecting words or phrases such as *because, as a result, therefore*?
- Are the causes or effects clearly described, and their connections clear?

Revise to meet written English-language conversions
- Are all sentences complete, with a subject and a verb?
- Are all the words spelled correctly?
- Are all proper nouns capitalized, including names of people and places?
- Did you use proper punctuation?

▶ Rubric for Self-Assessment

Evaluate your cause-effect essay using the following rating scale:

	Score 4	Score 3	Score 2	Score 1
Organization	Supports the thesis with logically ordered paragraphs linking a historical development to earlier events (its causes) or later ones (its effects)	Uses a reasonably clear organization, but occasionally fails to follow it or includes less relevant information (for example, events that are not really causes or effects of the subject)	Chooses an organization not suited to the topic (for example, presents causes or effects without showing how they are linked to the subject)	Shows lack of organizational strategy
Presentation	Clearly shows how the causes led to the development or how the effects grew from it; uses facts, examples, and reasons to support the thesis	Discusses the causes or effects of the development adequately but could go into greater depth; links most supporting information to the thesis	Does not discuss the causes or effects of the historical development adequately or in any detail; does not link supporting information to the thesis	Does not provide any facts, reasons, or examples about the causes or effects of the historical development being analyzed
Use of Language	Varies sentence structure and vocabulary successfully; includes no or very few mechanical errors	Uses some variety in sentence structure and vocabulary; includes few mechanical errors	Uses the same types of sentences without varying them; repeats words; includes many mechanical errors	Writes incomplete sentences; uses language poorly; includes many mechanical errors

Unit 5

Underground Railroad By the middle of the 1830s, opposition to slavery was rising among reformers. Abolitionists aided enslaved people who sought to escape via the Underground Railroad to the North or to Canada.

1830s

Lincoln's Gettysburg Address Lincoln's firm leadership inspired the Union side. In the Gettysburg Address, he vowed that "these dead shall not have died in vain . . . and that government of the people, by the people, for the people, shall not perish from the earth."

1863

Civil War and Reunion

Decision at Gettysburg All attempts at compromise having failed, the United States endured a bloody four-year civil war. After the Battle of Gettysburg, the war turned in favor of the Union army.

1863

A New Voice in Government Before the Civil War, African Americans had no voice in southern government. During Reconstruction, they became a powerful voting force in southern elections. African Americans were elected to public office as sheriffs, mayors, state legislators, and members of Congress.

1868

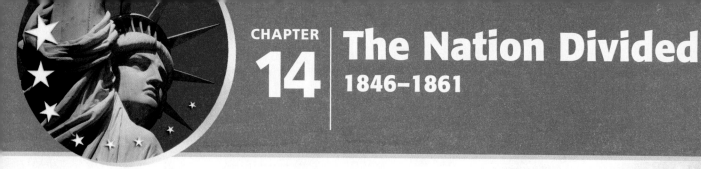

Chapter Preview

The conflict over the issue of slavery continued to divide the country. A series of events in the 1850s caused the crisis to deepen. Eventually the conflict erupted into war between North and South.

U.S. Events

1850
Fugitive Slave Act requires citizens to help catch runaway slaves.

1852
Harriet Beecher Stowe publishes *Uncle Tom's Cabin*.

1854
Kansas-Nebraska Act leads to violence.

1850

1853

1856

World Events

1853 Commodore Matthew Perry arrives in Japan to open trade.

Quick View Video
View the chapter video for a quick preview of the main ideas.

In Eastman Johnson's painting, *A Ride for Liberty—The Fugitive Slaves,* a mother holding a small child looks back for possible pursuers.

1857
Supreme Court declares Missouri Compromise unconstitutional.

1860
Abraham Lincoln is elected President.

1861
Civil War begins with bombardment of Fort Sumter.

1856

1859

1862

1857 Soldiers in India revolt against the British.

1861 Russian tsar frees serfs.

History Reading Skill Analyze Cause and Effect

What causes brought the Union to the brink of war in the 1850s?

In this chapter, you will learn how to analyze cause-and-effect relationships. Read the following speech by Senator John C. Calhoun in which he explains why he thinks the nation is so divided. The side notes show you how to analyze causes and effects.

Primary Source

In 1850, South Carolina Senator Calhoun wrote this speech in defense of slavery and gave his view of the reasons for the current division in the nation.

It is a great mistake to suppose that disunion can be effected by a single blow. The cords which bound these states together in one common union are far too numerous and powerful for that. Disunion must be the work of time. It is only through a long process that the cords can be snapped, until the whole fabric falls asunder. Already the agitation of the slavery question has snapped some of the most important and has greatly weakened all the others.

If the agitation goes on, the same force, acting with increased intensity, will finally snap every cord. Then nothing will be left to hold the states together except force.

So, the question again recurs—how can the Union be saved? To this I answer, there is but one way by which it can be—and that is by adopting such measures as will satisfy the states belonging to the southern section so that they can remain in the Union consistently with their honor and their safety.

—Senator John C. Calhoun, speech to the Senate, 1850

> Phrases such as "the work of" and "through a long process" highlight the cause-and-effect link.

> Two effects: The agitation of slavery has weakened some ties and destroyed others.

> Here is another example of cause and effect.

> Two causes: Southern states must be able to feel both safe and honorable in order to save the Union.

Analyze Cause and Effect

- Look for verbs and phrases that suggest how one event led to another: *lead to, snapped, saved, weakened.*
- Consider whether a cause has more than one effect and whether an effect has more than one cause.
- Confirm that one event actually results from another, rather than just occurring after it.

Document-Based Questions

1. Who gave this speech?
2. What issue does he say is dividing the Union?
3. How does he say the Union can be saved?

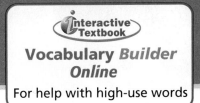

Vocabulary Builder Online
For help with high-use words

Vocabulary *Builder*

Previewing High-Use Academic Words

High-Use Word	Definition	Sample History Sentence
vital (VĪ tahl) (Section 1, p. 482)	*adj.* necessary for life; of great importance	The buffalo was <u>vital</u> to the way of life of the Plains Indians.
crisis (KRĪ sihs) (Section 1, p. 484)	*n.* turning point or deciding event in history	During the winter at Valley Forge, General Washington faced a <u>crisis</u> in keeping his force together.
deprive (dee PRĪV) (Section 2, p. 487)	*v.* to keep from happening; to take away by force or intent	During the administration of Andrew Jackson, many Native Americans were <u>deprived</u> of their homelands.
impose (ihm POHZ) (Section 2, p. 490)	*v.* to place a burden on someone or something	After the Boston Tea Party, the British <u>imposed</u> a harsh rule on Massachusetts.
embrace (ehm BRAYS) (Section 3, p. 496)	*v.* to hold tight; to readily accept	With the battles of Lexington and Concord, many Americans <u>embraced</u> the idea of independence from Britain.
clarify (KLAIR ih fī) (Section 3, p. 497)	*v.* to make the meaning of something clear	The Virginia and Tennessee resolutions <u>clarified</u> the reasons for opposing the Alien and Sedition acts.
accommodation (ak kom moh DAY shuhn) (Section 4, p. 501)	*n.* adjustment; adaptation	With the Treaty of Ghent, Britain and the United States reached an <u>accommodation</u> to end the War of 1812.
isolate (Ī sah layt) (Section 4, p. 503)	*v.* to set apart; to separate	With the French fleet in place, Cornwallis was <u>isolated</u> on the Yorktown peninsula.

Previewing Key Terms and People

Dred Scott

popular sovereignty, p. 483
secede, p. 484
fugitive, p. 484
Henry Clay, p. 484
John C. Calhoun, p. 485
Daniel Webster, p. 485
Harriet Beecher Stowe, p. 488

propaganda, p. 488
Stephen Douglas, p. 489
John Brown, p. 491
Dred Scott, p. 495
Roger B. Taney, p. 495
Abraham Lincoln, p. 495
civil war, p. 503

Growing Tensions Over Slavery

Objectives

1. Explain why conflict arose over the issue of slavery in the territories after the Mexican-American War.

2. Identify the goal of the Free-Soil Party.

3. Describe the compromise Henry Clay proposed to settle the issues that divided the North and the South.

Prepare to Read

 Reading Skill

Analyze Causes Causes are the reasons that events happen. As the United States struggled over the issue of slavery, events such as new laws or important speeches had dramatic effects on the struggle. Understanding how these events made such an impact will help you make sense of this turbulent time in American history.

Vocabulary *Builder*

High-Use Words

vital, p. 482

crisis, p. 484

Key Terms and People

popular sovereignty, p. 483

secede, p. 484

fugitive, p. 484

Henry Clay, p. 484

John C. Calhoun, p. 485

Daniel Webster, p. 485

Main Idea
The vast territory acquired as a result of the Mexican-American War reignited the controversy over slavery.

Vocabulary *Builder*
vital (vī tahl) *adj.* necessary for life; of great importance

⭐ **Background Knowledge** The Missouri Compromise of 1820 seemed to have quieted the differences between North and South. Then, the American victory in the Mexican-American War added new territory to the United States. In this section, you will learn how this development recharged the slavery issue.

Slavery and the Mexican-American War

Between 1820 and 1848, four new slaveholding states and four new free states were admitted to the Union. This maintained the balance between free and slaveholding states, with 15 of each. However, territory gained by the Mexican-American War threatened to destroy the balance.

The Wilmot Proviso The Missouri Compromise did not apply to the huge territory gained from Mexico in 1848. Would this territory be organized as states that allowed slavery? The issue was vital to northerners who wanted to stop slavery from spreading.

Fearing that the South would gain too much power, in 1846 Representative David Wilmot of Pennsylvania proposed that Congress ban slavery in all territory that might become part of the United States as a result of the Mexican-American War.

This proposal was called the Wilmot Proviso. The provision was passed in the House of Representatives, but it failed in the Senate.

Although the Wilmot Proviso never became law, it aroused great concern in the South. Many supporters of slavery viewed it as an attack on slavery by the North.

An Antislavery Party The controversy over the Wilmot Proviso also led to the rise of a new political party. Neither the Democrats nor the Whigs took a firm stand on slavery. Each hoped to win support in both North and South in the election of 1848.

The Democratic candidate for President in 1848, Senator Lewis Cass of Michigan, proposed a solution that he hoped would appeal to everyone. Cass suggested letting the people in each new territory or state decide for themselves whether to allow slavery. This process, called **popular sovereignty,** meant that people in the territory or state would vote directly on issues, rather than having their elected representatives decide.

Many Whigs and Democrats wanted to take a stronger stand against the spread of slavery. In August 1848, antislavery Whigs and Democrats joined forces to form a new party, which they called the Free-Soil Party. It called for the territory gained in the Mexican-American War to be "free soil," a place where slavery was banned.

The party chose former Democratic President Martin Van Buren as its candidate. Van Buren did poorly in the election. However, he won enough votes from the Democrats to keep Cass from winning. General Zachary Taylor, a Whig and a hero of the Mexican-American War, was elected instead.

☑**Checkpoint** Why was the Free-Soil Party founded?

The Election of 1848

Lewis Cass

That's you Dad! mere "FREE SOIL." We'll rat'em out yet . Long life to Davy Wilmot.

Martin Van Buren and his son

Reading Political Cartoons

Skills Activity

This 1848 cartoon reflects a view that members of the Free-Soil Party were "barnburners," ready to burn down the barn (the Democratic Party) to get rid of proslavery "rats."

(a) Identify Main Ideas How does the cartoon relate to the Election of 1848?

(b) Apply Information In the cartoon bubble (top right), what are the meanings of "FREE SOIL" and "Davy Wilmot"?

Calhoun Versus Webster

John C. Calhoun

"[If] something is not done to arrest it, the South will be forced to choose between abolition and secession. . . . If you are unwilling we should part in peace, tell us so; and we shall know what to do when you reduce the question to submission or resistance."

—John C. Calhoun, March 4, 1850

"I wish to speak today, not as a Massachusetts man, nor as a Northern man, but as an American. . . . I speak today for the preservation of the Union. . . . I speak today . . . for the restoration to the country of that quiet and that harmony which make the blessings of this Union so rich, and so dear to us all."

—Daniel Webster, March 7, 1850

Daniel Webster

Reading Primary Sources
Skills Activity

During the Senate debate on Clay's Compromise of 1850, John C. Calhoun and Daniel Webster wrote dramatic speeches evaluating the compromise.

(a) Detect Points of View For what region does Daniel Webster claim to be speaking?

(b) Apply Information Calhoun says "[If] something is not done to arrest it, the South will be forced to choose between abolition and secession." To what does "it" refer?

Main Idea

The compromise proposed by Henry Clay produced one of the greatest debates in American history.

Analyze Causes

What event did both southerners and northerners worry would destroy the balance of power between them?

Vocabulary *Builder*

crisis (KRĪ sihs) *n.* turning point or deciding event in history

A Bitter Debate

After the discovery of gold in California, thousands of people rushed west. California soon had enough people to become a state. Both sides realized that California's admission to the Union as a free state would upset the balance between free and slave states in the Senate.

Northerners argued that California should be a free state because most of the territory lay north of the Missouri Compromise line. But southerners feared that if free states gained a majority in the Senate, the South would not be able to block antislavery attacks like the Wilmot Proviso. Southern leaders began to threaten to secede, or withdraw, from the nation if California was admitted to the Union as a free state.

There were other issues dividing the North and South. Northerners wanted the slave trade abolished in Washington, D.C. Southerners wanted northerners to catch people who had escaped from slavery. Southerners called for a law that would force the return of fugitives, or runaway enslaved people.

For months it looked as if there was no solution. Then, in January 1850, Senator Henry Clay of Kentucky stepped forward with a plan to calm the crisis. Clay had won the nickname the Great Compromiser for working out the Missouri Compromise. Now, Clay made another series of proposals that he hoped would forever resolve the issues that bitterly divided northerners and southerners.

The Senate's discussion of Clay's proposals produced one of the greatest debates in American political history. South Carolina Senator John C. Calhoun was against compromise. Calhoun was gravely ill and just four weeks from death. He was too weak to give his speech, but he struggled to sit upright while his final speech was read to the Senate.

The admission of California as a free state, Calhoun wrote, would expose the South to continued attacks on slavery. There were only two ways to preserve the South's way of life. One was a constitutional amendment to protect states' rights. The other was secession.

Three days later, Massachusetts Senator Daniel Webster rose to support Clay's proposals and called for an end to the bitter sectionalism that was dividing the nation. Webster argued for Clay's compromise in order to preserve the Union.

Which view would prevail? The very existence of the United States depended on the answer.

✔Checkpoint How did California's proposed admission to the Union affect the debate between the North and the South over slavery?

⭐ **Looking Back and Ahead** With the territories acquired by the Mexican-American War, the nation could no longer overlook the slavery issue. Statehood for each of these territories would upset the balance between free states and slaveholding states. For a short while, it seemed to many that Henry Clay's proposed compromise gave concessions to both sides. But, as you will read in the next section, the compromise soon fell apart. When it did, the nation once again plunged down the road to all-out war between the regions.

Section 1 | Check Your Progress

Progress Monitoring Online
For: Self-test with instant help
Visit: PHSchool.com
Web Code: mya-5101

Comprehension and Critical Thinking

1. (a) Recall What was the Wilmot Proviso?
(b) Analyze Cause and Effect Did the Wilmot Proviso successfully address the nation's divisions over slavery? What effect *did* it have on the nation?

2. (a) List What were the main issues that led to Henry Clay's proposed compromise?
(b) Detect Points of View Write a sentence describing how you would feel about the need to compromise if you were a member of Congress from the North.

🔄 Reading Skill

3. Analyze Causes What did southerners want Congress to do about enslaved people who had fled to the North?

Vocabulary *Builder*

Complete these sentences so they clearly show your understanding of the key terms.
4. The status of new western territories would be decided by popular sovereignty, which is _____.
5. If southern states seceded from the Union, then _____.

6. Many northerners would not report fugitives, who were _____.

Writing

7. Consider the broad topic "Conflicts Between Slave States and Free States Before the Civil War." Divide it into four or five narrower topics. Each of these narrower topics should be covered in a research paper of a few pages.

Compromises Fail

Objectives

1. Summarize the main points of the Compromise of 1850.

2. Describe the impact of the novel *Uncle Tom's Cabin.*

3. Explain how the Kansas-Nebraska Act reopened the issue of slavery in the territories.

4. Describe the effect of the Kansas-Nebraska Act.

Prepare to Read

Reading Skill

Analyze Effects The important events of the 1850s had far-reaching effects around the nation. As you read Section 2, try to identify and understand these effects. Remember that two events do not necessarily have a cause-and-effect link just because they occur in sequence. Use signal words such as *result* to help you identify effects.

Vocabulary *Builder*

High-Use Words

deprive, p. 487

impose, p. 490

Key Terms and People

Harriet Beecher Stowe, p. 488

propaganda, p. 488

Stephen Douglas, p. 489

John Brown, p. 491

⭐ **Background Knowledge** In the previous section, you learned how many Americans hoped that Henry Clay's proposed compromise would quiet the controversy over slavery. Their hopes were soon dashed. In this section, you will learn how new disputes about slavery destroyed the compromise and led to new crises.

Main Idea

The key part of the Compromise of 1850 related to the Fugitive Slave Act.

The Compromise of 1850

In September 1850, Congress finally passed five bills based on Clay's proposals. This series of laws became known as the Compromise of 1850. President Zachary Taylor had opposed the Compromise. However, Taylor died in 1850. The new President, Millard Fillmore, supported the Compromise and signed it into law.

To Please the North The Compromise of 1850 was designed to end the crisis by giving both supporters and opponents of slavery part of what they wanted. To please the North, California was admitted to the Union as a free state. In addition, the Compromise banned the slave trade in the nation's capital. (However, Congress declared that it had no power to regulate the slave trade between slave states.)

To Please the South Under the terms of the Compromise, popular sovereignty would be used to decide the question of slavery in the rest of the Mexican Cession. People in the states created from that territory would vote whether to be a free state or a slave state when they requested admission to the Union. Also, in return for agreeing to outlaw the slave trade in Washington, D.C., southerners got a tough new fugitive slave law.

The Fugitive Slave Act of 1850 allowed special government officials to arrest any person accused of being a runaway slave. Suspects had no right to a trial to prove that they had been falsely accused. All that was required to <u>deprive</u> them of their freedom was for a slaveholder or any white witness to swear that the suspect was the slaveholder's property. In addition, the law required northern citizens to help capture accused runaways if authorities requested assistance.

Outrage in the North The Fugitive Slave Act became the most controversial part of the Compromise of 1850. Many northerners swore that they would resist the hated new law.

Northerners were outraged to see people accused of being fugitive slaves deprived of their freedom. An Indiana man was torn from his wife and children and given to an owner who claimed the man had escaped 19 years earlier. A wealthy African American tailor was carried back to South Carolina after living in New York for years. His friends quickly raised enough money to buy his freedom. But most who were shipped south remained there. Thousands of northern African Americans fled to the safety of Canada, including many who had never been enslaved.

In city after city, residents banded together to resist the Fugitive Slave Law. When two white Georgians arrived in Boston to seize fugitives, Bostonians threatened the slave catchers with harm if they did not leave the city right away. Another group rescued an accused runaway and sent him to safety in Canada. When the mob leaders were arrested, local juries refused to convict them.

John C. Calhoun had hoped that the Fugitive Slave Law would force northerners to admit that slaveholders had rights to their property. Instead, every time the law was enforced, it convinced more northerners that slavery was evil.

✓**Checkpoint** How did the Compromise of 1850 deal with the admission of California to the Union?

Vocabulary *Builder*
<u>deprive</u> (dee PRĪV) *v.* to keep from happening; to take away by force or intent

Returned to Slavery
Guarded by federal troops, fugitives Anthony Burns and Thomas Sims are captured in Boston and returned to enslavement in South Carolina. Below is a poster distributed by a southern slaveholder. **Critical Thinking:** *Draw Conclusions* *What details show the attitude of Bostonians to the return of Burns and Sims?*

Main Idea

Anger over the Fugitive Slave Act led Harriet Beecher Stowe to write the antislavery novel *Uncle Tom's Cabin.*

Uncle Tom's Cabin

One northerner deeply affected by the Fugitive Slave Act was Harriet Beecher Stowe. The daughter of an abolitionist minister, Stowe met many people who had escaped from slavery. She decided to write "something that will make this whole nation feel what an accursed thing slavery is."

In 1852, Stowe published *Uncle Tom's Cabin,* a novel about kindly Uncle Tom, an enslaved man who is abused by the cruel Simon Legree. In this passage, Tom dies after a severe beating:

> **"**Tom opened his eyes, and looked upon his master. . . . 'There an't no more ye can do! I forgive ye with all my soul!' and he fainted entirely away.
>
> 'I b'lieve, my soul, he's done for, finally,' said Legree, stepping forward, to look at him. 'Yes, he is! Well, his mouth's shut up, at last,—that's one comfort!'**"**
>
> —Harriet Beecher Stowe, *Uncle Tom's Cabin,* Chapter 38

Analyze Effects

What was one effect of Harriet Beecher Stowe's horror over slavery? What word in this paragraph highlights the cause-effect link?

Stowe's book was a bestseller in the North. It shocked thousands of people who previously had been unconcerned about slavery. As a result, readers began to view slavery as more than just a political conflict. It was a human, moral problem facing every American.

Many white southerners were outraged by Stowe's book. They criticized it as **propaganda,** false or misleading information that is spread to further a cause. They claimed the novel did not give a fair or accurate picture of the lives of enslaved African Americans.

☑**Checkpoint** **What impact did *Uncle Tom's Cabin* have?**

DISCOVERY SCHOOL

Explore More Video
To learn more about Harriet Beecher Stowe's book, view the video.

Uncle Tom's Cabin The novel *Uncle Tom's Cabin* had an impact that lasted long after slavery ended. An original illustration from the book and a scene on a decorative plate are shown here.
Critical Thinking: *Identify Costs You are a northerner during the 1850s. A fugitive comes to your door seeking help. Will you help her? List the costs and benefits of helping the person.*

Slavery After the Kansas-Nebraska Act

WASHINGTON TERRITORY

OREGON TERRITORY

UTAH TERRITORY

CA

NEW MEXICO TERRITORY

NEBRASKA TERRITORY

MINNESOTA TERRITORY

KANSAS TERRITORY

INDIAN TERRITORY

Missouri Compromise Line

MO

AR

TX

LA

MS AL GA

TN

KY

SC

NC

VA

WI

IA

IL IN OH

MI

PA

MD DE

NJ

NY

ME

VT NH MA CT RI

BRITISH TERRITORY

ATLANTIC OCEAN

PACIFIC OCEAN

MEXICO

FL

KEY

- Free states and territories
- Slave states and territories
- Open to slavery by popular vote, Compromise of 1850
- Open to slavery by popular vote, Kansas-Nebraska Act, 1854

0 km 500
0 miles 500
Albers Equal-Area Projection

MAP MASTER®
Skills Activity

The Compromise of 1850 and the Kansas-Nebraska Act threatened to upset the balance between slave and free states.

(a) Read a Map Key Which areas did the Kansas-Nebraska Act open to slavery?

(b) Clarify Problems What happened to the Missouri Compromise after 1854?

MapMaster Online

For: Interactive map
Visit: PHSchool.com
Web Code: myp-5012

The Kansas-Nebraska Act

The nation moved closer to war after Congress passed the Kansas-Nebraska Act in 1854. The act was pushed through by Senator Stephen Douglas. Douglas was eager to develop the lands west of his home state of Illinois. He wanted to see a railroad built from Illinois through the Nebraska Territory to the Pacific Coast.

In 1853, Douglas suggested forming two new territories—the Kansas Territory and the Nebraska Territory. Southerners at once objected. Both territories lay in an area closed to slavery by the Missouri Compromise. This meant that the states eventually created from these territories would enter the Union as free states.

To win southern support, Douglas proposed that slavery in the new territories be decided by popular sovereignty. Thus, in effect, the Kansas-Nebraska Act undid the Missouri Compromise.

As Douglas hoped, southerners supported the Kansas-Nebraska Act. They were sure that slave owners from Missouri would move across the border into Kansas. In time, they hoped that Kansas would enter the union as a slave state.

Northerners, however, were outraged by the Kansas-Nebraska Act. They believed that Douglas had betrayed them by reopening the issue of slavery in the territories. "The more I look at it the more enraged I become," said one northern senator of Douglas's bill. "It needs but little to make me an out-and-out abolitionist."

Main Idea

The Kansas-Nebraska Act allowed settlers in the territories to decide whether their territory would allow slavery.

KEY

← Movements of proslavery settlers	★ Capital of proslavery government
← Movements of antislavery settlers	★ Capital of antislavery government

Bleeding Kansas

The migration of proslavery and antislavery settlers into Kansas led to the outbreak of violence known as Bleeding Kansas. **Critical Thinking:** *Interpret Maps* *Why did some proslavery settlers take a more southerly route than did antislavery settlers?*

After months of debate, southern support enabled the Kansas-Nebraska Act to pass in both houses of Congress. President Franklin Pierce, a Democrat elected in 1852, then signed the bill into law. Douglas predicted that, as a result of the Kansas-Nebraska Act, the slavery question would be "forever banished from the halls of Congress." But events would soon prove how wrong he was.

☑**Checkpoint** **How did Stephen Douglas's plan undo the Missouri Compromise?**

Main Idea

Kansas suffered widespread violence as proslavery and antislavery settlers battled for control.

Bleeding Kansas

The Kansas-Nebraska Act left it to the white citizens of the territory to decide whether Kansas would be free or slave territory. Both proslavery and antislavery settlers flooded into Kansas within weeks after Douglas's bill became law. Each side was determined to hold the majority in the territory when it came time for the vote.

Thousands of Missourians entered Kansas in March 1855 to illegally vote in the election to select a territorial legislature. Although Kansas had only 3,000 voters, nearly 8,000 votes were cast on election day! Of 39 legislators elected, all but 3 supported slavery. The antislavery settlers refused to accept these results and held a second election.

Vocabulary *Builder*
impose (ihm POHZ) *v.* to place a burden on someone or something

Growing Violence Kansas now had two governments, each claiming the right to impose their government on the territory. Not surprisingly, violence soon broke out. In April, a proslavery sheriff was shot when he tried to arrest some antislavery settlers in the town of Lawrence. The next month, he returned with 800 men and attacked the town.

Three days later, John Brown, an antislavery settler from Connecticut, led seven men to a proslavery settlement near Pottawatomie (paht uh wah TOH mee) Creek. There, they murdered five proslavery men and boys.

These incidents set off widespread fighting in Kansas. Bands of proslavery and antislavery fighters roamed the countryside, terrorizing those who did not support their views. The violence was so bad that it earned Kansas the name Bleeding Kansas.

Bloodshed in the Senate Even before Brown's raid at Pottawatomie Creek, the violence in Kansas spilled over into the United States Senate. Charles Sumner of Massachusetts was the leading abolitionist senator. In a fiery speech, Sumner denounced the proslavery legislature in Kansas. He then attacked his southern foes, singling out Andrew Butler, an elderly senator from South Carolina.

Butler was not present the day Sumner made his speech. A few days later, however, Butler's nephew, Congressman Preston Brooks, marched into the Senate chamber. Using a heavy cane, Brooks beat Sumner until he fell to the floor, bloody and unconscious. Sumner never completely recovered from his injuries.

Many southerners felt that Sumner got what he deserved. Hundreds of people sent canes to Brooks to show their support. To northerners, however, Brooks's violent act was just more evidence that slavery was brutal and inhuman.

☑Checkpoint **What was the outcome of the election to select a legislature in the Kansas Territory?**

⭐ **Looking Back and Ahead** By 1856, all attempts at compromise had failed. The bitterness between the North and the South was about to alter the political landscape of the United States.

Analyze Effects
Describe the effect of the Kansas-Nebraska Act on Kansas.

Section 2 | **Check Your Progress**

Progress Monitoring ⓞnline
For: Self-test with instant help
Visit: PHSchool.com
Web Code: mya-5102

Comprehension and Critical Thinking

1. **(a) Recall** What parts of the Compromise of 1850 were included to please the North?
(b) Draw Conclusions Why do you think northerners were still not satisfied?

2. **(a) Recall** What was the Kansas-Nebraska Act?
(b) Evaluate Information How did the Kansas-Nebraska Act contribute to tension between the North and the South?

Reading Skill

3. **Analyze Effects** What was one effect of Harriet Beecher Stowe's book *Uncle Tom's Cabin*?

Vocabulary *Builder*

Complete the following sentence so that the second part further explains the first part and clearly shows your understanding of the key term.

4. Many white southerners considered *Uncle Tom's Cabin* propaganda; _____ an unfair picture of slavery.

Writing

5. Imagine that you are researching the effects of Harriet Beecher Stowe's book *Uncle Tom's Cabin*. Write down five questions that would help you focus your research on this topic. The questions should point you to areas where you need to find more information about the influence of Stowe's book.

Uncle Tom's Cabin

by Harriet Beecher Stowe

Prepare to Read

Introduction

Harriet Beecher Stowe rocked the nation in 1851 when she published *Uncle Tom's Cabin.* The novel won many converts to the antislavery cause. The excerpt below is from the opening chapter. Shelby, a Kentucky slave owner, must sell some of his enslaved servants to Mr. Haley, a slave trader. Haley is especially interested in buying a young woman named Eliza.

Reading Skill

Judging Characters In a work of fiction, characters may say things that the author thinks are wrong. We have to read carefully in order to understand how the author wants us to judge the characters. In the selection below, look for clues as to what Stowe really thinks of Mr. Haley, the slave trader.

Vocabulary *Builder*

As you read this literature selection, look for the following underlined words:

calculation (kal kyoo LAY shuhn) *n.* ability to figure out exactly what something is worth

humane (hyoo MAYN) *adj.* kind; considerate; merciful

candid (KAN dihd) *adj.* frank; honest

virtuous (VIR choo uhs) *adj.* highly moral

⭐ Background

Much of *Uncle Tom's Cabin* is written in dialect that reproduces how different types of characters speak. For example, to show the way Haley speaks, Stowe uses "ha'nt" for "haven't," "this yer" for "this here," "uns" for "ones," and "onpleasant" for "unpleasant."

"Come, how will you trade about the gal?—what shall I say for her—what'll you take?"

"Mr. Haley, she is not to be sold," said Shelby. "My wife would not part with her for her weight in gold."

"Ay, ay! women always say such things, cause they ha'nt no sort of <u>calculation</u>. Just show 'em how many watches, feathers, and trinkets, one's weight in gold would buy, and that alters the case, I reckon."

"I tell you, Haley, this must not be spoken of; I say no, and I mean no," said Shelby, decidedly.

"Well, you'll let me have the boy, though," said the trader; "you must own I've come down pretty handsomely for him."

"What on earth can you want with the child?" said Shelby.

"Why, I've got a friend that's going into this yer branch of the business—wants to buy up handsome boys to raise for the market. Fancy articles entirely—sell for waiters, and so on, to rich 'uns, that can pay for handsome 'uns. It sets off one of yer great places—a real handsome boy to open door, wait, and tend. They fetch a good sum; and this little devil is such a comical, musical concern, he's just the article!"

"I would rather not sell him," said Mr. Shelby, thoughtfully; "the fact is, sir, I'm a <u>humane</u> man, and I hate to take the boy from his mother, sir."

"O, you do?—La! yes—something of that ar natur. I understand, perfectly. It is mighty onpleasant getting on with women, sometimes, I al'ays hates these yer screechin', screamin' times. They are *mighty* onpleasant; but, as I manages business, I generally avoids

Slave auction

'em, sir. Now, what if you get the girl off for a day, or a week, or so; then the thing's done quietly,—all over before she comes home. Your wife might get her some ear-rings, or a new gown, or some such truck, to make up with her."

"I'm afraid not."

"Lor bless ye, yes! These critters ain't like white folks, you know; they gets over things, only manage right. Now, they say," said Haley, assuming a <u>candid</u> and confidential air, "that this kind o' trade is hardening to the feelings; but I never found it so. Fact is, I never could do things up the way some fellers manage the business. I've seen 'em as would pull a woman's child out of her arms, and set him up to sell, and she screechin' like mad all the time;—very bad policy—damages the article—makes 'em quite unfit for service sometimes. I knew a real handsome gal once, in Orleans, as was entirely ruined by this sort o' handling. The fellow that was trading for her didn't want her baby; and she was one of your real high sort, when her blood was up. I tell you, she squeezed up her child in her arms, and talked, and went on real awful. It kinder makes my blood run cold to think on 't; and when they carried off the child, and locked her up, she jest went ravin' mad, and died in a week. Clear waste, sir, of a thousand dollars, just for want of management,—there's where 't is. It's always best to do the humane thing, sir; that's been my experience." And the trader leaned back in his chair, and folded his arm, with an air of <u>virtuous</u> decision, apparently considering himself a second Wilberforce.

From *Uncle Tom's Cabin*, by Harriet Beecher Stowe

Analyze LITERATURE

Imagine that you are a northerner in 1851 reading *Uncle Tom's Cabin* for the first time. Write a letter to a friend explaining how this excerpt made you feel about the slave trade.

Judging Characters
Stowe has Haley refer to enslaved Africans as "critters," showing he does not think of them as human beings. Yet, he also claims that slave-trading has not hardened his feelings. What does this indicate about Stowe's view of Haley?

★ **Background**
William Wilberforce was a famous English clergyman who campaigned to end slavery.

If you liked this selection, you might want to read more about the antislavery movement in *Escape From Slavery: Five Journeys to Freedom* by Doreen Rappaport, illustrated by Charles Lilly. Harper Collins Publishers. 1991.

Objectives

1. Explain why the Republican Party came into being in the 1850s.

2. Summarize the issues involved in the Dred Scott decision.

3. Identify Abraham Lincoln's and Stephen Douglas's views on slavery.

4. Describe the differing reactions in the North and the South to John Brown's raid.

Prepare to Read

 Reading Skill

Analyze Causes and Effects
Historians often disagree over exactly what caused the Civil War. As you read Section 3, watch carefully for cause-and-effect links. Analyzing these links will help you answer this difficult question for yourself. Remember that sometimes the link is not directly stated. Identify an event, then ask yourself: What caused this event to happen? What were the effects of this event?

Vocabulary *Builder*

High-Use Words
embrace, p. 496
clarify, p. 497

Key People
Dred Scott, p. 495
Roger B. Taney, p. 495
Abraham Lincoln, p. 495

⭐ **Background Knowledge** You have learned that bitterness between northerners and southerners over slavery weakened the nation's two major political parties. In this section, you will learn about a new party that rapidly came to dominate northern politics.

Main Idea
The goal of the new Republican Party was to stop the spread of slavery into the western territories.

A New Antislavery Party

As the Whig Party split apart in 1854, many northern Whigs joined a new political party. It was called the Republican Party, and its main goal was to stop the spread of slavery into the western territories. The Republicans' antislavery stand also attracted northern Democrats and Free-Soil Party members.

The Republicans quickly became a powerful force in politics. The congressional elections of 1854 were held only months after the party was founded. Of the 245 candidates elected to the U.S. House of Representatives, 105 were Republicans. Republican victories in state races also cost the Democrats control of all but two northern state legislatures.

Two years later, in 1856, the Republican Party ran its first candidate for President. It chose John C. Frémont, the army officer who had helped California win independence during the Mexican-American War. The Republicans waged a strong antislavery campaign. Although the Democrat James Buchanan was elected, Frémont won in 11 of the nation's 16 free states.

Analyze Causes and Effects
How did growing northern concern about the growth of slavery affect the 1856 presidential election?

☑ **Checkpoint** What was the result of the election of 1856?

The Dred Scott Decision

In March 1857—only three days after Buchanan took office—the U.S. Supreme Court delivered a shattering blow to antislavery forces. It decided the case of *Dred Scott* v. *Sandford*.

Dred Scott was an enslaved person who had once been owned by a U.S. Army doctor. The doctor, and Scott, lived for a time in Illinois and in the Wisconsin Territory. Slavery was illegal in both places. After leaving the army, the doctor settled with Scott in Missouri.

With the help of antislavery lawyers, Scott sued for his freedom. He argued that he was free because he had lived where slavery was illegal. In time, the case reached the Supreme Court. Neither northerners nor southerners were prepared for what the Court decided.

The Court Decides Chief Justice Roger B. Taney wrote the decision for the Court. Scott was not a free man, he said, for two reasons. First, according to Taney, Scott had no right to sue in federal court because African Americans were not citizens. Second, Taney said, merely living in free territory did not make an enslaved person free. Slaves were property, Taney declared, and property rights were protected by the U.S. Constitution.

But the ruling went even further. Taney wrote that Congress did not have the power to prohibit slavery in any territory. Thus, the Missouri Compromise was unconstitutional.

Reaction Supporters of slavery rejoiced at the Dred Scott decision. The decision meant that slavery was legal in all territories—just as white southern leaders had been demanding all along.

Northerners, however, were stunned. African American leaders such as Frederick Douglass condemned the ruling. Still, Douglass declared, "my hopes were never brighter than now." He believed that outrage against the decision would bring more whites to the abolitionist cause.

Indeed, white northerners were also shocked by the ruling. Many had hoped that slavery would eventually die out if it were restricted to the South. Now, however, slavery could spread throughout the West.

One northerner who spoke out against the Dred Scott decision was an Illinois lawyer named Abraham Lincoln. The idea that African Americans could not be citizens, he said, was based on a false view of American history. In a very short time, Lincoln would become a central figure in the fight against the spread of slavery.

✔**Checkpoint** Why did Dred Scott claim he was no longer enslaved?

Main Idea
The Dred Scott ruling meant that all American territories were open to slavery.

Biography Quest

Abraham Lincoln
1809–1865

Abraham Lincoln was not yet a nationally known figure in 1857. But he was well known in Illinois as a clever, successful lawyer and politician.

People liked Lincoln for his quick wit and down-to-earth approach. He was known as a good, straightforward speaker. Even so, a listener once complained that he could not understand a speech of Lincoln's. "There are always some fleas a dog can't reach," was Lincoln's reply.

Biography Quest ⬤nline

Why was Lincoln voted out of Congress after one term?

For: The answer to the question about Lincoln

Visit: PHSchool.com

Web Code: myd-5013

Links Across Time

Elections and the Media

1858 Americans followed the Lincoln-Douglas debates as telegraph reports circulated around the country.

1960 Americans were for the first time able to watch presidential candidates debate live on television. Richard Nixon and John F. Kennedy debated before an enormous television audience. Many experts believe that the debates played a major role in Kennedy's victory.

Link to Today Online

Elections and the Media Today The digital revolution is again changing American political campaigns. What media do candidates use today?

For: Voting and the media
Visit: PHSchool.com
Web Code: myc-5103

Main Idea
Abraham Lincoln took a strong stand against slavery's expansion in the Lincoln-Douglas debates.

Vocabulary *Builder*
embrace (ehm BRAYS) *v.* to hold tight; to readily accept

The Lincoln-Douglas Debates

Lincoln had had only a brief career in politics. After serving in the Illinois state legislature, he was elected to Congress as a Whig. There, he voted for the Wilmot Proviso. After a single term, he returned to Illinois to practice law.

Lincoln's opposition to the Kansas-Nebraska Act brought him back into politics, this time embracing the Republican cause. He had long been a rival of Illinois Senator Stephen Douglas, the author of the Kansas-Nebraska Act. Their rivalry was personal as well as political. Both men had courted Mary Todd, who married Lincoln.

A House Divided In 1858, Illinois Republicans chose Lincoln to run for the Senate against Douglas. Accepting the nomination, Lincoln made a stirring speech in favor of the Union:

> "A house divided against itself cannot stand. I do not believe this government can endure, permanently, half slave and half free. I do not expect the Union to be dissolved—I do not expect the house to fall—but I do expect it will cease to be divided. It will become all one thing or all the other."
>
> —Abraham Lincoln, Springfield, Illinois, June 16, 1858

Lincoln did not state that he wanted to ban slavery. Still, many southerners became convinced that Lincoln was an abolitionist.

Debating Slavery Lincoln then challenged Douglas to a series of public debates. Thousands of people gathered to hear them speak. Newspapers throughout the nation reported what each man said.

Douglas strongly defended popular sovereignty. "Each state of this Union has a right to do as it pleases on the subject of slavery," he said. "In Illinois we have exercised that sovereign right by prohibiting slavery. . . . It is none of our business whether slavery exists in Missouri." Douglas also painted Lincoln as a dangerous abolitionist who wanted equality for African Americans.

Lincoln took a stand against the spread of slavery. He declared, "If slavery is not wrong, nothing is wrong." Lincoln predicted that slavery would die on its own. In the meantime, he said, it was the obligation of Americans to keep it out of the western territories.

In reply to Douglas, Lincoln stated: "I am not, nor ever have been in favor of bringing about in any way the social and political equality of the white and black races." But he did <u>clarify</u> this view. He insisted that "there is no reason in the world why the Negro is not entitled to all the rights enumerated in the Declaration of Independence, the right to life, liberty and the pursuit of happiness."

In the end, Douglas won the Senate election. However, the debates had made Lincoln known throughout the country. Two years later, the men would be rivals again—this time for the presidency.

Vocabulary *Builder*
<u>clarify</u> (KLAIR ih fī) *v.* to make the meaning of something clear

☑**Checkpoint** **What position did Douglas take on slavery?**

John Brown's Raid

The nation's attention soon was captured by the actions of John Brown. Driven out of Kansas after the Pottawatomie Massacre, Brown had returned to New England. There he hatched a plot to raise an army and free people in the South who were enslaved.

In 1859, Brown and a small band of supporters attacked the town of Harpers Ferry in Virginia. His goal was to seize guns the U.S. Army had stored there. He thought that enslaved African Americans would support him. He would then give them weapons and lead them in a revolt.

Brown quickly gained control of the arms. But troops commanded by Colonel Robert E. Lee surrounded Brown's force before it could escape. Ten of Brown's followers were killed. Brown was wounded and captured.

Main Idea
Northern support of John Brown shocked and angered southern slaveholders.

John Brown in Kansas
John Steuart Curry began painting this 10-foot-high mural in 1937. It shows John Brown as a fiery abolitionist with a rifle in one hand and a Bible in the other. **Critical Thinking:** *Detect Points of View Based on this painting, do you think Curry admired John Brown?*

Death of John Brown

Thomas Hovenden painted this portrait of a saintly John Brown. On his way to his death, Brown stops to kiss a child. Hovenden did not personally witness the events he showed here. **Critical Thinking: Contrast** *Compare this painting to the one on the previous page. How do these two paintings try to stir different emotions?*

At his trial, Brown sat quietly as the court found him guilty of murder and treason. Before hearing his sentence, he gave a moving defense of his actions. The Bible, he said, instructed him to care for the poor and enslaved. "If it is deemed necessary that I should forfeit my life for the furtherance of the ends of justice . . . I say, let it be done." He showed no emotion as he was sentenced to death.

When the state of Virginia hanged Brown for treason on December 2, 1859, church bells across the North tolled to mourn the man who many considered a hero. But southerners were shocked. People in the North were praising a man who had tried to lead a slave revolt! More than ever, many southerners were convinced that the North was out to destroy their way of life.

☑**Checkpoint** **What was John Brown's goal in launching the raid on Harpers Ferry?**

☆ **Looking Back and Ahead** The nation had suffered one dispute after another over the expansion of slavery since the end of the Mexican-American War in 1846. By the election of 1860, talk of the breakup of the United States was everywhere. In the next section, you will read how that breakup came about.

Section 3 | Check Your Progress

Progress Monitoring Online
For: Self-test with instant help
Visit: PHSchool.com
Web Code: mya-5103

Comprehension and Critical Thinking

1. **(a) Summarize** Which groups supported the newly formed Republican Party?
(b) Draw Conclusions How did the outcomes of the elections of 1854 and 1856 affect the Republican Party?

2. **(a) Identify** On what grounds did Dred Scott sue for his freedom in court?
(b) Draw Conclusions How did Taney's ruling further divide the North and the South?

3. **(a) Recall** What were the Lincoln-Douglas debates?
(b) Apply Information Why do you think the Lincoln-Douglas debates received national attention?

Reading Skill

4. **Analyze Causes and Effects** Identify one cause and one effect of John Brown's raid. Why did Brown and his followers attack Harpers Ferry? What happened as a result?

Writing

5. Reread the paragraphs in this section that describe the Lincoln-Douglas debates. When you have finished, paraphrase the excerpt from Lincoln's Springfield speech. Remember, when you paraphrase, you restate something said by someone else, using only your own words.

Objectives

1. Describe the results of the election of 1860.

2. Explain why southern states seceded from the Union.

3. Summarize the events that led to the outbreak of the Civil War.

Prepare to Read

 Reading Skill

Analyze Multiple Causes or Effects Many events in history have more than one cause, as the Civil War certainly did. Other events lead to more than one effect, which is also certainly true of the Civil War. As you read about this turning point in American history, look for causes with multiple effects and effects with multiple causes.

Vocabulary *Builder*

High-Use Words
<u>accommodation</u>, p. 501
<u>isolate</u>, p. 503

Key Term
civil war, p. 503

⭐ **Background Knowledge** John Brown's raid steadily increased tensions between North and South over slavery. In this section, you will learn how Abraham Lincoln's election as President created a crisis that shattered the nation and led to war.

The Nation Divides

As the election of 1860 drew near, Americans everywhere felt a sense of crisis. The long and bitter debate over slavery had left the nation seriously divided.

Election of 1860 The Republicans chose Abraham Lincoln as their presidential candidate. His criticisms of slavery during his debates with Douglas had made him popular in the North.

Southern Democrats wanted the party to support slavery in the territories. But northerners refused to do so. In the end, the party split in two. Northern Democrats chose Stephen Douglas as their candidate. Southern Democrats picked Vice President John Breckinridge of Kentucky.

Some southerners still hoped to heal the split between North and South. They formed the Constitutional Union Party and nominated John Bell of Tennessee. Bell promised to protect slavery *and* keep the nation together.

Stephen Douglas was sure that Lincoln would win the election. However, he believed that Democrats "must try to save the Union." He pleaded with southern voters to stay with the Union, no matter who was elected. However, when Douglas campaigned in the South, hostile southerners often pelted him with eggs and rotten fruit.

Main Idea
The election of 1860 led to the breakup of the Union.

Wood carving of Stephen Douglas

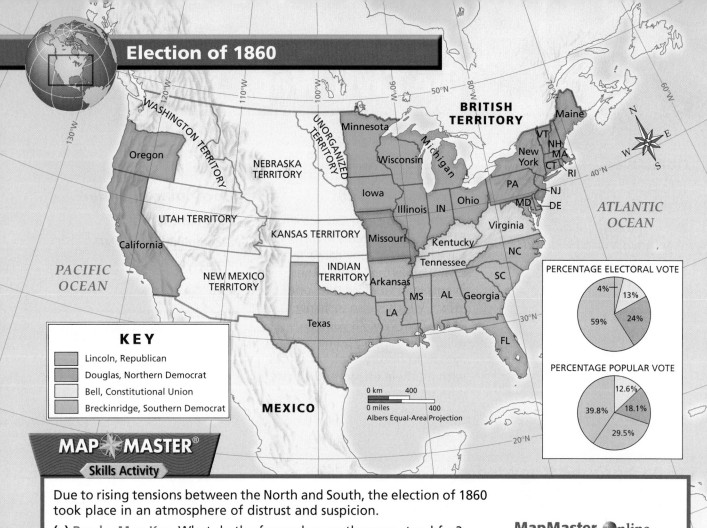

Election of 1860

BRITISH TERRITORY

WASHINGTON TERRITORY

Oregon

NEBRASKA TERRITORY

UNORGANIZED TERRITORY

Minnesota

Wisconsin

Michigan

Maine

VT
NH MA
New York
CT RI
PA
NJ

Iowa

Illinois IN Ohio

MD DE

UTAH TERRITORY

KANSAS TERRITORY

Missouri

Virginia

California

Kentucky

NC

PACIFIC OCEAN

NEW MEXICO TERRITORY

INDIAN TERRITORY

Arkansas

Tennessee

SC

ATLANTIC OCEAN

MS AL Georgia

LA

Texas

FL

MEXICO

KEY

- Lincoln, Republican
- Douglas, Northern Democrat
- Bell, Constitutional Union
- Breckinridge, Southern Democrat

0 km 400
0 miles 400
Albers Equal-Area Projection

PERCENTAGE ELECTORAL VOTE

4% 13%
59% 24%

PERCENTAGE POPULAR VOTE

12.6%
39.8% 18.1%
29.5%

MAP MASTER®
Skills Activity

Due to rising tensions between the North and South, the election of 1860 took place in an atmosphere of distrust and suspicion.

(a) Read a Map Key What do the four colors on the map stand for? Which party won nearly all the northern states? Which party won nearly all the southern states?

(b) Draw Conclusions How does the map show that sectionalism was important in the election?

MapMaster Online

For: Interactive map
Visit: PHSchool.com
Web Code: myp-5104

The election showed just how fragmented the nation had become. Lincoln won in every free state and Breckinridge in all the slave-holding states except four. Bell won Kentucky, Tennessee, and Virginia—all in the upper South. Douglas carried only Missouri. Although Lincoln got only 40 percent of the popular votes, he received enough electoral votes to win the election.

Southern States Secede Lincoln's election sent shock waves through the South. To many southerners, it seemed that the South no longer had a voice in the national government. They believed that the President and Congress were now set against their interests—especially slavery.

One Virginia newspaper expressed the feelings of many southerners. "A party founded on the single sentiment . . . of hatred of African slavery, is now the controlling power," it observed. "The honor, safety, and independence of the Southern people are to be found only in a Southern Confederacy."

South Carolina was the first southern state to secede from the Union. When news of Lincoln's election reached the state, the legislature called for a special convention. On December 20, 1860, the convention passed a declaration that "the union now subsisting between South Carolina and the other states, under the name of the 'United States of America' is hereby dissolved."

The Confederate States of America With hope of <u>accommodation</u> all but gone, six more states followed South Carolina out of the Union. However, not all southerners favored secession. Tennessee Senator Andrew Johnson and Texas Governor Sam Houston were among those who opposed it. Yet, the voices of the moderates were overwhelmed. "People are wild," said one opponent of secession. "You might as well attempt to control a tornado as attempt to stop them."

In early February, leaders from the seven seceding states met in Montgomery, Alabama, to form a new nation that they called the Confederate States of America. By the time Lincoln took office in March, they had written a constitution and named former Mississippi Senator Jefferson Davis as their president.

✓**Checkpoint** **Why did southern states secede from the Union?**

The Civil War Begins

On March 4, 1861, Abraham Lincoln became President of a nation facing the greatest crisis in its history. In his inaugural address, he assured the seceded states that he meant them no harm. "I have no purpose, directly or indirectly, to interfere with the institution of slavery where it exists," he promised. But he also warned them about continuing on the course they had chosen:

> ❝In your hands, my dissatisfied fellow countrymen, and not in mine, is the momentous issue of . . . war. The government will not assail [attack] you. . . . We are not enemies, but friends. We must not be enemies. Though passion may have strained, it must not break our bonds of affection.❞
>
> —Abraham Lincoln, Inaugural Address, March 4, 1861

Lincoln's assurance of friendship was rejected. The seceding states took over post offices, forts, and other federal property within their borders. The new President had to decide how to respond.

Fort Sumter Lincoln's most urgent problem was Fort Sumter, located on an island in the harbor of Charleston, South Carolina. The fort's commander would not surrender it. South Carolina authorities decided to starve the fort's 100 troops into surrender. They had been cut off from supplies since late December and could not hold out much longer.

Main Idea
President Lincoln's assurances of friendship in his inaugural address were rejected by the South.

Abraham Lincoln speaks at his first inauguration

Attack on Fort Sumter

History *Interactive*
Inside Fort Sumter
Visit: PHSchool.com
Web Code: myp-5107

America's most tragic conflict began early on the morning of April 12,1861, at Fort Sumter. The dark night was suddenly lit up by Confederate shells fired from the mainland. Within a few hours, the fort's wooden barracks had caught fire and portions of the fort had crumbled. At midday, a Confederate shell knocked over the fort's flagpole. The firing went on throughout the day and evening. By the next day, the Union garrison was exhausted and every wooden structure in the fort was ablaze. "The men lay . . . on the ground, with wet handkerchiefs over their mouths and eyes, gasping for breath."

Critical Thinking: Analyze Cause and Effect What was the cause of the Confederate attack on Fort Sumter? What were the effects?

◄ **Blueprint of the Fort**

This overhead diagram of the fort shows its pentagonal, or five-sided, shape. The square-shaped area on the left side of the diagram shows a small wharf. Prior to the Confederate attack, Union ships used this dock to unload supplies to the fort.

▼ **American flag from Fort Sumter**

▲ **Confederate Troops Fire on the Fort**

Confederate artillery pounded Fort Sumter for 34 hours. Fires raged out of control and threatened to ignite the fort's magazine, where many barrels of gunpowder were stored. Facing shortages of food and ammunition, the Union commander surrendered. The bloodiest of all American wars had begun.

Lincoln did not want to give up the fort. But he feared that sending troops might cause other states to secede. Therefore, he announced that he would send food to the fort, but that the supply ships would carry no troops or guns.

Confederate leaders decided to capture the fort while it was isolated. On April 12, Confederate artillery opened fire on the fort. After 34 hours, with the fort on fire, the U.S. troops surrendered.

Vocabulary *Builder*
isolate (ī sah layt) *v.* to set apart; to separate

Why War Came The Confederate attack on Fort Sumter marked the beginning of a long civil war. A **civil war** is a war between opposing groups of citizens of the same country.

The Civil War probably attracts more public interest today than any other event in American history. Americans continue to debate why the war took place and whether it could have been avoided.

In 1850, southerners might have been satisfied if they had been left alone. But by 1861, many Americans in both the North and the South had come to accept the idea that war could not be avoided. At stake was the nation's future. Four years later, a weary Lincoln looked back to the beginning of the conflict. He noted:

"Both parties [condemned] war, but one of them would *make* war rather than let the nation survive, and the other would *accept* war rather than let it perish, and the war came."

—Abraham Lincoln, Second Inaugural Address, March 4, 1865

Analyze Multiple Causes or Effects According to this section, what were two causes of the Civil War?

☑**Checkpoint** Why was Lincoln reluctant to give up Fort Sumter?

☆ **Looking Back and Ahead** Confederate cannons had nearly destroyed Fort Sumter. To many, it seemed like a huge fireworks display. No one knew that the fireworks marked the beginning of a terrible war that would last four years.

Section 4 | **Check Your Progress**

Progress Monitoring Online
For: Self-test with instant help
Visit: PHSchool.com
Web Code: mya-5104

Comprehension and Critical Thinking

1. **(a) Recall** How did divisions among the Democrats help lead to the election of Republican Abraham Lincoln in 1860?
   (b) Explain Problems What was the South's reaction to Lincoln's election? How did Lincoln try to reassure the South?

2. **(a) Identify** What event marked the start of war between the North and the South?

(b) Evaluate Information Explain what Abraham Lincoln meant by the following remark: "Both parties [condemned] war, but one of them would *make* war rather than let the nation survive. . . ."

Reading Skill

3. **Analyze Multiple Causes or Effects** What were three effects of Lincoln's warning to the South?

Vocabulary *Builder*

4. Write two definitions for the key term civil war. First, write a formal definition for your teacher. Second, write a definition in everyday English for a classmate.

Writing

5. Based on what you have read in this section, write a thesis statement for an essay explaining why the election of Abraham Lincoln caused the South to secede.

Not everything a writer includes in a selection is equally important. Some information is relevant because it is directly related to the subject of the text. Other information is less relevant because it does not directly relate to the subject. When you read, you must focus your attention on the main topic and the most relevant information. Read the fictional letter below to determine relevance.

The letter below is historical fiction. That means that it is based on history, but is not a primary source. In the letter, William, a farmer who had moved to Kansas Territory, writes to his brother Joseph in Vermont.

November 20, 1854
Dear Joseph,
   I was pleased to receive your last letter. The success of your store is a great achievement. Our new farm continues to prosper and little Sarah has recovered from the fever that had sickened her for a month. Of course, the issue of the Kansas-Nebraska Act continues to trouble me. I do not agree with your support of Senator Stephen Douglas of Illinois; however, I enjoy reading his speeches. Those who oppose slavery, as I do, do not want that cruel system in place in a territory where it had been banned. Under the terms of the Kansas-Nebraska Act, it is up to the people to decide the issue peacefully by voting their hearts. Yet, settlers who are for and against slavery in the territory seem intent on using force, instead of the ballot box. The elections next year will settle the issue once and for all.

Your loving brother,
William

Learn the Skill
Use these steps to determine which information is relevant and which is irrelevant.

1 **Identify the subject or topic.** What is the main topic of the selection?

2 **Identify your purpose for reading the selection.** Ask yourself: What am I trying to find out?

3 **Identify the information that is relevant to the topic.** What information is directly related to the subject? Why is it relevant?

4 **Identify the information that is irrelevant to the topic.** What information is not directly related to the subject? Why is it irrelevant?

Practice the Skill
Answer the following questions about the letter on the page.

1 **Identify the subject or topic.** What is the main topic of the letter?

2 **Identify the purpose for reading the selection.** Why am I reading this letter?

3 **Identify the information that is relevant to the subject.** (a) What are two statements that are directly related to the topic of the letter? (b) Why is each statement relevant?

4 **Identify the information that is irrelevant to the topic.** (a) What are two statements that are not directly related to the subject? (b) Why is each statement irrelevant?

Apply the Skill
See the Review and Assessment at the end of this chapter.

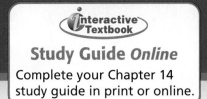

Study Guide Online
Complete your Chapter 14 study guide in print or online.

Chapter Summary

Section 1
Growing Tensions Over Slavery

- The acquisition of new territories in the West reopened the issue of slavery.
- Lawmakers debated how to keep a balance of power between free and slave-holding states.

Section 2
Compromises Fail

- The Compromise of 1850 attempted to settle the slavery question, but northerners refused to accept the Fugitive Slave Act.
- *Uncle Tom's Cabin* increased northern hatred of slavery and antagonized southern slaveholders.
- Popular sovereignty established by the Kansas-Nebraska Act triggered bloody fighting in Kansas.

Section 3
The Crisis Deepens

- The Republican Party was formed to oppose the spread of slavery.
- In the Dred Scott decision, the Supreme Court ruled that Congress could not ban slavery in any territory.
- Abraham Lincoln became a central political figure when he and Stephen Douglas debated slavery.
- John Brown, an abolitionist, and his followers attacked the federal arsenal at Harpers Ferry, Virginia, to protest slavery.

Section 4
The Coming of the Civil War

- After Lincoln won the presidential election of 1860, some southern states seceded from the Union.
- The Civil War began when Confederate troops fired on Fort Sumter.

Key Concepts

These notes will help you prepare for questions about key concepts.

Main Provisions of the Compromise of 1850

- California was admitted to the Union as a free state.
- Popular sovereignty would decide the issue of slavery in the territories won in the Mexican-American War.
- The slave trade was banned in Washington, D.C.
- Congress passed a strong Fugitive Slave Act.

Election of 1860

- Lincoln-Douglas debates attract attention to Lincoln.
- Republicans chose Lincoln as presidential candidate.
- Democratic Party splits.
- John Bell supports slavery and opposes secession.
- Lincoln wins every free state and is elected President.
- Southern states secede.

Events That Led to Civil War

- Compromise of 1850
- Publication of *Uncle Tom's Cabin*
- Kansas-Nebraska Act
- John Brown's raid on Harpers Ferry
- Dred Scott decision
- Election of Abraham Lincoln as President
- Secession of southern states and formation of the Confederate States of America
- Confederate attack on Fort Sumter

Vocabulary *Builder*

Key Terms

Fill in the blanks with the correct key terms.

1. Many southern states threatened to _____ from the Union if California was admitted as a free state.

2. Southerners claimed that *Uncle Tom's Cabin* was _____ because it did not give a fair picture of the lives of enslaved African Americans.

3. Slavery was the main issue that split the nation apart and led to a violent _____.

Comprehension and Critical Thinking

4. **(a) Recall** Why did Senator Stephen Douglas introduce the Kansas-Nebraska Act?
   (b) Understand Sequence How did the events in Kansas demonstrate the unrest that would eventually take shape throughout the nation?

5. **(a) Summarize** What was the Supreme Court's verdict in the Dred Scott case?
   (b) Detect Points of View How do you think Harriet Beecher Stowe reacted to the verdict?

6. **(a) Identify** What was the main goal of the Republican Party in the election of 1854?
   (b) Distinguish Relevant Information How did Abraham Lincoln represent Republican principles during the Lincoln-Douglas debates?

7. **(a) Identify** What is the subject of the painting below?
   (b) Draw Conclusions Do you agree with the artist's view of this person? Why or why not?

8. **(a) Describe** What happened at Fort Sumter?
   (b) Draw Conclusions Do you think southerners were justified in seceding despite Lincoln's assurances? Explain.

History Reading Skill

9. **Analyze Cause and Effect** Reread the text in Section 4 under the heading "The Nation Divides." How did the election of 1860 affect the unity of the United States?

Writing

10. **Choose one of the following topics for a research report:**
    - the Kansas-Nebraska Act
    - the Dred Scott decision
    - the early career of Abraham Lincoln

    List five questions you would want to pursue if you were going to research that topic. Write a thesis statement for the topic and find supporting evidence for that thesis from the chapter.

11. **Write a Narrative:**
    Imagine you are from a northern farm family and have just heard of the attack on Fort Sumter. Write a narrative describing your hopes and fears about the future.

Skills for Life

Determine Relevance

Use the fictional letter below to answer the questions that follow.

> October 18, 1856
>
> Dear Margaret,
>
> When the Republican Party was formed two years ago, we had no idea it would grow so quickly. I am so pleased with the party's choice of John Frémont as the Republican candidate for President. I know Mother would have agreed with me. I only hope you and I will be able to cast our votes in a presidential election soon.
>
> Your loving sister, Ellen

12. What is the letter about?

13. What is one statement directly related to the subject of the letter? Why is it relevant?

14. What is one statement that is irrelevant to the subject of the letter? Why is it irrelevant?

Test Yourself

1. All of the following were causes of the Civil War EXCEPT

   A John Brown's raid on Harpers Ferry.

   B the Dred Scott decision.

   C the use of child labor in northern factories.

   D the publication of Stowe's *Uncle Tom's Cabin.*

Refer to the quotation below to answer Question 2.

> "A house divided against itself cannot stand. . . . I do not expect the Union to be dissolved—I do not expect the house to fall—but I do expect it will cease to be divided. It will become all one thing or all the other."

2. What division does this quotation describe?

   A church and state

   B free states and slaveholding states

   C the House of Representatives and the Senate

   D Republicans and Democrats

Refer to the pie chart below to answer Question 3.

Percentage of Popular Vote, 1860

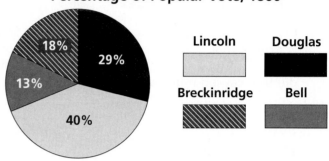

3. What conclusion can you draw from this pie chart?

   A Southerners voted for Douglas.

   B Lincoln won most of the popular vote.

   C Bell had little support in the North.

   D The two Democrats combined won more votes than Lincoln.

Document-Based Questions

Task: Look at Documents 1 and 2, and answer their accompanying questions. Then, use the documents and your knowledge of history to complete this writing assignment:

   Write a two-paragraph essay comparing the goals of the Fugitive Slave Law with its actual effects.

Document 1: In this speech, Senator John Calhoun of South Carolina explained the need for the Fugitive Slave Law. *According to Calhoun, what would happen if Congress did not pass the law?*

> "How can the Union be saved? . . . There is but one way . . . , and that is by adopting such measures as will satisfy . . . the southern section that they can remain in the Union consistently with their honor and their safety. . . .
>
>   But can this be done? Yes, easily. . . . The North has only . . . to conced[e] to the South an equal right in [newly] acquired territory, and to caus[e] the stipulations relative to fugitive slaves to be faithfully fulfilled—to cease the agitation of the slave question. . . ."

Document 2: This poster reveals Bostonians' commitment to protect runaways or kidnapped African Americans. *Why were posters like this illegal?*

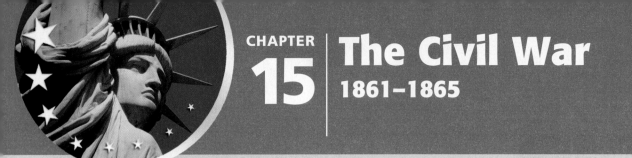

CHAPTER **15** | **The Civil War**
1861–1865

Chapter Preview

In 1861, war broke out between North and South. For more than four years, Americans fought other Americans. The Civil War was a long, difficult struggle that caused much suffering for both sides.

☑ **What You Will Learn**

As the war began and states took sides, the North and the South drew up plans and hoped for an early victory.

The early years of the war were indecisive, as neither side seemed able to defeat the other.

President Lincoln's decision to issue the Emancipation Proclamation opened the way for African Americans to join the Union army.

The war caused divisions in both North and South while changing the lives of civilians and soldiers alike.

Union victories at Gettysburg and Vicksburg in 1863 forced the South's surrender in April 1865.

U.S. Events

1861
Eleven states secede from the Union.

1862
President Lincoln announces plan of emancipation.

1863
Union wins victory at Gettysburg.

1861

1862

1863

World Events

1861 Napoleon III sends French troops to invade Mexico.

1862 Otto von Bismarck becomes prime minister of Prussia.

Quick View Video
View the chapter video for a quick preview of the main ideas.

All is peaceful now at Cemetery Hill in Gettysburg, Pennsylvania. But in July 1863, a terrible, bloody battle took place there that marked a turning point in the Civil War.

1864
Grant invades the South and lays siege to Petersburg.

1865
Lee surrenders at Appomattox.

1863

1864

1865

1864 French-backed Maximilian of Austria becomes emperor of Mexico.

History Reading Skill Understand Sequence

What was a Civil War battle like?

In this chapter, you will learn how to relate events in time and understand sequence. Read the following report about a major Civil War battle. The side notes show you how to relate events in time and identify their sequence.

> In 1862, George Washburn Smalley was a war journalist for a northern newspaper. Here, he describes the Battle of Antietam, a major battle during the early years of the Civil War.

Primary Source

> Fierce and desperate battle between 200,000 men has <u>raged since daylight. Finally, at four o'clock,</u> [Union General] McClellan was to advance . . . [at] . . . any cost. . . . [General] Burnside was to carry the woods next in front of him to the right, which the Rebels still held. . . .
>
> <u>There is a halt. The Rebel left gives way and scatters over the field.</u> The rest stand fast and fire. <u>More infantry comes up.</u> Burnside is outnumbered, flanked, compelled to yield the hill he took so bravely. His position is no longer one of attack. He defends himself with unfaltering firmness. . . .
>
> The sun is already down. Not half an hour of daylight is left. <u>None suspected how near was the peril of defeat. But the Rebels halted instead of pushing on. Before it was quite dark, the battle was over.</u>
>
> —*New York Daily Tribune*, September 20, 1862

Signal words—*since daylight, at four-o'clock*—show the sequence.

After new infantry shows up, the course of the battle is changed. These events are related in time.

Here, events are described in order: (1) There is a halt. (2) The Rebel left gives way.

The sequence of events—the Union is losing, but then the Rebels halt—causes the Union to unexpectedly win the battle.

Understand Sequence

- Sequence signal words and dates tell you when events happened.
- Look for events described in time, or chronological, order.
- Ask yourself how events are connected: Are they happening at the same time? Did one event cause another that follows?

Document-Based Questions

1. In which newspaper was this article published?
2. Describe the sequence of events in the battle.
3. Do you think this is a reliable account? Explain your answer.

Vocabulary *Builder*

Previewing High-Use Academic Words

High-Use Word	Definition	Sample History Sentence
distinct (dihs TIHNKT) (Section 1, p. 514)	*adj.* clear or definite; different in quality	Each Civil War general had his own distinct methods of fighting.
resource (REE sors) (Section 1, p. 514)	*n.* supply of something to meet a particular need	As the war dragged on, the South's war effort suffered from a lack of resources.
superior (sah PIR ee ahr) (Section 2, p. 519)	*adj.* of greater importance or value; above average	In some battles, a smaller force proved superior to a larger one.
reinforce (ree ihn FORS) (Section 2, p. 519)	*v.* to make stronger; to make more effective	Expecting an enemy attack, soldiers tried to reinforce their defenses.
restore (ree STOR) (Section 3, p. 524)	*v.* to bring back to a normal state; to put back; to reestablish	If a building was only damaged in the war, its owner might try to restore it by ordering repairs.
sustain (suh STAYN) (Section 3, p. 525)	*v.* to keep going; to endure; to supply with food; to support as just	Using horse carts to haul food and ammunition, the army was able to sustain its troops through a long campaign.
levy (LEHV ee) (Section 4, p. 531)	*v.* to impose by law	It is common for governments to levy a tax on imports.
currency (KER rehn see) (Section 4, p. 531)	*n.* money used to make purchases	The government prints paper currency that people can use for their purchases.
encounter (ehn KOWN ter) (Section 5, p. 534)	*v.* to meet in an unexpected way; to experience	Soldiers who entered enemy territory did not know what dangers they might encounter.
exceed (ehks SEED) (Section 5, p. 535)	*v.* to go beyond what is expected; to be greater than what was planned	The general had expected to win, but his victory exceeded his greatest hopes.

Previewing Key Terms and People

The Call to Arms

Objectives

1. Identify the states that supported the Union, the states that seceded, and the states whose loyalties were divided.

2. Describe the advantages each side had in the war.

3. Compare the different strategies used by the North and the South.

4. Summarize the results of the First Battle of Bull Run.

5. Describe the conditions soldiers in camp faced.

Prepare to Read

⊙ Reading Skill

Understand Sequence of Events The Civil War began as a result of a complex sequence of events. As that war proceeded in its early days, events continued at a furious pace. To form a full understanding of this phase of the war, pause regularly to summarize the sequence of events. Use your own words to recount the important events in the correct order.

Vocabulary *Builder*

High-Use Words

distinct, p. 514

resource, p. 514

Key Terms

border state, p. 513

neutral, p. 513

martial law, p. 513

blockade, p. 515

⭐ **Background Knowledge** In the previous chapter, you learned how tensions over slavery troubled the nation throughout the 1850s. Southern slaveholders became committed to protecting the system on which they depended. In this section, you will learn how this determination led to the Civil War.

Main Idea
As the war began and states chose sides, loyalties in the four border states were divided.

Taking Sides in the War

Two days after Fort Sumter's surrender, President Lincoln declared that a rebellion existed in the South. To put it down, he asked the nation's governors to raise 75,000 troops. Across the North, young men eagerly volunteered. Support was so widespread that the governors of Ohio, Indiana, and several other states begged to send more troops than the President had requested.

More States Secede Not all states were so enthusiastic, however. In Tennessee, the governor said that his state "will not furnish a single man" to fight against "our southern brothers." The governors of Kentucky and Missouri made similar replies to Lincoln's request. Maryland and Delaware did not respond at all.

The President's call for troops led more southern states to secede. On April 17, Virginia left the Union. In May, Arkansas, Tennessee, and North Carolina also joined the Confederacy. However, the western counties of Virginia, where there was little support for slavery, refused to secede. In 1863, these 50 counties were admitted to the Union as the state of West Virginia.

The Border States Loyalties remained divided in the border states—slave states that did not secede. Delaware had few enslaved people, and its support of the Union was strong. However, many people in Kentucky, Missouri, and Maryland favored the South. Kentucky and Missouri were important to controlling the Ohio and Mississippi rivers. And unless the Union could hold Maryland, Washington would be surrounded by the Confederacy.

At first, Kentucky declared itself **neutral,** or not favoring either side. Union generals wanted to occupy Kentucky, but Lincoln refused. He feared that such a move would push the state to secede. His strategy was wise. When Confederate forces invaded it in September 1861, Kentucky decided to support the North.

By contrast, the President acted forcefully to hold Missouri and Maryland. When Missouri's government sided with the South, Union supporters set up their own state government. Fighting broke out within the state. Finally, Lincoln sent troops, and the state stayed in the Union throughout the war.

In Maryland, southern sympathizers destroyed railroad and telegraph lines. So Lincoln placed eastern Maryland under **martial law.** This is a type of rule in which the military is in charge and citizens' rights are suspended. Maryland officials and others suspected of disloyalty were jailed without trials.

Understand Sequence of Events
Summarize the events as North and South geared up for full-scale conflict. Make sure to recount events in the correct sequence.

☑**Checkpoint** **How did the border states line up in the war?**

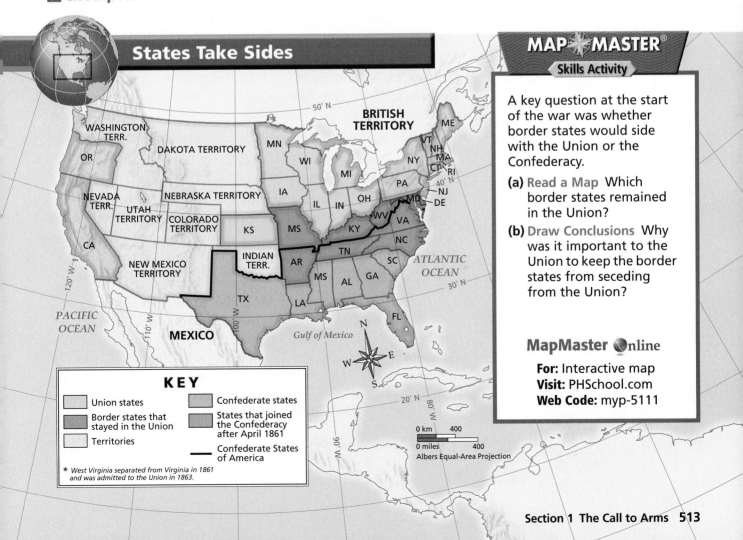

States Take Sides

MAP MASTER®

Skills Activity

A key question at the start of the war was whether border states would side with the Union or the Confederacy.

(a) Read a Map Which border states remained in the Union?

(b) Draw Conclusions Why was it important to the Union to keep the border states from seceding from the Union?

MapMaster Online

For: Interactive map
Visit: PHSchool.com
Web Code: myp-5111

KEY

- Union states
- Border states that stayed in the Union
- Territories
- Confederate states
- States that joined the Confederacy after April 1861
- Confederate States of America

West Virginia separated from Virginia in 1861 and was admitted to the Union in 1863.

0 km 400
0 miles 400
Albers Equal-Area Projection

Comparing Resources, 1861

Source: *The Times Atlas of World History*

Reading Charts

Skills Activity

The Union had an advantage over the Confederacy in a number of resources.

(a) **Read a Bar Graph** In which of the three comparisons is the Union's advantage the greatest?

(b) **Draw Conclusions** For each of these three resources, how would you expect the Union to benefit from its advantage?

(c) **Make Predictions** Based on the information in these graphs, which side would you expect to win the war? Explain.

Main Idea
Each side had its advantages and disadvantages, and each side was sure it would win.

Vocabulary *Builder*
distinct (dihs TIHNKT) *adj.* clear or definite; different in quality

Vocabulary *Builder*
resource (REE sors) *n.* supply of something to meet a particular need

North Against South

As the armies prepared, people on both sides were confident. A Union soldier declared that he was "willing . . . to lay down all my joys in this life to help maintain this government." Southerners compared themselves to Americans of 1776. A New Orleans poet wrote of Confederates: "Yes, call them rebels! 'tis the name/Their patriot fathers bore."

Southern Advantages Although outnumbered, the South had some <u>distinct</u> military advantages. To win, northern armies would have to invade and conquer the South. Confederates would be fighting on their own territory, with help from the local people.

In addition, most of the nation's experienced military officers were southerners. The Confederacy's three top generals—Albert Johnston, Joseph Johnston, and Robert E. Lee—all had resigned from the U.S. Army to fight for the South.

Northern Advantages In 1861, the United States had about 130,000 factories. Of those, 110,000 were in the North. The North had twice as much railroad track and almost twice as much farmland.

The North also had a population advantage. Some two thirds of the nation's people lived in states that remained in the Union, and in the South more than a third of the people were enslaved. With more <u>resources</u>, the North was able to field, feed, and equip larger armies.

✔**Checkpoint** What were each side's advantages?

The Two Sides Plan Strategies

Union leaders hoped to win a quick victory. To isolate the Confederacy, Lincoln had the navy blockade southern seaports. A **blockade** is a military action to prevent traffic from coming into an area or leaving it. Lincoln hoped to cut off the South's supply of manufactured goods and block overseas sales of cotton.

An important part of northern strategy was to gain control of the Mississippi River, the South's major transportation link. This would split the South in two. The Union also planned to invade Virginia and seize Richmond, the Confederate capital. It was just 100 miles from Washington, D.C.

The South's strategy was simpler. The Confederates did not need to invade the North. They had only to defend their land until northerners got tired of fighting. The Confederates sought aid from Britain and other European nations. They hoped that Britain's need of cotton for its textile mills would force the British to support the South.

☑Checkpoint **How did strategies on the two sides differ?**

Main Idea
While the North wanted to isolate the South and invade it, the South hoped to get help from Europe.

Americans Against Americans

On both sides, men rushed to be part of the fight. "I had never dreamed that New England . . . could be fired with so warlike a spirit," wrote Mary Ashton Livermore in Boston. In South Carolina, Mary Chesnut said that men rushed to enlist in the army for "fear the war will be over before they get a sight of the fun."

This war between Americans broke families apart, setting brother against brother, father against son. Kentucky Senator John Crittenden had two sons in the war fighting on different sides. Four brothers of Mary Lincoln, the President's wife, fought for the Confederacy.

Main Idea
The war often divided families as it drew most adult males on both sides into the military.

Old Enough for War
Soldiers in both the Union and Confederate armies might have been as young as 14. Nearly 4,000 Union troops were 16 or younger. **Critical Thinking: Draw Conclusions** *How do you think the experience of war affected young men?*

Fleeing Bull Run

Before the First Battle of Bull Run, both sides expected an easy victory. But they were wrong. Here, Union soldiers have panicked and are fleeing the Bull Run battlefield. Bull Run was an early sign that the war would be long and costly. **Critical Thinking: *Draw Conclusions*** *What reasons did each side have to think it would win an early victory? Why were both sides' expectations unreasonable?*

History *Interactive*
Explore the Lessons of a Battle
Visit: PHSchool.com
Web Code: myp-5177

The soldiers came from many backgrounds. Nearly half of the North's troops were farmers. One fourth were immigrants.

Three fourths of the South's 1 million white males between ages 18 and 45 served in the army. Two thirds of the 3.5 million northern males of the same age fought for the Union. Some soldiers were as young as 14.

☑**Checkpoint**   Who were the soldiers in this war?

First Battle of Bull Run

Main Idea
Expectations of a quick victory were dashed at Bull Run in July 1861.

Union General Irvin McDowell wanted time to turn his soldiers into an effective fighting force. But by July 1861, northern newspapers were demanding the capture of Richmond and a quick end to the war.

McDowell's 30,000 men left Washington and marched southwest into Virginia. About the same number of Confederates waited at Manassas, a railroad center about 25 miles away. Hundreds of people rode out from Washington to see the battle, expecting an easy Union victory.

The armies clashed along Bull Run, a river just north of Manassas, on July 21. At first, the Union army pushed forward. But a southern commander rallied his men to hold firm. "Look, there is Jackson with his Virginians, standing like a stone wall," he shouted. From then on, the general, Thomas Jackson, was known as "Stonewall" Jackson.

Slowly the battle turned in favor of the Confederates. The poorly trained Union troops began to panic. Soldiers and sightseers fled back to Washington. The Confederates were too exhausted to pursue them.

☑**Checkpoint**   What was the result of the First Battle of Bull Run?

A Soldier's Life

Most soldiers spent three fourths of their time in camp, not fighting. Training took up to 10 hours a day. When not training, soldiers stood guard, wrote home, and gathered firewood. A meal might be simply a dry, cracker-like product called hardtack.

Harsh Conditions Camp conditions were often miserable, especially when wet weather created muddy roads and fields. The lack of clean water was a major health threat. Outbreaks of smallpox, typhoid fever, and other diseases swept through the ranks. It was not unusual for half the men in a regiment to be too sick to fight.

Prisoners of War Both sides built prison camps for captured soldiers. Overcrowded prison camps became deathtraps. Nearly 10 percent of soldiers who died in the war perished in prison camps.

The camps at Elmira, New York, and Andersonville, Georgia, were the worst. Elmira camp, built to hold 5,000 Confederate prisoners, held 10,000. The camp cut rations to bread and water, forcing prisoners to eat rats to survive. Thousands died. At Andersonville, nearly 35,000 Union soldiers lived in a fenced, open field intended to hold 10,000 men. As many as 100 prisoners died each day, usually from starvation or exposure.

☑Checkpoint **What conditions did soldiers have to endure?**

⭐ **Looking Back and Ahead** The North's hopes for an early victory had been dashed. The war would be long and brutal. In the next section, you will read more about the early years of the war.

Main Idea
Rain, mud, disease, and crowded prison camps took a heavy toll on both sides.

Hardtack

Section 1 | **Check Your Progress**

Progress Monitoring ⬤nline
For: Self-test with instant help
Visit: PHSchool.com
Web Code: mya-5111

Comprehension and Critical Thinking

1. **(a) Recall** How did President Lincoln respond to the surrender of Fort Sumter?
   (b) Apply Information What caused three border states to remain in the Union?

2. **(a) List** What were three advantages held by the South? What were three advantages held by the North?
   (b) Analyze Cause and Effect How did the First Battle of Bull Run shatter the belief that the Civil War would be a quick Union victory?

🔁 Reading Skill

3. **Understand Sequence of Events** Choose a state that wavered about supporting the North or the South. Summarize the sequence of events that led this state to a final decision.

Vocabulary *Builder*

Complete each of the following sentences so that the second part explains the first and shows your understanding of the key term.

4. Union leaders planned a blockade; _____.

5. Lincoln placed Maryland under martial law; _____.

Writing

6. Create an outline that covers the information presented in this section, copying the form below. A few entries have been filled in.

   I. Taking sides in the war (first important topic)
      A. More states secede (first issue for that topic)
        1. A number of border states refused to send troops to support the Union (first point)
        2. _____ (second point)
      B.
        1.
        2.
   II.

Early Years of the War

Objectives

1. Explain how new weapons made fighting the war more dangerous.

2. Describe the course of the war in the East in 1862.

3. Describe the early days of the war in the West and at sea.

Prepare to Read

Reading Skill

Distinguish Events in Sequence As you read this section, it is important to keep events in sequence. Ask yourself: Which event happened first? Next? Last? You might number events to help you organize their sequence. This will help you to understand the unfolding drama of the Civil War.

Vocabulary *Builder*

High-Use Words

superior, p. 519
reinforce, p. 519

Key Terms and People

ironclad, p. 518
George McClellan, p. 519
casualty, p. 520
Ulysses S. Grant, p. 520

⭐ **Background Knowledge** The Union's crushing defeat at Bull Run made northerners realize that a long and difficult struggle lay ahead. In this section, you will learn how the bloody early years of war caused many to worry that the North might not win.

Main Idea
The use of new weapons forced commanders to rethink their tactics.

New Technology in the War

New weapons made the Civil War more deadly than any previous war. Traditionally, generals had relied on an all-out charge of troops to overwhelm the enemy. But new rifles and cannons were far more accurate and had a greater range than the old muskets and artillery. They could also be loaded much faster. As a result, the attacking army could be bombarded long before it arrived at the defenders' position.

Unfortunately, Civil War generals were slow to recognize the problem and change tactics. Thousands of soldiers on both sides were slaughtered by following orders to cross open fields against these deadly new weapons.

Both sides also made use of **ironclads.** These were warships covered with protective iron plates. Cannon fire bounced harmlessly off this armor. The most famous naval battle of the war occurred when two ironclads, the Union's *Monitor* and the Confederacy's *Merrimack,* fought to a draw in March 1862. The use of ironclads marked the end of thousands of years of wooden warships. The Confederates used ironclads against the Union's naval blockade. Ironclad Union gunboats played an important role in the North's efforts to gain control of the Mississippi River.

✔**Checkpoint** What new technologies were used in the Civil War?

The War in the East

After the Union's defeat at Bull Run, Lincoln removed McDowell and put General George McClellan in command. The general was a good organizer, but he was very cautious. For seven months, he trained his army but did not attack. "If General McClellan does not want to use the army," a frustrated Lincoln complained, "I would like to borrow it for a time."

In March 1862, McClellan was finally ready. He moved some 100,000 soldiers by boat along Chesapeake Bay to a peninsula southeast of Richmond. As McClellan advanced toward the Confederate capital, he discovered that his force was far <u>superior</u> to the 15,000 enemy soldiers blocking the way. However, McClellan still did not have as many soldiers as he wanted because Lincoln had ordered 37,000 soldiers to stay behind to guard Washington, D.C. The general stopped his advance and asked for more troops.

McClellan waited nearly a month before moving again. This delay gave the Confederates time to <u>reinforce</u> their small army of defenders. On May 31, 1862, the Confederates stopped McClellan's advance near Richmond. In late June, McClellan had to retreat.

With Richmond no longer threatened, Lee decided to invade the North. He hoped that a victory on Union soil would help win support for the South in Europe and turn northern public opinion against the war. In early September, he slipped his army into western Maryland.

Now McClellan had a stroke of luck. A Union officer found a paper showing Lee's battle plan. McClellan thus learned that the Confederate army had divided into two parts.

Main Idea
Each side suffered setbacks in the East in 1862.

Vocabulary *Builder*
<u>superior</u> (sah PIR ee ahr) *adj.* of greater importance or value; above average

Vocabulary *Builder*
<u>reinforce</u> (ree ihn FORS) *v.* to make stronger; to make more effective

Inset shows the recovery of the *Monitor*'s turret, or gun chamber, in 2002.

Explore More Video
To learn more about this historic battle, view the video.

Battle of Two Ironclads
The Civil War introduced ironclad warships. Here, an artist shows the battle between the Confederacy's *Merrimack* (left) and the Union's *Monitor* (right) off Hampton Roads, Virginia, in 1862. **Critical Thinking:** *Draw Conclusions* *How would you expect an ironclad ship to fare in a battle against an older warship that lacked armor? Explain.*

KEY

- ← Union troops
- ← Confederate troops
- ★ Union victory
- ★ Confederate victory

PA
OH
IN
MO
IL
KY
MD
DE
NJ
Antietam
Harpers Ferry
Bull Run
☆ Washington, D.C.
Potomac R.
Richmond
Seven Days
James R.
VA
Monitor versus Merrimack (no victor)
Chesapeake Bay
Cumberland R.
Fort Donelson
Fort Henry
TN • Nashville
Shiloh
Corinth
Tennessee R.
NC
SC
GA
AR
MS
AL
Mississippi R.
LA
Vicksburg
TX
Port Hudson
New Orleans
Gulf of Mexico
FL
ATLANTIC OCEAN

N W E S

0 km   200
0 miles   200
Albers Equal-Area Projection

MAP MASTER®
Skills Activity

In 1862, Union troops tried but failed to capture Richmond, the capital of the Confederacy. To the west, meanwhile, the Union's land and naval forces won some significant victories.

(a) Read a Map Which battles were Union victories? Which were Confederate victories?

(b) Interpret a Map Describe Grant's route to Shiloh. What city on the Mississippi River did Grant attack after the Battle of Shiloh?

MapMaster ⬤nline

For: Interactive map
Visit: PHSchool.com
Web Code: myp-5112

McClellan's troops attacked the larger part of Lee's army at Antietam Creek, near Sharpsburg, Maryland, on September 17, 1862. This was the bloodiest day of the Civil War. The Union army attacked again and again. It suffered about 12,000 **casualties**—the military term for persons killed, wounded, or missing in action. Lee lost nearly 14,000 men—almost one third of his army. He was forced to pull his battered army back into Virginia. To Lincoln's dismay, McClellan did not press his advantage by pursuing Lee.

Neither side won a clear victory at the Battle of Antietam. But because Lee had ordered a retreat, the North claimed victory.

✔**Checkpoint** How did McClellan's caution hurt the Union?

Main Idea
In the West, Union forces seized control of most of the Mississippi River in 1862.

The War in the West

As McClellan moved cautiously, Union armies in the West went on the attack. General **Ulysses S. Grant** led the most successful of these armies. McClellan and Grant were very different. McClellan wore carefully fitted uniforms. Grant, once a poor store clerk, wore rumpled clothes. McClellan was cautious. Grant took chances.

Union forces made major advances in western land and naval battles in 1862, seizing control of most of the Mississippi River. In February 1862, Grant moved his army south from Kentucky. First, he captured Fort Henry on the Tennessee River. Then, he captured Fort Donelson on the Cumberland River.

Two water routes into the western Confederacy were now wide open. Grant's army continued south along the Tennessee River toward Corinth, Mississippi, an important railroad center.

Before Grant could advance on Corinth, Confederate General Albert Sidney Johnston attacked. On April 6, 1862, he surprised Grant's troops at the Battle of Shiloh. (For more on this battle, see the Geography and History feature in this chapter.)

The Battle of Shiloh was costly yet important for both sides. The South suffered nearly 11,000 casualties and the North more than 13,000. However, the Union forced the Confederate army to withdraw from the railroad center. Union forces also gained control of western Tennessee and part of the Mississippi River.

Two weeks after the Battle of Shiloh, a Union fleet commanded by David Farragut entered the Mississippi River from the Gulf of Mexico. On April 26, Farragut captured New Orleans, Louisiana. By summer, nearly the entire river was in Union hands.

Distinguish Events in Sequence What was the sequence of battles in the West? When did these occur?

☑**Checkpoint** **What was the result of the Battle of Shiloh?**

⭐ **Looking Back and Ahead** Northern and southern generals both tried to carry the war into enemy territory. At first, neither side gained a decisive advantage. In the next section, you will read how the Emancipation Proclamation changed the nature of the war.

Section 2 | **Check Your Progress**

Progress Monitoring ⏻nline
For: Self-test with instant help
Visit: PHSchool.com
Web Code: mya-5112

Comprehension and Critical Thinking

1. **(a) Describe** Explain what life was like for a Civil War soldier.
(b) Evaluate Information How did harsh conditions and new technology result in a high number of casualties?

2. **(a) Summarize** Why was General McClellan considered to be an ineffective leader?
(b) Organize Information Make a chart that shows the place, casualties, leaders, outcome, and importance of the battles at Shiloh and Antietam Creek.

Reading Skill

3. **Distinguish Events in Sequence** During the Battle of Shiloh, which came first: Grant captured Fort Henry, Johnston attacked, Grant won a stunning victory? Identify the signal clues that you used.

Vocabulary *Builder*

Read each sentence. If the sentence is true, write YES. If the sentence is not true, write NO and explain why.
4. Both the Union and the Confederacy suffered many casualties.
5. Ironclads were of little importance in the war at sea.

Writing

6. Use library or Internet resources to find more information about one of the topics covered in this section. Suggestions for topics include the ironclad warships, the Battle of Shiloh, or the Battle of Antietam. Then, write a short introduction to a research paper that would present information about the topic.

The Battle of Shiloh

In April 1862, the Confederacy seized an opportunity to attack Union forces in the West. Two Union armies were attempting to join each other in south-western Tennessee. Confederate troops were camped close by in Corinth, Mississippi. The Confederates attacked near Pittsburgh Landing, Tennessee, on April 6, hoping to crush one Union force before the other could arrive.

KEY

← Union troops

← Confederate troops

Confederate troops attacked Union forces at the Battle of Shiloh.

1 A Sunken Road

The initial Confederate attack caught Union troops by surprise. They retreated a mile before establishing a defensive position along a sunken road. Troops crouched behind the road bank and fought off a dozen Confederate charges.

2 Exposed to Counterattack

Confederate troops marched toward the Union position without the protection of trees or foxholes. Every charge was met with a flurry of bullets from Union soldiers using vegetation and raised mounds of earth as cover.

Understand Effects:
A Bloody Victory

The Battle of Shiloh was one of the bloodiest engagements of the Civil War. Although the Union emerged the victor, both sides suffered heavy losses. Union General Ulysses S. Grant would continue to guide his army as it gradually seized control of the entire Mississippi Valley.

◀ Rifle bullets

Confederate jacket ▶

3 The "Hornet's Nest"

As the battle wore on, the Confederates nicknamed the Union position the "Hornet's Nest" because of the intense fire the Confederate soldiers encountered. Union bullets caused many Confederate injuries. One officer's jacket shows the devastating results of the battle.

Analyze **GEOGRAPHY AND HISTORY**

Write a paragraph explaining how northern troops used geography to give themselves an advantage over the Confederates.

SECTION 3 | The Emancipation Proclamation

Objectives

1. Explain why Lincoln issued the Emancipation Proclamation.
2. Identify the effects of the proclamation.
3. Describe the contributions of African Americans to the Union.

Prepare to Read

Reading Skill

Explain How Events Are Related in Time President Lincoln and others made many choices in fighting the war. They made these choices in the context of the events at the time. When reading about history, it is important to see how events in a period are related in time. Do events influence the attitudes and decisions of people going forward in time? Do they change people's actions and freedoms?

Vocabulary *Builder*

High-Use Words

restore, p. 524
sustain, p. 525

Key Terms and People

emancipate, p. 524
Horace Greeley, p. 524

Main Idea
Lincoln was slow to decide on emancipation but finally embraced it as a necessary war measure.

Vocabulary *Builder*
restore (ree STOR) *v.* to bring back to a normal state; to put back; to reestablish

⭐ **Background Knowledge** The first two years of war had not been good for the North. However, the North's victory at Antietam was a turning point. As you will now learn, that battle created the conditions that ended slavery and led to a Union victory.

Emancipating the Enslaved

Many abolitionists rejoiced when the war began. They urged Lincoln to end slavery and thus punish the South for starting the war.

Lincoln Changes His Mind At first, the President resisted. He knew most northerners did not want to end slavery. "You . . . overestimate the number in the country who hold such views," he told one abolitionist. He feared that any action to **emancipate,** or free, enslaved African Americans might make the border states secede.

Lincoln said his goal was to restore the Union, even if that meant letting slavery continue. He stated this very clearly in a letter to abolitionist newspaper publisher **Horace Greeley.**

> ❝If I could save the Union without freeing *any* slave, I would do it, and if I could save it by freeing *all* the slaves, I would do it. . . . What I do about slavery . . . I do because I believe it helps to save the Union.❞
>
> —Abraham Lincoln, letter to Horace Greeley, August 1862

Gradually, Lincoln began to change his mind. He realized how important slavery was to the South's war effort. He told his Cabinet that he intended to issue an Emancipation Proclamation. But Cabinet members advised him to wait until after a success on the battlefield.

A Famous Proclamation On September 22, 1862, a few days after Lee's retreat from Antietam, Lincoln met again with his Cabinet and issued a preliminary proclamation.

On January 1, 1863, Lincoln issued the final Emancipation Proclamation. This document had little immediate effect, however, because it freed enslaved people only in areas that were fighting the Union. Those were places where the Union had no power. The proclamation did not apply to parts of the South already under Union control. Nor did it free anyone in the border states.

The proclamation was both criticized and praised. Some abolitionists said it should be applied throughout the country. White southerners accused Lincoln of trying to cause a slave revolt. But many Union soldiers were enthusiastic. They welcomed anything that weakened the South. "This army will <u>sustain</u> the Emancipation Proclamation and enforce it with the bayonet," an Indiana soldier said.

Effects of the Proclamation Even though the proclamation freed few slaves at first, it had other important effects. Above all, it changed the Civil War into a struggle for freedom. This was no longer just a fight to save the nation. It was now also a fight to end slavery.

Vocabulary Builder
<u>sustain</u> (suh STAYN) v. to keep going; to endure; to supply with food; to support as just

The Emancipation Proclamation

❝That on the first day of January, in the year of our Lord [1863], all persons held as slaves within any State or designated part of a State, the people whereof shall then be in rebellion against the United States, shall be then, thenceforward, and forever free. . . . ❞

—Emancipation Proclamation, January 1, 1863

A Union general posted the announcement at right, declaring the freedom of enslaved African Americans in the part of Virginia occupied by his troops.

FREEDOM TO SLAVES!

Whereas, the President of the United States did, on the first day of the present month, issue his *Proclamation* declaring "that all persons held as *Slaves in certain designated States, and parts of States, are, and henceforward shall be free,*" and that the Executive Government of the United States, including the Military and Naval authorities thereof, would recognize and maintain the freedom of said persons. *And Whereas,* the county of Frederick is included in the territory designated by the Proclamation of the President, in which the *Slaves should become free,* I therefore hereby notify the citizens of the city of Winchester, and of said County, of said Proclamation, and of my intention to maintain and enforce the same.

I expect all citizens to yield a ready compliance with the Proclamation of the Chief Executive, and I admonish all persons disposed to resist its peaceful enforcement, that upon manifesting such disposition by acts, they will be regarded as rebels in arms against the lawful authority of the Federal Government and dealt with accordingly.

All persons liberated by said Proclamation are admonished to abstain from all violence, and immediately betake themselves to useful occupations.

The officers of this command are admonished and ordered to act in accordance with said proclamation and to yield their ready co-operation in its enforcement.

Winchester Va
Jan. 5th, 1863.

R. H. Milroy,
Brig. Gen'l Commanding.

Reading Primary Sources

Skills Activity

President Lincoln's proclamation specified that it applied only to certain parts of the United States.

(a) **Understand Sequence** In what order were these two declarations issued?

(b) **Compare** In what way is the declaration on the right more specific than the one by President Lincoln?

African American Soldiers

These are guards of the 107th Colored Infantry at Fort Corcoran in Washington, D.C. **Critical Thinking: *Apply Information*** *How did conditions for African American soldiers differ from those for white soldiers?*

Main Idea

African Americans fought for the Union and made other contributions to the war effort.

Explain How Events Are Related in Time

Explain why these two events are related in time: African American soldiers fought for the Union; President Lincoln issued the Emancipation Proclamation.

Also, the Emancipation Proclamation dashed any hopes that Britain would recognize the South's independence. Britain would not help a government that was fighting to keep people enslaved.

In both North and South, Lincoln's proclamation united African Americans in support of the war. "We shout for joy that we live to record this righteous decree," wrote Frederick Douglass.

☑**Checkpoint** **How did the proclamation affect the war?**

African Americans Help the Union

When the Civil War began, African American volunteers were not permitted to join the Union army. Northern African Americans appealed for the chance to help fight for the nation. However, not until after the Emancipation Proclamation were many allowed to serve.

Volunteering for Service The Emancipation Proclamation encouraged African Americans to enlist. Ultimately, 189,000 African Americans served in the Union army or navy. More than half were former slaves who had escaped or been freed by the fighting. All faced extra risks. If captured, they were not treated as prisoners of war. Most were returned to slavery and some were killed.

Black and white sailors served together on warships. In the army, however, African American soldiers served in all-black regiments under white officers. They earned less pay than white soldiers.

Despite these disadvantages, African American regiments fought with pride and courage. "They make better soldiers in every respect than any troops I have ever had under my command," a Union general said of an African American regiment from Kansas.

African American troops took part in about 40 major battles and hundreds of minor ones. The most famous was the attack on Fort Wagner in South Carolina by the 54th Massachusetts Infantry on July 18, 1863. The unit volunteered to lead the assault. As the soldiers charged, Confederate cannon fire rained down. Yet the 54th reached the top of the fort's walls before being turned back in fierce hand-to-hand fighting. The regiment suffered terrible losses. Nearly half of its soldiers were casualties.

Thousands of African Americans supported the Union in noncombat roles. Free northern and emancipated southern African Americans often worked for Union armies as cooks, wagon drivers, and hospital aides.

Resisting Slavery In the South, many enslaved African Americans did what they could to hurt the Confederate war effort. Some provided military and other kinds of information to Union armies. Enslaved people had always quietly resisted slavery by deliberately working slowly or damaging equipment. But with many slaveholders off fighting the war, large numbers of slaves refused to work.

✓**Checkpoint** **How did African Americans help the Union cause?**

⭐ **Looking Back and Ahead** The Emancipation Proclamation made the Civil War a fight to end slavery. After the war, the Thirteenth Amendment banned slavery throughout the nation. The next section tells how the war affected civilians on both sides.

Section 3 | Check Your Progress

Progress Monitoring ⬤nline
For: Self-test with instant help
Visit: PHSchool.com
Web Code: mya-5113

Comprehension and Critical Thinking

1. **(a) Identify** Why did Lincoln at first resist identifying slavery as an issue of the Civil War?
(b) Analyze Cause and Effect What effect did the Emancipation Proclamation have on slavery?

2. **(a) Recall** In what ways did African Americans participate in the Civil War?
(b) Explain Problems What were three problems faced by African American soldiers?

🔟 Reading Skill

3. **Explain How Events Are Related in Time** Identify events that happened after the Emancipation Proclamation. Explain how these events are connected.

Vocabulary *Builder*

4. Write two definitions for emancipate. First, write a formal definition for your teacher. Second, write a definition in everyday English for a classmate.

Writing

5. Use library or Internet resources to find information about the African American 54th Massachusetts Infantry. Then, list the subtopics to be included in a research paper about the regiment. Write a paragraph about one of those subtopics. Identify some photographs and other nontext items that you would include in a research report on the 54th.

The Civil War and American Life

Objectives

1. Explain how opposition to the war caused problems for both sides.
2. Identify the reasons that both sides passed draft laws.
3. Describe the economic hardships the war caused in the North and the South.
4. Describe the contributions of women to the war efforts.

Prepare to Read

Reading Skill

Explain How Events Are Related in Time As soldiers were fighting the Civil War on the battlefield, Americans in both the North and the South were facing other wartime challenges. You will have a better understanding of the Civil War Era if you can relate events on the battlefield to events in civilian life.

Vocabulary *Builder*

High-Use Words

<u>levy</u>, p. 531
<u>currency</u>, p. 531

Key Terms

habeas corpus, p. 529
draft, p. 530
income tax, p. 531
inflation, p. 531

⭐ **Background Knowledge** The Emancipation Proclamation ended the South's hope for help from Britain and France. It also encouraged African Americans to fight for the Union. However, it also increased tensions in both the North and the South. In this section, you will learn about the changes and strains the Civil War caused in American life.

Divisions Over the War

Main Idea
On both sides, pursuit of the war was hampered by disagreements among the people.

The Civil War not only divided the nation. It also caused divisions *within* the North and the South. Not all northerners supported a war to end slavery or even to restore the Union. Not all white southerners supported a war to defend slavery or secession.

Division in the South In the South, opposition to the war was strongest in Georgia and North Carolina. Barely half of Georgians supported secession. There were nearly 100 peace protests in North Carolina in 1863 alone. Yet only Virginia provided more troops to Confederate armies than did North Carolina. Generally, regions with large slaveholding plantations supported the war more strongly than poor backcountry regions, where there were fewer enslaved people.

Strong support for states' rights created other divisions. For example, South Carolina's governor objected to officers from other states leading South Carolina troops. And the governors of Georgia and North Carolina did not want the Confederate government to force men from their states to do military service.

Division in the North Northerners were also divided over the war. Many opposed the Emancipation Proclamation. Others believed that the South had a right to secede. Some northern Democrats blamed Lincoln and the Republicans for forcing the South into a war. Northern Democrats who opposed the war were called Copperheads, after the poisonous snake. Copperheads were strongest in Ohio, Indiana, and Illinois. They criticized the war and called for peace with the Confederacy.

Dealing With Disruptions Some people on both sides tried to disrupt the war effort. A common tactic was to encourage soldiers to desert. Some northerners helped Confederate prisoners of war to escape. In the South, peace groups tried to end the war by working against the Confederacy. They tried to prevent men from volunteering for military service and urged Confederate soldiers to desert.

To deal with such problems, both Lincoln and Confederate President Jefferson Davis suspended the right of habeas corpus in some places during the war. **Habeas corpus** is a constitutional protection against unlawful imprisonment. It empowers judges to order that imprisoned persons be brought into court to determine if they are being legally held. In the North, more than 13,000 people were arrested and jailed without trials.

Explain How Events Are Related in Time As the Civil War progressed on the battlefield, what was happening at home? Include information about both North and South in your answer.

☑**Checkpoint** How did the Civil War divide both North and South?

Copperheads

The Union at war

Copperheads, northern Democrats who oppose the war

Reading Political Cartoons
Skills Activity

Republicans in the North fiercely resented Democrats who favored a negotiated peace with the South. This cartoon takes a stand on the issue of war and peace.

(a) Detect Points of View Is the cartoonist more likely to be a Republican or a Democrat? Do you think the cartoonist is against the war? Explain.

(b) Draw Conclusions What is the cartoonist's opinion of Copperheads?

Join or Be Drafted

Volunteers rushed to enlist at first, but antiwar feeling soon grew. During the New York draft riots of 1863, a mob set fire to a home for African American orphans.
*Critical Thinking: **Detect Points of View** What motivated the people who rioted against the draft?*

Main Idea

Both sides found it necessary to draft men into military service.

The Draft Laws

Desertion was a problem for both sides. Between 300,000 and 550,000 Union and Confederate soldiers left their units and went home. About half returned after their crops were planted or harvested. However, at times, from one third to one half of an army's soldiers were away from their units without permission.

To meet the need for troops, each side established a **draft**, a system of required military service. The South, with its smaller population, was first to act. In April 1862, the Confederacy passed a law requiring white men between ages 18 and 35 to serve in the military for three years. Later, the age range expanded to cover men from 17 to 50. The North adopted a similar draft law in 1863, for men ages 20 to 45.

Exceptions existed, however. Wealthy people had many ways of escaping fighting. In the South, a man who held at least 20 enslaved people did not have to serve. Both sides allowed draftees to hire substitutes to serve in their place. Northerners could avoid the draft by paying the government $300. For many workers, however, this was about a year's pay.

People on both sides complained that the draft made the war "a poor man's fight." Anger against the draft led to violent riots in the North in July 1863. The worst took place in New York City. Mobs of factory workers and laborers rioted for several days, destroying property and attacking African Americans and wealthy white men.

☑ **Checkpoint** Why was the Civil War sometimes called a poor man's fight?

The War and Economic Strains

Northern industries boomed as they turned out goods the Union needed in the war. Plenty of jobs were available. But the draft drained away workers so there was a constant shortage.

To pay the costs of fighting the war, Congress <u>levied</u> the first income tax in American history in August 1861. An **income tax** is a tax on the money people receive. The Union also printed $400 million of paper money to help pay its expenses. This was the first federal paper money, or <u>currency</u>. Putting this additional money into circulation led to **inflation,** or a general rise in prices. In the North, the prices of goods increased an average of 80 percent during the war.

The South was less able than the North to sustain a war. The Union blockade prevented the South from raising money by selling cotton overseas. Shortages made goods more expensive. This led to much greater inflation than in the North. A pair of shoes that had cost $18 dollars in 1862 cost up to $800 in the South in 1864. The price of a pound of beef soared from 12 cents in 1862 to $8 in 1865.

Southern food production fell as invading Union armies destroyed farmland and crops. Shortages of food led to riots in some southern cities. In Richmond, more than 1,000 women looted shops for food, cloth, and shoes in 1863. A woman in North Carolina complained:

> **"**A crowd of we poor women went to Greensboro yesterday for something to eat as we do not have a mouthful of bread nor meat. . . . I have 6 little children and my husband in the army and what am I to do?**"**
>
> —farm woman in North Carolina, April 1863

Enslaved people also suffered from wartime shortages. What little they did have was often seized by Confederate soldiers.

☑**Checkpoint** **What strains did the war put on people?**

Women in the Civil War

Women in both the North and the South contributed to the war in many ways. At least 400 women disguised themselves as men and joined the Union or Confederate armies. Others became spies behind enemy lines. Many women took over businesses, farms, and plantations while their fathers, brothers, and husbands served on the battlefields.

In both North and South, women ran farms and plantations. Some southern women worked in the fields to help meet the needs of the Confederacy. They continued to work despite fighting that destroyed their crops and killed their livestock.

Women also ran many northern farms. "I saw more women driving teams [of horses] on the road and saw more at work in the fields than men," a traveler in Iowa reported in 1862.

Main Idea
The war strained the finances of governments and individuals.

Vocabulary _Builder_
levy (LEHV ee) *v.* to impose by law

Vocabulary _Builder_
currency (KER rehn see) *n.* money used to make purchases

Main Idea
The war opened many new opportunities for women, who contributed greatly to the war effort.

Women on both sides did factory work. Some performed dangerous jobs, such as making ammunition. Others took government jobs. For example, the Confederate government employed dozens of women to sign and number Confederate currency.

The war created many new opportunities for women. Some women became teachers. About 10,000 northern women became nurses. Men had dominated these professions before the war.

Barriers to women especially fell in the field of nursing. Elizabeth Blackwell, America's first female physician, trained nurses for the Union army. Social reformer Dorothea Dix became the head of Union army nurses. Harriet Tubman, who continued to lead enslaved people to freedom during the war, also served as a Union nurse. Clara Barton cared for wounded soldiers on the battlefield. Although nursing was not considered a "proper" job for respectable southern women, some volunteered anyway.

✔Checkpoint **How did the war affect women?**

⭐ **Looking Back and Ahead** Both sides suffered political and economic hardships during the war. Draft laws affected every family, while new jobs opened up for women. In the next section, you will read how the war finally ended in the defeat of the Confederacy.

Section 4 | **Check Your Progress**

Comprehension and Critical Thinking

1. **(a) Identify** What were two reasons some northerners opposed the war? What were two reasons some southerners opposed the war?
(b) Explain Problems Why did the military draft lead some people to describe the war as a poor man's fight?

2. **(a) Describe** Explain the changing role for women during the Civil War.
(b) Identify Costs What effects did the Civil War have on the economies of the North and of the South?

Reading Skill

3. **Explain How Events Are Related in Time** What was happening to the American economy as the Civil War raged on?

Vocabulary *Builder*

4. Draw a table with four rows and three columns. In the first column, list the key terms from this section: habeas corpus, draft, income tax, inflation. In the next column, write the definition of each term. In the last column, make a small illustration that shows the meaning of the term.

Writing

5. Reread the text under the heading "Women in the Civil War." Then, write a short paragraph about the role that women played in the Civil War. Include material directly quoted from this section. Be sure to copy the quotation exactly, to punctuate it correctly, and to identify the source.

Decisive Battles

⭐ **Background Knowledge** By 1865, four years of Civil War had produced hundreds of thousands of deaths. In this section, you will learn how the Civil War finally came to an end.

The Tide Turns

After the Union victory at the 1862 Battle of Antietam, the war again began to go badly for the North. As before, the problem was poor leadership. When McClellan failed to pursue Lee's beaten army, Lincoln replaced him with General Ambrose Burnside.

Confederate Victories Burnside knew McClellan had been fired for being too cautious. So Burnside decided on a bold stroke. In December 1862, he marched his army of 120,000 men directly toward Richmond. Lee massed 75,000 men at Fredericksburg, Virginia, to block their path. Using traditional tactics, Burnside ordered charge after charge. The Union suffered nearly 13,000 casualties in the Battle of Fredericksburg and the Confederates nearly 5,000.

Lincoln next turned to General Joseph Hooker, nicknamed "Fighting Joe." "May God have mercy on General Lee, for I will have none," Hooker boasted as he marched the Union army toward Richmond. In May 1863, Hooker's army was smashed at the Battle of Chancellorsville by a force that was half its size. But the victory was a costly one for the South. During the battle, Stonewall Jackson was shot and wounded. A few days later, Jackson died.

Main Idea
After suffering some defeats, Union forces gained the upper hand by winning major battles at Gettysburg and Vicksburg.

Union General Joseph Hooker

The Battle of Gettysburg

These Confederate victories made Lee bolder. He was convinced that a major victory on Union soil would force northerners to end the war. In June 1863, Lee's troops crossed Maryland and marched into Pennsylvania. The Union army, which was now commanded by General George Meade, pursued them.

On July 1, some Confederate soldiers approached the quiet town of Gettysburg. They were looking for shoes, which were in short supply in the South because of the Union blockade. Instead of shoes, the Confederates <u>encountered</u> part of Meade's army. Shots were exchanged. More troops joined the fight on both sides. By evening, the southerners had pushed the Union forces back through Gettysburg.

The next day, more than 85,000 Union soldiers faced some 75,000 Confederates. The center of the Union army was on a hill called Cemetery Ridge. The center of the Confederate position was nearly a mile away, on Seminary Ridge. The fighting raged into the next day as Confederate troops attacked each end of the Union line.

On the afternoon of July 3, Lee ordered an all-out attack on the center of the Union line. General George E. Pickett led about 15,000 Confederates across nearly a mile of open field toward Cemetery Ridge. As they advanced, Union artillery shells and rifle fire rained down on them. Only a few hundred men reached the Union lines, and they were quickly driven back. About 7,500 Confederates were killed or wounded in what is known as Pickett's Charge.

Vocabulary *Builder*
<u>encounter</u> (ehn KOWN ter) *v.* to meet in an unexpected way; to experience

Final Battles of the Civil War

KEY
- Union troops
- Confederate troops
- Union victory
- Confederate victory
- Union naval blockade

MAP MASTER®

Skills Activity

Union victories at Gettysburg and Vicksburg in July 1863 marked a turning point. This map shows the battles in the final years of the Civil War.

(a) Read a Map Which battles were fought in Confederate territory? In Union territory?

(b) Draw Inferences What can this map tell you about the damage suffered by North and South between 1863 and 1865?

MapMaster ⦿nline

For: Interactive map
Visit: PHSchool.com
Web Code: myp-5113

0 km 200
0 miles 200
Albers Equal-Area Projection

In all, the Confederacy suffered more than 28,000 casualties during the three-day Battle of Gettysburg. Union losses <u>exceeded</u> 23,000. For a second time, Lee had lost nearly a third of his troops. "It's all my fault," he said as he rode among his surviving soldiers. "It is I who have lost this fight."

The Fall of Vicksburg On July 4, 1863, as Lee's shattered army began its retreat from Gettysburg, the South suffered another major blow far to the south and west. Vicksburg surrendered to General Grant. It had been one of the last cities on the Mississippi River to remain in Confederate hands. Unable to take Vicksburg by force, Grant had begun a siege of the city in May 1863. A **siege** is an attempt to capture a place by surrounding it with military forces and cutting it off until the people inside surrender.

Day after day, Union guns bombarded Vicksburg. Residents took shelter in cellars and in caves they dug in hillsides. They ate mules and rats to keep from starving. After six weeks, the 30,000 Confederate troops at Vicksburg finally gave up. A few days later, the last Confederate stronghold on the Mississippi River, Port Hudson, Louisiana, also gave up. The entire river was now under Union control.

These events, coupled with Lee's defeat at Gettysburg, make July 1863 the major turning point of the Civil War. Now the Union had the upper hand.

The Gettysburg Address In November 1863, about 15,000 people gathered on the battlefield at Gettysburg to honor the soldiers who had died there. In what is now known as the Gettysburg Address, Lincoln looked ahead to a final Union victory. He said:

> **❝**We here highly resolve that these dead shall not have died in vain—that this nation, under God, shall have a new birth of freedom—and that government of the people, by the people, for the people, shall not perish from the earth.**❞**
> —Abraham Lincoln, Gettysburg Address, November 19, 1863

☑**Checkpoint** **Identify two events that marked turning points in the Civil War.**

Closing In on the Confederacy

In Ulysses S. Grant, President Lincoln found the kind of commander he had long sought. In 1864, the President gave him command of all Union forces. Grant decided that he must attack Richmond, no matter how large the Union losses.

Grant versus Lee Grant's huge army hammered at the Confederates in a series of battles in northern Virginia in the spring of 1864. Grant was unable to break through Lee's troops. But Grant did not retreat. Instead, he continued the attack.

Vocabulary *Builder*
exceed (ehks SEED) *v.* to go beyond what is expected; to be greater than what was planned

Union General Ulysses S. Grant

Main Idea
With Grant in command, Union forces carried the war to the heart of the Confederacy.

Cause and Effect

CAUSES
- Issue of slavery in the territories divides the North and South.
- Abolitionists want slavery to end.
- Southern states secede after Lincoln's election.

THE CIVIL WAR

EFFECTS
- Lincoln issues the Emancipation Proclamation.
- Total war destroys the South's economy.
- Hundreds of thousands of Americans killed.

Reading Charts
Skills Activity

The Civil War had multiple causes—and multiple effects.

(a) Analyze Cause and Effect Why did the North fear the extension of slavery to the West?

(b) Draw Conclusions Which effects were felt mainly in the South? Which effects were felt mainly in the North?

Relate Events in a Sequence

What happened first, the Union's victory in Atlanta or President Lincoln's reelection? Explain how these events are related in sequence.

Main Idea

Lee surrendered to Grant at Appomattox, putting an end to the long and bloody war.

After seven weeks of fighting, Grant had lost about 55,000 men; the Confederates had lost 35,000. Grant realized that his army could count on a steady stream of men and supplies. Lee, on the other hand, was running out of both.

The two armies clashed at Petersburg, an important railroad center south of Richmond. There, in June 1864, Grant began a siege, the tactic he had used at Vicksburg.

While Grant besieged Lee, another Union army under General **William Tecumseh Sherman** advanced toward Atlanta. Like Grant, Sherman was a tough soldier. He believed in **total war**—all-out attacks aimed at destroying an enemy's army, its resources, and its people's will to fight. Sherman later said:

> **"**We are not only fighting hostile armies, but a hostile people, and must make young and old, rich and poor, feel the hard hand of war.**"**
>
> —William T. Sherman,
> *Memoirs,* 1886

March to the Sea The Confederates could not stop Sherman's advance. The Union army marched into Atlanta on September 2, 1864. Atlanta's capture gave President Lincoln's reelection campaign a boost. In the months before the capture of Atlanta, many northerners had grown tired of the war. Support for Lincoln had been lagging. But after Atlanta's fall, Lincoln won a huge election victory over General George McClellan, the Democrats' candidate.

In November, Sherman ordered Atlanta burned. He then marched east toward the Atlantic Ocean. Along the way, Union troops set fire to buildings, seized crops and livestock, and pulled up railroad tracks. They left a path of destruction up to 60 miles wide. In February 1865, the army headed north across the Carolinas.

Checkpoint How did Sherman show "the hard hand of war"?

Peace at Last

In March 1865, Grant's army still waited outside Petersburg. For months, Grant had been extending his battle lines east and west of Petersburg. Lee knew it was only a matter of time before Grant would capture the city.

Lincoln, too, saw that the end of the war was near. In his Second Inaugural Address in March 1865, he asked Americans to forgive and forget. "With malice toward none; with charity for all; . . . let us strive together . . . to bind up the nation's wounds," said Lincoln.

Surrender at Appomattox On April 2, Grant's troops finally broke through Confederate lines. By evening, Richmond was in Union hands. Lee's army retreated to the town of Appomattox Court House. There, on April 9, 1865, his escape cut off, Lee surrendered.

Grant offered Lee generous surrender terms. The Confederates had only to give up their weapons and leave in peace. As Lee rode off, some Union troops started to celebrate the surrender. But Grant silenced them. "The war is over," he said. "The rebels are our countrymen again."

The War's Terrible Toll The Civil War was the bloodiest conflict the United States has ever fought. About 260,000 Confederate soldiers gave their lives in the war. The number of Union dead exceeded 360,000, including 37,000 African Americans. Nearly a half million men were wounded. Many returned home disfigured for life.

The war had two key results: It reunited the nation and put an end to slavery. However, a century would pass before African Americans would begin to experience the full meaning of freedom.

✔**Checkpoint** Why did Lee finally decide to surrender?

⭐ **Looking Back and Ahead** With Lee's surrender, the long and bitter war came to an end. In the next chapter, you will read how U.S. leaders tried to patch the Union together again.

Section 5 | Check Your Progress

Progress Monitoring ⊕nline
For: Self-test with instant help
Visit: PHSchool.com
Web Code: mya-5115

Comprehension and Critical Thinking

1. (a) Identify Why are the battles at Gettysburg and Vicksburg considered a turning point?
(b) Understand Sequence How did the advantages of the North at the start of the war continue to be advantages?

2. (a) Classify President Lincoln called for "charity for all." How would you classify his words to the country?
(b) Distinguish Facts From Opinions Write three facts and three opinions Grant might have stated about the Civil War.

Reading Skill

3. Relate Events in a Sequence What events led to the turning point of the Civil War in July 1863? How did those events change the war?

Vocabulary *Builder*

Complete each of the following sentences so that the second part further explains the first part and clearly shows your understanding of the key term.

4. Grant placed Vicksburg under a siege; _____.
5. Sherman pursued a total war; _____.

Writing

6. This section says that the Civil War took more than 620,000 American lives. Research and record the number of American deaths in World War I, World War II, Korea, and Vietnam. Compare the total number of American lives lost in these wars to the number lost in the Civil War. Then, write a paragraph to make a point about your findings. Also, credit the sources of published information you used.

A primary source is information about people or events presented by someone who lived through what is being described. Speeches are primary sources that can give important information about historical figures and events.

President Lincoln gave this speech at the dedication of the battlefield cemetery at Gettysburg.

Primary Source

"Fourscore and seven years ago our fathers brought forth on this continent a new nation, conceived in Liberty, and dedicated to the proposition that all men are created equal.

Now we are engaged in a great civil war, testing whether that nation, or any nation so conceived and so dedicated, can long endure. We are met on a great battlefield of that war. We have come to dedicate a portion of that field as a final resting place for those who here gave their lives that the nation might live. It is altogether fitting and proper that we should do this.

But in a larger sense, we cannot dedicate, we cannot consecrate, we cannot hallow, this ground. The brave men, living and dead, who struggled here have consecrated it, far above our poor power to add or detract. The world will little note, nor long remember, what we say here, but it can never forget what they did here. It is for us the living, rather, to be dedicated here to the unfinished work which they who fought here have thus far so nobly advanced. It is rather for us to be here dedicated to the great task remaining before us—that from these honored dead we take increased devotion to that cause for which they gave the last full measure of devotion—that we here highly resolve that these dead shall not have died in vain—that this nation, under God, shall have a new birth of freedom—and that government of the people, by the people, for the people, shall not perish from the earth."

—Abraham Lincoln, November 19, 1863

Learn the Skill

Use these steps to analyze a speech.

1 **Identify the source.** Find out who gave the speech, when it was given, and why it was given.

2 **Identify the main idea.** Read carefully to discover what the main idea of the speech is. What do you think the speaker wanted to tell his or her audience?

3 **Identify the point of view.** Often a speechmaker wants to persuade listeners to share his or her feelings. Read carefully to determine the point of view of the speechmaker. Look for language that expresses strong feelings.

Practice the Skill

Answer the questions about the speech above.

1 **Identify the source.** (a) Who wrote the speech? (b) When was the speech given? (c) Why was it given?

2 **Identify the main idea.** What is the most important idea in the speech?

3 **Identify the point of view.** (a) What is the speaker's opinion of the Civil War? (b) What words or phrases express his feelings? (c) Why do you think he feels this way?

Apply the Skill

See the Review and Assessment at the end of this chapter.

CHAPTER 15 | Quick Study Guide

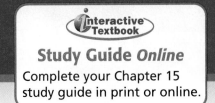

Study Guide *Online*
Complete your Chapter 15 study guide in print or online.

Chapter Summary

Section 1
The Call to Arms

- The Civil War was a war of Americans against Americans.
- Both the North and the South used their advantages in planning military strategy.

Section 2
Early Years of the War

- Civil War soldiers lived under harsh and dangerous conditions.
- Battles at Antietam Creek and Shiloh were important victories for the North.

Section 3
The Emancipation Proclamation

- The Emancipation Proclamation freed enslaved people in areas of rebellion.
- The Emancipation Proclamation changed the Civil War into a fight to end slavery.
- Approximately 189,000 African Americans served in the Union army and navy.

Section 4
The Civil War and American Life

- The Civil War caused divisions in both the North and the South.
- Draft laws that seemed to favor the wealthy led to protests and riots.
- The Civil War caused economic hardships and also led to changes in women's roles.

Section 5
Decisive Battles

- Major Confederate losses at Gettysburg and Vicksburg marked a turning point.
- Lee surrendered to Grant on April 9, 1865, at Appomattox Court House.
- Some 620,000 soldiers died in the Civil War.

Key Concepts

These notes will help you prepare for questions about key concepts.

Causes of the Civil War

- Spread of slavery in western territories divides North and South.
- Abolitionists want to end all slavery.
- South fears it will lose power in the federal government.
- Southern states secede after Lincoln's election.
- Confederates bomb Fort Sumter.

Effects of the Emancipation Proclamation

(Issued by President Abraham Lincoln on January 1, 1863)
- Freed enslaved people in areas that were in rebellion
- Turned war into a fight to end slavery
- Ended South's hopes for recognition of independence by Britain
- Encouraged African Americans to join Union army

Major Civil War Events, 1861–1865

- First Bull Run, July 1861
- Shiloh, April 1862
- Antietam Creek, September 1862
- Fredericksburg, December 1862
- Vicksburg, May–July 1863
- Gettysburg, July 1863
- Surrender of Confederate army, April 9, 1865, Appomattox Court House

Vocabulary *Builder*

Key Terms

Answer the following questions in complete sentences that show your understanding of the key terms.

1. Which army, the Union or the Confederate, sustained more casualties?

2. Why did Kentucky cease being neutral?

3. What was both Lincoln's and Davis's purpose in suspending habeas corpus?

4. How did Grant's siege of Vicksburg lead to the surrender of Confederate troops?

Comprehension and Critical Thinking

5. **(a) Recall** Why was it critical to keep Maryland in the Union?
   (b) Analyze Cause and Effect What was the effect of Lincoln's declaring martial law in Maryland?

6. **(a) Identify** Why did President Lincoln issue the Emancipation Proclamation?
   (b) Explain Problems What were two limitations of the Emancipation Proclamation?

7. **(a) Describe** What roles did women play in the Civil War?
   (b) Identify Economic Benefits In what way did the hardships of the Civil War provide new opportunities for women?
   (c) Link Past and Present Make a list of three opportunities that are open to women today that once were limited to men.

8. **(a) Classify** Create a chart of the battles fought at these places: Bull Run, Antietam Creek, Shiloh, Fredericksburg, Vicksburg, Gettysburg, Petersburg. Classify each battle as either a Union victory or a Confederate victory.
   (b) Detect Bias Reread the excerpt from Lincoln's Gettysburg Address found in Section 5. Do you think the address gave more comfort to northerners or to southerners? Why?

9. **(a) Summarize** Write three sentences that explain how the Civil War ended.
   (b) Make Predictions Do you think the surrender of the Confederate army at Appomattox Court House brought an end to the conflict between the northern and southern states? Explain.

History Reading Skill

10. **Understand Sequence** In a paragraph, summarize the events in the Civil War on the battlefield and on the home front. Use signal words to clarify the sequence. Where appropriate, show cause-effect links between events in sequence.

Writing

11. **Write on the following topic:**
    Find more information about a Civil War general. Write four paragraphs about him, using the guidelines below.
    • The first paragraph should introduce the general and present a thesis.
    • The second and third paragraphs should support this thesis by giving some background about the general's life, actions, and character.
    • The fourth paragraph should draw a conclusion about the general.

12. **Write a Narrative:**
    Choose one of the following roles: soldier, civilian, or nurse. Write two paragraphs of descriptive narrative telling about your experience in the Civil War.

Skills for Life

Analyze a Speech

Use the quotation below to answer the questions.

> ". . . the people of the Confederate States, in their conventions, determined that the wrongs which they had suffered and the evils with which they were menaced required that they should revoke the delegation of powers to the Federal Government which they had ratified in their several conventions. They consequently passed ordinances [laws] resuming all their rights as sovereign and independent States. . . ."
>
> —Jefferson Davis, April 29, 1861

13. **(a)** Who is the writer?
    (b) When was this written?

14. What is the main idea?

15. **(a)** What words or phrases show the writer's feelings?
    (b) Why do you think he feels this way?

Test Yourself

Refer to the quotation below to answer Question 1.

> "I now hold in contemplation of universal law and of the Constitution [that] the Union of these States is perpetual. . . . It follows from these views that no State upon its own mere motion can lawfully get out of the Union. . . ."
>
> —Abraham Lincoln, March 4, 1861

1. This quotation shows that Lincoln wanted to

A allow southern states to secede.

B amend the Constitution.

C abolish slavery.

D preserve the Union.

2. Which of the following granted freedom to all African Americans in areas of rebellion against the Union in 1863?

A Gettysburg Address

B Thirteenth Amendment

C Emancipation Proclamation

D surrender at Appomattox Court House

3. Which of the following was the North's most important advantage in the Civil War?

A Britain and other European nations sent economic aid.

B The nation's most experienced military leaders were northerners.

C The North had a larger population and more resources than the South.

D Northerners were united in their support for the war.

Document-Based Questions

Task: Look at Documents 1 and 2, and answer their accompanying questions. Then, use the documents and your knowledge of history to complete this writing assignment:

Write an essay describing the disagreement between the Copperheads and northern supporters of the Civil War. Include specific details about each side's position.

Document 1: Clement L. Vallandigham, an Ohio congressman, gave this speech in New York City in March 1863. *What does Vallandigham propose? How does that represent the Copperhead position?*

> "When I see that the experiment of blood has failed, . . . I am not one of those who proclaim . . . that we shall have separation and disunion. I am for going back to the instrumentality through which this Union was first made, and by which alone it can be restored.
>
> I am for peace, because it is the first step toward conciliation and compromise. You cannot move until you have first taken that indispensable preliminary—a cessation of hostilities. . . .
>
> Let men of intelligence judge: let history attest it hereafter. My theory . . . then, is this—stop this war."

Document 2: Copperheads were probably the most outspoken critics of the war in the North. *What opinion of Copperheads does this cartoon present?*

Chapter Preview

The Civil War was the bloodiest war fought on U.S. territory. The war ended slavery and reunited the North and the South. After the war, the nation faced the task of rebuilding the South—a region ruined by war.

Section 1

Rebuilding the Nation
Pages 546–549

☑ **What You Will Learn**

As the Civil War ended, Americans faced the problem of how to reunite the nation.

Section 2

The Battle Over Reconstruction
Pages 552–557

Disagreements over Reconstruction led to conflict in the government and in the South.

Section 3

The End of Reconstruction
Pages 558–563

With the end of Reconstruction, African Americans in the South lost many of the rights they had gained.

Northerners who moved south after the Civil War were called carpetbaggers. A carpetbag was a carpet rolled up or stitched together to hold belongings.

U.S. Events

1863
President Lincoln proposes mild Reconstruction plan.

1865
Lincoln is assassinated five days after war ends.

1867
Radical Reconstruction begins.

1860

1865

1870

World Events

1867 Dominion of Canada is formed.

Students and teachers pose outside the Freedmen's Bureau school in Beaufort, South Carolina.

1870
15th Amendment is ratified by the states.

1877
Rutherford B. Hayes becomes President after disputed election.

1896
Supreme Court upholds separate facilities for blacks and whites.

1870

1875

1900

1870 Italy becomes unified nation.

1873 Slave markets are abolished in Zanzibar, in Africa.

1876 Porfirio Díaz becomes leader of Mexico.

History Reading Skill   **Analyze and Evaluate Proposals**

How did the Civil War affect plantation owners?

Thomas Dabney's plantation lay in ruins after the Civil War. In the excerpt below, his daughter describes the way Dabney dealt with his personal crisis.

Primary Source

Thomas Dabney was a southern plantation owner. At the close of the Civil War, his property was in ruins and the plantation economic system had ended. His daughter, Susan Dabney Smedes, describes the proposals he made to face those challenges and the methods he used to carry out his proposals.

> He informed [former slaves] . . . that they were now free. His advice was that they should continue to work the crop as they had been doing. At the end of the year they should receive such pay for their labor as he thought just. . . .
>
> He owned nothing that could be turned into money without great sacrifice but five bales of cotton. There were yet two sons and two daughters to be educated. He decided to get a tutor for them and to receive several other pupils in his house in order to make up the salary.
>
> His chivalrous nature had always revolted from the sight of a woman doing hard work. He determined to spare his daughters all such labor as he could perform. General Sherman had said that he would like to bring every southern woman to the washtub. "He shall never bring my daughter to the washtub," Thomas Dabney said. "I will do the washing myself." And he did it for two years.

— Susan Dabney Smedes, *Memorials of a Southern Planter*

Here, he gives a reason to support his proposal: They will get paid at the end of the year.

Dabney proposes a way to get an education for his children.

Thomas Dabney proposes to his former slaves that they keep working.

Here, Dabney proposes how he will treat the women of his family.

He shows how he will carry out his proposal.

Analyze and Evaluate Proposals

- Ask yourself what goals Thomas Dabney has and how he proposes to meet those goals.
- You can identify Thomas Dabney's proposals in the decisions he makes. Support follows in the reasons for those decisions or the methods of carrying them forward.
- Evaluate Dabney's proposals. Do you think his proposals will help him meet his goals?

Document-Based Questions

1. Who is the author of this source?
2. What is the relationship of the author to Thomas Dabney?
3. How might the opinion of Dabney's former slaves compare with the author's opinion of Dabney?

Vocabulary _Builder_

Previewing High-Use Academic Words

High-Use Word	Definition	Sample History Sentence
voluntary (VAHL ahn tair ee) (Section 1, p. 547)	_adj._ not forced; done of one's own free will	The state of Virginia's ceding of western land to the U.S. government was <u>voluntary</u>.
resolve (ree SAHLV) (Section 1, p. 548)	_v._ to decide; to solve	The colonists <u>resolved</u> to fight the British.
critic (KRIHT ihk) (Section 2, p. 553)	_n._ someone who makes judgments on the value of objects or actions	The war hawks were <u>critics</u> of Madison's lenient policy toward the British.
impose (ihm POHZ) (Section 2, p. 555)	_v._ to place a burden on something or someone	The Tariff of 1816 <u>imposed</u> a high tax on certain goods imported into the country.
factor (FAK tor) (Section 3, p. 558)	_n._ condition or quality that causes something else to happen	Distance was the most important <u>factor</u> in the colonies developing cultures different from the British.
inferior (ihn FIR ee uhr) (Section 3, p. 561)	_adj._ of lower rank or status, or of poorer quality	At first, American manufactures were <u>inferior</u> in quality to British goods.

Previewing Key Terms and People

Abraham Lincoln, p. 546
amnesty, p. 547
freedman, p. 548
John Wilkes Booth, p. 549
Andrew Johnson, p. 552

black codes, p. 553
Hiram Revels, p. 555
Blanche Bruce, p. 555
scalawag, p. 555
carpetbagger, p. 555
impeachment, p. 556

Hiram Revels

poll tax, p. 560
literacy test, p. 560
grandfather clause, p. 560
segregation, p. 560
Homer Plessy, p. 561
sharecropper, p. 561

Abraham Lincoln

Andrew Johnson

Rebuilding the Nation

Objectives

1. Describe the postwar challenges that faced the nation.

2. Compare and contrast President Lincoln's plan for Reconstruction with the plan proposed by Congress.

3. Identify the goals of the Freedmen's Bureau.

4. Describe the immediate impact of Lincoln's assassination.

Prepare to Read

Reading Skill

Identify Proposals In turbulent times, such as after the Civil War, people may have many different ideas about how to move forward. They identify goals to achieve and propose solutions to problems. For example, each proposal made by a government leader was intended to achieve a specific goal. As you read Section 1, identify these proposals and goals.

Vocabulary *Builder*

High-Use Words

voluntary, p. 547

resolve, p. 548

Key Terms and People

Abraham Lincoln, p. 546

amnesty, p. 547

freedman, p. 548

John Wilkes Booth, p. 549

⭐ **Background Knowledge** After four years of bitter war, the Union finally had won the Civil War. Even though the fighting had ended, the nation remained divided. In this section, you will read of early plans for rebuilding national unity after the war.

Preparing for Reunion

As the Civil War ended, enormous problems faced the nation, especially the South. Vast stretches of the South lay in ruins. What provisions would be made for people who had been freed from slavery? Homeless refugees—both African American and white—needed food, shelter, and work. (For more on conditions in the South after the Civil War, see the Life at the Time feature at the end of this section.)

Somehow, though, Americans had to master their hard feelings and bring the North and the South together again. This process, known as Reconstruction, would occupy the nation for years to come.

Lincoln's Ten Percent Plan Abraham Lincoln wanted to make it easy for the southern states to rejoin the Union. His goal was to bind up the wounds of war as quickly as possible.

In December 1863, Lincoln introduced what was called the Ten Percent Plan. As soon as ten percent of a state's voters swore an oath of loyalty to the United States, the voters could organize a new state government. That government would have to declare an end to slavery. Then, the state could send members to Congress and take part in the national government again.

Main Idea

President Lincoln and Congress did not agree about how to bring the Union back together.

Lincoln's plan included amnesty for former Confederates who took the loyalty oath. An **amnesty** is a group pardon. The offer of amnesty did not apply to Confederate government leaders and top military officers.

The Wade-Davis Bill Six months later, Congress passed a much stricter plan for Reconstruction called the Wade-Davis Bill. Under that bill, 50 percent of voters would have to sign a loyalty oath before a state could return to the Union. Moreover, anyone who had <u>voluntarily</u> fought for the Confederacy would be barred from voting for delegates to a convention to write a new state constitution. The bill did not give them a right to vote. Lincoln would not sign the Wade-Davis Bill, so it never became law.

Lincoln and his fellow Republicans hoped to see a strong Republican Party in the new South. Lincoln thought that his "soft," or lenient, Reconstruction policy would win support from influential southerners. Supporters of a strict policy toward the South, known as Radical Republicans, disagreed. They argued that only a strict plan would keep the people who had led the South into secession from regaining power and weakening the control of the Radical Republicans.

✔**Checkpoint** How did Lincoln's plan for Reconstruction differ from that of the Radical Republicans in Congress?

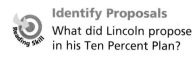

Identify Proposals
What did Lincoln propose in his Ten Percent Plan?

Vocabulary *Builder*
voluntary (VAHL ahn tair ee) *adj.* not forced; done of one's own free will

Destruction in the South
Parts of Richmond, capital of the Confederacy, lay in ruins at war's end. **Critical Thinking:** *Interpret Photographs* What do you think would be the most urgent need of the people of Richmond?

Main Idea
The Freedmen's Bureau
provided education and
economic help to freed slaves
and poor whites.

The Freedmen's Bureau

It was urgent to deal with the needs of freedmen, enslaved people who had been freed by the war, as well as other war refugees. Congress created the Freedmen's Bureau in March 1865. The bureau's first duty was to provide emergency relief to people displaced by the war.

Education The Freedmen's Bureau set up schools to teach freedmen to read and write. So great was the hunger for education that many African American communities started schools on their own. To pay a teacher, people pooled their pennies and dollars.

Many teachers were northern white women, but a large number were northern African American women. Edmonia Highgate, the daughter of freed slaves, taught at a Freedmen's Bureau school in Louisiana. "The majority of my pupils come from plantations, three, four and even eight miles distant," she wrote. "So anxious are they to learn that they walk these distances so early in the morning."

Most southern states had lacked systems of public education before the war. Now, public schools began to educate both blacks and whites. The Freedmen's Bureau helped to start schools at which African Americans could extend their education. These schools gave rise to such present-day institutions as Fisk University in Tennessee and Hampton University in Virginia.

Defending Freedmen The Freedmen's Bureau helped freedmen find jobs and resolved disputes between whites and blacks. Some people tried to cheat the freedmen. The Freedmen's Bureau set up its own courts to deal with such disputes.

☑**Checkpoint** What was the Freedmen's Bureau?

Vocabulary *Builder*
<u>resolve</u> (ree SAHLV) *v.* to decide; to
solve

Explore More Video
To learn more about Lincoln's life and presidency, view the video.

Assassinated!
Lincoln's assassination set off an intense hunt for the killer, John Wilkes Booth. **Critical Thinking:** *Make Predictions What effect do you think the assassination of Lincoln would have on the nation?*

Lincoln Is Murdered

As the war drew to a close, President Lincoln hoped for a peaceful Reconstruction. But Lincoln had no chance to put his plans into practice. He was shot dead on April 14, 1865, five days after Lee's surrender.

A Confederate sympathizer, John Wilkes Booth, slipped up behind Lincoln while he and his wife were attending a play at the Ford's Theatre in Washington. Booth fired a single pistol shot into the President's head. Lincoln died a few hours later.

Booth was shot dead two weeks later after pursuers trapped him in a barn and set it on fire. Eight people were convicted and four were hanged for their parts in the plot to kill Lincoln.

News of Lincoln's death shocked the nation. A special funeral train carried Lincoln's body back to Illinois for burial. In town after town, vast crowds paid their last respects.

Lincoln's successor was Vice President Andrew Johnson of Tennessee. Johnson was a southern Democrat who had remained loyal to the Union. Because Johnson had expressed bitterness toward the Confederates, many expected him to take a strict approach to Reconstruction.

Main Idea

Abraham Lincoln's assassination ended the chance of a lenient Reconstruction.

☑ **Checkpoint** **Why did many people expect Johnson to take a hard line on Reconstruction?**

⭐ **Looking Back and Ahead** Many people feared the effect of Lincoln's assassination on the process of Reconstruction. In the next section, you will learn how Reconstruction was affected by tensions between Lincoln's successor and members of Congress.

Section 1 | **Check Your Progress**

Progress Monitoring Online
For: Self-test with instant help
Visit: PHSchool.com
Web Code: mya-5121

Comprehension and Critical Thinking

1. **(a) Recall** How did the Civil War affect the North? How did the war affect the South?
(b) Contrast Why did the South have greater difficulty than the North in recovering from the Civil War?

2. **(a) Recall** How did Lincoln's plan for Reconstruction differ from the Wade-Davis Bill?
(b) Explain Problems What problems do you see for reuniting the nation in each plan?

Reading Skill

3. **Identify Proposals** Reread the paragraphs under the heading "The Freedmen's Bureau." What did the bureau propose to do to help the freedmen?

Vocabulary *Builder*

Answer the following questions in complete sentences that show your understanding of the key terms.
4. What did former Confederates have to do to get amnesty under Lincoln's plan to rebuild the Union?
5. Who were the freedmen?

Writing

6. Choose the best sentence to end a research paper about Abraham Lincoln. Explain your choice.
Sentences:
(a) Abraham Lincoln was humbly born on February 12, 1809, but he went on to be one of our greatest Presidents.
(b) Because Abraham Lincoln did not win a majority of the votes cast, his presidency turned out to be the nation's most turbulent period.
(c) His trials as President changed Lincoln into the steady leader who saved the Union in its darkest hour.

The South After the Civil War

The Civil War had a devastating impact on the South. All southerners—rich and poor, black and white—faced a long struggle to rebuild their lives and their land.

Confederate flag

Destroyed plantation

▲ Physical Destruction

Most of the fighting during the Civil War took place in the South. Cities and plantations lay in charred ruins. Two thirds of the railroads were destroyed.

▶ Wounded Soldiers

A quarter of a million Confederate soldiers died in the war. Thousands more were disabled by their wounds.

Returning Confederate veteran

Freedmen's school

Teaching people to read

▲ Freedmen

For nearly 4 million freedmen, the end of the Civil War was a time of both hope and fear. They were no longer enslaved. But most had no land, no jobs, and no education. The first task was to teach them to read.

Confederate money

◄ Financial Ruin

The economy of the South was ruined. Confederate money was suddenly worthless. Many banks closed, and people lost their life's savings.

Analyze LIFE AT THE TIME

Take one of the following roles: a wounded veteran; a planter whose plantation has been destroyed; a freedman. Write a paragraph explaining how you feel about the end of the war and the possibilities for the future.

The Battle Over Reconstruction

Objectives

1. Explain why conflicts developed over plans for Reconstruction.

2. Describe the changes in the South brought about by Radical Reconstruction.

3. Explain how Congress tried to remove President Johnson from office.

4. Describe how the Ku Klux Klan and other secret societies tried to prevent African Americans from exercising their rights.

Prepare to Read

 Reading Skill

Analyze Proposals Proposals must be carried out in order to be effective. The proposal must include details on how to put the proposal into action. As you read Section 2, look at the suggested ideas for carrying out proposals.

Vocabulary *Builder*

High-Use Words

critic, p. 553

impose, p. 555

Key Terms and People

Andrew Johnson, p. 552

black codes, p. 553

Hiram Revels, p. 555

Blanche Bruce, p. 555

scalawag, p. 555

carpetbagger, p. 555

impeachment, p. 556

☆ **Background Knowledge** You have read that Radical Republicans in Congress wanted a strict Reconstruction. In this section, you will learn how President Johnson's Reconstruction plans set the stage for a bitter battle between Johnson and Congress.

A Growing Conflict

Like President Lincoln, Andrew Johnson proposed a relatively lenient plan of Reconstruction. He followed Lincoln's example in putting his plan into effect himself, without consulting legislators.

The Thirteenth Amendment In January 1865, Congress approved a constitutional amendment to abolish slavery throughout the nation. The Thirteenth Amendment banned both slavery and forced labor. The amendment gave Congress the power to make laws to enforce its terms.

Johnson's Plan Like Lincoln, Johnson issued a broad amnesty to most former Confederates. Johnson allowed southern states to organize new governments and elect representatives to Congress. Each state, though, was required to abolish slavery and ratify the Thirteenth Amendment. By late fall, most of the states had met Johnson's requirements. When Congress met in December 1865, the representatives and senators elected by white southerners included many former Confederate leaders.

Main Idea
Andrew Johnson's lenient Reconstruction plan was rejected by Congress.

Andrew Johnson

Violence Against Freedmen
Popular magazines carried pictures of violence against freedmen, including the burning of a school (above) and the riots in Memphis (left). **Critical Thinking: *Make Predictions*** *How do you think northerners might have reacted to these pictures?*

Congress quickly rejected Johnson's approach. First, it refused to seat the southern senators and representatives. Next, the two houses appointed a committee to form a new plan for the South.

In a series of public hearings, the committee heard testimony about black codes—new laws used by southern states to control African Americans. Critics claimed that the codes replaced the system of slavery with near-slavery. In Mississippi, for example, African Americans could not vote or serve on juries. If unable to pay a fine as ordered by a court, they might be hired out by the sheriff to any white person who paid the fine.

Anger at these developments led Congress to adopt an increasingly hard line. The hardest line was taken by the Radical Republicans. The Radicals had two key goals. One was to prevent former Confederates from regaining control over southern politics. The other was to protect the freedmen and guarantee them a right to vote.

Vocabulary *Builder* <u>critic</u> (KRIHT ihk) *n.* someone who makes judgments on the value of objects or actions

✓**Checkpoint** **How did Congress respond to Johnson's plan for Reconstruction?**

The Fourteenth Amendment

The struggle over Reconstruction led to direct clashes between the President and Congress during 1866. At issue were two laws and a constitutional amendment.

Voicing alarm at the treatment of African Americans in the South, Congress passed the Civil Rights Act of 1866. It granted citizenship rights to African Americans and guaranteed the civil rights of all people except Native Americans.

President Johnson vetoed the bill and another one extending the life of the Freedmen's Bureau. Congress voted to overturn both vetoes. Under the Constitution, a vetoed bill becomes law if it wins the votes of two thirds of each house. Both bills received enough votes to become law.

Main Idea
Alarmed by violence against African Americans in the South, Congress approved the Fourteenth Amendment.

Opposing Plans for Reconstruction

I want a quick reunion. President Andrew Johnson	President Andrew Johnson (1865)	Radical Republicans (1867)	We want real change. Congressman Thaddeus Stevens
	• Majority of white men must swear oath of loyalty • Must ratify 13th Amendment • Former Confederate officials may vote and hold office	• Must disband state government • Must write new constitution • Must ratify 13th and 14th Amendments • Must allow African American men to vote	

Reading Charts
Skills Activity

President Andrew Johnson and Republican members of Congress, led by Thaddeus Stevens, disagreed about the process of Reconstruction.

(a) Read a Chart Which plan required states to write new constitutions?

(b) Detect Points of View Why did Radical Republicans think Johnson's plan was not strict enough?

Congress also drew up the Fourteenth Amendment to the Constitution, seeking to make sure that the Supreme Court did not strike down the Civil Rights Act. Republicans remembered the Court's Dred Scott decision. In that ruling, the Court declared that no one descended from an enslaved person could be a United States citizen.

The amendment failed at first to win the approval of three fourths of the states. It finally was approved in 1868, after Radicals took control of Reconstruction.

The Fourteenth Amendment says that all people born or naturalized in the United States are citizens. The amendment also declares that states may not pass laws that take away a citizen's rights. Nor can a state "deprive any person of life, liberty, or property, without due process of law; nor deny to any person . . . the equal protection of the laws."

Another provision declares that any state that denies the vote to any male citizen over the age of 21 will have its representation in Congress reduced. That provision was not enforced until the 1970s.

The Fourteenth Amendment became a powerful tool for enforcing civil rights. However, almost a century passed before it was used for that purpose.

Analyze Proposals
Congress proposed the Fourteenth Amendment to give freedmen a way to defend their rights. How would the amendment put that goal into action?

☑**Checkpoint** How did the Fourteenth Amendment seek to protect the freedmen?

Main Idea
During Radical Reconstruction, African Americans played an active part in the political life of the South.

Radical Reconstruction

Tempers rose as the elections of 1866 approached. White rioters and police attacked and killed many African Americans in two southern cities, Memphis and New Orleans. Outrage at this violence led Congress to push a stricter form of Reconstruction.

Radicals in Charge By early 1867, the Radical Republicans had won enough support from moderates to begin a "hard" Reconstruction. This period is known as Radical Reconstruction.

The Reconstruction Act of 1867 removed the governments of all southern states that had refused to ratify the Fourteenth Amendment. It then <u>imposed</u> military rule on these states, dividing them into five military districts. Before returning to the Union, each state had to write a new constitution and ratify the Fourteenth Amendment. Each state also had to let African Americans vote.

Under military rule, the South took on a new look. Soldiers helped register southern blacks to vote. In five states, African American voters outnumbered white voters. In the election of 1868, Republicans won all southern states. The states wrote new constitutions and, in June 1868, Congress seated representatives from seven "reconstructed" states.

Time of Hope and Advancement For the first time, African Americans in the South played an active role in politics. Prominent among them were free-born African Americans—carpenters, barbers, preachers—and former Union soldiers.

African Americans were elected as sheriffs, mayors, judges, and legislators. Sixteen African Americans served in the U.S. House of Representatives between 1872 and 1901. Two others, **Hiram Revels** and **Blanche Bruce,** served in the Senate.

Historians once took a critical view of Radical Reconstruction, focusing on the widespread corruption and excessive spending during this period. More recently, however, historians have written about important accomplishments of Reconstruction. They noted that during Reconstruction, southern states opened public schools for the first time. Legislators spread taxes more evenly and made fairer voting rules. They gave property rights to women. In addition, states rebuilt bridges, roads, and buildings destroyed by the war.

Radical Reconstruction brought other sweeping changes to the South. Old leaders lost much of their power. The Republican Party built a strong following based on three key groups. One group, called **scalawags** by their opponents, were southern whites who had opposed secession. Freedmen voters made up a second group.

The third group were **carpetbaggers,** a name given by southerners to northern whites who went south to start businesses or pursue political office. Critics claimed that these northerners were in such a rush to head south that they just tossed their clothes into cheap satchels called carpetbags.

Vocabulary *Builder*
impose (ihm POHZ) *v.* to place a burden on something or someone

Biography Quest

Hiram Revels
1822–1901

In his early years, Hiram Revels was a minister and preached to African American congregations across the Midwest. Throughout the Civil War, he was a staunch supporter of the Union.

In 1870, Revels was elected to the U.S. Senate and thus became the nation's first African American senator. He was elected to complete the unfinished term of former Confederate president Jefferson Davis.

Biography Quest ⬤nline

How did some senators try to keep Revels out of the Senate?

For: The answer to the question about Revels

Visit: PHSchool.com

Web Code: myd-5122

The Impact of Violence

The terror—
"WORSE THAN
SLAVERY"

Burning
school-
house

**Reading
Political Cartoons**

Skills Activity

The Ku Klux Klan used terror and violence to keep African Americans from voting. Northern cartoonist Thomas Nast shows his point of view about the Klan and other secret societies in this cartoon.

(a) Distinguish Relevant Information Point out two negative images in the cartoon. Give one word to describe the family.

(b) Detect Points of View What do you think is Nast's opinion of the Ku Klux Klan?

Targeting President Johnson Meanwhile, the Radicals mounted a major challenge against President Johnson. The Radicals tried to remove Johnson from office by impeachment. Impeachment is the bringing of formal charges against a public official. The Constitution says the House may impeach a President for "treason, bribery, or other high crimes and misdemeanors." After impeachment, there is a trial in the Senate. If convicted, the President is removed from office.

Johnson escaped removal—but barely. The House voted to impeach him in February 1868. The Senate trial took place from March to May. In the end, the votes went 35 for and 19 against Johnson. This was one vote short of the required two-thirds majority.

The Election of 1868 General Ulysses S. Grant, a war hero, won the presidential election for the Republicans in the fall of 1868. With southern states back in the Union under military rule, some 500,000 African Americans voted, mainly for Republicans. Grant won the electoral votes of 26 of the 34 states.

Grant was a moderate who had support from many northern business leaders. With his election, the Radicals began losing their grip on the Republican Party.

Fifteenth Amendment Over opposition from Democrats, Congress approved the Fifteenth Amendment in 1869. It barred all states from denying African American males the right to vote "on account of race, color, or previous condition of servitude."

Some African Americans said the amendment was too weak. It did not prevent states from requiring voters to own property or pay a voting tax. The amendment took effect in 1870, after three fourths of the states gave their approval.

The Ku Klux Klan Angry at being shut out of power, some whites resorted to violence. They created secret societies to terrorize African Americans and their white allies.

The best-known secret society was the Ku Klux Klan. Its members donned white robes with hoods that hid their faces. Klansmen rode by night to the homes of African American voters, shouting threats and burning wooden crosses. If threats failed, the Klan would whip, torture, shoot, or hang African Americans and white Republicans. Klan violence took hundreds of lives during the election of 1868.

The terror went on even after Congress responded with new laws. The Ku Klux Klan Acts of 1870 and 1871 barred the use of force against voters. Although the original Klan dissolved, new groups took its place. In the face of the terrorism, voting by African Americans declined. The stage was set for the end of Reconstruction.

☑**Checkpoint** **What were the key elements of Radical Reconstruction?**

⭐ **Looking Back and Ahead** Although Reconstruction guaranteed rights to more Americans, huge challenges remained. In the next section, you will learn more about the process of rebuilding the South. You will also learn that as time went on, Americans became less interested in Reconstruction. This set the scene for a return of power to former Confederates.

Terror and Violence

To spread terror, Ku Klux Klan members wore hoods like the one above when they attacked their victims. They also left miniature coffins as warnings. **Critical Thinking:** *Draw Conclusions Why do you think the hoods helped spread terror?*

Section 2 | **Check Your Progress**

Progress Monitoring ⬤nline
For: Self-test with instant help
Visit: PHSchool.com
Web Code: mya-5122

Comprehension and Critical Thinking

1. (a) Recall Which amendment guaranteed African Americans the right to vote: the Thirteenth, Fourteenth, or Fifteenth?
(b) Apply Information How did each of these three amendments help to expand democracy?

2. (a) Recall What was the Ku Klux Klan?
(b) Evaluate Information Why do you think the Klan was not formed before the Civil War?

🎯 Reading Skill

3. Analyze Proposals In 1867, the Radical Republicans in Congress proposed the Reconstruction Act. What actions did this proposal involve?

Vocabulary *Builder*

Complete each of the following sentences so that the second part clearly shows your understanding of the key term.
4. Radical Republicans in the House of Representatives tried to remove the President by impeachment, which is _____.

5. Former Confederates wanted to control the lives of freedmen through black codes, which were _____.

Writing

6. Rewrite the following passage to correct the grammar, spelling, and punctuation errors that you find. **Passage:** President Johnson wanting to show mercy to the defeated confederacy. Many of the republicans in Congress, however, opposed him. Because they wanted to protect the freedman. This conflict led congress to held impeachment hearings.

The End of Reconstruction

Objectives

1. Explain why support for Reconstruction declined.
2. Describe how African Americans in the South lost many newly gained rights.
3. Describe the sharecropping system and how it trapped many in a cycle of poverty.
4. Identify the signs that the South began to develop a stronger economy by the 1880s.

Prepare to Read

 Reading Skill

Evaluate Proposals When you read a proposal, ask yourself: Is the proposal likely to work as a way of advancing its goal?

Vocabulary *Builder*

High-Use Words

factor, p. 558

inferior, p. 561

Key Terms and People

poll tax, p. 560

literacy test, p. 560

grandfather clause, p. 560

segregation, p. 560

Homer Plessy, p. 561

sharecropper, p. 561

⭐ **Background Knowledge** You have read how Reconstruction brought both positive change and turmoil to the South. In this section, you will learn how Reconstruction's end led to new hardships for African Americans in the South.

Reconstruction's Conclusion

Main Idea
A deal between President Hayes and southern Democrats led to the end of Reconstruction.

Support for Radical Republicans declined as Americans began to forget the Civil War and focus on bettering their own lives. Scandals within President Grant's administration played an important role. Grant made poor appointments to public offices, often appointing personal friends. Many of the appointees proved to be corrupt. Although Grant himself had no part in the corruption that took place, his reputation suffered. Grant won reelection in 1872, but many northerners lost faith in the Republicans and their policies.

Self-rule for the South Meanwhile, many people in both North and South were calling for the withdrawal of federal troops and full amnesty for former Confederates. Starting with Virginia in 1869, opponents of Republicans began to take back the South, state by state. Slowly, they chipped away at the rights of African Americans.

In some states, campaigns of terror by secret societies were a major factor in restoring their power. By 1874, Republicans had lost control of all but three southern states. By 1877, Democrats controlled those, too.

The Election of 1876 The end of Reconstruction was a direct result of the presidential election of 1876. Because of disputes over election returns, the choice of the President was decided by

Vocabulary *Builder*
factor (FAK tor) *n.* condition or quality that causes something else to happen

Congress. There, a deal between the Republicans and Democrats settled the election—and sealed the fate of Reconstruction.

The candidates in 1876 were Rutherford B. Hayes of Ohio for the Republicans and Samuel J. Tilden of New York for the Democrats. The Republicans said they would continue Reconstruction, and the Democrats said they would end it.

Tilden won the popular vote by 250,000 votes. However, 20 electoral votes were in dispute. Without them, Tilden fell one vote short of the 185 needed to win in the electoral college.

To resolve the issue, Congress appointed a special commission of 15 members. Most of them were Republicans. The commission gave all 20 electoral votes to Hayes. Rather than fight the decision in Congress, Democrats agreed to accept it. Hayes had privately told them that he would end Reconstruction. Once in office, Hayes removed all federal troops from the South.

Evaluate Proposals
What proposal did Hayes make to the Democrats in order to end their opposition? How did this proposal meet the goals of both the Democrats and Republicans?

☑Checkpoint **What factors contributed to the end of Reconstruction?**

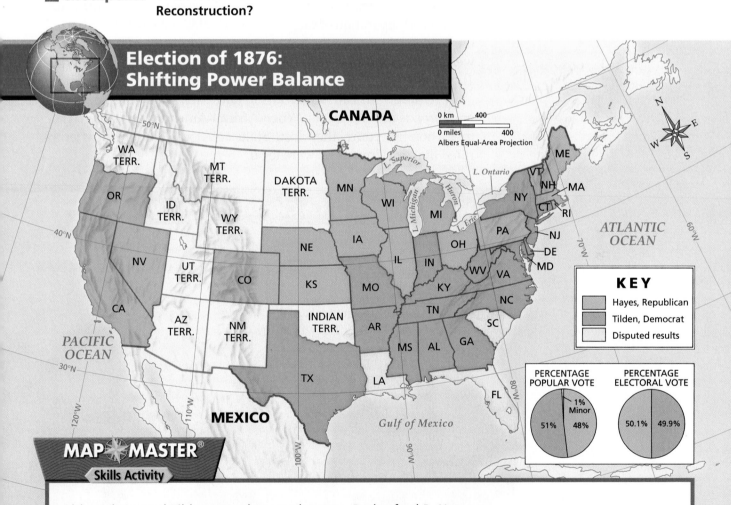

Election of 1876: Shifting Power Balance

0 km 400
0 miles 400
Albers Equal-Area Projection

KEY
- Hayes, Republican
- Tilden, Democrat
- Disputed results

PERCENTAGE POPULAR VOTE
51% | 48% | 1% Minor

PERCENTAGE ELECTORAL VOTE
50.1% | 49.9%

MAP MASTER®
Skills Activity

Although Samuel Tilden won the popular vote, Rutherford B. Hayes was declared the winner in the election.

(a) Read a Map Key In which region did Tilden have the most support?

(b) Draw Conclusions Based on this map, do you think the Civil War ended sectionalism? Explain.

MapMaster Online

For: Interactive map
Visit: PHSchool.com
Web Code: myp-5123

African Americans Lose Rights

With the end of Reconstruction, African Americans began to lose their remaining political and civil rights in the South. Southern whites used a variety of techniques to stop African Americans from voting. They passed laws that applied to whites and African Americans but were enforced mainly against African Americans.

One such law imposed a **poll tax**—a personal tax to be paid before voting. This kept a few poor whites and many poor freedmen from voting. Another law required voters to pass a **literacy test**, or a test to see if a person can read and write. In this case, voters were required to read a section of the Constitution and explain it.

However, a grandfather clause allowed illiterate white males to vote. The **grandfather clause** was a provision that allowed a voter to avoid a literacy test if his father or grandfather had been eligible to vote on January 1, 1867. Because no African American in the South could vote before 1868, nearly all were denied the right to vote.

Southern states created a network of laws requiring **segregation**, or enforced separation of races. These so-called Jim Crow laws barred the mixing of races in almost every aspect of life. Blacks and whites were born in separate hospitals and buried in separate cemeteries. The laws decreed separate playgrounds, restaurants, and schools. They required African Americans to take back seats or separate cars on railroads and streetcars. When African Americans challenged the restrictions in court, they lost. State and local courts consistently ruled that Jim Crow laws were legal.

Sharecropping Cycle of Poverty

1 **Planting the crop**
Landowners give the sharecropper land, seed, and tools in exchange for a share in the crop. Sharecroppers buy goods and supplies from the landowner on credit.

In 1896, the U.S. Supreme Court upheld segregation laws. **Homer Plessy** had been arrested for sitting in a coach marked "for whites only." In the case of *Plessy* v. *Ferguson,* the Court ruled in favor of a Louisiana law requiring segregated railroad cars. The Court said a law could require "separate" facilities, so long as they were "equal."

This "separate but equal" rule was in effect until the 1950s. In fact, facilities for African Americans were rarely equal. For example, public schools for African Americans were almost always <u>inferior</u> to schools for whites.

Vocabulary *Builder*
<u>inferior</u> (ihn FIR ee uhr) *adj.* of lower rank or status, or of poorer quality

☑**Checkpoint** **What methods did southern states use to deprive African Americans of their rights?**

A Cycle of Poverty

At emancipation, many freedmen owned little more than the clothes they wore. Poverty forced many African Americans, as well as poor whites, to become sharecroppers. A **sharecropper** is a laborer who works the land for the farmer who owns it, in exchange for a share of the value of the crop.

Main Idea
Freedmen farmers were forced into a cycle of poverty nearly impossible to escape.

The landlord supplied living quarters, tools, seed, and food on credit. At harvest time, the landlord sold the crop and tallied up how much went to the sharecroppers. Often, especially in years of low crop prices or bad harvests, the sharecroppers' share was not enough to cover what they owed the landlord for rent and supplies. As a result, most sharecroppers became locked into a cycle of debt.

History *Interactive*
Explore the Sharecropping Cycle
Visit: PHSchool.com
Web Code: myp-5127

Harvesting the crop and settling accounts
2 The sharecropper gives the landowner his crop. Landowner sells it and gives the tenant his share, minus the amount owed at the company store.

Farming land they did not own, sharecroppers were locked in a cycle of debt, as shown by the illustration. **Critical Thinking: Draw Conclusions** *Why was it hard for sharecroppers to escape the debt cycle?*

Cycle of debt
3 After a year of hard work, the sharecroppers often owed more than they had earned and had no choice but to offer the landlord a greater percentage of next year's crop.

Farms Rented for Shares of Products, 1880

(Bar graph. Y-axis: Farms Rented (tens of thousands), 0 to 60. X-axis: States — Connecticut, New Hampshire, Alabama, Texas, California, Oregon. Legend: Northeast, South, West)

- Connecticut (Northeast): about 1
- New Hampshire (Northeast): about 1
- Alabama (South): about 41
- Texas (South): about 53
- California (West): about 4
- Oregon (West): about 2

Source: *Inter-university Consortium for Political and Social Research*

Links Across Time

1963 Dr. Martin Luther King, Jr., speaks to Americans in Washington, D.C.

Fighting for Civil Rights

1896 In *Plessy* v. *Ferguson*, the Supreme Court upheld segregation laws in the South. These restrictions continued for more than 50 years.

1950s–1960s Some Americans launched a campaign to bring equal rights to African Americans. This civil rights movement used marches, petitions, and other public actions to end discrimination in education, use of public facilities, and voting.

Link to Today

Civil Rights Today Did the civil rights movement win equal rights for all Americans? Not everyone agrees. Go online to find out more about recent developments in civil rights.

For: Civil rights in the news
Visit: PHSchool.com
Web Code: myc-5123

Opportunities dwindled for African Americans in southern towns and cities, too. African American artisans who had been able to find skilled jobs during Reconstruction increasingly found such jobs closed to them. Those with some education could become schoolteachers, lawyers, or preachers in the African American community. But most urban African Americans had to take whatever menial job they could find.

☑**Checkpoint** **How did many freedmen and whites become locked in a cycle of poverty?**

Main Idea
By the 1880s, the South had begun to develop its own resources and industries.

Industrial Growth

It would be a long process, but during Reconstruction the South's economy began to recover. By the 1880s, new industries appeared. Southerners hailed a "New South," based on industrial growth.

The first element of the South's economy to begin recovery was agriculture. Cotton production, which had lagged during the war, quickly revived. By 1875, it was setting new records. Planters put more land into tobacco production, and output grew.

Southern investors started or expanded industries to turn raw materials into finished products. The textile industry came to play an important role in the southern economy.

The South had natural resources in abundance, but it had done little to develop them in the past. Atlanta newspaper editor Henry Grady described the funeral of a man from Georgia as follows:

> "They buried him in the heart of a pine forest, and yet the pine coffin was imported from Cincinnati. They buried him within touch of an iron mine, and yet the nails in his coffin and the iron in the shovel that dug his grave were imported from Pittsburgh."
>
> —Henry Grady to the Bay State Club of Boston, 1889

The South began to develop its own resources. New mills and factories grew up to use the South's iron, timber, and oil. Lumber mills and furniture factories processed yellow pine and hardwoods from southern forests.

Southern leaders took great pride in the region's progress. They spoke of a "New South" that was no longer dependent on "King Cotton." An industrial age was underway, although the North was still far more industrialized.

☑ Checkpoint What was the "New South" that was emerging by 1900?

⭐ **Looking Back and Ahead** When Reconstruction ended in 1877, its record showed many successes and some failures. Most importantly, all African Americans were finally citizens. Laws passed during Reconstruction, such as the Fourteenth Amendment, became the basis of the civil rights movement that took place almost 100 years later.

Factory in the "New South"

Section 3 | **Check Your Progress**

Progress Monitoring Online
For: Self-test with instant help
Visit: PHSchool.com
Web Code: mya-5123

Comprehension and Critical Thinking

1. (a) **Identify** Who were sharecroppers? How did they differ from landowners?
   (b) **Draw Conclusions** Why did so many sharecroppers live in poverty?

2. (a) **Recall** What is segregation?
   (b) **Analyze Cause and Effect** How did *Plessy* v. *Ferguson* make the fight against segregation more difficult?

Reading Skill

3. **Evaluate Proposals** In *Plessy* v. *Ferguson*, the Supreme Court proposed the idea of "separate but equal" facilities. Do you think this idea meets the goal of ensuring equal rights?

Vocabulary *Builder*

Complete each of the following sentences so that the second part clearly shows your understanding of the key term.

4. African Americans and whites had to pay a poll tax before _____.

5. Because of laws in the South requiring segregation, African Americans and whites _____.

Writing

6. Rewrite the following passage to correct the errors. **Passage:** The 1876 presidential election decided by a special commission. Samuel J. Tilden a democrat won the Popular vote over republican Rutherford B. Hayes. However, their were 20 disputed electorial votes. A special commission made an agreement with the democrats.

Thematic maps focus on special topics, such as food products, physical features, or political boundaries. Information presented in a visual way is easier to understand and absorb. One type of thematic map shows the migration or movement of people within a particular area.

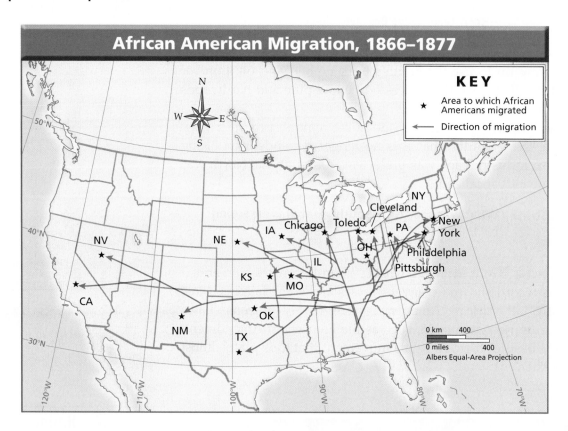

African American Migration, 1866–1877

KEY
★ Area to which African Americans migrated
← Direction of migration

Learn the Skill

Use these steps to learn how to trace migrations on maps.

1 **Identify the subject of the map.** Read the title of the map. Look for dates that identify the time period.

2 **Look at the map key.** The map key explains special symbols and colors used on the map.

3 **Determine direction.** To trace the route of a migration, use the direction arrows on the compass rose to identify north, south, east, and west. Then, identify the direction or directions of the route.

4 **Make a generalization.** Use the information on the map to make a general statement about the historic migration.

Practice the Skill

Answer the following questions about the map on this page.

1 **Identify the subject of the map.** What is the title of the map?

2 **Look at the map key.** What does the star symbol show?

3 **Determine direction.** In which direction did African Americans travel to migrate to New York?

4 **Make a generalization.** In general, to which areas of the country did African Americans migrate during Reconstruction?

Apply the Skill

See the Review and Assessment at the end of this chapter.

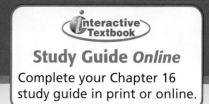

Study Guide *Online*
Complete your Chapter 16
study guide in print or online.

Chapter Summary

Section 1
Rebuilding the Nation

• The South faced major economic and social challenges at the end of the Civil War.

• Reconstruction plans and programs like the Freedmen's Bureau were designed to rebuild the South.

• The death of Abraham Lincoln threatened lenient plans for Reconstruction.

Section 2
The Battle Over Reconstruction

• President Andrew Johnson and the Radical Republicans clashed over Reconstruction plans.

• Conflict over Reconstruction led to Andrew Johnson's impeachment.

• During Reconstruction, African American males gained the right to vote. Republicans came to power in each southern state.

Section 3
The End of Reconstruction

• With the end of Reconstruction, African Americans in the South lost many rights they had gained after the Civil War.

• Many African Americans and poor whites were forced to become sharecroppers.

• The South's agriculture revived, and its industries expanded.

Key Concepts

These notes will help you prepare for questions about key concepts.

Freedmen Rights and Restrictions

Rights
• Were granted freedom from slavery
• Were given citizenship and the right to vote
• Could no longer be legally discriminated against

Restrictions
• Black codes
• Voting limited by laws and violence
• Legal segregation

The Civil War Amendments

Amendment 13
• Abolished slavery

Amendment 14
• Defined citizenship to include African Americans
• Guaranteed equal protection under the law

Amendment 15
• Guaranteed voting rights

Successes and Failures of Reconstruction

Successes
• The Union was restored, and the South began rebuilding.
• African Americans gained the right to vote.
• African Americans gained legal rights to equal treatment.

Failures
• Southern governments kept African Americans from voting.
• Federal troops were unable to stop the violence against African Americans.

Vocabulary *Builder*

Key Terms

Fill in the blanks with the correct key terms.

1. _____ were people who had been enslaved before emancipation.

2. Northerners who moved south after the Civil War were sometimes called _____.

3. Southern states gave _____, which required voters to read and explain part of the Constitution.

4. A _____ farmed land in return for a portion of the value of the crop.

Comprehension and Critical Thinking

5. **(a) Recall** How did the Wade-Davis Bill differ from Lincoln's plan for reuniting the country?
(b) Make Predictions How do you think southerners would have reacted to Reconstruction if Lincoln's plan had been followed?

6. **(a) Recall** How did Johnson and the Radicals come into conflict?
(b) Analyze Cause and Effect How effective do you think Johnson was after the failure of the impeachment process?

7. **(a) Recall** What right is guaranteed by the Fifteenth Amendment?
(b) Interpret Art How does the painting *His First Vote* (below) reflect how the Fifteenth Amendment affected African Americans?

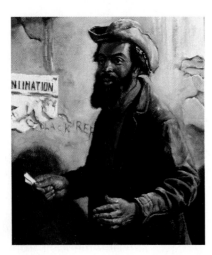

8. **(a) Recall** How did the Freedman's Bureau help African Americans after the Civil War?
(b) Make Predictions Which of the actions of the Freedmen's Bureau has probably had the longest lasting impact on African Americans? How?

9. **(a) Recall** What were the terms of the compromise that gave Rutherford B. Hayes the presidency in 1876?
(b) Draw Conclusions How were African Americans in the South affected by this compromise?

History Reading Skill

10. **Analyze and Evaluate Proposals** Review what you have read about the conflict between Johnson and Radical Republicans. What did each side propose? Which proposal makes the most sense to you? Explain.

Writing

11. **Write an essay on the following topic:**
Explain how events and developments during Reconstruction highlighted differences between North and South, even as the two tried to reunite.

Your essay should:
* state a thesis or purpose for writing;
* explain the subject you are writing about;
* offer evidence, examples, or details to support your explanation;
* conclude with a short summary of your main points.

12. **Write a Narrative:**
Imagine you are Hiram Revels. Write a narrative describing your first days in the Senate.

Skills for Life

Analyze a Migration Map
Use the map in the Skills for Life feature to answer the questions that follow.

13. What time period is covered in this map?

14. What does the arrow symbol show?

15. In which direction did African Americans travel to migrate to Oklahoma and New Mexico?

16. Based on the information in the map, what decision did many African Americans make during Reconstruction?

Test Yourself

Refer to the quotation below to answer Question 1.

"A system of oppression so rank that nothing could make it seem small except the fact that [African Americans] had already been ground under it for a century and a half."

1. Which system does this quotation refer to?

A amnesty

B Reconstruction

C sharecropping

D segregation

2. How did African Americans benefit from the passage of the Fourteenth Amendment?

A Their right to vote was protected.

B They became citizens.

C They were given land.

D They no longer had to pass literacy tests.

3. A chief goal of the Freedmen's Bureau was to promote

A abolition.

B industrial growth.

C education.

D segregation.

Document-Based Questions

Task: Look at Documents 1 and 2, and answer their accompanying questions. Then, use the documents and your knowledge of history to complete the following writing assignment:

Write a two-paragraph essay about the goals and methods of the Ku Klux Klan. Using specific details, draw a conclusion about whether Document 1 or Document 2 gives a more accurate description of the Klan.

Document 1: The "Organization and Principles" of the Ku Klux Klan, stated below, was written in 1868. It describes the goals of the Klan. *What does the Klan say is its attitude toward violence?*

"This is an institution of chivalry, humanity, mercy, and patriotism; embodying in its genius and its principles all that is chivalric in conduct, noble in sentiment, generous in manhood, and patriotic in purpose; its peculiar objects being:

First, to protect the weak, the innocent, and the defenseless from the [insults], wrongs, and outrages of the lawless, the violent, and the brutal; to relieve the injured and oppressed. . . .

Questions to be asked each [Klan] candidate:

• Are you in favor of a white man's government in this country? . . ."

Document 2: This political cartoon was published in a northern magazine in 1874. *Describe what has happened to the African American family.*

Writing Workshop

Research Paper

▶ Introduction

In a research paper, you gather information about a subject from several different sources. Then, you tie this information together with a single unifying idea and present it to your readers. A research paper should have the following characteristics:

- an interesting topic about which you need to find outside information

- information about that topic drawn from several different sources

- a thesis statement expressing an idea about the topic, based on the research

- information that identifies the sources used

Assignment On the following pages, you will learn how to plan, collect information for, and write a research paper. You will get step-by-step instructions. Each step will include an example from research about the Battle of Gettysburg.

Read the instructions and the examples. Then, follow each step to plan a research paper.

> **Write a research paper about a Civil War battle of your choice.**

For a review of the steps in the writing process, see the **Historian's Toolkit**, *Write Like a Historian.*

▶ Planning Your Research

Find a research subject. Start by listing subjects that interest you. Think about which of these subjects are likely to have information that you can readily find. Then, write a few questions you would like to answer about each subject.

Narrow your topic. One of the most important steps in writing a research paper is narrowing your topic to something you can cover in the space you have. If you have access to the Internet, you can use it to help you narrow your topic.

▶ Doing Your Research

Find your sources. A research paper involves consulting outside sources as you seek information you do not already have. Look for more recent sources to avoid relying on information that is out of date. Using library and Internet resources, keep researching until you have five good sources of information about your narrowed topic.

Take notes from your sources. As you read a source, write down and define key terms. Summarize longer passages and paraphrase important ideas, restating them in your own words. When you come across quotations you want to use, copy them exactly and identify their sources. Using someone else's words as if they were your own is called plagiarism, which is dishonest and can result in severe penalties.

Keep track of your sources. You need to identify each source that you use, whether the source is an encyclopedia, a book, a newspaper, a magazine, a television program, or an Internet site. In your final paper, you will create a bibliography that identifies all the sources you used.

▶ Writing Your Research Paper

Create a working thesis. After you review your notes, write a sentence that states the main idea of your paper.

Plan your organization. Depending on your topic, you can use various methods to organize your research paper. If you are discussing two items, one approach would be to compare and contrast them. If you are focusing on a complex event or a process, you could use a chronological organization.

> **Sample working thesis:**
> The Battle of Gettysburg consisted of a series of mistakes on the part of both North and South. Perhaps the greatest and most horrendous mistake of them all was Pickett's Charge.

Create an outline. Creating an outline can help you when you have a great deal of material to present. Decide the order that you think best suits your information and your thesis. Here is a portion of an outline for a research paper about Pickett's Charge at the Battle of Gettysburg.

> *Part of sample outline*
>
> I. Before Pickett's Charge
>   A. Status of Battle of Gettysburg on the morning of July 3
>   B. Lee's need to have decisive attack
>   C. Preparing Pickett's, Armistead's and Trimble's divisions
>   1. Pickett's was fullest division
>   2. Armistead and Trimble had lost many more men

Writing Workshop *continued*

Write your introduction. Write an introductory paragraph that grips your audience's attention. Set up your research topic, indicating what aspects of the topic you will cover. Lead up to your thesis statement.

Support your thesis with examples and details. Now write the body of your paper, presenting the best information that you found in your research. Writing a topic sentence for each paragraph will help you stay on target as you write. Keep the relationships between your ideas clear with transitions.

Write a strong conclusion. In your final paragraph, review the ground you have covered. Find a lively or powerful way to say what you found most interesting, moving, or surprising in what you learned.

▶ Giving Credit to Your Sources

You must identify the sources you use to support your ideas. Whenever you present statistics, little-known facts, direct quotations, or paraphrases of others' views, you need to give credit to the source of the information—both within your paper and in a bibliography listing the sources you used at the end of the paper.

Include citations within the paper. You have a few options for identifying sources within your paper. You can identify the source in parentheses. You can use a number corresponding to a footnote at the bottom of the page or an endnote at the end of the paper.

List your sources in a bibliography. At the end of your paper, you need to list the sources that you used. List them in alphabetical order by author, using accepted formats.

▶ Revising Your Research Paper

After completing your draft, read it again carefully, looking for ways to make your writing better. Here are questions to ask yourself.

Sample introduction

By the morning of July 3, 1863, the Battle of Gettysburg was two days old, and both armies were exhausted. The South had penetrated Northern defenses as far as Cemetery Ridge. The Union and Confederate armies were spread out over a large battlefield of rolling hills, and the ground in some places did not allow much visibility. Both sides had already made a number of mistakes in the two previous days of battle—mistaking the strength of the enemy and misrepresenting each other's positions. Perhaps the greatest, and most heroic, mistake of all was the one that was about to happen: the charge by General George Pickett, who led 15,000 Confederate soldiers with bayonets against the Union position on Cemetery Ridge.

Sample conclusion

Pickett's Charge is remembered as one of the most noble and tragic moments in military history. The Confederate soldiers fought bravely, but were no match for the Union weapons. Robert E. Lee had miscalculated, and his army paid the price. They staggered away from Gettysburg and never reached as far into the North again. The Civil War went on for almost two more years, but the tide had turned against the South. It turned on the heroic but mistaken charge by George Pickett and his men.

Revise to heighten interest and clarify research

- Does the first paragraph capture the reader's attention?
- Have you presented your information in the most compelling order?
- Are the relationships between ideas clear? Can you add any transitions to make them clearer?

Revise to meet written English-language conventions

- Are all sentences complete, with a subject and a verb?
- Are all the words spelled correctly?
- Are all proper nouns capitalized, including names of people and places?
- Did you use proper punctuation?

Revise to meet research-paper conventions

- Have you properly identified all of your sources?
- Are all quotations clearly marked, with credit given to the original writer or speaker?
- Is the bibliography complete and correctly formatted?

▶ Rubric for Self-Assessment

Evaluate your research paper using the following rating scale:

	Score 4	Score 3	Score 2	Score 1
Topic	Appropriate for a research paper, since it requires outside research; well focused and suits the scope of the paper	Appropriate for a research paper, requiring outside research; reasonably focused but may be a little too broad or too narrow	Barely appropriate for a research paper; not well focused, since it is too broad or too narrow	Not appropriate for a research paper; not focused at all
Organization	Uses order of importance correctly and makes the relationships between the items and the reasons for their relative importance clear	Uses order of importance and makes most of the reasons for their relative importance clear	Organization not suited to the topic	Shows lack of organizational strategy
Presentation	Develops ideas with relevant facts, details, or examples; links all information to the issue being analyzed	Develops most ideas with facts, details, or examples; links most information to the issue being analyzed	Does not give most ideas in depth; does not link some information to the issue being analyzed	Does not provide facts, details, or examples to support ideas
Use of Language	Varies sentence structure and vocabulary successfully; includes no or very few mechanical errors	Uses some variety in sentence structure and vocabulary; includes few mechanical errors	Uses the same types of sentences without varying them; does not vary vocabulary; includes many mechanical errors	Writes incomplete sentences; uses language poorly; sounds confused; includes many mechanical errors

Unit 6

Plains Farm Family Out on the Great Plains, settlers faced enormous challenges, including lack of schools and medical care. Families built their homes from sod, tightknit bricks of dirt and roots. Above all, Plains families had to face the terrible isolation of the western prairies.

1880s

Bull Moose Denied the Republican nomination for President in 1912, Theodore Roosevelt campaigned vigorously under the banner of the Bull Moose Party. Democrat Woodrow Wilson won the election.

1912

An Age of Industry

Geronimo The Apache chief Geronimo led the last important Native American defense against the military might of the United States. In 1886, Geronimo surrendered to a promise of peace. Instead, his people were exiled and imprisoned.

Picture Brides Japanese women entered the United States at Angel Island in San Francisco harbor. Many of them had exchanged photographs with potential husbands in the United States. By 1920, about 20,000 Japanese women had immigrated to the United States.

1886

EARLY 1900s

On the Assembly Line Henry Ford's use of the assembly line greatly reduced the time needed to build a car. The result was that Ford could sell his cars at a lower price than other automakers.

1920s

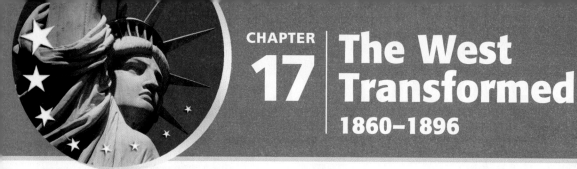

CHAPTER
17 | # The West Transformed
1860–1896

Chapter Preview

After the Civil War, Americans moved west in greater numbers. Miners, ranchers, and farmers settled on the Great Plains, changing the region forever. Meanwhile, Native Americans on the western lands struggled to keep their homelands.

1862
Congress passes Homestead Act.

1869
Transcontinental railroad is completed.

U.S. Events

1860

1868

1876

World Events

1864 Taiping Rebellion in China ends.

1869 Suez Canal opens.

Quick View Video
View the chapter video for a quick preview of the main ideas.

Cowhands drove cattle long distances along dusty trails to reach railroad towns where the cattle could be shipped east.

1876
Sioux defeat Custer's army at Little Big Horn.

1887
Dawes Act breaks up Native American tribal lands.

1889
Oklahoma opens to homesteaders.

1892
Populist Party organizes at national level.

1876

1884

1885 Indian National Congress forms to seek self-rule for India.

1888 Brazil bans slavery.

1892

History Reading Skill **Use Context Clues to Verify Meaning**

What was life like for Sioux families in the late 1800s?

In this chapter, you will practice using context clues to define unfamiliar words. Read the following account by Chief Standing Bear in which he describes the tasks and daily activities of a typical Lakota Sioux family. The side notes suggest ways to use context clues to define unfamiliar words.

Primary Source

Unfamiliar word

The Lakota Sioux were a large Plains Indian culture. They lived in tepees and hunted buffalo as their way of life. The buffalo provided many items for the Sioux, from clothing to shelter to tools.

Sinew was split for thread, coarse strands for heavy work and medium fine or very fine strands for decorative work, then folded into little bundles and placed in a sewing kit. . . .

Split for thread describes the use of the unfamiliar word _sinew_.

When the men came home from the hunt there were skins to be cleaned and tanned. . . . From rawhide were made moccasin soles, bags and trunks for holding ceremonial garments, headdresses, and other articles to be kept in neatness and order. . . .

Unfamiliar word

Here, examples give you information about the meaning of the unfamiliar word _rawhide_.

Grandmother, next to mother, was the most important person in the home. . . . As a storyteller, she was a delight. . . . Her sense of humor was keen, . . . she laughed as readily as we. . . .

Unfamiliar word

This phrase defines the unfamiliar word _keen_ as it applies to sense of humor.

— Chief Standing Bear, *Cry of the Thunderbird: The American Indian's Own Story*

Use Context Clues to Verify Meaning

- Restatements use different language to restate a word's meaning. Definitions tell you what a word means. Examples help you piece together a word's meaning by showing how the word is used.
- Also, look for comparison or contrast clues, in which unfamiliar words are described as similar to or different from familiar terms.

Document-Based Questions

1. Who wrote this account?
2. What were some of the daily activities of a Lakota Sioux family?
3. How do you think the roles of men and women in the family differed?

Vocabulary *Builder*

Previewing High-Use Academic Words

High-Use Word	Definition	Sample History Sentence
immigrate (IHM mah grayt) (Section 1, p. 581)	*v.* to move to a foreign region or country	Thousands of Chinese immigrated to the United States to work on western railroads.
manual (MAN yoo ahl) (Section 1, p. 581)	*adj.* involving work done by hand	The miners were exhausted after ten hours of manual labor.
transform (trans FORM) (Section 2, p. 584)	*v.* to change in appearance or form; to change the condition of something	The arrival of horses in Spanish times transformed the lives of Native Americans.
violate (VĪ ah layt) (Section 2, p. 589)	*v.* to break a rule or law; to disrespect; to disturb	Time after time, the government violated treaties it had made with Native Americans.
persist (per SIHST) (Section 3, p. 591)	*v.* to endure; to continue in the face of difficulty	Farmers on the frontier persisted despite the hardships they faced.
myth (mihth) (Section 3, p. 593)	*n.* story or legend; imaginary object; invented story	In discussing the "Wild West," it is difficult to separate fact from myth.
reside (ree ZĪD) (Section 4, p. 595)	*v.* to live (in or at); to dwell for a while; to exist (in)	The rancher resided in a large house with a view of distant mountains.
surplus (SER pluhs) (Section 4, p. 598)	*n.* excess; quantity that is left over	The company's expenses were very high that year; there was no surplus to invest in research.

Sitting Bull

Previewing Key Terms and People

Mining and Railroads

Objectives

1. Explain how the discovery of gold and silver affected the West.

2. Describe life in the western mining towns.

3. Summarize how railroads spread and helped the West to develop.

Prepare to Read

Reading Skill

Use Definition Clues As you read about history, you will come across unfamiliar words. In this textbook, definitions for many unfamiliar words are included in the text that surrounds the word. When you read a word that you do not know, look at nearby sentences. The unfamiliar word may be repeated and defined.

Vocabulary *Builder*

High-Use Words

<u>immigrate</u>, p. 581

<u>manual</u>, p. 581

Key Terms

vigilante, p. 580

subsidy, p. 580

transcontinental railroad, p. 581

⭐ **Background Knowledge** With the Civil War over, the nation turned its attention to its western frontier. This stretched from the Mississippi River to the Pacific Ocean. The frontier had prairies, mountains, and forests. Even though Americans thought of it as unsettled, it was the home of Mexican settlers and Native Americans.

Moving west, settlers first crossed the Great Plains. Most of the Plains receives little rainfall and has few trees. Thinking that crops could not grow there, settlers called the area the Great American Desert. In this section, you will learn how railroad builders and miners made the West a vital part of the nation's economy.

Main Idea
Settlement of the West often came in a rush, but many boomtowns soon died out.

Boom and Bust

In many parts of the West, settlement came in a rush. This was especially true in areas where prospectors found gold or silver. New mining towns sprang up in a flash—but many did not last long.

The gold rush of 1849 in California excited the nation. Before long, miners spread from California to the Sierra Nevada and the Rocky Mountains and to the Black Hills of the Dakota Territory.

Use Definition Clues
What is a lode? Write the sentence that provides a definition.

The Comstock Lode Just before the Civil War, prospectors began searching for gold in the Sierra Nevada. In 1859, two Irish prospectors found the gold they were looking for. However, a third man, Henry Comstock, said the claim was on his land. The find became known as the Comstock Lode. A lode is a rich vein of ore.

At the Comstock Lode, a blue-tinted sand stuck to all the equipment and made the gold hard to dig out. The blue mud turned out to be loaded with silver. In fact, the silver was far more valuable than the gold. This was one of the richest silver mines in the world.

In the next 20 years, the Comstock Lode produced $300 million worth of silver and made Nevada a center of mining. A tent city near the mines grew into the boomtown of Virginia City, Nevada.

The Boom Spreads After the Civil War, prospectors fanned out over the West. They found valuable ores in Montana, Idaho, and Colorado. They made a gold strike in South Dakota's Black Hills. In the 1890s, a gold find drew people from all over the world to Alaska.

Although each strike caused great excitement, few prospectors got rich. The ore was deep underground and expensive to extract. Comstock gave up and sold his mining rights for $11,000 and two mules. Many other prospectors sold their claims to large mining companies. By the 1880s, western mining had become a big business.

Boomtown Life Tent cities like Virginia City often arose around the diggings. Soon hotels, stores, and other wood-frame buildings appeared. Mining camps quickly grew into boomtowns.

Where prospectors went, others followed. Merchants brought mule teams hauling tools, food, and clothing. Nothing was cheap in the boomtown stores. Sometimes, miners paid high prices for bottles of pure drinking water. They did not want to drink from streams that might be polluted with chemicals, like arsenic, used in mining.

Women who joined the mining boom could make a good living. Some opened restaurants. Others washed clothes or took in boarders. One woman just baked pies. In a year, she became quite wealthy.

Nearly half the miners were foreign-born. The streets of the mining towns rang with Irish accents as well as Italian, German, Spanish, Chinese, and other languages. The foreign miners often faced hostility. For example, laws restricted Chinese miners to claims abandoned by others. Mobs often drove the Chinese from towns.

Discovery SCHOOL

Explore More Video
To learn more about boomtowns and ghost towns, view the video.

From Boomtown to Ghost Town In the 1870s, Virginia City, Nevada, had close to 30,000 inhabitants. When the Comstock Lode ran out, Virginia City became a ghost town. Today, it is a thriving tourist attraction. **Critical Thinking: *Identify Economic Alternatives*** *Why did Virginia City become a ghost town? How did it later restore its economy?*

Mining and Railroads in the West

MAP MASTER®

Skills Activity

Wherever prospectors discovered gold or silver, mines sprang up and people poured in. Railroads spread out to serve the new communities.

(a) Read a Map What railroad served Bozeman and Butte in Montana?

(b) Draw Conclusions Why were railroads eager to serve the new mining centers?

MapMaster ⬤nline

For: Interactive map
Visit: PHSchool.com
Web Code: myp-6131

KEY

┼┼┼┼ Railroads

⚒ Mining centers

Frontier Justice Mining towns sprouted so fast that law and order were hard to find. Miners formed groups of **vigilantes,** or self-appointed law keepers. Such groups hunted down bandits and imposed their own rough brands of justice.

As boomtowns grew, local residents began to seek more lasting forms of government. Sheriffs, marshals, and judges replaced vigilantes. Colorado, Dakota, and Nevada organized into territories in 1861, followed by Arizona and Idaho in 1863 and Montana in 1864.

In some mining towns, all the ore was soon extracted. Mines shut down and miners moved away. With few customers, businesses failed and merchants left. Boomtowns became ghost towns.

✓**Checkpoint** **Why did boomtowns use vigilante justice?**

Main Idea
Backed by federal aid, railroad companies had laid tracks from coast to coast by 1869.

The Railroad Boom

Railroads raced to lay track to the mines and boomtowns. They received generous help from the federal government.

Aid to Railroads Before 1860, railroad lines ended at the Mississippi River. Then, the federal government began to offer subsidies. **Subsidies** are grants of land or money. For every mile of track, the government gave the railroad 10 square miles of land next to the track. Railroads got more than 180 million acres, an area the size of Texas. They also received federal loans.

Spanning the Continent Many westerners dreamed of a transcontinental railroad, a railroad line that spanned the continent. In 1862, Leland Stanford and his partners won the right to build a line eastward from Sacramento. Their railroad was the Central Pacific. Another railroad, the Union Pacific, would build west from Omaha. When the lines met, tracks would stretch from coast to coast.

The railroads hired thousands of workers—native-born whites, Mexican Americans, and African Americans. Workers also immigrated to the United States from Mexico and Ireland. The Central Pacific brought 10,000 Chinese to the United States.

The work was hazardous; the pay low. Cutting through the Sierra Nevada, Chinese manual laborers were lashed by snow and winds. Avalanches buried weeks of work in moments and killed workers by the score. Daily progress sometimes came in inches. (For more on the building of the railroad, see the Geography and History feature.)

At last, on May 10, 1869, the two lines met at Promontory, Utah. Stanford drove the final spike into the last rail with a silver mallet.

Effects of the Railroads New towns sprang up in the West. People and supplies poured in. Gold and silver poured out.

Rapid population growth brought political changes. Nevada became a state in 1864; Colorado in 1876; North Dakota, South Dakota, Montana, and Washington in 1889; Idaho and Wyoming in 1890.

☑**Checkpoint** How did the railroads change the West?

⭐ **Looking Back and Ahead** Gold and silver discoveries brought boomtowns to the West. Then came railroads and more settlers. In the next section, you will read how these developments affected the Native Americans who lived in the West.

Vocabulary *Builder*
immigrate (IHM mah grayt) *v.* to move to a foreign region or country

Vocabulary *Builder*
manual (MAN yoo ahl) *adj.* involving work done by hand

Section 1 | Check Your Progress

Progress Monitoring ⊕nline
For: Self-test with instant help
Visit: PHSchool.com
Web Code: mya-6131

Comprehension and Critical Thinking

1. **(a) Recall** In 1850, what region of the United States was considered the western frontier?
(b) Detect Points of View Explain how each of the following groups viewed the western frontier: Americans, Spanish settlers, Native Americans.

2. **(a) Identify** Why did the government believe it was important to extend railroad lines west?
(b) Identify Economic Benefits What incentives did the government offer to railroad builders to extend railroad lines westward?

Reading Skill

3. **Use Definition Clues** Define the term subsidies in the following context, and describe the clue you used: Congress offered generous subsidies to railroads. Subsidies are grants of land or money.

Vocabulary *Builder*

Read each sentence. If the sentence is true, write YES. If the sentence is not true, write NO and explain why.

4. Vigilante groups in the West were replaced by homesteaders.

5. The transcontinental railroad connected the East with the West.

Writing

6. Persuasive writing always centers on an opinion—an idea about which there can be disagreement. Tell whether each of the following statements expresses an opinion or states a fact. **Statements:**

(a) A valuable gold strike was made in South Dakota's Black Hills.

(b) The unjust treatment of foreign miners was shameful.

(c) Creating a coast-to-coast railway was the most important factor in U.S. economic history.

(d) Some mining camps quickly grew into boomtowns.

Transcontinental Railroad

During the Civil War, Congress passed a bill that provided for the construction of a transcontinental railroad. The new law assigned two companies to build the railroad: the Central Pacific Railroad and the Union Pacific Railroad.

▼ **Two Railroads**
The Central Pacific headed east from Sacramento. The Union Pacific headed west from Omaha.

TRANSCONTINENTAL RAILROAD

KEY
⊢⊢⊢ Central Pacific Railroad
⊢⊢⊢ Union Pacific Railroad

Physical Obstacles ▶
Foul weather and rugged landscapes hampered construction efforts on both lines. The Central Pacific took almost five years to cross the Sierra Nevada.

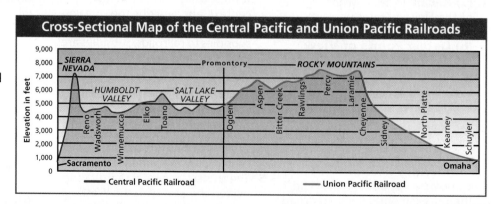

Cross-Sectional Map of the Central Pacific and Union Pacific Railroads

Central Pacific Railroad   Union Pacific Railroad

▲ **Blasting Through Mountains**

The Central Pacific recruited large numbers of Chinese workers to build the railroad. The workers would climb down steep cliffs in the Sierra Nevada and stuff explosives into the rocks to blast tunnels.

Understand Effects:
Moving West

The completion of the transcontinental railroad paved the way for increased settlement of the West. Additional railroads were built in the decades after 1869, and populations of western territories surged. Native Americans were increasingly hemmed in by steady tides of new settlers.

History *Interactive*

Travel the Transcontinental Railroad

Visit: PHSchool.com
Web Code: myp-6137

Leland Stanford

▲ **A Golden Spike**

With the engines No. 119 and Jupiter pulled nose to nose at Promontory, Utah, the railroads were joined by a golden spike on May 10, 1869. Leland Stanford, a railroad executive and later governor of California, supervised construction of the Central Pacific.

Analyze **GEOGRAPHY AND HISTORY**

Write a paragraph describing how geography affected the construction of the transcontinental railroad. Think about the physical obstacles each railroad company faced along the way.

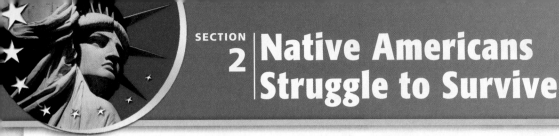

Native Americans Struggle to Survive

Objectives

1. Describe the importance of the buffalo to Native Americans of the Plains.

2. Explain how Native Americans and settlers came into conflict.

3. Summarize the struggles of Native American groups to maintain their traditional ways of life.

4. Explain why Congress passed the Dawes Act in 1887.

Prepare to Read

Reading Skill

Use Restatement Clues Like a definition clue, a restatement clue tells you what an unfamiliar word means. It restates in simple language what the word means. Restatement clues often follow the unfamiliar word, linked by a comma and the word *or.* This textbook often uses restatement clues to define key terms and highlights them in blue.

Vocabulary *Builder*

High-Use Words
transform, p. 584
violate, p. 589

Key Terms and People
travois, p. 584
tepee, p. 584
reservation, p. 586
Sitting Bull, p. 586

☆ **Background Knowledge** Mining and railroading brought people to the West and turned it into a booming region. But Native Americans struggled to survive there.

People of the Plains

At the end of the Civil War, some 360,000 Native Americans lived in the West, mainly on the Great Plains. Many, like the Arikaras and the Lakotas, had been there for centuries.

Main Idea
Native Americans of the Plains relied on the buffalo to meet many basic needs.

Life in Transition People of the Plains lived by gathering wild foods, hunting, and fishing. Some raised crops. Early Native Americans hunted buffalo and other game on foot. The arrival of the Europeans transformed their lives. Plains nations tamed herds of wild horses, descended from tough breeds brought by the Spanish. They also traded with the French and British for guns.

Vocabulary *Builder*
transform (trans FORM) *v.* to change in appearance or form; to change the condition of something

With guns, Native Americans could kill more game. On horseback, they could travel faster and farther. Some groups became wanderers, carrying belongings on **travois** (truh VOIZ), or small sleds. They lived in **tepees,** cone-shaped tents made of buffalo skins.

Many Plains nations followed the buffalo herds. In winter, they trailed the herds into protected valleys and forests. In summer, when grass on the Plains grew tall, hunters tracked the buffalo as they gathered to graze.

People found many uses for the buffalo. Its meat was a protein-rich food. Horns and bones could be made into tools, and tendons could be made into thread. Buffalo hunting thus played a key role in people's survival.

Division of Labors In many Plains nations, women managed village life. They cared for children and prepared food. They carved tools and made clothing and tepees. Sometimes they went to war. In 1876, a Crow woman named The Other Magpie rode against the Sioux for killing her brother. In some groups, a wise woman ruled.

Men were hunters and warriors. Often, they also led religious life. One important ritual was the Sun Dance. The four-day ceremony brought together thousands of Native Americans from many nations. Men would make pledges to the Great Spirit, or ruler of the universe.

✓**Checkpoint** **Why was the buffalo important to many groups?**

Broken Treaties

U.S. treaties promised to safeguard Native American lands. As miners and railroad crews pushed west, they broke those treaties.

Fort Laramie Treaty In 1851, ten thousand people from many Plains nations gathered near Fort Laramie in Wyoming for a "big talk" with U.S. officials. The officials wanted the nations to stop following the buffalo. If they would settle permanently, the government promised to protect their lands "as long as the grass shall grow."

No sooner had some Native American leaders signed the Fort Laramie Treaty than settlers moved onto their lands. In 1859, a gold strike at Pikes Peak in Colorado sent miners swarming to the region.

Main Idea
Treaties to protect Native American lands were quickly broken, and wars broke out.

Uses of the Buffalo
The buffalo was central to the life of Native Americans living on the Great Plains. It furnished not only food but also many other necessities of life. **Critical Thinking:** *Draw Conclusions Why did the nations of the Plains depend so heavily on the buffalo? How did they cope when the buffalo herds began to disappear?*

Covering Tepees Buffalo hides were used to cover the tepees in which the people of the Plains lived.

Keeping Warm The hairy hides of the buffalo provided clothing and warm coverings, such as this Cheyenne robe. Buffalo tendons made a strong thread for sewing garments together.

Sitting Bull
1831–1890

Sitting Bull's legend as a great Native American leader began at the age of 10, when he killed his first buffalo. During battle, a warrior would try to get close enough to the enemy to touch him. Sitting Bull excelled at this practice, called "counting coup." He was 14 when he touched his first enemy in battle. He soon became a leader known for his fearlessness in battle.

Biography Quest nline

What kind of education did Sitting Bull give his children?

For: The answer to the question about Sitting Bull

Visit: PHSchool.com

Web Code: myd-6132

Sand Creek Massacre In the early 1860s, new treaties forced Native Americans to give up land around Pikes Peak. Many warriors resisted. They attacked supply trains and homes.

In response, Colonel John Chivington and 700 volunteers attacked a band of Cheyennes at Sand Creek in eastern Colorado in 1864. These Cheyennes were friendly and under army protection. They raised a white flag to signal peace, but Chivington ordered his men to attack. In the end, more than 100 men, women, and children died.

Buffalo Soldiers The Sand Creek Massacre helped to ignite an era of war. Among the soldiers most feared on the Plains were African American veterans of the Civil War. The Native Americans called them Buffalo Soldiers. The Buffalo Soldiers fought on the Plains for 20 years. They also captured bandits from Texas to the Dakotas.

End of the Buffalo The giant herds of buffalo, so central to Native American life, began to shrink in the 1870s. Railroads had hunters kill the animals to feed their crews. Others also slaughtered buffalo because buffalo robes drew high prices in eastern cities. One hunter might kill 2,000 buffalo in a month.

✔**Checkpoint** Why did the buffalo begin to disappear?

Main Idea
Warfare continued even as some Native American nations tried to adapt to life on reservations.

Last Stand for Custer and the Sioux

New treaties in the late 1860s sought to end the wars on the Plains. Federal officials urged Plains nations to settle down and farm.

Reservations The southern Plains nations—the Kiowas, Comanches, and Arapahos—moved to reservations in Oklahoma. A reservation is land set aside for Native Americans to live on. Life there was a disaster. Poor soil in Oklahoma made farming difficult.

Many Sioux and Cheyennes gathered on land set aside for them in the Black Hills of the Dakotas. An 1874 gold strike brought a flood of miners. Sitting Bull and Crazy Horse led attacks to keep whites out.

Little Bighorn In June of 1876, under orders to force the Native Americans onto a reservation, Colonel George Armstrong Custer entered the Little Bighorn Valley in Montana Territory. Although outnumbered, he attacked a large band of Sioux and Cheyennes.

Custer and all his men died at the Battle of Little Bighorn. But the victory of Sitting Bull and Crazy Horse was fleeting. One Sioux recalled, "A winter or so later, more soldiers came to round us up on reservations. There were too many of them to fight now."

✔**Checkpoint** Why did Custer attack at Little Bighorn?

Native American Territory

KEY

Land lost by Indians

- Before 1850
- 1850–1870
- 1870–1890
- Indian reservations in 1890
- ✳ Battles
- ⚑ Fort

0 km 500
0 miles 500
Albers Conic Equal-Area Projection

MAP MASTER®
Skills Activity

By 1890, most Native Americans had been confined to reservations.

(a) Read a Map During what period did Native Americans lose most of their land in California?

(b) Draw Conclusions How did being restricted to reservations change the way of life of Native Americans on the Great Plains?

MapMaster Online

For: Interactive map
Visit: PHSchool.com
Web Code: myp-6132

Other Efforts at Resistance

Other Native American nations in the West also came under pressure. Among them were the Nez Percés to the north and the Navajos and Apaches to the south.

The Nez Percés The Nez Percés lived where Idaho, Oregon, and Washington now meet. They bred horses and cattle in the Snake River valley. Under pressure, many agreed to go to a reservation.

Rather than see his nation humiliated, Chief Joseph fled toward Canada with a large band of Nez Percés in 1877. The U.S. Army pursued them. In 75 days, the Nez Percés traveled 1,300 miles.

The army caught the Nez Percés near Canada's border. As Chief Joseph surrendered, he said, "I shall fight no more forever."

The Navajos Navajos raised sheep, horses, and cattle in the Southwest. Bands of Navajos also raided settlers' farms for livestock. To stop raids, white settlers called in the army. After a series of wars, the Navajos were defeated in 1864 in Arizona. Soldiers took them on what the Navajos called a "Long Walk" to a spot near the Pecos River. There, they suffered years of disease and hunger.

Main Idea

Efforts by Native Americans to preserve their traditional way of life did not succeed.

Links Across Time

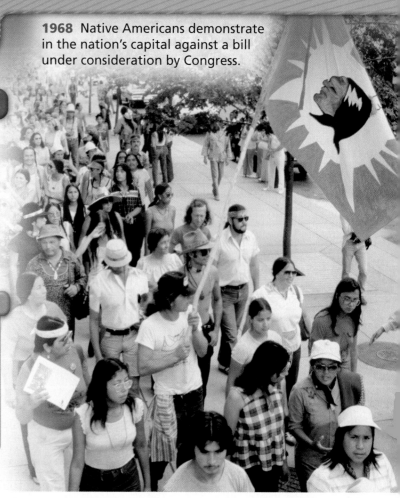

1968 Native Americans demonstrate in the nation's capital against a bill under consideration by Congress.

Civil Rights for Native Americans

1890 Some 200 Sioux were killed by soldiers at Wounded Knee. This incident brought the period of the Indian Wars to a violent close.

1960s Inspired in part by the civil rights movement, Native Americans organized to demand their rights. Groups such as the American Indian Movement sought to remind Americans of the history of broken treaties between Native Americans and the U.S. government.

Link to Today ⊙nline

Native American Rights Today Many Native American rights groups now focus their attention on the Supreme Court. What legal issues affect Native Americans in modern society?

For: Native American rights in the news
Visit: PHSchool.com
Web Code: myc-6132

Use Restatement Clues
What is a trance? Use a restatement clue in your answer.

The Apaches Fierce resistance came from Apaches like Geronimo, who refused to go to a reservation. From Mexico, Geronimo and his men attacked settlers in Arizona and New Mexico for 10 years. After his capture in 1886, he was sent to a reservation in Oklahoma.

The Ghost Dance Some Native Americans dreamed of returning to old ways. In the late 1880s, Native Americans across the Plains began performing a unique, swaying dance. Dancers fell into a trance, or dreamlike state. They believed they were talking to ghosts of their ancestors, so the dance was called the Ghost Dance. Dancers believed their ancestors and the buffalo would return and white people would leave the Plains. Soldiers guarding reservations saw the dance as the beginning of an uprising. In December 1890, Native American police went to a Sioux village to stop the dances. In a struggle to arrest Sitting Bull, police killed him.

Fearful of further violence, a band of Sioux tried to flee to safety. Army troops surrounded them at Wounded Knee Creek in South Dakota. As the Sioux were giving up their guns, a shot rang out. The troops opened fire with machine guns and rifles. Nearly 200 Sioux men, women, and children were killed. Some 30 soldiers died.

The Battle of Wounded Knee marked the end of the era of Indian Wars. "A people's dream died there," said one chief.

☑**Checkpoint** What was the purpose of the Ghost Dance?

The Failure of Reform

Reformers criticized the government for its harsh treatment of Native American nations. Criticism grew as more groups were forced onto reservations in the late 1800s.

Calls for Reform Susette La Flesche knew all about the calamity befalling Native Americans. Her father was an Omaha chief. In lectures and articles, she told of the destruction of native culture.

In 1881, inspired by La Flesche, the poet Helen Hunt Jackson wrote *A Century of Dishonor*. The book recorded the many treaties <u>violated</u> by the government at Native American expense. Alice Fletcher also promoted native rights. She became an agent for the U.S. Bureau of Indian Affairs, which dealt with Native Americans.

The Dawes Act Hoping to improve Native American life, Congress passed the Dawes Act in 1887. It tried to end Native Americans' wandering and turn them into farmers. Native American males each received 160 acres to farm. The act set up schools to make Native American children more like other Americans.

The Dawes Act failed. Few Native Americans took to farming. Many sold their land cheaply to dishonest whites. Federal agents replaced native leaders, and Native Americans had to give up traditional ways like the buffalo hunt. As a result, they remained poor. Many grew dependent on the government for food and supplies.

☑ **Checkpoint** What was the purpose of the Dawes Act?

⭐ **Looking Back and Ahead** As settlers poured into the West, buffalo grew scarce. Native Americans were moved onto reservations and forced to change their way of life. In the next section, you will read how some of the settlers made a living in the West.

Main Idea
The Dawes Act encouraged Native Americans to become farmers, but it failed.

Vocabulary *Builder*
<u>violate</u> (vī ah layt) *v.* to break a rule or law; to disrespect; to disturb

---

Section 2 | Check Your Progress

Progress Monitoring 🌐nline
For: Self-test with instant help
Visit: PHSchool.com
Web Code: mya-6132

Comprehension and Critical Thinking

1. **(a) Describe** How did guns and horses change the lives of Plains Native Americans?
   (b) Analyze Cause and Effect What were the short- and long-term effects of hunting buffalo on Native American life?

2. **(a) Identify** Who was Chief Joseph?
   (b) Detect Points of View In 1879, Chief Joseph appeared before Congress. He said, "Treat all men alike. Give them all the same law. Give them all an even chance to live and grow. All men were made by the same Great Spirit Chief." What was Chief Joseph trying to tell Congress? How do you think members of Congress responded to his words?

Reading Skill

3. **Use Restatement Clues** Use a restatement clue to define the term tepees in the following sentence: They lived in cone-shaped tepees, portable tents made of buffalo skins.

Vocabulary *Builder*

4. Write two definitions for each key term: travois, reservation. First, write a formal definition for your teacher. Second, write a definition in everyday English for a classmate.

Writing

5. Find three pieces of evidence in this section that support or refute the following opinion: In the nineteenth century, the U.S. government treated Native Americans in an unfair way.

Objectives

1. Explain how the cattle industry began.

2. Describe the life of a cowhand on the trail.

3. Discuss the myth of the Wild West.

4. Identify reasons for the end of the cattle boom.

Prepare to Read

 Reading Skill

Use Example Clues Writers may offer clues to a word's meaning by giving examples. Consider this sentence: "Canines such as poodles and spaniels make good companions." The examples show that *canines* means "dogs." A writer may describe an example in depth or tell what something does to help you visualize the unfamiliar word. Look for the phrases *such as* and *for example.*

Vocabulary *Builder*

High-Use Words

persist, p. 591

myth, p. 593

Key Terms

open range, p. 590

cattle drive, p. 590

vaquero, p. 592

cow town, p. 592

cattle kingdom, p. 593

⭐ **Background Knowledge** You have read how Native Americans were forced onto reservations. Now, you will learn how ranchers created a cattle industry that supplied beef to the nation.

The Rise of the Cattle Industry

For years, wild cattle wandered the **open range,** or unfenced land, of Texas. Called longhorns for their broad horns, they needed almost no care. They survived on prairie grass and watering holes.

Means and Markets The herds of cattle had grown from strays lost by Spanish ranchers. As American settlers moved in, they set up new ranches. But they did not bother to round up the stray herds because they had no means of getting the cattle to distant markets.

As railroads swept across the Plains in the 1860s, Texans at last saw a way to reach those markets. Protein-rich beef was in demand to feed city dwellers in the East and miners and soldiers in the West.

The Long Drives Ranchers began rounding up the cattle in the 1860s. They hired cowhands—skilled riders who know how to herd cattle—to move the cattle to rail lines in Kansas, Missouri, and Wyoming. Some rail lines were as far away as 1,000 miles.

Spring was an ideal time to begin a **cattle drive**—the herding and moving of cattle over long distances. Grass grew tall, and rivers flowed full from spring rains. The work was so demanding that cowhands brought a number of horses so that each day a fresh one would be available.

Main Idea
The coming of railroads gave western ranchers a way to get cattle to distant markets.

 Use Example Clues
What is an example of an open range? What does this term mean?

The long drives lasted two to three months. They followed well-worn trails. To the east lay the famous Chisholm Trail from San Antonio, Texas, to Abilene, Kansas. To the west, the Goodnight-Loving Trail led to rail towns in Wyoming. In just one year, as many as 600,000 cattle might be moved north.

☑**Checkpoint** **Why did cattle drives cover long distances?**

Life on the Trail

Life on the trail was hard and dangerous. The long cattle drives tested the nerve and skill of every cowhand.

A Risky Ride Andy Adams had driven many herds north. Never before had he seen cattle going blind with thirst. All he could do was "let them pass." When the crazed cattle finally sniffed out water and drank, their sight returned.

Cowhands such as Andy Adams kept the herds together as the cattle moved along the trails. The cowhands developed nerves of steel, staying calm even in times of extreme stress. Trip after trip, they persisted in performing their exciting but dangerous job.

Herding cattle was certainly risky. A lightning bolt could send a herd stampeding in all directions. Swift river currents sometimes carried the longhorns away, and cowhands would have to struggle to get the panicked animals back on solid ground. Cowhands also fought grass fires, pulled the cattle from swamps, and chased off thieves.

Main Idea
Cowhands, working long hours for low pay, learned skills developed earlier by Spanish and Mexican vaqueros.

Vocabulary *Builder*
persist (per SIHST) *v.* to endure; to continue in the face of difficulty

Cattle Trails in the West

MAP MASTER
Skills Activity

Cowhands drove great herds north to reach the rail lines. As settlements grew denser, these cattle drives came to an end.

(a) Read a Map Where did the Chisholm Trail start and end? Which trail on the map lay farthest west?

(b) Analyze Cause and Effect Why would an increase in population along the cattle trails help to bring the cattle drives to an end?

MapMaster Online

For: Interactive map
Visit: PHSchool.com
Web Code: myp-6133

KEY
— Cattle trails

saddle/
*silla de
montar*

spurs/
espoloñes

Outfitting a Vaquero

Cowhands borrowed much from early Spanish and Mexican vaqueros. The labels provide the English and Spanish names of the gear shown. **Critical Thinking:** *Frame Questions* What question would you want to ask a vaquero about the objects pictured here?

Main Idea

The West gained an exaggerated reputation for lawlessness and violence.

On the hot, dusty trails, cowhands could spend 18 hours a day in the saddle. Yet, for all their efforts, they earned wages of less than $1 a day. Like mining, cattle ranching relied on a workforce of low-paid laborers.

Spanish Roots The cowhands driving herds north owed much to Spanish and Mexican vaqueros (vah KAYR os). **Vaquero** (from *vaca*, meaning "cow") is the Spanish word for cowhand, or cowboy. Vaqueros tended cattle on ranches in Mexico, California, and the Southwest.

When Americans started to herd cattle, they learned from vaqueros how to ride, rope, and brand. Cowboys wore Mexican spurs and leather chaps that kept their legs safe from thorny shrubs. The broad-brimmed cowboy hat came from the Mexican *sombrero*, or "hat that provides shade." Cowboys used a leather lariat, or lasso (from the Spanish word *lazo*), to catch cattle and horses.

Approximately one third of all western cowhands were Mexican. Many others were African American and white veterans of the Civil War.

☑**Checkpoint** **What skills did American cowboys learn from Spanish and Mexican vaqueros?**

The Wild West

Cattle drives ended at towns along railroad lines. These towns—often unruly places—helped to create the fantasy of the Wild West.

Cow Towns In 1867, Joseph McCoy hit on an idea. The Illinois businessman figured that after months on the trail, cowboys were ready for a bath, a good meal, a soft bed, and some fun. Also, cattle needed to be penned as they awaited shipment east. So McCoy founded Abilene, Kansas, where the Chisholm Trail met the Kansas Pacific Railroad. Abilene was the first **cow town,** or settlement at the end of a cattle trail.

With money to be made from cowboys and their herds, rival cow towns such as Wichita and Dodge City, Kansas, soon sprang up along rail lines. Dance halls, saloons, hotels, and restaurants served the cowboys. Drinking and gambling often led to barroom brawls that spilled onto the streets. Gunfights were rare but common enough to lead towns such as Wichita to ban carrying pistols.

The Myth of the West Rough-and-tumble life in cow towns helped to spread the <u>myth</u> of the West as a place of violence, adventure, and endless opportunity. Easterners called it the Wild West.

No one did more to promote this fantasy than William "Buffalo Bill" Cody. A former buffalo hunter, Cody created a traveling Wild West show in 1883. Gun-slinging cowboys and Native Americans performed daring feats of sharp shooting and horseback riding. They staged performances depicting frontier events, including Custer's Last Stand. Annie Oakley broke the stereotype of the dainty woman with shooting as precise as any man's.

The myth of the Wild West had some basis in fact. But, as you have read, the West was also being transformed. Native Americans were being forced onto reservations. Mining and ranching were big businesses. Independent miners were becoming wage earners, like cowboys. Even wild cow towns were being quieted down by settlers and ministers who wanted peaceful communities for their families and their faiths.

☑ **Checkpoint**   **How true was the myth of the Wild West?**

Vocabulary *Builder*
<u>myth</u> (mihth) *n.* story or legend; imaginary object; invented story

Boom and Bust in the Cattle Kingdom

The cattle boom lasted from the 1860s to the 1880s. The region dominated by the cattle industry and its ranches, trails, and cow towns came to be called the **cattle kingdom.** Ranchers made large profits as herds and markets grew. But then the cattle industry collapsed.

The Cattle Boom At the height of the cattle boom, ranchers could buy a young calf for $5 and sell a mature steer for $60. Even after the expense of a cattle drive, profits were extremely high.

Main Idea
Overstocking and a spell of bad weather eventually put an end to the cattle boom.

Links to Art

Cold Morning on the Range, 1904

by Frederic Remington

Frederic Remington was a Yale-educated easterner who became a famous painter and sculptor of western scenes. His work highlighted such themes as self-reliance and mastery over nature. In *Cold Morning on the Range* (seen here), he portrays a rider in the process of taming a wild horse. **Critical Thinking:** *Evaluate Information How do you think Remington's work added to the myth of the Wild West?*

Profits rose still higher with the introduction of new breeds of cattle. These breeds caught fewer diseases and had more meat than longhorns. As a result, backers from the East and Europe invested millions in huge cattle companies. The ranches of one company alone covered almost 800 square miles in three states.

The Boom Ends By the mid-1880s, more than 7 million cattle roamed the open range. That was more than the land could feed. Then, beginning in 1886 and 1887, a cycle of scorching summers and frigid winters killed millions of cattle. Meanwhile, an economic depression threw many city dwellers out of work. Demand for beef dropped.

To make things worse, sheep began competing with cattle for prairie grasses across the Plains. Farmers fenced in the open range to keep cattle away from crops. Without free grazing for their herds, ranchers had to buy expensive feed.

Giant cattle ranches slowly gave way to smaller spreads that grew their own feed. As railroads expanded, their lines moved closer to the ranches. Large roundups and long cattle drives vanished. The cattle boom was over.

☑ **Checkpoint** **What factors ended the cattle boom?**

☆ **Looking Back and Ahead** As railroads pushed across the West, the cattle industry boomed. Cowhands moved herds north on long drives to meet trains that took the cattle east. The cattle boom lasted into the 1880s. In the next section, you will read how farming changed the West.

Texas Longhorn
The horns of longhorn cattle can be six feet wide or more. The cattle use them for both attack and defense.

Section 3 | **Check Your Progress**

Progress Monitoring ⬤nline
For: Self-test with instant help
Visit: PHSchool.com
Web Code: mya-6133

Comprehension and Critical Thinking

1. (a) Describe What dangers did cowhands face on cattle drives?
(b) Draw Conclusions Why do you think cowhands took these risks?

2. (a) Recall How did the expansion of railroads help to create a cattle boom?
(b) Identify Economic Benefits How did the cattle boom lead to economic prosperity for many new towns in the West?

↻ **Reading Skill**

3. Use Example Clues Reread the text following the subheading "Cow Towns." How do example and description help you understand the term cow town? What is a cow town?

Vocabulary *Builder*

Complete each of the following sentences so that the second part further explains the first and clearly shows your understanding of the key term.

4. Cattle drives brought thousands of cattle to rail lines; _____.

5. Vaqueros tended cattle herds; _____.

6. The cattle kingdom supplied meat to a growing nation; _____.

Writing

7. Based on what you have read in this section about the Wild West myth, write an opinion about the effects of this myth on American life. Back up your opinion with reasons and examples from the section and from your own knowledge.

Farming in the West

Objectives

1. Identify what attracted farmers to settle on the Great Plains.

2. Describe how people adapted to life on the Plains.

3. Summarize the result of the Oklahoma Land Rush.

4. Explain how economic issues led farmers to organize to seek reform.

Prepare to Read

 Reading Skill

Use Comparison or Contrast Clues Comparison and contrast can also help you define unfamiliar words. Comparison clues show how an unfamiliar word is similar to a familiar word, phrase, or example. Look for signal words such as *similar to* or *like* to highlight these clues. Contrast clues show how an unfamiliar word is different from a familiar word, phrase, or example. Look for signal words such as *unlike* or *instead* to highlight these clues.

Vocabulary *Builder*

High-Use Words

<u>reside</u>, p. 595

<u>surplus</u>, p. 598

Key Terms and People

homesteader, p. 595

sod, p. 596

sodbuster, p. 596

sooner, p. 598

grange, p. 598

farm cooperative, p. 598

inflation, p. 599

William Jennings Bryan, p. 599

⭐ **Background Knowledge** While ranchers and cowhands were building a cattle kingdom, hundreds of thousands of farmers were flooding onto the Great Plains.

Homesteading

By 1900, half a million farmers had settled on the Great Plains. Many were attracted by an offer of free land.

Homestead Act During the Civil War, Congress passed the Homestead Act of 1862. It offered a 160-acre plot to anyone who <u>resided</u> on the land for five years. Congress wanted to give the poor a chance to own farms. Thousands became homesteaders—settlers who acquired free land from the government—on the Great Plains.

But few had the money to move west and start a farm. Also, land companies took over large areas illegally. And on the dry Plains, 160 acres was too small to grow enough grain to profit. Only one homesteader in three lasted the required five years.

Railroads Promote Farming In fact, railroads promoted more farming than did the Homestead Act. More farms meant more shipping for western railroads. So the railroads gave away some of the 180 million acres they got from the government. They recruited thousands of people from the eastern United States, Ireland, Germany, and Scandinavia to settle on the Great Plains.

☑**Checkpoint** How did the Homestead Act help people gain land?

Main Idea
Would-be settlers could get a homestead from the government or land from railroad companies.

Vocabulary *Builder*
<u>reside</u> (ree ZĪD) *v.* to live (in or at); to dwell for a while; to exist (in)

Main Idea

New techniques and inventions helped settlers adapt to the difficult life on the Plains.

A Hard Life on the Plains

Life on the Great Plains was not easy. Water was scarce, and crops were hard to grow. Farmers struggled to make ends meet.

Busting Sod The first farmers on the eastern Plains staked out sites near water and trees. Later arrivals continued on to the treeless prairie. The farther west one went, the drier the climate became.

The soil of the Plains was fertile. It was covered with a thick **sod,** or a surface layer of earth in which the roots of grasses tangle with soil. With little rain, sod baked into a hardened mass. Early settlers, lacking wood, cut sod into bricks to build walls. Two rows of sod bricks made walls that kept homes cool in summer and warm in winter.

New Farming Methods Farmers broke through the tough sod with plows. The sod often cracked plows made of wood or iron. In 1877, John Deere of Illinois invented a sodbusting plow made of steel. Steel plows were stronger and lighter than other plows.

Plains farmers, or **sodbusters** as they were known, used machines called drills to plant crops. The drills buried seeds deep in the ground where there was moisture. Farmers used reapers to harvest crops and threshers to beat off the hard coverings of the grains.

Water often lay hundreds of feet below ground. Farmers used windmills to pump the water out. To keep cattle from trampling crops, farmers put up fences. Lacking wood, they used barbed wire. Joseph Glidden, an Illinois farmer, invented this twisted metal wire in 1874.

Sodbusters

Thickly matted grass roots held the fertile Plains soil in a tight grip. Even with a four-horse plow, sodbusting (breaking up the sod) was backbreaking work. Worse, once exposed by plowing, the fertile soil might be blown away by winds. **Critical Thinking: Clarify Problems** *What problems did settlers face on the Plains? How did they overcome their problems?*

◀ **Railroads Lure Settlers**
Railroads, eager for customers, offered free land to lure settlers to the Great Plains. People came from eastern cities and from many countries in Europe.

Sod ▶
Deep, thick roots allowed grasses to thrive in areas of the Great Plains that received limited amounts of moisture.

Farm Families Whole families worked on the farms. Men labored from dawn to dusk. Children tended animals and helped with other chores. Life was also hard for women. Besides keeping house, they helped plant and harvest. They educated children. They nursed the sick. They sewed clothing, preserved food, and made such basics as candles and soap.

Exodusters Thousands of African Americans, many of them former slaves, streamed onto the Plains. By the early 1880s, perhaps 70,000 African Americans had settled in Kansas. These settlers were known as Exodusters because they believed they were like the Jews fleeing slavery in Egypt, a biblical story told in the book of Exodus.

Some Exodusters took up farming. Others moved to towns. Men often worked as hired hands and women as laundresses.

The Spanish Southwest In the Southwest along the border with Mexico, arriving settlers found Spanish-speaking farmers and sheepherders. Many had been there since before the Mexican-American War, when the United States had acquired this territory.

The coming of the railroads brought more immigrants from Mexico. Many helped build the new lines. Some of the older Hispanic residents were large landowners, known as *ricos* (REE kos). They fought to keep their lands, deeded under Spanish or Mexican law.

☑**Checkpoint** Who were the sodbusters and the Exodusters?

Reading Skill **Use Comparison or Contrast Clues** What comparison clue is included in this paragraph to help you define the term *Exodusters*? What are Exodusters?

◀ **A Sod House**
Settlers cut sod into bricks that they used to construct sturdy sod houses like the one at left.

◀ **Care With Resources**
Like the Native Americans, early farm families had few resources to spare. The woman in this picture gathers dried buffalo manure to use as a fuel for heating or cooking, or to use as a fertilizer for crops.

Main Idea
A rush for land in Oklahoma in 1889 signaled the closing of the western frontier.

A Last Rush for Land

By the 1880s, few areas on the Plains remained free to settlers. The federal government agreed to open Oklahoma to homesteaders.

Boomers and Sooners In April 1889, nearly 100,000 people gathered at a line near present-day Oklahoma City. These were the "boomers." They had come to claim some of the 2 million acres of free homesteads in what was once Indian Territory.

At noon, a volley of gunfire signaled the start of the Oklahoma Land Rush. A few people, known as **sooners,** had already sneaked onto the land. They jumped from hiding and grabbed the best land. Other rushes followed until all 2 million acres had been claimed.

The Frontier Closes In 1890, the national census reported that the United States no longer had land available for homesteading. In the West, "there can hardly be said to be a frontier line," the report stated.

☑**Checkpoint** **Where was the last land rush in the West?**

Main Idea
Facing an economic crisis, farmers formed groups like the National Grange and the Populist Party.

Vocabulary *Builder*
<u>surplus</u> (SER pluhs) *n.* excess; quantity that is left over

Farmers Organize

Wheat and grain from Plains farms fed the growing cities of America and Europe. A few big farmers prospered. But small farmers faced an economic crisis and quickly organized to end it.

Crisis on the Farm The more grain that farmers hauled to market, the lower grain prices fell. Farmers were producing a <u>surplus</u> of crops. One Kansas farmer complained that "we are poorer by many dollars than we were years ago."

Small farmers were hit the hardest by low grain prices. Many had borrowed money for land and machinery. As prices fell, Plains farmers could not repay their loans and lost their land. In the South, tenants and sharecroppers fell deeper into debt as cotton prices fell.

Cooperatives and Political Parties Many farmers lived in poverty and isolation. Some communities began to form granges, groups of farmers who met for lectures, sewing bees, and other events. In 1867, local granges joined to form the National Grange.

What began as a social and educational movement evolved into an economic protest. In the 1870s and 1880s, Grangers demanded the same low rates from railroads and warehouses that were given to big farmers. They elected state officials who passed laws limiting rates.

A group called the Farmers' Alliance organized in the late 1870s to help farmers. It set up farm cooperatives—groups of farmers who pool their money to make large purchases of tools, seed, and other supplies at a discount. In the South, both whites and blacks joined the Alliance.

In 1892, unhappy farmers joined with members of labor unions to form the Populist Party. This was a political party that pushed for social reforms. It demanded public ownership of railroads and warehouses to control rates, a tax on income to replace property taxes, an eight-hour workday, and other reforms.

Populists wanted to use silver in addition to gold as a basis for the money supply. With more money circulating, Populists hoped to see **inflation,** or a general rise in prices. They believed rising grain prices would help farmers pay off their debts. In that way, the farmers could avoid foreclosure—the taking of property to settle a debt. Summing up Populist demands, Kansas activist Mary Elizabeth Lease said:

> ❝We want money, land, and transportation. We . . . want the power to make loans direct from the government. We want the accursed foreclosure system wiped out. . . .❞
>
> —Mary Elizabeth Lease, 1890 speech

The Election of 1896 In the presidential election of 1896, Populists supported Democrat William Jennings Bryan, known as the "Great Commoner." Bryan won the votes of farmers from the South and West for supporting the use of silver to raise prices.

Bankers and business owners claimed rising prices would ruin the economy. They backed Republican William McKinley and his gold-alone standard. McKinley won. Republicans took both the White House and Congress for the first time in decades. The Populists faded. Although the major parties absorbed many of their ideas, most Americans saw no link between farm problems and their own.

These presidential campaign buttons show the two major candidates in 1896. William McKinley (right) won for the Republicans. William Jennings Bryan (left) had the backing of Democrats and Populists but lost.

☑**Checkpoint** **What did the Populists demand?**

☆ **Looking Back and Ahead** Farmers found it hard to make a living, so they organized to demand reforms. In the next chapter, you will read about the rise of big business and labor.

Section 4 | **Check Your Progress**

Progress Monitoring ⦿nline
For: Self-test with instant help
Visit: PHSchool.com
Web Code: mya-6134

Comprehension and Critical Thinking

1. **(a) Recall** What was a homesteader?
   (b) Explain Problems What were three problems associated with the Homestead Act?

2. **(a) Recall** What is a surplus?
   (b) Clarify Problems How did a surplus of grain contribute to low grain prices? How did the National Grange, the Farmers' Alliance, and the Populist Party try to address the economic crisis caused by low prices?

Reading Skill

3. **Use Comparison or Contrast Clues** Define the term inflation in the following sentence: Like the wind under a child's runaway balloon, inflation pushed prices higher and higher.

Vocabulary *Builder*

Answer the following questions in complete sentences that show your understanding of the key terms.

4. How did tough sod make living on the Great Plains difficult?

5. Why were Great Plains farmers called sodbusters?

6. Who were the sooners?

7. How did forming a farm cooperative help farmers?

8. How did Populists think inflation would help them economically?

Writing

9. Imagine that you will be writing an editorial meant to influence readers of your school newspaper about coed sports teams. Write a few sentences creating an audience profile describing these readers. Think about who they are: How old are they? What types of interests do they have? What sports interest them the most?

As you learned in the Skills for Life in the previous chapter, thematic maps focus on topics such as agricultural products, migrations, or physical regions. The map below is a climate map. Climate refers to the average weather of a place over a period of time. The visual information included on a climate map can help you understand the economy of a region.

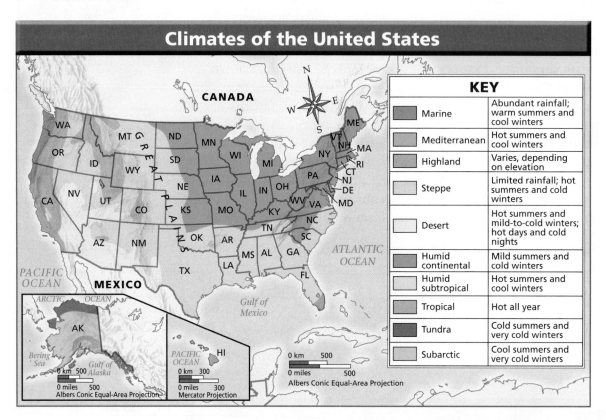

Climates of the United States

KEY	
Marine	Abundant rainfall; warm summers and cool winters
Mediterranean	Hot summers and cool winters
Highland	Varies, depending on elevation
Steppe	Limited rainfall; hot summers and cold winters
Desert	Hot summers and mild-to-cold winters; hot days and cold nights
Humid continental	Mild summers and cold winters
Humid subtropical	Hot summers and cool winters
Tropical	Hot all year
Tundra	Cold summers and very cold winters
Subarctic	Cool summers and very cold winters

Learn the Skill

Use these steps to interpret climate maps.

1 **Use the map key to read the map.** The map key explains special symbols and colors used on the map.

2 **Look for patterns on the map.** Study the information on the map to notice trends or patterns.

3 **Make inferences.** Make generalizations. Use the information on the map to make a general statement about the climate.

Practice the Skill

Answer the following questions about the map on this page.

1 **Use the map key to read the map.** What does the key on this map tell you? What do the colors tell you? What other information is on this key?

2 **Look for patterns on the map.** How does the climate change as you move across the Great Plains states from east to west?

3 **Make inferences.** How do you think the climate of the Great Plains affects farming?

Apply the Skill

See the Review and Assessment at the end of this chapter.

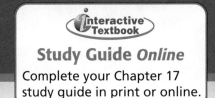

Interactive Textbook

Study Guide *Online*

Complete your Chapter 17 study guide in print or online.

Chapter Summary

Section 1
Mining and Railroads

- Gold and silver strikes in the West attracted many newcomers.
- Some mining towns became ghost towns after the metals were mined out.
- Immigrants came to the West from many countries to help build railroads.
- In 1869, a transcontinental railroad linked the East with the West.

Section 2
Native Americans Struggle to Survive

- Native Americans lost their lands, despite treaties aimed at protecting them.
- Native American nations were forced onto reservations.
- Native Americans fought for their way of life.
- The 1887 Dawes Act tried to promote new ways of living among Native Americans.

Section 3
The Cattle Kingdom

- Railroads provided a way for cattle ranchers to get their herds to distant markets.
- Unruly cattle towns helped to give rise to the myth of the Wild West.
- Economic depression, bad weather, and the fencing of crops brought the cattle boom to an end in the late 1800s.

Section 4
Farming in the West

- Free land for homesteaders helped to populate the Great Plains.
- Plains settlers faced a hard and isolated life.
- Disgruntled farmers and workers organized to demand reforms from government.
- The Populist Party shook up American politics in the 1890s.

Key Concepts

These notes will help you prepare for questions about key concepts.

The Western Frontier Disappears

Causes
- Gold and silver are discovered.
- A transcontinental railroad is built.
- The Homestead Act is passed.

Effects
- Mining towns rise and fall.
- More settlers, including immigrants, move west.
- Native American nations lose their lands.
- Wars break out between Native Americans and the U.S. Army.

Native Americans: A Chronology

- **1851** The Fort Laramie Treaty is signed.
- **1859** Miners discover gold at Pikes Peak, Colorado.
- **1864** The Sand Creek Massacre occurs in eastern Colorado.
- **1874** Gold is found in the Black Hills.
- **1876** Sioux and Cheyennes defeat Custer's forces at the Battle of Little Bighorn.
- **1887** Congress passes the Dawes Act.
- **1890** Nearly 200 Sioux die in the Battle of Wounded Knee.

Facts About Cowhands and Farmers

Cowhands
- Spanish and Mexican vaqueros passed on many skills.
- About one third of all western cowhands were Mexican.
- Cowhands worked long hours for low pay.

Farmers
- Farmers overcame great difficulties to survive on the Plains.
- Crop surpluses kept prices low.
- Farmers joined together to demand reforms.

Vocabulary *Builder*

Key Terms

Complete each of the following sentences so that the second part further explains the first part and clearly shows your understanding of the key term.

1. Plains Indians used travois in their travels; _____.

2. Farmers thought inflation would benefit farm prices; _____.

3. Vaqueros were important in cattle ranching; _____.

4. Railroads benefited from generous government subsidies; _____.

Comprehension and Critical Thinking

5. **(a) Describe** What difficulties did immigrants face in mining towns?
(b) Evaluate Information How did immigrants help to develop the West?

6. **(a) List** What types of changes did the transcontinental railroad bring to the West?
(b) Draw Inferences What were the effects of the building of railroads on Native Americans?

7. **(a) List** Describe three ways in which Native Americans made use of buffalo.
(b) Recall Why did the buffalo begin to disappear from the Great Plains in the 1870s?
(c) Draw Conclusions How did the disappearance of the buffalo change the lives of Native Americans?

8. **(a) Summarize** How did the U.S. government and settlers treat Native Americans?
(b) Detect Points of View What do you think the Native American chief meant when he said after the Battle of Wounded Knee, "A people's dream died there"?

9. **(a) Recall** Who was Buffalo Bill Cody?
(b) Apply Information Why do you think Americans characterize the West as "wild"?

10. **(a) Describe** What was life like for individuals who settled on the Great Plains?
(b) Draw Conclusions Why do you think families risked moving west?

History Reading Skill

11. **Use Context Clues** Choose four key terms or other unfamiliar words from this chapter. Write sentences that define these words. Include at least one of each clue type: example, comparison or contrast, definition, or restatement.

Writing

12. **Choose one of the following issues discussed in this chapter:**
    • the rise and fall of the cattle kingdom;
    • the settlement of the West and disappearance of the frontier;
    • relations between Native Americans and the U.S. government.

    State an opinion about the issue, and list several facts and reasons from the chapter to support your opinion.

13. **Write a Narrative:**
    Write one or two diary entries from the point of view of a family member who is moving west in the 1870s. Describe why your family is moving west and how you feel about it. Tell what you expect to see in the West and the type of life you think you will have.

Skills for Life

Interpret a Climate Map

Use the map below to answer the questions.

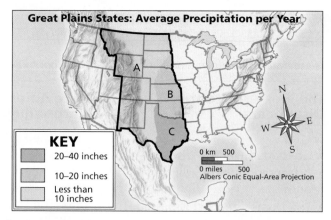

Great Plains States: Average Precipitation per Year

KEY
20–40 inches
10–20 inches
Less than 10 inches

0 km 500
0 miles 500
Albers Conic Equal-Area Projection

14. Study the key. What does the green color mean?

15. As you move east to west across the Great Plains states, how does the amount of precipitation change?

16. How do you think the amount of rain in the Great Plains states affects farming there?

Test Yourself

1. **Which of the following turned Virginia City, Nevada, into a boomtown?**

    A transcontinental railroad

    B Comstock Lode

    C Fort Laramie Treaty

    D Oklahoma Land Rush

Refer to the quotation below to answer Question 2.

> "Let me be a free man, free to travel, free to stop, free to work, . . . free to choose my own teachers, free to follow the religion of my fathers, free to think and talk and act for myself. . . ."
>
> —Chief Joseph of the Nez Percés, 1879

2. **Chief Joseph referred to which event?**

    A Reconstruction

    B Homestead Act

    C National Grange

    D Dawes Act

Refer to the photograph below to answer Question 3.

3. **The photograph best reflects which of the following?**

    A gold rush of 1849

    B Fort Laramie Treaty

    C Populist movement

    D Homestead Act

Document-Based Questions

Task: Look at Documents 1 and 2, and answer their accompanying questions. Then, use the documents and your knowledge of history to complete this writing assignment:

> Write an essay about the economic crisis facing farmers in the 1890s.

Document 1: Mary Elizabeth Lease gave this speech in 1890. *What hardship does Lease say farmers are suffering? What does she say is the cause?*

> "After all our years of toil . . . and hardships upon the Western frontier, monopoly is taking our homes from us by an infamous system of mortgage foreclosure. . . . How did it happen? The government, at the bid of Wall Street, repudiated its contracts with the people. . . . As Senator Stewart [of Nevada] puts it, 'For twenty years the market value of the dollar has gone up and the market value of labor has gone down, till today the American laborer . . . asks which is the worst—the black slavery that has gone or the white slavery that has come?'"

Document 2: The more farmers harvested, the less they earned. *How does this graph help to explain the farmers' problem?*

Wheat Prices, 1866–1896

Source: *Historical Statistics of the United States*

CHAPTER

18 | Industry and Urban Growth
1865–1915

Chapter Preview

After the Civil War, the United States continued to change in many ways. Cities grew, industry boomed, and vast numbers of immigrants came to the United States. With these changes came new challenges.

1869
Workers organize Knights of Labor.

1882
John D. Rockefeller forms Standard Oil.

1889
Jane Addams founds Hull House to help city poor.

U.S. Events

1860

1875

1890

World Events

1878 Salvation Army is formed in London.

1889 German engineers build first gas-powered automobile.

Quick View Video
View the chapter video
for a quick preview of the
main ideas.

Steel bridges like the Brooklyn
Bridge in New York, shown here,
helped change the face of
American cities.

1892
Ellis Island opens
as entry station
for immigrants.

1903
Wright Brothers
make first
airplane flight.

1913
Henry Ford sets up
assembly line to mass-
produce automobiles.

1890

1905

1920

1901 First wireless
radio message is
sent across Atlantic.

History Reading Skill Use Word Origins

How have immigrants changed America?

Many new words in English evolved from the languages of immigrants, as well as from the long-ago influences of Latin and Greek. In this chapter, you will practice using word origins to determine word meanings and to understand how other languages have affected the English language. Read the following account. The side notes suggest ways to use word origins.

Primary Source

Many immigrants came to America in the 1900s. One was Mary Antin, who came to Boston as a young girl. Here, she describes the adjustments her family made to their new home.

> The word *banana* comes to English from Spanish or Portuguese but probably was first used in West Africa.

"Our initiation into American ways began with the first step on the new soil. My father corrected us even on the way from the pier. . . . [W]e paid the strictest attention to my father´s instructions.

The first meal was an object lesson of much variety. . . . [My father] tried to introduce us to a . . . slippery kind of fruit which he called <u>banana</u>. . . . After the meal he had better luck with a curious piece of furniture on runners . . . called rocking chair. . . . [W]e found . . . ways of getting into the American <u>machine</u> of perpetual <u>motion</u>. . . . We laughed over . . . [its] novelty. . . .

> The words *motion* and *immigrant* both come from the Latin roots *mot* and *migr*, meaning "move."

> The word *machine* builds on the Greek root *mech*, meaning "machine."

[Next] we had to visit the stores and be dressed . . . in American clothing. . . . With our <u>immigrant</u> clothing we shed also our impossible Hebrew names."

—Mary Antin, *The Promised Land*

Use Word Origins

- Words may be built on Greek or Latin roots. Get to know those roots to help you recognize related English words.
- Some words come into English more or less the same as in their original language.
- Use context to adapt a root's meaning to modern usage.

Document-Based Questions

1. What new food did Mary's father want the family to try?
2. What did they think of the rocking chair?
3. What did Mary mean when she said: "With our immigrant clothing we shed also our impossible Hebrew names"?

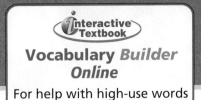
Vocabulary *Builder*

Previewing High-Use Academic Words

High-Use Word	Definition	Sample History Sentence
factor (FAK tor) (Section 1, p. 608)	**n.** condition or quality that causes something else to happen	Technology was one <u>factor</u> that led to the Industrial Revolution.
alter (AWL ter) (Section 1, p. 613)	**v.** to change; to make different	Bridges and tall buildings <u>altered</u> the look of American cities.
eliminate (ee LIHM ih nayt) (Section 2, p. 615)	**v.** to get rid of	For many Americans, the automobile <u>eliminated</u> the need for horses.
justify (JUHS tih fī) (Section 2, p. 616)	**v.** to give good reason for an action	Industrialists said that competition <u>justified</u> tough ways of doing business.
accelerate (ak SEL er ayt) (Section 3, p. 621)	**v.** to increase in speed	Immigration <u>accelerated</u> population growth in the United States.
clinic (KLIHN ihk) (Section 3, p. 622)	**n.** place where people receive medical treatment, often for free or for a small fee	Poor families went to free <u>clinics</u> because they could not afford medical care.
isolate (ī sah layt) (Section 4, p. 627)	**v.** to set apart; to separate	Many farmers felt <u>isolated</u> after moving to large, crowded cities.
exclude (ehks KLYOOD) (Section 4, p. 629)	**v.** to keep out, expel, or reject	All-white schools in the South <u>excluded</u> African American students.
minimum (MIHN ah muhm) (Section 5, p. 632)	**adj.** smallest amount possible or allowed	The law did not set a <u>minimum</u> wage for factory workers.
circuit (SIR kuht) (Section 5, p. 633)	**n.** route repeatedly traveled	Preachers followed a regular <u>circuit</u> as they traveled from state to state.

Previewing Key Terms and People

A New Industrial Revolution

Objectives

1. List reasons industry grew rapidly after the Civil War.

2. Identify inventions and inventors that changed the way Americans lived.

3. Describe the advances that revolutionized transportation.

Prepare to Read

Reading Skill

Use Greek Word Origins
English words may be built on several Greek roots, and each of these may be adapted to modern usage. Thus, once you know the roots of a word, you may need to experiment with different ways to shape an up-to-date word. Use the modern context as your final clue to a word's modern English meaning.

Vocabulary *Builder*

High-Use Words

factor, p. 608

alter, p. 613

Key Terms and People

patent, p. 610

Thomas Edison, p. 610

Alexander Graham Bell, p. 611

Henry Ford, p. 612

assembly line, p. 613

Wilbur and Orville Wright, p. 613

⭐ **Background Knowledge** You have seen how the Industrial Revolution of the early 1800s changed the way Americans lived and worked. In this section, you will learn how a new Industrial Revolution changed life after the Civil War.

Why Industry Boomed

Main Idea
Abundant resources, new technology, government aid to business, and a railroad boom all contributed to industrial growth.

As the nation expanded westward, conditions were ripe for industrial growth. Vast deposits of coal, iron, lead, and copper now lay within reach of the miner's pickax. The towering forests of the Pacific Northwest furnished lumber for building.

Government policy favored industrial growth. Congress gave generous land grants and other subsidies to railroads and other businesses. The government also kept high tariffs on imports. Tariffs helped American industry by making foreign goods more expensive.

Vocabulary *Builder*
factor (FAK tor) *n.* condition or quality that causes something else to happen

Steel and Oil Technology was another factor that spurred industrial growth. In the 1850s, inventors developed the Bessemer process, a method to make stronger steel at a low cost. Steel quickly replaced iron as the basic building material of cities and industry.

Pittsburgh became the nation's steel-making capital. Nearby coal mines and good transportation helped Pittsburgh steel mills thrive. Other steel mills sprang up across the Midwest.

Workers near Titusville, Pennsylvania, tapped a new source of energy in 1859. As they drilled into the ground, a stream of dark liquid gushed upward. It was the nation's first oil strike. The oil industry soon devised methods to refine crude oil into lubricants for machines—and, later, into gasoline to power engines and automobiles. Oil was so valuable it became known as "black gold."

A Railroad Boom Railroads fueled industrial growth. Trains carried people and goods to the West and raw materials to eastern factories. Companies improved service by adding sleeping and dining cars and laying down thousands of miles of new tracks.

As more lines were built, railroads sought ways to limit competition and keep prices high. Some big lines consolidated, or combined. They bought up smaller lines or forced them out of business. The Pennsylvania Railroad, for example, consolidated 73 smaller companies. Railroads also gave secret rebates, or discounts, to their best customers. In some places, rival rail lines made agreements to fix rates at a high level.

Such practices helped giant railroads control grain traffic in the West and South. However, high rates angered small farmers, who relied on the railroads to get their goods to market. As a result, many farmers joined the Granger and Populist movements.

☑ **Checkpoint** **How did the government support business?**

Industrial Centers, 1865–1914

KEY
✗ Iron mines   🛢 Oil wells
⛏ Coal mines   🏭 Steel industry

MAP MASTER®
Skills Activity

Resources such as iron, coal, and oil became vital to industry. Iron and coal were especially important resources for the production of steel.

(a) Read a Map Name two areas that had reserves of oil.

(b) Draw Conclusions Based on the map, why do you think Pittsburgh became a center of the steel industry?

MapMaster ◑nline

For: Interactive map
Visit: PHSchool.com
Web Code: myp-6141

609

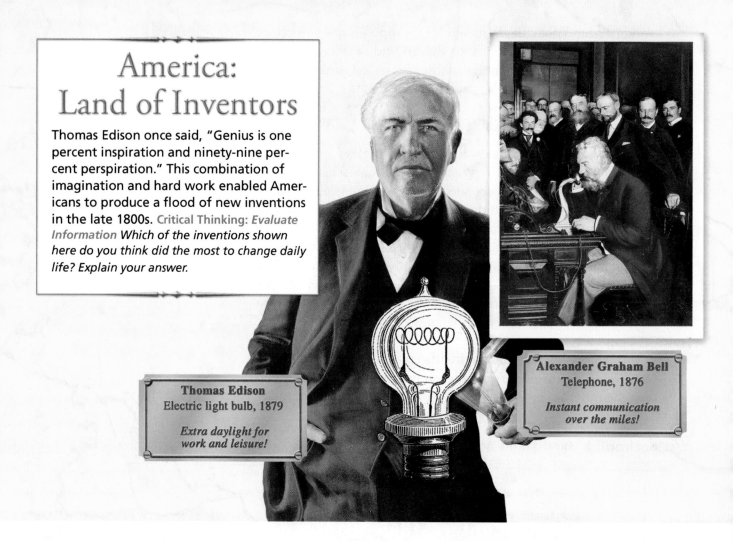

America: Land of Inventors

Thomas Edison once said, "Genius is one percent inspiration and ninety-nine percent perspiration." This combination of imagination and hard work enabled Americans to produce a flood of new inventions in the late 1800s. **Critical Thinking:** *Evaluate Information Which of the inventions shown here do you think did the most to change daily life? Explain your answer.*

Thomas Edison
Electric light bulb, 1879

Extra daylight for work and leisure!

Alexander Graham Bell
Telephone, 1876

Instant communication over the miles!

Inventors and Inventions

Main Idea
Thomas Edison and other inventors created hundreds of devices that made life easier.

In the late 1800s, enterprising Americans created an astonishing flood of new inventions. In fact, the government issued more patents in 1897 alone than in the ten years before the Civil War! A **patent** is a document giving someone the sole right to make and sell an invention.

Around the world, the United States became known as a land of invention. Almost every day, it seemed, American inventions made business and life easier.

Edison's Invention Factory In 1876, Thomas Edison set up a research laboratory in Menlo Park, New Jersey. At this "invention factory," Edison and other scientists produced the light bulb, the phonograph, the motion picture camera, and hundreds of other useful devices.

Still, such inventions would be worthless without a reliable source of energy. In 1882, Edison opened the nation's first electrical power plant in New York City. Other power plants soon sprang up all over the country. They supplied the electricity that lit up homes, powered city streetcars, and enabled factories to replace steam engines with safer electric engines. The modern age of electricity had begun.

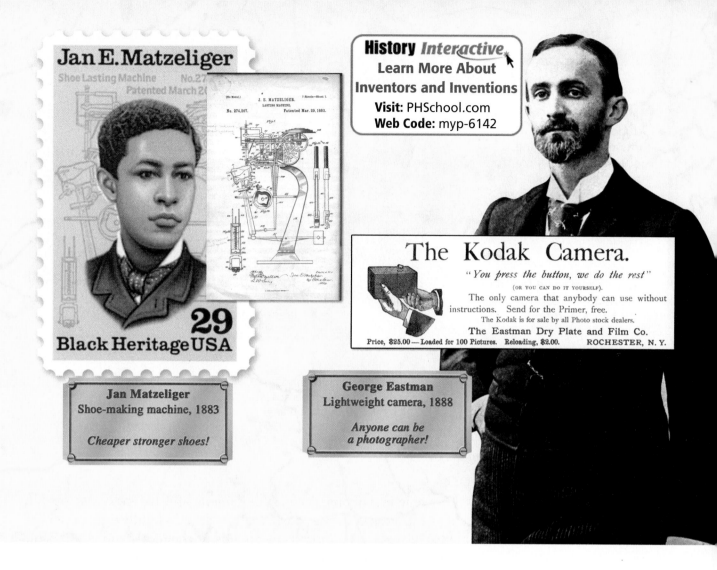

Jan E. Matzeliger
Shoe Lasting Machine No.27
Patented March 20

No. 274,207. Patented Mar. 20, 1883.

29
Black Heritage USA

History Interactive
Learn More About
Inventors and Inventions
Visit: PHSchool.com
Web Code: myp-6142

The Kodak Camera.
"You press the button, we do the rest"
(OR YOU CAN DO IT YOURSELF).
The only camera that anybody can use without
instructions. Send for the Primer, free.
The Kodak is for sale by all Photo stock dealers.
The Eastman Dry Plate and Film Co.
Price, $25.00 — Loaded for 100 Pictures. Reloading, $2.00.   ROCHESTER, N. Y.

Jan Matzeliger
Shoe-making machine, 1883

Cheaper stronger shoes!

George Eastman
Lightweight camera, 1888

*Anyone can be
a photographer!*

A Communications Revolution Improved communication was vital to growing American businesses. The telegraph, in use since 1844, helped people stay in touch with one another. But Americans still had to wait weeks for news from Europe to arrive by boat. In 1866, Cyrus Field had an underwater telegraph cable laid across the Atlantic Ocean that sped communications from Europe.

The telegraph used a code of dots and dashes. Alexander Graham Bell wanted to build a device that would carry the human voice. Bell worked for years inventing this device, which he called the telephone. Finally, in 1876, he sent the first telephone message to his assistant in another room: "Mr. Watson, come here. I want you."

Bell's patent for the telephone was the most valuable patent ever issued. By 1885, more than 300,000 phones had been sold, most of them to businesses. Instead of going to a telegraph office, people could buy, sell, and get information about prices or supplies simply by picking up the telephone. In time, Bell organized over 100 local companies into the giant American Telephone and Telegraph Company.

Devices for Home and Office Some inventions made office work faster and cheaper. In 1868, Christopher Sholes invented a letter-writing device called the "Type-Writer." Soon, female typists in offices were churning out letters at 60 words per minute.

Use Greek Word Origins
Phon means "sound" in Greek. *Tele* means "far away." Explain how Greek roots create the meaning we use for *telephone.*

The Wright brothers' design included a propeller, a lightweight gas engine, a rudder, and a set of controls that allowed the pilot to move the plane up, down, left, and right.

Orville had to lie face down, working the controls with his hands and feet.

The first flight lasted only 12 seconds and flew 120 feet—but the plane landed in one piece!

Human Flight

Until the Wright brothers invented the airplane, people had flown only by wind power, in balloons and gliders. The airplane was revolutionary because it powered itself. In addition, the pilot controlled the movement of the plane. This photograph shows the Wright brothers' first flight on December 17, 1903. **Critical Thinking: *Contrast*** *Identify two ways that the Wright brothers' airplane differed from modern airplanes.*

Some inventions, such as the camera, affected individuals more than businesses. George Eastman introduced a lightweight camera in 1888. It replaced hundreds of pounds of chemicals and equipment. Because Eastman's camera sold at a low price, ordinary people could record their lives on film.

African Americans contributed to the flood of inventions. Jan Matzeliger revolutionized the shoe industry with a machine that sewed the tops to the soles. Granville Woods devised a way to send telegraph messages between moving trains.

☑**Checkpoint** **Why was Edison's power plant important?**

Main Idea
The automobile and the airplane launched an age of fast transportation.

A Transportation Revolution

Technology also revolutionized transportation. For thousands of years, people had traveled by foot or by horse. Railroads went faster and farther but only where tracks ran.

Then, in the late 1800s, European engineers developed the automobile. Suddenly, people were able to travel almost anywhere and at any time. The development of the automobile ushered in an era of freer and faster transportation.

Henry Ford Only 8,000 Americans owned automobiles in 1900. Then, Henry Ford, an American manufacturer, made the automobile available to millions. Ford perfected a system to mass-produce cars and make them available at a lower price.

To speed construction and lower costs, Ford introduced the assembly line in 1913. The **assembly line** is a manufacturing method in which a product is put together as it moves along a belt. As each car frame moved along the belt, one set of workers hooked up the engine, another attached the wheels, and so on. The assembly line sliced production time in half. Lower costs allowed Ford to charge lower prices. By 1917, more than 4.5 million Americans owned cars.

Cars changed the nation's landscape. A web of roads spread across the country. Cities began sprawling into the countryside.

The Wright Brothers Another transportation revolution took place in 1903. Wilbur and Orville Wright tested a gas-powered airplane at Kitty Hawk, North Carolina. On its first flight, the plane stayed in the air for 12 seconds and flew 120 feet. Orville made four flights that day. His longest flight lasted 59 seconds.

Surprisingly, the first flights did not attract much interest. No one could see any practical use for a flying machine. The military uses of the airplane did not become clear until World War I (1914–1918). By the 1920s, the airplane had begun to <u>alter</u> the world by making travel quicker and trade easier.

Vocabulary *Builder*
alter (AWL ter) *v.* to change; to make different

✓**Checkpoint** **Why did the cost of automobiles decrease?**

⭐ **Looking Back and Ahead** Resources and technology set the stage for growth. In the next section, you will see how business leaders built on this foundation to create giant industries.

Section 1 | **Check Your Progress**

Progress Monitoring 🌐nline
For: Self-test with instant help
Visit: PHSchool.com
Web Code: mya-6141

Comprehension and Critical Thinking

1. **(a) Identify** What factors were in place at the end of the Civil War that helped create a surge in industrial growth?
(b) Analyze Cause and Effect What effect did the discovery of new energy sources have on the Industrial Revolution?

2. **(a) List** What inventions revolutionized American life in the late 1800s?
(b) Make Predictions What impact did Ford's assembly line have on changing American lifestyles?

Reading Skill

3. **Use Greek Word Origins** The Greek root *graph* means "writing," and the Greek root *phon* means "sound." The name of what Edison invention combines these roots?

Vocabulary *Builder*
Answer the following questions in complete sentences that show your understanding of the key terms.

4. How does a patent protect inventors?

5. How did the assembly line revolutionize factories?

Writing

6. Which of the following statements are logical, and which are not logical? Explain why.
Statements:

(a) Abundant natural resources aid economic growth because they provide energy and raw materials for manufacturing.

(b) Secret rebates are unfair because they encourage business but not the arts.

(c) Secret rebates are unfair because they were given to some customers but not to others.

(d) Inventions aid industrial growth because they show Americans' special ingenuity.

Big Business and Organized Labor

Objectives

1. Describe how new business methods helped American industry grow.

2. Identify the leaders of "big business" and the practices they used.

3. Summarize how working conditions changed as industry grew.

4. Describe workers' efforts to organize during the late 1800s.

Prepare to Read

Reading Skill

Use Latin Word Origins
English words may also combine several Latin roots or words to build one word. Knowledge of the several roots can help you make a general guess of the English word's meaning. Context offers confirming information. As you read Section 2, look for words built on Latin word origins. Notice how this ancient language continues to influence English today.

Vocabulary *Builder*

High-Use Words

<u>eliminate</u>, p. 615

<u>justify</u>, p. 616

Key Terms and People

entrepreneur, p. 614

corporation, p. 614

monopoly, p. 615

Andrew Carnegie, p. 615

John D. Rockefeller, p. 615

trust, p. 615

free enterprise, p. 616

Samuel Gompers, p. 618

collective bargaining, p. 618

⭐ **Background Knowledge** You have learned about the new Industrial Revolution that took place after the Civil War. In this section, you will see how this industrial boom had a very different impact on business owners and on workers.

New Ways of Doing Business

Main Idea
Business leaders developed new ways to raise money needed for expansion.

Business expansion was led by bold entrepreneurs (ahn treh preh NYOORZ). An **entrepreneur** is someone who sets up new businesses to make a profit. To raise capital, or money, entrepreneurs adopted new ways of organizing business.

The Corporation Many businesses became corporations, or businesses owned by many investors. Corporations raise large amounts of capital by selling stock, or shares. Stockholders receive a share of the profits and pick directors to run the company.

Corporations limited the risk of investors. Owners of other types of businesses could lose their savings, homes, and other property if the business failed. Stockholders risked only the amount of money they had invested.

Banking Banks lent huge amounts of capital to corporations. These loans helped American industry grow faster than ever before. They also made huge profits for the bankers.

One banker, J. Pierpont Morgan, made himself the most powerful force in the American economy. Morgan gained control of key industries, such as railroads and steel. In hard times, Morgan and his friends bought stock in troubled corporations. They then ran the companies in ways that <u>eliminated</u> competition and increased profits.

☑**Checkpoint**   How did corporations raise capital?

Vocabulary *Builder*
<u>eliminate</u> (ee LIHM ih nayt) *v.* to get rid of

Growth of Big Business

As in Jefferson's time, the government took a laissez-faire approach to business in the late 1800s. Congress rarely made laws to regulate business practices. This atmosphere of freedom encouraged the growth of what came to be known as "big business." Entrepreneurs formed giant corporations and monopolies. A **monopoly** is a company that controls most or all business in a particular industry.

Carnegie One of the giants of big business was Andrew Carnegie. A poor Scottish immigrant, he worked his way up in the railroad business. He then entered the growing steel industry. Slowly, Carnegie gained control of every step in making steel. His companies owned iron mines, steel mills, railroads, and shipping lines. In 1892, Carnegie combined his businesses into the giant Carnegie Steel Company. It soon produced more steel than all the mills of England.

As a business leader, Carnegie could be ruthless. Still, he believed that the rich had a duty to improve society. He called his philosophy the Gospel of Wealth. Carnegie donated hundreds of millions of dollars to build libraries and support other charities. "I started life as a poor man," he said, "and I wish to end it that way." Carnegie set up a foundation that continued to fund worthy causes after his death. Many business leaders followed his example.

Rockefeller Another business giant, John D. Rockefeller, also came from humble beginnings. Rockefeller was the son of a peddler in New York. At age 23, he invested in an oil refinery. He used the profits to buy other oil companies. Rockefeller was a brilliant entrepreneur. He also did not hesitate to crush competitors, slashing prices to drive rivals out of business.

In 1882, Rockefeller ended competition in the oil industry by forming the Standard Oil Trust. A **trust** is a group of corporations run by a single board of directors. Other industries followed his lead. By 1900, trusts dominated many of the nation's key industries, from meatpacking to sugar refining to the manufacture of copper wire.

Main Idea
By the late 1800s, many major industries were dominated by a few giant companies.

Biography Quest

John D. Rockefeller
1839–1937

John D. Rockefeller was one of the most hated and admired figures of his time. The ruthless tactics he used in building his oil empire won him many enemies. Yet, he also donated much of his fortune to charitable causes, funding parks and universities. Journalist Ida Tarbell described Rockefeller as "a man whose soul is built like a ship in air-tight compartments. . . . The life that goes on in compartment one has no relation to that of compartment two."

Biography Quest **Online**

What experience taught Rockefeller his first lesson as a businessman?

For: The answer to the question about Rockefeller

Visit: PHSchool.com

Web Code: myd-6142

Debate Over Trusts Was big business good or bad for the nation? Americans at the time hotly debated that issue. Today, many historians believe that both views are partly true.

Critics saw trusts as a threat to **free enterprise,** the system in which privately owned businesses compete freely. They saw leaders like Carnegie and Rockefeller as "robber barons" who unfairly eliminated competition. Critics also pointed out that business leaders used their wealth to influence politicians.

Others saw big business leaders as bold "captains of industry" who built up the economy and created jobs. They argued that limiting costly competition allowed companies to lower prices for their products. As a result, American consumers were able to afford more goods and services.

Social Darwinism A new philosophy called Social Darwinism also supported the trend toward trusts. Scientist Charles Darwin had said that, in nature, forms of animal and plant life survived if they could adapt to change better than others. Social Darwinism applied this idea of "survival of the fittest" to human affairs.

Big business leaders used Social Darwinism to <u>justify</u> efforts to limit competition. Businesses that drove out their competitors, they said, were "fittest" and deserved to survive. As you will see, Social Darwinism was also used to justify harsh working conditions.

✔**Checkpoint** How did Rockefeller control the oil industry?

Use Latin Word Origins
The Latin word *ducere* can mean "to draw out." Combine this with *pro-,* meaning "forth." Connect these word origins to the modern usage of the word *products.*

Vocabulary *Builder*
<u>justify</u> (JUHS tih fı) *v.* to give good reason for an action

Trusts and Monopolies: Good or Bad?

A newspaper editor, quoted below, defends the right of businesses to cooperate in forming trusts and monopolies.

❝The right to cooperate is as unquestionable as the right to compete. . . . The trust denies competition only by producing and selling more cheaply than those outside the trust can produce and sell.❞

—Benjamin R. Tucker,
Chicago Conference on Trusts

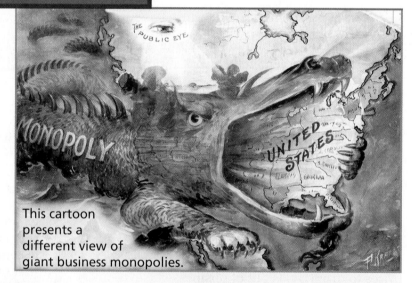

This cartoon presents a different view of giant business monopolies.

Reading Primary Sources
Skills Activity

By 1900, the question of trusts and monopolies had become one of the most hotly debated issues in the United States.

(a) Interpret Primary Sources According to Tucker, how does the public benefit from trusts?

(b) Detect Points of View How does the view of monopoly expressed in the cartoon differ from Tucker's view?

Changes in the Workplace

Before the Civil War, most factories were small. A boss knew every worker in the shop. As giant industries grew, however, the close relationships between owners and workers ended.

American industry attracted millions of new workers. Most were immigrants or native-born whites. Others were African Americans who left southern farms for northern factories.

Women and Children In some industries, the majority of workers were women. They outnumbered men in the textile mills of New England, the tobacco factories of the South, and the garment sweatshops of New York. A sweatshop is a manufacturing workshop where workers toil long hours under poor conditions for low pay.

Children also worked in industry, often in hazardous jobs. In bottle factories, eight-year-old boys ran with white-hot bottles to cooling racks. Children toiled in textile mills, tobacco factories, coal mines, and garment sweatshops. Most child laborers could not go to school. Therefore, they had little chance of improving their lives.

Dangerous Conditions Factory work could be dangerous. Breathing in fibers or dust all day, textile workers and miners came down with lung diseases. Steelworkers risked burns and death from vats of molten metal. Employers were not required to pay compensation for injuries suffered on the job. Social Darwinists claimed that such harsh conditions were necessary to cut costs, increase production, and ensure survival of the business.

An accident at a New York sweatshop tragically called attention to the dangers many workers faced. On March 25, 1911, fire broke out in the Triangle Shirtwaist Factory. Within minutes, the upper stories were ablaze. Hundreds of workers raced for the exits only to find them locked. The company had locked the doors to keep workers at their jobs. Panicked workers piled up against the exits.

Firetrucks rushed to the scene, but their ladders were too short to reach the fire. One after another, workers trying to escape the flames leaped to their deaths. Nearly 150 people, most of them young women, died in the Triangle Fire. As a result, New York and other states approved safety laws to help protect factory workers.

☑**Checkpoint** **What dangers did factory workers face?**

Workers Organize

Since the early days of the Industrial Revolution, factory workers had made attempts to organize. Most early efforts to form unions failed, however. Companies hired private security guards to attack strikers or union organizers. In addition, laws made it illegal for workers to go on strike. Still, workers continued their attempts to form unions, often in secret. Labor unions sought safer working conditions, higher wages, and shorter hours.

Main Idea
As industry grew, working conditions often got worse.

Child coal miners

Main Idea
Despite many obstacles, organized labor began to grow in the late 1800s.

A Violent Strike

Strikes often turned violent. This 1877 picture shows a confrontation between Maryland state militia and workers during a railroad strike. At least 10 strikers were killed. **Critical Thinking:** *Evaluate Information* How does this picture suggest that there was violence on both sides?

Knights of Labor In 1869, a group of Philadelphia clothing workers formed a union called the Knights of Labor. At first, the union was small and secret. Then, in 1879, the Knights elected Terence Powderly as president. Powderly rejected the use of strikes as a tool. Instead, he tried to win support by holding public rallies.

Under Powderly, the Knights of Labor admitted women, African Americans, immigrants, and unskilled workers. No earlier labor union had included all workers. For a time, the Knights became the biggest union in the country.

Union successes were undercut by a series of violent labor disputes. One of the worst episodes occurred in Chicago. On May 4, 1886, striking workers rallied in Haymarket Square. Suddenly, a bomb exploded and killed seven policemen. Police sprayed the crowd with bullets. As a result of such violence, public opinion turned against unions. The Knights of Labor, some of whom were at Haymarket Square, lost much of their influence.

Rise of the AFL In 1886, the year of the Haymarket Riot, Samuel Gompers formed a new union in Columbus, Ohio. It was called the American Federation of Labor, or AFL. The AFL soon replaced the Knights of Labor as the leading union in the country.

Unlike the Knights, the AFL admitted skilled workers only. Gompers argued that skilled workers could create a powerful union because their skills made it costly and difficult to train replacements. He also believed that the most effective way to win improvements was through collective bargaining. In **collective bargaining,** unions negotiate with management for workers as a group. Gompers believed in using strikes, but only if all else failed.

This practical approach worked well. By 1904, the AFL had grown to more than a million members. But because it barred African Americans, immigrants, and unskilled workers, the AFL still included only a tiny fraction of American workers.

Women in the Labor Movement Women played leading roles in building unions. Mary Harris Jones tirelessly traveled the country, campaigning for unions and giving support to striking miners. She called attention to the hard lives of children in textile mills. Because of her work with children, people began calling her Mother Jones.

Bitter Strikes In 1893, the nation was hit by a severe enconomic depression. Many business owners cut production, fired workers, and slashed wages. A wave of violent strikes swept the country. One of the worst occurred near Chicago. George Pullman, a manufacturer of railroad cars, cut his workers' pay by 25 percent. Still, he refused to lower rents on company-owned housing.

Angry workers struck the Pullman plant. Railroad workers walked off their jobs in support. By July, rail lines were shut down from coast to coast. President Grover Cleveland then sent federal troops to Chicago to end the strike. They were joined by deputies paid by the railroads. Marshals fired on the crowds, killing two protesters.

In such violent labor disputes, the public generally sided with the owners. Most Americans saw striking unions as radical and violent. By 1900, only about 3 percent of American workers belonged to a union.

☑ **Checkpoint** What methods did the AFL use?

☆ **Looking Back and Ahead** Big business grew at a rapid pace. Organized labor also grew but faced many obstacles. In the next chapter, you will learn how these trends began to shift.

Mother Jones

Section 2 | **Check Your Progress**

Progress Monitoring ⬤nline
For: Self-test with instant help
Visit: PHSchool.com
Web Code: mya-6142

Comprehension and Critical Thinking

1. **(a) Recall** What big business tactic did Rockefeller use to eliminate competition?
   (b) Compare and Contrast How were trusts viewed as both a threat and an advantage to the free enterprise system?

2. **(a) List** How did changes in the factory system affect workers in the late 1800s?
   (b) Draw Conclusions Why was there an effort to organize workers into labor unions?

🔄 **Reading Skill**

3. **Use Latin Word Origins** Connect the roots *ad-*, meaning "out," and *optare*, meaning "choose or wish," to the modern English word *adopted* as it is used in the following sentence: To raise capital, Americans adopted new ways of organizing business.

Vocabulary *Builder*

4. Draw a table with six rows and two columns. In the first column, list these terms: entrepreneur, corporation, monopoly, trust, free enterprise, collective bargaining. In the next column, write the definition of each word.

Writing

5. Which of the following statements seems the most emotional in its appeal? Which seems the most persuasive? Why?
   Statements:
   (a) One cause of the Pullman strike was George Pullman's failure to lower rents on company-owned housing.
   (b) One cause of the Pullman strike was George Pullman's unfair treatment of workers.
   (c) One cause of the Pullman strike was a conflict between George Pullman and his workers over wages and rent.

Cities Grow and Change

Objectives

1. Explain why cities grew in the late 1800s.

2. Describe the problems city dwellers faced and the efforts to improve city life.

3. Identify the attractions and leisure activities cities offered.

Prepare to Read

Reading Skill

Use Latin Word Origins Latin roots can be paired with different prefixes or suffixes to create related words. For example, the root *port* means "carry." Paired with the prefix *sub-,* meaning "beneath," it is the root of the English word *support,* meaning "carry from beneath." Paired with the prefix *im-,* meaning "in or toward," it is the root of the English word *import,* meaning "carry into." As you read, look for examples of words that share a Latin root.

Vocabulary *Builder*

High-Use Words

<u>accelerate</u>, p. 621

<u>clinic</u>, p. 622

Key Terms and People

urbanization, p. 620

tenement, p. 622

Jane Addams, p. 622

settlement house, p. 622

⭐ **Background Knowledge** You have seen how American industry boomed in the late 1800s. In this section, you will learn how the industrial age reshaped American cities.

Main Idea
Industrialization, migration, and technology all contributed to the growth of American cities.

Rapid Growth of Cities

"We cannot all live in cities," wrote journalist Horace Greeley, "yet nearly all seem determined to do so." Greeley was describing the growth of American cities in the late 1800s.

Urbanization The rate of urbanization was astonishing. **Urbanization** is the rapid growth of city populations. In 1860, only one American in five was a city dweller. By 1890, one in three lived in a city. For the first time, the United States had cities the sizes of London and Paris.

Use Latin Word Origins Use the Latin root *tract,* meaning "pull or drag," to define the word *attracting.* Then, name at least one other related word that shows the influence of this root.

The reason for this rapid urbanization was simple. Cities attracted industry, and industry attracted people. Farmers, immigrants, and African Americans from the South all migrated to cities in search of jobs and excitement.

Many fast-growing cities were located near waterways. New York and San Francisco had excellent ocean harbors. Chicago rose on the shores of Lake Michigan. Cities near waterways drew industry because they provided easy transport for goods.

Growing Out and Up New technology helped cities grow. Elevated trains carried passengers over crowded streets. In 1887, the first electric streetcar system opened in Richmond, Virginia. Ten years later, the nation's first electric subway trains began running beneath the streets of Boston.

Public transportation gave rise to suburbs, living areas on the outskirts of a city. People no longer had to live in cities to work in cities. Steel bridges also <u>accelerated</u> suburban growth. The Brooklyn Bridge, completed in 1883, linked the city center in Manhattan to outlying Brooklyn. As a result, New York City was able to spread out to house its growing population.

Cities began to expand upward as well as outward. In 1885, architects in Chicago constructed the first 10-story building. People called it a "skyscraper" because its top seemed to touch the sky. By 1900, steel-framed skyscrapers up to 30 stories high towered over cities. Electric elevators whisked office workers to the upper floors.

As cities grew outward from their old downtown sections, living patterns changed. Many cities took on a similar shape. Poor families crowded into the oldest sections at the city's center. Middle-class people lived farther out in row houses or new apartment buildings. The rich built fine homes on the outskirts of the city.

✓**Checkpoint** **How did technology change city life?**

> **Vocabulary *Builder***
> <u>accelerate</u> (ak SEL er ayt) *v.* to increase in speed

Problems of Urban Life

Rapid urbanization brought many problems. Fire was a constant threat in tightly packed neighborhoods. In 1871, fire engulfed Chicago. Winds blew flames across the city faster than a person could run. The Chicago Fire leveled 3 square miles of downtown, killed 300 people, and left 18,000 homeless.

> **Main Idea**
> As cities grew, they faced a variety of problems, especially in the poorest neighborhoods.

Explore More Video
To learn more about the changes in city life, view the video.

A Changing City Cities underwent great changes in the late 1800s. The photograph shows a Chicago street in 1900. **Critical Thinking:** *Link Past and Present Describe two ways a picture of this street today might look different.*

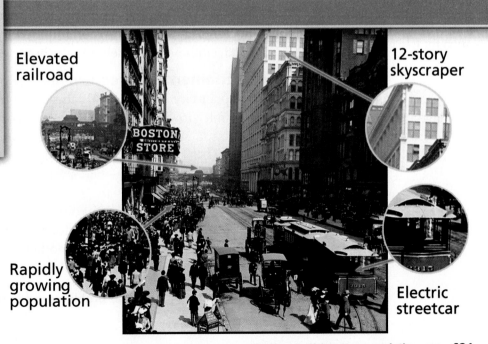

Elevated railroad

12-story skyscraper

Rapidly growing population

Electric streetcar

A Tenement Family
This photograph shows a family in their New York tenement apartment. **Critical Thinking: Clarify Problems** *Based on this photograph and your reading, identify one problem this family might face daily.*

Vocabulary *Builder*
clinic (KLIHN ihk) *n.* place where people receive medical treatment, often for free or for a small fee

Tenement Life In downtown slums, the poor lived in bleak conditions. People crowded into tenements, buildings divided into many tiny apartments. Many apartments had no windows, heat, or indoor plumbing. Often, 10 people might live in a single room. Several families shared a single bathroom.

Slum streets were littered with garbage. Outbreaks of cholera and other diseases were common. Babies ran the greatest risk. In one Chicago slum, half of all babies died before the age of one.

Improving City Life In the 1880s, cities began to improve urban life. They installed streetlights and set up fire, sanitation, and police departments. Public health officials waged war on disease.

Religious groups served the poor. Mother Cabrini, a Catholic nun, set up hospitals and clinics for people who could not afford a doctor. The Salvation Army, founded by a Methodist minister, gave food, clothing, and shelter to the homeless.

Settlement Houses Reformers like Jane Addams worked hard for poor city dwellers. Addams came from a well-to-do family, but she felt strong sympathy for the poor. In 1889, she opened Hull House, a settlement house in the slums of Chicago. A settlement house is a center offering help to the urban poor. Soon, reformers—most of them women—had started settlement houses in other major cities.

At settlement houses, volunteers taught English to immigrants, sponsored music and sports for young people, and provided nurseries for children of working mothers. Addams and other settlement house leaders also pressured state legislatures to outlaw child labor.

✔**Checkpoint** **What problems did tenement dwellers face?**

The Excitement of City Life

Despite hardships, cities offered attractions that were not available in the country. Newcomers were awed by electric lights that turned night into day, elevated railroads rumbling overhead, and tall buildings that seemed to pierce the clouds.

Department Stores Downtown shopping areas attracted hordes of people. People came to buy the goods pouring in from American factories. To meet the needs of shoppers, merchants developed a new type of store, the department store.

Earlier, people had bought shirts in one store, boots in another, and lamps in a third. A department store offered all of these goods in separate sections of the same store. Shoppers could wander from floor to floor, bathed in light from crystal chandeliers. Elegant window displays advertised the goods for sale.

Leisure Activities Long hours on the job made people value their free time. This strict division between work and play led to a new interest in leisure. To meet this need, cities provided a wealth of entertainment. Almost every museum, orchestra, art gallery, and theater was located in a city. Circuses drew audiences with elephants, lions, acrobats, and clowns.

In the 1850s, Frederick Law Olmsted planned Central Park in New York. Other cities followed suit. Parks, zoos, and gardens allowed urban dwellers to enjoy green grass and open air.

Main Idea

Cities lured newcomers with a wide variety of attractions and leisure activities.

Cause and Effect

CAUSES
- Growth of industries in cities attracted workers.
- African Americans from the South and immigrants sought a better life.
- Many cities near waterways attracted industries.
- Technological advances led cities to construct subways, trolleys, streetlights, bridges, and skyscrapers.
- Many leisure activities that cities provided drew people to urban areas.

URBANIZATION

EFFECTS
- Urban transportation systems enabled people to live in one part of the city and work in another.
- Flood of people into cities led to teeming neighborhoods that became slums.
- Improvements in transportation gave rise to suburbs.

Reading Charts
Skills Activity

The movement of large numbers of people to cities was one of the biggest social changes of the late 1800s.

(a) Interpret Charts How did technology encourage the growth of cities?

(b) Analyze Cause and Effect Why was the growth of industry a cause of urbanization?

Early baseball glove
and baseball card

Sports Americans had always enjoyed outdoor games. Not until after the Civil War, however, did professional sports teams begin to spring up in cities. The most popular sport by far was baseball. A guidebook of the time noted:

"Base ball first taught us Americans the value of physical exercise as an important aid . . . in cultivating the mind up to its highest point. It is to the introduction of base ball as a national pastime, in fact, that the growth of athletic sports in general in popularity is largely due."

—*Spalding's Official Base Ball Guide,* 1889

The first professional team, the Cincinnati Red Stockings, appeared in 1869. Only seven years later, teams from eight cities formed the National League of Professional Baseball Clubs. A game might draw as many as 5,000 fans, loudly rooting for their city's home team. African American players, banned from the majors in the 1880s, formed their own professional baseball league.

In 1891, James Naismith nailed two peach baskets to the walls of a gym in Springfield, Massachusetts. He handed players a soccer ball and challenged them to throw the ball in the basket. The new game, called basketball, became a favorite winter sport. Football was also popular. At the time, the sport was brutal and dangerous. Players wore no helmets. In one season, 44 college players died of injuries.

☑**Checkpoint** What leisure activities did city dwellers enjoy?

⭐ **Looking Back and Ahead** You have already learned that immigration contributed to the growth of cities. In the next section, you will take a closer look at immigrant life.

Section 3 | Check Your Progress

Progress Monitoring Online
For: Self-test with instant help
Visit: PHSchool.com
Web Code: mya-6143

Comprehension and Critical Thinking

1. (a) Describe Why did cities grow rapidly after the Civil War?
(b) Apply Information What role did technology play in urbanization? Give at least two examples.

2. (a) Identify What type of housing did poor city dwellers live in?
(b) Identify Benefits Why do you think many people wanted to live in cities in spite of harsh conditions?

Reading Skill

3. Use Latin Word Origins The Latin root *urb* means "city." How does this influence the meaning of the term suburb? What other word in Section 3 shows the influence of the root *urb*?

Vocabulary *Builder*

Read each sentence below. If the sentence is true, write YES. If the sentence is not true, write NO and explain why.
4. Urbanization was the result of people moving to western farms.

5. Tenements were apartments used by the wealthy.
6. Settlement houses provided needed services for city dwellers.

Writing

7. "Life in a city is more rewarding than life outside a city." List two or three arguments in favor of this opinion and two or three arguments opposing this opinion.

The New Immigrants

Objectives

1. Identify the reasons immigration to the United States increased in the late 1800s.

2. Describe the difficulties immigrants faced adjusting to their new lives.

3. Discuss how immigrants assimilated and contributed to American life.

4. Describe efforts to limit immigration.

Prepare to Read

 Reading Skill

Use Other Word Origins The English language reflects interactions with cultures from around the world. Some words have been adopted in their original form. Others have changed in spelling or pronunciation but still show the influence of the original language.

Vocabulary *Builder*

High-Use Words

<u>isolate</u>, p. 627

<u>exclude</u>, p. 629

Key Terms

steerage, p. 626

assimilation, p. 627

anarchist, p. 629

⭐ **Background Knowledge** The industrial age changed the face of cities with new buildings and bridges. It also changed the population. In this section, you will learn about the millions of people immigrating to the United States during this time.

A Fresh Start

Between 1865 and 1915, some 25 million immigrants entered the United States—more than the population of the entire country in 1850! They were part of a worldwide surge of migration.

Reasons for Migration There were many reasons for this vast migration. In European nations such as Italy, the amount of farmland was shrinking as populations swelled. Machines were replacing farmhands, forcing more people from the land. They looked to the United States as a "land of opportunity" where they could build a better life.

Other immigrants sought religious freedom. In the 1880s, Jews in Russia became targets of government-sponsored pogroms (POH grohmz), or violent attacks against Jews. Armenian Christians faced similar persecution in Turkey.

Finally, political unrest drove many from their native lands. In 1910, a revolution in Mexico pushed tens of thousands of refugees across the Rio Grande.

Jobs pulled immigrants to the United States. Steamship companies and railroads, which profited from immigration, sent agents to Asia and Europe to advertise cheap land and plentiful jobs. The promise of freedom also drew people from lands without traditions of democracy and liberty.

Main Idea

In the late 1800s, a new wave of immigrants came to the United States for economic and political reasons.

Poor Italian villager

Immigration, 1865–1915

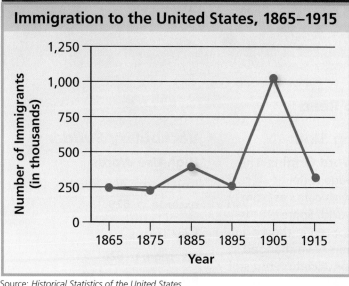

Immigration to the United States, 1865–1915

Source: *Historical Statistics of the United States*

Sources of Emigration, 1865–1915

46.1% Southern and Eastern Europe

43.8% Northern and Western Europe

2.5% Asia

7.1% Americas

0.5% Africa and elsewhere

Source: *Historical Statistics of the United States*

Reading Charts
Skills Activity

The line graph at left shows how immigration increased in the decades after the Civil War. The pie chart on the right shows where these "new immigrants" in the United States came from.

(a) Read a Graph Approximately how many immigrants entered the United States in 1875? In 1905?

(b) Draw Inferences Based on your reading, how would the pie chart have looked different in the 1830s?

The New Immigrants In the early 1800s, most immigrants were Protestants from northern and western Europe. Many spoke English and had experience in democracy.

By contrast, most of the "new immigrants" who began to arrive in the late 1800s came from nations of southern and eastern Europe, such as Italy, Poland, Russia, and Greece. Most were Catholic or Jewish. A smaller number came from Asia and the Pacific. Few understood English or had experience living in a democracy or in a city.

☑**Checkpoint**   **Why did many people leave their homelands?**

Main Idea
Immigrants faced many challenges to settle in the United States.

Starting a New Life

The decision to emigrate was difficult. It meant leaving home, family, and friends and starting a strange life. (For more on the immigrants' experiences, see the Life at the Time feature in this chapter.)

Coming to America The passage by boat was miserable. Immigrants were crammed below decks in steerage, large compartments that usually held cattle. The tight, airless berths were breeding grounds for disease. Rough seas sickened the travelers.

Most people coming from Europe landed in New York. After 1892, they went to the receiving center on Ellis Island. Asian immigrants entered through Angel Island in San Francisco Bay.

New arrivals faced a rigorous physical examination at the receiving centers. Did they limp? Were their eyes free of disease? Those judged to be disabled or seriously ill might be sent home.

Immigrant Neighborhoods Once admitted to the United States, about two thirds of immigrants settled in cities, near other people from the same country. Ethnic neighborhoods helped people feel less <u>isolated</u> in their new homes.

In immigrant neighborhoods, sidewalks rang with the sounds of Italian, Chinese, Yiddish, and other languages. Newcomers celebrated familiar holidays and cooked foods from the old country, such as kielbasa (Polish sausage) and goulash (Hungarian stew). Italians joined social groups such as the Sons of Italy. Greeks read newspapers in Greek. Small storefronts were turned into Jewish synagogues or Buddhist temples.

☑Checkpoint   **What hardships did immigrants face?**

Becoming American

Immigrant neighborhoods were springboards to a new life. Organizations called immigrant aid societies helped new arrivals with clothing, housing, and language classes.

Assimilation Newcomers often felt caught between the old world and new. Most clung to traditional modes of worship, family life, and community relations. At the same time, they worked hard to assimilate. **Assimilation** is the process of becoming part of another culture.

Children of immigrants assimilated more rapidly than their parents. Surrounded by English-speakers in school and on the street, they learned the language quickly. They played baseball and dressed like native-born Americans. Immigrant parents felt both pride and pain as they saw their children change.

Main Idea
For many immigrants, the goal was to become part of American life and culture.

Becoming American
Citizenship classes, like the one shown here, were an important step toward assimilation. **Critical Thinking:** *Draw Inferences What subjects do you think students like these might study in citizenship classes?*

This man is labeled *Russian Anarchist.*

This man is labeled *Italian Brigand.* A brigand is a bandit.

A Nativist View of Immigration

In this 1891 cartoon, the man in the suit tells Uncle Sam that he can get rid of anarchy, crime, and other ills by restricting immigration. **Critical Thinking: *Detect Bias*** *What details create a negative picture of immigrants?*

Still, the fondest dream of many immigrants was to educate their children so that the next generation could be better off. One Russian Jewish immigrant called education "the essence of American opportunity, the treasure that no thief could touch . . . surer, safer than bread or shelter."

Contributions of Immigrants The labor of immigrants was essential to the new American economy. Desperate for money, newcomers took whatever jobs they could find. Immigrants worked in steel mills, meatpacking plants, mines, and garment sweatshops. They helped build subways, skyscrapers, and bridges. Chinese, Irish, and Mexican workers laid down hundreds of miles of railroad track in the West.

Through hard work and saving, many immigrants slowly advanced economically. Often, they began by opening small businesses, such as stores or barbershops, to serve their communities. In time, their customers expanded beyond the neighborhood. Outsiders might bring their clothing to Chinese laundries or buy foods they had never tasted before. In this way, ethnic foods such as spaghetti, chow mein, and bagels became part of American life.

Individual immigrants made major contributions. Andrew Carnegie and Alexander Graham Bell were born in Scotland. Samuel Goldwyn and Louis Mayer, Jewish immigrants from Eastern Europe, established the motion picture industry in California. Italian-born Arturo Toscanini became a famous orchestra conductor. Belgian immigrant Leo Baekeland invented the first plastic.

☑Checkpoint **How did immigrants assimilate?**

Use Other Word Origins
Identify the words in this paragraph that came into English from the Yiddish word *beygl,* meaning "ring or bracelet," and the Italian word *spago,* meaning "string or cord."

A New Wave of Nativism

As in the 1840s, increased immigration led to a wave of nativism. Nativists sought to preserve the United States for native-born American citizens.

Nativists argued that the new immigrants would not assimilate because their languages, religions, and customs were too different. They also charged that immigrants took jobs away from Americans. Nativists associated immigrants with violence, crime, and anarchy. An **anarchist** is a person who opposes all forms of government.

On the West Coast, nativist feelings against Chinese immigrants ran high. Mobs drove Chinese from mining camps and cities and sometimes killed them. In 1882, Congress passed a law to exclude Chinese laborers from the United States. The Chinese Exclusion Act was the first law limiting immigration based on race. It was finally repealed in 1943.

In 1917, Congress passed a law that denied entry to immigrants who could not read their own languages. Since education at the time was usually restricted to the wealthy, this law barred most of the world's poor people from immigrating to the United States.

✓**Checkpoint** Why did nativists oppose immigration?

⭐ **Looking Back and Ahead** Although immigration slowed after 1917, it never stopped. In the 1960s, Congress finally eased restrictions on immigration.

Main Idea
Many Americans distrusted immigrants and called for limits on immigration.

Vocabulary *Builder*
exclude (ehks KLYOOD) *v.* to keep out, expel, or reject

Section 4 | Check Your Progress

Progress Monitoring ⓞnline
For: Self-test with instant help
Visit: PHSchool.com
Web Code: mya-6144

Comprehension and Critical Thinking

1. (a) **List** Why did people immigrate to the United States in the late 1800s?
   (b) **Frame Questions** What five questions could you ask one of those immigrants?

2. (a) **Describe** How did immigrants try to assimilate?
   (b) **Detect Bias** How did nativists feel about the ability of immigrants to assimilate?

🔄 **Reading Skill**

3. **Use Other Word Origins** The text lists *kielbasa* and *goulash*, food items introduced to America by immigrants. The Polish and Hungarian words are used because these foods have no English-word counterparts. On your own or with a partner, name foods from other cultures. Do we use the original name or an English word?

Vocabulary *Builder*

Complete each of the following sentences so that the second part explains the first part and shows your understanding of the term.

4. Many immigrants traveled across the ocean in steerage; _____.

5. Immigrants blended into American life through a process called assimilation; _____.

Writing

6. Imagine that you are writing an editorial in which you object to a bill that excludes immigrants who could not read their own languages. Which of the following arguments is most persuasive? Why? **Arguments:**

   (a) Many native-born American citizens do not know how to read, so the bill uses an unfair standard for immigrants.

   (b) Immigrants come to this country for a better life, which includes getting an education.

   (c) The bill is being used as a trick to restrict all immigration.

An Immigrant's Journey

From all over the world, immigrants poured into the United States. Wherever they came from, these newcomers shared many of the same hopes, fears, and challenges.

 Passage

Immigrants faced a long, difficult ocean crossing crowded into ship holds that were designed to carry cargo or cattle.

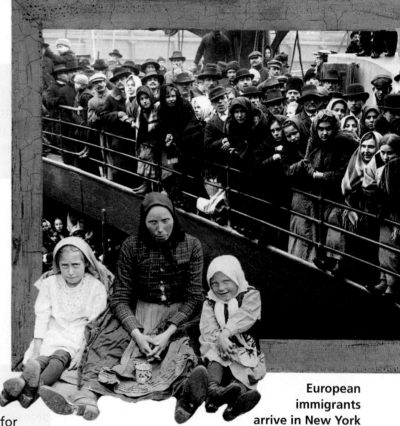

"Day after day the weather was bad and the sea stormy. The hatch was tightly closed and there was no circulation of air, so we were all tortured by the bad odor."

—Japanese immigrant describes the voyage

European immigrants arrive in New York

 Arrival

New York's Ellis Island was the point of entry for many European immigrants. Asians were detained on Angel Island outside San Francisco.

"Immigration officials slammed a tag on you with your name, address, country of origin, etc. . . . Then they pushed you and they'd point, because they didn't know whether you spoke English or not."

—Irish immigrant describes arrival at Ellis Island

3 ▶ Ethnic Neighborhoods

Crowded into ethnic neighborhoods, immigrants preserved familiar ways as they adjusted to their new culture.

"When we first arrived we still wore our wooden shoes. . . . We conquered the English language beautifully. My father spoke well. But in the home we spoke Frisian."

–Dutch immigrant describes life in America

A street in a Jewish neighborhood in New York

4 ▶ Citizenship

For many immigrants, becoming a citizen was the proudest moment of their lives.

"I am the youngest of America's children, and into my hands is given all her priceless heritage. . . . Mine is the whole majestic past, and mine is the shining future."

–Russian immigrant expresses pride in becoming U.S. citizen

A new citizen is sworn in

Analyze LIFE AT THE TIME

Suppose that you are an immigrant in 1900. For each stage of the journey from passage to citizenship, write a sentence describing your hopes or your fears.

Education and Culture

Objectives

1. Explain how public education changed after 1870.
2. Identify new American writers and the topics they wrote about.
3. Describe the growth of the American newspaper industry.

Prepare to Read

Reading Skill

Use Popular Word Origins
Some words and phrases do not come from formal languages. Instead, they arise from popular use. For example, in the previous section, you saw that *basketball* got its name because it was originally played using peach baskets. The term *basketball* remained even when people stopped using real baskets to play with. Other words and phrases also have origins in popular usage that have since gone out of date.

Vocabulary *Builder*

High-Use Words
minimum, p. 632
circuit, p. 633

Key Terms and People
compulsory education, p. 632
realist, p. 634
Mark Twain, p. 634
Joseph Pulitzer, p. 635
yellow journalism, p. 635

⭐ **Background Knowledge** You have learned how northern states established tax-supported public schools in the mid-1800s. In this section, you will learn how the expansion of public education was linked to other changes in American culture.

Educating Americans

Main Idea
States took steps to expand education, including requiring children to attend school.

Before 1870, fewer than half of American children went to school. Many attended one-room schoolhouses, with all age levels and only one teacher. As industry grew, people realized that the nation needed an educated workforce. As a result, states improved public schools at all levels.

Education Expands In 1852, Massachusetts passed the first compulsory education law. **Compulsory education** is the requirement that children attend school up to a certain age. Other states in the North, Midwest, and West followed. Most states required a minimum tenth-grade education.

Vocabulary *Builder*
minimum (MIHN ah muhm) *adj.*
smallest amount possible or allowed

In the South, which had no tradition of public schools, the Freedmen's Bureau built grade schools for both white and black students. Southern states were more reluctant to pass compulsory education laws than states in the North or West. Still, by 1918, every state required children to attend school.

After the Civil War, many cities and towns built public high schools. By 1900, there were 6,000 high schools in the country. Still, not until 1950 did the majority of Americans of high school age graduate.

Higher education also expanded. New private colleges for both women and men opened. Many states built universities that offered free or low-cost education.

The School Day For elementary school students, the typical school day lasted from 8:00 A.M. to 4:00 P.M. Pupils learned the "three Rs": reading, 'riting, and 'rithmetic.

The most widely used textbooks were *McGuffey's Eclectic Readers*. Students memorized and recited lessons that had titles like "Waste Not, Want Not." Such poems and stories taught not only reading but also moral values and the Christian religion.

Education for Adults Older Americans also got more opportunity to widen their knowledge. Wealthy individuals such as Andrew Carnegie gave money to towns and cities to build public libraries. Libraries offered more than books and magazines. Speakers often gave talks on important topics of the day.

In 1874, a Methodist minister opened a summer school for Bible teachers along Lake Chautauqua (shuh TAWK wuh) in New York. The next year, the camp was opened to the public. Mostly middle-class men and women gathered at Chautauqua to hear lectures on a wide variety of subjects. The Chautauqua Society later began sending out traveling companies on a wide <u>circuit</u>. In time, Chautauquas reached as many as 5 million people in 10,000 towns each year.

Vocabulary *Builder*
<u>circuit</u> (SIR kuht) *n.* route repeatedly traveled

✔**Checkpoint** **How did states expand public education?**

High School Enrollment, 1880–1910

Source: *Historical Statistics of the United States*

Reading Charts
Skills Activity

The late 1800s saw a dramatic rise in public high school enrollment.

(a) Read a Chart How many Americans attended public high schools in 1880? In 1910?

(b) Distinguish Relevant Information Which of the following might help you understand the reasons for the trend shown on the graph: a mathematics textbook from 1890; a list showing when states passed compulsory education laws; a population graph? Explain.

Main Idea

A new generation of American writers tried to describe real life as it was.

New American Writers

As learning became available to more people, Americans began to read more books and magazines. Many bestsellers were dime novels, low-priced paperbacks that often told thrilling tales of the "Wild West." One popular writer, Horatio Alger, wrote "rags-to-riches" stories about poor boys who became successful through hard work, courage, and honesty.

Realism Other American writers were realists, writers who try to show life as it is. They often emphasized the harsh side. Some, such as Stephen Crane, had been newspaper reporters. Crane depicted the hardships of slum life in his novel *Maggie: A Girl of the Streets.*

California-born Jack London wrote of miners and sailors who risked their lives in backbreaking jobs. Kate Chopin shocked readers with *The Awakening,* a novel about an unhappily married woman. The poems of Paul Laurence Dunbar described the joys and sorrows of black life. He was the first African American to earn a living as a writer.

Use Popular Word Origins

Based on context clues, what do you think the phrase *pen name* means? What do you think was the origin of this term?

Mark Twain The most popular author of the time was Mark Twain, the pen name of Samuel Clemens. Twain made his stories realistic by capturing the speech patterns of southerners who lived and worked along the Mississippi River.

Twain set his novel *Huckleberry Finn* in the days before the Civil War. Huck, an uneducated boy, and Jim, an escaped slave, raft down the Mississippi River together. Though brought up to believe slavery is right, Huck comes to respect Jim and decides to help him win his freedom.

Some parents complained that Huck was a crude character who would have a bad effect on children. But today, many critics consider *Huckleberry Finn* to be one of the greatest American novels.

✓**Checkpoint** What kinds of topics did realists write about?

Huckleberry Finn

In this passage from Mark Twain's *Huckleberry Finn,* shown below, Huck recounts a conversation with his friend Jim, an escaped slave.
Critical Thinking: *Evaluate Information* How does the language in this passage give a sense of realism?

Mark Twain

"He was saying how the first thing he would do when he got to a free State he would go to saving up money and never spend a single cent, and when he got enough he would buy his wife, which was owned on a farm close to where Miss Watson lived; and then they would both work to buy the two children, and if their master wouldn't sell them, they'd get an Ab'litionist to go and steal them."

Cover of an early edition of *Huckleberry Finn*

A Newspaper Boom

The number of American newspapers grew dramatically in the late 1800s. By 1900, half the newspapers in the world were printed in the United States.

Causes The spread of education was one reason for the growth of the newspaper industry. As more Americans could read, they bought more newspapers and magazines.

The newspaper boom was also linked to urbanization. In towns and villages, neighbors could share news face to face. In cities, people needed newspapers to stay informed.

A New Kind of Newspaper A Hungarian immigrant, Joseph Pulitzer, created the first modern, mass-circulation newspaper. In 1883, Pulitzer bought the *New York World.* He immediately cut the price so that more people could afford it.

Pulitzer added crowd-pleasing features to his newspaper, including color comics. The Yellow Kid, a tough but sweet slum boy, became the first popular American comic strip character.

The *New York World* became known for sensational headlines that screamed of crime and scandal. Readership skyrocketed, and other papers followed his lead. Because of the Yellow Kid, critics coined the term **yellow journalism** to describe the sensational reporting style of the *New York World* and other papers.

☑**Checkpoint** **Why did the newspaper industry grow?**

⭐ **Looking Back and Ahead** In this section, you saw how education increased the popularity and influence of newspapers. In the next chapter, you will see how newspapers and magazines contributed to a growing reform movement.

Main Idea
Education contributed to a rapid growth in American newspapers.

The Yellow Kid

Section 5 | **Check Your Progress**

Progress Monitoring ⬤nline
For: Self-test with instant help
Visit: PHSchool.com
Web Code: mya-6145

Comprehension and Critical Thinking

1. (a) Describe What were schools like before 1870?
(b) Draw Inferences Why do you think compulsory education laws were important for the industrialized North?

2. (a) Identify What were the goals of realists?
(b) Apply Information How did Mark Twain's use of language make his stories more realistic?

🔁 Reading Skill

3. Use Popular Word Origins The phrase "yellow journalism" is still used to describe one type of reporting. How has the meaning separated from its origin?

Vocabulary *Builder*

Read each sentence below. If the sentence is true, write YES and explain why. If the sentence is not true, write NO and explain why not.
4. Yellow journalism used sensational headlines to attract readers.

5. Mark Twain was not a realist because he wrote about people.
6. Compulsory education allowed parents to choose whether or not to send children to school.

Writing

7. Do you think memorizing and reciting lessons from books like *McGuffey's Readers* is a useful way for children to learn? Write a paragraph explaining your opinion. Give at least two reasons.

Economic and social factors often affect political decisions. A cost-benefit analysis is one tool that helps people make these decisions. A cost-benefit analysis compares the costs and benefits, or rewards, that would result if a certain choice were made.

This is an excerpt from the 1902 book *The Battle With the Slum* by Jacob Riis. He was a journalist, photographer, and reformer who focused attention on the conditions in the slums of New York City.

Primary Source

"The East Side, that had been orderly, became a hotbed of child crime. . . . Yesterday, Mayor Low's reform government voted $6 million for new schools. . . . In the most crowded neighborhood in all the world, where the superintendent lately pleaded in vain for three new schools, half a dozen have been built, the finest in this or any other land—great, light, and airy structures, with playgrounds on the roof; and all over the city the like are going up.

The briefest of our laws . . . says that never one shall be built without its playground. And not for the child's use only. The band shall play there yet and neighbor meet neighbor in such social contact as the slum has never known to its undoing . . . Clergymen applaud the opening of the school buildings on Sunday for concerts, lectures, and neighborhood meetings. Common sense is having its day. The streets are cleaned."

—Jacob Riis, *The Battle With the Slum*

Learn the Skill

Use these steps to conduct a cost-benefit analysis.

1 **Identify the issue.** What is the economic, social, or political issue being considered? Look for the main idea and important details.

2 **List the costs and benefits.** Make a two-column chart. List the benefits in the first column and the costs in the second column.

3 **Compare the costs and the benefits.** Are the benefits greater than the costs? Are the costs greater than the benefits?

4 **Make the best decision.** Based on the costs and benefits in the chart, choose the option that makes the best sense. Be able to give reasons for your choice.

Practice the Skill

Answer the following questions about the primary source on this page.

1 **Identify the issue.** (a) What issue is discussed? (b) What are two details relating to the issue?

2 **List the costs and benefits.** Make a chart listing the costs and benefits.

3 **Compare the costs and the benefits.** Are the benefits greater than the costs? Explain.

4 **Make the best decision.** Based on the information in your chart, what decision would you make about the issue? Explain your answer.

Apply the Skill

See the Review and Assessment at the end of this chapter.

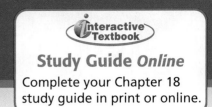

Study Guide *Online*
Complete your Chapter 18 study guide in print or online.

Chapter Summary

Section 1
A New Industrial Revolution

- The discovery of valuable resources fed a major growth in industry.
- Inventions such as the electric light, the telephone, and the automobile changed life.

Section 2
Big Business and Organized Labor

- Industrial growth gave rise to new forms of business, such as corporations and trusts.
- Harsh working conditions led to the formation of labor unions.

Section 3
Cities Grow and Change

- People migrated to cities to find jobs.
- Rapid urbanization created such problems as poor housing and sanitation.

Section 4
The New Immigrants

- Twenty-five million immigrants entered the United States between 1865 and 1915.
- The work of immigrants contributed to the growth of the American economy.
- A new wave of nativists sought to limit immigration.

Section 5
Education and Culture

- Education expanded in response to the needs of industry.
- As more people learned to read, popular books and newspapers boomed.

Immigrant family

Key Concepts

These notes will help you to prepare for questions about the key concepts.

The Growth of Big Business

Causes
- A growing network of railroads allows access to natural resources.
- U.S. government gives land grants and other subsidies to businesses.
- New inventions and the assembly line lower costs and raise profit.
- Banks loan corporations large amounts of money.
- Stockholders invest money in large corporations.

Effects
- Heads of corporations and bankers gain money and influence.
- Some business leaders use their wealth to set up charities.
- Corporations form trusts that get control of key industries and crush the competition.
- Facing hazardous conditions in large factories, workers begin to organize and demand better working conditions.

Facts About Immigration in the Late 1800s

Reasons for Coming to America
- Hope of gaining land or work
- Escape from religious persecution
- Desire to benefit from public education system

Hardships Faced
- Traveling in steerage
- Getting examined at the port of entry
- Learning a new language and a new culture
- Facing the prejudice of "nativists"

Vocabulary *Builder*

Key Terms

Answer the questions in complete sentences that show your understanding of the key terms.

1. Why did inventors apply for patents?

2. How did forming corporations help entrepreneurs raise capital?

3. Why did Samuel Gompers favor collective bargaining?

4. Why was assimilation a goal of many immigrants?

5. What services did settlement houses provide?

Comprehension and Critical Thinking

6. **(a) Describe** What government policies helped to spark industrial growth?
   (b) Clarify Problems How did the policies of the federal government create problems for small businesses?

7. **(a) Identify** Identify two devices invented by Thomas Edison.
   (b) Draw Conclusions Some people think Edison's creation of a research laboratory was more important than any of his inventions. Give one reason for this opinion.

8. **(a) Recall** What happened at Haymarket Square on May 4, 1886?
   (b) Analyze Cause and Effect How did the events at Haymarket Square and the Pullman plant affect public opinion toward unions?

9. **(a) Summarize** What did Horace Greeley mean when he said, "We cannot all live in cities, yet nearly all seem determined to do so"?
   (b) Identify Costs and Benefits How did the new Industrial Revolution affect the way of life in cities?

10. **(a) Describe** What jobs did immigrants hold after arriving in the United States?
    (b) Identify Economic Benefits Why do you think immigrants were willing to work long hours in dangerous conditions for little pay?

11. **(a) Describe** What was a typical school day like for a child in the 1880s?
    (b) Draw Conclusions What impact did the Industrial Revolution have on education in America?

History Reading Skill

12. **Use Word Origins** Choose an English word from this chapter, and trace its language influences. Use a print or online dictionary. Most entries will show the languages a word has passed through, in order from most recent to most distant. List the languages your chosen word has moved through.

Writing

13. **Write a Persuasive Paragraph:**
    Choose one headline from the list below and write a persuasive paragraph that gives your opinion on the issue. Remember to support your opinion with facts, examples, and reasons.
    • Captains of Industry: Heroes or Tyrants?
    • Immigration: A Benefit or a Danger?
    • The New Industrial Revolution: A Better Life or a Less Human One?

14. **Write a Narrative:**
    Imagine that you are a settlement house worker in a large city in the late 1800s. Write a letter to a friend describing why you have chosen to live among the poor.

Skills for Life

Conduct a Cost-Benefit Analysis

The document below describes piecework, a system in which garment workers are paid a certain amount for each piece of clothing they make. Use the document to answer the questions.

> "The differential rate system of piecework consists briefly in offering two different rates for the same job; a high price per piece, in case the work is finished in the shortest possible time and in perfect condition, and a low price, if it takes a longer time to do the job or if there are any imperfections in the work. . . . The advantages of this [system] are: First, that the manufactures are produced cheaper under it, while at the same time the workmen earn higher wages."
>
> —Frederick Taylor, "A Piece-Rate System," 1895

15. (a) What is the cost of the system discussed in the text? (b) What is one benefit of the system?

16. Do you think the benefits are greater than the costs? Explain.

Test Yourself

1. **Which of the following most benefited big business?**

   A creation of the Knights of Labor

   B passage of the Chinese Exclusion Act

   C laissez-faire government policies

   D yellow journalism

Refer to the quotation below to answer Question 2.

> "Give me your tired, your poor,
> Your huddled masses yearning to breathe free,
> The wretched refuse of your teeming shore,
> Send these, the homeless, tempest-tossed to me,
> I lift my lamp beside the golden door!"
>
> —poem by Emma Lazarus, inscribed
> on the Statue of Liberty pedestal

2. **To whom does the poem refer?**

   A inventors   C realists

   B nativists   D immigrants

Refer to the graph below to answer Question 3.

U.S. Rural and Urban Population, 1870–1920

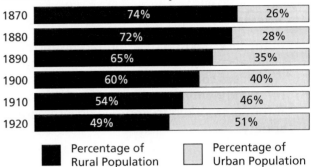

Year	Percentage of Rural Population	Percentage of Urban Population
1870	74%	26%
1880	72%	28%
1890	65%	35%
1900	60%	40%
1910	54%	46%
1920	49%	51%

Sources: *Historical Statistics of the United States* and *Statistical Abstract of the United States*

3. **In what year was the urban population larger than the rural population?**

   A 1870   C 1910

   B 1890   D 1920

Document-Based Questions

Task: Look at Documents 1 and 2, and answer their accompanying questions. Then, use the documents and your knowledge of history to complete this writing assignment:

> Write an essay analyzing the reasons for the success of the AFL.

Document 1: In a speech in 1898, Samuel Gompers described the need for trade unions. *State three purposes of trade unions cited by Gompers.*

> "The trade unions . . . were born of the necessity of workers to protect and defend themselves from encroachment, injustice and wrong. . . . To protect the workers in their inalienable rights to a higher and better life; to protect them, not only as equals before the law, but also in their health, their homes, their firesides, their liberties as men, as workers, and as citizens; to overcome and conquer prejudices and antagonism; to secure to them the right to life; the right to be full sharers in the abundance which is the result of their brain and brawn. . . . The attainment of these is the glorious mission of the trade unions."

Document 2: Unions enjoyed enormous growth in the late 1800s and early 1900s. *What was the increase in union membership between 1897 and 1915?*

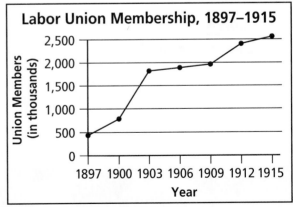

Labor Union Membership, 1897–1915

Source: *Historical Statistics of the United States*

Chapter Preview

In the late 1800s, the nation faced serious problems. Political corruption was common, and many Americans continued to face inequality. A period of reform known as the Progressive Era took shape as reformers worked to improve government and society.

U.S. Events

1874 Opponents of alcohol use form Woman's Christian Temperance Union.

1883 Civil service begins system of tests for government jobs.

1890 Sherman Antitrust Act is passed.

1865

1880

1895

World Events

1800s Pogroms against Russian Jews increase.

1893 New Zealand is first nation to give women the vote.

Photographs like this one by Jacob Riis called public attention to the problems of city slums.

1901
Theodore Roosevelt becomes President.

1909
Reformers found NAACP to promote rights of African Americans.

1920
19th Amendment guarantees women right to vote.

1905 Japanese navy wins victory in war with Russia.

1910

1910 Revolution breaks out in Mexico.

1925

History Reading Skill Identify and Explain Central Issues

What central problems and issues did America face in the late nineteenth century?

In this chapter, you will practice identifying and explaining central issues. You will also practice placing events in the context of the time and place in which they occurred. Read the following essay by Walt Whitman, in which he identifies the problems he sees in late nineteenth-century America. The side notes suggest ways to analyze central issues and orient them in time and place.

Primary Source

Here, Whitman outlines some specific problems that he believes industrialization is causing, for example, business and government corruption.

I say we had best look our times and lands searchingly in the face, like a physician diagnosing some deep disease. . . . Genuine belief seems to have left us. The underlying principles of the States are not honestly believed in nor is humanity itself believed in. What penetrating eye does not see through the mask?

We live in an atmosphere of hypocrisy throughout. . . . The depravity of the businesses classes of our country is not less than has been supposed, but infinitely greater. The official services of America, national, state, and municipal, . . . are deep in corruption, bribery, and falsehood.

I say that our New World democracy, however great a success in uplifting the masses and in developing products, is, so far, an almost complete failure in its social, religious, moral, [and] literary . . . results. It is as if we were somehow being endowed with more and more body, and left with little or no soul.

—Walt Whitman, *Democratic Vistas in Complete Prose*

To find a problem, identify the main idea: People no longer hold honest beliefs.

Orient events in the larger context: Whitman refers here to business and government corruption that was common in the late 1800s.

Reword text to explain problems: Whitman believes that Americans are sacrificing morality for material gain.

Identify and Explain Central Issues

- Look for important issues and problems of a historical period. What concerned people of the time?
- Restate problems to understand and explain them.
- Place the problems and issues in the context of other historical events you know about, such as westward expansion.

Document-Based Questions

1. What problems does Whitman see in business and government?
2. What is his opinion of democracy?
3. What do you think Whitman means by "the underlying principles of the States"?

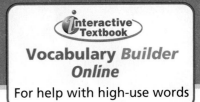

Vocabulary *Builder*
Online
For help with high-use words

Vocabulary *Builder*

Previewing High-Use Academic Words

High-Use Word	Definition	Sample History Sentence
enrich (ehn RIHCH) (Section 1, p. 644)	*v.* to make wealthy; to increase in quality or wealth	Industrial expansion after the Civil War <u>enriched</u> business leaders.
exert (ehks ZERT) (Section 1, p. 645)	*v.* to use; to put into action	Temperance leaders tried to <u>exert</u> pressure on lawmakers to ban alcohol.
efficient (ee FISH ehnt) (Section 2, p. 650)	*adj.* done in a way that minimizes waste and gets better results	During the Industrial Revolution, new machines and new sources of power made manufacturing more <u>efficient</u>.
rigid (RIH jihd) (Section 2, p. 653)	*adj.* strict; not easily bent or changed	When it came to women's rights, Susan B. Anthony was <u>rigid</u> and refused to compromise.
devise (dee VĪZ) (Section 3, p. 657)	*v.* to carefully think out; to invent	John D. Rockefeller <u>devised</u> a way to gain a monopoly on the oil business.
commit (kah MIHT) (Section 3, p. 658)	*v.* to make a pledge or promise	Some women <u>committed</u> themselves to ending child labor.
submit (sahb MIHT) (Section 4, p. 661)	*v.* to yield; to give up power or control	The reformer argued that people should not <u>submit</u> to injustice.
crisis (KRĪ sihs) (Section 4, p. 664)	*n.* turning point; situation involving great risk	The Civil War was the greatest <u>crisis</u> in American history.

Woodrow Wilson

Previewing Key Terms and People

Objectives

1. Identify the problems in American politics during the Gilded Age.
2. Describe the political reforms the Progressives supported.
3. Explain how journalists contributed to reform efforts.

Prepare to Read

🎯 Reading Skill

Place Events in a Matrix of Time and Place As you read this textbook, notice that chapters often cover overlapping time periods. History is complex and involves many continuing issues. To gain a better understanding of a period, place events from one chapter in the context of other events from the same time period. Think back to other chapters and to your own knowledge for these connections.

Vocabulary *Builder*

High-Use Words

enrich, p. 644
exert, p. 645

Key Terms

civil service, p. 645
primary, p. 646
recall, p. 647
initiative, p. 647
referendum, p. 647
graduated income tax, p. 647
muckraker, p. 648

☆ **Background Knowledge** As you have read, by the late 1800s giant corporations controlled much of American business. In this section, you will learn why many Americans began to demand that the government control the power of these huge trusts and monopolies.

Reform in the Gilded Age

The period after the Civil War came to be known as the Gilded Age. *Gilded* means "coated with a thin layer of gold paint." It suggests falseness beneath surface glitter. Some Americans worried that the glitter of American society was hiding serious problems. The Gilded Age lasted from the 1870s through the 1890s.

Two concerns shaped politics during the Gilded Age. Many Americans feared that industrialists and other wealthy men were <u>enriching</u> themselves at the expense of the public. The other worry was corruption, or dishonesty in government. Bribery and voter fraud appeared to be widespread.

Taming the Spoils System Critics said a key source of corruption was the spoils system, the practice of rewarding political supporters with government jobs. The spoils system had grown since the Age of Jackson. Whenever a new President took office, job seekers swarmed to Washington, demanding rewards for their political support.

Main Idea
Many Americans sought to fight corruption by ending the spoils system and controlling big business.

Vocabulary *Builder*
enrich (ehn RIHCH) *v.* to make wealthy; to increase in quality or wealth

In 1881, James Garfield became President. He was soon swamped with people seeking jobs. Four months later, Garfield was shot by a disappointed office seeker. He died two months later. The assassination sparked new efforts to end the spoils system.

Vice President Chester A. Arthur succeeded Garfield. Arthur, a New York politician, owed his own rise to the spoils system. Yet, he worked with Congress to reform how people got government jobs.

In 1883, Arthur signed the Pendleton Act. It created the Civil Service Commission. The **civil service** is a system that includes most government jobs, except elected positions, the judiciary, and the military. The aim of the Civil Service Commission was to fill jobs on the basis of merit. Jobs went to those with the highest scores on civil service examinations. At first, the Commission controlled only a few jobs. Over time, however, the civil service grew to include more jobs.

Controlling Big Business In the late 1800s, big business <u>exerted</u> a strong influence over politics. Railroad owners and industrialists bribed members of Congress in order to secure their votes. Outraged by such actions, many Americans demanded that something be done to limit the power of railroads and monopolies.

Under the Constitution, the federal government has the power to regulate interstate commerce, or trade that crosses state lines. In 1887, President Grover Cleveland signed the Interstate Commerce Act. It forbade practices such as rebates. It also set up the Interstate Commerce Commission to oversee railroads.

Vocabulary *Builder*
exert (ehks ZERT) *v.* to use; to put into action

The Problem of Corruption

The Capitol building is where Congress meets.

This hand is coming out of a window labeled "Trusts."

Reading Political Cartoons

Skills Activity

In many cities, illegal businesses often paid "protection" to police in order to avoid arrest. This 1894 cartoon compares this practice to corruption in the federal government.

(a) Interpret Cartoons Who is the man on the right? What is he getting from the man in the window?

(b) Draw Inferences What do you think the giver expects in return?

Thomas Nast cartoon of Boss Tweed

President Benjamin Harrison signed the Sherman Antitrust Act in 1890. It prohibited businesses from trying to limit or destroy competition. The law sounded tough but proved difficult to enforce. Judges sympathetic to business ruled in favor of trusts. Instead of regulating trusts, the Sherman Act was used to limit the power of labor unions. The courts said strikes blocked free trade and thus threatened competition.

Corruption in the Cities Corruption was a particularly serious problem in city governments. As cities grew, they needed to expand services such as sewers, garbage collection, and roads. Often, politicians accepted money to award these jobs to friends. As a result, corruption became a way of life.

In many cities, powerful politicians called bosses controlled work done locally and demanded payoffs from businesses. City bosses were popular with the poor, especially immigrants. The bosses handed out turkeys at Thanksgiving and extra coal in winter. Often, they provided jobs. In return, the poor voted for the boss or his chosen candidate.

William Tweed, commonly known as Boss Tweed, carried corruption to new extremes. During the 1860s and 1870s, he cheated New York City out of more than $100 million. Journalists exposed Tweed's crimes. Cartoonist Thomas Nast pictured Tweed as a greedy giant and as a vulture feeding on the city. Faced with prison, Tweed fled to Spain. There, local police arrested him when they recognized him from Nast's cartoons. Still, when Tweed died in jail in 1878, thousands of poor New Yorkers mourned for him.

☑**Checkpoint** How did the civil service system limit corruption?

Progressives and Political Reform

Opposition to corruption led to the rise of the Progressive movement. The Progressives were a diverse group of reformers united by a belief in the public interest, or the good of all the people. The public interest, they said, must not be sacrificed to the greed of a few huge trusts and city bosses.

Main Idea
Political reformers called Progressives worked to give more power to voters and expose social problems.

The Wisconsin Idea Wisconsin was one of the first states to adopt Progressive reforms. Wisconsin governor Robert La Follette, known as Battling Bob, introduced various Progressive reforms that became known as the Wisconsin Idea.

La Follette opposed political bosses. He appointed commissions of experts to solve problems. For example, his railroad commission recommended lowering railroad rates. As rates decreased, rail traffic increased, which helped both railroad owners and customers.

Since the Age of Jackson, party leaders had picked candidates for local and state offices. In 1903, Wisconsin was the first state to adopt a primary run by state government officials. A **primary** is an election in which voters, rather than party leaders, choose their party's candidate. By 1917, all but four states had followed Wisconsin's lead.

Progressive Political Reforms

Before		After
Party leaders pick candidates for state and local offices	**PRIMARY** →	Voters select their party candidates
Only members of state legislature can introduce bills	**INDIRECT INITIATIVE** →	Voters can propose bills to the legislature
Only legislators pass laws	**REFERENDUM** →	Voters can vote on bills directly
Only courts or legislature can remove corrupt officials	**RECALL** →	Voters can remove elected officials from office

Reading Charts

Skills Activity

During the Progressive Era, reforms put more power in the hands of voters.

(a) Read a Chart What was the recall? Which reform allowed voters to propose laws?

(b) Identify Benefits What were the benefits of the primary system?

(c) Draw Conclusions Which of these reforms would you say is most important? Why?

More Power to Voters Some states instituted reforms to put more power in the hands of voters. One such reform was the recall, a process by which people may vote to remove an elected official from office. The recall made it easier to get rid of corrupt officials.

Other reforms gave voters a direct say in the lawmaking process. The initiative is a process that allows voters to put a bill before a state legislature. In order to propose an initiative, voters must collect a certain number of signatures on a petition. The referendum is a way for people to vote directly on a proposed new law.

Two Constitutional Amendments Many Progressive reformers backed a graduated income tax, a method of taxation that taxes people at different rates depending on income. The wealthy pay taxes at a higher rate than the poor or the middle class. When the Supreme Court ruled that a federal income tax was unconstitutional, Progressives called for a constitutional amendment. The Sixteenth Amendment, which gave Congress the power to pass an income tax, was ratified in 1913.

Since 1789, United States senators had been elected by state legislatures. Powerful interest groups often bribed lawmakers to vote for certain candidates. Progressives wanted to end this abuse by having people vote for senators directly. The Seventeenth Amendment, ratified in 1913, required the direct election of senators.

Place Events in a Matrix of Time and Place In the 1890s, the Populists had also supported an income tax. How did the roots of Populism differ from the roots of Progressivism?

☑**Checkpoint** What reforms put more power in the hands of voters?

Main Idea

By exposing corruption and other problems, journalists won public support for Progressive reform.

The Muckrakers

The press played an important role in exposing corruption and other problems. President Theodore Roosevelt compared reporters who uncovered problems to men who raked up dirt, or muck, in stables. **Muckraker** became a term for a crusading journalist.

Some muckrakers targeted big business. Ida Tarbell's work led to demands for more controls on trusts. She accused oil baron John D. Rockefeller of unfair business methods. Tarbell wrote:

> "Every great campaign against rival interests which the Standard Oil Company has carried on has been inaugurated . . . to build up and sustain a monopoly in the oil industry."
>
> —Ida M. Tarbell, *History of the Standard Oil Company*

Others described how corruption in city government led to inadequate fire, police, and sanitation services. Jacob Riis (REES), a photographer and writer, provided shocking images of slum life.

In 1906, Upton Sinclair's novel *The Jungle* told grisly details about the meatpacking industry. Sinclair described how packers used meat from sick animals and how rats often got ground up in the meat.

✔**Checkpoint** How did muckrakers stir public opinion?

⭐ **Looking Back and Ahead** The Progressive movement began at local and state levels. In the next section, you will see how three Presidents brought Progressive ideas into the White House.

Section 1 | Check Your Progress

Progress Monitoring Online
For: Self-test with instant help
Visit: PHSchool.com
Web Code: mya-6151

Comprehension and Critical Thinking

1. (a) Recall How was the spoils system reformed during the Gilded Age?
(b) Analyze Cause and Effect What abuses do you think were occurring under the spoils system that made reform necessary?

2. (a) Identify Who were some of the principal muckrakers during the Progressive Era, and what did each try to do?
(b) Link Past and Present What impact do you think their efforts had on life in the United States today?

Reading Skill

3. Place Events in a Matrix of Time and Place Ida Tarbell wrote muckraking articles about the Standard Oil Company. Why did she think this was necessary? How had Standard Oil's business practices changed American industry? Think back to the previous chapter to answer these questions.

Vocabulary *Builder*

Answer the following questions in complete sentences that show your understanding of the key terms.
4. Which jobs are civil service positions?

5. What happens in a primary election?
6. What did muckrakers try to do?
7. What happens in a successful referendum?
8. How are tax rates structured under the graduated income tax?

Writing

9. Write a statement supporting the work of the muckrakers. Then, write a statement opposing their work. For each statement, write one question to ask the muckrakers about their methods and their goals.

The Progressive Presidents

Objectives

1. Describe how Theodore Roosevelt tried to limit the power of business.

2. Summarize the main points of Roosevelt's Square Deal.

3. Identify the reforms promoted by Presidents Taft and Wilson.

Prepare to Read

Reading Skill

Explain Issues From the Past Every era in history has its issues—the ideas or problems that people think about, argue about, and put their energies into. As you read about history, explain these issues to yourself as a way of understanding what mattered to people of that time. Use headings and main ideas to help you identify and explain the issues.

Vocabulary *Builder*

High-Use Words

efficient, p. 650

rigid, p. 653

Key Terms and People

Theodore Roosevelt, p. 649

trustbuster, p. 650

conservation, p. 651

national park, p. 651

William Howard Taft, p. 652

Woodrow Wilson, p. 652

⭐ **Background Knowledge** Although Progressives made many gains at the state and local levels, they had little success at the national level. William McKinley, who was elected President in 1896 and 1900, had the strong support of bankers and business leaders. Then, a shocking assassination thrust a Progressive into the presidency.

The First Progressive President

On September 6, 1901, an unemployed anarchist stood nervously in line at the world's fair in Buffalo, New York. He was waiting to shake the hand of President William McKinley. When McKinley extended his hand, the assassin fired two shots into the President. McKinley died eight days later.

Vice President Theodore Roosevelt then became President. At age 42, he was the youngest President to take office. He was also a strong supporter of Progressive goals.

Teddy Roosevelt Teddy Roosevelt—or TR, as he was called— came from a wealthy New York family. As a child, he suffered from asthma and often was sick. To build his strength, he lifted weights, ran, and boxed. For a time, he worked on a cattle ranch.

TR wanted to serve the public. At the age of 23, he was elected to the New York state legislature. Later, he served on the Civil Service Commission. He then headed New York City's police department and served as assistant secretary of the navy.

Main Idea
Theodore Roosevelt was the first President to support limits on the power of business.

Campaign tray showing Teddy Roosevelt as a soldier

In 1898, the United States went to war against Spain. (You will read about this in the next chapter.) Roosevelt led a unit of troops in some daring exploits that received widespread publicity. He returned home to a hero's welcome and was elected governor of New York. Two years later, Roosevelt was elected Vice President under McKinley.

TR and Big Business As President, Roosevelt won a reputation as a **trustbuster**, a person working to destroy monopolies and trusts. He was not against big business, he said. Indeed, he liked big business. But he saw a difference between "good trusts" and "bad trusts." Good trusts, he said, were <u>efficient</u> and fair and should be left alone. Bad ones took advantage of workers and cheated the public by eliminating competition. The government, he said, must either control bad trusts or break them up.

Roosevelt resolved to do just that. In 1902, he had the government bring a lawsuit against the Northern Securities Company. Northern Securities was a trust that had been formed to control competition among railroads. TR argued that the company used unfair business practices.

In 1904, the Supreme Court ruled that Northern Securities had violated the Sherman Antitrust Act. It ordered the trust to be broken up. The decision was a victory for Progressives. For the first time, the Sherman Antitrust Act had been used to break up trusts, not unions.

Roosevelt later launched suits against other trusts, including Standard Oil and the American Tobacco Company. In time, the courts broke up both trusts because they attempted to limit free trade.

A Boost for Organized Labor Roosevelt also clashed with mine owners. In 1902, Pennsylvania coal miners went on strike for better pay and a shorter workday. Mine owners refused to negotiate with the miners' union.

As winter approached, schools and hospitals ran out of coal. Furious at the owners, Roosevelt threatened to send in troops to run the mines. Finally, the mine owners sat down with the union and reached an agreement. Roosevelt was the first President to side with strikers.

☑ **Checkpoint** What was Theodore Roosevelt's attitude toward big business?

Vocabulary *Builder*
<u>efficient</u> (ee FISH ehnt) *adj.* done in a way that minimizes waste and gets better results

The Square Deal

Main Idea
Roosevelt's program of Progressive reform included measures to conserve natural resources and protect consumers.

Roosevelt ran for President in his own right in 1904. During the campaign, he promised Americans a Square Deal. By this, he meant that everyone from farmers and consumers to workers and owners should have the same opportunity to succeed. That promise helped Roosevelt win a huge victory.

Discovery SCHOOL

Explore More Video
To learn more about protecting wilderness areas, view the video.

Conserving Natural Resources Roosevelt took action to protect the nation's wilderness areas. To fuel the nation's surging industrial growth, lumber companies were cutting down entire forests. Miners were removing iron and coal at a frantic pace, leaving gaping holes in the earth.

Roosevelt loved the outdoors and worried about the destruction of the wilderness. He pressed for conservation, or the protection of natural resources. Roosevelt was not against using resources, but he believed they had to be used wisely, with an eye toward the future. For example, he urged lumber companies to plant new trees in the forests they were clearing. Roosevelt declared:

> "I recognize the right and duty of this generation to develop and use the natural resources of our land; but I do not recognize the right to waste them, or to rob, by wasteful use, the generations that come after us."
>
> —Theodore Roosevelt, "The New Nationalism"

Under Roosevelt, the U.S. Forest Service was formed in 1905 to conserve the nation's woodlands. Roosevelt also had thousands of acres of land set aside for national parks. A **national park** is a natural area protected and managed by the federal government.

Roosevelt and Conservation
In 1903, President Roosevelt (left) went camping in California's Yosemite Valley with conservationist John Muir (right). The trip strengthened Roosevelt's commitment to conservation. Today, you can still enjoy the wilderness areas of Yosemite National Park. **Critical Thinking: Link Past and Present** *What do the two pictures above suggest about the long-term effects of Roosevelt's conservation policies?*

Explain Issues From the Past
Explain Roosevelt's reasons for supporting conservation and how they affected his approach to big business.

Protecting Consumers Roosevelt also supported reforms to protect consumers. Upton Sinclair's novel *The Jungle* had shocked Roosevelt. The President made public a report exposing unhealthy conditions in meatpacking plants. The public outcry forced Congress to pass a law in 1906 allowing closer inspections of meatpacking houses.

Muckrakers had also exposed drug companies for making false claims about medicines and adding harmful chemicals to canned foods. In response, Congress passed the Pure Food and Drug Act, which required food and drug makers to list all the ingredients on packages.

☑**Checkpoint** **Why did Roosevelt support conservation?**

Taft and Wilson

Roosevelt did not want to run for reelection in 1908. Instead, he backed William Howard Taft, his secretary of war. Taft won easily.

Troubles for Taft Taft's approach to the presidency was far different from Roosevelt's. Unlike the energetic Roosevelt, Taft was quiet and cautious. Roosevelt loved power, Taft was wary of it.

Nevertheless, Taft supported many Progressive causes. He broke up even more trusts than TR. He favored the graduated income tax, approved new safety rules for mines, and signed laws giving government workers the eight-hour workday. He also oversaw the creation of a federal office to make regulations controlling child labor.

Despite such actions, Taft lost Progressive support. In 1909, he signed a bill that raised most tariffs. Progressives opposed the new law, arguing that tariffs raised prices for consumers. Also, Taft modified some conservation policies. Progressives accused the President of blocking conservation efforts.

Election of 1912 By 1912, Roosevelt had broken with Taft. He decided to run against Taft for the Republican nomination. Roosevelt had massive popular support, but Taft controlled the Republican Party leadership. At its convention, the Republican Party nominated Taft.

Roosevelt and his supporters stormed out of the convention. They set up a new party, called the Progressive Party, and chose Roosevelt as their candidate. He accepted, saying "I feel as strong as a bull moose." Roosevelt's Progressive Party became known as the Bull Moose Party.

Democrats chose Woodrow Wilson, also a Progressive, as their candidate. Wilson had served as president of Princeton University and as governor of New Jersey. Wilson was known as a brilliant

Main Idea
Roosevelt's successors also promoted reforms.

Three-Way Race
TR, the "bull moose" candidate, made the presidential election of 1912 a three-way race. **Critical Thinking:** *Draw Inferences* *Why does the cartoonist show the "moose" nipping at the elephant?*

scholar and a cautious reformer. Though honest and idealistic, he was often criticized for being <u>rigid</u> and unwilling to compromise with others.

Together, Taft and Roosevelt won more votes than Wilson. However, they split the Republican vote, and so Wilson won the 1912 presidential election.

Wilson and the New Freedom Wilson hoped to restore free competition among American corporations. He called his program to achieve this goal the New Freedom. To ensure fair competition, Wilson persuaded Congress to create the Federal Trade Commission (FTC) in 1914. The FTC had the power to investigate companies and order them to stop using unfair practices to destroy competitors.

Wilson signed the Clayton Antitrust Act in 1914. The new law banned some business practices that limited competition. In addition, it stopped antitrust laws from being used against unions.

To regulate banking, Congress passed the Federal Reserve Act in 1913. The act set up a system of federal banks and gave the government the power to raise or lower interest rates and control the money supply.

✓**Checkpoint** **How did a split among Republicans enable Woodrow Wilson to become President?**

⭐ **Looking Back and Ahead** Despite Wilson's successes, the Progressive movement slowed after 1914. By then, Progressives had achieved many of their goals. Also, in 1914, war broke out in Europe. Americans worried that the war might soon affect them. You will read about World War I in the next unit.

Vocabulary *Builder*
rigid (RIH jihd) *adj.* strict; not easily bent or changed

Woodrow Wilson

Progress Monitoring 🌐nline
For: Self-test with instant help
Visit: PHSchool.com
Web Code: mya-6152

Comprehension and Critical Thinking

1. **(a) Recall** Why did Theodore Roosevelt want to break up Northern Securities and Standard Oil?
   (b) Identify Benefits Which groups of people might have benefited from Roosevelt's actions as a trustbuster?

2. **(a) Recall** Why did the Republican Party split during the 1912 presidential election campaign?
   (b) Draw Conclusions What impact might a powerful third party such as the Bull Moose Party have on a presidential election?

🔄 **Reading Skill**

3. **Explain Issues From the Past** Reread the text following the subheading "A Boost for Organized Labor." Explain the central issues that moved Roosevelt. How did he interact with big business over these issues?

Vocabulary *Builder*

Read each sentence below. If the sentence is true, write YES. If the sentence is not true, write NO and explain why.

4. Theodore Roosevelt was called a trustbuster because he lost the trust of the people.

5. Roosevelt was a strong supporter of conservation, which is the protection of natural resources.

Writing

6. Write the opening paragraph to an editorial evaluating TR's presidency. Complete the following topic sentence, and introduce each point that follows with a transition word: Theodore Roosevelt's Square Deal created a number of reforms that were *(express your opinion here)*. For example, he _____. In addition, he _____. Most important *(OR worst of all)*, he _____.

The Jungle
by Upton Sinclair

Prepare to Read

Introduction

The main characters in *The Jungle* are a family of immigrants who have recently immigrated to Chicago from Eastern Europe. Several of them find jobs at a meatpacking plant. In this excerpt, Elzbieta, one family member, learns the gruesome details of the sausage-making process.

Reading Skill

Analyze Symbolism Symbolism is the use of concrete images or objects to represent abstract ideas. Upton Sinclair wrote *The Jungle* in order to make a statement about the excesses of unrestricted free enterprise. As you read this passage, consider what the practices Sinclair describes might represent.

Vocabulary *Builder*

As you read this literature selection, look for the following underlined words:

scheme (skeem) *n.* dishonest plan

hopper (HAH per) *n.* a bin in which material is temporarily stored

nuisance (NOO sehns) *n.* annoyance

enforce (ehn FORS) *v.* bring about by force

Background

This passage describes, among other things, the working conditions for laborers. Though Sinclair wrote *The Jungle* in order to speak out against working conditions for laborers, the public's reaction was not what Sinclair intended. The public outcry over this book's description of meat-packaging practices helped lead to the passage of the Pure Food and Drug Act of 1906.

The packers were always originating such schemes—they had what they called "boneless hams," which were all the odds and ends of pork stuffed into casings; and "California hams," which were the shoulders, with big knuckle joints, and nearly all the meat cut out; and fancy "skinned hams," which were made of the oldest hogs, whose skins were so heavy and coarse that no one would buy them—that is, until they had been cooked and chopped fine and labeled "head cheese"!

It was only when the whole ham was spoiled that it came into the department of Elzbieta. Cut up by the two-thousand-revolutions-a-minute flyers, and mixed with half a ton of other meat, no odor that ever was in a ham could make any difference. There was never the least attention paid to what was cut up for sausage; there would come all the way back from Europe old sausage that had been rejected, and that was mouldy and white—it would be dosed with borax and glycerine, and dumped into the hoppers, and made over again for home consumption. There would be meat that had tumbled out onto the floor, in the dirt and sawdust, where the workers had tramped and spit uncounted billions of consumption germs. There would be meat stored in great piles in rooms, and the water from leaky roofs would drip over it, and thousands of rats would race about on it. It was too dark in those storage places to see well, but a man could run his hands over these piles of meat and sweep off handfuls of the dried dung of rats. These rats were nuisances, and the packers would put out poisoned bread for them, they would die, and then rats, bread, and meat would go into the hoppers together. This is no fairy story and no joke: the meat would be shoveled into carts, and the man who did the shoveling would not trouble to lift out a rat even when he saw one—there were things that went into the sausage in comparison with which a poisoned rat was a tidbit. There was no place for the men to wash their hands before they ate their dinner, and so they made a practice of washing them in the water that was to be ladled into the sausage. There were the butt-ends of smoked meat, and the scraps of corned beef, and all the odds and ends of the waste of the plants, that would be dumped into old barrels in the cellar and left there. Under the system of rigid economy which the packers <u>enforced</u>, there were some jobs that it only paid to do once in a long time, and among these was the cleaning out of the waste barrels. Every spring they did it; and in the barrels would be dirt and rust and old nails and stale water—and cartload after cartload of it would be taken up and dumped into the hoppers with fresh meat, and sent out to the public's breakfast. Some of it they would make into "smoked" sausage—but as the smoking took time, and was therefore expensive, they would call upon the chemistry department, and preserve it with borax and color it with gelatine to make it brown. All of their sausage came out of the same bowl, but when they came to wrap it they would stamp some of it "special," and for this they would charge two cents more a pound.

From *The Jungle*, by Upton Sinclair. © 1981. Bantam.

Analyze Symbolism
Upton Sinclair wrote at a time when few laws controlled how people worked and what they produced. Sinclair blamed the capitalist system for these abuses, rather than the lack of laws. Knowing Sinclair's motivation for writing this book, what abstract idea might the "special" and "fancy" packaging of the meat represent?

☑ **Checkpoint**   **What was wrong with the way the packers cleaned out the waste barrels?**

Analyze LITERATURE
After reading this passage, what images are the most striking? Are the images powerful? Now imagine that you are a member of the general public reading this passage. Write a short letter to your local newspaper expressing your reaction to this passage.

If you liked this passage from *The Jungle*, you might enjoy reading more about the labor movement in America in *Ashes of Roses* by Mary Jane Auch. Henry Holt and Company, 2002.

Objectives

1. Describe how women won the right to vote.

2. Identify the new opportunities that women gained during the Progressive Era.

3. Explain how the temperance movement gained strength during the early 1900s.

Prepare to Read

Reading Skill

Identify Central Issues From the Past What changes did people of the past work to achieve? As you read Section 3, try to identify the central issues at the core of women's efforts for change. In your own words, answer the questions: What was this struggle about? What change did these people seek?

Vocabulary *Builder*

High-Use Words

<u>devise</u>, p. 657

<u>commit</u>, p. 658

Key Terms and People

Carrie Chapman Catt, p. 657

suffragist, p. 657

Alice Paul, p. 658

Frances Willard, p. 659

prohibition, p. 659

⭐ **Background Knowledge** The Progressives' desire for reform touched many parts of society. However, Progressives were not particularly interested in women's rights. In this section, you will learn how American women finally won the right to vote.

Women Win the Vote

Main Idea
After more than 70 years of effort, American women won the right to vote in all elections.

The Seneca Falls Convention of 1848 marked the start of an organized women's rights movement in the United States. After the Civil War, Elizabeth Cady Stanton and Susan B. Anthony formed the National Woman Suffrage Association. This group pushed for a constitutional amendment to give women the right to vote.

Anthony spoke all over the country for the cause. In 1872, she was arrested for trying to vote. At her trial, she told the judge:

> ❝My natural rights, my civil rights, my political rights, my judicial rights, are all alike ignored. Robbed of the fundamental privilege of citizenship, I am degraded from the status of a citizen to that of a subject.❞
>
> —*Proceedings of the Trial of Susan B. Anthony*

Women Vote in the West In most states, leading politicians opposed women's suffrage. Still, in the late 1800s, women won voting rights in four western states: Wyoming, Utah, Colorado, and Idaho. Pioneer women had worked alongside men to build farms and cities. By giving women the vote at least in local or state elections, these states recognized the women's contributions.

When Wyoming applied for statehood in 1890, many members of Congress wanted it to bar women from voting. Wyoming lawmakers stood firm. "We may stay out of the Union for 100 years, but we will come in with our women." Wyoming was admitted.

Growing Support In the early 1900s, support for women's suffrage grew. More than 5 million women worked outside the home. Although women were paid less than men, wages gave them some power. Many demanded a say in making the laws.

After Stanton and Anthony died, a new generation of leaders took up the cause. Carrie Chapman Catt <u>devised</u> a detailed strategy to win suffrage, state by state. Across the nation, **suffragists,** or people who worked for women's right to vote, followed her plan. Their efforts brought steady gains. One by one, states in the West and Midwest gave women the right to vote.

The Nineteenth Amendment Still, in some of these states, women could not vote in federal elections. More women joined the call for a federal amendment to allow them to vote in all elections.

Vocabulary *Builder*
devise (dee vīz) *v.* to carefully think out; to invent

Identify Central Issues From the Past
Identify the central issue, or goal, for suffragists.

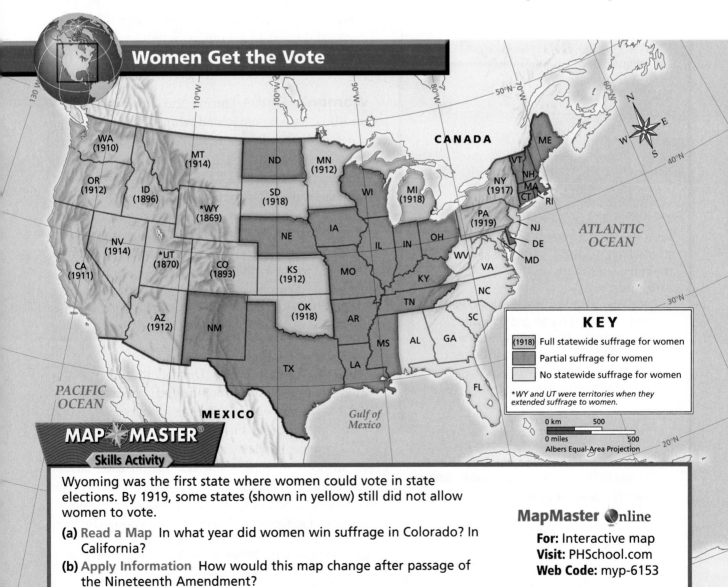

Women Get the Vote

KEY

(1918) Full statewide suffrage for women

Partial suffrage for women

No statewide suffrage for women

WY and UT were territories when they extended suffrage to women.

0 km 500
0 miles 500
Albers Equal-Area Projection

MAP MASTER®

Skills Activity

Wyoming was the first state where women could vote in state elections. By 1919, some states (shown in yellow) still did not allow women to vote.

(a) Read a Map In what year did women win suffrage in Colorado? In California?

(b) Apply Information How would this map change after passage of the Nineteenth Amendment?

MapMaster ●nline

For: Interactive map
Visit: PHSchool.com
Web Code: myp-6153

As the struggle dragged on, suffragists such as Alice Paul took more forceful steps. Paul met with President Woodrow Wilson in 1913. Paul told Wilson that suffragists had <u>committed</u> themselves to achieving such an amendment. Wilson pledged his support.

By 1919, the tide had turned. Congress passed the Nineteenth Amendment guaranteeing women the right to vote. By August 1920, three fourths of the states had ratified the amendment. The Nineteenth Amendment doubled the number of eligible voters.

☑**Checkpoint** **Why did suffragists want a constitutional amendment?**

Main Idea
During the Progressive Era, women fought for access to jobs and education.

New Opportunities for Women

Besides working for the vote, women struggled to gain access to jobs and education. Most states refused to grant women licenses to practice law or medicine.

Higher Education Despite obstacles, a few women managed to get the higher education needed to enter a profession. In 1877, Boston University granted the first Ph.D., or doctoral degree, to a woman. Slowly, more women earned advanced degrees. By 1900, the nation had 1,000 women lawyers and 7,000 women doctors.

Women's Clubs During the late 1800s, many middle-class women joined women's clubs. At first, most clubwomen read books and sought other ways to advance their knowledge. In time, many became reformers. They raised money for libraries, schools, and parks. They pressed for laws to protect women and children, to ensure pure food and drugs, and to win the vote.

Faced with racial barriers, African American women formed their own clubs, such as the National Association of Colored Women. They battled to end segregation and violence against African Americans. They also joined the battle for suffrage.

Biography Quest

Alice Paul
1885–1977

Alice Paul was an American who studied in England. There, she saw the radical methods used by English suffragists.

Returning to the United States, Paul formed a new suffrage group, which merged into the National Woman's Party in 1917. Paul called on President Wilson many times and worked tirelessly for the Nineteenth Amendment.

Biography Quest **nline**

How did Paul become involved in the struggle for a voting rights amendment?
For: The answer to the question about Paul
Visit: PHSchool.com
Web Code: myd-6153

Women Reformers During the Progressive Era, many women committed themselves to reform. Some entered the field of social work, helping the poor in cities.

Florence Kelley investigated conditions in sweatshops. In time, she was made the chief factory inspector for Illinois. Kelley's main concern was child labor. She organized a boycott of goods produced in factories that employed young children.

☑**Checkpoint** **What gains did women make in education?**

The Crusade Against Alcohol

You have read that reformers began a temperance movement, or campaign against alcohol abuse, in the 1820s. Women took a leading role in the temperance movement. In the late 1800s, the movement gained new strength.

In 1874, a group of women organized the Woman's Christian Temperance Union, or WCTU. Frances Willard became its president in 1879. Willard spoke tirelessly about the evils of alcohol. She called for state laws to ban the sale of liquor. She also worked to close saloons. In time, Willard joined the suffrage movement, bringing many WCTU members along with her.

Carry Nation was a more radical temperance crusader. After her husband died from heavy drinking, Nation often stormed into saloons. Swinging a hatchet, she smashed beer kegs and liquor bottles. Nation won publicity, but her actions embarrassed the WCTU.

After years of effort, temperance leaders persuaded Congress to pass the Eighteenth Amendment in 1917. The amendment enforced prohibition, a ban on the sale and consumption of alcohol. The amendment was ratified in 1919.

☑Checkpoint **How did supporters of temperance seek to influence public policy?**

⭐ **Looking Back and Ahead** For many women, the Nineteenth Amendment was a final victory. Others saw it as just one step on the road to full equality. Today, Americans still debate issues involving the roles of women in society, government, the family, and the workplace.

Main Idea

Temperance supporters won passage of a constitutional amendment banning alcohol.

Cartoon of a temperance supporter

Section 3 | Check Your Progress

Progress Monitoring Online

For: Self-test with instant help
Visit: PHSchool.com
Web Code: mya-6153

Comprehension and Critical Thinking

1. (a) Recall What did the Nineteenth Amendment to the Constitution do?
(b) Link Past and Present How has its passage helped women?

2. (a) Recall What did the Eighteenth Amendment to the Constitution do?
(b) Make Predictions What would be the results of the Eighteenth Amendment? Explain your reasoning.

Reading Skill

3. Identify Central Issues From the Past Reread the text under the heading "New Opportunities for Women." Identify the central issues for the women mentioned in those paragraphs.

Vocabulary *Builder*

Read each sentence below. If the sentence is true, write YES. If the sentence is not true, write NO and explain why.
4. Suffragists were people who worked to ban alcohol.

5. During prohibition, the sale and use of tobacco in the United States were outlawed.

Writing

6. Imagine that you are working with a group of people in 1912 promoting women's suffrage. Create four slogans for banners and leaflets supporting the right of women to vote. Then, write a short persuasive paragraph supporting and developing one of those slogans.

Struggles for Justice

Objectives

1. Describe the efforts of African American leaders to fight discrimination.

2. Describe the life of Mexican Americans and the challenges they faced.

3. Explain why some Americans called for limits on Japanese immigration.

4. Discuss the problems facing religious minorities.

Prepare to Read

Reading Skill

Identify Central Problems From the Past Understanding the problems of the past helps you understand the reactions of people from that time. As you read, identify problems and restate them in your own words. Think about how people of that time responded and how people today might respond to similar problems.

Vocabulary *Builder*

High-Use Words

submit, p. 661

crisis, p. 664

Key Terms and People

Booker T. Washington, p. 660

W.E.B. Du Bois, p. 661

lynching, p. 661

parochial school, p. 665

anti-Semitism, p. 665

⭐ **Background Knowledge** After Reconstruction, African Americans in the South lost many rights. Jim Crow laws led to segregation in public places. In this section, you will see how African Americans and other groups opposed discrimination.

African Americans

Main Idea
African American leaders took different approaches to the problems of segregation and discrimination.

African Americans faced discrimination in the North as well as in the South. Landlords often refused to rent homes in white areas to African Americans. Across the nation, they were restricted to the worst housing and the poorest jobs.

Booker T. Washington During this time, educator Booker T. Washington emerged as the most prominent African American. Born into slavery, Washington taught himself to read. Later, he worked in coal mines, attending school whenever he could. In 1881, Washington helped found the Tuskegee Institute in Alabama. The school offered training in industrial and agricultural skills.

Washington advised African Americans to learn trades and seek to move up gradually in society. Eventually, they would have money and the power to demand equality. Washington declared:

❝No race can prosper till it learns that there is as much dignity in tilling a field as in writing a poem. It is at the bottom of life we must begin, and not at the top. Nor should we permit our grievances to overshadow our opportunities.❞

—Booker T. Washington, speech to Atlanta Exposition

Washington's practical approach won the support of business leaders such as Andrew Carnegie and John D. Rockefeller. They helped him build trade schools for African Americans. At the same time, Presidents sought his advice on racial issues.

W.E.B. Du Bois W.E.B. Du Bois (doo BOYS) had a different view. A brilliant scholar, Du Bois was the first African American to receive a Ph.D. from Harvard University. He agreed with Booker T. Washington on the need for "thrift, patience and industrial training." However, Du Bois criticized Washington for being willing to accept segregation:

> **"**So far as Mr. Washington apologizes for injustice, North or South, does not rightly value the privilege and duty of voting . . . and opposes the higher training and ambition of our brighter minds,—so far as he, the South, or the Nation, does this,—we must unceasingly and firmly oppose them.**"**
> —W.E.B. Du Bois, *The Souls of Black Folk*

Du Bois urged blacks to fight discrimination rather than patiently <u>submit</u> to it. In 1909, he joined Jane Addams and other reformers in forming the National Association for the Advancement of Colored People, or NAACP. Blacks and whites in the NAACP worked for equal rights for African Americans.

Campaign Against Lynching In the 1890s, more than 1,000 African Americans in the South and elsewhere were victims of lynching, or murder by a mob. The epidemic of violence worsened after the depression of 1893. Often, jobless whites took out their anger on blacks.

Vocabulary *Builder*
<u>submit</u> (sahb MIHT) *v.* to yield; to give up power or control

Identify Central Problems From the Past
Identify the central problems facing African Americans in the late 1800s. How did people of the time respond to those problems?

History *Interactive*
Booker T. Washington and W.E.B. Du Bois
Visit: PHSchool.com
Web Code: myp-6152

Two African American Leaders

Two African American Leaders
Booker T. Washington (left) was the most prominent African American leader of his day. He urged African Americans to work patiently to move up in society. W.E.B. Du Bois (right) admired Washington but criticized many of his ideas. Rather than patiently accepting discrimination, Du Bois urged African Americans to fight it actively.
Critical Thinking: *Contrast* *How did Washington's and Du Bois's ideas about how to fight segregation differ?*

Booker T. Washington

W.E.B. Du Bois

Ida B. Wells Fights Against Lynching

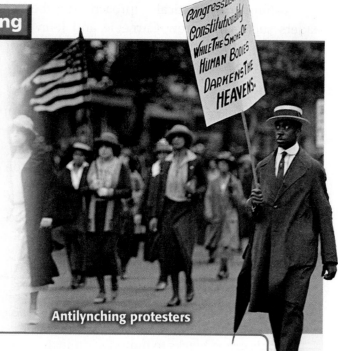

"The real purpose of these savage demonstrations is to teach the Negro that in the South he has no rights that the law will enforce. Samuel Hose [a lynching victim] was burned to teach the Negroes that no matter what a white man does to them, they must not resist. . . . The daily press offered reward for [Hose's] capture and . . . incited the people to burn him as soon as caught."

—Ida B. Wells, "Lynch Law in Georgia," 1899

Antilynching protesters

Reading Primary Sources
Skills Activity

In 1895, journalist Ida B. Wells published an analysis that exposed the truth about the lynching of African Americans.

(a) Interpret a Primary Source According to Wells, why do lynchings occur?

(b) Compare Ida Wells is often classified as a muckraker. How was her work similar to the work of Jacob Riis?

The murders outraged Ida B. Wells, an African American journalist. In her newspaper, *Free Speech,* Wells urged African Americans to protest the lynchings. She called for a boycott of segregated streetcars and white-owned stores. Wells spoke out despite threats to her life.

Setbacks and Successes Few white Progressives gave much thought to the problems faced by African Americans. President Wilson ordered the segregation of workers in the federal civil service. "Segregation is not humiliating, but a benefit," he told protesters who came to talk to him.

Despite obstacles, some African Americans succeeded. Scientist George Washington Carver discovered hundreds of new uses for peanuts and other crops grown in the South. Sarah Walker created a line of hair care products for African American women. She became the first American woman to earn more than $1 million.

Black-owned insurance companies, banks, and other businesses served the needs of African Americans. Black colleges trained young people for the professions. Churches like the African Methodist Episcopal Church became the training ground for generations of African American leaders.

✓**Checkpoint** On what grounds did W.E.B. Du Bois disagree with Booker T. Washington?

Mexican Americans

By 1900, about half a million Mexican Americans lived in the United States. Like African Americans, Mexican Americans often faced legal segregation. In 1910, the town of San Angelo, Texas, built new schools for its Anglo children. Mexican children were forced to go to separate, inferior schools. When Mexican children tried to attend one of the new schools, officials barred their way.

Increased Immigration In 1910, revolution and famine swept Mexico. Thousands of Mexicans fled into the United States. They came from all levels of Mexican society. Many were poor farmers, but some came from middle-class and upper-class families.

At first, 90 percent of Mexican immigrants settled in the Southwest. In time, the migration spread to other parts of the country. People who could not find work in the Southwest began moving to the Midwest and the Rocky Mountain region.

Daily Life Mexican immigrants often worked as field hands, built roads, or dug irrigation ditches. Some lived near the railroads they helped build. Still others worked in city factories under harsh conditions. They were paid less than Anglo workers and were denied skilled jobs.

Like other immigrants, Mexican Americans sought to preserve their language and culture. They created barrios, or ethnic Mexican American neighborhoods. Los Angeles was home to the nation's largest barrio. Its population almost tripled between 1910 and 1920.

Within the barrio, Mexican immigrants and Mexican Americans took many steps to help each other. Some formed mutualistas, or mutual aid groups. These groups worked like other immigrant aid societies. Members of mutualistas pooled money to pay for insurance and legal advice. They also collected money for the sick and needy.

☑️**Checkpoint** Why did emigration from Mexico rise after 1910?

Main Idea
The growing Mexican American population faced prejudice but found support in close-knit communities.

Mexican Americans Helping One Another

Like other groups, Mexican Americans formed mutual aid groups. Members of a mutualista in Arizona are shown marching in a parade (bottom left). Below is the symbol of the Cruz Azul Mexicana, or Mexican Blue Cross, which aided poor families.

Critical Thinking: *Draw Conclusions* *Why were mutual aid groups like these important to Mexican American communities?*

Japanese Brides Arrive in the United States

The Gentlemen's Agreement between President Roosevelt and Japan allowed Japanese wives to join their husbands who were already in the United States. Here, a group of Japanese women arrive at San Francisco. **Critical Thinking: *Clarify Problems*** *What problem was Roosevelt trying to solve by allowing Japanese women to enter the United States?*

Main Idea

As large numbers of immigrants arrived from Japan, some Americans called for limits on Japanese immigration.

Vocabulary *Builder*
crisis (KRĪ sihs) *n.* turning point; situation involving great risk

Asian Americans

As you learned in the previous chapter, the Chinese Exclusion Act of 1882 kept Chinese from settling in the United States. Employers on the West Coast and in Hawaii began hiring workers from other Asian countries, mainly the Philippines and Japan.

Japanese Immigrants More than 100,000 Japanese entered the United States in the early 1900s. Most went first to Hawaii to work on sugar plantations. When the United States annexed Hawaii in 1898, many Japanese decided to seek a better life on the mainland.

Many of the newcomers were farmers. They settled on dry, barren land that Americans thought was useless. Through hard work, the Japanese made their farms profitable. Soon, they were producing a large percentage of southern California's fruits and vegetables.

A Gentlemen's Agreement Prejudice against Asians was high. In 1906, San Francisco forced all Asian students, including Japanese children, to attend separate schools. When Japan protested the insult, the issue threatened to cause an international crisis.

Unions and other groups put pressure on President Theodore Roosevelt to limit immigration from Japan. Because Roosevelt did not want to antagonize a growing naval power, he tried to soothe Japanese feelings. He condemned the segregated schools and proposed that if San Francisco ended segregation, he would restrict Japanese immigration.

In 1907, Roosevelt reached a "Gentlemen's Agreement" with Japan. Japan would stop any more workers from going to the United States. The United States, in exchange, would allow Japanese women to join their husbands who were already in the country.

Anti-Japanese feeling remained high. In 1913, California banned Asians who were not American citizens from owning land.

☑**Checkpoint** What was the Gentlemen's Agreement?

Religious Minorities

Religious minorities also faced prejudice. As you have read, the immigration boom included large numbers of Roman Catholics and Jews. Nativist groups, such as the Anti-Catholic American Protective Association, worked to restrict immigration. Even Jews and Catholics who were not immigrants faced discrimination in jobs and housing.

Anti-Catholic feeling was common in schools. Some teachers lectured against the Pope, and textbooks contained references to "deceitful Catholics." In response, American Catholics set up their own **parochial schools,** or schools sponsored by a church.

The most notorious case of **anti-Semitism,** or prejudice against Jews, in the United States took place in Georgia in 1913. Leo Frank, a Jewish man, was falsely accused of murdering a young girl. Newspapers inflamed public feeling against "the Jew." Despite a lack of evidence, he was sentenced to death. When the governor of Georgia reduced the sentence, a mob took Frank from prison and lynched him.

In response to the lynching and other cases of anti-Semitism, American Jews founded the Anti-Defamation League. (Defamation is the spreading of false, hateful information.) The League worked to promote understanding and fight prejudice against Jews.

☑Checkpoint   **What problems did Jews and Catholics face?**

⭐ Looking Back and Ahead   Groups such as the NAACP and the Anti-Defamation League were formed to fight discrimination. Today, many Americans continue to work against prejudice.

Main Idea
Immigration also led to increased prejudice against Jews and Roman Catholics.

Section 4 | **Check Your Progress**

Progress Monitoring ⬤nline
For: Self-test with instant help
Visit: PHSchool.com
Web Code: mya-6154

Comprehension and Critical Thinking

1. (a) Contrast How did Booker T. Washington and W.E.B. Du Bois propose to improve life for African Americans?
(b) Draw Conclusions Whose ideas do you think would be more likely to help African Americans in the long run? Explain your reasons.

2. (a) Identify What was the Gentlemen's Agreement?
(b) Analyze Cause and Effect How did the Gentlemen's Agreement affect Japanese immigration?

🕗 Reading Skill

3. Identify Central Problems From the Past What central problems faced Asian Americans in the late 1800s? How did Japan respond to these problems? Can you connect their problems to the attitudes toward immigrants today?

Vocabulary *Builder*

4. Write two definitions for the key terms lynching and anti-Semitism. First, write a formal definition for your teacher. Second, write a definition in everyday English for a classmate.

Writing

5. Imagine that you are an editorial writer who attended a debate between Booker T. Washington and W.E.B. Du Bois about the best tactics for fighting discrimination. Write a topic sentence that states the central idea of each man's argument. Then, write a paragraph endorsing one of these points of view and explaining your position.

Photographs are one type of primary source. By capturing a moment in time, they can provide important details about a historical period or event. The photographs below were taken by Jacob Riis.

Baxter Street, New York
(From *Battle With the Slums*, 1902.)

Lodgers in a New York tenement
(From *How the Other Half Lives*, 1890.)

Learn the Skill
Use these steps to analyze photographs.

1. **Find out information about the photograph.** Read the caption to identify the time and place.

2. **Identify the subject.** Look carefully at the photograph. What does it show? If there are people in the photograph, what are they doing?

3. **Decide what the photograph tells about history.** Study the photograph to find out what it illustrates about the past. Try to determine the photographer's point of view or opinion about the scene.

4. **Decide if the photograph is a reliable source of information.** The photographer may have shot the photograph for a special reason or left out certain details in the scene. You should ask questions to determine the reliability of the photograph.

Practice the Skill
Answer the following questions about the photographs on this page.

1. **Find out information about the photograph.** (a) Where was the left photograph taken? (b) When was it published?

2. **Identify the subject.** (a) Who are the people in the right photograph? (b) What are they doing?

3. **Decide what the photograph tells about history.** (a) What do these photographs show about life in New York City slums at the time? (b) How do you think the photographer felt about these scenes? Explain.

4. **Decide if the photograph is a reliable source.** Do you think these photographs give a reliable idea of how poor people lived in New York City? Explain.

Apply the Skill
See the Review and Assessment at the end of this chapter.

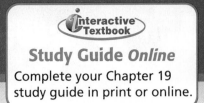

Chapter Summary

Section 1
The Gilded Age and Progressive Reform

- Corrupt political bosses sometimes gained power over cities during the Gilded Age.
- Progressives supported reforms that gave more power to the voters.
- Muckrakers exposed political, social, and business corruption.

Section 2
The Progressive Presidents

- Theodore Roosevelt tried to break up business trusts that hurt competition.
- Roosevelt's Square Deal called for conservation and consumer protection.
- Roosevelt and Progressive Republicans established the Bull Moose Party.
- Woodrow Wilson continued Progressive reforms in his New Freedom program.

Section 3
The Rights of Women

- The Nineteenth Amendment guaranteed women the right to vote.
- The Eighteenth Amendment banned the sale and consumption of alcoholic beverages.

Section 4
Struggles for Justice

- Booker T. Washington said African Americans should work patiently to move up in society, whereas W.E.B. Du Bois said blacks should actively fight discrimination.
- Mexican immigrants worked in low-paying jobs in the fields and factories and lived in ethnic neighborhoods called barrios.
- Asians faced discrimination, especially on the West Coast.
- Roman Catholics and Jews also faced different forms of discrimination.

Key Concepts

These notes will help you prepare for questions about key concepts.

Progressive Era Amendments

- **Sixteenth**—Congress gains power to pass an income tax
- **Seventeenth**—provides for direct election of senators
- **Eighteenth**—bans sale and consumption of alcohol nationally (later repealed)
- **Nineteenth**—gives women the right to vote in all elections

Major Reform Legislation During the Gilded Age

Date	Legislation	Major Purpose
1883	Pendleton Act	Fill government jobs on basis of merit
1887	Interstate Commerce Act	Regulate railroads, stop pools and rebates
1890	Sherman Antitrust Act	Prohibit attempts to destroy competition

Major Reform Legislation During the Progressive Era

Date	Legislation	Major Purpose
1906	Pure Food and Drug Act	Protect consumers from unsafe food and drugs; stop false advertising
1914	Federal Trade Commission	Investigate attempts to destroy competition
1914	Clayton Antitrust Act	Ban practices limiting free enterprise; stop use of antitrust laws against unions

Vocabulary *Builder*

Key Terms

Answer the following questions in complete sentences that show your understanding of the key terms.

1. Why would Upton Sinclair be considered a muckraker?

2. Why would William Howard Taft be considered a trustbuster?

3. Why would Alice Paul and Carrie Chapman Catt be considered suffragists?

4. What happened to the more than 1,000 African Americans who were lynched in the South during the 1890s?

Comprehension and Critical Thinking

5. **(a) List** Which legislation did Congress pass to curb big business, and what were the goals of the legislation?
   (b) Make Predictions How effective do you think the legislation was?

6. **(a) Describe** Which four reforms were instituted during the Progressive Era to give voters more power?
   (b) Apply Information How would voters in your state use each of these reforms to get what they want done?

7. **(a) Recall** What did Theodore Roosevelt do to protect the nation's natural areas?
   (b) Draw Conclusions How have Americans benefited from Roosevelt's actions?

8. **(a) Recall** How did the role of President change during the administration of Theodore Roosevelt?
   (b) Evaluate Information Suggest one reason for the change.

9. **(a) Recall** What was the principal goal of the women's rights movement after the Civil War?
   (b) Draw Inferences Why was that an important goal?

10. **(a) Summarize** What kind of discrimination did African Americans, Mexican Americans, and Asian Americans face during this period?
    (b) Link Past and Present How do these groups still face similar discrimination today? Which types of discrimination are no longer legal?

History Reading Skill

11. **Identify and Explain Central Issues** Explain the issues central to corruption in city government, placing them in the context of the nation's growth in the late 1800s. Give an example of a problem that resulted from this corruption. How did people respond to that corruption?

Writing

12. **Write a two-paragraph persuasive composition:**
    Choose one particular present-day problem that you feel needs to be corrected. (You do not need to provide a solution.) Express your opinion about this problem, explaining why it needs to be addressed. Include several facts and reasons supporting your opinion. Then, end with a strong statement meant to persuade your readers to take action against the problem.

13. **Write a Narrative:**
    Imagine you are a Japanese immigrant in California around 1910. Write a narrative describing your experiences since arriving in the state.

Skills for Life

Analyze Photographs

Use the photograph below by Jacob Riis to answer the questions that follow.

Seventh Avenue night school, New York
(From *Children of the Poor*, 1892.)

14. **(a)** Who are the people in the photograph?
    (b) What are they doing?

15. How do you think the photographer feels about the situation in the photograph? Explain.

16. In general, does the photograph give a reliable idea of how poor people lived in New York City? Explain.

Test Yourself

1. **The principal reason Theodore Roosevelt wanted to break up certain trusts was that he believed they**

   A were unfair to entrepreneurs.

   B hurt workers and the public.

   C made a few Americans rich and kept the majority poor.

   D threatened to slow the growth of foreign trade.

2. **Unlike Booker T. Washington, W.E.B. Du Bois believed that African Americans should**

   A work to achieve equal rights gradually.

   B accept racial segregation laws.

   C actively resist discrimination.

   D focus on gaining industrial and agricultural skills.

Refer to the quotation below to answer Question 3.

> "I recognize the right and duty of this generation to develop and use the natural resources of our land; but I do not recognize the right to waste them, or to rob, by wasteful use, the generations that come after us."

3. **The person who made the above statement would best be described as a**

   A muckraker.

   B suffragist.

   C prohibitionist.

   D conservationist.

Document-Based Questions

Task: Look at Documents 1 and 2, and answer their accompanying questions. Then, use the documents and your knowledge of history to complete this writing assignment:

> Write a short essay about the muckrakers of the late 1800s and early 1900s. Be sure to identify the different muckrakers and to describe their goals and accomplishments. Include information about how they got their name.

Document 1: The excerpt below is from journalist Ida Tarbell's *History of the Standard Oil Company. What does Tarbell say is the goal of a trust?*

> "Standard Oil Trust is the most perfectly developed trust in existence; that is, it satisfies most nearly the trust ideal of entire control of the commodity in which it deals. Its vast profits have led its officers into various allied interests, such as railroads, shipping, gas, copper, iron, steel, as well as into banks and trust companies. . . . It has led in the struggle against legislation directed against combinations. Its power in state and Federal government, in the press, in the college, in the pulpit, is generally recognized."

Document 2: In *How the Other Half Lives,* Jacob Riis called attention to the misery of tenement living. *What aspect of tenement living is Riis describing in this excerpt?*

> "It is said that nowhere in the world are so many people crowded together on a square mile as here. . . . In this house . . . there were fifty-eight babies and thirty-eight children that were over five years of age. In Essex Street, two small rooms in a six-story tenement were made to hold a "family" of father and mother, twelve children, and six boarders. These are samples of the packing of the population that has run up the record here to the rate of three hundred and thirty thousand per square mile.
>
> The densest crowding of Old London . . . never got beyond a hundred and seventy-five thousand. Even the alley is crowded out. Through dark hallways and filthy cellars, crowded, as is every foot of the street, with dirty children, the settlements in the rear are reached."

Writing Workshop

Persuasive Editorial

▶ Introduction

In a persuasive editorial, you express an opinion about an issue of public interest. You support that opinion with facts, reasons, and examples, and communicate your viewpoint to a particular audience. A persuasive editorial should have the following characteristics:

- a topic that involves a matter of opinion

- an issue of public (rather than personal) interest

- a thesis statement that clearly expresses an opinion about that issue

- specific facts, details, examples, and reasons that support the opinion

- reasonable tone and persuasive language

Assignment On the following pages, you will learn how to write a persuasive editorial. You will get step-by-step instructions. Each step will include an example from a sample editorial expressing an opinion about suffrage for women.

Read the instructions and the examples. Then, follow each step to plan and write a 500–700 word persuasive editorial.

Write about the settlement of the West and the disappearance of the frontier.

For a review of the steps in the writing process, see the **Historian's Toolkit, *Write Like a Historian.***

Sample thesis statement:
A constitutional amendment giving women the right to vote should be passed.

▶ Prewriting

Find a persuasive topic. A persuasive editorial presents an opinion about an issue of public interest. Opinions deal with matters of interpretation—with questions that can be viewed in more than one way.

Define your audience. When you plan to write a persuasive editorial, you need to know your audience. Ask the following questions to create an audience profile:

- What issues is my audience most concerned about?
- Where do they live?
- How much do they know about this issue? How are they likely to feel about it?

Sample supporting fact:
More than 5 million women are in the workforce.
Sample supporting reason:
It is only fair that women in the workforce, as well as homemakers, have a say in the laws that govern them.

Create a working thesis. Your thesis should express an informed opinion based on a knowledge of the facts and reflect logical thinking.

Brainstorm for supporting information. You need to find facts, details, examples, and reasons that support your opinion.

Think about opposing arguments. Your editorial will be especially persuasive if you pay attention to opposing arguments—opinions that are different from the one you are expressing. It is a good idea to mention such arguments and then answer them in support of your own opinion.

▶ Drafting

Decide how to organize your writing. Persuasive editorials may be organized in a number of different ways. Three effective methods of organization are order of importance, process of elimination, and contrast.

- **Order of importance** List three or four major reasons for supporting your opinion, and then support and develop each of these reasons, going from the least significant reason to the most important one.
- **Process of elimination** Lead the reader step by step through several possible interpretations. Show why each interpretation is not valid or does not fit the facts as well as your approach does.
- **Contrast** If you are focusing on just two alternative viewpoints, you could contrast them, hoping to persuade your audience that one is more valid than the other.

Introduce your thesis. Draft an introductory paragraph that sets up the issue you will be writing about. State your opinion on the matter and the main reasons that support your opinion.

Support your thesis with examples and details. Use your notes to write paragraphs supporting your opinion with facts and reasons. The more specific and concrete your supporting details are, the more convincing your essay will be.

Use a persuasive tone. As you write your draft, keep in mind that you are addressing an audience that does not necessarily agree with you. Present your ideas tactfully. Acknowledge but do not insult opposing opinions.

Write a strong conclusion. In your final paragraph, restate your opinion as forcefully as you can.

Writing Workshop *continued*

▶ Model Essay

Read the following model of a persuasive essay. Notice how it includes the characteristics you have learned about.

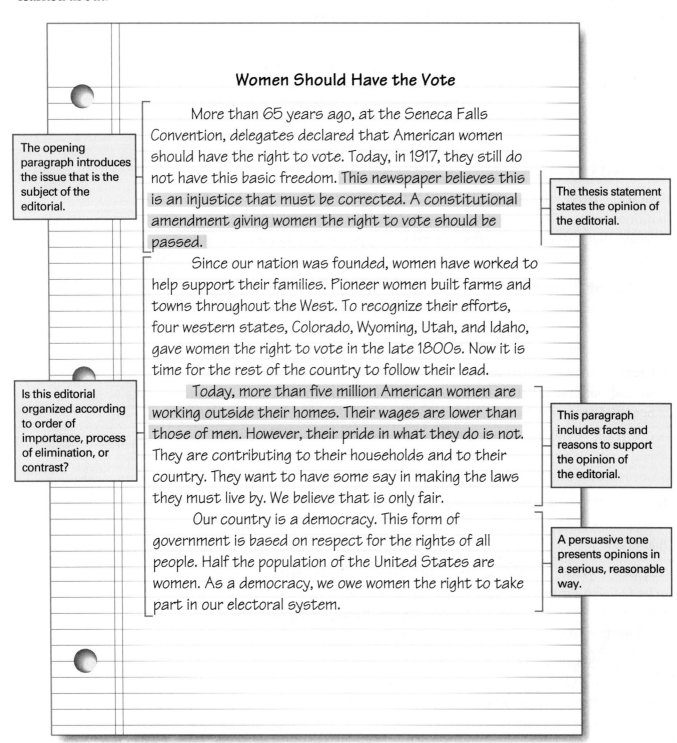

Women Should Have the Vote

The opening paragraph introduces the issue that is the subject of the editorial.

More than 65 years ago, at the Seneca Falls Convention, delegates declared that American women should have the right to vote. Today, in 1917, they still do not have this basic freedom. This newspaper believes this is an injustice that must be corrected. A constitutional amendment giving women the right to vote should be passed.

The thesis statement states the opinion of the editorial.

Since our nation was founded, women have worked to help support their families. Pioneer women built farms and towns throughout the West. To recognize their efforts, four western states, Colorado, Wyoming, Utah, and Idaho, gave women the right to vote in the late 1800s. Now it is time for the rest of the country to follow their lead.

Is this editorial organized according to order of importance, process of elimination, or contrast?

Today, more than five million American women are working outside their homes. Their wages are lower than those of men. However, their pride in what they do is not. They are contributing to their households and to their country. They want to have some say in making the laws they must live by. We believe that is only fair.

This paragraph includes facts and reasons to support the opinion of the editorial.

Our country is a democracy. This form of government is based on respect for the rights of all people. Half the population of the United States are women. As a democracy, we owe women the right to take part in our electoral system.

A persuasive tone presents opinions in a serious, reasonable way.

▶ Revising

After completing your draft, read it again carefully to find ways to make your writing better. Here are some questions to ask yourself.

Revise to strengthen your thesis and support
- Does the thesis state your opinion clearly and strongly?
- Does each paragraph offer valid reasons and solid facts that support that opinion?

Revise to be more convincing
- Is the tone of the editorial reasonable but persuasive?
- Are the opposing arguments dealt with effectively and respectfully?
- Does the editorial make the reader feel that the issue is important?

Revise to meet written English-language conventions
- Are all sentences complete, with a subject and a verb?
- Are all the words spelled correctly?
- Are all proper nouns capitalized, including names of people and places?
- Did you use proper punctuation?

▶ Rubric for Self-Assessment

Evaluate your persuasive editorial using the following rating scale:

	Score 4	Score 3	Score 2	Score 1
Organization	Supports the thesis with a series of paragraphs guided by a reason stated in a topic sentence	Uses order of importance or some other effective way of organizing the composition; uses a reasonably clear organization to present the supporting information	Chooses an organization not suited to the topic	Shows lack of organizational strategy
Presentation	Supports the opinion effectively with relevant facts, details, or examples; links all information to the opinion being supported	Supports the opinion adequately with several facts, details, or examples; links most information to the opinion being supported	Does not support the opinion adequately; does not link supporting information to the opinion	Does not provide facts, details, or examples to support the opinion
Use of Language	Uses persuasive language and reasonable tone; varies sentence structure and vocabulary successfully; includes no or very few mechanical errors	Is often persuasive and usually reasonable; uses some variety in sentence structure and vocabulary; includes few mechanical errors	Is not respectful of opposing views; repeats sentence style; does not vary vocabulary; includes many mechanical errors	Does not have a persuasive tone; is not respectful of opposing views; includes incomplete sentences; uses language poorly; includes many mechanical errors

Unit 7

Think Like a Historian

As you read this unit, think about this question: *How did a more powerful United States expand its role in the world?*

Americans Look Overseas By 1900, the United States Navy had enlarged and modernized its naval fleet. The nation showed growing interest in overseas trade and in playing a larger role in world affairs.

1900

1917

United States Enters World War I America joined with France and the other Allies to push back Germany and Austria-Hungary in the First World War. President Wilson hoped this would be the war to make the world "safe for democracy."

A New Role in the World

Panama Canal The United States began building a canal across a narrow strip of land in Central America. The new canal made it possible for oceangoing ships to sail more quickly between the west and east coasts of the United States.

1904

America's Diverse Population The U.S. population continues to grow more diverse, as immigrants come to America from all parts of the world. In recent years, Hispanics have become the largest minority.

21ST Century

Chapter Preview

By the late 1800s, the United States was taking a larger role in world affairs. The nation acquired new territories in the Pacific and strengthened its trade ties with Asia. In addition, the Spanish-American War led to increased involvement in Latin America.

✓ What You Will Learn

During the last half of the 1800s, the United States acquired territories and built up trade in the Asia-Pacific region.

A quick U.S. victory in the Spanish-American War of 1898 gave the United States an overseas empire.

The United States expanded the Monroe Doctrine and became more involved in Latin America.

When World War I began in Europe, the United States at first tried to remain neutral.

U.S. Events

1854 United States signs trade treaty with Japan.

1850

1893 American planters stage revolt in Hawaii.

1890

1898 United States wins Spanish-American War.

1900

World Events

1858 France begins conquest of Indochina.

1880s European powers carve up Africa.

1900 Boxer Rebellion breaks out in China.

President Theodore Roosevelt followed a "big stick" policy as he sought to block European nations from interfering when Latin American nations could not pay their debts.

1904
United States begins to build Panama Canal.

1914
United States Navy occupies port of Veracruz, Mexico.

1900

1910 Japan annexes Korea.

1910

1920

1914 World War I begins in Europe.

History Reading Skill **Frame Research Questions**

What questions could you ask to learn more about the Panama Canal?

In this chapter, you will practice framing, or asking, questions that can be answered through research. Read the following account of the history of the Panama Canal. The side notes show you how to frame research questions.

> **Primary Source**
>
> In 1914, the United States completed the Panama Canal after overcoming many challenges. The waterway across Central America's narrowest point connected the Pacific and Atlantic oceans.
>
> For at least 400 years people dreamed about digging a canal across the Isthmus of Panama. . . .
>
> The first dreamer was King Charles V of Spain. In 1534 his soldiers had to struggle across the Isthmus on a bumpy stone road . . . with the stolen riches of Bolivia and Peru piled on the backs of mules and horses. . . .
>
> By 1855, despite many deaths from malaria and yellow fever, an American company succeeded in completing a railroad across the Isthmus to transport [gold] prospectors and their families. . . .
>
> In 1882 the French began digging a great trench . . . across the Isthmus. It had been the dream of Ferdinand de Lesseps, but his canal company ultimately collapsed because of disease, corruption, and mismanagement.
>
> —Nancy Winslow Parker, *Locks, Crocs, & Skeeters: The Story of the Panama Canal*

Ask questions to extend the text: How did the Spanish interact with local populations?

Ask questions to solve puzzles: Why build this railroad? How did the risks balance with the likely rewards?

Ask questions to connect across time periods: How did Americans overcome the challenges that defeated Lesseps?

Frame Research Questions

- Ask questions that are narrow enough to realistically answer. For example, questions should focus on a specific time period.
- Ask questions about *who* and *what* to find out important details. Then, ask *why* and *how* to go even further.
- Ask questions that require you to extend into related topics of interest to you.

Document-Based Questions

1. According to the excerpt, who was the first European to think about building a canal across the Isthmus of Panama?
2. How would a canal have benefited the Spanish?
3. What challenge faced both the railroad builders and the canal builders?

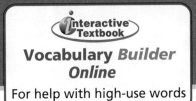
Vocabulary *Builder*

Previewing High-Use Academic Words

High-Use Word	Definition	Sample History Sentence
critic (KRIHT ihk) (Section 1, p. 681)	*n.* someone who makes judgments about objects or actions	<u>Critics</u> are often quick to find fault with a president's actions.
exclude (ehks KLYOOD) (Section 1, p. 684)	*v.* to keep out or expel; to reject or not be considered	The United States objected to the attempts by some nations to <u>exclude</u> U.S. merchants from trade in China.
revolt (ree VOHLT) (Section 2, p. 688)	*n.* uprising; rebellion	Spain struggled to put down <u>revolts</u> in Cuba and the Philippines.
prospect (PRAHS pehkt) (Section 2, p. 690)	*n.* expectation; likely outcome	American businesses wanted to invest in China, lured by the <u>prospect</u> of great profits.
hostile (HAHS tihl) (Section 3, p. 694)	*adj.* unfriendly; intending to do harm; like an enemy	U.S. forces had little trouble defeating <u>hostile</u> forces in Puerto Rico.
invest (ihn VEHST) (Section 3, p. 697)	*v.* to supply money for a project in order to make a profit	If you <u>invest</u> in a stock today, you are hoping that its value will grow so that you can sell it at a profit later.
stationary (STAY chuh nair ee) (Section 4, p. 700)	*adj.* not moving; having a fixed place; not changing in position, size, or number	The battle lines remained <u>stationary</u> for months at a time, and neither side was able to gain any ground.
clause (klaws) (Section 4, p. 703)	*n.* part of a law, treaty, or other written agreement	One widely criticized <u>clause</u> of the treaty required Germany to pay large sums for war damages.

Liliuokalani

Previewing Key Terms and People

Matthew C. Perry, p. 680
isolationism, p. 681
imperialism, p. 681
Frederick Jackson Turner, p. 682
Liliuokalani, p. 683
sphere of influence, p. 684
reconcentration, p. 688
José Martí, p. 688
William Randolph Hearst, p. 689

Emilio Aguinaldo, p. 690
protectorate, p. 692
isthmus, p. 693
William C. Gorgas, p. 695
corollary, p. 697
dollar diplomacy, p. 697
Francisco Villa, p. 698
nationalism, p. 699
militarism, p. 699

trench warfare, p. 700
propaganda, p. 701
reparations, p. 703

Eyes on the Pacific

Objectives

1. Describe early attempts by the United States to expand in the Pacific.

2. List the reasons many Americans came to favor expansion.

3. Explain how the United States gained the territories of Samoa and Hawaii.

4. Describe how the United States protected its trading rights in China.

Prepare to Read

Reading Skill

Ask Extension Questions In discussing one central event, history books will often mention a related event. You may find yourself interested in the related event. Why did it happen? What made it important? How did it affect those involved? Framing questions in specific language will help you research to find the answers.

Vocabulary *Builder*

High-Use Words
critic, p. 681
exclude, p. 684

Key Terms and People
Matthew C. Perry, p. 680
isolationism, p. 681
imperialism, p. 681
Frederick Jackson Turner, p. 682
Liliuokalani, p. 683
sphere of influence, p. 684

⭐ **Background Knowledge** You have seen how the United States extended its borders under the banner of Manifest Destiny. In this chapter, you will learn how the United States began to seek new opportunities overseas.

The United States Looks Overseas

In the mid-1800s, the United States was ready to take on new challenges. It found new trading partners and acquired more land.

Opening Japan to Trade U.S. merchants longed to engage Japan in a profitable trade. However, for 250 years, Japan had blocked outside trade and barred foreigners from entering or leaving the country.

In 1853, a squadron of heavily armed U.S. warships, commanded by Commodore Matthew C. Perry, sailed into Tokyo Bay. Perry presented the Japanese with a letter from the President calling for Japan to grant trading rights to Americans. The Japanese were awed by Perry's powerful ships and menacing guns. When Perry returned in 1854, they signed a treaty opening Japan for trade.

Perry's visit had another important effect. Faced with the technology and power of the United States, the Japanese recognized their own weakness. They set out to transform their feudal society into an industrial nation that could compete in the modern world.

Purchasing Alaska In 1867, Alaska was a Russian colony. Russia told U.S. Secretary of State William Seward that it wanted to sell Alaska. Seward strongly favored U.S. expansion. He saw Alaska as a stepping stone for trade with Asia and the Pacific.

Main Idea
The United States opened trade with Japan and purchased Alaska from Russia.

Japanese statuette of Commodore Perry

Alaska is twice the size of Texas. The United States purchased the territory for $7.2 million, about 2 cents an acre. The purchase increased the area of the United States by almost one fifth.

Many Americans opposed the purchase. Some saw Alaska as a frozen wasteland—"Seward's Folly" or "Seward's Icebox." But the <u>critics</u> changed their tune when valuable discoveries of gold led to the Klondike and Alaska gold rushes of 1897–1898. Alaska, it turned out, was rich in an amazing array of resources.

Vocabulary *Builder*
<u>critic</u> (KRIHT ihk) *n.* someone who makes judgments about objects or actions

✔**Checkpoint** **How did the United States get Japan to open trade?**

The Expansionist Mood

Until the late 1800s, Americans heeded George Washington's advice to "steer clear of permanent alliances." The nation generally pursued a policy of **isolationism**—that is, avoiding involvement in other countries' affairs. Americans stood aside as the nations of Europe undertook a policy of **imperialism**—building empires by imposing political and economic control over peoples around the world.

In the late 1800s, however, a new spirit of expansion gripped the nation. Americans began to consider a new sort of Manifest Destiny that would extend overseas. Supporters of expansion offered a variety of arguments for increased involvement in world affairs. These included promoting economic growth and spreading American values. A new view of history also encouraged expansionism.

Main Idea
In the late nineteenth century, the United States began to turn away from isolationism in a bid to acquire overseas territories.

Seward's Folly

Russia offers Alaska.

Will "Billy" Seward trade?

Reading Political Cartoons

Skills Activity

The cartoonist shows a Russian stranger offering to trade "bears, seals, icebergs," and more.

(a) Recognize Points of View What is the cartoonist's opinion about the purchase of Alaska? What symbols does the cartoonist use to make the point?

(b) Apply Information What did people learn about Alaska after 1898? How would you change the cartoon, based on that information?

Cause and Effect

CAUSES

- Western frontier closes.
- European nations acquire overseas colonies and compete for resources and markets.
- U.S. industry needs to acquire raw materials and to find new markets in which to sell its products.
- Some in the United States want to spread American culture and values to other parts of the world.

U.S. OVERSEAS EXPANSION

EFFECTS

- U.S. Navy grows in size and power.
- United States gains control of territories in the Caribbean and the Pacific.
- The United States issues Open Door Policy, which allows all nations to trade with China.
- U.S. builds Panama Canal.
- United States sends troops to Latin American nations to protect its interests.

Reading a Chart

Skills Activity

American expansionists wanted an overseas empire. By 1900, they had achieved their goal.

(a) Read a Chart Which causes listed on the chart relate to benefits for the U.S. economy?

(b) Apply Information How was a strong navy related to the expansionists' goals?

The Turner Thesis In 1893, historian Frederick Jackson Turner put forth the thesis, or idea, that the western frontier had defined American history. Westward movement, he said, had built individualism and democratic values. Turner concluded:

> "And now, four centuries from the discovery of America, at the end of a hundred years of life under the Constitution, the frontier has gone, and with its going has closed the first period of American history."
>
> —Frederick Jackson Turner, *The Significance of the Frontier in American History*

Today, few historians accept Turner's thesis. But the idea of a closing frontier influenced expansionists such as Theodore Roosevelt. Overseas expansion, they said, was the new frontier that would help the nation renew its vitality and strength.

Ask Extension Questions

Isolationism and expansionism each had their advantages and disadvantages for the United States. Suggest a possible research question that builds on this topic.

Promoting Economic Growth The United States had a powerful industrial economy. It produced far more than Americans would buy. U.S. leaders watched nervously as European powers seized land in Africa and Asia. If the United States did not act soon, it might be shut out of global markets and denied raw materials.

A top supporter of expansion was Alfred T. Mahan, naval captain and author. Mahan said that future U.S. prosperity depended on building up trade. The key to strong trade, he argued, was a powerful navy that would control the world's sea lanes and thus protect U.S. access to foreign markets.

Spreading American Values In the late 1800s, many Americans believed that Americans of the "Anglo-Saxon race" were superior to "lesser races" in other nations. Therefore, the argument went, Americans had a divine duty to spread Christian values and western civilization around the world.

☑**Checkpoint** **What arguments did expansionists make?**

Gaining Footholds in the Pacific

Supporters of expansion expressed interest in various Pacific islands. They saw them as essential for expanding U.S. influence and trade.

Rivalry for Samoa U.S. steamship companies and missionaries fanned interest in Samoa, a chain of islands in the South Pacific. The steamship companies and the U.S. Navy wanted to set up coaling stations, where ships could stock up on coal.

Britain and Germany also wanted Samoa. Armed conflict loomed in 1889, as Britain, Germany, and the United States all sent warships to Samoa. But fighting was averted when a typhoon struck, disabling or destroying most of the warships. Ten years later, in 1899, the United States and Germany divided the islands of Samoa between them. The people of Samoa, however, had no say in the matter.

Interest in Hawaii Expansionists also eyed Hawaii, a group of islands in the North Pacific. The islands have great natural beauty, sunshine, beaches, and rolling surf. But beauty was secondary. Located between Asia and the United States, Hawaii could serve as a "military and commercial outpost in the Pacific."

The first people to settle Hawaii arrived by canoe from other islands in the Pacific around the 600s. They lived undisturbed until 1778, when Captain James Cook, an English explorer, arrived.

In 1820, the first American missionaries came, hoping to convert Hawaiians to Christianity. Later, other Americans acquired land and set up huge sugar plantations.

As the sugar industry in Hawaii grew, so did the power of American planters. In 1887, planters forced the Hawaiian king, Kalakaua, to accept a new constitution that gave them great influence.

When Kalakaua died in 1891, his sister Liliuokalani (lih lee oo oh kah LAH nee) succeeded him. The new queen was a strong advocate of Hawaiian independence. She refused to recognize the 1887 constitution. She wanted to restore the power of the monarchy and reduce foreign influence in Hawaii.

Main Idea
The United States gained Pacific footholds in Samoa and Hawaii.

Biography Quest

Liliuokalani
1838–1917

Queen Liliuokalani championed several women's causes during her long life. She supported the establishment of a college that would train young Hawaiian women to be scholars. Other efforts led to the 1890 founding of a maternity home to help mothers and to provide care for newborns. She also championed the idea of a women's bank for Hawaii.

Biography Quest ●**nline**

In what other field is Liliuokalani remembered for her contributions?

For: The answer to the question about Liliuokalani
Visit: PHSchool.com
Web Code: myd-6162

Boxer Rebellion

U.S. troops joined soldiers from other powers in crushing the Boxer Rebellion of 1900 in China. **Critical Thinking:** *Detect Points of View This painting shows the event from the foreigner's point of view. Describe how a Chinese artist's painting would have differed.*

Annexing Hawaii In 1893, American planters organized an uprising. Without consulting the U.S. government, they persuaded a U.S. official to land 50 U.S. Marines to help overthrow the queen and set up a pro-American government. But President Grover Cleveland rejected a proposal to annex Hawaii. He argued that the revolt had been illegal and was not supported by the people of the islands.

Cleveland's successor, William McKinley, however, favored annexation and supported a treaty to achieve it. On July 7, 1898, Congress voted to make Hawaii a territory of the United States.

☑**Checkpoint** **How did the United States acquire Hawaii?**

Carving Up China

Main Idea

After other powers grabbed spheres of influence in China, the United States campaigned for equal trading rights there.

In the late 1800s, China had just emerged from an unsuccessful war. Taking advantage of China's weakness, European powers and Japan forced the Chinese empire to grant them land and trading rights. They set about dividing China into **spheres of influence,** or areas where another nation has economic and political control.

Vocabulary *Builder*
<u>exclude</u> (ehks KLYOOD) *v.* to keep out or expel; to reject or not be considered

Open Door Policy At first, Americans were not part of this activity. But as the other powers carved up China, U.S. leaders feared that Americans would be <u>excluded</u> from the China trade.

In 1899, U.S. Secretary of State John Hay issued a message to the other powers. He called on them to keep an "open door" in China. By this, he meant that he wanted them to guarantee the rights of all nations to trade with China on an equal basis. The various nations responded cautiously, most saying neither yes nor no. But Hay declared publicly that the Open Door Policy had been accepted.

Boxer Rebellion Many Chinese resented foreign influences in their country. They organized a secret society to combat the foreigners. The society called itself the Righteous and Harmonious Fists. Europeans called this society and its members Boxers, because they performed ceremonial exercises that resembled shadowboxing.

In the spring of 1900, the Boxers began a rebellion to expel the foreigners. Backed by China's government, they attacked and killed westerners and Chinese Christians. Mobs burned churches and the homes of foreigners. Hundreds of foreigners and some 2,000 Chinese sought safety in a walled section of Beijing, the Chinese capital.

Eventually, the outside powers, including the United States, sent in 18,000 troops armed with modern weapons. The troops freed the trapped foreigners, crushed the rebellion, looted the capital, and killed thousands of Chinese.

The Open Door Again Secretary Hay feared that the other powers would use the Boxer Rebellion as an excuse to seize more Chinese territory. To prevent this, he issued a second Open Door note. In it, he repeated the principle of open trade and made an even stronger statement about American intentions to preserve trade. He also said that China should remain one country and not be broken up into separate pieces.

☑ **Checkpoint** What was the goal of the U.S. Open Door Policy?

☆ **Looking Back and Ahead** Under the urging of expansionists, the government promoted U.S. trade and began to acquire territories overseas. In the next section, you will read of how the Spanish-American War gave the United States an empire.

Section 1 | **Check Your Progress**

Progress Monitoring ⬤nline
For: Self-test with instant help
Visit: PHSchool.com
Web Code: mya-6161

Comprehension and Critical Thinking

1. (a) Recall What benefit did Seward see in acquiring Alaska?
(b) Detect Points of View Why did people call the purchase of Alaskan lands "Seward's Folly"?

2. (a) Summarize In what three ways did U.S. supporters of expansion justify increased involvement in world affairs?
(b) Identify Economic Benefits How did the division of Samoa and the annexation of the Hawaiian Islands benefit the United States?

Reading Skill

3. Ask Extension Questions American acquisition of territory in the Pacific region was controversial. Suggest a possible research question building on this topic.

Vocabulary *Builder*

Complete each of the following sentences so that the second part further explains the first part.

4. During much of the 1800s, the nation followed a policy of isolationism; _____.

5. Competing European nations followed policies of imperialism; _____.

6. China was divided into spheres of influence; _____.

Writing

7. In an essay contrasting U.S. policy toward China with the policies of other world powers, which of the following would you focus on, and why?

(a) the similarities between U.S. policies and those of other nations toward China

(b) the differences between U.S. policies and those of other nations toward China

(c) the change in U.S. policies toward China over time

Economic Interests in the Pacific

After the Civil War, the United States became a world leader in industry and agriculture. American leaders believed that expansion was essential in order to compete with European factories. They favored expansion across the Pacific to gain resources, open new markets, and encourage trade.

RUSSIA

ALASKA
[PURCHASED, 1867]

CANADA

UNITED STATES

P A C I F I C

JAPAN
TOKYO

MIDWAY ISLAND
[ANNEXED, 1867]

O C E A N

CHINA

N

HAWAII
[ANNEXED, 1898]

0   1000   2000 MILES

0   1000   2000   KILOMETERS

UNITED STATES IN THE PACIFIC

1 **A New Market in Asia**

Seeking to pressure Japan into opening its ports to trade, Commodore Matthew C. Perry led a fleet of warships that entered Tokyo Bay in 1853. Japan realized it could not compete with American naval power. It decided to open trade relations with the United States.

2 "Seward's Folly"

Critics called Alaska "Seward's Folly" because they thought it was an icy wasteland. However, a gold rush in the 1890s proved the critics wrong. These miners pose for a photograph next to their Alaskan claim.

Understand Effects:
America Expands Its Influence

By the start of the Spanish-American War in 1898, the United States had expanded its influence across the entire Pacific Ocean. It acquired valuable raw materials from its new territories and increased its influence on global trade.

Secretary of State William Seward

3 A Commercial and Naval Outpost

American planters were attracted to Hawaii because its soil and climate yielded crops year-round. The United States also leased Pearl Harbor from Hawaii as a fueling and repair station for ships.

Analyze GEOGRAPHY AND HISTORY

What were American goals in the Pacific and Asia? Write a paragraph describing how Hawaii's climate and location made it vital to reaching those goals.

The Spanish-American War

Objectives

1. Describe how Americans reacted to the revolt in Cuba.

2. Identify the reasons the United States declared war on Spain.

3. Explain how the Spanish-American War led to the creation of an American overseas empire.

Prepare to Read

 Reading Skill

Ask Analytical Questions
Reading about history may sometimes leave you puzzled. Ask questions that focus on these puzzles, then research to find answers. Start by looking at what doesn't make sense to you, such as why people acted in a particular way. Use the question starters *who, what, when, why,* and *how* to begin. Then, think about how events changed over time and what caused the changes.

Vocabulary *Builder*

High-Use Words
revolt, p. 688
prospect, p. 690

Key Terms and People
reconcentration, p. 688
José Martí, p. 688
William Randolph Hearst, p. 689
Emilio Aguinaldo, p. 690
protectorate, p. 692

⭐ **Background Knowledge** In the previous section, you read how the United States took its first steps on the world stage in the late 1800s. In this section, you will learn how it fought a war that transformed it into a major world power.

Main Idea
Americans sympathized with rebels who sought to gain Cuba's independence.

Vocabulary *Builder*
revolt (ree VOHLT) *n.* uprising; rebellion

Ask Analytical Questions
Revolts in Cuba interested many Americans. Suggest a possible research question on this topic.

War Clouds Loom

Cuba, 90 miles off the coast of Florida, had been under Spanish rule since Columbus came in 1492. Over the centuries, Cubans grew increasingly discontented with Spain's harsh rule. In 1868, the Cubans began an uprising that was finally put down 10 years later.

Rebellion in Cuba Cubans rose up again in 1895. To suppress this new revolt, the Spanish began a policy of reconcentration. Reconcentration is the forced movement of large numbers of people into detention camps for military or political reasons. In the Spanish camps, food was scarce and sanitation poor. As a result, an estimated 200,000 Cubans died.

Cuban exiles in the United States, led by José Martí, urged the United States to help the rebels. Martí, Cuba's greatest poet, had long dreamed of an independent Cuba. However, he was killed in a skirmish in Cuba before he could see his dream come true.

Americans React Many Americans were sympathetic to the Cuban rebels. They called on the U.S. government to intervene to oust the Spanish. Other Americans wanted to intervene for economic reasons, to safeguard American investments in Cuba. At the time,

Americans had about $50 million invested in Cuban sugar and rice plantations, railroads, and iron mines.

President Cleveland ignored the calls for intervention. He remarked that "there seems to be an epidemic of insanity in the country." When William McKinley became President in 1897, he also tried to maintain neutrality. Still, the clamor for war continued.

Some of the loudest cries came from the New York press. As you have read, Joseph Pulitzer of the *New York World* had developed a style of reporting that became known as yellow journalism. Pulitzer's rival, William Randolph Hearst of the *New York Journal*, tried to outdo Pulitzer in the use of sensational stories and headlines.

The two publishers focused much of their attention on Cuba. "FEEDING PRISONERS TO THE SHARKS," read one headline in the *Journal*. The *World* called Cuba a land of "blood on the roadsides, blood in the fields, blood on the doorsteps, blood, blood, blood." This daily barrage of horror stories fed American outrage against Spain.

"Remember the *Maine*" Early in 1898, fighting broke out in Havana, Cuba's capital. President McKinley ordered the battleship *Maine* to Havana harbor to protect American lives and property.

On February 15, at 9:40 P.M., a great explosion sank the *Maine* and killed 260 men. To this day, no one knows what caused the explosion. However, the press and the public blamed Spain. With cries of "Remember the *Maine*," Americans demanded revenge.

✓**Checkpoint** Why was the *Maine* in Havana harbor?

Explore More Video
To learn more about the sinking of the *Maine*, view the video.

The Yellow Press Reports on the *Maine* Sensational coverage of the explosion of the battleship *Maine* by New York's yellow press helped feed the fever for war.
Critical Thinking:
Distinguish Facts From Opinions From these examples and from what you have read, state two facts and two opinions that appeared in coverage of the Maine.

Vocabulary *Builder*
<u>prospect</u> (PRAHS pehkt) *n.* expectation; likely outcome

The United States Goes to War

War fever swept the United States. At first, President McKinley favored a peaceful settlement between Spain and the rebels. He feared that war would disrupt the U.S. economy. In the end, though, McKinley gave in to the public pressure. On April 11, 1898, he asked Congress to declare war on Spain. Nine days later, Congress did so.

Surprise in the Philippines The first great battle of the war was not fought in Cuba. It took place halfway around the world.

Assistant Secretary of the Navy Theodore Roosevelt was eager to expand U.S. naval power. After the *Maine* blew up, Roosevelt saw the <u>prospect</u> of war growing. Roosevelt telegraphed Commodore George Dewey, head of the Pacific fleet. He ordered Dewey to move his ships so as to strike the Philippines when war broke out. On May 1, Dewey, with a small fleet of American warships, sank the entire Spanish squadron at Manila Bay, in the Philippines. The Americans did not lose a single ship or life.

Fall of Manila Like the Cubans, many Filipinos were in rebellion against the Spanish. Dewey enlisted Emilio Aguinaldo, a rebel leader, to help him seize Manila from the Spanish. Soon, the United States found itself in control of the Philippine Islands. Aguinaldo was a major help to the Americans. But the Americans overlooked the fact that Aguinaldo was fighting for Philippine independence. Soon he would be fighting against the Americans.

War in the Caribbean The war's focus next shifted to Cuba. The main fighting took place around Santiago and at sea. American ground forces arrived in Santiago in late June. They were poorly trained and poorly equipped—but eager to fight.

One of the best known units was the Rough Riders, led by Theodore Roosevelt. Roosevelt had given up his navy post to join the war. On July 1, Roosevelt helped lead his men in a successful charge up San Juan Hill that became the most celebrated event of the war.

Americans—both black and white—fought in the Santiago campaign. First Lieutenant John J. Pershing wrote:

> **"**White regiments, black regiments . . . fought shoulder to shoulder, unmindful of race or color . . . and mindful only of their common duty as Americans.**"**
> —First Lieutenant John J. Pershing, speech, November 27, 1898

Meanwhile, U.S. ships had trapped the Spanish fleet in Santiago harbor. When the fleet tried to escape, U.S. ships destroyed it. The 24,000 Spanish soldiers at Santiago surrendered two weeks later.

After the Spanish surrendered Cuba, American troops invaded Puerto Rico, another Spanish possession in the Caribbean. They quickly brought the island under U.S. control.

Theodore Roosevelt, Rough Rider

☑ **Checkpoint** What lands did Spain lose in the Caribbean?

Spanish-American War

War in the Caribbean

War in the Pacific

KEY
- - → U.S. Navy
- → U.S. Army
- → Spanish fleet
- ★ U.S. victories
- Spanish colonies

ATLANTIC OCEAN

Gulf of Mexico

Tampa FL

Key West

Havana

CUBA

Santiago

HAITI

DOMINICAN REPUBLIC

San Juan

PUERTO RICO

JAMAICA (Br.)

BAHAMAS (Br.)

Caribbean Sea

CHINA

PACIFIC OCEAN

Hong Kong (Br.)

Dewey

Manila Bay

Manila

PHILIPPINE ISLANDS

South China Sea

BRITISH NORTH BORNEO

0 km 300
0 miles 300
Polyconic Projection

0 km 300
0 miles 300
Azimuthal Equal-Area Projection

MAP MASTER®
Skills Activity

The two fronts in the Spanish-American War were on opposite sides of the world.

(a) Read a Map Locate these places: Philippine Islands, Manila Bay, Santiago, San Juan. Which are located in the Pacific Ocean? Which are in the Atlantic Ocean or the Caribbean Sea?

(b) Interpret Maps Describe the different routes taken by the U.S. Navy and the U.S. Army to reach Santiago.

MapMaster Online

For: Interactive Map
Visit: PHSchool.com
Web Code: myp-6162

An American Empire

In December 1898, Spain and the United States signed a peace treaty. Spain accepted Cuban independence. It granted Puerto Rico, the Philippines, and the Pacific islands of Guam and Wake to the United States. In return, the United States paid Spain $20 million.

Debating the Treaty The treaty triggered an angry debate in the United States. Many Americans said taking colonies violated the principle of the Declaration of Independence—that all people had a right to self-government. Besides, they said, acquiring colonies brought the risk of future wars.

Expansionists, by contrast, welcomed the treaty. It gave the United States important bases, they said, and provided new business opportunities. Also, they argued, the United States had a duty to spread the ideas of democratic government to other parts of the world.

In a close vote, the Senate ratified the treaty on February 6, 1899. The United States now had an overseas empire.

Main Idea

Over opposition from some Americans, the United States took on an overseas empire.

Governing Cuba and Puerto Rico The United States replaced Spain as the leading Caribbean power. As a result, Cuba did not gain the true independence it sought. In 1902, Congress forced Cuba to include the Platt Amendment in its new constitution. The amendment limited Cuba's power to make treaties or borrow money. It gave the United States a right to intervene in Cuban affairs. It also allowed the United States to keep a naval base at Guantánamo Bay. In effect, it made Cuba a protectorate of the United States. A **protectorate** is an independent country whose policies are controlled by an outside power. Wrote one Cuban journalist, "The Americans have made our country free. As free as a dog on a leash."

The Foraker Act of 1900 set up a government in Puerto Rico, with a U.S.-appointed governor. The act gave Puerto Ricans limited self-rule. Americans developed Puerto Rico's economy and educational system. In 1917, Puerto Ricans were made citizens of the United States. Still, many Puerto Ricans wanted to be free of outside control.

Revolt in the Philippines When the United States took control of the Philippines, many Filipinos felt betrayed. Led by Emilio Aguinaldo, they renewed their fight for independence. In a three-year war, about 4,000 Americans and 20,000 Filipinos were killed. Finally, in 1901, Aguinaldo was captured and fighting came to an end. Not until 1946 did the Philippines gain independence.

Emilio Aguinaldo

✓Checkpoint How did the treatment of Cuba, Puerto Rico, and the Philippines differ?

⭐ **Looking Back and Ahead** The Spanish-American War gave the United States an overseas empire. Next, you will read how the United States extended its influence in Latin America.

Section 2 | **Check Your Progress**

Progress Monitoring 🌐nline
For: Self-test with instant help
Visit: PHSchool.com
Web Code: mya-6162

Comprehension and Critical Thinking

1. (a) Identify What role did the press play in rallying American support for a war in Cuba?
(b) Draw Inferences What motivated the United States to enter into a war with Spain?

2. (a) List What were the terms of the peace treaty between the United States and Spain?
(b) Analyze Cause and Effect How had the United States replaced Spain as a colonial power in the world?

Reading Skill

3. Ask Analytical Questions Reread the text following the subheading "Debating the Treaty." What were the arguments in the debate? Suggest a possible research question on this topic.

Vocabulary *Builder*

Answer the following questions in complete sentences that show your understanding of the key terms.
4. How did reconcentration suppress the people of Cuba?

5. Why did a Cuban describe protectorate status as like being a "dog on a leash"?

Writing

6. Write a sentence in response to each of the following essay prompts. Then choose one of the prompts and write a few notes listing some facts you would include in the essay.

(a) Describe the fighting during the Spanish-American War.
(b) Analyze why the U.S. entered the Spanish-American War.
(c) Take a stand on the merits of the U.S. entry into the Spanish-American War.

The United States and Latin America

Objectives

1. Explain why and how the United States built the Panama Canal.

2. Discuss how Presidents expanded the Monroe Doctrine to intervene in the affairs of Caribbean nations.

3. Describe how relations between the United States and Mexico became strained under President Wilson.

Prepare to Read

🔄 Reading Skill

Focus Research Topics
Research topics must be specific. Frame questions to a particular time and place. Avoid questions that would require yes or no answers. Connect questions to the context of your history reading. Work toward asking questions that can be answered with evidence from available and reliable research sources.

Vocabulary *Builder*

High-Use Words
hostile, p. 694
invest, p. 697

Key Terms and People
isthmus, p. 693
William C. Gorgas, p. 695
corollary, p. 697
dollar diplomacy, p. 697
Francisco Villa, p. 698

⭐ **Background Knowledge** By 1902, the United States was a world power, with colonies overseas and a strong economy. In this section, you will learn how it used its new-found power in Latin America.

Linking the Oceans

During the Spanish-American War, the U.S. Navy sent the battleship *Oregon* from San Francisco to Cuba to bolster the American fleet. The trip—14,000 miles around the tip of South America—was long and dangerous. The journey took more than two months.

Clearly, a shorter route was needed. A canal across Central America would link the Atlantic and Pacific oceans. President Theodore Roosevelt was determined to build that canal. Not only would it improve global shipping. It would also make it easier for the U.S. Navy to defend the United States's new colonial empire.

Choosing a Site The Isthmus of Panama was the ideal location for a canal. An **isthmus** is a narrow strip of land joining two larger areas of land. The Isthmus of Panama is 50 miles wide.

In 1902, Panama was a province of the South American nation of Colombia. President Roosevelt offered Colombia $10 million in cash and $250,000 yearly in rent to allow the United States to build a canal through Panama. Without consulting his government, a Colombian diplomat agreed to the offer.

Main Idea
In order to build a canal between the oceans, Teddy Roosevelt helped Panama to break away from Colombia.

Route of the USS *Oregon*

Links Across Time

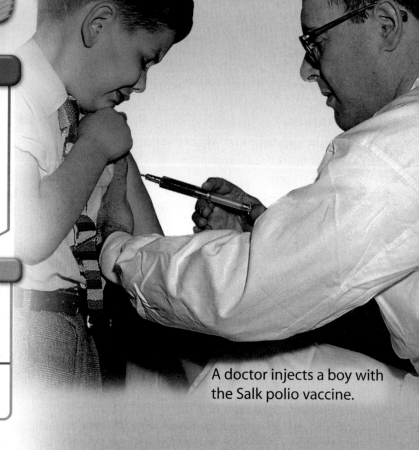

A doctor injects a boy with the Salk polio vaccine.

Medical Breakthroughs

1940–Today A long string of medical advances followed Colonel William C. Gorgas's success in controlling yellow fever and malaria in the Canal Zone.

Penicillin (1941), then other antibiotics
Vaccines against polio (1954, 1960)
Elimination of smallpox (1979)
Decoding of the human genome (genetic "blueprints"), allowing hereditary diseases to be targeted (2000)

Link to Today nline

Medical Advances Today What are the latest advances in fighting cancer or heart disease? Go online to learn more about medical breakthroughs.

For: Medical breakthroughs
Visit: PHSchool.com
Web Code: myc-6163

Vocabulary *Builder*
hostile (HAHS tihl) *adj.* unfriendly; intending to do harm; like an enemy

---

The proposed deal outraged many Colombians. Some said it was against Colombia's constitution, because the United States would be gaining permanent control over a 6-mile-wide stretch of Colombian territory. Other Colombians were willing to negotiate but claimed the rights were worth far more than the United States had offered. Consequently, Colombia's government held out for more money.

However, Roosevelt was impatient. He did not want to lose time in bargaining. Moreover, he knew that many Panamanians disliked Colombian rule. Secretly, he let Panamanians know that the United States would help if they claimed independence from Colombia. The Panamanians, of course, would then reap the rewards of a canal.

Revolt in Panama A revolt took place on November 3, 1903. U.S. gunboats waited in the harbor to provide support for the rebels. U.S. Marines landed in Colón to prevent <u>hostile</u> Colombian troops from reaching Panama City. Many Americans were alarmed by Roosevelt's role in the revolt, criticizing his "gunboat diplomacy."

The United States immediately recognized the independent Republic of Panama. Three days later, a Frenchman acting for Panama signed a treaty giving the United States permanent use and control of a 10-mile-wide zone across the Isthmus of Panama. The United States agreed to pay $10 million plus $250,000 a year in rent.

✓**Checkpoint** How did the United States help rebels in Panama?

The Panama Canal

In 1904, the U.S. government began to build a canal across Panama. President Roosevelt urged the engineers to "Make the dirt fly!"

Fighting Disease   The first great obstacle to building the canal was not an engineering problem. It was disease. Malaria and yellow fever were widespread in Panama. Real work on the canal could not begin until those diseases were controlled.

William C. Gorgas, an American expert on tropical diseases, took up the problem. Most people at the time believed that the damp night air caused yellow fever and malaria. A major breakthrough came when a Cuban doctor, Carlos Juan Finlay, discovered that yellow fever was transmitted by a certain kind of mosquito. An English doctor, Ronald Ross, found that a different kind of mosquito carried malaria. Gorgas had already made significant progress toward wiping out disease-carrying mosquitoes in Cuba. Now he turned to Panama.

At Gorgas's direction, workers cleared brush and drained swamps where mosquitoes lived. The huge effort paid off. By 1906, Gorgas had nearly wiped out yellow fever and reduced malaria in Panama.

The "Big Ditch"   Construction of the canal involved three major tasks. Workers had to cut through a mountain, dam a river, and erect the canal's giant locks. By raising or lowering the water level, the locks would allow ships to cross Panama's Cordillera Mountains.

The most challenging job was digging the Gaillard Cut, a 9-mile ditch through the mountains. Thousands of men worked day after day under the tropical sun or in drenching rainstorms. Mudslides were a constant problem. To many workers, it seemed that the digging would never end. One later recalled:

> "I load cement, I unload cement. I carry lumber until my shoulders peel."
>
> —laborer Albert Banister, quoted in David McCullough, *The Path Between the Seas*

While engineers and supervisors came from the United States, most of the laborers were West Indians of African descent. Some 20,000 were from Barbados. More than 6,000 workers lost their lives during the construction of the canal.

Despite unexpected costs and delays, work on the canal was finished six months ahead of schedule. The Panama Canal opened on August 15, 1914. On that day, the SS *Ancon*, brightly decorated with flags, made the first official passage through the canal. After years of work, the Atlantic and the Pacific were joined.

✔**Checkpoint**   **What problems did canal builders have to overcome?**

Main Idea

Despite many obstacles, construction was completed and ships began traveling through the Panama Canal in 1914.

Teddy at the Controls

President Theodore Roosevelt posed for a picture at the controls of a steam shovel in Panama. He told the canal builders: "Make the dirt fly!" **Critical Thinking: Apply Information** What actions by President Roosevelt made the canal possible?

THE Panama Canal

History *Interactive*
Tour the Panama Canal
Visit: PHSchool.com
Web Code: myp-6163

The building of the Panama Canal was one of the greatest engineering feats of all time. Construction of the canal began in 1904 and was finished in 1914. When it was completed, the Atlantic and Pacific oceans were linked. **Critical Thinking:** *Synthesize Information* What were the costs and benefits of building the canal?

Panama Canal

KEY
- Canal Zone
-)(Locks
- ••• Canal

Caribbean Sea

Colón

PANAMA

Gatún Lake

80°W

PANAMA

9°N

Gaillard Cut

Panama City

Balboa

0 km 10
0 miles 10
Conformal Conic Projection

PACIFIC OCEAN

N W E S

Locks Under Construction ▲
Because of the uneven elevation in the Canal Zone, the canal planners designed a system of locks to raise and lower the water level. This photograph shows construction of a lock in 1913. The huge gates open and close to let water in and out.

▲ Ships passing through the canal from the Pacific to the Caribbean are actually traveling northwest.

FAST FACTS

Length: 50 miles

Cost to build: $375 million

Time to build: 10 years

Amount of earth removed during construction: more than 230 million cubic yards

Source: Panama Canal Authority

Locks in ▶ **Use Today**
Locks were built in pairs, allowing ships to pass in both directions at the same time.

Wielding a "Big Stick" in Latin America

Theodore Roosevelt was fond of quoting an old West African proverb: "Speak softly and carry a big stick; you will go far." Roosevelt sought to resolve many problems through diplomacy. But he wanted the world to know that if diplomacy failed, the United States would not hesitate to use military force.

Policing the Hemisphere President Roosevelt applied his "big stick" policy in Latin America. He was eager to assert the claim of the United States to be the leader in the Western Hemisphere. He especially wanted to prevent European nations from becoming too powerful in the United States's "back yard."

In 1904, European nations considered using military force to collect overdue debts from the Dominican Republic, a small Caribbean nation. Roosevelt wanted to prevent any such action. In his annual message to Congress, he announced a new policy. It came to be known as the Roosevelt Corollary to the Monroe Doctrine. A corollary is a logical extension of a doctrine or proposition.

Roosevelt pointed out that the neighbors of the United States sometimes got into disputes with foreign nations. When that happened, argued Roosevelt, the United States had the right to "exercise . . . an international police power" to restore order.

Roosevelt sent marines to the Dominican Republic and took over the country's finances. Thereafter, the United States often cited the Roosevelt Corollary when intervening in Latin America.

Dollar Diplomacy William Howard Taft, who followed Roosevelt as President, had a different approach to foreign affairs. His policy became known as dollar diplomacy. Taft's dollar diplomacy was a policy based on the idea that economic ties were the best way to expand American influence. Responding to Taft's urging, U.S. bankers and businesses <u>invested</u> heavily in Asia and Latin America.

Taft's dollar diplomacy led to as many military interventions in Latin America as Roosevelt's "big stick." When a revolution broke out in Nicaragua, where Americans had invested in land and businesses, the United States sent in marines. Later, American troops also occupied Haiti and Honduras. The United States argued that it needed to protect its citizens. However, many Latin Americans bitterly resented interference in their economic and political affairs.

☑**Checkpoint** How did Roosevelt build on the Monroe Doctrine?

Relations With Mexico

Woodrow Wilson, who became President in 1913, had his own ideas about foreign relations. Earlier Presidents argued that the United States had to compete with other nations for trade, power, and prestige. Wilson added a further goal: U.S. foreign policy should aim to support and nurture democracy throughout the world.

Main Idea
Under Presidents Roosevelt and Taft, the United States often sent soldiers into Latin American nations.

Focus Research Topics
Suggest a more focused research question that builds on the following topic: How did Latin Americans respond to U.S. actions under the Roosevelt Corollary?

Vocabulary *Builder*
invest (ihn VEHST) *v.* to supply money for a project in order to make a profit

Main Idea
Under Woodrow Wilson, the United States used military force in Mexico.

Revolution in Mexico Wilson's foreign policy got its first test in relations with Mexico. In 1911, Mexicans had overthrown their longtime dictator, Porfírio Díaz. The country was plunged into a violent revolution that went on until 1917.

Wilson at first followed a policy that he called "watchful waiting." He said he hoped Mexico would develop a democratic government.

In 1914, a minor incident led Wilson to intervene in Mexico. U.S. sailors who went ashore in Tampico were briefly arrested. Although they were released promptly with an apology, Wilson sent the navy to occupy the port of Veracruz. More than 100 Mexicans died. The incident brought Mexico and the United States close to war. Tempers cooled after South American nations arranged for peace talks.

Chasing Villa Wilson was drawn into Mexican affairs again by the actions of Francisco Villa, a Mexican rebel general nicknamed Pancho. In 1916, Villa's rebels crossed into New Mexico. They raided and burned the town of Columbus, killing 18 Americans.

Mexico's president reluctantly let the United States pursue Villa into Mexico. On Wilson's orders, General John J. Pershing led several thousand soldiers across the border. Mexicans saw this as a full-scale invasion and demanded that the Americans leave. After 11 months, Wilson ordered Pershing to withdraw without capturing Villa.

Pancho Villa

☑ **Checkpoint** What was Wilson's policy toward Mexico?

⭐ **Looking Back and Ahead** World events provided the backdrop for Wilson's withdrawal of troops from Mexico. In 1917, the United States was facing likely involvement in a world war that was raging in Europe and parts of Africa, Asia, and the Pacific. In the next section, you will learn about that war and the U.S. role in it.

Section 3 | Check Your Progress

Progress Monitoring Online
For: Self-test with instant help
Visit: PHSchool.com
Web Code: mya-6163

Comprehension and Critical Thinking

1. (a) Recall Why was the building of a canal important to the United States?
(b) Understand Sequence What events led to the eventual building of the Panama Canal?

2. (a) Describe According to President Wilson, what was the goal of U.S. foreign policy?
(b) Compare and Contrast How did the foreign policies of Presidents Roosevelt and Taft differ?

Reading Skill

3. Focus Research Topics Reread the text following the heading "Fighting Disease." Suggest a more focused research question that is based on the following: How do science and economics work together?

Vocabulary *Builder*

Read the sentence below. If the sentence is true, write YES. If the sentence is not true, write NO and explain why.
4. The United States planned to build a canal through an isthmus river bed.

Writing

5. Write a few sentences defining one of the following terms. Then, analyze its effect on relations between the U.S. and Latin America during the early twentieth century.
• gunboat diplomacy
• dollar diplomacy
• "big stick" policy
• Roosevelt Corollary
• Monroe Doctrine
• Veracruz incident

World War I

Objectives

1. Explain the causes of World War I.
2. Discuss how the United States became involved in World War I.
3. Describe the three clauses of the Treaty of Versailles that Germany resented.

Prepare to Read

Reading Skill

Ask Questions That Connect to the Present Does history repeat itself? Investigate by asking questions that connect history to the present. Compare or contrast a historical situation with a current situation. Or look at ways that historical situations have led to current situations. Ask questions that require research to answer.

Vocabulary *Builder*

High-Use Words

stationary, p. 700
clause, p. 703

Key Terms and People

nationalism, p. 699
militarism, p. 699
trench warfare, p. 700
propaganda, p. 701
reparations, p. 703

⭐ **Background Knowledge** Although the United States had abandoned isolationism, it tried to steer clear of Europe's conflicts. In 1914, a European war put U.S. isolationism to a stern test.

War in Europe

In 1914, tensions in Europe erupted into the largest war the world had yet seen. There were many different causes for the conflict that later became known as World War I.

Imperial Rivalries The great powers of Europe were competing for territory and trade in Africa, Asia, and the Pacific. In particular, France and England looked on distrustfully as Germany aggressively expanded its overseas holdings.

Nationalism A surge of nationalism, or pride in one's own nation or ethnic group, boosted tensions. France sought to reclaim territory it had lost to Germany in 1870. Russia encouraged Serbian and other Balkan nationalists to break free from Austria-Hungary.

The Alliance System To protect themselves, European nations made defensive alliances with one another. Germany formed an alliance with Austria-Hungary. France, Britain, and Russia pledged to come to one another's aid if attacked. The alliance system meant that any conflict between two powers would quickly involve others.

Military Buildup Another factor that led to war was militarism, or the glorification of the military. For glory and for self-protection, nations built up their armed forces. Military leaders gained great influence in European governments.

Main Idea
World War I broke out in August 1914, pitting the Allies against the Central Powers.

Ask Questions That Connect to the Present

Ask a question that connects the text to the present and requires research to answer. You might focus on how nationalism has continued to influence international relations.

Gassed, 1919
by John Singer Sargent

John Singer Sargent, an American painter, created this large mural (7 ft × 20 ft) after witnessing a mustard gas attack during World War I. The gas causes skin blisters, choking, and blindness. **Critical Thinking:** *Draw Conclusions What evidence can you see in the painting of the effects of mustard gas?*

Vocabulary *Builder*
stationary (STAY shuh nair ee) *adj.* not moving; having a fixed place; not changing in position, size, or number

War Begins   The spark that set off the war came on June 28, 1914, in Sarajevo (sa ruh YAY voh), in Bosnia. A Serbian nationalist assassinated Archduke Franz Ferdinand, heir to Austria-Hungary's throne. Austria-Hungary accused the government of independent Serbia of supporting terrorism. On July 29, Austria-Hungary invaded Serbia.

The alliance system drew one country after another into war. Russia backed Serbia. Germany declared war on Russia and France. Britain declared war on Germany. Soon, more than 20 countries had been drawn in. Britain, France, and Russia were known as the Allies. Germany and Austria-Hungary were called the Central Powers.

The Deadliest War   Fighting took place mainly on two fronts, or zones, of battle. On the western front, Britain, France, and Italy faced Germany and Austria-Hungary. On the eastern front, the Central Powers faced Russia.

The western front settled into a bitter stalemate, or deadlock. After some early German successes, the eastern front also stalemated.

With stalemate came trench warfare. In **trench warfare,** soldiers take shelter in opposing lines of ditches. Between the <u>stationary</u> positions of the two sides was "no man's land," or contested territory. After days of shelling the enemy, officers would order troops to charge into "no man's land" and attack the enemy trenches. There, they were mowed down by enemy fire. As death tolls mounted, the two sides fought back and forth over the same patches of land.

New technology made the war more violent. Airplanes were used for scouting and support of ground forces. The tank appeared in battle. Improved machine guns and heavy artillery raised the death toll. Perhaps the most feared of the new weapons was poison gas.

✓**Checkpoint**   How did new technology affect the war?

The United States Enters the War

President Woodrow Wilson proclaimed "strict and impartial neutrality." He said the United States would stay out of the war.

Neutrality Most Americans backed Wilson's policy. They saw no reason to get involved in "a European problem." But, in time, U.S. opinion shifted in favor of the Allied side. The shift was aided by skillful British propaganda. **Propaganda** is information that is used to sway public opinion. Americans were sickened to read accounts from the British side of Germany's brutal treatment of conquered lands.

Both the Allies and the Central Powers sought assistance from the United States, with its vast industrial capacity. However, most U.S. trade was with the Allies. A British naval blockade of German ports prevented important supplies from reaching German ports.

Toward War On May 7, 1915, a German submarine, or U-boat, sank the *Lusitania,* a British passenger liner. Nearly 1,200 people died, 124 of them American. U.S. protests led Germany to halt U-boat attacks on passenger liners. In 1916, Wilson was reelected on the slogan, "He kept us out of war."

Germany resumed U-boat warfare on February 1, 1917. When U-boats sank four U.S. merchant ships, Wilson shed neutrality. In April 1917, he asked Congress to declare war on Germany. War had been "thrust upon" the United States, Wilson said. He added: "The world must be made safe for democracy."

Supporting the War Effort Americans quickly prepared for war. The nation faced an enormous task. It would have to raise, train, and equip an army of millions and send it thousands of miles across the Atlantic.

The United States began the war with the world's sixteenth-largest army, numbering 125,000 men. By war's end, almost four million Americans from diverse ethnic backgrounds had served in uniform.

American factories quickly converted to make weapons and supplies. To conserve food, officials urged Americans to observe wheatless Mondays and meatless Tuesdays. People planted "victory gardens." Americans bought Liberty Bonds to help pay for the war.

☑**Checkpoint** Why did the United States enter the war?

Main Idea
After three years of official neutrality, the United States entered the war in 1917 on the side of the Allies.

The Western Front

KEY

— Farthest German advance, 1914
→ Allied offensive, 1918
----- Armistice line, 1918
★ Major battles
▮ Allies
▮ Central Powers
▯ Neutral nations

0 km 100
0 miles 100
Azimuthal Equal-Area Projection

MAP MASTER®
Skills Activity

For most of World War I, neither side could push back the other. Then, in 1917, the Allies threw back a German offensive.

(a) Understand a Map Approximately how close did the Germans get to Paris?

(b) Interpret Evidence
Why was the Battle of Verdun significant for the French?

MapMaster ●nline
For: Interactive map
Visit: PHSchool.com
Web Code: myp-6164

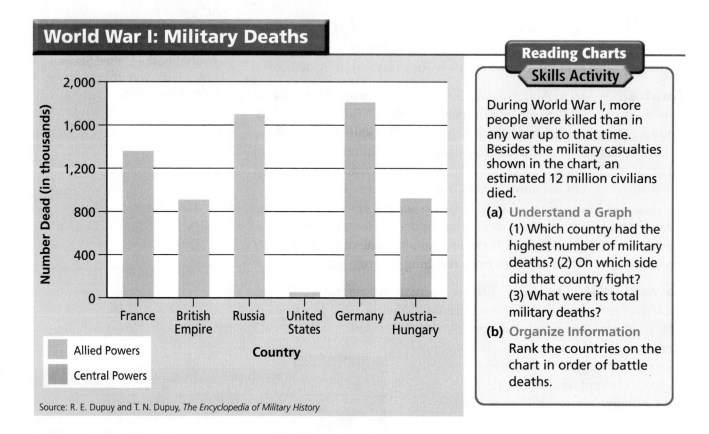

World War I: Military Deaths

Number Dead (in thousands) / **Country**

- Allied Powers
- Central Powers

Source: R. E. Dupuy and T. N. Dupuy, *The Encyclopedia of Military History*

During World War I, more people were killed than in any war up to that time. Besides the military casualties shown in the chart, an estimated 12 million civilians died.

(a) Understand a Graph
(1) Which country had the highest number of military deaths? (2) On which side did that country fight? (3) What were its total military deaths?

(b) Organize Information
Rank the countries on the chart in order of battle deaths.

Americans at War

Main Idea
U.S. troops helped to turn the tide, and the exhausted Germans called an end to fighting in November 1918.

U.S. troops reached France in June 1917, when things looked bad for the Allies. Russia had withdrawn from the war after a revolution broke out there in March 1917. The Germans were on the offensive in France. By early June, Germans had reached the Marne River, less than 50 miles from Paris.

In intense combat, U.S. Marines cleared the Germans from heavily fortified Belleau Wood. Their victory helped prevent the Germans from taking Paris. Then, an Allied offensive pushed the Germans back.

Germany's military and political leaders decided the cause was lost. Beset by illness and short on supplies, Germany's army was losing the will to fight. It had no reserves. The Allies had fresh American troops. Germany agreed to an armistice, or halt in fighting. The armistice took effect at 11 A.M. on the eleventh day of the eleventh month—November 11, 1918. The Central Powers had lost the war.

☑**Checkpoint** Why did German leaders decide to stop fighting?

Searching for Peace

Main Idea
The peace settlement was harsher than Wilson wanted but included his plan for a League of Nations.

In January 1918, with war still raging, Wilson proposed a plan for shaping a peace settlement. It became known as the Fourteen Points. In the first thirteen points, Wilson said that nations should end secret treaties. They should agree to freedom of the seas, arms reduction, and settlement of various colonial claims.

For Wilson, the fourteenth point was the most important. It called for an international organization to help nations settle disputes peacefully.

The victorious powers arranged a peace conference in Paris. When Wilson arrived in December 1918, two million war-weary people turned out to cheer him and his Fourteen Points.

European leaders did not share Wilson's idealism. They had signed secret treaties for dividing up territory. And while Wilson called for "peace without victory," European leaders wanted to punish Germany.

In the end, Wilson compromised on many issues. The Treaty of Versailles (ver SI) contained many harsh <u>clauses</u>. It took away territory on Germany's borders, stripped Germany of colonies, and forced it to pay huge **reparations,** or war damages. Wilson agreed to these clauses because the treaty also set up the League of Nations, the peacekeeping organization he wanted.

The Versailles Treaty created great bitterness in Germany. In time, German extremists would exploit that bitterness to win support.

Vocabulary *Builder*
<u>clause</u> (klawz) *n.* part of a law, treaty, or other written agreement

An American soldier

☑**Checkpoint** **Why did Wilson accept such a harsh treaty?**

☆ **Looking Back and Ahead** In November 1919, the U.S. Senate voted not to ratify the Versailles Treaty and refused to let the United States join the League of Nations. Without the United States, the League could do little when crises shook the world in the 1930s. At Versailles, a French general made a prediction that proved tragically accurate. "This isn't a peace," he said, "it's a twenty-year truce."

Section 4 | **Check Your Progress**

Progress Monitoring ⦿nline
For: Self-test with instant help
Visit: PHSchool.com
Web Code: mya-6164

Comprehension and Critical Thinking

1. **(a) Identify** What were the four main causes of World War I?
   (b) Evaluate Information How did each cause help to draw the world into a global war?

2. **(a) Recall** What were the reasons the United States entered World War I on the Allied side?
   (b) Draw Conclusions Do you think the United States could have avoided getting involved in the war? Explain.

Reading Skill

3. **Ask Questions That Connect to the Present** World War II engulfed the world's nations barely 20 years after the end of World War I. Ask a question that connects the text to the later time period and requires research to answer. You might focus on the role of the United States in the two wars.

Vocabulary *Builder*

4. Write two definitions for each key term: trench warfare, propaganda, reparations. First, write a formal definition for your teacher. Second, write a definition in everyday English for a classmate.

Writing

5. Revise the following passage about World War I for errors in sentence structure, grammar, and mechanics. **Passage:** World war I was called "the war to end ali Wars it took place from nineteen fourteen to 1918. There were many soldiers who were killed. Especially soldiers from European countries. The united states did not enter World war 1 until 1917. Trying to remain neutral but we couldnt. Fighting stopped on november 11 1918 at 11 in the am. The eleventh hour of the Eleventh day of the eleventh month. We honor those who lost there lives in this war on armistice Day in November.

History is the story of change. Changes can result from a combination of causes, including war, natural or human disasters, economic needs, or new political ideas. Over time, new patterns of historical events develop. Identifying them will help you understand historical change.

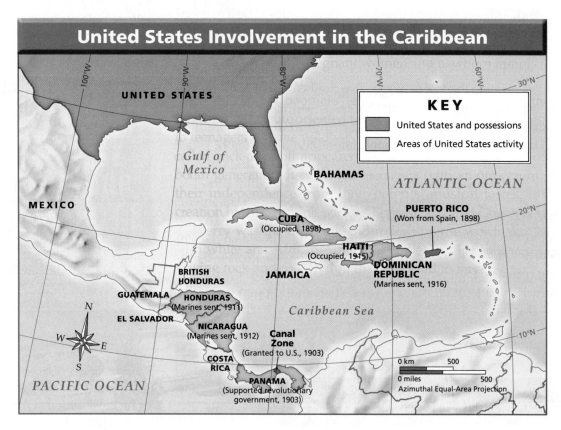

United States Involvement in the Caribbean

KEY
United States and possessions
Areas of United States activity

UNITED STATES

Gulf of Mexico

MEXICO

BAHAMAS

ATLANTIC OCEAN

PUERTO RICO
(Won from Spain, 1898)

CUBA
(Occupied, 1898)

HAITI
(Occupied, 1915)

DOMINICAN
REPUBLIC
(Marines sent, 1916)

BRITISH
HONDURAS

JAMAICA

GUATEMALA HONDURAS
(Marines sent, 1911)

EL SALVADOR

Caribbean Sea

NICARAGUA
(Marines sent, 1912)

Canal
Zone
(Granted to U.S., 1903)

COSTA
RICA

PANAMA
(Supported revolutionary
government, 1903)

PACIFIC OCEAN

0 km   500
0 miles   500
Azimuthal Equal-Area Projection

Learn the Skill

Use these steps to recognize new historical patterns.

1 **Identify the main idea.** Look at the title of the map or chart to determine the subject.

2 **Evaluate information.** How is the information presented? Look for dates of specific events. What important facts do you find out about the events? Framing questions can help you better evaluate the information.

3 **Look for a historical pattern.** Make generalizations about the events. Add information from other sources to determine and extend the historical pattern.

4 **Draw conclusions.** Use the information to draw conclusions about the historical pattern.

Practice the Skill

Answer the following questions about the map on this page.

1 **Identify the main idea.** What is the subject of the map?

2 **Evaluate information.** (a) What happened in 1903? (b) What happened as a result?

3 **Look for a historical pattern.** (a) What do the events on this map show about the change in U.S. foreign policy during this period? (b) What information about the Panama Canal can you add to this map from Section 3?

4 **Draw conclusions.** How did the events on this map affect U.S. power in the Caribbean?

Apply the Skill

See the Review and Assessment at the end of the chapter.

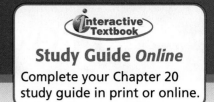

Chapter Summary

Section 1
Eyes on the Pacific

- The United States purchased Alaska and acquired Pacific territories.
- The United States recognized the Pacific islands as important military outposts.
- The Open Door Policy was meant to give the United States equal trading opportunities with other nations in China.

Section 2
The Spanish-American War

- The United States went to war against Spain over Cuba and the Philippines.
- Naval and land battles in the Philippines and in Cuba and Puerto Rico resulted in victory for the United States.
- The United States took control of lands from which it had evicted Spain.

Section 3
The United States and Latin America

- The United States built the Panama Canal to improve global shipping and to strengthen American defense.
- Disease and tough terrain made building the Panama Canal very difficult.
- Foreign policy in the early 1900s aimed to build U.S. influence in Latin America.

Section 4
World War I

- World War I was caused by a combination of international rivalries and alliances.
- The war pitted the Allies and the United States against the Central Powers.
- The Treaty of Versailles imposed a harsh peace and created the League of Nations.

Key Concepts

These notes will help you prepare for questions about key concepts.

U.S. Influence in Asia

Japan
- U.S. Navy warships under Matthew C. Perry sail into Tokyo Bay in 1853.
- Japan opens its ports in 1854.
- Japan begins to modernize.

China
- European powers carve China into spheres of influence.
- U.S. Open Door Policy claims the right of all nations to trade with China.
- Western powers crush Chinese rebels in the Boxer Rebellion.

U.S. Territorial Gains

Territory Acquired or Controlled by the United States in the Pacific
- Alaska: purchased in 1867
- Hawaii: annexed in 1898
- Samoa: a portion annexed in 1899

Territory Gained in Spanish-American War
- Puerto Rico
- Cuba
- Philippines
- Guam

United States in Latin America

- United States backs Panamanians and builds the Panama Canal.
- President Theodore Roosevelt issues the Roosevelt Corollary to the Monroe Doctrine.
- President William Howard Taft promotes dollar diplomacy.
- United States sends troops to many Latin American nations.
- President Woodrow Wilson has U.S. Navy seize Mexican port.
- U.S. General Pershing pursues Pancho Villa into Mexico.

Vocabulary *Builder*

Key Terms

Answer the questions in complete sentences that show your understanding of the key terms.

1. How did imperialism conflict with isolationism in U.S. foreign policy?

2. Why did foreign nations want to establish spheres of influence in China?

3. Why was Theodore Roosevelt's foreign policy seen as a corollary to the Monroe Doctrine?

4. Why was an isthmus a good place to build a canal?

5. How did British propaganda influence American opinion about World War I?

Comprehension and Critical Thinking

6. **(a) Recall** Why was Secretary of State Seward interested in buying Alaska?
   (b) Detect Points of View How does the cartoon below reflect what many Americans thought of the purchase at first?
   (c) Identify Economic Benefits How did buying Alaska provide economic benefits?

7. **(a) Identify** In which regions of the world did European powers gain control by 1900?
   (b) Evaluate Information What impact did the expansion policies of European countries have on the foreign policy of the United States?

8. **(a) Recall** What event was the immediate cause of the Spanish-American War?
   (b) Draw Conclusions Do you think this event by itself was enough to start the war? Why or why not?

9. **(a) Explain** How did the United States gain an overseas empire?
   (b) Detect Points of View Why do you think some critics felt that having an empire was against American ideals?

10. **(a) Summarize** How did Roosevelt apply his "big stick" policy to Latin America?
    (b) Compare How was Taft's dollar diplomacy like the Roosevelt Corollary?

History Reading Skill

11. **Frame Research Questions** Frame one research question for each section in this chapter. Remember to frame questions that go beyond the text and require research to answer.

Writing

12. **Write a paragraph about one of these issues:**
    - Take a stand on American expansion in the Pacific.
    - Analyze U.S. relations with Latin America from the 1890s to 1915.
    - Summarize the Spanish-American War.

    Your paragraph should:
    - Begin with a sentence that states the main idea about your subject.
    - Include facts, reasons, and example from the chapter to develop your ideas.

    When you are finished, exchange papers with another student. Correct errors. Try to connect the supporting information as much as possible.

13. **Write an Editorial:**
    Imagine that you are a newspaper editor who either strongly agrees or disagrees with President Roosevelt's policy of gunboat diplomacy. Write a brief editorial that expresses your views.

Skills for Life

Recognize New Historical Patterns
Create a list of key events related to the Spanish-American War, based on this chapter. Use your list and the map in Section 2 to answer the questions.

14. What is the subject of the map?

15. **(a)** What key event took place on February 15, 1898?
    (b) What happened as a result of this event?

16. Based on the events on your list, what historical pattern can you identify?

17. Why did this pattern emerge at this time?

Test Yourself

1. **The chief goal of the Open Door Policy was to**

    A divide China into spheres of influence.

    B open Japan for trade.

    C put down the Boxer Rebellion.

    D protect U.S. trading rights in China.

2. **In the late 1800s, expansionists argued that the United States**

    A should avoid involvement with other nations.

    B needed new markets for its products.

    C should reject the Turner thesis.

    D should accept the Roosevelt Corollary.

Refer to the cartoon below to answer Question 3.

THE BIG STICK IN THE CARIBBEAN SEA

3. **What is the subject of this cartoon?**

    A yellow journalism

    B the Spanish-American War

    C the Roosevelt Corollary

    D the war in the Philippines

Document-Based Questions

Task: Look at Documents 1 and 2, and answer their accompanying questions. Then, use the documents and your knowledge of history to complete this writing assignment:

> Write a short essay comparing the viewpoints of supporters and opponents of overseas expansion. Evaluate the validity of the arguments on each side.

Document 1: In January 1899, Senator Orville H. Platt explained why he supported annexing the Philippines. *What arguments does Platt give?*

"I believe the same force was behind . . . our ships in Manila Bay that was behind the landing of Pilgrims on Plymouth Rock. . . . [We] have been chosen to carry forward this great work of uplifting humanity . . . . From the time of the landing on Plymouth Rock in the spirit of the Declaration of Independence, in the spirit of the Constitution, believing that all men are equal and endowed by their Creator with inalienable rights, believing that governments derive their just powers from the consent of the governed, we have spread that civilization . . . until it stood at the Pacific Ocean looking ever westward."

Document 2: Senator George F. Hoar responded to Platt's argument in favor of annexing the Philippines. *Why does Senator Hoar oppose annexing the Philippines?*

"You have no right at the cannon's mouth to impose on an unwilling people your Declaration of Independence and your Constitution and your notions of freedom and notions of what is good. . . . Now the people of the Philippine Islands are clearly a nation— a people three and one-third times as numerous as our fathers were when they set up this nation. . . . The people there have got a government, with courts and judges . . . and it is proposed to turn your guns on them and say, 'We think that our notion of government is better than the notion you have got yourselves.'"

Writing Workshop

Writing for Assessment

▶ Introduction

In writing for assessment, you write an essay in response to a test question. To write a successful essay, you need to understand what is being asked in the question, answer the question clearly, and support your answer with examples or details. You also need to do all these things within a stated time limit. Essays written for assessment should have the following characteristics:

- a clearly worded thesis statement that answers the question
- strong supporting information that backs up the thesis statement
- a clear, logical organization
- a conclusion that sums up your views

Assignment On the following pages, you will learn how to write for assessment by responding in an essay to a test question. You will get step-by-step instructions. Each step will include an example from a sample test essay tracing U.S. involvement in World War I from 1914 to 1917.

Read the instructions and the examples. Then, follow each step to plan and write an essay of 300 to 400 words.

> **Write an essay that summarizes U.S. foreign policies from 1853 to 1915.**

▶ Prewriting

Budget your time. Before you begin to write an essay, note how much time you have. If the essay question is part of a larger test, check to see what percentage of the test's grade the essay represents. In other words, if the essay counts for 20 percent of the total score, plan to spend 20 percent of your time to write the essay. If you have 30 minutes for your essay, spend about 5 minutes on prewriting (understanding the question, writing a thesis statement, and creating a rough outline); from 20 to 25 minutes on actually writing the essay; and from 2 to 5 minutes on reading over the essay and making revisions and corrections.

Understand the essay-question prompt. Begin by looking closely at the essay-question prompt and identifying the key words. The chart on the facing page shows examples of key words most often used in essay prompts.

For a review of the steps in the writing process, see the **Historian's Toolkit, *Write Like a Historian.***

Essay Question Prompts	
Key Word	**What It Means**
analyze	break the topic down into its parts; show causes and effects
compare	show how two or more things are similar
contrast	show how two or more things are different
defend	support an argument or position with facts, reasons, examples, and logic
define	state the meaning of a term; describe the basic nature of something
discuss	make observations about a subject in detail (similar to *examine* and *explain*)
evaluate	judge the significance, condition, or worth of something
summarize	give a condensed account or overview of an issue, event, or sequence of events
trace	describe a sequence of events; follow the development or progress of something

When you read the essay question, underline or circle the key words, as well as the subject and time period you are to discuss and any special areas the prompt asks you to cover.

Sample essay question:

key word   *subject*   *areas to cover*
Trace the U.S. involvement in World War I, from neutrality to entrance

           time period
into the war, from 1914 to 1917.

Write a thesis statement. Based on your knowledge, write a sentence that clearly responds to the prompt. As in any other piece of writing, your thesis statement should present the main idea of your essay.

Note your main points in a rough outline. Create a quick outline that lists the main points you expect to cover in the order that you expect to follow. Be sure that your outline reflects the essay question prompt. For example, if the prompt asks you to "trace" something, you may want to use chronological order.

Sample thesis statement:
The United States had been neutral when war broke out in 1914, but entry to the war seemed inevitable by the spring of 1917 because a series of incidents had pushed the nation into the conflict.

► Drafting

Write a short introductory paragraph. In the first paragraph of your essay, introduce your subject and write your thesis statement.

Support your thesis with examples and details. Devote one body paragraph to each of the main points in your outline. Make sure you cover everything that the prompt requests. Include relevant, accurate information to develop each point you discuss.

Write a strong conclusion. In your final paragraph, sum up your support of your thesis statement.

Writing Workshop *continued*

▶ Model Essay

Read the following model of an essay discussing the involvement of the United States in World War I from 1914 to 1917. Notice how it includes the characteristics you have learned about.

The United States and the War in Europe, 1914–1917

The thesis statement identifies the main idea about U.S. isolationism before WW I and hints at why the United States entered the war.

In the fall of 1914, Americans felt far removed from the European rush to war. By the spring of 1917, however, everything had changed. In less than three years, a string of events had pulled a reluctant United States into joining the battle in Europe.

Before the war, the United States had followed a policy of isolationism, keeping itself out of the complicated system of European alliances. President Wilson insisted on U.S. neutrality when the war started.

Despite its neutrality, the United States traded more with the Allies than with the Central powers. When Germany began to blockade Britain with U-boats, American ships were affected. In 1915, the sinking of the *Lusitania*, a British passenger ship with more than 100 Americans aboard, increased anti-German sentiment in the United States.

Examples and details in these paragraphs support the thesis. Words highlighted in yellow show how chronology was used to trace the events.

In 1916, President Woodrow Wilson was reelected with the campaign slogan, "He kept us out of war." Wilson tried to convince the warring European countries to end the fighting. However, Wilson's efforts failed.

The tide in America turned toward war in early 1917 when the Zimmermann telegram came to light. Germany had secretly offered to help Mexico seize southwestern U.S. states if Mexico joined the Central powers. Americans were outraged.

The conclusion reviews the content of the essay and restates the thesis.

So, it is not surprising that Congress voted overwhelmingly in favor of entering the war in April, 1917. The nation discovered that the ocean separating it from Europe could not guarantee protection from war.

▶ Revising

After completing your draft, read it again carefully to find ways to make your writing better. Here are some questions to ask yourself.

Revise to strengthen your thesis

- Do the introduction and the thesis statement clearly respond to the prompt?
- Do the body paragraphs cover the issues set forth in the prompt and develop the thesis statement?
- Does the conclusion tie up the essay?

Revise to use varied and clear vocabulary and helpful transitions

- Does the essay avoid repetition?
- Does the essay include transitions showing relationships appropriate to the key words in the prompt?

Revise to meet written English-language conventions

- Are all sentences complete, with a subject and a verb?
- Are all the words spelled correctly?
- Are all proper nouns capitalized?
- Are all sentences punctuated properly?

▶ Rubric for Self-Assessment

Evaluate your essay written for assessment using the following rating scale:

	Score 4	Score 3	Score 2	Score 1
Organization	Supports the thesis with logically ordered paragraphs covering the areas specified in the prompt; paragraphs have an organizing principle that suits the prompt	Uses a reasonably clear organization but occasionally fails to follow it or includes less relevant information	Chooses an organization not suited to the topic (for example, uses chronological order for a comparison-and-contrast essay)	Shows lack of organizational strategy
Presentation	Clearly and accurately responds to the prompt and covers the areas specified in the prompt; uses facts, examples, and reasons intelligently to support the thesis; clearly links all supporting information to the thesis	Responds to the prompt accurately and covers the areas specified but does not go into greater depth; links most but not all supporting information to the thesis; could use more support	Responds to the prompt accurately but does not cover all the areas requested; includes some incorrect supporting information; does not link supporting information to the thesis	Does not respond accurately to the prompt; does not include a thesis; fails to provide any facts, reasons, or examples to support the thesis
Use of Language	Varies sentence structure and vocabulary successfully; includes almost no mechanical errors	Uses some variety in sentence structure and vocabulary; includes several mechanical errors	Uses the same types of sentences without varying them; repeats words; includes many mechanical errors	Writes incomplete sentences; uses language poorly; sounds confused; includes many mechanical errors

LINKING PAST TO PRESENT
THE UNITED STATES IN THE MODERN WORLD

Table of Contents

Key Terms

baby boom, p. 720
benevolent association, p. 715
creativity, p. 722
diversity, p. 714
ghetto, p. 731

refugee, p. 740
satellite city, p. 718
services, p. 726
suburbanite, p. 719

Immigrants have made our population and economy grow and refreshed our traditions. Their hopes and dreams for a better life have become an important part of the history of our nation.

A New Wave of Immigration

When Christopher Columbus reached the Americas in 1492, his crew included English, Irish, African, and Jewish sailors. Since Columbus's voyage, immigration to the United States has followed the same pattern of **diversity,** or differences. You learned that waves of immigration drew millions of immigrants to the United States in the early 1800s. Another great wave of immigration began in the 1880s. Before it ended in the 1920s, it drew millions of people from southern and eastern Europe to the East Coast of the United States. At the same time, many Asians crossed the Pacific Ocean. Most of the Asians settled in the American West.

As the wave of immigration continued, so, too, did anti-immigrant feeling. You have read how most Asian immigration was banned in the early 1900s. In the 1920s, Congress passed laws restricting most other immigration from outside the Americas. This limited the wave of immigration to the United States for more than 40 years.

Immigrants from Europe wait to be processed at Ellis Island, Upper New York Bay, in the 1920s.

Chinese immigrants passing through immigration at Angel Island, San Francisco, in the 1920s.

A Latino wedding in
the United States, 1929

San Francisco's
Chinatown

Emigration From the Americas and Asia

Meanwhile, emigration continued from the Americas. In the early years of the 1900s, unrest drove many Mexicans to the barrios, or Latino neighborhoods of cities in the American Southwest. Barrios offered newcomers a sense of security. Here the newcomers lived among relatives and friends from the same Mexican community. They formed social clubs and became proprietors of Mexican American grocery stores, bakeries, restaurants, and barber shops.

The largest barrio was in Los Angeles. By 1925, Los Angeles had a larger Mexican population than any other city in the world except Mexico City.

Thriving immigrant neighborhoods grew up in other American cities. San Francisco's Chinatown became the largest Asian neighborhood in the United States. It had newspapers, schools, and places of worship familiar to the Chinese immigrants. It also had **benevolent associations**—groups that looked after the welfare of their members. The associations fought discriminatory laws, provided aid to needy families, and ensured that workers were cared for properly. They also helped immigrants locate people from their home regions of China.

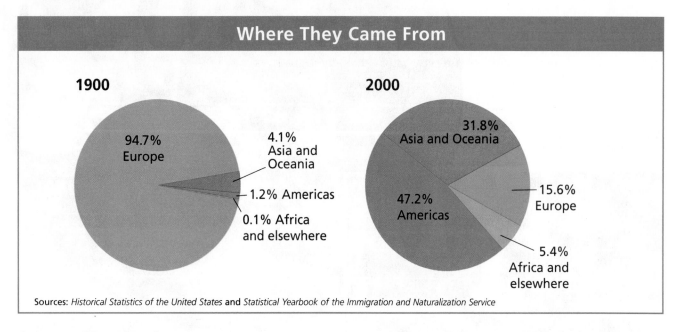

Where They Came From

1900

- 94.7% Europe
- 4.1% Asia and Oceania
- 1.2% Americas
- 0.1% Africa and elsewhere

2000

- 31.8% Asia and Oceania
- 15.6% Europe
- 47.2% Americas
- 5.4% Africa and elsewhere

Sources: *Historical Statistics of the United States* and *Statistical Yearbook of the Immigration and Naturalization Service*

Sources of Immigration

Between 1900 and 2000, there has been a dramatic shift in the source of immigration to the United States. **Critical Thinking: *Interpret Graphs*** *From what region of the world did most immigrants to the United States come in 1900? From what region did most come one hundred years later?*

American businesses benefit from people whose roots are from all corners of the world.

New Sources of Immigration

In 1965, Congress ended the old quota system that favored European immigration. New laws made it easier for non-Europeans to enter the country. Since then, immigrants from around the world have been arriving in the United States at a rate faster than at any time since the early 1900s.

As in the past, new immigrants generally make their first American home in urban areas with others who speak their native language. This has led to the growth of ethnic neighborhoods such as San Francisco's Chinatown and "Little Havana" in Miami, Florida. People from Eastern Europe, Southeast Asia, Central America, the Middle East, and Southern Asia have also established immigrant neighborhoods in American cities.

Today, as in the past, immigrants face many challenges. However, in the past few years, many recent immigrants have risen to leadership positions in American business, culture, government, and the military.

Immigration Policy

Although most immigrants enter the United States legally, others do so without permission. In recent years, Americans have become very concerned with the issue of illegal immigration. In 1986, Congress passed a law that allowed people who had arrived illegally before 1982 to apply for citizenship. At the same time, it increased penalties for employers who hired workers who had entered the country illegally.

By some estimates, one third of the illegal immigrants in the country live in California. In 1994, California voters passed a law that banned schooling and health services for illegal immigrants. However, the law was immediately challenged in state courts and has never gone into effect. The nation still struggles with the question of how to control illegal immigration without depriving legal immigrants of their rights.

The American Identity

In an auditorium in Austin, Texas, a woman from Costa Rica has just become an American citizen. Interviewed by a reporter, she says:

> " When I first came, I felt like a stranger, but now I feel like I am part of America. That's all I wanted—the American dream. "
>
> —Karolyn Mora, interview, April 6, 2001

Mora was among 473 immigrants from 73 countries who had just become American citizens. Officials at the ceremony had never seen so many nations represented before.

Today, people from every corner of the globe flock to the United States. Rather than melting away our differences, the American experience has led us to accept differences.

Americans today feel comfortable retaining important parts of their diverse cultures and accepting parts of our national culture. Increasing diversity has brought new challenges, as groups have struggled to protect their rights. But diversity has given us strength. Among the most important of these is the acceptance of differences. This has helped greatly enrich American culture.

As President Lyndon Johnson said:

> " [Our] land flourished because it was fed from so many sources—because it was nourished by so many cultures and traditions, and people. "
>
> —President Lyndon B. Johnson, 1965

This Mexican American girl commemorates her culture with traditional dress and flags.

Korean Americans celebrate their joint heritage with the flags, symbols, and dress of two cultures.

Assessment

1. **Recall:** How did sources of immigration change after 1965?

2. **Make Inferences:** Do you think life is harder for new immigrants than it was for immigrants a century ago? Explain your answer.

A Changing Population

Big, shiny cars
on a Philadelphia
street in the 1950s

American cities lured more than immigrants in the early 1900s. As you have learned, a new Industrial Revolution resulted in a massive migration of Americans from farm to city. That migration continued into the 1950s. People flooded to the cities because there were jobs there. Urban industries provided millions of jobs for people whose employment opportunities were limited in poor rural areas.

Growth of the Middle Class

The new city dwellers found many attractions in city life. They attended sporting events, bought newspapers, shopped at department stores, and supported urban economies in many other ways. They used new means of transportation—buses, subways, or cable cars—to reach their jobs. For the first 50 years of the century, their activities created a thriving economy in the cities of the United States.

That trend reversed itself in the middle of the twentieth century. By the millions, middle-class Americans were moving out of the cities to settle in the surrounding suburbs. The migration fed new growth in the suburbs, and suburban communities spread farther out from city centers, creating huge areas with their own satellite cities—smaller cities located near large ones.

A historic government program helped spur middle-class growth. Near the end of World War II, the federal government acted to help the generation of soldiers whose lives had been interrupted by the conflict. A GI Bill of Rights helped returning veterans set up farms and businesses. It also granted loans to veterans to pay for college.

The leafy suburb of
Fairfax, Delaware, in
the 1950s

The GI Bill helped fuel a remarkable long-term economic boom during the 1950s. With a college education, graduates were able to command more responsible jobs. With growing families and larger incomes, more people were able to buy houses. Many bought homes in suburbs. Shopping centers with modern department stores sprang up near the new suburban housing. No longer did consumers have to travel to the city to buy what they wanted.

During the 1950s, automobiles became an important part of middle-class life. By 1960, for example, nine out of ten **suburbanites**, people who lived in suburbs, owned a car. To accommodate the increase in automobiles, the federal government built thousands of miles of highways. The new highway system gave a special boost to the automobile and trucking industries. With good highways, Americans could travel more easily for business or pleasure.

Aided by the GI Bill of Rights, American veterans enroll at Indiana University, 1947.

Those Left Behind

Despite the growing prosperity, poverty remained a problem for many Americans. Many rural areas lagged behind in income, education, and health care. Also, as more middle-class Americans began to move out of cities to the suburbs, conditions grew worse in the slum areas at the center of many large cities. People who lived in these "inner cities" faced poverty, overcrowding, and high rates of crime and drug abuse.

The 1960s saw new efforts to improve these conditions. The federal government set up sweeping programs such as Head Start, which was designed to help poor children acquire the skills they needed to do well in school. Many state governments expanded welfare programs, which provided payments to jobless families.

Critics objected that many of these programs were too expensive and did not always work. In the 1980s, the federal government sought to scale down many social programs. But Americans continued to seek ways to help the significant minority of people left behind by the nation's growing prosperity.

An urban slum, 1960s

The Baby Boom

The prosperity of the 1950s increased Americans' confidence in the future. This, in turn, helped lead to a **baby boom,** a soaring birth rate, in the United States.

How important was the baby boom to American society? Consider these statistics: During the whole of the 1930s, the population of the United States grew by only 9 million. In the 1950s, it grew by 29 million people.

Improvements in health care and nutrition sustained the baby boom. Better care for pregnant women and newborn infants meant that more babies survived.

As the "baby boomers" grew to their teenage years, they helped create a new culture oriented toward youth. Television shows appealing to teenagers became wildly popular. In the 1950s, a new type of music called rock-and-roll appeared, which became the sound of the baby boom generation. It provided teenagers with an opportunity to show their independence from their parents' musical tastes. It led to the creation of teenage idols such as Elvis Presley and Chuck Berry.

Berry was the first rock-and-roller to write words that entertained both white and African American audiences. He achieved this with a driving rock-and-roll rhythm that was hard to forget.

Evidence of the baby boom: full hospital nursery, 1951

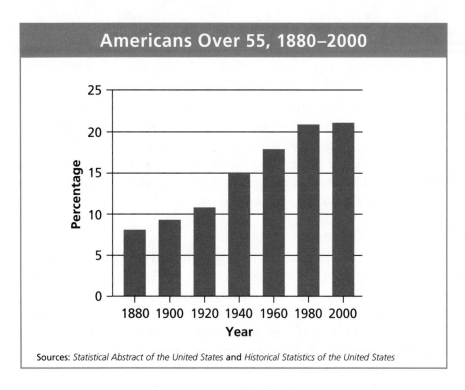

Americans Over 55, 1880–2000

Percentage (y-axis: 0, 5, 10, 15, 20, 25)

Year (x-axis: 1880, 1900, 1920, 1940, 1960, 1980, 2000)

Sources: *Statistical Abstract of the United States* and *Historical Statistics of the United States*

Americans Age

The percentage of Americans over the age of 55 has steadily increased since 1880. **Critical Thinking:** *Interpret Graphs Between what years did the percentage of Americans over the age of 55 increase the most?*

Baby Boomers Grow Older

Let's spring ahead a half century. By the early 2000s, the first baby boomers were approaching retirement. The birthrate had dropped. Overall, the U.S. population was aging. This situation was labeled "the graying of America."

Our aging population presents challenges to both older and younger Americans. Today, the baby boomers are still young enough to be active. However, as they age, who will care for them? How will they pay their medical bills? How will they find appropriate housing?

Fortunately, a number of organizations focus on issues that concern older Americans. These organizations include government agencies such as Social Security and Medicare, which provide pensions and medical assistance to the elderly. They include private groups, such as the American Association of Retired Persons (AARP).

Older Americans have political clout. A greater proportion of older Americans than younger ones vote and participate in the political process.

Still active: baby boomers in the twenty-first century

Assessment

1. **Recall:** How did the GI Bill of Rights contribute to economic growth?

2. **Draw Conclusions:** What do you think led to the steady increase in the percentage of Americans over the age of 55 during the 1900s? Explain.

You have learned that the Industrial Revolution transformed the United States from a farming economy into a manufacturing economy. That process continued well into the twentieth century. During these years, Americans built the world's leading industrial economy. Railroads and highways crisscrossed the nation. Skyscrapers became a symbol of the American urban landscape.

American Creativity

An important element in building the massive American economy was **creativity**—the ability to use imagination to develop new and original ideas or things. As you have learned, American creativity helped develop the assembly line. The assembly line enabled the Ford Motor Company to build an automobile at a price that the average American could afford. Auto sales spurred growth in other parts of the economy. This provided employment for millions of Americans in steel mills, oil refineries, auto plants, and other factories.

By 1929, the United States had the world's mightiest industrial economy. But even this industrial power could not protect Americans from the disaster that was just over the horizon.

Assembly line at the Ford company, 1920s

The Great Depression

The United States never experienced an economic setback quite as bad as the one that struck at the end of the 1920s. For the whole of the 1930s, the United States suffered through a drastic downturn that left tens of millions of people jobless and some of them homeless. In 1933, the worst year of the Great Depression, one out of every four U.S. workers was unemployed.

Franklin Delano Roosevelt took office as President in 1933. He believed that the government had the obligation to use all its powers to end the Great Depression. Roosevelt won approval in Congress for a series of programs aimed at restoring the country's economic health. These programs were called the New Deal.

The New Deal was a turning point in the relationship between the federal government and individual citizens. Since the 1930s, the federal government has taken more responsibility for controlling the economic cycles. Its efforts are aimed at ensuring that the U.S. economy never again suffers a downturn like that of the Great Depression.

Still, many critics argued that the New Deal went too far. It ran counter to the tradition of laissez faire, which was based on the idea that the government should play a limited role in the economy. Instead, the New Deal increased the size of the federal government and the role of government in people's lives. Today, people still disagree about the impact of the New Deal.

Families of the unemployed on the road to California, 1937

The hard life: vegetable harvesters in Calipatria, California, 1939

A New Deal poster celebrates farm and industrial employment.

Workers Fight for Better Conditions

The hardships of the Great Depression gave a major boost to the union movement. Under the New Deal, a law called the Wagner Act protected American workers from unfair management practices, such as firing a worker for joining a union. It also guaranteed workers the right to collective bargaining. As you have learned, collective bargaining is the right of a union to negotiate for its members as a group.

The Wagner Act helped union membership grow from 3 million to 9 million during the 1930s. Still, it took many bitter strikes in the 1930s and 1940s before unions were accepted in many basic industries. By the 1950s, American factory workers benefited from the general prosperity of the nation.

In the 1950s, the struggle for union recognition turned to agricultural workers. They were among the poorest-paid workers in the United States.

One of those poorly paid workers was César Chávez. For much of his early life, Chávez labored in California fruit and vegetable fields. Then, in 1952, he decided to devote his life improving the lot of his fellow farm workers. For years, Chávez traveled from camp to camp, getting workers to join the union. When farm owners refused to recognize the union, Chávez led workers on strike. By the late 1970s, Chávez's union, the United Farm Workers of America, had become the leading voice of farm workers in the United States.

César Chávez leads united farmers on strike, 1966. At right, a button urges people not to purchase grapes picked by nonunion labor.

Construction workers on strike during the Great Depression

Working conditions for young people today are vastly different from what they were at the beginning of the 1900s.

Fighting Child Labor

Until the 1930s, young children often worked long hours in the nation's factories. They were expected to supplement their parents' low incomes by doing work that was hard and dirty, and often dangerous.

In 1916, Congress passed an act banning goods produced by child labor from interstate commerce. The law forbade any manufacturer or dealer from shipping to another country or state any item produced by children under the age of 14. However, in 1918, the Supreme Court declared that the law violated the U.S. Constitution.

The Great Depression changed attitudes toward the role of government in the economy. More Americans came to demand that government power be used to reduce the evils of child labor. Adults who could not find jobs also saw the new laws as a way of opening up more jobs to them.

In 1938, the Fair Labor Standards Act put real limits on child labor. The law prohibits employment of young people under the age of 16 except in certain after-school jobs. It also requires employers to pay young workers the legal minimum wage. In addition, it limits the age of child laborers to 16 and over, or to 18 if the occupation is hazardous. This time, the Supreme Court upheld the law.

Despite the law, child labor remains a problem in industries that employ migrant farmworkers. It is also an issue because some American companies import products that may have been made in foreign countries by child workers.

Assessment

1. **Recall:** How did the role of children in the economy change?

2. **Draw Conclusions:** Why do you think the Great Depression increased support for the union movement?

At its founding, the United States was a nation of farmers. As you have learned, the Industrial Revolution transformed the nation into an industrial powerhouse. By 1915, heavy industry dominated the U.S. economy. Later, new technologies and increasing prosperity focused the economy on consumer goods. The United States soon became the world's leading manufacturer of consumer goods.

From Manufacturing to Services

By the late 1940s, a boom in electronics—led by radio and television—produced many more factory jobs. Job growth centered in the urban centers of the Northeast and Midwest.

From the 1960s, the U. S. economy underwent a historic shift. The economy began losing manufacturing jobs—but gaining service jobs at the same time. **Services** are economic actions that one person performs for another. Today, the United States is the world's leading producer of services. Teachers, barbers, lawyers, engineers, police, and salespeople all perform services. Other jobs in the service section include financial services (banking, insurance, investment), online services (Web design, online marketing, advertising), and health care.

Economic Change
Between 1960 and 2000, there was a dramatic change in the nature of the United States economy. **Critical Thinking:** *Interpret Graphs In what decade did the value of services produced in the U.S. first exceed the value of goods produced?*

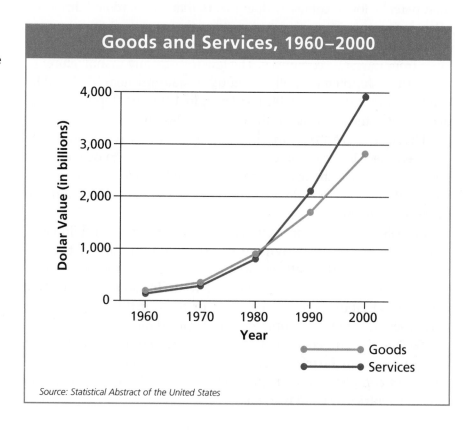

Goods and Services, 1960–2000

Source: Statistical Abstract of the United States

New Technologies

By the 1980s, the U.S. economy was becoming deeply influenced by a new technology: computers. The first electronic computers were built in the 1940s. They were huge. One early model, called ENIAC, weighed 30 tons and took up as much room as a railroad car. Despite its vast size, however, ENIAC was very slow, and its computing powers were limited. Early computers were generally limited to the government, the military, and large businesses.

Computers took a giant leap forward in the 1960s with the invention of the microchip. One tiny chip can contain millions of bits of information. The chip allowed scientists to build smaller, faster, and less expensive computers. By the 1980s, scientists had introduced the personal computer. Now, ordinary Americans could buy computers for home use.

Today, no part of American society has been left untouched by this new technology. As computers play increasingly important roles in business, government, and homes, computer-related careers are booming. Many of the new jobs involve the storage, use, and transfer of information. For this reason, economists refer to our times as the "information age."

New technologies create new challenges and new jobs.

Even such traditional jobs as trucking and farming now require computer skills. At the beginning of the twenty-first century, well over half of all American workers reported some use of computers on the job.

The revolution in personal computers has created exciting opportunities for careers. In the process, it has transformed the location of work itself. Many Americans are no longer bound by the commute to and from work. Today's computers and the Internet have made it possible for many people to make a living from their homes.

The computer is not the only new technology that has transformed the American economy and daily life. The laser, invented in the 1950s, has a wide variety of uses, from CD players to supermarket scanners to surgery. The development of atomic energy has also had a major impact on both industry and the military.

Computers and the Internet have made it possible for more people to make a living from their homes.

Inside an industrial powerhouse: heavy industry supported the booming U.S. economy in the middle of the 1900s.

Skilled Workers in Demand

In the 1950s, a typical American worker was a white male who had graduated from high school. Such a worker often had a secure 40-hour-a-week job where he would hope to stay until retiring at age 65.

Today, someone entering the work force can expect to have four or five different jobs during his or her working life. The face of the U.S. labor force has changed.

Computers have affected the nature of work and the status of American workers. As we have seen, they have given a boost to many new service occupations. As the number of service jobs has increased, the number of manufacturing jobs has declined. Much factory work has shifted to overseas plants, where labor costs are lower.

The loss of these unskilled and semiskilled jobs has cost many workers their jobs. Today, there are fewer job openings for workers who do not have a specific skill. To compete in the job market today, many unskilled workers find they must gain new skills. More and more workers enter job-training programs or to return to school to secure degrees.

In recent years, political leaders in both parties have focused on improving education. "Public schools are America's great hope," said President George W. Bush, "and making them work for every child is America's great duty."

The Importance of Education

There is a clear relationship between level of education and level of income. **Critical Thinking:** *Interpret Graphs Based on the information in the graph, write a general statement about the relationship between education and income.*

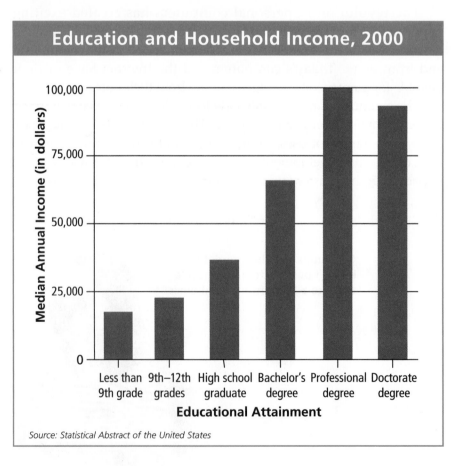

Education and Household Income, 2000

Median Annual Income (in dollars)

Educational Attainment: Less than 9th grade, 9th–12th grades, High school graduate, Bachelor's degree, Professional degree, Doctorate degree

Source: Statistical Abstract of the United States

These young people volunteered to clean up a local beach.

Volunteers working at a Los Angeles soup kitchen help feed the hungry.

Prosperity and Poverty

Even though the United States has the world's most productive economy, the benefits of new technology have not reached all Americans. Although many Americans prosper, many others are still held back by the hand of poverty.

This is especially true of people who live in areas once dominated by major industries. During the 1970s, industries in New England and the Midwest began a steady decline. The industries were unable to compete with goods produced in foreign factories. Numerous American factories closed down, throwing people out of work.

In time, the areas of declining factory production came to be known as the rust belt. The term calls to mind aging and abandoned factories. In the rust belt, large numbers of Americans were looking for work, trying their best to get by on limited funds.

At the same time, economic misfortune hit other Americans. Older citizens, Native Americans, and some residents of inner cities struggled to make ends meet. Many inner-city residents did not own cars. Mass-transit systems were often not an efficient means of commuting from the inner city to the suburbs. As a result, people who lived in the inner city earned less than people living outside the inner city.

Americans have long prided themselves at living in a land of plenty. However, poverty cast a long shadow across the land of plenty.

Assessment

1. **Recall:** What is a service job?

2. **Analyze Cause and Effect:** Why was it harder today for someone without an education to earn a good living than it was in the past?

The Era of Civil Rights

As you have seen, the Civil War amendments to the Constitution were a major step forward for African Americans. The Thirteenth Amendment ended slavery. The Fourteenth Amendment guaranteed citizenship rights to African Americans and others. The Fifteenth Amendment protected the right to vote.

By themselves, the Thirteenth, Fourteenth, and Fifteenth Amendments did not bring equal rights for African Americans. As you read in Chapter 12, the 1896 Supreme Court ruling in *Plessy* v. *Ferguson* was a huge step backward for civil rights in the United States. For the first half of the 1900s, the Plessy ruling supported widespread legalized segregation in the South.

The Era of Segregation

Although segregation existed in all parts of the country, it was especially damaging in the South. There, African Americans and whites could not ride in the same streetcars or railway cars. They could not drink from the same water fountains. They could not eat in the same restaurants, be treated in the same hospitals, or be buried in the same cemeteries.

Segregation took many forms. In many public places, African Americans were permitted to drink only from restricted water fountains.

FOR COLORED ONLY

Partly to escape these restrictions, large numbers of African Americans moved from the South to the North and the West in the years after 1910. This movement became known as the great migration. African Americans migrated in hopes of getting good jobs and living in a society free of segregation. Their hopes were not always met. In the North and West, African Americans often found themselves closed out of many jobs. They encountered housing discrimination often. Many ended up living in **ghettos,** poor sections of cities.

In the 1920s, large numbers of African American musicians, artists, and writers settled in Harlem, in New York City. "Harlem was like a great magnet for the negro intellectual," said one black writer. This gathering of African American artists and musicians led to the Harlem Renaissance, a rebirth of African American culture.

During the Great Depression of the 1930s, African Americans were especially hard hit. They were often the last to be hired and the first to be fired from their jobs. Because African Americans were often poorer than most other Americans, they had smaller savings to help them through the difficult times.

World War II, which the United States fought from 1941 to 1945, spurred attempts to win equal rights. Fighting in segregated units, African American soldiers contributed to victory. After the war, they were ready to challenge discrimination at home. In recognition of their service, President Harry Truman ended segregation in the military.

African American painter Jacob Lawrence created a series of paintings that he called *The Migration of the Negro.* Of this painting, Lawrence explained: "In every town, Negroes were leaving by the hundreds to go North and enter into Northern industry."

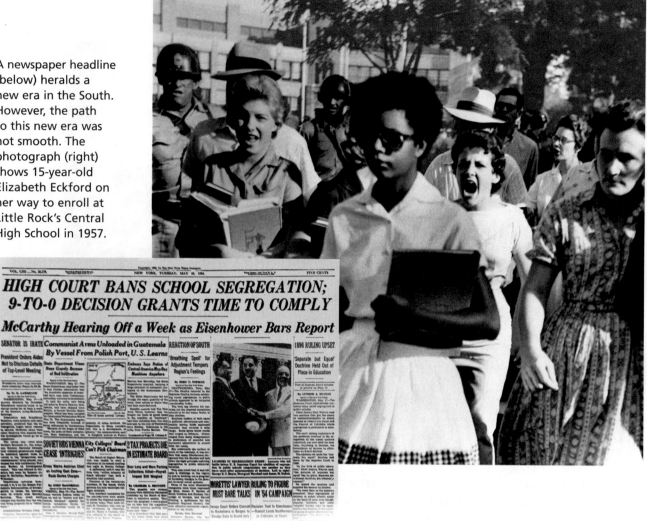

A newspaper headline (below) heralds a new era in the South. However, the path to this new era was not smooth. The photograph (right) shows 15-year-old Elizabeth Eckford on her way to enroll at Little Rock's Central High School in 1957.

HIGH COURT BANS SCHOOL SEGREGATION; 9-TO-0 DECISION GRANTS TIME TO COMPLY

McCarthy Hearing Off a Week as Eisenhower Bars Report

The Movement Gains Force

A major breakthrough in the fight for civil rights came in 1954 with a Supreme Court ruling known as *Brown* v. *Board of Education of Topeka*. Lawyers for the NAACP argued that school segregation violated the Fourteenth Amendment, which promised all citizens "equal protection of the laws." The Court agreed. Overturning the decision in *Plessy* v. *Ferguson*, the court ordered that school segregation was unconstitutional. Chief Justice Earl Warren wrote:

> "We conclude that in the field of public education the doctrine of 'separate but equal' has no place. Separate educational facilities are inherently unequal."
> —Earl Warren, *Brown* v. *Board of Education of Topeka*

Despite the Brown ruling, many southern schools were slow to integrate. Central High School in Little Rock Arkansas, became a battleground for integration. In 1957, federal troops had to be sent to the high school to protect the African American students trying to enroll at the schools.

A second turning point came in 1955. Rosa Parks, a seamstress in Montgomery, Alabama, refused to give up her seat in a bus to a white person. Her arrest led to an African American boycott of Montgomery's buses. It was led by a young minister named Martin Luther King, Jr. The boycott lasted 382 days and brought Rosa Parks, Dr. King, and their cause to the attention of the world.

After Montgomery, Dr. King led many nonviolent protests against segregation. Often, the protests were met with violence. Dr. King encouraged his followers to maintain their peaceful efforts. "If we protest courageously, and yet with dignity and Christian love, when the future history books are written, somebody will have to say, 'There lived a race of people, . . . who had the moral courage to stand up for their rights.'"

King and other civil rights leaders inspired other Americans. Many young northerners traveled south to join in the struggle. White and black protesters called Freedom Riders rode together on buses throughout the South. Other protesters sat at segregated lunch counters, where they were often taunted and pelted with food.

It took courage to participate in nonviolent demonstrations. Police sometimes used attack dogs or water hoses against protesters. More than once, mobs bombed the houses and churches of African American leaders. Many civil rights workers, both black and white, were attacked or killed.

Martin Luther King, Jr., muses in his cell after his arrest for protesting segregation in Birmingham, Alabama, in 1963.

Peaceful protests like this one gained nationwide attention and growing support for the civil rights movement.

Malcolm X was one of a new generation of more radical civil rights leaders. He argued that African Americans could succeed only if they separated from white society.

Signs of Change

By the 1960s, some African Americans were turning away from Dr. King's ideas of nonviolence. Leaders such as Malcolm X demanded more rights and more power immediately.

In the 1960s, Congress passed civil rights laws to help end racial segregation and discrimination. The Voting Rights Act of 1965 protected African Americans who wanted to register to vote. The result was dramatic. In 1960, only 29 percent of southern African Americans were registered to vote. By 1969, almost 65 percent were registered. The new voting clout of African Americans was shown in the increasing numbers of African Americans holding public office. By 2000, there were 39 members in the Congressional Black Caucus, a group made up of African American members of the Senate and the House of Representatives.

Voter Registration in the South

In the 1960s, the percentage of African Americans registered to vote in the South changed dramatically. **Critical Thinking: *Interpret Graphs*** *Write a general statement that explains the difference between the two pie graphs.*

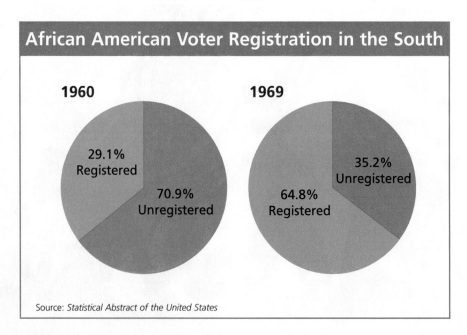

African American Voter Registration in the South

1960

29.1% Registered

70.9% Unregistered

1969

35.2% Unregistered

64.8% Registered

Source: *Statistical Abstract of the United States*

African American Household Income, 1950–2000

Source: *U.S. Census Bureau*

Income Rises

Household income of African Americans climbed during the last half of the 1900s. **Critical Thinking: *Interpret Graphs*** What was the median income of African American families in 1950? What was the median income in 1970? What factors would explain this rate of change?

In the media: author Toni Morrison (left), the first African American woman to win the Nobel Prize for Literature, appears on *The Oprah Winfrey Show.*

New Directions in Civil Rights

The civil rights movement toppled many of the barriers to African American advancement. African Americans began to make rapid advances in politics, government, and business.

Many businesses and universities adopted affirmative action programs. These programs sought to hire and promote minorities, women, and others who had faced discrimination. By the 1970s, more African Americans were entering such professions as medicine and law.

Despite these advances, many African Americans were still trapped by poverty in urban slums. Many still had to contend with discrimination in hiring, promotions, and pay. Civil rights leaders warned that the nation's commitment to equality seemed to be slipping. They urged renewed attention to the problems of inner-city poverty.

Assessment

1. **Recall:** What did the Supreme Court decide in *Brown* v. *Board of Education of Topeka?*

2. **Draw Conclusions:** Why is the Constitution an important tool in fighting discrimination?

Expanding Opportunities

As you have learned, American women began their long fight to win the vote during the mid-1800s. Unfortunately, pioneers of the suffragist movement such as Susan B. Anthony did not live to see the day when women were granted the right to vote in national elections. But that day did arrive.

Demanding Equal Treatment

In 1919, Congress passed the Nineteenth Amendment. The amendment stated that the "right of citizens of the United States to vote shall not be denied or abridged by the United States or by any state on account of sex." By the next year, the amendment had been ratified by enough states to make it part of the Constitution. American women cast their first presidential votes during the election of 1920. Exactly 130 years after the first presidential election, American women had won the right to vote.

American women cast their first presidential votes during the election of 1920. The same year, women's suffrage leader Carrie Chapman Catt founded the League of Women Voters. The organization worked to educate voters and encourage women to vote. "Everybody counts in applying democracy," Catt noted. The League of Women Voters also worked to guarantee other rights, such as the right of women to serve on juries.

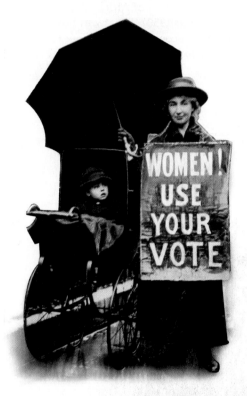

Suffragist urges women to use a hard-won right.

In 2004, 14 women were serving in the U.S. Senate.

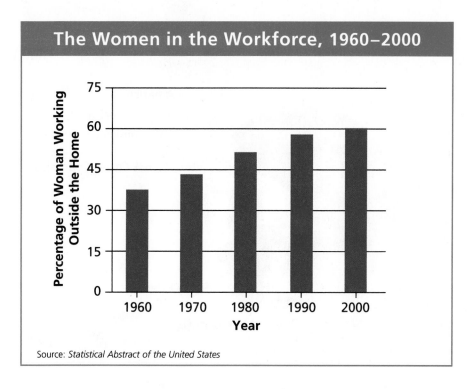

The Women in the Workforce, 1960–2000

Percentage of Woman Working Outside the Home (vertical axis: 0, 15, 30, 45, 60, 75)

Year (horizontal axis): 1960, 1970, 1980, 1990, 2000

Source: *Statistical Abstract of the United States*

Women in the Workforce

During the last half of the 1900s, women were an increasingly important force in the workforce. **Critical Thinking:** *Interpret Graphs When did more than half of all women first participate in the workforce?*

The women's movement has claimed many successes. Women slowly began to win posts in government, including:

- **First woman elected to Congress:** Jeannette Rankin of Montana, 1916

- **First woman elected as a state governor:** Nellie Tayloe Ross of Wyoming, 1924

- **First woman in the Cabinet:** Frances Perkins, Secretary of Labor, 1933

- **First woman appointed to the Supreme Court:** Sandra Day O'Connor, 1981

Much progress has been made in employment. Women now hold many important positions in corporations and in public service organizations, such as police forces. For the first time, women hold large numbers of management and professional jobs in the United States. Today, a growing percentage of the lawyers and doctors in the United States are women.

Some people believe that the women's movement has gone far enough. They claim that some laws give women unfair preferences in such areas as hiring and college admissions. However, others argue that much remains to be done. Though women's incomes continue to rise, on average, women still earn less than 75 percent of what men earn. Single women who are heads of households face particular challenges. More than half the children in these households live in poverty. Working mothers also have the problem of finding affordable, adequate day care.

Meg Whitman, chief executive officer of eBay, with her executive team

Latino Diversity

The Latino population of the United States is quite diverse. This chart includes both immigrants and descendants of immigrants. It also includes Mexican Americans whose ancestors already lived in places like California when those lands became part of the United States. Puerto Rico is a United States territory, so its people are citizens from birth. **Critical Thinking:** *Interpret Graphs* *What is the largest group shown on the graph? Where on the graph would immigrants from Argentina be included?*

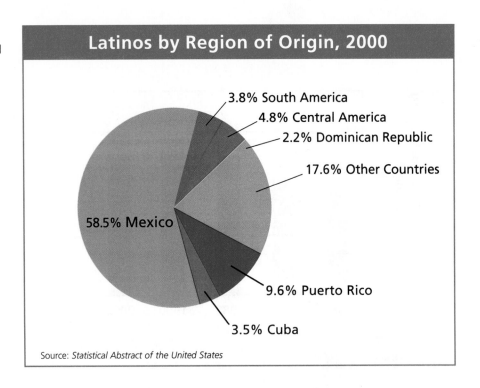

Latinos by Region of Origin, 2000

- 3.8% South America
- 4.8% Central America
- 2.2% Dominican Republic
- 17.6% Other Countries
- 58.5% Mexico
- 9.6% Puerto Rico
- 3.5% Cuba

Source: *Statistical Abstract of the United States*

New Mexico Governor Bill Richardson with Arizona Governor Janet Napolitano at the Hispanic Leadership Summit, 2003

Latinos in the United States

The largest single ethnic group in the United States today consists of people whose ancestors lived in Mexico or the Spanish-speaking countries of Central and South America and the Caribbean. Census figures for 2000, for example, show that almost one third of the people in California call themselves either Latino or Hispanic.

Making a place for themselves in this country has been easier for some Latinos than for others. Not surprisingly, those with training in business or other professions have often made the quickest adjustment. For example, the largest wave of Cuban immigrants came to the United States after a Communist revolution in 1959. Many of these Cubans were well educated, including former government and business leaders. As a result, they had little trouble adapting to their new home and building a successful life. Like other Americans, many Latinos who do not have employment skills find the transition to the United States most difficult.

The story of how Latinos helped pioneer an end to school segregation in the United States is not widely known. In 1946, eight years before the *Brown* v. *Board of Education of Topeka*, a federal district court issued a decision in a little-known case, *Mendez* v. *Westminster*. The California court ruled that young Latinos could not be forced to attend separate "Mexican" schools in Orange County, California. In *Mendez* v. *Westminster*, the federal court ruled for the first time that segregation based on national origins violated the "equal protection" clause of the Fourteenth Amendment.

Helped by rulings such as these, Latinos have made great advances in recent years. A number of Latinos held high positions in the administrations of Presidents Bill Clinton and George W. Bush. Bill Richardson, for example, was U.S. ambassador to the United Nations and Secretary of Energy in the administration of Bill Clinton. Richardson later became governor of New Mexico.

Just as Latinos have made great progress in government, Latino business leaders have made their mark in many major corporations. For example, Nancy E. Archuleta founded her own company in 1985. MEVATEC is the nation's fastest-growing Latino-owned business. Nilza Serrano is CEO of The Media Shop in Hollywood, California. It is a leading media center for the entertainment industry. Oscar de la Renta became one of the world's top clothing designers. Joseph A. Unanue turned the company he founded, Goya Foods, into the nation's largest privately owned Latino enterprise.

Nilza Serrano, CEO of The Media Shop

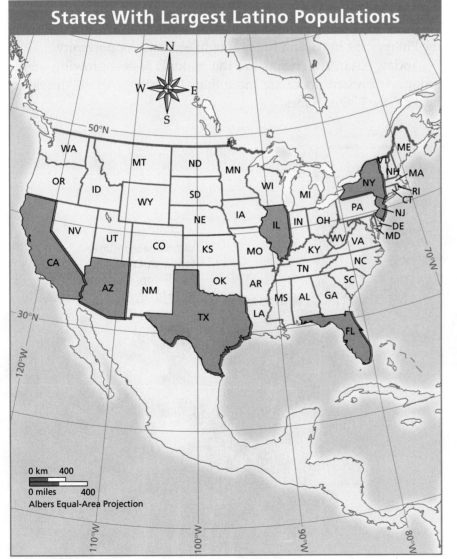

States With Largest Latino Populations

0 km 400
0 miles 400
Albers Equal-Area Projection

Latino Population in the United States

Seven states in the United States are home to more than 27 million Latinos. **Critical Thinking: Interpret Maps** *Which two U.S. states have the largest populations of Latinos?*

Latino Populations	
California	10,966,556
Texas	6,669,666
New York	2,867,583
Florida	2,682,715
Illinois	1,530,262
Arizona	1,295,617
New Jersey	1,117,191

Source: *U.S. Census Bureau, 2000*

Asian Americans Surmount Challenges

As you have learned, Asians made substantial contributions to the growth of the nation during the late 1800s. For example, you learned about the key role played by Chinese people in building the transcontinental railroad. Despite their achievements, Asians have struggled to gain acceptance. "Exclusion" laws passed by Congress in 1882 and 1907 prohibited further emigration from China and Japan.

During World War II, many Japanese Americans were imprisoned as security risks—even though they had shown no proof of disloyalty. In 1942, President Franklin Roosevelt issued an order placing more than 100,000 Japanese Americans in internment camps. In 1988, Congress officially apologized for these actions and partially compensated the surviving internees.

The last of the Asian "exclusion" laws was repealed in 1952. Since then, Asians have immigrated to the United States in increasing numbers. War and famines pushed many Asians into other parts of the world. After the Vietnam War, many Southeast Asians came to the United States. Many were **refugees,** people who flee their home country and seek refuge elsewhere. Many immigrants from the Philippines, India, and Korea sought economic opportunity.

Today, Asian Americans are the nation's fastest-growing ethnic group. At present, there are more than 10 million Asian Americans living in the United States.

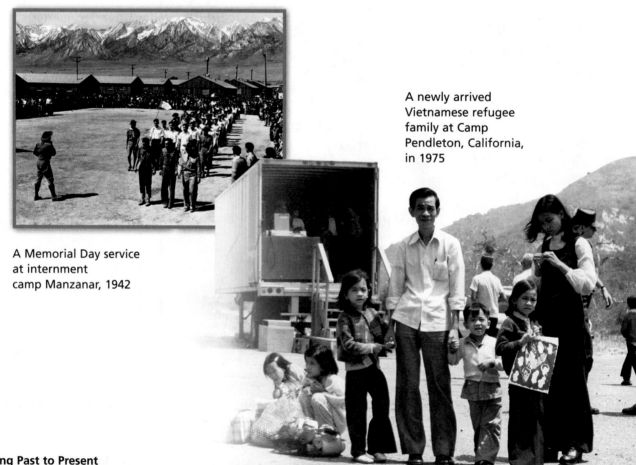

A Memorial Day service
at internment
camp Manzanar, 1942

A newly arrived
Vietnamese refugee
family at Camp
Pendleton, California,
in 1975

In 2001, leaders of different religions came together to pray for the nation and for the victims of the September 11 terrorist attacks.

Protecting Religious Diversity

The First Amendment guarantees freedom of religion. Yet, as you have read, in the late 1800s, religious minorities such as Jews and Roman Catholics often faced discrimination. Such instances are less common today than they were 100 years ago. Still, anti-Semitism and prejudice against Roman Catholics still exist.

Today, the United States is more religiously diverse than ever before. In addition to Christians and Jews, there are increasing numbers of Muslims, Buddhists, and Hindus. As in the past, this diversity has sometimes led to mistrust and conflict.

Still, after the terrorist attacks on New York and Washington, D.C., on September 11, 2001, Americans reaffirmed their belief in freedom of religion and religious diversity. Religious leaders of all faiths stood side by side at a national memorial service in Washington, D.C. Isolated incidents of religious bigotry were widely condemned by political leaders.

President George W. Bush said:

" We have seen . . . the saying of prayers in English, Hebrew and Arabic. . . . I ask you to uphold the values of America, and remember why so many have come here. We are in a fight for our principles, and our first responsibility is to live by them. No one should be singled out for unfair treatment or unkind words because of their ethnic background or religious faith. "

—George W. Bush, address to Congress, September 20, 2001

Assessment

1. **Recall:** What did a federal court rule in *Mendez* v. *Westminster*? What was its significance?

2. **Draw Conclusions** What can individual citizens do to oppose discrimination against ethnic and religious minorities?

Reference Section

Table of Contents

Primary Source Readings in American History

Primary Source Readings in American History *(continued)*

The Creation of Cherokee Country

Background

The Cherokees were one of the dominant Native American groups of the Southeast culture region. They originally lived in the area that is now North Carolina, South Carolina, and Georgia. Other major groups in the Southeast included the Natchez and Creeks.

Like other Native Americans, the Cherokees had a strong tradition of oral literature.

History, folk tales, and religious beliefs were memorized and recited, passing from one generation to the next. Creation stories were an important part of this oral tradition. The following story tells how the Cherokee lands in Georgia and the surrounding area were created. The mountains described are the Appalachians.

Vocabulary *Builder*

suspend (suh SPEND) *v.* to hang from

cardinal (KAHRD uh nuhl) *adj.* main; most important

vault (vawlt) *n.* arched roof or ceiling

dart (dahrt) *v.* to move suddenly or rapidly

alight (uh LIT) *v.* to come to rest from the air

buzzard (BUHZ uhrd) *n.* any of various breeds of vultures

The earth is a great island floating in a sea of water, and <u>suspended</u> at each of the four <u>cardinal</u> points by a cord hanging down from the sky <u>vault</u>, which is of solid rock. When the world grows old and worn out, the people will die and the cords will break and let the earth sink down into the ocean, and all will be water again. The Indians are afraid of this.

When all was water, the animals were above . . . beyond the arch, but it was very much crowded, and they were wanting more room. They wondered what was below the water and at last . . . the little Water-beetle, offered to go and see if it could learn. It <u>darted</u> in every direction over the surface of the water, but could find no firm place to rest. Then it dived to the bottom and came up with some soft mud, which began to grow and spread on every side until it became the island which we call the earth. It was afterward fastened to the sky with four cords, but no one remembers who did this.

At first the earth was flat and very soft and wet. The animals were anxious to get down, and sent out different birds to see if it was yet dry, but they found no place to <u>alight</u> and came back again to [the world above]. At last it seemed to be time, and they sent out the Great <u>Buzzard</u>, the father of all the buzzards we see now. He flew all over the earth, low down near the ground, and it was still soft. When he reached the Cherokee country, he was very tired, and his wings began to flap and strike the ground, and wherever they struck the earth there was a valley, and where they turned up again there was a mountain. When the animals above saw this, they were afraid that the whole world would be mountains, so they called him back, but the Cherokee country remains full of mountains to this day.

Nineteenth Annual Report of the Bureau of American Ethnology, 1897–1898

Comprehension and Critical Thinking

1. Why did the animals want dry land?
2. According to this creation story, how were the Appalachian Mountains formed?
3. Critical Thinking: *Apply Information* Why do you think animal figures play an important role in this and other creation stories?

Pericles, *Funeral Oration*

Background

Ancient Greece was divided into many small city-states, among them Athens and Sparta. Today, we consider Athens the birthplace of democracy.

In the fifth century B.C., a great conflict called the Peloponnesian War broke out between Athens and an alliance of city-states under the leadership of Sparta. At the time, the most respected leader in Athens was Pericles.

While the war was going on, Pericles was asked to deliver a speech honoring the city's war dead. He chose the occasion to also praise Athens, its government, its military, and its way of life. In the following selection from the speech, Pericles explains why he thinks the government of Athens is superior to those of other city-states.

Vocabulary *Builder*

capacity (kuh PAS ih tee) *n.* ability; skill

obscurity (ahb SKYOOR uh tee) *n.* state of being unclear or unknown

surveillance (suhr VAIL uhns) *n.* careful watching

injurious (ihn JYOOR ee uhs) *adj.* harmful

magistrate (MAJ uh strayt) *n.* official who enforces the law

statute (STACH oot) *n.* formal written law

Our constitution does not copy the laws of neighboring states; we are rather a pattern to others than imitators ourselves. Its administration favors the many instead of the few; this is why it is called a democracy. If we look to the laws, they afford equal justice to all in their private differences; if to social standing, advancement in public life falls to reputation for <u>capacity</u>, class considerations not being allowed to interfere with merit; nor again does poverty bar the way, if a man is able to serve the state, he is not hindered by the <u>obscurity</u> of his condition.

The freedom which we enjoy in our government extends also to our

Bust of Pericles

ordinary life. There, far from exercising a jealous <u>surveillance</u> over each other, we do not feel called upon to be angry with our neighbor for doing what he likes, or even to indulge in those <u>injurious</u> looks which cannot fail to be offensive, although they inflict no positive penalty. But all this ease in our private relations does not make us lawless as citizens. Against this fear is our chief safeguard, teaching us to obey the <u>magistrates</u> and the laws, particularly such as regard the protection of the injured, whether they are actually on the <u>statute</u> book, or belong to that code which, although unwritten yet cannot be broken without acknowledged disgrace.

Thucydides, *History of the Peloponnesian War*

Comprehension and Critical Thinking

1. According to Pericles, what makes Athens a democracy?

2. What freedoms do Athenians enjoy in their private lives?

3. Critical Thinking: *Compare* Based on this description, in what ways was the government of Athens similar to the government of the United States today?

Bartolomé de Las Casas, *The Destruction of the Indies*

Background

Bartolomé de Las Casas was a Roman Catholic priest born in Seville, Spain, in 1484. In his youth, he met Christopher Columbus and traveled to the West Indies. There, he observed the conquest of the Americas and was horrified by the treatment of Native Americans by the conquistadores.

Las Casas dedicated his long life to protecting Native Americans from Spanish abuse.

On several occasions, he returned to Spain to plead their case before the Spanish throne. His writings and discussions shocked Spanish leaders who attempted to pass laws to protect the Indians. The conquistadores' friends at court, however, often had the policies reversed. Below is an excerpt from a 1542 work detailing the abusive policies of the Spanish.

Vocabulary *Builder*

tyrannical (tih RAN ih kuhl) *adj.* harsh; using power unjustly

instrumental (ihn struh MEHN tuhl) *adj.* serving as an important tool; very helpful

annihilation (uh nī uh LAY shuhn) *n.* complete destruction

Sacrament (SAK ruh mehnt) *n.* sacred rite of the Christian church

indigenous (ihn DIHJ uh nehs) *adj.* native to a region or counry

tribulation (trihb yoo LAY shuhn) *n.* great sorrow or trouble

---

There are two main ways in which those who have traveled to this part of the world pretending to be Christians have uprooted these pitiful peoples and wiped them from the face of the earth. First, they have waged war on them: unjust, cruel, bloody and <u>tyrannical</u> war. Second, they have murdered anyone and everyone who has shown the slightest sign of resistance. . . . This latter policy has been <u>instrumental</u> in suppressing the native leaders, and, indeed, given that the Spaniards normally spare only women and children, it has led to the <u>annihilation</u> of all adult males. . . .

The reason the [Spanish] have murdered on such a vast scale and killed anyone and everyone in their way is purely and simply greed. They have set out to line their pockets with gold. . . . The Spaniards have shown not the slightest consideration for these people, treating them (and I speak from first-hand experience, having been there from the outset) not as brute animals—indeed, I would to God they had done and had shown them the consideration they afford their animals—so much as piles of dung in the middle of the road. They have had as little concern for their souls as for their bodies, all the millions that have perished having gone to their deaths with no knowledge of God and without the benefit of the <u>Sacraments</u>. . . .

The <u>indigenous</u> peoples never did the Europeans any harm whatever; on the contrary, they believed them to have descended from the heavens, at least until they or their fellow-citizens had tasted, at the hands of these oppressors, a diet of robbery, murder, violence, and all other manner of trials and <u>tribulations</u>.

Bartolomé de Las Casas, *The Destruction of the Indies*

Comprehension and Critical Thinking

1. What warning did the Menominee give Marquette and Joliet?

2. How long was the journey from St. Ignatius to the Mississippi?

3. Critical Thinking: *Predict* What dangers do you think Marquette and Joliet will face as they continue their journey?

Jacques Marquette, *Reaching the Mississippi*

Background

Jacques Marquette was born in northern France in 1637. He joined the Jesuits at the age of 17 and worked as a priest in France for more than a decade.

In his late twenties, Marquette was sent to Quebec, in the heart of France's North American empire. Marquette served as a missionary to the native people of the continent. There, he heard rumors of a great river southwest of Quebec, which the French hoped would be a "Northwest Passage" to the Pacific Ocean. In 1673, Marquette joined Canadian-born explorer Louis Joliet and five other adventurers to find the river. Here, he describes reaching the Mississippi River.

Vocabulary *Builder*

dissuade (dihs WAYD) *v.* to advise against; discourage

salvation (sal VAY shuhn) *n.* saving of a person's soul, especially referring to life after death

embark (ehm BAHRK) *v.* to start on a journey

depute (dee PYOOT) *v.* to select someone for a task or mission

---

On the 17th day of May, 1673, we started from the mission of St. Ignatius. . . . [T]he first nation that we came to was that of the Folle Avoine [Menominee]. . . . I told these people . . . of my design to go and discover those remote nations, in order to teach them the mysteries of our holy religion. They . . . did their best to <u>dissuade</u> me. They represented to me that I would meet nations who never show mercy to strangers. . . .

I thanked them for their advice . . . but told them that I could not follow it, because the <u>salvation</u> of souls was at stake. . . .

We left the waters flowing to Quebec . . . to float on those that would thenceforward take us through strange lands.

. . . [W]e arrived at . . . the Mississippi on the 17th of June, with a joy that I cannot express.

Finally on the 25th of June we perceived on the water's edge some tracks of men, and a narrow . . . beaten path. . . . [A]fter walking about two leagues, we discovered a village. . . . We . . . decided to reveal ourselves. . . . by shouting with all our energy, and stopped without advancing any farther. On hearing the shout, the savages [the Illinois] . . . having probably recognized us as Frenchmen, especially when they saw a black gown—or, at least, having not cause for distrust, as we were only two men, and had given them notice of our arrival—they <u>deputed</u> four old men to come and speak to us. . . . They afterward invited us to enter their village.

Jacques Marquette, *The Jesuit Relations*, Vol. LIX

Comprehension and Critical Thinking

1. What warning did the Menominee give Marquette and Joliet?

2. How long was the journey from St. Ignatius to the Mississippi?

3. **Critical Thinking: Predict** What dangers do you think Marquette and Joliet will face as they continue on their journey?

Marquette and Joliet on the Mississippi

Primary Sources

William Bradford, *History of Plimoth Plantation*

Background

On September 6, 1620, the Pilgrims departed from Plymouth, England, on board the *Mayflower*. The journey across the Atlantic Ocean took 66 days. Their intended destination was the mouth of the Hudson River, site of present-day New York City. During the second half of the trip, they encountered rough weather. The threat of shipwreck if they continued on to the Hudson led them to halt, explore Cape Cod, and settle in Massachusetts.

Among the passengers was William Bradford. He later served as governor of the Plymouth Colony for more than 25 years. Bradford also wrote *History of Plimoth Plantation*, a valuable source of information about the colony. In this excerpt, Bradford describes the arrival of the Pilgrims at Cape Cod.

Vocabulary *Builder*

succor (SUHK uhr) *n.* help or aid

barbarian (bahr BEHR ee uhn) *n.* uncivilized person

desolate (DEHS uh liht) *adj.* empty; lacking in life or comfort

sustain (SUH stayn) *v.* support; keep alive

Being thus arrived in a good harbor and brought safe to land, they fell upon their knees and blessed the God of Heaven who had brought them over the vast and furious ocean and delivered them from all the perils and miseries thereof, again to set their feet on the firm and stable, their proper element.

But here I cannot but stay and make a pause and stand half amazed at this poor people's present condition; and so I think will the reader too, when he well considers the same. Being thus past the vast ocean and a sea of troubles before in their preparation . . . they had now no friends to welcome them, nor inns to entertain or refresh their weather-beaten bodies, no houses or much less towns to repair to, to seek for succor. . . . These savage barbarians, when they met with them (as after will appear) were readier to fill their sides of arrows than otherwise. And for the season, it was winter, and they that know the winters of that country know them to be sharp and violent and subject to cruel and fierce storms, dangerous to travel to known places, much more to search an unknown coast. Besides, what could they see but a hideous and desolate wilderness full of wild beasts and wild men? And what multitudes there might be of them they knew not. . . . What could now sustain them but the spirit of God and his grace?

William Bradford, *History of Plimoth Plantation*

Pilgrims of Plymouth Colony

Comprehension and Critical Thinking

1. What does Bradford mean when he speaks of the Pilgrims' "proper element"?
2. What fears do the Pilgrims face? According to Bradford, what is their one source of hope?
3. *Critical Thinking: Detect Bias* What is Bradford's view of Native Americans? How do you think Native Americans viewed the Pilgrims?

Maryland Act of Toleration

Background

Lord Baltimore was the founder of the Maryland Colony and served as Lord Proprietary, or head of the government. He had hoped to make Maryland a Catholic colony. However, the majority of colonists turned out to be Protestants. Nevertheless, Catholic settlers got the large grants and held the positions of power in the colony. Protestant settlers were unhappy with those conditions.

In 1649, Lord Baltimore encouraged the Maryland legislature to pass an act of toleration. The law gave the colony a measure of religious freedom. The act was designed to protect Protestants but, in fact, protected the Catholic minority as well. The following excerpt from the Act of Toleration identifies some of the people and actions that would and would not be tolerated in the colony.

Vocabulary *Builder*

blaspheme (blas FEEM) *v.* to speak against God or holy matters

confiscation (kahn fihs KAY shuhn) *n.* seizure of property by a government

forfeiture (FOR fuh chuhr) *n.* act of giving up something as a penalty

amity (AM ih tee) *n.* peaceful relations

discountenance (dihs KOWNT uhn ehns) *v.* make to feel shame

Forasmuch as, in a well-governed and Christian commonwealth, matters concerning religion and the honor of God ought in the first place to be taken into serious consideration, . . . be it therefore ordered and enacted by the Right Honorable Cecilius Lord Baron of Baltimore, absolute Lord and Proprietary of this Province with the advise and consent of this General Assembly:

That whatsoever person or persons within the Province thereunto belonging shall from henceforth blaspheme God, that is, curse Him; or deny our Savior Jesus Christ to be the son of God, or shall deny the Holy Trinity, the Father, Son, and Holy Ghost . . . shall be punished with death and confiscation or forfeiture of all his or her lands and goods to the Lord Proprietary and his heirs.

And be it also enacted . . . that whatsoever person or persons shall from henceforth use or utter any reproachful words or speeches concerning the Blessed Virgin Mary, the Mother of our Savior, or the Holy Apostles . . . shall in such case for the first offense forfeit to the said Lord Proprietary and his heirs . . . the sum of five pounds sterling. . . . And that every person or persons before mentioned offending herein the third time, shall for such third Offence forfeit all his lands and Goods and be for ever banished and expelled out of this Province. . . .

And for the more quiet and peaceable government of this Province, and the better to preserve mutual love and amity amongst the Inhabitants thereof, be it therefore [enacted] that no person or persons whatsoever within this Province . . . professing to believe in Jesus Christ, shall from henceforth be any ways troubled, molested or discountenanced for or in respect of his or her religion nor in the free exercise thereof within this Province or the Islands thereunto belonging nor any way compelled to the belief or exercise of any other Religion against his or her consent.

An Act Concerning Religion, April 24, 1649

Comprehension and Critical Thinking

1. What actions were punishable by death under the Maryland Act of Toleration?

2. What people were given religious freedom in Maryland? Why?

3. Critical Thinking: *Contrast* Based on your reading, how did colonial Maryland differ from Puritan New England in terms of religious toleration?

Primary Sources

The Magna Carta

Background

King John ruled England from 1199 to 1216. During his troubled reign, he found himself in conflict with England's feudal barons. The nobles especially resented John's attempts to tax them heavily.

In 1215, the barons forced John to sign the Magna Carta, or Great Charter. Most of this document was intended to protect the rights of the barons.

However, over time, the document came to guarantee some basic rights of English citizens. When English colonists came to North America, they brought these ideas with them. Eight of the 63 clauses of the Magna Carta are printed here.

Vocabulary *Builder*

counsel (KOWN suhl) *n.* advice; consent

bailiff (BAY lihf) *n.* tax collector in medieval England

credible (KREHD uh buhl) *adj.* believable

peer (peer) *n.* person of equal rank

realm (rehlm) *n.* kingdom

enjoin (ehn JOIN) *v.* to order; to enforce

---

12. No [tax] nor aid shall be imposed on our kingdom, unless by common counsel of our kingdom, except for ransoming our person, for making our eldest son a knight, and for once marrying our eldest daughter; and for these there shall not be levied more than a reasonable aid. . . .

30. No sheriff or bailiff of ours, or other person, shall take the horses or carts of any freeman for transport duty, against the will of the said freeman.

31. Neither we nor our bailiffs shall take, for our castles or for any other work of ours, wood which is not ours, against the will of the owner of that wood. . . .

38. No bailiff for the future shall, upon his own unsupported complaint, put any one to his "law," without credible witnesses brought for this purpose.

39. No freeman shall be taken or imprisoned . . . or exiled or in any way destroyed, nor will we go upon him nor send upon him, except by the lawful judgment of his peers or by the law of the land.

40. To no one will we sell, to no one will we refuse or delay, right or justice. . . .

45. We will appoint as justices, constables, sheriffs, or bailiffs only such as know the law of the realm and mean to observe it well. . . .

63. Wherefore it is our will, and we firmly enjoin, that the English Church be free, and that the men in our kingdom have and hold all the aforesaid liberties, rights, and concessions, well and peaceably, freely and quietly, fully and wholly, for themselves and their heirs, of us and our heirs, in all respects and in all places for ever, as is aforesaid.

The Magna Carta, in *Source Problems in English History,* ed. White and Notestein

Comprehension and Critical Thinking

1. Which clauses of the Magna Carta listed here protect the right of people to their own private property?

2. What promise is made in clause 12?

3. Critical Thinking: *Link Past and Present* How do the principles expressed in clauses 38–40 apply to the United States today?

Jonathan Mayhew, *On Unlimited Submission to Rulers*

Background

During the Great Awakening, American preachers spoke out on both political and religious issues. One of these preachers was Jonathan Mayhew, the Congregationalist minister at Boston's West Church. In a 1750 sermon, Mayhew argued against the idea that people owed complete submission, or obedience, to their rulers. Mayhew based his argument on the teachings of an early Christian leader, the apostle Paul.

Mayhew's lengthy sermon was printed and widely read in the colonies. In this excerpt, he explains his view of the purpose of government.

Vocabulary *Builder*

welfare (WEHL fair) *n.* well-being

parity (PAR ih tee) *n.* similarity

allegiance (uh LEE jehntz) *n.* loyalty

implicit (ihm PLIH siht) *adj.* by suggestion; not stated directly

---

The [goal of government] is the good of civil society. . . .

If it be our duty, for example, to obey our king merely for this reason, that he rules for the public <u>welfare</u> (which is the only argument the apostle makes use of), it follows, by a <u>parity</u> of reason, that when he turns tyrant and makes his subjects his prey to devour and to destroy instead of his charge to defend and cherish, we are bound to throw off our <u>allegiance</u> to him and to resist. . . . Not to discontinue our allegiance, in this case, would be to join with the sovereign in promoting the slavery and misery of that society, the welfare of which we ourselves, as well as our sovereign, are indispensably obliged to secure and promote as far as in us lies.

It is true the apostle puts no such case of such a tyrannical prince; but, by his grounding his argument for submission wholly upon the good of civil society, it is plain he <u>implicitly</u> authorizes and even requires us to make resistance whenever this shall be necessary to the public safety and us to make happiness.

Jonathan Mayhew, *A Discourse Concerning Unlimited Submission and Non-Resistance to the Higher Powers*

Jonathan Mayhew

JONATHAN MAYHEW, D.D. PASTOR OF THE WEST CHVRCH IN BOSTON, IN NEW ENGLAND. AN ASSERTOR OF THE CIVIL AND RELIGIOVS LIBERTIES OF HIS COVNTRY AND MANKIND, WHO, OVERPLIED BY PVBLIC ENERGIES, DIED OF A NERVOVS FEVER.

Comprehension and Critical Thinking

1. According to Mayhew, what is the chief goal of a government?

2. What does Mayhew think people should do if a ruler becomes tyrannical?

3. Critical Thinking: *Make Predictions* How do you think ideas like Mayhew's might contribute to a spirit of resistance and revolution in the colonies?

Primary Sources

Patrick Henry, *Speech in the House of Burgesses*

Background

Patrick Henry was born in Virginia in 1735. Trained as an attorney while a young man, he became known for his speaking skills. Henry was elected to the Virginia House of Burgesses in 1765 and strongly opposed the Stamp Act. In a speech related to the crisis, he spoke against Parliament and the king, declaring, "If this be treason, make the most of it." Bitter criticism from delegates forced him to apologize for the statement and affirm his loyalty to the king.

In March 1775, Henry made the following speech, which became his best known. Some credit this speech with being the deciding act in gaining Virginia's troops for the Revolutionary cause. At the end of the speech, members of the assembly jumped from their seats and shouted, "To Arm! To Arms!"

They tell us, sir, that we are weak; unable to cope with so formidable an <u>adversary</u>. But when shall we be stronger? Will it be the next week, or the next year? Will it be when we are totally disarmed, and when a British guard shall be stationed in every house? Shall we gather strength by <u>irresolution</u> and inaction? Shall we acquire the means of effectual resistance by lying <u>supinely</u> on our backs and hugging the <u>delusive</u> phantom of hope, until our enemies shall have bound us hand and foot?

Sir, we are not weak if we make a proper use of those means which the God of nature hath placed in our power. Three millions of people armed in the holy cause of liberty, and in such a country as that which we possess, are invincible by any force which our enemy can send against us. . . . The battle, sir, is not to the strong alone; it is to the <u>vigilant</u>, the active, the brave.

Besides, sir, we have no election. If we were base enough to desire it, it is now too late to retire from the contest. There is no retreat but in submission and slavery! Our chains are forged! Their clanking may be heard on the plains of Boston! The war is inevitable—and let it come! I repeat, sir, let it come!

It is vain, sir, to <u>extenuate</u> the matter. The gentlemen may cry, Peace, peace! But there is no peace. The war has actually begun! The next gale that sweeps from the north will bring to our ears the clash of resounding arms! Our brethren are already in the field! Why stand we here idle? What is it that gentlemen wish? What would they have? Is life so dear or peace so sweet as to be purchased at the price of chains and slavery? Forbid it, almighty God. I know not what course others may take, but as for me, give me liberty or give me death!

Patrick Henry, speech to the Virginia Assembly, March 23, 1775

Comprehension and Critical Thinking

1. According to Henry, why would the Americans be difficult to defeat?

2. Why does Henry think the Americans have no "election," or choice, but to fight?

3. Critical Thinking: *Detect Points of View* How do you think a colonist who did not want to break away from Britain might respond to Henry's argument?

William Sutherland, *The Battle of Lexington*

Background

After the Boston Tea Party, the British government passed the Intolerable Acts. The acts were designed to punish Massachusetts for the crime of its colonists. Massachusetts became an armed camp, with British control limited to Boston. Parliament declared the colony in rebellion.

On April 18, 1775, some 700 British troops left Boston to march on Concord and seize arms stored there by the colonists. One of these British soldiers was William Sutherland. Along the way, the troops passed through the town of Lexington. In this letter, Sutherland describes what happened next.

Vocabulary *Builder*

instantaneous (ihn sten TAY nee uhs) *adj.* immediate; at once

grenadier (grehn uh DIR) *n.* member of a European military force formerly armed with grenades

consequence (KAHN suh kwehns) *n.* result of an action

On coming within gunshot of the village of Lexington, a fellow from the corner of the road, on the right hand, [aimed his weapon] at me. . . . I immediately called to Mr. Adair and the party to observe this circumstance, which they did, and I acquainted Major Pitcairn of it immediately.

We still went on farther when three shots more were fired at us, which we did not return, this is sacred truth as I hope for mercy. These three shots were fired from a corner of a large house to the right of the church. When we came up to the main body, which appeared to me to exceed four hundred in and about the village, who were drawn up in a plain opposite to the church, several officers called out, "Throw down your arms and you shall come to no harm," or words to that effect. Which, they refusing to do, <u>instantaneously</u> the gentlemen who were on horseback rode in amongst them, of which I was one, at which instant I heard Major Pitcairn's voice call out, "Soldiers, don't fire; keep your ranks; form and surround them." Instantly some of the villains, who got over the hedge, fired at us, which our men for the first time returned, which set my horse a-going, who galloped with me down a road above six hundred yards among the middle of them before I turned him. And in returning, a vast number who were in a wood at the right of the <u>grenadiers</u> fired at me, but the distance was so great that I only heard the whistling of the [musket balls], but saw a great number of people in the wood. In <u>consequence</u> of their discovering themselves by firing, our grenadiers gave them a smart fire.

William Sutherland, letter, April 27, 1775

Comprehension and Critical Thinking

1. What do the British want the colonists gathered in Lexington to do? What do the British promise in return?

2. According to Sutherland, who started the shooting?

3. Critical Thinking: *Evaluate Information* Do you think Sutherland's version of the events is believable? Why or why not?

Statue of a minuteman

Thomas Paine, *Common Sense*

Background

Born in England in 1737, Thomas Paine left school at the age of 12. Later, he unsuccessfully tried a variety of careers, from sailor to tax collector. Then, he met Benjamin Franklin in London. Franklin helped Paine come to the American colonies and find work as a journalist.

Two years later, in 1776, Paine published *Common Sense* in order to stir up support for American independence. In different parts of the pamphlet, Paine gives political, military, and moral arguments for breaking away from Britain. In the excerpt below, Paine discusses economic reasons.

Vocabulary *Builder*

advocate (AD vuh kiht) *n.* person who speaks in favor of something

reconciliation (rehk uhn sihl ee AY shuhn) *n.* making peace after a disagreement

renounce (ree NOWNS) *v.* to promise to give up

variance (VAIR ee uhns) *n.* quarrel; dispute

contention (kuhn TEHN shun) n. disagreement; conflict

I challenge the warmest <u>advocate</u> for <u>reconciliation</u>, to show a single advantage that this continent can reap, by being connected with Great Britain. I repeat the challenge, not a single advantage is derived. Our corn will fetch its price in any market in Europe, and our imported goods must be paid for, buy them where we will.

But the injuries and disadvantages we sustain by that connection, are without number; and our duty to mankind at large, as well as to ourselves, instruct us to <u>renounce</u> the alliance: Because, any submission to, or dependence on Great Britain, tends directly to involve this continent in European wars and quarrels; and sets us at <u>variance</u> with nations, who would otherwise seek our friendship,

and against whom, we have neither anger nor complaint. As Europe is our market for trade, we ought to form no partial connection with any part of it. It is the true interest of America to steer clear of European <u>contentions</u>. . . .

Europe is too thickly planted with kingdoms to be long at peace, and whenever a war breaks out between England and any foreign power, the trade of America goes to ruin, because of her connection with Britain.

Thomas Paine, *Common Sense*

Thomas Paine

Comprehension and Critical Thinking

1. According to Paine, what advantages can the colonies gain by remaining connected with Britain?

2. What effect does Paine say Britain has on American trade?

3. Critical Thinking: *Evaluate Information* Paine's purpose was to persuade colonists to support independence. Which colonists do you think would be most persuaded by the arguments given above?

Joseph J. Ellis, *His Excellency George Washington*

Background

George Washington gained his first real military experience during the French and Indian War in the 1750s. He was credited with saving the remains of a large American and British army that had been cut to pieces by the French and their Indian allies early in the war.

When the American Revolution started in 1775, Washington was the obvious choice to command American forces. Compared to the best British generals, Washington was inexperienced. But John Adams felt that choosing a Virginian would secure the loyalty of that important colony. It turned out to be a wise decision.

In the following excerpt, a modern historian discusses Washington as a military leader.

Vocabulary *Builder*

protracted (proh TRAKT ehd) *adj.* drawn out; lasting a long time

indefatigable (ihn dih FAT ih guh buhl) *adj.* impossible to tire out; energetic

arrogant (AR uh gehnt) *adj.* full of pride

align (uh LĪN) *v.* to bring into close agreement; to fit

decisive (dee SĪ sihv) *adj.* leading to a final outcome or decision

Washington spent the entire war in the field with the Continental army. He was not, by any standard, a military genius. He lost more battles than he won; indeed, he lost more battles than any victorious general in modern history. Moreover, his defeats were frequently a function of his own overconfident and aggressive personality, especially during the early stages of the war, when he escaped to fight another day only because the British generals opposing him seemed choked with the kind of caution that, given his resources, Washington should have adopted as his own strategy. But in addition to being fortunate in his adversaries, he was blessed with personal qualities that counted most in a protracted war. He was composed, indefatigable, and able to learn from his mistakes. He was convinced that he was on the side of destiny—or, in more arrogant moments, sure that destiny was on his side. Even his critics acknowledged that he could not be bribed, corrupted, or compromised. Based on his bravery during several battles, he apparently believed he could not be killed. Despite all his mistakes, events seemed to align themselves with his own instincts. He began the war at the siege of Boston determined to deliver a decisive blow against more disciplined and battle-tested British regulars. He ended it at the siege of Yorktown doing precisely that.

Joseph J. Ellis, *His Excellency George Washington*

Comprehension and Critical Thinking

1. According to the author, why was Washington able to survive early defeats in battle?

2. How did Washington's army at Boston differ from his army at Yorktown?

3. Critical Thinking: *Support Opinions* (a) Make a table with two columns, one listing Washington's strengths and the other listing his weaknesses as a general. (b) Based on the information in your table, discuss why Washington was or was not the right man to lead the American army in the Revolutionary War.

Primary Sources

Thomas Jefferson, *Virginia Statute for Religious Freedom*

Background

In 1786, the Virginia legislature adopted the Statute for Religious Freedom, written by Thomas Jefferson. The law is still part of the Virginia state constitution.

Other states followed Virginia's lead. The Statute for Religious Freedom later became the basis for the First Amendment to the United States Constitution, which guarantees freedom of religion.

Jefferson himself recognized the importance of this document. Later in life, he directed that his tombstone list what he considered his three greatest accomplishments: writing the Declaration of Independence, founding the University of Virginia, and writing the Virginia Statute for Religious Freedom.

Vocabulary *Builder*

propagation (prahp uh GAY shuhn) *n.* spread

abhor (ab HOR) *v.* to hate

civil (SIHV uhl) *adj.* relating to citizenship

diminish (dih MIHN ihsh) *v.* to lessen

irrevocable (ih REHV uh kuh buhl) *adj.* unchangeable

infringement (ihn FRIHNJ mehnt) *n.* violation

I. *Whereas* Almighty God hath created the mind free . . . that to compel a man to furnish contributions of money for the propagation of opinions which he disbelieves and abhors, is sinful and tyrannical . . . that our civil rights have no dependence on our religious opinions, any more than our opinions in physics or geometry . . .

II. *Be it . . . enacted by the General Assembly*, that no man shall be compelled to frequent or support any religious worship, place, or ministry whatsoever, nor shall be enforced, restrained, molested, or burdened in his body or goods, nor shall otherwise suffer, on account of his religious opinions or belief; but that all men shall be free to profess, and by argument to maintain, their opinions in matters of religion, and that the same shall in no wise diminish, enlarge, or affect their civil capacities.

III. And although we well know that this Assembly, elected by the people for the ordinary purpose of legislation only, have no power to restrain the acts of succeeding assemblies, constituted with powers equal to our own, and that therefore to declare this act to be irrevocable would be of no effect in law; yet we are free to declare, and do declare, that the rights hereby asserted are of the natural rights of mankind, and that if any act shall hereafter be passed to repeal the present, or to narrow its operation, such an act will be infringement of natural right.

Thomas Jefferson, Virginia Statute for Religious Freedom

Comprehension and Critical Thinking

1. According to Jefferson, what is the relationship between civil rights and religious belief?

2. What does Jefferson mean when he calls freedom of religion a "natural right"?

3. Critical Thinking: *Compare* Read the First Amendment to the Constitution. How does the First Amendment reflect ideas similar to those in the Virginia Statute for Religious Freedom?

James Madison, *The Federalist, No. 39*

Background

The *Federalist Papers* is a name given to a series of 85 essays written in 1787 by Alexander Hamilton, James Madison, and John Jay. Their goal was to win support for the Constitution.

Originally, the three authors did not sign the essays with their own names. Instead, they used the Roman name *Publius*, from the Latin word for "public." Using such pen names was a common practice in political writing of the time. It indicated the great respect the early leaders of the United States had for the ancient Roman Republic.

The following excerpt is from *The Federalist* No. 39. Here, James Madison shows that the government formed by the Constitution is a republic.

Vocabulary *Builder*

bestow (bee STOH) *v.* to give

inconsiderable (ihn kuhn SIHD uhr uh buhl) *adj.* small; unimportant

standard (STAN duhrd) *n.* something against which other things are judged

conformable (kuhn FORM uh buhl) *adj.* in harmony or agreement

magistrate (MAJ ihs trayt) *n.* official who enforces the law

We may define a republic to be, or at least may <u>bestow</u> that name on, a government which derives all its powers directly or indirectly from the great body of the people, and is administered by persons holding their offices during pleasure, for a limited period, or during good behavior. It is ESSENTIAL to such a government that it be derived from the great body of the society, not from an <u>inconsiderable</u> proportion, or a favored class of it. . . .

On comparing the Constitution planned by the convention with the <u>standard</u> here fixed, we perceive at once that it is, in the most rigid sense, <u>conformable</u> to it. The House of Representatives, like that of one branch at least of all the State legislatures, is elected immediately by the great body of the people. The Senate, like the present Congress, and the Senate of Maryland, derives its appointment indirectly from the people. The President is indirectly derived from the choice of the people, according to the example in most of the States. . . . The Senate is elective, for the period of six years; which is but one year more than the period of the Senate of Maryland, and but two more than that of the Senates of New York and Virginia. The President is to continue in office for the period of four years; as in New York and Delaware, the chief <u>magistrate</u> is elected for three years, and in South Carolina for two years.

James Madison, *The Federalist* No. 39

James Madison

Comprehension and Critical Thinking

1. What does Madison consider to be the most important quality of a republic?

2. Describe two examples Madison uses to show that the government under the Constitution fits the definition of a republic.

3. Critical Thinking: *Draw Inferences* Why do you think Madison tries to show that the proposed new government has many similarities to the state governments?

Thomas Jefferson, *On Majority Rule*

Background

The early leaders of the United States thought long and hard about the meaning of republican government.

One of the key issues was the question of the majority versus the minority. In a republic, the people who make laws have to be elected. They therefore represent the views of the largest number of people. How can the rights of the minority—especially those who hold unpopular views—be protected in a nation where the majority rules? This issue is still debated today.

In these two excerpts, Thomas Jefferson talks about what he calls *lex majoris partis*—Latin for "the law of the majority." The first reading is from a letter written by Jefferson to a friend. The second is from his First Inaugural Address.

Vocabulary *Builder*

fundamental (fuhn duh MEHNT uhl) *adj.* basic

enounce (ee NOWNS) *v.* to express

unanimous (yoo NAN uh muhs) *adj.* agreed upon by everyone

despotism (DEHS puh tihz uhm) *n.* rule by a tyrant

prevail (pree VAIL) *v.* to win out; to gain the advantage

countenance (KOWN tuh nehns) *v.* to approve or accept

The first principle of republicanism is that the *lex majoris partis* is the <u>fundamental</u> law of every society of individuals of equal rights; to consider the will of the society <u>enounced</u> by the majority of a single vote as sacred as if <u>unanimous</u> is the first of all lessons in importance, yet the last which is thoroughly learnt. This law once disregarded, no other remains but that of force, which ends necessarily in military <u>despotism</u>.

Thomas Jefferson, letter to Alexander von Humboldt, 1817

All, too, will bear in mind this sacred principle, that though the will of the majority is in all cases to <u>prevail</u>, that will to be rightful must be reasonable; that the minority possess their equal rights, which equal law must protect, and to violate would be oppression. . . . Having banished from our land that religious intolerance under which mankind so long bled and suffered, we have yet gained little if we <u>countenance</u> a political intolerance as despotic, as wicked, and capable of as bitter and bloody persecutions.

Thomas Jefferson, First Inaugural Address, 1801

Comprehension and Critical Thinking

1. In his letter to Humboldt, what does Jefferson say about the importance of majority rule in a republic?

2. Restate in your own words what Jefferson says in his First Inaugural Address about people who hold minority or unpopular opinions.

3. Critical Thinking: *Apply Information* Based on the above, do you think Jefferson would agree with the following statements? Explain.
   (a) "The President is still the President, even though he won by only a few votes."
   (b) "She lost the election, so we can ignore the opinions of the people who voted for her."

Thomas Jefferson

Hillary Rodham Clinton, *The Importance of Voting*

Background

The right to vote is one of the most basic rights guaranteed by the Constitution. Over the years, different groups of Americans—such as women and African Americans—have struggled long and hard to secure their right to vote. Yet, many Americans have failed to exercise this right. This drop in voter turnout has worried leaders of all political parties, including Hillary Rodham Clinton.

Clinton served as First Lady of the United States and, later, as a senator from New York. In this column, written before the presidential election of 2000, Clinton urges young people to go out and vote.

Vocabulary *Builder*

cite (sīt) *v.* to mention or refer to

survey (SER vay) *n.* process for gathering public opinion

factor (FAK tor) *n.* condition or quality that causes something else to happen

aspect (AS pehkt) *n.* single part or element among many

incumbent (ihn KUHM behnt) *adj.* required as a duty

privilege (PRIHV uh lihj) *n.* special right not shared by everybody

In 1998, fewer than one in five 18- to 24-year-olds voted. When asked why . . . they cite a number of reasons: They feel ignored by politicians; they feel their vote doesn't really count; and they say that they don't get the kind of information they need to make an informed decision.

The survey concludes that the single factor that most influences whether a young person will vote is whether his or her parents vote. But almost half of this group reported that they never—or almost never—talked about politics, government, or current events with their parents.

There is at least one hopeful sign that might help us bring this generation into the process: More than half of them volunteer on a regular basis, and 94 percent define the most important aspect of citizenship as "helping others." I hope that the trend toward service learning in the schools will provide the opportunity for young people to see that the work they do in their communities, and the issues they care about as a result, can be and are affected by what happens in the voting booth.

There are 70.2 million people in this country under 20. The thought that this huge segment of the population might never bother to vote for President or governor, state legislator or town clerk, is extraordinarily alarming. It is incumbent on those of us who do vote, who do believe in the power of one vote to change history, and who do believe in our system of government, to consider very carefully how best to bring them into the political process. . . .

It doesn't matter if you're black or white, old or young, rich or poor, male or female, Republican or Democrat. Don't throw this precious privilege away. When you wake up next Tuesday, please go vote.

Hillary Rodham Clinton, *Talking It Over*, November 1, 2000

Comprehension and Critical Thinking

1. What major concern or worry does Clinton express?

2. According to Clinton, in what way are the majority of young Americans good citizens?

3. Critical Thinking: *Draw Conclusions* Why do you think Clinton calls voting a precious privilege? Do you agree with this view? Explain.

Primary Sources

Washington Irving, *Rip Van Winkle*

Background

Washington Irving was born in New York City in 1783. He was the first American to make a living as a popular writer, as well as the first American writer to win a wide readership in Europe. Irving is best known for *The Sketch Book* (1819), a collection of essays that also contains two famous short stories, "The Legend of Sleepy Hollow" and "Rip Van Winkle."

"Rip Van Winkle" is a humorous fantasy about a lazy New York farmer who goes to sleep in the mountains before the American Revolution—and does not wake up for 20 years! In this selection, Rip returns to his village for the first time since his long nap.

He now hurried forth, and hastened to his old resort, the little village inn—but it too was gone. A large rickety wooden building stood in its place, with great gaping windows, some of them broken, and mended with old hats and petticoats, and over the door was painted, "The Union Hotel, by Jonathan Doolittle." Instead of the great tree that used to shelter the quiet little Dutch inn of yore, there now was reared a tall naked pole, with something on the top that looked like a red night-cap, and from it was fluttering a flag, on which was a singular assemblage of stars and stripes—all this was strange and <u>incomprehensible</u>. He recognized on the sign, however, the ruby face of King George . . . but even this was singularly [changed]. The red coat was changed for one of blue and buff, a sword was held in the hand instead of a sceptre, the head was decorated with a cocked hat, and underneath was painted in large characters, GENERAL WASHINGTON.

There was, as usual, a crowd of folk about the door, but none that Rip recollected. The very character of the people seemed changed. There was a busy, bustling, <u>disputatious</u> tone about it,

instead of the accustomed . . . drowsy tranquility. He looked in vain for the sage Nicholas Vedder, with his broad face, double chin, and fair long pipe, uttering clouds of tobacco smoke instead of idle speeches; or Van Bummel, the schoolmaster, doling forth the contents of an ancient newspaper. A lean, <u>bilious</u>-looking fellow, with his pockets full of handbills, was <u>haranguing vehemently</u> about rights of citizens—elections—members of congress—liberty—Bunker's Hill—heroes of seventy-six—and other words, which were a perfect Babylonish <u>jargon</u> to the bewildered Van Winkle.

Washington Irving, *The Sketch Book*

Comprehension and Critical Thinking

1. Identify two objects Rip sees at the hotel that he does not understand.

2. What are the men talking about when Rip arrives? Why doesn't Rip understand them?

3. Critical Thinking: *Draw Inferences*
   Rip thinks that "the very character of the people seemed changed." How did the people change? What do you think caused this change?

George Washington, *Farewell Address*

Background

As he prepared to leave office, President George Washington made a speech describing his vision of the nation's future. The speech became known as Washington's Farewell Address.

The speech deals with a wide range of topics, from the need to keep down the nation's debt to the importance of education. Washington also warns against the dangers of forming political parties, which began during his presidency.

The following excerpt from Washington's Farewell Address deals with relations between the United States and other countries. Washington's ideas about foreign relations influenced American foreign policy for generations.

Vocabulary *Builder*

commercial (KUH MER shuhl) *adj.* relating to trade

caprice (kuh PREES) *n.* sudden change

patronize (PAY truh nīz) *v.* to support

infidelity (ihn fuh DEHL uh tee) *n.* disloyalty; unfaithfulness

maxim (MAK sihm) *n.* wise saying

The great rule of conduct for us in regard to foreign nations is, in extending our commercial relations, to have with them as little political connection as possible. So far as we have already formed engagements, let them be fulfilled with perfect good faith. Here let us stop. Europe has a set of primary interests which to us have none; or a very remote relation. Hence she must be engaged in frequent controversies, the causes of which are essentially foreign to our concerns. . . . Why, by interweaving our destiny with that of any part of Europe, entangle our peace and prosperity in the toils of European ambition, rivalship, interest, humor or caprice?

It is our true policy to steer clear of permanent alliances with any portion of the foreign world; so far, I mean, as we are now at liberty to do it; for let me not be understood as capable of patronizing infidelity to existing engagements. I hold the maxim no less applicable to public than to private affairs, that honesty is always the best policy. I repeat, therefore, let those engagements be observed in their genuine sense. But, in my opinion, it is unnecessary and would be unwise to extend them.

George Washington, Farewell Address

George Washington

Comprehension and Critical Thinking

1. Restate the main point of the first sentence of the excerpt in your own words.

2. How does Washington think the United States should deal with agreements that it has already made with other nations?

3. Critical Thinking: *Identify Costs* Based on the above, what is one way the United States might suffer from forming permanent alliances with a European country?

Primary Sources

Tecumseh, *Speech at Vincennes*

Background

The great Shawnee leader Tecumseh was born in 1768 in what is now the state of Ohio. In the early 1800s, Tecumseh became the chief spokesman for Native Americans who opposed white settlement of western lands. Along with his brother, known as the Prophet, Tecumseh sought to organize Native Americans into a united league.

In 1810, Tecumseh was outraged that some Indians near the Wabash River had sold land to the United States government. In 1810, he met at Vincennes, Indiana, with the territorial governor, William Henry Harrison, to protest the sale. The following excerpt is from the speech Tecumseh gave that day.

Vocabulary *Builder*

traverse (truh VERS) *v.*
to travel over or across

encroach (ehn KROHCH) *v.*
to intrude upon the rights or property of another

stationary (STAY shuh nair ee) *adj.* fixed; unmoving

Until lately, there was no white man on this continent; that it then all belonged to red men, children of the same parents, placed on it by the Great Spirit that made them, to keep it, to traverse it, to enjoy its productions, and to fill it with the same race, once a happy race, since made miserable by the white people who are never contented but always encroaching. The way, and the only way, to check and to stop this evil, is for all the red men to unite in claiming a common and equal right in the land, as it was at first, and should be yet; for it never was divided, but belongs to all for the use of each. For no part has a right to sell, even to each other, much less to strangers—those who want all, and will not do with less.

The white people have no right to take the land from the Indians, because they had it first; it is theirs. They may sell, but all must join. Any sale not made by all is not valid. The late sale is bad. It was made by a part only. Part do not know how to sell. It requires all to make a bargain for all. All red men have equal rights to the unoccupied land. The right of occupancy is as good in one place as in another. There can not be two occupations in the same place. The first excludes all others. It is not so in hunting or traveling; for there the same ground will serve many, as they may follow each other all day; but the camp is stationary, and that is occupancy. It belongs to the first who sits down on his blanket or skins which he has thrown upon the ground; and till he leaves it no other has a right.

Tecumseh, speech at Vincennes, in *The World's Famous Orations*, ed. William Jennings Bryan

Comprehension and Critical Thinking

1. Why does Tecumseh object to the recent sale of land by Native Americans?

2. What solution does Tecumseh suggest for the increase in white settlement?

3. Critical Thinking: *Detect Points of View* Based on this speech, how does Tecumseh's view of property differ from that of the Americans who settled in the West?

Francis Scott Key, *The Star-Spangled Banner*

Background

The War of 1812 gave birth to an enduring American tradition. On September 13, 1814, British ships bombarded Fort McHenry near Baltimore. A young lawyer, Francis Scott Key, waited anxiously to find out if the fort would fall. The next morning, Key was relieved to see the American flag still flying over the fort.

Key described his feelings in the poem "The Star-Spangled Banner." The poem was then set to a traditional English tune and quickly became popular. In 1889, it was officially chosen to be played at all military flag raisings. The tradition of performing the song at Major League baseball games began in 1918. Finally, in 1931, Congress adopted "The Star-Spangled Banner" as the national anthem of the United States.

Vocabulary Builder

twilight (TWĪ līt) *n.* dim light between sunset and dark

perilous (PEHR uh luhs) *adj.* dangerous

rampart (RAM pahrt) *n.* defensive wall

haughty (HAWT ee) *adj.* overly proud

repose (ree POHZ) *v.* to rest

fitful (FIHT ful) *adj.* at irregular intervals

Oh, say, can you see by the dawn's early light
  What so proudly we hailed at the <u>twilight</u>'s
last gleaming,
Whose broad stripes and bright stars through
the <u>perilous</u> fight,
  O'er the <u>ramparts</u> we watched were so
gallantly streaming?
And the rockets' red glare, the bombs bursting
in air,
Gave proof through the night that our flag
was still there.
Oh, say, does that star-spangled banner yet wave
O'er the land of the free and the home of
    the brave?

On the shore, dimly seen through the mists
of the deep,
  Where the foe's <u>haughty</u> host in dread silence
<u>reposes</u>,
What is that which the breeze, o'er the
towering steep,
  As it <u>fitfully</u> blows, half conceals,
half discloses?
Now it catches the gleam of the morning's
first beam,
In full glory reflected, now shines on
the stream.
'Tis the star-spangled banner; oh long
may it wave
O'er the land of the free and the home of
the brave!

Francis Scott Key, "The Star-Spangled Banner"

**The flag as it
was in 1812**

Comprehension and Critical Thinking

1. How did Key know that Fort McHenry had not fallen to the British?

2. What words does Key use to describe the people of the United States?

3. Critical Thinking: *Apply Information* Based on what you have read, why would Key have been concerned about the safety of Fort McHenry?

Primary Sources

John Marshall, *Gibbons v. Ogden*

Background

In 1824, the Supreme Court decided the case of *Gibbons* v. *Ogden*.

The case involved steamboat traffic between different states. The state of New York had granted Aaron Ogden a license giving him the sole right to operate steamboats on state waterways between New York and New Jersey. When Thomas Gibbons began operating steamboats on the same waterways, Ogden sued him. Gibbons had a license granted by the federal government.

In his decision, Chief Justice John Marshall upheld the constitutional right of Congress to regulate interstate commerce. In this excerpt, Marshall discusses the meaning of the "commerce clause" of the Constitution, which is also reprinted below.

Vocabulary *Builder*

comprehend (kahm pree HEHND) *v.* to include

inconvenient (ihn kuhn VEEN yehnt) *adj.* causing difficulty or trouble

commence (kuh MEHNS) *v.* to begin

terminate (TER muh nayt) *v.* to end

jurisdiction (joor ihs DIHK shuhn) *n.* area in which a government has legal and political authority

From the Constitution of the United States ("commerce clause")

Article 1, Section 8.
The Congress shall have the power . . .
3. To regulate commerce with foreign nations, and among the several states, and with the Indian tribes.

From *Gibbons* v. *Ogden*

Commerce among the states cannot stop at the external boundary line of each state, but may be introduced into the interior. It is not intended to say that these words comprehend that commerce which is completely internal, which is carried on between man and man in a state, or between different parts of the same state, and which does not extend to or affect other states. Such a power would be inconvenient and is certainly unnecessary. Comprehensive as the word "among" is, it may very properly be restricted to that commerce which concerns more states than one. . . .

[States] either join each other, in which case they are separated by a mathematical line, or they are remote from each other, in which case other states lie between them. What is commerce "among" them, and how is it to be conducted? Can a trading expedition between two adjoining states commence and terminate outside of each? And if the trading intercourse be between two states remote from each other, must it not commence in one, terminate in the other, and probably pass through a third? Commerce among the states must, of necessity, be commerce with the states. . . . The power of Congress, then, whatever it may be, must be exercised within the territorial jurisdiction of the several states.

Gibbons v. Ogden, in *The Annals of America*, Volume 5

Comprehension and Critical Thinking

1. According to Marshall, what kind of trade does Congress not have the power to regulate?

2. Does Marshall believe that Congress can control certain kinds of trade within a state? Explain.

3. Critical Thinking: *Identify Benefits* How might the constitutional power of Congress to regulate interstate commerce benefit the nation's economy?

Alexis de Tocqueville, *Democracy in America*

Background

Alexis de Tocqueville, a young French writer, visited the United States in 1831. During his travels, he observed firsthand the impact of Jacksonian democracy. After returning to France, Tocqueville began writing *Democracy in America,* a detailed look at American politics, society, economics, religion, and law. The first volume was published in 1835. The book is still studied and quoted by historians and politicians today.

Following are two excerpts from *Democracy in America*. In the first, Tocqueville discusses the role of the American people in their government. In the second, he gives his view of the American character.

Vocabulary *Builder*

infraction (ihn FRAK shuhn) *n.* violation

random (RAN duhm) *adj.* chosen without plan or control

ardent (AHRD uhnt) *adj.* intense; enthusiastic

enterprising (EHNT uhr prī zihng) *adj.* full of energy; willing to undertake new projects

innovator (IHN uh vayt uhr) *n.* person who creates a new way of doing something

From Part Two, Chapter 1

In America the people name those who make the law and those who execute it; they themselves form the jury that punishes <u>infractions</u> of the law. Not only are the institutions democratic in their principle, but also in all their developments; thus the people name their representatives directly and generally choose them every year in order to keep them more completely under their dependence. It is therefore really the people who direct. . . . This majority is composed principally of peaceful citizens who, either by taste or by interest, sincerely desire the good of the country. Around them parties constantly agitate. . . .

From Part Two, Chapter 10

The American taken <u>randomly</u> will therefore be a man <u>ardent</u> in his desires, <u>enterprising</u>, adventurous—above all, an <u>innovator</u>. This spirit is in fact found in all his works; he introduces it into his political laws, his religious doctrines, his theories of social economy, his private industry; he brings it with him everywhere, into the depths of the woods as into the heart of towns.

Alexis de Tocqueville, *Democracy in America*, trans. by Harvey C. Mansfield and Delba Winthrop

Alexis de Tocqueville

Comprehension and Critical Thinking

1. According to Tocqueville, who controls the American government?

2. How does Tocqueville's view of American government fit what you have learned about the Jackson era?

3. Critical Thinking: *Link Past and Present* How does Tocqueville describe what he sees as the typical American? What people today might fit Tocqueville's description?

Primary Sources

Fredrika Bremer, *A Day Among the Swedes at Pine Lake*

Background

Like Ireland and Germany, Sweden became a great source of immigrants to the United States in the mid-1800s. Many Swedish immigrants left home because Sweden did not have enough good farmland to support its growing population. The majority of Swedish immigrants settled in the Midwest, especially in Minnesota, where the land and climate were similar to those in their homeland.

Fredrika Bremer was a Swedish writer who traveled extensively in the United States. In 1853, she described her travels in the book *Homes of the New World: Impressions of America.* In this excerpt, she describes her visit to a community of Swedish immigrants in Minnesota.

Mrs. Petterson, a large woman, who in her youth must have been handsome, came out to receive me, bent double and supported on a crutch-stick, but her open <u>countenance</u> beaming with kindness. She is not yet fifty, but is aged and broken down before her time by severe labor and trouble. . . .

Her husband began here as a farmer, but neither he nor his wife were accustomed to hard work; their land was poor (with the exception of Bergvall's farm, all the land around Pine Lake appears to be of a poor quality), they could not get help, and they were without the conveniences of life; they had a large family, which kept increasing; they endured incredible hardships. Mrs. Petterson, while [nursing] her children, was compelled to do the most <u>laborious</u> work; bent double with <u>rheumatism</u>, she was often obliged to wash for the whole family on her knees. Her husband was at last obliged to give up farming; he then took to shoemaking, and at this trade succeeded in making a livelihood for himself and his family.

He had now been dead a few years, and his widow was preparing to leave the little house and garden, which she could no longer look after, and remove to her son-in-law, Bergvall's. She felt herself worn out, old, and finished before her time, as she said; but still did not regret having come to America, because, as regarded her children and their future, she saw a new world opened to them, richer and happier than that which the mother country could have offered them, and she would have been glad to have purchased this future for them at the sacrifice of her own life; she would be well contented to go down to the grave, even before her time, and there to have done with her crutch.

Fredrika Bremer, *Homes of the New World: Impressions of America*

Comprehension and Critical Thinking

1. What hardships did Mrs. Petterson and her husband face when they first came to the United States?

2. Why is Mrs. Petterson glad that they decided to immigrate?

3. Critical Thinking: *Identify Costs and Benefits* Based on this selection and your reading, make a chart showing some of the costs and benefits of coming to the United States in the 1840s.

Solomon Northrup, *Twelve Years a Slave*

Background

Solomon Northrup was a free African American in New York State. But in 1841, he was kidnapped by slave traders. Separated from his wife and three children, he ended up on a plantation in Louisiana. After 12 years, he finally regained his freedom, thanks to the efforts of a group of white and black New Yorkers.

In 1853, Northrup published *Twelve Years a Slave*, a book about his experiences under slavery. In this excerpt, Northrup describes a slave auction. Eliza, an enslaved woman, watches as her son Randall is sold by the slave dealer, Freeman.

Vocabulary *Builder*

besought (bee SAWT) *v.*
begged (past tense of *beseech*)
paroxysm (PAR uhks ihz uhm) *n.*
sudden, violent outburst
plaintive (PLAYN tihv) *adv.*
sad; sorrowful
afflict (uh FLIHKT) *adj.*
to cause pain
avail (uh VAYL) *n.*
help; usefulness

All the time the trade was going on, Eliza was crying aloud, and wringing her hands. She besought the man not to buy him, unless he also bought her self and Emily. She promised, in that case, to be the most faithful slave that ever lived. The man answered that he could not afford it, and then Eliza burst into a paroxysm of grief, weeping plaintively. Freeman turned round to her, savagely, with his whip in his uplifted hand, ordering her to stop her noise, or he would flog her. . . .

All the frowns and threats of Freeman, could not wholly silence the afflicted mother. She kept on begging and beseeching them, most piteously not to separate the three. Over and over again she told them how she loved her boy. A great many times she repeated her former promises—how very faithful and obedient she would be; how hard she would labor day and night, to the last moment of her life, if he would only buy them all together. But it was of no avail; the man could not afford it. The bargain was agreed upon, and Randall must go alone. Then Eliza ran to him; embraced him passionately; kissed him again and again; told him to remember her—all the while her tears falling in the boy's face like rain.

Solomon Northrup, *Twelve Years a Slave: Narrative of Solomon, a Citizen of New-York, Kidnapped in Washington City in 1841*

Slave auction

Comprehension and Critical Thinking

1. What does Eliza want? How does she try to get it?

2. How does the slave dealer respond to Eliza?

3. Critical Thinking: *Draw Conclusions* Northrup's book was widely read in the North. What effect do you think descriptions like this one had on readers?

Primary Sources

Elizabeth Cady Stanton, *Letter From Seneca Falls*

Background

Elizabeth Cady Stanton was the leading figure of the early women's rights movement. In 1848, she and Lucretia Mott organized the first American women's rights convention at Seneca Falls, New York. She also authored the Declaration of Sentiments, issued by the Seneca Falls convention. Echoing the Declaration of Independence, the Declaration of Sentiments stated that "all men and women are created equal." Until her death in 1902, Stanton worked to win the right for women to vote.

Stanton also spoke out in support of education for women. She believed that education was needed to prepare women for full citizenship. In the following passage, she describes a new approach to educating women.

Vocabulary *Builder*

untrammeled (uhn TRAM uhld) *adj.* without limitations; free

romp (rahmp) *v.* to play actively and noisily

metropolis (muh TRAHP uh lihs) *n.* large city

melancholy (MEHL ehn kahl ee) *adj.* sad; depressing

drone (drohn) *n.* male bee that does no work

lucrative (LOO kruh tihv) *adj.* well-paying; profitable

The great work before us is the proper education of those just coming on the stage. Begin with girls of this day, and in twenty years we can revolutionize this nation. The childhood of women must be free and <u>untrammeled</u>; the girl must be allowed to <u>romp</u> and play, climb, skate, and swim. Her clothing must be more like those of the boy—strong, loose-fitting garments, thick boots, etc.—that she may be out in all seasons and enter freely into all kinds of sports. Teach the girls to go alone, by night and day—if need be, on the lonely highway or through the busy streets of the <u>metropolis</u>.

The manner in which all courage and self-reliance is early educated out of the girl—her path portrayed with danger and difficulties that never exist, is <u>melancholy</u> indeed. Better, far, suffer occasional insults, or die outright, than live the life of a coward, or never more without a protector. The best protection that any woman can have, one that will serve her at all times and in all places, is courage, and this she must get by experience. . . .

The girl must early be impressed with the idea that she is to be "a hand and not a mouth"—a worker, and not a <u>drone</u>—in the great hive of human action. She must be taught to look forward to a life of self-dependence, and like the boy, prepare herself for some <u>lucrative</u> trade or profession.

Elizabeth Cady Stanton, *History of Suffrage*

Comprehension and Critical Thinking

1. In what ways does Stanton think the education of girls should be like that of boys?

2. What does Stanton mean when she says that a woman should be "a hand and not a mouth"?

3. Critical Thinking: *Make Generalizations* Summarize in one sentence Stanton's goal for women.

Ralph Waldo Emerson, *Self-Reliance*

Background

Ralph Waldo Emerson was not only the most influential thinker of the transcendentalist movement, he was also one of the most admired Americans of his day. His essays and poems won a wide readership. In his lifetime, Emerson was best known for his popular lectures. He traveled across the country, especially the Northeast, addressing large crowds on a wide variety of topics. His early training as a minister helped make him a powerful speaker—especially when he was speaking out against slavery.

In one of his most important essays, *Self-Reliance,* Emerson warned against conformity, or blind following of standards set by others. Instead, he argued in favor of individualism.

Vocabulary *Builder*

envy (EHN vee) *n.* desire for or resentment of what others have

bestow (bee STOH) *v.* to give as a gift

integrity (ihn TEHG ruh tee) *n.* state of being true and sincere

arduous (AHR joo uhs) *adj.* very difficult

solitude (SOL uh tood) *n.* state of being alone

There is a time in every man's education when he arrives at the conviction that <u>envy</u> is ignorance; that imitation is suicide; that he must take himself for better for worse as his portion; that though the wide universe is full of good, no kernel of nourishing corn can come to him but through his toil <u>bestowed</u> on that plot of ground which is given to him to till. . . .

Trust thyself: every heart vibrates to that iron string. . . . Nothing is at last sacred but the <u>integrity</u> of your own mind. . . .

What I must do is all that concerns me, not what the people think. This rule, equally <u>arduous</u> in actual and in intellectual life, may serve for the whole distinction between greatness and meanness. It is the harder because you will always find those who think they know what is your duty better than you know it. It is easy in the world to live after the world's opinion; it is easy in <u>solitude</u> to live after our own; but the great man is he who in the midst of the crowd keeps with perfect sweetness the independence of solitude.

Ralph Waldo Emerson, *Self-Reliance*

Ralph Waldo Emerson

Comprehension and Critical Thinking

1. According to Emerson, who has the right to judge a person's actions?

2. How does Emerson define greatness?

3. Critical Thinking: *Apply Information* If you were designing a T-shirt devoted to the idea of individualism, what words from *Self-Reliance* would you put on it? Why?

John O'Sullivan, *Manifest Destiny*

Background

John O'Sullivan was a very influential journalist. In 1837, he founded the *United States Magazine and Democratic Review*. This monthly publication became highly popular among Jacksonian Democrats. In fact, the first person to subscribe to the magazine was Andrew Jackson himself!

In 1839, O'Sullivan published a series of newspaper editorials in which he outlined his view of the United States and its destiny or mission. He called the United States the "Great Nation of Futurity" because he believed the rise of America marked the beginning of a great new era in human history. O'Sullivan's editorials gave rise to the phrase "manifest destiny," the idea that the United States was meant to extend its borders to the Pacific Ocean.

Vocabulary *Builder*

domain (doh MAYN) *n.*
area under someone's rule

inevitable (ihn EHV ih tuh buhl) *adj.* certain; unable to be stopped

smite (smīt) *v.* to strike dead

hierarch (HĪ uhr ahrk) *n.* chief priest in ancient times

oligarch (AHL uh gahrk) *n.* one of a small group of rulers

myriad (MEER ee uhd) *n.* extremely large number

Our national birth was the beginning of a new history, the formation and progress of an untried political system, which separates us from the past and connects us with the future only; and so far as regards the entire development of the natural rights of man, in moral, political, and national life, we may confidently assume that our country is destined to be the great nation of futurity. . . .

The far-reaching, the boundless future will be the era of American greatness. In its magnificent <u>domain</u> of space and time, the nation of many nations is destined to manifest to mankind the excellence of divine principles; to establish on earth the noblest temple ever dedicated to the worship of the Most High—the Sacred and the True. . . .

Yes, we are the nation of progress, of individual freedom, of universal enfranchisement. . . . We must onward to the fulfillment of our mission—to the entire development of the principle of our organization—freedom of conscience, freedom of person, freedom of trade and business pursuits, universality of freedom and equality. This is our high destiny, and in nature's eternal, <u>inevitable</u> decree of cause and effect we must accomplish it. . . .

For this blessed mission to the nations of the world, which are shut out from the life-giving light of truth, has America been chosen; and her high example shall <u>smite</u> unto death the tyranny of kings, <u>hierarchs</u>, and <u>oligarchs</u>, and carry the glad tidings of peace and good will where <u>myriads</u> now endure an existence scarcely more enviable than that of beasts of the field. Who, then, can doubt that our country is destined to be *the great nation* of futurity?

John O'Sullivan, "The Great Nation of Futurity"

Comprehension and Critical Thinking

1. Identify three words in the above essay which show that O'Sullivan takes a religious viewpoint.

2. According to O'Sullivan, what is the mission of the United States?

3. **Critical Thinking:** *Apply Information* How could O'Sullivan's ideas be used to support the idea that the United States should expand to the Pacific Ocean?

David Rohrer Leeper, *Gold Rush Journal*

Background

In 1848, gold was discovered in California. The gold rush that followed attracted fortune-seekers from all over the nation and all over the world. Many of these forty-niners recorded their experiences in letters, diaries, and memoirs. One of the forty-niners was David Rohrer Leeper. Leeper was barely 17 years old when he left Indiana to try his luck in the California gold fields. He spent five years in California.

In 1894, when he was 62, he retold his experiences in the book *The Argonauts of '49, some recollections of the plains and the diggings.* In this excerpt, Leeper describes how it felt to be a teenager leaving home in search of gold and adventure.

Vocabulary *Builder*

<u>yoke</u> (yohk) *n.* pair of pack animals bound together by a wooden collar

<u>pang</u> (pang) *n.* sudden physical or emotional pain

<u>wrought</u> (rawt) *adj.* made; fashioned

<u>intensify</u> (ihn TEHN suh fī) *v.* to make stronger or sharper

On February 22, 1849, our little party of six set out from South Bend, Indiana, for the newly discovered gold-fields of California. . . . All were young—the oldest twenty-five, the youngest seventeen. Our equipment consisted of two wagons, seven <u>yoke</u> of oxen, and two years' supplies. The long journey before us, the comparatively unknown region through which it lay, and the glamour of the object for which it was undertaken, lent our adventure considerable local interest, so that many friends and spectators were present to witness our departure, our two covered wagons being objects of much curious concern as they rolled out of Washington street, with their three thousand miles chiefly of wilderness before them.

But for us the occasion had few <u>pangs</u>. The diggings had been discovered but a twelve-month before, and the glowing tales of their marvelous richness were on every tongue. Our enthusiasm was <u>wrought</u> up to the highest pitch, while the hardships and perils likely to be incident to such a journey were given scarcely a passing thought. Several parties of our acquaintance had already gone, and others were preparing to go, which still further <u>intensified</u> our eagerness.

David Rohrer Leeper, "The Argonauts of '49" from *California as I Saw It*, Library of Congress

California forty-niner

Comprehension and Critical Thinking

1. According to Leeper, what was the mood of him and his friends as they left for California?

2. What were their reasons for going?

3. **Critical Thinking:** *Make Predictions* Based on your reading, do you think Leeper and his friends would have faced any unexpected challenges? Explain.

Defiance of the Fugitive Slave Law

Background

In the North, the most hated part of the Compromise of 1850 was the Fugitive Slave Law. The law required all citizens to help catch runaway slaves. Anyone who let a fugitive slave escape could be fined $1,000 and jailed.

Some northern abolitionists banded together to form "vigilance committees." Their purpose was to resist efforts to return African Americans to slavery. The *Liberator*, the abolitionist newspaper founded by William Lloyd Garrison, published this list of instructions for vigilance committees. Garrison strongly opposed the use of violence but suggested other ways to interfere with slave catchers.

Vocabulary *Builder*

induce (ihn DOOS) *v.* to persuade

infamous (IHN fuh muhs) *adj.* having a bad reputation; disgraced

resolute (REZ uh loot) *adj.* determined; firm

loathe (lohth) *v.* to hate

detest (dee TEHST) *v.* to hate

As soon as the kidnappers arrive in any town, large handbills should be posted in all public places, containing their names, with a description of their persons and the business on which they come.

An attempt should be made to <u>induce</u> the landlord of any hotel or boardinghouse to which they may go, to refuse them entertainment, on the ground of their being persons <u>infamous</u> by profession, like pick-pockets, gamblers, or horse-stealers. . . .

Two <u>resolute</u>, unarmed men should follow each of them wherever he goes, pointing him out from time to time with the word SLAVE-HUNTER. . . . He should not have a moment's relief from the feeling that his object is understood, that he cannot act in secret, that he is surrounded by those who <u>loathe</u> his person and <u>detest</u> his purpose, and who have means always at hand to prevent the possibility of success.

"Reception and Treatment of Kidnappers," *Liberator*,
January 31, 1851

Poster defying the Fugitive Slave Law

Comprehension and Critical Thinking

1. In one sentence, describe this writer's approach to opposing the Fugitive Slave Law.

2. How can you tell that the writer of this article does not favor the use of violence?

3. Critical Thinking: *Detect Points of View* How does the writer of this article use emotionally charged words to express strong feelings about the Fugitive Slave Law? Give three examples.

Abraham Lincoln and Stephen Douglas, *Debate at Alton, Illinois*

Background

The 1858 Illinois Senate race pitted Democratic candidate Stephen Douglas against Republican candidate Abraham Lincoln. During the campaign, Lincoln challenged Douglas to a series of debates. Over the course of two months, the candidates held seven fiery debates in different towns. Thousands of people came from miles around to listen.

The main issue of the debates was the extension of slavery into the western territories. The Lincoln-Douglas debates set out in clear terms the difficult issue of slavery in the territories. These excerpts are from their final debate.

Vocabulary *Builder*

controversy (KAHN truh ver see) *n.* debate; argument

sentiment (SEHN tuh mehnt) *n.* feeling

proposition (prahp uh ZIHSH uhn) *n.* basic principle or argument

radiate (RAY dee ayt) *v.* to spread outward

LINCOLN: The real issue in this <u>controversy</u>—the one pressing upon every mind—is the <u>sentiment</u> on the part of one class that looks upon the institution of slavery as a wrong, and of another class that does not look upon it as a wrong. The sentiment that contemplates the institution of slavery in this country as a wrong is the sentiment of the Republican Party. It is the sentiment around which all their actions, all their arguments, circle, from which all their <u>propositions</u> <u>radiate</u>. They look upon it as being a moral, social, and political wrong; and while they contemplate it as such, they nevertheless have due regard for its actual existence among us, and the difficulties of getting rid of it in any satisfactory way and to all the constitutional obligations thrown about it. Yet, having a due regard for these, they desire a policy in regard to it that looks to its not creating any more danger. They insist that it should, as far as may be, be treated as a wrong; and one of the methods of treating it as a wrong is to make provision that it shall grow no larger. They also desire a policy that looks to a peaceful end of slavery at some time, as being wrong.

DOUGLAS: He says that he looks forward to a time when slavery shall be abolished everywhere. I look forward to a time when each state shall be allowed to do as it pleases. If it chooses to keep slavery forever, it is not my business, but its own; if it chooses to abolish slavery, it is its own business, not mine. I care more for the great principle of self-government, the right of the people to rule, than I do for all the Negroes in Christendom. . . . Hence, I say, let us maintain this government on the principles that our fathers made it, recognizing the right of each state to keep slavery as long as its people determine, or to abolish it when they please.

The Lincoln-Douglas Debates, in *Annals of America*, Volume 9

Comprehension and Critical Thinking

1. According to Lincoln, what is the basic idea behind the Republican Party?

2. Summarize Douglas's attitude toward the abolition of slavery.

3. Critical Thinking: *Detect Points of View* Did Lincoln favor the immediate abolition of slavery? Why or why not?

Robert E. Lee, *Letter to His Sister*

Background

The Lees were one of the most respected families in Virginia as well as in the United States. In 1776, Richard Henry Lee had introduced the resolution in the Continental Congress calling for independence. His cousin, Harry Lee, was a cavalry commander in the Revolutionary War.

Harry's son, Robert E. Lee, also had a distinguished career in the U.S. military. He served in the Mexican War and acted as superintendent of the Military Academy at West Point. But when Virginia seceded from the Union in April 1861, Lee faced a difficult choice. He had to decide whether to keep his position or remain loyal to Virginia. In this letter, he tells his sister of his decision. He later agreed to accept command of the Confederate army.

Vocabulary *Builder*

forborne (for BORN) *v.* to stop or avoid (*past tense of* forbear)

redress (ree DREHS) *n.* fair settlement

commission (kuh MIHSH uhn) *n.* official document making someone a military officer

endeavor (ehn DEHV uhr) *v.* to try

The whole South is in a state of revolution, into which Virginia, after a long struggle, has been drawn; and though I recognize no necessity for the state of things, and would have <u>forborne</u> and pleaded to the end for <u>redress</u> of grievances, real or supposed, yet in my own person I had to meet the question whether I should take part against my native State.

Robert E. Lee

With all my devotion to the Union, and the feeling of loyalty and duty of an American citizen, I have not been able to make up my mind to raise my hand against my relative, my children, my home. I have, therefore, resigned my <u>commission</u> in the Army, and save in defense of my native State (with the sincere hope that my poor services may never be needed) I hope I may never be called upon to draw my sword.

I know you will blame me, but you must think as kindly as you can, and believe that I have <u>endeavored</u> to do what I thought right.

The Wartime Papers of Robert E. Lee

Comprehension and Critical Thinking

1. Based on this reading, was Lee in favor of secession?

2. What reason does he give for resigning his commission with the Union army?

3. Critical Thinking: *Draw Conclusions* How would you describe Lee's feelings about his decision? Would you consider him a traitor? Why or why not?

James Henry Gooding, *Letters From an African American Soldier*

Background

James Henry Gooding was a free African American born in New York. At the age of 19, he went to Massachusetts to find work on a whaling ship. He made a good living, married, and settled down in Massachusetts. Then, in February 1863, he became one of the first people to volunteer for the 54th Massachusetts, the famous African American regiment of the Union army. He soon rose to the rank of corporal.

From March 1863 until he was killed in battle in February 1854, Gooding wrote a series of letters that were published in a Massachusetts newspaper. The first excerpt here was written while the 54th was still in training camp. The second was written after the assault on Fort Wagner.

Vocabulary *Builder*

vie (vī) *v.* to compete

ignoble (ihg NOH buhl) *adj.* shameful

parapet (PAR uh peht) *n.* barrier used to shield troops from enemy fire

bayonet (bay uh NEHT) *n.* short blade attached to the end of a rifle

battery (BAT uhr ree) *n.* set of heavy guns, such as cannons

May 24, 1863

We have received marching orders; the order was read at dress parade last Thursday, so next Sunday I think we shall be on our way to Dixie. . . .

It seems that most every man in the regiment <u>vies</u> with each other in excellence in whatever they undertake. It is, I think, one of the best guarantees that the 54th will be a credit to old Massachusetts wherever it goes. The citizens of this Commonwealth need not be ashamed of the 54th now; and if the regiment will be allowed a chance, I feel confident the Colored Volunteers will add glory to her already bright name. There is not a man in the regiment who does not appreciate the difficulties, the dangers, and maybe <u>ignoble</u> death that awaits him, if captured by the foe, and they will die upon the field rather than be hanged like a dog; and when a thousand men are fighting for their very existence, who dare say them men won't fight determinedly? The greatest difficulty will be to stop them.

July 20, 1863

The 54th, the past week, has proved itself twice in battle. . . .

Gen. Strong asked us if we would follow him into Fort Wagner. Every man said, yes—we were ready to follow wherever we were led. . . . We went at it, over the ditch and on to the <u>parapet</u> through a deadly fire; but we could not get into the fort. We met the foe on the parapet of Wagner with the <u>bayonet</u>—we were exposed to a murderous fire from the <u>batteries</u> of the fort, from our Monitors and our land batteries, as they did not cease firing soon enough. Mortal men could not stand such a fire, and the assault on Wagner was a failure.

On the Altar of Freedom: A Black Soldier's Civil War Letters From the Front, ed. Virginia M. Adams

Comprehension and Critical Thinking

1. What is Gooding's attitude about going into battle? What prediction does he make?

2. Does Gooding's prediction come true?

3. **Critical Thinking:** *Draw Inferences* Why do you think the men of the 54th Massachusetts were unwilling to be captured alive?

Primary Sources

Walt Whitman, *O Captain! My Captain!*

Background

Walt Whitman was born in 1819 on Long Island and grew up in Brooklyn. In 1855, he published his greatest collection of poems, *Leaves of Grass*. He kept adding to the collection for the rest of his life. During the Civil War, Whitman volunteered to care for men in military hospitals.

After the assassination of Abraham Lincoln, Whitman wrote two poems honoring the fallen President that became very famous. "When Lilacs Last in the Dooryard Bloom'd" is considered one of his best works. "O Captain! My Captain!" is a shorter poem and one of the few Whitman wrote using rhyme. The poem was greatly loved by the American people. Whitman was so often asked to recite it, he said he almost regretted writing it.

Vocabulary *Builder*

rack (rak) *n.* cause of pain or upset

exult (ehg ZUHLT) *v.* to leap for joy

keel (keel) *n.* main piece of steel or timber extending along the bottom of a ship

trill (trihl) *n.* rapid repeat of the same tone by a musical instrument

O Captain! my Captain! our fearful trip is done,
The ship has weather'd every <u>rack</u>, the prize we
   sought is won,
The port is near, the bells I hear, the people all
   <u>exulting</u>,
While follow eyes the steady <u>keel</u>, the vessel
   grim and daring;
     But O heart! heart! heart!
      O the bleeding drops of red,
       Where on the deck my Captain lies,
        Fallen cold and dead.

O Captain! my Captain! rise up and hear the bells;
Rise up—for you the flag is flung—for you the
   bugle <u>trills</u>,
For you bouquets and ribbon'd wreaths—for you
   the shores a-crowding,
For you they call, the swaying mass, their eager
   faces turning;
     Here Captain! dear father!

This arm beneath your head!
   It is some dream that on the deck,
     You've fallen cold and dead.

My Captain does not answer, his lips are pale
   and still,
My father does not feel my arm, he has no pulse
   nor will,
The ship is anchor'd safe and sound, its voyage
   closed and done,
From fearful trip the victor ship comes in with
   object won;
     Exult O shores, and ring O bells!
      But I with mournful tread,
       Walk the deck my Captain lies,
        Fallen cold and dead.

Walt Whitman, *Leaves of Grass*

Comprehension and Critical Thinking

1. Who is the Captain in the poem? What is the ship?
2. Why does Whitman write "our fearful trip is done" and "the prize we sought is won"?
3. Critical Thinking: *Detect Points of View* What is Whitman's attitude toward the Captain and the events discussed in the poem?

Walt Whitman

Frederick Douglass, *What the Black Man Wants*

Background
Frederick Douglass was born into slavery in Maryland in 1817. Escaping to the North, he became a leading abolitionist. He spoke at antislavery conventions, published the antislavery newspaper the *North Star,* and wrote a best-selling autobiography that awakened many people to the injustices of slavery. In addition, Douglass was a delegate to the 1848 women's rights convention at Seneca Falls.

Only a few days after the end of the Civil War, Douglass addressed the annual meeting of the Massachusetts Anti-Slavery Society. He discussed one of the key issues of Reconstruction: the enfranchisement of, or giving the vote to, African Americans. This is an excerpt from that speech.

Vocabulary *Builder*
unconditional (uhn kuhn DIHSH uhn uhl) *adj.* without limits or reservations

mockery (MAHK uhr ee) *n.* false imitation

sufficient (suh FIHSH uhnt) *adj.* enough

deprivation (deh prih VAY shuhn) *n.* act of taking something away

incapacity (ihn kuh PAS ih tee) *n.* lack of ability

I am for the "immediate, <u>unconditional</u>, and universal" enfranchisement of the black man, in every State in the Union. Without this, his liberty is a <u>mockery</u>; without this, you might as well almost retain the old name of slavery for his condition; for in fact, if he is not the slave of the individual master, he is the slave of society, and holds his liberty as a privilege, not as a right. He is at the mercy of the mob, and has no means of protecting himself. . . .

It may be asked, "Why do you want it? Some men have got along very well without it. Women have not this right." Shall we justify one wrong by another? This is the <u>sufficient</u> answer. Shall we at this moment justify the <u>deprivation</u> of the Negro of the right to vote, because some one else is deprived of that privilege? I hold that women, as well as men, have the right to vote, and my heart and voice go with the movement to extend suffrage to woman; but that question rests upon another basis than which our right rests.

We may be asked, I say, why we want it. I will tell you why we want it. We want it because it is our right, first of all. No class of men can, without insulting their own nature, be content with any deprivation of their rights. We want it again, as a means for educating our race. Men are so constituted that they derive their conviction of their own possibilities largely by the estimate formed of them by others. If nothing is expected of a people, that people will find it difficult to contradict that expectation. By depriving us of suffrage, you affirm our <u>incapacity</u> to form an intelligent judgment respecting public men and public measures; you declare before the world that we are unfit to exercise the elective franchise, and by this means lead us to undervalue ourselves.

Frederick Douglass, *What the Black Man Wants*

Comprehension and Critical Thinking

1. According to Douglass, when should the government grant African Americans the right to vote? Under what conditions?

2. What is Douglass's view of women's suffrage?

3. Critical Thinking: *Evaluate Information* Summarize one argument Douglass uses in favor of granting the vote to African Americans. Explain whether you find that argument persuasive and why.

Chief Joseph, *I Will Fight No More Forever*

Background

In 1877, the U.S. government ordered members of the Nez Percé Nation to move off their lands in western Oregon onto a reservation in Idaho. Instead, about 800 Nez Percés tried to escape to Canada. This group included Hin-mah-too-yah-lat-kekt, more commonly known as Chief Joseph.

The Nez Percé traveled over 1,500 miles of mountainous terrain in their attempt to escape. They fought many battles with pursuing U.S. troops, only to be halted just forty miles from the safety of the Canadian border. On October 5, the exhausted survivors surrendered. Chief Joseph's speech has become a famous symbol of the resistance and conquest of Native Americans in the West.

I am tired of fighting. Our chiefs are killed. Looking Glass is dead. Toohulhulsote is dead. The old men are all dead. It is the young men who say yes or no. He who led the young men is dead.

Chief Joseph

It is cold and we have no blankets. The little children are freezing to death. My people, some of them, have run away to the hills and have no blankets, no food. No one knows where they are—perhaps freezing to death. I want to have time to look for my children and see how many I can find. Maybe I shall find them among the dead.

Hear me, my chiefs. I am tired. My heart is sick and sad. From where the sun now stands, I will fight no more forever.

Chief Joseph's Surrender,
in *New Perspectives on the West* (PBS)

Comprehension and Critical Thinking

1. How would you describe the mood of this speech?

2. What does Chief Joseph want to do after the surrender? What promise does he make?

3. Critical Thinking: *Evaluate Information* Why do you think this short speech has become so admired and famous?

Laura Ingalls Wilder, *Grasshoppers Walking*

Background

Laura Ingalls Wilder was born in 1867. When she was a child, her family moved westward. In the 1930s, Wilder began writing a series of children's novels based on her family's experiences as homesteaders. When she began to write her classic "Little House" book series, she had no intention of creating fame for herself or the places she lived.

She wrote simply to preserve her memories of her childhood on the Midwestern frontier.

The books are still in print and are published in over 40 languages worldwide. In this excerpt from the fourth novel, *On the Banks of Plum Creek*, Wilder describes one of the hardships of prairie life: grasshoppers.

Vocabulary *Builder*

thicket (THIHK iht) *n.* a thick growth of shrubs or small trees

dooryard (DOR yahrd) *n.* yard just outside the door of a house

Day by day more and more grasshoppers hatched out of the ground. Green grasshoppers of all sizes were swarming everywhere and eating. The wind could not blow loud enough to hide the sound of their jaws, nipping, gnawing, chewing.

They ate all the green garden rows. They ate the green potato tops. They ate the grass, and the willow leaves, and the green plum <u>thickets</u> and the small green plums. They ate the whole prairie bare and brown. And they grew. . . .

"Oh, Charles," Ma said one morning, "seems to me I just can't bear one more day of this."

Ma was sick. Her face was white and thin, and she sat down tired as she spoke.

Pa did not answer. For days he had been going out and coming in with a still, tight face. He did not sing or whistle anymore. It was worst of all when he did not answer Ma. He walked to the door and stood looking out. . . .

All across the <u>dooryard</u> the grasshoppers were walking shoulder to shoulder and end to end, so crowded that the ground seemed to be moving. Not a single one hopped. Not one

turned its head. As fast as they could go, they were all walking west. . . .

They all stood looking at that strange sight. Only Carrie climbed onto her high chair and beat the table with her spoon. . . . "There, you shall have your breakfast," Ma said, turning around. Then she cried out. "My goodness."

Grasshoppers were walking over Carrie. They came pouring in the eastern window, side by side and end to end, across the window sill and down the wall and over the floor. They went up the legs of the table and the benches and Carrie's high stool. Under the table and benches, and over the table and benches and Carrie, they were walking west.

Laura Ingalls Wilder, *On the Banks of Plum Creek*

Comprehension and Critical Thinking

1. Why is the grasshopper invasion a threat to the family's farm?

2. What are the emotional effects on Pa and Ma?

3. Critical Thinking: *Draw Conclusions* What personal qualities do you think homesteaders like Ma and Pa need to survive on the prairie?

Primary Sources

Lewis Hine, *Child Labor in the Coal Mines*

Background

Lewis Hine was a journalist and photographer. He spent much of his early career photographing immigrants with the same dignity and respect given to the first European settlers in this country. Later, his efforts focused on the horrors and injustices of child labor.

In 1911, Hine investigated child labor in the coal-mining regions of Pennsylvania. Here, he reports on the working conditions of "breaker boys," whose job was to sit on benches and sort coal as it passed below them on a swiftly moving belt.

Vocabulary *Builder*

monotony (mu NAH tuh nee) *n.* boring, repetitive sameness

persist (pehr SIHST) *v.* to refuse to stop

coroner (KAW ruh nuhr) *n.* legal official who investigates causes of deaths not due to natural causes

The boys working in the breaker are bent double, with little chance to relax; the air at times is dense with coal-dust, which penetrates so far into the passages of the lungs that for long periods after the boy leaves the breaker, he continues to cough up the black coal dust. Fingers are calloused and cut by the coal and slate, the noise and <u>monotony</u> are deadening; and, worse still, grave danger from the machinery to those boys who <u>persist</u> in playing about the breaker, and even for those at their regular work.

While I was in the region, two breaker boys of 15 years, while at work assigned to them, fell or were carried by the coal down into the car below. One was badly burned and the other was smothered to death. . . . This boy who was killed was Dennis McKee. The <u>Coroner</u> told me that this boy had reached his fifteenth birthday only a few days before his death and the evidence seemed to prove that he was working in another breaker before he was 14 years old.

Lewis Hine, "Child Labor in the Coal Mines,"
in *Child Labor: An American History,* Hugh D. Hindman

Coal-mining boys

Comprehension and Critical Thinking

1. What are some of the physical effects of working in the breaker?

2. Describe the accident that killed Dennis McKee.

3. Critical Thinking: *Draw Inferences* Based on this reading, what do you think might be the psychological effects of working as a breaker boy?

McGuffey's Second Eclectic Reader

Background

Nearly every American child who attended public school in the late 1800s learned lessons from *McGuffey's Eclectic Readers.* First published in 1836, the six readers taught moral and religious lessons along with reading and writing. Since then, children have been delighted by these books filled with exotic adventures, exciting tales, beautiful poems, and humorous fables. The following two stories are from *McGuffey's Second Eclectic Reader,* intended for very young children.

A Kind Brother

1. A boy was once sent from home to take a basket of things to his grandmother.

2. The basket was so full that it was very heavy. So his little brother went with him, to help carry the load.

3. They put a pole under the handle of the basket, and each then took hold of an end of the pole. In this way they could carry the basket very nicely.

4. Now the older boy thought, "My brother Tom does not know about this pole.

5. "If I slip the basket near him, his side will be heavy, and mine light; but if the basket is in the middle of the pole, it will be as heavy for me as it is for him.

6. "Tom does not know this as I do. But I will not do it. It would be wrong, and I will not do what is wrong."

7. Then he slipped the basket quite near his own end of the pole. His load was now heavier than that of his little brother.

8. Yet he was happy; for he felt that he had done right. Had he deceived his brother, he would not have felt at all happy.

At Work

1. A little play does not harm any one, but does much good. After play, we should be glad to work.

2. I knew a boy who liked a good game very much. He could run, swim, jump, and play ball; and was always merry when out of school.

3. But he knew that time is not all for play; that our minutes, hours, and days are very precious.

4. At the end of his play, he would go home. After he had washed his face and hands, and brushed his hair, he would help his mother, or read in his book, or write upon his slate.

5. He used to say, "One thing at a time." When he had done with work, he would play; but he did not try to play and to work at the same time.

McGuffey's Second Eclectic Reader

Comprehension and Critical Thinking

1. What is the main lesson in "A Kind Brother"?

2. What is the main lesson in "At Work"?

3. Critical Thinking: *Link Past and Present* Do you think schools today should teach lessons like these to young children? Why or why not?

Primary Sources

Jacob Riis, *How the Other Half Lives*

Background

Jacob Riis immigrated to the United States from Denmark in 1870. After living for several years in extreme poverty, he found a job as a police reporter for the *New York Tribune*. He became one of the leading muckrakers of the Progressive Era. Riis's writing and photographs helped expose the harsh living conditions in the crowded tenements of New York City. This excerpt is from Riis's 1890 book *How the Other Half Lives*.

Vocabulary *Builder*

aghast (uh GAST) *adj.* horrified

array (ur RAY) *n.* orderly arrangement

apex (AY pehks) *n.* highest point

truant (TROO uhnt) *n.* pupil who misses school without permission

The problem of the children becomes, in these swarms, to the last degree perplexing. Their very number make one stand <u>aghast</u>. I have already given instances of the packing of the child population in East Side tenements. They might be continued indefinitely until the <u>array</u> would be enough to startle any community. For, be it remembered, these children with the training they receive—or do not receive—with the instincts they inherit and absorb in their growing up, are to be our future rulers, if our theory of government is worth anything. More than a working majority of our voters now register from the tenements.

I counted the other day the little ones, up to ten years or so, in a Bayard Street tenement that for a yard has a triangular space in the center with sides fourteen or fifteen feet long, just room enough for a row of ill-smelling closets at the base of the triangle and a hydrant at the <u>apex</u>. There was about as much light in this "yard" as in the average cellar. I gave up my self-imposed task in despair when I had counted one hundred and twenty-eight in forty families. . . . Bodies of drowned children turn up in the rivers right along since summer whom no one seems to know anything about. When last spring some workmen, while moving a pile of lumber on a North River pier, found under the last plank the body of a little lad crushed to death, no one had missed a boy, though his parents afterward turned up. The <u>truant</u> officer assuredly does not know, though he spends his life trying to find out, somewhat illogically, perhaps, since the department that employs him admits that thousands of poor children are crowded out of the schools year by year for want of room.

Jacob Riis, *How the Other Half Lives*

Comprehension and Critical Thinking

1. According to Riis, why should all Americans be concerned about tenement children?

2. What point does Riis make about education received by tenement children?

3. Critical Thinking: *Draw Conclusions* What details would have shocked readers? Why do you think muckrakers sought to shock their audience?

J. M. Lizarras, *A Japanese-Mexican Labor Union*

Background

In 1903, Mexican and Japanese farm workers in California joined together to form the Japanese-Mexican Labor Association (JMLA). The JMLA was the first labor union comprised of members from different racial groups. They held a successful strike against beet growers known as the Oxnard Strike of 1903. The JMLA then applied for a charter to join the American Federation of Labor. AFL president Samuel Gompers refused unless the union banned Asian workers. J. M. Lizarras, head of the Mexican branch of the union, wrote this response to Gompers.

Vocabulary *Builder*

counsel (KOWN suhl) *v.* to exchange views and advice

rations (RA shuhnz) *n.* fixed daily allowance of food or other necessities

accord (uh KORD) *v.* to grant or give

We beg to say in reply that our Japanese brothers here were the first to recognize the importance of co-operating and uniting in demanding a fair wage scale. . . .

In the past we have <u>counseled</u>, fought and lived on very short <u>rations</u> with our Japanese brothers, and toiled with them in the fields, and they have been uniformly kind and considerate. We would be false to them and to ourselves and to the cause of Unionism if we, now, accepted privileges for ourselves which are not <u>accorded</u> to them. . . .

We will refuse any other kind of charter, except one which will wipe out race prejudices and recognize our fellow workers as being as good as ourselves. I am ordered by the Mexican union to write this letter to you and they fully approve its words.

in *A Different Mirror: A History of Multicultural America*, Ronald Takak

Japanese farmworkers in California

Comprehension and Critical Thinking

1. According to Lizarras, why are the Mexicans unwilling to separate from the Japanese workers?

2. What promise does Lizarras make on behalf of the union?

3. Critical Thinking: *Identify Benefits* What benefits might the union have gained from joining the AFL? Do you agree with its decision? Why or why not?

Primary Sources

Alfred Thayer Mahan, *The Influence of Sea Power Upon History*

Background

In 1890s, naval historian Alfred Thayer Mahan published *The Influence of Sea Power Upon History.* Although the book focused on the 1600s and 1700s, it had a great impact on American foreign policy at the time. Mahan argued that industrial growth and increased overseas trade went hand in hand with military expansion.

He convinced two U.S. Presidents: William McKinley and Theodore Roosevelt to follow his policies. The taking of Caribbean islands, Hawaii, and the Philippines as U.S. military bases was a direct result of Mahan's influence.

Vocabulary *Builder*

common (KAHM uhn) *n.* large area of public land that can be used by all

beset (bee SEHT) *v.* to attack from all sides

maritime (MAR uh tīm) *adj.* relating to sea navigation and shipping

---

The first and most obvious light in which the sea presents itself from the political and social point of view is that of a great highway; or better, perhaps, of a wide <u>common</u>, over which men may pass in all directions but on which some well-worn paths show that controlling reasons have led them to choose certain lines of travel rather than others. These lines of travel are called trade routes; and the reasons which have determined them are to be sought in the history of the world. . . .

Home trade is but a part of the business of a country bordering on the sea. Foreign necessities or luxuries must be brought to its ports, either in its own or in foreign ships, which will return bearing in exchange the products of the country, whether they be the fruits of the earth or the work of men's hands; and it is the wish of every nation that this shipping business should be done by its own vessels. The ships that thus sail to and fro must have secure ports to which to return and must, as far as possible, be followed by the protection of their country throughout the voyage. . . .

The needs of commerce, however, were not all provided for when safety had been secured at the far end of the road. The voyages were long and dangerous, the seas often <u>beset</u> with enemies. In the most active days of colonizing there prevailed on the sea a lawlessness, the very memory of which is now almost lost, and the days of settled peace between <u>maritime</u> nations were few and far between. Thus arose the demand for stations along the road, like the Cape of Good Hope, St. Helena, and Mauritius, not primarily for trade but for defense and war; the demand for possession of posts like Gibraltar, Malta, Louisburg, at the entrance of the Gulf of St. Lawrence—posts whose value was chiefly strategic, though not necessarily wholly so.

Alfred Thayer Mahan, *The Influence of Sea Power Upon History, 1660–1783*

Comprehension and Critical Thinking

1. What does Mahan say is the primary importance of the sea in history?

2. According to Mahan, why must seagoing nations have military stations overseas?

3. Critical Thinking: *Distinguish Relevant Information* Mahan wanted to encourage the United States to build up its naval power. Do you think his use of examples from past history was relevant? Explain.

Theodore Roosevelt, *Corollary to the Monroe Doctrine*

Background

In his annual address to Congress in 1905, President Theodore Roosevelt argued that the Monroe Doctrine had to be adapted to changing times. In particular, Roosevelt was concerned about growing American military and economic interests in Latin America, especially in the Panama Canal.

To keep other powers out of Latin America and to ensure economic security, he issued his corollary. This policy allowed the United States to exercise force if needed to protect the Western Hemisphere from unrest and wrongdoing.

Vocabulary *Builder*

aggression (uh GREHSH uhn) *n.* policy of unjustified warlike action against another nation

endure (ehn DYOOR) *v.* to bear without complaint; to put up with

reluctance (ree LUHK tuhns) *n.* unwillingness

As a mere matter of self-defense we must exercise a close watch over the approaches to this canal; and this means we must be thoroughly alive to our interests in the Caribbean Sea.

It must be understood that under no circumstances will the United States use the Monroe Doctrine as a cloak for territorial aggression. We desire peace with all the world, but perhaps most of all with the other peoples of the American continent. There are, of course, limits to the wrongs which any self-respecting nation can endure. It is always possible that wrong actions toward this nation or toward citizens of this nation in some state unable to keep order among its own people, unable to secure justice from outsiders, and unwilling to do justice to those outsiders who treat it well, may result in our having to take action to protect our rights; but such action will not be taken with a view to territorial aggression, and it will be taken at all only with extreme reluctance and when it becomes evident that every other resource has been exhausted.

Theodore Roosevelt, "Corollary to the Monroe Doctrine," in *Annals of America*, Volume 13

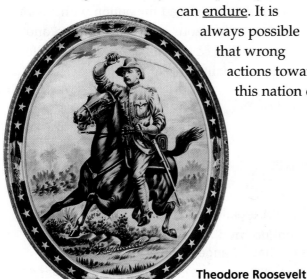

Theodore Roosevelt

Comprehension and Critical Thinking

1. According to Roosevelt, why would the United States be concerned about political developments in the Caribbean?

2. What promise does Roosevelt make about American foreign policy goals?

3. Critical Thinking: *Apply Information* How could the arguments given here be used to justify military intervention in the Caribbean region?

Primary Sources

John F. Kennedy, from *A Nation of Immigrants*

Background

President John F. Kennedy understood well the importance of immigration to the United States. His ancestors had come to the United States from Ireland to escape the potato famine. In his book *A Nation of Immigrants*, which was written a few years before he became President, Kennedy wrote the passage that follows. During his presidency, Kennedy revised immigration laws. He decided to revise the book as well to reflect the changes in the laws. Kennedy was working on the book at the time of his assassination in 1963.

Vocabulary *Builder*

conviction (con vihk shun) *n.* strong belief

realization (reel ih ZAY shun) *n.* the coming to full understanding; sudden awareness

infused (ihn FUZD) *v.* put into

One of America's characteristics has always been the lack of a rigid class structure. It has traditionally been possible for people to move up the social and economic scale. Even if one did not succeed in moving up oneself, there was always the hope that one's children would. Immigration is by definition of gesture of faith in social mobility. It is the expression of action of a positive belief in the possibility of a better life. It has thus contributed greatly to developing the spirit of personal betterment in American society and to strengthening the national confidence in change and the future. Such confidence, when widely shared, sets the national tone. The opportunities that America offered made the dream real, at least for a good many, but the dream itself was in large part the product of millions of plain people beginning a new life in the <u>conviction</u> that life could indeed be better, and each new wave of immigration rekindled the dream. . . .

The *continuous* immigration of the nineteenth and early twentieth centuries . . . gave every old [established] American a <u>realization</u> of how far he might go. It reminded every American, old and new, that change is the essence of life, and that American society is a process, not a conclusion. The abundant resources of this land provided the foundation for a great nation. But only people could make the opportunity a reality. Immigration provided the human resources. More than that, it <u>infused</u> the nation with a commitment to far horizons and new frontiers, and thereby kept the pioneer spirit of American life, the spirit of equality and of hope, always alive and strong.

John F. Kennedy, from *A Nation of Immigrants*, 1958

John F. Kennedy

Comprehension and Critical Thinking

1. According to Kennedy, how does immigration benefit established Americans?

2. What do you think Kennedy means when he says that "change is the essence of life"?

3. Critical Thinking: *Draw Conclusions* In what ways do you think immigration affects the "spirit of hope" in the United States?

Richard Wright, *Black Boy*

Background

The African American author Richard Wright was born and raised in Mississippi. His grandparents had been enslaved. In 1927, when he was 19, Wright and his aunt moved to Chicago, Illinois. Like many African Americans in the South, Wright and his aunt migrated north in hopes of getting good jobs and escaping segregation. What they found often did not match their expectations. Jobs and housing were scarce. In his autobiography, *Black Boy,* Wright recalls his first impressions of the city of Chicago.

Vocabulary *Builder*

mythical (MITH ih kul) *adj.* imaginary, fictitious

depot (DEE poh) *n.* station

intent (ihn TENT) *adj.* determined; resolved

My first glimpse of the flat black stretches of Chicago depressed and dismayed me, mocked all my fantasies. Chicago seemed an unreal city whose <u>mythical</u> houses were built of slabs of black coal wreathed in . . . gray smoke. . . .

The train rolled into the <u>depot</u>. Aunt Maggie and I got off and walked slowly through the crowds into the station. I looked about to see if there were signs saying: FOR WHITE—FOR COLORED. I saw none. Black people and white people moved about, each seemingly <u>intent</u> upon his private mission. There was no racial fear. Indeed, each person acted as though no one existed but himself. It was strange to pause before a crowded newsstand without having to wait until a white man was served. And yet, because everything was so new, I began to grow tense again, although it was a different sort of tension than I had known before. I knew that this machine city was governed by strange laws, and I wondered if I would ever learn them.

Richard Wright, *Black Boy*

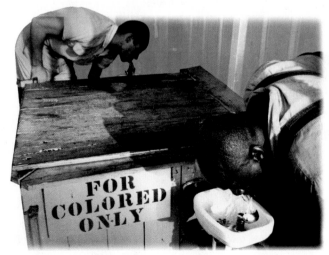

A segregated water fountain in the South

Comprehension and Critical Thinking

1. What is Wright's first reaction to the city of Chicago?

2. How does his impression change in this selection?

3. **Critical Thinking:** *Make Inferences* Lifestyles in Chicago were different from what Wright was used to in the South. How do you know this is true?

John Steinbeck, *The Grapes of Wrath*

Background

On October 29, 1929, the stock market crashed, spurring the Great Depression, a period of economic downturn that lasted nearly ten years. During this time, a severe drought in the Great Plains turned 150,000 square miles of farmland into a dust bowl. With their crops buried under layers of dust, many farmers and their families set off to find work in California.

In his novel *The Grapes of Wrath,* John Steinbeck presents ordinary people striving to save their humanity in desperate times. When the Joads lose their farm in Oklahoma, they join thousands of others, traveling the narrow highways toward California and chasing the dream of a piece of land to call their own.

Vocabulary *Builder*

scuttled (SKUT tuld) *v.* to run or move quickly, especially to get away from danger

perplexed (pur PLEXT) *adj.* full of doubt or uncertainty; puzzled or confused

The cars of the migrant people crawled out of the side roads onto the great cross-country highway, and they took the migrant way to the West. In the daylight they <u>scuttled</u> like bugs to the westward; and as dark caught them, they clustered like bugs near to shelter and to water. And because they were lonely and <u>perplexed</u>, because they had all come from a place of sadness and worry and defeat, and because they were all going to a new mysterious place, they huddled together; they talked together; they shared their lives, their food, and the things they hoped for in the new country. . . .

In the evening a strange thing happened: the twenty families became one family, the children were the children of all. The loss of home became one loss, and the golden time in the West was one dream. And it might be that a sick child threw despair into the hearts of twenty families, of a hundred people; that a birth there in a tent kept a hundred people quiet and awestruck through the night and filled a hundred people with the birth-joy in the morning.

John Steinbeck, *The Grapes of Wrath,* 1939

A family of migrants makes its way to California in 1937.

Comprehension and Critical Thinking

1. Where were the migrant people going?
2. Why were they going there?
3. Critical Thinking: *Analyze Symbolism* What might the birth of a new baby symbolize for the migrant people?

César Chávez, *Address to the Commonwealth Club of California*, 1984

Background

In the 1950s, the struggle for union recognition turned to agricultural workers. One of those poorly paid workers was César Chávez. In 1962, Chávez founded the National Farm Workers Association, later to become the United Farm Workers (UFW).

By 1970, the UFW convinced grape growers to accept union contracts and had effectively organized most of the industry. Through nonviolent tactics, such as boycotts, pickets, and strikes, Chávez made people aware of the struggles of farm workers and fought for better pay and safer working conditions. César Chávez and the union sought recognition of the importance and dignity of all farm workers. Below is an excerpt from one of Chávez's many speeches on the topic.

Vocabulary *Builder*

union (YOON yuhn) *n.* an organization uniting various individuals or political units with common interests and goals

collective bargaining (cah LEC tiv bar gah ning) *n.* negotiations between organized workers and their employer for wages, working conditions, and other benefits

rhetoric (RET ar ik) *n.* language that is showy and elaborate but largely empty of ideas of sincere emotion

All Hispanics—urban and rural, young and old—are connected to the farm workers' experience. We had all lived through the fields—or our parents had. We shared that common humiliation.

How could we progress as a people, even if we lived in the cities, while the farm workers—men and women of our color—were condemned to a life without pride?

How could we progress as a people while the farm workers—who symbolized our history in this land—were denied self-respect? . . .

Those who attack our <u>union</u> often say, "It's not really a union. It's something else: A social movement. A civil rights movement. It's something dangerous."

They're half right. The United Farm Workers is first and foremost a union. A union like any other. A union that either produces for its members on the bread and butter issues or doesn't survive.

But the UFW has always been something more than a union—although it's never been dangerous if you believe in the Bill of Rights.

The UFW was the beginning! We attacked that historical source of shame and infamy that our people in this country lived with. We attacked that injustice, not by complaining; not by seeking hand-outs; not by becoming soldiers in the War on Poverty. We organized!

Farm workers acknowledged we had allowed ourselves to become victims in a democratic society—a society where majority rule and <u>collective bargaining</u> are supposed to be more than academic theories or political <u>rhetoric</u>. And by addressing this historical problem, we created confidence and pride and hope in an entire people's ability to create the future.

César Chávez, President
United Farm Workers of America, AFL-CIO
Address to the Commonwealth Club of California, 1984

Comprehension and Critical Thinking

1. According to Chávez, to what experience are all Hispanics connected?

2. What tactics did Chávez and the UFW use to bring about change?

3. Critical Thinking: *Identify Cause and Effect* What were two positive effects of the forming of the UFW?

Background

On May 17, 1954, Chief Justice Warren read the U.S. Supreme Court's decision to desegregate schools in the United States. According to this ruling, African Americans must be allowed to attend the same schools as white students. Stiff resistance to desegregation quickly developed in the deep South.

Three years later, the pressure to integrate Little Rock, Arkansas, boiled over. On one side were the forces of violence and racism. On the other were nine African American students who planned to attend Central High School. Elizabeth Eckford was one those students. Because of a mix-up, she faced the full anger of a mob alone. Below is her account of what happened on that first day of school.

I saw a large crowd of people standing across the street from the soldiers guarding Central. As I walked on, the crowd suddenly got very quiet. . . . I looked at all the people and thought, "Maybe I will be safer if I walk down the block to the front entrance behind the guards."

For a moment all I could hear was the shuffling of their feet. Then someone shouted, "Here she comes, get ready!" I moved away from the crowd on the sidewalk and into the street. If the mob came at me, I could then cross back over so the guards could protect me.

The crowd moved in closer and then began to follow me, called me names. . . .Then my knees started to shake and all of a sudden I wondered whether I could make it to the center entrance a block away. It was the longest block I ever walked in my whole life.

Even so, I still wasn't too scared because all the time I kept thinking that the guards would protect me. . . .

The crowd was quiet. I guess they were waiting to see what was going to happen. When I was able to steady my knees, I walked up to the guard who had let the white students in. He too didn't move. When I tried to squeeze past him, he raised his bayonet and then the other guards closed in and they raised their bayonets.

Elizabeth Eckford, "First Day at Central High School," from Daisy Bates, *The Long Shadow of Little Rock,* 1962

Elizabeth Eckford in 1957

Comprehension and Critical Thinking

1. What was Eckford's first thought when she got off the bus and saw the mob waiting for her?

2. Why do you suppose Eckford, who was calm at first, suddenly got so nervous that her "knees started to shake"?

3. Critical Thinking: *Draw Conclusions* Based on these events, what personal characteristics do you think Elizabeth Eckford possessed?

Robert G. Kaiser, *America and the Aftermath of September 11*

Background

September 11, 2001, was a day of incredible horror and incredible bravery. Terrorists flew planes into both towers of New York's World Trade Center. Within a short time, both buildings crumbled to the ground, killing thousands of people. In Washington, D.C., a third plane, under the command of another terrorist, crashed into the Pentagon, destroying a large part of the building and killing hundreds more.

A fourth hijacked airplane might have brought more destruction on the nation's capital. However, heroic passengers took action. Following is the story of the passengers of United Airlines Flight 93, as reported in an essay for the *Encyclopaedia Britannica 2001 Year in Review.*

Vocabulary *Builder*

symbolic (sihm BAHL ihk) *adj.* standing for or in place of something else

devastating (DEHV uh stay tihng) *adj.* causing great physical or emotional damage

resourceful (ree SORS fuhl) *adj.* able to deal with problems in a creative way

scuffle (SKUHF uhl) *v.* to struggle with disorder at close quarters

---

The horror planned for September 11 was supposed to be worse, and very nearly was. The fourth hijacked airplane was evidently aimed at the Capitol or the White House in Washington—we may never know its target for certain. A direct hit on either would have been <u>symbolically</u> <u>devastating</u>, adding enormously to the impact of the attacks. But a group of brave and <u>resourceful</u> passengers on United Airlines Flight 93 prevented its hijackers from fulfilling their mission. . . .

Passengers on board the flight, who thought they were flying . . . to San Francisco, made calls to relatives on the ground with cellular telephones and learned that a hijacked plane already had been flown into the World Trade Center. . . . One of them was Jeremy Glick, 31, sales manager for a technology firm, who told his wife to "have a good life" and promised to go down fighting against the terrorists. Glick and several other passengers . . . were plotting to rush the cockpit . . . to disrupt whatever plan their hijackers had in mind. One of the other plotters, Todd Beamer, told a telephone operator whom he had reached via an onboard "airfone" about this plan. The operator heard him shout to his comrades, "Are you guys ready? Let's roll!" The operator then heard screams and sounds of a <u>scuffle</u> before the line went dead. In the next few moments, the plane took a series of sharp turns and then plunged into the Pennsylvania countryside. . . . Somehow, the passengers had disrupted the hijackers and forced the plane to Earth.

In that case, the technological wizardry of the age contributed to heroism and self-sacrifice that may have saved many lives in Washington.

Encyclopaedia Britannica 2001 Year in Review: The Events of 2001 and How They Shaped the World

Comprehension and Critical Thinking

1. What did the terrorists plan to do with United Airlines Flight 93?

2. What role did technology play in the passengers' plan?

3. Critical Thinking: *Identify Alternatives* What other course of action might the passengers on Flight 93 have followed? Why do you think people like Glick and Beamer chose to act as they did?

1 George Washington (1732–1799)

Years in office:
1789–1797
Party:
none
Elected from:
Virginia
Vice President:
John Adams

2 John Adams (1735–1826)

Years in office:
1797–1801
Party:
Federalist
Elected from:
Massachusetts
Vice President:
Thomas
    Jefferson

3 Thomas Jefferson (1743–1826)

Years in office:
1801–1809
Party:
Democratic
    Republican
Elected from:
Virginia
Vice President:
1) Aaron Burr,
2) George Clinton

4 James Madison (1751–1836)

Years in office:
1809–1817
Party:
Democratic
    Republican
Elected from:
Virginia
Vice President:
1) George Clinton,
2) Elbridge Gerry

5 James Monroe (1758–1831)

Years in office:
1817–1825
Party:
Democratic
    Republican
Elected from:
Virginia
Vice President:
Daniel Tompkins

6 John Quincy Adams (1767–1848)

Years in office:
1825–1829
Party:
National
    Republican
Elected from:
Massachusetts
Vice President:
John Calhoun

7 Andrew Jackson (1767–1845)

Years in office:
1829–1837
Party:
Democratic
Elected from:
Tennessee
Vice President:
1) John Calhoun,
2) Martin Van
    Buren

8 Martin Van Buren (1782–1862)

Years in office:
1837–1841
Party:
Democratic
Elected from:
New York
Vice President:
Richard Johnson

9 William Henry Harrison* (1773–1841)

Years in office:
1841
Party:
Whig
Elected from:
Ohio
Vice President:
John Tyler

10 John Tyler (1790–1862)

Years in office:
1841–1845
Party:
Whig
Elected from:
Virginia
Vice President:
none

11 James K. Polk (1795–1849)

Years in office:
1845–1849
Party:
Democratic
Elected from:
Tennessee
Vice President:
George Dallas

12 Zachary Taylor* (1784–1850)

Years in office:
1849–1850
Party:
Whig
Elected from:
Louisiana
Vice President:
Millard Fillmore

*Died in office

13 Millard Fillmore (1800–1874)

Years in office:
1850–1853
Party:
Whig
Elected from:
New York
Vice President:
none

14 Franklin Pierce (1804–1869)

Years in office:
1853–1857
Party:
Democratic
Elected from:
New Hampshire
Vice President:
William King

15 James Buchanan (1791–1868)

Years in office:
1857–1861
Party:
Democratic
Elected from:
Pennsylvania
Vice President:
John Breckinridge

16 Abraham Lincoln** (1809–1865)

Years in office:
1861–1865
Party:
Republican
Elected from:
Illinois
Vice President:
1) Hannibal Hamlin,
2) Andrew Johnson

17 Andrew Johnson (1808–1875)

Years in office:
1865–1869
Party:
Republican
Elected from:
Tennessee
Vice President:
none

18 Ulysses S. Grant (1822–1885)

Years in office:
1869–1877
Party:
Republican
Elected from:
Illinois
Vice President:
1) Schuyler Colfax,
2) Henry Wilson

19 Rutherford B. Hayes (1822–1893)

Years in office:
1877–1881
Party:
Republican
Elected from:
Ohio
Vice President:
William Wheeler

20 James A. Garfield** (1831–1881)

Years in office:
1881
Party:
Republican
Elected from:
Ohio
Vice President:
Chester A. Arthur

21 Chester A. Arthur (1829–1886)

Years in office:
1881–1885
Party:
Republican
Elected from:
New York
Vice President:
none

22 Grover Cleveland (1837–1908)

Years in office:
1885–1889
Party:
Democratic
Elected from:
New York
Vice President:
Thomas Hendricks

23 Benjamin Harrison (1833–1901)

Years in office:
1889–1893
Party:
Republican
Elected from:
Indiana
Vice President:
Levi Morton

24 Grover Cleveland (1837–1908)

Years in office:
1893–1897
Party:
Democratic
Elected from:
New York
Vice President:
Adlai Stevenson

**Assassinated

Presidents of the United States

25 William McKinley** (1843–1901)

Years in office:
1897–1901
Party:
Republican
Elected from:
Ohio
Vice President:
1) Garret Hobart,
2) Theodore Roosevelt

26 Theodore Roosevelt (1858–1919)

Years in office:
1901–1909
Party:
Republican
Elected from:
New York
Vice President:
Charles Fairbanks

27 William Howard Taft (1857–1930)

Years in office:
1909–1913
Party:
Republican
Elected from:
Ohio
Vice President:
James Sherman

28 Woodrow Wilson (1856–1924)

Years in office:
1913–1921
Party:
Democratic
Elected from:
New Jersey
Vice President:
Thomas Marshall

29 Warren G. Harding* (1865–1923)

Years in office:
1921–1923
Party:
Republican
Elected from:
Ohio
Vice President:
Calvin Coolidge

30 Calvin Coolidge (1872–1933)

Years in office:
1923–1929
Party:
Republican
Elected from:
Massachusetts
Vice President:
Charles Dawes

31 Herbert C. Hoover (1874–1964)

Years in office:
1929–1933
Party:
Republican
Elected from:
California
Vice President:
Charles Curtis

32 Franklin D. Roosevelt* (1882–1945)

Years in office:
1933–1945
Party:
Democratic
Elected from:
New York
Vice President:
1) John Garner,
2) Henry Wallace,
3) Harry S Truman

33 Harry S Truman (1884–1972)

Years in office:
1945–1953
Party:
Democratic
Elected from:
Missouri
Vice President:
Alben Barkley

34 Dwight D. Eisenhower (1890–1969)

Years in office:
1953–1961
Party:
Republican
Elected from:
New York
Vice President:
Richard M. Nixon

35 John F. Kennedy** (1917–1963)

Years in office:
1961–1963
Party:
Democratic
Elected from:
Massachusetts
Vice President:
Lyndon B. Johnson

36 Lyndon B. Johnson (1908–1973)

Years in office:
1963–1969
Party:
Democratic
Elected from:
Texas
Vice President:
Hubert Humphrey

*Died in office
**Assassinated

37 Richard M. Nixon*** (1913–1994)

Years in office:
1969–1974
Party:
Republican
Elected from:
New York
Vice President:
1) Spiro Agnew,
2) Gerald R. Ford

38 Gerald R. Ford (b. 1913)

Years in office:
1974–1977
Party:
Republican
Appointed from:
Michigan
Vice President:
Nelson
    Rockefeller

39 Jimmy Carter (b. 1924)

Years in office:
1977–1981
Party:
Democratic
Elected from:
Georgia
Vice President:
Walter Mondale

40 Ronald W. Reagan (b. 1911–2004)

Years in office:
1981–1989
Party:
Republican
Elected from:
California
Vice President:
George H.W.
    Bush

41 George H.W. Bush (b. 1924)

Years in office:
1989–1993
Party:
Republican
Elected from:
Texas
Vice President:
J. Danforth
    Quayle

42 William J. Clinton (b. 1946)

Years in office:
1993–2001
Party:
Democratic
Elected from:
Arkansas
Vice President:
Albert Gore, Jr.

43 George W. Bush (b. 1946)

Years in office:
2001–
Party:
Republican
Elected from:
Texas
Vice President:
Richard Cheney

***Resigned

State	Date of Entry to Union (Order of Entry)	Land Area in Square Miles	Population (In Thousands)	Number of Representatives in House*	Capital	Largest City
Alabama	1819 (22)	50,750	4,447	7	Montgomery	Birmingham
Alaska	1959 (49)	570,374	627	1	Juneau	Anchorage
Arizona	1912 (48)	113,642	5,131	8	Phoenix	Phoenix
Arkansas	1836 (25)	52,075	2,673	4	Little Rock	Little Rock
California	1850 (31)	155,973	33,872	53	Sacramento	Los Angeles
Colorado	1876 (38)	103,730	4,301	7	Denver	Denver
Connecticut	1788 (5)	4,845	3,406	5	Hartford	Bridgeport
Delaware	1787 (1)	1,955	784	1	Dover	Wilmington
Florida	1845 (27)	53,997	15,982	25	Tallahassee	Jacksonville
Georgia	1788 (4)	57,919	8,186	13	Atlanta	Atlanta
Hawaii	1959 (50)	6,423	1,212	2	Honolulu	Honolulu
Idaho	1890 (43)	82,751	1,294	2	Boise	Boise
Illinois	1818 (21)	55,593	12,419	19	Springfield	Chicago
Indiana	1816 (19)	35,870	6,080	9	Indianapolis	Indianapolis
Iowa	1846 (29)	55,875	2,926	5	Des Moines	Des Moines
Kansas	1861 (34)	81,823	2,688	4	Topeka	Wichita
Kentucky	1792 (15)	39,732	4,042	6	Frankfort	Louisville
Louisiana	1812 (18)	43,566	4,469	7	Baton Rouge	New Orleans
Maine	1820 (23)	30,865	1,275	2	Augusta	Portland
Maryland	1788 (7)	9,775	5,296	8	Annapolis	Baltimore
Massachusetts	1788 (6)	7,838	6,349	10	Boston	Boston
Michigan	1837 (26)	56,809	9,938	15	Lansing	Detroit
Minnesota	1858 (32)	79,617	4,919	8	St. Paul	Minneapolis
Mississippi	1817 (20)	46,914	2,845	4	Jackson	Jackson
Missouri	1821 (24)	68,898	5,595	9	Jefferson City	Kansas City
Montana	1889 (41)	145,556	902	1	Helena	Billings
Nebraska	1867 (37)	76,878	1,711	3	Lincoln	Omaha
Nevada	1864 (36)	109,806	1,998	3	Carson City	Las Vegas
New Hampshire	1788 (9)	8,969	1,236	2	Concord	Manchester
New Jersey	1787 (3)	7,419	8,414	13	Trenton	Newark
New Mexico	1912 (47)	121,365	1,819	3	Santa Fe	Albuquerque
New York	1788 (11)	47,224	18,976	29	Albany	New York
North Carolina	1789 (12)	48,718	8,049	13	Raleigh	Charlotte
North Dakota	1889 (39)	68,994	642	1	Bismarck	Fargo
Ohio	1803 (17)	40,953	11,353	18	Columbus	Columbus
Oklahoma	1907 (46)	68,679	3,451	5	Oklahoma City	Oklahoma City
Oregon	1859 (33)	96,003	3,421	5	Salem	Portland
Pennsylvania	1787 (2)	44,820	12,281	19	Harrisburg	Philadelphia
Rhode Island	1790 (13)	1,045	1,048	2	Providence	Providence
South Carolina	1788 (8)	30,111	4,012	6	Columbia	Columbia
South Dakota	1889 (40)	75,898	755	1	Pierre	Sioux Falls
Tennessee	1796 (16)	41,220	5,689	9	Nashville	Memphis
Texas	1845 (28)	261,914	20,852	32	Austin	Houston
Utah	1896 (45)	82,168	2,233	3	Salt Lake City	Salt Lake City
Vermont	1791 (14)	9,249	609	1	Montpelier	Burlington
Virginia	1788 (10)	39,598	7,079	11	Richmond	Virginia Beach
Washington	1889 (42)	66,582	5,894	9	Olympia	Seattle
West Virginia	1863 (35)	24,087	1,808	3	Charleston	Charleston
Wisconsin	1848 (30)	54,314	5,364	8	Madison	Milwaukee
Wyoming	1890 (44)	97,105	494	1	Cheyenne	Cheyenne
District of Columbia		61	572	1 (nonvoting)		

Self-Governing Areas, Possessions, and Dependencies	Land Area in Square Miles	Population (In Thousands)	Capital
Puerto Rico	3,515	809	San Juan
Guam	209	155	Agana
U.S. Virgin Islands	132	121	Charlotte Amalie
American Samoa	77	65	Pago Pago

Sources: Department of Commerce, Bureau of the Census

*As of 108th Congress.

Alabama
 Alaska
 Arizona
 Arkansas
 California

 Colorado
 Connecticut
 Delaware
 Florida
 Georgia

 Hawaii
 Idaho
 Illinois
 Indiana
 Iowa

 Kansas
 Kentucky
 Louisiana
 Maine
 Maryland

 Massachusetts
 Michigan
 Minnesota
 Mississippi
 Missouri

 Montana
 Nebraska
 Nevada
 New Hampshire
 New Jersey

 New Mexico
 New York
 North Carolina
 North Dakota
 Ohio

 Oklahoma
 Oregon
 Pennsylvania
 Rhode Island
 South Carolina

 South Dakota
 Tennessee
 Texas
 Utah
 Vermont

 Virginia
 Washington
 West Virginia
 Wisconsin
 Wyoming

English and Spanish Glossary

The glossary defines all high-use words and many key historical words and terms. The high-use words appear underlined the first time that they are used in the text. The key words and terms appear in blue type the first time that they are used. Each word in the glossary is defined in both English and Spanish. The page number(s) after the English definition refers to the page(s) on which the word or phrase is defined in the text. For other references, see the index.

Pronunciation Key

When difficult names or terms first appear in the text, they are respelled to help you with pronunciation. A syllable printed in small capital letters receives the greatest stress. The pronunciation key below lists the letters and symbols that will help you pronounce the word. It also includes examples of words using each of the sounds and shows how each word would be pronounced.

Symbol	Example	Respelling
a	hat	(hat)
ay	pay, late	(pay), (layt)
ah	star, hot	(stahr), (haht)
ai	air, dare	(air), (dair)
aw	law, all	(law), (awl)
eh	met	(meht)
ee	bee, eat	(bee), (eet)
er	learn, sir, fur	(lern), (ser), (fer)
ih	fit	(fiht)
ī	mile	(mīl)
ir	ear	(ir)
oh	no	(noh)
oi	soil, boy	(soil), (boi)
oo	root, rule	(root), (rool)
or	born, door	(born), (dor)
ow	plow, out	(plow), (owt)

Symbol	Example	Respelling
u	put, book	(put), (buk)
uh	fun	(fuhn)
yoo	few, use	(fyoo), (yooz)
ch	chill, reach	(chihl), (reech)
g	go, dig	(goh), (dihg)
j	jet, gently bridge	(jeht), (JEHNT lee), (brihj)
k	kite, cup	(kīt), (kuhp)
ks	mix	(mihks)
kw	quick	(kwihk)
ng	bring	(brihng)
s	say, cent	(say), (sehnt)
sh	she, crash	(shee), (krash)
th	three	(three)
y	yet, onion	(yeht), (UHN yuhn)
z	zip, always	(zihp), (AWL wayz)
zh	treasure	(TREH zher)

A

abolitionist (a boh LIH shuhn ihst) person who wanted to end slavery (p. 423)
abolicionista persona que quería abolir la esclavitud

accelerate (ak SEL er ayt) to increase in speed (p. 621)
acelerar aumentar la velocidad

accommodation (ak kom moh DAY shuhn) adjustment; adaptation (p. 501)
acomodo ajuste; adaptación

accumulate (uh KYOOM yoo layt) to collect slowly; to increase in amount over time (pp. 81, 753)
acumular reunir lentamente; aumentar una cantidad con el tiempo

adobe (uh DOH bee) sun-dried, unburned brick made of clay and straw (p. 12)
adobe seco al sol, ladrillo no quemado hecho de arcilla y paja

alien (AY lee ihn) outsider; someone from another country (pp. 298, 392)
extranjero persona que no pertenence a un grupo; persona de otro país

alliance (ah LĪ ans) agreement between countries to aid and support one another (pp. 57, 141, 183)
alianza convenio entre países por el que se comprometen a ayudarse y apoyarse mutuamente

alter (AWL ter) to change; to make different (pp. 315, 613)
alterar cambiar; hacer algo diferente

amend (ah MEHND) to change or revise (p. 264)
enmendar cambiar o revisar

amendment (ah MEHND mehnt) revision or addition to a bill, law, or constitution (p. 221)
enmienda revisión o adición a un proyecto de ley, ley o constitución

amnesty (AM nehs tee) government pardon (p. 547)
amnistía indulto que otorga el gobierno

anarchist (AN ahr kehst) person who opposes all forms of government (p. 629)
anarquista persona que se opone a todas las formas de gobierno

annex (an NEHKS) to add on or take over (p. 456)
anexar agregar o apoderarse de algo

anti-Semitism (an tee SEH mih tihz uhm) prejudice against Jews (p. 665)
antisemitismo prejuicio contra los judíos

appeal (ah PEEL) to ask that a court decision be reviewed by a higher court (p. 262)
apelar pedir que una decisión de un tribunal sea revisada por un tribunal superior

apprentice (uh PREHN tihs) person who learns a trade or craft from a master (p. 110)
aprendiz persona que aprende un oficio o destreza de un maestro

assembly line (ah SEHM blee līn) manufacturing method in which a product is put together as it moves along a conveyor belt (p. 613)
línea de montaje método de manufactura por el cual se arma un producto a medida que se desplaza en una banda transportadora

assimilation (ah sih mih LAY shuhn) process of becoming part of another culture (p. 627)
asimilación proceso de convertirse en parte de otra cultura

B

baby boom (BAY bee boom) large increase in the birthrate from the late 1940s through the early 1960s (p. 720)
baby boom gran aumento de la tasa de natalidad entre la segunda mitad de la década de 1940 y la primera mitad de la década de 1960

backcountry (bak KUHN tree) frontier region located along the eastern slope of the Appalachian Mountains (p. 81)
backcountry región fronteriza ubicada a lo largo de la ladera oriental de los montes Apalaches

barrio (BAHR ree oh) Latino neighborhood in the United States (p. 663)
barrio vecindario latino de Estados Unidos

benevolent association (beh NE vo lehnt a so see AY shun) group that looks after the welfare of its members (p. 715)
asociación benevolente grupo que se preocupa del bienestar de sus miembros

bill (bihl) proposed law (p. 259)
proyecto de ley ley propuesta

bill of rights (bihl uhv rīts) written list of freedoms that a government promises to protect (pp. 103, 205)
declaración de derechos lista escrita de las libertades que un gobierno se compromete a proteger

black codes (blak kohds) southern laws that severely limited the rights of African Americans after the Civil War (p. 553)
códigos negros leyes sureñas que limitaron severamente los derechos de los afroamericanos después de la Guerra Civil

blockade (BLAHK ayd) shutting a port or roadway to prevent people or supplies from coming into or leaving an area (pp. 161, 328, 515)
bloqueo cierre de un puerto o camino para impedir que entren o salgan personas o provisiones en cierta zona

bond (bahnd) certificate issued by a government for a certain amount of money that the government promises to pay back with interest (p. 284)
bono certificado emitido por un gobierno por cierta cantidad de dinero que el gobierno promete devolver con intereses

borderland (BOR der land) land along a frontier (p. 90)
tierra limítrofe tierra a lo largo de una frontera

border state (BOR der stayt) slave state that remained in the Union during the Civil War (p. 513)
estado fronterizo estado esclavista que permaneció en la Unión durante la Guerra Civil

boycott (BOI kaht) organized campaign to refuse to buy or use certain goods and services (p. 147)
boicot campaña organizada para rehusar comprar o usar ciertos bienes y servicios

C

canal (kah NAHL) artificial waterway dug across land to improve transportation (p. 403)
canal vía navegable artificial excavada a lo largo de un terreno para mejorar el transporte

capitalism (KA piht ahl ihz uhm) economic system in which people put money, or capital, into a business or project in order to make a profit later on; economic system in which privately owned businesses compete in a free market (p. 344)
capitalismo sistema económico en el que las personas invierten dinero (capital) en un negocio o proyecto para obtener ganancias más adelante; sistema económico en el que los negocios de propiedad privada compiten en un mercado libre

capitalist (KA piht ahl ihst) person who invests capital, or money, in a business to earn a profit (p. 383)
capitalista persona que invierte capital (dinero) en un negocio para obtener ganancias

carpetbagger (KAHR peht BAG er) uncomplimentary nickname for a northern white who went to the South after the Civil War to start a business or pursue a political career (p. 555)
carpetbagger sobrenombre despreciativo dado a los norteños blancos que se mudaron al Sur después de la Guerra Civil para emprender un negocio o seguir una carrera política

casualty (KA su ahl tee) military term for a person killed, wounded, or missing in action (p. 520)
baja término militar que describe a una persona muerta, herida o desaparecida en combate

cattle drive (KAT tl drīv) herding and moving of cattle over long distances, usually to railroads (p. 590)
arreo de ganado conducción y traslado de ganado a grandes distancias, por lo regular hacia los ferrocarriles

cattle kingdom (KAT tl KING duhm) region dominated by the cattle industry and its ranches, trails, and cow towns (p. 593)
región ganadera región donde predomina la industria ganadera y sus ranchos, sendas y pueblos vaqueros

caucus (KAW kuhs) private meeting of members of a political party (p. 352)
reunión de comité encuentro privado de los integrantes de un partido político

cavalry (KAV uhl ree) units of troops on horseback (p. 183)
caballería unidades de tropas a caballo

cease (sees) to stop; to come to an end (pp. 296, 313, 388)
cesar detenerse; llegar a su fin

cede (seed) to give up (pp. 144, 345, 457)
ceder entregar

censorship (SEHN sor shihp) the power to review, change, or prevent the publication of news (p. 267)
censura poder de revisar, cambiar o evitar la publicación de noticias

charter (CHAHR ter) official document that gives certain rights to an individual or a group (pp. 67, 342)
carta de privilegio documento oficial que confiere ciertos derechos a un individuo o grupo

checks and balances (chehks and BAL an sez) a principle of the U.S. Constitution that gives each branch of government the power to check, or limit, the actions of the other branches (p. 257)
control y equilibrio principio de la Constitución de Estados Unidos que otorga a cada rama del gobierno el poder de controlar o limitar las acciones de las otras ramas

circuit (SIR kuht) route repeatedly traveled; circular trip around an area (pp. 340, 633)
circuito trayecto que se recorre una y otra vez; un recorrido circular en torno a un área

circumnavigate (ser kuhm NAV ih gayt) to travel all the way around Earth (p. 40)
circunnavegar hacer un recorrido completo alrededor de la Tierra

citizen (SIHT ih zehn) person who owes loyalty to a particular nation and is entitled to all its rights and protections (p. 270)
ciudadano persona que debe lealtad a una determinada nación y que tiene derecho a recibir todos sus derechos y protecciones

civil disobedience (SIHV ihl dih soh BEE dee ehns) idea based on nonviolence that people have a right to disobey a law they consider unjust, if their consciences demand it (p. 433)
desobediencia civil idea de que las personas tienen derecho, sin usar la violencia, a desobedecer una ley que consideren injusta, si su conciencia así lo exige

civil service (SIHV uhl SER vihs) system that includes most government jobs, except elected positions, the judiciary, and the military (p. 784)
administración pública sistema que incluye a la mayoría de los trabajos del gobierno, excepto a los cargos elegidos, a los judiciales y a los militares

civil war (SIHV ihl wor) war between people of the same country (p. 503)
guerra civil guerra entre habitantes de un mismo país

civilian (suh VIHL yuhn) person not in the military (p. 187)
civil persona que no pertenece a las fuerzas armadas

civilization (sihv uh luh ZAY shuhn) advanced culture in which people have developed cities, science, and industries (p. 8)
civilización cultura avanzada en la cual la gente ha desarrollado ciudades, la ciencia y la industria

clan (klan) group of families that are related to one another (p. 15)
clan grupo de familias que están relacionadas entre sí

clarify (KLAIR ih fī) to make the meaning of something clear (p. 497)
aclarar explicar el significado de algo

clause (klawz) part of a law, treaty, or other written agreement (pp. 430, 703)

cláusula parte de una ley, tratado u otro acuerdo escrito

clinic (KLIHN ihk) place where people receive medical treatment, often for free or for a small fee (p. 622)
clínica lugar donde las personas reciben asistencia médica, en muchos casos gratuitamente o a cambio de un pago reducido

collective bargaining (koh LEHK tihv BAHR gehn ing) negotiation between company management and a union representing a group of workers about wages, benefits, and working conditions (p. 618)
negociación colectiva negociación entre un sindicato que representa a un grupo de trabajadores y la dirección de una compañía acerca de los salarios, prestaciones y condiciones de trabajo

collide (koh LĪD) to come together with great force or violence; to crash (p. 140)
colisionar encontrarse con gran fuerza o violencia; chocar

commit (kuh MIHT) to make a pledge or a promise (pp. 491, 658)
comprometerse hacer un voto o una promesa

compromise (KAHM proh mīz) agreement in which each side gives up part of what it wants to end a disagreement (p. 214)
acuerdo compromiso por el que cada una de las partes renuncia a una parte de lo que desea con el fin de acabar con una desavenencia

compulsory education (kuhm PUHL sor ee ehd jyoo KAY shuhn) requirement that children attend school up to a certain age (p. 632)
educación obligatoria exigencia de que los niños asistan a la escuela hasta una edad determinada

confine (kuhn FĪN) to keep within certain limits; to shut or imprison (p. 188)
confinar mantener dentro de ciertos límites; encerrar o encarcelar

conquistador (kahn KWIHS tuh dor) conqueror, especially one of the sixteenth-century Spanish soldiers who defeated the Indian civilizations of Mexico, Central America, or Peru (p. 44)
conquistador persona que conquista, especialmente uno de los soldados españoles del siglo XVI que derrotaron a las civilizaciones indígenas de México y América Central o Perú

conservation (kahn ser VAY shuhn) protection of natural resources (p. 651)
conservación protección de los recursos

constitution (kahn stih TYOO shuhn) document in which the laws, principles, organization, and processes of a government are established (p. 204)
constitución documento que establece las leyes, principios, organización y procedimientos de un gobierno

continental (kahn tihn EHN tuhl) form of paper money printed during the American Revolution (p. 188)
continental forma de papel moneda impreso durante la Guerra de la Independencia

continental divide (kahn tihn EHN tuhl dih VĪD) mountain ridge that separates river systems flowing toward opposite sides of a continent (p. 318)
divisoria continental cadena montañosa que separa sistemas fluviales que corren hacia lados opuestos de un continente

contract (KAHN trakt) agreement between two or more parties that can be enforced by law (p. 346)
contrato convenio entre dos o más partes que se puede hacer valer por ley

contrast (KAHN trast) difference shown between things when compared (pp. 89, 214)
contraste diferencia que se manifiesta entre dos cosas cuando son comparadas

convert (kuhn VERT) to change from one purpose or function to another; to change from one political party or religion to another (pp. 91, 357, 415)
convertir cambiar de un propósito o función a otro; cambiar de un partido político o de una religión a otra

Copperhead (KAHP er hehd) northerner who opposed using force to keep the southern states in the Union (p. 531)
Copperhead norteño que se oponía al uso de la fuerza para mantener a los estados sureños dentro de la Unión

corduroy road (KOR der oi rohd) road made of sawed-off logs, laid side by side (p. 403)
camino de troncos camino hecho de troncos aserrados y colocados uno al lado de otro

corollary (KOR oh lair ee) a logical extension of a doctrine or proposition (p. 697)
corolario una extensión lógica de una doctrina o proposición

corporation (kor por AY shuhn) business owned by many investors (p. 614)
compañía empresa que es propiedad de muchos inversionistas

cotton gin (KAHT tuhn jihn) machine that used a spiked wooden cylinder to remove seeds from cotton fibers (p. 396)
despepitadora de algodón máquina que servía para quitar las semillas a las fibras de algodón por medio de un cilindro de madera con púas

coureur de bois (koo REHR duh BWAH) French term for "runner of the wood" (p. 54)
coureur de bois término francés para "corredor del bosque" o contrabandista de pieles

cow town (kow town) settlement at the end of a cattle trail (p. 592)
pueblo vaquero asentamiento situado al final de una ruta de ganado

creativity (kree ay TIHV ih tee) ability to use one's imagination to develop new and original ideas or things (p. 722)
creatividad capacidad de usar la imaginación para desarrollar ideas o cosas para hacer nuevas y originales

crisis (KRĪ sihs) turning point or deciding event; situation involving great risk (pp. 156, 315, 484, 664)
crisis momento crucial o acontecimiento decisivo; una situación que implica un gran riesgo

critic (KRIHT ihk) someone who makes judgments about objects or actions (pp. 331, 553, 681)
crítico persona que hace juicios sobre objetos o acciones

culture (KUHL cher) way of life (p. 10)
cultura forma de vida

culture area (KUHL cher AIR ee uh) region in which groups of people have a similar way of life (p. 11)
área cultural región en la cual grupos de personas tienen una forma de vida similar

currency (KER rehn see) money used to make purchases (pp. 11, 531)
moneda dinero que se usa para realizar compras

D

dame school (daym skool) school run by a woman, usually in her own home (p. 119)
escuela de señoritas escuela administrada por una mujer, generalmente en su propia casa

debtor (DEH tor) person who cannot pay his or her debts (p. 87)
deudor persona que no puede pagar sus deudas

decline (dee KLĪN) to lose strength or power over a period of time (pp. 54, 324)
decaer perder fuerza o poder a lo largo de cierto tiempo

deprive (dee PRĪV) to keep from happening; to take away something needed by force or intent (pp. 7, 487)
privar impedir que suceda; tomar por la fuerza o con intención algo que se necesita

devise (dee VĪZ) to carefully think out; to invent (pp. 206, 657)
idear hacer planes cuidadosamente; inventar

devote (dee VOHT) to commit; to apply time and energy (p. 397)
dedicar comprometer; destinar tiempo y energía

dictatorship (dihk TAY tor shihp) government in which one person or a small group holds complete authority (pp. 252, 455)
dictadura gobierno en el que una persona o un grupo pequeño ejerce una autoridad total

direct democracy (dir EHKT deh MAH kra see) system of government in which ordinary citizens have the power to govern (p. 24)
democracia directa sistema de gobierno en el que los ciudadanos comunes tienen poder para gobernar

discrimination (dihs krihm ihn AY shuhn) denial of equal rights or equal treatment to certain groups of people (p. 395)
discriminación negación de igualdad de derechos o de un tratamiento igualitario a ciertos grupos de personas

dissent (dihs SEHNT) disagreement (p. 267)
disensión desacuerdo

distinct (dihs TIHNKT) clear or definite; clearly different in its quality (pp. 12, 466, 514)
distinto claro o definido; que difiere claramente en cuanto a su calidad

diversity (dih VER sih tee) differences (p. 714)
diversidad diferencias

divine right (dih VĪN rīt) belief that a ruler's authority comes directly from God (p. 122)
derecho divino creencia en que la autoridad de un gobernante proviene directamente de Dios

domestic (doh MEHS tihk) having to do with the home or household; pertaining to a country's internal affairs (p. 108)
doméstico relacionado con la casa o el hogar; relativo a los asuntos internos de un país

draft (draft) system of required military service (p. 530)
leva sistema del servicio militar obligatorio

dumping (DUHMP ing) selling goods in another country at very low prices (p. 342)
inundación de mercado venta de productos en otro país a precios muy bajos

duty (DOOT ee) import tax (p. 146)
aranceles impuestos a las importaciones

E

economic depression (eh koh NAH mihk dee PREH shuhn) period when business activity slows, prices and wages drop, and unemployment rises (p. 208)
depresión económica período en el que la actividad comercial disminuye, los precios y los salarios bajan y el desempleo aumenta

economy (ee KAHN uh mee) system governing the production, use, and distribution of goods; system of business and personal transactions by which people in a region or nation earn their livings (p. 404)
economía sistema que gobierna la producción, el uso y la distribución de bienes; sistema de transacciones comerciales y personales mediante las cuales los habitantes de una región o país se ganan la vida

efficient (ee FISH ehnt) acting effectively, without wasted cost or effort (pp. 191, 386, 463, 650)
eficiente que actúa con eficacia, sin desperdiciar costos ni esfuerzos

eliminate (ee LIHM ih nayt) to get rid of (pp. 422, 615)
eliminar deshacerse de algo

emancipate (ee MAN sih payt) to set free (p. 524)
emancipar liberar

embargo (ehm BAHR goh) government order that forbids foreign trade (p. 324)
embargo orden gubernamental que prohíbe el comercio exterior

embrace (ehm BRAYS) to accept; to hold tight to; to readily accept (p. 496)
abrazar aceptar; aferrarse a; aceptar sin dificultad

emotion (ee MOH shuhn) strong feeling such as sadness, anger, or love (pp. 214, 432)
emoción sentimiento intenso; por ejemplo, tristeza, ira o amor

emotional (ee MOH shuh nuhl) appealing to the emotions, or feelings, of people (p. 147)
emocional relativo a las emociones o sentimientos de la gente

emphasize (EHM fah sīz) to stress; to make more important (p. 389)
recalcar destacar; dar más importancia

encomienda (ehn koh mih EHN dah) land granted to Spanish settlers that included the right to demand labor or taxes from Native Americans (p. 147)
encomienda terreno otorgado a los colonos españoles, que incluía el derecho a exigir trabajo o impuestos de los indígenas americanos

encounter (ehn KOWN ter) to meet in an unexpected way; to experience (p. 534)
tropezar con encontrar de modo inesperado; experimentar

enlightened (ehn LĪT ehnd) to be freed from the superstitions and ignorance of the Middle Ages and embrace reason and experience (p. 4)
ilustrado liberado de las supersticiones e ignorancia de la Edad Media y que ha abrazado la razón y la experiencia

enlist (ehn LIHST) to sign up for military duty (p. 187)
enlistarse inscribirse para el servicio militar

enrich (ehn RIHCH) to make wealthy; to improve or increase in quality or wealth (pp. 362, 644)
enriquecer hacer rico; mejorar o aumentar en cuanto a calidad o riqueza

entrepreneur (ahn treh preh NEWR) someone who sets up new businesses to make a profit (p. 614)
empresario persona que establece negocios nuevos para obtener ganancias

exceed (ehks SEED) to go beyond what is expected; to outdo or be greater than what was planned (p. 535)
exceder ir más allá de lo esperado; superar lo proyectado

excise tax (EHKS īz tax) tax placed on the making of or use of a product (p. 379)
impuesto sobre consumos impuesto que se aplica a la manufactura o uso de un producto

exclude (ehks KLOOD) to keep out or expel; to reject or not be considered (pp. 428, 629, 684)
excluir mantener fuera o expulsar; rechazar o no considerar

executive (ehks ZEHK yoo tihv) in government, person who runs the government and sees that the laws are carried out (p. 205)
ejecutivo en un gobierno, persona que dirige el gobierno y hace cumplir las leyes

exert (ehks ZERT) to use; to put into action (p. 645)
ejercer utilizar; poner en acción

expansion (ehks PAN shuhn) extending of a nation beyond its existing borders (p. 447)
expansión acto de extender un país más allá de sus fronteras existentes

expedition (ehks peh DIH shuhn) journey undertaken by a group of people with an objective (p. 317)
expedición viaje que emprende un grupo de personas con un objetivo concreto

extended family (ehks TEHN dehd FAM ih lee) close-knit family group that includes parents, children, grandparents, aunts, uncles, and cousins (pp. 107, 400)
familia extensa grupo familiar unido que incluye a los padres, hijos, abuelos, tías, tíos y primos

F

faction (FAK shuhn) organized political group (pp. 290, 382)
facción grupo político organizado

factor (FAK tor) condition or quality that causes something else to happen (pp. 45, 558, 608)
factor condición o cualidad que provoca que ocurra algo distinto

factory system (FAK tor ee SIHS tehm) methods of production that bring workers and machinery together in one place (p. 383)
sistema de fábricas métodos de producción que reúnen trabajadores y maquinaria en un mismo lugar

famine (FAM ihn) widespread starvation (p. 394)
hambruna escasez generalizada de alimentos

farm cooperative (fahrm koh AH per at ihv) group of farmers who pool their money to make large purchases of tools, seeds, and other supplies at a discount (p. 598)
cooperativa agrícola grupo de agricultores que forman un fondo común con su dinero para hacer compras grandes de herramientas, semillas y otras provisiones a precio con descuento

federalism (FEHD er uhl ihz uhm) principle of the U.S. Constitution that establishes the division of power between the federal government and the states (p. 257)
federalismo principio de la Constitución de Estados Unidos que establece la división de poderes entre el gobierno federal y los estados

feudalism (FYOOD uhl ihz uhm) system in which a ruler grants parts of his land to lords in exchange for military service and financial assistance (p. 25)
feudalismo sistema en el cual el gobernante otorga parte de su tierra a los señores a cambio de servicio militar y ayuda financiera

finance (FĪ nans) to pay for; to supply with money (p. 120)
financiar pagar por algo; proveer dinero

flexible (FLEHKS ah bahl) capable of change (p. 221)
flexible capaz de cambiar

forty-niner (FOR tee NĪ ner) person who came to California in search of gold (p. 464)
los del cuarenta y nueve personas que vinieron a California en busca de oro

fragment (FRAG mehnt) broken part or piece; small section of something (p. 501)
fragmento parte rota o pieza de algo; sección pequeña de algo

free enterprise (free EHN ter prīz) economic system in which each privately owned business decides what to produce, how much to produce, and what prices to charge (p. 616)
libre empresa sistema económico en el que cada empresa de propiedad privada decide qué producir, cuánto producir y qué precios cobrar

freedmen (FREED mehn) men and women who were legally freed from slavery after the Civil War (p. 548)
libertos hombres y mujeres liberados jurídicamente de la esclavitud después de la Guerra Civil

freedom of the press (FREE duhm uhv thuh prehs) right of newspapers and other public media to publish articles believed to be accurate (p. 105)
libertad de prensa derecho de los diarios y otros medios públicos de comunicación a publicar artículos cuyo contenido consideran como cierto

frontier (fruhn TIR) land that forms the furthest extent of a nation's settled regions (p. 444)
frontera territorio que constituye la extensión más lejana de las regiones establecidas de un país

fugitive (FYOO jih tihv) runaway (p. 484)
fugitivo persona que huye

function (FUHNK shuhn) purpose; proper use; official duty (p. 90)
función propósito; uso adecuado; responsabilidades que conlleva un cargo

fundamental (fuhn duh MEHN tahl) most important part; foundation of an idea or action; the essential quality (pp. 78, 293, 385)
fundamental lo más importante; la base de una idea o acción; la cualidad esencial

G

gentry (JEHN tree) upper class of colonial society (p. 110)
alta burguesía clase alta de la sociedad colonial

ghetto (GEHT oh) poor run-down neighborhood where one group of people live due to poverty or prejudice (p. 731)
gueto vecindario pobre y decadente donde vive un grupo de gente por motivos de pobreza o prejuicios

glacier (GLAY sher) thick sheet of ice (p. 6)
glaciar gruesa capa de hielo

graduated income tax (GRAD yoo ay tehd IHN kuhm taks) tax on earning that charges different rates for different income levels (p. 647)
impuesto sobre la renta escalonado impuesto sobre las ganancias que aplica tasas diferentes a los distintos niveles de ingreso

grandfather clause (GRAND fah ther klawz) law that excused a voter from a literacy test if his father or grandfather had been eligible to vote on January 1, 1867 (p. 560)
cláusula del abuelo ley que eximía a un votante de la prueba de alfabetización si su padre o abuelo había tenido derecho a votar el 1 de enero de 1867

grange (graynj) group of farmers who met for lectures, sewing bees, and other events (p. 598)
grange grupo de agricultores que se reunían para participar en conferencias, círculos de costura y otras actividades

grievance (GREE vans) formal complaint (p. 172)
querella queja formal

guerrilla (guh RIHL uh) fighter who works as part of a small band to make hit-and-run attacks (p. 191)
guerrillero combatiente dentro de un pequeño grupo que realiza ataques relámpago

H

habeas corpus (HAY bee ihs KOR puhs) the right not to be held in prison without first being charged with a specific crime; constitutional protection against unlawful imprisonment (pp. 104, 252, 529)
habeas corpus derecho a no ser encarcelado sin antes haber sido acusado de un delito específico; protección constitucional contra el encarcelamiento ilegal

homesteader (HOHM steh der) settler who acquired free land offered by the government (p. 595)
finquero colono que adquirió tierras gratis ofrecidas por el gobierno

hostile (HAHS tihl) unfriendly; intending to do harm (pp. 291, 383, 450, 694)
hostil poco amistoso; que se propone hacer daño

I

immigrate (IHM mah grayt) to move into a foreign region or country (p. 581)
inmigrar mudarse a una región o país extranjero

impeachment (ihm PEECH mehnt) process of bringing formal charges against a public official (p. 556)
juicio político proceso que consiste en presentar una acusación formal contra un funcionario público

impose (ihm POHZ) to place a burden on something or someone (pp. 66, 285, 490, 555)
imponer colocar una carga sobre algo o alguien

impressment (ihm PREHS mehnt) act of forcing a person into service; practice of seizing sailors on American ships and forcing them to serve in the British navy (pp. 296, 388)
leva práctica de obligar a una persona a prestar servicio militar; captura de marineros de navíos estadounidenses para obligarlos a servir en la armada británica

impulse (IHM puhls) sudden push or driving force; sudden action; driving force behind an action (p. 415)
impulso empujón repentino o fuerza motriz; acción repentina; la fuerza motriz detrás de una acción

inauguration (ihn awg er AY shuhn) ceremony in which the President officially takes the oath of office (pp. 282, 374)
toma de mando ceremonia en la que el presidente hace el juramento propio de su cargo

income tax (IHN kuhm taks) tax on the money people earn (p. 531)
impuesto a los ingresos impuesto sobre el dinero que la gente gana

indentured servant (ihn DEHN cherd SER vehnt) person who signs a contract to work for a set number of years in exchange for ocean passage to the colonies (p. 111)
sirviente contratado persona que firma un contrato para trabajar durante un número determinado de años a cambio de un pasaje oceánico a las colonias

individualism (ihn dih VIHD yoo uhl ihz uhm) concept that stresses the importance of each individual (p. 432)
individualismo concepto que hace hincapié en la importancia de cada individuo

Industrial Revolution (ihn DUHS tree uhl rehv oh LYOO shuhn) gradual replacement of many hand tools by machines (p. 382)
Revolución Industrial sustitución gradual de muchas herramientas manuales por máquinas

inferior (ihn FIR ee uhr) less worthy; less valuable; of lower rank; of poorer quality (pp. 395, 561)
inferior menos digno; menos valioso; de categoría más baja; de menor calidado

inflation (ihn FLAY shuhn) general rise in prices (pp. 531, 599)
inflación aumento generalizado de los precios

infrastructure (IHN frah struhk cher) basic public works needed for a society to function, including the systems of roads, bridges, and tunnels (p. 343)
infraestructura obras públicas básicas necesarias para el funcionamiento de una sociedad, como los sistemas de carreteras, puentes y túneles

integrate (IHN teh grayt) to bring together; to join parts so they become a whole; to bring together individuals of different races to achieve equality (p. 60)
integrar reunir; juntar partes para que formen un todo; reunir individuos de diferentes razas para lograr igualdad

interchangeable parts (ihn ter CHAYNJ ah buhl pahrts) identical pieces that can be assembled quickly by unskilled workers (p. 386)
partes intercambiables piezas idénticas que pueden ser ensambladas con rapidez por trabajadores no calificados

interest group (IHN trehst groop) organization that represents the concerns of a particular group (p. 271)
grupo de intereses organización que representa los asuntos que conciernen a un grupo en particular

interstate commerce (IHN ter stayt KAHM mers) trade between two or more states (p. 344)
comercio interestatal intercambio comercial entre dos o más estados

invest (ihn VEHST) to purchase something with money with the hope that its value will grow; to supply money for a project in order to make a profit (pp. 284, 383, 697)
invertir adquirir algo a cambio de dinero con la esperanza de que su valor aumente; facilitar dinero para un proyecto para que dé ganacias

ironclad (ī ern klad) warship covered with protective iron plates (p. 518)
acorazado barco de guerra cubierto con placas protectoras de hierro

irrigate (IR uh gayt) to water crops by channeling water from rivers or streams (p. 7)
irrigar regar los cultivos canalizando el agua de los ríos o arroyos

isolate (ī soh layt) to set apart; to separate (pp. 403, 503, 627)
aislar apartar; separar

isolated (ī soh lay tehd) set apart; separated (p. 449)
aislado apartado; separado

J

joint resolution (joint reh soh LYOO shuhn) agreement approved by a majority of members in both houses (p. 458)
resolución conjunta convenio aprobado por una mayoría de los integrantes de las dos cámaras

judicial branch (jyoo DIH shuhl branch) system of courts to settle disputes involving national issues (p. 213)
poder judicial sistema de tribunales para dirimir pleitos referentes a cuestiones nacionales

judicial review (jyoo DIH shuhl ree VYOO) principle that the Supreme Court has the right to decide whether acts of Congress are constitutional or not (p. 313)
revisión judicial principio según el cual la Corte Suprema tiene derecho a decidir si los actos del Congreso son constitucionales

jurisdiction (jer ihs DIHK shuhn) power of a court to hear and decide cases (p. 262)
jurisdicción potestad de un tribunal para conocer y resolver sobre casos

justify (JUHS tih fī) to give good reason for an action (p. 616)
justificar dar buenas razones para una acción

K

kayak (KĪ ak) boat consisting of a light wooden frame covered with watertight skins except for a single or double opening in the center, and propelled by a double-bladed paddle (p. 12)
kayac bote que consta de una ligera estructura de madera cubierta de pieles impermeables a excepción de una única o doble abertura en el centro, y que se impulsa por medio de un remo de dos paletas

L

laissez faire (LAY seh fair) idea that government should not interfere in the economy (p. 311)
laissez faire idea de que el gobierno no debe entrometerse en la economía

land grant (land grant) government gift of land (p. 446)
concesión de tierras donación de tierras por parte del gobierno

legislature (LEHJ ihs lay cher) part of a government that makes laws (pp. 103, 205)
legislatura parte de un gobierno que se encarga de elaborar leyes

levy (LEHV ee) to impose a tax by law; to force to be paid (pp. 102, 454, 531)
gravar imponer una contribución por ley; obligar a que se pague

libel (LĪ behl) publishing of false statements that unjustly damage a person's reputation (pp. 105, 267)

libelo publicación de afirmaciones falsas que dañan injustamente la reputación de una persona

limited government (LIHM ih tehd GUHV ern mehnt) the principle that the government has only the powers that the Constitution gives it (p. 256)
gobierno limitado el principio de que el gobierno tiene únicamente los poderes que la Constitución le otorga

literacy test (LIH ter ah see tehst) examination to see if a person can read and write; used in the past to restrict voting rights (p. 560)
prueba de alfabetización examen para establecer si una persona sabe leer y escribir, se usaba en el pasado para restringir el derecho al voto

lode (lohd) large deposit of precious metal that reaches from deep underground toward the surface (p. 466)
filón depósito grande de un metal precioso que se extiende desde un punto profundo bajo tierra hacia la superficie

logic (LAH jihk) reason; good sense; careful thought (p. 171)
lógica razón; buen juicio; reflexión cuidadosa

lynching (LIHNCH ihng) when a mob illegally seizes and executes someone (p. 661)
linchamiento cuando una multitud captura y ejecuta ilegalmente a una persona

M

manual (MAN yoo ahl) involving work done by hand (pp. 444, 581)
manual referente al trabajo que se hace con las manos

martial law (MAHR shuhl law) type of rule in which the military is in charge and citizens' rights are suspended (p. 513)
ley marcial tipo de gobierno en el que los militares están al mando y se suspenden los derechos de los ciudadanos

mass production (mas proh DUHK shuhn) manufacturing of large numbers of identical products quickly and cheaply (pp. 386, 612)
producción en masa manufactura rápida y a bajo costo de un gran número de productos idénticos

maximum (MAK suh muhm) largest; highest; greatest (p. 113)
máximo el más extenso; más alto; mayor o mejor

mercantilism (MER kan tihl ihz uhm) economic policy that held that a nation prospered by exporting more goods to foreign nations than it imported from them (p. 50)
mercantilismo principio económico según el cual una nación prospera exportando más bienes a países extranjeros que los que importa de ellos

mercenary (MER sehn air ee) soldier who fights merely for pay, often for a foreign country (pp. 161, 181)
mercenario soldado que combate tan sólo por una paga, casi siempre en favor de un país extranjero

middle class (MIHD uhl klas) in the 13 colonies, a portion of the colonial population that included small planters, independent farmers, and skilled craftsworkers (p. 111)
clase media en las 13 colonias, parte de la población colonial que incluía a los pequeños cultivadores, a los granjeros independientes y a los artesanos

militarism (MIHL uh tuh rihz uhm) glorification of the military (p. 699)
militarismo glorificación de los militares

militia (mih LIH shah) organized body of armed volunteers (p. 140)
milicia cuerpo organizado de voluntarios armados

minimize (MIHN ah mīz) to reduce to the lowest possible amount (p. 204)
reducir al mínimo disminuir a la cantidad más pequeña posible

minimum (MIHN ah muhm) smallest amount possible or allowed (pp. 146, 632)
mínimo cantidad más pequeña posible o permitida

minuteman (MIHN uht man) colonial militia volunteer who was prepared to fight at a minute's notice (p. 152)
miliciano de la Guerra de Independencia voluntario de la milicia colonial que estaba siempre preparado para luchar

mission (MIHSH uhn) religious settlement run by Catholic priests and friars; settlement that aims to spread a religion into a new area (p. 47)
misión colonía religiosa administrada por sacerdotes católicos y frailes; asentamiento cuya finalidad es diseminar la religión en una nueva zona

monopoly (muhn AH poh lee) company that controls all or nearly all business in a particular industry (pp. 150, 615)
monopolio compañía que controla toda o casi toda la actividad de una industria en particular

monotheism (MAHN oh thee ihz uhm) belief that there is only one god (p. 22)
monoteísmo creencia de que solamente hay un dios

motive (MOH tihv) thought or feeling behind an action (p. 55)
motivo pensamiento o sentimiento detrás de una acción

mountain man (MOWN tehn man) fur trapper of the Northwest (p. 449)
hombre de montraña cazador de pieles del Noroeste

muckraker (MUHK rak er) crusading journalist (p. 648)
muckraker periodista que busca poner en evidencia las ruindades de las personas

mutualista (myoo chew LEES tah) Mexican American mutual aid group (p. 663)
mutualista grupo de ayuda mutua de los estadounidenses de origen mexicano

myth (mihth) story or legend; imaginary object; invented story (pp. 37, 593)
mito cuento o leyenda; objeto imaginario; relato inventado

N

national park (NA shuhn uhl pahrk) natural area protected and managed by the federal government (p. 651)
parque nacional extensión natural protegida y administrada por el gobierno federal

nationalism (NA shuhn uhl ihz uhm) devotion to the interests of one's own country; pride in one's own nation or ethnic group (pp. 327, 699)
nacionalismo lealtad a los intereses del propio país; orgullo respecto a la propia nación o grupo étnico

nativist (NAY tihv ihst) person who wanted to preserve the United States for white, American-born Protestants and who was opposed to immigration (p. 394)
nativista persona que buscaba reservar Estados Unidos para los protestantes blancos nacidos en el país, y que se oponía a la inmigración

natural rights (NA cher uhl rīts) rights that belong to every human being from birth (p. 122)
derechos naturales derechos de los que goza todo ser humano desde el momento de su nacimiento

naturalization (na cher uhl ih ZAY shuhn) legal process guaranteeing citizenship (p. 270)
naturalización procedimiento jurídico que garantiza la ciudadanía

navigation (nav uh GAY shuhn) science of locating the position and plotting the course of ships (p. 19)
navegación ciencia de ubicar la posición y de trazar el trayecto de los barcos

negative (NEHG ah tihv) in opposition to an idea; not positive (p. 41)
negativo opuesto a una idea; no positivo

neutral (NEW truhl) not favoring either side in a dispute (pp. 295, 387, 513)
neutral que no favorece a ninguna de las partes en un pleito

nominating convention (NAHM ih nay ting kuhn VEHN shuhn) large meeting of party delegates to choose candidates for office (p. 352)
convención de postulación gran encuentro de delegados de un partido para elegir candidatos a un cargo

northwest passage (NORTH wehst PAS saj) water route through or around North America (p. 51)
paso del noroeste ruta navegable a través o alrededor de América del Norte

nullification (nuhl ih fih KAY shuhn) idea that a state has the right to nullify, or cancel, a federal law that the state leaders consider to be unconstitutional (p. 364)

anulación idea de que un estado tiene derecho a anular o cancelar una ley federal que los dirigentes del estado consideran inconstitucional

nullify (NUHL ih fī) to cancel a federal law; to deprive of legal force (pp. 301, 393)
anular cancelar una ley federal; privar de fuerza jurídica

O

open range (OH pehn raynj) unfenced land (p. 590)
campo abierto terreno no cercado

option (AHP shuhn) choice; possible course of action (p. 192)
opción elección; posible manera de actuación

override (OH ver rīd) set aside; disregard; overrule; replace (pp. 259, 553)
invalidar dejar de lado; no tener en cuenta; no admitir; sustituir

P

parochial school (pah ROH kee uhl skool) school sponsored by a church (p. 665)
escuela parroquial escuela auspiciada por una iglesia

participate (pahr TIHS ah payt) to take part in; to share in an activity (pp. 24, 349)
participar tomar parte en algo; compartir una actividad

patent (PAT ehnt) document that gives someone the sole right to make and to sell an invention (p. 610)
patente documento que otorga a una persona el derecho exclusivo a fabricar y vender un invento

peninsular (peh nihn suh LAR) Spanish colonist who was born in Spain (p. 48)
peninsular colono español nacido en España

persecute (PER suh kyoot) to mistreat due to one's religion, race, or political beliefs (p. 69)
perseguir maltratar a alguien por razón de su religión, raza o creencias políticas

persist (per SIHST) to endure; to continue in the face of difficulty (p. 591)
resistir soportar; continuar a pesar de la dificultad

petition (peh TIH shuhn) formal written request to someone in authority that is signed by a group of people (p. 147)
petición solicitud formal por escrito, firmada por un grupo de personas y dirigida a una autoridad

pilgrim (PIHL gruhm) person who takes a religious journey (p. 69)
peregrino persona que emprende un viaje religioso

plantation (plan TAY shuhn) large estate farmed by many workers (pp. 47, 87)
plantación finca grande cultivada por muchos trabajadores

poll tax (pohl taks) personal tax to be paid before voting (p. 560)
impuesto al voto impuesto personal que debía pagarse para poder votar

polygamy (poh LIHG ah mee) practice of having more than one wife at a time (p. 463)
poligamia práctica de tener más de una esposa al mismo tiempo

pool (pool) agreement to divide up business in an area and fix rates at a high level (p. 609)
mancomunidad convenio para dividirse el negocio de una zona y fijar tarifas altas

popular sovereignty (PAH pyoo lahr SAH ver ehn tee) the idea that the people are the key source of a government's authority; right of people in a territory or state to vote directly on issues rather than have their elected representatives decide (pp. 256, 483)
soberanía popular la idea de que la gente es la fuente clave de la autoridad del gobierno; derecho de los habitantes de un territorio o estado a votar directamente sobre ciertas cuestiones en vez de que sus representantes electos decidan

potlatch (PAHT lach) ceremony held by some Native American groups at which the hosts showered their guests with gifts such as woven cloth, baskets, canoes, and furs (p. 12)
potlach ceremonia realizada por algunos grupos de indígenas americanos en la cual los anfitriones agasajaban a sus huéspedes con regalos como tejidos, cestas, canoas y pieles

preamble (PREE am buhl) introduction to a declaration, constitution, or other official document (p. 172)
preámbulo introducción a una declaración, constitución u otro documento oficial

precedent (PREH seh dehnt) example to be followed by others in the future (pp. 283, 375)
precedente ejemplo a seguir por otros en el futuro

precise (pree SĪS) exact; accurate (p. 27)
preciso exacto; acertado, certero

predestination (pree dehs tihn AY shuhn) idea that God decides the fate of a person's soul even before birth (p. 415)
predestinación idea de que Dios decide el destino del alma de una persona incluso antes de su nacimiento

presidio (prih SIHD ee oh) military post where soldiers lived in the Spanish colonies (p. 92)
presidio puesto militar donde vivían los soldados en las colonias españolas

primary (PRĪ mair ee) election in which voters, rather than party leaders, choose their party's candidate for an election (p. 646)
primaria elección donde los votantes, y no los dirigentes de un partido, eligen el candidato de su partido para una elección

prior (PRĪ or) preceding in time; earlier; former (p. 150)
previo que precede en tiempo; anteriormente; antiguo

private property (PRĪ veht PRAH per tee) property owned by an individual (p. 252)
propiedad privada propiedad que pertenece a una persona

privateer (prī vuh TEER) armed civilian ship that had the government's permission to attack enemy ships and keep goods seized (p. 190)
corsario barco civil armado con el permiso del gobierno para atacar a los barcos enemigos y quedarse con los bienes capturados

prohibition (proh ih BIH shuhn) total ban on the sale and consumption of alcohol (pp. 416, 659)
ley seca prohibición total de la venta y consumo de alcohol

propaganda (prah peh GAN dah) false or misleading information that is spread to further a cause; information used to sway public opinion (pp. 488, 701)
propaganda información falsa o engañosa que se difunde para apoyar una causa; información usada para influir en la opinión pública

proprietary colony (proh PRĪ eh tair ee KAHL uhn ee) English colony in which the king gave land to one or more proprietors, or owners, in exchange for a yearly payment (p. 78)
colonia de propietarios colonia inglesa donde el rey concedía tierras a uno o más propietarios o dueños a cambio de un pago anual

proprietor (proh PRĪ ah tor) owner of a business or colony (p. 86)
propietario dueño de una empresa o colonia

prospect (PRAHS pehkt) expectation; something to look forward to happening (pp. 110, 170, 310, 464, 690)
prospecto expectativa; algo que se desea que ocurra

province (PRAHV ahns) governmental division of a country, similar to a state (pp. 51, 346)
provincia división gubernamental de un país, semejante a un estado

provoke (prah VOHK) to cause to anger; to excite; to cause an action (pp. 301, 393, 457)
provocar incitar al enojo; excitar; dar lugar a una acción

public school (PUHB lihk skool) school supported by taxes (pp. 118, 417)
escuela pública escuela financiada con impuestos

pueblo (PWEHB loh) town in the Spanish colonies; Anasazi village (p. 93)
pueblo asentamiento en las colonias españolas; aldea anasazi

pursue (per SYOO) to chase after; to try to capture (pp. 331, 402, 851, 950)
perseguir ir tras de algo; tratar de capturar

Q

quote (kwoht) to repeat the exact words spoken or written (p. 357)
citar repetir las palabras exactas habladas o escritas

R

racism (RAY sihz uhm) belief that one race is superior or inferior to another (p. 116)
racismo creencia de que una raza es superior o inferior a otra

ranchero (ran CHAIR oh) owner of a ranch (p. 446)
ranchero dueño de un rancho

ratify (RAT ih fī) to approve (pp. 218, 264)
ratificar aprobar

rationing (RASH uhn ihng) limits set on the amount of certain goods people can buy (p. 817)
racionar establecer límites sobre la cantidad de ciertos bienes que la gente puede comprar

react (ree AKT) to act in response to an action; to respond (pp. 152, 298, 350, 390)
reaccionar actuar en respuesta a una acción; responder

realist (REE uhl ihst) writer or artist who tries to show life as it is (p. 634)
realista escritor o artista que intenta mostrar la vida tal como es

referendum (reh fer EHN duhm) process by which citizens vote directly on a bill (p. 647)
referéndum procedimiento por el cual los ciudadanos votan directamente respecto a un proyecto de ley

refugee (REHF yoo jee) person who flees his or her homeland to seek safety elsewhere (p. 740)
refugiado persona que escapa de su país de origen en busca de seguridad en otro lugar

reign (rayn) period of dominance or rule (p. 393)
reinado período de dominación o gobierno

reinforce (ree ihn FORS) to make stronger; to strengthen; to make more effective (pp. 122, 328, 519)
reforzar hacer más fuerte; fortalecer; hacer más eficaz

religious freedom (ree LIHJ uhs FREE duhm) right of all individuals to follow their own religious belifes (p. 24)
liberetad de religión derecho de todas los individuos a seguir sus propias creencias religiosas

rendezvous (RAHN day voo) yearly meeting where trappers would trade furs for supplies (p. 449)
rendezvous encuentro anual en el que los tramperos intercambiaban pieles por provisiones

reparation (reh pahr AY shuhn) payment for war damages (p. 703)
reparación pago por los daños ocasionados por una guerra

repeal (ree PEEL) to cancel (pp. 152, 255)
revocar cancelar

representative government (reh pree SEHN tah tihv GUHV ern mehnt) political system in which voters elect others to make laws (p. 69)
gobierno representativo sistema político en el que los votantes eligen a otras personas para que elaboren las leyes

reproduce (ree prah DOOS) to make a copy (p. 435)
reproducir hacer una copia

republic (ree PUHB lihk) system of government in which the people choose representatives to govern them (pp. 25, 252)
república sistema de gobierno en el que la gente elige representantes que los gobernarán

reservation (reh zer VAY shuhn) area set aside by the government for Native Americans to live on (p. 586)
reservación territorio que el gobierno destina a ser habitado por indígenas americanos

reside (ree ZĪD) to live in; to dwell for a while; to exist in (pp. 8, 595)
residir vivir en algún lugar; habitar por un tiempo; existir

resolution (rehz uh LOO shuhn) formal statement of opinion or policy (p. 171)
resolución declaración formal de una opinión o política

resolve (ree SAHLV) to decide; to solve (pp. 143, 364, 548)
resolver decidir; dar solución

resource (REE sors) supply of something to meet a particular need (pp. 188, 514)
recurso abasto de algo que satisface una necesidad en particular

restore (ree STOR) to bring back to a normal state; to put back; to reestablish (p. 50, 188, 326, 524)
restaurar devolver a una condición normal; reponer; restablecer

restrict (ree STRIHKT) to confine; to keep within a certain boundary or limit; to place limitations on something or somebody (p. 75)
restringir confinar; mantener dentro de ciertas fronteras o límites; poner limitaciones a algo o alguien

retain (rih TAYN) to keep (p. 103)
retener mantener

revival (ree VĪ vuhl) huge outdoor religious meeting (p. 415)
reunión evangelista encuentro religioso de grandes proporciones al aire libre

revolt (ree VOHLT) uprising; rebellion; to rebel (pp. 116, 400, 688)
revuelta sublevación; rebelión

rigid (RIH jihd) strict; not easily bent or changed (pp. 48, 653)
rígido estricto; que no se dobla o cambia con facilidad

royal colony (ROI uhl KAHL uh nee) colony under direct control of the English crown (p. 78)
colonia real colonia bajo control directo de la corona inglesa

S

sachem (SAY chuhm) member of the tribal chief council in the League of the Iroquois (p. 15)
sachem (representante en tiempo de paz) miembro del consejo del jefe tribal de la Liga de los iroqueses

salvation (sal VAY shuhn) in Christianity, the means for saving one from evil; everlasting afterlife (p. 23)
salvación en la cristiandad, la manera para librarse del mal; la vida eterna

satellite (SAT uhl īt) nation that is dominated politically and economically by a more powerful nation (p. 718)
satélite nación dominada política y económicamente por otra más poderosa

scalawag (SKAL eh wag) southern white who opposed secession (p. 555)
scalawag blanco sureño que se oponía a la secesión

secede (seh SEED) to withdraw from membership in a group (pp. 331, 484)
separarse retirarse como miembro de un grupo

sedition (seh DIH shuhn) stirring up of rebellion against a government (pp. 300, 392)
sedición acto de fomentar la rebelión contra un gobierno

segregation (sehg reh GAY shuhn) enforced separation of races (p. 560)
segregación separación obligada de dos razas

self-government (sehlf GUHV ern mehnt) right of people to rule themselves independently (p. 348)
autogobierno derecho de las personas a gobernarse a sí mismas de forma independiente

separation of powers (seh pahr AY shuhn uhv POW ers) principle by which the powers of government are divided among separate branches (pp. 123, 253)
separación de poderes principio por el cual los poderes del gobierno se dividen entre sus distintas ramas

service (SER vihs) economic action that one person performs for another (p. 726)
servicio acción económica que una persona lleva a cabo en favor de otra

settlement house (SEHT ehl mehnt hows) center offering help to the urban poor (p. 622)
centro comunitario centro que ofrece ayuda a los habitantes pobres de una ciudad

sharecropper (SHAIR krah per) person who rents a plot of land and farms it in exchange for a share of the crop (p. 561)
aparcero persona que alquila un terreno y lo cultiva a cambio de una parte de la cosecha

siege (seej) military blockade or bombardment of an enemy town or position in order to force it to surrender (pp. 455, 535)
sitio cerco militar o bombardeo de una población o posición enemiga a fin de obligarla a rendirse

slave code (slayv kohd) one of a group of laws that controlled every aspect of enslaved African Americans' lives and denied them basic rights (pp. 116, 399)
código de la esclavitud una de un grupo de leyes que regulaban la vida de los esclavos afroamericanos y les negaban los derechos fundamentales

smuggling (SMUH glihng) act of illegally importing or exporting goods (p. 324)
contrabando importación o exportación ilegal de mercancías

social reform (SOH shuhl ree FORM) organized attempts to improve conditions of life (p. 414)
reforma social intentos organizados de mejorar las condiciones de vida

sod (sahd) soil held together by the tangled roots of grasses (p. 596)
tepe pedazo de tierra sujetado por las raíces enmarañadas del pasto

sodbuster (SAHD buhs ter) farmer on the Great Plains in the late 1800s (p. 596)
sodbuster granjero de las Grandes Llanuras de la segunda mitad del siglo XIX

sooner (SOO ner) person who sneaked onto the land before the start of the Oklahoma land rush (p. 598)
sooner persona que se introdujo a escondidas en las tierras antes de que comenzara la carrera por las tierras de Oklahoma

specify (SPEHS uh fī) to describe or to point out in detail (p. 73)
especificar describir o señalar en detalle

speculator (SPEHK yoo lay tor) person who invests in a risky venture in the hope of making a large profit (p. 284)
especulador persona que invierte en una empresa arriesgada con la esperanza de tener grandes ganancias

sphere (sfeer) rounded shape; area of interest or influence (p. 17)
esfera figura redondeada; zona de interés o influencia

spirituals (SPIR ih chyoolz) religious folk songs that blended biblical themes with the realities of slavery (p. 400)
canto espiritual canto religioso tradicional que combinaba temas bíblicos con las realidades de la esclavitud

spoils system (spoilz SIHS tehm) act of replacing government officials with supporters of a newly elected President (p. 354)
sistema de sinecuras sustitución de funcionarios gubernamentales por partidarios del presidente recién electo

states' rights (stayts rīts) the right of states to limit the power of the federal government (pp. 301, 393)
derechos de los estados derecho de los estados a limitar el poder del gobierno federal

stationary (STAY chuh nair ee) not moving; having a fixed place; not changing in position, size or number (p. 700)
estacionario que no se mueve; que tiene un lugar fijo; que no cambia de posición, tamaño o número

steerage (STIR ihj) large compartments of ships that usually held cattle (p. 626)
tercera clase grandes compartimientos de los barcos en los que normalmente se transportaba ganado

stock (stahk) share of ownership in a corporation (p. 614)
acción participación en la propiedad de una compañía

strait (strayt) narrow passage that connects two large bodies of water (p. 40)
estrecho travesía estrecha que conecta dos grandes masas de agua

submit (suhb MIHT) to give up power and control (p. 661)
someterse ceder el poder y el control

subsidy (SUHB sih dee) grant of land or money (p. 580)
subsidio concesión de tierras o dinero

suburbanite (suh BER ban īt) person who lives in the suburbs (p. 719)
suburbano persona que viva in los suburbios

suffrage (SUH frihj) right to vote (p. 351)
sufragio derecho al voto

suffragist (SUH frihj ihst) person who worked for women's right to vote (p. 657)
sufragista persona que luchaba por el derecho al voto de las mujeres

superior (suh PIR ee er) of greater importance or value; above average in quality; higher in position or rank (p. 519)

superior de mayor importancia o valor; por encima del promedio en cuanto a calidad; que ocupa una posición o categoría más alta

surplus (SER pluhs) excess; quantity that is left over (pp. 7, 598)
superávit excedente; cantidad sobrante

survey (ser VAY) to measure an area using special instruments and the techniques of mathematics (p. 84)
medir estudiar y medir una zona por medio de instrumentos especiales y técnicas matemáticas

sustain (suh STAYN) to keep going; to support as just (pp. 68, 525)
sostener mantener en marcha; apoyar como justo

T

tariff (TAIR ihf) tax placed on goods entering a country from another country (pp. 286, 379)
arancel impuesto con que se gravan las mercancías que entran en un país provenientes de otro

telegraph (TEHL eh graf) invention that allows messages to be sent quickly over long distances by sending electrical signals along a wire (p. 391)
telégrafo invento que permite enviar mensajes rápidamente a grandes distancias por medio de señales eléctricas que viajan por un cable

temperance movement (TEHM per ehns MOOV mehnt) organized effort to end alcohol consumption (p. 416)
movimiento por la temperancia esfuerzo organizado en contra del consumo de alcohol

tenement (TEHN eh mehnt) building divided into many tiny apartments (p. 622)
conventillo un edificio dividido en muchos apartamentos pequeños

tepee (TEE pee) portable tent made of buffalo skins (p. 584)
tipi tienda portátil construida con pieles de búfalo

toleration (tahl er AY shuhn) recognition that other people have the right to different opinions (p. 73)
tolerancia reconocimiento de que otras personas tienen el derecho de mantener opiniones distintas

total war (TOH tuhl wor) all-out attacks aimed at destroying not only an enemy's army but also its resources and its people's will to fight (p. 536)
guerra total ataques masivos encaminados a destruir no sólo al ejército enemigo, sino también sus recursos y la voluntad de luchar de la población

town meeting (town MEET ing) meeting in colonial New England during which settlers discussed and voted on issues; form of direct democracy in which residents meet to make decisions for the community (p. 75)
cabildo abierto reunión en la Nueva Inglaterra colonial donde los colonos discutían y votaban sobre sus asuntos; forma de democracia directa en la que los residentes se reúnen para tomar decisiones que conciernen a la comunidad

traitor (TRAY ter) person who betrays his or her country (p. 192)
traidor persona que traiciona a su país

transcendentalism (trans sehn DEHN tuhl ihz uhm) movement that sought to explore the relationship between humans and nature through emotions rather than through reason (p. 432)
trascendentalismo movimiento que se proponía explorar la relación entre los seres humanos y la naturaleza mediante las emociones en vez de la razón

transcontinental railroad (trans kahn tihn EHN tuhl RAYL rohd) rail line that spans the continent (p. 581)
ferrocarril transcontinental sistema ferroviario que cruza un continente de costa a costa

transform (trans FORM) to change in appearance or form; to change the condition of something (pp. 183, 584)
transformar cambiar la apariencia o la forma; cambiar la condición de algo

transmit (trans MIHT) to pass along; to send (p. 16)
trasmitir pasar, circular; enviar

travois (trav OI) small sled (p. 584)
travois trineo pequeño

triangular trade (trī ANG yuh ler trayd) three-way colonial trade route between the colonies, the islands of the Caribbean, and Africa (p. 115)
comercio triangular ruta de comercio colonial a tres bandas entre las colonias, las islas del Caribe y África

tribute (TRIH byoot) money paid by one country to another in return for protection (p. 295)
tributo dinero que un país paga a otro a cambio de protección

trust (truhst) group of corporations run by a single board of directors (p. 615)
trust grupo de compañías dirigidas por un solo consejo directivo

trustbuster (TRUHST buhs ter) person who worked to destroy monopolies and trusts (p. 650)
trustbuster persona que lucha para destruir los monopolios y trusts

turnpike (TERN pīk) road built by a private company that charges a toll to use it (p. 492)
camino de peaje camino construido por una compañía privada que cobra una cuota por su uso

U

unconstitutional (uhn kahn stih TOO shuhn uhl) contrary to what is permitted by the U.S. Constitution (pp. 263, 285)
inconstitucional contrario a lo que permite la Constitución de Estados Unidos

urbanization (er ban ihz AY shuhn) movement of large numbers of people from rural areas to cities; rapid growth of city populations (pp. 390, 620)
urbanización desplazamiento de un gran número de personas de las zonas rurales a las ciudades; crecimiento rápido de la población de las ciudades

V

vague (vayg) uncertain; not precise or exact (p. 819)
vago incierto; no preciso o exacto

vaquero (vah KAIR oh) Spanish word for cowboy (p. 592)
vaquero término que se aplica a los ganaderos mexicanos o hispanos

veto (VEE toh) to reject, as when the President rejects a law passed by Congress (p. 259)
vetar rechazar, como cuando el Presidente rechaza una ley aprobada por el Congreso

via (VEE ah) by way of (p. 424)
vía paso por algún lugar

vigilante (vihj ihl AN tee) self-appointed law enforcer (pp. 465, 580)
vigilante persona que se designa a sí misma para hacer cumplir la ley

violate (VĪ ah layt) to break a rule or law; to disrespect; to disturb (p. 589)
violar no cumplir una regla o ley; ofender; molestar

vital (VĪ tuhl) necessary for life; of great importance; spirited; lively (pp. 183, 482)
vital necesario para la vida; de gran importancia; lleno de vida; animado

voluntary (VAHL ahn tair ee) not forced; done of one's free will (pp. 357, 547)
voluntario no forzado; hecho por voluntad propia

W

war hawk (wor hawk) one of the members of Congress from the South and the West who called for war with Britain prior to the War of 1812 (p. 327)
halcón de guerra uno de los miembros del Congreso de representantes del Sur y del Oeste que instaban a la guerra con Gran Bretaña antes de la guerra de 1812

water rights (WAW ter rīts) legal right to use water from a river, stream, or other body for a purpose (p. 464)
derecho de aguas derecho jurídico a utilizar el agua de un río, arroyo u otra masa de agua con un fin determinado

women's rights movement (WOO mehns rīts MOOV mehnt) organized campaign to win property, education, and other rights for women (p. 429)
movimiento por los derechos femeninos campaña organizada para obtener el derecho a la propiedad, a la educación y otros derechos para la mujer

women's suffrage (WOO mehns SUH frihj) right of women to vote (p. 428)
sufragio femenino derecho de las mujeres a votar

writ of assistance (riht uhv uh SIHS tehns) court order that allowed officials to make searches without saying for what they were searching (p. 148)
auto de asistencia orden judicial que permitía a determinados funcionarios a realizar registros sin tener que revelar lo que andaban buscando

Y

yellow journalism (YEHL oh JER nahl ihz uhm) style of reporting and displaying news in a sensational way that distorts the truth (p. 635)
periodismo amarillista estilo de reseñar y presentar noticias de un modo sensacionalista que deforma la verdad

Critical Thinking Skills

Critical Thinking Skills

Acknowledgments

Staff Credits

The people who made up the America: History of our Nation team—representing design services, editorial, editorial services, education technology, manufacturing and inventory planning, market research, marketing services, planning and budgeting, product planning, production services, publishing processes, and rights and permissions—are listed below. Boldface type denotes the core team members.

Mary Aldridge, Helene Avraham, Renee Beach, Kerry Lyn Buckley, **Libby Forsyth, Joe Galka, Holly Gordon, Monduane Harris, John Kingston, Marian Manners,** Kathleen Mercandetti, **Xavier Niz, Carrie O'Connor,** Kim Ortell, Ryan Richards, Kirsten Richert, **Laura Ross,** Colleen Searson, Donna Schindler, **Frank Tangredi,** Rachel Winter

Additional Credits

Penny Baker, Claudio Barriga, Lois Brown, Pradeep Byram, Rui Camarinha, Sarah Carroll, Jennifer Ciccone, Jim Doris, Doreen Galbraith, Barbara Hall, Beth Hyslip, Daniela Mastria, Michael McLaughlin, Karen Mancinelli Paige, John McClure, Mark O'Malley, Lesley Pierson, Matt Raycroft, Maureen Raymond, Rose Sievers, Mildred Schulte, Ann Shea

Map and Art Credits

Maps: Mapping Specialists Limited, except where noted and with additional type set by Justin Contursi

Illustrated Maps: Anthony Morse: **20, 82, 210, 320-321, 425, 460-461, 582, 686, 788,** with additional type set by Artur Mkrtchyan

Illustrations: Kevin Jones Associates: **13, 451**

Art: Keithley and Associates (all charts, graphs, instructional art, and photo composites except where noted) with additional type set by Ernest Albanese and Justin Contursi

Justin Contursi: Atlas design and photo treatments for Skills Activities

gdps: **200-203, 278-281, 302, 305, 306-309, 332, 336-339, 364, 378-381, 410-413, 436, 440-443, 468, 478-481, 504, 507, 508-511, 538, 542-545, 574-577, 604-607, 636, 640-643, 667, 676-679**

Brainworx: **210-211, 216, 286, 288-289, 320-321, 341, 420-421, 425, 432-433, 450-451, 460-461, 502, 522-523, 550-551, 582-583, 596-597, 610-611, 630-631, 686-687**

Photo Credits

Photo Research: Omni-Photo Communications, Inc.; **Cover** © Bob Gelberg/Masterfile; **A1** Getty Images, Inc.; **A2** Esbin/Anderson/Omni-Photo Communications, Inc.; **A3 b.** Dallas and John Heaton/CORBIS; **A3 t.** AP/Wide World Photos; **A4** Tom & Susan Bean; **A5** Julie Habel/CORBIS; **A5** Marvin Newman; **A6** Grant Heilman Photography; **A7 b** Bill Ross/CORBIS; **A7 t.** Giancarlo de Bellis/Omni-Photo Communications, Inc.; **A10** Larry Downing/Reuters/CORBIS; **A11** CORBIS; **A12 m.** Connie Ricca/CORBIS; **A12 t.** Smithsonian American Art Museum, Washington, DC / Art Resource, NY; **A12 b.** Bettmann/CORBIS; **A13 t.** Bettmann/CORBIS; **A13 b.** Jay Dorin/Omni-Photo Communications, Inc.; **A15 l.** Anaheim Public Library; **A15 r.** D. Boone/CORBIS; **A16 backgrnd** © Royalty-Free/Corbis; **A16** CORBIS; **i** © Bob Gelberg/Masterfile; **iv-v** John Guthrie, Guthrie Studios; **vii** The Granger Collection, New York; **viii** Courtesy National Archives, **ix** O.C. Seltzer, Lewis and Clark with Sacagawea, at the Great Falls of the Missouri River, #0137.871. From the Collection of Gilcrease Museum, Tulsa, Oklahoma; **x** Collection of The New-York Historical Society, negative no. 26280; **xi** AP/Wide World Photos; **xii** The Granger Collection, New York; **xiii** Bettmann/CORBIS; **xiv** Bettmann/CORBIS; **xvi** Courtesy of the Library of Congress; **HT 1** Omni-Photo Communications, Inc.; **HT 2 l.** Courtesy National Archives; **HT 2 r.** Omni-Photo Communications, Inc.; **HT 3** Lawrence Migdale/Pix; **HT 4** CORBIS/Bettmann; **HT 5** © David Young-Wolff/PhotoEdit inc.; **HT 8 l.** David Stoecklein/CORBIS; **HT 8 r.** Sime s.a.s./eStock/PictureQuest; **HT 12** Copyright © North Wind/North Wind Picture Archives; **HT 13** CC Lockwood/Animals Animals; **HT 14** Mary Evans Picture Library; **HT 15** The Granger Collection, New York; **HT 19** KAL/The Baltimore Sun/CartoonArts International/CWS; **HT 21** Brand X Pictures/PictureQuest; **HT 22** © Jeff Greenberg/PhotoEdit Inc.; **1 t.r.** Jamestown-Yorktown Educational Trust, VA, USA/The Bridgeman Art Library, London/New York; **1 t.l.** Hair Comb (Seneca Iroquois) late 17th century, carved moose antler, 4 1/2 " H (11.4 cm.). From the collections of the Rochester Museum & Science Center, Rochester, New York (RM 2932); **1 b.** CORBIS/Bettmann; **2-3** Tom Bean/CORBIS; **5 l.** Tinglit kayak (wood), Inuit School (19th century)/Private Collection, Boltin Picture Library/Bridgeman Art Library; **5 r.** IND 123 0784502/2 *Vasco da Gama* (c.1469-1525) Portuguese navigator, Spanish School, (16th century)/Private Collection, Index;/www.bridgeman.co.uk; **6** Jonathan Blair/CORBIS; **8** Charles & Josette Lenars/CORBIS; **8 inset** The Granger Collection, New York; **9** Jorge Ianiszewski/Art Resource, NY; **10** Werner Forman/Art Resource, NY; **11 r.** The Granger Collection, New York; **11 l.** Michel Zabe/© Dorling Kindersley; **11 m.** Michel Zabe/© Dorling Kindersley; **13 r.** Stock Montage, Inc.; **13 b.l.** PhotoDisc, Inc./Getty Images; **13 t.l.** Andy Deering/Omni-Photo Communications, Inc.; **14** Hair Comb (Seneca Iroquois) late 17th century, carved moose antler, 4 1/2 " H (11.4 cm.). From the collections of the Rochester Museum & Science Center, Rochester, New York (RM 2932); **15** The Art Archive/Cherokee Indian Museum North Carolina/Mireille Vautier; **17 l.** Courtesy of the Freer Gallery of Art, Smithsonian Institution, Washington, D.C.: Purchase, F1946.12, f. 38b; **17 t.r.** Peter Chadwick/© Dorling Kindersley; **17 b.r.** Roger Phillips /© Dorling Kindersley; **17 m.r.** Philip Dowell© Dorling Kindersley; **18** Giraudon/Art Resource, NY; **19** Figure of Shou Lao (jade), Chinese School, (17th century) /Fitzwilliam Museum, University of Cambridge, UK/ Bridgeman Art Library; **20 l.** photolibrary.com; **20 r.** © Tom Stoddart/Woodfin Camp & Associates; **21 r.** The Granger Collection, New York; **21 t.l.** © Markus Matzel/Peter Arnold, Inc.; **21 b.l.** Philip Dowell© Dorling Kindersley; **23** Tissot, James Jacques Joseph (1836-1902) *Moses and the 10 Commandments* c. 1896-1902. Gouache on board. 10 11/16 x 5 5/8". Gift of the Heirs of Jacob Schiff, x1952-190. Photo by John Parnell. The Jewish Museum, New York, NY, U.S.A./Art Resource, NY; **24** Bildarchiv Preussischer Kulturbesitz/Art Resource, NY; **25** AP/Wide World Photos; **26** The Granger Collection, New York; **29** Bildarchiv Preussischer Kulturbesitz/Art Resource, NY; **30** Figure of Shou Lao (jade), Chinese School, (17th century) /Fitzwilliam Museum, University of Cambridge, UK/ Bridgeman Art Library; **31** © Royalty-Free/CORBIS; **32-33** Amos Zemer/Omni-Photo Communications, Inc.; **36** The Granger Collection, New York; **37** Ridolfo Ghirlandaio (1483-1561) *"Christopher Columbus."* Museo Navale di Pegli, Genoa, Italy. Scala/Art Resource, NY.; **38** Astrolabe, copper, by Ahmad Ibn Khalaf an Iraqi Arab, 9th century, NO_DATA / Bibliotheque Nationale de Cartes et Plans, Paris, France/ Bridgeman Art Library; **39 t.** John Cabot (c. 1450-c. 1499), Genoese navigator. Image

Select/Art Resource, NY; **39 b.** The Art Archive/Museo de la Torre del Oro Seville/Dagli Orti/The Picture Desk; **40 t.l.** Corel Professional Photos CD-ROM™; **40 b.r.** Corel Professional Photos CD-ROM™; **40 m.l.** Corel Professional Photos CD-ROM™; **40 t.r.** Corel Professional Photos CD-ROM™; **40 b.l.** Corel Professional Photos CD-ROM™; **40 m.r.** Roger Phillips/© Dorling Kindersley; **42 b.** National Gallery Collection; by kind permission of the Trustess of the National Gallery, London/CORBIS; **42 t.** Copyright © North Wind/North Wind Picture Archives—All rights reserved.; **43 t.l.** Mary Evans Picture Library; **43 t.r.** The Granger Collection, New York; **43 b.** James Stevenson /© National Maritime Musuem, London,©Dorling Kindersley; **45** The Granger Collection, New York; **47** The Granger Collection, New York; **49** *Portrait of Henry VIII* (1491-1547), Holbein, Hans the Younger (1497/8-1543) / Belvoir Castle, Leicestershire, UK/ Bridgeman Art Library; **50 r.** Peter M. Fisher/Corbis; **50 t.** © Dorling Kindersley; **50 b.** Bettmann/CORBIS; **51** *Queen Elizabeth I playing the lute* (miniature, Hilliard, Nicholas (1547-1619) / Berkeley Castle, Gloucestershire, UK/ Bridgeman Art Library; **52** Tate Gallery, London / Art Resource, NY; **55** The Granger Collection, New York; **56** ©Monica Graff/The Image Works; **57** The Granger Collection, New York; **60** Copyright © North Wind/North Wind Picture Archives - - All rights reserved.; **62-63** CORBIS/Bettmann; **68** State Capitol, Commonwealth of Virginia. Courtesy The Library of Virginia.; **69** Courtesy of the Library of Congress. Art © Romare Bearden Foundation/Licensed by VAGA, New York, NY; **70** Head of Squanto (d.1622), an American Indian of the Pawtuxet tribe who became a good friend to the Pilgrims (wood), American School, (17th century) / Private Collection/ Bridgeman Art Library; **71** T11999 *The Spermaceti Whale,* DETAIL, engraved by William Home Lizars (1788-1859) plate 10 from Vol 12 of Sir William Jardine's 'Naturalist's Library', pub. 1833-45 (hand-coloured engraving), Stewart, James (1791-1863) (after)/Natural History Museum, London, UK,/Bridgeman Art Library; **72 t.l.** Courtesy, American Antiquarian Society; **72 b.l.** CORBIS; **72-73** Courtesy of The Salem Witch Museum, Salem, Massachusetts; **75** Courtesy of the Library of Congress; **76** Mary Evans Picture Library; **79** The Granger Collection, New York; **83 t.** Roy Rainford/Robert Harding World Imagery; **83 m.** © Charles E. Rotkin/CORBIS; **83 b.** © Philip Gould/CORBIS; **84** Courtesy of the Library of Congress; **85** The Granger Collection, New York; **87** *Portrait of General James Edward Oglethorpe* (1696-1785) founder of the State of Georgia, copy of original portrait in Atlanta, c.1932 (oil on canvas), Ravenet, Simon Francois (1706/21-74) (after) / Corpus Christi College, Oxford, UK/ Bridgeman Art Library; **89** Hulton Archive/Getty Images Inc.; **90** Everett C. Johnson/eStock Photography, LLC; **92** *Tumacacori Mission,* 1855 (oil on canvas), Pratt, Henry Cheever (1803-80) / © Phoenix Art Museum, Arizona, Francis Hover Stanley and Carolanne Smurthwaite/Bridgeman Art Library; **92 inset** Jack Dykinga /Getty Images; **96** The Granger Collection, New York; **98-99** Embroidered by: Eunice Bourne, Massachusetts (Barnstable), 1732- before 1781. Overmantel (detail). American, Colonial, mid-18th century. Plain weave linen embroidered with wool, silk and metallic yarns, glass beads, and wood frame with glass. 63 x 129 cm (24 13/16 x 50 13/16 in) (Including frame). Museum of Fine Arts, Boston. Seth K. Sweetser Fund, 21.2233. Photograph © 2006 Museum of Fine Arts, Boston; **101** CORBIS; **103** The Granger Collection, New York; **105 r.** The New York Public Library, Rare Book Division/Art Resource; **105 l.** Copyright © North Wind/North Wind Picture Archives - - All rights reserved.; **106** Courtesy of the Library of Congress; **107 m.** Geoff Brightling © Dorling Kindersley, Courtesy of the Museum of English Rural Life, The University of Reading; **107 r.** Andy Crawford © Dorling Kindersley, Courtesy of the Museum of the Revolution, Moscow; **107 l.** Geoff Dann © Dorling Kindersley,

Courtesy of the Barleylands Farm Museum and Animal Centre, Billericay; **109 b.r.** CORBIS/Bettmann; **109 b.l.** © Richard T. Nowitz/CORBIS; **109 t.l.** The Granger Collection, New York; **109 t.r.** Colonial Williamsburg Foundation, gift of Frances Matthews.; **bkgd 109** Corel Professional Photos CD-ROM™; **110 r.** Victoria & Albert Museum, London/Art Resource, NY; **110 l.** Wenham Museum; **111** The Granger Collection, New York; **112** The Granger Collection, New York; **115** The Granger Collection, New York; **116** *Slaves preparing tobacco, Virginia, America,* c.1790, from 'Le Costume Ancien et Moderne', Volume II, plate 50, by Jules Ferrario, engraved by Angelo Biasioli (1790-1830), published c.1820s-30s (colour litho), Bramati, G. (19th century) (after) / Private Collection, The Stapleton Collection/Bridgeman Art Library; **117** CORBIS; **119 b.** CORBIS/Bettmann; **119 t.l.** The Granger Collection, New York; **119 t.r.** The Granger Collection, New York; **120** Schomburg Center/Art Resource, NY; **121** Copyright © North Wind/North Wind Picture Archives - - All rights reserved.; **123** Archivo Icongrafico, S.A/CORBIS; **125 t.** Collection of The New-York Historical Society (1938.312); **125 b.** Pearson Education/PH School Division; **128** The Granger Collection, New York; **129** The Granger Collection, New York; **134 t.** Tony Freeman /PhotoEdit; **134-35 b.** Courtesy National Archives.; **134-35 t.** The Granger Collection, New York; **135 b.r.** Copyright © North Wind/North Wind Picture Archives - - All rights reserved.; **136-37** *The Fight on Lexington Common, April 19, 1775,* from 'The Story of the Revolution' by Woodrow Wilson (1856-1924), published in Scribner's Magazine, January 3, 1898 (oil on canvas), Pyle, Howard (1853-1911)/© Delaware Art Museum, Wilmington, USA, Howard Pyle Collection;/Bridgeman Art Library; **139 r.** CORBIS; **139 l.** CORBIS/Bettmann; **141** The Granger Collection, New York; **143** Robert Griffing/Paramount Press, Inc.; **144** Mary Evans Picture Library; **147** Copyright © North Wind/North Wind Picture Archives - - All rights reserved.; **148** The Granger Collection, New York; **149** The Granger Collection, New York; **151 r.** The Granger Collection, New York; **151 l.** Boston Tea Party tea leaves in a glass bottle, collected by T.M. Harris, Dorchester Neck, December 1773, American School, (18th century)/© Massachusetts Historical Society, Boston, MA, USA/Bridgeman Art Library; **151 m.** Courtesy, American Antiquarian Society; **153** Jim Conaty/Omni-Photo Communications, Inc.; **154 t.** Courtesy of the Library of Congress; **154 b.l.** John Singleton Copley (American, 1738-1815), *Mrs. James Warren (Mercy Otis)* ca.1763. Oil on canvas. 49 5/8 x 39 1/2 in. (126 x 100.3 cm). Bequest of Winslow Warren. Courtesy, Museum of Fine Arts, Boston. Reproduced with permission. ©2000 Museum of Fine Arts, Boston. All Rights Reserved. Photograph © 2006 Museum of Fine Arts, Boston.; **154 b.r.** Jim Barber/StockRep, Inc.; **154 m.** The Granger Collection, New York; **155** The Granger Collection, New York; **157** The Granger Collection, New York; **158** Fort Ticonderoga Museum; **159** Fort Ticonderoga Museum; **160 t.r.** Copyright © North Wind/North Wind Picture Archives - - All rights reserved.; **160 b.** Copyright © North Wind/North Wind Picture Archives - - All rights reserved.; **160 t.l.** American 18th Century, *Attack on Bunker's Hill, with the Burning of Charles Town,* oil on canvas, .533 x .708 (21 x 27 7/8); framed: .603 x .774 x .038 (23 3/4 x 30 1/2 x 1 1/2). Gift of Edgar Williams and Bernice Chrysler Garbisch, Photograph © 2000 Board of Trustees, National Gallery of Art, Washington, 1783 or after, oil on canvas.; **166-67** Corel Professional Photos CD-ROM™; **171** Bettmann/CORBIS; **172** The Granger Collection, New York; **173** Maryland Historical Society, Baltimore; **174** Courtesy National Archives and Records Administration, College Park, Maryland, photo no. (USH001TF 011 004); **175** Index Stock Imagery, Inc.; **179** The Granger Collection, New York; **181** The Granger Collection, New York; **182 l.** Uniforms of the American Revolution: 1777 Private Field

Wind Picture Archives—All rights reserved.; **391** New York Historical Society, New York, USA/The Bridgeman Art Library, London/New York; **392** Matthew Brady/Library of Congress, Washington, D.C. USA/The Bridgeman Art Library, London/New York; **393** The Granger Collection, New York; **394** CORBIS; **398 t.** Hunter Museum of Art; **398 b.** Liz McAulay © Dorling Kindersley; **399 t.** Collection of The New-York Historical Society; **399 b.** New-York Historical Society, New York, USA/The Bridgeman Art Library, London/New York; **400** The Granger Collection, New York; **403** Courtesy of the Library of Congress; **410-11** Shelburne Museum, Shelburne, Vermont (cat #27.1.5-25) Photograph by Ken Burris.; **415** Courtesy of the Library of Congress; **415** Courtesy of the Library of Congress; **416** © New Bedford Whaling Museum. detail; **417 r.** The Granger Collection, New York; **418** Brooke/Topical Press Agency/Getty Images; **420 t.** ©Kevin Fleming/CORBIS; **420 b.** Fine Art Photograhic Library/CORBIS; **421 t.l.** Culver Pictures, Inc.; **421 t.r.** The Granger Collection, New York; **421 m.t.** CORBIS; **421 b.r.** CORBIS; **421 b.l.** The Metropolitan Museum of Art, The Elisha Whittelsey Collection, The Elisha Whittelsey Fund, 1951. MM 55138 Photograph, all rights reserved, The Metropolitan Museum of Art.; **423** Getty Images Inc. - Hulton Archive Photos; **424** Image by courtesy of the Wedgwood Museum Trust Limited, Barlaston, Staffordshire, England.; **425 l.** Harriet Tubman Quilt made by the Negro History Club of Marin City and Sausalito, CA, 1951, 120 x 96 inches, cotton appliqued. Designed by Ben Irvin. Gift of the Howard Thurman Educational Trust to the permanent collection of the Robert W. Woodruff Library, Atlanta; **425 r.** Levi Coffin House Association - Indiana State Museum and Historic Sites; **427** Courtesy of the Library of Congress; **428** CORBIS; **430** Maria Mitchell Association; **432 l.** Courtesy of the Library of Congress; **432 r.** Copyright ©1930 by R.R. Donnelly & Sons, Inc. and Plattsburgh College Foundation, Inc. All rights reserved.; **433** Corbis/Bettmann; **434** Thomas Cole Oil on Canvas 23 3/4x 31 1/2. The Minneapolis Institute of Arts; **439** © New Bedford Whaling Museum.; **440-41** 59.21 Benjamin Franklin Reinhart, *The Emigrant Train Bedding Down for the Night,* 1867, oil on canvas, 40 x 70 in. Corcoran Gallery of Art, Washington, D.C. Gift of Mr. and Mrs. Lansdell K. Christie; **446** CLAVER CARROLL /photolibrary.com; **449 r.** The Granger Collection, New York; **449 t.l.** Kenneth Lilly © Dorling Kindersley; **449 b.l.** The Granger Collection, New York; **450** The Granger Collection, New York; **451 t.l.** Tria Giovan/CORBIS; **451 b.l.** Oregon Historical Society, Negative No. Object 473; **451 r.** Courtesy of the Lane County Historical Museum. photo by John Zimmerman; **453** PhotoDisc, Inc./Getty Images; **455 r.** The Granger Collection, New York; **455 l.** John M. Roberts/CORBIS; **457** Bettmann/CORBIS; **460 b.** Corel Professional Photos CD-ROM™; **460 t.** Bettmann/CORBIS; **461 r.** Chicago Historical Society; **461 l.** Color lithograph by unknown artist, Landing of the Troops at Vera Cruz, 1847. Anne S.K. Brown Military Collection, John Hay Library, Brown University; **463 r.** Used by permission, Utah State Historical Society, all rights reserved; **463 l.** *Handcart Pioneers* by CCA christensen © by Intellectual Reserve, Inc. Courtesy of Museum of Church History and Art Used by Permission.; **464 l.** Courtesy History Division, Los Angeles County Museum of Natural History; **464 r.** Andrew McKinney/© Dorling Kindersley; **465** USC Regional History Center; **466** *San Francisco, general view,* ca. 1850-52; detail, engraving by S. Frank Marryat, Collection of The New-York Historical Society, negative no. 26280; **470** The Granger Collection, New York; **476 b.** CORBIS; **476 t.** The Granger Collection, New York; **477 t.** Mary Evans Picture Library; **477 b.** *His First Vote,* 1868 (oil on canvas), Wood, Thomas Waterman (1823-1903)/Private Collection, Christie's Images/www.bridgeman.co.uk/The Bridgeman Art Library, London/New York; **478-79** The Granger Collection, New York; **481** The Granger Collection, New York; **483** Courtesy of the Library of Congress; **484 l.** Clemson University; **484 r.** The Granger Collection, New York; **487 l.** Copyright © North Wind/North Wind Picture Archives—All rights reserved.; **487 r.** Illinois State University; **488 l.** Bettmann/CORBIS; **488 r.** Réunion des Musées Nationaux/Art Resource, NY; **490** The Granger Collection, New York; **493 b.** Pearson Education/PH School Division; **493 t.** The Granger Collection, New York; **495** John Henry Brown, *"Abraham Lincoln"* (1809-1865), Sixteenth US President. Watercolor on ivory, c. 1860. National Portrait Gallery, Smithsonian Institution/Art Resource, NY. (detail); **496** CORBIS/Bettmann; **497** Kansas State Historical Society; **498** The Granger Collection, New York; **499** National Portrait Gallery, Smithsonian Institution/Art Resource, NY (NPG.71.29); **501** Hulton-Deutsch Collection/CORBIS; **502 m.** The Granger Collection, New York; **502 b.** United States Department of the Interior; **502 t.** Courtesy of the Library of Congress, Geography and Map Division; **506** Kansas State Historical Society; **507** The Granger Collection, New York; **508-09** David Muench/Muench Photography Inc.; **515 l.** Omni-Photo Communications, Inc.; **515 r.** Omni-Photo Communications, Inc.; **516** Courtesy Beverley R. Robinson Collection, US Naval Academy Museum; **517** Dave King / Dorling Kindersley © Confederate Memorial Hall, New Orleans; **519** Bettmann/CORBIS; **519 inset** Steve Helber/AP/Wide World Photos; **522-23** from Great Battles of the Civil War by kind permission of Marshall Editions Ltd; **523 l.** Publisher's Press, Inc.; **523 r.** Collection of Picture Research Consultants, Inc. Photo © Collection of David and Kevin Kyle; **525** Collection of the personal papers of General Robert H. Milroy, Courtesy of the Jasper County Public Library, Rensselaer, Indiana (detail); **526** AP/Wide World Photos; **529** The Granger Collection, New York; **530 r.** The Granger Collection, New York; **530 l.** Getty Images Inc. - Hulton Archive Photos; **532** AP/Wide World Photos; **533** Courtesy National Archives and Records Administration, College Park, Maryland, photo no. (NWDNS-111-B-326); **535** Courtesy of the Library of Congress; **541** The Granger Collection, New York; **542** Antique Textile Resource; **542-43** CORBIS; **545 m.** Courtesy of the Library of Congress; **545 r.** The Granger Collection, New York; **545 l.** John Henry Brown, *Abraham Lincoln* (1809-1865), Sixteenth US President. Watercolor on ivory, c. 1860. National Portrait Gallery, Smithsonian Institution/Art Resource, NY.; **547** CORBIS/Bettmann; **548 r.** CORBIS/BETTMANN; **548 l.** Getty Images - Hulton Archive Photos; **550 m.** The Charleston Museum; **550 b.** The Granger Collection, New York; **550 t.** Dave King/ Dorling Kindersley © Confederate Memorial Hall, New Orleans; **551 t.l.** Copyright © North Wind/North Wind Picture Archives—All rights reserved.; **551 m.** Douglas Mudd, National Numismatic Collection, The Smithsonian Institution; **551 t.r.** neg. #86-113-74, Rudolf Eickmeyer, National Museum of American History, Smithsonian Institution; **551 b.** The Museum of the Confederacy, Richmond, Virginia, Photography by KATHERINE WETZEL; **552** Courtesy of the Library of Congress; **553 l.** The Granger Collection, New York; **553 r.** Courtesy of the Library of Congress; **554 r.** Courtesy of the Library of Congress; **554 l.** Courtesy of the Library of Congress; **555** The Granger Collection, New York; **556** The Granger Collection, New York; **557 t.** Old Court House Museum, Vicksburg, Photo by Bob Pickett; **557 b.** Collection of Mississippi State Historical Museum/Mississippi Department of Archives and History; **560 l.** Courtesy of the Library of Congress; **560-61** CORBIS; **562** CORBIS/Bettmann; **563** CORBIS; **565** CORBIS; **566** *His First Vote,* 1868 (oil on canvas), Wood, Thomas Waterman (1823-1903)/Private Collection, Christie's Images/www.bridgeman.co.uk/The Bridgeman Art Library, London/New York; **567** The Granger Collection, New York; **572 t.** Solomon D. Butcher Collection, Nebraska State Historical Society; **572 b.l.** Corbis-

Collection, New York; **774** Omni-Photo Communications, Inc.; **778** CORBIS/Bettmann; **780** Snark/Art Resource, NY; **783** Bancroft Library, University of California; **785** The Museum of American Political Life, University of Hartford; **792 01** © National Portrait Gallery, Smithsonian Institution/Art Resource, NY; **792 02** © National Portrait Gallery, Smithsonian Institution/Art Resource, NY; **792 03** White House Collection, copyright White House Historical Association; **792 04** ©National Portrait Gallery, Smithsonian Institution/Art Resource, NY; **792 05** ©National Portrait Gallery, Smithsonian Institution/Art Resource, NY; **792 06** National Portrait Gallery, Smithsonian Institution/Art Resource, NY; **792 07** White House Collection, copyright White House Historical Association; **792 08** White House Collection, copyright White House Historical Association; **792 09** © National Portrait Gallery, Smithsonian Institution/Art Resource, NY; **792 10** © National Portrait Gallery, Smithsonian Institution/Art Resource, NY; **792 11** White House Collection, copyright White House Historical Association; **792 12** © National Portrait Gallery, Smithsonian Institution/Art Resource, NY; **793 13** White House Collection, copyright White House Historical Association; **793 14** © National Portrait Gallery, Smithsonian Institution/Art Resource, NY; **793 15** © National Portrait Gallery, Smithsonian Institution/Art Resource, NY; **793 16** White House Collection, copyright White House Historical Association; **793 17** White House Collection, copyright White House Historical Association; **793 18** ©National Portrait Gallery, Smithsonian Institution/Art Resource, NY; **793 19** White House Collection, copyright White House Historical Association; **793 20** ©National Portrait Gallery, Smithsonian Institution/Art Resource, NY; **793 21** © National Portrait Gallery, Smithsonian Institution/Art Resource, NY; **793 22** White House Collection, copyright White House Historical Association; **793 23** White House Collection, copyright White House Historical Association; **793 24** White House Collection, copyright White House Historical Association; **794** White House Collection, copyright White House Historical Association; **794 25** © National Portrait Gallery, Smithsonian Institution/Art Resource, NY; **794 26** ©National Portrait Gallery, Smithsonian Institution/Art Resource, NY; **794 27** © National Portrait Gallery, Smithsonian Institution/Art Resource, NY; **794 28** White House Collection, copyright White House Historical Association; **794 29** White House Collection, copyright White House Historical Association; **794 30** White House Collection, copyright White House Historical Association; **794 31** White House Collection, copyright White House Historical Association; **794 32** White House Collection, copyright White House Historical Association; **794 33** White House Collection, copyright White House Historical Association; **794 34** White House Collection, copyright White House Historical Association; **794 35** © National Portrait Gallery, Smithsonian Institution/Art Resource, NY; **795 36** and **795 37** White House Collection, copyright White House Historical Association; **795 38** White House Collection, copyright White House Historical Association; **795 39** White House Collection, copyright White House Historical Association; **795 40** White House Collection, copyright White House Historical Association; **795 41** White House Collection, copyright White House Historical Association; **795 42** White House Historical Association (White House Collection) (6196) (detail); **795 43** Bob Daemmrich/Stock Boston Inc. /PictureQuest

Text Credits

Grateful acknowledgment is made to the following for copyrighted material:

Robert A. Freedman Dramatic Agency
Excerpt from *Valley Forge* by Maxwell Anderson from *America On Stage, Ten Great Plays of American History* by Stanley Richards. Copyright © 1934 by Maxwell Anderson. Copyright renewed © 1962 by Gilda Oakleaf Anderson, Alan Anderson, Terence Anderson, Quentin Anderson, and Hesper A. Levenstein. All rights reserved. CAUTION: Professionals and amateurs are hereby warned that *Valley Forge,* being fully protected under the Copyright Laws of the United States of America, the British Commonwealth, including the Dominion of Canada, and all other countries of the International Copyright Union and the Universal Copyright Convention, is subject to Royalty. All rights, including professional, amateur stage rights, motion picture, recitation, lecturing, public reading, radio and television broadcasting, video or sound recording, all other forms of mechanical or electronic reproduction, information storage and retrieval systems and photocopying and the right of translation into foreign languages, are strictly reserved. Particular emphasis is laid on the question of reading, permission for which must be secured from the author's agent in writing. All inquiries concerning rights should be addressed to Robert A. Freedman Dramatic Agency, Inc. at 1501 Broadway, Suite 2310, New York, New York 10036.

Library of Congress, Manuscript Division
Excerpt from the "Samuel F.B. Morse Papers at the Library of Congress, 1793–1919" from *The Library of Congress.*

From Letter to His Sister by Robert E. Lee from the Wartime Papers of R. E. Lee. Copyright © 1961 by Commonwealth of Virginia. Used by permission of Little, Brown and Company. All rights reserved

Note: Every effort has been made to locate the copyright owner of material reprinted in this book. Omissions brought to our attention will be corrected in subsequent editions.